GUIDE TO CURRENT BRITISH JOURNALS

Second edition

edited by

DAVID P. WOODWORTH
Lecturer, School of Librarianship, Loughborough

Vol. 1

LONDON

THE LIBRARY ASSOCIATION

1973

The Library Association
7 Ridgmount Street, London, WC1E 7AE

© David Woodworth, 1973

Vol. 1.

First edition 1970

Second edition 1973

Vol 1. ISBN: 0 85365 356 9
Vol 2. ISBN: 0 85365 097 7

PRINTED BY Unwin Brothers Limited
THE GRESHAM PRESS OLD WOKING SURREY ENGLAND

Produced by 'Uneoprint'
A member of the Staples Printing Group

CONTENTS

Numbers refer to inclusive entry numbers of titles within a subject field and to relative pages concerned.

			Page
INTRODUCTION			vii
0 GENERAL		1-3	1
01 Bibliography		4-24	1-2
02 Libraries, Librarianship		25-78, 4586-4589	2-6, 346
03 Dictionaries		79	6
04 Interviews		80	6
05 General periodicals		81-332, 4590-4604	7-23, 346-347
06 Organisations		333-348	23-24
07 Journalism. Newspapers		349-354	24
09 Archives. Rare Books		355-358	24-25
1 PHILOSOPHY		359-374	25-26
13 Occult		375-376	26
14 Philosophical systems		377-378	26
15 Psychology		379-404	26-28
16 Logic		405-409, 4605	28-29, 347
17 Ethics		410-412	29
18 Aesthetics		413	29
2 RELIGION. THEOLOGY		414-427, 4606-4607	30, 347
21 Theology		428	31
22 Bible. Christian religion		429-440, 4608-4609	31, 347
23 Prophecy		441	32
24 Practical theology		442	32
26 Christian church. Christianity		443-478	32-34
27 Christian church history		479-482	34-35
28 Christian churches. Sects		483-559, 4610-4613	35-40, 347-348
29 Non-christian religions		560-579	40-42
3 SOCIAL SCIENCES		580-595	42-43
30 Sociology		596-622	43-45
31 Statistics		623-644	45-46
32 Current affairs. Politics.		645-749, 4614-4620	46-54, 348
33 Economics		750-887, 4621-4630	54-64, 348-349
34 Law		888-961, 4631-4633	64-70, 349
35 Public administration		962-1014, 4634-4636	70-74, 349
36 Social welfare		1015-1107, 4637-4640	74-81, 349
37 Education		1108-1295, 4641-4644	81-95, 349-350
38 Commerce. Trade		1296-1443, 4645-4648	95-107, 350
39 Customs. Folklore		1444-1457, 4649-4652	107-108, 350
4 LANGUAGES. PHILOLOGY		1458-1474, 4653	108-109, 350
41 Linguistics		1475-1477, 4654	109, 350
420 English		1478-1481	110

iii

				Page
	440 French	1482		110
	460 Spanish	1483		110
	47 Classical	1484-1486		110
	49 African and other languages	1487-1492		110-111
5	**SCIENCE**	1493-1522, 4655		111-113, 351
	502 Natural history	1523-1562		113-116
	51 Mathematics	1563-1586		116-118
	52 Astronomy. Surveying	1587-1610		118-120
	53 Physics	1611-1706, 4656-4657		120-128, 351
	54 Chemistry	1707-1790		128-135
	55 Geology. Meteorology	1791-1849, 4658-4659		135-139, 351
	56 Palaeontology. Fossils	1850-1851		139
	57 Anthropology. Biology	1852-1940, 4660-4661		139-146, 351
	58 Botany	1941-1969		146-148
	59 Zoology	1970-2025, 4662		148-152, 351
6	**TECHNOLOGY**	2026-2040		152-153
	608 Patents. Trade marks	2041-2046		153-154
	61 Medical sciences	2047-2354, 4663-4669		154-177, 351-352
	62 Engineering	2355-2794, 4670-4684		178-211, 352-353
	63 Agriculture. Forestry. Fisheries	2795-3014, 4685-4686		211-228, 353
	64 Catering. Domestic Science	3015-3071, 4687		228-232, 353
	65 Business. Management	3072-3312, 4688-4694		232-250, 353-354
	66 Industrial chemistry	3313-3516, 4695-4696		250-267, 354
	67 Manufactures	3517-3593		267-273
	68 Industries. Trades	3594-3749, 4697-4704		273-284, 354
	69 Building	3750-3810		284-289
7	**THE ARTS**	3811-3841		289-291
	71 Town and country planning	3842-3864, 4705		291-293, 354
	72 Architecture	3865-3900		293-296
	73 Craft art. Masonry. Sculpture	3901-3918		296-297
	74 Design. Needlework	3919-3924		297
	75 Art. Painting	3925		298
	77 Photography. Cinematography	3926-3950		298-299
	78 Music	3951-4002		300-303
	79 Entertainment. Sport	4003-4182		303-316
8	**LITERATURE**	4183-4259		316-321
	820 English	4261-4293		321-323
	830 German	4294-4295		323
	839 Scandinavian	4296		323
	840 French	4297-4298		323-324
	87 Greek	4299		324
	883 Ukrainian	4300		324
	891 Welsh	4301		324
	892 Hebrew. Jewish	4302		324

9	**GEOGRAPHY. HISTORY**	4303-4349	*Page* 324-327
	91 Geography	4350-4361	327-328
	92 Biography. Genealogy	4362-4370	328-329
	93 Archaeology	4371-4443	329-334
	94 Modern history	4444-4538	334-341
	95 Asia	4539-4556, 4706	341-342, 355
	96 Africa	4557-4571	342-343
	97 N. America	4572-4576	344
	98 S. America	4577-4580	344
	99 Oceania. Polar regions	4581-4585	344-345

APPENDICES	1	Journals carrying abstracts	357
	2	Discontinued journals	359
	3	Societies and their publications	361
INDEX			377

INTRODUCTION

The second edition of this work includes very many more titles than was included in the first edition and the scope of the work has been widened in order to include certain categories previously excluded. With the exception of slight alterations, similar format of entry is maintained to provide a quick reference source for the speedy assessment and identification of British journals.

Two additional appendices are included which, I hope, will enhance the usefulness of the work; one listing those journals discontinued since publication of the first edition of the Guide and the Directory of Publishers and one listing publications of Societies/institutions.

The Directory of Publishers of British Journals, previously published separately, is now included as Volume 2 of this work but has been compiled as a self contained publication in order to be available separately if so desired.

While the greatest care has been taken to ensure accuracy, no responsibility can be taken for changes in subscription rates etc which may have changed since going to print.

AREA

'British' refers to England, Wales, Scotland, Northern Ireland and the Isle of Man and Channel Islands. Some journals from the Irish Republic have also been included.

SCOPE

Exclusions have been kept to a minimum but the following fields are, at present, omitted:-

(a) Parish magazines

(b) Some 'pin-up' journals

(c) Daily Press

(d) Some children's periodicals, especially comics

(e) Student publications, unless containing serious material

BASIS OF COMPILATION

Questionnaires were sent out during the Summer of 1972 and Winter of 1972/3 to as many publishers as could be traced. In addition to questions about journals a specimen copy was requested, where possible, for monitoring purposes at first hand. Where this has been possible I have noted the date of the issue seen, but where publishers were not able to send a copy of their publication the information supplied has had to be relied upon for accuracy although, wherever possible, titles have been checked if they were taken by local libraries.

Where no reply was received, as many as possible have been included after personal assessment and in a few cases entries carry minimum information. This is usually the case for new titles recently announced or where it has proved impossible to see titles and inclusion has been made for completeness.

Unfortunately, for various private reasons, a limited number of publishers specifically requested that their journals be excluded.

ARRANGEMENT

(a) Contents page refers to classified contents by the Universal Decimal Classification (UDC), and inclusive page and entry numbers. This should/may be used as a primary guide to the main sequence.

(b) Main sequence, classified broadly by U.D.C.

(c) Appendices

(d) Index referring *to*:
  (i) Numbers assigned to individual periodical titles
  (ii) Inclusive numbers assigned to all journals in a subject field (italicized).

from:
  (iii) previous titles to entry numbers relating to titles currently used.

FORM OF ENTRY

TITLE, as on title page (no inversion, following the practice of the National Lending Library) with sub-titles where relevant.

DATE OF FIRST ISSUE, under present title.

PREVIOUS TITLES AND DATES, in curves

PUBLISHER (and Group where appropriate) and **ADDRESS**

FREQUENCY, number per year

LEVEL OF APPEAL (see list of symbols)

COVERAGE, compiled from information supplied by the publisher, specialists or personal assessment

FEATURES. A factual statement of the more important features of the journal, such as book reviews, letters, monographic articles etc.

INDEX. Divided into four sections
  (a) frequency of issue, ie quarterly, annually etc.
  (b) date actually issued where possible
  (c) whether a title page is supplied with the index (for binding purposes)
  (d) whether the index is cumulated, with details where possible.

BIBLIOGRAPHICAL DATA:
  (a) which issue has been seen (evidence of currency of entry)
  (b) number of text pages (T.p) in issue seen
  (c) number of Advertisement pages (Ad.p.) in issue seen
  (d) circulation.

SUBSCRIPTION: Per copy and per year, where possible

INDEXED IN: whether the journal is indexed by any/either of the following:-

  BEI   British Education Index
  BHI   British Humanities Index
  BTI   British Technology Index
  IBZ   Internationale Bibliographie der Zeitschriftenliteratur.

LATE ENTRIES

Entries for journals received, or traced, after going to print have a special section at the end of the main sequence, but similarly classified. This includes entries, some only with minimum information, up to the end of March 1973.

SYMBOLS

The following symbols have been used to denote Level of Appeal, these are repeated frequently throughout the work and also on the book mark:-

- ○ Popular.
- ‡ Technical.
- + Research.
- = Trade/Professional.
- * Society/Institution.
- † House journal.

INTERNATIONAL STANDARD SERIAL NUMBERS (ISSN)

The inclusion of those ISSN's adopted by the Bowker Co. was considered but eventually I decided to omit such references until some future edition when their formal adoption has been agreed.

APPENDICES

1. **ABSTRACTS**: This provides details of those journals carrying abstracts of the literature of their field. Numbers refer to individual entries in the main sequence.

2. **DISCONTINUED TITLES**: Information for which definite information has been received to this effect, excluding amalgamations with other journals.

3. **SOCIETIES/INSTITUTIONS AND THEIR PUBLICATIONS**: This has been introduced because a number of journals sponsored by Societies are, in fact, published by Commercial firms on their behalf. This section is confined to those organisations professionally based and reference to the Directory of Publishers will be necessary for other organisations, such as Research Associations.

UP-DATING

Future editions are planned at approximately 3 year intervals and I would be pleased to receive details of omissions, data alterations, notes of new journals and suggestions at any time. *No charge is made for such entries.*

ACKNOWLEDGMENTS

I would like to thank: Mr A. J. Illes of Cambridge University Library for his continuing co-operation in supplying information on new and discontinued titles: those publishers who have supplied such a vast amount of information: my wife for her forbearance and assistance throughout, without which the work would have taken considerably longer to complete.

D. P. Woodworth
Ashby-de-la-Zouch
April 1973.

0
GENERAL

002
DOCUMENTATION

1 BULLETIN OF CURRENT DOCUMENTATION. 1971.
Association of Commonwealth Universities, 36 Gordon Square, London, WC1.
3, =
No Index.
Per year 75p.

2 JOURNAL OF DOCUMENTATION. 1944.
Aslib, 3 Belgrave Square, London, SW1.
4, = ‡ +   Recording, organizing and disseminating information.
Book reviews, letters, monographic articles.
A, January, Yes, None.
July 1972, T.p. 97, Ad. p. 3.   4000.
Subscription on application.
Indexed in: IBZ, LISA.

009
HUMANITIES

3 BRITISH HUMANITIES INDEX. 1962.
(Subject Index to Periodicals, 1915-1962, excl. 1923-1925).
The Library Association, 7 Ridgmount Street, London, WC1E 7AE.
4, + = ‡   Index to 380 periodicals in the arts fields.
A, No, None.
1: 1972, T.p. 33.   1301.
Per year £15.

01
BIBLIOGRAPHY

4 ASLIB BOOK LIST. A monthly list of recommended scientific and technical books. 1936.
Aslib, 3 Belgrave Square, London, SW1.
12, = + ‡
Book reviews.
A, February, Yes, None.
T.p. 12.   3000.
Per year £2.

5 THE BIBLIOTHECK: A Scottish Journal of bibliography and allied topics. 1956.
Scottish Group of the University, College and Research Section of the Library Association, University Library, Stirling.
2, + =   Bibliography and related subjects embodying original material based on manuscripts or printed books of Scottish interest or association.
Book reviews, monographic articles.
Index to Vol. 1-5 (1956-70) to be published.
T.p. 34, Ad. p. 5.
Per copy 60p, per year £1.20.

6 THE BOOK COLLECTOR. 1952.
The Collector Ltd., 58 Frith Street, London, W1V 6BY.
4, + =   Any aspect of book collecting & bibliography.
Book notices, book reviews, letters, articles.
A, Spring, No, None.
Per year £3.

7 BOOKS FOR YOUR CHILDREN. 1965.
Anne and Barrie Wood, 14 Stoke Road, Guildford, Surrey.
4, ○   Information on favourite children's authors, new books, constant themes in children's literature and up to date children's book information and lists for parents and teachers.
Book notices, book reviews, letters, monographic articles.
A, October, No, None.
Vol 7, No. 3, T.p. 18, Ad. p. 6.   5000.
Per copy 17½p, per year 60p.

8 BRITISH BULLETIN OF PUBLICATIONS ON LATIN AMERICA, THE WEST INDIES, PORTUGAL AND SPAIN. 1949.
Hispanic Council/Luso Brazilian Council, 2 Belgrave Square, London, SW1.
2, =
No Index.
April 1972, T.p. 20.   1700.
Per copy £1.25, per year £2.50.

9 THE BRITISH NATIONAL BIBLIOGRAPHY. 1950.
The Council of the British National Bibliography Ltd., 7 & 9 Rathbone Street, London, W1P 2AL.
52, = * ‡   A list of new British books received by the Agent for the Copyright Libraries, arranged according to the Dewey Decimal Classification and catalogued according to the British Text of the Anglo-American Cataloguing Rules (1967).
A, —, Yes, 5 year.
May 31, 1972, T.p. 176.   5000.
Per copy 45p, per year £20. Full Service £48.50.

10 BRITISH UNION CATALOGUE OF PERIODICALS: New Periodical Titles. 1964.
Butterworths, 88 Kingsway, London, WC2B 6AB.
4, ‡ +   The recording of new periodical titles of all subjects for the period in and after 1960. This embraces periodicals and serials beginning publication for the first time, changing their titles or beginning a new series.
A, Yes, 5 year/10 year.
June 1972, T.p. 40.   1200.
Per year £10.50.

11 CHILDREN'S BOOK REVIEW. 1971.
Five Owls Press Ltd., Widbury, 67 High Road, Wormley, Broxbourne, Herts, EN10 6JJ.
6, ○ =   Articles on children's literature and reading; reviews of recent children's books; list of forthcoming titles.
Book notices, book reviews, articles.
A, December, No, None.
June 1972, T.p. 29, Ad. p. 10.   1900.
Per copy 25p, per year £1.25.

12 CURRENT BIBLIOGRAPHY OF PUBLISHED MATERIAL RELATING TO NORTH STAFFORDSHIRE AND SOUTH CHESHIRE. 1964.
Stoke-on-Trent City Libraries, Horace Barks Reference Library, Bethesda Street, Hanley, Stoke-on-Trent, ST1 3RS.
4, +   Lists items, including periodical articles, published in, or concerning the area of Staffordshire, North of Stafford, and Southern Cheshire, or by or about local authors, organisations, firms, etc.
No Index.
Jan-March 1971, T.p. 32.   c. 100.
Per copy Gratis.

13 EAST MIDLANDS BIBLIOGRAPHY. 1970.
(North Midland Bibliography 1963-1969).
Library Association, East Midlands Branch, c/o The Library, College of Art & Technology, Kedleston Road, Derby, DE3 1GB.

Key to reference symbols

○ popular   ‡ technical   = trade/professional

+ research   * society/institution   † house journal

4, + = Lists new publications with interest to East Midlands of England (Derbyshire, Nottinghamshire, Lincolnshire, Rutland, Leicestershire, Northamptonshire, and former Soke of Peterborough).
Book notices*
A, January/February, Yes, None.
9(4), 1971, T.p. 65.   120.
Per copy 75p, per year £3.

14 GROWING POINT. 1962.
Mrs. Margery Fisher, Ashton Manor, Northampton, NN7 2JL.
9, ○ = Children's books from picture books to novels for young adults, certain adult books recommended for 'teens'.
Book notices, book reviews, monographic articles.
A, —, No, None.
May 1972, T.p. 20.
Per copy 20p, per year £1.50.

15 INDEX TO FORTHCOMING RUSSIAN BOOKS: (Novyye Knigi SSSR). No. 1, 1970.
(Index to Forthcoming Russian Books, Series A: Technical Sciences, No. 1, 1965-No. 12, 1969, Series B: Life Sciences, No. 1, 1965-No. 12, 1969.)
Scientific Information Consultants Ltd., 661 Finchley Road, London, NW2 2HN.
12, ‡ + The only publication in English which gives advance information on books being published in the USSR. Contains selected titles and bibliographical data extracted from Soviet weekly "Novyye Knigi SSSR". Covers technical and life sciences, economics, law, social sciences, humanities, political sciences, etc.
Book notices.
Subject index in each issue.
No 3, 1971, T.p. 72.
Per year £22.

16 THE JOURNAL OF THE WELSH BIBLIOGRAPHICAL SOCIETY. 1910.
The Welsh Bibliographical Society, c/o The National Library of Wales, Aberystwyth, SY23 3BU.
1, + * = History of printing, book trade & libraries; topics of Welsh bibliographical interest.
Monographic articles.
4 yearly, At end of volume (vol. = 4 issues), Yes, None.
June 1971, T.p. 82.
50p (individual), £1 institutions.

17 THE JUNIOR BOOKSELF. 1936.
The Junior Bookshelf, Marsh Hall, Thurstonland, Huddersfield, HD4 6XB, Yorks.
6, = + * Reviews of new children's books, also articles on children's writers and illustrators.
A, February, with No. 1 of next volume, No, None.
August 1971, T.p. 56, Ad. p. 18.   2750.
Per copy 25p, per year £1.25.
Indexed in: BEI

18 LIBRARY: Published for the Bibliographical Society. 1889.
Oxford University Press, Press Road, Neasden, London, NW10.
4, + Printing and publishing, printing types, book illustration, rare books, the book trade, and all aspects of descriptive and historical bibliography, both English and foreign.
Book reviews, monographic articles.
A, March, Yes, None.
March 1972, T.p. 80, Ad. p. 10.   500.
Per copy £1.35, per year £5.
Indexed in: IBZ.

19 LIBRARY AND INFORMATION BULLETIN. 1967.
The Library Association, 7 Ridgmount St., London, WC1E 7AE.
3/5, * + Librarianship. Reports of library surveys; notices of additions to L.A. Library. Technical in bias. Theses abstracted, equipment described. Abstracts, book notices, commodity prices, monographic articles, new products.
None yet, possibly after 20 issues.
No. 17, T.p. 67.   700.
Per copy £1.

20 THE LITERARY REPOSITORY: Devoted to the printing of unpublished manuscripts and original articles; also a catalogue of rare and scholarly books and manuscripts.
Toucan Press, Mount Durand, St. Peter Port, Guernsey, C.I.
3/4, + = Book notices, book reviews, commodity prices, letters, monographic articles, obituaries.
No Index.
No. 1/1972, T.p. 16.   10000.
Per copy 7p, per year 12p.

21 LONG ROOM: bulletin of the Friends of the Library. 1970.
(Bulletin of the Friends of the Library, 1946-58.)
Friends of the Library, Trinity College, Dublin. The Library, Trinity College, Dublin.
2, * + Specializes in the publication of bibliogs. of Irish authors, checklists, material relating to Anglo-Irish studies and to Irish printing, esp. in 18th cent. Contains studies based on collns. in other Irish libraries and in libraries abroad.
Letters, monographic articles.
No index pub. yet, but prob. one after 10 issues.
Spring 1972, T.p. 26, Ad.p. 2.   650.
Free to members.

22 PERIODICALS NEWS. 1970.
British Museum, c/o Periodicals News, N.R.L.S.I. (Holborn Division), 25 Southampton Bdgs., London, WC2.
13, Lists changes of titles, closures, etc. and selected additions to the periodicals stock of the National Reference Library of Science and Invention.
No Index.
No. 2, 1972, T.p. 10.
Free.

23 TRANSACTIONS OF THE CAMBRIDGE BIBLIOGRAPHICAL SOCIETY. 1949.
Cambridge University Press, PO Box 92, London, NW1.
1, + * Bibliographies with particular reference to Cambridge.
Monographic articles.
5 year, —, Yes, None.
T.p. 82, Ad.p. 4.
Free to members.
Indexed in: BHI.

24 TRANSPORT BOOKMAN. 1970.
Chater & Scott, Ltd., 530 High Road, Chiswick, London, W4.
6, =
No Index.
Per copy 15p, per year 90p.

02

LIBRARIES. LIBRARIANSHIP

25 AN LEABHARLANN. IRISH LIBRARY: Journal of the Library Association of Ireland and the Library Association, Northern Ireland Branch. 1972.
(Northern Ireland Libraries 1960-1971).
N.I. Branch of the Library Association, c/o The Library, Queen's University, Belfast.
4, = * Libraries & Librarianship in Ireland.
Book notices, book reviews, letters, monographic articles.
No Index.
T.p. 30, Ad.p. 4.
Free to members.

26 ARLIS (Art Libraries Society) NEWSLETTER. 1969.
Editor ARLIS Newsletter, St. Albans School of Art Library, 7 Hatfield Road, St. Albans, Herts.
4,* =   Exists to further the purposes of ARLIS, i.e. "To promote art librarianship particularly by acting as a forum for the interchange of information and materials."
Book notices, book reviews, letters, articles, new products.
No Index.
October 1971, T.p. 22.   140.
Per copy 30p, per year £1. Available to members only. £1 membership fee-includes Newsletter.

27 ASLIB INFORMATION. 1973.
Aslib, 3 Belgrave Square, London, SW1X 8PL.
12, =
No Index.
Per copy 80p, per year £8. Members 20p; £2.

28 ASLIB PROCEEDINGS. 1949.
Aslib, 3 Belgrave Square, London, SW1.
12, = + ‡   Special librarianship & information work.
Book reviews, letters, monographic articles.
A, February, Yes, None.
T.p. 60, Ad.p. 10.
Subscription on application.

29 ASLIB TRANSPORT AND PLANNING GROUP NEWSLETTER. 1971.
(Transport 1967-1971)
Aslib T & P Group, 3 Belgrave Square, London, SW1.
4, ○ =   News sheet aimed at information work in libraries dealing with transportation and planning.
No Index.
December 1971, T.p. 4.   200.
Free to Aslib members.

30 ASSISTANT LIBRARIAN. Official journal of the Association of Assistant Librarians. 1953.
(Library Assistant 1898-1952).
Association of Assistant Librarians, c/o Central Library, Manor Park Road, Sutton, Surrey.
= *   All aspects of librarianship & library education.
Book notices, book reviews, letters, monographic articles, new products.
A, February, Yes, None.
T.p. 16, Ad.p. 8.
Free to members.

31 BODLEIAN LIBRARY RECORD. 1938.
(Bodleian Quarterly Record 1914-1938).
Bodleian Library, Oxford, OX1 3BG.
1/2, + =   Bibliographical, both manuscripts and printed books; library & printing history. Based mainly on, but not restricted to, Bodleian and its holdings.
Monographic articles.
Per vol. (of 6 nos.) often with first no. of next vol., Yes, None.
June 1971, T.p. 56.   2000.
Per copy 17½p.
Indexed in: BHI, IBZ.

32 THE BOOK TROLLEY: Quarterly journal of the Hospital Libraries & Handicapped Readers Group of the Library Association. 1965.
The Editor. Book Trolley, c/o Scottish Hospital Centre, Crewe Road South, Edinburgh, EH4 2LF.
4, * =   Articles and comment on library work in hospitals, homes, prisons and with the handicapped in the community. Also library services to professional staff engaged in such work.
Book notices, book reviews, letters, obituaries.
2 year, in preparation, No, None.
June 1972, T.p. 22, Ad.p. 2.   Approx. 900.
Per year £3. Free to members.

33 BOOKS AND BOOKMEN. 1955.
Hansom Books, Artillery Mansions, 75 Victoria Street, London, SW1H OHZ.
12, ○   Current literature, poetry, authors.
Book notices, book reviews, commodity prices, letters, monographic articles, new products, obituaries.
No Index.
July 1972, T.p. 88, Ad.p. 10.
Per copy 30p, per year £4.05.

34 BRIO: Journal of the United Kingdom Branch of the International Association of Music Libraries. 1964.
IAML (UK Branch), Michael Short, Hon. Secretary IAML (UK Branch), Haldane Library, Imperial College, London, SW7 2AZ.
2, *   Music librarianship and bibliography.
Book notices, book reviews, monographic articles.
No Index.
Spring 1970, T.p. 22, Ad.p. 6.   450.
Per copy 50p, per year £1.

35 CADIG NEWSLETTER. 1964.
CADIG [Coventry and District Information Group], Reference Library, Bayley Lane, Coventry.
4, †   Reports the activities of CADIG, other similar groups, lists members' surplus stock, comments on any interesting new publications, and generally tries to communicate with CADIG's scattered membership.
No Index.
January 1972, T.p. 4.
Free to members

36 CIIG BULLETIN: Journal of the Construction Industry Information Group. 1970.
(CIIG Newsletter).
Construction Industry Information Group, BCM/Box 693, London, WC1V 6XX.
4, * ‡   Handling and use of information in the construction industry, including national and organisational systems, library operation, documentation, etc.
Book reviews, letters, monographic articles, obituaries.
A, October (with last issue of each vol.), Yes, None.
Jan 1972, T.p. 28, Ad.p. 8.   300.
Per copy £1, per year £4. Free to members.

37 COUNTY NEWSLETTER. 1956.
(County Libraries Section Newsletter 1949-1955)
County Libraries Group of the Library Association, c/o Central Library, Southgate, Stevenage, Herts.
4, =   Current information on County Library affairs in Great Britain and on the activities of the Group Committee.
Monographic articles.
No Index.
June 1972, T.p. 8.   3000.
Per year £1. Free to members.

38 CYLCHGRAWN LLYFRGELL GENEDLAETHOL CYMRU/ THE NATIONAL LIBRARY OF WALES JOURNAL, 1939.
The National Library of Wales, Aberystwyth, Cardiganshire, SY23 3BU.
2, +   Articles on historical, literary, palaeographical, genealogical, and artistic subjects based on the library's resources.
Monographic articles.
No Index.
Summer 1972, T.p. 104.
Per copy 30p, per year 70p.
Indexed in: BHI

39 THE EASTERNER. 1959.
Library Association (Eastern Branch), County Library, Rope Walk, Ipswich, Suffolk, IP4 1LX.
Irregular, * =   Librarianship in the locality, accounts of meetings, new library openings, individual library developments.
Articles, obituaries.
No Index.
May 1972, T.p. 8.
Free to members.

40 EDUCATION LIBRARIES BULLETIN. 1958.
(University of London Institute of Education Library Bulletin 1949-1957).
University of London Institute of Education Library, 11-13 Ridgmount Street, London, WC1E 7AH.
3, + * = Topics of interest to librarians, academic staff, and students of educational institutions. Pays particular attention to problems of libraries in colleges, institutes and schools of education.
Book notices, book reviews, letters, monographic articles, obituaries.
4 year, last issue of fourth year, No, None.
Spring 1972, T.p. 51, Ad.p. 1.   700.
Per copy 40p, per year £1.20.

41 FOCUS ON INTERNATIONAL AND COMPARATIVE LIBRARIANSHIP. 1967.
International and Comparative Librarianship Group, Library Association, 7 Ridgmount St., London, WC1E 7AE.
4, * = Description of all types of library and documentation services in all parts of the world with emphasis on the problems of cross-cultural communication.
Book notices, book reviews, letters, monographic articles.
3 year, 1970, No, 10 year.
July 1972, T.p. 16.   950.
Per year £1.

42 INTERNATIONAL CATALOGUING: Quarterly bulletin of the IFLA Committee on Cataloguing. 1972.
IFLA Committee on Cataloguing, c/o Department of Printed Books, The British Museum, London, WC1B 3DG.
4, ‡ + News about cataloguing activities; articles on specific cataloguing problems.
No Index.
January/March 1972, T.p. 8.
Per year £2. Free to members.

43 INTERNATIONAL LIBRARY REVIEW. 1969.
Academic Press Inc. (London) Ltd., 24-28 Oval Road, London, NW1.
4, ‡ +
Monographic articles.
A, —, Yes, None.
T.p. 125.
Per year £10.

44 JOURNAL OF LIBRARIANSHIP: Quarterly of the Library Association. 1969.
The Library Association, 7 Ridgmount Street, London, WC1E 7AE
4, * = Theoretical and applied librarianship.
Book reviews, letters, monographic articles.
A, January, Yes, None.
April 1972, T.p. 61.   1100.
Per year £5.

45 KENT NEWSLETTER. 1950.
Kent Sub-Branch Library Association, c/o Kent County Library, Maidstone, Kent.
2, * = Items & news for libraries in Kent.
Letters, articles, obituaries, news.
No Index.
Winter 1970-71, T.p. 19.
Free to members.

46 LEG NEWS. 1972.
Library Education Group, the Library Association, School of Librarianship, Polytechnic of North London, Essex Street, London, NW1.
3, = Education and training in librarianship.
No Index.
Free to members.

47 THE LAW LIBRARIAN: Bulletin of the British and Irish Association of Law Librarians. 1970.
Sweet & Maxwell Ltd. (for British and Irish Association of Law Librarians.) 11 New Fetter Lane, London, EC4P 4EE.
3, * = Law libraries, Librarianship and bibliography (no geographical restrictions); BIALL activities.
Book notices, book reviews, legal notes, letters, articles, obituaries.
2 year, December, Yes, None.
April-July 1972, T.p. 16.   400.
Per copy 75p, per year £2.

48 LIBER BULLETIN. 1972.
Ligue des bibliothèques européennes de recherche. The Main Library, University of Birmingham, P.O. Box 363, Birmingham B15 2TT and Bibliothèque cantonale et universitaire, CH-1005 Lausanne, Switzerland.
2, ‡ + Covers the activities of the Ligue des bibliothèques européenes de recherche, with additional information and news on European libraries.
Book notices, book reviews, monographic articles.
2 yearly, —, Yes, None.
No. 1, 1971, T.p. 80.   250.
Per year 90DM.

49 LIBRARIANS FOR SOCIAL CHANGE. 1972.
John Noyce, 67 Vere Road, Brighton.
4, = Librarianship in general.
Book reviews, letters, articles.
No Index.
No. 1, T.p. 30, Ad.p. 46.   300.
Per copy 20p.

50 LIBRARY ACTION: Quarterly Journal of the Library Action Group. 1971.
Library Action Group, 21 Bainbrigge Rd., Leeds LS6 3AD.
4, ○ = Librarianship, particularly controversial or taboo aspects.
Book notices, book reviews, letters, articles, parliamentary reports.
No Index.
September 1971, T.p. 18.   200.
Per copy 25p, per year £1.

51 LIBRARY ASSOCIATION RECORD. Official Journal of the Library Association. 1899.
(Library Chronicle 1884; The Library 1889).
Library Association, 7 Ridgmount Street, London, WC1E 7AE.
12, = + ‡ All aspects of library & information work. **Liaison** as insert.
Book notices, book reviews, letters, monographic articles, new products, news.
A, February, Yes, None.
May 1972, T.p. 24, Ad.p. 24.   17500.
Per year £8. Free to members.

52 LIBRARY & INFORMATION SCIENCE ABSTRACTS. 1969.
(Library Science Abstracts. 1950-1968).
The Library Association, 7 Ridgmount Street, London, WC1E 7AE.
6, + = International abstracting service, placing particular emphasis on currency of material.
Abstracts.
A, February, Yes, None.
2: 1972, T.p. 52.   1905.
Per year £10.

53 LIBRARY HISTORY: Journal of the Library History Group of the Library Association. 1967.
(Newsletter of the Library History Group 1963-1966).
Library History Group, Library Association, 54 George Lane, Marlborough, Wiltshire, SN8 4BY.
2, ‡ * + The history of all types of library, general and special, academic and popular, national, institutional, municipal and private, in any part of the world.
Book notices, book reviews, legal notes, letters, monographic articles, obituaries, parliamentary reports.

3 year. At the end of a volume, which covers 3 calendar years. Yes, None.
Spring 1972, T.p. 50, Ad.p. None yet; to be decided. 1600.
Per copy 75p, per year £1.50. Free to members.
Indexed in: BHI.

54 LIBRARY REVIEW: A quarterly magazine on libraries and literature. 1927.
W. & R. Holmes (Books), 98-100 Holm Street, Glasgow, G2 6SN.
4, ○ ‡   Popular appeal for librarians, educationists and readers generally.
Book notices, book reviews, letters, articles.
2 yearly, Spring, Yes, None.
Spring 1972, T.p. 42, Ad.p. 5.
Per year £1.80.

55 NEW LIBRARY WORLD. 1971.
(The Library World 1898-1971).
Clive Bingley (Journals) Ltd., 16 Pembridge Road, London, W11.
12, ‡   News, comment and current affairs coverage in professional librarianship and information science.
Book reviews, letters, monographic articles, new products, obituaries.
A, March/April, Yes, None.
May 1972, T.p. 241, Ad.p. 71.   1400.
Per copy 35p, per year £4.

56 MEDICAL SECTION OF THE LIBRARY ASSOCIATION BULLETIN. 1947.
Library Association, 7 Ridgmount Street, Store Street, London, WC1E 7AE.
4, * +   Medical librarianship.
No Index.
T.p. 8.
Free to members.

57 NORTH WESTERN NEWSLETTER. 1950.
North Western Branch of the Library Association, c/o T. F. Houghton, Hon. Editor, County Branch Library, Cross St., Standish, Nr. Wigan.
6, * =   News, information, notices of meetings, calendar of events, articles on aspects of librarianship.
Letters, new libraries, new methods, obituaries.
No Index.
April 1972, T.p. 12, Ad.p. 3.   2000.
Per copy 21p, per year £1.25. Free to branch members.

58 NORTHERN IRELAND LIBRARIES. 1960.
Northern Ireland Branch of the Library Association, c/o The Library, Queen's University, Belfast, BT7 1LS.
4, = *   Librarianship in general.
Book notices, book reviews, letters, monographic articles.
No Index.
T.p. 29, Ad.p. 3.   260.
Free to members.

59 OPEN ACCESS: A News-Sheet for West Midland Librarians. 1951.
(Periodical of this title 1929-1939 published by Midland Division of Association of Assistant Librarians).
Library Association, West Midland Branch, Reference Library, Birmingham. B3 3HQ.
4, *   West Midland Libraries and Librarianship.
Book notices, book reviews, letters, monographic articles, obituaries.
Periodically, —, No, None.
Winter 1972, T.p. 15.   1500.
Free to members; others £1 per year.

60 OSTI NEWSLETTER. 1966.
Office for Scientific and Technical Information, D E S, Elizabeth House, 39 York Road, London, SE1 7PH.
4, ‡ +   Information about new grants and contracts, progress with existing ones, new policy developments and new activities with which OSTI is associated.
A, December, No, None.
December 1971, T.p. 8.
Free.

61 OUTPOST. 1947.
(Dacaal 1937).
Association of Assistant Librarians, Devon & Cornwall Branch, c/o Public Library, Plymouth.
3, =   News & reports of meetings.
None.
T.p. 24.
Free to members.

62 THE PRIVATE LIBRARY: Quarterly Journal of the Private Libraries Association. 1958.
(PLA Quarterly 1957-1959).
Private Libraries Association, 41 Cuckoo Hill Road, Pinner, Middlesex.
4, * +   Book-collecting; book illustration; author collections and bibliographies; bookplates.
Book notices, book reviews, monographic articles.
None.
Autumn 1969, T.p. 48.   1000.
Per copy £1. Free to members.

63 PROGRAM. News of computers in libraries. 1969.
Aslib, 3 Belgrave Square, London SW1.
4, = + ‡   Reports on new projects & developments in library computerization.
Book reviews, monographic articles.
A, November, Yes, None.
T.p. 49, Ad.p. 1.   750.
Subscription: on application.

64 RESEARCH IN LIBRARIANSHIP. 1965.
Edward R. Reid-Smith, 34 Norfolk Street, Werneth, Oldham, Lancs.
3, + =   Research results, methodology, abstracts of theses, book reviews, current projects. Mainly British but some articles from other countries.
Abstracts, book reviews, monographic articles, tests.
2 years, End of each volume, Yes, None.
T.p. 32.   650.
Per copy 50p, per year £1.50.

65 SLA NEWS. Official Journal of the Scottish Library Association. 1950.
c/o Dept. of Librarianship, University of Strathclyde, Livingstone Tower, Richmond Street, Glasgow C1.
6, = * +   All aspects of Scottish librarianship.
Book notices, book reviews, letters, monographic articles.
2 year, with last issue of volume, Yes, Vols 1-82 (1950-1967).
T.p. 31, Ad.p. 8.
Free to members.

66 THE SCHOOL LIBRARIAN. 1937.
The School Library Association, Premier House, 150 Southampton Row, London, WC1B 5AR.
4, * =   School librarianship at all levels: books, etc. for school libraries, their organization and use; Association and related news.
Book reviews, monographic articles.
A, December, Yes, None.
June 1972, T.p. 96, Ad.p. 24.   7400.
Per copy £1.20, per year £4.80. Free to members.
Indexed in: BEI

67 SERVICE POINT. 1972.
c/o J. G. Fleming, St. James Branch Library, Laird Street, Birkenhead.
3, =   News, articles & ideas about branch & mobile libraries.
None.
Per copy 25p, Free to members of LA Branch & Mobile Libraries Group.

68 SOLANUS: Bulletin of the Slavonic & East European Group of SCONUL. 1966.
National Central Library, Store Street, London, WC1E 7DG.
Irregular, + =   Library materials for Slavonic and East European Studies.
Book notices, book reviews, monographic articles.
None.
February 1972, T.p. 26.
Free to members.

69 YLG NEWS. 1962.
(Spotlight 1955-1957; YLS Activity, 1958-1960; YLS News 1960-1961).
Library Association (Youth Libraries Group), c/o Mrs. C. Kloet, Comprehensive School, Hattersley, Cheshire.
3, * =   Matters of interest to those interested in or working with children and libraries.
Book notices, book reviews, letters, articles.
Complete Index (Duplicated) 1955-1970 inclusive.
Winter 1971, T.p. 24.
Free to members.

70 Y DDOLEN: The magazine for librarians in Wales. 1970.
Welsh Library Assocation; AAL, N & S Wales Divisions, c/o Central Library, The Hayes, Cardiff, CF1 2QU.
2, * =   News and views on librarianship in Wales and related topics.
Book notices, letters, articles, obituaries.
None.
June 1972, T.p. 11.   750.
Circulation limited to LA members in Wales.

71 YORKSHIRE LIBRARIAN. 1956.
Library Association, Yorkshire Branch, c/o Regional College of Art, Anlaby Road, Hull.
2, =   Libraries and librarianship with special reference to Yorkshire.
Book notices, book reviews, letters, articles.
None.
Free to members.

025.3

INDEXING

72 CATALOGUE AND INDEX. 1966.
Library Association, Cataloguing and Indexing Group, 7 Ridgmount Street, Store Street, London, WC1E 7AE.
4, =   Cataloguing, indexing and classification in libraries
Book notices, book reviews, letters, articles.
2 year, c. October, Yes, None.
T.p. 16.   2000.
Free to members

73 THE INDEXER. Journal of the Society of Indexers. 1958.
Society of Indexers, c/o Barclays Bank Ltd., 1 Pall Mall East, London, SW1.
2, = *   Book and periodical indexing.
Book notices, book reviews, letters, monographic articles
2 year, —, No, None.
T.p. 54.
Free to members

74 INFORMATION STORAGE AND RETRIEVAL. Theory and practice. 1963.
Pergamon Press Ltd., Headington Hill Hall, Oxford, OX3 0BW.
6, = +   Advances in theory, technique and practice in information storage and retrieval.
Book reviews, letters, monographic articles.
A, Last issue of volume, Yes, None.
T.p. 67.
Per copy £3, per year £16.

028

BOOK REVIEWS

75 BOOKS. Journal of the National Book League. 1929-1968, 1970.
National Book League, 7 Albemarle Street, London, W1X 4BB.
4, ○ = ‡ +   All aspects of the book world.
No Index.
T.p. 32.
Free to members.
Indexed in: BEI

76 BRITISH BOOK NEWS. 1944.
British Council, 59 New Oxford Street, London, WC1A 1BP.
12, ‡   Review of new books published in Britain: each issue contains about 230 reviews of books on all subjects, annotated lists of forthcoming books and paperbacks, bibliographical articles and publishing news.
Book reviews.
A, —, Yes, None.
June 1972, T.p. 91, Ad.p. 13.   10000.
Per copy 20p, per year £2.40.

77 READING: a journal for the study and improvement of reading and related skills. 1967.
(UKRA Bulletin. 1965/66)
United Kingdom Reading Association, c/o 63 Laurel Grove, Sunderland, Co. Durham SR2 9EE.
3, + *   New developments in reading, including classroom methods and more formal research; reviews/evaluations of new materials and books. Reading and associated skills from infant to adult levels.
Book notices, book reviews, letters, monographic articles.
No, None.
March 1972, T.p. 44.
Per copy 37½p. Free to members.

78 TIMES LITERARY SUPPLEMENT. 1902.
Times Newspapers Ltd, Printing House Square, London, EC4.
52, = ‡ ○ +   Book reviews from all fields. Articles on cultural and academic interest.
Book notices, book reviews, letters, monographic articles.
A, —, No, None.
T.p. 20, Ad.p. 3.
Per copy 12p, per year £3.50.

03

DICTIONARIES

79 GEIRIADUR PRIFYSGOL CYMRU/UNIVERSITY OF WALES DICTIONARY. 1950.
University of Wales Press, Merthyr House, James Street, Cardiff, CF1 6EU, Glam
1   Dictionary issues and up dated in parts.
Parts 1 to 21 Bound in 1 Volume.
37p per Part.   3500.

049

INTERVIEWING

80 ORAL HISTORY: an occasional newsletter. 1970.
Paul Thompson, Department of Sociology, University of Essex, Colchester, Essex.
1/2, +   Techniques of interviewing for historical purposes, reports on research, articles on archives, reviews, conference reports, and list of current research in progress in Britain.
No Index.
Per year £2.

05
GENERAL PERIODICALS

81 AJR INFORMATION. 1946.
Association of Jewish Refugees in Great Britain, 8 Fairfax Mansions, London, NW3 6JY.
12, *   Articles and news on subjects of interest to Jews who came to this country before the war as victims of Nazi persecution.
Book reviews, letters, articles, obituaries, parliamentary reports.
No Index.
July 1972, T.p. 12, Ad.p. 3.   4500.
Per year £3 minimum.

82 AWRE NEWS. 1953.
Atomic Weapons Research Establishment, UKAEA, AWRE, Aldermaston, Reading, RG7 4PR.
12, +   Reports activities at AWRE not covered by security restrictions, recreational societies, and general interest articles.
Articles, obituaries.
No Index.
June 1972, T.p. 20, Ad.p. 20.   6000 app.
Free.

83 AION: Journal of St. Symeon's Fellowship. 1968.
St. Symeon's Fellowship, St. Symeon's House, Oswaldkirk, York, YO6 5YT.
2, ○ * +
Book notices, book reviews, letters, articles, obituaries.
No Index.
December 1971, T.p. 20.   1500
Per copy 10p, per year £1.

84 AMPLEFORTH JOURNAL. 1895.
(Ampleforth Diary, 1890-1894)
Ampleforth Abbey, Ampleforth College, Yorks, YO6 4EN.
3, = *   Varying topics with emphasis on theology.
Book notices, book reviews, letters, articles, obituaries.
No Index.
T.p. 192.
Per copy 50p, per year £1.20.

85 ANNABEL. 1966.
D. C. Thomson Co. Ltd., 80 Kingsway East, Dundee.
12, ○   People and personalities, fashion, knitting, crochet, cookery, beauty, fiction, travel, motoring, crosswords, health, books, home, children, housing, films, sewing, dress-making.
No Index.
July 1972, T.p. 60, Ad.p. 20.
Per copy 12½p, per year £2.60.

86 ANTHOS. 1972.
Whitehall Musical & Dramatic Society, 135 Griffith Avenue, Dublin 9.
4,   Poetry, reviews, stories, articles.
No Index.
Per copy 25p.

87 AQUARIUS: A Religio-Cultural Review. 1971.
(Everyman 1968-1970).
Servite Priory, Benburb, Co. Tyrone, N. Ireland.
1, * ○   Articles, interviews, poetry, poems, mainly on Irish life, literature, arts, social and political and religious (card enclosed with contents list).
No Index.
No. 5 1972, T.p. 140, Ad.p. 11.   7000.
Per copy 35p.

88 THE ARCHER: Works Journal of Robert Fletcher and Son, Ltd. 1920.
Robert Fletcher & Son, Ltd., Kearsley Paper Works, Stoneclough, Radcliffe, Manchester, M26 9EH.
4, †   Internal company topics of interest to employees and pensioners. Items of interest to customers, agents friends of the company.
3 year,—, No, None.
Free.

89 ATOM NEWS. 1962.
UK Atomic Energy Authority, 11 Charles II Street, London, SW1Y 4QP.
12, †   Activities of UK Atomic Energy Authority and associated organisations and their employees; significant events in nuclear energy world-wide.
Book reviews, letters, new companies, new products, obituaries, parliamentary reports, patents.
No Index.
June 1972, T.p. 12.   8000.
Per copy 1p, per year 30p.

90 BA NEWS. 1971.
British Aluminium Co. Ltd., Norfolk House, St. James's Square, London, SW1.
6, †
No Index.
Free.

91 BEA MAGAZINE. 1946.
British European Airways, West London Air Terminal, Cromwell Road, London, S.W.7.
12, ○ ‡ = + †   Colour supplement to the weekly 'BEA News'.
Book notices, book reviews, articles, new products.
No Index.
July 1972, T.p. 20, Ad.p. 4.
Free.

92 BOAC NEWS. 1967.
BOAC, Air Terminal, Victoria, London, SW1.
†   Worldwide activities of BOAC and its staff.
No Index.
May 26, 1972, T.p. 8, Ad.p. Most.   29500.
Free.

93 BARCLAYCARD MAGAZINE. 1971.
Juxon House, 94 St. Paul's Churchyard, London, EC4M 8EH.
6, ○
Book notices, book reviews, letters, articles.
No Index.
September/October 1972, T.p. 20, Ad.p. 20.
Free

94 THE BELMONT STANDARD: the house magazine of Peglers Ltd. 1947.
Peglers Ltd., Belmont Works, St. Catherine's Ave., Doncaster.
4, †   Employees, retired employees, local schools and colleges, local press, agents and selected customers.
Letters, articles, new companies, new products, obituaries, patents, standards, tests.
No Index.
April 1972, T.p. 46, Ad.p. 1.   3750.
Free.

95 BITMAN. 1970.
Bitman, 141 Westbourne Park Road, London, W11 1BQ.
2   Reports on the various activities of BIT Information Service as it develops; prints out some of the more valuable information that flows through the BIT office; and primarily carries information on the growth of alternative structures in this country + occasional reprints of articles from the alternative media of other countries.
Book reviews, legal notes, letters, articles, tests.
No Index.
Subscription on application.

96 BLACK FLAG. 1971.
10 Gilbert Place, London, WC1.
12, ○   Anarchist underground publication.
No Index.
Subscription on application.

97 BLACK VOICE. 1971.
   31 Belgrave Road, London, N16.
   12, ○   Underground paper.
   No Index.
   Subscription on application.

98 BLACKWOOD'S MAGAZINE. 1804.
   William Blackwood & Sons Ltd., 32 Thistle Street, Edinburgh, EH2 1EN
   12, ○ +   Short stories, poems, biography, memoirs, history, literature, military, travel, politics.
   6m, June/December, Yes, None.
   June 1972, T.p. 96, Ad.p. 6,   11500.
   Per copy 25p, per year £3.

99 BLUE RAT. 1971.
   64 Constance Road, Twickenham, Middx.
   12, ○   Underground paper.
   No Index.
   Subscription on application.

100 THE BOOK OF JOB: the house magazine of Job's dairy. 1929.
   H. A. Job Ltd., Raleigh Way, Hanworth, Feltham, Middlesex.
   4, †   Internal, free to all employees and pensioners.
   No Index.
   Spring 1972, T.p. 22   1000+.
   Gratis.

101 BOOTS NEWS. Staff newspaper for all employees of The Boots Co., Ltd.
   Granby PR International Ltd., c/o East Midland Litho Ltd., Peterborough, Northants.
   26, ○
   No Index.
   T.p. 16.
   Free.

102 BOURNVILLE REPORTER. 1969.
   Bournville Works Magazine 1902-69.
   Cadbury Schweppes Ltd., Bournville, Birmingham 30.
   12, †   Local newspaper for factory community covering Company, union, human interest stories.
   No index.
   14500.
   Per copy Gratis.

103 BOWMAKER MAGAZINE. 1962.
   Bowmaker Limited, Bowmaker House, Lansdowne, Bournemouth. BH1 3LG.
   4, †   News and views of the Company's activities for the staff.
   No Index.
   Spring/Summer 1972, T.p. 48.
   Free.

104 BRIG: University of Stirling. 1970.
   Publications Board, University of Stirling.
   12, ○   Items that interest students and general news coverage.
   Book reviews, letters, articles, patents, standards, tests.
   No Index.
   T.p. 8, Ad.p. 1½.   1000.
   Per copy 3p.

105 BRIGHTON FOLK DIARY. 1970.
   c/o Flat 4, 1 Sillwood Place, Brighton, Sussex.
   6, ○   News and views of folk music activity in and around Sussex. Articles of local interest on the subject. Record reviews.
   No Index.
   July/August 1972, T.p. 20, Ad.p. 16.   2500.
   Free.

106 THE BRITANNIC MAGAZINE: The Staff Magazine of Britannic Assurance Co., Ltd. 1930.
   (Onward 1922-29).
   Britannic Assurance Co. Ltd., Moor Green, Birmingham, B13 8QF.
   3, †   To keep the staff informed of social activities and also of the achievements of their colleagues in the business field.
   Letters, articles.
   No Index.
   Spring 1972, T.p. 32.
   Free.

107 BRITISH FLEET NEWS. 1968.
   Shell Tankers (UK) Ltd., Shell Centre, London, SE1 7NA.
   12, †   Activities by and affecting crew members aboard ST(UK) ships.
   No Index.
   February 1972, T.p. 8.
   Free.

108 BROOK '72. 1947.
   Publicity Department, Brook Motors Ltd. (A Hawker-Siddeley Company) Empress Works, Huddersfield, HD1 3LJ.
   12, †   Works newspaper, covering works features, social events, management communications.
   No Index.
   April/May 1972, T.p. 6.   3800.
   Free.

109 CALIBAN. 1962.
   (Diocesan Magazine of William of Wykeham).
   The College, Winchester, Hants.
   2, +   Poetry, short stories, drawings, etc.
   No Index.
   November 1971, T.p. 34, Ad.p. 9.   500.
   Per copy 30p, per year 55p.

110 CAMBRIDGE QUARTERLY. 1964
   H. A. Mason, Newhayes, Huntingdon Road, Cambridge.
   4, +   Essays, literary criticism, poetry, sociology, etc.
   Letters, articles.
   A, Last issue of volume, Yes, None.
   T.p. 108.
   Per copy 40p, per year £2.
   Indexed in: BHI

111 CAMBRIDGE REVIEW: a journal of University life and thought. 1879.
   Barrie and Jenkins Ltd., 2 Clement's Inn, London, WC2.
   6, = +   Current affairs and general interest articles for students.
   A, June, No, None.
   T.p. 25, Ad.p. 7.
   Per copy 10p, per year 75p.

112 CAMDEN JOURNAL. 1965.
   London Borough of Camden (Libraries and Arts Department). St. Pancras Library, 100 Euston Road, London, NW1 2AJ.
   6, ○   Lists of recent additions to stock; matters of literary or local interest.
   No Index.
   April/May 1972, T.p. 16, Ad.p. 2.   5000.
   Free.

113 CANDIDA. 1972.
   IPC Magazines Ltd., Tower House, Southampton Street, London WC2E 9QX.
   52, ○   All purpose woman's journal.
   Book reviews, articles.
   No Index.
   300000.
   Per copy 10p.
   Ceased after going to print.

114 CANNING QUARTERLY NEWS. 1952.
   W. Canning & Company, Limited, Great Hampton Street, Birmingham, B18. 6AS.
   4   Employees of Group and Overseas Agents.
   New products, obituaries.
   No Index.
   T.p. 28.   2200.
   Per copy 1p.

115 CAPE NEWS. 1969.
(Cape Magazine 1952-1969).
Cape Asbestos Company Limited, 114 Park Street, London, W. 1.
6, † Cape Group employees, pensioners, etc.
Book reviews, letters, new companies, new products, obituaries, tests.
No Index.
April/May 1972, T.p. 8p.   11500.
Free.

116 CAPELLA.
Tara Telephone Publications, 30 Thorncliffe Park, Rathgar, Dublin, 14.
3, =
No Index.
Per copy 15p.

117 CARA: The Inflight magazine of Aer Lingus-Irish Airlines. 1968.
Publicity Department, Head Office, Aer Lingus-Irish, Dublin Airport.
4, ○ † For Aer Lingus passengers and dealing mainly with articles on Ireland, places served by the Airline and articles of general interest.
Book reviews, articles.
No Index.
April/June 1972, T.p. 27, Ad.p. 21.
300000.
80p per year and Free to passengers.

118 CARTHUSIAN. 1872.
Langhams Herald Press, Farnham, Surrey.
5, ○ Accounts of school events, news of young people's views on politics and everyday life.
No Index.
T.p. 28, Ad.p. 8.
Per copy 25p, per year £1. 50.

119 CERES.
269a Portobello Road, London, W11.
○ Underground journal.
No Index.
Subscription on application.

120 CHARACTER AND ENERGY. 1971.
David Boadella, Abbotsbury, Dorset.
3, ○
None.
Per year £2.

121 CHARRILOCK. 1923.
Charrington, Gardner, Locket & Co., Ltd., Tower House, 40 Trinity Square, London, EC3P 3AA.
4, † Business and social news relating to the employees' operations and installations of the Charringtons Group of Companies which is scattered from Glasgow to Kent and from the Midlands to East Anglia. Anything to do with the various trades carried out by the several divisions of the Charringtons Group of Companies.
No Index.
Spring 1972, T.p. 3.   4800.
Free.

122 CHILDREN'S RIGHTS. 1971.
Children's Rights Publications Ltd., 24 Manor View, London, N3.
○
No Index.
Per copy 18p.

123 CIRCUIT MAGAZINE. 1965.
Editorial Board, 8 Chelmsford Square, London.
3, = ○ Art, Sociology, Politics, Theatre, Literature, etc.
Book reviews, articles.
No Index.
T.p. 42, Ad.p. 6.   5000.
Per copy 15p, per year 55p.

124 THE CIRCULATOR. 1927.
Babcock & Wilcox Ltd., Cleveland House, St. James's Square, London, SW1Y 4LN.
4, † Company product news, application stories, interest articles and company and subsidiary sports and social activities.
No Index.
Christmas 1971, T.p. 36.   15000.
Free.

125 CLARE MARKET REVIEW. 1906.
The London School of Economics and Political Science (University of London), St. Clements Building, Clare Market, London, WC 2A 2AE.
2, ○ Best of contemporary poetry and fiction, whether in the original or in translation, as well as relevant and topical economic and international political comment.
Book notices, book reviews, monographic articles.
No Index.
May 1971, T.p. 130, Ad.p. 3.   1000.
Per copy 50p, £2 for four issues.

126 THE COMMON CRIER: the house magazine of the Common Brothers Group. 1953.
Common Brothers Ltd., Exchange Bldgs, Quayside, Newcastle upon Tyne, NE1 3AB.
4, = † To seafarers employed by the Company and also to their families. Also to firms with whom we do business and the Company's shore-based staff.
Obituaries.
No Index.
No. 72, T.p. 47, Ad.p. 6.
Free.

127 CONTACT. 1968.
Avon Cosmetics Ltd., Nunn Mills Road, Northampton.
17, + News about the company—progress, plans and activities—and its employees.
Articles, letters, new products, standards.
No Index.
June 9, 1972, T.p. 8.   3000.
Free.

128 CONTEMPORARY COMMUNICATIONS: the journal of the Communications Guild. 1972.
Communications Guild Ltd., 21 Highfield Avenue, St. Austell, Cornwall.
2, = Science of communication in all areas.
Monographic articles.
No Index.
September 1972, T.p. 38, Ad.p. 2.
Per year 45p.
Free to members.

129 CONTEMPORARY REVIEW: Incorporating The Fortnightly. 1866.
Contemporary Review Co. Ltd., 37 Union Street, London, S. E. 1.
12, + ○ History, literature, the arts, religion, politics, philosophy, theology, book reviews including quarterly review of current fiction. Poetry and short stories are occasionally published.
Book notices, book reviews, legal notes, letters, articles.
6 — Yes, None.
June 1972, T.p. 55.
Per copy 30p, per year £4. 02.
Indexed in: BHI, IBZ.

130 COSMOPOLITAN. 1972.
National Magazine Co. Ltd., 680 Garrett Lane, London, SW17

Key to reference symbols

○ popular   ‡ technical   = trade/professional

+ research   * society/institution   † house journal

12, ○   Fiction, fashion beauty, domestic subjects.
Book reviews.
No Index.
June 1972, T.p. 81, Ad.p. 59.   250000.
Per copy 20p, per year £3.60.

131 THE COTTSMAN. 1916.
The Mitchell Cotts Group Ltd., Cotts House, Camomile
   St., London, EC3P 3AJ.
2/3, ○ = †   Group employees world wide and
   ex-employees. Clients and Prospects world wide.
Articles, new companies, new products, obituaries,
   tests.
No Index.
June 1972, T.p. 36.   6000.
Free.

132 COUNTERTALK. 1969.
The Royal Bank of Scotland Ltd., Staff Magazine
   Committee, 42 St. Andrew Sq., Edinburgh, EH2 2YE.
4, †   Royal bank staff + pensioners + subscribers +
   complimentaries mainly to other banks in Britain
   and overseas.
Letters, articles, obituaries, standards.
No Index.
Summer 1972, T.p. 37, Ad.p. 11.   4500.
Per copy 10p, per year 40p.

133 CROSSLINK: Quarterly newspaper of Bakelite Xylonite
   Ltd. 1971.
Bakelite Xylonite Limited, Enford House, 139
   Marylebone Road, London, NW1 5QE
4, †
Articles, new products, obituaries.
Spring 1972, T.p. 8
Free.

134 CUNARD TRAFALGAR. 1971
Pearl & Dean Ltd., 33 Dover Street, London W1X 4AJ.
†
No Index.
Free.

135 CURRENT. 1968.
Mary Glasgow Publications Ltd., 140 Kensington
   Church Street, London, W8
9, ○   Interest magazine for teenagers.
Book reviews, articles.
No Index.
No. 9, 1971, T.p. 16.
Per year 65p.

136 THE DARK HORSE: Lloyds Bank Staff Magazine. 1919.
Lloyds Bank, Elizabeth House, 9-11 Bush Lane, London,
   EC4R OAR
12, †
Book reviews, letters, articles, new products.
No Index.
February 1972, T.p. 43, Ad.p. 20.   17200
Per copy 5p, per year 60p.

137 David Brown TRACTOR NEWS (Publication suspended).
   1955.
David Brown Tractors Ltd., Meltham, Huddersfield
   HD7 3AR.
6, †
Activities of the company.
No Index.
T.p. 8.   50000.
Free.

138 DICKINSON NEWS. 1937.
John Dickinson & Co. Ltd., (part of Dickinson Robinson
   Group Ltd.), Apsley, Hemel Hempstead, Herts.
2, †   Company news, employee interests, retirement
   biographies, etc.
No Index.
T.p. 20.   12000
Free.

139 DOE WORLD. 1971.
(Works World 1968-1971).
Department of the Environment, 2 Marsham, Street,
   London, SW1P 3EB.
12, ‡ ○ †   Communication journal for staff of
   c. 70,000 world wide.
Letters, articles, new products, obituaries, standards,
   tests.
No Index.
July 1972, T.p. 16.   c. 15000.
Per copy 3p.

140 DOOMLORE. 1971.
Steve Moore, 7 Hilend, Shooters Hill, London, SE18 3NH.
Ireg, ○
Fantasy.
No Index.
No. 1, 1971, T.p. 20.   200.
Per copy 10p.

141 DRAWDOWN: The House Magazine of Coates Brothers
   and Company Limited. 1951
(CB Magazine 1946-1951)
Coates Group of Companies, Easton Street, London
   WC1X 0DP.
1, †   News of Coates Brothers and Company Limited
   and Coates associated companies.
No Index.
1971, T.P. 36.   4000.
Free.

142 DREAMER (New series). 1972.
(Dreamer, 1970-1971).
Brian Mills, 3 Ilford Road, High West Jesmond,
   Newcastle-upon-Tyne 3.
4, ○   Pictorial Collage.
No Index.
Per copy 10p. per year £1.25.

143 DURHAM UNIVERSITY JOURNAL. 1876
The University of Durham, Old Shire Hall, Durham,
   DH1 3HP.
3, = +   Aims, to keep open the frontiers between
   subjects and to provide a forum for the discussion
   of ideas. The main emphasis is on literature,
   history, philosophy and theology, but articles on
   science, sociology and political thought are also
   included. Ample space is given to specialist
   reviews of books which cover a wide range of
   topics.
Book reviews, letters, monographic articles.
A, December, Yes, None.
March 1972, T.p. 109, Ad.p. 2.
Per copy 20p, per year 60p.
Indexed in: BHI, IBZ.

144 EMGAS. 1951.
East Midlands Gas Board, di Montfort Street,
   Leicester, LE1 9DB
4, †   News, features relating to Board's activities,
   also employee news and features.
No Index.
Spring 1972, T.p. 36.   13000.
Free to employees and pensioners.

145 EAST KENT OMNIBUS. 1947.
East Kent Road Car Co. Ltd., Station Road West,
   Canterbury, Kent.
4, †
No Index.
March/April 1971, T.p. 24.
Free.

146 ECHOING TIMES. 1957.
(Echograms, 1925-1938).
Southern Newspapers Ltd., Southampton, 45 Above Bar,
   Southampton.

4, † For distribution to all members of the staff and pensioners of Southern Newspapers Ltd., Southernprint Ltd. and W. H. Hallett Ltd. Covers developments within the group, social, sporting and personal stories of members of the staffs.
No Index.
Spring, 1972. T.p. 36. 1570.
Free.

147 EDINBURGH GAZETTE. 1699.
H.M. Exchequer, 102 George Street, Edinburgh 2.
104, State intelligence, public and legal notices.
A, —, Yes, None.
T.p. 8.
Per year £7.

148 ELIZABETHAN. 1947.
(Young Elizabethan 1947).
6 Lansdown, Stroud Glos.
12, ○ A literary magazine aimed to interest, inform and amuse children 12-17.
Articles of current interest and short stores.
No Index.
May 1972, T.p. 28.
Per copy 20p, per year £2.40.

149 ENCOUNTER. 1953.
Encounter Ltd., 25 Haymarket, London, SW1.
12, = ○ Current affairs review.
Book notices, book reviews, letters, articles.
6, January/July, No, None.
T.p. 96, Ad.p. 11. 26500.
Per copy 40p, per year £4.50.
Indexed in BHI.

150 ENSIGN: House Journal of NI Group Ltd. 1965.
(Entaco News 1939-1965)
Needle Industries Stationery Office, Studley, Warwickshire.
11, ○ † To Employees generally throughout organisation ie Studley Group-Redditch-Port Glasgow-India. Complimentary copies to Shareholders-pensioners Local Press and Local Government offices ie Ministry of Labour etc.
Letters, articles, new companies, new products, obituaries.
No Index.
May 1972, T.p. 32.
Free.

151 ETONIANA. 1904-1955, 1965.
Alden & Blackwell (Eton) Ltd., Eton College, Windsor SL4 6DF.
2, + * History, biographies, bibliographies of Eton College & Etonians; incl. reprints of relevant letters and MSS in private possession as well as original research articles.
MS one to 1955.
c. 120.
Per year 60p.

152 EXPORT NEWS. 1952.
Unilever Export Limited, Lever House, Port Sunlight, Wirral, Cheshire.
3, † ○ News and comment—largely personal—on home and overseas members of publishing company. Overseas pictures featured.
Letters, articles, new companies, new products, obituaries.
No Index.
June 1972, T.p. 24.
Free.

153 EXPRESSION: The House Journal of the William Press Group of Companies.
The William Press Group of Companies, Publicity Department, 22 Queen Anne's Gate, London, SW1.
4, ○, ‡ = † Major projects, developments and activities of the Group companies plus social news.
No Index.
T.p. 32. 5000
Free.

154 FABULOUS 208. 1964.
I.P.C. Magazines Ltd., Tower House, Southampton Street, London, WC2E 9QX.
52, ○ Pop/fashion/beauty/fiction Pin-ups. Features of young female interest eg dressmaking personal problems. Music reviews, personalities-pop/film/football.
Letters, articles.
No Index.
T.p. 32, Ad.p. 6. 208438.
Per copy 6p, per year £4.25.

155 FASTENER NEWS: The newspaper for the GKN Screws and Fasteners Sub-Group. 1972
(Nettlefolds News 1952-1971)
G.K.N. Screws & Fasteners Limited, Smethwick, Warley, Worcestershire.
4, † News about the various member companies in the Sub-Group. Also articles and contributions.
Letters, articles, new companies, new products, obituaries, patents, standards, tests.
No Index.
Spring, 1972, T.p. 12.
Free.

156 FLAMBEAU. 1963.
W.P.R. Ltd. (for Gas Council), Rex House, Hampton Road West, Hanworth, Middx.
4, ○ =
No Index.
Free.

157 FREE FORM. 1972.
(Informer.)
Circle Books, 16 Davenant Road, Oxford OX2 8BX.
Irreg. ‡ = ○ Reviews, small press/mags, lists. advertisements.
Book notices, book reviews, letters, notes new products, standards, tests.
No Index.
Ad.p. 3. 1200.
Free.

158 THE FREEMAN. 1908.
Guild of Freemen of the City of London, 4 Dowgate Hill, London EC4.
1, * Freemen of the City of London.
No Index.
3000.
Free.

159 FRENDZ. 1971.
(Friends 1969-1971).
Echidna Epics Co. Ltd., 307 Portobello Road, London, W10.
26, ○ Alternative life-style in all its varied aspects. As well as news, reviews etc, music, books, films, the activities of radical political and social groups, drugs, comics etc also covered.
Book notices, book reviews, letters, articles, new products, obituaries, parliamentary reports.
No Index.
23 June 1972, T.p. 18, Ad.p. 3. 20000.
Per copy 15p, per year £3.25.

160 FULCRUM: Journal of the Oxford Society for Social Responsibility in Science. 1972.
Oxford Society for Social Responsibility in Science, 27 Wytham Street, Oxford.
4/6, ○ ‡ * Social effects of science and technology; uses and abuses of science; social, political and economic factons involved. Factual articles, analysis, and opinion.
Book notices, book reviews, letters, articles, standards, tests.

No Index.
May 1972, T.p. 20.   2000.
Per copy 7p and Free to members.

161 GIRL ABOUT TOWN. 1972.
Girl About Town Company, 47 Victoria Street, London, SW1.
26, =   Secretarial advertising medium.
No Index.
8 August 1972, T.p. 14, Ad.p. 14.
Free.

162 GIROSCOPE. 1970.
Leyden Pulishing Co. Ltd., Sheraton House, 14 Great Chapel Street, London, W1.
4, ○   Magazine of GPO Giro.
No Index.
Free.

163 GLOBAL TAPESTRY JOURNAL & VEGAN ACTION. 1969.
BB Bks, 1 Spring Bank, Salesbury, Blackburn, Lancs, BB1 9EU.
3, ○   Alternative Society. Creative Living. Ecology. Veganism. Non-Violent revolution. Poetry and prose. Methods of change or alteration of human consciousness (yoga, tantra, organic and chemical enstatics, meditation, diet, deep rhythmic breathing).
Book notices, book reviews, legal notes, letters, articles.
No Index.
Per copy 25p, per year £1.

164 GONGSTER. 1939.
Nottingham University Students' Union, Portland Building, Nottingham.
13, *   Covers new/opinions concerned with Nottingham University Students' Union
Letters.
No Index.
March 6, 1972, T.p. 12, Ad.p. 1.   2000.
Per copy 4p, per year £1.

165 GOODWILL. 1946.
Rubery Owen Holdings Ltd., Darlaston, PO Box 10, Wednesbury, Staffordshire, WS10 8JD.
2, †   Means of communication to keep customers, suppliers, Embassies, Overseas companies etc. up to date with company progress.
No Index.
February 1972, T.p. 24.   8000
Per copy 10p.

166 GRANTA. 1889.
21A Silver Street, Cambridge.
3, ○   Cultural and intellectual—covers ground of interest to students which is overlooked in the national press.
Book reviews, articles, reports.
No Index.
Easter, 1972, T.p. 33, Ad.p. 5.   1500.
Per copy 20p, per year 60p.

167 HARLEQUIN: Leisure Magazine of Harwell and associated Atomic Research Organisations. 1948.
AERE Harwell, Didcot, Berks.
12, †
Articles.
No Index.
June, 1972, T.p. 8, Ad.p. 8.
Per copy 3p.

168 H. R. OWEN, LTD., REPORTS.
H. R. Owen, Ltd., 17 Berkeley Street, London, W1.
4, †   News and Comment for the Staff.
Articles.
No Index.
Spring, 1972. T.p. 16.
Free.

169 HARPERS BAZAAR AND QUEEN. 1970.
(Harpers Bazaar. 1929; The Queen 1861).
National Magazine Co. Ltd., 680 Garratt Lane, London, SW17 0NP.
12, ○   Fashion, Beauty, Art, Theatre, Films, Decoration, Travel, Cookery.
No Index.
June 1972, T.p. 75, Ad.p. 57.   860919.
Per copy 30p, per year £4.25.

170 HERS. 1966.
IPC Magazines Ltd., Tower House, Southampton Street, London, W.C.2.
12, ○   True life story magazine for young women.
No Index.
Per copy 10p.

171 HIBERNIA: Fortnightly Review. 1968.
(Hibernia, the Nation's Review, 1936-1968).
Hibernia National Review Ltd., 179 Pearse Street, Dublin 2.
24, ○   Independent review of Irish current affairs: politics, economics, finance; literature, theatre, music, cinema and the visual arts; Spring and Autumn book supplements, and Irish political directory (annually, January).
Book notices, book reviews, letters, articles.
No Index.
23-6-1972, T.p. 28, Ad.p. Most.   c. 14000.
Per copy 10p, per year £2.50.

172 HONEY. 1960.
IPC Magazines Ltd., Tower House, Southampton Street, London, W.C.2.
12, ○   Fashion magazine aimed at girls in late teens and early twenties.
Book notices, book reviews, letters, articles.
No Index.
T.p. 57, Ad.p. 99.
Per copy 15p.

173 HOOVER NEWS. 1948.
Hoover Limited, Perivale, Greenford, Middlesex.
6, †   For the information and amusement of employees. Facts about the company, its performance, its plans for the future. Employee conditions, pay and benefits.
No Index.
January/February 1972, T.p. 12, Ad.p. Most.   13500
Free.

174 HOTEL.
Guest Publications Ltd., (for Strand Hotels Group), 318 Earls Court Road, London, SW5.
4, †   For the information of guests staying with the Strand Hotels Group.
No Index.
Summer 1972, T.p. 42, Ad.p. Most.
Free.

175 HOTLINE. 1969.
British Road Services Limited, Northway House, High Road, London, N20 9ND.
10, †   Internal news only.
No Index.
Free.

176 THE HUMAN WORLD: A quarterly review of English letters. 1970.
Brynmill Publishing Co. Ltd., 130 Bryn Rd., Brynmill, Swansea, SA2 0AT.
4, ○   Literary criticism, philosophy, linguistics, political commentary and criticism, fiction and poetry, theology, wide-ranging reviews, moral questions, history.
Book reviews, letters, monographic articles.
No Index.
May 1972, T.p. 94, Ad.p. 4.
Per copy 50p, per year £1.50.

177 HUNTING FLEET MAGAZINE. 1954.
(Hunting Fleet Newsletter, 1951-1954).
Hunting & Son Ltd., P.O. Box I.T.A., Milburn House,
   Newcastle-upon-Tyne, NE99 1TA.
4, ‡ =   Internal staff magazine, prime object for
   seagoing personnel, to give news of colleagues,
   vessels and group companies, thereby fostering a
   closer ship/shore relationship.
No Index.
December 1971, T.p. 20, Ad.p. 500.
Free.

178 HYDDGEN. 1972.
Gwasg Gwenffrwd, Talwrn Glas, Afonwen, Caerwys,
   Flintshire, CH7 5UB.
1, ○ + *   Cultural, political, historical, and socio-
   logical topics of Welsh and international relevance
   (Bi-lingual).
Book notices, book reviews, letters, monographic
   articles, obituaries.
5 year, —, No, None.
Per copy £1 per year.

179 THE IDLER: An Entertainment. 1968.
The Old Crown, Wheatley, Oxford.
4, ○   Uses extracts from medieval to modern writing
   to show the continuity of human experience; illu-
   strations by Albrecht Durer to modern illustrators
   (Ardizzonne) for this aim. Promotes the essay.
   Serious intention but not solemn.
Letters, articles.
No Index.
Vol. I, No. 4, T.p. 8.   2500.
Per copy $12\frac{1}{2}$p, per year 50p.

180 ILLUSTRATED LONDON NEWS. 1842.
Illustrated London News and Sketch Ltd., 10 Elm
   Street, London, WC1.
52, ○   World affairs, science and theatre.
Book reviews, legal notes, letters, articles, obituaries,
   parliamentary reports.
6m, June/December, No, None.
T.p. 33, Ad.p. 5.   59000.
Per copy 20p, per year £8.

181 IMAGES. 1972.
Dept. of Communication Studies, Polytechnic of Central
   London, Regent Street, London W1.
4, ○   Communications media.
No Index.
Summer 1972, T.p. 12.
Free.

182 IN PRINT: Journal of the Swindon public libraries,
   museums and art gallery.
Public Library, Swindon, Wilts.
12, ○   General information concerning accessions
to, and activities organised by, the Swindon libraries,
   etc.
No Index.
July 1972, T.p. 6.
Free.

183 THE IRISH POST: The weekly newspapers of the Irish
   in Britain. 1970.
Irish Post Ltd., 2/4 The Broadway, Southall, Middlesex.
52, ○   News, sport, comment and reviews for the Irish
   in Britain.
None.
June 24, 1972, T.p. 20, Ad.p. Most.
Per copy 5p.

184 ISIS. The Oxford University Magazine. 1892.
Pergamon Press Ltd., Headington Hill Hall, Oxford
   OX3 0BW.
24, ○   Current political and artistic issues on the
   university and natural scene.
Book reviews, letters, articles.
None.
T.p. 24, Ad.p. 1.
Per copy 5p.

185 JAMAICAN WEEKLY GLEANER. 1964.
The Gleaner Company Ltd., London Office:
   122 Shaftesbury Avenue, London, W1V 8HA.
52, ○   West Indian immigrants resident in the United
   Kingdom.
Letters, articles, news, obituaries, parliamentary
   reports.
None.
June 14, 1972, T.p. 40, Ad.p. Most.   27000.
Per copy 4p.

186 JOURNAL AND GRAPHIC REVIEW. 1970.
National Society of Operative Printers Graphical and
   Media Personnel, 13-16 Borough Road, London,
   SE1 0AL.
12, = †   Printing trade interest; members' activities;
   correspondence; book reviews; official union notices;
   topical items of interest from politics to gardening.
None.
June 1972, T.p. 16.   23000.
Subscription per copy: 3p; 72p per year.

187 JOURNAL OF THE WILLIAM MORRIS SOCIETY.
William Morris Society, 25 Lawn Crescent, Kew,
   Surrey.
4, ○
None.
Free to members.

188 KWA NEWS. 1966.
(K-W-A News Magazine)
Kalamazoo Ltd., Mill Lane, Northfield, Birmingham,
   B31 2RW.
6, †   All employees, retired employees, overseas
   distributors etc, to communicate information about
   the organisation, new products, changes, activities of
   employees.
Letters, new products, obituaries.
None.
May 1972, T.p. 8.
Free.

189 KRAFTSMAN. 1957.
Kraft Foods Limited, Regina House, 259/269 Old
   Marylebone Road, London, NW1 5RB.
6, †   Activities of Kraft marketing, production and
   managerial staff.
Letters, new products, obituaries.
None.
July 1971, T.p. 16.   4500.
Free.

190 LAMBETH LOCAL. 1972.
London Borough of Lambeth Town Hall, Brixton Hill,
   SW2 1RW.
4   Lambeth Council and its activities reflecting con-
   troversy in Lambeth and posing local problems as
   well as offering solutions.
None.
Spring 1972, T.p. 8.   120000.
Free.

191 LEEDS LOCAL.
10 Burkett Terrace, Leeds, 6.
13-26, ○   News of Community progress in Leeds.
None.
Subscription on application.

192 LEEDS STUDENT. 1970.
(Union News 1946-1970)
Leeds University Union and Leeds Polytechnic Union
155 Woodhouse Lane, Leeds, 2.
c. 22, † ○   News, features, reviews of interest to the
   students of Leeds.
Book reviews, letters, articles, obituaries.
None.
May 5, 1972, T.p. 12.   3500.
Per copy $2\frac{1}{2}$p, per year £1.75.

193 LENSBURY CLUB NEWS. 1948.
Lensbury Club, Shell Centre, London, SE1 7NA.

12, † Activities by and affecting members of Lensbury Club, the sports and social club of the Shell Group of companies in London.
None.
June 1972, T.p. 8.
Free.

194 LIBRARY BULLETIN. 1971.
(Index to Periodical Articles; Classified Accessions List)
Headquarters Library, Department of the Environment, 2 Marsham Street, London, SW1P 3EB.
24, ‡ + Current awareness service covering all aspects of the environment except construction.
Abstracts, book notices, new products, standards, tests.
A, Towards end of year <u>after</u> the last issue to which it refers, No, None.
1 June 1972, T.p. 72. c. 1800.
Per copy 50p, per year £9.

195 LISTENER. 1929.
BBC Publications, 35 Marylebone High Street, London W1.
52, = + Reproduction of broadcast talks, reviews and surveys of radio and TV.
6m, July/January, Yes, None.
T.p. 32, Ad.p. 4. 68000.
Per copy 10p, per year £5.
Indexed in: BHI, IBZ

196 LLÊN CYMRU. 1950.
University of Wales Press, Merthyr House, James Street, Cardiff, CF1 6EU, Glam.
1 double issue, +
Abstracts, book notices, book reviews, monographic articles, obituaries.
4 years, —, No, None.
800.
Per copy 50p per double issue.

197 LLYFRAU NEWYDD/NEW BOOKS. 1970.
Gwasg Gwenffrwd, Talwrn Glas, Afonwen, Caerwys, Flintshire, CH7 5UB.
6, ○ + Book reviews, notes and critical review articles (Bi-lingual).
Book notices, book reviews, monographic articles.
5 year — No, None.
Per copy £1, per year £6.
Private circulation.

198 LONDON GAZETTE. 1665.
(Oxford Gazette 1665)
H.M. Stationery Office, 1st Avenue House, High Holborn, London, WC1V 6HB.
250/300, ○ ‡ = Medium through which government departments, local authorities and individuals place notices that are required by statute.
Q, 6 mths after the end of quarter, No, None.
28.6.72, T.p. 90. 2000.
Per copy 10p, per year £23.87.

199 LONDON MAGAZINE. 1954.
30 Thurloe Place, London, SW7.
6, ○ Magazine of the arts, literature, short stories, poetry, criticism, cinema, theatre, art, architecture, memoirs.
Book reviews, letters.
A, June/July, No, None.
June/July 1972, T.p. 170, Ad.p. 5.
Per copy 90p, per year £5.
Indexed in: BHI

200 LONDON SHELL. 1950.
Shell International Petroleum Co., Shell Centre, London, SE1 7NA.
17, † All activities by and affecting SIPCo London Office Staff.
No Index.
June 2, 1971, T.p. 8.
Free.

201 LONDON WEEKLY DIARY OF SOCIAL EVENTS. 1921.
London Diary Publications Ltd., 39 Hertford Street, London, W1Y 8HR.
52, = ○ Events in London; theatre, cinema and restaurant reviews; items of interest to visitors to London.
21-5-72, T.p. 38, Ad.p. 9.
Quantity subscriptions—5p per copy
Single subscriptions—11p per copy.

202 LOOK NOW. 1972.
I.P.C. Magazines Ltd., Tower House, Southampton Street, London, WC2E 9QX.
12, ○ Fashion, beauty, fiction, features—young feminine interest inc. music, dressmaking, rooms, crafts, competitions and offers.
Letters, articles.
No Index.
T.p. 32, Ad.p. 76.
Per copy 15p, per year £2.70.

203 LOVE AFFAIR. 1971.
IPC Magazines Ltd., Tower House, Southampton Street, London, WC2.
52, ○ True life story magazine aimed at middle teens to twenties girls.
No Index.
Per copy 15p.

204 LOVING. 1970.
IPC Magazines Ltd., Tower House, Southampton Street, London, WC2.
52, ○ True life story weekly magazine aimed at mid teenage girls.
No Index.
Per copy 10p.

205 LUCAS REFLECTIONS. 1929.
Joseph Lucas Limited, Reflections Office, J.2., Joseph Lucas Limited, Great King Street, Birmingham, B19 2XF.
6, † 'Link' publication between the Company, employees and pensioners.
Letters, articles, new companies, new products, obituaries, patents, standards, tests.
2 year, —, Yes, None.
20000.
Free

206 LYONS MAIL. J. Lyons club magazine. 1911.
J. Lyons & Company Ltd., Cadby Hall, London, W14 OPA.
12, † Circulated only to staff of J. Lyons Group of companies and pensioners—food factories, hotels, restaurants, laundries, car selling and maintenance, etc in British Isles and abroad.
No Index.
July 1972, T.p. 11, Ad.p. 2. 35000.
Free.

207 M.E.B. NEWS. 1966.
(Midlands Electricity News 1964-1966)
Press Services, 184 Corporation St., Birmingham, 4.
12, † News and features of interest to the staff of the Midlands Electricity Board.
Book reviews, letters, monographic articles, new products, obituaries, parliamentary reports, tests.
No Index.
Free.

208 MABON. 1969.
Cymdeithas y Celfyddydau yng Ngogledd Cymru (North-Wales Association for the Arts), 9-11 Wellfield House, Bangor, Sir Gaernarfon, North Wales.
2, ○ Short stories, poems, articles on various topics including literature in general and the arts. Works by school pupils and students are published alongside well established authors.
Book notices, book reviews.
No Index.
Spring 1972, T.p. 50, Ad. p. 1. 1400.
Per copy 20p, per year 40p.

209 MAC MATTERS. 1920.
Mac Fisheries Ltd., Ocean House, Bracknell, Berks.
12, †   Company events, developments and news of general interest to staff.
No Index.
December 1971, T.p. 4.
Free.

210 MACE FORUM. 1971.
(Mace Bulletin)
Mace Marketing Services, 113 Upper Richmond Road, London, SW15 2TL.
25, †   Mace retailers, to Mace wholesalers and other officials in the Mace marketing organisation.
Commodity prices, letters, new products, obituaries, standards, tests.
No Index.
27 May 1972, T.p. 8.   5000.
Free.

211 MAYFAIR incorporating King. 1966.
Fisk Publishing Co. Ltd., 95A Chancery Lane, London, WC2.
○
Book reviews, letters, articles.
No Index.
240000.
Per year £3.60.

212 MERCURY: Staff newspaper of the Cable and Wireless Group of Companies. 1972.
(The Zodiac 1906-1972)
The Zodiac Publishing Co. Ltd., (associated with Cable and Wireless Ltd.), Mercury House, Theobalds Road, London, WC1X 8RX.
12, + ○ ‡ =   Worldwide News, features about, by staff of Cable and Wireless and telecommunication organisations generally.
Book reviews, letters, obituaries.
No Index.
No. 1, T.p. 8.   10000.
Free.

213 MIDBANK CHRONICLE: The Midland Bank Staff Magazine. 1951.
(The Midland Venture. 1920-1951)
Midland Bank Ltd., Bucklersbury House, (1st Floor), 83 Cannon St., London, EC4N 8DS.
12, †   Active and retired staff of the Midland Bank Group.
Book reviews, letters, articles, obituaries.
No Index.
June 1972, T.p. 40, Ad.p. 11.   15766
Per year £1.

214 MINUS ONE. 1963.
S. E. Parker, 2 Orsett Terrace, London, W2 6AH.
2, ○   Concerned with exposition of the philosophy of anarchist individualism, particularly as based on conscious egoism.
Book notices, book reviews, letters, articles, obituaries.
No Index.
Subscription on application.

215 MIRABELLE. c1967.
IPC Magazines Ltd., Tower House, Southampton Street, London, WC2.
52, ○   Picture story magazine for early teenage girls.
No Index.
Per copy 10p.

216 MODERN LIVING: Customer relations magazine of the North Thames Gas Board. 1939.
North Thames Gas Board, 30 Kensington Church Street, London, W8 4HB.
4, ○   Gas in domestic use, fashion, beauty, cookery, children, the home, personality interviews, competitions.
No Index.
Winter 1971, T.p. 14, Ad.p. 2.   c. 100000.
Free, Controlled circulation

217 MOLE EXPRESS
19 New Brown Street, Manchester, 4.
13, ○
No Index.
Per copy 12½p.

218 MONDAY SCOT. 1972.
G. Warner, Monday Club of Scotland, 59 Ravelston Road, Bearsden, Glasgow.
4, ○
No Index.
Per copy 5p.

219 MORGANS WORLD. 1969.
(Morgans Magazine)
The Morgan Crucible Company Limited, 98 Petty France, London, SW1H 9EG.
1, †   Product and market development of Morgan companies.
Articles, new companies, new products, obituaries, standards, tests.
A, −, Yes, None.
T.p. 24.   20000.
Free.

220 MYSL POLSKA (Polish Thought). 1941.
A. Dargas, 8 Alma Terrace, London, W8.
23, = +   Political and cultural life of Poland and world affairs.
Book notices, book reviews, letters, articles, obituaries, parliamentary reports.
No Index.
T.p. 4.   1200
Per copy 10p, per year £2.40.

221 NAAFI NEWS. 1945.
Naafi, Public Relations Dept., London, SE11 5QX.
12, †   Communications journal.
May 1972, T.p. 20.   10000.
Free.

222 NC NEWS. 1971.
(Thorncliffe News, 1940-1970)
Newton Chambers Group, Chapeltown, Sheffield, S30 4YP.
12, †   News, views and comment on the activities, products and people in the Newton Chambers Group.
No Index.
May 1972, T.p. 4.   3250.
Per copy ½p.

223 NCR POST. 1946.
The National Cash Register Co. Ltd., 206/216 Marylebone Road, London, N.W.1.
11, †   News for employees
No Index.
June 1972, T.p. 4.   10000.
Free.

224 NORWEB NEWS. 1971.
North Western Electricity Board, Cheetwood Road, Manchester.
12, †
Book reviews, letters, new products, obituaries, parliamentary reports, standards, tests.
No Index.
June 1972, T.p. 8.
Free.

225 NU NORWICH NEWSLETTER. 1970.
(NU Newsletter 1964-1970).
Norwich Union Insurance Group, Surrey Street, Norwich, NOR 88A.
12, †   Sports and social activities at the Group's Head Office, Norwich.
Letters, articles.

No Index.
June 1972, T.p.12.   2500.
Free to Norwich Union Norwich staff only.

226 NAŠA REČ (Our Word). 1948.
Union Oslobodjenje (Liberation), 53 Hawthorn Drive, Harrow, Middlesex, HA 2 7NU.
10, + ○   Political, literary, informative of current political and cultural events in Yugoslavia.
Book notices, book reviews, letters, articles.
No Index.
November 1972, T.p.16.   1843.
Per copy 10p, per year £1.

227 NESTLÉ GROUP NEWS, 1965.
The Nestlé Company Ltd., St George's House, Park Lane, Croydon, Surrey, CR9 1NR.
6, †   Mainly concerned with activities of employees of Nestlé's and associated companies, plus a certain amount of information on company activities and organisation in the UK.
New products, obituaries.
No Index.
March, 1972, T.p.12.   c.12000.
Free.

228 THE NEW ADVANCE. 1947.
Woolwich Equitable Building Society, Equitable House, Woolwich, London, SE18 6AB.
4, †   Staff, Business connections, etc.
Articles, obituaries, parliamentary reports, standards, tests, news.
No Index.
Spring 1972, T.p.32.   5500.
Free.

229 NEW DIRECTION: The magazine of the sexual revolution. 1971.
Gold Star Publications Ltd., Gadoline House, Godstone Road, Whyteleafe, Surrey.
12, ○   Human relationships, adult sex.
Letters, articles.
No Index.
Vol.1, No.9, T.p.62, Ad.p.6.   75000.
Per copy 40p, per year £4.

230 NEW EDINBURGH REVIEW. 1969.
Edinburgh University Student Publications Board, 1 Buccleuch Place, Edinburgh, EH8 8LW.
6, ○   Articles on Literary, Political, Social, Arts topics. Now covers one theme in each issue e.g. Ireland, Science, Women, Law.
Book reviews, articles.
No Index.
April 1972, T.p.36, Ad.p.2.   800.
Per copy 15p, per year 75p.

231 NEW EPOCH—Ruskin College Magazine. 1948.
Ruskin College Students' Association, Ruskin College, Oxford.
1, + * ○   General Student experiences.
Book reviews, notes, letters, articles.
No Index.
T.p.32, Ad.p.6.   2000.
Per copy 10p.

232 NEW WINDOW. 1948.
Department of Health and Social Security, Editorial Office, Room 010, State House, High Holborn, London, WC1R 4SX.
12, † =   News, pictures and articles by members of the staff on personal interests and hobbies, features about the Department's work, news on staff and Civil Service in general.
Letters.
No Index.
June 1972, T.p.20, Ad.p.5.   20000.
Per copy 3p, per year 36p.

233 NEWS AND VIEWS. 1960.
Post Office London Telephones, Camelford House, Albert Embankment, London, SE1 7TS.
4, †   Information about the achievements and policies of London Telephones and news about the people employed therein. Readers' letters and ready reference to who's who in the organization, plus articles of interest about the London scene.
Book reviews, commodity prices, letters, articles, new products.
No Index.
T.p.28.   c.60000.
Free.

234 19. 1968.
IPC Magazines Ltd., Tower House, Southampton Street, W.C.2.
12, ○   Fashion, beauty, social features, personalities, problem features i.e. medical, legal and sexual problems, careers, travel, entertainment, reviews, competitions, offers, home features and patterns.
Book reviews, commodity prices, legal, letters, articles, new companies, new products.
No Index.
c.200000.
Per copy 17½p, per year £2.75.

235 THE NOR'-EASTER: Staff magazine of the North Eastern Electricity Board. 1948.
The North Eastern Electricity Board, Carliol House, Newcastle upon Tyne, NE99 1SE.
4, †   Principally a medium for publicising the activities of the employees of NEEB and featuring the Board's developments—new service centres, offices and depots, training courses and activities of Local Advisory Committees. There are also semi-technical articles on electricity.
Commodity prices, articles, new products, obituaries.
No. Index.
Summer 1972, T.p.68.
Issued free to Board's staff.

236 NORWICH UNION GROUP MAGAZINE. 1964.
(Staff Gazette 1888-91; The Norwich Union 1891-1910; The Norwich Union Magazine 1911-1964)
Norwich Union Insurance Group, Surrey Street, Norwich, NOR 88A.
4, †   Activities, both business and social, of the Norwich Union Group of Companies and its employees throughout the world.
Articles, new companies, new products, obituaries, reports, tests.
Editorial use only.
Summer 1972, T.p.56.   8500.
Per copy 2½p, per year 10p
(available to Norwich Union staff only).

237 NOVA. 1965.
IPC Magazines Ltd., Tower House, Southampton Street, London, WC2E 9QX.
12, ○   General interest intelligent women's magazine.
Book notices, book reviews, letters, articles, new products.
No Index.
T.p.60.
Per copy 25p, per year £4.

238 OPPORTUNITY. c.1930.
Vernons Organisation, Vermail House, Ormskirk Road, Liverpool.
2, ○ †   General features and news items concerning employees in all companies within the group.
Book reviews, letters, articles, new companies, obituaries.
No Index.
Spring 1972, T.p.48.   5000.
Free.

239 ORE: The magazine which remembers the Island of Britain and those who first came to it. 1954.

Eric Ratcliffe (Ore Publications), 11 High Plash, Cuttys Lane, Stevenage, Herts.
Irregular
* Poetry, articles and artwork relevant to the theme of our ancient Royal House, Celtic history, Arthurian legend, Druidism and similar subjects.
Book reviews, poems, monographic articles.
Irregular
No Index.
No. 15, 1972, T.p. 48.   600.
Per copy 15p.

240 ORGANICS NEWS. 1971.
(Hexagon Courier)
ICI Organics Division, Hexagon House, Blackley, Manchester.
12, † Newspaper of ICI Organics Division and Caters for the Division's employees. The accent is on people and their activities, with coverage of product successes and other division achievements.
No Index.
28 June 1972, T.p. 8.
Free.

241 ORPHEUS. 1971.
(Aspect. 1969-1970).
Steve Moore, 7 Hilend, Shooters Hill, London, SE18 3NH.
Irregular, ○ Articles, stories and comic strips pertaining to, and/or containing a fantasy element.
Letters, monographic articles.
No Index.
March 1971, T.p. 51, Ad.p. 1.   750.
Per copy 25p.

242 OXFORD MAGAZINE: a forum for University opinion. 1883-1971, 1972.
Modino Press Ltd. (for Oxford Magazine Ltd.), 6 Conduit Street, London, W1R 9TG.
26, ○ Comment and discussion on topical events affecting the University.
Book reviews, letters, articles.
No Index.
28 April 1972, T.p. 16, Ad.p. 3.
Per copy 10p, per year £1.50.
Free to members of congregation.

243 OZ. 1969.
(London Oz 1967)
OZ Publications Ink Ltd., 19 Gt. Newport St., W.C.2.
9/12, ○ ‡ + Broad alternative society coverage.
Irregular.
No Index.
July/August 1972, T.p. 55.   80000.
Per copy 25p, per year £2.50.

244 PM NEWSLETTER. 1967.
BB Bks, 1 Spring Bank, Salesbury, Blackburn, Lancs, BB1 9EU.
3, ○ News, information, reviews, listings, concerning (mainly) little magazines, small press publications, underground newspapers, counter-culture reading matter. Including books, pamphlets, newsletters, leaflets, posters, records, badges, booklets, folders.
Book notices, book reviews, letters.
No Index.
Free.

245 PELICAN. 1969.
(The Pelican Record 1891-1969).
Corpus Christi College, Oxford.
3, † Matters of interest to past and present members of the college.
Book reviews, letters, articles, obituaries.

246 PEN AND INK. 1960
The Parket Pen Company Ltd., 15 Grosvenor Gardens, London, SW1W 0BL.
6, † News about the company and employees, for internal circulation.
No Index.
Free.

247 PENNANT: The House Newspaper of the British Oxygen Co. Ltd. 1957.
British Oxygen Co. Ltd., Hammersmith House, Hammersmith, London, W6.
12, ○ † Company affairs and items of interest to BOC employees.
Book reviews, commodity prices, letters, articles, new companies, new products, obituaries.
No Index.
April 1972, T.p. 8.   22000.
Free.

248 PENTHOUSE: The International Magazine for Men. 1965.
Penthouse Publications Ltd., 2 Bramber Road, London, W14 9PB.
12, ○ Male interests, especially sexual topics.
Book reviews, letters, articles.
No Index.
September 1972, T.p. 79, Ad.p. 37.   237210.
Per copy 35p, per year £4.20.

249 PETTICOAT. 1966.
I.P.C. Magazines Ltd., Tower House, Southampton Street, London, WC2E 9QX.
52, ○ Fashion, Fiction, Beauty, Pop, Features—young female interest inc. emotional interest, personalities, crafts, horoscopes.
Letters, monographic articles.
No Index.
T.p. 48, Ad.p. 20.   203498.
Per copy 6p, per year £4.45.

250 PORT SUNLIGHT NEWS. 1922.
(Port Sunlight Monthly Journal 1895-1922).
UML Limited, the Unilever services company on Merseyside, Lever House, Port Sunlight, Wirral, Cheshire.
12, † ○ News, features, comment and pictures of <u>particular</u> interest to local Unilever employees and pensioners.
Book reviews, letters, articles, new companies, obituaries.
No Index.
June 1972, T.p. 8.
Free.

251 THE PRESS ASSOCIATION LINK: House Journal. 1966.
(The Link: Magazine of the P.A. Fellowship 1959-1960; The Link: The House Journal of The Press Association and Associated Companies 1960-1965; The Link: The House Journal of the Press Association, 1965-1966).
The Press Association Ltd., 85 Fleet Street, London, EC4P 4BE.
3, † = Stories and pictures reflecting developments of the national news agency through news of the men and women engaged in them.
No Index.
Feb-March 1972, T.p. 20.   1500.
Free to staff, annuitants, and members.

252 PREVIEW. 1971.
Preview Magazine (Bristol) Ltd., 77 Park St., Bristol 1.
12, ○ Information articles reviews about arts and entertainments in Bristol and the West: films, popular and classical music, theatre, art, poetry, environment.
Book reviews, articles.
No Index.
May 1972, T.p. 50.   9000.
Per copy 10p, per year £1.20.

253 PRINTER'S PROPHET: The Abbot House Magazine. 1924.

Key to reference symbols

○ popular   ‡ technical   = trade/professional

+ research   * society/institution   † house journal

Abbot Duplicate Book Co. Ltd., Abbot Works, Kings
  Langley, Herts, WD4 8JD
3/4, †   Products and activities of the Company.
Commodity prices, legal notes, letters, articles, new
  products, obituaries.
No Index.
February 1972, T.p. 12.   9000.
Free.

254 PRIVATE EYE. 1961.
Pressdram Ltd., 34 Greek Street, London, W1.
26, ○   Political satire, news and comment.
No Index.
T.p. 17, Ad.p. 5.   52000.
Per copy 10p.

255 PROFILE. 1967.
Hackney Library Services Central Library, Mare St.,
  Hackney, London, E8 1HG.
12, ○   Local history, local authors, exploitation of
  library stock and services. Temporarily suspended.
Book notices, letters, articles.
No Index.

256 PUNCH. 1841.
Punch Publications Ltd., Watling Street, Bletchley,
  Bucks.
52, ○   Humour, books, cinema, theatre and TV reviews.
  Reports on current affairs.
Book reviews, letters, articles.
6m, June/December, No, None.
T.p. 43, Ad.p. 22.   125000.
Per copy 15p, per year £6.

257 THE QUARTERLY REVIEW. 1809.
John Murray, 50 Albemarle Street, London, SW1.
4, = ○   Social, national and economic affairs.
Book reviews, articles.
A, Last issue of year, No, None.
T.p. 119, Ad.p. 3.
Per copy 50p, per year £2.15.
Indexed in: IBZ.

258 QUEST: The Journal of The City University, London.
  1967.
The City University, St. John Street, London, EC1V 4PB.
3, = ‡ +   All educational matters relating to the
  University in particular and the world of education
  in general. The contents have a special relevance
  for The City University and its development, but
  also have a wider significance among educationists,
  industrialists and industrial training organisations.
Book reviews, letters, monographic articles.
No Index.
Spring 1972, T.p. 32, Ad.p. 1.
Per copy 25p.

259 RACAL GRAPEVINE.
Racal Group Services Limited, 26 Broad Street, Woking-
  ham, Berkshire.
6, †   Company and staff news.
Articles, new products, patents, standards, tests.
No Index.
September 1971, T.p. 10.
Free.

260 THE RAMSBURY TREE. 1962.
Ramsbury Building Society, The Square, Ramsbury,
  Marlborough, Wilts.
2, †   Investing Members of the Society.
Abstracts, legal notes, letters, articles, new products.
No Index.
November 1971, T.p. 12.
Free.

261 READER'S DIGEST.
First published in Britain in 1938.
The Reader's Digest Association Limited, 25 Berkeley
  Square, London, W1X 6AB.
12, ○   International articles of general interest, con-
  densed books (mostly non-fiction), profiles, medical
  reports, humour items, etc.
Letters, articles, new products.
No Index.
May 1972, T.p. 137, Ad.p. 103.   1.5 million.
Per copy 25p, per year £3.58.

262 READERS NEWS.
Readers Union Group of Book Clubs, P.O. Box 6, Newton
  Abbot, Devon, TQ12 1XD.
12, ○
No Index.
Free.

263 THE RED MOLE: Journal of International Marxist
  Group (British section of Fourth International).
  1970.
(Black Dwarf. 1968-1970.)
Relgocrest Ltd., 182 Pentonville Road, London, N.1.
25, ○   Gives news and views on the world-wide
  revolutionary struggle against capitalism and
  imperialism, the national liberation struggles and
  the anti-bureaucratic struggles in the workers'
  states.
Book notices, book reviews, obituaries.
No Index.
5 June 1972, T.p. 10.   15000.
Per copy 10p, per year £3.

264 RED RAT.
197 Goldhurst Terrace, London, NW6.
12, ○   Underground journal.
No Index.
Per copy 10p.

265 ROWNTREE MACKINTOSH NEWS. 1971.
(C.W.M. 1902-1971).
Rowntree Mackintosh Ltd., York.
10, †   Company news and employee activities.
No Index.
May 1972, T.p. 8.   26500.
Free.

266 RUBERY OWEN NEWS. 1972.
(Owen News 1971).
Rubery Owen Holdings Ltd., Darlaston, PO Box 10,
  Wednesbury, Staffordshire, WS10 8JD.
5, †   Means of Communication to keep Employees of
  parent firm and Group companies at home and over-
  seas up to date with company developments.
No Index.
T.p. varies 8/12.   9500.

267 SERHB NEWS: Newspaper of the South-Eastern Regional Hospital Board, Scotland. 1970.
(The SERHB Magazine, 1968-1970)
South-Eastern Regional Hospital Board, Scotland,
  11 Drumsheugh Gardens, Edinburgh, EH3 7QQ.
4/6, †   Circulated to nurses, doctors and other health
  service staff, press, M.P.s, local authority health
  officials.
Informs employees and the public of the work of the
  hospital service in the South-Eastern Region, Scotland.
Articles, obituaries, parliamentary reports.
No Index.
December 1971, T.p. 12.   23500.
Free.

268 SSEB NEWS. 1971.
(Kelvin Magazine)
South of Scotland Electricity Board, Cathcart House,
  Glasgow, S.4.
12, † ○   To inform and entertain 14000 staff of a ser-
  vice vital to the industrial and social well-being of
  South Scotland.
No Index.
June 1972, T.p. 8.   16000.
Free

269 SALEMAKER. 1960.
Lyons Maid Ltd., Glacier House, Hammersmith Grove, London, W6 0NG.
6, = Main medium of printed communication between Lyons Maid, manufacturers of ice cream and iced lollies, and their dealers—owners and proprietors of confectionery, tobacco and paper shops, snackbars, cafes, restaurants, holiday camps, etc.
No Index.
April/May 1972, T.p. 12 Ad.p. None.   60000.
Free

270 SCHUSS. 1968.
Mary Glasgow Publications Ltd., 140 Kensington Church Street, London, W8.
9, O Covers practical subjects like: crafts, recipes and puzzles—up-to-date topics from Germany, Austria and Switzerland.
No Index.
No. 7, 1971, T.p. 8.
Per year 45p.

271 SCOTIA REVIEW. 1972.
(Scotia 1970-1972)
Scotia, 33A Huddart Street, Wick, Caithness.
3, O Scottish life and literature—political bias towards Scottish Nationalism—poetry, essays on poets, novelists, short stories.
annum, postage paid.
No Index.
April 1972, T.p. 6.
Per copy 5p, per year £1.

272 SEAL: House Journal of Serck Audio Valves. c. 1947.
Serck Audio Valves, Newport, Shropshire.
3, = Background stories on SAV customers and applications of the company's products. Company news for external consumption.
Articles, new companies, new products.
No Index.
Free.

273 SEED: Journal of Organic Living. 1972.
Seed Publications, 88 Boileau Road, Ealing, London W5.
12, O Aspects of natural living, including organic foods, pollution control, natural medicine, traditional recipes, folk wisdom, nature hints, self-improvement, through meditation and group contacts, natural handicrafts, wildlife preservation and organic gardening and farming.
No index.
June, 1972, T.p. 16, Ad.p. 3.   3000.
Per copy 10p, per year £1.20.

274 SEVEN ARTS. 1957.
Hansom Books, Artillery Mansions, 75 Victoria Street, London, SW1.
12, O Combines issues of Art and Artists, Books and Bookmen, Dance and Dancers, Films and Filming, Music and Musicians, Plays and Players and Records and Recording.
Book notices, book reviews, commodity prices, legal notes, letters, articles, new products, obituaries, standards, tests.
No index.
Per copy £2.08, per year £25.

275 SHE. 1955.
The National Magazine Co. Ltd., Chestergate House, Vauxhall Bridge Road, London, SW1V 2HF.
12, O Fiction, fashion and beauty. Tough controversial factual and general interest articles rather than 'feminine'.
No index.
June 1972, T.p. 76, Ad.p. 88.   298950.
Per copy 15p, per year £2.25.

276 SHORT STORY: The house journal of SHORTS. 1950.
Nicholson & Bass Ltd., 34 Alfred St., Belfast, N. Ireland.
10, + General news on company affairs, production, contracts, sports and social activities.
No index.
May 1972, T.p. 4.   6000.
Free.

277 SIGNATURE: magazine of the Diners' Club of Gt. Britain, 1966
(Diners' Club Magazine.)
Diners' Club of Gt. Britain, 214 Oxford St., London, W1.
12, + Wining, dining and travel
Book reviews, articles.
No index.
June, 1972, T.p. 32, Ad.p. 8.   103000.
Per copy 10p, per year £1.20.

278 SKEFKO NEWS. 1966.
The Skefko Ball Bearing Company Ltd., Leagrave Road, Luton, Beds.
6, + Information sheet for Skefko employees and pensioners.
No index.
June 1972, 4.
Free.

279 SMITH EXPRESS: for the Employees of Jas Smith & Sons (Cleaners) Ltd. 1958.
Jas Smith & Sons Ltd., Dewsbury, Yorkshire.
4, + Working conditions, personalities, leisure activities, promotions and pensioner appeal; changes in methods and routine and branch news to the benefit of the works.
Letters, articles, new branches, obituaries, standards, tests.
No index.
1972, T.p. 11.   1200.
Free.

280 SOLIDARITY: for workers' power. 1961.
Solidarity (London), c/o 27 Sandringham Rd, London, NW11.
Irregular, O Problems of everyday life—and discusses what an alternative society might be like.
Book reviews, letters, articles.
No index.
Vol. 7, No. 1, T.p. 32.
Per copy 5p.

281 SPARE RIB. 1972.
9 Newburgh Street, London, W1A 4XS.
12, O Women's news journal.
Book reviews, letters, articles, new products.
No index.
Per year £2.

282 THE SPECTATOR. 1828.
Spectator Ltd., 99 Gower Street, London, WC1.
52, O = Politics, books, finance and the arts.
Book notices, book reviews, legal notes, letters, articles, obituaries, parliamentary reports.
6m, c. 4 months after each volume, Yes, 15 year.
T.p. 24, Ad.p. 7.
Per copy 10p, per year £5.

283 SPOTLIGHT: newspaper of H.M. Naval Base, Rosyth. 1969.
Ministry of Defence Navy Dept., Personnel Dept., H.M. Dockyard, Rosyth, Inverkeithing.
12, O
Letters, articles, obituaries.
No index.
June 1972, T.p. 12.
Per copy 3p, per year 36p.

284 SPREAD EAGLE: The Staff magazine of Barclays Bank Limited. 1926.
Barclays Bank Limited, 54 Lombard Street, London, EC3P 3AH.
12, †

285-299

Book reviews, letters, articles, new companies, new products, obituaries, tests.
No index.
March 1972, T.p. 47 Ad.p. 19.
(75p to pensioners) per year £1.

285 SRUTH. 1967.
(An Deo-Greine 1905-1923 An Gaidheal 1923-1967)
An Comunn Gaidhealach, Abertarff House, Inverness.
13, (Published as a supplement to the Stornoway Gazette), ○ †   Reports on the activities of the Association and articles in Gaelic and English of cultural, social and economic and general interest to the Gaelic Highlands.
Book notices, book reviews, letters, articles.
No index.
27th May 1972, T.p. 2.   12000.
Per copy 4p, per year 90p.

286 STAYBRITE CHRONICLE. 1956.
Firth-Vickers Stainless Steels Ltd., Staybrite Works, Weedon Street, Sheffield S9 2FU.
3, †   Domestic news regarding personnel and new applications of company products.
General interests/hobbies, letters, new products, obituaries.
No index.
December 1971, T.p. 24.
Per copy 1p.

287 STREET FARMER: incorporating Amateur Architecture. 1971.
Street Farm Collective, 63 Patshull Rd., London, NW5.
2, ○   Analysis of state manifestation in, and control of environment and development of, plots for altering the state by modifying environment, propagation of alternative weapons as a process and product of the rising revolution.
No index.
Spring 1972, T.p. 32.   700.
Per copy 20p.

288 TR JOURNAL. 1951.
Telephone Rentals Ltd., 197 Knightsbridge, London, SW7.
4, †   Produced for the members of the organisation and subsidiary companies to bring into focus their common interests.
Letters, articles, new companies, new products, obituaries, tests.
No index.
Spring 1972, T.p. 36.   4000.
Free.

289 TV ACTION & Countdown. 1972.
(Countdown, 1971-1972)
Polystyle Publications (part of Argus Press, which is a BET company), 382-386 Edgware Road, London W2 1EP.
52, ○   Television series in strip form, plus scientific information in the form of features. Largely space and futuristically orientated. Age group 7-14.
Letters, articles, new products.
No index.
June 17, 1972, T.p. 22.
Per copy 5p, per year £3.90.

290 TABLEWARE TIMES. 1971.
(Burslem Bulletin 1946-1971)
Royal Doulton Tableware Ltd., Mile Street, Burslem, Stoke-on-Trent, Staffs.
2, †   Circulated to employees.
Prices, articles, new companies, new products, obituaries.
No index.
Summer 1972, T.p. 4.   4500.
Free.

291 TARMAC WORLD. 1967.
Tarmac Limited, Ettingshall, Wolverhampton, WV4 6JP.
6, †   Items of general interest news concerning all Group employees, including contractual activities and sporting and social events.
New companies, new products, obituaries.
No index.
T.p. 16.   26000.
Free.

292 TATE AND LYLE NEWS. 1970.
Tate & Lyle Group, Leon House, High Street, Croydon, CR9 3NH.
8, ○ †   News items and short features related to Group's interests.
No index.
June 1972, T.p. 12.   7000.
Free.

293 TATE & LYLE TIMES. 1949.
Tate & Lyle Group, Leon House, High Street, Croydon, CR9 3NH.
4, †   Subjects directly or indirectly related to Group's interests, inc. shipping, sugar, engineering, etc.
Book reviews, letters, articles, new companies, new products, obituaries, parliamentary reports, standards, tests.
No index.
April 1972, T.p. 28.   9000
Free.

294 THAMES GAS. 1950.
(Co-Partners Magazine 1911-1949)
North Thames Gas Board, 30 Kensington Church Street, London W8 4HB.
12, ○ †   News and events of happenings concerning North Thames Gas, its employees and pensioners.
Letters, articles, obituaries, parliamentary reports,
A, January/Yes, None.
May 1972, T.p. 20.   25000.
Free.

295 THE THREE CROWNS. 1962.
Coutts & Co., 440 Strand, London WC2.
2, †
Letters, new products, obituaries.
No index.
Spring 1972, T.p. 44.   1600.
Free.

296 THROB. 1972.
Edinburgh University Student Publications, 1 Buccleuch Place, Edinburgh EH8 9LW.
1,   Contains poetry, music etc., written by students of Edinburgh University.
No index.
1972, T.p. 22.   400.
Per copy 15p.

297 TIM: (The Ingersoll Message). 1950.
Ingersoll Group Ltd., 202 New North Road, London N1 7BL.
4, †   All Ingersoll employees and all jeweller customers.
No index.
Free.

298 TIME AND TIDE. 1920.
Time & Tide, Classified House, New Bridge Street, London EC4.
52, ○   General current affairs.
Book reviews, letters, articles.
No index.
T.p. 12, Ad.p. 12.
Per copy 10p, per year £4.

299 TIME OUT. 1968.
Time Out in London Ltd., 374 Grays Inn Road, London WC1X 8BB
52, ○

No index.
30000.
Per copy 10p.

300 TIMKEN. 1960.
(Timken Times, 1946-1960)
British Timken, Division of The Timken Company,
Duston, Northampton, NN5 6UL.
7, †   News for Company employees.
No index.
Vol 13, No 1, 1972, T.p. 34.
Free.

301 toomUCH: the newspaper from the Medical School,
University College Hospital Medical School, London,
WC1.
10, ○ * + house journal
No index.
June 1972, T.p. 20.
Per copy 2p.

302 TRAVELLING, 1972.
Leyden Publishing Co. Ltd., 5-7 Carnaby Street,
London W1A 4XT.
4, ○   Aspects of modern travel and related general
topics.
Book notices, book reviews, letters.
No index.
Spring 1972, T.p. 36, Ad.p. 10
Free.

303 TRUE MAGAZINE. 1953.
IPC Magazines Ltd., Tower House, Southampton St.,
London WC2E 9QX.
12, ○   Real Life fiction—romantic interest for women
aged 18 to 27
No index.
T.p. 68, Ad.p. 21.   215000
Per copy 15p, per year £2.50.

304 TRUMAN TIMES. 1971.
Truman Ltd., 91 Brick Lane, London E1 6QN.
6, † =   Circulated to all Truman Licensees and free
trade outlets.
Book reviews, commodity prices, legal notes, letters,
new products, obituaries.
No index.
May/June 1972, T.p. 8.
Free.

305 TUESDAY PAPER. 1972.
Tuesday Press Ltd., 8 Garrick Street, London WC2E
9DH.
36, ○   Weekly newspaper for children aged 10-14.
No index.
20 June 1972, T.p. 8.
Per copy 5p, per year £1.80.

306 TWENTIETH CENTURY. 1900.
(Nineteenth Century 1877-1899)
Dennis Hackett, 5 Plough Place, Fetter Lane, London,
EC4.
4, ○   literary/social articles. Each issue devoted to
different theme, economic sections, reviews, poetry.
Book reviews, articles.
No index.
T.p. 58.   3000.
Per copy 50p, per year £2.25.
Indexed in: BHI.

307 TWICE: University of East Anglia Student Union
Newspaper. 1971.
(Mandate Chips)
Students Union UEA, University Village, Wilberforce
Rd., Norwich. NOR 88C Norfolk.
30, ○ *   Students Union activities—Sport, social,
Societies, Politics, information (wotson), general
news, and views, etc.
Book reviews, commodity prices, letters, notes, new
products, tests.

No index.
June 9, 1972, T.p. 10.   1300.
Per copy 3p.

308 UKAPIAN. 1936.
United Kingdom Provident, 33 Gracechurch Street,
London EC3P 3DY
6, †   Matters of interest about the work of the office
to staff and to related groups i.e. pensioners,
brokers, agents etc.
Book reviews, letters, new branches, new products,
obituaries.
No index.
June 1972, T.p. 8.   2000.
Free.

309 UNILEVER INTERNATIONAL. 1960.
Unilever Limited, Unilever House, Blackfriars, London
EC4.
2, †   Describes the activities of the business and
its people for company employees.
New companies, new products.
No index.
Summer 1972, T.p. 40.   60000
Free.

310 UNISON. 1960.
Public Relations Dept, The British United Shoe
Machinery Company Limited, PO Box 88, Belgrave
Road, Leicester LE4 5BX.
12, †   Employees, pensioners and other retired per-
sonnel as well as associated companies within the
group.
No index.
May 1972, T.p. 4.   5500.
Free.

311 UNIVERSITY OF EDINBURGH JOURNAL. 1925.
Scottish Academic Press Ltd., (for University of
Edinburgh Graduates Association), 25 Perth Street,
Edinburgh.
2, + *   Academic matters in general
Book notices, book reviews, letters, monographic
articles, obituaries, parliamentary reports.
No index.
June 1972, T.p. 96.   2700.
Per copy 80p, per year £1.60.

312 THE UNIVERSITY OF LEEDS GAZETTE. 1971.
The University of Leeds, Central Printing Services,
Woodhouse Lane, Leeds LS2 9JT.
3, * †   Diary of events—meetings, public lectures
etc., personalia section on members of staff; grants
and donations; financial policy; constitutional
matters; new schemes of study; new buildings,
honorary degrees; new departments and institutes;
any organisational changes.
News, obituaries.
No index.
January 1972, T.p. 40.
Free.

313 THE UNIVERSITY OF LEEDS REPORTER. 1971.
(The University of Leeds New Reporter, 1971)
University of Leeds Central Printing Services, Woodhouse Lane, Leeds LS2 9JP.
c. 20, ○ * †   Reports from University Committees,
announcements of coming events, news from departments, readers' letters and general news of interest
to members of the University.
Letters, news, obituaries.
No Index.
24 May 1972, T.p. 4.
Free to members of the University

314 VALENTINE. 1957.
IPC Magazines Ltd., Tower House, Southampton St.
London WC2E 9QX.

52,○ For teenage girls with strip and text romantic/
female interest fiction plus lively features on
beauty, fashion and romance.
Book reviews, letters, articles.
No index.
T.p. 32, Ad.p. 4.   164000.
per copy 4p, per year £3.50.

315 VEGAN ACTION NEWSLETTER. 1967.
BB Bks, 1 Spring Bank, Salesbury, Blackburn, Lancs,
BB1 9EU.
Irregular,○ News of activities and ideas concerned
with defence of all animal species (including hu-
manity) against exploitation, injury (and involuntary
death). Living in harmony with the environment.
No index.
Free.

316 VICKERS NEWS. 1919.
Vickers Ltd., Vickers House, Millbank Tower, Millbank,
London SW1.
12, † Providing news and features on and about the
Vickers group of companies. Internal circulation
only aimed at all levels from shop floor to middle
and top management.
No index.
June 1972, T.p. 16.   30000.
Free.

317 VICTOR MAGAZINE. 1947.
Victor Products Ltd., P.O. Box, Wallsend, Northumberland. NE28 6PP.
4, † 8 Progress and news of personal and social
events through the organisation. Including managerial review and technical articles.
No index.
April 1972, T.p. 16.   1750.
Free.

318 VOICE. 1972.
Morris International, 4 Vincent Square, Westminster,
London SW1.
26, ○
No index.
per year £3.

319 WATNEYS NEWS. 1972.
(Red Barrel)
Watney Mann Ltd., Palace Street, London, SW1.
12, † All company activities.
Book reviews, articles, new companies, new products,
obituaries.
No index.
June 1972, T.p. 8.   27000
Free.

320 WEEKEND. 1957.
(Overseas Daily Mail 1904; Weekly Overseas Daily
Mail 1950; Weekend Mail 1953)
Associated Newspapers Group Limited, Carmelite
House, Carmelite Street, London, EC4 Y0JA.
52, ○ Popular family magazine with dramatic, humo-
rous and glamour photographs (colour and mono),
entertainment, personality interviews, true adven-
ture stories, fiction, general interest features,
cartoons—aimed at appealing equally to men and
women.
Book reviews, letters, new products.
No index.
June 7th-13th, T.p. 33, Ad.p. 15.   1170577.
Per copy 4p, per year £4.16.

321 WEIR BULLETIN. 1919.
The Weir Group Limited, Cathcart, Glasgow, G44 4EX.
4, † General interest. Articles on company topics
for employees and customers, with some works
news.
Book reviews, articles, new companies, new products,
obituaries.

No index.
Spring 1972, T.p. 40.   12800
Free.

322 WEST LONDON FREE PRESS. 1971.
(Itch, 1970)
West London Free Press, c/o 22 Cedars Drive,
Hillingdon, Middlesex.
12, ○ * Local Politics, community action. Guide
to local events and entertainments.
Book reviews, legal notes, letters, articles.
No index.
March 1972, T.p. 40, Ad.p. 3.   3000.
Per copy 5p, per year 75p).

323 WHERE TO GO: in London and around. 1966.
G.D. Shaw, Where To Go Ltd., 191 Kings Cross Road,
W.C.1.
52, ○ Information for tourists and visitors on
theatres, clubs, restaurants, also historical land-
marks, places to see, river trips, etc.
No Index.
June 8, 1972, T.p. 31, Ad.p. 31.   28000.
Per copy 10p.

324 THE WHIP.
The Civil Service Union, 17-21 Hatton Garden, London,
EC1.
12, * Members of the Civil Service Union.
No Index.
T.p. 8.   23000.
Free to members.

325 WHITE AND RED: the staff magazine of the Provincial
Insurance Company.
Provincial Insurance Company Limited, Stramongate,
Kendal, Westmorland.
2, † Official company statistics and news.
No Index.
May 1968, T.p. 37.   1000.
Free.

326 WIADOMOSCI GOSPODARCZE. 1950.
Association of Polish Merchants & Industrialists, 47
Earls Court Rd, London, W8 6EE.
12, ‡ = † Legal notes, new products, prices, practical
hints, properties, management economic review.
Book reviews, commodity prices, legal notes, letters,
articles, new companies, new products, obituaries,
tests.
No Index.
May 1972, T.p. 14, Ad.p. 2.   600.
Per copy 8p, members only.

327 WILLS WORLD. 1965.
W.D. & H.O. Wills, East Street, Bedminster, Bristol,
BS99 7UJ.
12, † News of the Tobacco Industry and W.D. & H.O.
Wills as it affects the firm's employees and pen-
sioners.
Letters, new products, obituaries, parliamentary reports.
No Index.
T.p. 16.   17500.
Free.

328 WIMPY TIMES. 1962.
Wimpy International Ltd., 214 Chiswick High Road,
London, W4.
4, = † Wimpy Bar owners and operators in the UK
and in more than 30 other countries, all of whom
hold the Wimpy franchise from Wimpy International
Ltd.
No Index.
Summer 1972, T.p. 12.   1700.
Free.

329 WOMAN. 1937.
IPC Women's Magazines Group, Tower House,
Southampton Street, London, WC2E 9QX.

52, ○ All subjects with feminine angle, behind the headline features, medical, psychological miscellaneous personalities, fiction, practical housekeeping, emotional human interest, service.
Book notices, book reviews, commodity prices, letters, articles, new products, standards, tests.
No Index.
T.p. 56, Ad.p. 53.   1980000.
Per copy 6p, per year £6.50.

330 WRITERS JOURNAL. 1971.
(Djnn and Writers World. 1969-1971)
James Bird, 102 Finchale Green, Spennymoor, County Durham.
6, ○ =
Book notices, book reviews, legal notes, letters, monographic articles, obituaries.
No Index.
June 1972, T.p. 29.
Per copy 15p, per year 90p.

331 Y GWYDDONYDD. 1962.
University of Wales Press, Merthyr House, James Street, Cardiff, CF1 6EU, Glam.
4, ‡ +
Abstracts, book notices, book reviews, legal notes, letters, monographic articles, tests.
A, No, None.
1200.
Per copy 25p, per year £1.

332 ZERO ONE: Journal of anarchism and the arts. 1971.
Dancing Patch Publications, 39 Minford Gardens, West Kensington, London, W. 14 OAP.
4, ○ Elitist, destructive in its criticism, ill mannered and non apologetic to those it attacks in the fields of Art, Politics, Literature
Book notices, book reviews, letters, obituaries, parliamentary reports.
No Index.
June 1972, T.p. 150, Ad.p. 10.   350.
Per copy £1, per year £4.

061.3

CONFERENCES

333 FORTHCOMING INTERNATIONAL SCIENTIFIC AND TECHNICAL CONFERENCES. 1950.
Aslib, 3 Belgrave Square, London, SW1X 8PL.
4, ‡ + Lists in chronological order forthcoming conferences in all fields of science and technology, both international and British national. Exhibitions included only when held in conjunction with a conference. Previously issued by D.S.I.R./D.E.S.
Index supplied at end of each issue.
February 1972, T.p. 81.   550.
Per year £8.

069

MUSEUMS

334 AMGUEDDFA: Bulletin of the National Museum of Wales. 1969
National Museum of Wales, Cathays Park, Cardiff. CF1 3NP.
3, ○ * Archaeology, Art, Botany, Geology, Industry, Zoology, Welsh Folk Life and Language.
Book notices, monographic articles.
2 yearly, December, No, None.
Summer/Autumn 1971, T.p. 40.
Per copy 30p, per year 85p.

335 ANNUAL REPORT AND BULLETIN OF THE WALKER ART GALLERY, LIVERPOOL. 1970.
(Liverpool Bulletin and Walker Art Gallery, Annual Report 1951-1970).
Walker Art Gallery, William Brown Street, Liverpool, L3 8EL.
1, + † Activities of, and acquisitions by, the gallery.
Monographic articles.
No Index.
1970, T.p. 76.   c. 1000.
Per copy 50p.
Indexed in: BHI.

336 BRITISH MUSEUM QUARTERLY. 1926.
British Museum, Bloomsbury, London, WC1.
4, ○ = ‡ + Aspects of acquisitions in the British Museum.
Monographic articles.
6m, —, Yes, 10 year.
T.p. 80.
Per copy 25p, per year £1.
Indexed in: BHI, 1BZ.

337 BRITISH MUSEUM SOCIETY BULLETIN. 1969.
British Museum Society, 6A Bedford Square, London, W.C.1.
3, * Society news; Museum information on current exhibitions, acquisitions and events for Society members.
Monographic articles.
No Index.
June 1972, T.p. 20.   c. 5000
Per year £3.

338 EXETER MUSEUMS BULLETIN. 1972.
City of Exeter Museums and Art Gallery, Exeter.
4, ○
No Index.
On application.

339 JOURNAL OF THE MANX MUSEUM. 1924.
Manx Museum and National Trust, Douglas, I.O.M.
1, ○ + * Manx Studies, Principally History, Archaeology, Folk-Life, Natural History and Language.
Monographic articles.
Every 8 years, volume, Yes, None.
1971, T.p. 32.   c. 600.
Per copy 30p.

340 JOURNAL OF THE SCUNTHORPE MUSEUM SOCIETY. 1964.
Scunthorpe Museum Society, Museum & Art Gallery, Oswald Road, Scunthorpe, Lincs.
irreg. * +
Monographic articles.
No Index.

341 MUSEUMS ASSOCIATION MONTHLY BULLETIN. 1961.
Museums Association, 87 Charlotte Street, London, W1P 2BX.
12, ‡ + * News and notices.
Book notices, letters, new products, obituaries.
A, September, No, None.
May 1972, T.p. 5, Ad.p. 7.   c. 2500.
Per copy 10p, per year £1.

342 MUSEUMS CALENDAR. 1955.
Museums Association, 87 Charlotte Street, London, W1P 2BX.
1, + * Directory of museums and art galleries of U.K. and their staffs; information on activities, committees, affiliated bodies etc, of the Association; membership lists; overseas museums associations; useful addresses.
No Index.
1972, T.p. 126, Ad.p. 6.   c. 1400.
Per copy £1.25, per year £1.25.

343 MUSEUMS JOURNAL. 1901.
Museums Association, 87 Charlotte Street, London, W1P 2BX.

4, ‡ + *   Any aspect of museum or art gallery activity, development, practice or technique.
Book notices, book reviews, letters, monographic articles, new products.
A, September, Yes, Occasional.
June 1972, T.p. 34, Ad.p. 6.   c. 2500.
Per copy £1.25, per year £5.
Indexed in: BHI.

344 PREVIEW: City of York Art Gallery Quarterly. 1948.
York Art Gallery, Exhibition Square, York, YO1 2EW.
4, + †   International museums, art historians, universities, dealers, Friends of the gallery.
No Index.
3000.
Free.

345 765 JOURNAL. 1965.
(765 Plans and Progress 1962. 765 News 1963).
Manchester Transport Museum Society, 1020 Manchester Road, Castleton, Rochdale, Lancs.
4, * ○   Activities of the Society also includes historical remembrances and articles on Manchester Tramways.
Brief articles.
No Index.
March 1972, T.p. 4.   Average 77 per issue. 1970-71.
Per copy c.5p, per year 20p.

346 STUDIES IN CONSERVATION. 1952.
International Institute for Conservation of Historic and Artistic Works, 176 Old Brompton Road, London, SW5.
4, = ○ ‡ +   Maintenance, restoration of museum pieces, relics and artistic works.
Letters, monographic articles.
A, November, Yes, None.
T.p. 44.
Free to members.

347 TAYMAG: quarterly newsletter of the Dundee City Museums.
City Museums & Art Galleries Dept., Albert Square, Dundee.
4, ○ +   Provides notes and information on the Art galleries and museums in Dundee on Tayside. Studies on local archaeology, history.
No Index.
January-March 1972, T.p. 12.
Free.

348 VICTORIA AND ALBERT MUSEUM BULLETIN.
Victoria & Albert Museum, South Kensington, London SW7
4, ○ = +   Monographic articles.
No Index.
T.p. 39.
Per copy 40p, per year £2.
Indexed in: BHI.

07

JOURNALISM
NEWSPAPERS

349 CAMPAIGN: The newspaper of the communications business. 1968.
(World's Press News 1931-1968).
Haymarket Publishing Ltd., Gillow House, 5 Winsley Street, London, W1A 2HG.
52, =   News and features dealing with advertising, marketing and related industries—ie, the media film production companies, public relations etc.
Book notices, book reviews, legal notes, letters, monographic articles, new companies, new products, obituaries, parliamentary reports, patents, standards, tests.
Q, 2 months after last issue indexed, Yes, A.
14.7.72, T.p. 22, Ad.p. 22.   14096.
Per copy 20p, per year £10.

350 COMMUNICATION. 1972.
British Association of Industrial Editors, 2a Elm Bank Gardens, London, SW13.
4, *   Industrial editing.
Monographic articles.
5 year, 1977, No, None.
July 1972, T.p. 9, Ad.p. 3.   1000.
Per year £2.50.

351 GREAT NEWSPAPERS REPRINTED.   1971.
Peter Way Ltd., 28 James St, Covent Garden, London, WC2E 8PA.
12, ○   Each issue is a full size facsimile of a complete newspaper from notable dates in British history. A wrap-round provides background articles by historians to the events described in the newspaper.
No Index.
4 July 1972, T.p. 14, Ad.p. 3.   1400.
Per copy 15p, per year £1.80.

352 PRODUCTION JOURNAL. 1958.
Newspaper Society, 6 Carmelite St., London, EC4Y 0BL.
4, ‡ =   All newspaper Production Techniques.
Abstracts, letters, new products.
No Index.
April 1972, T.p. 22, Ad.p. 22.   3000.
Per copy 12p. Free to members.

353 THEN. 1972.
Peter Way Ltd, 28 James St., Covent Garden, London, WC2E 8PA.
6, ○   Reprinted letters, reports and journalism from one year from the past. Each issue is devoted to one year only.
No Index.
27 May 1972, T.p. 105.   4500.
Per copy 60p, per year £3.60.

354 WORLDWIDE NEWSPAPER COLLECTING AND PRESS HISTORY. 1970.
Peter Wild, Pheasant Walk, High Legh, Nr. Mere, Cheshire.
6, ○ + *   Subscribers' advertisements for 17th/20th century newspapers. Learned articles on press history. Used by Professors of Journalism for course notes. Unusual/interesting 17th/20th century newspaper reports/Advertisements, Wide coverage all aspects.
No Index.
T.p. 40, Ad.p. 18.   500.
Per year £2.

09

ARCHIVES
RARE BOOKS

355 ARCHIVES: the journal of the British Records Association. 1949.
British Records Association, The Charterhouse, Charterhouse Square, London, E.C.1.
2, + *   Preservation, use and publication of archives and manuscripts; research and other topics of interest to archivists, historians and librarians.
Book notices, book reviews, letters, monographic articles, obituaries.
2 year, with first issue in alternate years, Yes, None.
April 1972, T.p. 56, Ad.p. 8.   1100.
Members £1.50, Non-members £2.25.
Indexed in: BHI.

356 CAERNARVONSHIRE RECORD OFFICE BULLETIN. 1968.
Caernarvonshire County Record Office, County Offices, Caernarvon.
1, ○ +   Review of year's accessions and account of some recent work on records at the Caernarvonshire Record Office.

Monographic articles.
A,—,Yes,None.
1971, T.p. 30.   500.
Price varies.

357 IRISH ARCHIVES BULLETIN. 1971.
Irish Society for Archives, University College, Dublin.
2, ‡ *   All matters relating to Archives including State Papers, Local Government Records, Business records, Legal Records and Estate Papers as well as private papers.
Monographic articles.
No Index.
May 1972, T.p. 7.   300.
Per copy 50p, per year £1.

358 JOURNAL OF THE SOCIETY OF ARCHIVISTS. 1955. (Bulletin of the Society of Local Archivists 1947-1954).
The Society, c/o Guildhall Library, Basinghall Street, London, EC2P 2EJ.
2, + ‡ =   Archive Theory and Practice, Archive Administration and Records Management, Administrative History, Historical Manuscript Studies. Technical (Conservation, Document Repair, Housing and Storage).
Book notices, book reviews, legal notes, monographic articles, obituaries.
4 year,—, Yes, None.
April 1972, T.p. 50, Ad.p. 6.   1200.
Per copy £1.25, per year £1.80.

1
PHILOSOPHY

359 AMERICAN PHILOSOPHICAL QUARTERLY. 1964.
Basil Blackwell & Mott Ltd., 5 Alfred Street, Oxford, OX1 4HB.
4, +   All aspects of philosophy, substantive or historical.
Articles.
A, No. 4, Yes, None.
T.p. 84.   1500.
Per year £3.

360 ANALYSIS. 1933.
Basil Blackwell & Mott Ltd., 5 Alfred Street, Oxford, OX1 4HB.
6, +   Philosophical questions, treated in an elucidatory rather than a speculative manner.
Articles.
A, June, Yes, Vols. 1-26.
T.p. 30.   1600.
Per year £2.
Indexed in: BHI.

361 THE BEACON. 1922.
Lucis Press Ltd., 128 Finchley Road, Hampstead, London, NW3.
6, =   Esoteric philosophy presenting the principles of the Ageless Wisdom as a Contemporary Way of Life.
Book notices, book reviews, monographic articles.
No Index.
T.p. 32.   1500.
Per copy 25p, per year £1.50.

362 EFRYDIAU ATHRON YDDOL. 1937.
University of Wales Press, Merthyr House, James Street, Cardiff, CF1 6EU, Glam.
1, +   Philosophy.
Abstracts, book reviews.
No Index.
400.
Per copy 37p.

363 HERMATHENA. A Dublin University review.
Hodges Figgis & Co. Ltd., Dublin.
2, +   Literature, Science and philosophy.
Book reviews, monographic articles.
No Index.
T.p. 107, Ad.p. 6.
Per copy £1, per year £2.
Indexed in: BHI.

364 THE HUMAN CONTEXT: Le Domaine Humain. 1968.
Chaucer Publishing Co. Ltd., Chaucer House, 13-4 Cork Street, London, WIA 2AF.
3, = + *   Explores the philosophical assumptions and the methodology of the human sciences. It aims at a critical dialogue between different orientations in philosophy itself and at a confrontation with science.
Book notices, book reviews, letters, monographic articles, obituaries.
A,—, Yes, 3 year.
May 1972, T.p. 200, Ad.p. 5.   800 +.
Per copy £2, per year £5.25.

365 THE LOCKE NEWSLETTER. 1970.
Roland Hall, Dept. of Philosophy, University of York, Heslington, York, England.
1, +   Any aspect of the life or work of the philosopher John Locke (1632-1704), or related authors; work in progress, bibliography, etc.
Book notices, book reviews, letters, monographic articles.
5 year,—, No, None.
Summer 1971, T.p. 39, Ad.p. 1.   c. 500.
Free of charge, to Locke Scholars and appropriate institutions.

366 METAPHILOSOPHY. 1970.
Basil Blackwell & Mott Ltd., 5 Alfred Street, Oxford, OX1 4HB
4, +   Stresses considerations about philosophy or some particular school, method or field.
Articles and reviews.
A, October, Yes, None.
T.p. 96.
On Application.

367 MIND: a quarterly review of psychology and philosophy. 1876.
Basil Blackwell & Mott Ltd., 5 Alfred Street, Oxford, OX1 4HB.
4, +   Completely independent of all schools of philosophy, it covers the entire field of contemporary philosophical discussion.
Articles, discussion notes, reviews.

Key to reference symbols

○ popular   ‡ technical   = trade/professional

+ research   * society/institution   † house journal

A, October, Yes, None.
T.p. 160, Ad.p. 16.   c. 5000.
Per copy 50p, per year £1.50.

368 PHILOSOPHICAL BOOKS. 1960.
Leicester University Press, 2 University Road, Leicester. LE1 7RB.
3, + =   Comprises solely reviews of books in philosophy. The aim is to provide reviews that are reasonably prompt and of a high professional standard, to assist librarians and individuals in their choice.
No Index.
May 1972, T.p. 36, Ad.p. 3.   750.
Per copy 35p, per year £1.

369 PHILOSOPHY FORUM. 1971.
Gordon and Breach, 41/42 William 4th Street, London, W.C.2.
4, +   Discussion, on a philosophical level, on issues of primary importance to mankind.
Book notices, book reviews, letters, monographic articles, tests.
No Index.
On application.

370 THE PHILOSOPHICAL QUARTERLY. 1949.
University of St. Andrews (for the Scots Philosophical Club), St. Andrews, Fife.
4, = +   All branches of philosophy.
Book notices, book reviews, monographic articles.
A, October, Yes, None.
T.p. 96, Ad.p. 6.
Per year £2.
Indexed in: BHI.

371 PHILOSOPHY. Journal of the Royal Institute of Philosophy. 1931.
(Journal of Philosophical Studies 1926-1930).
Macmillan (Journals) Ltd., Brunel Road, Basingstoke, Hants.
4, * = +   Non-technical philosophy.
Book notices, book reviews, monographic articles.
A, October, Yes, None.
T.p. 86, Ad.p. 12.
Per year £2.50.
Free to members.
Indexed in: BHI IBZ.

372 RADICAL PHILOSOPHY. 1972.
Radical Philosophy Group, c/o R.J. Norman, Darwin College, University of Kent, Canterbury.
3, ○ + *   Philosophical writing of a kind which avoids the academicism of the existing philosophical journals; criticism of orthodox philosophy in its role as social ideology.
Book notices, book reviews, letters, monographic articles.
No Index.
Summer 1972, T.p. 34.
Per copy 35p, per year £1.

373 RATIO. 1957.
Basil Blackwell & Mott Ltd., 5 Alfred Street, Oxford, OX1 4HB.
2, +   All branches of pure and applied philosophy, from logic and philosophy of nature to ethics and philosophy of religion. Is opposed to scepticism and irrationalism.
Reviews, articles.
A, December, Yes, None.
T.p. 88, Ad.p. 4.   580.
Per copy £1, per year £1.80.
Indexed in: BHI.

374 STUDIES. An Irish quarterly review of letters, philosophy and science.
Talbot Press, Dublin, 1.
4, = +
Book notices, book reviews, monographic articles.
A, Last issue of volume, Yes, None.

T.p. 117, Ad.p. 10.
Per copy 50p, per year £2.
Indexed in: BHI.

133

OCCULTISM

375 FATE AND HOROSCOPE. 1954.
Athol Publications, Athol St., Douglas, Isle of Man.
12, ○   Stories of the unknown and unexplained, the occult, lost civilisations, para-psychology, ufology, prediction, healing, graphology, spiritualism, graphology and the supernatural.
No Index.
T.p. 84, Ad.p. 12.   11000.
Per copy 15p, per year £1.90.

133.9

SPIRITUALISM

376 SPIRITUALIST NEWS. 1968.
Spiritualist News Agency Co. Ltd., Bankside, 42 High Street, Barnet, Herts.
12, ‡ + * ○   National and international news and feature coverage on all occult, Spiritualistic and allied matter.
Book notices, book reviews, letters, articles, new products, obituaries, tests.
No Index.
June 1972, T.p. 8, Ad.p. 1½.   18000.
Per copy 3½p, per year 80p.

141.332

THEOSOPHY

377 THE THEOSOPHICAL JOURNAL. 1960.
(Theosophical News and Notes 1941-1959).
Theosophical Society in England, 50 Gloucester Place, London, W1H 3HJ.
6, *   Religion, philosophy, science, psychical research, occultism.
Book notices, book reveiws, letters, monographic articles, obituaries.
No Index.
T.p. 28, Ad.p. 2.
Free to members.

141.333

ANTHROPOSOPHY

378 ANTHROPOSOPHICAL QUARTERLY. 1956.
Anthroposophical Society in Gt. Britain, Rudolf Steiner House, 35 Park Road, London, NW1 6XT.
4, *   Translations of Lectures not otherwise in print. Articles relating to Anthroposophy.
Book reviews, letters, monographic articles.
A, Winter number, No, None.
Winter 1971, T.p. 22.   2100.
Per copy 20p, per year £1.

159.9

PSYCHOLOGY

379 BEHAVIOUR RESEARCH AND THERAPY. 1963.
Pergamon Press Ltd., Headington Hill Hall, Oxford, OX3 0BW.
4, = +   Development of behaviour therapy in psychiatry, modern learning theory etc.
Book reviews, letters, monographic articles.
A, Last issue of volume, Yes, None.
T.p. 100.
Per copy £5, per year £18.

380 BEHAVIOURAL ENGINEERING ASSOCIATION CONFERENCE PROCEEDINGS. 1969.
Behavioural Engineering Association, c/o Department of Mental Health, Queen's University, Belfast.
1, ‡ +   Aspects of current trends in behavioural modification.
Monographic articles.
No Index.
1969, T.p. 130, Ad.p. 2.   200.
Per copy £1.50, per year £1.50.

381 BRITISH JOURNAL OF MATHEMATICAL AND STATISTICAL PSYCHOLOGY. 1948.
John Wright & Sons Ltd., 44 Triangle West, Bristol, 8.
2, ‡
Monographic articles, tests.
A, —, Yes, None.
No Index.
May 1972, T.p. 128, Ad.p. 2.   900.
Per copy £3.25, per year £6.

382 BRITISH JOURNAL OF PSYCHOLOGY. 1904.
Cambridge University Press (for the British Psychological Society), PO Box 92, London, NW1 2DB.
4, +   General and experimental psychology.
Book reviews, monographic articles.
A, November, Yes, Vols. 1-20 (1929).
May 1972, T.p. 177, Ad.p. 10.   3550.
Per copy £2.50, per year £7.50.
Indexed in: BHI, IBZ.

383 BRITISH JOURNAL OF SOCIAL AND CLINICAL PSYCHOLOGY. 1962.
Cambridge University Press (for the British Pyschological Society, PO Box 92, London, NW1 2DB.
4, +   Social psychology, criminology, personality measurement and related topics.
Book notices, book reviews, monographic articles.
A, December, Yes, None.
June 1972, T.p. 99, Ad.p. 4.   2560.
Per copy £2.25, per year £6.50.
Indexed in: BEI

384 INDIVIDUAL PSYCHOLOGY NEWS LETTER: Organ of the International Association of Individual Psychology. 1950.
The Association, 6 Vale Rise, London, NW11 8SD.
6, *   Propagation of Alfred Adler's School of Thought, dealing with psychology, education, sociology, literature.
Book notices, book reviews, letters, articles, obituaries.
Yes,
No Index.
May/June 1972, T.p. 20.   500.
Per year £1.20.

385 INTERNATIONAL JOURNAL OF PSYCHOLOGY. 1966.
Gordon & Breach, 41/42 William 4th Street, London WC2.
4, +   Cross-cultural studies in all areas of psychology.
Book notices, book reviews, commodity prices, letters, monographic articles, patents, standards, tests.
No Index.
Subscription on application.

386 INTERNATIONAL REVIEW OF APPLIED PSYCHOLOGY: Journal of the International Association of Applied Psychology. 1968.
(Bulletin of International Association of Applied Psychology. 1952-1967).
Liverpool University Press, 123 Grove Street, Liverpool, L7 7AF.
2 +   Any field of applied psychology, particularly surveys of work in different countries and areas of psychology.
Monographic articles.
No Index.
April 1972, T.p. 72, Ad.p. 2.   3200.
Per copy £1.50, per year £3.00.

387 THE IRISH JOURNAL OF PSYCHOLOGY. 1971.
The Psychological Society of Ireland, Woodlands, Renmore, Galway, Ireland.
2, + * ‡   General, experimental, applied and theoretical psychology.
Book notices, book reviews, monographic articles.
18m, —, Yes, None.
Per year £3.

388 THE JOURNAL OF ANALYTICAL PSYCHOLOGY. 1955.
The Society of Analytical Psychology Ltd., 30 Devonshire Place, London W1.
2, + =   Current psychology especially from the Jungian point of view and literature, philosophy, anthropology, religion and all allied fields.
Book notices, book reviews, letters, monographic articles, obituaries.
A, July, Yes, None.
January 1972, T.p. 128, Ad.p. 4.   1200.
Per copy £1.50, per year £3.

389 JOURNAL OF THE BALINT SOCIETY. 1971.
The Balint Society, 150 Lady Margaret Road, Southall, Middlesex.
Irregular, ‡   Psychosomatic Research. Psychological aspects of general medical practice.
Book notices, book reviews, monographic articles, obituaries.
No Index.
June 1971, T.p. 36.
Free to members.

390 MAN: RESEARCH ABSTRACTS. 1972
Institute of Psychology, Roebuck Park House, Dundrum, Dublin 14.
Irreg., ○ + ‡   Research in all specialities of the behavioural sciences.
Abstracts.
A, —, Yes, None.
May 1972, T.p. 35.
Per copy 30p, per year £2.50 per 10 issues. Reduction for Institute Members.

391 PROCEEDINGS OF THE INSTITUTE OF PSYCHOPHYSICAL RESEARCH. 1968.
Hamish Hamilton for Institute of Psychophysical Research, 118 Banbury Road, Oxford, OX2 6JU.
Irregular, ○ +   Original research and discussion in psychology.
Monographic articles.
Integral with each volume.
1972, T.p. 190.
Per copy £2.25.

392 PSYCHOLOGIST MAGAZINE. A guide to happy living. 1933.
Psychologist Magazine, Manfield House, 1 Southampton Street, London WC2.
12, ○   Practical help and guidance to assist the man in the street with all problems.
No Index.
T.p. 30, Ad.p. 2.   22000.
Per year £1.50.

393 QUARTERLY JOURNAL OF EXPERIMENTAL PSYCHOLOGY. 1948.
Academic Press Inc. (London) Ltd., 24-28 Oval Road, London, NW1.
4, *   Experimental not clinical psychology.
Scientific papers, book notices, book reviews.
A, February, Yes, None.
May 1972, T.p. 119, Ad.p. 7.   1300.
Per year £6.50.

394 RED RAT. 1971.
42 Essendine Mansions, Essendine Road, London W9.
4, =   Journal of abnormal psychologists, the role of psychology in Society.
No Index.
Per copy 15p.

395 THORNFIELD JOURNAL: Organ of the U.C.D. Student
    Psychological Society. 1967.
  University College, Dublin, Student Psychological
    Society. c/o Thornfield Laboratory, University
    College, Stillorgan Road, Dublin 4.
  1, ‡ + *   Recent and original work in all branches of
    Psychology, contributed by students of the Department of Psychology, University College, Dublin, and
    by professional psychologists working in the field.
  Book notices, book reviews, monographic articles,
    tests.
  A, —, Yes, None.
  T.p. 100.   250.
  Per copy 50p.

159.922.7

CHILD PSYCHOLOGY

396 JOURNAL OF CHILD PSYCHOLOGY AND PSYCHIATRY AND ALLIED DISCIPLINES: official organ
    of The Association of Child Psychology and
    Psychiatry. 1960.
  Pergamon Press Ltd., Headington Hill Hall, Oxford
    OX3 0BW.
  4, = + *   Mental life and behaviour of children.
  Book reviews, letters, monographic articles.
  A, Last issue of volume, Yes, None.
  Per copy £3.50, per year £12.
  Indexed in: BEI

159.953

LEARNING

397 JOURNAL OF STRUCTURAL LEARNING. 1967.
  Gordon & Breach, 41/42 William 4th Street, London
    WC2.
  4, +   Learning of any structures such as linguistic
    structure, scientific structure or even artistic structure, the study of those being classed as mathematical learning, under the definition that mathematics
    is the study of relationships.
  Book notices, book reviews, letters monographic
    articles.
  No Index.
  Subscription on application.

159.956

PERCEPTION

398 PERCEPTION. 1972.
  Pion Limited, 207 Brondesbury Park, London, NW2 5JN.
  4, + *   Physiological mechanisms, clinical neurological disturbances. Psychological data on perception: experience, skills, culture, illusions—their
    theoretical significance. Cognitive experiments;
    interpretations of sensory patterns by organisms,
    machines. Philosophical implications for epistemology, art.
  Book reviews, letters, monographic articles, tests.
  A, last issue of each volume, Yes, None.
  T.p. 120.
  Per copy £3.50, per year £10.

159.96

PSYCHIC PHENOMENA

399 INSIGHT MAGAZINE. 1969.
  Deric R. James, Esq., 118 Windham Road, Bournemouth, Hampshire.
  4, +   Witchcraft, Black Magic, Ceremonial and Hermetic Magic, Psychical Research, Archeology, Comparative Religions, Alchemical lore, Tantric Yoga
    and Sexual aspects of esoteric knowledge.
  Book notices, book reviews, letters, monographic
    articles, tests.
  No Index.
  April 1972, T.p. 40, Ad.p. 6.   1200.
  Per copy 25p, per year £1.

400 JOURNAL OF THE SOCIETY FOR PSYCHICAL
    RESEARCH. 1884.
  Society for Psychical Research, 1 Adam and Eve Mews,
    London W8.
  4, + *   Investigation of psychic phenomena.
  Book notices, book reviews, letters, monographic
    articles.
  A, —, Yes, None.
  T.p. 52.
  Free to members.
  Indexed in: BHI, IBZ.

401 LIGHT: A journal of psychic studies. 1881.
  College of Psychic Studies, 16 Queensberry Place,
    London, SW7.
  4, * ○ +   All aspects of spiritual and psychic exploration and experience.
  Book reviews, letters, articles, obituaries.
  No Index.
  Spring 1972, T.p. 52, Ad.p. 2.   1400.
  Per copy 20p, per year 90p.

402 PREDICTION. 1935.
  Link House Publications Ltd., Link House, Dingwall
    Avenue, Croydon, Surrey CR9 2TA.
  12, ○   Deals generally with the occult sciences—
    astrology, palmistry, graphology. Dream interpretation, Spiritualism, Tarot.
  Book reviews, letters, articles.
  No Index.
  T.p. 46, Ad.p. 16.   48000.
  Per copy 15p, per year £2.

403 PROCEEDINGS OF THE SOCIETY FOR PSYCHICAL
    RESEARCH. 1882.
  Society for Psychical Research, 1 Adam and Eve Mews,
    London W8.
  Irregular, + *   Investigation of psychic phenomena.
  Book notices, book reviews, monographic articles.
  A, —, Yes, None.
  T.p. 100.
  Free to members.
  Indexed in: BHI

159.964.2

PSYCHO-ANALYSIS

404 INTERNATIONAL JOURNAL OF PSYCHOANALYSIS
    and Bulletin of the International Psycho-Analytical
    Association. 1920.
  Bailliere, Tindall & Cassell Ltd. (for the Institute of
    Psycho-Analysis), 7-8 Henrietta Street, London
    WC2 8QE.
  4,   Medical and theoretical aspects of psychoanalysis.
  Book notices, book reviews, letters, monographic
    articles, obituaries.
  A, Pt 4 each year, Yes, None.
  Pt 1, 1972, T.p. 161, Ad.p. 4.
  Per copy £2.10, per year £5.
  Indexed in: IBZ

165.62

PHENOMENOLOGY

405 JOURNAL OF THE BRITISH SOCIETY FOR
    PHENOMENOLOGY. 1970.
  Haigh & Hochland Ltd., Precinct Centre, Oxford Road,
    Manchester 13.
  3, * +   Phenomenology and existential philosophy,
    especially that produced by younger thinkers.
  Book notices, book reviews, letters, monographic
    articles, obituaries.
  No Index.
  May 1972, T.p. 110, Ad.p. 6. c. 500.
  Per copy £1.50, per year £3.50.

165.63
RATIONALISM

406 NEW HUMANIST: journal of the Rationalist Press
    Association Ltd. 1972.
(Humanist 1956-1972. The Literary Guide 1899-1956).
Pemberton Publishing Co. Ltd., 88 Islington High Street,
    London, N1 8EL.
12, ○   Social problems and issues.
Book reviews, letters, articles.
A, December, No, None.
June 1972, T.p. 40, Ad.p. 4.   20000+.
Per copy 15p, per year £2.25.
Indexed in: BHI

407 QUESTION. 1968.
(Rationalist Annual 1884-1968)
Pemberton Publishing Co. Ltd., 88 Islington High Street,
    London N1.
1, ○   Annual journal of the Rationalist Press
    Association. Keeps pace with the broadening of
    scope which rationalist thinking has undergone
    since the first publication in 1884.
Monographic articles.
No Index.
1972, T.p. 100, Ad.p. 4.
Per copy Cloth 75p, Paper 25p.

167.2
ANALYSIS

408 APPLICABLE ANALYSIS. 1971.
Gordon and Breach, 41/42 William 4th Street, London
    WC2.
4, + ‡   Analysis that has been applied, or is potenti-
    ally applicable to the solution of scientific,
    technical, engineering and social problems. To
    encourage the development of applicable analysis,
    rather than of generalizations merely for the
    purposes of abstraction.
Book notices, book reviews, letters, monographic
    articles, new products, tests.
No Index.
Subscription on application.

168
SYSTEMATIZATION

409 SYSTEMATICS. The journal of the Institute for the
    Comparative Study of History, Philosophy and the
    Sciences. 1963.
The Institute, 23 Brunswick Road, Kingston-on-Thames,
    Surrey.
4, = ‡ + *   Interdisciplinary research in human
    development.
Book notices, book reviews, letters, monographic
    articles.
A, March, Yes, None.
T.p. 84, Ad.p. 2.
Per year £2.50.

17
ETHICS

410 ETHICAL RECORD. 1965.
(South Place Magazine 1895-1909; Monthly Lists 1909-
    1920; Monthly Record 1929-1964).
South Place Ethical Society, Red Lion Square, London
    WC1R 4RL.
10, †   Humanism, education, psychology, sociology,
history, literature etc.
Book reviews, letters, monographic articles, obituaries.
No Index.
June 1972, T.p. 23.
Per year 75p, free to members.

178.2
TEMPERANCE

411 ALERT: journal of better living. 1954.
International Temperance Assoc., 119 St. Peter's
    Street, St. Albans, Herts.
4, ○ + *
Book notices, book reviews, letters, articles, new
    products, parliamentary reports, tests.
No Index.
April 1972, T.p. 22, Ad.p. 2.   10000.
Per copy 10p, per year 50p.

179.2
CRUELTY TO CHILDREN

412 THE CHILD'S GUARDIAN. 1887.
National Society for the Prevention of Cruelty to
    Children, 1 Riding House Street, London W1.
6, *   Intended to keep members up to date on the
    latest developments in the field of child welfare. Case
    histories published of action taken by the NSPCC.
Book reviews, letters, monographic articles.
No Index.
T.p. 16.   57000.
Free to members.

18.01
AESTHETICS

413 THE BRITISH JOURNAL OF AESTHETICS. 1960.
Thames & Hudson Ltd (for The British Society of
    Aesthetics), 30 Bloomsbury Street, London WC1.
4, +   General aesthetics, theory of art, including
    psychological, sociological educational approach,
    theory and principles of criticism.
Book notices, book reviews, letters, monographic
    articles.
No Index.
Per copy 80p, per year £3.
Indexed in: BHI

2
RELIGION. THEOLOGY

414 BACK TO GODHEAD: the magazine of the Hare Krishna Movement.
The International Society for Krishna Consciousness, 7 Bury Place, Bloomsbury, London WC1.
12, ○.

415 CHANGE.
The Scientology Foundation, Saint Hill Manor, East Grinstead, Sussex, RH19 4JY.
12, ○   News and views of Scientology.
No Index.
No. 49, T.p. 6, Ad.p. 6.
Free to members.

416 CRUCIBLE. 1962.
C of E Board for Social Responsibility of the General Synod, Church House, Dean's Yard, Westminster, London, SW1P 3NZ.
6, *   Social issues designed to help Christians to work out for themselves a mutual interpretation between the Church and the social order.
Book notices, book reviews, legal notes, letters, articles.
A, November, Yes, None.
May/June 1972, T.p. 32.   c. 2000.
Per copy 15p, per year £1.

417 JOURNAL OF THEOLOGICAL STUDIES. 1899, New Series 1950.
Oxford University Press, Press Road, Neasden, London NW10.
2, +
Book reviews, letters, monographic articles.
No Index.
April 1972, T.p. 340, Ad.p. 8.   1300.
Per copy £2.50, per year £4.
Indexed in: BHI, IBZ.

418 RELIGION: journal of religion and religions. 1971.
Oriel Press Limited, 32 Ridley Place, Newcastle upon Tyne, NE1 8LH.
2, ○ =   Of particular interest to teachers and students of theology, comparative religion, anthropology, social science, hermeneutics and allied subjects.
Book notices, book reviews, monographic articles.
No Index.
Spring 1972, T.p. about 90.   c. 300.
Per copy £2, per year £3.

419 RELIGIOUS STUDIES. 1965.
Cambridge University Press, PO Box 92, London NW1 2DB.
4, +   Nature and meaning of religious experience.
Book reviews, monographic articles.
A, last issue of volume, Yes, None.
July 1972, T.p. 95, Ad.p. 2.   1400.
Per copy £1.30, per year £4.
Indexed in: BHI

420 SCOTTISH JOURNAL OF THEOLOGY. 1948.
Cambridge University Press, PO Box 92, London, NW1 2DB.
4, +   Biblical and applied theology.
Book reviews, monographic articles.
A, last issue of volume, Yes, None.
May 1972, T.p. 127, Ad.p. 2.   1525.
Per copy 90p, per year £2.50.

421 STUDIES IN COMPARATIVE RELIGION. 1967.
(Tomorrow 1941 in U.S.A. Transferred to this country in 1962).
Perennial Books Ltd., Pates Manor, Bedfont, Middlesex, TW14 8JP.
4, =   Devoted to the study of the great religions of the world, together with the civilizations, traditional arts and sciences that have sprung from those religions.
Book notices, book reviews, letters, articles, obituaries.
A, October, No, None.
Autumn 1971, T.p. 64, Ad.p. 4.
Per copy 50p, per year £2.16.

422 TSF BULLETIN. 1961.
Theological Students' Fellowship, 39 Bedford Square, London, WC1B 3EY (affiliated to Inter-Varsity Fellowship).
3, *   Theology—expanding and defending the Christian faith.
Book notices, book reviews, letters, articles.
A, Summer, No, None.
Spring 1972, T.p. 24, Ad.p. 1.   c. 3000.
Including RE Bulletin per copy 15p (students) 20p (others) per year 45p/60p.

423 TEILHARD REVIEW. 1966.
The Teilhard Centre for the Future of Man, 3 Cromwell Place, London, SW7 2JE.
3, ‡ * +   Integrated studies concerned with the Future of Man, in which the insights of scientists, theologians and others are brought together in the search for a more unified view of Man.
Book notices, book reviews, letters, monographic articles.
First six years in preparation.
June 1972, T.p. 40, Ad.p. 2.   ca. 3500.
Per copy 50p, per year £1.50.
Free to Members.

424 THEOLOGICAL AND RELIGIOUS INDEX. 1971.
Theological Abstracting and Bibliographical Services (TABS). 22, Dragon Terrace, Harrogate, Yorkshire, HG1 5DN.
4, +   Indexing service, special emphasis placed on material in non-theological journals and books.
A, with each fourth issue, No, None.
Vol. 1, No. 2, T.p. 44.
Per copy 35p, per year £1.25.

425 THEOLOGY. A monthly review. 1920.
S.P.C.K. Holy Trinity Church, Marylebone Road, London, NW1.
12, =   All aspects of theology.
Book notices, book reviews.
A, December, No, None.
T.p. 46, Ad.p. 4.   5500.
Per year £1.50.
Indexed in: IBZ, BHI.

426 TYNDALE BULLETIN. 1966.
(Tyndale House Bulletin 1956-65).
Tyndale Press, 39 Bedford Square, London, WC1B 3EY.
1, +   Biblical and theological studies.
Monographic articles.
A, At back of each volume, Yes, None.
1971, T.p. 128.   400/500.
Per copy £1.25.

427 VISION.
Association for Promoting Retreats, Church House, Newton Road, London, W2.
2, *
Articles; List of Retreat Houses, Anglican and R.C.
No Index.
June 1972, T.p. 22, Ad.p. 2.   7000-7500.
Per copy 15p, per year 30p.

211

FREETHINKING

428 THE FREETHINKER. 1881.
G. W. Foote & Co. Ltd., 103 Borough High Street, London, SE1 1NL.
52, ○ + *   Caters essentially for humanists, rationalists, atheists and agnostics, both in U.K. and abroad.
Book notices, book reviews, letters, monographic articles, obituaries.
No index in recent years. It is hoped to issue an index annually, starting with the 1972 vol., and if so, title page will be included.
24-6-1972, T.p. 8.
Per copy 3p, per year £2.55.

22

BIBLE. CHRISTIAN RELIGION

429 BIBLE IMPACT. 1970.
Society for Proclaiming Britain is Israel, 87 St. Barnabas Road, Woodford Green, Essex.
4, ○ *   All aspects of Christian philosophy, doctrine, prophecy and Old and New Testament history. Comment on the world situation, satire, cartoons, children's stories.
Book notices, book reviews, letters, articles, obituaries.
No Index.
March 1972, T.p. 28, Ad.p. 1.   1500.
Free.

430 BIBLE TRANSLATOR. 1950.
Headley Brothers, Invicta Works, Ashford, Kent.
4, = + ‡   World wide aspects of Bible translation.
Book notices, book reviews, letters, monographic articles.
A, January, Yes, 10 year.
T.p. 148.
Per year 50p.

431 BIRTH. 1965.
The Society for Proclaiming Britain is Israel, Birth Lodge, 78 St Barnabas Road, Woodford Green, Essex.
12, =   To teach the Bible as truth.
T.p. 32.   5500.
Free.

432 CHRISTIAN ACTION. 1964.
Christian Action Publications, 104/5 Newgate Street, London, EC1A 7AP.
4, * †   Economic, sociological and political issues examined from a Christian perspective, together with reports and correspondence on work of Christian Action and its associated organisations.
Book notices, book reviews, letters, monographic articles.
No Index.
Spring 1972, T.p. 28, Ad.p. 4.   2500.
Per copy 22½p, per year £1.

433 EXPOSITORY TIMES. 1889.
T. & T. Clark, 38 George Street, Edinburgh, EH2 2LQ.
12, ‡ +   To record the results of the best study of the Bible in the present day in an interesting and practically useful form; for both ministers and laymen.
Book notices, book reviews.
A, September, Yes, None.
June 1972, T.p. 32, Ad.p. 3.
Per copy 16p, per year £2.34.

434 NEW TESTAMENT STUDIES. 1954.
Cambridge Univerisity Press, P.O. Box 92, London, NW1 2DB.
4, +   Doctrine, theology and language of the New Testament.
Book reviews, monographic articles.
A, Last issue of volume, Yes, None.
April 1972, T.p. 135, Ad.p. 1.   2200.
Per copy £1.50, per year £4.50.

435 REDEMPTION TIDINGS. 1924.
Assemblies of God in Great Britain and Ireland, 106-114 Talbot Street, Nottingham, NG1 5GH.
52, ○   Mainly British Isles: but quite a number of subscribers overseas—U.S.A., Canada, Australia, S. Africa and other English-speaking places.
Book notices, book reviews, commodity prices, letters, articles, obituaries.
No Index.
6th July 1972, T.p. 20, Ad.p. 4.   8900.
Per copy 5p, per year £3.90.

436 SCRIPTURE BULLETIN. 1969.
Catholic Biblical Assn. of G.B. (in collaboration with S.P.C.K. and Bible Reading Fellowship), St Mary's, Strawberry Hill, Twickenham, London.
2, ○ + *   Bible news, articles and reviews at both an academic and a popular level. Special attention to ecumenical role of the Bible.
Book reviews, letters, monographic articles, obituaries.
No Index.
Spring 1972, T.p. 24.
Per copy 50p, per year £1.

437 WORD IN ACTION: The Bible in the World. 1972.
(Bible Society News)
The British & Foreign Bible Society, 146 Queen Victoria Street, London, EC4V 4BX.
4, ○ *   Gives up to date news of the work being done by the Bible Societies at home as well as overseas.
No Index.
No. 2, 1972, T.p. 8.   150000.
Free but donations of 20p a year cover costs.

226

EVANGELISM

438 JAPAN NEWS: The Magazine of the Japan Evangelistic Band. 1968.
(Magazine of the Japan Evangelistic Band. 1903-1968)
The Japan Evangelistic Band, 26 Woodside Park Road, London, N12 8RR.
6, *   Reports and plans of the Mission's Activity.
No Index.
May 1972, T.p. 4.
Per Year 50p.

439 THE KINGDOM VOICE: British Monthly News-letter. 1939.
Kingdom Revival Crusade, Riverside Cottage, Bridgend, Harpford, Sidmouth, Devon, EX10 0NG.
12, +   Propogation of the Gospel.
No Index.
1, 1972, T.p. 4.
Per year £1.

440 SUNRISE NEWS: The Magazine of the Sunrise Band. 1969.
(Heralds of Sunrise—1964/69; Magazine of the Sunrise Band 1906-1964)
The Sunrise Band, 26 Woodside Park Road, London, N12 8RR.
6, *   Reports and plans of the Mission's Activity.
No Index.
January 1972, T.p. 4.
Per year 50p.

231.75
PROPHECY

441 PROPHETIC WITNESS. 1957.
(Advent Witness 1917-1956).
Prophetic Witness Publishing Co., 2 Upperton Gardens, Eastbourne, Sussex.
12   Religious—primarily eschatological.
Book notices, book reviews, letters, articles.
No Index.
6, 1972, T.p. 19, Ad.p. 4.   6000.
Per copy 5p, per year 90p.

247
CHURCH FURNISHING

442 CHURCH AND SCHOOL EQUIPMENT NEWS.
Trade and Technical Press Ltd., Crown House, Morden, Surrey.
12, =   Upkeep and maintenance of churches of all denominations.
No Index.
T.p. 8, Ad.p. 8.
Free, Controlled circulation.

26
CHRISTIAN CHURCH. CHRISTIANITY.

443 ADVANCE. 1971.
(Christian Endeavour 1930-1971.(approx.) Christian Endeavour Times 1896-1930 (approx.))
Christian Endeavour Union of Gt. Britain & Ireland, 31 Lampton Road, Hounslow, TW3 1JD.
4,* †   News and articles of interest to members within the Movement.
Book notices, book reviews, monographic articles, obituaries.
April 1972, T.p. 8, Ad.p. ¼ (limited).   2000.
Per copy 7p, per year 25p.

444 APOSTOLIC HERALD. 1922.
The Puritan Press Ltd., (for Apostolic Church Missionary Movement), 353 Great Horton Road, Bradford, Yorks, BD7 3BZ.
12, ○ *   General missionary and evangelical news with particular emphasis on the work of the Apostolic Church Missionary Movement. Includes section for children.
Articles.
No Index.
May 1972, T.p. 19.   4400.
Per copy 3p, per year 66p.

445 BROADSHEET. 1971.
(Coming Alive—1969)
Christian Alliance, 157 Waterloo Road, London, SE1 8UU.
4, *   Activities of the Christian Alliance in its Hostels, Holiday Houses and Clubs. Its aims being to place the claims of God before people and to win them to a personal acceptance of Jesus Christ as Lord and Saviour.
Letters, obituaries.
No Index.
July/Sept, 1972, T.p. 8.   c. 1500.
Free.

446 CATENA: Journal of the Catenian Association. 1917.
The Catenian Association, 8 Chesham Place, London, SW1.
12, †   Activities of the Catenian Association and its 260-odd Circles in the UK, Ireland and Overseas and of its members in public, business and professional life.
Book notices, book reviews, letters, articles, obituaries.
No Index.
April 1972, T.p. 32, Ad.p. 10.   11000.
Per copy 9p, per year £1.

447 CHRISTIAN GRADUATE: Quarterly Journal of the Graduates' Fellowship. 1948.
Inter-varsity Fellowship, 39 Bedford Square, London, WC1B 3EY.
4,*   General and specialist articles for christian graduates.
Book notices, book reviews, letters, articles.
Irregular, —, No, None
March 1972, T.p. 32.   11000.
Per copy 15p, per year 75p.

448 DIALOGUE. 1964.
(St. Nicholas Review 1957-1964)
The Guild of St. Nicholas, 27 Knighton Rd., Leicester.
12,* ○   Academic Christian opinion in the University and colleges of Leicester.
Notices, reports, book reviews, letters, articles, obituaries.
10 years, —, Yes, None.
August 1972, T.p. 14, Ad.p. 1.   120.
Per copy 3p, per year 75p.

449 EMERGENCY POST. 1939.
The Paternoster Press, Paternoster House, 3 Mount Radford Crescent, Exeter, Devon, EX2 4JW.
12, =   Evangelistic inset for broadcast distribution.
No Index.
No. 3, 1972, T.p. 8.   130000.
Per year 72p.

450 THE EVANGELICAL QUARTERLY. 1931.
The Paternoster Press, Paternoster House, 3 Mount Radford Crescent, Exeter, Devon, EX2 4JW.
4, =   Biblical, theological and historical subjects.
Book notices, book reviews, monographic articles.
A, October-December, Yes, None.
April-June 1971, T.p. 64, Ad.p. 1.   1700.
Per copy 30p, per year £1.30.

451 GUIDEPOSTS: A practical guide to successful living. 1966.
Guideposts Associates Inc., The Witney Press Ltd., Marlborough Lane, Witney, Oxon OX8 7DZ.
6, ○   Interdenominational, interfaith publication for Britain and the Commonwealth, seeking to point the way to deeper faith and more creative living.
No Index.
June/July 1972, T.p. 40.   15000.
Per copy 10p, per year 75p.

452 THE HARVESTER. 1920.
The Paternoster Press, Paternoster House, 3 Mount Radford Crescent, Exeter, Devon, EX2 4JW.
12, =   Evangelism in the UK and overseas.
Book notices, book reviews, letters, articles, obituaries.
No Index.
May 1972, T.p. 13, Ad.p. 6.   5000.
Per copy 8p, per year £1.30.

453 MADONNA formerly Direction. 1897.
Irish Messenger Office, 37 Lr. Leeson St., Dublin, 2.
12, ○   Official publication of the Christian Life Community Groups and Parish Sodalities of Our Lady. The object of the magazine is to link the faith with ordinary life and to apply the understanding of it to present day circumstances.
Obituaries, religious articles.
No Index.
August 1972, T.p. 32.   20000.
Per copy 3½p, per year 72p.

454 NEWSPEACE. 1970.
Fellowship of Reconciliation, 9 Coombe Rd., New Malden, Surrey, KT3 4QA.

12, † Articles on peace and nonviolent techniques and allied subjects, letters, calendar of forthcoming events and meetings of Fellowship and local meetings, conference information and reports, etc.
Book notices, book reviews, letters, obituaries.
No Index.
T.p. 12.   750.
Per copy 7½p, per year £1.
Free to members.

455 REALITY. 1936.
(Redemptorist Record—1926)
Redemptorist Publications, 75 Orwell Road, Rathgar, Dublin, 6.
12, ○   Current religious, moral and social problems with a view to creating a better understanding of them and inspiring its readers to become involved in working for their solution. Its pages provide a forum for discussion concerning Christian living in our times.
Book reviews, letters, articles, reports, standards, tests.
No Index.
June 1972, T.p. 48, Ad.p. 8.   51400.
Per copy 5p, per year 80p.

456 RECONCILIATION QUARTERLY. 1967.
(Reconciliation 1920-1939, 1947-1967, Christian Pacifist 1939-1946)
Fellowship of Reconciliation, 9 Coombe Rd., New Malden, Surrey, KT3 4QA.
4, =   Church, peace, political, race, social, environmental and many other matters of importance to society, both topical and far reaching. And then one specific subject is dealt with in depth, usually by about four or five experts in the field chosen.
Book notices, book reviews.
No Index.
June 1972, T.p. 60.   1600.
Per copy 20p, per year 90p.

457 SERVICE. 1930.
Civil Service Christian Union, 27 Jacqueline Gardens, Billericay, Essex.
4, ○   News of activities of Civil Service Christian Union and information of interest to members, with devotional articles.
Book reviews, letters.
Free to members.

458 THE STANDARD OF TRUTH. 1946.
(The Standard of Truth and Call to Pentecost 1945-1946)
Churches of God in Great Britain and Ireland, 16 Newal Road, Ballymoney, Co. Antrim.
6, =   Religion in its widest context.
No Index.
July-August 1972, T.p. 12.   1525.
Per copy 5p, per year 48p.

459 VOICE: A Christian magazine for students. 1970
Inter-Varsity Fellowship, 39 Bedford Square, London, WC1B 3EY.
3, ○   A popular magazine of a serious kind providing Christian comment on today's issues.
Book reviews, letters, articles.
No Index.
Summer 1972, T.p. 24.   15000.
Per copy 10p, per year 40p.

460 ZION'S HERALD: Journal of the Goshen Fellowship. 1965.
c/o Mr. F. L. Brown, 4 Canberra Road, Bexleyheath, DA7 5SG, Kent.
12, *   Spirit of prophecy.
Articles.
A, With last issue of June each year, No, None.
May 1972, T.p. 20.   180.
Per copy 7½p, per year £1.

261.6
MORAL REARMAMENT.

461 MRA INFORMATION SERVICE. 1952.
(New World News)
45 Hays Mews, London, W1X 7RT.
52, ○   Comment on current affairs. World-wide news, Moral Re-Armament films, plays, literature, conferences, campaigns.
Book notices, book reviews.
A, —, Yes, None.
24. 6. 1972, T.p. 4-8.
Per year £2.50.

263
SUNDAY. SABBATH (OBSERVANCE)

462 JOY AND LIGHT: Lord's Day Magazine. 1952.
(Lord's Day Magazine 1926 Quarterly Publications 1843)
The Lord's Day Observance Society, 55 Fleet Street, London, EC4Y 1LQ.
3, = + *   Churches and Christians of various denominations.
Book notices, book reviews, legal notes, articles, parliamentary reports.
No Index.
June-Sept. 1972, T.p. 35.   35000.
Per copy 2½p, per year 15p.

264
LITURGY

463 LITURGICAL STUDIES: Journal of the Church Service Society. 1971.
Scottish Academic Press, 25 Perth Street, Edinburgh.
2, =
No Index.
T.p. 70.
Per year £1.25.

464 LITURGY BULLETIN. 1972.
Diocese of Southwark, Commission for Liturgy, Archbishop's House, St. George's Road, London, SE1.
4, =
No Index.
Per year 50p.

266
MISSIONS

465 BULLETIN OF THE SCOTTISH INSTITUTE OF MISSIONARY STUDIES. 1967.
Scottish Institute of Missionary Studies, c/o Dept. of Religious Studies, University of Aberdeen, King's College, Taylor Building, Aberdeen AB9 2UB.
2, + *   Review of current literature on Christianity in the non-western world and on missions: news, notes and queries on missionary studies: archives and missionary records.
Book notices, book reviews, letters, articles.
No Index.
No. 9, 1971, T.p. 21.   250.
Per year £1.50.

466 CMS MAGAZINE. 1972.
Church Missionary Society, 157 Waterloo Road, London, SE1L 8UU.
4, *

Key to reference symbols

○ popular   ‡ technical   = trade/professional

+ research   * society/institution   † house journal

Book notices, letters.
No Index.
40000.
Per copy 24p.

467 DIVINE LIGHT. 1971.
Divine Light Mission, 3 Woodside Avenue, London, N6.
12, ○   Spiritual discourses of Param Hans Satgurudev Shri Sant Ji Maharaj, who reveals the Knowledge of Truth to all seekers, and of His Holy Family.
No Index.
April 1972, T.p. 30.   5000.
Per copy 30p.

468 THE HEALING HAND. 1966.
Edinburgh Medical Missionary Society, 12 Mayfield Terrace, Edinburgh.
4,* ○   Medical missionary work.
Book notices, book reviews.
No Index.
T.p. 31, Ad.p. 2.
Free.

469 IN: incorporated into Buzz. 1969.
Church Missionary Society, 157 Waterloo Road, London, SE1L 8UU.
12, ○   Missionary activity of all kinds for Teenagers.
No Index.
May 1972, T.p. 17, Ad.p. 5.   2000.
Per copy 10p, per year £1.20.

470 MISSION. 1964.
(Missionary Messenger 1923-1963)
Bible Churchmen's Missionary Society, 157 Waterloo Road, London, SE1 8XN.
4,*   Missionary work and the Church overseas, especially in Africa and North India.
No Index.
Winter 1972, T.p. 16.   8850.
Per copy 6p, per year 24p.

471 PACEMAKER. 1971.
(Satellite)
Church Missionary Society, 157 Waterloo Road, London, SE1L 8UU.
6, ○   News sheet mainly for children.
No Index.
May-June 1972, T.p. 11.   5530.
Per copy 2½p, per year 15p.

472 PURPOSE. c1965.
(Venture c1964)
Youth Crusade Worldwide, Bulstrode, Gerrards Cross, Bucks, SL9 8SZ.
4, †   Young People's missionary magazine giving up-to-date worldwide coverage.
Book reviews, articles, reports.
No Index.
23rd June 1972, T.p. 20, Ad.p. 3.   1400.
Per copy 6p, per year 24p.

473 SWIFT. 1971.
(Satellite)
Church Missionary Society, 157 Waterloo Road, London, SE1L 8UU.
6, ○   News of missionary activities for sunday school children.
No Index.
May-June 1972, T.p. 11.   6750.
Per copy 2½p, per year 15p.

267

CHURCH ARMY.

474 THE CHURCH ARMY REVIEW.
Church Army, 185 Marylebone Road, London, NW1 5QL.
6, ○   Work of Church Army officials.
Book notices, book reviews, articles.

No Index.
June-July 1972, T.p. 24.   18000.
Per copy 2½p.

267.3

Y.M.C.A.

475 YMCA WORLD. 1966.
(The British YMCA Review 1907).
National Council of Y.M.C.A.', 112 Great Russell Street, London, WC1
4, †   Pictorial, YMCA news items. Articles concerning particular YMCAs. General articles. Viewpoint column, etc.
No Index.
Spring 1972, T.p. 34, Ad.p. 6.   32000.
Per copy 10p, per year 30p.

268

SUNDAY SCHOOLS

476 SCOTTISH PRIMARY QUARTERLY. 1926.
Scottish Sunday School Union for Christian Education, 70 Bothwell Street, Glasgow, G2 7JE.
4,   Articles and lesson material for Primary Sunday school teachers.
No Index.
Feb. 1972, T.p. 40, Ad.p. 2.   5000.
Per copy 25p, per year £1.

477 SCOTTISH SUNDAY SCHOOL TEACHER. 1926.
The Scottish Sunday School Union for Christian Education, 70 Bothwell Street, Glasgow, G2 7JE.
3,   Articles and lessons for Junior Sunday School teachers.
No Index.
Dec. 1971-Mar. 1972, T.p. 40, Ad.p. 2.   5200.
Per copy 25p, per year 75p.

478 SENIORSCOPE. 1968.
The Scottish Sunday School Union for Christian Education, 70 Bothwell Street, Glasgow, G2 7JE.
3,   Articles and lesson material for Senior Sunday school teachers.
No Index.
Jan-Mar. 1972, T.p. 37, Ad.p. 1.   2000.
Per copy 25p, per year 75p.

27

CHRISTIAN CHURCH HISTORY

479 BULLETIN OF THE SOCIETY FOR AFRICAN CHURCH HISTORY. 1962.
Marcham Manor Press (for Society for African Church History). c/o Department of Religious Studies, University of Aberdeen, Aberdeen AB9 2UB Scotland.
1, + *   History of Christianity in Africa and the sources for its elucidation.
Book notices, book reviews, monographic articles.
10 year intended, 1973
3 (2) 1970, T.p. 110.   300.
Per copy £1.05, per year £1.05.

480 JOURNAL OF ECCLESIASTICAL HISTORY. 1966.
Cambridge University Press, PO Box 92, London, NW1 2DB.
4, +   Church and liturgical history—all denominations in all parts of the World.
Book reviews, monographic articles.
A, December, Yes, None.
July 1972, T.p. 79, Ad.p. 3.   2150.
Per copy £1.50, per year £5.
Indexed in: BHI, IBZ

271

MONASTICISM

481 CISTERCIAN STUDIES. 1966.
The Cistercian Order. Caldey Abbey, Caldey Island, off Tenby, Pembrokeshire.
4, =   Dealing with monastic spirituality.
Monographic articles.
None.
No 1, 1972, T.p. 120.
Per copy 55p, per year £2.20.

271.2

DOMINICANS

482 NEW BLACKFRIARS. 1964.
(Blackfriars; Life of the Spirit).
New Blackfriars, St. Dominics Priory, Southampton Road, London, NW5.
12, =   Theology, philosophy, sociology.
Book reviews, monographic articles.
A, December, No, None.
T.p. 56.   1700.
Per copy 25p, per year £2.50.
Indexed in: BHI

28

CHRISTIAN CHURCHES AND SECTS

483 CHURCH NEWS. 1947.
Home Words Printing & Publishing Co. Ltd., 11 Ludgate Square, London, EC4M 7AY.
12, ○   Parish magazine inset.
No Index.
August 1972, T.p. 16.   c. 350000.
Per copy 2p, per year 60p.

484 CHURCH QUARTERLY. 1968.
(London Quarterly & Holborn Review 1853-1968; Church Quarterly Review 1875-1968).
Epworth Press/SPCK, 27 Marylebone Road, London, NW1.
4, =   All aspects of Christian doctrine.
Book reviews, monographic articles.
A, April, No, None.
T.p. 9, Ad.p. 4.   2500.
Per year £2.

485 CRUSADE MAGAZINE. 1955.
Thirty Press Ltd., 19 Draycott Place, London, SW3 2SJ.
12, ○ =   Current topics of significance to Christians in all major denominations—both British and international news. Articles on devotional, domestic and national interest topics.
No Index.
T.p. 14.   15744.
Per copy 12p, per year £1.86.

486 THE ELIM EVANGEL. 1919.
Elim Publications Board, P.O. Box 38, Cheltenham, Glos.
52,   Elim Pentecostal Church giving news and views as well as Christian material.
Book reviews, letters, monographic articles, obituaries.
No Index.
24 June 1972, T.p. 20, Ad.p. 1.
Per copy 5p.

487 LIFE AND WORSHIP. 1971.
(Liturgy 1932-1970).
Fowler Wright Books Ltd., Tenbury Wells, Worcs.
4, ‡   Liturgy and worship in Christian Churches.
Book notices, book reviews, letters, articles.
A, —, Yes, None.

488 THE MODERN CHURCHMAN. 1912.
The Modern Churchmen's Union, Caynham Vicarage, Ludlow, Salop.
4, ○   Theology and related topics; Church affairs; and each issue includes editorial comment on a wide range of events and ideas from the liberal Christian point of view.
Book notices, book reviews, monographic articles.
A, July, Yes, None.
April 1972, T.p. 56, Ad.p. 1.   1000.
Per copy 45p, per year £1.25. Free to members

489 NEW CONTACT: The family Church newspaper for the West. 1971.
(Contact 1964-1971).
The Bristol & West Church Newspaper Co. Ltd., 279 Gloucester Rd., Bristol 7.
12, ○   Church and general news features.
Book reviews, letters, articles.
No Index.
July 1972, T.p. 13, Ad.p. 3.
Per copy 4p, per year 65p.

490 POINT THREE. Monthly magazine of Toc H. 1967.
(Toc H Journal).
Toc H, 15 Trinity Square, London, EC3
12, *   Community work in general.
Book notices, book reviews, letters, articles, news.
A, January/February, No, None.
T.p. 20, Ad.p. 1.   1500.
Per copy 5p.

491 THE PROCLAIMER. 1965.
Pentecostal Holiness Church, 35 Dongola Rd., Bristol, BS7 0HW
4, * +   Christian work at home and overseas.
Book reviews, letters, articles.
No index.
April/June 1972, T.p. 12.
Free.

492 WHITE CANONS.
(The Norbertine).
Our Lady of England Priory, Storrington, Pulborough, Sussex.
4, ○   General religious subjects and information of the Norbertine Order in England and Abroad.
Book notices, book reviews, letters, monographic articles, obituaries.
No index.
March 1972, T.p. 24, Ad.p. 11.   1000.
Per copy 5p, per year 30p.

493 WORLD PENTECOST. 1971.
The City Temple, Cowbridge Road, Cardiff.
4, ○ + *   Reports of world Pentecostal Movements and churches. Articles on matters of religious importance. Theses on doctrinal subjects.
Articles, reports.
No index.
Issue 2, 1972, T.p. 28.
Per copy 20p, per year 75p.

281

PRIMITIVE AND EASTERN CHURCHES

495 CHRYSOSTOM. Bulletin of the Society of St. John Chrysostom. 1960.
Society of St. John Chrysostom, Marion House, Holden Avenue, London, N12.
3, =   Ecumenism with special reference to Eastern Churches.
Book reviews, monographic articles.
No index.
T.p. 24.
Free to members.

496 EASTERN CHURCHES REVIEW: A Journal of Eastern
    Christendom. 1966.
  Clarendon Press, Oxford (for The House of St Gregory
    and St Macrina, 1 Canterbury Road, Oxford
    OX2 6LU)
  2, +   Past history and contemporary situation of the
    Churches of the Christian East; theology, spirituality,
    liturgy and art of Eastern Christendom; questions of
    Christian reunion.
  Book reviews, letters, monographic articles, obituaries.
  2 years, Spring, Yes, None.
  Autumn 1971, T.p. 124, Ad.p. 4.   900.
  Per copy £1, per year £2.
  Indexed in: BHI

282

ROMAN CATHOLIC CHURCH

497 APPROACHES. 1965.
  Approaches, Casa Garcia Moreno, 1 Waverley Place,
    Saltcoats, Scotland, KA21 5AX.
  4,   Promotes lay initiative in the temporal order that
    is juridically distinct from the Hierarchy yet in a
    spirit of uncompromising fidelity to the social doc-
    trine of the Teaching Church.
  Book notices, book reviews, letters, monographic arti-
    cles.
  No index.
  March 1972, T.p. 132, Ad.p. 2.   1500.
  Per copy 20p, per year £2.

498 CATHOLIC CITIZEN. 1911.
  St. Joan's Alliance, Newman House, 15 Carlisle Street,
    London, W1.
  6, ○   All mothers having relevance to the elimination
    of discrimination based on sect.
  Book notices, book reviews, articles, parliamentary
    reports.
  No index.
  T.p. 9, Ad.p. 1.
  Per year £1.

499 CATHOLIC FIRESIDE: The Weekly Magazine for All
    the Family. 1879.
  Catholic Fireside Ltd., Station Road, Hinckley, Leics.
  53, ○   Background to matters of interest to Christian
    families; travel, information, comment, etc. Short
    stories and serials; a home section, medical column.
  Book notices, book reviews, letters, articles, obituaries.
  No index.
  16 June 1972, T.p. 19, Ad.p. 3.   31000.
  Per copy 4p, per year £3.50.

500 CATHOLIC HERALD. 1934.
  Catholic Herald Ltd., 67 Fleet Street, London, EC4.
  52, = ○   News and comment mainly from Roman
    Catholic Standpoint.
  No index.
  T.p. 10.   85500.
  Per copy 5p.

501 THE INNES REVIEW. 1950.
  Scottish Catholic Histories Association, 25 Finlas
    Street, Glasgow, N2.
  2, = +   Cultural and religious history of Scotland.
  Monographic articles.
  6m, —, Yes, vols. 1-20.
  T.p. 104, Ad.p. 2.   450.
  Per copy 75p, per year £1.50.

502 IRISH MESSENGER. 1888.
  Irish Messenger Office, 37 Lower Leeson St., Dublin 2,
    Ireland.
  12, ○   Devotional magazine, and is the official publica-
    tion of the 'Apostleship of Prayer' which is a world
    wide union of the Catholic laity who, by their daily
    offerings and good works, co-operate with Christ in
    the salvation of the World.
  Letters, obituaries, Articles on Religion.
  No index.
  August 1972, T.p. 32.   180000.
  Per copy 3½p, per year 72p.

503 THE LIBERAL CATHOLIC: a quarterly magazine of
    religious thought and practice in the world today.
    1924.
  St Alban's Press, Drayton House, 30 Gordon Street,
    London, WC1H 0BE.
  4, ○ ‡ = +   Religious thought and practice in the con-
    temporary world. Mysticism, ritual, sacramentalism,
    catholic and ecumenical movements, both general
    and popular treatment, with some attention to
    scholarship and research for clerical readers (i.e.
    priests and clergymen).
  Book notices, book reviews, monographic articles,
    reports.
  5 year, —, No, None.
  March 1972, T.p. 28.   950.
  Per copy 40p, per year £1.50.

504 LONDON RECUSANT. 1971.
  The London Recusant Society, 21 Merryhills Drive,
    Enfield, Middlesex, EN2 7NS.
  3, +   Studies covering the post-Reformation Catholic
    history of London—London in its widest senses—and
    recusant historical problems which could be illus-
    trated from sources in London.
  Book reviews, monographic articles.
  A, January, No, None.
  May 1972, T.p. 44.   150.
  Per year £1.

505 THE MONTH: A Review of Christian Thought and
    World Affairs, incorporating Dublin Review; Herder
    Correspondence. 1864.
  Month Publications, 114 Mount Street, London, W1Y 6AH.
  12, ‡ =   In-depth reporting of Church events, especi-
    ally RC, throughout the world; impact of Christian
    thinking on political life, psychology and interdis-
    ciplinary fields; theology.
  Book notices, book reviews, articles.
  A, December, No, None.
  June 1972, T.p. 30.   4500.
  Per copy 25p, per year £2.50.

506 NOVENA. 1951.
  Redemptorist Publications, Alphonsus House, Chawton,
    Alton, Hants.
  12, =   Catholic family life, articles of interest to
    Christian Families.
  No index.
  June 1972, T.p. 26, Ad.p. 6.   28348.
  Per copy 7½p, per year £1.20.

507 OLD CATHOLIC CHURCH HERALD. 1970.
  Old Catholic Church in Britain, 267 Beechings Way,
    Rainham, Kent.
  6, ○ +   Events within the Old Catholic Church in Bri-
    tain and in other countries, plus items of general
    religious interest.
  Mar/April 1972, T.p. 12, Ad.p. 2.   500.
  Per year 50p.

508 RECUSANT HISTORY: Journal of Research into post-
    Reformation Catholic history in England and Wales.
    1951.
  (Bibliographical Studies, c. 1944-1951).
  Catholic Record Society, c/o 114 Mount Street, London
    W1.
  3, + *   Post Reformation Catholic history in England
    and Wales.
  Book notices, book reviews, monographic articles.
  2 yearly, October, Yes, None.
  T.p. 60.   c. 700.
  Per copy 75p, per year £1.25.
  Indexed in: BHI

509 ROC NEWS: A magazine for the Religious of Scotland. 1971.
Council of Major Religious Superiors (Scotland), 'Bellfield', 26 Manse Rd., Edinburgh, EH12 7SP.
6, = *.
Book reviews, letters, articles, obituaries.
No index.
April/May 1972, T.p. 40.   400.
Per copy 30p, per year £2.

510 SCRIPTURE IN CHURCH. 1971.
Dominican Publications, St. Saviour's, Upper Dorset Street, Dublin 1.
4, ‡ =   Commentaries on the Bible based on the readings at the Roman Catholic Mass.
No index.
No 5, 1972, T.p. 138.   7000.
Per copy 60p, per year £2.50.

511 THE TABLET: The International Catholic Weekly. 1840.
The Tablet Publishing Co. Ltd., 48 Great Peter Street, London, SW1P 2HB.
52, = ○   Politics, literature, social problems, ecclesiastical affairs, history.
Book notices, book reviews, letters, articles, obituaries, parliamentary reports.
A, February, Yes, None.
24th June 1972, T.p. 18, Ad.p. 5.   c. 50000 (Readership).
Per copy 10p, per year £4.

512 USHAW MAGAZINE. 1891.
Ushaw College, Durham.
2, *   Reflects the theological teaching now going on in a Roman Catholic Major Seminary. It also contains news of activities in the College and the adjoining school.
Book notices, book reviews, letters, monographic articles, obituaries.
A, Discontinued December 1966, Yes, None.
June 1972, T.p. 56, Ad.p. 12.   1100.
Per copy 55, per year £1.

513 WESTMINSTER CATHEDRAL JOURNAL. 1971.
Westminster Cathedral, Archbishop's House, London, SW1.
12, ○ =.
No index.
Per copy 5p.

283

ANGLICAN CHURCH

514 CANTERBURY CATHEDRAL CHRONICLE. 1928.
The Friends of Canterbury Cathedral, Flat 1, 8 The Precincts, Canterbury.
1, * ○.
Book notices, book reviews, monographic articles, obituaries.
No Index.
Autumn 1971, T.p. 52.
Free to members.

515 CHRISM: the St. Raphael Quarterly. 1965.
(St. Raphael Quarterly)
Guild of St. Raphael, 16 Lincoln's Inn Fields, London WC2A 3ED.
4, *   Church's Ministry of Healing. News on the Guild and its movement.
Book notices, book reviews, letters, articles, obituaries, reports.
None.
May 1972, T.p. 30.   approx 2000.
Per copy 15p, per year 50p.

516 CHRISTIAN RECORD. 1969.
Church of England Newspaper Ltd., 182 Fleet Street, London EC4.
52, =   Interdenominational evangelical.
No index.
T.p. 20, Ad.p. Most.
Per copy 5p, per year £3.50.

517 CHURCH OF ENGLAND NEWSPAPER.
Church of England Newspaper Ltd., 182 Fleet Street, London EC4.
52, =   Anglican evangelical.
Book reviews, letters, articles.
No index.
T.p. 16, Ad.p. Most.
Per copy 5p, per year £3.50.

518 CHURCH TIMES: An ecclesiastical and general newspaper. 1863.
G. J. Palmer & Sons Ltd., 7 Portugal Street, London WC2A 2HP.
52, ‡ =   News and views of the Church of England, plus Christian comment on national and international affairs. Reviews of all important religious books.
Book notices, book reviews, letters, monographic articles, obituaries.
A, March or April, Yes, None.
16th June 1972, T.p. 13, Ad.p. 7.   48686.
Per copy 4p, per year £3.40.

519 HOME AND FAMILY: Journal of the Mothers' Union. 189?.
The Mothers' Union, St. Mary's House, 125 Herne Hill, London SE24.
4, *   Concerned with home and family life especially care of children and their Christian training.
Book notices, book reviews, letters, articles, new products.
No index.
June 1972, T.p. 16, Ad.p. 3.   250000 +.
Per copy 3p, per year 12p.

520 HOME MISSION NEWS. 1937.
(Home Mission Field 1886-1936).
Additional Curates Society, 14 Rothamsted Avenue, Harpenden, Herts.
4, *   Church of England and Church in Wales affairs.
Book notices, book reviews, articles, obituaries.
No index.
Spring 1972, T.p. 16.   20000.
Per copy 2½p, per year 10p.

521 HOME WORDS. 1870.
Home Words Printing & Publishing Co. Ltd., 11 Ludgate Square, London EC4M 7AY.
12, ○   Parish magazine insets: home and abroad.
No index.
August 1972, T.p. 16.   750000.
Per copy 2p, per year 60p.

522 LOYALIST LINKS: the magazine of the League of Anglican Loyalists. 1968.
League of Anglican Loyalists, 11 Cumberland Mansions, West Hampstead, London NW6 1LL.
3, =   Defence of the Catholic heritage of the Church of England and encouragement of the ecumenical movement for corporate reunion with the holy see. Articles dealing with Church affairs.
Book notices, book reviews, letters, articles, obituaries.
No index.
April 1972, T.p. 20.
Per copy 15p, per year 45p.

523 THE NET.: Mackenzie Memorial Mission to Zululand. 1866.
Zululand Swaziland Association. Editor. Rev. Peter Burtwell, The Rectory, Hanwood, Shrewsbury, Salop.

2,* Provides supporters of the work of the Anglican Dioceses of Zululand and Swaziland in U.K. with information concerning progress.
Letters, articles, obituaries.
No index.
June 1972, T.p. up to 30.   1700.
Per year 30p.

524 THE READER: official organ of the Central Readers' Board. 1904.
Central Readers' Board, Church House, Dean's Yard, Westminster, London SW1.
6, ‡   All matters concerning the lay ministry of the Anglican communion, including training, examinations and development.
Book notices, book reviews, legal notes, letters, articles, obituaries.
A, January, No, None.
June 1972, T.p. 24, Ad.p. 2.   5800.
Per copy 6p, per year 50p.

525 TOGETHER: For all concerned with religious education. 1972.
(The Church Teacher: 1956-1972).
Church Information Office, Church House, Dean's Yard, Westminster, London SW1P 3NZ.
12, ○ *   Religious education of children and younger teenagers, both in day and Sunday schools and at home (basically C. of E., but with contributions from other denominations).
Book notices, book reviews, articles.
No index.
April 1972, T.p. 20, Ad.p. 2.   5500.
Per copy 10p, per year £1.25.

526 WESTMINSTER ABBEY OCCASIONAL PAPER.
Westminster Abbey, London, SW1.
Irregular, ○   News and information about the Abbey, etc.
Articles.
No Index.
June 1972, T.p. 24.
Per copy 10p.

283.41

CHURCH OF SCOTLAND

527 LIFE AND WORK. 1879.
Church of Scotland, 121 George Street, Edinburgh, EH2 4YN.
12, =   Church of Scotland at home and throughout the world.
No Index.
T.p. 26, Ad.p. 13.   200000.
Per copy 5p, per year £1.

528 SCAN: News magazine of the Scottish Episcopal Church.
James Paton J & J Cook Ltd., 18/20 Gordon Street, Paisley.
11,*   All members of the Scottish Episcopal Church.
Book notices, book reviews, letters, articles, obituaries.
No Index.
July/August 1972, T.p., 12, Ad.p. 1.   36000.
Per copy 2p, per year 50p.

283.429

CHURCH IN WALES

529 HIGHLIGHTS.
Church in Wales Publications, 8 Hickman Road, Penarth, Glam.
1/2   Broadsheet on Report of the Governing Body Meeting.
No Index.
May 1972, T.p. 4.   800.
Per copy 5p.

530 IMPACT. 1969.
(Province 1949-1968).
Church in Wales Publications, 8 Hickman Road, Penarth, Glam.
4,   Church in Wales theology.
Letters.
No Index.
No. 5, 1970, T.p. 20.   600.
Per copy 12½p, per year 50p.

531 WELSH CHURCHMAN.
Church in Wales Publications, 8 Hickman Road, Penarth, Glam, CF6 2YO.
12, ○   News of the Six dioceses of the Church of Wales.
No Index.
March 1972, T.p. 11, Ad.p. 1.

532 Y LLAN: Weekly paper of the Church in Wales (in Welsh). 1870.
Church in Wales Press, Hickman Road, Penarth CF6 2YQ.
52, ○ *   Church affairs, some attention to secular current affairs, theology, devotional material. Particular attention to Welsh affairs; Aimed at Anglican clergy and laity but with interdenominational interest also.
Book notices, book reviews, letters, articles, obituaries.
No Index.
16 July 1972, T.p. 8.   1000.
Per copy 3p, per year £1.56.

284.5

HUGUENOTS

533 HUGUENOT SOCIETY OF LONDON QUARTO SERIES. 1888.
Huguenot Society of London, Barclays Bank Ltd., 1, Pall Mall East, London, SW1.
Irregular, +   Each issue devoted to a specific subject.
No Index.
Subscription on application.

534 PROCEEDINGS OF THE HUGUENOT SOCIETY OF LONDON. 1885.
Herguenot Society of London, Barclays Bank Ltd., 1 Pall Mall East, London, SW1.
1, +   All aspects of Huguenot interest: historical, economic, art-historical, genealogical etc. Area covered is mainly British Isles from 16th Century to date.
Book reviews, monographic articles, obituaries.
6 year, At end of volume, Yes, Vols. 1-20.
Vol. 22, No. 1, T.p. 70.   c. 800.
Free to members.

285

PRESBYTERIAN CHURCHES

535 EVANGELICAL PRESBYTERIAN. 1964.
(Irish Evangelical 1928-1964).
Evangelical Presbyterian Church, c/o Evangelical Book Shop, 15 College Sq. East, Belfast, BT1 6DD.
12, ○   Proclamation of the historic Christian faith as set forth in the great creeds of the Christian Church.
Book notices, book reviews, letters, articles, obituaries.
3 yearly, —, Yes, None.
June 1972, T.p. 14, Ad.p. 1.   1000.
Per copy 4p, per year 48p.

536 FREE CHURCH CHRONICLE. 1948.
Free Church Federal Council, 27 Tavistock Square, London, WC1H 9HH.
10, * =
Free Church and related theological, moral and social subjects.
Book reviews, articles.

No Index.
May/June 1972, T.p. 16, Ad.p. 3.   3200.
Per copy 4p, per year 44p.

537 JOURNAL OF THE HISTORICAL SOCIETY OF THE PRESBYTERIAN CHURCH OF WALES. 1916.
The Society, c/o 61 Blaenau Rd., Llandybie, Carms., SA18 3YT.
3, +   Research into the history of Methodism in Wales.
Book notices, book reviews, letters, monographic articles.
A, Last issue of each volume, Yes, None.
October 1971, T.p. 32.   650.
Per year 50p.

538 THE JOURNAL OF THE PRESBYTERIAN HISTORICAL SOCIETY OF ENGLAND. 1914.
Presbyterian Historical Society of England, 86 Tavistock Place, London, WC1H 9RT.
1, *   History of World Presbyterianism.
Book reviews, letters, monographic articles, obituaries.
4 year, –, Yes, None.
May 1972, T.p. 44.   400.
Per copy 30p. Free to members.
Indexed in: BHI.

539 PRESBYTERIAN HERALD. 1943.
(Missionary Herald 1843; Irish Presbyterian 1856).
Presbyterian Church in Ireland, Church House, Belfast, BT1 6DW.
11, =   Book reviews, letters, news.
No Index.
T.p. 20, Ad.p. 4.   24500.
Per copy 5p, per year 50p.

540 REFORM: the magazine of the United Reformed Church. 1972.
(Presbyterian Outlook; Congregational Monthly 1926-1972; Enterprise 1968-1972).
The United Reformed Church, 86 Tavistock Place, London, WC1H 9RT.
12, * †   News, articles, reports—affairs of local churches and regional groups, national organisation of the URC, accounts of work overseas, comment on social and national affairs.
Book reviews, letters, news, reports.
No Index.
Per copy 7p, per year £1.17.

541 Y TYST. 1871.
(Y Tyst Cymraeg 1867-1870).
Union of Welsh Independents, 11 St. Helens Road, Swansea.
52, =   Church in Wales countrywide.
Book notices, book reviews, letters, articles.
No Index.
T.p. 12.   3500.
Per copy 5p.

286
BAPTIST CHURCHES

542 BAPTIST QUARTERLY. Journal of the Baptist Historical Society. 1922.
(Transactions of the Baptist Historical Society 1908-1921).
Baptist Union of Great Britain and Ireland, 4 Southampton Road, London, WC1B 4AB.
4, + =   Continuing study and recording of Baptist History.
Book notices, book reviews, monographic articles.
2 year, January, Yes, None.
T.p. 47.
Free to members.
Indexed in: BHI, IBZ.

543 BAPTIST TIMES. 1902.
(Freeman 1855; Baptist 1872).
Baptist Times Ltd., 4 Southampton Row, London WC1B 4AB.
52, =   Baptist and Free Church World wide.
Book notices, book reviews, letters, monographic articles.
No Index.
T.p. 12, Ad.p. Most.   20000.
Per copy 5p, per year £2.50.

544 EUROPEAN BAPTIST.
European Baptist Federation, 4 Southampton Row, London, WC1B 4AB.
4, =   Articles, news.
No Index.
T.p. 19.
Subscription on application.

545 IRISH BAPTIST HISTORICAL SOCIETY JOURNAL. 1968.
Baptist Union of Ireland, 3 Fitzwilliam Street, Belfast, BT9 6AW.
1, *   The history of Baptists, Baptist churches and Baptist work in Ireland.
Monographic articles.
A, –, Yes, None.
1970/71, T.p. 65.
Per copy $62\frac{1}{2}$p.

546 THE QUEST: The magazine for Young Baptists. 1926.
Baptist Missionary Society, 93 Gloucester Place, London, W1H 4AA.
4,   For young people in Baptist churches.
No Index.
T.p. 30, Ad.p. 2.   6000.
Per copy 4p, per year 16p.

547 REFORMATION TODAY. 1970.
Cuckfield Baptist Chapel, 4 Gander Hill, Haywards Heath, Sussex, RH16 3RY.
4, ○   Persons throughout the world with an interest in the teachings and practices of Reformed (Calvinistic) Baptists.
Book notices, book reviews, letters, articles.
No Index.
T.p. 40.
Per copy $12\frac{1}{2}$p, per year 50p.

548 WONDERLANDS: The junior magazine of the Baptist Missionary Society. 1909.
(Juvenile Missionary Herald 1845-1908).
Baptist Missionary Society, 93 Gloucester Place, London, W1H 4AA.
12,   For children in 8/12 age group attached to Baptist churches.
No Index.
18500.
Per copy 1p, per year 12p.

287
METHODIST CHURCHES

549 BATHAFARN. Journal of the Historical Society of the Methodist Church in Wales. 1946.
The Society, c/o Llys Myfyr, Pwllheli, Caern.
1, + =   All aspects of history of English and Welsh Methodism.
Book notices, book reviews, monographic articles, obituaries.
Vols. 1-21 published in 1966.
T.p. 43.
Free to members.

550 CHRISTIAN WORDS and missionary outlook: monthly magazine of the Wesleyan Reform Union. c. 1869.
Wesleyan Reform Union, Wesleyan Reform Church House, 123 Queen Street, Sheffield, S1 2DU, Yorks.

12.
Church news and religious articles.
No Index.
June 1972, T.p. 23.   2400.
Per copy 2½p, per year 30p.

551 JOURNAL OF THE CORNISH METHODIST HISTORICAL ASSOCIATION.
c/o 1 Penventon Terrace, Redruth, Cornwall.
2, *
Book reviews, short articles.
No Index.
May 1972, T.p. 24.
Free to members.

552 JOURNAL OF THE LANCASHIRE AND CHESHIRE BRANCH OF THE WESLEY HISTORICAL SOCIETY. 1965.
Lancashire & Cheshire Branch of W.H.S., 4 Brecon Close, Royton, Oldham, Lancs.
2, *   History of Methodism in Lancashire and Cheshire, plus associated parts of Derbyshire and the West Riding.
Book notices, book reviews, letters, monographic articles, obituaries.
5 year, 1969, No, None.
August 1970, T.p. 20.   130.
Per copy 15p, per year 25p.

553 NOW: incorporating Women's Work and Kingdom Overseas. 1970.
Methodist Missionary Society, 25 Marylebone Road, London, NW1 5JR.
10, ○   Information concerning the Christian Church in Europe, Asia, India, Africa, New Guinea and the Caribbean, together with geographical and political background etc.
No Index.
June 1972, T.p. 24.   80000.
Per copy 5p, per year 60p.

554 PROCEEDINGS OF THE WESLEY HISTORICAL SOCIETY. 1893.
Wesley Historical Society, c/o A. A. Taberer Ltd., Bankhead, Broxton, Chester.
3, + ○   18th and 19th century Methodist history.
Book notices, book reviews, letters, monographic articles.
2 yearly, —, Yes, Vols. 1-XXX.
December 1971, T.p. 30.   950.
Free to members and per year 75p.
Indexed in: BHI.

288

UNITARIANISM

555 TRANSACTIONS OF THE UNITARIAN HISTORICAL SOCIETY. 1915.
The Society, c/o 13 Devonshire Road, West Bridgford, Nottingham.
1, + * =   History of Unitarianism and Dissent and other material relevant to the interests of a learned society.
Book reviews, monographic articles.
4 year, as supplement to fourth part of each volume, Yes, None.
October 1971, T.p. 39, Ad.p. 3.   240.
Per year personal 80p, Institutions £1.25.
Indexed in: BHI.

556 THE UNITARIAN. 1903.
c/o 27 Gladstone Road, Altrincham, Cheshire.
12, ○ =   News of contemporary movements and relevant historical aspects.
Book reviews, letters, articles.
No Index.
Per copy 3p, per year 66p.

289.6

SOCIETY OF FRIENDS (QUAKERS)

557 THE FRIEND: A Quaker Weekly Journal. 1843.
The Friends Publications, Ltd., Drayton House, 30 Gordon Street, London, WC1H OBQ.
52, *   News relevant to the Society of Friends; articles on religious and social topics, peace and international relations.
Book notices, book reviews, letters, articles, obituaries.
A, —, Yes, None.
May 26, T.p. 26, Ad.p. 4.
Per copy 7p, per year £4.94.

558 FRIENDS QUARTERLY. 1947.
(Friends Quarterly Examiner 1867).
Headley Brothers Ltd., Invicta Press, Ashford, Kent.
4, =   Quakerism.
3 year, —, No, None.
T.p. 48.   1000.
Per year £1.
Indexed in: BHI.

559 JOURNAL OF THE FRIENDS HISTORICAL SOCIETY. 1903.
Friends Historical Society, Friends House, Euston Road, London, NW1.
12, + =   Quaker history.
Book reviews, monographic articles.
3 year, —, Yes, 50 year.
T.p. 64.
Free to members.
Indexed in: BHI.

294.3

BUDDHISM

560 THE MUSLIM HERALD. 1960.
The London Mosque, 16 Gressenhall Road, London, SW18 5QL.
12, +   Articles on Islam, Christianity, Hinduism, Judaism, Buddhism etc.
Book reviews, letters, monographic articles.
No Index.
July 1971, T.p. 32.   1000.
Per copy 15p, per year £1.50.

561 THE MIDDLE WAY: journal of the Buddhist Society. 1943.
(Buddhism in England 1926-1943).
The Buddhist Society, 58 Eccleston Square, London, SW1V 1PH.
4, *   Buddhism and other philosophies and religions in relation to Buddhism.
Book notices, book reviews, letters, monographic articles.
A, May, No, None.
May 1972, T.p. 47, Ad.p. 4.   3000.
Per copy 25p, per year £1.12.
Free to members.

562 THE WESTERN BUDDHIST: Journal of the Full Buddhist Tradition. 1954.
100 Roundwood Way, Banstead, Surrey.
Irregular, * =   Buddhist teaching and practice, traditional and modern.
Book notices, book reviews, letters, articles, obituaries.
No Index.
Per copy c. 50p.

294.527

YOGA

563 YOGA AND HEALTH. 1971.
Astrian Public Relations Ltd., 344 South Lambeth Road, London, SW8.

12, ○
No Index.
Per copy 20p.

564 YOGA QUARTERLY REVIEW. 1971.
Yoga Research Association, 79 Addison Way, London, NW11.
4, ○
No Index.
T.p. 51.
Per copy £1.20, per year £4.

296

JUDAISM

565 CHRISTIAN ATTITUDES ON JEWS AND JUDAISM: A Bi-monthly Survey. 1968.
Institute of Jewish Affairs, 13-16 Jacob's Well Mews, George Street, London, W1H 5PD.
6, +   Review of the more important statements and publications relevent to the Churches' new approach.
Abstracts, book notices, book reviews, monographic articles.
No Index.
Feb 1972, T.p. 18.   1200.
Per copy 35p, per year £2.

566 EUROPEAN JUDAISM. 1971.
European Judaism, 34 Upper Berkeley Street, London, W1.
2, =
No Index.
Per year £1.30.

567 HAMAOR. (The Light). 1962.
Federation of Synagogues, 64 Leman St., London, E.1.
3, *
Book notices, book reviews, letters, articles, obituaries.
No Index.
March/April 1972, T.p. 26, Ad.p. 6.   5000.
Per copy 12½p.

568 THE HERALD. 1973.
(The Jewish Missionary Herald 1842-1972).
International Society for the Evangelization of the Jews, 45 Gildredge Road, Eastbourne, Sussex.
6, *   Spread of the Gospel of Jesus Christ amongst Jewish people throughout the world.
No Index.
May 1972, T.p. 16, Ad.p. None.   12000.
Free to subscribers to the Society.

569 JEWISH GAZETTE (Manchester and Leeds). 1928.
Jewish Gazette Ltd., 18 Cheetham Parade, Manchester, M8 6DJ.
52, ○   General all purpose newspaper.
No Index.

570 THE JEWISH QUARTERLY. 1953.
Jewish Literary Publications Ltd., 68 Worcester Crescent, London, NW7 4NA.
4, ○ + *   Current trends in literature and art with particular reference to Jewish writers and artists. General surveys of cultural and social problems, historical research, communal affairs, education, reviews.
Book notices, book reviews, letters, monographic articles, obituaries.
Index for the first 20 years in preparation.
Spring 1972, T.p. 50.   5000.
Per copy 40p, per year £1.50.

571 JEWISH TELEGRAPH. 1950.
Jewish Telegraph Ltd., Levi House, Bury Old Road, Manchester, 8.
52, ○   A local news weekly covering Lancashire and Cheshire.
Book notices, book reviews, letters, obituaries, parliamentary reports.
No Index.
June 9, 1972, T.p. 18, Ad.p. Most.   c. 10000.
Per copy 3p.

572 JEWISH TRIBUNE: Organ of Anglo-Jewish Orthodoxy. 1962.
Agudas Israel of Gt Britain, 97 Stamford Hill, London, N.16.
26, ○   World Jewish News and Interests.
Book notices, book reviews, letters, articles, obituaries, parliamentary reports.
No Index.
Per copy 5p, per year £1.50.

573 JOURNAL OF SEMITIC STUDIES. 1956.
Manchester University Press, 316-324 Oxford Road, Manchester, M13 9NR.
2, +   Interprets Semitic studies in the broadest sense, including articles of linguistic, literary, historical, archeological, legal, philosophical and anthropological interest—Semitic languages, Islamica, post-biblical Jewish studies, etc are also covered.
Book reviews, monographic articles.
No Index.
Spring 1972, T.p. 172, Ad.p. 2.   c. 750.
Per copy £2.70, per year £4.80.

574 NEW VISION. 1969.
(British Israel Quarterly).
British Israel World Federation, 6 Buckingham Gate, London, SW1.
4, + =   Furthering beliefs that the Celto-Saxons are the descendants of Ancient Israel.
Book notices, book reviews, letters, articles, obituaries.
No Index.
T.p. 30.
Free to members.

575 PATTERNS OF PREJUDICE. 1967.
Institute of Jewish Affairs, 13-16 Jacob's Well Mews, George Street, London, W1H 5PD.
6, + *   Study of causes and manifestations of racial, religious and ethnic discrimination and prejudice, with particular reference to antisemitism.
Book notices, book reviews, letters, monographic articles.
A, Jan-Feb issue, Yes, None.
Jan-Feb. 1972, T.p. 32.   1200.
Per copy 35p, per year £2.

576 POINTER. Quarterly Journal of the Union of Liberal and Progressive Synagogues. 1965.
The Union, 28 St. John's Wood Road, London, NW8.
4, ○   Judaism and Jewish life in Britain and abroad.
Book reviews, letters, articles.
No Index.
T.p. 18, Ad.p. 2.   6000.
Per copy 10p, per year 50p.
Indexed in: BHI.

577 THE SCRIBE: Journal of Descendants of Babylonian Jewry. 1972.
11 Russell Road, London, W14.
6, ○.
No Index.
Per year £1.50.

578 SOVIET JEWISH AFFAIRS: A Journal on Jewish Problems in the USSR and Eastern Europe. 1971.

Key to reference symbols

○ popular   ‡ technical   = trade/professional

+ research   * society/institution   † house journal

Bulletin on Soviet and East European Jewish Affairs 1968-1970).
Institute of Jewish Affairs, 13-16 Jacob's Well Mews, George Street, London, W1H 5PD.
2, +   Historical and broad contextual aspects as well as current developments and analyses.
Abstracts, book notices, book reviews, legal notes, letters, monographic articles.
A, —, Yes, None.
Nov. 1971, T.p. 146, Ad.p. 6.   850.
Per copy £1, per year £2.

579 WORLD JEWRY: Review of the World Jewish Congress.
World Jewish Congress, 55 New Cavendish Street, London, W1M 8BT.
6, ○ *   Review of activities and policies of World Jewish Congress.
Book notices, book reviews, letters, monographic articles, obituaries.
No Index.
May 1972, T.p. 30, Ad.p. 2.   3000.
Per copy 20p, per year £1.20.

3
SOCIAL SCIENCES

580 AMERICAN BEHAVIOURAL SCIENTIST. 1957.
Sage Publications Ltd., St George's House, 44 Hatton Garden, London, EC1N 8ER.
6, = +   Social and behavioural sciences.
Book reviews, monographic articles.
A, —, Yes, None,
May/June 1972, T.p. 157.
Per year £8, Individual £5.46.

581 COMPARATIVE GROUP STUDIES. 1970.
Sage Publications Ltd., St. George's House, 44 Hatton Garden, London, EC1N 8ER.
4, = +   Social science of group work.
Book reviews, monographic articles.
A, —, Yes, None.
August 1971, T.p. 100.
Per year £7, Individual £4.70.

582 COMPARATIVE STUDIES IN SOCIETY AND HISTORY. 1959.
Cambridge University Press, P.O. Box 92, London, NW1 2DB.
4, +   New research into problems of Change and stability that rear in human societies through time or in the contemporary world.
Book reviews, monographic articles.
A, October, Yes, None.
March 1972, T.p. 119, Ad.p. 5.   2100.
Per copy £2, per year £5.

583 CURRENT AWARENESS BULLETIN: Human Sciences and Management. 1969.
University of Surrey, Library, Guildford.
26, +   Annotated references to articles from about 150 journals taken by the library mainly on behavioural, social and educational sciences topics of interest to the university.
No Index.
9th June, 1972, T.p. 8.   100.
£10 per year.

584 ECONOMY AND SOCIETY. 1972.
Routledge and Kegan Paul Ltd., 68-74 Carter Lane, London, EC4V 5EL.
4, + =   An international forum for scholarship and analysis in the social sciences.
Book notices, book reviews, monographic articles.
A, —, Yes, None.
February 1972, T.p. 116.
Per copy £1.25, per year £4.50.

585 ESSRA MAGAZINE. 1972.
Economic & Social Science Research Association, 177 Vauxhall Bridge Road, London, SW1.
12, =
No Index.
Per copy 7½p.

586 FEEDBACK: Journal of Loughborough University Social Science Society. 1971.
L.U.T. Social Science Society, Loughborough University, Students' Union, Loughborough, Leics. LE11 3TU.
2, *   General social science interest e.g. political science, sociology, economic history, and economics, written by undergraduate students at L.U.T.
Monographic articles.
No Index.
Winter 1971, T.p. c. 40.   200.
Per copy 25p, per year 50p.

587 JOURNAL OF LATIN AMERICAN STUDIES. 1969.
Cambridge University Press, P.O. Box 92, London, NW1 2DB.
2, +   Latin America from the Standpoint of the Social Sciences.
Book reviews, monographic articles.
A, October, Yes, None.
May 1972, T.p. 159, Ad.p. 6.   1200.
Per copy £2.50, per year £4.

588 NEW SOCIETY. 1962.
New Science Publications, 128 Long Acre, London, WC2.
52, ○ =   The social sciences, social policy, the social services, and social action; plus social reportage, reviews of the arts seen socially, and reviews of social science and general books. For the interested layman as well as for the actual or student specialist.
Book reviews, legal notes, letters, monographic articles.
Q, during ensuing quarter, No, None.
22 June 1972, T.p. 31, Ad.p. 21.   37000.
Per copy 12p, per year £6.50.

589 PHILOSOPHY OF THE SOCIAL SCIENCES. 1971.
Aberdeen University Press (Scotland) for York University, Toronto (Canada), The Aberdeen University Press Ltd., Farmers Hall, Aberdeen, Scotland, AB9 2XT.
4, +   Philosophy of the social sciences, i.e. issues in general methodology (metascience rather than research techniques) and the application of philosophy to the social sciences.
Book reviews, monographic articles.
A, With first issue of following year, Yes, None.
March 1972, T.p. 88.
Per year £3.

590 SSRC NEWSLETTER. 1967.
State House, High Holborn, London, WC1R 4TH.
4, +   Information on the SSRC's activities and policies, lists of latest grants, results of SSRC studentship scheme. Descriptions of selected research projects supported by SSRC, discussion articles on research policy and methods.
Book notices, book reviews, articles.

No Index.
No. 15, June 1972, T.p. 36.   11000.
Free.

591 SHIELD. 1870.
Josephine Butler Society, 'Candida', 49 Hawkshead Lane, North Mimms, Hatfield, Herts.
2, ‡ * =   Promotion of high standards of morality and sexual responsibility.
Book notices, book reviews, legal notes, monographic articles, obituaries, parliamentary reports.
A, –, Yes, None.
Nov. 1970, T.p. 32.   350.
Per copy 77p.

592 SOCIAL SCIENCE AND MEDICINE. 1967.
Pergamon Press Ltd., Headington Hill Hall, Oxford, OX3 0BW.
6, = +   All areas of socio-behavioural sciences and medicine.
Book reviews, monographic articles.
A, Last issue of volume, Yes, None.
Per copy £3, per year £16.

593 THEORIA TO THEORY. 1965.
Macmillian, Co. Ltd., Houndmills, Basingstoke, Hants.
4, +   Questions of science and religion and philosophical interpretations. Frontier questions in natural and social science which can be of interest in religion. Social science as dealing with man and his environment.
Book reviews, letters, monographic articles.
A, October, Yes, None.
T.p. 96, Ad.p. 2.   500.
Per copy 75p, per year £3.

3-053.7

YOUTH

594 YOUTH AND SOCIETY. 1969.
Sage Publications Ltd., St. Georges House, 44 Hatton Garden, London, EC1N 8ER.
4, + =   Broad social and political implications of youth culture and youth development.
Book reviews, monographic articles.
A, –, Yes, None.
December 1971, T.p. 116.
Per year £7, Individual £4.70.

595 YOUTH SERVICE. 1960.
Youth Service Information Centre, 37 Belvoir St., Leicester, LE1 6SL.
6, O   Topics of general interest to those concerned with the youth service and allied fields. Articles by by and interviews with professionals concerned with young people.
Letters, articles.
No Index.
May/June 1972, T.p. 16.   24000.
Per copy 5p, per year 50p.

301

SOCIOLOGY

596 AFRICAN SOCIAL RESEARCH. 1966.
(Rhodes-Livingstone Institute Journal 1944-1965).
Manchester University Press, 316-324 Oxford Road, Manchester M13 9NR.
2, +, *   Covers the general field of social research in Africa, especially sociology and social anthropology, psychology, economics, human geography and demography, history and political science.
Book notices, book reviews, monographic articles.
5 years, December 1970, No, None.
Dec. 1971, T.p. 76, Ad.p. 9.   c. 1000.
Per copy £1.44, per year £2.88.

597 BRITISH JOURNAL OF SOCIOLOGY. 1950.
Routledge & Kegan Paul Ltd., 68 Carter Lane, Ludgate Hill, London, EC4.
4, +
Book reviews, monographic articles.
A, December, Yes, 10 year.
T.p. 120, Ad.p. 8.
Per copy £1, per year £3.
Indexed in: BHI, IBZ.

598 COMMUNES: Journal of Commune Movement. 1968.
(Ahimsa Communities 1965-1968).
Commune Movement, 88 Strathmore Avenue, Hull.
6, *   Communal life styles in Britain.
Book reviews, letters, articles.
No Index.
June 1972, T.p. 28.   3500.
Per copy 20p, per year £1.

600 ENVIRONMENT AND BEHAVIOR. 1969.
Sage Publications Ltd., St. George's House, 44 Hatton Garden, London, EC1N 8ER.
= +   Influence of the physical environment on human behaviour.
Book reviews, monographic articles.
A, –, Yes, None.
March 1972, T.p. 121.
Per year £8. Individual £5.40.

601 FORUM: Journal of human relations. 1968.
2 Bramber Rd, London, W14 9PB.
13, O ‡   Up-to-date, expert information and advice on all aspects of sexuality: psychological, sociological, physiological.
Book reviews, legal notes, letters, articles, new products, tests.
No Index.
T.p. 82.   75000.
Per copy 40p.

602 HUMAN RELATIONS. A quarterly journal of studies towards the integration of the social sciences. 1947.
Plenum Publishing Co. Ltd., Antvar House, London Road, Wembley, Middlesex.
4, +
Monographic articles.
A, Last issue of year, Yes, None.
T.p. 92, Ad.p. 3.
Per copy £1.50, per year £4.20.
Indexed in: BHI, IBZ.

603 JOURNAL FOR THE THEORY OF SOCIAL BEHAVIOUR. 1971.
Basil Blackwell & Mott Ltd., 5 Alfred Street, Oxford OX1 4HB.
2, +   A co-operative effort between all whose fields of study impinge on human behaviour, with philosophers contributing conceptual analyses.
Articles.
A, –, Yes, None.
Subscription on application.

604 JOURNAL OF DEVELOPMENT STUDIES: A Quarterly Journal devoted to Economic, Political and Social Development. 1964.
Frank Cass & Co. Ltd., 67 Great Russell Street, London WC1B 3BT.
4, +   All aspects of development—economic, political, sociological, and anthropological—in the less developed countries.
Book notices, book reviews, letters, monographic articles.
A, Last issue of each vol—July, No, None.
Jan. 1972, T.p. 340, Ad.p. 6.
Per copy £1.75, per year £6.

605 JOURNAL OF MATHEMATICAL SOCIOLOGY. 1971.
Gordon & Breach, 41/42 William 4th street, London, WC2.

2, + ‡   Logic of measurement, particularly the
relationship of measurement problems to sociological and social psychological phenomena.
Book notices, book reviews, letters, monographic articles, new products, tests.
No Index.
Subscription on application.

606 JOURNAL OF SOCIAL POLICY. 1972.
Cambridge University Press, P.O. Box 92, London, NW1 2DB.
4, +   Aspects of social policy and its implementation.
Book reviews, monographic articles.
A, Last issue of volume, Yes, None.
1-1 January 1972, T.p. 96.
Per copy £1.50, per year £5.

607 PACIFIC SOCIOLOGICAL REVIEW. 1957.
Sage Publication Ltd., St. George's House, 44 Hatton Garden, London, EC1N 8ER.
4, =
Monographic articles.
A, —, Yes, None.
April 1972, T.p. 124.
Per year £7, Individual £4.70.

608 POVERTY AND HUMAN RESOURCES ABSTRACTS. 1965.
Sage Publications Ltd., St. George's House, 44 Hatton Garden, London, EC1N 8ER.
4, =   Human, social and manpower problems.
Abstracts.
Q, Each issue, Yes, A.
March 1972, T.p. 157.
Per year £20, Individual £13.40.

609 PROBLEMS OF SOCIETY. 1972.
New Educational Press & Angus & Robertson Ltd., Pekes, Hellingley, Hailsham, Sussex.
4, =   School and tertiary level interests.
Book reviews, letters, articles.
A, —, Yes, None.
T.p. 64.
Per year £4.

610 QUEST. 1970.
209, Abbey House, Victoria Street, London SW1H 0LD.
26, ○ =   News and information service on the voluntary movement and social change.
Book notices.
6m, Jan and Jul, No, None.
16.5.1972, T.p. 30.
Per year £5.

612 SOCIAL STUDIES: Irish Journal of Sociology. 1972. (Christus Rex Journal 1947-1971).
St. Patrick's College, Maynooth, Co. Kildare, Ireland.
6, +   Applied sociology aiming at giving Irish society an awareness of itself and the world in which it exists.
Book notices, book reviews, monographic articles
A, —, Yes, None.
March 1972, T.p. 145.   2500.
Per copy 30p, per year £2.

613 SOCIETY FOR THE STUDY OF LABOUR HISTORY BULLETIN. 1960.
Society for the Study of Labour History, c/o University of Sheffield, Department of Extramural Studies, 85 Wilkinson St. Sheffield, S10 2GS.
2, * + =   All aspects of working class history, mainly British history but selective coverage of other countries.
Book notices, book reviews, letters, monographic articles, obituaries.
1st cumulative appearing Autumn 1972. Planned to produce index every four issues and cumulative every twenty. No, 10 year.
Spring 1972, T.p. 100, Ad.p. 1.   800.
Per year varies, Free to members.

614 SOCIOLOGICAL ANALYSIS: A discussion journal of research and ideas. 1970.
Department of Sociological Studies, University of Sheffield, Sheffield, S10 2TN.
3, +   Discussion of theoretical questions in the fields of sociology, social anthropology and history considered as one related aspect of social-scientific knowledge.
Book reviews, letters, monographic articles.
Not decided yet: Will be considered after 5 years.
Easter Term 1972, T.p. 16.
Per year £3.15.

615 THE SOCIOLOGICAL REVIEW.
(Old Series 1908 New Series 1953).
University of Keele, Keele, Staffordshire, ST5 5BG.
4, + *   Sociology and Social anthropology.
Book reviews, monographic articles.
A, with the November issue, Yes, None.
Feb. 1972, T.p. 135, Ad.p. 7.   1700.
Per copy £1, per year £3.
Indexed in: BHI.

616 SOCIOLOGY: The Journal of the British Sociological Association. 1967.
Oxford University Press, Press Road, Neasden, London, NW10.
3, +   Sociology of economic development, education, the family, industry, leisure, occupations, political relations, population, race relations, and of rural and urban life, as well as the applications of sociology in medicine, social administration and other fields.
Book reviews, letters, articles.
A, September, Yes, None.
May 1972, T.p. 166, Ad.p. 16.   1400.
Per copy £2, per year £4.50.

617 WELSH SOCIOLOGIST. 1972.
Gwasg Gwenffrwd, Talwrn Glas, Afonwen, Caerwys, Flintshire, CH7 5UB.
1, ○ +   Sociology, social anthropology, linguistics, material culture, folk life, folklore.
Book notices, book reviews, legal notes, letters, monographic articles, obituaries.
5 year, —, No, None.
Per year £3.

618 WOMEN'S REPORT. 1972.
Women's Report, Fawcett House, 27 Wilfred Street, London, SW1.
6, ○   Women's liberation, anti-discrimination and equal pay.
No Index.
T.p. 16.
Per year £1.

301.153

PUBLIC OPINION

619 NOP BULLETIN. 1963.
National Opinion Polls Ltd., 76/86 Strand, London, WC2R 0DZ.
12, +   Summary of findings of the regular NOP political polls and ad hoc surveys conducted for the Daily Mail and other bodies for publication (post-publication releases).
Monographic articles.
A, January, Yes, None.
May 1972, T.p. 23.   175.
Per copy £1, per year £7.50.

301.16

SOCIAL RELATIONS

620 COMMUNITY. 1971.
Printing Services Partnership, 82 High Road, East Finchley, London, N. 2.

3, ○   News and comment on new expressions of community (eg. communes, community houses, wider intentional communities, house groups, work camps, team ministry, community development groups, etc.) emerging on the Christian scene in (mainly) British society.
Book reviews, articles.
No Index.
Summer, 1972, T.p. 16.   c. 1000.
Per copy 15p, per year 50p.

621   COMMUNITY DEVELOPMENT JOURNAL. 1966.
Oxford University Press, Press Road, Neasden, NW10.
3, +   Community development in both 'developed' and 'developing' countries. Also deals with related aspects of development such as agricultural extension, social education and functional adult literacy, and techniques of adult teaching and communication.
Book notices, book reviews, letters, monographic articles.
A, October, No, None.
April 1972, T.p. 77, Ad.p. 1.   1000.
Per copy £1, per year £3.

622   COMMUNITY FORUM. 1971.
N. Ireland Community Relations Commission, Bedford House, Bedford St, Belfast, BT2 7FD.
4, + *
Book notices, book reviews, legal notes, letters, articles, tests.
No Index.
Spring, 1972, T.p. 28.   2500.
Free.

31

STATISTICS

623   BRITISH AID STATISTICS: statistics of economic aid to developing countries. 1963-1967; 1964-1968; 1965-1969; 1966-1970; 1968.
(British Aid, 1966-1967).
H.M.S.O., P.O. Box 569, London, SE1.
1, ‡, +   Official Financial aid flows, and private aid flows to developing countries. Statistics on Technical Assistance.
No Index.
Per copy £2.10.

624   BULLETIN OF THE OXFORD UNIVERSITY INSTITUTE OF ECONOMICS AND STATISTICS. 1939.
Basil Blackwell & Mott Ltd., 5 Alfred Street, Oxford, OX1 4HB.
4, +   Application of statistical methods to economic and social problems, including study of theory of statistics.
Articles
A, November, Yes, None.
T.p. 92.   1400.
Per year £3.
Indexed in: BHI.

625   CIVIL JUDICIAL STATISTICS: Statistics relating to the committee of the Privy Council, House of Lords, the supreme court of judicature, county courts and other civil courts.
H.M.S.O., P.O. Box 569, Atlantic House, Holborn, Viaduct, London, EC1P 1BN.
1, ‡ +
No Index.
T.p. 100.   1250.
Per copy 85p.

626   DIGEST OF STATISTICS, NORTHERN IRELAND. 1954.
H M Stationery Office, 80 Chichester Street, Belfast BT1 4JY.
2, +   Reference book of economic and social change in Northern Ireland.
No Index.

627   DIGEST OF WELSH STATISTICS/CRYNHOAD O YSTADEGAU CYMRU. 1954
HMSO, Cardiff.
1, +   Population and vital statistics—Social conditions Education—Labour—Production—Transport and Communications—Finance—Area and Climate. All statistics relate to Wales (including Monmouthshire) except where otherwise indicated.
No Index.
No. 17, 1970 T.p. 133.
Per copy £1.10.

628   JOURNAL OF THE ROYAL STATISTICAL SOCIETY
Series A—1834.
Series B—1934.
Series C—1952.
Royal Statistical Society, 21 Bentinck Street, London, W1M 6AR.
Series A—4, Series B and C—3, *   All aspects of statistics, statistical methodology and statistical applications and statistical algorithms. The proceedings of the Society with discussion of the papers.
Abstracts, book notices, book reviews, letters, obituaries, tests.
A, —, Yes, 10 year.
Per copy £1, per year £6, depending on Series.
Free to members.

629   MONTHLY DIGEST OF STATISTICS. 1946.
HMSO, P.O. Box 569, London, SE1.
12, = ‡ +   Digest of all main economic and Social Statistics collected by Government departments.
No Index.
T.p. 156.
Per copy 50p, per year £6.

630   THE REGISTRAR GENERAL'S QUARTERLY RETURN FOR ENGLAND AND WALES. 1849.
Her Majesty's Stationery Office, P.O. Box 569, London, SE1.
4, +   Quarterly marriages, live and stillbirths, deaths; infant, neonatal, and perinatal mortality; deaths from certain causes; accidental deaths; notifications of abortions; meteorological report; insured persons absent from work owing to sickness or industrial injury; migration. Annual population estimates for England and Wales by sex and age.
No Index.
Per copy 23p, per year £1.10.

631   THE REGISTRAR GENERAL'S STATISTICAL REVIEW OF ENGLAND AND WALES: Tables: Part I, Medical; Part II Population, Part III, Commentary. 1921.
(Annual Report of the Registrar General for England and Wales. 1837-1920.)
Her Majesty's Stationery Office, P.O. Box 569, London, SE1.
One of each Part, + ‡ =
Part I; Mortality statistics; notifications of infectious diseases; meteorological data.
Part II: Statistics of population, marriages, births, divorces, adoptions, fertility, Parliamentary and local government electors, local elections.
Part III: Detailed analyses of statistics in Parts I and II, with comment on the trend of mortality from different causes of death, notifications of infectious diseases, population trends, marriage, birth and fertility rates.
No Index.
Subscription on application.

632   THE REGISTRAR GENERAL'S WEEKLY RETURN FOR ENGLAND AND WALES. 1970.
(A Table of Mortality for the Metropolis. 1840-45; Births and Deaths registered in London. 1846-1869; Weekly Return of Births and Deaths in London and

in other Large Towns in the United Kingdom. 1870-1921; Weekly Return of Births and Deaths Registered in County Boroughs and other Great Towns and of Cases of... Infectious Diseases. 1922-1948; Registrar General's Weekly Return for England and Wales, Births and Deaths, Infectious Diseases, Weather Report. 1949-1969).
Her Majesty's Stationery Office, P.O. Box 569 London, SE1.
52/53, + =   Weekly births, stillbirths and deaths, infant deaths, deaths from certain diseases; deaths in Greater London by sex and age; notifications of infectious diseases; new claims to sickness benefit; meteorological data.
No Index.
Per copy 18p, per year £10.66.

633 SCOTTISH ABSTRACT OF STATISTICS. 1971.
(Digest of Scottish Statistics).
HMSO, Bankhead Avenue, Sighthill, Edinburgh.
1, ‡ +   Statistics, including social economic, labour industrial activity, incomes and earnings, finance and population.
A, With each issue, Yes, None.
Subscription on application.

634 STATISTICAL RECORD. 1971.
149 Fleet Street, London, EC4.
4, =
No Index.
Per year £15.

635 THE STATISTICIAN: Journal of the Institute of Statisticians.
(The Incorporated Statistician 1950-1961).
Longmans Group Ltd., (for the Institute of Statisticians), 5 Bentinck Street, London, W.1.
4, ‡ + *   Applied statistics in research, business, and government.
Book reviews, monographic articles.
A, —, Yes, None.
March 1972, T.p. 98, Ad.p. 7.
Per copy £1.25, per year £4.

312

DEMOGRAPHY

636 ANNUAL ESTIMATES OF THE POPULATION OF SCOTLAND.
HMSO, Atlantic House, Holborn Viaduct, London EC1P 1BN.
1, +   Estimates of the Population of Scotland, Regional Divisions, Planning Regions, conurbations, Counties of Cities Large and Small burghs, Landward areas by d.c.s' and New Towns.
A, With issue, Yes, None.
Subscription on application.

637 ANNUAL REPORT OF THE REGISTRAR GENERAL FOR SCOTLAND.
HMSO, Atlantic House, Holborn Viaduct, London.
1, +   Mortality, population and vital statistics.
A, With issue, Yes, None.
Subscription on application.

638 LOCAL POPULATION STUDIES. 1970.
(Local Population Studies, Magazine and Newsletter. 1968-1969).
Nottingham University, Department of Adult Education, 14-22 Shakespeare St., Nottingham.
2, +   Historical demography and social structures, especially as applied to individual parishes or small regions.
Book notices, letters, monographic articles.
No Index.
Autumn 1971, T.p. 74, Ad.p. 2.   650.
Per copy 37p, per year 75p.

639 POPULATION PROJECTIONS. 1970-2010: England and Wales, Scotland, Northern Ireland, Great Britain, United Kingdom. 1971.
Her Majesty's Stationery Office, P.O. Box 569, London, SE1.
1, +   Projections based on mid-year estimates, by sex and age; some marital condition projections are included. There is also a detailed discussion of all aspects of the projections, the method used, and the variations from earlier projections.
No Index.

640 POPULATION REGISTRATION. 1962.
The Institute of Population Registration, Peter J. Butt, Esq., 11 Selborne Road, Littlehampton, Sussex.
4, *   News and items dealing with population matters and the registration thereof, including Census etc. Legal notes, letters, obituaries, parliamentary reports.
No Index.
March 1972, T.p. 24.   c. 550.
Free to members.

641 POPULATION STUDIES: a journal of demography. 1947.
The Population Investigation Committee, London School of Economics, Houghton Street, Aldwych, London, WC2A 2AE.
3, ‡ = +   All aspects of demographic research, demography, techniques of analysis and reviews of research.
Abstracts, book notices, book reviews, monographic articles.
A, November, Yes, 25 years.
July 1971, T.p. 166, Ad.p. 8.   2660.
Per copy £1.80, per year £4.50.
Indexed in: BHI.

642 QUARTERLY RETURN OF THE REGISTRAR GENERAL, SCOTLAND.
HMSO, Atlantic House, Holborn Viaduct, London.
4, +   Mortality, population and vital statistics.
Q, with issue, Yes, None.
Subscription on application.

643 THE REGISTRAR GENERAL'S ANNUAL ESTIMATES OF THE POPULATION OF ENGLAND AND WALES AND OF LOCAL AUTHORITY AREAS. 1948.
Her Majesty's Stationery Office, P.O. Box 569, London, SE1.
1, +   An estimate of the population of each local authority area and, for England and Wales as a whole, an estimate divided by sex and age groupings.
No Index.

644 WEEKLY RETURN OF THE REGISTRAR GENERAL, SCOTLAND.
HMSO, Atlantic House, Holborn Viaduct, London.
52, +
No Index.
Subscription on application.

32

CURRENT AFFAIRS. POLITICS

645 ALLIANCE: The Newspaper of the Alliance party of Northern Ireland. 1971.
(Alliance Bulletin 1970).
The Alliance Party of Northern Ireland, Alliance Headquarters, 6 Cromwell Road, Belfast, BT7 1JW.
12, ○   News, features and photographs relating to the growth of non-sectarian centre politics in Northern Ireland, as shown in the activities of the Alliance Party—already the province's second-largest party and committed to an outright challenge for power.
Book reviews, letters, articles.
No Index.
June 1972, T.p. 8.
Per copy 5p, per year 60p.

646 ALTERNATIVE. 1972.
   Union Movement, 76A Rochester Road, London, SW1.
   ○
   Per copy 5p.

647 ARAB REPORT AND RECORD. 1966.
   Arab Report and Record, 84 Chancery Lane, London, WC2A 1DL.
   24, +   Record of events and opinions in the Arab states and world events concerning them.
   Book reviews, articles.
   A, Index of persons, Subject index, April/May, Yes, None.
   16-31 March 1972, T.p. 27, Ad.p. 1.   575.
   Per year £40.

648 BRETON NEWS: Bulletin of the Breton Information Bureau. 1960.
   Breton Information Bureau, 9 Br Cnoc Sion, Ath Cliath 9, Eire.
   4, ‡ +   News of events concerning the struggle of the Bretons in the economic, cultural and political field, to maintain and develop their identity as a national community.
   No Index.
   Winter 1971-1972, T.p. 6.   1000.
   Per year 50p.

649 BRITAIN AND ISRAEL. 1970.
   Britain and Israel, 15 Uxbridge St., London W8.
   10, ○   Anglo/Israel/Middle East Affairs.
   Brief articles.
   No Index.
   April 1972, T.p. 4.
   Per copy 5p, per year £1.

650 BRITISH JOURNAL OF POLITICAL SCIENCE. 1971.
   Cambridge University Press, P.O. Box 92, London, NW1 2DB.
   4, +   All branches of political science.
   Book reviews, monographic articles.
   A, Last issue of volume, Yes, None.
   January 1972, T.p. 132, Ad.p. 1.   800.
   Per copy £2 per year £6.

651 CELTIC NEWS. 1963.
   Celtic League, 9 Br Cnoc Sion, Ath Cliath 9, Eire.
   4, *   News of the struggle of the Celtic peoples for the maintenance and development of their national identity.
   No Index.
   Spring 1972, T.p. 12.   1300.
   Per year 30p.

652 THE CHRISTIAN SOCIALIST. 1850.
   (Socialist Christian in 1950s).
   Christian Socialist Movement, Kingsway Hall, Kingsway, London, WC2.
   4, ○   Social, economic, industrial questions from a Christian and Socialist point of view. Articles, book reviews, obituaries from time to time. Letters. Occasional advts.
   Book reviews, letters, articles.
   No Index.
   October 1971, T.p. 16.   800.
   Per copy 6p, per year 50p.

653 COMPARATIVE POLITICAL STUDIES. 1969.
   Sage Publications Ltd., St. George's House, 44 Hatton Garden, London EC1N 8ER.
   4, = +
   Book reviews, monographic articles.
   A, —, Yes, None.
   July 1971, T.p. 124.
   Per year £8, Individual £5.40.

654 CONCORD: news bulletin of the English-Speaking Union of the Commonwealth. 1962.
   (The English-Speaking World).
   The English-Speaking Union, Dartmouth House, 37 Charles Street, London, W1X 8AB.
   4, *
   No Index.
   March 1972, T.p. 8.   37000.
   Per copy 2½p, per year 20p.

655 CORRESPONDENTS WORLD WIDE: The continual updated service in World Affairs.
   Correspondents World Wide Limited, (for the Atlantic Education Trust), 23/25 Abbey House, 8 Victoria Street, London SW1H 0LA.
   3, ○ +   An expert service enabling non-specialists to inform themselves on all important aspects of the current world scene.
   Book Notices, articles.
   No Index.
   T.p. 300.   1400.
   Per year £12.60.

656 CRISIS PAPER. 1968.
   Atlantic Information Centre for Teachers, 23/25 Abbey House, 8 Victoria Street, London, SW1H 0LA.
   7, + *   Produced rapidly, when needed, to provide immediate coverage of a topical issue currently in the news. Each one includes a brief analysis, a chronology, a short reading list and a wide and representative selection of world press comment on the topic.
   No Index.
   T.p. 20.   1000.
   Per copy 20p, per year £1.

657 CROSSBOW. Bow Group Quarterly. 1957.
   Bow Publications Ltd., 240 High Holborn, London WC1.
   4, = +   Politics.
   Book reviews, letters, articles.
   No Index.
   T.p. 54, Ad.p. 11.   4000.
   Per copy 25p, per year £1.

658 DAY BY DAY: News Commentary and Digest of National and International Affairs. 1962.
   Loverseed Press, Woolacombe House, 141 Woolacombe Rd., Blackheath, London, S.E.3.
   15, ○
   Comments on and reports serious national and international affairs, with stress on construction, peacemaking and opposition to war and other violence. Reviews the arts.
   Film reviews, art reviews, book reviews, occasional poetry, letters, obituaries, parliamentary, reports, opera and play reviews. Reports cricket.
   No Index.
   T.p. 16.   11700.
   Per copy 9p, per year £1.40.

659 DEVELOPMENT NEWS DIGEST. 1971.
   (Development News).
   Voluntary Committee on Overseas Aid and Development, 69 Victoria Street, London, SW1.
   52, * +   Digest of news relating to development of poor countries which has appeared in the national press and other media.
   No Index.
   May 5-11, 1972, T.p. 15.   c. 300.
   Per year £3.50.

660 EAST-WEST DIGEST. 1965.
   Foreign Affairs Publishing Co., 139 Petersham Rd., Richmond, Surrey.
   24, †   Subversion, defence, politics, international affairs, East-West realtions, disruption in industry, Communism, New Left, Sino-Soviet bloc.
   Book reviews, letters, articles, parliamentary reports.
   A, January, No, None.
   June 1972, T.p. 40, Ad.p. 1.   5000.
   Per year £5.
   Free to M.P.

661 FLEET STREET LETTER. 1938.
Fleet Street Letter Ltd., 72 Fleet Street, London, EC4 1JH.
48, ‡ Investment. British politics, World affairs, political and economic, business, in short article format.
A, January, No, None.
15 June 1972, T.p. 4.
Per year £12.

662 FOCUS. 1971.
ESL Bristol, St. Lawrence House, 29/31 Broad Street, Bristol, BS1 2HF.
18, * FOCUS is a children's national newspaper in wallchart form. A round up of the most significant news items over a given fortnight with features which concentrate on issues behind the news.
Articles.
No Index.
Per year £8.50. (18 issues).

663 FORTNIGHT: An Independent Review for Northern Ireland. 1970.
Fortnight Publications Ltd., 15 James Street South, Belfast BT2 7GA.
23, ○ Irish politics, emphasis on the North.
Book reviews, letters, articles, parliamentary reports.
A, December, No, None.
8 June 1972,
T.p. 20, Ad.p. 3,   3000.
Per copy 10p, per year £2.50.

664 GOVERNMENT AND OPPOSITION: Journal of Comparative Politics. 1965.
Government and Opposition Ltd., London School of Economics and Political Science, Houghton Street, London, WC2A 2AE.
4, = + Comparative study of problems of government and opposition in the internal and international fields.
Book notices, book reviews, monographic articles.
A, Last issues of volume, No, 5 year.
Summer 1971, T.p. 137.
Per copy £1.40, per year £5.
Indexed in: BHI.

665 IMPACT: international fortnightly. 1971.
News and Media Ltd., 33 Stroud Green Road, London, N4 3EF.
24, ○ Middle East, Afro-Asian and general world affairs.
Book notices, book reviews, letters, articles, obituaries, parliamentary reports.
No Index.
23 June-13 July 1972, T.p. 14, Ad.p. 1.   2000.
Per copy 10p. per year £3.50.

666 THE INDIVIDUALIST. Journal of the Personal Rights Association. 1870.
Personal Rights Association, 31 Parkside Gardens, London SW19.
6, + ○ Opposition to state interference in banking and the supply of money.
Book reviews, letters, articles.
No Index.
T.p. 12, Ad.p. 1.   500.
Per year £1.

667 INTERNATIONAL AFFAIRS: A Quarterly Review published for the Royal Institute of International Affairs. 1922.
Oxford University Press, Press Road, Neasden, London, NW10.
4, ○ + Contains significant articles on matters of broad international interest. The principal article in each issue is often contributed by a world statesman or other leading international personality.
Book notices, book reviews, letters, monographic articles.
A, October, Yes, None.
April 1972, T.p. 184, Ad.p. 14.   4000.
Per copy £1, per year £3.50.
Indexed in: BHI, IBZ.

668 INTERNATIONAL DEMOCRATIC REVIEW: a world review of politics, philosophy and literature. 1973.
International Democratic Action, 143a Croydon Road, Beckenham, Kent, BR3 3RB.
4, ○ * Political, philosophical and literary contributions reflecting a spirit of moderation and understanding.
Book notices, book reviews, letters, monographic articles, obituaries, parliamentary reports.
A, April, Yes, None.
April 1973, T.p. 180, Ad.p. 20.   c. 3000.
Per copy 75p, per year £2.80.

669 INTERNATIONAL POLITICAL SCIENCE ABSTRACTS. 1951.
Basil Blackwell & Mott Ltd., 5 Alfred Street, Oxford, OX1 4HB.
4, + Abstracts of articles and books on political science from all over the world.
No Index.
T.p. 148.   1500.
Per copy £1.50, per year £4.

670 INTERNATIONAL STUDIES QUARTERLY.
Sage Publications Ltd., 44 Hatton Garden, London E.C.1.
4, = Cross national interdisciplinary research; features a wide variety of comparative cross cultural studies.
Monographic articles.
A, —, Yes, None.
June 1972, T.p. 126.
Per year £7.

671 INTERNATIONALIST. 1971.
The Internationalist, Britwell Salome, Oxford, OX9 5BR.
3, ○ Magazine of world development.
No Index.
36000.
Per year 85p.

672 IRISH DEMOCRAT.   1945.
(Irish Freedom 1939-1944).
Connolly Publications Ltd., 283 Grays Inn Road, London, W.C.1.
12, ○ Irish politics from Labour-Republican angle, political activities of Irish in Britain, Irish culture.
No Index.
T.p. 8.   8000.
Per copy 7p, per year £1.14.

673 JOURNAL OF COMMONWEALTH POLITICAL STUDIES. 1961.
Leicester University Press, 2 University Road, Leicester LE1 7RB.
3, + = Comparative politics and recent history, on individual countries in the Commonwealth and general themes.
Book reviews, monographic articles.
A, Last issue of year, Yes, None.
March 1972, T.p. 92, Ad.p. 4.   700.
Per copy £1.10, per year £2.75.

674 JOURNAL OF INTERAMERICAN STUDIES AND WORLD AFFAIRS. 1958.
Sage Publications Ltd., St. George's House, 44 Hatton Garden, London EC1N 8ER.
4, = +
Book reviews, monographic articles.
A, —, Yes, None.
February 1972, T.p. 127.
Per year £10.

675 JOURNAL OF MODERN AFRICAN STUDIES. 1963.
Cambridge University Press, P.O. Box 92, London, NW1 2DB.

4, + Politics, economics and related topics in contemporary Asia.
Book reviews, monographic articles.
A, a part of next volume, Yes, None.
9-3 October 71, T.p. 166, Ad.p. 8.   2600.
Per copy £1.50, per year £5.
Indexed in: BHI

676 NEW STATESMAN. 1913.
The Statesman & Nation Publishing Co. Ltd., Great Turnstile, London, WC1V 7HJ.
52, ○ = +   Current Affairs, Literature, the Arts and Entertainment.
Book reviews, articles, letters.
6m, Jan-June, Yes, None.
16 June 1972, T.p. 45.   70000.
Per copy 10p, per year £6.

677 NEWSLETTER FROM SCOTLAND. c.1950.
Scottish Information Office, St. Andrew's House, Edinburgh, EH1 3DQ.
12, ○   Scottish affairs generally.
No Index.
Subscription on application.

678 ORZEL BIALY (White Eagle): Polish Political and Cultural Monthly. 1941.
Gryf Ltd., 171 Battersea Church Road, London, SW11.
11, ○   World current affairs.
Book notices, book reviews, letters.
No Index.
June 1972, T.p. 40, Ad.p. 3.   5000.
Per copy 20p, per year £2.40.

679 OVERSEAS DEVELOPMENT, 1966.
Overseas Development Administration Foreign and Commonwealth Office, Eland House, Stag Place, London, SW1.
6, ○ ‡ = + *   News items, pictures and articles covering widest possible range of development subjects, including international aid.
No Index.
May 1972, T.p. 12.   10500.
Per year 57p.

680 PLANET.
Llangeitho, Tregavon, Cardigan.
6, =   Review of current affairs and the arts dealing with all aspects of life in Wales and the world today.
No Index.
Per copy 25p, per year £1.50.

681 POLICY AND POLITICS, 1972.
Macmillan Journals Ltd., Brunel Road, Basingstoke, RG21 2XS, Hants.
4, =   Book reviews, letters, monographic articles.
A, –, Yes, None.
Per year £6.50.

682 THE POLITICAL QUARTERLY. 1930.
Political Quarterly Publishing Co. Ltd., 49 Park Lane, London, W1.
4, * = +   Politics and public administration at home and abroad.
Book reviews, monographic articles.
A, December, Yes, None.
T.p. 115, Ad.p. 14.
Per copy 60p, per year £2.50.
Indexed in BHI, IBZ.

683 POLITICAL STUDIES: The Journal of the Political Studies Association of the United Kingdom. 1953.
Oxford University Press, Press Road, Neasden, London, NW10.
4, +   Political questions on a wide front, including both institutional and theoretical political studies and studies of allied questions in the legal, historical, philosophical, sociological and other fields.
Book reviews, monographic articles.
A, –, Yes, None.

June 1972, T.p. 135, Ad.p. 8.   1800.
Per copy £1.50, per year £4.50.
Indexed in: BHI, IBZ.

684 PORTUGUESE AND COLONIAL BULLETIN. 1961.
c/o 10 Fentiman Road, London, SW8.
4, ○, +   Events in Portugal and colonies principally in the political, economical and social fields. Reports on the anti-fascist and anti-colonialist struggles.
Legal notes, articles, new companies.
No Index.
October 1971, T.p. 10.
Per year 75p.

685 RED FLAG. 1963.
Revolutionary Workers Party, (Trotskyist) British Section of The IV International, 24 Cranbourn Street, London, WC2.
24, =   A Marxist analysis and orientation of the world class struggle which goes towards the overthrow of capitalism and the construction of socialism.
No Index.
T.p. 6.   5000.
Per copy 3p, per year 80p.

686 THE REPORT ON WORLD AFFAIRS. 1947.
(Report on Foreign Affairs 1919)
Report on World Affairs Ltd., 32 St. James's Street, London SW1A 1HR.
4, ○ = ‡   Report, factual, objective, compiled from large panel of experts, on world affairs (UK included) of current, past quarter.
Parliamentary reports.
Q, Cumulative, up to and including previous issue of volume to final Annual Index.
July 1972, T.p. 83.   2000.
Per copy £1.25, per year £5, 3 years £12.

687 ROUND TABLE: The Commonwealth Quarterly. 1910.
Oxford University Press, Press Road, Neasden, London, NW10.
4, ○ +   International and Commonwealth affairs.
Book reviews, articles, letters.
A, January, Yes, None.
July 1972, T.p. 130, Ad.p. 14.   2300.
Per copy £1, per year £4.

688 THE SCHILTROM: The Magazine for the Scottish Nationalist.
Schiltrom Publications, c/o 4c Lusset View, Radnor Street, Clydebank, Scotland.
5, ○   Deals with all subjects (mostly of a political nature) likely to be of interest to people concerned with the future of Scotland, the nation.
Articles.
No Index.
Spring 1972, T.p. 13, Ad.p. 1   c.200.
Per year 65p.

689 SCOTTISH JOURNAL OF POLITICAL ECONOMY. 1954.
Longman Group Ltd., 43/49 Annandale Street, Edinburgh EH7 4AT.
3, = * +
Economic and social affairs, general political economy, economic history.
Book notices, monographic articles.
A, Last issue of year, Yes, None.
June 1972, T.p. 100, Ad.p. 5.   1000.
Per copy £2, per year £5.
Indexed in: BHI, IBZ.

Key to reference symbols

○ popular   ‡ technical   = trade/professional

+ research   * society/institution   † house journal

690 SPEARHEAD. 1964.
Albion Press, 50 Pawsons Road, Croydon CRO 2QF, Surrey.
12, ○   Comment on political affairs.
Letters, articles.
No Index.
July 1972, T.p. 18, Ad.p. 2.   4000.
Per copy 12p, per year £1.50.

691 SURVEY OF CURRENT AFFAIRS. 1971.
(Commonwealth Survey, 1955-66; Survey of British and Commonwealth Affairs, 1967-70),
Central Office of Information (Reference Division), Hercules Road, London, SE1.
12, +   British domestic affairs (political, economic and social) and international relations. Texts or summaries of speeches, communiques, reports, etc.
6m, January/July, No, A.
June 1972, T.p. 52.   6000
Per year £2.97.

692 SWINTON JOURNAL. c.1950.
Swinton Conservative College, Masham, Nr. Ripon, Yorkshire.
4, + *   Economics, politics, social studies, history.
No Index.
1200.
Per copy 20p, per year 60p.

693 TWO NATIONS. 1970.
Worker's Association for the Democratic Settlement of the National Conflict in Ireland, 10 Athol Street, Belfast 12.
10, ○   Politics of Irish and Ulster nationalism from an anti-nationalist point of view.
No Index.

694 WORLD SURVEY. 1969.
(British Survey 1939-1968)
Atlantic Education Trust, 23/25 Abbey House, 8 Victoria Street, London SW1H 0LA.
12, + *   Each 'Survey' is a monograph on a particular country or a subject of international importance, written by an author with personal knowledge of it, with a map and a reading list.
Monographic articles.
A, January, No, None.
T.p. 18.   5000.
Per copy 20p, per year £1.90.

695 WORLD TODAY: Published for the Royal Institute of International Affairs. 1945.
Oxford University Press, Press Road, Neasden, London, NW10.
12, ○ +   Provides factual and up-to-date information for the general reader on current world problems. Internal political and economic conditions in foreign countries are also analysed.
No Index.
December 1971, T.p. 45, Ad.p. 4.   3500.
Per copy 28p, per year £3.25.

323.1

RACE RELATIONS

696 ANTI-APARTHEID NEWS: Newspaper of the Anti-Apartheid Movement. 1965.
Anti-Apartheid Movement, 89 Charlotte Street, London W1P 2DQ.
10, * ○ +   In-depth reports on the facts of the situation in Southern Africa, and the campaigns being waged in Britain and internationally against white supremacy.
Book reviews, letters, articles.
No Index.
June 1972, T.p. 11, Ad.p. 1.   7500.
Per copy 5p, per year 75p.

697 AZANIA COMBAT: Organ of the PAC Mission to Europe and the Americas. 1969.
Pan Africanist Congress of Azania (South Africa), 22a Hillview Gardens, London, NW4 2JH.
4, +   Current affairs of Pan Africanist Congress and broad struggle against apartheid in South Africa as well as commentary on global struggle against imperialism.
Book reviews, letters, articles, reports.
No Index.
No. 4, 1971, T.p. 10.   1000.
Per copy 7½p, per year 30p.

698 EDUCATION AND COMMUNITY RELATIONS. 1970.
Community Relations Commission, 10-12 Russell Square, London, WC1.
11, ‡ =
Book notices, book reviews, notes.
No Index.
June 1972, T.p. 8.   14000.
Free.

699 GARAVI GUJARAT. 1968.
Garavi Gujarat Publications, 22 Rosoman Street, London, EC1R 0NH.
26, ○ *   News on Indians/Asians in this country with articles on laws of this country, such as Immigration laws, literature, book review, women's page, Our Gujaratis, Biography of prominent Gujarati, news on India and Britain, and rest of the world; for better community relations.
No Index.
15.8.72, T.p. 26, Ad.p. 14.   21509.
Per copy 8p, per year £3.

700 INTERNATIONAL DEFENCE AND AID FUND INFORMATION SERVICE MANUAL. 1967.
Christian Action Publications, 104/5 Newgate Street, London, E.C.1.
2, * + ‡   Records on all aspects of Apartheid: Economic-Political-Social-Religious-Educational-Cultural-Sport-etc. Complete data on all Laws and Practices relating to Racial Discrimination. Reports and details on: Political Prisoners and Trials, Detainees, Resettlement and Trade Unions.
A, —, Yes, None.
Per year £6.

701 JOURNAL OF BLACK STUDIES. 1971.
Sage Publications Ltd., St. George's House, 44 Hatton Garden, London, EC1N 8ER.
4, + =   Forum for the open discussion of the colour problem.
Monographic articles, book reviews.
A, —, Yes, None.
June 1971, T.p. 130.
Per year £7, Individual £4.70.

702 THE MANCUNIAN INDIAN. 1971.
The Indian Association, Gandhi Hall, Brunswick Road, Manchester M20 9QB.
12, ○ =   To foster good relations between various communities.
No Index.
Per copy 3p.

703 NEW COMMUNITY: Journal of the Community Relations Commission. 1971.
(Community, 1971)
Community Relations Commission, Russell Square House, 10-12 Russell Square, London, WC1B 5EH.
4, *   Covers applied and theoretical approaches to the associated fields of community relations, ethnic and race relations and migration.
Abstracts, book notices, book reviews, letters, monographic articles, parliamentary reports.
Not yet decided.
No. 1 Oct. 1971, T.p. 83, Ad.p. 2.   7500.
Per copy 50p, per year £2.

704 RACE: A Journal of Race and Group Relations. 1958.
Oxford University Press (for Institute of Race Relations), Press Road, Neasden Lane, London, NW10.
4, +   World social situations and problems; sociological, anthropological, political, historical, legal etc.
Book notices, book reviews, letters, monographic articles.
A, July, Yes, None.
January 1972, T.p. 112, Ad.p. 6.   c. 1300.
Per copy £1, per year £3.50.
Indexed in: BHI.

705 RACE RELATIONS: quarterly Bulletin of the Race Relations Board. 1967.
Race Relations Board, 5 Lower Belgrave Street, London, SW1W, 0NR.
4, *   Work of the Race Relations Board.
No Index.
Summer 1972, T.p. 8.
Free.

706 RACE RELATIONS ABSTRACTS. 1968.
Institute of Race Relations, 36 Jermyn Street, London, SW1.
3, = + *
Abstracts.
Author index with each issue.
T.p. 22.
Subscription on application.

707 RACE RELATIONS BULLETIN. 1969.
The Runnymede Trust, Stuart House, 1 Tudor Street, London, EC4Y 0AD.
11, + *   Survey of the field of Race Relations in Great Britain with news and summaries of publications and research. The Industrial Supplement is of particular interest in the field of employment.
Book notices, book reviews, reports.
No Index.
June 1972, T.p. 6.   6000.
Per year £1.

708 RACE TODAY. 1969.
(Newsletter, 1960-1969)
Institute of Race Relations, 36 Jermyn Street, London, SW1Y 6DU.
12, * ○ + =   Race and community relations in Britain in an international context with reports and articles from overseas.
Book notices, book reviews, legal notes, letters, articles.
No Index.
June 1972, T.p. 32, Ad.p. 3.   3000.
Per copy 10p, per year £1.20.

323.2

CONFLICT

709 CONFLICT STUDIES. 1969.
Institute for the Study of Conflict, RUSI Building, Whitehall, London, SW1.
Irregular, + *   Studies on violence, revolutionary warfare, guerrillas, conflict in society.
No Index.
No. 7, T.p. 24.
Per copy 75p, per year £5.

323.33

WORKING CLASS

710 HANES GWEITHWYR CYMRU/WELSH LABOUR HISTORY. 1970.
Gwasg Gwenffrwd, Talwrn Glas, Afonwen, Caerwys, Flintshire CH7 5UB.
2, + ○ *   History of working-class and popular movements in Wales (Bilingual content).
Book notices, book reviews, letters, monographic articles.
5 year — No, None.
Per copy 50p, per year £1.

328

PARLIAMENTS

711 DEBATE: A digest of Parliamentary Debates and questions. 1971.
New Educational Press, Pekes, Hellingly, Hailsham, Sussex.
10, +   Contains an overview of all important matters raised in the UK Parliament. Only verbatim extracts from the official record are used. Includes summary of all proceedings and comprehensive index.
Monthly — No, A.
No. 6, T.p. 64.
Per year £10.

712 EUROPEAN PARLIAMENT DIGEST: a digest of Parliamentary Debates and questions. 1973.
New Educational Press, Pekes, Hellingly, Hailsham, Sussex.
10, +   All important matters raised in the European Parliament.
M, —, No, A.
Per year £10.

713 THE PARLIAMENTARIAN: Journal of the Parliaments of the Commonwealth. 1919.
Commonwealth Parliamentary Assocn., 7 Old Palace Yard, London, SW1.
4.   Parliamentary/Commonwealth topics.
Book notices, book reviews, monographic articles, parliamentary reports.
A, January, Yes, None.
April 1972, T.p. 80.   5500.
Per copy 75p, per year £2.50.

714 PARLIAMENTARY AFFAIRS. 1947.
Hansard Society for Parliamentary Govt., 162 Buckingham Palace Road, London, SW1.
4, +   All aspects of parliamentary democracy and history.
Book notices, monographic articles.
A, Last issue of year, Yes, None.
T.p. 93, Ad.p. 2.
Per copy 75p, per year £3. Free to members.
Indexed in: BHI, IBZ.

715 THE POLITICAL COMPANION. 1969.
Political Reference Publications, 18 Lincoln Green, Chichester, Sussex.
4, ○ +   A pocket-size compendium of facts and figures on the British Parliament, politics and elections. Exclusive listing of prospective parliamentary candidates and an analysis of the division lobby and questions record of each Member of Parliament.
Book notices, book reviews.
No Index.
April/June 1972, T.p. 150.   8000+.
Per copy 60p, per year £2.

716 REVIEW OF PARLIAMENT AND PARLIAMENTARY DIGEST. 1972.
Parliamentary Digest, 171 Queen Victoria Street, London, EC4.
Weekly during sessions, =
No Index.
Per year £35.

717 VACHER'S EUROPEAN COMPANION. 1972.
A. S. Kerswill Ltd., 15 Cochrane Mews, St. John's Wood, London, NW8.

4, + = Supplies names, addresses, telephone numbers of wide range of senior individuals throughout European Communities and European Free Trade area, also Governments, the Communities and Diplomatic representation, also Commercial organisations and other European Institutions.
No Index.
April 1972, T.p. 80, A.p. 8.   2000.
Per copy 75p, per year £2.50.

718 VACHER'S PARLIAMENTARY COMPANION. 1832.
A.S. Kerswill Ltd., 15 Cochrane Mews, St. John's Wood, London, NW8.
4, + = Parliamentary and Public Offices reference book.
No Index.
January/March 1972, T.p. 180, Ad. p. 12.   9500.
Per copy 60p, per year £2.

719 WESTMINSTER SUMMARY. 1971
New Educational Press, Pekes, Hellingly, Hailsham, Sussex.
10, + Digest of Parliamentary Debates.
No Index.
Per year £1.

329

POLITICAL PARTIES

720 WELSH NATION. 1956.
(Welsh Nationalist. 1932-1955)
Plaid Cymru, 8 Heol y Frenhines, Cardiff.
50, ○ Political, economic and cultural life of Wales and other Celtic nations.
Book notices, book reviews, legal notes, letters, articles, obituaries, parliamentary reports.
No Index.
16. 6. 72, T.p. 8.   5000.
Per copy 4p, per year £3.25.

721 Y DRAIG GOCH. 1926.
Plaid Cymru, Heol y Dŵr., Caerfyrddin (Carmarthen.)
12, ○ Semi-official organ of Plaid Cymru.
Welsh politics, economics and cultural life. Book notices, book reviews, letters, articles, parliamentary reports.
No Index.
May 1972, T.p. 7, Ad.p. 1.   4000.
Per copy 3p, per year 75p.

722 Y FANER: Baner ac Amserau Cymru. 1843.
County Press, County Press Buildings, Bala, N. Wales.
52, ○ * ‡ Welsh nationalism.
Book notices, book reviews, legal notices, letters, articles, new products, obituaries, parliamentary reports.
No Index.
May 16, 1972, T.p. 4, Ad.p. 2.
Per copy 5p, per year £2.60.

329.12

LIBERALS

723 FRINGE: Oxford University Liberal Society Newsletter. 1969.
(Oxford Guardian. 1920-1968)
Oxford University Liberal Society, c/o President, O.U.L.S., Oxford University.
20, * OULS items; Oxford University affairs; politics in Oxford and beyond; Liberal approaches to political issues in general.
No Index.
Summer 1972, T.p. 6.   250+.
Via donation.

724 LIBERAL NEWS. 1970.
(Liberal News Commentary)
Anglia Echo Newspapers Ltd., 2-6 High Street, Haverhill, Suffolk.
26, ○
No Index.
T.p. 16, Ad. p. 4.
Per copy 5p.

725 NEW OUTLOOK: A Radical Quarterly. 1961.
Lord Beaumont of Whitley, 59 West Heath Road, London, NW3.
4, ○ Depth articles on matters of interest to radicals and liberals.
Book reviews, letters, articles.
No Index.
No. 2, 1972, T.p. 84.
Per copy 25p, per year £1.

726 NORTHERN RADICAL. c. 1969.
Ulster Liberal Party, 5 Windsor Ave., Belfast, BT9 6EE.
4, ○ Politics.
Book notices, book reviews, letters, articles, parliamentary reports.
6m — Yes, None.
July 1972, T.p. 8.
Per copy 5p.

329.14

SOCIALISM

727 FURTHER LEFT. 1971.
12 Fulham Park Road, London, SW6.
○ Socialist magazine for teachers in further education.
No Index.
Per copy 10p, per year 80p.

728 HYDE PARK SOCIALIST. 1968.
Hyde Park Socialists, c/o J. Hughes, 48 Gilbey Road, London, SW17 0QF.
4, ○ Political activity on the left, especially the libertarian left and grass roots politics.
Book notices, book reviews, letters, articles, obituaries.
No Index.
Spring 1972, T.p. 8.   600.
Per copy 5½p, per year 22p.

729 INTERNATIONAL MARXIST. 1971.
Revolutionary Marxist Tendency of the 4th International, IMR Publications, 16A Holmdale Road, London, NW6.
4, ○
No Index.
Per copy 20p.

730 INTERNATIONAL SOCIALISM. 1960.
Socialist Review Publishing Co. Ltd., 6 Cottons Gardens, London, E2.
6, ○ Contemporary Marxist Socialist analysis.
Book reviews, letters, monographic articles.
No Index.
T.p. 40.   6000.
Per copy 15p, per year £1.

731 KEEP LEFT: Official weekly paper of the Young Socialists. 1952.
Aileen Jennings, 186a Clapham High St., London, SW4.
50, ○ All aspects of the political and social concern to youth—unemployment, education, jobs, youth clubs, sport, etc. Activities of Young Socialists and young people in general.
Book reviews, letters.
No Index.
June 17, 1972, T.p. 8.   7000.
Per copy 3p, per year £2.86.

732 LABOUR WEEKLY. 1971.
The Labour Party, Transport House, Smith Square, London, SW1P 3JA.
52, ○ News and comment about the Labour Party and trade unions at local and national level, plus coverage of general political and industrial news.
Book reviews, letters, parliamentary reports.
No Index.
June 16, 1972, T.p. 11, Ad.p. 1.
Per copy 5p.

733 LEFT: Paper of the Labour Party Young Socialists. 1968.
Labour Party Young Socialists National Committee, Transport House, Smith Square, London, SW1.
10, ○
Book notices, book reviews, legal notes, letters, articles, obituaries, parliamentary reports.
No Index.

734 M.L.Q. (Marxist Leninist Quarterly). 1971.
Communist Federation of Great Britain, 65 Sisters Avenue, London, SW11.
4, ○
No Index.
Per copy 20p.

735 NEW LEFT REVIEW. 1959.
7 Carlisle Street, London, W1.
6, + * = Marxist review of international stature and world wide circulation covering questions of politics, theory, economics, social development, psychology and revolution.
Book reviews, letters, monographic articles.
A, End of year, Yes, None.
March/April 1972, T.p. 105, Ad.p. 3.   10000.
Per copy 35p, per year £1.85.
Indexed in: BHI.

736 SCOTTISH MARXIST. 1972.
Scottish Committee of the Communist Party of Great Britain, Gallacher House, 69 Albert Road, Glasgow, S2.
4, ○
No Index.
Per copy 25p.

737 SOCIALIST AFFAIRS. 1971.
(Socialist International Information 1951-1970)
Socialist International, 88a St John's Wood High Street, London, NW8.
Irreg., * Affairs of democratic socialist parties throughout the world. Articles relating to international politics and the labour movement in general.
Book reviews, letters, monographic articles, obituaries, parliamentary reports.
A, January, Yes, None.
May 1972, T.p. 25, Ad.p. None.   3000.
Per year £3, and £4 for non-party members.

738 SOCIALIST COMMENTARY. 1942.
(Socialist Vanguard 1934-1941)
Socialist Commentary Publications Ltd., 11 Great Russell Street, London, WC1.
12, =
Book reviews, letters, articles, obituaries, parliamentary reports, patents.
No Index.
T.p. 32, Ad.p. 2.   5000.
Per copy 15p, per year £2.

739 SOCIALIST STANDARD: Official journal of the Socialist Party of Great Britain and the World Socialist Party of Ireland. 1904.
The Socialist Party of Great Britain, 52 Clapham High Street, London, SW4.
12, ○ * Political analysis, discussion and commentary with a view to developing a movement for a democratic world community.
Book reviews, letters, articles.

A, — No, None.
June 1972, T.p. 16.   5000.
Per copy 5p, per year 80p.

740 SOCIALIST WOMAN: National paper of the Socialist Woman Groups. 1971.
Socialist Woman, 182 Pentonville Road, London, N1.
6, ○ For the women's liberation movement; trade unionists etc.
Book notices, book reviews, letters, articles, obituaries.
No Index.
March/April 72, T.p. 16.   2000.
Per copy 5p, per year 50p.

741 SOCIALIST WORKER. 1968.
(Labour Worker)
International Socialists, 6 Cottons Gardens, London, E2 8DN.
52, ○ Left wing political analysis of news and events.
No Index.
June 1972, T.p. 12.   25000.
Per copy 4p, per year £3.40.

742 THE SPOKESMAN. 1970.
(London Bulletin 1967-1969)
Bertrand Russell Peace Foundation Ltd., Bertrand Russell House, Gamble Street, Forest Road West, Nottingham, NG7 4ET.
6, ○ Political, economic, sociological analyses. British Labour Movement, Socialist thought, anti-imperialist struggle; political prisoners: news and analyses.
Book notices, book reviews, letters, monographic articles.
No Index.
April/May 1972, T.p. 100, Ad.p. 4.   3000.
Per copy 35p, per year £2.

743 THIRD WORLD. 1972.
Fabian Society, 11 Dartmouth Street, London, SW1.
12, = ○ Socialist news sheet.
No Index.
Subscription on application.

744 TRIBUNE. 1937.
Tribune Publications Ltd., 24 St. John Street, London, EC1.
52, ○ = + Independent socialist weekly.
Book notices, book reviews, letters, articles, obituaries, parliamentary reports.
No Index.
T.p. 13, Ad.p. 3.   36000.
Per copy 5p, per year £3.50.

745 VENTURE. 1949.
(Empire 1938-1948)
Fabian Society, 11 Dartmouth Street, London, SW1.
11, = + ‡ Problems of the developing world.
Letters, articles.
No Index.
T.p. 28, Ad.p. 3.   3000.
Per copy 10p, per year £1.50.

746 VOICE OF THE PEOPLE: incorporating Irish Liberation Press. 1972.
(Irish Liberation Press 1970-1972)
Voice of the People, 194 Hackney Road, London, E2.
6, ○ Revolutionary socialist paper for the working class and other oppressed people.
No Index.
May-June 1972, T.p. 16.
Per copy 10p, per year £1.

329.15

COMMUNISM

747 IRISH COMMUNIST. 1972.
British and Irish Communist Organisation, 10 Athol Street, Belfast, 12.

12, ○
No Index.
Per copy 10p.

748 RED FRONT: For working class power, for a socialist Britain. 1968.
Marxist-Leninist Organisation of Britain, 18 Camberwell Church Street, London, SE5.
Irregular, + *
Book reviews, letters, articles.
No Index.
Subscription on application.

749 RED VANGUARD: A journal of theory and practice. 1970.
Marxist-Leninist Organisation of Britain, 18 Camberwell Chruch Street, London, SE5.
Irregular, + *   Communist movement, Marxist theory and practice, national liberation problems, revolution.
Book reviews, articles.
No Index.
Subscription on application.

33
ECONOMICS

750 BRITISH ECONOMY SURVEY. 1971.
Oxford University Press, Press Road, Neasden, London, NW10.
3, =   Provides information about the current state of the British economy. Designed to stimulate economics students to observe for themselves how the economy works and to discuss it with greater insight.
No Index.
Summer 1972, T.p. 48, Ad.p. 1.   3000.
Per copy 40p, per year £1.

751 BULLETIN OF ECONOMIC RESEARCH. 1971.
(Yorkshire Bulletin of Economic & Social Research 1948-1970 (inc.))
Depts. of Economics of the Universities of Hull, Leeds, Sheffield, York and Bradford, Department of Economics, University of York, Heslington, York, YO1 5DD, for correspondence.
2, +
Monographic articles.
A, November, Yes, None.
November 1971, T.p. 52, Ad.p. 4.   c. 700.
Per copy 75p, per year £1.50.
Indexed in: BHI.

752 THE BUSINESS ECONOMIST. 1969.
Basil Blackwell & Mott Ltd., 5 Alfred Street, Oxford, OX1 4HB.
3, + =   Application of economics, in industry and commerce.
Articles and reviews.
No Index.
Subscription on application.

753 BUSINESS FORECAST. 1966.
The Charterhouse Group Limited, 1 Paternoster Row, St Pauls, London, EC4P 4HP.
4, ‡   Analyses the outlook for the economy and for business in the following months.
No Index.
22nd June 1972, T.p. 6.   5000.
Free.

754 CONTENTS OF RECENT ECONOMICS JOURNALS. 1971.
H.M.S.O., P.O. Box 569, London, SE1 9NA.
52, +   Current awareness service covering over 170 journals in theoretical and applied economics, concentrating on English language journals. Also lists working papers in economic subjects recently received in the library of the University of Warwick.

No Index.
30 June 1972, T.p. 8.   520.
Per year £6.

755 ECONOMIC AGE. 1968.
Economic Age Ltd., 10 Upper Berkeley Street, London, W1.
6, = ○   Economic and social affairs.
Book notices, book reviews, monographic articles.
No Index.
T.p. 44, Ad.p. 4.
Per copy 50p, per year £2.50.

756 ECONOMIC AND SOCIAL REVIEW. 1969.
Economic & Social Studies, 4 Burlington Road, Dublin, 4, Ireland.
4, + =   Economics, sociology, anthropology, demography, political science and related fields.
Book notices, book reviews, monographic articles.
A, October, Yes, None.
January, 1972, T.p. 215.   450.
Per copy £1.25, per year £3.50, libraries £5.

757 ECONOMIC JOURNAL: Quarterly journal of the Royal Economic Society. 1890.
Macmillan Journals Ltd., Basingstoke, Hants.
4, ‡ + = *   Economics and related subjects.
Book reviews, monographic articles.
A, December, Yes, None.
December 1971, T.p. 320, Ad.p. 15.   10000.
Per copy £1.50, per year £6, Free to members.
Indexed in: BHI, IBZ.

758 ECONOMIC PROGRESS REPORT. 1970.
Circulation Section (H), Central Office of Information, Hercules Road, London, SE1.
12, ○   Explains changes in economic policies of the government, effect of new measures and gives a monthly summary of economic situation.
A, December, No, None.
July 1972, T.p. 8.
Free.

759 ECONOMIC REVIEW. 1971.
Confederation of Irish Industry, 28 Fitzwilliam Place, Dublin, 2.
4, =   Current economic comment in the form of interviews and short articles on National and International Economic Affairs with specific emphasis on Business Economics.

760 ECONOMIC SELECTIONS: An International Bibliography. 1967.
Gordon & Breach, 41/42 William 4th Street, London, WC2.
4   International guide to new books published on economics. Each publication is evaluated in terms of the category and budget of the teaching or research libraries that would be interested in its purchase.
Book notices, book reviews, commodity prices, letters, monographic articles, new companies, patents, standards, tests.
Each issue, has index.
Subscription on application.

761 ECONOMIC TRENDS. 1953.
H.M.S.O., P.O. Box 569, London, SE1.
12, = + ‡   Trends in the UK economy as seen from official statistics.
Monographic articles.
No Index.
T.p. 44.
Per copy 40p, per year £5.20.

762 ECONOMICA. 1934.
(Economica, a Journal of the Social sciences 1921-1933)

London School of Economics and Political Science, Univ. of London, Houghton Street, Aldwych, London, WC2A 2AE.
4, ‡ +   Economics, economic history, statistics and related problems.
Book notices, book reviews, monographic articles.
A, November, No, (one consolidated index publ. 1959— Vols 1-25, 1934-1958).
May 1972, T.p. 117, Ad.p. 8.   3400.
Per copy £1.80, per year £5.
Indexed in: BHI, IBZ.

763 ECONOMICS: The Journal of The Economics Association. 1949.
Economics Association, 101 Hatton Garden, London, EC1.
3, + *   Section A. Economics Section B Teaching Methodology in Economics Section C Book Reviews Economics.
Book notices, book reviews, monographic articles.
No Index.
Summer 1972, T.p. 60, Ad.p. 7.   2500.
Per copy 70p, per year £2.

764 THE ECONOMIST. 1843.
Economist Newspaper Co. Ltd., 25 St. James's Street, London, SW1.
52, = + ‡ ○   Major political, social and business developments internationally.
Book notices, book reviews, commodity prices, legal notes, letters, articles, new companies, new products, parliamentary reports.
Q, — No, None.
T.p. 50, Ad.p. 37.   100000.
Per copy 12½p, per year £6.50.
Indexed in: BHI, IBZ.

765 HISTORY OF ECONOMIC THOUGHT NEWSLETTER. 1968.
c/o Mr. D. Collard, Dept. Economics, University of Bristol, Bristol, BS8 1HY.
2, +   Current and prospective research in the history of economic thought in all languages; bibliographical features; reports of conferences; occasional book reviews; communications among specialists.
Book reviews, letters, articles, obituaries.
No Index.
Autumn 1971, T.p. 28.   300.
Per year 50p.

766 LSE: The magazine of the London School of Economics and Political Science. 1950.
London School of Economics and Political Science, Houghton Street, Aldwych, London, WC2A 2AE.
2, †   Activities at L.S.E., personalities, news of former students and staff, purely of internal interest. No academic.
Articles, obituaries.
No Index.
June 1972, T.p. 18.   3500.
Free.

767 THE MANCHESTER SCHOOL OF ECONOMIC & SOCIAL STUDIES. 1930.
University of Manchester, Dept. of Economics, Dover Street, Manchester, M13 9PL.
4, ‡ +   Economics and social fields.
Book notices, book reviews, monographic articles.
A, December, Yes, None.
March 1972, T.p. 122, Ad.p. 2.   1400.
Per copy £1, Library/institution rate £4, personal subscriptions £3.
Indexed in: BHI.

768 NATIONAL INSTITUTE ECONOMIC REVIEW. 1959.
National Institute of Economic & Social Research, 2 Dean Trench Street, Smith Square, London, SW1P 3HE.
4, +   Comprehensive view of the general economic situation and the outlook for 1 to 2 years ahead. In addition it includes special articles of interest to academic, government and business economists.
Calendar of economic events.
A, February, No, None.
T.p. 120.   5000.
Per copy £3.50.

769 NEDDY IN PRINT. 1970/71.
NEDO, Millbank Tower, Millbank, London, SW1P 4QX.
4, ‡ = + ○ *   A free quarterly catalogue listing the reports and films produced by and for the National Economic Development Council (known as NEDC or Neddy), the Economic Development Committees (EDCs or Little Neddies) and the National Economic Development Office (NEDO). These published works result from research and discussion aimed at improving performance and efficiency in industry and commerce.
No Index.
Spring 1972, T.p. 40.   15000.
Free.

770 NORTHERN IRELAND ECONOMIC REPORT. 1964.
H M Stationery Office, 80 Chichester Street, Belfast, BT1 4JY.
1, +   Review of economic situation in Northern Ireland.
No Index.

771 OXFORD ECONOMIC PAPERS. 1938, New Series 1949.
Oxford University Press, Press Road, Neasden, London, NW10.
3, +   Economics, both theoretical and applied, and of a relatively non-mathematical character.
Book reviews, monographic articles.
A, —, Yes, None.
March 1972, T.p. 136, Ad.p. 4.   2000.
Per copy £1.25, per year £3.
Indexed: BHI.

772 QUARTERLY ECONOMIC COMMENTARY. 1968.
The Economic and Social Research Institute, 4 Burlington Road, Dublin, 4.
4, ○ = +   Commentary on current economic trends and forecasts for the coming year of National Accounts and other major economic variables. Most issues feature an article on some problem or series of economic statistics relevant to economic forecasting. Serves also as medium of publication for Joint Quarterly Industrial Survey conducted by the Confederation of Irish Industries along with the Institute and for seasonally corrected economic series.
No Index.
Winter 1971/72, T.p. 44.   600/700.
Per copy 75p, per year £2.50.

773 REVIEW OF ECONOMIC STUDIES. 1933.
Longman Group Limited, 43/49 Annandale Street, Edinburgh, EH7 4AT.
4, = +
Book notices, monographic articles.
A, Last issue of year, Yes, None.
January 1972, T.p. 116.   3000.
Per copy £1.60, per year £5.

774 SCOTTISH ECONOMIC BULLETIN. 1971.
HMSO, Bankhead Avenue, Sighthill, Edinburgh.
2, ○   Charts and statistics illustrating the trends in the Scottish economy and articles commenting on these trends.
Abstracts, monographic articles.
Subscription on application.

775 VITAL ECONOMIC TRENDS IN THE UNITED KINGDOM. 1964.
Interstats Limited, Brockhill House, Pinemount Road, Camberley, Surrey.

331
LABOUR ECONOMICS

777 CHANGES IN RATES OF WAGES AND HOURS OF WORK. 1966.
HMSO, P.O. Box 569, London, SE1.
12, +   Provides information about changes in the basic rates of wages or minimum entitlements and the normal hours of work of manual workers.
Tables.
No Index.
March 1972, T.p. 6.
Per copy 13½p, per year £1.92.

778 DEPARTMENT OF EMPLOYMENT GAZETTE. 1971.
Board of Trade Labour Gazette 1905-1916; Labour Gazette 1893-1904; Labour Gazette 1917-1921; Ministry of Labour Gazette 1922-1968; Employment and Productivity Gazette 1968-1970.
HMSO, P.O. Box 569, London, SE1.
12, +   Work of the Department including articles on labour, industrial relations, manpower planning, strikes etc. Statistics on unemployment, employment, earnings, hours of work, overtime, retail prices, stoppages of work.
Monographic articles
A, February, Yes, None.
May 1972, T.p. 93 Ad. p. 3.
Per copy 52½p, per year £7.

779 EMPLOYMENT AND PRODUCTIVITY GAZETTE. 1968.
Labour Gazette 1893-1904; Board of Trade Labour Gazette 1905-1916; Labour Gazette 1917-1921; Ministry of Labour Gazette 1922-1968.
HMSO, P.O. Box 569, London, SE1.
12, +   Work of the Department including articles on labour, industrial relations, manpower planning, strikes etc. Statistics on unemployment, employment, earnings, hours of work, overtime, retail prices, stoppages of work.
Legal notes, monographic articles.
A, February, yes, none.
December 1970, T.p. 124, Ad. p. 4.
Per copy 35p, per year £1.60.

780 FAMILY EXPENDITURE SURVEY. 1957.
HMSO, P.O. Box 569, London, SE1.
1, +   Analysis of returns of survey into family expenditure, including information on the contributions of individual members of the family.
Tables.
Included in each annual vol.
1970, T.p. 141.
Per copy £2.30.

781 INTERNATIONAL JOURNAL OF MAN-MACHINE STUDIES. 1969.
Academic Press Inc. Ltd., 24 Oval Road, London, SW1.
4, = + ‡   Mathematical and engineering approaches to study of man.
Book reviews, monographic articles.
A, – yes, none.
T.p. 128.
Per year £9

782 NEW EARNINGS SURVEY. 1968.
HMSO, P.O. Box 569, London, SE1.

12, ‡ = + *   Each monthly volume contains a complete set of consistent colour-coded charts illustrating current trends in all the inter-relating sections of the economy, ranging from Advertising (expenditure analysis) to Zinc (consumption, production, price and stocks).
No Index.
May 1972, T.p. 2 + 100 charts.   2000.
Per copy £5, per year £50.

1, +   Results of a periodic sample survey of the earnings of employees in employment in Great Britain.
Tables.
No Index.
1970, T.p. 269.
Per copy £2.80.

331.1
INDUSTRIAL RELATIONS

783 BRITISH JOURNAL OF INDUSTRIAL RELATIONS. 1963.
London School of Economics, Aldwych. London, WC2A 2AE.
3, ‡ +   All aspects of industrial relations; covering psychological, economic, sociological, political and legal studies of management and labour everywhere. Includes chronicle of industrial relations statistics and events in Britain.
Book notices, book reviews, legal notes, monographic articles, parliamentary reports.
Included in November issue each year. A, Yes, None.
March 1972, T.p. 164, Ad. p. 7.   2000.
Per copy £2, per year £5.50.

784 BULLETIN OF NORTH EAST GROUP FOR THE STUDY OF LABOUR HISTORY. 1967.
North East Group for the Study of Labour History, c/o Dept. of Humanities, Newcastle upon Tyne Polytechnic, NE1 8ST.
1, + *   Research into all aspects of labour history and the preservation of such records as exist.
Book notices, book reviews, monographic articles, obituaries.
A, – yes, none.
October 1971, T.p. 40.   150-200.
Per copy 50p.

785 CBI INDUSTRIAL RELATIONS BULLETIN.
Confederation of British Industry, 21 Tothill St., SW1.
12, ‡ = + *   Newsletter.
Book notices, book reviews, legal notes, articles, parliamentary reports.
No Index.
31 March 1972, T.p. 4.
Per year £4 (£2 to members).

786 INDUSTRIAL PARTICIPATION. 1972.
(Co-Partnership 1894-1971)
Industrial Co-Partnership Association, 60 Buckingham Gate, London, SW1.
4, * =   Participation in industry: Consultation, communication, job enrichment Management by consent profit-sharing, collective bargaining: Conflict and cooperation; ownership; co-operation rough articles, case studies, research reports etc.
Book notices, book reviews, letters, monographic articles.
No Index.
Spring 1972, T.p. 24, Ad. p. 8   5000.
Per copy 40p, per year £2.

787 INDUSTRIAL RELATIONS BULLETIN. 1971.
Fabian Society, 11 Dartmouth Street, London, SW1.
4, ○ =
No Index.
Per year £1.

788 INDUSTRIAL RELATIONS REVIEW AND REPORT. 1971.
Industrial Relations Enterprises Ltd. 286, Kilburn High Road, London, N.W.6.
24, ‡ +   Industrial Relations law and interpretation, Procedures, News and details of recent pay settlements. Original research on all aspects of industrial relations. Unique league table of basic weekly rates.

No Index.
April 1972, T.p. 31, Ad. p. 1.   2000.
Per copy £2.50, per year £40.

789   INDUSTRIAL SOCIETY. 1967.
(Industrial Welfare 1918-1967)
The Industrial Society, 48 Bryanston Sq., London W1H 8AH.
12, ‡ =   Man-management, industrial relations, communication and participation, leadership, development of young employees, conditions of employment.
Book notices, book reviews, legal notes, letters, monographic articles, new products, parliamentary reports.
A, December, No, Index.
June 1972, T.p. 26, Ad. p. 6   10000
Per copy 40p, per year £4.50.

331.2

SALARIES. WAGES

790   INCOMES DATA REPORTS. 1966.
Incomes Data Services Ltd., 140 Gt Portland St., London W1.
24, + =   Industrial relations. Providing comprehensive information on wages, salaries and conditions of employment, coverage of national and company agreements.
A, February, Yes, None.
May 1972, T.p. 36,   3000.
Per year £60.

791   INCOMES DATA STUDIES. 1971.
Incomes Data Services Ltd., 140 Gt. Portland Street, London W1.
24, + =   Industrial relations. Providing comprehensive information on wages, salaries, conditions of employment, coverage of national and company agreements.
A, February, Yes, None.
June 1972, T.p. 20.   3000.
Per year £25.

331.82

INDUSTRIAL HYGIENE AND SAFETY

792   ANNALS OF OCCUPATIONAL HYGIENE. 1958.
Pergamon Press Ltd., (for British Occupational Hygiene Society) Headington Hill Hall, Oxford OX3 0RW.
4, = + ‡ *   All aspects of the health of the working man and woman.
Book reviews, monographic articles,
A, October, Yes, 10 year.
T.p. 61, Ad. p. 2.
Per copy £4.50, per year £16.

793   BRITISH JOURNAL OF OCCUPATIONAL SAFETY. 1967.
(British Journal of Industrial Safety 1946-1966)
Royal Society for the Prevention of Accidents, 52 Grosvenor Gardens, London SW1.
4, = + ‡   Practical applications and research for improvement of safety and health of employees.
Legal notes, letters, monographic articles, new products.
3 year, Winter 1971 etc., No, None.
T.p. 36, Ad. p. 15.
Free to members.

794   INDUSTRIAL SAFETY. 1960.
(Uniform and Industrial Clothing 1955-1956; Safety Equipment and Industrial Clothing 1957-1959)
United Trade Press Ltd., 9 Gough Square, Fleet Street, London EC4.
12, + ‡   All aspects of work accident prevention, health and welfare.
Book notices, legal notes, letters, monographic articles, new companies, new products, patents, standards, tests.
No Index.
T.p. 27, Ad. p. 28.
Per copy 25p, per year £3.

795   SAFETY AT SEA INTERNATIONAL. 1967.
Rhodes Marine Publications Ltd., 54/5 Wilton Road, London SW1.
6, = + ‡   All aspects of safety in the design, construction, operation and management of shipping.
Book notices, book reviews, legal notes, letters, articles, new companies, new products, reports, patents, standards, tests.
No Index.
T.p. 39, Ad. p. 7.   5000.
Per year £2.50

796   TRANSACTIONS OF THE SOCIETY OF OCCUPATIONAL MEDICINE. 1967.
(Transactions of the Association of Industrial Medical Officers. 1966)
The Longman group Ltd., 33 Montgomery Street, Edinburgh EH7 5JX.
4, = *   Administrative, environmental and clinical aspects of health at work.
Book notices, book reviews, letters, monographic articles, obituaries,
A, Last issue of each volume, Yes, None.
T.p. 34, Ad. p. 6.   1700.
Per copy 75p per year £2.50.

797   VIGILANCE: The Journal of National Vulcan Engineering Insurance Group Ltd. 1967.
(The Vulcan Journal - 1904-1966)
National Vulcan Engineering Insurance Group Ltd., St Mary's Parsonage, Manchester M60 9AP.
3, ‡ =   Safety in industry
Monographic articles.
No Index.
Spring 1972, T.p. 14, Ad. p. 1.   c. 30000.
Free.

331.88

TRADE UNIONS

798   CONTACT. 1969.
(Electron)
Electrical, Electronics, Telecommunication and Plumbing Union, Hayes Court, West Common Road, Bromley, BR2 7AU.
4, = ○ ‡   Contact is circulated by direct mail to members. It covers Union policy, technical pages, principally in electronics, social events involving members and items of general and political interest.
Book reviews, letters, parliamentary reports.
No Index.
May 1972, T.p. 23, Ad. p. 1   420000.
Free.

799   COUNTRY STANDARD. 1935.
J. Dunman, 27 Bedford Street, London, WC2E 9EE.
3/4, ○   Politics, trade unionism for agriculture and the countryside, usually one or two articles on foreign countries, especially socialist or developing.
Book notices, book reviews, letters, articles, obituaries, parliamentary reports.
No Index.
Autumn 1971, T.p. 12,
Per year 20p.

Key to reference symbols

○ popular   ‡ technical   = trade/professional

+ research   * society/institution   † house journal

800 EQUITY. 1971,
(Equity Letter 1947-1970)
British Actors' Equity Association (Incorporating the Variety Artistes' Federation), 8 Harley Street, London W1N 2AB.
4, * Union activity and matters of general and/or trade union interest in the entertainment industry.
Book reviews, legal notes, letters, articles, new companies, obituaries, parliamentary reports.
No Index.
June 1972, T.p. 16, Ad. p. 1. 24000.

801 RECORD: News and Views Paper of the Tranport and General Workers Union. 1922.
T.G.W.U. Transport House, Smith Square, London SW1.
12, ○ = Industrial/pay news and policy, social and political companies.
Book notices, book reviews, letters, articles, parliamentary reports.
No Index.
October 1972, T.p. 16,
Per copy 2½p.

332

BANKING. FINANCIAL ECONOMICS

802 APPROPRIATION ACCOUNTS: Classes I-V: Civil and Classes VI-XI: Civi (2 Vols). 1970-71.
(Civil appropriation accounts 1861-62 1969-70)
HMSO, P.O. Box 569, London SE1.
1.
A, with each volume, Yes, none.
1970-71, T.p. 298,
Per copy £2. 10.

803 BANK OF ENGLAND STATISTICAL ABSTRACT. 1971.
Bank of England, London, EC2R 8AH.
1, + = Statistics covering most of the financial series which appear regularly in the annex to the Quarterly Bulletin, together with the sector financial accounts, wherever possible, for the period 1945 to the end of 1969.
No Index.
March 1971, T.p. 193
Per copy £3.

804 THE BANKER. 1926.
The Banker Limited, Bracken House, Cannon Street, London EC4P 4BY.
12, + = Banking, financial and economic developments in Britain and overseas - coverage and editorial appraisal.
Book notices, book reviews, legal notes, monographic articles, new banks,
A, December, yes, none.
June 1972, T.p. 115, Ad. p. 118
Per copy 50p, per year £7.
Indexed in: BHI, IBZ

805 THE BANKERS' MAGAZINE. 1844.
Waterlow & Sons, 12 Vandy Street, London EC2.
12, ‡ * + = Banking, Finance, the economy, model answers to banking diploma questions.
Book reviews, legal notes, letters, monographic articles, 6m, Jan/July, Yes, None.
June 1972, T.p. 45, Ad. p. 11. 6000.
Per copy 30p, per year £4.

806 THE CASHIER. Journal of the Association of Cashiers. 1955.
Association of Cashiers, Old Rectory, Tallington, Stamford, Lincs.
6, = * Monetary news.
Book reviews, legal notes, articles, new products, reports.
No Index.
T.p. 21.
Free to members.

807 EUROMONEY. 1969.
Euromoney Publications Ltd., (Subsidiary of Associated Newspapers), 14 Finsbury Circus, London EC2.
12, ‡ = All aspects of international banking and money movements from the practical to the academic (but concentrating on the former) including international money, foreign exchange and bond markets.
Book reviews, letters, monographic articles.
A, June, Yes, None.
June 1972, T.p. 68, Ad. p. 34 5000.
Per copy £1. 25, per year £15.

808 FINANCIAL STATEMENT AND BUDGET REPORT. 1969-70
(Financial statement 1880-)
HMSO, P.O. Box 569, London SE1.
1, =
No Index.
1972-73, T.p. 40
Per copy 52p.

809 INTERNATIONAL CURRENCY REVIEW Incorporating Money Management. Journal of the World Financial Community. 1969.
Currency Journals Ltd., 11 Regency Place, London SW1P 2EA.
6, = Currency, monetary and economic affairs, finance, exchange rates, controls etc.
No Index.
September-October 1972, T.p. 122.
Per year £16.

810 INTERNATIONAL FINANCIAL BULLETIN: Quarterly review. 1972.
International Economic Services, Foremarke House, Thorpe Green, Egham, Surrey. TW20 8QL.
4, =
No Index.
Per year £25.

811 THE JOURNAL OF THE INSTITUTE OF BANKERS. 1879.
The Institute of Bankers, 10 Lombard Street, London, E.C. 3.
6, * = Current trends in banking and matters of interest.
Book notices, book reviews, legal notes, letters, monographic articles,
A, February, Yes, None.
April 1972, T.p. 70, Ad. p. 9 90000.
Per copy 40p, per year £2. 40, Free to members.

812 LOANS FROM THE NATIONAL LOANS FUND. 1968-69.
(Loans from the consolidated fund 1965-6; Government expenditure below the line 1960-1)
HMSO, P.O. Box 569, London SE1.
1,
No Index.
1972-73, T.p. 22
Per copy 21p.

813 MONEY MATTERS. 1972.
Barclay's Bank Trust Co. Ltd., Juxon House, 94 St. Pauls' Churchyard, London EC4M 8EH.
Irreg., ○
Free.

814 MONEYMAKER. 1972.
Mendip Publications Ltd., 7 Swans Lane, Draycott, Somerset BS27 3SS.
12, ○ News, advice and ideas for turning spare time to profit; the 'hows' of starting up a small business.
Book reviews, commodity prices, legal notes, letters, monographic articles, new companies, new products.
No Index.
T.p. 9, Ad. p. 11
Per copy 14p, per year £1. 68.

815 MONTHLY STATEMENT OF BALANCES OF LONDON CLEARING BANKS.
Committee of London Clearing Bankers, 10 Lombard Street, London EC3.
12, +
No Index.
Free, Controlled circulation.

816 MOORGATE AND WALL STREET: A Review Issued by Hill Samuel & Co. Ltd.
Hill Samuel & Co. Ltd., 100 Wood St., London EC2.
2, ○ = + Topics of interest - financial, economic etc., - to friends and clients of Hill Samuel.
Monographic articles.
No Index.
Spring 1972, T.p. 95
Free.
Indexed in: BHI

817 POLITICS AND MONEY: An Analysis of Current Trends. 1970.
Politics and Money Publishing Co., 14 South Hill, Park Gardens, London N.W.3.
10, + ○ Current economic, monetary and political developments here and internationally are analysed: their interconnections shown; their significance assessed; and the likely trends arising from them examined.
Articles.
No Index.
May-June 1972, T.p. 26
Per year £1.75.

818 PUBLIC EXPENDITURE. 1969.
HMSO, P.O. Box 569, London SE1.
1, + Forecasts of government public spending policy for about 4 or 5 years ahead.
No Index.
1975-76, T.p. 103,
Per copy 68p.

819 SCOTTISH BANKERS MAGAZINE. 1909.
Institute of Bankers in Scotland, 62 George Street, Edinburgh.
4, =
Book reviews, articles, news.
A, −, Yes, None.
T.p. 53, Ad. p. 17.
Per copy 15p, per year £1.
Indexed in: BHI

820 SOURCES OF FINANCE. 1970.
Scottish Council (Development and Industry), 1 Castle Street, Edinburgh EH2 3AJ.
Every 2nd year, = Breakdown of all sources of finance in Scotland.
No Index.
Per year £1.25.

821 TSB GAZETTE: Journal of the Trustee Savings Banks Assn. 1927.
TSB Association, Knighton House, 52-66 Mortimer St., London W1.
4, = *
Articles, new products, obituaries.
2 years, December 1971, Yes, None.
T.p. 64 et seq 5000.
Free-controlled cirulation.

332.2

SAVINGS

822 PLANNED SAVINGS: A Commentary on Unit Trusts, Life Assurance and Savings. 1966.
Wootten Publications Ltd., 150/152 Caledonian Road, London N1 9RD.
12, = All aspects of saving, insurance policies, property bonds, insurance funds, building societies and unit trusts.
Book reviews, letters, new companies, new products.
A, January, No, None.
1, 1971, T.p. 24, Ad. p. 24.
Per copy £1, per year £6.30.

332.4

CURRENCY. MONEY

823 INTERNATIONAL BANK NOTE SOCIETY. 1961.
International Bank Note Society, 19/21 Great Tower Street, London E.C.3.
4, * Specialised articles on paper currency of the world. Directed at the collector only specialising in "notaphily".
Book reviews, letters, monographic articles.
No Index.
September 1971, T.p. 50, Ad. p. 18.   1200.
Per year £2.80.

332.6

INVESTMENT FINANCE

824 THE INVESTMENT ANALYST. JOURNAL OF THE SOCIETY OF INVESTMENT ANALYSTS. 1961.
Society of Investment Analysts, 21 Godliman Street, London EC4.
3, = * All aspects of investment analysis.
Book reviews, monographic articles.
No Index.
T.p. 40.
Per copy 50p, per year £1.50, Free to members.

825 INVESTORS GUARDIAN. 1863.
Haymarket Publishing Ltd., Gillow House, 5 Winsley Street, London W.1.
52, ○ ‡ Analysis and news for private and professional investors.
Book notices, book reviews, commodity prices, legal notes, letters, new companies, new products, parliamentary reports,
No Index.
9.6.72, T.p. 57, Ad. p. 7
Per copy 20p, per year £10.40.

826 THE STOCK EXCHANGE JOURNAL. 1896.
The Finanical Times/Stock Exchange Council, Old Broad Street, London, EC2N 1HP.
4, ○ = History of Stock Exchange, general finance, etc.
Book reviews, legal notes, letters, monographic articles, obituaries, parliamentary reports.
No Index.
March 1972, T.p. 32, Ad.p. 10.   5000.
Per copy 25p, per year £1.

827 STOCK EXCHANGE WEEKLY OFFICIAL INTELLIGENCE.
Council of the Stock Exchange, 14 Austin Friars, London, EC2N 2EU.
52, = Dividends, New Issues, Company Information.
New companies.
No Index.
June 3, 1972, T.p. 21.   2020.
Per copy 43p, per year £18.

332.7

CREDIT

828 BUSINESS CREDIT and Hire Purchase Journal. 1952. (Hire Purchase Journal 1935-1951).
Quaintance & Co. (Publishers), Ltd., 24A Chertsey Street, Guildford.

12, = Entire field of credit, banking, finance, insurance.
No Index.
June 1972, T.p. 21, Ad.p. 3.
Per copy 25p, per year £2.50.

829 CREDIT: Finance Houses Association Quarterly Review. 1960.
Finance Houses Association, 14 Queen Anne's Gate, London, S.W.1.
4, = Instalment Credit Industry, together with regular statistical information on instalment credit.
Book reviews, monographic articles.
No Index.
March 1972, T.p. 24.

830 CREDIT RETAILER: Incorporating Credit Retail & Credit Retailing. 1970.
Credit Retailer (Publishers), Ltd., 1 Kenilworth House, Grosvenor Road, London, W4 4EJ.
12, = Retail or Consumer credit.
Book reviews, legal notes, letters, articles, new companies, new products, obituaries, standards, tests.
No Index.
May 1972, T.p. 18, Ad.p. 6.
Per copy 50p, per year £6.

831 HIRE TRADING.
Hire Purchase Trade Association, 3 Berners Street, London, W1.
4, = Legal and trade information for the instalment credit industry.
Legal notes, new companies, parliamentary reports.
No index.
T.p. 24, Ad.p. 2.
Per year 50p.

333

LAND. PROPERTY

832 COUNTRY GENTLEMEN'S MAGAZINE. 1900.
Country Gentlemen's Association, 54-62 Regent Street, London, W1.
12, * All aspects of country living.
Book notices, book reviews, legal notes, letters, articles, new products.
No index.
T.p. 38, Ad.p. 26.   36000.
Per year £2.10.
Per year £2.10. Free to members.

833 COUNTRY LANDOWNER: Journal of the Country Landowners' Association. 1949.
(Journal of the Central Landowners' Association 1920-49).
Country Landowners' Association, 7 Swallow Street, London, W1R 8EN.
6, * All aspects of the ownership of agricultural land.
Book reviews, commodity prices, legal notes, letters, articles, new products, obituaries, parliamentary reports, standards.
A, February, Yes, None.
April 1972, T.p. 32, Ad.p. 32.   42000.
Per year £2.10.
Free to members.

834 DALTON'S WEEKLY, 1869.
E. & S. Herbert Ltd., 27 South Lambeth Road, London, SW8.
52, = ○ Adverts of hotels, boarding houses, businesses, etc.
No index.
Ad.p. 70.
Per copy 5p.

835 THE ESTATES GAZETTE. Incorp. Property Market Review and Auction Chronicle; The Estates Journal; The Auctioneer. 1858.
The Estates Gazette Ltd., 151 Wardour Street, London, W1V 4BN.
52, ¼ = + Real property—ownership, use, management, valuation, disposal and development; estate agency; auctioneering; valuation surveying; land agency; estate management; land economy; transactions in land and buildings; values and prices; property companies.
Book notices, book reviews, commodity prices, legal notes, letters, monographic articles, obituaries, parliamentary reports.
Q, No fixed date. No, 10 year.
June 17, 1972, T.p. 35, Ad.p. 165.   21250.
Per copy 15p, per year £12.

836 EUROPROPERTY MAGAZINE. 1967.
European Property Owners Association, 51 Brompton Road, London, SW3.
12, * Ownership of property in Europe.
No index.
T.p. 5, Ad.p. 3.   1500.
Free to members.

837 HOMEFINDER: the national property magazine. 1910.
Homefinders (1915) Ltd., 199 Strand, London, WC2.
12, ○ = Homes for sale throughout Britain.
Book reviews, commodity prices, legal notes, letters, articles, new products, parliamentary reports.
No index.
July 1972, T.p. 24, Ad.p. 76.
Per copy 25p, per year £3.

838 THE HOME OWNER.
Halifax Building Society, Permanent Buildings, Halifax.
3, †
Articles.
No index.
May 1972, T.p. 32.   135000.
Free.

839 HOMES OVERSEAS. 1965.
Homefinders (1915) Ltd., 199 Strand, London, WC2.
6, ○ = Residential property for sale in Europe, the West Indies and South Pacific. Also property to rent and for sale for holidays investment and retirement.
Book reviews, commodity prices, legal notes, letters, articles.
A, February, No, None
June 1972, T.p. 40, Ad.p. 40.   12000.
Per copy 21p, per year £1.25.

840 HOUSEBUYER. 1968.
(Houses and Estates-1955-1968)
Haymarket Publishing Limited, Gillow House, 5 Winsley Street, London, W1.
12, ○ Coverage of property (private) for sale, especially new property.
No index.
Per copy 17½p, per year £3.11.

841 HOUSING. 1936.
Institute of Housing Managers, Victoria House, Southampton Row, London WC1B 4EB.
6, * = Housing management.
Book notices, book reviews, legal notes, letters, monographic articles, new products, obituaries, parliamentary reports.
No index.
May 1972, T.p. 44, Ad.p. 2.
Per copy 25p, per year £1.50.

842 HOUSING RETURN FOR SCOTLAND. 1946.
H.M.S.O. Bankhead Avenue, Sighthill, Edinburgh.
4, ‡ + Progress of house building in Scotland by public and private agencies, with figures of slum

clearance and of house conversions and improvements.
Subscription on application.

843 HOUSING REVIEW. 1957.
(Housing Centre Review 1951-1956)
Housing Centre Trust, 13 Suffolk Street, Pall Mall East, London, SW1Y 4HG.
6, ‡ + *   Housing and closely related subjects of interest to all concerned with the improvement of housing conditions.
Book reviews, letters, monographic articles, new products, obituaries, parliamentary reports, standards.
A, November/December, No, None.
January/February 1972, T.p. 43, Ad.p. 5.   2200.
Per copy 30p, per year £5.

844 PROPERTY AND INVESTMENT REVIEW. 1970.
Newman Books Limited, 48 Poland Street, London, W1V 4PP.
12, =   Property and investment and the news of commerce and industry.
Book reviews, legal notes, letters, articles, new companies, obituaries.
No index.
June 1972, T.p. 31, Ad.p. 30.   4000.
Per copy 50p, per year £6.

845 PROPERTY JOURNAL. 1970.
(Real Estate Journal 1950-1969)
National Association of Property Owners, 14-16 Bressenden Place, London, SW1.
12, = *   Property management, town and country planning, rating, taxation.
Book reviews, legal notes, articles, news, obituaries, parliamentary reports.
A, —, Yes, None.
T.p. 40, Ad.p. 10.   5000.
Free to members.

846 PROPERTY SURVEY. 1967.
Forth Publishing Group, 45 Moray Place, Edinburgh, EH3 6DD
26, =   Advertisements for users of industrial and commercial property seeking/selling property or sites.
No index
23.6.1972, T.p. 1, Ad.p. 15.   20000.
Per copy Free, Controlled circulation.

847 SSHA JOURNAL. 1970.
(Housing Special, 1968-1969)
Scottish Special Housing Association, 15/21 Palmerston Place, Edinburgh, EH12 5AJ
4, =.

334

CO-OPERATIVE SOCIETIES

848 THE BULLETIN: the Society for Co-operative Studies. 1967.
Society for Co-operative Studies, Stanford Hall, Loughborough, Leics.
3, * +   Promotion of studies and research on co-operative problems.
Monographic articles.
No index.
March 1972, T.p. 27.   500
Per copy 8p. Free to members.

849 CONSUMER AFFAIRS BULLETIN. 1945.
International Co-operative Alliance, 11 Upper Grosvenor Street, London, W1X 9PA.
12, ○ = * +   Consumer information and protection of co-operatives and the consumer.
Commodity prices, legal notes, new companies, new products, parliamentary reports, patents, standards, tests.
A, December, Yes, None.
T.p. 15.
Subscription on application.

850 CO-OPERATIVE NEWS SERVICE. 1945.
International Co-operative Alliance, 11 Upper Grosvenor St., London, W1X 9PA.
12, + *   International co-operative news.
New companies, news, obituaries.
A, December, Yes, None.
T.p. 14,   800.
£1 per year.

851 CO-OPERATIVE REVIEW. Official Organ of the Co-operative Union Ltd. 1926.
Co-operative Union Ltd., Holyoake House, Hanover Street, Manchester M60 0AS.
12, ○ = + * ‡   Reflects the policy of the Co-operative Union to member-societies. Directed to co-operative society boards of directors, chief officials, managers, staff, educationists, lay-activists, students and co-operative society members.
Book notices, book reviews, legal notes, letters, articles, new products, obituaries.
No index.
May 1972, T.p. 8.   40000.
per copy 4p.

852 REVIEW OF INTERNATIONAL CO-OPERATION: the official organ of the International Co-operative Alliance. 1907.
(International Co-operative Bulletin, 1905-1928)
International Co-operative Alliance, 11 Upper Grosvenor Street, London, W1X 9PA.
6, = + ‡ *   All forms of international co-operative activities.
Book reviews, monographic aritcles, obituaries.
A, November, Yes, None.
T.p. 38, Ad.p. 2.   c. 8000.
Per copy £1.50.

853 SCOTTISH CO-OPERATOR. Official journal of the co-operative movement in Scotland. 1869.
Co-operative Press Ltd., 418 Chester Road, Manchester, M16 9HP.
52, =.
Book notices, book reviews, commodity prices, letters, articles, new products, parliamentary reports.
No index.
T.p. 8, Ad.p. 8.
Per copy 3p.

334.1

BUILDING SOCIETIES

854 BUILDING SOCIETIES INSTITUTE QUARTERLY. 1947.
Building Society Institute, Fanhams Hall, Ware, Hertfordshire.
4, ‡ =   Building society business and related topics.
Book notices, book reviews, legal notes, letters, monographic articles, obituaries, standards, tests.
A, October, Yes, None.
April 1972, T.p. 54, Ad.p. 4.   5500.
Per copy 25p, per year £1.

855 BUILDING SOCIETY AFFAIRS. 1960.
Building Societies Association, Fanhams Hall, Ware, Herts.
4, = ○   News and comments of society progress.
Commodity prices, legal notes, news.
No index.
T.p. 4.
Free.

856 BUILDING SOCIETY STATISTICS. 1960.
Building Societies Association, Fanhams Hall, Ware, Herts.
4, ‡ = ○   News of society finance.
No index.
T.p. 1.
Free.

857 OCCASIONAL BULLETIN. 1952.
Nationwide Building Society, New Oxford House, Holborn, WC1V 6PW.
Irregular.
○ + *   House prices, housing and allied subjects; halfyearly and annual results of Nationwide Building Society.
Commodity prices, articles,
No index.
February 1972, T.p. 4.   40000.
Free.

858 PERMANENT LIGHT. 1946.
Leeds Permanent Building Society. Permanent House, The Headrow, Leeds, 1.
4 †   News of members of staff and articles thought likely to be of interest to them.
Book notices, book reviews, letters, articles, new products, obituaries.
No index.
Second Quarter 1972, T.p. 60,   2700.
Free.

859 ROUND THE TABLE: The Staff Magazine of the Halifax Building Society.
Halifax Building Society, Permanent Buildings, Commercial St., Halifax.
3 †.
Articles, obituaries.
No index.
January 1972, T.p. 36.   7000.

335.8

ANARCHISM

860 ANARCHY. 1961.
Freedom Press, 84b Whitechapel High Street, London, E1.
12, = +   Anarchist principles.
Book reviews, letters, articles.
A, December, No, None.
T.p. 32,   4000.
Per copy 15p, per year £1.80.

336.2

TAXATION

861 BRITISH TAX REVIEW. 1956.
Sweet & Maxwell (Associated Book Publishers), 11 New Fetter Lane, London, EC4P 4EE
6, ‡ =   Current notes of interest on tax matters plus practical problems, authoritative articles, notes of cases and book reviews. A special feature is Current Tax Intelligence which contains a note of everything of importance, to tax practitioners, that has happened during the previous two months.
Book notices, book reviews, legal notes, monographic articles.
A, last issue of year, Yes, 1956-1965.
Per copy 90p, per year £4.75.

862 INLAND REVENUE STATISTICS. 1970.
(Previously included in the annual Report of the Commissioners of H.M. Inland Revenue.)
H.M.S.O., Atlantic House, Holborn Viaduct, EC1.
1, ‡   Statistics of taxation, incomes analysed by trade status and region, wealth, rateable values, regional non-domestic floor space and agricultural land prices.
A, —, Yes, None.
T.p. 160.   2500.
Per copy £1.75.

863 LAND & LIBERTY: Politics—Economics—Philosophy. 1919.
(The Single Tax 1894-1902; Land Values 1902-1919)
Land & Liberty Press Ltd., 177 Vauxhall Bridge Road, London SW1.
6 † =   Advocates the rating and taxation of land values, free trade and the market economy. Opposed to all forms of monopoly and state privileges. Of interest to planners, architects, land economists, surveyors and land reformers.
Book notices, book reviews, letters, articles, parliamentary reports.
A, Yes, 2 year.
May/June 1972, T.p. 24.   1700.
Per copy 15p, per year £1.

864 LOCAL FINANCIAL RETURNS (SCOTLAND) 1947-48.
(Local Taxation Returns (Scotland) 1880-1946/7).
Her Majesty's Stationery Office, 13A Castle Street, Edinburgh EH2 3AR.
1, +   Transactions of counties, counties of cities, burghs and district councils, joint boards, and committees of such authorities, local harbour and dock authorities and district fishery boards.
1969/70, T.p. 15.
Per copy 35p.

865 REPORT OF THE COMMISSIONERS OF H.M. INLAND REVENUE. 1857.
H.M.S.O., Atlantic House, Holborn Viaduct, London, EC1.
1, ‡   Developments in legislation and policy; organisation and personnel; information services; statistics.
A, —, Yes, None.
T.p. 75.   2500.
Per copy 68p.

866 TAXATION. 1927.
Taxation Publishing Co. Ltd., 98 Park Street, London, W1Y 4BR.
52, =   Law, practice and administration of direct taxation.
Book reviews, legal notes, letters, news, parliamentary reports.
6m, April/October, Yes, 2 year.
T.p. 15, Ad.p. 36.   13000.
Per copy 10p, per year £6.

867 TAXES: The Journal of the Inland Revenue Staff Federation. 1922.
(Tax Clerks Journal-1912-1921).
Inland Revenue Staff Federation, 7 St. George's Square, London, SW1V 2HY.
12, ‡ * †   Items of relevance to the trade union and professional interests of Inland Revenue staff concerned with the assessment and collection of income tax; and with the valuation of properties.
Book notices, book reviews, letters, articles, obituaries, parliamentary reports.
A, December, No, None,
June 1972, T.p. 39, Ad.p. 12.   c. 21000.
Per year £1.50, and Free to members.

868 VAT NEWSLETTER: and information service to commerce and industry. 1972.
Newsletters for Business, 139 Northolt Road, South Harrow, Middx. HA2 0LX.
24, =   VAT issues in general and associated problems.
No index.
Per year £20.

337
CUSTOMS. EXCISE

869 REPORT OF THE COMMISSIONERS OF HER MAJESTY'S CUSTOMS AND EXCISE.
H.M.S.O., PO Box 569, London, SE1.
1, ‡ Review of the year's activity in HM Customs and Excise and statistics of the various duties.
No index.
Per copy £1.10.

337.1
COMMON MARKET. FREE TRADE

870 COMMON MARKET LAW REPORTS. 1962.
Illustrated Newspapers Ltd.,/Common Law Reports Ltd., 49 Park Lane, London W1.
6, = Edited translations of decisions made by the European Court of Justice etc.
A, April, Yes, None.
T.p. 80, Ad.p. 1.
Subscription on application.

871 THE COMMON MARKET NEWS LETTER: The Fortnightly Business, Industrial and Political Information Service on the European Community. 1971.
European Economic Data Publishing Co. Ltd., 32 St. James's Street, London, SW1A 1HR.
26, = ○
Legal notes, parliamentary reports.
Fortnightly, Every third issue, Cumulative to Annual, Yes, A.
7 July 1972, T.p. 8.
Per year £18.50

872 EUROPEAN TRENDS. 1964.
(EEC Supplement—1959-1964).
The Economist Intelligence Unit Ltd., Spencer House, 27 St. James's Place, London, SW1A 1NT.
4, ‡ + Provides a wide range of background information on European integration. Thoroughly researched reports in depth seek out the vital data on which sound and profitable decisions can be based.
No index.
T.p. 50,
Per copy £6, per year £20.

873 JOURNAL OF COMMON MARKET STUDIES. 1962.
Basil Blackwell & Mott Ltd., 5 Alfred Street, Oxford, OX1 4HB.
4, + Provides a forum of high-level exchange between scholars and administrators on the political and economic problems of federation in all parts of the world.
Articles, Registers of Current Research, Documents, book reviews.
A, June, Yes, Vols. 1-4, 5-8.
T.p. 68, Ad.p. 4. c. 1200.
Per copy £1, per year £2.50.
Indexed in: BHI.

338
INDUSTRY. INDUSTRIAL ECONOMICS

874 CBI: INDUSTRIAL TRENDS SURVEY. 1958.
The Confederation of British Industry, 21 Tothill Street, London, SW1.
4, + * Latest trends in output, orders, employment, investment plans. Stocks of raw materials, costs, prices, export orders export deliveries, the factors limiting output and the factors limiting new export orders.
Monographic articles.
No index.
March 1972, T.p. 47.
Per copy 75p, per year £14.

875 CBI: MEMBERS BULLETIN.
Confederation of British Industry, 21 Tothill Street, London, SW1.
24, = * †
No index.
16.6.1972, T.p. 4.
Members only—free.

876 CBI REVIEW. 1971.
Confederation of British Industry, 21 Tothill Street, London, SW1.
4, + * Comment on complex issues of modern industrial society, not necessarily official views of CBI.
Monographic articles.
No Index.
Per copy 75p, per year £3.

877 CBI SMALLER FIRMS BULLETIN.
Confederation of British Industry, 21 Tothill Street, London, SW1.
4, ‡ = * News sheet.
Book notices, legal notes, parliamentary reports.
No Index.
April 1972, T.p. 4.
Per copy 20p, per year 80p.
Free to members.

878 CRAFTWORK. 1972.
Smaller Industries Council for Rural Areas of Scotland, 27 Walker Street, Edinburgh, EH3 7H2.
4, =
No Index.
Per copy 15p.

879 FANFARE FOR BRITAIN.
Confederation of British Industry, 21 Tothill Street, London, SW1.
2, ○ ‡ = * Success stories from British commerce and industry.
No Index.
May 1972, T.p. 8.
Free.

880 INTERNATIONAL LICENSING. 1964.
International Licensing Limited, 92 Cannon Lane, Pinner, Middx. HA5 1HT.
12, + = Particulars of products/processes available for manufacture under licence or joint venture arrangements, and products for which licences and know-how are sought. Covers all branches of industry and circulates worldwide.
New products, patents.
No Index.
March 1972, T.p. 16. c. 7500.
Per year £10.

881 IRISH INDUSTRY: the business and industrial Journal of Ireland. 1932.
McEvoy Press Ltd., 58 Middle Abbey Street, Dublin I.
12, = Annual Gen. Meetings—Annual Reviews—Building Ind.—Spring Show—Horse Show—Printing—Publishing—Packaging. Electrification—Banking—Insurance—Freight Transport—General News and Views.
Book reviews, legal notes, letters, monographic articles, new companies, new products, obituaries, parliamentary reports, patents, standards, tests.
No Index.
August 1971, T.p. 29, Ad.p. 3.
Per copy 15p.

882 JOURNAL OF INDUSTRIAL ECONOMICS. 1952.
Basil Blackwell & Mott Ltd., 5 Alfred Street, Oxford, OX1 4HB.
3, = + Individual business and its relation to the economy.
Monographic articles.
A, July, Yes, None.
T.p. 84. 1500.
Per copy 75p, per year £1.50.
Indexed in: BHI.

883 THE MANUFACTURERS' AGENT. 1952.
The Manufacturers' Agents Association, P.O. Box 8, Majestic House, Staines, Middx.
12, =   General agents information and advertisements.
No Index.
June 1972, T.p. 9, Ad.p. 5.   1600.
Per copy 15p, per year £3.

884 PRODUCT LICENSING JOURNAL AND RESEARCH DISCLOSURE. 1965.
(Lapis Industrial Opportunities 1958-1964).
Industrial Opportunities Ltd., Homlarch, Havant, Hants.
12, =   Details products and processes available for manufacture under licence; also research disclosed to obviate need for patenting. For directors of medium size companies; patent/licensing managers large companies.
Book reviews, letters, articles, new products, patents.
No Index.
T.p. 32, Ad.p. 1.
Per copy £1, per year £10.50.

885 REPORT ON THE CENSUS OF PRODUCTION OF NORTHERN IRELAND. 1949.
H.M.S.O., Belfast.
1, = +   Statistics on production in manufacturing industries, construction, gas, electricity and water undertakings.
A, —, No, None.
Per year 75p.

338.984

ECONOMIC PLANNING

886 FUTURES. The journal of forecasting and planning. 1968.
Iliffe Science & Technology Publications Ltd., 32 High Street, Guildford, Surrey.
4, ‡ =   Book reviews, letters, monographic articles.
A, March, Yes, None.
T.p. 97.   1200.
Per copy £3, per year £12.

887 SOCIO-ECONOMIC PLANNING SCIENCES.
Pergamon Press Ltd., Headington Hill Hall, Oxford OX3 0BW.
6, + =   All aspects relating to education, transportation, housing, pollution and economic planning.
Book reviews, monographic articles.
A, Last issue of volume. Yes, None.
Per copy £3, per year £14.

34

LAW

888 ALL ENGLAND LAW REPORTS. 1936.
(Law Times Reports, 1843)
Butterworths, 88 Kingsway, London, WC2B 6AB.
48, ‡ +   Full (verbatim) reports of judicial decisions of the House of Lords, Court of Appeal, High Court and other superior courts of England and Wales which establish new, or modify and apply existing principles of law.
Law reports.
4m, April, August, January each year, Yes, A.
11.7.72, T.p. 131, Ad.p. 2.   14393.
Per year £13.20.

889 ANGLO-AMERICAN LAW REVIEW. 1972.
Justice of the Peace Ltd., Little London, Chichester, Sussex.
4, =   Anglo/American law.
Book notices, book reviews, legal notes, letters, monographic articles, obituaries.
A, February/March, Yes, None.
Jan-March 1972, T.p. 142, Ad.p. 6.   600.
Per copy £1.50, per year £6.

890 CAMBRIAN LAW REVIEW. 1970.
The Committee of the Cambrian Law Review, Department of Law, U.C.W., Aberystwyth, Wales.
1, ○ ‡ + *   Book notices, book reviews, legal notes, letters, monographic articles, obituaries.
5 year, —, Yes, None.
1972, T.p. 114, Ad.p. 7.   700.
Per copy 50p.

891 CAMBRIDGE LAW JOURNAL. 1921.
Cambridge University Press, P.O. Box 92, London, NW1 2DB.
2, +   All aspects of civil, criminal, constitutional and international law and legal history.
Book reviews, legal notes, monographic articles.
A, November, Yes, None.
April 1972, T.p. 92, Ad.p. 3.   1700.
Per copy £1.50, per year £2.80.
Indexed in: BHI, IBZ.

892 CIVIL JUDICIAL STATISTICS (SCOTLAND). c.1939.
HMSO, Bankhead Avenue, Sighthill, Edinburgh.
1, +   Statistics relating to the House of Lords (Scottish Appeals); Court of Session; Sheriff Courts and other Civil Courts; Licensing Courts: Certain Legal and Public Departments; Bankruptcy; Court Fees and Fees taken in the Departments during the current year.
A, with each issue, Yes, 5 year.
Subscription on application.

893 COMMON MARKET LAW REVIEW. 1963.
Stevens (Associated Book Publishers), 11 New Fetter Lane, London, EC4P 4EE.
4, ‡ =   Published in co-operation with the British Institute of International and Comparative Law and the Europa Instituut of the University of Leyden.
Presents a balanced and comprehensive survey of the evolution of the law of the European Communities to English language readers throughout the world. Each issue contains a number of leading articles, a group of shorter articles, comments and notes, a survey of the case law of the European Court of Justice and of important national court decisions, a review of legislation, surveys of literature, a new section on negotiations, and book reviews.
A, October, Yes, None.
Per copy £3, per year £10.

894 THE CONVEYANCER AND PROPERTY LAWYER. 1936.
Sweet & Maxwell (Associated Book Publishers), 11 New Fetter Lane, London, EC4P 4EE.
6, ‡ =   Contemporary aspects of conveyancing practice.
Book notices, book reviews, legal notes, letters, monographic articles.
A, November/December, Yes, None.
Per copy 90p, per year £7.

895 CURRENT LAW. 1947.
Sweet & Maxwell (Associated Book Publishers), 11 New Fetter Lane, London, EC4P 4EE.
Irregular, = ‡
The current law service comprises: The Monthly Parts, issued on the 8th of every month; The Year Book, published each April; The Citator Volume, issued each year with The Year Book; The Statutes, issued in parts, shortly after receiving the Royal Assent. At the end of each year a bound volume is provided free as part of the service. Every source of legal information is monitored and checked by the *Current Law* Editors. The information is completely up-to-date, is reliable and all the important indexes, citators and references are cumulative from part to part and from year to year. The complete 1972 service is £21 (delivery charge £1.60 extra) but subscribers who do not wish to take advantage of all the available services have a choice of five other services, ranging from Service D (monthly parts only) at £8 (delivery charge 60p).

A descriptive leaflet is available on request. A full explanatory booklet—*How to Use Current Law*—is available free.

896 EUROLAW COMMERCIAL INTELLIGENCE. 1972.
Common Law Reports Ltd., 49 Park Lane, London, W1Y 3LB.
24, =
No Index.
Per year £10.

897 EUROPEAN LAW DIGEST. 1973.
Common Law Reports Ltd., 49 Park Lane, London, W1Y 3LB.
12, =
No Index.
Per copy £2.50.

898 FAMILY LAW. 1971.
Justice of the Peace Ltd., Little London, Chichester, Sussex.
6, ○ =   Lawyers, social workers, etc.
Book notices, book reviews, legal notes, letters, articles, obituaries, parliamentary reports.
A, February/March, Yes, None.
May/June 1972, T.p. 32.   2000.
Per copy 50p, per year £3.

899 FINANCIAL TIMES—EUROPEAN LAW NEWSLETTER. 1972.
Financial Times Ltd., Bracken House, Cannon Street, London, EC4.
4, =
No Index.
Subscription on application.

901 INDUSTRIAL RELATIONS LAW REPORTS. 1972.
I.R.L.R., 286 Kilburn High Road, London, NW6.
12, =
Per year £30.

902 INTERNATIONAL BAR JOURNAL. 1971.
(International Bar News)
International Bar Association, 14 Waterloo Place, London, SW1Y 4AR.
2, ‡ =
Book notices, book reviews, legal notes, monographic articles.
No Index.
May 1972, T.p. 138.
Per year £5. Free to members.

903 THE IRISH LAW TIMES AND SOLICITORS JOURNAL. 1867.
Hely Thom Ltd., P.O. Box 138, Botanic Road, Dublin 9.
50, * =
Legal notes.
A, c. October, Yes, None.
T.p. 8, Ad.p. 1.   1000.
Free to members.

904 JOURNAL OF THE LAW SOCIETY OF SCOTLAND. 1956.
The Law Society of Scotland, Law Society's Hall, 26 Drumsheugh Gardens, Edinburgh, EH3 7YR.
12, = *
Abstracts, book notices, book reviews, legal notes, letters, monographic articles, obituaries, parliamentary reports.
A, February, Yes, None.
May 1972, T.p. 35, Ad.p. 21.   4000.
Free to members.

905 JOURNAL OF PLANNING AND PROPERTY LAW. 1948.
Sweet & Maxwell (Associated Book Publishers), 11 New Fetter Lane, London, EC4P 4EE.
12, = ‡
Most parts comprise: Editorial; articles of current interest; Parliamentary intelligence; Ministerial Information and circulars; notes of cases; Lands Tribunal decisions; enforcement notice appeal decisions; reviews; correspondence; notes of planning decisions; Statutory Instruments; practical points; and a cumulative index.
A, December, Yes, None.
Per copy 50p, per year £5.25.

906 THE JURIDICAL REVIEW: The Law Journal of Scottish Universities. 1956.
(The Juridical Review (without sub-title) 1889-1955)
W. Green & Son Ltd., St. Giles Street, Edinburgh, EH1 1PU.
3, ‡ =   Legal and historical with the emphasis on Scots Law.
Book notices, book reviews, legal notes, monographic articles.
A, —, Yes, None.
April 1972, T.p. 96, Ad.p. 2.
Per year £3.

907 LAW NOTES. 1881.
Law Notes, 25/26 Chancery Lane, London, WC2.
12, =   Legal cases for the profession, news.
Book notices, book reviews, legal notes, letters, news, obituaries, parliamentary reports.
A, December, Yes, None.
T.p. 28, Ad.p. 12.   8500.
Per copy 12½p, per year £1.75.

908 THE LAW QUARTERLY REVIEW. 1885.
Stevens (Associated Book Publishers), 11 New Fetter Lane, London, EC4P 4EE.
4, ‡ =   Searching and detailed expositions of various aspects of the law.
Book notices, book reviews, legal notes, monographic articles.
A, October, Yes, Vols. 1-80 (1885-1964).
April 1969, T.p. 151, Ad.p. 23.
Per copy £1.50, per year £5.
Indexed in: BHI, IBZ.

909 THE LAW REPORTS. 1865.
Incorporated Council of Law Reporting for England and Wales, 3 Stone Buildings, Lincoln's Inn, London, WC2.
11, = ‡   Decisions of cases heard in the High Courts, House of Lords and Privy Council.
A, December, Yes, 10 year.
T.p. 135.
Per copy £1.50, per year £24.

910 THE LAW SOCIETY'S GAZETTE. 1903.
The Law Society, 113 Chancery Lane, London, WC2.
47, = *   All aspects of law.
Abstracts, book notices, book reviews, legal notes, letters, monographic articles, occasionally new products, obituaries, parliamentary reports.
A, January, Yes, None.
T.p. 18, Ad.p. 14.   34200.
Per copy 12½p, per year £6.50.

911 MEDICINE, SCIENCE AND THE LAW. 1971.
John Wright & Sons Ltd., 42-44 Triangle West, Bristol BS8 1EX.
=
Monographic articles.

912 MODERN LAW REVIEW. 1937.
Stevens (Associated Book Publishers), 11 New Fetter Lane, London, EC4P 4EE.
6, ‡ =   Thorough and exhaustive examination of any new development while it is still of topical interest.

Key to reference symbols

○ popular   ‡ technical   = trade/professional

+ research   * society/institution   † house journal

Book notices, book reviews, legal notes, monographic articles.
A, November, Yes. Vols. 1-33 (1937-1970).
January 1969, T.p. 120, Ad.p. 19.
Per copy £1, per year £4.75.
Indexed in: BHI, IBZ.

913 NEW LAW JOURNAL. 1965.
(Law Journal, 1822)
Butterworths, 88 Kingsway, London, WC2B 6AB.
+ = Provides an up-to-date and practical service for the practitioner to include all the day to day information that he requires together with reasoned comment on legal affairs.
Book notices, book reviews, legal notes, letters, monographic articles, parliamentary reports.
A, Jan/Feb, Yes, None.
13.4.72, T.p. 24, Ad.p. 24. 8491.
Per copy 20p, per year £7.

914 NIGERIAN LAW JOURNAL. 1964.
Sweet & Maxwell (Associated Book Publishers), 11 New Fetter Lane, London, EC4P 4EE.
1, ‡ = African law and sociology, and anthropology.
Book notices, book reviews, letters, monographic articles.
A, —, Yes, None.
Per copy £4.50 (Bound) £2.90 (Paperback).

915 OYEZ NOTES
Solicitors Law Stationery Society, Breams Buildings, London, EC4.
=

916 PATENT LAW REVIEW. 1969
Sage Hill/Clark Boardman/Sweet & Maxwell,
Sweet & Maxwell (Associated Book Publishers), 11 New Fetter Lane, London, EC4P 4EE.
1, = Collects for quick and convenient reference the thinking of the best contemporary writers in the patent field. The leading articles published in the U.S.A. during the year are selected for inclusion and, for effective use, they are arranged according to subject-matter and comprehensively indexed.
Monographic articles, patents.
A, —, Yes, None.
Per copy £12.50.

917 PROPERTY AND COMPENSATION REPORTS. 1949.
Sweet & Maxwell (Associated Book Publishers), 11 New Fetter Lane, London, EC4P 4EE.
3 parts per vol, 2 vols. per year, ‡ =
Important property, planning and compensation cases which come before the House of Lords, Court of Appeal and High Court, and also all the decisions of the Lands Tribunal on these subjects. The latter include claims for compensation, for refusal of planning permission, for compensation following the compulsory acquisition of land, and for compensation for loss from land drainage works by river boards, as well as claims for payments for loss of land values and applications for the discharge or modification of restrictive covenants.
6m, 3rd part each year, Yes, None
Per copy £3, per year £16.

918 PUBLIC LAW. 1956.
(The British Journal of Administrative Law 1954-56)
Stevens (Associated Book Publishers), 11 New Fetter Lane, London, EC4P 4EE.
4, ‡ = Authoritative and critical comments on topical questions in the field of constitutional and administrative law.
Book notices, book reviews, monographic articles.
A, Last issue of year, Yes, None.
Per copy £1.50, per year £5.50.

919 SWEET & MAXWELL'S STUDENTS' LAW REPORTER. 1970.
Sweet & Maxwell (Associated Book Publishers), 11 New Fetter Lane, London, EC4P 4EE.
3, ‡ = Provides students with full and detailed information of current cases and legislation.
Legal notes.
No Index.
Free via Colleges only on application.

920 THE WEEKLY LAW REPORTS. 1953.
Incorporated Council of Law Reporting for England and Wales, 3 Stone Buildings, Lincoln's Inn, London, WC2.
47, = Cases heard in the High Courts.
A, December, Yes, 10 year.
T.p. 116.
Per copy 50p, per year £10.

340.6

FORENSIC MEDICINE

921 JOURNAL OF THE FORENSIC SCIENCE SOCIETY. 1959.
The Forensic Science Society, 107 Fenchurch Street, London, EC3M 5JB.
4, ‡ + Covers the entire field of production and use of expert evidence in both Criminal and Civil Courts.
Book notices, book reviews, legal notes, letters, monographic articles, obituaries, standards, tests.
A, —, Yes, None.
Jan. 1972, T.p. 54, Ad.p. 3. 2000.
Per copy £1.25, per year £5.

922 MEDICO-LEGAL JOURNAL. 1901.
W. Heffer & Sons Ltd. (for Medico Legal Society), Cambridge.
4, * =
Legal aspects of medical crimes and cases.
Book reviews, monographic articles.
A, Last issue of year, Yes, None.
T.p. 49.
Per copy 50p, per year £2.
Indexed in: BHI.

341

INTERNATIONAL LAW

923 THE INTERNATIONAL AND COMPARATIVE LAW QUARTERLY. 1952.
(Journal of the Society of Comparative Legislation and International Law 1896-1951, Transactions of the Grotius Society 1915-1959)
The British Institute of International and Comparative Law, 32 Furnival Street, London, EC4A 1JN.
4, + * ‡ Public international law, private international law, comparative law, Commonwealth law and Law of the European Communities. Also covers Current Legal Developments all over the world.
Book notices, book reviews, legal notes, monographic articles, obituaries.
A, October, Yes, None.
April 1972, T.p. 194, Ad.p. 24. 3250.
Per copy £2, per year £6.50.

341.67

ARMS CONTROL. DISARMAMENT

925 SANITY: Voice of CND. 1960.
CND, 14 Grays Inn Road, London, WC1.
12, * Peace, nuclear and general disarmament, foreign affairs, international coverage.
Book reviews, letters, articles, obituaries, parliamentary reports, tests.

No Index.
July 1972, T.p. 8, Ad.p. 8.
Per copy 5p, per year 75p.

341.8

CONSULS

926 DIPLOMATIC BOOKSHELF. Monthly List of Arrivals and Departures. 1966.
Arthur H. Thrower Limited, 44-46 South Ealing Road, Ealing, London, W5.
12, =   News of interest to Diplomatic Corps, arrivals and departures of diplomats, book reviews.
Notices, book reviews, letters.
No Index.

927 HER MAJESTY'S CONSULS LIST. 1903.
L. V. Josephi, National Mutual House, South Park, Sevenoaks, Kent.
6, =   The British Diplomatic service throughout the world; Overseas diplomats in London.
1. Geographical list of Diplomatic Officers.
2. Magazine section, predominantly export subjects.
No Index.
T.p. 48, Ad.p. 16.   2000.
Per year £3.75.

342.36

MONARCHY

928 THE MONARCHIST: Journal of the Monarchist League. 1967.
(The Monarchist Guardian. 1960-1966)
The Monarchist League, 29 York Street, London, W1.
4, + *   Modern and historical Monarchical questions; recording and publicising events of Monarchical interest; reviewing Monarchist and historical works.
Book notices, book reviews, letters, monographic articles, obituaries, parliamentary reports.
No Index.
Winter 1972, T.p. 48.
Per copy 15p, per year 75p. Free to Members.

342.7

HUMAN RIGHTS

929 THE AUDITOR: The monthly journal of Scientology. 1964.
The Hubbard College of Scientology, Saint Hill Manor, East Grinstead, Sussex.
12, †   Scientology in general.
Book notices, letters, articles, new products, obituaries.
No Index.
No. 75, T.p. 8.   c. 125000.
Free to members.

930 CAFD NEWSLETTER. 1971.
Council for Academic Freedom and Democracy, 152 Camden High St., London, NW1.
6, ○ *   Report of activities of CAFD covering case work, campaigns, publications, etc. Also general news on academic freedom and democracy.
No Index.
May-June 1972, T.p. 2.   700.
Per year £2.50.

931 FREEDOM: Scientology. 1968.
The Church of Scientology World Wide, Saint Hill Manor, East Grinstead, Sussex.
10/12, ○ ‡ *   Human rights, abuses in Society, justice, with particular emphasis on rights for mental patients and opposition to involuntary institutionalisation—the role of the individual in Society and his betterment is also included.

Book notices, book reviews, legal notes, letters, articles, new products, obituaries, parliamentary reports, standards, tests.
No Index.
April-May 1972, T.p. 8.   150000.
Per copy 5p.

932 NCCL BULLETIN. 1960.
(Civil Liberty 1934-1959)
National Council for Civil Liberties, 152 Camden High St., London, NW1.
6, * ○   Record of the activities of the National Council for Civil Liberties covering case work, research, education, pressure group activities.
Book notices, legal notes, parliamentary reports etc., etc.
No Index.
June/July 1972, T.p. 12.   6000.
Per year £2.

933 SPEAK-OUT. 1969.
National Council for Civil Liberties, 152 Camden High St., London, NW1.
Irregular, ○ *   A broadsheet on a particular issue published as part of major N.C.C.L. campaigns.
Legal notes, parliamentary reports.
No Index.
January 1972, T.p. 4.   30000.
Per copy 2p.

342.8

ELECTORAL LAW

934 REPRESENTATION. 1908.
Electoral Reform Society, 6 Chancel Street, London, SE1.
4, = +   Electoral systems in all countries.
Articles, news, obituaries, parliamentary reports.
No Index.
T.p. 4, Ad.p. 4.
Free to members.

343

CRIMINAL LAW

935 CRIMINAL APPEAL REPORTS. 1908.
Sweet & Maxwell (Associated Book Publishers), 11 New Fetter Lane, London, EC4P 4EE.
4, ‡ =   Arguments on points of law and practice, but also accounts of hearings on questions of fact and sentence. Every judgment is carefully revised by the Court of Appeal itself which attaches the highest importance to the series.
A, Part Four, Yes, None.
Per copy £2.25, per year £8.

936 CRIMINAL LAW REVIEW. 1954.
Sweet & Maxwell (Associated Book Publishers), 11 New Fetter Lane, London, EC4P 4EE.
12, ‡ ○ =   Authoritative comments, opinions and insights on current topics. It reports on every important case in criminal law, many not reported elsewhere, classified and indexed. There are many other useful features expressly designed for all working in the criminal law.
Book notices, book reviews, legal notes, letters, monographic articles.
A, December, Yes, None.
November 1969, T.p. 55, Ad.p. 6.
Per copy 40p, per year £4.20.
Indexed in: BHI.

937 CRIMINAL STATISTICS SCOTLAND: Statistics relating to police apprehensions and criminal proceedings for the year 19–. 1939.
(Judicial Statistics Scotland (Criminal Statistics)

H.M.S.O., Government Buildings, Bankhead Drive,
    Sighthill, Edinburgh.
1, ‡ +
Subscription on application.

343.58
ANIMAL WELFARE

938 ANIMAL WORLD: Official organ of the RSPCA. 1869.
    RSPCA, 105 Jermyn Street, London, SW1.
    12, *   Animal welfare.
    Book notices, book reviews, parliamentary reports.
    No Index.
    T.p. 14, Ad.p. 1.   8000.
    Free to members.

939 CRUEL SPORTS. 1959.
    Cruel Sports (1927-47), League Doings (1947-58).
    League Against Cruel Sports Ltd., 1 Reform Row,
        London, N17 9TW.
    3, *   Presents information and the case against fox-
        hunting, deerhunting, otterhunting, harehunting and
        coursing, badger digging and baiting.
    Book reviews, legal notes, letters, articles, obituaries,
        parliamentary reports.
    No Index.
    Vol. 13, No. 3, 1972, T.p. 6.   20000.
    Per copy 4p, per year 50p.

940 ISPA NEWS. 1965.
    International Society for the Protection of Animals,
        106 Jermyn Street, London, SW1.
    4, *   To keep members informed of ISPA's work
        overseas for the protection of animals.
    No Index.
    Summer 1971, T.p. 8.   3000.
    Free to members.

343.81
PRISONS

941 THE PRISON OFFICERS MAGAZINE. Official journal
        of the Prison Officers Association. 1921.
    Prison Officers Association, 245 Church Street,
        Edmonton, London, N9.
    12, =   All aspects of prison work.
    Book reviews, letters, articles, news, obituaries,
        parliamentary reports.
    No Index.
    T.p. 20, Ad.p. 5.
    Free to members.

942 PRISON SERVICE JOURNAL. 1960.
    Home Office Prison Department, c/o H.M. Borstal,
        Hewell Grange, Redditch, Worcs.
    4, =   Penology, including the study of delinquency.
    Book notices, book reviews, letters, monographic
        articles, obituaries.
    No Index.
    July 1972, T.p. 24, Ad.p. 2.
    Per copy 7½p, per year 25p.

343.82
PROBATION

943 PROBATION: Journal of the National Association of
        Probation Officers. 1955.
    National Assoc. of Probation Officers, 6 Endsleigh
        Street, London, WC1H 0DZ.
    3, ‡ * +   All matters concerning general reform and
        treatment of offenders mainly in England and Wales
        but also internationally.
    Book notices, book reviews, legal notes, letters, mono-
        graphic articles, obituaries, parliamentary reports,
        standards, tests.

No Index.
March 1972, T.p. 32, Ad.p. 1.   4250.
Per copy 20p, per year 60p.
Free to members.

343.9
CRIMINOLOGY

944 THE BRITISH JOURNAL OF CRIMINOLOGY. 1960.
    (The British Journal of Deliquency 1950-1960)
    Stevens (Associated Book Publishers), (For the
        Institute for the Study and Treatment of delinquency),
        11 New Fetter Lane, London, EC4P 4EE.
    4, ‡ =   Current developments in various countries,
        together with a calendar of individual research
        projects undertaken in the United Kingdom and
        abroad, giving information of use to research
        workers contemplating the study of similar or
        related problems.
    Book notices, book reviews, legal notes, monographic
        articles.
    A, October, Yes, 1950-1970.
    April 1969, T.p. 103, Ad.p. 9.
    Per copy £1.50, per year £5.25.
    Indexed in: BHI, IBZ.

945 THE CRIMINOLOGIST. 1967.
    (Crime & Detection 1966-1967)
    Forensic Publishing Company, 9 Old Bailey, London,
        EC99 1AA.
    4, ‡ + =   All aspects of police, criminology, forensic
        science, law, penology &c.
    Book reviews, legal notes, letters, monographic articles
    A, February, Yes, None.
    Winter 1972, T.p. 93, Ad.p. 3.   10000.
    Per year £3.

946 CRIMINOLOGY. 1962.
    Sage Publications Ltd., St. George's House, 44 Hatton
        Garden, London, EC1N 8ER.
    4, = +   Crimes and deviant behavior as found in
        sociology, psychology, psychiatry, law and social
        work.
    Book reviews, monographic articles.
    A, —, Yes, None.
    May 1971, T.p. 124.
    Per year £7, Individual £4.70.

947 HOWARD JOURNAL OF PENOLOGY & CRIME
        PREVENTION. 1952.
    (Howard Journal 1921-1951)
    Butterworth & Co. Ltd., (for the Howard
        League for Penal Reform), 88 Kingsway, London,
        WC2B 6AB.
    1, = *   Preventive measures; treatment and after-
        care of offenders; theoretical and practical.
    Book reviews, monographic articles.
    1972, T.p. 96.
    Per copy £1.60, 60p (members).
    Indexed in: BHI, IBZ.

347.4
BONDS. CONTRACTS.

948 BONDHOLDER'S REGISTER. 1872.
    A. B. Filby, Kenwards, Piltdown, Uckfield, Sussex.
    24, =   Covers matters regarding Bonds and Bearer
        Securities; particular sinking fund operations and
        coupon payments.
    A, January, No, None.
    13 June 1972, T.p. 12, Ad.p. as required.   6500.
    Per year £12.

347.7

BUSINESS LAW

949 INDUSTRIAL LAW JOURNAL. 1972.
(Bulletin of the Industrial Law Society)
Sweet & Maxwell (Associated Book Publishers) (for the Industrial Law Society), 11 New Fetter Lane, London, EC4P 4EE.
4, ‡ * Every aspect of industrial law.
Book notices, book reviews, legal notes, monographic articles.
A, December, Yes, None.
Per copy £1, per year £3.

950 THE JOURNAL OF BUSINESS LAW. 1957.
Stevens (Associated Book Publishers), 11 New Fetter Lane, London, EC4P 4EE.
‡ Every aspect of the law connected with the conduct of business: everything is done to forewarn the business-man so that he can safeguard his interests. It is particularly directed at everyone who is responsible for management and commercial policy.
Book notices, book reviews, legal notes, monographic articles.
A, October, Yes, None.
January 1969, T.p. 92, Ad.p. 10.
Per copy £1.25, per year £5.

951 JOURNAL OF WORLD TRADE LAW. 1967.
Vincent Press, 60 Cole Park Road, Twickenham, Middx.
6, + = Legal and economic issues involved in international trade.
Book reviews, monographic articles.
A, with Nov./Dec. issue, No, None.
Per copy £2.50, per year £15.
Indexed in: BHI.

952 THE MEDICAL SECRETARY: Journal of the Association of Medical Secretaries.
Association of Medical Secretaries, 22 Manchester Street, London, W1.
4, ‡ + * Educational articles, professional articles related to medical secretarial work in all spheres, hospital, practice health authority, industry. Current reports.
Book notices, book reviews, legal notes, letters, monographic articles, new products, parliamentary reports.
No Index.
No. 21, 1972, T.p. 23, Ad.p. 1. 4000.
Free to members.

953 PROFESSIONAL ADMINISTRATION: The official journal of the Institute of Chartered Secretaries and Administrators. 1971.
(Incorporating The Chartered Secretary, The Secretaries Journal, Incorporated Secretaries Journal, The Secretary & Secretaries Chronicle.)
FT Business Publications Ltd., (Pearson-Longman), 388/389 Strand, London, WC2.
11/12, = * Chartered secretaries and others involved in company and public administration, including company secretaries, financial controllers and public service officers. Law, tax, pension, insurance, property government and business systems and services.
Book reviews, legal notes, letters, monographic articles, new products, parlimantary reports, standards.
A, December/January, Yes, None.
June 1972, T.p. 36, Ad.p. 30. 49000.
Per copy 25p, per year £3.

347.962

MAGISTRATES

954 THE MAGISTRATE: Journal of The Magistrates' Association. 1921.
The Editor, E. R. Horsman Esq., Court House, Leigh Road, Eastleigh, Hants. SO5 4ZN.
12, ‡ * Work of magistrates' courts, the law they administer and the problems they encounter.
Book reviews, legal notes, letters, monographic articles, obituaries, parliamentary reports.
A, Each year, No, None.
June 1972, T.p. 16, Ad.p. 3. 20000.
Per year £2, and free to members.

347.964

LEGAL PERSONNEL.

955 J.P. WEEKLY LAW DIGEST. 1972.
(J.P. Supplement)
Justice of the Peace Ltd., Little London, Chichester, Sussex.
52, = All those engaged in legal practice.
Abstracts.
A, February, Yes, None.
15.7.72, T.p. 4, Ad.p. None. 1000.
Per copy 5p, per year £3.12.

956 JUSTICE OF THE PEACE. 1971.
(Justice of the Peace and Local Government Review. 1837-1971)
Justice of the Peace Ltd., Little London, Chichester, Sussex.
52, = Magistrates, Clerks to Justices, Solicitors, Police, Probation, Prison Officers, etc.
Book notices, book reviews, legal notes, letters, monographic articles, obituaries, parliamentary reports.
A, February/March, Yes, 10 year.
29.7.1972, T.p. 27, Ad.p. 8.
Per copy 17½p, per year £9.75.

957 JUSTICE OF THE PEACE REPORTS. 1837.
Justice of the Peace Ltd., Little London, Chichester, Sussex.
52, = Lawyers, all those engaged in legal practice.
A, February/March, Yes, None.
15.7.72, T.p. 24, Ad.p. None. 2500.
Per copy 15p, per year £7.35.

958 THE JUSTICES' CLERK: The journal of the Justices' Clerks' Society. 1947.
(The Bulletin. 1943-46)
The Justices' Clerks' Society, P. J. Halnan, Hon. Sec. J.C.S. County Hall, Cambridge.
3, * = Professional news re the Society and members. Articles and information for members.
Book notices, book reviews, legal notes, letters, monographic articles, obituaries.
A, January, No, None.
May 1972, T.p. 30, Ad.p. 2.
Per year £1.25.

959 THE LEGAL EXECUTIVE. 1963.
The Institute of Legal Executives, Ilex House, Barrhill Road, London, SW2 4RW.
6, = * Features and general information of a legal nature.
Abstracts, book notices, book reviews, legal notes, letters, obituaries, parliamentary reports.
A, March, Yes, None.
May 1972, T.p. 32, Ad.p. 11. 1370.
Per copy 35p, per year £2. Free to members.

960 LOCAL GOVERNMENT REVIEW. 1971.
(Justice of the Peace and Local Government Review 1927-1971)
Justice of the Peace Ltd., Little London, Chichester, Sussex.
52, = All those engaged in Local Government Administration/finance etc., for the professional rather than the amateur.

Book notices, book reviews, legal notes, letters, monographic articles, new products, obituaries, parliamentary.
A, February/March, Yes, None.
1.7.72, T.p. 24, Ad.p. 4.   2000.
Per copy 17½p, per year £9.75.

347.964.3
BAILIFFS

961 BAILIFF JOURNAL.
Certified Bailiffs' Association of England and Wales, 26 Park Place, Stevenage, Herts.
=
No Index.
Subscription on application.

35
PUBLIC ADMINISTRATION

962 APPROPRIATION ACCOUNTS. 1922.
H.M.S.O., Chichester St., Belfast, BT1 4JY.
1, ‡   Expenditure of Government departments in N.I.
Parliamentary reports.
A, With volume, Yes, None.
December 1971, T.p. 204.
Per copy £1.72.

963 PUBLIC ADMINISTRATION: Journal of the Royal Institute of Public Administration. 1923.
(The Journal of Public Administration. 1923-1925)
Royal Institute of Public Administration, Hamilton House, Mabledon Place, London, WC1H 9BD.
4,*   Study and practice of public administration in the United Kingdom and overseas countries.
Book notices, book reviews, letters, monographic articles.
A, —, Yes, 10 yr subject and author 1953-1962.
Spring 1972, T.p. 116, Ad.p. 4.   9300.
Per copy 75p, per year £2.75.
Indexed in: BHI.

964 PUBLIC ADMINISTRATION BULLETIN. 1972.
(PAC Bulletin 1964-1972)
Joint University Council for Social and Public Administration, Royal Institute of Public Administration, Hamilton House, Mabledon Place, London, WC1H 9BD.
2, +   To serve the needs of teachers, researchers and students of public administration in universities and colleges for information on developments in their subject. It is sponsored by the Public Administration Committee of the Joint University Council for Social and Public Administration.
Book reviews, monographic articles.
No Index.
June 1972, T.p. 38.   150.
Per copy 50p, per year 90p.

965 REPORT ON THE ADMINISTRATION OF HOME OFFICE SERVICES.
HMSO, Chichester House, Chichester Street, Belfast, BT1 4PS.
1, = +   Account of the various services coming within the ambit of Home Office Service.
Parliamentary reports.
A, —, Yes, None.
T.p. 90.
Per copy 85p.

35.08
CIVIL SERVICE

966 CIVIL SERVICE OPINION. 1922.
Society of Civil Servants, 19 Surrey Street, London, WC2.
12,*   Civil service and public administration.
Book notices, book reviews, letters, articles, obituaries.
No Index.
T.p. 25, Ad.p. 10.   65000.
Per copy 5p.

967 CIVIL SERVICE STATISTICS. 1970.
HMSO, 49 High Holborn, London, WC1V 6HB.
1, +   A statistical description of the Civil Service: brief introduction to location, structure, manpower, administration and tables concentrating on non-industrial staff of the civil service.
Statistical tables.
A, —, Yes, None.
1971, T.p. 53.
Per copy 75p.

968 EMBASSY: the international magazine for the diplomatic world. 1971.
Novel Publishers Ltd., 132 Wardour Street, London, W1.
12, =
No Index.
Per year £6.

969 STATE SERVICE. 1921.
(State Technology 1919-1920)
Institution of Professional Civil Servants, 3-7 Northumberland Street, London, WC2N 5BS.
12,* =   Civil service trade union matters.
Book reviews, legal notes, letters, articles, news, obituaries, parliamentary reports.
A, January, Yes, None.
T.p. 24, Ad.p. 10.   87000.
Free to members.

351.713
RATING. VALUATION

970 RATES AND RATEABLE VALUES IN SCOTLAND. 1959.
H.M.S.O., Annandale Street, Edinburgh.
1, O   Figures for Population, Area, Rate Poundages, Produce of Rates and Valuation, Receipts from Rates and Rateable Values as per Rating Authorities for the year in question.
A, With issue, Yes, None.
Subscription on application.

971 RATING AND VALUATION REPORTER. 1961.
(Rating and Income Tax 1924-1960)
Rating Publishers Ltd., 2 Paper Buildings, Temple, London, EC4.
51/52, ‡   All aspects of Land Rating, Valuation, compensation for compulsory purchase, lease-hold reform etc.
Book notices, book reviews, legal notes, letters, articles, obituaries, parliamentary reports.
A, January-February, Yes, None.
15 June 1972, T.p. 12.   3000.
Per copy 20p, per year £9.

972 THE VALUER: Journal of The Incorporated Society of Valuers & Auctioneers. January, 1927.
The Society, 3 Cadogan Gate, London, SW1.
10,* =
Book notices, book reviews, legal notes, articles, obituaries, parliamentary reports.
A, —, No, None.
June 1972, T.p. 33, Ad.p. 6.
Per year £2.50, and Free to members.

351.74
POLICE

973 POLICE: The Magazine of the Police Federation. 1968.
(Police Federation Newsletter)

Police Federation, 15-17 Langley Road, Surbiton, Surrey, KT6 6LP.
12, = *   Entire police service from cadet to chief constable and all individuals connected with it.
Book notices, book reviews, legal notes, letters, monographic articles, parliamentary reports.
June 1972, T.p. 32, Ad.p. 15.   22280.
Per copy 50p. Free to members.

974 POLICE COLLEGE MAGAZINE. 1949.
M & W Publications Ltd., 42 Stanley Street, Liverpool, L1 6AW.
2, =   Progress and activities of the Police College and general police matters.
Book notices, book reviews, legal notes, letters, articles, news, obituaries.
No Index.
T.p. 69, Ad.p. 3.
Free to members.

975 POLICE JOURNAL: a quarterly review for the Police of the World. 1929.
Little London, Chichester, Sussex.
4, =   All matters pertaining to police.
Book notices, book reviews, legal notes, letters, new products, obituaries, tests.
A, February/March, Yes, Occasional.
July/August, T.p. 83, Ad.p. 15.   3000.
Per copy 75p, per year £3.

976 POLICE RESEARCH BULLETIN. 1966.
Home Office Police Planning Organisation, Horseferry House, Dean Ryle Street, London, SW1.
4, =
No Index.
Subscription on application.

977 POLICE REVIEW: The weekly news magazine of the British police. 1893.
Police Review Publishing Co. Ltd., 67 Clerkenwell Road, London, ECLR 5BJ.
52, ‡   Covers all matters relating to police work in Britain.
Abstracts, book reviews, commodity prices, legal notes, letters, monographic articles, new products, obituaries, parliamentary reports, patents, standards, tests.
No Index.
9.6.1972, T.p., 22, Ad.p. 10.   35000.
Per copy 5p, per year £4.50.

978 POLICE WORLD: quarterly journal of the International Police Association.
M & W Publications Ltd., 42 Stanley Street, Liverpool, L1 6AW.
4, =   Police and general interest matters.
Book reviews, legal notes, letters, news, obituaries.
No Index.
T.p. 46, Ad.p. 20.
Free to members.

351.75

SECURITY

979 SECURITY AND PROTECTION: official journal of the Industrial Police and Security Association. 1969.
Trade News Ltd., (for the I.P.S.A.), Pembroke House, Campsbourne Road, Hornsey, London, N8.
12, = ‡ *   All aspects of industrial security.
Book reviews, legal notes, letters, monographic articles, new companies, new products.
No Index.
July 1972, T.p. 20, Ad.p. 8.
Per year £2.75. Free to members.

980 SECURITY GAZETTE: Fire and Safety Management. 1958.
Security Gazette Ltd., 326 St John Street, London, EC1V 4QD.

12, =   All aspects of National and Industrial Security Fine and Safety.
Book notices, book reviews, legal notes, letters, articles, new companies, new products, obituaries, parliamentary reports, standards.
A, December, Yes, None.
June 1972, T.p. 21, Ad.p. 22.   4200.
Per year £3.

981 SECURITY SURVEYOR: Journal of the Association of Burglary Insurance Surveyors. 1972.
Victor Green Publications Ltd., 44 Bedford Row, London, WC1R 4LL.
6, ‡ = + *   All aspects of security.
Book notices, book reviews, legal notes, letters, monographic articles, new companies, new products, obituaries, parliamentary reports, patents, standards, tests.
6m, –, No, None.
March 1972, T.p. 55, Ad.p. 55.   3500.
Per copy 30p, per year £1.80.

351.77

PUBLIC HEALTH

982 ENVIRONMENTAL HEALTH: The Journal of the Association of Public Health Inspectors. 1969.
(Public Health Inspector 1964-1969; Sanitarian 1932-1964)
The Association of Public Health Inspectors, 19 Grosvenor Place, London, S.W.1.
12, ‡ *   All aspects of environmental health. The control of those factors in man's physical environment which have a significant effect on his health and well-being.
Book notices, book reviews, legal notes, letters, monographic articles, new products, obituaries, parliamentary reports, standards.
A, February/March, No, None.
January 1972, T.p. 35, Ad.p. 8.   6500.
Per copy 20p, per year £3.25.

352

LOCAL GOVERNMENT

983 COUNTY COUNCILS GAZETTE. 1957.
(Supplement to County Council Times 1896-1908;
Official Circular of the County Councils Association 1908-1913; Official Gazette 1913-1936; County Councils Association Gazette 1937-1957).
County Councils Association, 66A Eaton Sq., London, SW1W 9BH.
12, * =   County councils in England and Wales, Government departments, universities, local authority associations and public bodies in UK and abroad.
Book notices, book reviews, legal notes, letters, monographic articles, obituaries, parliamentary reports.
A, January, No, None.
April 1972, T.p. 32, Ad.p. 7.   6713.
Per copy 5p, per year 90p.

984 LOGA (Local Government Annotations Service). 1968.
Reference library, London Borough of Havering, (On behalf of the Advisory Body of librarians—London Boroughs Association), c/o Central Library, Romford, Essex.
12, ○ ‡   Abstracts of articles and pamphlets which have a direct or background interest to all those working in or studying Local Government in its widest meaning.
Abstracts, tests.
No Index.
March 1972, T.p. 32.   800.
Per copy 17p, per year £2.30.

985 LOCAL GOVERNMENT CHRONICLE: The journal for management in local government. 1872.
(Knight's Official Advertiser of Local Management in England and Wales 1855-1871).
Brown Knight & Truscott Ltd., 11-12 Bury Street, London, EC3A 5AP.
52, ‡ * =   Management of local authorities, their financing, local government law, housing, planning, social services and general administration.
Book notices, book reviews, legal notes, letters, articles, new products, obituaries, parliamentary reports.
A, February, Yes, None.
16 June 1972, T.p. 34, Ad.p. 22.   6407.
Per copy 15p, per year £7.80.

986 LOCAL GOVERNMENT FINANCE. 1936.
(Financial Circular).
Institute of Municipal Treasurers and Accountants, 1 Buckingham Place, London, SW1.
12, =   All fields of finance as relative to local government.
Book reviews, letters, monographic articles, obituaries, reports, standards.
A, December, Yes, None.
August 1970, T.p. 35, Ad.p. 16.
Free to members.

987 LOCAL GOVERNMENT STUDIES. 1971.
Charles Knight & Co. Ltd., 11-12 Bury Street, London, EC3A 5AP.
2, = +   Local government problems from all disciplines and professions which have contributions to make to the management of local affairs.
Book notices, book reviews, monographic articles.
None.
April 1972, T.p. 82, Ad.p. 9.   c. 1100.
Per copy £2, per year £3.

988 MUNICIPAL AND PUBLIC SERVICES JOURNAL. 1966.
(London, 1893; Municipal Journal, 1899).
Municipal Journal Ltd., 178-202 Great Portland Street, London, W1N 6NH.
52, ‡   Special interests of local and public authorities, placing emphasis on interdepartmental and multi-professional matters, and management in particular.
Book notices, book reviews, commodity prices, legal notes, letters, monographic articles, new products, obituaries, parliamentary reports, standards.
A, January/February, No, None.
30 June 1972, T.p. 22, Ad.p. 33.   7062.
Per copy 15p, per year £7.

989 MUNICIPAL ENGINEERING. 1956.
(Sanitary Record 1874; Municipal Engineering and Sanitary Record 1916).
Municipal Group of Companies, 178-202 Great Portland Street, London W1N 6NH.
52, ‡ *   The entire field of environmental technology: construction and maintenance of roads and bridges; traffic engineering and control; town and country planning; building; sewerage, sewage disposal; refuse collection and disposal; public health.
Book notices, book reviews, legal notes, letters, monographic articles, new companies, new products, obituaries, parliamentary reports, standards, tests.
A, —, Yes, None.
19 May 1972, T.p. 50, Ad.p. 50.   6500.
Per copy 15p. per year £6.
Indexed in: BTI

990 MUNICIPAL REVIEW. 1930.
Association of Municipal Corporations, 36 Old Queen Street, London, SW1.
12, ‡ *   Local government and urban administration.
Book notices, book reviews, letters, new products, parliamentary reports.
A, April, Yes, None.
T.p. 39, Ad. p. 6.   11500.
Per copy 10p, per year £1.50.

991 NOTTINGHAM CITY NEWS AND CALENDAR. 1971.
(Diary of Entertainments and Events 1946-1961; Nottingham Civic News 1961-1971).
Nottingham Corporation Publicity and Information Department, 54 Milton Street, Nottingham.
12, ○   Diary of Entertainments and events, summaries of committee decisions, articles of local interest.
No index.
June 1972, T.p. 30, Ad.p. 2.   4000.
Per copy 3p, per year 66p.

992 OPPORTUNITIES. 1963.
Link House Publications Ltd., 45 Moray Place, Edinburgh, EH3 6DD.
50, =   Advertisements only, for local authority and other public service staff.
No index.
T.p. 36.   16000
992+
Free.

993 PARISH COUNCILS' REVIEW: A Countryside Magazine. 1950.
National Association of Parish Councils, 100 Great Russell Street, London, WC1.
4, * =   Rural administrators, esp. members and clerks of parish councils, and rural electors.
Book notices, book reviews, legal notes, letters, articles, obituaries, parliamentary reports.
No index.
Summer 1972, T.p. 56, Ad.p. 8.   22056.
Per copy 15p, per year 55p.

994 PUBLIC SERVICE. 1953.
(Local Government Officer 1906-1911; Municipal Officer 1911-1920; Local Government Service 1920-1952).
NALGO, 8 Harwood Row, London, NW1.
12, * =   Local government matters in general.
Letters, articles, news, obituaries.
Index for internal use only.
T.p. 14, Ad.p. 5.
Free to members.

995 QUARTERLY BULLETIN OF THE INTELLIGENCE UNIT, GREATER LONDON COUNCIL. 1970.
(Quarterly Bulletin of the Research and Intelligence Unit, Greater London Council, 1967-1970).
Greater London Council, GLC Bookshop, The County Hall, London, SE1 7PB.
4, +   Broad fields of research and current problems of general interest with special reference to London local government, statistics, population, urban and regional planning, transportation, social services, architecture and civic design, housing, employment.
Abstracts, book notices, book reviews, monographic articles, reports, tests.
Irregular cumulative indexes.
March 1972, T.p. 64.   4000.
Per copy 50p, per year £2.

996 RURAL DISTRICT REVIEW: Journal of the Rural District Councils Association. 1949.
Municipal Publications, 3 Clement's Inn, London, WC2.
12, = ‡   Local government administration.
Book notices, book reviews, letters, articles, new products, obituaries, parliamentary reports.
A, January, No, None.
T.p. 24, Ad.p. 3.   12000.
Per year £1.50.

997 SCOTLAND 72. 1970.
Scottish Council (Development and Industry), 1 Castle Street, Edinburgh, EH2 3AJ.
1, +   List of local authorities and public bodies in Scotland.
No index.
Per year £2.10.

WOODWORTH

Guide to Current British Journals

Key to symbols appearing in entries referring to LEVEL OF APPEAL

- ○ Popular
- ‡ Technical
- + Research
- = Trade/Professional
- * Society/Institution
- † House journal

354
CENTRAL GOVERNMENT

998 JOURNAL OF ADMINISTRATION OVERSEAS. 1966.
(Journal of African Administration 1949-61; Journal of Local Administration Overseas 1962-8).
Her Majesty's Stationery Office, 49 High Holborn, London, WC1V 6HB.
4, ‡ * =   All aspects of administration overseas at central and local level—also land tenure, social development, training, manpower planning, development planning, adult education, rural development.
Book notices, book reviews, legal notes, monographic articles.
A, January, Yes, 5 year.
April 1972, T.p. 60.   2000.
Per copy 32½p, per year £1.50.

355.1
ARMY

999 AN COSANTÓIR: The Irish Defence Journal. 1940.
An Cosantóir, Red House, Infirmary Road, Dublin 7, Ireland.
12, ○   Contemporary military affairs: historical; humorous.
Book reviews, letters, articles.
A, January, Yes, None.
June 1972, T.p. 30, Ad.p. 6.   1000.
Per copy 10p, per year £1.20.

1000 ARMY ORDERS.
H.M.S.O., PO Box 569, London, SE1.
12, ‡ =   Legal notices etc. concerning the Army.
A, —, Yes, None.
Per copy varies, per year 70p.

1001 THE ARMY QUARTERLY AND DEFENCE JOURNAL. 1920.
West of England Press Publishers Ltd., Tavistock, Devon.
4, = +   International affairs relating to defence; strategic and defence studies; current Service problems; tactical, administrative and organizational aspects of land warfare including guerilla and urban warfare; book reviews and correspondence on defence matters; military history; weapons.
Book notices, book reviews, letters, monographic articles.
A, July, Yes. There is one cumulative index: 1920-1970.
April 1972, T.p. 128, Ad.p. 8.   1500.
Per copy 88p, per year £3.
Indexed in: IBZ.

1002 CADET JOURNAL AND GAZETTE. 1935.
Army Cadet Force Association, 58 Buckingham Gate, London, SW1.
12, †   The Army Cadet Force at home and abroad.
Book reviews, letters, articles, obituaries.
No index.
June 1972, T.p. 20, Ad.p. 3.   4000.
Per copy 12½p, per year £1.50.

1003 THE CORMORANT: Gazette of the Joint Services Staff College. 1947.
Chesham Press, 18 Germain Street, Chesham, Bucks.
2, =   Activities and progress of the College.
No index.
T.p. 48, Ad.p. 20.
Controlled circulation to past and present members of staff and students.

1004 THE COVENANTER: The Regimental Journal of the Cameronians (Scottish Rifles). 1921.
The Hamilton Advertiser, Press Buildings, Hamilton, Lanarkshire.
2, * ○   Notices and reports of regimental events, and items of interest to members of the regiment.
Letters, articles, obituaries.
No index.
Summer 1971, T.p. 40, Ad.p. 4.   c. 500 copies.
Per copy 25p, per year 50p, for ex-other ranks, and 75p for ex-officers.

1005 JOURNAL OF THE QUEEN'S REGIMENT. 1967.
RHQ, The Queen's Brigade, Howe Barracks, Canterbury, Kent.
4, =   Regimental news.
Book notices, book reviews, letters, articles, obituaries.
No index.
January 1967, T.p. 60, Ad.p. 5.
Per copy 10p, per year £1.

1006 JOURNAL OF THE SOCIETY FOR ARMY HISTORICAL RESEARCH. 1921.
The Society for Army Historical Research, c/o The Library, Old War Office Building, Whitehall, London, SW1.
4, + =   History and traditions of the British Army and of the law forces of the Empire and Commonwealth.
Book notices, book reviews, letters, monographic articles.
A, Yes, Vols 1-XL 1921-1962.
Summer 1972, T.p. 64.   1150.
Per year £2.10. Free to members.

1007 SOLDIER. 1945.
HMSO, Clayton Barracks, Aldershot, Hants.
12, ○ †   British Army activities worldwide.
Book reviews, letters, articles.
No index.
June 1972, T.p. 38, Ad.p. 10.   37500.
Per copy 7½p, per year £1.05.

355.2
RECRUITMENT

1008 COMPULSORY MILITARY SERVICE AND THE OBJECTOR. 1970.
Lansbury House Trust Fund, 3 Caledonian Road, London, N1.
4, + ‡   Legal and sociological aspects of military service regulations with special reference to legislative provisions for conscientious objection and the response and activities of objectors.
Legal notes, letters, parliamentary reports.
No index.
No. 8, 1971, T.p. 4.   3000.
Per year 50p.

355.4
WAR

1009 THE IRISH SWORD. 1949.
The Three Candles, Aston Place, Dublin 2.
2, +   To encourage research into the history of a. warfare in Ireland, and b. Irishmen in war.
Book reviews, letters, monographic articles.
2 years, —, Yes, None.
Free to members.

Key to reference symbols

○ popular   ‡ technical   = trade/professional

+ research   * society/institution   † house journal

355.58
CIVIL DEFENCE

1010 JOURNAL OF THE INSTITUTE OF CIVIL DEFENCE. 1938.
(Civil Defence 1949).
Air Raid Protection Institute Co., 316 Vauxhall Bridge Road, London, SW1.
4, * = ‡ +   Civil defence in general.
Book notices, book reviews, legal notes, letters, news, new products, obituaries, parliamentary reports, standards, tests.
No index.
T.p. 32.   2500.
Free to members.

359
NAVY

1011 FLIGHT DECK: Fleet Air Arm Quarterly.
Directorate of Naval Air Warfare, Ministry of Defence, c/o Wykeham Hall, Lee-on-Solent, Hants.
4, =
No index.
Free.

1012 THE MARINER'S MIRROR. 1911.
Cambridge University Press, PO Box 92, London, NW1.
4, +   Nautical history.
Book notices, book reviews, monographic articles, obituaries.
A, January, Yes, None.
T.p. 130, Ad.p. 2.   1800.
Per copy £1, per year £3. Free to members.
Indexed in: BHI.

1013 NAVAL REVIEW. 1913.
Naval Review, Hill Cross, Swanmore, Southampton.
4, =
No index.
T.p. 96, Ad.p. 8.
Controlled circulation to commissioned officers.

1014 NAVY INTERNATIONAL. 1972.
(Navy: the journal of the Navy League 1895).
Maritime World Ltd., 24 Petworth Road, Haslemere, Surrey.
12, ‡ = + *   Naval matters—naval strategy, ships, equipment, technology.
Book reviews, letters, monographic articles, new products, obituaries.
A, —, No, None.
6, 1972, T.p. 30, Ad.p. 2.   4000.
Per copy $17\frac{1}{2}$p, per year £1.75.

361
SOCIAL WORK

1015 BENEFITS INTERNATIONAL. 1971.
Pension Publications Ltd., Management Office, 14 Finsbury Circus, London, EC2.
12, ‡ =   Comment and interpretation on developments and trends in employee benefits around the world.
Letters, monographic articles.
A, June, No, None.
June 1972, T.p. 18.   500.
Per year £25.

1016 BRITISH ASSOCIATION OF RETIRED PERSONS: Members' Quarterly Bulletin. 1970.
B.A.R.P., 1 Albyn Place, Edinburgh, EH2 4NG.
4, *   Information of political-pressure actions taken on members' behalf, also general information on concessions and benefits available to older people in UK.
No index.
8-14 March 1972, T.p. 4.   c. 2500.
Free to members.

1017 BRITISH JOURNAL OF PSYCHIATRIC SOCIAL WORK. 1947.
Association of Psychiatric Social Workers, Oxford House, Derbyshire Street, London, E2.
2, = *
Abstracts, book reviews, monographic articles.
2 year, —, No, None.
T.p. 50, Ad.p. 2.
Per year £1.50.

1018 BRITISH JOURNAL OF SOCIAL WORK. 1971.
British Association of Social Workers, Oxford House, Derbyshire Street, London, E2 6HG.
4, =
Book reviews, letters, articles.
A, —, Yes, None.
Per year £4.

1019 CASE CON: A revolutionary magazine for social workers. 1970.
Case Con, Basement, 110 Lansdowne Way, London, SW8.
4, =   All social work matters and their political context.
Book reviews, letters, articles.
No index.
April 1972, T.p. 20.   4000.
Per copy 10p, per year 50p.

1020 CHESHIRE SMILE: The quarterly magazine of the Cheshire Homes. 1954.
Cheshire Foundation for the Sick, Greenacres, 39 Vesey Road, Sutton Coldfield, Warwicks.
4, †   To maintain contact between Homes, and to inform the general public about their activities and future plans.
Book reviews, commodity prices, articles, new products, obituaries.
c. 5 years.
Spring 1972, T.p. 36, Ad.p. 4.   5500.
Per copy 10p, per year 50p.

1021 CLAYMORE: Official journal of the Royal British Legion, Scotland. 1951.
Herald Press, Arbroath.
4, *   British Legion activities.
Letters, articles, news.
No index.
T.p. 45, Ad.p. 3.   4500.
Per copy $7\frac{1}{2}$p, per year 50p.

1022 FOCUS on Social Work and Service in Scotland. 1972.
Published by an Editorial Board representing 14 statutory and voluntary organisations. Editor: c/o 19 Claremont Crescent, Edinburgh, 7.
12, = ○   Trends and developments in social work and service and the related fields of housing, education, planning, environment etc.
News items, coming events, book notices, letters, articles.
No index.
June 1972, T.p. 20, Ad.p. 4.
Per copy 20p, per year £2.

1023 HEARTS OF OAK JOURNAL. 1906.
Hearts of Oak Benefit Society, 155 Charing Cross, Road, London, WC2.
4, *   Insurance and Friendly Society news.
Book notices, book reviews, letters, articles, news, obituaries, parliamentary reports.
No index.
T.p. 31, Ad.p. 3.   12000.
Free to members.

1024 NACRO INFORMATION BULLETIN. 1966.
National Association for the Care and Resettlement of Offenders (NACRO), 125 Kennington Park Road, London, SE 11.
4, *   Penal and After-care field.
Book notices, book reviews, monographic articles.
No index.
June 1972, T.p. 12.
Per copy 20p, per year 50p. Free to members.

1025 N.F.C.U. JOURNAL.
National Federation of Claimants Unions, 74A Stratford Road, Sparkbrook, Birmingham, B11 1AN.
Irreg., ○   History and politics of Social Security and claimants unions.
Book reviews, articles.
No index.
No. 2, T.p. 30.   600.
Per copy 25p, £1 per 4 issues.

1026 PARLIAMENT AND SOCIAL WORK.
British Association of Social Workers, Oxford House, Derbyshire Street, London, E2 6HG.
Weekly during sessions.
=   Digest of proceedings in both Houses affecting the Social Services.
No Index.
Per year £3.

1027 SOCIAL ACTION Incorporating Simon Star, 1972.
(Simon Star 1964; Social Action 1969.)
Simon Community Trust, Simon House, Grange Road, Ramsgate, Kent.
12, + *   Spotlights work being done, and research carried out, by organisations concerned and caring for homeless and rootless people.
Book notices, book reviews, letters, short articles, obituaries, parliamentary reports, tests.
No Index.
June, 1972, T.p. 4, Ad.p. 1.   5000.
Per copy 3p, per year 80p.

1028 SOCIAL SERVICE QUARTERLY. 1920.
(Social Service: a quarterly survey.)
National Council of Social Service, 26 Bedford Square, London, WC1B 3HU.
4, ○ +   Survey of social welfare work, in public and voluntary fields, in Gt Britain, and overseas; authoritative book reviews.
Book notices, book reviews, letters, monographic articles, parliamentary reports.
A, Autumn or Winter, No, None.
Spring, 1972, T.p. 40, Ad.p. 10   2200
Per copy 20p, per year 85p.

1029 SOCIAL WORK. 1944.
Association of Child Care Officers, Oxford House, Derbyshire Street, London, E2.
4, =   All aspects of social work.
Book reviews, letters, monographic articles.
A, October, Yes, None.
T.p. 26, Ad.p. 6.   4400
Free to members.

1030 SOCIAL WORK TODAY. 1970.
British Association of Social Workers, 42 Bedford Square, London, WC1B 3DP.
24, * + =   All matters of interest to the social work profession, including theory and practice, social policy and administration, casework, group work and community work. Contents include a regular Parliamentary column and book reviews.
Book notices, book reviews, legal notes, letters, monographic articles, obituaries, parliamentary reports.
A, May, No, None.
15.6.72, T.p. 24, Ad.p. 24.   13000
Per copy 25p, per year £4.

1031 THE VILLAGE.
National Council of Social Service, 26 Bedford Square, London, WC1B 3HU.
4, ○   Rural social affairs.
Book notices, book reviews, parliamentary reports.
A, December, No, None.
Spring 1972, T.p. 23½, Ad.p. 3½.   4000
Per copy 5p, per year 20p.

1032 WRVS MAGAZINE. 1970.
(WRVS Bulletin c. 1939-1970.)
Women's Royal Voluntary Service, 17 Old Park Lane, London, W1Y 4 AJ.
12, †   Work of the Women's Royal Voluntary Service in England, Scotland and Wales, and subjects of allied interest in field of community service.
Book reviews, articles.
No Index.
June 1972, T.p. 29, Ad.p. 6.   10000.
Per copy 2½p, per year 30p.

1033 THE WELFARE OFFICER. 1945.
Institute of Welfare Officers, Red Cross House, 73 Penrhyn Road, Kingston Upon Thames, Surrey. KT 12EQ.
6, = + *   Matters of interest to Welfare and Social Workers in industry, commerce, local and national government, hospitals, old people's homes and voluntary and statutory organisations.
Book notices, book reviews, legal notes, letters, monographic articles, new products, obituaries.
No Index.
May 1972, T.p. 24, Ad.p. 10.   1200
Per copy 20p, per year £1.50. Free to members.

361.191

RED CROSS

1034 CROSSTALK: The monthly magazine of the British Red Cross Society. 1972.
(News Review 1957-1971)
The British Red Cross Society, 9 Grosvenor Crescent, London, SW1X 7EJ.
12, *   The work and allied matters of the British Red Cross Society at home and overseas and International Red Cross affairs; International Committee of the Red Cross and League of Red Cross Societies.
Letters, articles.
No Index.
February 1972, T.p. 23.   c. 8000.
Per copy 10p, per year, £1.20.

1035 JUNIOR JOURNAL. 1923.
British Red Cross Society, 9 Grosvenor Crescent, London SW1X 7EJ.
4, †
No Index.
Summer 1972, T.p. 16.   11000
Per copy 4p, per year 16p.

362.1

MEDICAL WELFARE SERVICES

1036 MEDICAL RECORD. 1949.
Assocn. of Medical Records Officers, Shotley Bridge General Hospital, Consett, Co. Durham.
4, ‡   Planning of records systems and documents; computer research and statistical analysis, normal anatomy and physiology.
Book notices, book reviews, legal notes, letters, monographic articles, new products, obituaries.
A, May, Yes, None.
May 1972, T.p. 31, Ad.p. 4.   1300.
Per copy 30p, per year £1.

362.11

HOSPITALS

1037 BRITISH HOSPITAL EQUIPMENT DIRECTORY. 1969.
Philip King Ltd, 54/55 Wilton Road, London SW1.
6, = ‡
News, new products.
No Index.
10000.
Free.

1038 BRITISH HOSPITAL JOURNAL. 1966.
(Hospital & Social Service Journal 1892-1965),
Law & Local Government Publications Ltd,
27-29 Furnival Street, London EC4.
52, = * ‡   National Health Service administration.
Book reviews, commodity prices, legal notes, letters, articles, new companies, new products, parliamentary reports, standards, tests.
2 year, —, Yes, 5 year.
T.p. 27, Ad.p. 25.   10000.
Per copy 5p, per year £3.75.

1039 THE BULLETIN. Official organ of the Association of Hospital & Welfare Administrators. c. 1940
The Association, Bensted House, Faversham, Kent.
Irregular, =   Homes & hospital administration
Legal notes, letters, news, obituaries, parliamentary reports.
No Index.
T.p. 53.
Free to members.

1040 E.R.H.B. MAGAZINE. 1962.
Eastern Regional Hospital Board, Vernonholme, Riverside Drive, Dundee.
4, †   Articles of interest to all grades of hospital staff.
Letters, articles, new products, obituaries, tests.
No Index.
No. 2, 1972, T.p. 32.
Free.

1041 HOSPITAL ABSTRACTS: A monthly survey of world literature 1961.
H.M. Stationery Office, P.O. Box 569, London, SE1.
12, ‡   The whole field of hospitals and their administration, with the exception of strictly medical and related professional matters.
Abstracts.
A, June, Yes, None.
June 1972, T.p. 64, Ad.p. 4.   1500
Per copy 45p, per year £5.70.

1042 HOSPITAL & HEALTH SERVICES PURCHASING: Guide to Equipment and Suppliers. 1972.
(Hospital Purchasing Guide 1967-1968; Hospital Purchasing 1969-1971)
Institute of Health Service Administrators, 75 Portland Place, London W1N 4AN.
12, ‡ = *   Guide to new developments in equipment, supplies, and services. Also discusses current topics in the supplies field.
Book notices, monographic articles, new companies, new products.
A, January, No, None.
Jan 1972, T.p. 24.   10313.
Controlled circulation. Also available on subscription to The Hospital & Health Services Review.

1043 THE HOSPITAL AND HEALTH SERVICES REVIEW. 1972.
(The Hospital Gazette 1904-1929; The Hospital 1930-1971).
The Institute of Health Service Administrators, 75 Portland Place, London W1N 4AN.
12, = ‡ † *   Management, policy, planning, finance & personnel management.
Book notices, book reviews, legal notes, letters, monographic articles, obituaries, parliamentary reports.
A, January, No, None.
Jan 1972, T.p. 38, Ad.p. 22.   6049
Per copy 36p, per year £4.

1044 HOSPITAL MANAGEMENT.
(Hospital & Health Management; Hospital & Nursing Home Management)
Whitehall Press Limited, 29 Palace Street, London SW1.
6 =   Design, building, equipping, commissioning, managing and operating of hospitals in Britain and abroad.
Book notices, book reviews, letters, monographic articles, new products, parliamentary reports.
A, —, Yes, None.
May/June 1972, T.p. 29, Ad.p. 10.   c. 4000
Per copy 50p, per year £3.

1045 MEDICAL OFFICER. 1908.
Pergamon Press Ltd, Headington Hill Hall, Oxford, OX3 0BW.
52, =   Public health & community medicine.
Book reviews, letters, articles, news, new products.
A, Last issue of volume, Yes, None.
Per copy 10p, per year £4.50.

1046 REGIONAL REVIEW: Journal of the Western Regional Hospital Board. 1964.
WRHB. 351 Sauchiehall St, Glasgow, G2 3HT.
4, † =   All asspects of hospital work in the region.
No Index.
Summer 1971, T.p. 32.
Free.

1047 ST. GEORGE'S HOSPITAL GAZETTE. 1892.
St. George's Hospital Medical School, Hyde Park Corner, London SW1X 7NA.
3, † *   Articles by and on St. George's men. Current work at St. George's Hospital and Medical School. Editorials of current interest. Historical articles. Reports of clubs.
Book reviews, letters, articles, obituaries.
No Index.
Spring 1972, T.p. 43, Ad. p. 8.   1800.
Per copy £1.05.   Free to members.

1048 ST. THOMAS' HOSPITAL GAZETTE. 1891.
St. Thomas' Hospital Medical School, London SE1.
3, ‡ =   Medical, financial & historical. Social news.
Book reviews, letters, monographic articles.
No Index.
Spring 1972, T.p. 32, Ad.p. 6.   1400.
Per year 50p.

362.15

MATERNITY SERVICES

1049 MATERNAL AND CHILD CARE. 1965.
Bouverie Publishing Co. Ltd, 2 Salisbury Court, Fleet Street, London EC4.
12, = ‡ +   Gynaecology, obstetrics etc.
Book reviews, letters, articles, new products.
A, December, No, None.
T.p. 8, Ad.p. 6.   15000.
Controlled circulation.

1050 NATIONAL CHILDBIRTH TRUST NEWSLETTER.
National Childbirth Trust, 9 Queensborough Terrace, Bayswater, London W2 3TB.
2, ○ *
Letters, articles.
No Index.
Spring 1972, T.p. 16.
Free to members.

362.4

WELFARE SERVICES TO THE PHYSICALLY HANDICAPPED

1051 BLESMAG: quarterly journal of the British Limbless Ex-Service Men's Association. 1946.
British Limbless Ex-service Men's Association, Frankland Moore House, 185/187 High Road, Chadwell Heath. Romford. Essex.
4,*   News magazine.
No Index.
Spring 1972, T.p. 28, Ad.p. 2.   15000.
Free to members.

1052 BRITISH DEAF NEWS. 1955.
(Deaf Quarterly Times 1901-1902; Deaf News 1902-1954)
British Deaf & Dumb Association, 3 Compton Street, Carlisle CA1 1HO.
6, * = ‡
2 year, —, Yes, None.
T.p. 34.
Per copy 5p, per year 45p.

1053 BRITISH JOURNAL OF AUDIOLOGY. 1973.
(Sound 1967-1972).
Royal National Institute for the Deaf, 105 Gower Street, London WC1E 6AH.
4, ‡   Technical & scientific aspects of audiology as opposed to the sociological & educational aspects.
Book notices, book reviews, commodity prices, letters, monographic articles, obituaries, tests.
A, November, Yes, Vol 1-6 as 'Sound'.
T.p. 25, Ad.p. 3.
Per copy 50p, per year £2.

1054 GLAD NEWS: News Sheet of the Greater London Association for the Disabled. 1972.
Eyre and Spottiswoode, 2 Serjeants Inn, Fleet Street, London, EC4.
4, *   To local authorities, voluntary organisations, some medical personnel or anyone concerned with the disabled in Greater London.
Book notices, book reviews, articles, new products, reports.
No Index.
July 1972, T.p. 6   3500
Per copy 5p, per year 20p.

1055 THE NEW BEACON: Journal of blind welfare. 1930.
(The Beacon, 1917-1929).
Royal National Institute for the Blind, 224 Great Portland St., London W1N 6AA.
12,*   All aspects of blind welfare throughout the world and causes and prevention of blindness, news items (home and abroad), original material (prose and verse) by blind authors, letters. Advertisements are accepted.
Abstracts, book notices, book reviews, commodity prices, letters, monographic articles, new companies, new products, obituaries, parliamentary reports, standards, tests.
A, —, Yes, None.
May 1972, T.p. 27, Ad.p. 2.   2500 print, 1500 braille.
Per copy 9p, per year £1. braille edition per year: 55p

1056 PENSIONERS' VOICE: official publication of the National Federation of Old Age Pensions Association. 1940.
National Federation of Old Age Pensions Asscns., 91 Preston New Road, Blackburn.
12, ○ *
Letters, articles.
No Index.
July 1972, T.p. 7, Ad.p. 1.   50000
Per copy 2p, per year 55p.

1057 PROGRESS (in braille type)
Royal National Institute for the Blind, 224 Great Portland Street, London W1N 6AA.
12, ○   Articles of general interest, mostly from letterpress periodicals, letters, pen-friends, exchange & mart, competitions, advertisements.
No Index.
1465.
Per year 35p.

1058 REHABILITATION. 1956.
British Council for Rehabilitation of the Disabled, Tavistock House, South Tavistock Square, London WC1H 9LB.
4, ‡ + =   Rehabilitation of the disabled, social, medical, therapeutic.
Book notices, book reviews, monographic articles, new products, parliamentary reports.
No Index.
October/November 1971, T.p. 50, Ad.p. 6.   5000
Per copy 35p, per year £1.40.

1059 TALK. 1954.
The National Deaf Children's Society, 31 Gloucester Place, London W1H 4EA
4, ○ ‡ + =   Welfare of deaf children.
Book notices, book reviews, letters, articles, obituaries, parliamentary reports.
No Index.
T.p. 32, Ad.p. 6.   16000.
Free.

362.5

WELFARE SERVICES TO THE POOR.

1060 THE ALMSHOUSES GAZETTE: the official organ of the National Association of Almshouses. 1952.
The National Association of Almshouses, Billingbear Lodge, Wokingham, Berkshire.
4, * =   Disseminates information, advice and current legislation. Gives examples of current work applicable.
No Index.
March 1972, T.p. 4.   5600.
Per copy 2½p.

1061 THIRD WORLD. 1969.
Save the Children Fund, 29 Queen Anne's Gate, London, SW1.
3, ○   Problems of the underprivileged aimed at secondary school level.
No Index.
No. 8, T.p. 4.
Per copy 1p.

1062 TODAY'S CHILDREN. 1961.
Save the Children Fund, 29 Queen Anne's Gate, London SW1.
3   Aimed at primary school children describing the work of SCF.
No Index.
January-April 1972, T.p. 4.
Per copy 1p.

362.7

CHILD WELFARE

1063 CHILD ADOPTION. 1950.
(Bulletin of Standing Conference of Societies Registered for Adoption 1950)
Association of British Adoption Agencies, 27 Queen Anne's Gate, London SW1.
4, ‡ *   Adoption in Britain and overseas, of interest to workers in British adoption agencies and others concerned with adoption.

Book reviews, legal notes, letters, monographic articles, obituaries, parliamentary reports, standards.
A, Yes, None.
No. 1, 1972, T.p. 64.   1500
Per copy 35p, per year £1.40.

1064 GATEWAY. 1953.
Church of England Children's Society, Old Town Hall, Kennington, London SE11 4QD.
4, ○ * †   All aspects of the Society's work. Childcare and fund-raising intended to stimulate interest among supporters and general public.
No Index.
Summer 1972, T.p. 20.   160000
Free.

1065 THE WORLD'S CHILDREN. 1923.
(Record of The Save the Children Fund 1920-1923)
The Save the Children Fund, 29 Queen Anne's Gate, London, SW1H 9DH.
4, * †   Aspects of Child Welfare in general and the work of The Save the Children Fund in particular.
Letters, articles.
No Index.
June 1972, T.p. 23, Ad.p. 1.   105000.
Per year 30p.

362.8

YOUTH ORGANISATIONS

1066 HOSTELLING NEWS. 1972.
Youth Hostels Association, Trevelyan House, St. Albans, Herts.
4, * ○   Hostelling activities in Britain and abroad.
Book notices, book reviews, letters, articles, obituaries.
No Index.
Spring 1972, T.p. 8, Ad.p. 2.   200000.
Free to members.

366.1

FREEMASONS

1067 THE MASONIC RECORD. 1922.
(Freemasons Magazine 1793-1853; Masonic Mirror 1854-1921)
Masonic Record Co. Ltd, 38 Great Queen Street, London WC2.
12, *
Book notices, book reviews, letters, articles, news, obituaries.
No Index.
T.p. 16, Ad.p. 16.
Per year £1.50.

367

ASSOCIATIONS

1068 A'BHRATACH UR (The New Banner): The Newsletter of the Celtic League in Glasgow. 1971.
(An Bratach (The Flag) 1970)
Stanley K. Hunter, 34 Gray Street, Glasgow, Scotland, G3 7TY.
12, ○ *   News of Gaelic events in Glasgow and of the campaigns for the Freedom of the Celtic Nations—Scotland, Ireland, Wales, Isle of Man, Cornwall and Brittany.
Book notices, book reviews, letters, articles.
No Index.
T.p. 7.   100
Per copy 10p, per year 75p.

1069 BUSINESS AND PROFESSIONAL WOMAN. Journal of the National Federation of Business & Professional Women's Clubs of Great Britain & N. Ireland. 1938.
The Federation, 54 Bloomsbury Street, London WC1.
4, * =   All matters concerning working women.
Book reviews, letters, articles, obituaries, parliamentary reports.
No Index.
T.p. 32.
Per year 50p. Free to members.

1070 CLUB & INSTITUTE JOURNAL. 1875.
Club & Institute Union Ltd, Club Union House, 251/256 Upper Street, London N1.
12, * =   Circulation to all Social Clubs affiliated to Club & Institute Union. Covers officers and committee members in 4000 clubs.
Book notices, book reviews, commodity prices, legal notes, letters, articles, new products, obituaries.
No Index.
July 1972, T.p. 27, Ad.p. 24.   48797
Per copy 5p, per year 90p.

1071 CLUB COMMITTEE. 1970.
(Northern Club Trade News 1967-1970)
Provincial Trade Press Ltd, 320 Higher Lane, Lymm, Cheshire.
12, =   Club management & leisure activities.
Legal notes, letters, new products.
No Index.
T.p. 22, Ad.p. 24.
Per copy $17\frac{1}{2}$p, per year £2.75.

1072 CLUB MIRROR. The National Club Trade Newspaper. 1968.
St. Martin's Press, 18 Queens Road, Brighton, Sussex.
12, ○ =   All matters relevant to the club trade.
Commodity prices, letters, articles, new companies, new products.
No Index.
6, 1972, T.p. 20, Ad.p. 20.   25000
Per copy 10p, per year £1.52.

1073 ENGLISH TEMPLAR YOUTH. International Organisation of Good Templars.
c/o 124 Sternhold Avenue, Streatham Hill, London SW2 4PP.
4, ○
News, articles.
No Index.
Summer 1972, T.p. 20.
Free to members.

1074 FORESTERS' MISCELLANY. 1836.
Ancient Order of Foresters, 136 High St., Southampton.
12, *   Official monthly journal of the Ancient Order of Foresters Friendly Society.
Letters, articles, obituaries.
No Index.
July 1972, T.p. 28.   12500.
Free to AOF members only.

1075 THE GOOD TEMPLAR WATCHWOOD: Journal of the International Order of Good Templars.
International Order of Good Templars, 11 Warstone Lane, Birmingham B18 6JE.
4, ○   News of the Order.
No Index.
Summer 1972, T.p. 22.
Per copy 5p, per year 25p.

1076 HOME AND COUNTRY. 1919.
National Federation of Women's Institutes, 11a King's Road, Sloane Square, London, SW3.
12, *   W.I. reports and general matters of interest to women.
Book reviews, letters, new products, reports.
No Index.
T.p. 27, Ad.p. 21.   153000.
Per copy 3p, per year 35p.

1077 THE JUVENILE TEMPLAR.
International Order of Good Templars, 11 Warstone Lane, Birmingham, B18 6JE.
4, ○ News of the Juvenile Section of the Order.
No Index.
March 1972, T.p. 12.
Free to members.

1078 LADIES CIRCLE MAGAZINE.
National Association of Ladies' Circles, Devonshire Buildings, Devonshire Street, Keighley, Yorks.
4, * News of happenings and other general material.
No Index.
T.p. 32, Ad.p. 8.
10p (Past members). Free to members.

1079 MARRIED WOMEN'S ASSOCIATION BULLETIN. 1960.
(Wife and Citizen).
Married Women's Association, 87 Redington Road, London, NW3 7RR.
4, ○ * Legal reform and the legal and economic position of a wife.
Book notices, book reviews, legal notes, letters, new companies, parliamentary reports.
No Index.
September 1972, T.p. 8. c. 1500.
Per year £1.

1080 NEWS AND VIEWS. Official journal of the National Association of Round Tables of Great Britain and Ireland. 1928.
The Association, 78 Old Broad Street, London, EC3.
4, *
No Index.
Autumn 1972, T.p. 23, Ad.p. 9. 30000.
Free to members.

1081 ROTARY: official publication of Rotary International in Great Britain and Ireland. 1958.
(The Rotary Wheel 1917. Rotary Service 1939).
Rotary International in G.B. and I., Sheen Lane House, Sheen Lane, London, SW14 8AF.
4, * Community services, vocational and international topics.
Letters, articles, obituaries.
A, February, No, None.
T.p. 18, Ad.p. 6. 50000.
Per copy 12½p, per year 60p.

1082 SCOTTISH HOME AND COUNTRY: Magazine of the Scottish Women's Rural Institutes. 1924.
Central Council of the Scottish Women's Rural Institutes, 42 Heriot Row, Edinburgh, EH3 6EU.
12, * ○ News of activities of Scottish Women's Rural Institutes and subjects of interest to countrywomen: handcrafts, housewifery, country life etc.
Book reviews, commodity prices, letters, new products, obituaries.
No Index.
March 1972, T.p. 14, Ad.p. 12. 19583.
Per copy 5p, per year 90p.

368

INSURANCE

1083 BONUS: A periodical commentary published from the Insurance Advice Centre. 1971.
Stocker Hocknell Limited, 4 Market Square, Amersham, Buckinghamshire.
4, ○ The need to undertake appropriate insurances with the aid of skilled unprejudiced advice.
No Index.
No. 2 1972, T.p. 8. 8000.
Free.

1084 COVER. 1948.
Provincial Insurance Company Ltd., Stramongate, Kendal, Westmorland.
3, = Information on the company's contracts—developments in the insurance market generally.
Legal notes, articles, new products.
No Index.
T.p. 16. 22000.
Free.

1085 GEN. 1972.
General Accident Fire & Life Assurance Corporation Ltd., General Buildings, Perth.
12, † Staff only, new products.
No Index.
No. 3, 1972, T.p. 4. 10000.
Free.

1086 GENERALITIES. 1949.
General Accident Fire & Life Assurance Corporation Limited, General Buildings, Perth, Scotland.
4, † Staff and pensioners.
No Index.
Spring 1972, T.p. 40. 11500.
Free.

1087 GENERAL'S REVIEW. 1906.
General Accident Fire & Life Assurance Corporation Limited, General Buildings, Perth, Scotland.
4, ‡ For agencies (insurance brokers etc) only.
No Index.
No 3, 1972, T.p. 8. 42000.
Free.

1088 INSURANCE BROKERS' MONTHLY. 1950.
Insurance Publishing & Printing Co., 9 Market Street, Stourbridge, Worcs.
12, ‡ = Insurance Brokers in U.K. and abroad; Insurance Companies UK and abroad.
Book reviews, legal notes, letters, monographic articles, obituaries, parliamentary reports.
No Index.
June 1972, T.p. 50, Ad.p. 45. 7500.
Per year £3.

1089 INSURANCE RECORD. 1863.
The Tudor Press Ltd., 75 Carter Lane, London EC4V 5ET.
12, ‡ = Accident, Fire and Life insurance current information and security matters of special interest to brokers and purchasers of insurance.
Book reviews, letters, monographic articles, new companies, new products, obituaries.
No Index.
May 1972, T.p. 40, Ad.p. 32. 5006.
Per copy 15p, per year £1.50.

1090 JOURNAL OF THE CHARTERED INSURANCE INSTITUTE. 1912.
(Federation of Insurance Institutes of Great Britain and Ireland. Journal. 1899-1907; The Insurance Institute of Great Britain and Ireland. Journal. 1908-1911.)
The Chartered Insurance Institute, 20 Aldermanbury, London, EC2V 7HY.
1, + * ‡ Insurance and related subjects.
Book notices, book reviews, legal notes, monographic articles.
A, incorporated in the volume, Yes, None.
1972, T.p. 332. 23000.
Per copy £1.10.

1091 JOURNAL OF THE INSTITUTE OF ACTUARIES. 1866.
(The Assurance Magazine and Journal of the Institute of Actuaries, 1852-1866; The Assurance Magazine 1850-1852).
Institute of Actuaries, Staple Inn Hall, High Holborn, London, WC1V 7QJ.
3, + * Applications of actuarial science and method.
Legal notes, letters, monographic articles, obituaries, standards, book reviews.
A, —, November, Yes.
T.p. 135. 4500.
Per copy £1.25, per year £3.75.

1092 JOURNAL OF THE INSURANCE INSTITUTE OF LONDON. 1908.
Insurance Institute of London, 20 Aldermanbury, London EC2.
1, ‡ +   All aspects of insurance.
Monographic articles.
In each issue.
1970/71, T.p. 120.   6000.
Per copy 63p and Free to members.

1093 LEGAL AND GENERAL GAZETTE. 1971.
Legal & General Assurance Society Ltd., Temple Court, 11 Queen Victoria Street, London EC4.
6, †   Technical and business information concerning the Society's business and business environment.
Legal notes, articles, new products.
No Index.
June 1972, T.p. 12.   7000.
Free to the Staff of the Society.

1094 POLICY. 1964.
(Policy Insurance Weekly 1948).
Stone & Cox Ltd., 44 Fleet Street, London EC4.
12, + ‡ =   Underwriting and marketing insurance of all types.
Book notices, book reviews, legal notes, letters, monographic articles, new companies, new products, obituaries, parliamentary reports.
A, December, Yes, None.
T.p. 55, Ad.p. 56.
Per copy 30p, per year £3.60.

1095 POLICY HOLDER INSURANCE JOURNAL. 1873.
PH Press Ltd., 231 Strand, London WC2R 1DA.
52, ‡ =   Current developments throughout the insurance world.
Book reviews, legal notes, letters, articles, new companies, new products, obituaries, parliamentary reports.
A, —, Yes, None.
June 16, 1972, T.p. 27, Ad.p. 23.
Per copy 10p, per year £6.

1096 POST MAGAZINE & INSURANCE MONITOR. 1854.
(Post Magazine 1840-1853)
Buckley Press Ltd., 12/13 Henrietta St., London WC2E 8LP.
52, ‡ = +   All aspects of insurance.
Book notices, book reviews, commodity prices, legal notes, letters, monographic articles, new companies, new products, obituaries, parliamentary reports, standards, tests.
A, varies, according to work on hand. Yes, None.
T.p. 40, Ad.p. 40.   14000
Per copy 15p, per year £10.66.

1097 REINSURANCE: the monthly international reinsurance magazine. 1969.
Buckley Press Ltd., 12/13 Henrietta St., London WC2E 8LP.
12, ‡ +   All aspects of reinsurance, worldwide.
A, varies, according to work on hand. Yes, None.
T.p. 36, Ad.p. 16.   2500.
Per copy 25p, per year £3.58.

1098 TEMPLE BAR. 1955.
Franey & Co., Ltd., Burgon Street, London, EC4.
4, †   A general interest magazine devoted largely to the social activities of the Society and its Staff.
Articles, obituaries.
No Index.
Spring 1972, T.p. 28.   9500.
Free to Staff, pensioners and certain business connections.

1099 THE TRANSACTIONS OF THE FACULTY OF ACTUARIES. 1901.
The Faculty of Actuaries, 23 St. Andrew Square, Edinburgh EH2 1AQ.
Irreg.*   Consists mainly of papers presented on actuarial subjects at Sessional Meetings of the Faculty, together with the relevant discussions.
Book reviews, letters, monographic articles, obituaries.
2 yearly, —, Yes, None.
Vol 32, Pt. 4, T.p. 108.   1100.
Per copy £1.25. Free to members.

369.4

YOUNG PEOPLE'S SOCIETIES

1100 THE BOYS' BRIGADE GAZETTE. Official Magazine for Officers of the Boy's Brigade. 1895.
Boys' Brigade, Brigade House, Parson's Green, London, SW6.
6, *
Book reviews, letters, news obituaries.
No Index.
T.p. 25, Ad.p. 7.   11000.
Per year 50p.

1101 THE BRIGADE. 1892.
Church Lads Brigade, 58 Gloucester Place, London, W1.
2, *
Book reviews, articles, news, obituaries.
No Index.
T.p. 20.
Free to members.

1102 THE BROWNIE. 1962.
The Girl Guides Association, 17-19 Buckingham Palace Road, London, SW1W 0PT.
52, O *   Members of the Movement ages 7-10 years.
Book reviews, letters, articles.
No Index.
June 1972, T.p. 24, Ad.p. 1.   33750.
Per copy 3p, per year £3.90.

1103 THE 'D' TROOPER MONTHLY. 1964.
'D' Troop, 1st Glasgow Scouts, 4 Victoria Circus, Glasgow, Scotland G12 9LD.
12, *   Scouting activities.
Book reviews, letters, articles.
No Index.
T.p. 10.   120
Per copy 10p, per year £1.

1104 THE GUIDER, 1927.
(Girl Guide Gazette 1913-1926).
The Girl Guides Association, 17-19 Buckingham Palace Road, London, SW1W 0PT.
12, O *   Adult Members of the Movement (Leaders).
Book notices, book reviews, letters, articles, obituaries, standards, tests.
No Index.
July 1972, T.p. 40, Ad.p. 11.   33500.
Per copy 9p, per year £1.50.

1105 THE RANGER. 1946.
Girl Guides Association, 17-19 Buckingham Palace Road, London, SW1W 0PT.
12, * O   Members of the Movement ages 14-20.
Book reviews, articles.
No Index.
July 1972, T.p. 20, Ad.p. 1.   4900.
Per copy 3p, per year 66p.

1106 THE SCOUTER. 1922.
(Headquarters' Gazette 1908-1921).
Scout Association, 25 Buckingham Palace Road, London, SW1.
12, *
Book reviews, letters, articles, news,
A, April, Yes, None.
T.p. 36, Ad.p. 17.   40000.
Per copy 10p, per year £1.50.

1107 TODAY'S GUIDE. 1970.
(The Guide 1917-1969).
The Girl Guides Association, 17-19 Buckingham Palace Road, London, SW1W 0PT.
52, ○ *   Members of the Movement, age group 10-14.
Book reviews, letters, articles, new products.
No Index.
23.6.1972, T.p. 12, Ad.p. 2.   23000.
Per copy 5p, per year £3.90.

37

EDUCATION

1108 ASPECTS OF EDUCATION: Journal of the Institute of Education, University of Hull. 1964.
University of Hull, Institute of Education, 173 Cottingham Road, Hull, HU5 4AY.
2, =   Each issue has a theme, drawn alternately from general educational problems and classroom practice.
Monographic articles,
Bibliography and index in each issue.
No. 13, 1971, T.p. 135.
Per copy 50p.
Indexed in: BEI.

1109 BRITISH EDUCATION INDEX. 1954.
British National Bibliography, 7 & 9 Rathbone Street, London, W1P 2AL.
4, +   An index to articles of permanent educational interest in about 140 British periodicals, covering all levels of education and related topics such as child psychology and delinquency.
A, –, Yes, None.
January-March 1972, T.p. 52.   896.
Per year £7.

1110 BRITISH JOURNAL OF EDUCATIONAL STUDIES. 1952.
Basil Blackwell, 5 Alfred Street, Oxford OX1 4HB.
3, + =   Historical, philosophical, social, psychological, pedagogic studies in education at an advanced academic level.
Book notices, book reviews, monographic articles, obituaries.
A, November, Yes, None.
June 1972, T.p. 116, Ad.p. 4.   1250.
Per copy 80p, per year £2.
Indexed in: BEI.

1111 BRTISH JOURNAL OF EDUCATIONAL TECHNOLOGY. 1971.
(Journal of Educational Technology 1970).
Councils & Education Press Ltd (for National Council for Educational Technology), 10 Queen Anne Street, London W1M 9LD.
3, + *   Theory, application and development of educational technology and communications.
Book reviews, monographic articles.
No Index.
January 1972, T.p. 84.   1500.
Per copy £1.60, per year £4.40.

1112 BRITISH MENSA ACTIVITIES BULLETIN. 1966.
British Mensa Limited, 13 George Street, Wolverhampton, Staffs.
12, *   Circulated within British Mensa mainly as a vehicle of communication between members, including notices of meetings and other announcements and relevant articles and letters.
Letters, articles.
No Index.
July 1972, T.p. 12.   2800.
Free to members only.

1113 BULLETIN OF THE GENERAL STUDIES ASSOCIATION. 1963
General Studies Association, Longmans House, Harlow, Essex.
2, =   Problems of general education and specialisation.
Book notices, book reviews, letters, monographic articles.
2 year, –, Yes, None.
T.p. 79, Ad.p. 9.
Free to members
Indexed in: BEI

1114 CBI EDUCATION AND TRAINING BULLETIN.
Confederation of British Industry, 21 Tothill Street, London, SW1.
4 = + *   Newsheet.
Book notices, book reviews, articles, parliamentary reports.
No Index.
May 1972, T.p. 24.
Per copy 25p, per year £2. £1 for members and educ. estab.)

1115 CAMBRIDGE JOURNAL OF EDUCATION. 1971.
Cambridge Institute of Education, Shaftesbury Road, Cambridge.
3, = +   Questions of educational interest, chiefly those concerning professional education of teachers. Contributions by members of education bodies in Cambridge ATO.
Monographic articles.
A, No 1 of each volume, No, None.
Lent 1972, T.p. 63.   800.
Per copy 35p, per year £1.

1116 CHILD AND MAN: A Journal for contemporary education. 1964.
Steiner Schools Followship, 4 Cavendish Avenue, London, NW8 9JE.
2, ○ +   Medium for expression and discussion of the ideas underlying what is known as Steiner and Waldorf education.
Book reviews, letters, monographic articles.
No Index.
Winter 1971, T.p. 48, Ad.p. 4.   1500.
Per copy 35p, per year 70p.

1117 CHILDREN'S LITERATURE IN EDUCATION. 1970.
Ward Lock Educational, 116 Baker Street, London, W1M 2BB.
3, ○   Children's literature and the rôle it can play in the classroom.
No Index.
Per year £1.50.

1118 CHOWANNA (in Polish). 1968.
Kazimierz Obtulowicz, 76 Cleveland Street, London, W1P 5DS.
26, +   Problems of education, emphasis on child-centres and scouting methods.
Book notices, book reviews, letters, reports, tests.
No Index.
T.p. 6.   130.
Per copy 5p.

1119 THE COMMERCIAL TEACHER. 1963.
J. L. White, Falkland Cottage, Mottram St. Andrew, Nr. Macclesfield, Ches., SK10 4RA.
4, * =   Teaching of commercial subjects.
Book reviews, letters, articles, obituaries.
No Index.
July 1972, T.p. 36, Ad.p. 4p.   3500.
Free to members and year 50p.

Key to reference symbols

○ popular   ‡ technical   = trade/professional

+ research   * society/institution   † house journal

1120 COMPREHENSIVE EDUCATION. 1965.
The Campaign For Comprehensive Education (formerly the Comprehensive Schools Committee), 123 Portland Road, London W11.
4, ○ +   All aspects of comprehensive education—teaching, running, and organizing the schools; administration of, by local authorities; government policy towards; research results. Articles by teachers, parents, researchers, administrators, and pupils.
Abstracts, book reviews, letters, articles, new products.
3 years, 1970 et seq, Yes, None.
T.p. 40.   c. 3000.
Per copy 50p, per year £1.50.
Indexed in: BEI.

1121 DURHAM RESEARCH REVIEW. 1950.
Institute of Education, University of Durham in association with the Institute of Education, University of Newcastle upon Tyne. Institute of Education, 48 Old Elvet, Durham.
2, +   Research and scholarship on the subject of education. Research papers employ mainly the psychological, sociological, comparative and historical methods, whilst the range of topics is wide.
Book notices, book reviews, monographic articles.
5 year, Spring 1970, Yes, None.
Spring 1972, T.p. 51.   c. 500.
Per copy 50p, per year £1.
Indexed in: BEI, BHI.

1122 EDUCATION: Journal of the Association of Education Committees. 1903.
Councils & Education Press Ltd., 10 Queen Anne Street, London, W.1.
52, ‡ = +   Educational administration in England and Wales, including policy issues and LEA and school management.
Book notices, book reviews, commodity prices, legal notes, letters, articles, new products, parliamentary reports, patents, standards, tests.
6m, January/July, No, None.
28-4-1972, T.p. 11, Ad.p. 25.   7834.
Per copy 10p, per year £6.80.
Indexed in: BEI.

1123 EDUCATION AND URBAN SOCIETY. 1969.
Sage Publications Ltd., St. George's House, 44 Hatton Garden, London EC1N 8ER.
4 = +   Social scientific research on education as a social instruction within urban environments.
Book reviews, monographic articles.
A, —, Yes, None.
February 1972, T.p. 124.
Per year £7. Individual £4.70.

1124 EDUCATION EQUIPMENT. 1959.
Benn Brothers Ltd., Lyon Tower, 125 High Street, Colliers Wood, London, S.W. 19.
12, =
Book reviews, new products.
No Index.
Free, Controlled circulation.

1125 EDUCATION FOR DEVELOPMENT: Journal of the Faculty of Education, University College, Cardiff. 1970.
Faculty of Education, University College, Cardiff.
2, =   Primarily designed for those engaged professionally and administratively in the field of education.
Research Notices; Communication Media Notes; book reviews, monographic articles.
4 years, October 1973, Yes, None.
March 1972, T.p. 57, Ad.p. 8.   1200.
Per copy 24p, per year 48p.

1126 EDUCATION FOR TEACHING: Journal of the Association of Teachers in Colleges and Departments of Education. 1944.
(Bulletin of Education 1943-1953).
Association of Teachers in Colleges and Departments of Education, 3 Crawford Place, London, W1H 2BN.
3, = *   Education of teachers and allied topics.
Book notices, book reviews, monographic articles.
No Index.
Summer 1972, T.p. 80, Ad.p. 7.   8000.
Per copy 25p, per year 70p.
Indexed in: BEI.

1127 EDUCATION IN THE NORTH. 1965.
Waverley Press (for Aberdeen College of Education), Hilton Place, Aberdeen, AB9 1FA.
1, ○ +   Aims at giving those concerned with education in Scotland an opportunity of sharing ideas, methods and research findings with their colleagues and the general public.
Monographic articles.
No Index.
1972, T.p. 96.
Per copy 35p.

1128 EDUCATION 3-13. 1973.
William Collins Sons & Co. Ltd., 144 Cathedral Street, Glasgow, C4 0NB.
2, ○ + *   Articles of professional classroom interest by and for teachers of the development group 3-13; a means of communication and contact.
Book reviews, letters, monographic articles.
A, October, Yes, None.
T.p. 64.
Per copy 50p, per year £1.

1129 EDUCATION TODAY. International digest of current educational literature. 1950.
(Educational Times 1847-1949).
J.V. Chapman, College of Preceptors, 2/3 Bloomsbury Square, London, WC1.
6, *
3 year, —, Yes, None.
T.p. 32, Ad.p. 1.   3000.
Per year £1.

1130 EDUCATIONAL AND CHURCH EQUIPMENT. 1969.
(Church & Educational Equipment Digest 1965-1969).
Westbourne Publishing Group, Crown House, Morden, Surrey.
12, = ‡
No Index.
T.p. 40, Ad.p. 24.   15000.
Free, Controlled circulation.

1131 EDUCATIONAL BROADCASTING INTERNATIONAL: A Journal of the Centre for Educational Development Overses. 1971.
(CETO News, 1963-1966; Educational Television International, 1967-1970).
Wynn Williams Ltd., Centenary Buildings, King Street, Wrexham.
4, ‡, +, *, †   Educational broadcasting: information from all round the world, aimed primarily at readers in developing countries. All levels of education from primary to University, also non-formal education.
Abstracts, book notices, book reviews, monographic articles, new products.
A, March, Yes, None.
March 1971, T.p. 72, Ad.p. 2½.   c. 1500.
Per copy £1.50, per year £5. (individuals £3; currently under review).

1132 EDUCATIONAL MEDIA INTERNATIONAL. 1971.
International Council for Educational Media, Modino Press Ltd., 68 Queen Street, London EC4 1SL.
4, =
No Index.
Per year £3.

1133 EDUCATIONAL RESEARCH: A review for teachers and all concerned with progress in education. 1958.
National Foundation for Educational Research in England and Wales, The Mere, Upton Park, Slough, Bucks.
3, + =   All aspects of education: research notes, which are outlines of an individual survey or experiment, or abstracts of theses, reviews.
Book reviews, monographic articles.
A, June, No, Subject index every 3 years.
February 1972, T.p. 80, Ad.p. 6.   5000.
Per copy 75p, per year £2.
Indexed in: BEI.

1134 ESSEX EDUCATION. 1947.
Essex Education Committee, County Hall, Chelmsford.
6, =   Development of education in Essex.
Book notices, book reviews, letters, monographic articles.
A, March, Yes, None.
T.p. 25, Ad.p. 2.   5500.
Controlled circulation.

1135 EUROPEAN STUDIES TEACHERS SERIES. 1971.
European Communities Information Service, 23 Chesham Street, London, SW1.
4,   Folder of essays, charts, diagrams and maps about contemporary Europe.
No Index.
Per year 50p.

1136 EUROPEAN TRAINING: Professional review of theory and practice.
MCB (European Training) Ltd., 200 Keighley Rd, Bradford, BD9 4JZ.
3, ○ = + *   Commentaries by international training authorities; Current developments in research on training; Case studies of training efforts and their impacts; Underlying trends in training in different parts of Europe.
Book reviews, monographic articles.
A, —, Yes, None.
Spring 1972, T.p. 112, Ad.p. 61.   1000.
Per year £10.75.

1137 FORUM FOR THE DISCUSSION OF NEW TRENDS IN EDUCATION. 1958.
P.S.W. Publications, 11 Pendene Road, Leicester, LE2 3DQ.
3, *   Education (secondary and primary) with especial reference to new methods and ideas, the furtherance of comprehensive education and non-streaming.
Book reviews, letters, monographic articles.
A, Subsequent volume (3rd No.), No, None.
June 1972, T.p. 16, Ad.p. 3.   1800.
Per copy 35p, per year £1.

1138 GENERAL EDUCATION. 1971.
Longman Group Ltd., 5 Bentinck Street, London, W1.
4, =
No Index.
Per copy 40p.

1139 GRIFFIN: The Journal of the British American Alumni and the British American Educational Foundation Inc. 1963.
British American Alumni, c/o 17 Queen's Road, Beckenham, Kent, BR3 4JN.
2, *   Covers activities of those students who have crossed the Atlantic on an English Speaking Union exchange scholarship and includes articles about participating schools and education and Anglo-American relations generally.
Book reviews, letters, articles, obituaries.
No Index.
Christmas 1971, T.p. 212, Ad.p. 2.   1300.
Per copy 15p.

1140 HISTORY OF EDUCATION. 1972.
David & Charles (Publishers) Ltd., South Devon House, Newton Abbot, Devon.
2, + ○   Sponsored by the History of Education Society to promote study of subjects in all aspects.
Book reviews, monographic articles.
A, Last issue of year, Yes, None.
Per copy £1, per year £2.

1141 HISTORY OF EDUCATION SOCIETY BULLETIN. 1968.
History of Education Society, c/o Department of Education University of Cambridge, 17 Brookside, Cambridge, CB2 1JG.
2 + = *   Reports of meetings, short articles, bibliographical information, reports on research in the field, and some short notices of books and all other information of interest to members.
No Index.
Spring 1971, T.p. 60.   450.
Per copy 50p, per year £1. Free to members.

1142 ITV EDUCATION NEWS: News of ITV School and Adult Education Programmes. 1970.
Independent Broadcasting Authority, 70 Brompton Road, London, SW3.
2, ○ +   Latest information on Independent Television's school and adult education programmes.
Book notices, articles, new products.
No Index.
February 1972, T.p. 4.
Free.

1143 IDEAS: A curriculum magazine published termly by University of London Goldsmiths' College. 1972.
(Ideas—The magazine of The Curriculum Laboratory University of London Goldsmiths' College 1967-1972).
University of London Goldsmiths' College, Lewisham Way, New Cross, London, SE14 6NW.
3, *   Curriculum development in all areas of education including community education, descriptive and action-research based.
Book reviews, letters, monographic articles, new products.
No Index.
December 1971, T.p. 40.
Per copy 45p.

1144 THE INDEPENDENT SCHOOL: Magazine of the I.S.A.I.
Independent Schools Association, 49 Gordon Road, Whitstable, Kent.
3, * + ○   Policy and events of independent education especially this Association. History of schools and personalities. Legislation for education. Occasional supplements.
Book reviews, legal notes, letters, articles, new schools, new products, obituaries, parliamentary reports, standards, tests.
No Index.
March 1972, T.p. 24, Ad.p. 8.   800.
Per copy 15p, per year 50p.

1145 IRISH JOURNAL OF EDUCATION: Iris Eireannach an Oideachais. 1967.
Educational Research Centre, St. Patrick's College, Dublin 9.
2, ‡ + =   Any aspect of education. Reports of experimental research and articles which have a particular relevance to education in Ireland.
Book reviews, monographic articles.
2 yearly, Winter of even years, Yes, None.
Winter 1970, T.p. 75, Ad.p. 5.   1000.
Per copy 40p, per year 80p.
Indexed in: BEI.

1146 JOURNAL OF CURRICULUM STUDIES. 1968.
William Collins Sons & Co. Ltd., 144 Cathedral Street, Glasgow C4 0NB.

2, + * Description, discussion, analysis of the practice and theory of curriculum study at all levels of education.
Book notices, book reviews, monographic articles, tests.
A, November, Yes, None.
November 1971, T.p. 92.
Per copy £1, per year £2.
Indexed in: BEI.

1147 JOURNAL OF EDUCATIONAL ADMINISTRATION AND HISTORY. 1968.
Dept. of Education, The University of Leeds, Leeds, LS2 9JT.
2, = + To publish work and stimulate interest in the fields of the administration and history of education. Mainly United Kingdom, but not exclusively so.
Book notices, book reviews, monographic articles.
2 yearly, —, Yes, None.
December 1971, T.p. 68.   750.
Per copy 60p, per year £1.
Indexed in: BEI.

1148 JOURNAL of the Institutes of Education of Durham and Newcastle Universities. 1948.
Newcastle University Institute of Education, Newcastle upon Tyne, NE1 7RU.
5 = ○ To interest all teachers in the problems encountered by other teachers in the North-East of England and their attempts at solutions.
Book notices, book reviews, articles.
A, November, Yes, None.
May 1972, T.p. 22, Ad.p. 4.   2800.
Per copy 2½p, per year 12½p, and Free to members.

1149 JOURNAL OF MORAL EDUCATION. 1971.
Pemberton Publishing Co. Ltd., 88 Islington High Street, London, N1 8EN.
3 + Caters for primary and secondary schools, for college and university departments of education and for psychology and sociology research departments by providing a medium for communicating new information in this developing field.
Abstracts, book reviews, monographic articles.
A, —, No, None.
October 1971, T.p. 90, Ad.p. 2.   1000+
Per copy £1, per year £2.50.

1150 JOURNAL OF VERBAL LEARNING AND VERBAL BEHAVIOR. 1972.
Academic Press, 15 Cavendish Square, London, W1M 0HT.
6, =
Book reviews, monographic articles.
A, —, Yes, None.
Per year £10.

1151 JUNIOR EDUCATION EQUIPMENT. 1966.
Benn Brothers Ltd, Lyon Tower, 125 High Street, Colliers Wood, London, SW19.
3, =
Book reviews, new products.
No Index.
Free, controlled circulation.

1152 KENT EDUCATION GAZETTE: official journal of the Kent Education Committee. 1920.
Kent Education Committee, Springfield, Maidstone.
11, =
Book notices, articles, news.
No Index.
T.p. 9, Ad.p. 3.
Free, controlled circulation.

1153 LONDON EDUCATIONAL REVIEW. 1972.
Institute of Education, University of London, London, WC1.
3, = + Ideas and research in areas of current educational interest.
Book reviews, letters, monographic articles, obituaries.

A, October/November, No, None.
T.p. 80.   1100.
Per copy 60p, per year £1.50.

1154 MENSA JOURNAL: A Communication Network for International Mensa. 1968.
(Intelligence).
Mensa Journal, 1 Carlingford Rd., Hampstead, London, NW3.
8/12, ○ * + ‡
Book notices, book reviews, commodity prices, legal notes, letters, monographic articles, obituaries, tests.
No Index.
July/August 1972, T.p. 12.   18000.
Free to members.

1155 NCET NEWS. 1971.
National Council for Educational Technology, 160 Great Portland Street, London, W1N 5TB.
Irregular, = Educational technology and communications news sheet.
Articles.
No Index.
Spring 1972, T.p. 8.
Free.

1156 NEW ERA: Incorporating World Studies Quarterly Bulletin. 1921.
World Education Fellowship, 55 Upper Stone Street, Tunbridge Wells, Kent.
10, + Every aspect of education—parent, teacher etc.
Book notices, book reviews, letters, monographic articles, obituaries.
A, March, No, None.
April 1972, T.p. 38.
Per copy 20p, per year £2.
Indexed in: BEI.

1157 NEW SIXTH.
Eye to Eye Publications, 107-111 Fleet Street, London, EC4.
4, ○
No Index.
Subscription on application.

1158 NEWS AND VIEWS: Journal of Society of Assistants Teaching in Preparatory Schools. 1963.
(SATIPS Newsletter 1953-1963).
SATIPS Ltd., Kilvington, Ringley Avenue, Horley, Surrey.
3, * Educational matters both at the practical classroom level and in wider aspects.
Book notices, book reviews, letters, monographic articles, obituaries, parliamentary reports, standards, tests.
No Index.
March 1972, T.p. 21, Ad.p. 4.   1500.
Per copy 30p, per year 90p.

1159 NORTHERN IRELAND EDUCATION STATISTICS. 1965.
Her Majesty's Stationery Office, 80 Chichester Street, Belfast, BT1 4JY.
2, * Series of publications of statistics relating to education in Northern Ireland—finance, school leavers, examinations, further education, schools, pupils, teachers, scholarships and awards.
Statistical tables.
No Index.
T.p. 115.
Per copy 87½p.

1160 ON COURSE: Journal of education for industry and commerce. 1966.
Department of Education & Science, Curzon St., London, W1Y 8AA.
3, = Liaison between schools and colleges and industry and commerce.
Book notices, articles.

No Index, No.
Summer 1972, T.p. 24.   50000.
Free.

1161 PNEU: Journal of the Parents National Educational Union. 1966
(Parents' Review January 1891-1966).
Holywell Press Ltd, 9 Alfred St, Oxford.
6, * =   Educational problems, articles of general interest of famous people, places, artists & composers fitting in with the PNEU school syllabus.
Book notices, book reviews, letters, articles.
A, —, Yes, None.
January/February 1972, T.p. 48, Ad.p. 8.   1600.
Per copy 20p, per year £1.20.

1162 PRACTICAL EDUCATION: Journal of the Institute of Craft Education. 1902.
Institute of Craft Education, 23 Brimburn Drive, Darlington.
11, * =   Teaching techniques & aids to workshop efficiency for the craft educationalist.
Book notices, book reviews, letters, monographic articles.
A, —, No, None.
T.p. 19, Ad.p. 9.
Free to members.

1163 PROGRAMMED LEARNING AND EDUCATIONAL TECHNOLOGY: Journal of the Association for Programmed Learning & Educational Technology. 1964.
Sweet & Maxwell (Associated Book Publishers), 11 New Fetter Lane, London, EC4P 4EE.
6, ‡ *   Every aspect of educational innovation other than the purely curricular.
Abstracts, book notices, book reviews, letters, monographic articles, new products.
A, November, Yes, None.
Per copy £1, per year £5.
Indexed in: BEI.

1164 RAEC GAZETTE. 1967.
Royal Army Educational Corps, Eltham Palace, Eltham, London, SE9 5QE.
3, =
No Index.
Subscription on application.

1165 RANK & FILE: Journal of Socialist Teachers. 1968.
Rank & File Teachers, 28 Manor Road, London, N16.
5, =   Covers education and affairs of the National Union of Teachers from the point of view of left-wing and progressive teachers.
Book reviews, legal notes, letters, articles.
Occasional, —, No, None.
Summer 1972, T.p. 20.   7500.
Per copy 9p, per year 45p.

1166 RECALL: review of educational cybernetics and applied linguistics. 1969.
Longmac Ltd, Research Publications Services, Victoria Hall, East Greenwich, London SE10 0RF.
3, * ‡ + =   Cybernetic and mathematical approaches to educational technology and applied linguistics; programmed learning, use of computers for teaching purposes, modelling of teaching processes through automata theory.
Book notices, book reviews, letters, monographic articles, new products, patents, standards, tests.
4 year, —, No, None.
T.p. 32, Ad.p. 4.   400
Per copy 75p, per year £1.75.

1167 REMEDIAL EDUCATION: Journal of the National Association for Remedial Education. 1966.
Longman Group Ltd., Journals Division, 43/45 Annandale Street, Edinburgh EH7 4AT.
3, + *   Presents practical information and research findings over the whole range of learning disability likely to be experienced by children whose handicap is not so severe as to exclude them from the ordinary school system. Particular interest in the teaching of the basic subjects and particularly of literacy in all its aspects, which includes a consideration of children's imaginative literature and the publication of appropriate book-lists. Most issues contain a section on non-English speaking children and a feature for teachers-in-training.
Book notices, book reviews, articles.
No Index.
June 1972, T.p. 48, Ad.p. 3.   3000.
Per copy £1.10, per year £2.50.

1168 RESEARCH IN EDUCATION. 1969.
Manchester University Press, 316-324 Oxford Road, Manchester M13 9NR.
2, + =   The main emphasis is on empirical research in any of the recognised fields of education, together with interdisciplinary studies; also included are papers on research in education at any level from primary to higher.
Book reviews, monographic articles.
No Index.
May 1972, T.p. 86, Ad.p. 4.   700.
Per copy £1.44, per year £2.50.
Indexed in: BEI.

1169 RESEARCH IN EDUCATION: The Newsletter of the Scottish Council for Research in Education. 1968.
Scottish Council for Research in Education, 16 Moray Place, Edinburgh EH3 6DR.
2, ○ +   Research results & topics of general interest in the field of education.
Book reviews, monographic articles.
No Index.
T.p. 4.   63000.
Free.

1170 RESOURCES. 1971.
Educational Resources Ltd., 6 Hartington Road, London W4 3UA.
12, =
No Index.
Per year £3.

1171 SCOTTISH EDUCATIONAL JOURNAL: Official Organ of the Educational Institute of Scotland. 1876.
Pergamon Press Ltd., Headington Hill Hall, Oxford, OX3 0BW.
46, =
Book notices, book reviews, letters, articles, new products, obituaries, parliamentary reports.
A, —, Yes, None.
T.p. 15, Ad.p. 7.   5000.
Per copy 4p, per year £2.

1172 SCHOOL TECHNOLOGY. 1971.
(Schools Council Project Technology Bulletin. 1968-1970)
National Centre for School Technology, Trent Polytechnic, Nottingham.
4, ○ ‡ * †   Provides a forum for discussion among educationalists and industrialists having general concern for the development of technological activities at school.
Book reviews, letters, monographic articles, new products.
4 year, —, Yes, None.
June 1972, T.p. 40, Ad.p. 1.   4000.
Per year £1.50.

1173 SEAR: The Magazine of Manchester Mensa. 1968.
Manchester Mensa, Sear House, Sear Square, 212 Buxton Rd., Stockport, Cheshire.
12, *   General interest by & for people with IQ greater than 148.
Letters, articles.
No Index.
May 1972, T.p. 16.
Per copy 8p, per year 75p.

1174 SOCIOLOGY OF EDUCATION ABSTRACTS.
Pergamon Press Ltd., Headington Hill Hall, Oxford, OX3 0BW.
6, =   All areas of social science & education.
Abstracts.
A, —, Yes, None.
Subscription on application.

1175 SPECTRUM: A magazine for Christians in education. 1968.
Association of Christian Teachers, 47 Marylebone Lane, London W1M 6AX.
3, ○ =   Christian comment on education, (philosophy, theory, practice), forum for ideas, classroom experience, news and review of current developments within education.
Book reviews, letters, articles.
3 years, —, No, None.
May 1972, T.p. 36, Ad.p. 5.   3400.
Per copy 40p, per year £1.

1176 STUDIES IN DESIGN EDUCATION AND CRAFT: a journal of new approaches in design education. 1970.
(Studies in Education and Craft).
Studies in Education, Nafferton, Driffield, Yorkshire.
2, ‡ + =   Developments in the whole field of design and craft education ranging from art through the crafts to applied science and technology.
Book reviews, monographic articles.
No Index.
Spring 1972, T.p. 75, Ad.p. 5.   1200
Per copy 75p, per year £1.50.

1177 STUDIES IN EDUCATION. 1970
St. Luke's College of Education, Institute of Education, University, Exeter.
Irregular, =
No Index.
Per copy 13p.

1178 TIMES EDUCATIONAL SUPPLEMENT. 1910.
Times Newspapers Ltd., Printing House Square, London EC4.
52, =   News & comment on all aspects of education.
Book notices, book reviews, commodity prices, letters, articles, new products, parliamentary reports, tests.
6m, July/January, Yes, None.
T.p. 35, Ad.p. 29.   100000.
Per copy 12p, per year £7.
Indexed in: BEI.

1179 TRAINING OFFICER: Offical journal of the Institute of Training Officers. 1965.
Marylebone Press Ltd., 276/282 Corn Exchange, Fennel Street, Manchester M4 3HF.
12, * =
Book notices, book reviews, letters, articles, news, new products.
A, January, Yes, None.
T.p. 30, Ad.p. 4.   4000.
Free to members.

1180 TRENDS IN EDUCATION. 1966.
HMSO, PO Box 569, Atlantic House, Holborn Viaduct, London, EC1.
4, =
Book reviews, letters, articles.
2 years, —, Yes, None.
Subscription on application.
Indexed in: BEI

1181 URBAN EDUCATION. 1966.
Sage Publications Ltd., St. George's House, 44 Hatton Garden, London Ec1N 8ER.
4, =
Monographic articles.
A, —, Yes, None.
April 1971, T.p. 115.
Per year £7, individual £4.70.

1182 WEA NEWS. 1959.
Workers' Educational Association, Temple House, 9 Upper Berkeley Street, London W1H 8BY.
2, *
Book notices, book reviews, letters, articles.
No Index.
January 1972, T.p. 10, Ad.p. 2.   27000.
Per copy 5p, per year 10p.

1183 WHERE: information on education. 1960.
Advisory Centre for Education, 32 Trumpington Street, Cambridge, CB2 1QY.
12, ○   Factual, up-to-date reports on all aspects of education, informing parents and teachers about opportunities for children, helping them to set their experience in a wider context.
Monographic articles.
A, cumulated, January, No, None.
December 1971, T.p. 22.   23000.
Per copy 35p, per year £3.75, and free to members.
Indexed in: BEI.

1184 THE WORLD AND THE SCHOOL: A review for teachers of international affairs. 1963.
Atlantic Information Centre for Teachers, 23/25 Abbey House, 8 Victoria Street, London, SW1H 0LA.
3, ○ *   Aims to assist teachers of current affairs in secondary schools. Each number has a main teaching topic, discussed by experts, whose articles are followed by comment on the use of the material, a bibliography, articles on education policy and curriculum development in social studies, and reviews of books and teaching aids.
Book notices, book reviews, articles.
A, January, No, None.
T.p. 80.   1200.
Per copy 70p, per year £2.

37:2

RELIGIOUS EDUCATION

1185 LEARNING FOR LIVING: a journal of Christian Education. 1961.
(Religion in Education).
SCM Press Ltd., 63 Bloomsbury Street, London, WC1B 3QX.
5, *   Inteded for teachers of religious education in schools and colleges of education, discusses recent developments in this field, passes information about CEM activities.
Book notices, book reviews, letters, articles.
No Index.
May 1972, T.p. 40, Ad.p. 5.   6000.
Per copy 25p, per year £1.50.
Indexed in: BEI.

1186 RE BULLETIN. 1971.
Theological Students' Fellowship, 39 Bedford Square, London WC1B 3EY.
3, *   Bulletin for students doing religious education in colleges & universities. (Insert to TSF Bulletin)
No Index.
T.p. 4.
Per copy 2p.

37:282

CATHOLIC EDUCATION

1187 CATHOLIC EDUCATION TODAY. 1967.
(Catholic Teachers' Journal 1958-1966).
St. Mary's College, Strawberry Hill, Twickenham, Middlesex.
6, =   All aspects of education, but with special reference to religious education.
Book reviews, letters, monographic articles, news.
No Index.
T.p. 19, Ad.p. 12.   3500.
Per copy $12\frac{1}{2}$p, per year £1.

37:32
CATHOLIC EDUCATION

1188 TEACHING POLITICS: Journal of the Politics Association. 1972.
Longman Group Ltd., 5 Bentinck Street, London W1M 5RN.
=
Book reviews, letters, monographic articles.
A, —, Yes, None.
Subscription on application.

37:34
LEGAL EDUCATION

1189 THE LAW TEACHER 1971.
(Journal of the Association of Law Teachers 1967-1970).
Sweet & Maxwell (Associated Book Publishers), 11 New Fetter Lane, London EC4P 4EE.
3, † * =   Current matters affecting legal education, important articles analysing legal development for integration into teaching courses and reporting on new methods, a comprehensive section dealing with recent developments by way of case law statutes, statutory instruments and all reports of bodies concerned with law and law reform and, not the least important, a comprehensive book review section which presents rapid coverage in depth of the latest key publications, together with a shorter note-form coverage of other material which may also be relevant.
A, —, No, None.
Per copy £1.25, per year £3.

37:38
COMMERCIAL EDUCATION

1190 TEACHER IN COMMERCE. 1916.
(Shorthand Teacher 1882-1915).
Educational Publishing Co. (for Faculty of Teachers in Commerce Ltd.), King Street, Wrexham.
4, =   All aspects of commercial teaching.
Book reviews, letters, articles, obituaries.
No Index.
T.p. 28, Ad.p. 15.   3000.
Free to members.

37:4
LANGUAGE TEACHING

1191 IRAL: INTERNATIONAL REVIEW OF APPLIED LINGUISTICS IN LANGUAGE TEACHING.
Oxford University Press, Press Road, Neasden, London, NW10.
4, +   Combination of theoretical linguistic research and its practical application to language teaching. Carries both synoptic articles on different aspects of applied linguistics and reports on completed or continuing research projects.
Book reviews, articles.
No Index.
February 1972, T.p. 103, Ad.p. 10.   300.
Per copy £1.75, per year £6.40.

1192 LANGUAGE-TEACHING ABSTRACTS. 1968.
(English-Teaching Abstracts 1961-1967).
Cambridge University Press, Bentley House, 200 Euston Road, London, NW1 2DB.
4, + =   Objective summaries of articles from 300 worldwide journals on linguistics, psychology, language studies, teaching methodology and technology and experimental teaching. Brief notes on relevant new books, and on current research in Britain.
Abstracts, book notices, tests.
A, October, No, None.
April, 1972, T.p. 70, Ad.p. 2.   1700
Per copy 70p, per year £2.

1193 MODERN LANGUAGES. 1919.
(Modern Language Teaching 1905-1918).
The Modern Language Association, 2 Manchester Square, London W1M 5RF.
4, * =   Language, literature teaching methods, as well as review of books and courses, bibliography and Association News.
Book reviews, letters, monographic articles, reports.
A, —, Yes, None.
June 1972, T.p. 48, Ad.p. 18.   2500.
Per copy 75p, per year £3.
Indexed in: BEI.

37:420
ENGLISH TEACHING

1194 THE ARELS JOURNAL. 1972.
Association of Recognised English Language Schools, 43 Russell Square, London WC1B 5DH.
2, * =   Teaching of English to foreign students with particular references to the private schools providing tuition.
Book notices, book reviews, letters, monographic articles, parliamentary reports.
2 year, —, No, None.
Summer 1972, T.p. 12, Ad.p. 2.   500.
Per copy 13p, per year 25p.

1195 ENGLISH: Published for the English Association. 1935.
Oxford University Press, Press Road, Neasden, London NW10.
3, ○ +   Contains literary articles, articles on various aspects of the teaching of English, poetry, reviews of books, and booklists of recent literary and educational publications.
Book reviews, letters, articles.
A, —, Yes, None.
Spring 1972, T.p. 39, Ad.p. 10.   500.
Per copy 53p, per year £1.50.

1196 ENGLISH IN EDUCATION. 1967.
(N.A.T.E. Bulletin. 1965-1967).
Oxford University Press, Press Road, Neasden, London, NW10. (for National Association for the Teaching of English).
3, ‡ + =   To improve the teaching of English & act as a medium for exchange of ideas & co-operation.
Book notices, book reviews, monographic articles.
No Index.
Summer 1968, T.p. 82, Ad.p. 14.
Free to members.
Indexed in: BEI.

1197 ENGLISH LANGUAGE TEACHING: Published in association with the British Council. 1946.
Oxford University Press, Press Road, Neasden, London, NW10.
3, + =   For the teacher of English as a foreign or second language.
Book reviews, letters, articles.
3 year, —, No, None.
February 1972, T.p. 104, Ad.p. 7.   7000.
Per copy 40p, per year £1.
Indexed in: BEI.

1198 MODERN ENGLISH TEACHER. 1973.
International Language Centre, International House, 40 Shaftesbury Avenue, London W1V 8HJ.
3, =   Practical suggestions of methods for teaching certain English structures in the classroom.
Book reviews, letters, monographic articles.
None.
Per year £3 (incl. Modern English) and 25p; 75p individually.

1199 MULTIRACIAL SCHOOL: The Journal of the Associations for the Education of Pupils from Overseas (ATEPO). 1971
(English for Immigrants 1967-1971)
Oxford University Press, Press Road, Neasden, London, NW10.
3, = Suggestions for teaching multiracial classes, with news of developments in organisation, training and research.
Book reviews, letters, articles.
No Index.
Summer 1972, T.p. 29, Ad.p. 5.   600.
Per copy 40p, per year £1.

1200 TEACHING ENGLISH: CITE Newsletter. 1969.
(CITE Newsletter: Teaching English 1967-1968).
Centre for Information on the Teaching of English, Moray House College of Education, Holyrood Road, Edinburgh, EH8 8AQ.
3, = All aspects of teaching English (language and literature) as mother-tongue, with special reference to current work in Scotland. Currently focussing on ROSLA and inter- and multi-disciplinary work involving English.
Book notices, book reviews, articles.
A, October, No, None.
May 1972, T.p. 47, Ad.p. 5.   2500.
Per copy 15p, per year 45p.

37:43

GERMAN TEACHING

1201 TREFFPUNKT: Journal of the Association of Teachers of German. 1958.
Association, 27 Wood Lane End, Adeyfield, Hemel Hempstead, Herts.
4, =
Book notices, book reviews, letters, news, obituaries, tests.
No Index.
T.p. 20, Ad.p. 2.
Free to members.

37:482

RUSSIAN TEACHING

1202 JOURNAL OF RUSSIAN STUDIES. 1969.
(ATR. Association of Teachers of Russian Journal 1962-1969).
Association of Teachers of Russian. Editor: J. M. Kirkwood, Department of Russian and Soviet Studies, University of Lancaster, Bailrigg, Lancaster.
2, + = Language, literature, history of Russia/Soviet Union.
Book reviews, monographic articles.
No Index.
No. 20, 1970, T.p. 27, Ad.p. 5.   800.
Per year £2.

37:5

SCIENCE TEACHING

1203 EDUCATION IN SCIENCE. Bulletin of the Association for Science Education. 1963.
The Association, College Lane, Hatfield, Herts.
5, = Science teaching in schools.
No Index.
T.p. 41, Ad.p. 14.
Free to members.

1204 SCHOOL SCIENCE REVIEW: The Journal of the Association for Science Education. 1919.
John Murray (for the Association for Science Education), 50 Albemarle Street, London, W1X 4BD.
4, ‡ * = Teaching of science in secondary schools.
Book notices, book reviews.
A, September, Yes, None.
March 1972, T.p. 202, Ad.p. 84.   1600.
Per year £4.
Indexed in: BEI.

1205 SCIENCE. Official journal of the Irish Science Teachers' Association. 1962.
General Publications, 59 Merrion Square, Dublin, 2.
3, = School science teaching in Ireland.
Book notices, book reviews, letters, articles, news, obituaries, tests.
No Index.
T.p. 30, Ad.p. 11.
Free to members.

1206 SCIENCE TEACHER. 1959.
(Science Teaching 1956-1959).
Junior Club Publications Ltd, 36 Craven Street, London, WC2N 5NG.
6, + ‡ = Studies in methodology of science and maths teaching, plus original question papers and answers for British and International Mathematical Olympiads.
Book notices, book reviews, letters, monographic articles, new products, standards, tests.
A, June, No, None.
T.p. 25, Ad.p. 10.
Per copy 10p, per year 40p.

1207 SCIENCE TEACHING EQUIPMENT.
Milton Publishing Co. Ltd., 28 Craven Street, London, WC2N 5PD.
4, ‡ All types of science teaching equipment.
No Index.
April/May 1972, T.p. 4, Ad.p. 7.   8021.
Per copy 75p, per year £3.

37:51

MATHEMATICS TEACHING

1208 INTERNATIONAL JOURNAL OF MATHEMATICAL EDUCATION IN SCIENCE AND TECHNOLOGY. 1970.
John Wiley & Sons Ltd., Baffins Lane, Chichester, Sussex, PO19 1UD.
4, = † Mathematical education.
Book reviews, letters, monographic articles.
A, —, No, None.
April-June 1972, T.p. c. 100.
Per year £6.

1209 MATHEMATICS TEACHING. 1955.
Association of Teachers of Mathematics, Market Street Chambers, Nelson, Lancs. BB9 7LN.
4, + Teaching of mathematics at all levels.
Book notices, book reviews, letters, monographic articles.
2 yearly, Inserted in Summer edition odd years for previous two, No, None.
Summer 1972, T.p. 64, Ad.p. 5.   6000.
Per copy 75p, per year £3.
Indexed in: BEI.

37:53

PHYSICS TEACHING

1210 PHYSICS EDUCATION. 1966.
The Institute of Physics, London and Bristol, Netherton House, Marsh St., Bristol, BS1, 4BT.
7, ‡ + Teaching methods, new courses and curriculum developments, new apparatus, teaching kits, educational technology, physics in industry, the history and philosophy of physics, book and film reviews, reports on conferences, meetings and exhibitions, news, announcements and details of forthcoming events.

Book notices, book reviews, letters, monographic articles, new products, tests.
No Index.
March 1972, T.p. 63, Ad.p. 4.   3681.
Per copy £1.50, per year £9.
Indexed in: BEI.

37:54
CHEMISTRY TEACHING

1211 EDUCATION IN CHEMISTRY. 1964.
The Chemical Society, Burlington House, London, W1V 0BN.
6, ‡ =   Covers the problems of chemical education at all levels from the secondary school to the university.
Book reviews, letters, monographic articles, new products, obituaries, tests.
A, November, Yes, None.
May 1972, T.p. 29, Ad.p. 11.   5579.
Per copy £1.50, per year £6.
Indexed in: BEI.

37:55
GEOLOGY TEACHING

1212 GEOLOGY: Journal of The Association of Teachers of Geology. 1969.
Edward Roberts Ltd. (for The Association of Teachers of Geology), Cardiff.
1, *   Syllabuses on the matters connected with geology teaching.
Book notices, book reviews.
No Index.
1971, T.p. 128.   750.
Per copy £1.50.

37:574
BIOLOGY TEACHING

1213 JOURNAL OF BIOLOGICAL EDUCATION. 1967.
Academic Press Inc. (London) Ltd. (for Institute of Biology), 24-28 Oval Road, London, NW1.
6, ‡ *   Biology teaching at all levels—theory, practice, administrative.
Book notices, book reviews, commodity prices, letters, monographic articles, new products, tests.
A, December, Yes, None.
June 1972, T.p. 75, Ad.p. 7.   1600.
Per year: £4.

37:613
HEALTH EDUCATION

1214 HEALTH EDUCATION JOURNAL. 1943.
Health Education Council, Middlesex House, Ealing Road, Wembley, Middx. HAO 1HH.
4, =   All aspects of health education.
Book reviews, monographic articles.
A, –, Yes, None.
Winter/Spring 1972, T.p. 35.   2400.
Per copy $17\frac{1}{2}$p, per year £1.
Indexed in: BEI.

37:655
PRINTING TEACHING

1215 ATPAS BULLETIN. 1951.
Association of Teachers of Printing & Allied Subjects, 132 Cheviot Road, West Norwood, London, SE 27.
3, * = ‡   Educational developments at all levels in industrial environment.
Book notices, book reviews, letters, articles, new products, obituaries, reports, tests.
No Index.
T.p. 11, Ad.p. 5.
Free to members.

37:658
MANAGEMENT EDUCATION

1216 MANAGEMENT EDUCATION AND DEVELOPMENT: Journal of the Association of Teachers of Management. 1970.
(A.T.M. Bulletin. 1960-1969).
Association of Teachers of Management, c/o Dept. of Management, Polytechnic, 77, Whitworth Street, Manchester, 1.
3, ‡ = + *   Research and current practice dealing with every aspect of the education and development of managers.
Book notices, book reviews, monographic articles.
No Index.
August 1972, T.p. 60, Ad.p. 2.   650.
Per copy £2, per year £5.

37:7
ART EDUCATION

1217 ATHENE. Journal of the Society for Education through Art. 1939.
The Society, 29 Great James Street, London, WC1.
2/3, * =
Book notices, book reviews, letters, articles.
No Index.
T.p. 22, Ad.p. 4.
Free to members.
Indexed in: BEI.

1218 COLOUR REVIEW: Art Teachers Journal. 1960.
Winsor & Newton Limited, Wealdstone, Harrow, Middlesex.
3, = †   Features on art materials and art education.
Book reviews, commodity prices, monographic articles, new products.
No Index.
Summer 1972, T.p. 16.   12500.
Circulation limited to educational institutions Secondary level and above.

37:78
MUSIC EDUCATION

1219 MUSIC IN EDUCATION. 1944.
(School Music Review 1892, School Music Record 1930, Music in Schools 1937).
Novello & Co. Ltd. (Granada Group), 27 Soho Square, London, W1V 6BR.
6, ‡ +   Musicians, particularly those concerned with music at school, college or university.
Book notices, book reviews, letters, monographic articles, new products.
A, March, Yes, None.
May/June 1972, T.p. 40, Ad.p. 15.
Per copy 15p, per year £1.05.
Indexed in: BEI.

1220 MUSIC TEACHER. 1921.
(Music Student 1908-1921).
Evans Brothers Limited, Montague House, Russell Square, London, WC1B 5BX.

Key to reference symbols

○ popular   ‡ technical   = trade/professional

+ research   * society/institution   † house journal

12, = *   For professional teachers of music. Teaching notes on various piano examinations; analyses of the set works of all the examining boards, and new teaching material are included.
Book reviews, articles.
A, January, No, None.
July 1972, T.p. 28, Ad.p. 22.   6186.
Per copy 20p, per year £2.90.

37:792

DRAMA EDUCATION

1221 SPEECH AND DRAMA. 1951.
Society of Teachers of Speech & Drama, St. Bride Institute, Bride Lane, London, EC4.
3, * =   Whole range of speech and drama in education and research. Ranging from professional theatre, through non-professional, verse-speaking, oratory, examinations, research, to linguistics.
Book notices, book reviews, letters, monographic articles, new products, reports, tests.
A, Spring Issue, Yes, None.
Summer 1972, T.p. 50, Ad.p. 7.   2000.
Per copy 50p, per year £1.50.

37:793.3

DANCE TEACHING

1222 DANCE: journal of the Imperial Society of Teachers of Dancing. 1972.
(Dance Journal 1907-1972).
Imperial Society of Teachers of Dancing, 70 Gloucester Place, London, W1H 4AJ.
6, ‡ = *   Developments in dancing.
Book notices, book reviews, letters, articles, new products, obituaries.
No Index.
May 1972, T.p. 12, Ad.p. 4.
Free to members.

1223 DANCE TEACHER. 1952.
International Dance Teachers Association, 76 Bennett Rd., Brighton BN2 5JL.
12, ‡ = + *   Teaching of all forms of dancing.
Book reviews, legal notes, letters, articles, new products, obituaries.
No Index.
June 1972, T.p. 16, Ad.p. 4.   4500.
Per year £1.50.

37:9

HISTORY TEACHING

1224 HISTORY TEACHERS NEWS LETTER. 1970.
Historical Association, 59a Kennington Park Road, London, SE11 4VH.
Ireg, * =
No Index.
September 1970, T.p. 12.
Free.

1225 TEACHING HISTORY. 1969.
The Historical Association, 59a Kennington Park Road, London, SE11 4JH.
2, ‡ * =   Interchange of experience on contemporary methods of teaching history in the classroom with evaluation of experiments.
Book notices, book reviews, letters, monographic articles.
2 yearly (4 parts to vol.), Issue 4, 8, etc., No.
May 1972, T.p. 80, Ad.p. 16.   c.5000.
Per copy 60p, per year £1 (Nonmembers) 30p, 50p (Members).
Indexed in: BEI.

371

TEACHING

1226 CENTRE POINT: Incorporating The London Teacher. 1967.
(London Teacher & Schools Review. 1883-1967).
Inner London Teachers' Association, Hamilton House, Mabledon Place, London WC1H 9BD.
3, * =   Matters of professional and educational interest to teachers, particularly those teaching in the area of the inner London Education Authority and are members of the National Union of Teachers.
Book notices, book reviews, letters, articles, obituaries, parliamentary reports.
No Index.
June 1972, T.p. 11, Ad.p. 4.   14000.
Per copy 10p, per year 30p.

1227 CRAFT TEACHER NEWS. 1971.
Elliott Publications Limited, 9 Queen Victoria Street, Reading RG1 1SY, Berks.
4, ‡   Devoted entirely to conveying information about equipment, supplies, teaching aids, etc. of direct interest to those concerned with teaching practical subjects in schools.
Book notices, book reviews, new products.
No Index.
June 1972, T.p. 10, Ad.p. 10.   7500.
Free.

1228 DIDASKALOS: Journal of the Joint Association of Classical Teachers. 1963.
Basil Blackwell & Mott Ltd., 5 Alfred Street, Oxford OX1 4HB.
1, = +   Teaching the classics both at school and university level. Each issue is arranged around one specific aspect of classics teaching.
Articles.
3 years, June, No, None.
No. 3 1972, T.p. 206, Ad.p. 10.   2500.
Per year £2.
Indexed in: BEI.

1229 THE NEW SCHOOLMASTER. Journal of the National Association of Schoolmasters. 1921.
Pergamon Press Ltd., Headington Hill Hall, Oxford, OX3 OBW.
9, = *
Book reviews, legal notes, letters, articles, news, new products, obituaries, parliamentary reports.
No Index.
T.p. 16, Ad.p. 8.
Free to members.

1230 OVERSEAS CHALLENGE: bulletin of the National Council for the Supply and Training of Teachers Overseas. 1963.
Overseas Development Administration of the Foreign and Commonwealth Office, Eland House, Stag Place, London, SW1.
3, =   All aspects of school teaching in the developing world.
Letters, articles.
No Index.
Spring 1972, T.p. 32.
Free.

1231 THE PARENT-TEACHER. Official journal of the NFPTA. 1963.
(Parent-Teacher National Bulletin 1956-1962).
National Federation of Parent-Teacher Associations, 5 Ransley Green, Ruckinge, Ashford, Kent.
2, * = ○
Book notices, book reviews, letters, articles, news, new products, obituaries, parliamentary reports.
No Index.
T.p. 14, Ad.p. 6.
Free to members.

1232 PICTORIAL EDUCATION. 1926.
   Evans Brothers Limited, Montague House, Russell
      Square, London, WC2B 5BX.
   12, =   Large size pages, 8 in full colour are designed
      as attractive visual teaching aids, and provide junior
      and secondary school teachers of history, geography,
      English, social studies, religion, art and science with
      valuable authoritative material.
   A, September, No, None.
   July 1972, T.p. 24.   37000.
   Per copy 25p, per year £3.50.

1233 PICTORIAL EDUCATION QUARTERLY. 1926.
   Evans Brothers Limited, Montague House, Russell
      Square, London, WC1B 5BX.
   4, =   Each issue is devoted to one topic and provides a
      wealth of visual material and background informa-
      tion for class teaching or group work, and includes
      a full colour wall picture 24 × 40 inches and a
      frieze 12 × 40 inches.
   A, Included with Pictorial Education, September issue,
      No, None.
   Summer 1972, T.p. 2 large pictures plus text, folded.
      24000.
   Per copy 20p, per year £1.

1234 RANK AND FILE: Journal of Socialist Teachers.
   17 Dingle Road, Ashford, Middx.
   5, =   Pressure group within N.U.T. to force change
      and progress within the profession.
   Articles.
   No Index.
   Summer 1972, T.p. 20.
   Per copy 5p, per year 45p.

1236 SCOTTISH SCHOOLMASTER. 1950.
   Scottish Schoolmasters Association, 41 York Place,
      Edinburgh, 1.
   5, * =   Education, teachers' interests.
   Book notices, book reviews, legal notes, letters, articles,
      obituaries, parliamentary reports.
   No Index.
   May 1972, T.p. 16, Ad.p. 8.   3500.
   Per copy 10p, and Free to members.

1237 THE TEACHER: Journal of the National Union of
      Teachers. 1963.
   (The Schoolmaster 1872-1924; Schoolmaster and Woman
      Teachers Chronicle 1925-1962).
   Schoolmaster Publishing Co. Ltd., Derbyshire House,
      St. Chad's Street, London, WC1H 8AJ.
   52, * =   All aspects of teaching.
   Book notices, book reviews, letters, articles, obituaries,
      parliamentary reports.
   6m, January/July, No, None.
   T.p. 20, Ad.p. 8.   65000.
   Per copy 3p, per year £3.
   Indexed in: BEI.

1238 TEACHER IN WALES. 1960.
   Wales & Border Newspapers, Caxton Press, Oswestry,
      Salop.
   11, =   All aspects of education in Wales.
   Book reviews, letters, articles, news, obituaries.
   No Index.
   T.p. 40, Ad.p. 18.
   Per copy 5p, per year 60p.
   Indexed in: BEI.

371.048

CAREERS

1239 CAREER. 1968.
   Dominion Press Ltd., Grand Buildings, Trafalgar Square,
      London WC2.
   6, =   Career advice and guidance for final year under-
      graduates.
   No Index.
   Free, Controlled circulation.

1240 CAREERS QUARTERLY. 1969.
   (Youth Employment).
   Institute of Careers Officers, c/o Kent Training College
      for the Youth Employment Service, College Road,
      Hextable, Swanley, Kent.
   4, * = +   Vocational guidance, careers, education, em-
      ployment and training of young people, guidance in
      other countries, some research papers.
   Book reviews, letters, monographic articles.
   No Index.
   Spring 1972, T.p. 48, Ad.p. 8.
   Per copy 40p, and Free to members.

1241 CAREER SCOTLAND. 1971.
   Dominion Press Ltd., Grand Buildings, Trafalgar Square,
      London, WC2.
   1, = ○
   No Index.
   Per copy £1.25, and Free to final year undergraduates.

1242 HOSPITAL CAREER. 1969.
   Dominion Press Ltd., Grand Buildings, Trafalgar Square,
      London WC2.
   4, =   Advice and information for school leavers.
   No Index.
   T.p. 18, Ad.p. 15.   10000.
   Free, Controlled circulation.

1243 P.S.A.B. NEWS BULLETIN. 1967.
   (Bulletin 1946-1967).
   Public Schools Appointments Bureau, 17 Queen Street,
      Mayfair, London, W1X 8BL.
   3,   Careers information of all kinds, with special
      coverage of careers activities in public schools, and
      aspects of careers likely to interest parents with
      sons at school.
   Book notices, book reviews, monographic articles.
   2 year, September, No, 10 year.
   Spring 1972, T.p. 52.   4250.
   Per copy 25p, per 2 years £1.50.

1244 PUBLIC SCHOOL LEAVER. 1969.
   Dominion Press Ltd., Grand Buildings, Trafalgar Square,
      London, WC2.
   4, =   Vocational advice and information for public
      school sixth formers.
   No Index.
   T.p. 26, Ad.p. 30.   12000.
   Free, Controlled circulation.

1245 SCHOOL LEAVER. 1969.
   Dominion Press Ltd., Grand Buildings, Trafalgar Square,
      London, WC2.
   4, =   Vocational advice and guidance for school
      leavers.
   No Index.
   T.p. 23, Ad.p. 20.   25000.
   Free, Controlled circulation.

1246 SCOTTISH YOUTH REVIEW. 1962.
   8 Palmerston Place, Edinburgh EH12 5AA.
   4, =
   No Index.
   Per copy 12½p, per year 45p.

371.33

VISUAL AIDS

1247 SCREEN. 1969.
   (Screen Education 1959-1968).
   Society for Education in Film and Television, 63 Old
      Compton Street, London W1V 5PN.
   4, * +   Film and television theory and criticism.
   Book reviews, letters, monographic articles.
   3 year, March 1972 et seq, Yes, None.
   Spring 1972, T.p. 126, Ad.p. 6.
   Per copy 50p, per year £1.90.

1248 VISUAL EDUCATION. 1951.
National Committee for Audio Visual Aids in Education, 33 Queen Anne St., London, W1M 0AH.
11, All aspects of audio-visual media and their use in schools, colleges and universities plus reviews of new films, film strips and other teaching aids.
Book notices, book reviews, commodity prices, letters, monographic articles, new companies, new products, tests.
A, July, Yes, None.
June 1972, T.p. 31, Ad.p. 11.   7111.
Per copy 20p, per year £2.40.
Indexed in: BEI.

371.7

PHYSICAL EDUCATION

1249 BRITISH JOURNAL OF PHYSICAL EDUCATION. 1970.
(1899-1969 Ling Association Leaflet; 1908-1922 J. of Scientific Physical Training; 1923-1941 J. of School Hygiene & P.E.; 1942-1954 Journal of Physical Education; 1955-1969 Physical Education.)
The Physical Education Association of G.B. & N.I., Ling House, 10 Nottingham Place, London W1M 4AX.
6, * = Physical education teachers and all interested in the subject.
Abstracts, book notices, book reviews, commodity prices, legal notes, letters, monographic articles, new products, obituaries.
A, Autumn, Yes, None.
May 1971, T.p. 48, Ad.p. 4.   1200.
Free to members.

1250 BULLETIN OF PHYSICAL EDUCATION. 1946.
British Association of Organisers and Lecturers in Physical Education, Department of Physical Education, St. Paul's College, Cheltenham, Gloucestershire, GL50 4AZ.
4, + = * All aspects of physical education, sport and recreation.
Book notices, book reviews, letters, monographic articles, new products, obituaries, tests.
No Index.
April 1972, T.p. 66, Ad.p. 22.   1000.
Per year £1.75. Free to members.

1251 LABAN ART OF MOVEMENT GUILD MAGAZINE. 1948.
Laban Art of Movement Guild, 3 Beech Grove, Burton-on-Stather, Scunthorpe, Lincolnshire, DN15 9DB.
2, ‡ * ○ Human movement applied to education, art, industry, sport or, therapeutically, to medicine.
Book notices, book reviews, letters, monographic articles, obituaries.
No index.
May 1972, T.p. 35.   1200.
Per copy 40p, per year 80p.

1252 OUTDOORS. 1970.
The Physical Education Association of G.B. & N.I., Ling House, 19 Nottingham Place, London, W1M 4AX.
4, * ○ Outdoor Education aimed particularly at Physical Educationalists who with larger classes, and better facilities are becoming more involved with all aspects of outdoor activities.
Book notices, commodity prices, legal notes, letters, articles, new products.
No index.
May 1972, T.p. 11, Ad.p. 1.   1200.
Free to members.

371.9

EDUCATION OF SPECIAL CLASSES

1253 THE GUILD OF TEACHERS OF BACKWARD CHILDREN. 1957.
The Guild of Teachers of Backward Children, Minster Chambers, Southwell, Notts.
3, = ‡ Educationists in universities, colleges, school, mental hospitals, especially those involved in work with retarded, backward and educationally subnormal children.
Book notices, book reviews, letters, monographic articles, tests.
No Index.
April 1972, T.p. 32, Ad.p. 5.   2500.
Per copy 75p, per year £2.

1254 RESEARCH IN SPECIAL EDUCATION: Abstracts and Information. 1967.
The Association for Special Education, Publications Dept., Beaconwood, Bordon Hill, Stratford-upon-Avon.
2, + Abstracts and information of research work in special education in progress or reported.
Abstracts.
No Index.
No. 3, 1971, T.p. 75.   1000.
Per copy 75p.

1255 SPECIAL EDUCATION: Education Journal of The Spastics Society: incorporating Spastics Quarterly. 1965.
(Special Schools Journal 1911-1957).
The Spastics Society and the Association for Special Education, 12 Park Crescent, London, W1N 4EQ.
4, ‡ + * The education of all handicapped children including physically and mentally handicapped, maladjusted and socially deprived.
Book notices, book reviews, letters, monographic articles.
A, March, Yes, None.
June 1972, T.p. 27, Ad.p. 8.   6750.
Per copy 50p, per year £1.50.
Indexed in: BEI.

1256 THE TEACHER OF THE BLIND: The Organ of the College of Teachers of the Blind. 1907.
College of Teachers of the Blind, Royal School for the Blind, Church Road North, Wavertree, Liverpool, LI5 6TQ.
4, + * Aspects of the development of the visually-handicapped child and adolescent, and of contemporary educational and welfare thinking.
Book notices, book reviews, commodity prices, letters, monographic articles, new products, obituaries, tests.
No Index.
April 1972, T.p. 35, Ad.p. 1.
Per copy 30p. Free to members.

1257 THE TEACHER OF THE DEAF: The Journal of the National College of Teachers of the Deaf (incorporated). 1903.
National College of Teachers of the Deaf, c/o 32 Merston Dr., Manchester, M20 0WT.
6, ‡ + The principles and methods of teaching children with impaired hearing. Relevant educational, audiological, psychological, linguistic and medical research.
Book notices, book reviews, letters, monographic articles, new products, obituaries.
A, January, No, None.
March 1972. T.p. 75, Ad.p. 10.   1800.
Per copy 50p, per year £2.90.

1258 TEACHING & TRAINING. 1962.
National Association of Teachers of the Mentally Handicapped, 1 Beechfield Avenue, Urmston, Manchester 31 3 RT.
4, + * All aspects of teaching the mentally handicapped.
Book notices, book reviews, legal notes, letters, monographic articles, obituaries, parliamentary reports.
No Index.
Autumn 1971, T.p. 35.
Per copy 15p, per year 60p.

372

ELEMENTARY EDUCATION

1259 ART AND CRAFT IN EDUCATION. 1936.
Evans Brothers Limited, Montague House, Russell Square, London, WC1B 2BX.
12, =   An aid to teachers of creative studies, written by a team with a practical approach to such subjects as music, peotry, puppetry, ceramics, crayons, picture making.
No Index.
July 1972, T.p. 24, Ad.p. 6.   20506.
Per copy 20p, per year £2.90.

1260 CHILD EDUCATION. 1924.
Evans Brothers Limited, Montague House, Russell Square, London, WC1B 2BX.
12, =   Written for infant and nursery school teachers; contains attractive wall pictures, short stories, poetry, music, art and craft activities.
Book notices, book reviews, new products.
A, January, No, None.
July 1972, T.p. 21, Ad.p. 12.   73816.
Per copy 20p, per year £2.90.

1261 CHILD EDUCATION QUARTERLY. 1924.
Evans Brothers Limited, Montague House, Russell Square, London WC1B 2BX.
4, =   Each issue deals with a single topic illustrated in a large full colour wall picture. It is a valuable source of classroom material.
A, In the January issue of Child Education, No, None.
Summer 1972, T.p. 18.   50000.
Per copy 15p, per year 80p.

1263 FROEBEL JOURNAL. 1965.
(Froebel Bulletin)
The National Froebel Foundation, Froebel Institute, Grove House, Roehampton Lane, London, SW15
3, + *   Articles and book reviews of interest to teachers and anyone interested in the education of children under 13. Also notices of forthcoming courses, new publications and advertisements.
Book notices, book reviews, monographic articles.
No Index.
Spring 1972, T.p. 50, Ad.p. 2.
Per copy 25p, per year £2.10.
Indexed in: BEI.

1264 NURSERY JOURNAL, 1948.
(Crêche News 1915; Day Nursery Journal 1940-1947).
National Society of Children's Nurseries, 45 Russell Square, London WC1.
12, =   Child care.
Book reviews, letters, articles, new products.
No Index.
T.p. 20.
Per copy 10p, per year £1.

1265 TEACHERS WORLD. 1911.
Evans Brothers Limited, Montague House, Russell Square, London WC1B 2BX.
52, =   Imaginative yet practical approach to classroom teaching. Articles by practising teachers give help on a variety of subjects, and is stimulating to all interested in the broader aspects of education.
Book reviews, new products.
No Index.
30 June 1972, T.p. 26, Ad.p. 26.   28202.
Per copy 6p, per year £4.70.
Indexed in: BEI.

373

SECONDARY EDUCATION

1266 AMA: Journal of the Incorporated Association of Assistant Masters in Secondary Schools.
Gordon House, 29 Gordon Square, London WC1H 0PT.
12, =.
Book reviews, letters, articles.
A, —, Yes, None.
Per copy 8p.

1267 HOUSECRAFT: Official magazine of the Association of Teachers of Domestic Science. 1928.
Hamilton House, Mabledon Place, London WC1H 9BB.
12, * =   Home economics and needlework in schools, further education, colleges of education and universities. Technical background information needed by specialist teachers and students and the wider educational context.
Book reviews, letters, monographic articles, new products, obituaries, conference reports, news and comment.
A, December, No, None.
May 1972, T.p. 21/22, Ad.p. 17.   12845.
Per copy 21p, per year £2.50.

1268 SCOTTISH SECONDARY TEACHERS' ASSOCIATION BULLETIN. 1947.
Scottish Secondary Teachers' Association, 15 Dundas Street, Edinburgh, EH3 6QG.
10, *   Information to members on matters pertaining to the Association.
Legal notes, parliamentary reports.
No Index.
10 April 1972, T.p. 11.
Free to members only.

1269 TECHNICAL EDUCATION ABSTRACTS. 1960.
Information for Education Ltd., School of Education, University of Liverpool, 19-23 Abercromby Square, Liverpool 7.
4, ‡ = *   Technical education and industrial training. Only British sources are covered.
Abstracts, book reviews.
Q, —, Yes, A.
11(1), T.p. 29.   500.
Per year £5.50.

1270 THE TECHNICAL JOURNAL: Magazine of the Association of Teachers in Technical Institutions. 1904.
A.T.T.I., Hamilton House, Mabledon Place, London, WC1.
9, * =   All aspects of further and higher education.
Book reviews, letters, monographic articles, new products.
A, February/March, No, None.
T.p. 25, Ad.p. 12.   30000.
Free to members.

373.6

COMMERCIAL TRAINING

1271 INDUSTRIAL AND COMMERCIAL TRAINING. 1969.
Wellens Publishing, The Sun, Guilsborough, Northampton, NN6 8PY.
12, =   Comprehensive information service in whole training and technical education area. Range of interest from craft, operator and clerical training at one end to professional and managerial training at the other.
Book notices, book reviews, legal notes, letters, monographic articles, new products.
No Index.
3, 1972, T.p. 41, Ad.p. 6.   3500.
Per copy 50p, per year £5.

374

ADULT EDUCATION

1272 ADULT EDUCATION. 1926.
NIAE, 35 Queen Anne Street, London, W1M 0BL.
6, + *   Record of contemporary activities and a

professional forum for the discussion of new developments in adult education.
Book notices, book reviews, letters, monographic articles, obituaries, standards.
A, March, Yes, None.
T.p. 64-72, Ad.p. 2-4.   2500.
Per copy 50p, per year £2.70.
Indexed in: BEI.

1274 HOME STUDY. 1966.
National Extension College, Shaftesbury Road, Cambridge.
4,*   Advice and information for adults studying at home with the National Extension College.
No Index.
February 1972, T.p. 30, Ad.p. 2,   7000.
Per year £1.

1275 LINK: Guildford Journal of Adult Education. 1968.
Adult Education Centre, 73 Farnham Road, Guildford.
3,*   For and by adult education students, mainly evening class students, and tutors.
Book notices, book reviews, letters, articles.
No Index.
March 1972, T.p. 28.
Per copy 3p.

1276 ONE AND ALL. 1891.
National Adult School Union, Drayton House, Gordon Street, London, WC1H 0BE.
12, ○ * †   Topical subjects—educational, social, religious, moral, scientific, etc. And News of the Movement, etc., book notices, letters, etc.
M, —, Yes, 5 year,
6, 1972, T.p. 16,   1600.
Per copy 4p, per year 78p.

1277 STUDIES IN ADULT EDUCATION. 1969.
David and Charles (Publishers) Ltd., South Devon House, Newton Abbot, Devon.
2, = +   Theory of adult education in Britain, with relevant reports of developments abroad.
Book reviews, monographic articles.
A, Last issue of year, Yes, None.
Per copy 90p, per year £1.75.

1278 TEACHING ADULTS. 1966.
NIAE, 35 Queen Anne Street, London W1M 0BL.
4 (during autumn and winter months) * +   Magazine for, and predominantly by, part-time teachers of adults. Covers teaching methods and techniques in both specialised and general subject areas, and new products, equipment, aids, audio-visual material and books useful to such teachers.
Book notices, book reviews, letters, monographic articles, new products, standards.
No Index.
T.p. 20, Ad.p. 4.   10000.
Per copy 25p, per year £1.

378

HIGHER EDUCATION

1280 AUT BULLETIN. 1962.
Association of University Teachers, Bremar House, Sale Place, London W2.
6, = *   All aspects of education.
No Index.
T.p. 17, Ad.p. 6.
Free to members.

1281 BACIE JOURNAL. 1947.
(BACIE Bulletin).
British Association for Commercial and Industrial Education, 16 Park Crescent, London W1N 4AP.
4,* =   An authoritative guide to training practice and policy.
Monographic articles.

No Index.
March 1972, T.p. 34, Ad.p. 12.   5000.
Per copy 50p, per year £3 and free to members.
Indexed in: BEI.

1282 BACIE NEWS. 1970.
(BACIE Memoranda)
British Association for Commercial and Industrial Education, 16 Park Crescent, London W1N 4AP.
7,* =   A concise summary of current events in the training field.
Book notices, book reviews, new companies, new products, obituaries.
No Index.
February 1972, T.p. 8, Ad.p. 6.   5000.
Free to members.

1283 EDUCATION & TRAINING. 1968.
(Technical Education, c. 1950-1968).
Macmillan Journals Ltd., 4 Little Essex St., London, WC2.
12, + ‡   Further education in general.
Book notices, book reviews, letters, articles, new products, obituaries, parliamentary reports.
No Index.
June 1972, T.p. 32, Ad.p. 6.   4500.
Per copy 30p, per year £4.
Indexed in: BEI.

1284 FIRST EMPLOYMENT OF UNIVERSITY GRADUATES. 1963.
H.M.S.O., Atlantic House, High Holborn, London, EC2.
1, =   First destinations of University Graduates. Further training, (home/overseas) full-time permanent U.K. employment with employer category (Public service, education, industry/commerce etc.)
No Index.
1969-70, T.p. 51.
Per copy 68p.

1285 FURTHER EDUCATION. 1969.
Careers Research & Advisory Centre, Bateman Street, Cambridge.
6, ‡   Developments in further education of interest to schools, colleges, and employers. Information on research on FE. Designed to increase knowledge and understanding of FE System.
Book reviews, letters, articles.
No Index.
Spring 1972, T.p. 30, Ad.p. 20.
Per copy 40p, per year £1.50.

1286 HIGHER EDUCATION BULLETIN: (New Series). 1972.
(Higher Education Bulletin, 1968-1970)
Department of Educational Research, University of Lancaster, Bailrigg, Lancaster.
3, = + * †   National and international developments in higher education and recent research relevant to the responsibilities of the college, university or polytechnic lecturer as teacher, tutor and scholar.
Book notices, book reviews, articles.
A, February, Yes, None.
May 1972, T.p. 56.   1000
Per copy 35p, per year £1.

1288 HIGHER EDUCATION REVIEW. 1968.
Cornmarket Press Ltd., 42/3 Conduit Street, London W1R 0NL.
3, =   Higher education in the UK.
Book notices, book reviews, monographic articles, parliamentary reports.
No Index.
T.p. 82, Ad.p. 8.
Per copy 50p, per year £1.50.
Indexed in: BEI.

1289 RESEARCH INTO HIGHER EDUCATION ABSTRACTS. 1966.
Society for Research into Higher Education, 25 Northampton Square, London, EC1V 0HL.

4, + *   Abstracts of articles and books reporting results of research into all aspects of higher education.
A, June, Yes, None.
October 1970, T.p. 44, Ad.p. 2,   900.
Per copy £1, per year £4.

1290 SECONDARY EDUCATION. 1970.
(Higher Education Journal, 1936-1970)
National Union of Teachers, Hamilton House, Mabledon Place, London, WC1H 9BD.
3, * † +   Secondary and higher education.
Book notices, book reviews, monographic articles.
No Index.
Spring, 1972, T.p. 44, Ad.p. 7.   30000.
Per copy 25p, per year 75p, and supplied free on ratio basis to NUT members in secondary schools etc.

1291 SESAME: the newspaper of the Open University. 1972.
The Open University, Walton Hall, Beltchley, Bucks.
9, *   Educational subjects of interest to students, full-time staff and part-time staff of the Open University.
Letters, articles.
No Index.
May 1972, T.p. 10, Ad.p. 2.
Free.

1292 TIMES HIGHER EDUCATION SUPPLEMENT. 1971.
Times Publishing Co., Printing House Square, London, EC4.
52, = .
Book reviews, letters, articles.
No Index.
Per copy 8p.

1293 UNIVERSITY EQUIPMENT. 1968.
Benn Brothers Ltd., Lyon Tower, 125 High Street, Colliers Wood, London, SW19 2JN.
6, =.
Book reviews, new products.
No Index.
Free, controlled circulation.

1294 THE VOCATIONAL ASPECT OF EDUCATION. 1969.
(The Vocational Aspect of Secondary and Further Education, 1948-1968).
V.A. Dept., Bolton College of Education (Technical), Chadwick St., Bolton, Lancs. BL2 1JW.
3, ‡ +   All aspects of technical, vocational and further education and vocational guidance. Reports on research projects and reviews of books in these fields.
Book reviews, monographic articles.
A, Autumn, No, None.
Autumn 1970, T.p. 60, Ad.p. 2.   2000.
Per copy 75p, per year £1.75.
Indexed in: BEI.

1295 WHICH COURSE? 1972.
Dominion Press Ltd., Grand Buildings, Trafalgar Square, London, WC2.
○   For school leavers entering further education.
No Index.
Free, controlled circulation.

38
COMMERCE. TRADE

1296 ACHIEVEMENT: A business link between Britain and the United States. 1939.
World Trade Magazine Limited, 13 New Bridge Street, London, EC4V 6HH.
12, =   To interest the American industrialist in the goods and services available from Britain. Stories of what British companies are doing, particularly in relation to the American market.
Book notices, book reviews, letters, articles, new companies, new products, tests.
No Index.
June 1972, T.p. 20, Ad.p. 18.   10000.
Per copy 20p, per year £2.40.

1297 BANK OF ENGLAND QUARTERLY BULLETIN. 1960.
Economic Intelligence Department, Bank of England, London, EC2R 8AH.
4, + ‡ ○   Includes a regular commentary on the current economic and financial situation, an analysis of financial flows between sectors and a statistical annex, together with articles on related topics including research.
A, March, Yes, 10 year.
June 1972, T.p. 150.
Free.

1298 BARCLAYS INTERNATIONAL QUARTERLY. 1972.
(D C O Quarterly, 1966-1971)
Barclays Bank International Ltd., 54 Lombard Street, London, EC3P 3AH.
4, = †
Book reviews, letters, articles, obituaries.
2 yearly, —, Yes, None.
February 1972, T.p. 80.   16500.
Per copy 25p.

1299 BARCLAYS INTERNATIONAL REVIEW: a monthly economic and trade review. 1971.
(Barclays Oversease Review, 1947-Oct. 1971).
Barclays Bank International Ltd., 54 Lombard Street, London, EC3P 3AH.
12, =   Trade, economic and financial trends in some 33 countries.
Commodity prices, new companies, new products.
No Index.
June 1972, T.p. 64,   29000.
Free.

1300 BARCLAYS REVIEW. 1971.
(Barclays Bank Review, 1919-1971).
Barclays Bank, 54 Lombard Street, London, EC3.
4, =   A review, through articles, notes and statistical tables of current economic and financial affairs, both of the United Kingdom and the world.
2 year, —, Yes, None.
May 1972, T.p. 48.   43000.
Free.
Indexed in: BHI.

1301 BUSINESS MONITOR. 1962.
H.M.S.O., P.O.Box 569, London, SE1 9NH.
Irregular, = + ‡   Collective title of over 130 separately available statistical bulletins published monthly (M), quarterly (Q), or annually (A) in the following four series: Production Series—114 titles; Civil Aviation Series—8 titles; Service and Distributive Series—8 titles; Miscellaneous Series—7 titles. New titles added to the series are announced in 'Trade and Industry' when they first appear.
No Index.
Subscription varies with each series.

1303 COMPANY INFORMATION: Jordan's Selected Service. 1971.
(Jordan's Daily Register 1895-1971).
Jordan & Sons Limited (Jordan's Group Limited), Wilec House, 82 City Road, London, EC1Y 2BX.
254, = +   Detailing every new English or Welsh company, showing principal objects, registered office, management and division of capital; Limited Partnerships; Overseas Companies trading in Great Britain. Selected abstracts available as required.
Abstracts, new companies.
No Index.
5.6.72, T.p. 41.   200.
£30-£120 p.a. according to selection.

1304 FOCUS ON INDUSTRY AND COMMERCE. 1952.
North Staffordshire Chamber of Commerce & Industry, Winton House, Stoke Road, Stoke-on-Trent.
12, =
Book notices, book reviews, legal notes, monographic, articles, news, new products.
No Index.
T.p. 20, Ad.p. 32.
Free, Controlled circulation.

1305 JOURNAL OF COMMERCE. 1826.
(Journal of Commerce & Shipping Telegraph).
Journal of Commerce, Liverpool.
Daily, = ‡ Transport news, insurance, shipbuilding.
Book notices, book reviews, commodity prices, legal notes, letters, articles, new companies, new products.
No Index.
T.p. 8, Ad.p. Most.
Per copy 5p.

1306 KNIGHT'S INDUSTRIAL REPORTS.
Charles Knight & Co. Ltd., 11-12 Bury Street, London, EC3A 5AP.
12, = + Texts/Summaries of legal decisions, statutory Instruments and statutes which affect industry in any way.
6m, —, Yes, None.
Per year £16.

1307 LLOYDS BANK REVIEW. 1946.
(Lloyds Bank Monthly Financial Report 1917-1921; Lloyds Bank Monthly 1921-1930; Lloyds Bank Monthly Review 1930-1939).
Lloyds Bank Limited, 71 Lombard Street, London, EC3.
4, ○ General economic matters.
Articles, charts.
Cumulative index 1946-1966.
April 1972, T.p. 84.
Free.
Index in: BHI.

1308 MARKET PLACE. 1972.
Traden Publications, Charlton Place, Downing Street, Manchester.
52, ○
No Index.
Subscription on application.

1309 MERCANTILE GUARDIAN. 1885.
Benn Brothers Ltd., Lyon Tower, 125 High Street, Colliers Wood, SW19 2JN.
12, ‡ = Britain's leading export sales journal promoting the sale of consumer & industrial products, circulating to over 8,000 leading importers of British goods in important World market areas.
Monographic articles, new companies, new products.
No Index.
August 1972, T.p. 28, Ad.p. 44.   9830.
Per copy 40p, per year £3.50.

1310 MIDLAND BANK REVIEW. 1916.
Midland Bank Ltd., Economics Dept., Poultry, London. EC2P 2BX.
4, ‡ + World economics.
Articles.
A, —, Yes, 10 year.
May 1972, T.p. 36.   50000.
Free.
Indexed in: BHI

1311 MOODIES INFORMATION SERVICES.
BRITISH SERVICES:
MOODIECARDS. Full particulars of the financial records of some 4500 U.K. quoted companies. £260.
MOODIES REVIEW. Weekly London market letter. £12.75.
CHARTS. Charts of earnings, dividends and prices on some 1000 companies. £24.20.
INDUSTRIES & COMMODITIES. Surveys and statistics on some 70 industries and commodities. £27.50.
TAXATION. Updated Budget Day Price adjustments on quoted shares and fixed interest stocks. £15.
SHARE ISSUES. Details of all issues, acquisitions, etc. £11.
EQUITY DIVIDEND RECORD. Updated dividend details on all quoted companies in U.K. £10.
FIXED INTEREST AND PREFERENCE PAYMENTS. Full details of all Fixed Interest Payments and Preference Dividends relating to U.K. quoted stocks. £10.
INVESTMENT HANDBOOKS. Two convenient quarterly volumes covering 1000 companies. £18.50.
AUSTRALIAN SERVICES:
AUSTRALIAN CARDS: MoodieCards on some 350 Australian companies. £26.40.
AUSTRALIAN REVIEW. Monthly Australian market letter. £6.60.
AUSTRALIAN DIVIDEND RECORD. Updated Dividend details on Australian companies. £5.50.
SOUTH AFRICAN SERVICES:
SOUTH AFRICAN CARDS. MoodieCards on some 250 South African companies. £24.20.
SOUTH AFRICAN REVIEW. Monthly South African market letter. £6.60.
SOUTH AFRICAN DIVIDEND RECORD. Updated Dividend details on South African companies. £5.50.
EUROPEAN SERVICE:
INTERNATIONAL BONDS. Full information on International Bond Issues. £48.40.
AMERICAN AND CANADIAN SERVICES:
CANADIAN CARDS. MoodieCards on some 150 Canadian companies. £17.60.
INDUSTRIAL MANUAL. Covers every industrial firm listed on American Stock Exchanges, plus some important unlisted companies + weekly updating supplements (published July). £98.
OTC INDUSTRIAL MANUAL. Contains information on 3300 actively traded over-the counter industrial corporations + weekly updating supplements. (published July). £89.
BANKS & FINANCE MANUAL. Facts, statistics and pertinent details on over 9300 financial enterprises in U.S. + weekly updating supplements. (published April). £77.
PUBLIC UTILITIES MANUAL. Detailed descriptions of approx. 600 public utility corporations in U.S. + weekly updating supplements. (published August). £75.
TRANSPORTATION MANUAL. Reliable source of information on over 900 U.S. and Canadian corporations + weekly updating supplements. (published September). £75.
MUNICIPAL & GOVERNMENTS MANUAL. Comprehensive data on over 13000 U.S. and foreign government agencies, etc., + weekly updating supplements. (published January). £124.
STOCK SURVEY. Weekly American newsletter. £50.
BOND SURVEY. Weekly report on all developments affecting U.S. Bonds. £60.
HANDBOOK OF COMMON STOCKS. Quarterly volume on over 2000 Common Stocks. £24.
DIVIDEND RECORD. Updated Dividend details on over 9500 issues. £40.

Moodies Services, 6-8 Bonhill Street, London, EC2A 4BU.
=

1312 MULTINATIONAL BUSINESS. 1971.
The Economist Intelligence Unit Ltd., Spencer House, 27 St. James's Place, London, SW1A 1NT.
4, ‡ + A guide to multinational corporate enterprise intended for those who are engaged in—or need to keep pace with—its rapid development.

No Index.
T.p. 44.
Per copy £15, per year £40.

1313 NATIONAL WESTMINSTER. 1968.
(The Westminster).
National Westminster Bank, 75 Shaftesbury Avenue, London W1V 8AT.
6, + =   Staff journal giving news and view of banking and social activities.
Book reviews, letters, articles, obituaries.
No Index.
June 1970, T.p. 66, Ad.p. 20.
Free.

1314 NATIONAL WESTMINSTER BANK QUARTERLY REVIEW. 1968.
National Westminster Bank Ltd., 41 Lothbury, London, EC2.
4, ‡ =   Financial, economic and political affairs.
Monographic articles.
A, −, Yes, None.
May 1972, T.p. 60.
Free.
Indexed in: BHI

1315 QUARTERLY ECONOMIC REVIEWS. 1952.
The Economist Intelligence Unit Ltd., Spencer House, 27 St. James's Place, London, SW1A 1NT.
4, ‡ = +   Current economic and business intelligence, backed by comment and statistical analysis, for about 150 countries in 70 sections.
No Index.
T.p.c. 20
Per copy £4.50, per year varies according to numbers taken.

1316 SUPPLY ESTIMATES. 1970-71.
(Civil Estimates, 1853-4 to 1969-70).
H.M.S.O., P.O. Box 569, London, SE1.
1, +   12 separate classes are issued separately during the Spring of each year and are republished in one gathering together with index in May or June.
No Index.
1972-73, T.p. 780.
Per copy £6.50.

1317 THE THREE BANKS REVIEW. 1949.
National and Commercial Banking Group Ltd., 3 Bishopsgate, London EC2N 3AA.
4, +   General economic, government and financial topics of interest to the official and business world and to academic economists and students. UK banking history.
Monographic articles.
No Index.
June 1972, T.p. 78.   39000.
Free.

1318 TOWER TIMES. 1971.
World Trade Centre, 52 St. Katharine's Way, London, E1.
4, = *   Journal of World Trade Centre London, the British member of the World Trade Centers Association; circulates to industrialists, bankers, chambers of commerce, Members of Parliament, trade missions, UK embassies, etc.
Summer 1972, T.p. 5, Ad. p. 1.   7500.
Free.

1319 TRADE AND INDUSTRY: incorporating the Board of Trade Journal and New Technology. 1970.
(Board of Trade Journal, 1886-1970).
H.M.S.O., P.O. Box 569, London SE1 9NH.
52, = ‡   Official announcements relating to trade and industry; overseas trade and exports; information on customs duties and import regulations of overseas countries; statistics of trade, production and prices. Incorporates *New Technology* as a monthly supplement.
Book notices, book reviews, commodity prices, monographic articles, new companies, new products, parliamentary reports, standards, tests.
Q, 5th issue of following volume, Yes, None.
13 July 1972, T.p. 46, Ad.p. 4.   12000.
Per copy 10p, per year £7.60.

1320 TRADING ACCOUNTS AND BALANCE SHEETS: accounts and balance sheets of certain trading or commercial services conducted by government departments in the year. 1920.
H.M.S.O., P.O. Box 569, London, SE1.
1, +
No Index.
1970-71, T.p. 90.
Per copy 74p.

1321 TRADING AND OTHER ACCOUNTS. 1922.
H.M.S.O., Chichester St., Belfast, BT1 4JY.
1, ‡   Trading accounts of the government departments in N.I.
Parliamentary reports.
A, With Volume, Yes, None.
December/January 1972, T.p. 80.
Per copy 89p.

1322 THE U.K. EXPORTER'S GUIDE TO PAYMENTS RISKS & IMPORT REGULATIONS ABROAD. 1971.
(A Guide to Payments Risks & Import Regulations Abroad).
Barclays Bank, Economic Intelligence Department, 54 Lombard Street, London EC3.
3, =   Those factors essential in making an initial appraisal of an overseas market (viz. economic prospects, exchange rates, import regulations) for each of 130 countries.
No Index.
May 1972, T.p. 60.   22000.
Free.

1323 VISION: European Business Magazine. 1971.
17 Stratton Street, London W1X 5FD.
6, =
No Index.
Subscription on application.

380.8

TOURISM

1324 INTERNATIONAL TOURISM QUARTERLY. 1971.
The Economist Intelligence Unit Ltd., Spencer House, 27 St. James's Place, London, SW1A 1NT.
4, + =   Data, comment and analysis for the world tourism industry. A practical guide for those whose business it is to isolate trends in tourism and plan for its growth.
No Index.
T.p. 52.
Per copy £6, per year £20.

381

CHAMBERS OF COMMERCE

1325 ABERDEEN CHAMBER OF COMMERCE JOURNAL. 1919.
15 Union Terrace, Aberdeen, AB9 1HF.
4, ○ ‡ = +
Articles, new products.

Key to reference symbols

○ popular   ‡ technical   = trade/professional

+ research   * society/institution   † house journal

4 year, 1967, Yes, None.
T.p. 27, Ad.p. 28.   1650.
Per copy 10p, per year 40p.
Free to members.

1326 BARNSLEY. Offical journal of Barnsley & District Chamber of Commerce. 1964
Marylebone Press, 276/282 Corn Exchange, Manchester, M4 3HF.
4, =
No Index.
T.p. 18, Ad.p. 14.
Free to members.

1327 C & T: LUTON COMMERCE & TRADE JOURNAL. 1947.
White Crescent Press Ltd., Crescent Road, Luton, Beds.
6, =
No Index.
T.p. 13, Ad.p. 11.   2000.
Free to members.

1328 COVENTRY COMMERCE: Monthly Publication of Coventry Chamber of Commerce, Inc. 1965.
(Coventry Chamber of Commerce Journal 1930-1964).
Coventry Chamber of Commerce, Station Tower, Station Square, Coventry, CV1 2GG.
12, =
Book notices, book reviews, letters, articles, new companies, parliamentary reports.
No Index.
May 1972, T.p. 16, Ad.p. 20.   1000.
Per copy 25p, per year £3.

1329 DUNDEE CHAMBER OF COMMERCE JOURNAL: Industry in the Tayside Region. 1958.
Dundee Chamber of Commerce, Chamber of Commerce Buildings, Panmure Street, Dundee DD1 1ED.
4, =   Trade & industrial activities in the region.
Book reviews, articles, obituaries.
2 year, —, No, None.
March 1972, T.p. 46, Ad.p. 52.   2000.
Per copy 20p, per year £1.

1330 EASTERN EUROPE. 1971.
London Chamber of Commerce & Industry, 69 Cannon Street, London EC4N 5AB.
26, =
No Index.
Per year £24.

1331 EDINBURGH CHAMBER OF COMMERCE AND MANUFACTURERS QUARTERLY JOURNAL.
Featherhall Press Ltd., Featherhall Avenue, Edinburgh 22.
4, =
Book reviews, monographic articles, news, obituaries.
No Index.
T.p. 12, Ad.p. 44.   2200.
Free to members.

1332 FORUM. 1971.
(North West Lancashire Chambers of Commerce Journal).
Mather Bros. Ltd., 1 Garstang Road, Preston.
12, =   Management in the area covering Preston, Wigan, Chorley, Fylde Coast, Lancaster & Kendal. Trade unions, foreign embassies and chambers of commerce in UK and British commercial posts overseas.
Book notices, book reviews, legal notes, articles, patents, standards, tests.
No Index.
May 1972, T.p. 14, Ad.p. 10.
Free to members.

1333 HOME & ECONOMIC AFFAIRS NEWSLETTER. 1969.
London Chamber of Commerce & Industry, 69 Cannon St., EC4N 5AB.
23, =   Digest of up-to-date factual information of interest to the businessman and notes on London Chamber activities.
Book notices, legal notes, new companies, parliamentary reports, standards.
No Index.
May 1972, T.p. 2. c. 9000.
Free to members.

1334 THE HUB: Journal of the Sheffield Junior Chamber of Commerce. 1950.
(The Anvil ?-1950).
Sheffield Junior Chamber of Commerce, Cutler's Hall, Sheffield 1.
12, ‡ = +   Activities & interests of members of the Chamber.
Letters, articles, tests.
No Index.
April 1972, T.p. 12, Ad.p. 12.   800.
Per copy 12½p, per year £1.50.

1335 INDUSTRIAL NOTTINGHAM. 1916.
Nottingham Chamber of Commerce & Industry, 395 Mansfield Road, Nottingham, NG5 2DL.
12, = †   News and events in Nottingham area.
Book notices, book reviews, legal notes, letters, monographic articles, new products, obituaries, parliamentary reports.
No Index.
April 1972, T.p. 64, Ad.p. 57.   1800.
Per year £1.

1336 INDUSTRIAL TYNESIDE.
Tyne & Wear Chamber of Commerce, 4 St. Nicholas Buildings, Newcastle on Tyne, NE1 1RR.
12, =   News & comment on the industrial & commercial scene.
No Index.
August 1970, T.p. 15, Ad.p. 2.
Per copy 5p.

1337 THE JOURNAL: Glasgow Chamber of Commerce. 1966.
(Glasgow Chamber of Commerce Journal 1917-1965).
Glasgow Chamber of Commerce, 30 George Square, Glasgow G2 1EQ.
12, =   Industrial & commercial affairs.
Book notices, book reviews, legal notes, letters, articles, new companies, new products, obituaries, parliamentary reports, patents.
No Index.
June 1972, T.p. 26, Ad.p. 20.   4020.
Per copy 15p, per year £2.50.

1338 JOURNAL OF THE LEICESTER AND COUNTY CHAMBER OF COMMERCE AND INDUSTRY. 1928.
Leicester and County Chamber of Commerce and Industry, 4 Horsefair Street, Leicester LE1 6EA.
12, =   Topics of a commercial and industrial nature of general interest to members of a mixed industry/profession association.
Book reviews, legal notes, letters, articles, new companies, new products, obituaries, parliamentary reports, patents, standards, tests.
No Index.
May 1972, T.p. 24, Ad.p. 16.
Per copy 5p, per year 60p.
Free to members.

1339 THE LEEDS JOURNAL: Journal of the Leeds Chamber of Commerce and Industry. 1929.
Leeds Chamber of Commerce & Industry, 9 Quebec Street, Leeds, LS1 2HD.
12, * —
Book reviews, legal notes, letters, articles, new companies, new products, parliamentary reports, patents, standards, tests.

A, April, Yes, None.
June 1972, T.p. 17, Ad.p. 38.   3312.
Per copy 15p, per year £2.88.

1340 THE LINK: the news journal of the Hornchurch and District Chamber of Commerce and Industry. 1949.
c/o Harold Wood Printing Co. Ltd., 115 Victoria Road, Romford, Essex, RM1 2NH.
6, =   News for members.
No Index.
August 1972, T.p. 10, Ad.p. 6.
Free to members.

1341 MEDWAY: The quarterly journal of the Medway Chamber of Commerce. 1947.
Medway Chamber of Commerce, 21 Railway Street, Chatham, Kent.
4, =   Industrial, trade & professional news of the Chamber covering the Medway Area (Chatham, Rochester, Gillingham, Strood, Rainham & outlying villages).
No Index.
Spring 1972, T.p. 10, Ad.p. 14.   1000.
Per copy 10p, per year 40p.

1342 MERSEYSIDE BUSINESS NEWS. 1970.
(Merseyside Industrial & Commercial News 1967-1970).
Kershaw Publications (Gordon Kerr Ltd), 46 The Albany, Liverpool, L3 9EG.
12, =   Developments on Merseyside relating to Commerce & Industry & News of the Merseyside Chamber of Commerce.
Book reviews, letters, new companies, new products.
No Index.
May 1972, T.p. 18, Ad.p. 20.   6500.
Per copy 10p, per year £2.20.

1343 MIDLANDS INDUSTRY & COMMERCE: The Birminham & West Midlands Chambers of Commerce Journal. 1958.
(Birmingham Chamber of Commerce Journal 1901-1957).
Birmingham Chamber of Commerce & Industry, 75 Harborne Road, Edgbaston, Birmingham, B15 3DH.
12, ‡ = *   Chamber of Commerce affairs; industrial and commercial matters; international matters, including exports; subjects of importance to firms in the West Midlands area.
Book notices, book reviews, legal notes, articles, new products, obituaries.
A, –, No, None.
June 1972, T.p. 33, Ad.p. 65.   7428.
Per year £2.50.

1344 NATIONAL CHAMBER OF TRADE JOURNAL. 1939.
National Chamber of Trade, Enterprise House, Henley-on-Thames, Oxon.
4, =   Retail trading throughout U.K. also services trading.
Book reviews, commodity prices, legal notes, letters, articles, obituaries, parliamentary reports, standards, tests.
No Index.
May 1972, T.p. 31.   20000.
Per year 30p.
Free to members.

1345 PRODUCTION EXCHANGE: Northern Executive. 1969.
Engineering Industries Association, 15 Walker Terrace, Prince Consort Road, Gateshead-on-Tyne, 8.
6, ‡ = + *   Information & news of Northern business.
Book notices, book reviews, letters, monographic articles, new companies, new products, patents, standards, tests.
No Index.
No. 12, 1971, T.p. 40, Ad.p. 30.   4000.
Free.

1346 RECORD. 1971.
(Monthly Record—1870-1970).
Manchester Chamber of Commerce & Industry, P.O. Box 559, Ship Canal House, King Street, Manchester, M60 2HB.
12, = + †   News of topical interest to industry, commerce and the professions, including statistics.
Book notices, book reviews, commodity prices, legal notes, articles, new companies, new products, obituaries, parliamentary reports, patents.
A, January, Yes, None.
June 1972, T.p. 16, Ad.p. 24.   4000.
Per copy 25p, per year £3.

381.5

RETAIL TRADE

1347 SHOP PROPERTY. 1967.
Newman Books Limited, 48 Poland Street, London, W1V 4PP.
12, =   Shopping facilities and premises.
Book notices, book reviews, legal notes, letters, articles.
No Index.
May 1972, T.p. 18, Ad.p. 18.   5500.
Per copy 25p, per year £3.

382

INTERNATIONAL TRADE

1348 AFRICAN DEVELOPMENT. 1966.
African Buyer & Trader Ltd., Wheatsheaf House, Carmelite Street, London EC4Y OAX.
12, = + ‡   Economic and business affairs throughout the African continent, featuring commercial information, projects, contracts, mining, communications, and general economic surveys on African countries.
Book notices, book reviews, commodity prices, letters, monographic articles, new companies, new products.
No Index.
June 1972, T.p. 50, Ad.p. 40.
Per year £5.50.

1349 ANGLO AMERICAN TRADE NEWS.
American Chamber of Commerce (U.K.), 73 Brook Street, London, W1Y 2EB.
12, =   Developments in British-American trade, trade legislation, new products, company news, personnel movement, speeches by government or industrial spokesmen, tax legislation (British or American).
Book notices, book reviews, legal notes, letters, monographic articles, new companies, new products, obituaries.
No Index.
T.p. 26, Ad.p. 18.   2500.
Per year £2.40.

1350 BRAZILIAN BULLETIN. 1972.
Brazilian Embassy, Commercial Section, 15 Berkeley Street, London, W1X 5AE.
12, =   Aspects of the Brazilian economy and outstanding topical subject. News of trade and industrial development in Brazil. Anglo-Brazilian trade news and commercial opportunities. Legal notices. Selected indicators.
No Index.
June 1972, T.p. 17, Ad.p. 11.   950.
Free.

1351 BRITAIN AND OVERSEAS. 1971.
(Monthly Bulletin—Commonwealth Industries Association. 1941-1970).
Commonwealth Industries Association, 6/14 Dean Farrar Street, London, SW1H ODX.

6, = News and views on Britain's economy and our role in overseas trade payments with special emphasis on the need to maintain our traditional open seas policy in the interests of the Commonwealth and other overseas connections.
No Index.
May/June 1972, T.p. 16.

1352 CHINA TRADE AND ECONOMIC NEWSLETTER. 1955.
Monitor Consultants, 35 John Street, London WC1N 2AT.
12, + = ‡ Exclusive information service drawing directly on the experience of firms regularly involved in the trade and on first-hand study of economic conditions in China, with supporting statistics from official sources and commodity notes from market specialists.
Book notices, book reviews, commodity prices, articles, new companies.
No Index.
May 1972, T.p. 12. 300.
Per copy 75p, per year £9.

1353 COMMONWEALTH TRADE. 1949.
Commonwealth Secretariat, Marlborough House, Pall Mall, London, SW1Y 5HX.
1, + Statistical and textual accounts of trade.
No Index.
1970, T.p. 131.
Per copy £1.50.

1354 EUROPEAN REVIEWS. 1962.
(European-Atlantic Review 1956-1961).
Birkett Press Ltd., 64 Kingsway, London, WC2.
4, = + ‡ All aspects of trade with Europe.
Book notices, book reviews, letters, articles, news.
No Index.
T.p. 22, Ad.p. 12. 7000.
Per copy 12½p, per year 50p.

1355 FAR EAST TRADE & DEVELOPMENT. 1946.
Laurence French Publications Ltd., 3 Belsize Crescent, London, NW3 5QZ.
12, ‡ = + East/West trade and development relations. Reports on Asian, including Chinese, development, East/West business activities, trade and industrial trends.
Letters, articles, new companies.
No Index.
March 1972, T.) T.p. 29, Ad.p. 14. 10000.
Per copy 25p, per year £4.

1356 MIDDLE EAST ECONOMIC DIGEST: MEED. 1957.
Economic Features Limited, 84-86 Chancery Lane, London, WC2A 1DL.
52, ‡ = + Economic and commercial and industrial news, reviews, statistics of Middle East.
Book notices, book reviews, commodity prices, monographic articles.
A, —, Yes, None.
2.6.1972, T.p. 23, Ad.p. 5. 2000.
Per copy 75p, per year £37.50.

1357 OVERSEAS TRADE STATISTICS OF THE UNITED KINGDOM. 1971.
(Overseas Trade Accounts of the United Kingdom, 1965-1970; Accounts Relating to Trade and Navigation of the United Kingdom, 1848-1964.)
H.M.S.O., P.O. Box 569, London, SE1 9NH.
12, + Statistics of the overseas trade of the United Kingdom compiled from declarations made to H.M. Customs & Excise. Detailed statistics of imports and exports are given by both commodity and country.
M, —, No, None.
May, 1972, T.p. 506. 1500.
Per copy £1.85, per year £25.05.

1358 SINO BRITISH TRADE. 1964.
Sino British Trade Council, 25 Queen Anne's Gate, London, SW1H 9BU.
12, = UK/China trade and other countries' trade with China. China's economy in general.
No Index.
March 1972, T.p. 8, 600.
Per year £5.

1359 TRADE PARTNERS: Journal of East-West Trade. 1962.
Hill and Tyler Limited, Nottingham.
4, ‡ = British products, techniques, business projects and companies likely to be of interest to works managers, specialists and trade officials in the USSR, China, Poland, Czechoslovakia, Hungary, Romania, Bulgaria, Eastern Germany, Albania, Mongolia, North Korea, North Vietnam and Cuba.
Book notices, commodity prices, articles, new companies, new products, patents, standards, tests.
No Index.
April 1972, T.p. 11, Ad.p. 9. 5000.
Per copy 25p, per year £1.

1360 VOX. 1966.
Voluntary Committee on Overseas Aid and Development, 69 Victoria Street, London, SW1.
12, ○ * News and features about world development issues and about activities (especially in Britain) designed to promote development, with relevant comment, correspondence and book and film reviews.
Book notices, book reviews, letters, articles, parliamentary reports.
No Index.
June 1972, T.p. 16. 1600.
Per copy 7p, per year 80p.

1361 WEST INDIAN REVIEW. 1972.
(Jamaican & West Indian Review).
Arawak Press Ltd., The Penthouse, Glenwood House, Dorking, Surrey.
4, =
No Index.
Per copy 18p.

1362 WEST INDIES CHRONICLE. 1966.
(Chronicle of the West India Committee 1959-1966; West India Committee Circular 1886-1959).
The West India Committee, 18 Grosvenor Street, London, W1X 0HD.
12, = ○ ‡ + Business, politics, history and general news on the West Indies.
Book notices, book reviews, commodity prices, letters, articles, new companies, new products, obituaries, parliamentary reports.
A, —, Yes, None.
June 1972, T.p. 30, Ad.p. 19. 3500.
Per copy 50p, per year £6.

382.5

IMPORT TRADE

1363 IMPORT: for export import and mail order. 1963.
James Pike Ltd., St. Ives, Cornwall.
6, ‡ Products, new and established, available for importing to any country from any country.
New products.
No Index.
12500.
Per year £2.50. Controlled circulation

382.6

EXPORT TRADE

1364 BRITISH EXPORT GAZETTE. 1892.
British Export Gazette, Flat 2, 1f Oval Road, Regents Park, London NW1.

12, = + ‡   Exporting of British products world-wide.
Book notices, book reviews, commodity prices, letters, new companies, new products, patents, standards, tests.
No Index.
T.p. 48, Ad.p. 24.
Per copy 20p, per year £2.25.

1365 BRITISH TRADE JOURNAL AND EXPORT WORLD. 1863.
Benn Bros. Ltd., 154 Fleet Street, London EC4.
12, =   Specifications of new British capital goods for export only.
No Index.
T.p. 14, Ad.p. 18.   9000.
Per copy 25p, per year £2.75.

1366 CRONER'S EXPORT DIGEST. 1958.
Croner Publications Ltd., 46/50 Coombe Road, New Malden, Surrey.
12, =
Book reviews, new companies, news, new products.
No Index.
T.p. 30, Ad.p. 28.   12000
Subscription on application.

1367 EXPORT COURIER: Product information for international buyers. 1967.
Stokes & Lindley-Jones Limited., 21 Montpelier Row, Blackheath, London, SE3 0SR.
16, =   Colourful exposure of British consumer goods among buyers abroad. Each issue concentrates on one class of product. Circulation is appropriately directed.
New Products.
No Index.
3/72, T.p. 4, Ad.p. 96.   10334.

1368 EXPORT DIRECTION: The Journal for export decision makers. 1970.
Special Interest Publications Ltd., 196 Shaftesbury Avenue, London WC2.
12, ‡ =   For senior export management talking about exporting techniques in relation to direct selling, overseas subsids, licensing. Coverage and evaluation of export services: shipping, financial promotional, marketing, translation etc.
Book notices, book reviews, legal notes, letters, monographic articles, new companies, new products, standards.
No Index.
30000.
Per year £4.50.

1369 HUMBERSIDE EXPORT NEWS. 1972.
Treharne Publications (Hull) Ltd., Midland Bank Chambers, 9 Lairgate, Beverley, East Yorkshire.
6, =   Humber and worldwide business connections.
Book notices, commodity prices, legal notes, letters, articles, new companies, new products, parliamentary reports, patents, standards, tests.
No Index.
T.p. 16, Ad.p. 4.
Per copy 10p, per year £2.

383/388

COMMUNICATIONS. TRANSPORT

1370 ABC GOODS TRANSPORT GUIDE.
Illife Transport Publications Ltd., Dorset House, Stamford Street, London, SE1
2, =
No Index.
Subscription on application.

1371 ABC GUIDE TO INTERNATIONAL TRAVEL.
(International Travel Requirements.)
ABC Travel Guides Ltd., (IPC Business Press Ltd.) Oldhill, London Road, Dunstable, Beds.
4, = ‡   Guide containing essential information on the passport, visa, health and currency regulations, together with customs import allowances, climate, business hours and languages for every country in the world.
No Index.
T.p. 60.
Subscription on application.

1372 BUSINESS TRAVEL WORLD. 1972.
(Business Travel, 1961-1972, Travel World 1950-1972.)
Blandford Press Ltd., 167 High Holborn, London, WC1V 6PH.
=   New services, in air, sea, rail, road transportation. Accommodation for business man worldwide. Conference and convention facilities. Commentaries. Appointments. Institutional and Guild news.
Book reviews, letters, articles, new companies, new products, obituaries, tests.
No Index.
June 1972, T.p. 15, Ad.p. 17.   15000.
Per copy 10p, per year £1.25.
Free, Controlled circulation.

1373 THE CHARTERED INSTITUTE OF TRANSPORT JOURNAL. 1971
(Institute of Transport Journal, 1962-1971; Journal of the Institute of Transport 1920-1961)
The Chartered Institute of Transport, 80 Portland Place, London W1N 4DP.
6 * = ‡   All forms of transport broadly organisational operational or commercial.
Book notices, book reviews, legal notes, letters, monographic articles.
2 year, —, Yes, None
May 1972, T.p. 42, Ad.p. 6.   16000.
Per copy 42p, per year £2.50.

1374 COOK'S CONTINENTAL TIMETABLE: A simple guide to the principal rail services of Europe, North Africa and the Near East, with local shipping services in the North Sea, the Baltic and the Mediterranean. 1873.
Cooks/Midland Bank, 45 Berkeley Street, London, W1A 1EB.
12,   Designed for quick and accurate use. Each country's tables are preceded by a diagram map with table numbers on every line.
No Index.
6, 1973, T.p. 472, Ad.p. 12.   12185.
Per copy £1, per year £11.50.

1375 EXPEDITION NEWS. 1970.
World Expeditionary Association, 22 Beauchamp Place, London, SW3.
3, O   Information of general interest to expedition organisers.
No Index.
Summer 1972, T.p. 6.
Free to members.

1376 ITF JOURNAL.
International Transport Workers' Federation Maritime House, Old Town, Clapham, London, SW4 0JR.
4, = *
No Index.
T.p. 24.
Per year £1.50.

1377 ITF NEWSLETTER.
International Transport Workers' Federation, Maritime House, Old Town, Clapham, London, SW4 0JR.
12, = *
No Index.
Per year £2.

1378 INTER-CITY ABC.
ABC Travel Guides Ltd., (Member of IPC Business Press Ltd.), Oldhill, London Road, Dunstable, Beds.
12, =   Timetable giving in one volume nationwide Inter-City services in Great Britain. Other information includes fares, pullmans, sleepers, meals and refreshments on trains and rail/air links Heathrow and Gatwick.
No Index.
July 1972, T.p. 192.
Per copy 30p, per year £4.38.

1379 INTERNATIONAL TOURISM QUARTERLY. 1971.
Economist Intelligence Unit Ltd., 27 St. James's Place, London, SW1.
4, ‡ +   Collation and analysis of tourism problems and in depth surveys.
Monographic articles, statistical data.
No Index.
No. 1, 1971, T.p. 80.
Subscription on Application.

1380 JOURNAL OF TRANSPORT ECONOMICS AND POLICY 1967.
London School of Economics and Political Science, Houghton Street, Aldwych, London, WC2A 2AE.
3, ‡ +   All forms of transport, also traffic engineering, planning and economic aspects.
Book notices, book reviews, monographic articles,
A, January, Yes, None.
May 1972, T.p. 123, Ad.p. 5.
Per copy £1.50, per year £3.50

1381 THE JOURNAL OF TRANSPORT HISTORY: New Series. 1971.
(First Series 1953-1966).
Leicester University Press, 2 University Road, Leicester LE1 7RB.
2, + =   History of transport as a whole, embracing all periods and all countries, whilst giving particular attention to the United Kingdom.
Book reviews, monographic articles, bibliography.
2 yearly, September (with No. 4 of each vol.), Yes, None.
February 1972, T.p. 64.   500.
Per copy £1.25, per year £2.
Indexed in: BHI.

1382 KNOW BRITAIN.
Educational Productions Ltd., 27/28 Maunsel Street, London, SW1.
Seasonal, ○   Travel magazine.
Book reviews, articles.
No Index.
Free, controlled circulation.

1383 TRANSPORT HISTORY. 1968.
David & Charles (Publishers) Ltd., South Devon House, Newton Abbot, Devon.
3, ○ +   History of all methods of transport with special emphasis on economic and social history affected by transport change.
Book reviews, monographic articles.
A, November, Yes, None.
Per copy 75p, per year £2.25.

1384 YOUTH TRAVELS. 1968.
Educational Interchanges Council, 43 Russell Square, London, WC1B 5DG.
1, ○   Details of youth travel facilities including family exchanges.
No Index.
1972, T.p. 16.
Per copy 2p.

383

POSTAL SERVICES

1385 POSTAL HISTORY INTERNATIONAL. 1972.
Proud-Bailey Company Limited, 96 Queen's Road, Brighton.
12, ○   Postal history and associated fields.
Book reviews, letters, monographic articles.
No Index.
June 1972, T.p. 30, Ad.p. 4.
Per copy 40p, per year £3.

385

RAILWAYS

1386 ABC RAIL GUIDE. 1966.
(ABC Railway Guide 1853-1965).
ABC Travel Guides Ltd., (Member of IPC Business Press Ltd.), Oldhill, London Road, Dunstable, Beds.
12, = ‡   Routes and fares from London to principal stations in Great Britain with quick reference timetables. Timetables of all rail services in South-Eastern England. Details of local and continental shipping services and recommended hotels and guest houses throughout Gt. Britain.
No Index.
T.p. 654, Ad.p. 102.   23000.
Subscription on application.

386

CANALS. INLAND WATERWAYS

1387 BULLETIN of the Inland Waterways Association. 1946.
Inland Waterways Association, 114 Regents Park Road, London NW1.
4, ○ * + =   All aspects of the inland waterways.
Book reviews, letters, monographic articles, new products, obituaries, parliamentary reports.
No Index.
June 1972, T.p. 50, Ad.p. 30.
Free to members.

1388 LOCK GATE.
Great Ouse Restoration Society, c/o Bedfordshire County Record Office, Bedford.
4, ○ ‡
No Index.
Free to members.

1389 WATERWAYS NEWS: Staff newspaper of the British Waterways Board. 1971.
British Waterways Board, Press and Publicity Office, Melbury House, Melbury Terrace, London NW1 6JX.
11, † ○   Inland waterways under the jurisdiction of BWB; canals and canal people, rallies and unusual events held on the canals.
Book reviews, letters, articles, new companies, obituaries.
No Index,
May/June 1972, T.p. 12.   6000.
Per copy 4½p, per year 50p.

1390 WATERWAYS WORLD. 1972.
Waterways Productions Ltd., 26 Chaseview Road, Alrewas, Burton-on-Trent, Staffs.
12, ○ =   National and international on all aspects of inland waterways (rivers and canals) in Britain and abroad.
Book notices, book reviews, commodity prices, letters, articles, new companies, new products, obituaries, standards, tests.
No Index.
Spring 1972, T.p. 8, Ad.p. 10.   10000.
per copy 20p, per year £1

387

SEA TRANSPORT

1391 BALTIC EXCHANGE MAGAZINE.
Turret Press Ltd., 65/66 Turnmill Street, London EC3M 5RA.
4, † =   All aspects of transportation, mainly shipping.
Features, book reviews, legal notes, letters, monographic articles, new companies, new products, obituaries, patents, standards, tests.
No Index.
Summer 1972, T.p. 26, Ad.p. 10.
Per year £2.

1392 BRISTOL PORTS JOURNAL. 1967.
Leaderpress Ltd., Thomas Street, Hull.
4, =   Trade and commerce.
No Index.
Per copy 25p, per year £1.

1393 FAIRPLAY INTERNATIONAL SHIPPING JOURNAL. 1966.
Fairplay Publications Ltd., 51 Bishopsgate, London EC2.
52, = ‡   Worldwide developments in shipping, shipbuilding, marine equipment etc.
Book reviews, monographic articles, new companies, new products, parliamentary reports.
No Index.
T.p. 38, Ad.p. 37.   4500.
Per copy 20p, per year £12.

1394 FLYING ANGEL NEWS. 1972.
(The Flying Angel, 1962-1971).
The Missions to Seamen, St. Michael Paternoster Royal, College Hill, London EC4R 2RL.
6, * =   News of the society's activities in Britain and overseas, aimed primarily at supporters of The Missions to Seamen.
Book reviews, articles.
No Index.
March/April, 1972, T.p. 8.   15000.
Per copy 5p, per year 30p.

1395 THE HANDY SHIPPING GUIDE. 1887.
Wilkinson Bros. Ltd., 12-16 Laystall Street, London EC1R 4PB.
52, =   To exporters and shipping and forwarding agents.
Each issue, Weekly, No, None.
17.6.1972, T.p. 140, Ad.p. 102.
Per copy 10p, per year £9.15.

1396 LLOYD'S LIST. 1969.
(Lloyd's List, 1734-Lloyd's List and Shipping Gazette, 1922-1969).
Corporation of Lloyd's, Lloyd's, Lime Street, London, EC3M 7HA.
Daily Monday to Saturday incl, ‡ =   Provides a worldwide service of news and shipping intelligence for the shipping and insurance communities and to commerce.
Book notices, book reviews, legal notes, letters, articles, new companies, new products, obituaries, parliamentary reports, standards, tests.
No Index.
5.7.1972, T.p. 13, Ad.p. 3.
Per copy 5p, per year £15.60.

1397 LLOYD'S LOADING LIST. 1920.
(General Weekly Shipping List 1853-1919).
Corporation of Lloyd's, Lloyd's, Lime Street, London, EC3M 7HA.
52, =   A weekly exporters guide giving details of vessels loading at United Kingdom and near continental ports for all parts of the world.
No Index.
3.7.1972, T.p. 240.
Per copy 11p, per year £5.72.

1398 LLOYD'S LOG. 1932.
(Monthly Notes, 1930-1932).
The Corporation of Lloyd's, Lime Street, London, EC3M 7HA.
12, †   Circulates widely amongst the Lloyd's insurance market at home and abroad. Records functions (receptions etc.) at Lloyd's together with articles of insurance and general interest mostly contributed by people in the market.
Abstracts, book reviews, monographic articles, new companies, obituaries,
No Index.
May 1972, T.p. 24
Per copy 10p, per year £1.20.

1399 MARITIME HISTORY. 1971.
David & Charles (Publishers) Ltd., South Devon House, Newton Abbot, Devon.
2, ○ + =   History of merchant shipping.
Monographic articles.
A, Final issue of year, Yes, None.
Per copy 90p, per year £1.75.

1400 NATIONAL PORTS COUNCIL BULLETIN. 1972.
National Ports Council, Commonwealth House, 1-19 New Oxford Street, London WC1A 1DZ.
4, ‡ +   The research and technical work by the council in all its aspects.
Monographic articles.
No Index.
Spring 1972, T.p. 56.   1000.
Per copy £2.

1401 THE NAUTICAL MAGAZINE. 1832
Brown Son & Ferguson Ltd., 52 Darnley Street, Glasgow, G41 2SG.
12, = ‡ +   Merchant navy, navigation, astronomy.
Book reviews, legal notes, letters, articles, new products, obituaries, tests.
6m, December/June, Yes, None.
June 1972, T.p. 76, Ad.p. 16.   3000.
Per copy 20p, per year £3.

1402 POLANEWS: the journal for all employees of the P.L.A. 1970.
(Staff Supplement 1927-1966, Port Watch 1967-1969).
Port of London Authority, World Trade Centre, London, E1.
12, ○
Letters, articles, obituaries.
No Index.
June 1972, T.p. 8.   11600.
Free.

1403 PORT OF HULL & HUMBER PORTS JOURNAL. c.1961.
Leaderpress Ltd., Thomas Street, Hull.
4, =   Trade and commerce.
No Index.
Per copy 25p, per year £1.

1404 PORT OF LONDON: Magazine of the Port of London Authority. 1970.
(PLA Monthly 1925-1970).
Port of London Authority, World Trade Centre, London, E1.
12, † =   Shipping, trade and history of the port.
Book notices, book reviews, monographic articles, new companies, new products.
A, September, Yes, 40 year.
June 1972, T.p. 36, Ad.p. 11.   6400.
Per copy $12\frac{1}{2}$p, per year £1.50.
Free, controlled circulation.

1405 REGISTRY OF SHIPS: monthly supplement to the Mercantile Navy List. 1857.
H.M.S.O., P.O. Box 569, London, SE1 9NH.
12, ‡   Lists additions to, and deletions from, the Mercantile Navy List, and changes of name and ownership of vessels registered in the United Kingdom and elsewhere in the Commonwealth.

Information given for each vessel: official number, name, ship type, port and year of registry, where and when built, material of construction, registered net and gross tonnage, owner, and manager (if recorded). Loose-leaf.
No Index.
May 1972, T.p. 20.
Per copy 69p, per year £8.82.

1406 SEA BREEZES: The magazine of ships and the sea. 1919.
The Journal of Commerce and Shipping Telegraph Ltd., 19 James Street, Liverpool, L2 7PE.
12, ○   Ships and seafaring matters generally, past and present. Designed to appeal to all who have an interest in maritime affairs, whether seagoing people or not, and all age groups.
Book notices, book reviews, letters, articles, new companies, obituaries.
A, As early as possible each year, Yes, None.
May 1972, T.p. 67, Ad.p. 10.   18000.
Per copy 15p, per year £2.25.

1407 THE SEAFARER. 1934.
Seafarers' Education Service, Mansbridge House, 207 Balham High Road, London, SW17 7BH.
4, *   British merchant seafaring.
Book reviews, letters, articles.
No Index.
Winter 1971, T.p. 27, Ad.p. 8.   3500.
Per copy 25p, per year £1.

1408 THE SEAMAN. 1887.
National Union of Seamen, Maritime House, Old Town, Clapham, London, SW4.
12, * =   News items relative to shipping, seamen, trade unions, industrial relations.
Letters, articles, obituaries, parliamentary reports.
No Index.
May 1972, T.p. 16.   16000.
Per copy 2½p.
Free to members.

1409 SHIPPING STATISTICS & ECONOMICS. 1970.
H.P. Drewry (Shipping Consultants) Ltd., 87/91 New Bond Street, London, W1Y 9LA.
12, + 2 Six Monthly Reviews, ‡ = +   World developments in shipping, shipbuilding, seaborne trade are reviewed and analysed, particular emphasis being placed on charter market trends and tanker/dry cargo freight rates.
No Index.
T.p. 72.   1050.
£22 p.a.—UK and Europe.

1410 SHIPPING STUDIES. 1971.
Research Division, H.P. Drewry (Shipping Consultants) Ltd., 87-91 New Bond Street, London, W1Y 9LA.
Irregular (c.10 p.a.), = ‡ +   Independent monographs covering one aspect of the subject at a time—technical, economic, financial, statistical.
No Index.
No. 1, 1971, T.p. 41.
Series rate £40 per 10, Additional copies £4 each.

1411 SHIPPING WORLD & SHIPBUILDER: Incorporating Syren & Shipping. 1965.
Benn Brothers Ltd., Lyon Tower, 125 Colliers Wood, High Street, London, SW19.
12, ‡ =
Book notices, book reviews, commodity prices, legal notes, letters, articles, new companies, new products, obituaries, parliamentary reports, patents, standards, tests.
6m, January/July, Yes, 2 year.
T.p. 67, Ad. p. 87.   6000
Per year £5.
Indexed in: BTI.

1412 SOUTHAMPTON & SOLENT PORTS JOURNAL. c.1968.
Leaderpress Ltd., Thomas Street, Hull.
4, =   Trade and commerce.
Per copy 25p, per year £1.

1413 THE TELEGRAPH: Incorporating The Merchant Navy Journal & Ships' Telegraph. 1969.
(Merchant Navy Journal 1937-1969, Ships' Telegraph 1958-1969)
Merchant Navy & Airline Officers' Association, 133-137 Whitechapel High Street, London E1 7PU.
12, ‡ = *   Ships' officers of all departments in the Merchant Navy, navigating and engineer officers in civil aviation, management and administrative staff in shipping and civil aviation and others interested in these industries.
Book reviews, legal notes, letters, monographic articles, new companies, new products, obituaries, parliamentary reports, patents, standards, tests.
No Index.
June 1972, T.p. 20, Ad.p. Most.   21548.
Per copy 10p, per year £1.20.

388.1

ROAD TRANSPORT

1414 ROAD TRAFFIC REPORTS. 1970.
K. Mason, Industrial Opportunities Ltd., Homewell, Havant, Hants.
10, =   Road traffic reports in high courts and relevances to magistrates, solicitors etc.
Monthly cumulative index.
T.p. 64.
Per year £20.

1415 ROAD WAY: Journal of the Road Haulage Association. 1934.
Road Haulage Association, 22 Upper Woburn Place, London, WC1.
12, = + ‡   All aspects of road haulage in general—operating, political, legal, industrial relations, insurance, commercial and technical—and of RHA activities in particular.
Book reviews, legal notes, letters, articles, new products, obituaries, parliamentary reports, standards.
No Index.
June 1972, T.p. 42, Ad.p. 34.   18000.
Per copy 17p, per year £2.70.
Free to members.

1416 STEERING WHEEL. Journal of the British taxi industry. 1921.
Steering Wheel Publications Ltd., Fulwood House, High Holborn, London WC1.
24, =
Letters, news.
No Index.
T.p. 23, Ad.p. 8.   6000.
Per copy 4p, per year £1.50.

1417 TRAFFIC ENGINEERING & CONTROL. 1960.
Printerhall Ltd., 34/40 Ludgate Hill, London EC4.
12, = + ‡   All aspects of transportation etc.
Book reviews, monographic articles, news.
A,—, Yes, None.
T.p. 48, Ad.p. 20.
Per copy 25p, per year £3.
Indexed in: BTI.

1418 THE TRANSPORT ENGINEER: The Journal of the Institute of Road Transport Engineers. 1969.
(The Journal and Proceedings of the I.R.T.E. 1949-1968)
The Institute of Road Transport Engineers, 1 Cromwell Place, London, SW7 2JF.
4, * = ‡   All aspects of road transport and engineering.
Book notices, book reviews, legal notes, letters, monographic articles, new products, obituaries, patents, standards, tests.

No Index.
June 1972, T.p. 36, Ad.p. 12.   7000.
Per copy 40p, per year £2. Free, controlled circulation.

1419 TRANSPORT TRAINING: The Newspaper of the Road
   Transport Industry Training Board. 1968.
   The RTITB, Capitol House, Empire Way, Wembley,
   Middx.
   6, ‡ =   Passenger operation, road haulage and the
   retail motor trade.
   Book reviews, letters, articles, new companies.
   No Index.
   May/June 1972, T.p. 8.   32000.
   Free.

388.4

PASSENGER TRANSPORT BY ROAD

1420 APPTO: Journal of the Association of Public Passen-
   ger Transport Operators. 1971.
   (MPTA Journal. 1939-1970)
   Hirst, Kidd & Rennie Ltd., 172 Union Street, Oldham,
   Lancs.
   11, = + † ‡   Various aspects of public passenger
   transport.
   Book reviews, letters, articles, new products, obitua-
   ries, parliamentary reports.
   A, January, No, None.
   May 1972, T.p. 64, Ad.p. 2.
   Per copy 25p, per year £2.60. Free to members.

1421 BULLETIN OF THE TRAMWAY & LIGHT RAILWAY
   SOCIETY. 1956.
   The Society, 102 Marlborough Lane, London, SE7.
   4, ‡ *   Tramways, technical and historical.
   Book notices, book reviews, letters, monographic
   articles, news.
   No Index.
   T.p. 24, Ad.p. 1.
   Free to members.

1422 BUSES: Incorporating PASSENGER TRANSPORT
   (founded 1898). 1968.
   (Buses Illustrated 1949)
   Ian Allan Ltd., Terminal House, Shepperton, Middlesex.
   TW17 8AS
   12, ○ ‡   Road passenger transport operation from
   the viewpoints of the operator and the enthusiast.
   Particular emphasis on current news and historical
   material.
   Book notices, book reviews, letters, articles, new pro-
   ducts, tests.
   A, December, No, None.
   July 1972, T.p. 38, Ad.p. 6.   14000.
   Per copy 20p, per year £2.75.

1423 COACHING JOURNAL & BUS REVIEW. 1931.
   Travel & Transport Ltd., 4 Milk Street, London,
   EC2V 8AT.
   12, ‡ =   Public passenger transport by road.
   Book notices, book reviews, legal notes, letters, arti-
   cles, new companies, new products, obituaries,
   parliamentary reports, standards, tests.
   No Index.
   June 1972, T.p. 31, Ad.p. 41.   4500.
   Per copy 20p, per year £2.50.

1424 THE JOURNAL OF THE TRAMWAY MUSEUM
   SOCIETY. 1961.
   (Newsletter 1955-1960)
   The Tramway Museum Society, 29 Old Hall Avenue,
   Duffield, Derbys.
   4, * †   Recording the history and achievements of the
   society. Also articles of general tramway interest
   and of a house magazine nature.
   Book reviews, letters, monographic articles, obituaries
   No Index.
   April 1972, T.p. 18, Ad.p. 8.   1200.
   Per copy 10p, per year 40p.

1425 MODERN TRAMWAY AND LIGHT RAILWAY REVIEW:
   official organ of the Light Railway Transport
   League. 1937.
   Ian Allan Ltd. and Light Railway Transport League,
   Terminal House, Shepperton, Middlesex. TW17 8AS.
   12, ○ * ‡   Tramway operation with particular atten-
   tion to possible rapid transit development. Histori-
   cal aspects of tramways, especially with extensive
   or unusual operating features.
   Book notices, book reviews, letters, monographic
   articles.
   A, December, No, None.
   July 1972, T.p. 36, Ad.p. 4.   5300.
   Per copy 20p, per year £2.75.

1426 THE PUBLIC ROAD TRANSPORT ASSOCIATION
   JOURNAL. 1943.
   The Public Road Transport Association, 172 Bucking-
   ham Palace Road, London, SW1.
   13, = * ‡   Passenger road transport industry.
   Book notices, legal notes, obituaries.
   A, December, Yes, None.
   May 1972, T.p. 20, Ad.p. 3.   800.
   Per copy 15p, per year £1.50p. Free to members.

1427 TRAMWAY REVIEW. Historical journal of the Light
   Railway Transport League. 1955.
   The League, 14 Cudlow Avenue, Rustington, Littlehamp-
   ton, Sussex.
   4, * ‡
   Book reviews, letters, monographic articles.
   2 year, December, No, None.
   T.p. 23.   1200.
   Per copy 12½p, per year 50p.

1428 TROLLEYBUS MAGAZINE: Journal of the National
   Trolleybus Association. 1966.
   (Newsletter of the National Trolleybus Association.
   1963-1966)
   National Trolleybus Association, 12 Coltsfoot Drive,
   Burpham, Guildford, Surrey.
   6, * ○   Documentation of all facets of history, past
   and present operation of trolleybuses of all ages
   all over the world, with special coverage of current
   trends.
   Book notices, book reviews, letters, monographic
   articles, new products, obituaries.
   A, November, No, None.
   March 1972, T.p. 20, Ad.p. 4.   800.
   Per copy 37p, per year £2.20.

388.9

AIR TRANSPORT

1429 ABC AIR CARGO GUIDE.
   ABC Travel Guides Ltd., (Member of IPC Business
   Press), Oldhill, London Road, Dunstable, Beds.
   12, = ‡
   Worldwide International and domestic general cargo
   rates, all I.A.T.A. Specified specific commodity
   rates, Import regulations for countries throughout
   the world, etc., AIRIMP cargo reservation codes
   and comprehensive air cargo flight information.
   No Index.
   Subscription on application.

1430 ABC AIRWAYS: International tourism and travel
   marketing magazine. 1969.
   IPC Transport Press (a member of IPC Business
   Press Ltd.), Dorset House, Stamford Street, London,
   SE1 9LU.
   12, =   Air travel worldwide.
   Letters, monographic articles, new companies.

Key to reference symbols

○ popular   ‡ technical   = trade/professional

+ research   * society/institution   † house journal

A, —, No, None.
July 1972, T.p. 41, Ad.p. 18.   40838.
Per copy 35p, per year £4.
Free with ABC World Airways Guide.

1431 ABC WORLD AIRWAYS GUIDE. 1972.
(ABC Airways 1969-1971)
ABC Travel Guides Ltd. (Member of IPC Business Press Ltd.), Oldhill, London Road, Dunstable, Beds.
12, ‡ =   Timetable and fares information for the airlines of the world. Contains a Quick Reference section, airlines feature section and section giving supplementary information on route maps, sector mileages, local taxes, baggage charges, currency and exchange rates, etc. etc.
No Index.
Subscription on application.

1432 AIR AND TRAVEL TRAINING WORLD. 1972.
(ITB News)
Air Transport & Travel Industry Training Board, Staines House, 158-162 High Street, Staines, Middx.
6, = +   To keep those involved in the practice of training in the industry, and those affected by it, informed of what is going on in the field.
Book notices, book reviews, articles.
No Index.
May 1972, T.p. 8.   4000.
Free.

1433 AIRPORTS INTERNATIONAL: Official journal of the International Civil Airport Association. 1968.
(Airport and Ground Services. 1967)
IPC Transport Press (A member of IPC Business Press Ltd.), Dorset House, Stamford Street, London, SE1 9LU.
4, ‡   World wide coverage with readers at key management level; airport managers and administrators, planning, specifying and purchasing executives, at airports, airlines and government depts. in over 200 countries and associated territories.
Letters, monographic articles, new companies, new products.
No Index.
June 1972, T.p. 52, Ad.p. 25$\frac{1}{6}$.   6000.
Per copy 50p, per year £2. Free, controlled circulation

1434 JETLINE SCHEDULES. 1966.
Jetline Schedules Ltd., Golden House, 29 Gt. Pulteney Street, London, W1.
12, =   Timetable guide of the sixty-three airlines flying to and from London to all parts of the world, and continental connecting flights by national airlines.
No Index.
June 1972, T.p. 38, Ad.p. 10.   30000.
Per copy 33$\frac{1}{2}$p, per year £4.

1435 SKY TRADER & AIR MARKETING INTERNATIONAL. International air cargo magazine. 1962.
Skylink Ltd., 6 Adam Street, London, WC2.
12, =   All aspects of air cargo.
Letters, articles, news, new products, parliamentary reports, standards.
A, —, No, None.
T.p. 19, Ad.p. 17.   10000.
Free, controlled circulation.

389.1

METROLOGY. WEIGHTS & MEASURES.

1436 MONTHLY REVIEW of the Institute of Weights and Measures Administration. 1892.
Institute of Weights and Measures Administration, Weights and Measures Office, Tredegar Street, Cardiff CF1 2FB.
12, * ‡ =   Legal and technical data relating to metrology, food and drugs, petroleum and other Acts of Parliament administered by Inspectors of Weights and Measures in the United Kingdom together with news of members.
Legal notes, letters, articles, obituaries, standards, tests.
A, January, Yes, None.
May 1972, T.p. 32, Ad.p. 8.   2000.
Per copy 35p, per year £4. Free to members.

389.151

METRICATION

1437 CBI METRICATION BULLETIN.
Confederation of British Industry, 21 Tothill Street, London, SW1.
4, ‡   * =
News sheet.
No Index.
21.4.1972, T.p. 4.
Per copy 20p. Free to members.

1438 GOING METRIC. 1971.
Metrication Board, 22 Kingsway, London, WC2B 62E.
4, ○   Covers all sectors of industry, trade and education, providing an up to date flow of information on the progress of metrication in Britain and overseas.
Abstracts, book notices, book reviews, standards.
No Index.
April 1972, T.p. 4.   140000.
Free.

1439 METRIC INFORMATION SERVICE BULLETIN. 1969.
Metric Information Service, Triumph House, 189 Regent Street, London, W1R 7WF.
26, ‡ = +   Particular emphasis upon metrication, its introduction in UK and abroad, technical problems arising from its introduction, advice upon technical aspects of metrication. Provision of technical data sheets, news of manufacturers products. This Bulletin is backed up by an enquiry service.
Abstracts, book notices, book reviews, commodity prices, letters, monographic articles, new companies, new products, parliamentary reports, patents, standards, tests.
No Index.
June 1972, T.p. 18.   3000.
Full subscription £21 p.a. Individual sections issued at reduced rates.

1440 METRICATION NEWS: Incorporating Decimal Currency News. 1971.
(Decimal Currency News. 1969-1970)
Metric Information Service, Triumph House, 189 Regent Street, London, W1R 7WF.
5, ‡ = +   Particular emphasis upon metrication in UK and overseas, technical information, product information, trade information, overseas product and trade information. Technical and metric training information.
Abstracts, book notices, book reviews, commodity prices, letters, monographic articles, new companies, new products, parliamentary reports, patents, standards, tests.
No Index.
Feb 1972, T.p. 8, Ad.p. 2.   3000.
Per year £4. Price includes access to back-up enquiry service.

389.2

UNIVERSAL TIME

1441 GREENWICH TIME REPORT. 1968.
(Contained in the Royal Observatory Bulletins, Time and Latitude Service 1956-1967)

Royal Greenwich Observatory, Herstmonceux Castle,
   Hailsham, Sussex.
4, ‡ +   Tabulated data of Universal Time, Atomic
   Time and Radio time signals.
No Index.

389.6

STANDARDIZATION

1442 BSI NEWS.
British Standards Institution, 2 Park Street, London, W1.
12, + ‡ =   All aspects of standardisation.
Monographic articles, news, standards, tests.
No Index.
T.p. 32.   30000.
Free to members.

1443 THE QUARTERLY BULLETIN. 1971.
British Standards Institution, Maylands Avenue,
   Hemel Hempstead, Hertfordshire.
4, ‡ = +   Information on workings and current
   developments in Technical Help to Exporters service. Topical news of available services and advance information on overseas investigatory trips to identify technical problems for exporters.
Book notices, legal notes, letters, monographic
   articles, new products, standards, tests.
No Index.
June 1972, T.p. 4.   1500.
Free to members and enquirers.

39

CULTURAL ANTHROPOLOGY

1444 NEW DIFFUSIONIST. 1971.
C.E. Joel, 39 West Street, Great Gransden, Sandy, Beds.
4, =   Study of inter-relationships in cultural anthropology.
No Index.
Per copy 10p, per year 50p.

391

COSTUME

1445 COSTUME. 1967.
The Costume Society, c/o Victoria & Albert Museum,
   London, SW7. Address for enquiries: 251 Popes
   Lane, London, W5.
1, + *   History and technology of costume.
Monographic articles.
A, —, No, None.
Per year £2.
Indexed in: BHI.

1446 PROCEEDINGS OF THE SCOTTISH TARTANS
   SOCIETY. 1966.
Scottish Tartans Society, Broughty Castle Museum,
   Broughty Ferry, Dundee DD5 2BE.
1, ‡ + *   Notes and articles on the history of tartans
   and Highland dress etc.
No Index.
No. 5, 1971-72, T.p. 12.
Free to members.

396

WOMEN

1447 NEWSLETTER OF THE WOMEN'S GROUP ON PUBLIC
   WELFARE AND THE STANDING CONFERENCES
   OF WOMEN'S ORGANISATIONS.
National Council of Social Service for Women's Group
   on Public Welfare, 26 Bedford Square, London,
   WC1B 3HU.
4, *   Channel of information for women's organisations about relevant legislation; and of new developments in social welfare affecting women and children.
Book notices, book reviews.
No Index.
Spring 1972, T.p. 5, Ad.p. 2.   3500.
Subscription: 75p for 12 copies of each issue per year.

1448 WOMEN SPEAKING. 1958.
(Speaking of Women. 1953-1958)
C.E. Hodge, The Wick, Roundwood Avenue, Hutton
   Mount, Brentwood, Essex.
4, ○   Women's views on current affairs and news of
   women in world affairs.
Book reviews, legal notes, letters, articles, parliamentary reports.
No Index.
October 1971, T.p. 23. Ad.p. 1.
Per copy 15p, per year 70p.

397

GYPSIES

1449 JOURNAL OF THE GYPSY LORE SOCIETY. 1888.
T. & A. Constable Ltd., Hopetoun Street, Edinburgh.
4, *
Book notices, book reviews, monographic articles.
A, January, Yes, None.
T.p. 80.
Per year £2.10.

398

FOLKLORE

1450 BALTHUS: Folk-lore and fantasy. 1971.
Jon M. Harvey, 18 Cefn Road, Cardiff, CF4 3HS.
2, ○   Fantasy: articles, fiction, poetry and artwork
   on the subjects of the Supernatural, the Macabre,
   Swords and Sorcery and Folk-Lore, (also the
   Occult, if dealt with in a non-sensational manner).
Book reviews, letters, articles.
No Index.
Winter 1971, T.p. 34.   300.
Per copy 20p. 60p for 3 issues.

1451 FOLK REVIEW. 1972.
(Folk and Country 1970—1972).
Hanover Books Ltd., 61 Berners Street, London
   W1P 3AE.
12, ○
No Index.
T.p. 32.
Per copy 20p.

1452 FOLKLORE. 1890.
(Folk-Record 1878-1882: Folk-Lore Journal 1883-1889).
The Folklore Society, c/o University College London,
   Gower Street, London, WC1E 6BT.
4, * +   The study of folk traditions and cultures:
   covering oral traditions, material cultures and
   song and dance.
Book notices, book reviews, letters, monographic articles, obituaries.
A, In winter issue (usually published February of
   following year), No, None.
winter 1971, T.p. 80, Ad.p. 2.   1000
Per copy 90p, per year £3.25.
Indexed in: BHI, IBZ.

1453 LORE AND LANGUAGE: The Journal of the Survey of
   Language and Folklore. 1969.
The Survey of Language and Folklore, Department of
   English Language, The University, Sheffield,
   SI0 2TN.

2, ○ + Research in language, folklore and kindred topics.
Book notices, book reviews, monographic articles.
No Index.
January 1972, T.p. 14.   500.
Per copy 15p, per year 30p.

1454 ORE: The magazine which remembers the Island of Britain and those who first came to it. 1954.
Ore Publications, 11 High Plash, Cuttys Lane, Stevenage, Herts.
2, ○   Poetry and prose on Arthurian Britain, British folklore and legend, the Roman/British period, and prehistory. Plus poetry reviews of unrestricted subject matter.
Book notices, book reviews, articles.
No Index.
No. 16 1972, T.p. 40, Ad.p. 1.
Per copy 17p.

1455 ROS: Journal of Kerry folk life. 1972.
Trustees of Muckross House, Killarney, Co. Kerry.
2, ○.
No Index.
Subscription on application.

398.4
WITCHCRAFT

1456 QUEST: The Journal of Practical Occultism. 1970.
Spook Enterprises, 38 Woodfield Avenue, London, W5.
4, ○   All aspects of occultism, magic, witchcraft, paganism, and the British Mysteries.
Book notices, book reviews, letters, articles.
No Index.
September 1970, T.p. 29, Ad.p. 3.   c. 1000.
Per copy 20p, per year 75p.

1457 THE WAXING MOON: Journal of Pagan Movement in Britain and Ireland. 1970.
Pagan Movement in Britain and Ireland Cymdeithas Selene, Cân y Lloer, Ffarmers, Llanwrda, Sir Gaerfyrddin, South Wales.
4, ○ *   Pagan and poetic, heathen magic and the old religion. Paganism and the Craft of the Wise (Witchcraft).
Book reviews, letters, articles, reports.
No Index.
2nd August 1971, T.p. 20.   1000.
Per copy 20p, per year 70p.

4
LANGUAGES
PHILOLOGY

1458 ARCHIVUM LINGUISTICUM. 1949-1969; (New Series) 1970-.
Scolar Press Ltd., 20 Main Street, Menston Yorks, LS29 6EZ.
1, =   General Linguistics and Comparative Philology.
Articles, review articles, book reviews.
No Index.
Subscription on application.

1459 AUDIO-VISUAL LANGUAGE JOURNAL. 1963.
Audio-Visual Language Association, Dept. of Modern Languages, University of Salford, Salford, 5.
3, = ‡ * +   Linguistics, applied linguistics and language reading with particular reference to technology.
Book reviews, letters, monographic articles, new products.
A, November, No, None.
T.p. 55, Ad.p. 9.
Per year £2. Free to members.

1460 THE INCORPORATED LINGUIST. 1962.
(The Linguists' Review 1924-1961).
The Institute of Linguists, Lloyds Bank Chambers, 91 Newington Causeway, London, SE1 6BN
4, ‡ †=   Transactions of the Institute. All aspects of modern languages and their use.
Book reviews, legal notes, letters, monographic articles, new products, obituaries, standards, tests.
A, January, Yes, None.
April 1972, T.p. 33, Ad.p. 2.   4000.
Per copy 60p, per year £2. Free to members.

1461 JOURNAL OF LINGUISTICS. 1965.
Cambridge University Press, PO Box 92, London, NW1 2DB.
2, +   All branches of linguistics including phonetics.
Book reviews, monographic articles.
A September, Yes, None.
October 1971, T.p. 157, Ad.p. 12.   2600.
Per copy £2.50, per year £4.

1462 LANGUAGE & SPEECH. 1959.
Robert Draper Ltd., 85 Udney Park Rd., Teddington, Middx.
4, +   All aspects of language and speech: language structure, psychology of language and speech, transmission and reception of speech, mechanical speech recognition and synthesis, mechanical translation, language statistics and abnormalities of language and speech.
Book notices, book reviews, monographic articles.
A, October-December, No, None.
Jan-March 1972, T.p. 104.
Per copy £2.75, per year £10.

1463 LANGUAGE IN SOCIETY. 1972.
Cambridge University Press, PO Box 92, London NW1 2DB.
2, +   All aspects of the study of language in its social setting.
Book reviews, monographic articles.
A, Last issue of volume, Yes, None.
April 1972, T.p. 176, Ad.p. 1.
Per copy £2.50, per year £4.

1464 MEDIUM AEVUM. 1932.
Basil Blackwell & Mott Ltd., 5 Alfred Street, Oxford OX1 4HB.
3, +   Entire field of medical studies from Romanesque to 16th Century.
Book reviews, monographic articles.
A, No. 3, Yes, None.
T.p. 118, Ad.p. 5.   900.
Per copy £1.50, per year £2.50.
Indexed in: BHI, IBZ

1465 MODERN LANGUAGE REVIEW. 1905.
Modern Humanities Research Association, c/o Bedford College, Regents Park, London NW1.
4, = + *   Modern and medieval languages and literature.
Book reviews, monographic articles.
A, October, Yes, 10 year.
T.p. 240.
Free to members.
Indexed in: BHI, IBZ.

1466 TRANSACTIONS OF THE PHILOLOGICAL SOCIETY. 1854.
(Proceedings 1842-1853)
Basil Blackwell & Mott Ltd., 5 Alfred Street, Oxford OX1 4HB.
1, * + =   Scientific study of language.
Monographic articles.
Irregular, —, Yes, None.
T.p. 200.
Per copy £2.10. Free to members.
Indexed in: IBZ.

408.7

DIALECTS

1467 THE JOURNAL OF THE LANCASHIRE DIALECT SOCIETY. 1951.
The Lancashire Dialect Society.
c/o Professor G. L. Brook, Department of English, The University, Manchester M13 9PL.
1, ○ + *   Articles, stories and poems in Lancashire dialects. Dialectology. Articles on dialects, not merely those of Lancashire.
Book notices, book reviews, letters, monographic articles.
15 years.
January 1972, T.p. 32.   c. 200.
Per year 50p. Free to members.

1468 TRANSACTIONS OF THE YORKSHIRE DIALECT SOCIETY. 1897.
Yorkshire Dialect Society, School of English, The University, Leeds, Yorkshire, LS2 9JT.
1, *   The origins and history of dialect and kindred subjects; dialect verse, prose and literature.
Book notices, book reviews, monographic articles, obituaries.
5 year, Usually New Year, No, None.
1971, T.p. 64.   700.
Per copy 50p.

408.9

ARTIFICIAL LANGUAGES

1469 IDO-LETRO: Journal of the International Language (Ido) Society of Great Britain. 1947.
(Monatala Letro, 1936 to 1946;
Monthly Letter, ? to 1935.)
International Language (Ido) Society of Great Britain, 1 Hillside Road, Darlington, Co. Durham, DL3 8HB.
4, *   A news-letter keeping supporters of the international language informed of progress of the movement and helping to further contacts and collaboration. In addition to Society news, includes reading matter in Ido (poems and prose). Language used: almost entirely Ido.
No Index.
April 1972, T.p. 4.   180.
Per copy 25p and Free to members.

408.92

ESPERANTO

1470 THE BRITISH ESPERANTIST. International language journal. 1905.
(The Esperantist 1903).
British Esperanto Association, 140 Holland Park Avenue, London W11.
11, * = + ○   Progress of the international language.
2 year, January, Yes, None.
T.p. 24, Ad.p. 3.   3810.
Free to members.

1471 ĈE NI. 1961
(Half Yearly Bulletin 1953-1960).
British Association of Blind Esperantists, 10 Windsor Avenue, Gatley, Cheadle, Cheshire SK8 4DU.
2, *   In Braille.
Book notices, book reviews, letters, monographic articles, obituaries.
No Index.
Winter 1971-2, T.p. 16.   c. 50.
Free to members.

1472 ESPERANTO CONTACT. 1971.
British Esperanto Association, 140 Holland Park Avenue, London W11.
12, ○.
No Index.
Free to members.

1473 ESPERANTO EN SKOTLANDO: oficiala bulteno de la skota Federacio Esperantista. 1945.
Scottish Esperanto Federation.
The Editor, Esperanto en Skotlando, 2 Lady Helen Street, Kirkcaldy, Fife.
4, *   Matters relating to Esperanto and Esperantists in Scotland and abroad; international language problems generally. In Esperanto.
Book notices, book reviews, letters, articles, obituaries.
Q, None, Yes, None.
Summer 1972, T.p. 12.   250.
Per year 25p.

1474 THE ESPERANTO TEACHER: Official organ of Esperanto Teachers Association. 1967.
(The Esperantist Teacher 1962-1966).
Esperanto Teachers Association, 87 Sebastian Ave., Shenfield, Essex.
3, ‡ =.
Book notices, book reviews, commodity prices, legal notes, letters, articles, obituaries, standards, tests.
No Index.
May 1972, T.p. 13.   600.
Per copy 20p, per year 50p. Free to members.

413.11

NAMES

1475 VIZ: Newsletter of The Names Society. 1969.
(From January, 1968 with no title).
The Names Society, 7 Aragon Avenue, Thames Ditton, Surrey KT7 0PY.
6, *   Information and anecdotes about personal, place, street, house, boat, field, pub and trade names. Book reviews, results of surveys conducted by members.
Book reviews, letters, articles.
Planned to be issued yearly.
March 1972, T.p. 17.   400.
Per year £1. Free to members.

1476 JOURNAL OF THE ENGLISH PLACE-NAME SOCIETY. 1969.
English Place Name Society, University College, Gower St., London WC1.
1, + *   Place-names of England, and relevant historical, archaeological and topographical studies.
Book notices, book reviews, monographic articles.
No Index.
Members only.

414

PHONETICS

1477 JOURNAL OF THE INTERNATIONAL PHONETIC ASSOCIATION. 1971.
(Dhi Fonetik Titčer 1886-1888; Le Maître Phonétique 1889-1970.)

International Phonetic Association, University College, Gower Street, London WC1E 6BT.
2, * = All aspects of phonetics and phonology.
Book reviews, letters, articles, obituaries.
A, December, Yes, None.
Dec. 1971, T.p. 52, Ad.p. 2.   650.
Per copy £1, per year £2.

420

ENGLISH LANGUAGE

1478 CRITICAL QUARTERLY. 1959.
Oxford University Press, Press Road, Neasden, London NW10.
4, + = * Critical comment on drama, poetry, literature.
Book notices, book reviews, letters.
No Index.
T.p. 95, Ad.p. 4.   5000.
Per copy 25p, per year £1.
Indexed in: BHI.

1479 MODERN ENGLISH: a magazine for foreign students and teachers of English. 1961.
International Language Centre, International House, 40 Shaftesbury Ave., London W1V 8HJ.
10, = ○ Educational magazine taken by European students who want to improve their knowledge of English language. Topics of interest to young people aged 15 to 23 approx. Pop music, politics, fashion, sport. Language exercises.
Book reviews, letters, articles.
A, January, No, None.
No 2, 1972, T.p. 20, Ad.p. 7.
Per copy 20p, per year £2.25.

1480 NOTES AND QUERIES: For Readers and Writers, Collectors and Librarians. 1849.
Oxford University Press, Press Road, Neasden, London NW10.
12, + Devoted principally to English language and literature, lexicography, history and scholarly antiquarianism. Emphasis is on the factual rather than speculative.
Book reviews, letters.
A, —, Yes, None.
May 1972, T.p. 38.   1500.
Per copy 50p, per year £5.

1481 REVIEW OF ENGLISH STUDIES: A Quarterly Journal of English Literature and English Language. 1925, New Series 1950.
Oxford University Press, Press Road, Neasden, London NW10.
4, + Historical and critical studies in English literature and the English language.
Book reviews, monographic articles.
A, —, Yes, None.
May 1972, T.p. 127, Ad.p. 16.   2000.
Per copy £1.25, per year £3.50.

440

FRENCH LANGUAGE

1482 FRENCH STUDIES. 1946.
Basil Blackwell & Mott Ltd., 5 Alfred Street, Oxford OX1 4HB.
4, + All aspects of French literature and criticism, both in mediaeval and modern periods.
Book reviews, monographic articles.
A, October, Yes, Volumes 1-20.
T.p. 112, Ad.p. 4.   1400.
Per year £3.50.
Indexed in: BHI.

460

SPANISH LANGUAGE

1483 BULLETIN OF HISPANIC STUDIES. 1923.
Liverpool University Press, 123 Grove Street, Liverpool, L7 7AF.
4, + Devoted exclusively to the languages and literatures of Spain, Portugal and Latin America.
Book notices, book reviews, monographic articles.
A, October, Yes, None.
October 1971, T.p. 95, Ad.p. 4.   975.
Per copy £1.25, per year £4.
Indexed in: BHI.

47

CLASSICAL LANGUAGES

1484 CLASSICAL QUARTERLY: Published under the auspices of the Classical Association and the Oxford and Cambridge Philological Societies. 1907, New Series 1951.
Oxford University Press, Press Road, Neasden, London NW10.
2, + Greek and Latin language and literature, but also includes some papers on ancient history, ancient philosophy, and classical archaeology.
Book reviews, monographic articles.
A, —, Yes, None.
May 1972, T.p. 198, Ad.p. 4.   1300.
Per copy £1.40, per year £2.25. Combined sub with Classical Review-£4.40.
Indexed in: BHI.

1485 CLASSICAL REVIEW. 1887, New Series 1951.
Oxford University Press, Press Road, Neasden, London NW10.
3, + For the classical scholar and general classical reader, including shorter articles on all branches of classical learning, reviews of recent English and foreign books which deal with classical subjects, summaries of foreign classical periodicals, and notes of current events in the classical world.
Book notices, book reviews, letters, articles.
A, —, Yes, None.
December 1971, T.p. 173, Ad.p. 8.   1600.
Per copy £1.20, per year £2.50. Combined sub with Classical Qtly—£4.40.
Indexed in: BHI.

1486 PROCEEDINGS OF THE CLASSICAL ASSOCIATION. 1904.
John Murray (for the Classical Association), 50 Albemarle Street, London, W1X 4BD.
1, * = Coverage consists of:- Reports on activities including the Annual General Meeting of the year within the association and reports from allied branches overseas, on classical studies in general.
No Index.
1971, T.p. 62, Ad.p. 13.   4795.
Per copy 50p.
Indexed in: BHI.

49

AFRICAN LANGUAGES

1487 AFRICAN LANGUAGE REVIEW. 1966.
(Sierra Leone Language Review 1962-1965).
Frank Cass & Co. Ltd., 67 Great Russell Street, London WC1B 3BT.
1, + African and Creole language studies.
Book notices, book reviews, monographic articles.
A, —, Yes, None.
Per copy £3.75.

1488 AFRICAN LANGUAGE STUDIES. 1960.
School of Oriental and African Studies, University of London, London WC1E 7HP.
1, +   Collected papers dealing with various aspects of the study of African languages, both descriptive and comparative, and including literature and oral literature.
A, with each issue 300, Yes, None.
1968, T.p. 197.
Per copy £3.
Subscription on application.

1489 JOURNAL OF WEST AFRICAN LANGUAGES. 1964.
Cambridge University Press, PO Box 92, London NW1.
2, +   Research into the distribution phonology, morphology and grammar.
Monographic articles.
No Index.
T.p. 62, Ad.p. 2.   500.
Per copy £1.50, per year £2.
Indexed in: BHI.

491.6

CELTIC LANGUAGES

1490 BULLETIN OF THE BOARD OF CELTIC STUDIES. 1932.
University of Wales Press, Merthyr House, James Street, Cardiff, CF1 6EU.
2, + ‡.
Book reviews, monographic articles, obituaries.
2 year, —, No, None.
Per copy 50p, per year £1.

1491 STUDIA CELTICA. 1966.
University of Wales Press, Merthyr House, James Street, Cardiff, CF1 6EU, Glam.
1, ‡ +.
A, with each volume, Yes, None.
Per copy £1.50.

491.62

GAELIC LANGUAGES

1492 CRANN-TARA: Newsletter of Comunn na Canain Albannaich (The Scottish Language Society). 1971.
Comunn na Canain Albannaich, 27 Lyttleton, East Kilbride, Glasgow.
3, †   Progress of the Gaelic language in Scotland. Also serves as a publicity medium to advertise what the Society is doing on behalf of the language.
Book notices, book reviews, letters, articles.
5 year, Not yet issued, Yes, None.
June 1972, T.p. 6, 250.
Per copy 6p, per year 20p.

5
SCIENCE

1493 B A RECORD: A review of the activities of the British Association for the Advancement of Science. 1967.
British Association for the Advancement of Science, 3 Sanctuary Buildings, 20 Great Smith Street, London SW1.
3/4, †   News of Annual Meetings, Projects Division, staff changes, constitutional matters, changes of offices, etc.
No Index.
April 1972, T.p. 4.
Free.

1494 BASRA JOURNAL. 1962
J. England, 'Houndel', Ounsdale Road, Wombourne, Wolverhampton, Staffs.
4, ○ +   Original scientific ideas and conjectures, the results of amateur research, and factual articles to stimulate interest in unsolved problems of science and mathematics.
Book reviews, letters, monographic articles.
No Index.
Subscription on application.

1495 'FT' ABSTRACTS IN SCIENCE AND TECHNOLOGY: a monthly review of significant events and developments. 1972.
Microinfo Ltd. (By agreement with the Financial Times, London), 4 High Street, Alton, Hampshire.
12, ‡ +   Indexed coverage in almost 40 subject categories ranging from aerospace and agriculture through business systems, communications, data processing, all aspects of engineering and materials, to paper/print, coatings, pollution and surface transport systems.
Based on abstracts of material previously published in the Financial Times.
A, January, No, None.
April 1972, T.p. 24.
Per year £25.

1496 GEC JOURNAL OF SCIENCE AND TECHNOLOGY. 1972.
(GEC Journal—1930-1961; GEC Journal of Science and Technology 1962-1967; GEC-AEI Journal of Science and Technology 1968; Journal of Science & Technology 1969-72).
The General Electric Co. Ltd., 1 Stanhope Gate, London W1A 1EH.
4, ‡ + †   Science and technology within GEC, for worldwide circulation.
Monographic articles.
A, With first number of next year, No, None.
T.p. 44.
Free, controlled circulation.

1497 ICI MAGAZINE. 1927.
ICI Limited, IC House, Millbank, London SW1.
12, †   Company news, events and personalities, plus articles submitted by employees.
New companies, new products, obituaries, reports.
A, March, Yes, None.
T.p. 24.   80000.
Per copy 1p, per year 12p.

1498 SATIS: Science and technology information sources for teachers. 1969.
(Teachers Abstracts.)
National Centre for School Technology, Trent Polytechnic, Nottingham.
4, ‡ * =   Science and technology abstracts for secondary school teachers.
Abstracts, book reviews, letters.

A, —, Yes, None.
March 1972, T.p. 30.   1000.
Per year £1.75.

1499 ADVANCE. 1966.
University of Manchester Institute of Science and Technology, Sackville Street, Manchester M60 1QD.
2, ‡ = +   Current technical and management research work in the Institute likely to be of interest to industry.
Monographic articles.
No Index.
June 1971, T.p. 64.   5000.
Free.

1500 ADVANCEMENT OF SCIENCE. 1939.
Academic Press Inc. (London) Ltd., 24-28 Oval Road, London NW1.
4, ‡ + =   Science in general.
Book notices, book reviews, monographic articles.
A, June, No, None.
T.p. 128.
Per year £3.
Indexed in: BEI, BHI, BTI.

1501 BIOGRAPHICAL MEMOIRS OF FELLOWS OF THE ROYAL SOCIETY. 1955.
(Obituary Notices of Fellows of the Royal Society 1932-1954).
The Royal Society, 6 Carlton House Terrace, London, SW1Y 5AG.
1, + *   An authoritative record of some of the most important developments in science and the men responsible for them. Each contains a bibliography of the subject's writings.
Author index published as appendix to Author Index Proceedings and Transactions. Last issue 1961-1970.
Volume 17, T.p. 756.   1350.
Price of each part varies in accordance with the number of pages it contains.

1502 BRITISH JOURNAL FOR THE HISTORY OF SCIENCE. 1962.
Headley Brothers Ltd., The Invicta Press, Ashford, Kent.
2, + = *   The history of science and mathematics in all periods.
Book reviews, monographic articles.
2 years, Last issue of volume, Yes, None.
1000.
Per copy £1.50, per year £3.
Indexed in: BHI.

1503 THE BRITISH JOURNAL FOR THE PHILOSOPHY OF SCIENCE. 1950.
Cambridge University Press (for the British Society for the Philosophy of Science), P.O. Box 92, London, NW1 2DB.
4, +   Logic, the method and the philosophy of science.
Book reviews, monographic articles.
A, Last issue of volume, Yes, 20 year, 1970.
May 1972, T.p. 101, Ad.p. 9.   1840.
Per copy £1.50, per year £4.50.
Indexed in: BHI, IBZ.

1504 BULLETIN OF THE BRITISH SOCIETY FOR SOCIAL RESPONSIBILITY IN SCIENCE. 1971.
The Society, 70 Great Russell Street, London, WC1.
4, = ‡
No Index.
Per copy 5p, Free to members.

1505 CZECHOSLOVAK SCIENCE AND TECHNOLOGY DIGEST. 1970.
Scientific Information Conservants Ltd., 661 Finchley Road, London, NW2 2HN.
6, = + ‡
Book reviews, monographic articles.
No Index.
Per year £26.

1506 ENDEAVOUR. 1942.
Imperial Chemical Industries Ltd., Millbank, London, SW1.
3, + =   Reviews of current advances in pure and applied sciences with regular contributions on history of science.
Book notices, book reviews, monographic articles.
A, —, Yes, None.
September 1971, T.p. 56.
Free, controlled circulation.
Indexed in: BTI, IBZ.

1507 FIBRES POST. 1966.
(Signpost 1957).
ICI Fibres, Hookstone Road, Harrogate, Yorkshire.
26, †   Company policy, products developments and activities.
Letters, new companies, new products, obituaries.
No Index.
19.5.1972, T.p. 8.   14000.

1508 MEMOIRS & PROCEEDINGS: Manchester Literary & Philosophical Society. 1788.
Manchester Literary & Philosophical Society, 36 George Street, Manchester, M1 4HA.
1, + *   Literature and science and the education of the public in these fields.
Monographic articles.
A, —, Yes, None.
1970/71, T.p. 120.   800.
Per copy £2.10.
Indexed in: IBZ.

1509 NATURE. 1869.
Macmillan (Journals) Ltd., 4 Little Essex Street, London, WC2.
52, = +   Pure Science.
Book notices, book reviews, letters, monographic articles, obituaries, parliamentary reports.
Q, —, No, None.
T.p. 99, Ad.p. 40.   17000.
Per copy 25p, per year £15.
Indexed in: BEI, BHI, IBZ.

1510 NEW SCIENTIST AND SCIENCE JOURNAL. 1956.
New Science Publications, 128 Long Acre, London, WC2E 9QH.
52, ○ = + ‡   Applied science.
Book notices, book reviews, letters, monographic, articles, new products.
No Index.
50000.
Per copy 10p, per year £3.75.
Indexed in: BTI.

1511 NOTES AND RECORDS OF THE ROYAL SOCIETY. 1938.
The Royal Society, 6 Carlton House Terrace, London, SW1Y 5AG.
2, ○ ‡ *   History of science, history of the Royal Society and on the lives and scientific achievements of its past Fellows.
Irregular, Last issue covers volumes 1-20, Yes.
Vol. 26 (1971), T.p. 258.   850.
Per part £1.25, per year £2.50.

1512 PSI: Popular and Amateur Science Index. 1969.
Marjan Press, Bedwell Community Centre, Bedwell Crescent, Stevenage.
6, ‡ ○   Science and technology for the layman including do-it-yourself and hobbies.
No Index.
T.p. 19.
Per year £3.15.

1513 THE PROCEEDINGS OF THE ROYAL INSTITUTION
OF GREAT BRITAIN. 1851.
Applied Science Publishers Ltd., 22 Rippleside
Commercial Estate, Barking, Essex.
1, ○   Contains versions of most of the Friday Evening
Discourses and some other lectures given at the
Royal Institution, mainly of scientific or technical
interest, and intended for non-specialist readers.
Monographic articles.
A, –, Yes, None
1972, T.p. 360.   2500/3000.
Per copy £4.
Indexed in: BHI, BTI.

1514 PROCEEDINGS OF THE ROYAL SOCIETY OF
EDINBURGH: Section A Mathematical & Physical
Sciences, Section B Biology. 1940.
(Proceedings of the Royal Society of Edinburgh
1832-1939).
Royal Society of Edinburgh, 22/24 George Street,
Edinburgh, EH2 2PQ.
Irregular, * + ‡   All branches of science.
Monographic articles.
Each volume, Last issue of each volume, Yes, None.
T.p. Varies.   c. 1250 per section.
Per copy UK £1.75, per vol. £6.

1515 SCIENCE FOR PEOPLE. 1972.
(BSSRS Newsheet 1969-1972)
British Society for Social Responsibility in Science, 9
Poland Street, London, W1V 3DG.
6, *   Exploration of all issues raised by consideration
of the relationship between science and technology
and society at large.
Book notices, book reviews, letters.
No Index.

1516 SCIENCE POLICY. 1972.
(Science Policy News).
Science Policy Foundation, 2A Station Road, Frimley,
Surrey.
6, ‡
No Index.
Per year £8.

1517 SCIENCE PROGRESS: A review journal of current
scientific advance. 1894.
Blackwell Scientific Publications, Osney Mead, Oxford,
OX2 0EL.
4, ○ + =   Reviews of a particular region of research,
not for specialists in that field, but for professional
scientists in quite different disciplines and for
undergraduate students of the science in question.
Book notices, book reviews, monographic articles.
A, December, Yes, None.
Spring 1972, T.p. 150. Ad.p. 6.
Per copy £1.75, per year £6.
Indexed in: BTI, IBZ.

1518 SCIENTIFIC ERA. 1972.
Scientific Era Publications, 5/6 Maiden Lane, Stamford,
London, PE9 2AZ.
12, ‡ + *   Digest of scientific and technical news.
Aimed at bridging gap between man-in-street and
scientific authorities and industry.
New products, articles, patents, standards, tests.
No Index.
May 1972, T.p. 34.
Per copy 15p, per year £2.10.

1519 SCOTTISH SCHOOLS SCIENCE EQUIPMENT
RESEARCH CENTRE. BULLETIN. 1965.
S.S.S.E.R.C., 103 Broughton Street, Edinburgh,
EH1 3RZ.
8, +
Tests, ideas and descriptions of new equipment.
Commodity prices, articles, new products, tests.
No Index.
June 1972, T.p. 12.
Free.

1520 SOVIET SCIENCE REVIEW. 1971.
IPC Science and Technology Press Ltd., IPC House,
32 High Street, Guildford, Surrey.
6, ‡
No Index.
Per year £15.

1521 TRANSACTIONS OF THE ROYAL SOCIETY OF
EDINBURGH. 1783.
Royal Society of Edinburgh, 22, 24 George Street,
Edinburgh, EH2 2PQ.
Irregular, * + ‡ =   Research contributions in all
branches of biological science, including medicine
and geology.
Monographic articles.
Each volume, Last issue of each volume, Yes, None.
T.p. 42.   c. 1000.
Per copy varies, Per volume UK 12 gns.

1522 WALES SCIENCE BULLETIN. 1968.
Schools Council, Committee for Wales, 129 Cathedral
Road, Cardiff, CF1 9SX.
2, =   General scientific interest to primary and
secondary schools in Wales.
Letters, articles.
No Index.
March 1972, T.p. 55.
Free.

502

NATURAL HISTORY

1523 BULLETIN OF THE BRITISH MUSEUM (NATURAL
HISTORY) HISTORICAL SERIES. 1953.
British Museum (Natural History), Cromwell Road,
London, SW7 5BD.
Irregular, +   History, natural history.
Monographic articles.
Volume indexes are published, Yes, None.
500.
Subscription varies.

1524 BULLETIN OF THE CROYDON NATURAL HISTORY
AND SCIENTIFIC SOCIETY LTD. 1967.
Croydon Natural History & Scientific Society Ltd., 96a
Brighton Road, South Croydon, CR2 6AD.
6, ○ + *   Information on current research, recent
publications and domestic matters.
Book notices, obituaries.
No Index.
600.
Free to members.

1525 CARDIFF NATURALISTS' SOCIETY REPORTS AND
TRANSACTIONS. 1867.
The Society, c/o National Museum of Wales, Cardiff,
CF1 3NP.
1, ○ + *
Monographic articles, obituaries.
A, Yes, Vols. 1-70 in 1938.
T.p. 156.
Per copy £1.05p. Free to members.

1526 COUNTRY LIFE. 1897.
IPC Magazines Ltd., Tower House, Southampton Street,
London, WC2E 9QX.
52, ○   Architecture, art treasures, sport, travel. The
countryside in all its moods and pursuits—fine
houses and old towns, antiques, gardening and wild
life.
Book reviews, letters, articles.
6m, Spring/Autumn, Yes, None.

Key to reference symbols

○ popular   ‡ technical   = trade/professional

+ research   * society/institution   † house journal

T.p. 60, Ad.p. 45.   48497.
Per year £15.
Indexed in: BHI.

1527 COUNTRY-SIDE: A Magazine devoted to Nature. 1905.
The British Naturalists' Association, 'Willowfield', Boyneswood Road, Four Marks, Alton, Hants.
3, * ○ ‡ +   All aspects of natural history.
Book notices, book reviews, letters, monographic articles, obituaries.
4-yearly, June 1972, No, None.
June 1972, T.p. 50, Ad.p. 6.   2250.
Per copy 25p, per year 75p.

1528 CROYDON BIBLIOGRAPHIES FOR REGIONAL SURVEY. 1968.
Croydon Natural History & Scientific Society Ltd., 96a Brighton Road, South Croydon, CR2 6AD.
Irregular, +   Exhaustive bibliographies of published and other works relating to the geology, geography, natural history, archaeology and history of Croydon and adjacent parts of N.E. Surrey and N.W. Kent.
No Index.
1969, T.p. 21.   600.
Free to members.

1529 EAST AFRICAN WILDLIFE JOURNAL. 1963.
Blackwell Scientific Publications (for the East African Wild Life Society), Osney Mead, Oxford, OX2 EL.
4, +   Study of wildlife from any part of Africa, and also includes comprehensive reviews and brief communications.
Monographic articles.
A, December, Yes, None.
May 1972, T.p. 76, Ad.p. 4.   1500.
Per copy £2.50, per year £8.

1530 ESSEX NATURALISTS' TRUST BULLETIN. 1959.
The Trust, 9 Bury Fields, Felsted, Dunmow, Essex.
2, *   Natural history.
No Index.
T.p. 24.
Free to members.

1531 THE GLASGOW NATURALIST: journal of the Andersonian Naturalists of Glasgow. 1908.
(Proceedings of the Natural History Society of Glasgow 1852-1883; Proceedings and Transactions of the Natural History Society of Glasgow (New Series) 1883-1908; Annals of the Andersonian Naturalists' Society 1893-1925)
c/o B. W. Ribbons, Editor, Department of Botany, The University, Glasgow, G12 8QQ.
1, ○ + *   Natural history in Scotland. Proceedings of the Andersonian Naturalists of Glasgow.
Monographic articles, obituaries.
10 year, October, 1971, Yes, None.
October 1971, T.p. 80.   550.
Per copy £1.50.

1532 THE GREBE: Journal of the Hertfordshire and Middlesex Trust for Nature Conservation. 1970.
Hertfordshire and Middlesex Trust for Nature Conservation Ltd., 24 Castle Street, Hertford.
1, ○ ‡ *   Nature conservation in Hertfordshire and Middlesex, with particular reference to nature reserves owned and/or managed by the Trust, and to field studies carried out by local schools.
Book notices, book reviews, letters, monographic articles, obituaries.
4 year, —, Yes, None.
1970, T.p. 32.   1500.
Per copy 20p.

1533 HABITAT. 1965.
Council for Nature, Zoological Gardens, Regent's Park, London, NW1 4RY.
12, ○ *   Newsletter sent to all interested individuals and natural history societies affiliated to the Council for Nature.
Book notices, book reviews, obituaries, parliamentary reports.
No Index.
April 1972, T.p. 8.   2500.
Per copy 5p, per year £1.50.

1534 HAMPSHIRE FIELD CLUB PROCEEDINGS.
Hampshire Field Club, Dept. of Archaeology, University, Southampton.
1, * =   Archaeology, history in Hampshire.
Monographic articles.
A, —, Yes, None.
T.p. 150.
Free to members.

1535 JOHN PEEL JOTTINGS. 1954.
S. Redmayne & Sons Ltd., Station Road, Wigton, Cumberland.
2/3   Deals with Cumbrian countryside subjects, sent out to customers only, few copies to prospective customers.
No Index.

1536 JOURNAL OF NATURAL HISTORY: An International journal of taxonomic and general biology. 1967.
(Annals and magazine of Natural History 1838-1966)
Taylor & Francis Ltd., 10-14 Macklin Street, London, WC2B 5NF.
6, + = *   Taxonomic and general biology.
Book notices, book reviews, monographic articles.
A, In last issue of volume, Yes, None.
July-August 1972, T.p. 118.
Per copy £3.50, per year £18.50.
Indexed in: IBZ.

1537 JOURNAL OF THE CAMBORNE-REDRUTH NATURAL HISTORY SOCIETY. 1969.
Camborne-Redruth Nat. Hist. Soc., c/o 'Shang-ri-la', Reskadinnick, Camborne, Cornwall.
1, *   Local and Cornish natural history—mammals, birds, amphibia, flowering plants, ferns, bryophytes and lichens, also insects,—ecology, distribution in Cornwall, any new records.
Book reviews, monographic articles, obituaries.
No Index.
Vol. 2, part 2, Sept. 1970, T.p. 32.
Per year 75p.

1538 JOURNAL OF THE SOCIETY FOR THE BIBLIOGRAPHY OF NATURAL HISTORY. 1935.
Society for the Bibliography of Natural History, c/o British Museum (Natural History), London, SW7 5BD.
2, + =   All fields of the bibliography of natural history (including earth sciences), and the history of the natural sciences also contains review articles in these fields.
Book reviews, letters, monographic articles, obituaries.
3 year, —, Yes, None.
April 1972, T.p. 66.   500.
Per copy £3, per year £6, Free to members.

1539 THE KIST: The magazine of the Natural History and Antiquarian Society of Mid Argyll. 1971.
The Secretary, N.H.A.S.M.A., Harbour House, Crinan Lochgilphead, Argyll.
2, ○ *   All aspects of mid Argyll.
Book notices, book reviews, letters, monographic articles.
No Index.
T.p. 23.   500.
Per copy 15p, per year 30p, Free to members.

1540 NATURE IN CAMBRIDGESHIRE. 1958.
Cambridgeshire & Isle of Ely Naturalists' Trust Limited, 1 Brookside, Cambridge.
1, * =   Annual Report and Accounts of CAMBIENT plus scientific articles on wildlife of Cambs & Isle of Ely. Occasional Membership lists.
Book reviews, monographic articles, obituaries.

A, with each issue
1972, T.p. 45, Ad.p. 3.   2000.
Per copy 25p, and free to members.

1541 NATURE IN WALES: The journal of the Naturalists' Trusts of West Wales, North Wales & Radnor. 1955.
West Wales Naturalists' Trust, 4 Victoria Place, Haverfordwest.
2, ○ + *   Natural history in Wales.
Book notices, book reviews, letters, monographic articles.
5 year, —, No, None.
March 1972, T.p. 64, Ad.p. 4.   3000.
Per copy 55p, per year £2, Free to members.

1542 NEWSLETTER. 1958.
Cambridgeshire & Isle of Ely Naturalists' Trust Limited, 1 Brookside, Cambridge.
2, * =   Nature reserve news, excursion and meeting programmes. County activities in wildlife conservation.
Book notices, book reviews, letters, brief articles, new products, obituaries, parliamentary reports.
No Index.
January 1972, T.p. 6.   2000.
Free to members.

1543 NEWSLETTER.
Leicestershire & Rutland Trust for Natural Conservation, 68 Outwoods Road, Loughborough.
4, ○
No Index.
Free to members.

1544 NEWSLETTER OF THE SURREY NATURALISTS' TRUST.
Surrey Naturalists' Trust Ltd., 96a Brighton Road, South Croydon, CR2 6AD.
3-4, ○ *   Information on current conservation work in the County, domestic matters &c.
Book notices, letters, articles, obituaries.
Free to members.

1545 NORTH STAFFORDSHIRE JOURNAL OF FIELD STUDIES: incorporating the Transactions of the North Staffordshire Field Club. 1961.
University of Keele, Keele, Staffordshire, ST5 5BG.
1, *   All matters concerning North Staffs. Archaeology, history, field studies etc.
Monographic articles.
A, Dec., Yes, None.
1971, T.p. 152.   1000
Per copy £1.75.
Indexed in: BHI.

1546 PROCEEDINGS AND REPORTS. Belfast Natural History and Philosophical Society. 1871.
Belfast Natural History & Philosophical Society, 7 College Square North, Belfast, 1.
2 year, *   Natural, local, scientific history.
Monographic articles.
No Index.
1961-4, T.p. 67.   100.
Per copy 50p, Free to members.

1547 PROCEEDINGS OF THE BRISTOL NATURALISTS SOCIETY. 1863.
The Society, City Museum, Bristol, 8.
1, +
Monographic articles.
No Index.
T.p. 113, Ad.p. 6.
Per copy 75p, Free to members.

1548 PROCEEDINGS OF THE COTTESWOLD NATURALISTS' FIELD CLUB. 1853.
Society, Editor, Dr. M. West, Bunch of Grapes, Painswick, Glos.
1, ‡ + *   Geological, botanical, zoological and antiquarian interests.
Book reviews, monographic articles, obituaries.
No Index.
1970-71, T.p. 46.
Per copy £1.50, Free to members.
Indexed in: BHI.

1549 PROCEEDINGS OF THE CROYDON NATURAL HISTORY AND SCIENTIFIC SOCIETY. 1900.
(Reports of the Croydon Microscopical Club, Proceedings of the Croydon Microscopical and Natural History Club 1879-99)
Croydon Natural History & Scientific Society Ltd., 96a Brighton Road, South Croydon, CR2 6AD.
2/4, ‡ + *   Articles on any of the following aspects of Croydon or the adjacent 200 square miles of N.E. Surrey and N.W. Kent: geology; geography; archaeology; industrial archaeology; history; natural history &c.
Monographic articles, obituaries.
Approx. 5-8 years, On completion of each volume, Yes, None.
1970, T.p. 40.   600.
Per year £2.

1550 PROCEEDINGS OF THE DORSET NATURAL HISTORY AND ARCHAEOLOGICAL SOCIETY. 1928.
The Society, County Museum, High West Street, Dorchester.
1, * ‡ + =   History, archaeology, natural history, fine arts.
Book notices, book reviews, letters, monographic articles, obituaries.
Each issue, cumulated approx. each 40 vols.
T.p. 320.
Per copy varies, Free to members.
Indexed in: BHI.

1551 PROCEEDINGS OF THE LANCASHIRE AND CHESHIRE FAUNA SOCIETY.
c/o 11 Ashmore Avenue, Stockport, Cheshire, SK3 0QY.
○
No Index.
Free to members.

1552 SCOTTISH WILDLIFE TRUST NEWSLETTER. 1965.
The Scottish Wildlife Trust Ltd., 8 Dublin Street, Edinburgh, EH1 3PP.
3, ○ ‡ *   Work of the Trust and progress in nature conservation generally, throughout Scotland.
Reports, book reviews, articles.
No Index.
April 1972, T.p. 30.   4500.
Subscription to Trust £1 per year. Journal issued free to members.

1553 SELBOURNE MAGAZINE. 1963.
Selbourne Society, 57 Carlton Road, Ealing, London, W5.
4, ○ *   Conservation of places of interest and natural beauty.
Book notices, book reviews, articles, obituaries.
No Index.
T.p. 12, Ad.p. 1.
Per copy 35p.
Free to members.

1554 THE STARFISH: journal of the Association of School Natural History Societies. 1947.
The Society, c/o N. J. Mussett, Seaford College, Petworth, Sussex.
1, ‡ *   All aspects of school natural history, especially field work.
Book reviews, monographic articles, obituaries.
Index only available internally.
T.p. 42.   c. 500.
Free to members.

1555 THE SURREY NATURALIST: Annual Report of the Surrey Naturalists' Trust.
The Surrey Naturalists' Trust Ltd., 96a Brighton Road, South Croydon, Surrey, CR2 6AD.

1, ‡ ○ + *   Field biology and biological and geological conservation in the historical county of Surrey, and reports on practical conservation work on nature reserves and sites of special scientific interest.
Monographic articles.
No Index.
T.p. 43, Ad.p. 2.   1500.
Free to members.

1556 TRANSACTIONS OF THE CARDIFF NATURALISTS' SOCIETY. 1903.
(Cardiff Naturalists' Society Report and Transactions, 1867-1902.)
Cardiff Naturalists' Society, National Museum of Wales, Cathays Park, Cardiff.
1, ○ * +   Natural history of Cardiff and district.
Monographic articles.
General index only Volumes I to LXX
1867-8 to 1937.
Vol. 95, 1968/70, T.p. 76.
Per copy £1.25.   Free to members.

1557 TRANSACTIONS OF THE LINCOLNSHIRE NATURALISTS' UNION. 1895.
Lincolnshire Naturalists' Union, City & County Museum, Lincoln.
1 in two parts, ○ ‡ +   Results of investigations of geology, fauna and physical features of Lincolnshire.
Monographic articles.
4 year, —, No, None.
1971, T.p. 40.
Free to members.

1558 TRANSACTIONS OF THE NORFOLK & NORWICH NATURALISTS' SOCIETY. 1869.
Soman Wherry Press, Norwich
2, * +   Natural history.
Irregularly, c. 10 years.
T.p. 50.
Free to members.

1559 TRANSACTIONS OF THE NATURAL HISTORY SOCIETY OF NORTHUMBERLAND, DURHAM AND NEWCASTLE UPON TYNE. 1904.
(Transactions of the Natural History Society of Northumberland, Durham and Newcastle on Tyne 1831-1838; Transactions of the Tyneside Naturalists' Field Club 1846-1864; Natural History Transactions of Northumberland and Durham 1867-1913.
The Society, The Hancock Museum, Newcastle upon Tyne, NE2 4PT.
2, * + =   Local natural history including geology, mammals and other aspects of zoology, ornithology and botany.
Monographic articles.
No Index.
T.p. 230. c. 700
Free to members paying £4 subscription and on exchange.
Indexed in: BHI, IBZ.

1560 TRANSACTIONS OF THE WOOLHOPE NATURALISTS' FIELD CLUB. 1865.
Woolhope Naturalists Field Club, c/o J.W. Tonkin, Chy an Whyloryon, Wigmore, Leominster, Herefordshire, HR6 9UD.
1, +   Research in archaeology, architecture, history, geology, botany, natural history in Herefordshire and surrounding area.
Monographic articles, obituaries.
3 year, 1872 etc., Yes, None.
1970, T.p. 180.
Per copy £1.50. Free to members.
Indexed in: BHI.

1561 THE WORCESTERSHIRE NATURALISTS' CLUB NEWS LETTER Incorporating TRANSACTIONS. 1968.
(Transactions of the Worcs. Nat. Club 1847 to 1962-65).
The Worcestershire Naturalists' Club, 202 Pickersleigh Road, Malvern, Worcs. WR14 2QX.
2, * +   General natural history and conservation. Reports of Field Meetings and Winter Meetings. Sections—Ornithological—Botanical—Mammals—Lepidoptera—Conservation—Junior—Book Reviews—etc.
Book reviews.
No Index.
February 1972, T.p. 42.
Per year £1.

1562 WORLD WILDLIFE NEWS. 1967.
World Wildlife Fund, 7 Plumtree Court, London EC4.
3, ○   Conservation, wildlife and environment, WWF projects and regional news in UK.
Book reviews.
No Index.
Autumn 1971, T.p. 22.
Free to members.

51

MATHEMATICS

1563 BULLETIN OF THE LONDON MATHEMATICAL SOCIETY. 1969.
C.F. Hodgson & Son Ltd., 23 Pakenham Street, London WC1.
3, + =   Research in mathematics.
Articles.
A, Last issue of volume, No, None.
T.p. 192.
Per copy £2.25, per year £6.   Free to members.
Indexed in: IBZ.

1565 INTERNATIONAL JOURNAL OF SYSTEMS SCIENCE. 1971.
Taylor & Francis Ltd., 10-14 Macklin St., WC2B 5NF.
6, ‡ = +   Theory and practice of mathematical modelling, simulation, optimization and control.
Book notices, book reviews, monographic articles.
A, in last issue, Yes, None.
July 1972, T.p. 111.
Per copy £3, per year £22.

1566 JOURNAL OF STRUCTURAL LEARNING. 1968.
(ISGML Bulletin).
Gordon & Breach Ltd., (for the International Study Group for Mathematics Learning), 41/42 William 4th Street, London WC2.
4, +   Research into mathematics teaching.
Monographic articles.
No Index.
T.p. 81.
Per year £7.50.

1567 JOURNAL OF THE INSTITUTE OF MATHEMATICS AND ITS APPLICATION. 1965.
Academic Press Inc. (London) Ltd., 24/28 Oval Road, London NW1.
4, * ‡ +   All areas of mathematical application.
Book reviews, monographic articles.
A (Author only), —, Yes, None.
T.p. 100.
Per year £7.50.

1568 JOURNAL OF THE LONDON MATHEMATICAL SOCIETY. 1926.
C.F. Hodgson & Son Ltd., 23 Pakenham Street, London WC1.
4, = +
Research papers.
A, Last issue of year, Yes, Irregular.
T.p. 192.   2500.
Per copy £2.75, per year £10.
Indexed in: IBZ.

1569 MANIFOLD: A mathematics magazine. 1968.
Manifold Publications, Mathematics Institute,
University of Warwick, Coventry CV4 7AL.
3, ○ ‡ +   Aims to present mathematics as it is being practised by present-day mathematicians, but with the minimum of technicality, in a form suitable for the 'interested layman'. Plus games, cartoons, etc.
Book notices, book reviews, letters, monographic articles, obituaries.
No Index.
Spring 1971, T.p. 42, Ad.p. 1.   700.
Per copy 15p, per year 50p.

1570 THE MATHEMATICAL GAZETTE: The Journal of the Mathematical Association. 1894.
G. Bell & Sons, Ltd., York House, Portugal Street, London WC2A 2HL.
4, * ‡   Mathematics, and in particular the teaching of mathematics, at high school and college level.
Book notices, book reviews, letters, monographic articles, obituaries.
A, February, Yes, None.
December 1971, T.p. 127, Ad.p. 8.
Per copy 90p, per year £3.60. Free to members.

1571 MATHEMATICAL PIE. 1950.
Mathematical Pie Ltd., Alpha House, The Avenue, Rowington, Warks.
3, ○   Mathematical problems, curiosities etc., for schools etc.
No Index.
Summer 1972, T.p. 8.   50000.
Per copy 6p, per year 18p.

1572 MATHEMATICAL SPECTRUM: A Magazine of Contemporary Mathematics. 1968.
The Editor, Mathematical Spectrum, Hicks Building, The University, Sheffield S3 7RH.
2, =   Pure mathematics, applied mathematics, statistics, operational research, computing science. Also educational, opportunities, career prospects, and historical topics.
Book reviews, letters, articles.
No Index.
No. 2 1971/2, T.p. 46.   2000.
Per copy 23p, per year 40p.

1573 MATHEMATICS IN SCHOOL. 1971.
Longman Journals (for the Mathematical Association), 5 Bentinck Street, London W1M 5RN.
6, * †   Written for teachers of mathematics, especially those who teach 7-16 year olds.
Book reviews, letters, monographic articles, new products, tests.
A, —, Yes, 10 year.
March 1972, T.p. 34, Ad.p. 9.   5000.
Per copy 50p, per year £3.

1574 PHILOSOPHICAL TRANSACTIONS OF THE ROYAL SOCIETY. SERIES A (MATHEMATICAL & PHYSICAL SCIENCES). 1887.
(Philosophical Transactions of the Royal Society 1665-1886).
The Royal Society, 6 Carlton House Terrace, London, SW1Y 5AG.
2, +   Papers, normally exceeding 24 printed pages, containing results or methods of critical importance.
A, Last issue, Yes, 10 year Author index.
1545.
Per volume £14.25: The price of each part varies in accordance with the number of pages and illustrations it contains. Each volume is closed when the price of its constituent parts is not less than £17.50.

1575 PROCEEDINGS OF THE CAMBRIDGE PHILOSOPHICAL SOCIETY. 1843.
Cambridge University Press, PO Box 92, London NW1 2DB.
6, +   Research in all branches of mathematics including applications in the natural sciences.
Book reviews, monographic articles.
6m, May/November, Yes, 10 year.
May 1972, T.p. 146.   1050.
Per copy £4, per year £20.
Indexed in: IBZ.

1576 PROCEEDINGS OF THE EDINBURGH MATHEMATICAL SOCIETY. 1886.
Oliver & Boyd Ltd., Tweeddale Court, 14 High Street, Edinburgh, 1.
2, +   Pure and applied mathematics.
Book reviews, papers, obituaries.
2 year, —, None.
T.p. c. 88, Ad.p. 2.
Free to members.

1577 PROCEEDINGS OF THE LONDON MATHEMATICAL SOCIETY. 1865, New Series 1951.
Oxford University Press, Press Road, Neasden, London NW10.
8, +   Pure and applied mathematics.
Book reviews, research papers.
Every 4 issues (2 vols per year), —Yes, None.
April 1972, T.p. 191.   1600.
Per copy £3.60, per year £26.

1578 PROCEEDINGS OF THE ROYAL SOCIETY. SERIES A MATHEMATICAL AND PHYSICAL SCIENCES. 1905.
(Proceedings of the Royal Society 1854-1904; Abstracts of papers published in Phil. Trans. 1800).
The Royal Society, 6 Carlton House Terrace, London, SW1Y 5AG.
6, +   Papers, not normally exceeding 24 printed pages, containing results or methods of critical importance.
A, —, Yes, 10 year.
13 June 1972, T.p. 144.   3250.
Per copy £1.75, per year £6.25.
Indexed in: IBZ.

1579 QUARTERLY JOURNAL OF MATHEMATICS. 1930.
Oxford University Press, Press Road, Neasden, London NW10.
4, +   Pure mathematics and its applications.
Book reviews, monographic articles.
A, —, Yes, None.
March 1972, T.p. 112, Ad.p. 2.   1000.
Per copy £2, per year £7.

1580 USSR COMPUTATIONAL MATHEMATICS AND MATHEMATICAL PHYSICS [Cover-to cover translation of Zhurnal Vychislitel 'noi Matematiki i Matematicheskoi Fiziki]. 1969.
Pergamon Press Ltd., Headington Hill Hall, Oxford OX3 0BW.
6, + =   Computational mathematics and branches of mathematical physics.
Book reviews, short articles.
A, Last issue of volume, Yes, None.
Per copy £10.50, per year £60.

512

ALGEBRA

1581 LINEAR AND MULTILINEAR ALGEBRA. [in preparation].
Gordon & Breach, 41/42 William 4th Street, London WC2.
4, +   Linear and multilinear algebra and certain cognate areas.
Book notices, book reviews, letters, monographic articles.
A, —, No, None.
Per year £17.25.

513.83
TOPOLOGY

1582 TOPOLOGY. 1961.
Pergamon Press Ltd., Headington Hill Hall, Oxford OX3 0BW.
4, + = Mathematics with special emphasis on topology.
Monographic articles.
A, First issue of succeeding volume, Yes, None.
T.p. 100.
Per copy £4, per year £14.

519.24
PROBABILITY

1583 ADVANCES IN APPLIED PROBABILITY. 1969.
Applied Probability Trust, Dept. of Probability & Statistics, The University, Sheffield S3 7RH.
3, + Review and expository papers in applied probability, as well as mathematical and scientific papers of interest to probabilists.
Abstracts, letters, monographic articles.
5 year, —, Yes, None.
April 1972, T.p. 192.   800.
Per year £5.25.

1584 JOURNAL OF APPLIED PROBABILITY. 1964.
Applied Probability Trust, Dept. of Probability & Statistics, The University, Sheffield S3 7RH.
4, + Applications of probability theory to the biological, physical, social and technological sciences.
Letters, articles.
5 year, —, Yes, None.
March 72, T.p. 234, Ad.p. 1.   1500.
Per year £10.

519.28
OPERATIONS RESEARCH

1585 CYBERNETICS ABSTRACTS. Referativnyy zhurnal Kibernetika No. 1, 1964.
(Theoretical Cybernetics Abstracts).
Scientific Information Consultants Ltd., 661 Finchley Road, London NW2 2HN.
12, ‡ † English translation of about 10000 bibiliogr. entries and abstracts on the theory and application of control systems, information theory, operations research and mathematical economics, programming and computer theory, application of mathematics and cybernetics in biology, psychology, medicine, linguistics.
Abstracts, book notices, new products, patents.
Author index only.
10, 1970, T.p. 200.
Per year £70.

1586 OPERATIONAL RESEARCH QUARTERLY. 1950.
Pergamon Press Ltd., Headington Hill Hall, Oxford OX3 0BW.
4, = + Application of O.R. topics in management, business, government and defence.
Book notices, book reviews, monographic articles.
A, March, Yes, None.
T.p. 120, Ad.p. 6.
Per copy £2.50, per year £7.50.
Indexed in: BTI

521
ASTRONOMY

1587 ASTRONOMY & SPACE. 1971.
David & Charles (Publishers) Ltd., South Devon House, Newton Abbot, Devon.
4, ○ ‡ * Study of astronomy and space, mainly intended for the amateur astronomer.
Book notices, book reviews, letters, monographic articles, obituaries.
A, June, No, None.
June 1972, T.p. 88, Ad.p. 4.   1500.
Per copy 65p, per year £2.50.

1588 HERMES: Journal of the Junior Astronomical Society. 1960.
(The Junior Astronomer 1953-60).
Junior Astronomical Society, 58 Vaughan Gardens, Ilford, Essex.
4, ○ * Astronomy and spaceflight, many written by specialists and professional astronomers but designed for a non-technical audience.
Book reviews, letters, monographic articles.
No Index.
October 1971, T.p. 26, Ad.p. 6.   1600.
Per year £1.50. Free to members.

1589 MONTHLY NOTICES OF THE ROYAL ASTRONOMICAL SOCIETY. 1827.
Blackwell Scientific Publications Ltd., Osney Mead, Oxford OX2 0EL.
20, ‡ + * Results of original research in positional and dynamical astronomy, astrophysics, radio astronomy, cosmology, space research, and the design of astronomical instruments.
Short communications.
Per volume (4 issues), Last part of each volume, Yes, None.
May 1972, T.p. 120.   1865.
Per copy £3.50, per volume £12.50.

1590 THE OBSERVATORY: a review of astronomy. 1876.
The Observatory Magazine, Royal Greenwich Observatory, Herstmonceux Castle, Hailsham, Sussex.
6, + Professional astronomy in general.
Book notices, book reviews, letters, monographic articles, obituaries.
A, December, Yes, 15 yr.
April 1972, T.p. 43, Ad.p. 3.   3500.
Per copy 60p, per year £3.

1591 QUARTERLY JOURNAL OF THE ROYAL ASTRONOMICAL SOCIETY. 1960.
Blackwell Scientific Publications Ltd., Osney Mead, Oxford OX2 0EL.
4, * = Reports of Society's meetings.
Monographic articles, obituaries.
A, December, Yes, None.
March 1972, T.p. 114.   3900.
Per copy £1.25, per year £4.

1592 ROYAL OBSERVATORY ANNALS. 1956.
(Greenwich Observations 1836-1955).
Royal Greenwich Observatory, Herstmonceux Castle, Hailsham, Sussex.
1/2, + Astronomical research and allied subjects.
No Index.
Subscription on application.

1593 ROYAL OBSERVATORY BULLETINS. 1956.
(Greenwich Observations 1836-1955).
Royal Greenwich Observatory, Herstmonceux Castle, Hailsham, Sussex.
6, + Astronomical research and allied subjects.
Irregular, End of volume, Yes, None.
Subscription on application.

1594 WEBB SOCIETY QUARTERLY JOURNAL. 1968.
The Webb Society, K. Glyn Jones, Wild Rose, Church Road, Winkfield, Windsor, Berks.
4, * Amateur astronomy, specializing in observations and history of nebulae, star-clusters, and double stars.
Book reviews, letters, monographic articles, standards, tests.

No Index.
400.
Per year £1.

523.03
ASTROPHYSICS

1595 ASTROPHYSICAL LETTERS. 1967.
Gordon & Breach, 41/42 William 4th Street, London WC2.
4, + ‡   New views and discoveries in all branches of astrophysical research.
Book notices, book reviews, letters, monographic articles, tests.
6m, At close of each volume, No, None.
Subscription on application.

1596 COMMENTS ON ASTROPHYSICS AND SPACE PHYSICS. 1969.
Gordon & Breach, 41/42 William 4th Street, London WC2.
6, + ‡   Critical commentaries on significant current developments appearing in scientific literature.
Book notices, book reviews, legal notes, letters, monographic articles, new products, patents, standards, tests.
No Index.
Subscription on application.

1597 EARTH AND EXTRATERRESTRIAL SCIENCES: Conference reports and professional activities. 1969.
Gordon & Breach, 41/42 William 4th Street, London WC2.
8, + ‡   Reports on important new results and developments in basic research advances in earth, space, and astronomical sciences.
Book notices, book reviews, letters, monographic articles, tests.
No Index.
Subscription on application.

523.4
PLANETS. SPACEFLIGHT.

1598 JOURNAL OF THE BRITISH INTERPLANETARY SOCIETY. 1934.
British Interplanetary Society, 12 Bessborough Gardens, London SW1 2JJ.
12, ‡ + *   All areas of space research and technology.
Book notices, book reviews, monographic articles.
A, December, Yes, None.
June 1972, T.p. 64.   1500.
Per year £12. Free to members.
Indexed in: IBZ

1599 PLANETARY AND SPACE SCIENCE. 1959.
Pergamon Press Ltd., Headington Hill Hall, Oxford OX3 0BW.
12, + =   Sun and planets, their atmospheres and related space.
Book reviews, monographic articles.
A, Last issue of volume, Yes, None.
T.p. 125.
Per copy £4, per year £44.

523.72
SOLAR ENERGY

1600 SOLAR ENERGY.
Pergamon Press Ltd., Headington Hill Hall, Oxford OX3 0BW.
4, + =   Science and technology of solar energy application.

Short articles.
A, Last issue of volume, Yes, None.
Per copy £4, per year £12.

526.8
CARTOGRAPHY

1601 SUC BULLETIN. 1964.
Society of University Cartographers, Department of Geography, Social Studies Building, PO Box 147, University of Liverpool, Liverpool, L69 3BX.
2, ‡ *   General cartographical matters. Reviews of maps and atlases. Cartographic notes dealing with matters of topical interest.
Book reviews, letters, monographic articles,
No Index.
Summer 1971, T.p. 121.
Per copy 75p, per year £1.25. Free to members.

1602 THE CARTOGRAPHIC JOURNAL. 1964.
The British Cartographic Society, c/o 4 Tamesa Ho., Chertsey Road, Shepperton, Middlesex.
2, ‡ = +   All aspects of map making, map librarianship, map use, history of maps.
Book reviews, commodity prices, letters, monographic articles, new products, obituaries, standards, tests.
4 year, 1968, Yes, None.
December 1971, T.p. 85, Ad.p. 6.
Per copy £1.25, per year £2.50. Free to members.

526.9
SURVEYING

1603 CHARTERED SURVEYOR: Journal of the Royal Institution of Chartered Surveyors. 1955.
(Journal of the Surveyors Institution 1921-1930; Journal of the Chartered Surveyors Institution 1930-1946; Journal of the Royal Institution of Chartered Surveyors 1946-1955).
Royal Institution of Chartered Surveyors, 12 Great George Street, London, SW1P 3AD.
12, ‡ *   Surveying specialisations: land agency and agriculture, quantity surveying, building surveying, land surveying, estate agency, planning, minerals surveying, valuations.
Abstracts, book notices, book reviews, legal notes, letters, monographic articles, new products, obituaries, parliamentary reports.
A, 3 months after end of volume, Yes, None.
June 1972, T.p. 57, Ad.p. 47.   45000.
Per copy 50p, per year £5.

1604 CONSTRUCTION SURVEYOR. Journal of the Construction Surveyors' Institute. 1970.
(Building Surveyor).
The Institute, Temple Chambers, Temple Avenue, London, EC4.
6, * ‡ = +   All aspects of surveying.
Book reviews, legal notes, letters, articles, new companies, new products, parliamentary reports, standards, tests.
No Index.
T.p. 24, Ad.p. 12.   3500.
Free to members.

1605 ENGINEER SURVEYOR: Journal of the Engineer Surveyor's Association. 1933.
Engineer Surveyor's Association, 4 Hall Street, Manchester, 2.
10, ‡ = *   Mainly affairs of the Association.
Book reviews, letters, articles, new products, obituaries, patents, standards, tests.
No Index.
June 1972, T.p. 24, Ad.p. 7.   2500.
per copy 12½p, per year £1.50.

1606 SURVEY: Journal of the Guild of Surveyors.
Guild of Surveyors, 90 Camberwell Road, London, SE5.
4, = ‡ *   All branches of surveying, new techniques, instrumentation, case studies.
Book reviews, legal notes, letters, articles, new products, parliamentary reports.
No Index.
Spring 1972, T.p. 24.
Per copy 37½p. Free to members.

1607 SURVEY REVIEW. 1963.
(Empire Survey Review 1931-62).
Directorate of Overseas Surveys, Kingston Road, Tolworth, Surrey.
4, ‡   Land surveying including mapping and legal or cadastral surveys and the computation of these.
Abstracts, book notices, book reviews, letters, monographic articles, new products, obituaries, standards, tests.
2 year, April 1971, Yes, None.
April 1971, T.p. 48, Ad.p. 12.   1200.
Per copy 63p, per year £2.50.

1608 SURVEYOR—LOCAL GOVERNMENT TECHNOLOGY.
IPC Building & Contract Journals Ltd., 40 Bowling Green Lane, London, EC1.
52, = ‡   All aspects of surveying in the field of local government.
Book reviews, letters, monographic articles.
No Index.
Per year £7.80.
Indexed in: BTI.

526.918

PHOTOGRAMMETRY

1609 PHOTOGRAMMETRIC RECORD. Official Journal of the Photogrammetric Society.
The Society, 5 Ashbourne Grove, London, NW7.
2, = ‡ +
Book reviews, letters, monographic articles, obituaries.
3 year, —, Yes, None.
T.p. 80, Ad.p. 19.
Indexed in: BTI.

527

NAVIGATION

1610 THE JOURNAL OF NAVIGATION. 1972.
(The Journal of the Institute of Navigation—1948-1971)
John Murray (Publishers) Ltd., 50 Albemarle Street, London, W1.
4, * + = ‡   Science of navigation including those presented at meetings of the Institute, and discussion. A record of current navigational work, reviews of important books and matters of concern to those interested in navigation.
Book notices, book reviews, letters, monographic articles, obituaries.
A, October, Yes, 1948-1963.
T.p. 124, Ad.p. 8.
Per copy £2.
Indexed in: BTI.

53

PHYSICS

1611 ADVANCES IN PHYSICS. 1952.
Taylor & Francis Ltd., 10-14 Macklin Street, London, WC2B 5NF.
6, ‡ +   Experimental and theoretical work in all major branches of physics.
Book notices, book reviews, monographic articles.
A, in last issue of volume, Yes, None.
January 1972, T.p. 198.
Per copy £4.50, per year £24.50.
Indexed in: BTI.

1612 CONTEMPORARY PHYSICS. 1959.
Taylor & Francis Ltd., 10-14 Macklin Street, London, WC2B 5NF.
6, ‡ + =   A review of physics and associated technologies.
Book notices, book reviews, monographic articles.
A, in last issue of volume, Yes, None.
May 1972, T.p. 95, Ad.p. 4.
Per copy £2.50, per year £13.

1613 CURRENT PAPERS IN PHYSICS. 1966.
INSPEC, The Institution of Electrical Engineers, Savoy Place, London, WC2R 0BL.
24, + ‡ =   Current awareness tool for dissemination within laboratories and development organisations, and provides the title, authors and bibliographic reference for every entry published in its companion. Abstracts Journal, with same classification system.
Current titles.
No Index.
Per copy 70p, per year £7. Non-members £14.

1614 EUROPHYSICS NEWS. 1970.
European Physical Society, c/o Church Gate Press, Leicester.
12, ‡ * +   Items of current interest to the physics community throughout Europe.
Articles.
No Index.
April 1972, T.p. 12.
Free to members.

1615 JOURNAL OF PHYSICS A: Mathematical Nuclear and General Physics. 1968.
(Proceedings of the Physical Society 1874-1967).
The Institute of Physics, London and Bristol, Netherton House, Marsh Street, Bristol BS1 4BT.
12, ‡ +   Relativity, quantum optics, fundamental particle physics, nuclear physics, statistical mechanics, theoretical physics, mathematical methods, astrophysics, space physics, cosmic rays, plasma and discharge physics, magnetohydrodynamics.
Book notices, book reviews, letters, monographic articles.
A, December, Yes, None.
January 1972, T.p. 188.   2174.
Per copy £3, per year £36.
Indexed in: IBZ.

1616 JOURNAL OF PHYSICS D: Applied Physics. 1968.
(British Journal of Applied Physics 1950-1968.
The Institute of Physics, London and Bristol, Netherton House, Marsh Street, Bristol BS1 4BT.
18, ‡ +   Crystal growth, texture and morphology of solids, their relation to properties of materials, applied metal semi-conductor, dielectric, radio physics, acoustics, electron optics, wave propagation. Applied discharge physics, plasma physics, magnetohydrodynamics, masers, laser neutron transport.
Book notices, book reviews, letters, monographic articles.
A, December, Yes, None.
December 1971, T.p. 223.   2717.
Per copy £2.50, per year £39.
Indexed in: BTI.

1617 THE JOURNAL OF PHYSICS AND CHEMISTRY OF SOLIDS.
Pergamon Press Ltd., Headington Hill Hall, Oxford OX3 0BW.
12, + =   All aspects of the fundamental physics and chemistry of the solid state.
Book reviews, monographic articles.
A, Last issue of volume, Yes, None.
Per copy £5.50, per year £64.

1618 JOURNAL OF PLASMA PHYSICS. 1967.
Cambridge University Press, PO Box 92, London NW1 2DB.
6, +   Behaviour and uses of ionized media.
Book reviews, monographic articles.
A, November, Yes, None.
February 1972, T.p. 188.   800.
Per copy £5, per year £24.

1619 JOURNAL OF THE FRANKLIN INSTITUTE. 1826
Pergamon Press Ltd., Headington Hill Hall, Oxford OX3 0BW.
12, + =   All branches of the physical sciences, pure and applied.
Book reviews, monographic articles.
A, Last issue of volume, Yes, None.
Per copy £2, per year £20.

1620 METAL PHYSICS.
Institute of Physics, 1 Lowther Gardens, Prince Consort Road, London SW7 2AB.
6, = ‡
A, —, Yes, None.
Per year £18.

1621 PATTERN RECOGNITION. 1968.
Pergamon Press Ltd., Headington Hill Hall, Oxford OX3 0BW.
4, = +   All aspects of pattern recognition in theory and hardware and software.
Book reviews, monographic articles.
A, Last issue of volume, Yes, None.
Per copy £5.50, per year £20.

1622 THE PHILOSOPHICAL MAGAZINE. 1798.
Taylor & Francis Ltd., 10-14 Macklin Street, London, WC2B 5NF.
12, ‡ = +   Experimental, theoretical and applied physics.
Monographic articles.
6m, in last issue of volumes (2 per year), Yes, None.
July 1972, T.p. 263.
Per copy £3.75, per year £41.
Indexed in: BTI, IBZ.

1623 PHYSICS ABSTRACTS. 1898.
INSPEC, The Institution of Electrical Engineers, Savoy Place, London, WC2R 0BL.
24, + ‡ =   c. 200 classified subject codes which cover the whole of physics, from elementary particles to astrophysics. The subject index has about 1700 alphabetical subject headings under which relevant entries are listed. The number of items currently included is approx. 85000 per year.
Abstracts.
6m, —, No, 4 year.
Per copy £6, per year £130. Journal available in either paper or microfiche editions. Combined sub. to paper and microfiche £195 p.a.

1624 PHYSICS BULLETIN. 1968.
(Bulletin of the Institute of Physics and the Physical Society 1949-1967)
The Institute of Physics (London and Bristol), Netherton House, Marsh Street, Bristol BS1 4BT.
12, ‡ + * =   All aspects of physics.
Book notices, book reviews, letters, monographic articles, new products.
A, December, Yes, None.
June 1972, T.p. 56, Ad.p. 9.
Per copy £1, per year £12.

1625 PROGRESS OF PHYSICS 1967.
Gordon & Breach, 41/42 William 4th Street, London, WC2.
12, + ‡   Reports on the latest research results from all branches of physics, emphasizing problems of high energy physics, relativity theory and other disciplines.
Book notices, book reviews, letters, monographic articles, tests.
A, —, Yes, None.
Subscription on application.

1626 REPORTS ON PROGRESS IN PHYSICS. 1934.
The Institute of Physics, Netherton House, Marsh Street, Bristol, BS1 4BT.
12, ‡ + =   All branches of physics.
Monographic articles.
5 year, —, Yes, None.
No. 6, 1971, T.p. 108, Ad.p. 4.   1500.
Per copy £2.50, per year £30.

1627 REVIEW OF PHYSICS IN TECHNOLOGY. 1970.
The Institute of Physics (London and Bristol), Netherton House, Marsh Street, Bristol BS1 4BT.
3, ‡ +   Emphasises the interaction between basic research and technology, caters for the industrial physicist, engineer and technologist wanting information on new developments and provides an effective assessment of how the academic physicists work is implemented by the technologist.
Book notices, book reviews, letters, monographic articles, new products.
No Index.
Spring 1971, T.p. 48.   390.
Per copy £1.50, per year £6.

531

MECHANICS

1628 INTERNATIONAL JOURNAL OF NON-LINEAR MECHANICS.
Pergamon Press Ltd., Headington Hill Hall, Oxford OX3 0BW.
6, = +   Theoretical and applied mechanics of solids and fluids.
Book reviews, monographic articles.
A, Last issue of volume, Yes, None.
Per copy £4.50, per year £24.

1629 INTERNATIONAL JOURNAL OF SOLIDS AND STRUCTURES.
Pergamon Press Ltd., Headington Hill Hall, Oxford OX3 0BW.
12, + = ‡   Mechanics of solids and structures as a field of applied science and engineering.
Book reviews, monographic articles.
A, Last issue of volume, Yes, None.
Per copy £3.50, per year £36.

1630 JOURNAL OF APPLIED MATHEMATICS AND MECHANICS. Cover-to-cover translation of Prikladnaia Matematika i Mekhanika. 1969.
Pergamon Press Ltd., Headington Hill Hall, Oxford OX3 0BW.
6, = +   High level mathematical investigations of modern physical and mathematical problems. Special emphasis on aero and space science.
Book notices, book reviews, letters, monographic articles.
A, Last issue of volume, Yes, None.
T.p. 70.
Per copy £6.50, per year £36.

1631 JOURNAL OF BIOMECHANICS.
Pergamon Press Ltd., Headington Hill Hall, Oxford OX3 0BW.
6, = +   All aspects of biomechanics.
Book reviews, monographic articles.
A, Last issue of volume, Yes, None.
Per copy £4, per year £20.

Key to reference symbols

○ popular   ‡ technical   = trade/professional

+ research   * society/institution   † house journal

1632 JOURNAL OF THE MECHANICS AND PHYSICS OF SOLIDS. 1952.
Pergamon Press Ltd., Headington Hill Hall, Oxford OX3 0BW.
6, = + Theoretical and applied mechanics and the physics of solids.
Monographic articles.
A, Last issue of volume, Yes, None.
T.p. 70.
Per copy £4.50, per year £24.

1633 MECCANICA. 1966.
Pergamon Press Ltd., Headington Hill Hall, Oxford OX3 0BW.
4, = + Theoretical mechanics, mathematical physics, solid mechanics, strength of materials, design etc.
Book reviews, monographic articles.
A, Last issue of volume, Yes, None.
Per copy £2.50, per year £8.75.

1634 QUARTERLY JOURNAL OF MECHANICS & APPLIED MATHEMATICS. 1948.
Oxford University Press, Press Road, Neasden, London, NW10.
4, + General field of mechanics, particularly theoretical mechanics. Main subjects are continum mechanics (including mechanics of fluids and solids), classical electromagnetism, nonlinear dynamics, and combined fields such as magnetohydrodynamics, together with relevant mathematical and numerical methods.
Book reviews, monographic articles.
A, —, Yes, None.
May 1972, T.p. 119. 1400.
Per copy £2, per year £6.50.
Indexed in: IBZ.

531.32

PARTICLE DYNAMICS

1635 PARTICLE ACCELERATORS. 1970.
Gordon & Breach, 41/42 William 4th Street, London, WC2.
4, + ‡ Theoretical and experimental work on a variety of topics including particle orbit theory, high voltage techniques, magnet design, vacuum system engineering, radiation shielding, accelerator instrumentation, applications of cryogenics to accelerators, beam transport and new accelerator ideas.
Book notices, book reviews, commodity prices, letters, monographic articles, new products, tests.
A, —, No, None.
Subscription on application.

1636 PARTICULATE INFORMATION. 1973.
(L.U.T. Chemical Engineering Particle Abstracts 1968-1969; Particle Science and Technology Information Service Current Titles Bulletin 1969-1972)
PSTIS, University of Technology, Loughborough, Leics LE11 3TU.
12, ‡ + Particle characteristics, part.-part. systems, part.-gas systems, part.-liquid systems, part. production, size enlargement, air and water pollution, aerosols, droplets and powders. References from 200 journals, papers, patents, books, theses.
Abstracts, reports, patents, standards.
No Index.
April 1972, T.p. 26. c. 150.
Free to members, per year £16.

532

FLUID MECHANICS

1637 PHYSICS AND CHEMISTRY OF LIQUIDS. 1968.
Gordon & Breach, 41/42 William 4th Street, London, WC2.
4, + ‡ Research in the study of liquids from the different disciplines. It provides a single source of experimental and theoretical papers for those seeking to understand metallic and nonmetallic liquids.
Book notices, book reviews, letters, monographic articles, new products, standards, tests.
No Index,
Subscription on application.

1638 CHANNEL: A current information guide. 1968.
BHRA Fluid Engineering, Cranfield, Bedford.
12, + Announces and abstracts world's scientific and technical literature on the applications of fluid mechanics to civil and structural engineering.
Abstracts, patents, standards, tests.
6m, 3/6 months after end of period concerned, No, None.
March 1972, T.p. 32, Ad.p. 2.
Per year £20—UK.

1639 FLUIDICS FEEDBACK. 1967.
BHRA Fluid Engineering, Cranfield, Bedford.
12, ‡ + = All aspects of fluidics including pure fluidics devices, moving part devices, circuits and systems, components and applications.
Abstracts, book notices, book reviews, monographic articles, new companies, new products, patents, standards.
6m, July/January, No, None.
January 1972, T.p. 19, Ad.p. 1. 400.
Per year £20.

1640 HEAT AND FLUID FLOW. 1971.
Thermodynamics and Fluid Mechanics Group, The Institution of Mechanical Engineers, 1 Birdcage Walk, London SW1H 9JJ.
2, ‡ + Selected subject matter covering the full range of flow problems and various areas of thermodynamics, such as heat exchangers, heat transference, etc.
Abstracts, monographic articles.
A, —, No, None.
T.p. 80. 250.
Per copy £1.50, per year £2.50.

1641 JOURNAL OF FLUID MECHANICS. 1956.
Cambridge University Press, PO Box 92, London, NW1 2DB.
24, + Fundamental aspects of fluid mechanics and its applications.
Book reviews, monographic articles.
6 times a year, Last part of each volume, Yes, None.
July 1972, T.p. 190. 2500.
Per copy £2.50, per year £48.
Indexed in: BTI.

1642 THE JOURNAL OF NONMETALS. 1971.
Gordon & Breach, 41/42 William 4th Street, London, WC2.
4, + Electronic and structural properties of ionic, covalent, van der Waals and hydrogen bonded crystalline and noncrystalline solids and liquids. Typical substances which fall into these categories are oxides, nitrides, halides, carbides, etc., as well as semiconducting compounds and more complex minerals and salts.
Book notices, book reviews, letters, monographic articles, tests.
A, —, No, None.
Per year £19.60.

1643 SOLID-LIQUID FLOW ABSTRACTS. 1968.
Gordon & Breach, 41/42 William 4th Street, London, WC2.
4, + ‡ Flow of solids in pipes, such as slurry flow of coal, sand, minerals and ores, food products and the like, and the flow of blood 'in vitro' and 'in vivo' and the flow of plastic materials such as muds and sludges.

Abstracts.
Q, –, No, None.
Per year £15.50.

533.6
AERODYNAMICS

1644 INDUSTRIAL AERODYNAMICS ABSTRACTS: World literature of non-aeronautical aerodynamics. 1970.
BHRA—Fluid Engineering, Cranfield, Bedford.
6, ‡ + *   Fluid mechanics; the atmosphere—general, wind structure, air pollution; aerodynamics—surface features: general, structures and natural—vehicles and ships, internal flows; instrumentation and experimental techniques—velocity measurements, model tests, wind tunnel techniques; related topics.
Abstracts, book notices, book reviews, monographic articles, patents, standards.
6m, May/June and Nov/Dec, No, None.
March/April 1972, T.p. 24.   c. 200.
Per year £20.

534
ACOUSTICS

1645 ACOUSTICS ABSTRACTS. 1967.
Multi Science Publishing Co. Ltd., 28 Greville Street, London, EC1.
6, ‡ + *   Physical acoustics and vibration application of acoustic techniques. Physiological and bio acoustics, Noise and architectural acoustics.
Abstracts, book notices, book reviews.
A, –, Yes, None.
March-April 1972, T.p. 52.
Per copy £4, per year £24.

1646 APPLIED ACOUSTICS. 1968.
Applied Science Publishers Ltd., Ripple Road, Barking, Essex.
4, + ‡   Application of acoustic principles to design problems and the materials used in their solution. Intended for engineers, technologists, architects, public health inspectors, occupational hygienists.
Book reviews, letters, monographic articles, new products.
A, October, Yes, None.
January 1972, T.p. 79.   800.
Per year £10.

1647 JOURNAL OF SOUND AND VIBRATION. 1964.
Academic Press Inc. (London) Ltd., 24-28 Oval Road, London, NW1.
24, + ‡ * =   All aspects of sound and/or vibration, inclusive of reports on theoretical and experimental research work on practical work in noise and vibration control and on human response to sound and vibration.
Announcements of and reports on technical meetings, book reviews, letters, monographic articles, standards.
A, End of each volume, Yes, None.
Per year £57, British Acoustical Society members reduced rate of £36 per year.
Indexed in: BTI.

1648 NOISE AND VIBRATION BULLETIN. 1970.
Multiscience Publishing Company Ltd., 28 Greville Street, London, EC1.
12, ‡ + ○ =   Noise and vibration, its effects, methods of reduction and treatment, in structural engineering, transport, architecture and biological fields.
Book notices, book reviews, letters, new companies, new products, parliamentary reports, standards.
A, 2 months after end of year, Yes, None.
April 1972, T.p. 29.
Per year £10.50.

535
OPTICS

1649 ELECTRO OPTICS.
Milton Publishing Co. Ltd., 28 Craven Street, London, WC2N 5PD.
4, ‡   Equipments and systems designed for the following technologies: Character recognition; Electro-optical communications; Electro-optical data storage; Electro-optical medical instruments; Electro-optics in Military systems; Fibre optics; Guidance and Navigation systems; High speed photography; Holography; Information storage and transmission; Infra-red detection; Interferometry; Lasers; Low light level detection and intensification; Microscopy; Non-destructive testing; Optical instrumentation; Photocomposition; Photographic systems; Reprographics; Satellite photography; Spectrometry; Spectrophotometry; Television; Thin films; Tracking and X-ray.
New products.
No Index.
February 1972, T.p. 8, Ad.p. 15.   7094.
Per copy 75p, per year £3.

1650 OPTICA ACTA. 1953.
Taylor & Francis Ltd., 10-14 Macklin Street, London, WC2B 5NF.
12, ‡ = +   Theoretical and applied optics.
Book notices, book reviews, monographic articles.
A, in last issue, Yes, None.
April 1972, T.p. 82.
Per copy £2.75, per year £29.

1651 OPTICAL WORLD. 1972.
Optical World Ltd., 65 Brook Street, London, W1Y 2DT.
6, = ‡
Book reviews, commodity prices, letters, articles, new companies, new products, obituaries, parliamentary reports, patents, standards, tests.
No Index.
May 1972, T.p. 26, Ad.p. 6.
Per year £5.

1652 OPTO-ELECTRONICS. 1969.
Chapman & Hall, Associated Book Publishers, 11 New Fetter Lane, London, EC4P 4EE.
4, ‡ + =   All fields related to opto-electronics.
Book reviews, letters, monographic articles.
A, November, No, None.
February 1972, T.p. 68.   700.
Per copy £3, per year £10.50.

1653 VISION RESEARCH.
Pergamon Press Ltd., Headington Hill Hall, Oxford, OX3 0BW.
12, + =   All aspects of vision but principally the visual process.
Book reviews, letters, monographic articles.
A, Last issue of volume, Yes, None.
T.p. 200.
Per copy £3, per year £32.

535-1
INFRA-RED PHYSICS

1654 INFRARED PHYSICS. 1961.
Pergamon Press Ltd., Headington Hill Hall, Oxford, OX3 0BW.
4, = +   Infrared radiation: its generation, transmission, detection & applications.
Letters, book reviews, monographic articles.
A, Last issue of volume, Yes, None.
T.p. 60, Ad.p. 3.
Per copy £4, per year £14.

535.33

SPECTROSCOPY

1655 ATOMIC ABSORPTION & FLAME EMISSION SPECTROSCOPY ABSTRACTS. 1969.
Dr. P. R. Masek, Science & Technology Agency, 3 Dyer's Bldgs., Holborn, London, EC1.
6, ‡
Abstracts, book notices, letters, new products, patents, standards, tests.
A, —, No, None.
No 6, 1971, T.p. 50.
Per year £24.

1656 ELECTRON SPIN RESONANCE (Specialist Periodical Reports). 1973.
The Chemical Society, Burlington House, London, W1V 0BN.
1, +   An annual critical review of the literature on the subject.
Monographic articles.
A, —, Yes, None.
1971/72, T.p. 300.
Subscription on application.

1657 JOURNAL OF QUANTITATIVE SPECTROSCOPY AND RADIATIVE TRANSFER. 1961.
Pergamon Press Ltd., Headington Hill Hall, Oxford, OX3 0BW
12, = +   All aspects relative to pure & applied science.
Monographic articles.
A, Last issue of volume, Yes, None.
T.p. 100.
Per copy £4, per year £46.

1658 LASER-RAMAN SPECTROSCOPY ABSTRACTS. 1972.
Science & Technology Agency, 3 Dyer's Buildings, London, EC1.
4, ‡ = +
Abstracts.
A, —, Yes, None.
January/March 1972, T.p. 69.
Per year £30.

1659 MAGNETIC RESONANCE REVIEW. 1972.
Gordon & Breach, 41/42 William 4th Street, London, WC2.
4, + ‡   Surveys the magnetic resonance literature on a calendar year basis.
Review articles only.
A, —, No, None.
Per year £17.25.

1660 MASS SPECTROMETRY (Specialist Periodical Reports). 1970.
The Chemical Society, Burlington House, London, W1V 0BN.
2 year, +   Critical review of the literature on the mass spectrometry of organic and organometallic compounds.
Monographic articles.
2 year, —, Yes, None.
1970/71, T.p. 323.
Per copy £7.

1661 MASS SPECTROMETRY BULLETIN. 1966.
Mass Spectrometry Data Centre, A.W.R.E., Aldermaston, Reading, RG7 4PR.
12, ‡ =   Literature references, books, reports, patents etc, on mass spectrometry and allied topics.
A, January, No, None, N.B. 6 indexes also in each issue.
May 1972, T.p. 53.
Per year £35.

1662 NUCLEAR MAGNETIC RESONANCE (Specialist Periodical Reports). 1972.
The Chemical Society, Burlington House, London, W1V 0BN.
1, +   An annual critical review of the literature on the subject covering different phenomena in N.M.R. studies.
A, —, Yes, None.
1971.
Per copy £7.

1663 NUCLEAR MAGNETIC RESONANCE SPECTROMETRY ABSTRACTS. 1971.
Dr. P. R. Masek, Science & Technology Agency, 3 Dyer's Bldgs., Holborn, EC1.
6, ‡
Abstracts, book notices, letters, new products, patents, standards, tests.
A, —, No, None.
No 6, 1971, T.p. 90.
Per year £28.

1664 OMS-ORGANIC MASS SPECTROMETRY. 1968.
Heyden & Sons Limited, Spectrum House, Alderton Crescent, London NW4 3XX.
12, ‡ + =   Mass spectrometry problems in organic chemistry.
Book reviews, monographic articles, new products.
A, January, Yes, None.
April 1972, T.p. 116.
Per year £35. Reductions for personal subscribers.

1665 PERKIN-ELMER NMR QUARTERLY. 1971.
Perkin-Elmer Limited, Post Office Lane, Beaconsfield, Buckinghamshire HP9 1QA.
4, ‡ +   Nuclear magnetic resonance spectrometry.
Book notices, book reviews, letters, monographic articles, new products, obituaries, patents, standards, tests.
No Index.
December 1971, T.p. 12.   4000.
Free.

1666 SPECTROCHIMICA ACTA. Part A Molecular spectroscopy, Part B Atomic Spectroscopy. 1939.
Pergamon Press Ltd., Headington Hill Hall, Oxford, OX3 0BW.
12, + =
Book reviews, monographic articles.
A, Last issue of volume, Yes, None.
Part A £4.50, per year £46. Part B £2.50, per year £28.

1667 SPECTROSCOPIC PROPERTIES OF INORGANIC AND ORGANOMETALLIC COMPOUNDS (Specialist Periodical Reports). 1968.
The Chemical Society, Burlington House, London, W1V 0BN.
1, +   An annual critical review of the literature on the subject.
Monographic articles.
A, —, Yes, None.
1971, T.p. 604.
Per copy £10.

1668 X-RAY FLUORESCENCE SPECTROMETRY ABSTRACTS. 1970.
Dr. P. R. Masek, Science & Technology Agency, 3 Dyer's Bldgs., Holborn, EC1.
4, ‡
Abstracts, book notices, letters, new products, patents, standards, tests.
A, —, Yes, None.
No 4, 1971, T.p. 65.
Per year £24.

1669 XRS-X-RAY SPECTROMETRY. 1972.
Heyden & Son Limited, Spectrum House, Alderton Crescent, London, NW4 3XX.
4, ‡ +   Applications and theory of X-ray Spectrometry and the application of X-ray methods for

structural analysis, data handling methods and instrumentation.
Book notices, book reviews, monographic articles, new products, obituaries.
A, —, Yes, None.
April 1972, T.p. 33, Ad.p. 14.
Per copy £2.50, per year £10.

535.82
MICROSCOPY

1670 JOURNAL OF MICROSCOPY. 1969.
(Journal of the Royal Microscopical Society, 1878-1968).
Blackwell Scientific Publications, Osney Mead, Oxford, OX2 0EL.
6, ‡ + = * All branches of microscopy and related sciences, with particular interest in the optical, mechanical and electronic features of design of all types of microscopes and accessories.
Book reviews, monographic articles.
6 m, June/December, Yes, None.
June 1971, T.p. 86, Ad.p. 6.   1500.
Per copy £4, per year £20.
Indexed in: IBZ.

1671 ROYAL MICROSCOPICAL SOCIETY PROCEEDINGS. 1965.
The Society, Clarendon House, Cornmarket Street, Oxford, OX1 3HA.
6, = ‡ + *
Book reviews, letters, monographic articles.
A, —, Yes, None.
Part 3 1972, T.p. 43, Ad.p. 10.
Per year £4.
Free to Fellows.

536.2
HEAT TRANSFER

1672 INTERNATIONAL JOURNAL OF HEAT AND MASS TRANSFER. 1960.
Pergamon Press Ltd., Headington Hill Hall, Oxford, OX3 0BW.
12, = +   Analytical & experimental research in the field.
Book reviews, letters, monographic articles.
A, With first issue of succeeding volume, Yes, None.
T.p. 150.
Per copy £4.50, per year £48.

536.45
HIGH TEMPERATURE PHYSICS

1673 HIGH TEMPERATURES—HIGH PRESSURES: international journal of research. 1969.
Pion Limited, 207 Brondesbury Park, London, NW2 5JN.
6, + ‡   Interdisciplinary experimental and theoretical study of matter under extreme thermal and mechanical conditions, including properties of gases, liquids, and solids, fluid-dynamics, equipment, plasmas, magneto-hydrodynamics, combustion, explosions, energy conversion, and applications.
Abstracts, book reviews, letters, monographic articles, new products, standards, tests.
A, last issue of each volume, Yes, None.
T.p. 120.
Per copy £3.50, per year £18 inland.

536.48
LOW TEMPERATURE PHYSICS

1674 CRYOGENICS. The international journal of low temperature engineering & research. 1960.

IPC Science & Technology Publications Ltd., 32 High St., Guildford, Surrey.
6, ‡   Basic & applied low temperature research and development in all aspects.
Book reviews, letters, monographic articles, new products, patents.
A, February, Yes, None.
T.p. 76, Ad.p. 4.   1700.
Per copy £2.50, per year £15.
Indexed in: BTI.

537.2
ELECTROSTATICS

1675 ELECTROSTATICS ABSTRACTS. 1971.
Electrical Research Association, Cleeve Rd., Leatherhead, Surrey.
12, ‡ +   Covers the specialised field of static electrification of solids and fluids, its hazards, applications and devices; antistatics; and the phenomenon of conduction in solids and liquids.
Abstracts.
A, With last issue of the year, Yes, None.
April, 1972, T.p. 17.   c. 70.
Per year £10 to members, £12 to non-members.

537.3
ELECTRICITY

1676 SOLID-STATE ELECTRONICS. 1960.
Pergamon Press Ltd., Headington Hill Hall, Oxford, OX3 0BW.
12, + =   Applied solid-state physics, including transistor technology in all its aspects, transistor theory & design etc.
Book reviews, monographic articles.
A, December, Yes, None.
T.p. 100, Ad.p. 10.
Per copy £3, per year £32.

537.5
RADIATION

1677 CARRIER FREE: An occasional publication of The Radiochemical Centre of interest to biochemists and chemists using radioactive materials. 1971.
The Radiochemical Centre, Amersham, Bucks.
2/3, +   Radioactive chemicals and labelled compounds, especially their properties and uses likely to be of interest to biochemists and chemists.
Monographic articles, new products.
No Index.
No. 2, 1972, T.p. 5.   25000.
Free.

1678 INTERNATIONAL JOURNAL FOR RADIATION PHYSICS AND CHEMISTRY. 1969.
Pergamon Press Ltd., Headington Hill Hall, Oxford, OX3 0BW.
4, = +   Physical & chemical effects of ionizing radiation & related topics.
Letters, monographic articles.
A, Last issue of volume, Yes, None.
Per copy £5, per year £16.

1679 THE INTERNATIONAL JOURNAL OF APPLIED RADIATION AND ISOTOPES. 1969.
Pergamon Press Ltd., Headington Hill Hall, Oxford, OX3 0BW.
12, + =   Isotopic & radiation techniques.
Letters, monographic articles.
A, Last issue of volume, Yes, None.
Per copy £3.50, per year £36.

1680 NON-IONIZING RADIATION. 1969.
IPC Science & Technology Publications Ltd., 32 High Street, Guildford, Surrey.
4, + =   Effects, use & safety of electromagnetic radiation, from r.f. through microwaves & infrared to the optical region.
Book reviews, letters, monographic articles, new products, patents.
A, March, Yes, None.
T.p. 56.
Per copy £2.50, per year £10.

1681 RADIATION EFFECTS. 1969.
Gordon & Breach, 41/42 William 4th Street, London, WC2.
4, + ‡   Experimental and theoretical papers of both a fundamental and applied nature in the field of radiation.
Book notices, book reviews, letters, monographic articles, tests.
No Index.
Subscription on application.

1682 RADIONIC-MAGNETIC CENTRE NEWSLETTER. 1967.
Radionic-Magnetic Centre Organisation, Raleigh Park Road, Oxford, OX2 9BE.
4, + *   The science of radionics and biomagnetism, in connection with the treatment of animals and humans also other forms of therapeutic healing methods. Includes case studies, philosophy of Radionics etc.
Book reviews, letters, articles, new products, tests.
No Index.
Winter 1971, T.p. 20.   450.
Per year £3.

1683 TECHNICAL BULLETIN.
The Radiochemical Centre, Amersham, Bucks.
12, ‡ +
Technical data, product information and availability of groups of The Radiochemical Centre's products.
New products.
No Index.
72/3 April 1972, T.p. 4.   Between 6000 and 30000, according to subject, are mailed of each issue.
Free.

1684 UKCIS MACROPROFILES: Radiation & Photochemistry.
(Chemscan—Radiation & Photochemistry 1968-1970).
Service Department, UKCIS, The University, Nottingham, NG7 2RD.
26, ‡ +   References on the topic, selected by computer from the secondary publication, Chemical Titles.
References to papers in 700 important chemical journals.
No Index.
Issue 3, 1972, T.p. 49 (150 refs.).   60.
Per copy £1, per year £27.

537.59

COSMIC PHYSICS

1685 FUNDAMENTALS OF COSMIC PHYSICS (in preparation].
Gordon & Breach, 41/42 William 4th Street, London, WC2.
4, + ‡   Cosmic physics including general relativity, astronomy and astrophysics, space and planetary physics, and geophysics.
Book notices, book reviews, letters, monographic articles, tests.
A, —, No, None.
Per year £17.25.

538

MAGNETISM

1686 INTERNATIONAL JOURNAL OF MAGNETISM. 1970.
Gordon & Breach, 41/42 William 4th Street, London, WC2.
4, + ‡   Theoretical and experimental papers dealing with original research in all aspects of magnetism, emphasizing fundamental rather than applied aspects. Also provides data concerning conferences and meetings on magnetism.
Book notices, book reviews, letters, monographic articles, tests.
A, —, No, None.
Subscription on application.

539

PHYSICAL STRUCTURES

1687 FIBRE SCIENCE AND TECHNOLOGY. 1968.
Applied Science Publishers Ltd., Ripple Road, Barking Essex.
4, +   Original papers on fibre and whisker preparation, their structure and related physical properties, forming methods and application to products. Textile, polymer, ceramic and metallic fibres are covered in detail.
Book notices, book reviews, letters, monographic articles, standards, tests.
A, January, Yes, None.
January 1972, T.p. 83, Ad.p. 4.   500.
Per year £12.

1688 MATERIALS RESEARCH BULLETIN. 1967.
Pergamon Press Ltd., Headington Hill Hall, Oxford, OX2 0BW.
12, = +   Research on crystal growth, materials preparation and characterization.
Book reviews, monographic articles.
A, Last issue of volume, Yes, None.
Per copy £2.50, per year £26.

1689 TEXTURE. 1972.
Gordon & Breach, 41/42 William 4th Street, London, WC2.
4, + ‡   Medium of communication for scientists and engineers of various disciplines working in the field of texture or preferred orientation of crystalline solids including metals, polymers, ceramics and natural or synthetic rocks.
Book notices, book reviews, letters, monographic articles, new companies, new products, tests.
A, —, No, None.
Per year £12.05.

539.1

NUCLEAR PHYSICS

1690 COMMENTS ON ATOMIC AND MOLECULAR PHYSICS. 1969.
Gordon & Breach, 41/42 William 4th Street, London, WC2.
6, + ‡   Critical commentaries on significant current development appearing in scientific literature.
No Index.
Subscription on application.

1691 COMMENTS ON PLASMA PHYSICS AND CONTROLLED FUSION. 1972.
Gordon & Breach, 41/42 William 4th Street, London, WC2.
6, + ‡   Critical commentaries of significant developments in plasma physics and controlled fusion as they appear in scientific literature.

Book notices, book reviews, letters, monographic articles, new companies, new products, standards, tests.
No Index.
Per year £12.85.

1692 JOURNAL OF NUCLEAR ENERGY. 1954.
Pergamon Press Ltd., Headington Hill Hall, Oxford, OX3 0BW.
12, = + Science and technology of nuclear power.
Book reviews, letters, monographic articles.
A, Last issue of volume, Yes, None.
T.p. 100.
Per copy £2.50, per year £24.
Indexed in: BTI, IBZ.

1693 JOURNAL OF PHYSICS: B: Atomic and molecular physics. 1968.
(Proceedings of the Physical Society 1874-1968).
The Institute of Physics, London and Bristol, Netherton House, Marsh Street, Bristol, BS1 4BT.
12, ‡ + Study of atoms, ions, molecules, spectroscopy, surface physics, astrophysics, plasma, discharge and maser and laser physics, quantum optics, non linear optics, other investigations where the objects of study are elementary atomic, ionic or molecular properties or processes.
Book notices, book reviews, letters, monographic articles.
A, December, Yes, None.
December 1971, T.p. 240. 2142.
Per copy £3, per year £46.

1694 NEUTRON ACTIVATION ANALYSIS ABSTRACTS. 1971.
Science & Technology Agency, 3 Dyers Buildings, London, EC1.
4, ‡ + = All aspects of neutron activation analysis.
Abstracts.
A, —, Yes, None.
January/March 1972, T.p. 73.
Per year £30.

1695 PLASMA PHYSICS. 1967.
Pergamon Press Ltd., Headington Hill Hall, Oxford, OX3 0BW.
12, + = All fields of plasma physics and magneto-hydrodynamics.
Book reviews, letters, monographic articles.
A, Last issue of volume, Yes, None.
T.p. 100.
Per copy £2.50, per year £26.

539.12
MOLECULAR PHYSICS

1696 MOLECULAR CRYSTALS AND LIQUID CRYSTALS.
Gordon & Breach, 41/42 William 4th Street, London, WC2.
4, + ‡ Original experimental and theoretical papers on such topics as energy and charge transfer processes; photo and radiation effect; optical properties; advanced structure and bonding; NMR studies of liquid crystals, molecular, structural and phase transitions.
Book notices, book reviews, letters, monographic articles, patents, standards, tests.
6m, —, No, 5 year.
Subscription on application.

1697 MOLECULAR PHYSICS. 1959.
Taylor & Francis Ltd., 10-14 Macklin St., London, WC2B JNF.
12, ‡ = + All aspects of the physics of molecules.
Monographic articles.
6m, in last issue of volume. (2 per year), Yes, None.
May 1972, T.p. 198.
Per copy £3.75, per year £42.00.

539.2
SOLID STATE PHYSICS.

1699 COMMENTS ON SOLID STATE PHYSICS. 1968.
Gordon & Breach, 41/42 William 4th Street, London, WC2.
6, + ‡ Critical commentaries on significant current developments appearing in scientific literature.
Book notices, book reviews, letters, monographic articles, new products, tests.
No Index.
Subscription on application.

1700 FIELDS AND QUANTA. 1971.
Gordon & Breach, 41/42 William 4th Street, London, WC2.
4, + ‡ Nature of the fundamental interactions of matter. The emphasis is on subjects in the general area of particle physics but solid state theory, gravitation, and other subjects, which utilize field and quanta as a basis and add to our understanding of these topics, are also discussed.
Book notices, book reviews, commodity prices, letters, monographic articles, new products, tests.
A, —, No, None.
Subscription on application.

1701 JOURNAL OF PHYSICS C: Solid State Physics. 1968.
(Proceedings of the Physical Society 1874-1968).
The Institute of Physics, London and Bristol, Netherton House, Marsh Street, Bristol, BS1 4BT.
24, ‡ + All aspects of solid state physics other than the applied aspects and those wholly concerned with metals, also liquid state theory, experiment and superfluids.
Book notices, book reviews, letters, monographic articles.
A, December, Yes, None.
March 1972, T.p. 111. 2162.
Per copy £3, per year £65.

1702 SOLID STATE COMMUNICATIONS.
Pergamon Press Ltd., Headington Hill Hall, Oxford, OX3 0BW.
26, + = Original, experimental and theoretical research on the physical and chemical properties of solids and condensed systems.
Short articles.
A, Last issue of volume, Yes, None.
Per copy £1.50, per year £30.

539.5.01
RHEOLOGY

1703 BIORHEOLOGY. 1962.
Pergamon Press Ltd., Headington Hill Hall, Oxford, OX3 0BW.
4, = + Studies of flow and deformation in all biological systems, especially blood.
Book notices, book reviews, letters, monographic articles.
A, Last issue of volume, Yes, None.
T.p. 75.
Per copy £5.50, per year £20.

1704 BULLETIN OF THE BRITISH SOCIETY OF RHEOLOGY. 1941.
The Society, c/o Fuller's Earth Union Ltd., Patteson Court, Nutfield Road, Redhill, Surrey.
4, = + ‡ Notices, news.
No Index.
T.p. 20, Ad.p. 2.
Free to members.

1705 RHEOLOGY ABSTRACTS. 1958.
(Bulletin, British Society of Rheology 1940-1957).
Pergamon Press Ltd. (for British Society of Rheology), Headington Hill Hall, Oxford, OX3 0BW.

1706-1716

 4, = + * Abstracts.
 A, Last Issue of volume, Yes, None.
 T.p. 30, Ad.p. 3.
 Per copy £4, per year £14.

539.61
ADHESION

1706 THE JOURNAL OF ADHESION. 1969.
 Gordon & Breach, 41/42 William 4th Street, London, WC2.
 4, + ‡ Phenomenon of adhesion and the practical applications of adhesives.
 Book notices, book reviews, letters, monographic articles, new products, standards, tests.
 A, —, No, None.
 Subscription on application.

54
CHEMISTRY

1707 ALIPHATIC ALICYCLIC AND SATURATED HETEROCYCLIC CHEMISTRY (Specialist Periodical Reports). 1972.
 The Chemical Society, Burlington House, London, W1V 0BN.
 1, + An annual critical review of the literature on the subject.
 Monographic articles.
 A, —, Yes, None.
 1971, T.p. 600.
 Subscription on application.

1708 AMBIX: Journal of the Society for the Study of Alchemy and Early Chemistry. 1937.
 The Society for the Study of Alchemy and Early Chemistry, Dept. of Hist. & Phil. of Science, University College, Gower Street, London, WC1.
 3, + * History of alchemy and chemistry from earliest times to the 20th century.
 Book notices, book reviews, letters, monographic articles, obituaries.
 A, November, Yes, None.
 November 1971, T.p. 80, Ad.p. 2.   450.
 Per year £3.25. Free to members.

1709 ANNUAL REPORTS ON THE PROGRESS OF CHEMISTRY. 1904.
 The Chemical Society, Burlington House, London, W1V 0BN.
 1, + Provides the general reader with critical coverage of significant advances in major areas of chemistry. Two sections: A (Physical and Inorganic) and B (Organic).
 Monographic articles.
 A, —, Yes, None.
 1970, T.p. A504, B622.
 A £6. B £7.

1710 BIBLIOGRAPHIES OF CHEMISTS. 1971.
 Gordon & Breach, 41/42 William 4th Street, London, WC2.
 4, Bibliographies selected are those of organic and inorganic chemists; physical, analytical and polymer chemists; biochemists and medicinal chemists. Bibliographies of leading industrial chemists and academic scientists are included, the complete references being given for each article.
 Abstracts, letters.
 No Index.
 Subscription on application.

1711 CHEMICAL SOCIETY REVIEWS. 1972.
 (Quarterly Reviews 1947-1971; RIC Reviews 1968-1971)
 The Chemical Society, Burlington House, London, W1V 0BN.
 4, + Whole of chemistry and its interfaces with other disciplines of interest to a wide readership.
 Monographic articles.
 A, December, Yes, 5 year.
 No. 1 1972, T.p. 144, Ad.p. 2.
 Per copy £2.50, per year £8.

1712 CHEMISTRY IN BRITAIN. 1965.
 (Proceedings of the Chemical Society)
 The Chemical Society, Burlington House, London W1V 0BN.
 12, * = ‡ Keeps the chemist up to date on economic, political, and social factors affecting him together with a wide range of articles on professional and industrial matters.
 Book reviews, letters, monographic articles, new products, obituaries, tests.
 A, December, Yes, None.
 June 1972, T.p. 46, Ad.p. 38.   47000.
 Per copy £1, per year £10.
 Indexed in: BTI.

1713 IUPAC INFORMATION BULLETIN. 1956.
 International Union of Pure & Applied Chemistry, Bank Court Chambers, 2-3 Pound Way, Cowley Centre, Oxford OX4 3YF.
 3, * † News medium for the various activities of the International Union of Pure and Applied Chemistry, especially of chemical topics which need regulation, standardization or codification. It includes details of forthcoming international symposia which are to be sponsored by IUPAC together with reports of such meetings which have recently taken place. Two series of Appendices to the Bulletin are published, viz. (i) Appendices on Tentative Nomenclature, symbols, Units, and Standards, (ii) Technical Reports.
 No Index.
 Nos. 42/43 July 1972, T.p. 82, Ad.p. 2.
 Per year £1.

1714 JOURNAL OF THE CHEMICAL SOCIETY: Chemical Communications. 1972.
 (Journal of Chemical Society: Section D 1965-1971)
 The Chemical Society, Burlington House, London, W1V 0BN.
 + Short urgent research articles from all branches of chemistry.
 Monographic articles.
 A, February, Yes, None.
 No. 11 1972, T.p. 79, Ad.p. 4.
 Per year £30.

1715 THE JOURNAL OF COLOUR AND APPEARANCE. 1971.
 Gordon & Breach, 41/42 William 4th Street, London, WC2.
 6, ‡ Science and technology of colorant usage and color vision and appearance. Main emphasis is on color chemistry and physics, but other aspects such as psychology, biology (the mechanism of color vision), and mathematics (as related to calculation and computation of color differences and color measurements) are also covered.
 Book notices, book reviews, monographic articles.
 A, —, No, None.
 Subscription on application.

1716 JOURNAL OF COORDINATION CHEMISTRY. 1971.
 Gordon & Breach, 41/42 William 4th Street, London, WC2.
 4, + ‡ Reports original investigations on the synthesis, structure, and the physical and chemical properties of coordination compounds of metals. Deals primarily with basic phenomena such as equilibria, kinetics, mechanisms, and catalytic effects.
 Book notices, book reviews, letters, monographic articles, new products, tests.
 A, —, No, None.
 Subscription on application.

1717 PURE AND APPLIED CHEMISTRY: Official journal of the International Union of Pure and Applied Chemistry. 1969.
Butterworths, 88 Kingsway, London, WC2B 6AB.
Four volumes each of 4 parts averaging 12 issues.
+ *   Invited lectures at international symposia sponsored by IUPAC in all aspects of pure and applied chemistry at research level.
Monographic articles.
No Index.
Vol. 31, 1972, T.p. 320.   c. 1200.
Per volume £13.50.

1718 RETORT. Journal of Birmingham University Chemical Society. 1924.
Bartle & Son Ltd., Station Road, Scunthorpe, Lincs.
2, * ‡   Applications and research in all fields of chemistry.
Book reviews, letters, monographic articles, obituaries.
No Index.
T.p. 21, Ad.p. 8.
Free to members.

1719 RUSSIAN CHEMICAL REVIEWS (Uspekhi Khimii). 1960.
The Chemical Society, Burlington House, London, W1V 0BN.
12, +   A cover to cover English translation of the Russian review journal (Uspekhi Khimii).
Monographic articles.
No Index.
Subscription on application.

1720 UKCIS MACROPROFILES: ESR—Chemical Aspects. 1971.
Service Department, UKCIS, The University, Nottingham NG7 2RD.
26, ‡ +   References on the topic, selected by computer from the secondary publication, CA Condensates.
References to papers in 15000 journals.
No Index.
Vol. 2 Iss 4 (Feb. 1972), T.p. 15 (45 refs).   10.
Per copy £1, per year £27.

1721 UKCIS MACROPROFILES: NMR—Chemical Aspects. 1971.
Service Department, UKCIS, The University, Nottingham NG7 2RD.
26, ‡ +   References on the topic, selected by computer from the secondary publication, CA Condensates.
References to papers in 15000 journals.
No Index.
Volume 2 Iss 4 (Feb. 1972), T.p. 36 (110 refs).   20.
Per copy £1, per year £27.

541.1

PHYSICAL CHEMISTRY

1722 GENERAL DISCUSSIONS OF THE FARADAY SOCIETY.
The Chemical Society, Burlington House, London, W1V 0BN.
2, +   Cover the broad aspects of a physico-chemical topic thereby encouraging scientist of different disciplines to contribute to a common theme.
Monographic articles.
6m, published in the discussion (June, December), Yes, None.
No. 52 June 1972, T.p. 381
Per copy £8, per year approx £16 (each issue varies in price).

1723 JOURNAL OF THE CHEMICAL SOCIETY: Faraday Transactions 1. 1972.
(Transactions of the Faraday Society).
The Chemical Society, Burlington House, London, W1V 0BN.
12, +   Research articles in physical chemistry.
Book reviews, monographic articles.
A, March, Yes, None.
No. 5 1972, T.p. 190, Ad.p. 6.
Per year £18.

1724 JOURNAL OF THE CHEMICAL SOCIETY: Faraday Transactions II. 1972.
(Transactions of the Faraday Society).
The Chemical Society, Burlington House, London, W1V 0BN.
12, +   Research articles in chemical physics.
Book reviews, monographic articles.
A, March, Yes, None.
No. 1 1972, T.p. 192, Ad.p. 2.
Per year £12.

1725 RUSSIAN JOURNAL OF PHYSICAL CHEMISTRY (Zhurnal Fizicheskoi Khimii). 1959.
The Chemical Society, Burlington House, London, W1V 0BN.
12, +   A cover to cover English translation of the Russian journal, Zhurnal Fizicheskoi Khimii.
Monographic articles, obituaries.
No Index.
Per copy £6, per year £46.

1726 SYMPOSIA OF THE FARADAY SOCIETY. 1968.
The Chemical Society, Burlington House, London, W1V 0BN.
1, +   Discussion of a specialised physico-chemical topic with particular reference to recently rapidly developing lines of research.
Monographic articles.
A, —, Yes, None.
No. 4, 1971, T.p. 200.
Per copy £2.20, per year £2.20.

541.11

THERMOCHEMISTRY

1727 CHEMICAL THERMODYNAMICS (Specialist Periodical Reports). 1972.
The Chemical Society, Burlington House, London, W1V 0BN.
1, +   A critical review of the practical and theoretical aspects of the subject.
Monographic articles.
A, —, Yes, None.
1970, T.p. 300.
Subscription on application.

1728 THE JOURNAL OF CHEMICAL THERMODYNAMICS. 1969.
Academic Press Inc. (London) Ltd., 24-28 Oval Road, London, NW1.
6, +   New measurements of thermochemical and equilibrium quantities and thermodynamic properties of new theoretical approaches and comment.
Book reviews, monographic articles.
A, Last issue of year, Yes, None.
3 May 1972, T.p. 180, Ad.p. 5.   900.
Per year £12.50.

541.13

ELECTROCHEMISTRY

1729 ELECTROCHIMICA ACTA. 1959.
Pergamon Press Ltd., Headington Hill Hall, Oxford OX3 0BW.
12, = +   Pure and applied electrochemistry.
Book reviews, monographic articles.
A, Last issue of volume, Yes, None.

Key to reference symbols

○ popular   ‡ technical   = trade/professional

+ research   * society/institution   † house journal

T.p. 166.
Per copy £4.50, per year £50.
Indexed in: BTI.

1730 ELECTROCHEMISTRY (Specialist Periodical Reports). 1971.
The Chemical Society, Burlington House, London, W1V 0BN.
1, + An annual critical review of the literature on the subject, covering the most significant advances.
Monographic articles.
A, —, Yes, None.
1970/71, T.p. 307.
Per copy £7.

1731 ELECTROCHEMISTRY IN INDUSTRIAL PROCESSING AND BIOLOGY [English translation of Elektronnaya Obrabotka Materialov] 1970.
(Applied Electrical Phenomena 1966-1969)
Plenum Publishing Co. Ltd., Antvar House, London Road, Wembley, Middx.
6, ‡ + Fundamental research; precision (spark and electroerosion) machining; surface alloying; hardening and treatment; use of electric fields in industrial (chemical) processing and ore beneficiation, in biology, food processing and effluents treatment; development and design of electrical machining systems; etc.
Monographic articles.
No Index.
Subscription on application.

541.14

PHOTOCHEMISTRY

1732 PHOTOCHEMISTRY (Specialist Periodical Reports). 1970.
The Chemical Society, Burlington House, London, W1V 0BN.
1, + An annual critical review of the literature on the subject divided into 4 sections: physical, inorganic, organic and polymer.
Monographic articles.
A, —, Yes, None.
1970/71, T.p. 900.
Per copy £12.

1733 PHOTOCHEMISTRY AND PHOTOBIOLOGY. 1962.
Pergamon Press Ltd., Headington Hill Hall, Oxford OX3 0BW.
12, = + Photochemistry of biological materials and related substances.
Book reviews, monographic articles.
A, Last issue of volume, Yes, None.
Per copy £3, per year £32.

541.182.2

AEROSOLS

1734 JOURNAL OF AEROSOL SCIENCE. 1970.
Pergamon Press Ltd., Headington Hill Hall, Oxford OX3 0BW.
6, = + All aspects of aerosol research.
Monographic articles.
A, Last issue of volume, Yes, None.
T.p. 75.
Per copy £3, per year £16.

541.64

POLYMERISM

1735 EUROPEAN POLYMER JOURNAL. 1965.
Pergamon Press Ltd., Headington Hill Hall, Oxford OX3 0BW.
12, = ‡ + Polymer science in general.
Book reviews, letters, monographic articles.
A, —, Yes, None.
Per copy £3.50, per year £40.

1736 INTERNATIONAL JOURNAL OF POLYMERIC MATERIALS. 1971.
Gordon & Breach, 41/42 William 4th Street, London, WC2.
4, + ‡ Mechanisms and the interaction of engineering properties with chemical structure, morphology, processing techniques, end use applications and environment.
Book notices, book reviews, letters, monographic articles, new products, tests.
A, —, No, None.
Subscription on application.

1737 POLYMER NEWS. 1970.
Gordon & Breach, 41/42 William 4th Street, London, WC2.
12, + ‡ Current developments in the field, interpreted by polymer scientists and engineers as well as business executives and financial analysts. It provides regular coverage of: Research Review, Technological Review, Market Analysis, New Polymer Products, New Applications, New Measurement, Testing Techniques, Education News, Industry News, Government News and International News.
Book notices, book reviews, commodity prices, letters, monographic articles, new companies, new products, obituaries, patents, standards, tests.
A, —, No, None.
Subscription on application.

1738 POLYMER. 1960.
IPC Science & Technology Publications Ltd., 32 High Street, Guildford, Surrey.
12, + Physics, chemistry and application of polymer research.
Book reviews, letters, monographic articles.
A, December, Yes, None.
T.p. 81, Ad.p. 1.
Per year £14.
Indexed in: BTI.

542

EXPERIMENTAL CHEMISTRY

1739 COLLECTIVE PHENOMENA. 1972.
Gordon & Breach, 41/42 William 4th Street, London, WC2.
4, + ‡ Original theoretical and experimental work on all aspects of cooperative phenomena.
Book notices, book reviews, letters, monographic articles, tests.
A, —, No, None.
Per year £17.25.

542.2

LABORATORY PRACTICE

1740 THE GAZETTE OF THE INSTITUTE OF MEDICAL LABORATORY TECHNOLOGY. 1951.
Institute of Medical Laboratory Technology, 12 Queen Anne Street, London, W1M 0AU.
12, * = ‡ Medical laboratory technology.
Book notices, letters, articles.
No Index.
T.p. 14, Ad.p. 22.   14000.
Per copy $12\frac{1}{2}$p, per year £1.50.
Free to members.

1741 LAB. 1966.
Milton Publishing Co. Ltd., 28 Craven Street, London, WC2N 5PD.
12, ‡ All new laboratory equipments.
New products.

No Index.
March 1972, T.p. 10, Ad.p. 5.   16115.
Per copy 50p, per year £6.

1742 LABORATORY EQUIPMENT DIGEST. 1963.
Gerard Mann Ltd., 1-3 Astoria Parade, Streatham High Road, London, SW16 1PP.
12, ‡, +   Laboratory instrumentation, apparatus and techniques. Details of new equipment brought to the market, manufacturers' literature, authoritative contributed articles. Discussion of specific techniques and instruments.
Book reviews, letters, monographic articles, new companies, new products, tests.
No Index.
June 1972, T.p. 27, Ad.p. 105.   11500.
Per year £4 and Free, controlled circulation.

1743 LABORATORY PRACTICE. 1952.
United Trade Press Ltd., 9 Gough Square, Fleet Street, London, EC4.
12, + ‡   New techniques and instrumentation for laboratories in all branches of science.
Book reviews, letters, monographic articles, new products.
A, December, No, 10 year.
T.p. 44, Ad.p. 60.   6000.
Per copy 30p, per year £3.50.
Indexed in: BTI.

542.6

FILTRATION

1744 STOCHASTICS. 1972.
Gordon & Breach, 41/42 William 4th Street, London, WC2.
4, + ‡   Theory and applications of stochastic processes to problems of filtering, modelling, and identification, with particular emphasis on papers in the areas of biomedical modelling and identification, economic modelling and identification, and the realization of optimal nonlinear filters.
Book notices, book reviews, letters, monographic articles, tests.
A, —, No, None.
Per year £15.50.

542.91

SYNTHESIS

1745 BIOSYNTHESIS (Specialist Periodical Reports). 1972.
The Chemical Society, Burlington House, London, W1V 0BN.
1, +   An annual critical review of the biosynthesis of naturally occurring compounds.
Monographic articles.
A, —, Yes, None.
1970/71, T.p. 300.
Subscription on application.

543

ANALYTICAL CHEMISTRY

1746 THE ANALYST: Journal of the Society for Analytical Chemistry. 1876.
Society for Analytical Chemistry, 9/10 Savile Row, London, W1X 1AF.
12, + * ‡   All aspects of the theory and practice of analytical chemistry, fundamental and applied, inorganic and organic, including chemical, physical and biological methods, as original work or reviews critically evaluating existing knowledge.
Book reviews, monographic articles.
A, February, Yes, 10 year.

May 1972, T.p. 88, Ad.p. 16.   7151.
Per year £37. Including Analytical Abstracts.
Indexed in: BTI, IBZ.

1747 ANALYTICAL ABSTRACTS. 1954.
Society for Analytical Chemistry, 9/10 Savile Row, London, W1X, 1AF.
12, ‡ +   Abstracts of the world's literature dealing with all branches of analytical chemistry including biochemistry, pharmaceutical chemistry, food, agriculture, air, water, effluents, techniques, apparatus.
Abstracts.
6m, April/October, Yes, 5 year. One 10-yr. already published.
April 1972, T.p. ≃ 100.   6600.
Per copy £3, per year £28.

1748 INTERNATIONAL JOURNAL OF ENVIRONMENTAL ANALYTICAL CHEMISTRY. 1971.
Gordon & Breach, 41/42 William 4th Street, London, WC2.
4, + ‡   Provides information on the concentrations and distribution of environmental pollutants and their analysis by modern research methods. A wide variety of fields, including analytical aspects of organic, inorganic, physical, industrial chemistry, medical sciences and food chemistry are covered.
Book notices, book reviews, letters, monographic articles, new products, tests.
A, —, No, None.
Subscription on application.

1749 PROCEEDINGS OF THE SOCIETY FOR ANALYTICAL CHEMISTRY: ANALYTICAL DIVISION, CHEMICAL SOCIETY. 1972.
(Proceedings of the Society for Analytical Chemistry 1964-1971)
The Society, 9/10 Savile Row, London, W1X 1AF.
12, *   Reports in detail of meetings of the Society, including short technical and general papers on analytical chemistry.
Book notices, monographic articles, obituaries.
A, February, Yes, None.
June 1972, T.p. 22.   10000.
As supplement to Analyst (q.v.)

1750 TALANTA. 1958.
Pergamon Press Ltd., Headington Hill Hall, Oxford OX3 0BW.
12, + =   All aspects of analytical chemistry.
Book reviews, letters, monographic articles.
6m, June/December, Yes, None.
T.p. 125.
Per copy £3.50, per year £40.

545.844

CHROMATOGRAPHY

1751 CHROMATOGRAPHIA. 1972.
Pergamon Press Ltd., Headington Hill Hall, Oxford, OX3 0BW
= +   Chromatographic and related techniques.
Book reviews, letters, monographic articles.
A, —, Yes, None.
Per copy £2.50, per year £25.

1752 GAS AND LIQUID CHROMATOGRAPHY ABSTRACTS. 1958.
Institute of Petroleum, 61 New Cavendish Street, London, W1M 8AD.
4, ‡   Abstracts of gas and liquid chromatography literature worldwide.
Abstracts.
Q, —, Yes, A.
1971, No. 1, T.p. 84.   1200.
Members only—not available on subscription.

1753 GAS-CHROMATOGRAPHY-MASS SPECTROMETRY ABSTRACTS. 1970.
Dr. P. R. Masek, Science & Technology Agency, 3 Dyer's Bldgs., Holborn, EC1.
4, ‡
Abstracts, book notices, letters, new products, patents, standards, tests.
A, —, No, None.
No. 4, 1971, T.p. 96.
Per year £37.

1754 PERKIN-ELMER ANALYTICAL NEWS (PELAN). 1968.
Perkin-Elmer Limited, Post Office Lane, Beaconsfield, Buckinghamshire, HP9 1QA.
4, ‡ +   Gas/or liquid chromatography
Book notices, book reviews, letters, monographic articles, new products, obituaries, patents, standards, tests.
No Index.
September 1972, T.p. 8.   12600.
Free.

1755 THIN-LAYER CHROMATOGRAPHY ABSTRACTS. 1971.
Dr. P. R. Masek, Science & Technology Agency, 3 Dyer's Bldgs., Holborn, London, EC1.
6, ‡
Abstracts, book notices, letters, new products, patents, standards, tests.
A, —, No, None.
No. 6, 1971, T.p. 50.
Per year £24.

1756 UKCIS MACROPROFILES: Gas Chromatography. 1971.
Service Department, UKCIS, The University, Nottingham, NG7 2RD.
26, ‡ +   References on the topic, selected by computer from the secondary publication, CA Condensates.
References to papers in 15, 000 journals.
No Index.
Vol. 2 Issue (Feb. 1972), T.p. 20 (60 refs).   10.
Per copy £1, per year £27.

1757 UKCIS MACROPROFILES: Paper & Thin-layer Chromatography. 1971.
Service Department, UKCIS, The University, Nottingham, NG7 2RD.
26, ‡ +   References on the topic, selected by computer from the secondary publication, CA Condensates.
References to papers in 15, 000 journals.
No Index.
Vol. 2, Issue 4 (Feb 1972), T.p. 8 (24 refs).   10.
Per copy £1, per year £27.

546

INORGANIC CHEMISTRY

1758 ELECTRONIC STRUCTURE AND MAGNETISM OF INORGANIC COMPOUNDS (Specialist Periodical Reports). 1972.
The Chemical Society, Burlington House, London, W1V 0BN.
1, +   An annual critical review of the theoretical and chemical aspects of the subject.
Monographic articles.
A, —, Yes, None.
1971, T.p. 225.
Per copy £5.50.

1759 INORGANIC AND NUCLEAR CHEMISTRY LETTERS: Supplement to Journal of Inorganic & Nuclear Chemistry. 1971.
Pergamon Press Ltd., Headington Hill Hall, Oxford, OX3 0BW.
12, + =
No Index.
Per copy £2.50, per year £28.

1760 INORGANIC CHEMISTRY OF THE TRANSITION ELEMENTS (Specialist Periodical Reports). 1972.
The Chemical Society, Burlington House, London, W1V 0BN.
1, +   An annual critical review of the literature on the subject.
Monographic articles.
A, —, Yes, None.
1970/71, T.p. 400.
Per copy £7.

1761 INORGANIC REACTION MECHANISMS (Specialist Periodical Reports). 1970.
The Chemical Society, Burlington House, London, W1V 0BN.
18 month, +   A critical review of the literature on the subject.
Monographic articles.
A, —, Yes, None.
1969/70, T.p. 338.
Per copy £7.

1762 JOURNAL OF THE CHEMICAL SOCIETY: Dalton Transactions. 1972.
(Journal of The Chemical Society: Section A 1966-1971).
The Chemical Society, Burlington House, London, W1V 0BN.
24, +   Research articles in inorganic chemistry.
Monographic articles.
A, March, Yes, None.
No. 11, 1972, T.p. 95.
Per year £40.

1763 JOURNAL OF INORGANIC AND NUCLEAR CHEMISTRY. 1955.
Pergamon Press Ltd., Headington Hill Hall, Oxford, OX3 0BW.
12, = +   Inorganic chemistry, nuclear chemistry and radiochemistry.
Book reviews, letters, monographic articles.
A, Last issue of volume, Yes, None.
T.p. 275.
Per copy £6.50, per year £75.

1764 RUSSIAN JOURNAL OF INORGANIC CHEMISTRY (Zhurnal Neorganicheskoi Khimii). 1959.
The Chemical Society, Burlington House, London, W1V 0BN.
12, +   Cover to cover English translation of the Russian Journal, Zhurnal Neorganicheskoi Khimii.
Monographic articles, obituaries.
No Index.
Per copy UK £6, per year £46.

546.18

PHOSPHORUS

1765 PHOSPHORUS: and the Heavier Group Va elements. 1971.
Gordon & Breach, 41/42 William 4th Street, London, WC2.
6, + ‡   Forum for the review and discussion of synthetic and mechanistic problems common to investigators with widely different applied and theoretical objectives.
Book notices, book reviews, letters, monographic articles, new products, tests.
A, —, No, None.
Subscription on application.

546.22

SULPHUR

1766 INTERNATIONAL JOURNAL OF SULFUR CHEMISTRY. 1971.
Gordon & Breach, 41/42 William 4th Street, London, WC2.

Part A 4 issues per volume;
Part B 4 issues per volume;
Part C 1 issue per volume.
+ ‡ All aspects of sulfur and selenium chemistry. The last part contains review articles on topics of interest for mechanic studies in sulfur chemistry and selenium.
Book notices, book reviews, commodity prices, letters, monographic articles, new products, tests.
A, —, Yes, None.
Subscription on application.

546.26

CARBON

1767 CARBON.
Pergamon Press Ltd., Headington Hill Hall, Oxford, OX3 0BW.
6, = + Physics, chemistry and technology of carbons.
Book reviews, monographic articles.
A, Last issue of volume, Yes, None.
Per copy £5, per year £28.

1768 FLUOROCARBON AND RELATED CHEMISTRY (Specialist Periodical Reports). 1972.
The Chemical Society, Burlington House, London, W1V 0BN.
2 year, + A biennial critical review of the literature on the subject.
Monographic articles.
2 year, —, Yes, None.
1969/71, T.p. 307.
Per copy £7.

547

ORGANIC CHEMISTRY

1769 INDEX OF REVIEWS IN ORGANIC CHEMISTRY. 1971.
The Chemical Society, Burlington House, London, W1V 0BN.
1, + A compilation of review articles that have appeared in journals, books, conference proceedings, symposia and technical trade literature on organic chemistry.
A, Summer, Yes, 3 years.
1971, T.p. 296.
Per copy £3.

1770 INTRA-SCIENCE CHEMISTRY REPORTS. 1967.
Gordon & Breach, 41/42 William 4th Street, London, WC2.
4, + ‡ Each issue of this journal is generally devoted to a single topic of special interest to organic chemists and allied scientists, such as the aspects of fluorine chemistry, homoaromaticity and related studies, and new aspects of peptide chemistry.
Book notices, book reviews, letters, monographic articles, new products, tests.
A, —, Yes, None.
Per year £11.67.

1771 JOURNAL OF THE CHEMICAL SOCIETY: Perkin Transactions I. 1972.
(Journal of The Chemical Society Section C).
The Chemical Society, Burlington House, London, W1V 0BN.
24, + Research articles in organic and bio-organic chemistry.
Monographic articles.
A, March, Yes, None.
No. 11, 1972, T.p. 137.
Per year £42.

1772 JOURNAL OF THE CHEMICAL SOCIETY: Perkin Transactions II. 1972.
(Journal of the Chemical Society: Section B)
The Chemical Society, Burlington House, London, W1V 0BN.
15, + Research articles in the field of physical organic chemistry.
Monographic articles.
A, March, Yes, None.
No. 8, 1972, T.p. 121.
Per year £25.

1773 OMR—ORGANIC MAGNETIC RESONANCE. 1969.
Heyden & Son Limited, Spectrum House, Alderton Crescent, London, NW4 3XX.
6, ‡ + = Application of NMR, ESR and NQR to problems or organic chemistry.
Book reviews, monographic articles, new products.
A, —, Yes, None.
April 1972, T.p. 171.
Per year £10 for private subscriptions: £29 for corporate organisations.

1774 ORGANOMETALLIC CHEMISTRY (Specialist Periodical Reports). 1972.
The Chemical Society, Burlington House, London, W1V 0BN.
1, + An annual critical review of the literature on the subject.
Monographic articles.
A, —, Yes, None.
1971, T.p. 400.
Subscription on application.

1775 SURFACE AND DEFECT PROPERTIES OF SOLIDS (Specialist Periodical Reports). 1972.
The Chemical Society, Burlington House, London, W1V 0BN.
1, + An annual critical review of the literature on the subject.
Monographic articles.
A, —, Yes, None.
1971, T.p. 264.
Per copy £6.

1776 TETRAHEDRON. 1957.
Pergamon Press Ltd., Headington Hill Hall, Oxford, OX3 0BW.
24, + = All aspects of organic chemistry.
Monographic articles.
A, Last issue of volume, Yes, None.
T.p. 70.
Per copy £4.50, per year £85.

1777 TETRAHEDRON LETTERS. 1960.
Pergamon Press Ltd., Headington Hill Hall, Oxford, OX3 0BW.
52, + = Letters journal for the publication of research results in the field of organic chemistry.
A, Last issue of volume, Yes, None.
T.p. 30.
Per copy £1.50, per year £70.

547.45

CARBOHYDRATES.

1778 CARBOHYDRATE CHEMISTRY (Specialist Periodical Reports). 1968.
The Chemical Society, Burlington House, London, W1V 0BN.
1, + An annual critical review of the literature on the subject.
Monographic articles.
A, —, Yes, None.
1970, T.p. 278.
Per copy £7.

547.46
AMINO ACIDS

1779 AMINO-ACIDS PEPTIDES AND PROTEINS (Specialist Periodical Reports). 1969.
The Chemical Society, Burlington House, London, W1V 0BN.
1, +   A critical review of the literature on the synthetic and structural aspects of the subject.
Monographic articles.
A, —, Yes, None.
1970, T.p. 294.
Per copy £6.

547.52
AROMATIC CHEMISTRY

1780 AROMATIC AND HETEROAROMATIC CHEMISTRY (Specialist Periodical Reports). 1973.
The Chemical Society, Burlington House, London, W1V 0BN.
1, +   An annual critical review of the literature on the subject.
Monographic articles.
A, —, Yes, None.
1971/72, T.p. 300.
Subscription on application.

547.59
TERPENES

1781 TERPENOIDS AND STEROIDS (Specialist Periodical Reports). 1971.
The Chemical Society, Burlington House, London, W1V 0BN.
1, +   An annual critical review of the literature on all aspects of the subjects.
Monographic articles.
A, —, Yes, None.
1970, T.p. 557.
Per copy £11.

547.92
STEROIDS

1782 UKCIS MACROPROFILES: Steroids. 1971.
(CHEMSCAN—Steroids).
Service Department, UKCIS, The University, Nottingham, NG7 2RD.
26, ‡ +   References on the topic, selected by computer from the secondary publication, Chemical Titles.
References to papers in 700 important chemical journals.
No Index.
Issue 3, 1972, T.p. 33 (100 refs.).   30.
Per copy £1, per year £27.

547.94
ALKALOIDS

1783 THE ALKALOIDS (Specialist Periodical Reports). 1971.
The Chemical Society, Burlington House, London, W1V 0BN.
1, +   An annual critical review of the literature on the subject by an international team of experts.
Monographic articles.
A, —, Yes, None.
1970/71, T.p. 293.
Per copy £7.50.

548
FILMS

1784 THIN FILMS. 1968.
Gordon & Breach, 41/42 William 4th Street, London, WC2.
4, + ‡   Experimental and theoretical work, in the fields of superconductivity, magnetism, optics, crystal growth and structure, electron emission, lattice defects, order-disorder phenomena, electron diffraction, and mechanical effects in thin films.
Book notices, book reviews, letters, monographic articles, new products, tests.
No Index.
Subscription on application.

548.7
MOLECULAR CHEMISTRY

1785 DIELECTRIC AND RELATED MOLECULAR PROCESSES (Specialist Periodical Reports). 1972.
The Chemical Society, Burlington House, London, W1V 0BN.
2 year, +   A biennial critical review of selected major aspects of the field.
Monographic articles.
2 year, —, Yes, None.
1971, T.p. 350.
Subscription on application.

548.71
CRYSTALLOGRAPHY

1786 CRYSTAL LATTICE DEFECTS. 1969.
Gordon & Breach, 41/42 William 4th Street, London, WC2.
4, + ‡   Experimental and theoretical work concerning lattice defects in metals, semi-conductors, covalent crystals, ionic crystals, ceramics, complex inorganic crystals, molecular crystals, etc...
Book notices, book reviews, letters, monographic articles, new products, tests.
A, —, No, None.
Subscription on application.

549
MINERALOGY

1787 BULLETIN OF THE BRITISH MUSEUM (NATURAL HISTORY) MINERALOGY SERIES. 1950.
British Museum (Natural History), Cromwell Road, London, SW7 5BD.
Irregular, +   Mineralogy and Petrology.
Monographic articles
Volume indexes are published.
500.
Subscription varies.

1788 MINERALOGICAL ABSTRACTS. 1959.
(Vols. 1-13, 1920-1958 integral with Mineralogical Magazine).
The Mineralogical Society, 41 Queen's Gate, London, SW7 5HR.
4, ‡ = *   World coverage of mineralogy, crystallography, petrology, geochemistry, meteorites etc.
Abstracts, book notices, book reviews.
A, January, Yes, None.
June 1972, T.p. 86.   c.2000.
Per year £10. Free to members.

1789 MINERALOGICAL MAGAZINE. 1876.
The Mineralogical Society, 41 Queen's Gate, London, SW7 5HR.
4, ‡ + =   Scientific mineralogy & allied subjects.
Book reviews, monographic articles.

2 yearly, December, Yes, None.
March 1972, T.p.107, Ad.p. 8.   2000.
Per copy £2.25, per year £10. Free to members.

549.091
GEMMOLOGY

1790 JOURNAL OF GEMMOLOGY AND PROCEEDINGS OF THE GEMMOLOGICAL ASSOCIATION OF GT. BRITAIN. Journal of Gemmology. 1947.
Gemmological Association of Gt. Britain, Saint Dunstan's House, 2/4 Carey Lane, London, EC2V 8AB.
4, ‡ = +   Technical and educational journal dealing with the study of gemstones and their detection from synthetic and imitation counterparts.
Abstracts, book notices, book reviews.
Every 2 years, October issue every other year, No, None.
Approx 2800.
Per copy £1, per year £4.

55
GEOLOGY

1791 AMATEUR GEOLOGIST.
c/o J. N. Diggens, Liverpool Geological Society, Geology Dept., University, Liverpool.
○ = +
No Index.
Subscription on application.

1792 BRITISH GEOLOGICAL LITERATURE (NEW SERIES). 1972.
(British Geological Literature 1964-1968).
Bibliographic Press Ltd., 10 Montague Place, Worthing, Sussex, BN11 3BG.
4, ‡ +   Lists new papers on the geology and physical geography of the British Isles (including S. Ireland) and surrounding seas.
Abstracts.
Q, —, Yes, 5 year, 10 year.
August, 1972, T.p. 38.   c.100.
Per year £4.

1793 BROWN'S GEOLOGICAL INFORMATION BULLETIN. 1972.
Brown's Geological Information Service Ltd., 160 North Gower Street, London, NW1 2ND.
12, + = * ‡   Current activity in geology, especially in Britain: research, publications, exploration, meetings.
Book notices, book reviews, new companies, new products, obituaries.
A, (early 1973), Yes, None.
Restricted circulation, not sold separately.

1794 BULLETIN OF THE BRITISH MUSEUM (NATURAL HISTORY) GEOLOGY SERIES. 1949.
British Museum (Natural History), Cromwell Road, London, SW7 5BD.
Irregular, +   Taxonomic Palaeontology and Geology.
Monographic articles.
Volume indexes are published, Yes, None.
500.
Subscription varies.

1795 BULLETIN OF THE GEOLOGICAL SURVEY OF GREAT BRITAIN. 1939.
HMSO, P.O. Box 569, Atlantic House, High Holborn, London, EC1P 1BN.
Irregular, +   Geology of Great Britain and Northern Ireland.
Subscription varies.

1796 **GEOFORUM.**
Pergamon Press Ltd., Headington Hill Hall, Oxford, OX3 0BW.
4, + =   Forum for the evaluation of knowledge of our environment.
Book reviews, monographic articles.
A, Last issue of volume, Yes, None.
Per copy £3.50, per year £12.

1797 GEOLOGICAL JOURNAL. 1964.
(Liverpool and Manchester Geological Journal 1951-1963).
Geology Dept., University, Liverpool.
1, * + =   Geology with palaeontology, stratigraphy, structural geology, petrology, mineralogy, aerial geology.
Book reviews, monographic articles.
No Index.
T.p. 150, Ad.p. 2.
Free to members.

1798 GEOLOGICAL MAGAZINE. 1864.
Cambridge University Press, P.O. Box 92, London, NW1 2DB.
6, + =   All aspects of earth science.
Book reviews, monographic articles.
A, —, Yes, None.
Per copy £2, per year £8.

1799 GEOLOGICAL SOCIETY SPECIAL REPORTS. 1971.
Scottish Academic Press Ltd. (for Geological Society). 25 Perth Street, Edinburgh, EH3 5DW.
2, +   Monographs of shorter length than *Memoirs* series on special topics.
Monographic articles, reports.
No Index.
Priced individually.

1800 JOURNAL OF EARTH SCIENCES. 1970.
(Transactions of Leeds Geological Association).
Leeds Geological Association, c/o Dept. of Earth Sciences, University, Leeds, LS2 9JT.
2 yearly, = ‡ +
No Index.
Per copy £1.50.

1801 JOURNAL OF THE GEOLOGICAL SOCIETY. 1971.
(Quarterly Journal of the Geological Society 1845-1970).
Scottish Academic Press (for Geological Society), 25 Perth Street, Edinburgh, EH3 5DW.
6, + *   Medium primarily for original research by Fellows of the Society in all branches of geological science; includes Proceedings of Society activities.
Letters, monographic articles.
A, Last issue of volume, Yes, None.
March 1972, T.p. 108, Ad.p. 2.   4250.
Per year £10.

1802 JOURNAL OF THE HARKER GEOLOGICAL SOCIETY.
c/o D. R. Parker, Dept. of Geology, University, Hull, Yorks.
4, = + ‡
No Index.
Subscription on application.

1803 MEMOIRS OF THE GEOLOGICAL SOCIETY. 1958.
Geological Society, Burlington House, London, W1V 0JU.
Irregular, +   Monographs on geological topics of current interest and importance.
Monographic articles.
No Index.
Subscription on application.

1804 MERCIAN GEOLOGIST: Journal of the East Midlands Geological Society. 1964.
East Midlands Geological Society, 54 Cyprus Road, Mapperley Park, Nottingham, NG3 5EB.
1/2, * +   Primarily intended to publish original papers on English Midlands geology, but will accept other papers and review articles of interest to the Society Membership.
Book notices, book reviews, letters, monographic articles, obituaries, reports.

2/3 years, with the last part of the volume, Yes, None.
January 1972, T.p. 80.   700.
Ordinary Membership £2. annually. Institutional Membership £3. annually.

1805 MODERN GEOLOGY. 1969.
Gordon & Breach, 41/42 William 4th Street, London, WC2.
4, + ‡   Experimental and theoretical work on mathematical and statistical geology, isotype geology, radiation damage, thermoluminescence, new aspects of geochemistry and geophysics, remote sensing, lunar and planetary geology.
Book notices, book reviews, letters, monographic articles, new products, tests.
A, —, No, None.
Subscription on application.

1806 OVERSEAS GEOLOGY AND MINERAL RESOURCES.
HMSO, PO Box 569, Atlantic House, High Holborn, London, EC1P 1BN.
Irregular, +   Geology and mineral resources of territories overseas.
No Index.
Subscription varies.

1807 PROCEEDINGS OF THE CUMBERLAND GEOLOGICAL SOCIETY.
c/o R.E.O. Pearson, 123 High Road, Kells, Whitehaven, Cumberland.
= + ‡
No Index.
Subscription on application.

1808 PROCEEDINGS OF THE GEOLOGICAL SOCIETY OF GLASGOW.
Geological Department, University, Glasgow, W2.
= + ‡
No Index.
Subscription on application.

1809 PROCEEDINGS OF THE GEOLOGISTS' ASSOCIATION. 1859.
Benham and Company Limited, (for the Geologists Association), Colchester.
4, + *   All fields of Earth Science. Also record meetings, including Field Meetings, of the Association in Britain and abroad.
Letters, monographic articles, obituaries.
A, December, Yes, 10 year.
Per year £2. £5 non-members.
Indexed in: IBZ.

1810 QUARTERLY JOURNAL OF ENGINEERING GEOLOGY. 1967.
Scottish Academic Press (for the Geological Society), 25 Perth Street, Edinburgh, EH3 5DW.
4, + ‡ *   Geology as applied to civil engineering and mining practice, including rock mechanics, soil mechanics, geotechnics, applied sedimentology, pedology, mineralogy, petrology, geohydrology, hydrogeology and engineering applications of geophysics.
Book reviews, letters, monographic articles, obituaries, reports, tests.
A, with final part of volume, Yes, None.
Vol. 4, no. 3, 1972, T.p. 117, Ad.p. 1.   2000.
Per year £6.

1811 TERTIARY TIMES. 1970.
Tertiary Research Group, c/o 4 Yewdale Close, Bromley, Kent, BR1 4JJ.
1, + =   All aspects of tertiary geology in Britain, *especially* stratigraphy and palaeontology.
Book notices, book reviews, letters, monographic articles, obituaries.
A, in prospect, Yes, None.
June 1971, T.p. 48.   about 100.
Per copy varies, per year £1.

1812 TRANSACTIONS OF THE INSTITUTION OF MINING AND METALLURGY. B—Applied Earth Science. 1966.
(Transactions... Metallurgy 1892).
Institution of Mining & Metallurgy, 44 Portland Place, London, W1N 4BR.
4, * = ‡ +   All aspects of economic geology.
Book notices, book reviews, letters, monographic articles, obituaries.
A, April/June, Yes, None.
T.p. 169, Ad.p. 7.
Free to members. Non-members on application.
Indexed in: BTI, IBZ.

1813 TRANSACTIONS OF THE ROYAL GEOLOGICAL SOCIETY OF CORNWALL.
Royal Geological Society of Cornwall, Penzance.
1, ‡ * +   Geology of South West England with special reference to Cornwall.
Monographic articles.
2 yearly, —, Yes, None.
Vol. 20, Pt. 2, 1967-68, T.p. 79.
Per copy £1. 50.

550.3

GEOPHYSICS

1814 COMMENTS ON EARTH SCIENCES: GEOPHYSICS. 1970.
Gordon & Breach, 41/42 William 4th Street, London, WC2.
6, + ‡   Cross-communication of ideas between the various branches of geophysics and closely related sciences, which will inform not only specialists in the field, but also teachers and those researching into the wider areas of geophysics.
Book notices, book reviews, letters, monographic articles, new products.
No Index.
Subscription on application.

1815 GEOPHYSICAL FLUID DYNAMICS: Mechanics and energetics of atmospheres and oceans. 1969.
Gordon & Breach, 41/42 William 4th Street, London, WC2.
4, + ‡   Dynamics of the atmosphere of the earth and other planets and of the ocean, on air-sea interaction, theoretical and experimental studies of rotating, stratified and convecting fluids, laboratory and numerical models of geophysical flows, and related phenomena.
Book notices, book reviews, letters, monographic articles, tests.
A, —, No, None.
Subscription on application.

1816 THE GEOPHYSICAL JOURNAL OF THE ROYAL ASTRONOMICAL SOCIETY. 1958.
Blackwell Scientific Publications (for the Royal Astronomical Society), Osney Mead, Oxford, OX2 0EL.
c. 20 (3/4 vols.) ‡ = *   Physics of the earth and its internal structure.
Book reviews, monographic articles.
A, —, Yes, None.
May 1972, T.p. 96.
Per copy £3, per year £12. 50.

550.34

EARTHQUAKES. SEISMOLOGY

1817 BIBLIOGRAPHY OF SEISMOLOGY. 1965.
International Seismological Centre, 6 South Oswald Road, Edinburgh, EH9 2HX.
2, + ‡ =
No Index.
Per year £12. 50.

1818 BULLETIN OF THE INTERNATIONAL SEISMOLOGI-
CAL CENTRE. 1964.
(International Seismological Summary 1918-1963).
International Seismological Centre, 6 South Oswald
Road, Edinburgh, EH9 2HX.
12, + ‡ =
A, —, Yes, None.
Per year £50.

1819 INTERNATIONAL JOURNAL OF EARTHQUAKE
ENGINEERING AND STRUCTURAL DYNAMICS:
The Journal of the International Association for
Earthquake Engineering. 1972.
John Wiley & Sons Limited, Baffins Lane, Chichester,
Sussex, England.
4, +   All aspects of engineering related to earth-
quakes.
Monographic articles.
A, End of volume, Yes, None.
No. 1, 1972, T.p. 104.
Per year £13.

1820 REGIONAL CATALOGUE OF EARTHQUAKES. 1964.
International Seismological Centre, 6 South Oswald
Road, Edinburgh, EH9 2HX.
2, + ‡ =
No Index.
Per year £12.50.

550.4

GEOCHEMISTRY

1821 GEOCHIMICA ET COSMOCHIMICA ACTA. 1950.
Pergamon Press Ltd., Headington Hill Hall, Oxford,
OX3 0BW.
12, = +   Geochemistry and cosmochemistry.
Book reviews, letters, monographic articles.
A, Last issue of volume, Yes, 10 year.
T.p. 117.
Per copy £3, per year £30.

550.87

DOWSING

1822 JOURNAL OF THE BRITISH SOCIETY OF DOWSERS.
1956.
(Radio Perception 1933-1956).
British Society of Dowsers, 19 High Street, Eydon,
Daventry, Northants, N11 6PP.
4, ○ = +   The use of dowsing for geophysical medical,
agricultural and other purposes such as the tracing
of objects, animate and inanimate. To keep a Register of Dowsers.
Book notices, book reviews, letters, monographic
articles, new products, obituaries, reports, tests.
2 year, March 1972 et seq. Yes, None.
T.p. 48.   c.1025.
Per copy 30p, per year £1.20.
Free to members.

551.3.051

SEDIMENTATION

1823 SEDIMENTOLOGY. Official journal of the International
Association of Sedimentologists. 1953.
Blackwell Scientific Publications, Osney Mead, Oxford,
OX2 0EL.
4, = +   Sedimentology in all aspects and geological
implications of the subject.
Book reviews, monographic articles.
A, —, No, None.
Per copy £2.75, per year £10.

551.31

GLACIOLOGY. ICE

1824 ICE: News Bulletin of the International Glaciological
Society. 1958.
International Glaciological Society, Lensfield Road,
Cambridge, CB2 1ER.
3, ‡ + † *   News of recent field and laboratory work
into any aspect of snow and ice: geology, geophysics,
engineering, meteorology and climatology, oceanography, hydrology, physics, chemistry, &c. Conference news. News of members of the Society.
Issued free to members.
1st. issue 1972, No. 38, T.p. 24.   1400.
Per copy 50p, per year £1.50.
Free to members of the Society.

1825 JOURNAL OF GLACIOLOGY. 1947.
International Glaciological Society, Lensfield Road,
Cambridge, CB2 1ER.
3, ‡ + † *   All aspects of research into snow and ice:
geology, geophysics, engineering, meteorology and
climatology, oceanography, hydrology, physics,
chemistry, &c.
Abstracts, book notices, book reviews, letters, mono-
graphic articles, tests.
A, Middle of year following termination of volume.
Yes, None.
No. 61, 1972, T p. 171.   1700.
Per copy £3.34, per year £10.
Members of the Society—special rates.

551.44

CAVES. SPELEOLOGY

1826 BULLETIN OF THE BRITISH SPELEOLOGICAL
ASSOCIATION. 1940.
The Association, Duke Street, Settle, Yorks.
4, ○ ‡   News and minor articles on caves.
No Index.
T.p. 26.
Free to members only.

1827 THE CAVE DIVING GROUP NEWSLETTER: New
Series. 1964.
('Old Series' 1946-1963).
Cave Diving Group of Great Britain, c/o Mr. Colin
Priddle, 40 Ralph Rd., Bristol 7.
4, ‡ ○   Definitive accounts of original explorations by
cave divers with maps, practical cave diving.
Accounts of meetings of C.D.G. and of its required
sections.
Book reviews, legal notes, letters, articles, new products,
obituaries, standards, tests.
Irregular, April 1972 for years 1969, 70, 71, Yes, None.
April 1972, T.p. 24 + 2 maps.   140.
Per copy 20p.

1828 JOURNAL OF THE BRITISH SPELEOLOGICAL ASSO-
CIATION: Cave Science. 1967.
(Cave Science 1949-1965).
The Association, Duke Street, Settle, Yorks.
2, * ‡ +   All aspects of cave discovery, archaeology
and research, limestone, geomorphology and hydro-
logy.
Monographic articles.
4 year, Every 8 issues, No, None.
T.p. 45.
Free to members.

Key to reference symbols

○ popular   ‡ technical   = trade/professional

+ research   * society/institution   † house journal

1829 JOURNAL OF THE CRAVEN POTHOLE CLUB. 1949.
The Craven Pothole Club, Castle Chambers, Millbridge, Skipton, Yorkshire.
1, ‡ + *   The activities of the Craven Pothole Club, general caving articles and notes.
Book reviews, monographic articles, obituaries.
6 year, —, Yes, None.
1971, T.p. 66, Ad.p. 3.   500.
Per copy 65p.

1830 NEWSLETTER OF THE CAVE RESEARCH GROUP OF GREAT BRITAIN. 1946.
Cave Research Group, Lindum, The Homend, Ledbury, Herefordshire.
4, = * + ‡   Cave discovery and research.
Book notices, book reviews, letters, monographic articles, obituaries, reports, standards, tests.
No Index.
T.p. 35.
Per year 80p. Free to members.

1831 PROCEEDINGS OF THE BRITISH SPELEOLOGICAL ASSOCIATION. 1963.
The Association, Duke Street, Settle, Yorks.
1, ‡ +   All aspects of speleology and limestone geomorphology.
Monographic articles.
No Index.
T.p. 63.
Free to members.

1832 SPELEOLOGICAL ABSTRACTS. 1964.
British Speleological Association, Duke Street, Settle, Yorks.
1, = +   British speleology and limestone geomorphology.
Abstracts.
3 year, —, No, None.
T.p. 128.
Free to members.

1833 STUDIES IN SPELEOLOGY. 1964.
Pengelly Cave Studies Trust Ltd.
(Formerly Association of the Pengelly Cave Research Centre), c/o British Museum (Nat. Hist.), Cromwell Road, London, SW7 5BD.
1, + *   All aspects of cave studies, especially review articles on cave studies and conservation and new methods and results of cave research.
Book reviews, monographic articles.
A, —, Yes, 5 year approx.
1971, T.p. 68.   c.500.
Per copy £1.50.
(Members annual subscription (£2) also entitles to 4 duplicated newsletters.)

1834 TRANSACTIONS OF THE CAVE RESEARCH GROUP OF GREAT BRITAIN. 1948.
Cave Research Group, Lindum, The Homend, Ledbury, Herefordshire.
4, * = + ‡   Current and past research and science in all aspects of cave science.
Monographic articles.
A, December/January, No, None.
T.p. c.60.
Free to members.

551.46

OCEANOGRAPHY

1835 DEEP-SEA RESEARCH AND OCEANOGRAPHIC ABSTRACTS. 1953.
Pergamon Press Ltd., Headington Hill Hall, Oxford, OX3 0BW.
12, = +   Marine sciences in general.
Abstracts.
A, Last issue of volume, Yes, None.
T.p. 200.
Per copy £3, per year £34.

1836 OCEAN ENGINEERING.
Pergamon Press Ltd., Headington Hill Hall, Oxford, OX3 0BW.
6, = + ‡   Underwater engineering and design.
Book reviews, monographic articles.
A, Last issue of volume, Yes, None.
Per copy £3.50, per year £18.

1837 UNDERWATER SCIENCE AND TECHNOLOGY INFORMATION BULLETIN. 1969.
IPC Science & Technology Publications Ltd., 32 High Street, Guildford, Surrey.
12, ‡   References to u/w activity, edited, indexed and categorized.
A, January, Yes, None.
T.p. 42.   700.
Per year £14.

1838 UNDERWATER SCIENCE AND TECHNOLOGY JOURNAL. 1969.
IPC Science & Technology Publications Ltd., 32 High Street, Guildford, Surrey.
4, + ‡   All aspects of underwater science and exploration.
Book reviews, letters, monographic articles, new products, patents, standards.
A, March, Yes, None.
T.p. 55, Ad.p. 3.   700.
Per copy £2, per year £8.

551.48

HYDROLOGY

1839 HYDROLOGICAL SCIENCES BULLETIN. 1972.
International Association of Hydrological Science, Wallingford.
= ‡
No Index.
Subscription on application.

551.5

METEOROLOGY

1840 CONTRIBUTIONS TO ATMOSPHERIC PHYSICS.
Pergamon Press Ltd., Headington Hill Hall, Oxford, OX3 0BW.
4, = +   Experimental and theoretical work in all branches of meteorology.
Book reviews, monographic articles.
A, Last issue of volume, Yes, None.
T.p. 100.
Per copy £3.50, per year £12.

1841 ESTIMATED SOIL MOISTURE DEFICIT AND POTENTIAL EVAPOTRANSPIRATION OVER GREAT BRITAIN. 1962.
Director-General, Meteorological Office, Met 08, London Road, Bracknell, Berkshire, RG12 2SZ.
12/24 (depending on estimates of soil moisture).
‡ + =   Maps and tables of areal estimates of soil moisture deficit and tables of point estimates of monthly totals of potential evapotranspiration.
No Index.
14-6-1972, T.p. 8.
Per year £4.

1842 JOURNAL OF ATMOSPHERIC AND TERRESTRIAL PHYSICS. 1950.
Pergamon Press Ltd., Headington Hill Hall, Oxford, OX3 0BW.
12, = +   Characteristics of the earth's atmosphere at all heights.
Book reviews, monographic articles.
A, Last issue of volume, Yes, None.
T.p. 166.
Per copy £4.50, per year £50.
Indexed in: IBZ.

1843 THE MARINE OBSERVER: A quarterly journal of
 maritime meteorology. 1924.
 Her Majesty's Stationery Office, Atlantic House,
  Holborn Viaduct, London, EC1P 1BN.
 4, ‡   Meteorology, oceanography etc of interest to
  seamen. Reports of meteorological phenomena or
  of general scientific interest, extracted from
  meteorological logbooks of ships of the British
  Commonwealth.
 Abstracts from ships' meteorological logbooks, book
  reviews, monographic articles, obituaries.
 A, October, Yes, None.
 January 1972, T.p. 43, Ad.p. 1.   2125.
 Per copy 42½p, per year £1.88.

1844 METEOROLOGICAL MAGAZINE. 1920.
 (Symons's Meteorological Magazine, 1866-1920).
 Her Majesty's Stationery Office, Atlantic House,
  Holborn Viaduct, London, EC1P 1BN.
 12, ‡ +   Widespread meteorological coverage, e.g. in
  relation to aviation, industry, agriculture and hydro-
  logy. Reports of theoretical and laboratory re-
  searches, instrument development and meteorologi-
  cal events.
 Book reviews, letters, monographic articles, obituaries.
 A, December, Yes, None.
 June 1972, T.p. 32, Ad.p. 2.   2000.
 Per copy 21p, per year £2.52.

1845 QUARTERLY JOURNAL OF THE ROYAL METEORO-
  LOGICAL SOCIETY. 1856.
 Royal Meteorological Society, 49 Cromwell Road,
  London, SW7.
 4, = + ‡ *
 Book reviews, monographic articles, obituaries.
 A, October, No, None.
 T.p. 160, Ad.p. 8.
 Per copy £3.75, per year £12.
 Free to members.

1846 WEATHER. 1946.
 Royal Meteorological Society, 49 Cromwell Road,
  London, SW7.
 12, * ‡ =   All aspects of meteorology.
 Book reviews, letters, monographic articles.
 A, December, Yes, None.
 T.p. 51, Ad.p. 4.
 Per copy 15p, per year £1.80.
 Free to members.

1847 WEATHER REPORT. 1884.
 (Quarterly Weather Report 1869-1880).
 HMSO, PO Box 569, London, SE1.
 12, + ○   Summary of reports made daily from 600
  stations in the U.K.
 No Index.
 T.p. 33.
 Per copy 25p.
 Free to reporters.

552

PETROLOGY

1848 INTERNATIONAL JOURNAL OF ROCK MECHANICS
  AND MINING SCIENCES. 1964.
 Pergamon Press Ltd., Headington Hill Hall, Oxford,
  OX3 0BW.
 6, = +   All aspects of rock mechanics and mine
  environmental engineering.
 Book reviews, monographic articles.
 A, Last issue of volume, Yes, None.
 T.p. 83.
 Per copy £4, per year £20.

1849 JOURNAL OF PETROLOGY. 1960.
 Oxford University Press, Press Road, Neasden, London,
  NW10.
 3, +   Physics and chemistry of rocks, their mineralogy
  and textures, and certain aspects of their dating by
  natural radioactivity. Quantitative studies of rock-
  forming minerals, experimental physical chemistry
  relevant to petrology, and parts of isotope geology.
 Book reviews, monographic articles.
 A, —, Yes, None.
 October 1971, T.p. 212, Ad.p. 2.   1400.
 Per copy £3, per year £7.

56

PALAEONTOLOGY

1850 PALAEONTOLOGY. 1957.
 The Palaeontological Association, c/o Dr W.D.I.
  Rolfe, Hunterian Museum, The University, Glasgow,
  G12 8QQ.
 4, ‡ + *   All aspects of palaeontology.
 Monographic articles.
 A, November, Yes, 10 year,
 June 1972, T.p. 194.   2032.
 Per copy £5, per year £10. (£5 per year to individual
  members).

1851 SPECIAL PAPERS IN PALAEONTOLOGY. 1967.
 The Palaeontological Association, c/o Dr W.D.I.
  Rolfe, Hunterian Museum, University, Glasgow,
  G12 8QQ.
 2/3, + * ‡   Substantial separate works on all aspects
  of palaeontology and stratigraphical palaeontology.
 Monographic articles.
 No Index.
 No 6, 1970, T.p. 82   250.
 Per copy varies, per year £8. (£4 to individual
  members).

572

ANTHROPOLOGY

1852 JOURNAL OF THE ANTHROPOLOGICAL SOCIETY
  OF OXFORD. 1970.
 Institute of Social Anthropology, 51 Banbury Road,
  Oxford.
 3, + =   Research work in progress at the Institute.
  Of interest to philosophers, anthropologists and
  social scientists generally.
 Articles, book reviews, letters.
 No Index.
 Hilary 1972, T.p. 52, Ad.p. 1.   400.
 Per copy 75p, per year £1.

574

BIOLOGY

1853 AMINO ACIDS, PEPTIDE & PROTEIN ABSTRACTS.
  1972.
 Anthony G. Woolcott, Publisher, Information Retrieval
  Limited, 1 Falconberg Court, London, W1V 5FG.
 12, +   Abstracting and indexing services, covering
  biological sciences generally in particular, biophysics, biology, biochemistry and organic chemistry.
 Abstracts, book notices, book reviews, new products.
 A, 6-9 months after end of volume, No, None.
 T.p. 100.   1000.
 £40 Europe: £67 Airmail per year

1854 ANNALS OF APPLIED BIOLOGY. 1914.
 Biochemical Society (Publications)
  (for the Association of Applied Biologists)
 P.O. Box No. 32, Commerce Way, Whitehall Industrial
  Estate, Colchester, Essex.
 9, ‡ *   Crop and animal pests and diseases, crop
  physiology; crop protection; control of harmful birds
  and mammals.
 Book reviews, monographic articles.

A,—, Yes, 50 year index (1914-1962).
May 1972, T.p. 90.
Per copy £2.80, per year £5.

1855 AQUATIC SCIENCES & FISHERIES ABSTRACTS. 1971.
(Aquatic Biology Abstracts 1969-1971)
Anthony G. Woolcott, Publisher, Information Retrieval Limited, 1 Falconberg Court, London W1V 5FG.
12, ‡ + Abstracting and indexing services covering air and water pollution, fish and fisheries, and biological sciences; also limnology and oceanography, and water and water supply.
Abstracts, book notices, book reviews, new products.
A, 6-9 mths., after end of volume, No, None.
T.p. 160.   1000.
Per year £50, Europe Airmail £67.

1856 BEHAVIOURAL BIOLOGY ABSTRACTS. 1973.
Information Retrieval Ltd., 1 Falconberg Court, London W1V 5FG.
4, = ‡   2000 abstracts p.a.
M,—, No, A.
Subscription on application.

1857 BIOLOGICAL JOURNAL OF THE LINNEAN SOCIETY. 1969.
(Proceedings of the Linnean Society 1838-1968)
Academic Press Inc. (London) Ltd., 24-28 Oval Road, London, NW1.
4, * + =   General field of experimental and descriptive biology, palaeontology and systematics, as well as reports upon ecological and conservation studies and expeditions, and papers of a historical nature. Reports of the proceedings of the Society.
A, Following year, Yes, None.
T.p. 100, Ad.p. 3.
£10 per year, including index. Free to members.

1858 BIOLOGICAL MEMBRANE ABSTRACTS. 1973.
Information Retrieval Ltd., 1 Falconberg Court, London W1V 5FG.
12, = ‡   6000 abstracts p.a.
M,—, No, A.
Subscription on application.

1859 BIOLOGICAL REVIEWS OF THE CAMBRIDGE PHILOSPHICAL SOCIETY. 1933.
(Proceedings of the Cambridge Philosphical Society Biological Sciences 1923-1925, Biological Reviews and Biological Proceedings of the Cambridge Philosophical Society 1926-1934).
Cambridge University Press, P.O. Box 92, London, NW1 2DB.
4, +   Current progress and problems in particular areas of reseach.
Monographic articles.
A, November, Yes, 10 year.
May 1972, T.p. 130.   16900.
Per copy £2.60, per year £8.
Indexed in: IBZ.

1860 BIOLOGICAL RHYTHMS. 1972.
(Circadian Rhythms 1970-1971)
Biomedical Information Project, Dept., of Physiology, The University, Sheffield, S10 2TN.
12, ‡ +   Current awareness service, titles, authors addresses, references
No Index.
July 1972, T.p. 6.
Per copy 60p, per year £6.

1861 BIOLOGIST: Journal of the Institute of Biology 1970.
(Journal of Institute of Biology 1953-1969)
Institute of Biology, 41 Queens Gate, London, SW7.
4, * = ‡   Biology and its applications.
Book reviews, letters, monographic articles, parliamentary reports,
No Index
May 1972, T.p. 54, Ad.p. 12.   8500.
Per copy 50p, per year £2. Free to members.

1863 CALCIFIED TISSUE ABSTRACTS. 1969.
Anthony G. Woolcott, Publisher, Information Retrieval Limited, 1 Falconberg Court, London W1V 5FG, England.
12, +
Abstracts, book notices, book reviews, new products,
A, 6-9 months after end of volume, No, None.
Jan. 1972, T.p. 126.   1000.
Per year £20.

1864 CHEMORECEPTION ABSTRACTS. 1973.
Information Retrieval Ltd., 1 Falconberg Court, London W1V 5FG.
4, = ‡   2000 abstracts p.a.
M,—, No, A.
Subscription on application.

1865 ENVIRONMENTAL BIOLOGY AND MEDICINE. 1971.
Gordon & Breach, 41/42 William 4th Street, London WC2.
4, + ‡   Interaction of physical and biological phenomena as they affect man and the universe; the intention is to establish a medium for the advancement and dissemination of new and/or pertinent findings emanating from the many diverse areas associated with environmental biomedicine.
Book notices, book reviews, letters, monographic articles, new products, tests.
Irregular — No, None.
Subscription on application.

1866 FORMA ET FUNCTIO
Pergamon Press Ltd., Headington Hill Hall, Oxford OX3 0BW.
4, + =   Interaction of form and function in biology.
Book reviews, monographic articles.
A, Last issue of volume, Yes, None.
Per copy £4, per year £12.

1867 FRESHWATER BIOLOGY. 1971.
Blackwell Scientific Publications (in consultation with the Freshwater Biological Association), Osney Mead, Oxford, OX2 0EL.
4, + =   All aspects of freshwater biology.
Book reviews, monographic articles.
A, December, Yes, None.
March 1972, T.p. 86, Ad.p. 2.   280.
Per copy £2.50, per year £8.

1868 INTERNATIONAL ABSTRACTS OF BIOLOGICAL SCIENCES. 1954.
Pergamon Press Ltd., Headington Hill Hall, Oxford OX3 0BW.
12, + =   Survey of world literature in the fields of anatomy, biochemistry, biophysics, immunology pathology, microbiology, zoology, botany.
Abstracts.
A, Last issue of volume, No, None.
T.p. 230.
Per copy £8, per year £90

1870 JOURNAL OF BIOSOCIAL SCIENCE. 1969.
Blackwell Scientific Publications (for the Galton Foundation), Osney Mead, Oxford, OX2 0EL.
4, ○ + =   Social aspects of human biology, including reproduction and its control, gerontology, ecology, genetics and applied psychology; with biological aspects of the social sciences, including sociology, social anthropology, education and criminology; and biosocial aspects of demography.
Book reviews, letters, monographic articles, obituaries.
A, October, Yes, None.
April 1972, T.p. 118, Ad.p. 6.
Per copy £2.75, per year £10.

1871 JOURNAL OF EXPERIMENTAL BIOLOGY. 1930.
(British Journal of Experimental Biology 1923-1929).
Cambridge University Press, PO Box 92, London NW1 2DB.

6, + Experimental zoology with an emphasis on invertebrates.
Monographic articles.
6m, Last issue of volume, Yes, None.
June 1972, T.p. 282, Ad.p. 1.   2300.
Per copy £4, per year £18.

1872 JOURNAL OF THE MARINE BIOLOGICAL ASSOCIATION OF THE UNITED KINGDOM. 1887 (Old Series) 1889 (New Series)
Cambridge University Press, PO Box 92, London NW1 2DB.
4, +   All aspects of marine biology, oceanography and marine science.
Book reviews, monographic articles.
A, First part of next volume, Yes, None.
May 1972, T.p. 215, Ad.p. 5.   2800.
Per copy £6, per year £22.

1873 JOURNAL OF MOLECULAR BIOLOGY. 1959.
Academic Press Ltd., 24-28 Oval Road, London NW1.
24, +
Letters, monographic articles.
8 year, End of each volume, Yes, Every 20 volumes.
T.p. 200.
Per year £68.

1874 JOURNAL OF THEORETICAL BIOLOGY. 1961.
Academic Press Inc. (London) Ltd., 24-28 Oval Road, London NW1.
12, +   Theoretical work in all fields of biology, e.g. (a) generalized theories, (b) theories of specific processes or phenomena, (c) theoretical discussion of specific projects, (d) theoretical discussion of methods.
Letters.
Q, End of each volume, Yes, None.
June 1972, T.p. 207.   1600.
Per year £43.80.

1875 NUCLEIC ACIDS ABSTRACTS. 1971.
Anthony G. Woolcott, Publisher Information Retrieval Limited, 1 Falconberg Court, London W1V 5FG.
12, +   Abstracting and indexing services: covering Biological Sciences, chemistry.
Abstracts, book notices, book reviews, new products.
A, 6-9 months after end of volume, No, None.
T.p. 170.   1000.
Per year £40 Europe: £67 Airmail.

1876 PHILOSOPHICAL TRANSACTIONS OF THE ROYAL SOCIETY SERIES B (BIOLOGICAL SCIENCES). 1887.
(Philosophical Transactions of the Royal Society 1665-1886).
The Royal Society, 6 Carlton House Terrace, London SW1Y 5AG.
2, +   Papers, exceeding 24 printed pages in length, containing results or methods of critical importance.
A, Last issue, Yes, 10 year author.
1150.
Per volume £14.25: The price of each part varies in accordance with the number of pages and illustrations it contains. Each volume is closed when the price of its constituent parts is not less than £17.50.

1877 PROCEEDINGS OF THE ROYAL SOCIETY SERIES B BIOLOGICAL SCIENCES. 1905.
(Proceedings of the Royal Society 1854-1904; Abstracts of Papers Published in Phil. Trans 1800-1853).
The Royal Society, 6 Carlton House Terrace, London SW1Y 5AG.
3, +   Papers, not normally exceeding 24 printed pages, containing results or methods of critical importance.
A, Last part of each volume, Yes, 10 year authors.
No. 1064, T.P. 138.   2280
Per copy £1.75, per volume £6.25.

1878 PROCEEDINGS OF THE ROYAL SOCIETY OF EDINBURGH. B—BIOLOGY. 1941.
(Proceedings of the Royal Society of Edinburgh 1832-1940).
Royal Society of Edinburgh, 22-4 George Street, Edinburgh EH2 2PQ.
2, = + ‡
Monographic articles.
2 year, End of each volume, Yes, None.
T.p. 45.   1200.
Free to members.

575

HEREDITY

1879 ANNALS OF HUMAN GENETICS. 1955.
(Annals of Eugenics 1925-1954).
Cambridge University Press, PO Box 92, London NW1 2DB.
4, +   Observations on human heredity and related genetical and statistical problems.
Book notices, book reviews, monographic articles.
A, April, Yes, None.
July 1972, T.p. 128, Ad.p. 2.   1180.
Per copy £3, per year £10.

1880 BEHAVIOR GENETICS. 1971.
Plenum Publishing Co. Ltd., Davis House, 8 Scrubs Lane, Harlesden, London NW10 6SF.
4, = ‡ +   Research in the inheritance of behavior in animals and man.
Book reviews, letters, monographic articles.
A, —, Yes, None.
Per year £8.50.

1881 BIOLOGY AND HUMAN AFFAIRS. 1935.
British Social Biology Council, 69 Eccleston Square, London SW1.
3, = ‡   Social and human biology, population, nutrition, natural history etc.
Book reviews, monographic articles.
No Index.
Spring 1971, T.p. 53, Ad.p. 6.   700.
Per copy 50p, per year £1.25.
Indexed in: BEI.

1882 GENETICAL RESEARCH. 1960.
Cambridge University Press, PO Box 92, London NW1 2DB.
6, +   All aspects of genetics.
Book reviews, monographic articles.
6m, June/December, Yes, None.
April 1972, T.p. 80, Ad.p. 3.   1300.
Per copy £2.60, per year £12.

1883 GENETICS ABSTRACTS. 1968.
Anthony G. Woolcott, Publisher Information Retrieval Limited, 1 Falconberg Court, London W1V 5FG.
12, +   Biological sciences, medical sciences and veterinary science.
Abstracts, book notices, book reviews, new products.
Monthly, 6-9 months after end of volume, No, None.
March 1972, T.p. 400.   1000.
Per year £50.

1884 HEREDITY: Journal of the Genetical Society of Great Britain. 1947.
Longman Group Limited, 43/45 Annandale Street, Edinburgh, EH7 4AT.
6, = +   Research into experimental breeding, cytology, genetics, etc.
Book reviews, monographic articles.
A, —, Yes, None.
April 1972, T.p. 128, Ad.p. 2.   1500.
Per copy £2, per year £12.
Indexed in: IBZ.

1885 JOURNAL OF MEDICAL GENETICS. 1964.
British Medical Association, BMA House, Tavistock Square, London WC1H 9JR.
4, ‡ = + *   Clinical, statistical, pathological, cytological and biochemical aspects of medical genetics.
Book reviews, letters, monographic articles, obituaries.
A, December, Yes, None.
June 1972, T.p. 114, Ad.p. 2.
Per year £6.

576.3

CYTOLOGY

1886 CELL AND TISSUE KINETICS. 1968.
Blackwell Scientific Publications, Osney Mead, Oxford OX2 0EL.
6, + =   Studies of cell proliferation in normal and abnormal states; of control systems and mechanisms operating at inter- and intracellular and molecular levels; their modification by chemical and physical agents.
Book reviews, monographic articles.
A, November, Yes, None.
May 1972, T.p. 86, Ad.p. 2.
Per copy £1.75, per year £10.

1887 CELL MEMBRANES. 1970.
Biomedical Information Project, Dept., of Physiology, University of Sheffield, Sheffield S10 2TN.
12, + ‡   Biological studies, transport, immunology, physical and chemical studies, enzymes, organelle membranes, artificial membranes.
Current awareness service, titles, references, addresses.
No index,
April 1972, T.p. 13.   400-500.
Per copy 60p, per year £6.

1888 CONNECTIVE TISSUE RESEARCH. 1972.
Gordon & Breach, 41/42 William 4th Street, London WC2.
4, + ‡
Book notices, book reviews, letters, monographic articles, new products, tests.
A, —, No, None.
Per year £15.50.

1889 CYTOBIOS: Prestige International Journal of Cell Biology. 1969.
The Faculty Press, 88 Regent Street, Cambridge.
2, +   Original investigations into all aspects of cell biology.
Monographic articles.
6m, —, Yes, None.
April 1971, T.p. 71.
Per copy £5, per year £40.

1890 JOURNAL OF CELL SCIENCE. 1966.
(Quarterly Journal of Microscopical Science 1853).
Cambridge University Press, PO Box 92, London NW1 2DB.
6, +   Structure and function of plant and animal cells ranging from the molecular structure of cell components to the movement and interactions of whole cells.
Monographic articles.
6m, May/November, Yes, None.
January 1972, T.p. 265, Ad.p. 2.   1790.
Per copy £4.50, per year £22.

1891 JOURNAL OF MECHANOCHEMISTRY AND CELL MOBILITY. 1971.
Gordon & Breach, 41/42 William 4th Street, London WC2.
4 +   Mechanochemical energy conversions. Stresses the general principles underlying the operation of mechanochemical systems and the common denominators of the various types of motility in living cells, and encourages the application of biological designs to man-made mechanochemical energy conversions.
Book notices, book reviews, letters, monographic articles, tests.
A, —, No, None.
Per year £17.50.

1892 JOURNAL OF NEUROCYTOLOGY. 1972.
Chapman & Hall Ltd., 11 New Fetter Lane, London EC4.
4, = ‡
Book reviews, monographic articles.
A, —, Yes, None.
Per year £12.

1893 TISSUE & CELL. 1968.
Longman Group Limited, 43/49 Annandale Street, Edinburgh, EH7 4AT.
4, + =
Book notices, book reviews, monographic articles.
A, Last issue of year, Yes, None.
March 1972, T.p. 184, Ad.p. 2.   600.
Per copy £4, per year £15.

576.8

MICROBIOLOGY. PARASITOLOGY

1894 BIODETERIORATION RESEARCH TITLES. 1972.
(International Biodeterioration Bulletin Reference Index Supplement 1967; IBBRIS 1968-1971).
Biodeterioration Information Centre, University of Aston in Birmingham, 80 Coleshill Street, Birmingham, B4 7PF.
4, + ‡   Classified index of current literature on the biological deterioration of materials.
No Index.
Autumn 1971, T.p. 36.   500.
Per year £10.

1895 INTERNATIONAL BIODETERIORATION BULLETIN. 1965.
Biodeterioration Information Centre, University of Aston in Birmingham, 80 Coleshill Street, Birmingham B4 7PF.
4, † ‡ *   Deterioration of materials by living organisms, including fungal, bacterial, insect and rodent attack on wood, textiles, plastics, etc., marine fouling, rotting and infestation of stored food products, aircraft bird-strikes.
Book reviews, letters, monographic articles, new products.
A, With final issue for year, No, None.
Summer 1971, T.p. 47.   750.
Per year £10.

1896 INTERNATIONAL JOURNAL FOR PARASITOLOGY.
Pergamon Press Ltd., Headington Hill Hull, Oxford OX3 0BW.
4, = +   All aspects of the phenomenon of parasitism.
Book reviews, letters, monographic articles.
A, Last issue of volume, Yes, None.
Per copy £3, per year £10.

1897 JOURNAL OF APPLIED BACTERIOLOGY. 1954.
(Proceedings. Society of Agricultural Bacteriologists 1938-1944; Proceedings of the Society for Applied Bacteriology 1945-1953).
Academic Press Inc. (London) Ltd., 24-28 Oval Road, London NW1.
4, +   Microbiology, especially bacteriology in its application to agriculture and other industries.
Book reviews, monographic articles, obituaries.
A, With Part 4, Yes, None.
Per year £9.05, Free to members.

1898 THE JOURNAL OF GENERAL MICROBIOLOGY. 1947.
Cambridge University Press, PO Box 92, London NW1 2DB.
12, +   All aspects of the biology of micro-organisms except virology.
Monographic articles.
Q, Last issue of each volume, Yes, about 4 year.
July 1972, T.p. 207, Ad.p. 4.   5000.
Per copy £5.50, per year £48.

1899 JOURNAL OF MEDICAL MICROBIOLOGY. 1969.
(Journal of Pathology and Bacteriology).
Longman Group Limited, 43/49 Annandale Street, Edinburgh EH7 4AT.
4, = +
Book notices, monographic articles.
A, Last issue of year, Yes, None.
February 1972, T.p. 164, Ad.p. 4.   2200.
Per copy £2.25, per year £8.

1900 MICROBIOLOGY ABSTRACTS: Section A: Industrial and Applied Microbiology. 1965.
Anthony G. Woolcott, Publisher, Information Retrieval Limited, 1 Falconberg Court, London W1V 5FG.
12, + ‡   Abstracting and indexing services covering agriculture, biological sciences; patents; feed, flour and grain; food and food industries; foresty; medical sciences, pharmacology; and the textile industries.
Abstracts, book notices, book reviews, new products, patents.
A, 6-9 months after end of volume, No, None.
T.p. 190.   1000.
Per year £40 Europe: £67 Airmail.

1901 MICROBIOLOGY ABSTRACTS: Section B: Bacteriology & General Microbiology. 1966.
Anthony G. Woolcott, Publisher, Information Retrieval Limited, 1 Falconberg Court, London, W1V 5FG.
12, ‡ +   Abstracting and indexing services covering biological sciences, medical sciences and veterinary science.
Abstracts, book notices, book reviews, new products, patents.
4, 6-9 months after end of volume, No, None.
T.p. 200.   1000.
Per year £40 Europe: £67 Airmail.

1902 MICROBIOLOGY ABSTRACTS, Section C: Algology, mycology & protozoology. 1972.
Anthony G. Woolcott, Publisher, Information Retrieval Limited, 1 Falconberg Court, London, W1V 5FG.
12, ‡ +   Abstracting and indexing services, covering biological sciences, medical sciences and veterinary science.
Abstracts, book notices, book reviews, new products, patents.
A, 6-9 months after end of volume, No, None.
T.p. 120.   1000.
Per year £40 Europe: £67 Airmail.

1903 MICROBIOS: Prestige International Journal of Chemical & General Microbiology. 1969.
The Faculty Press, 88 Regent Street, Cambridge, England.
2, +   General and chemical microbiology.
Monographic articles.
6m, —, Yes, None.
April 1971, T.p. 71.
Per copy £5, per year £40.

1904 PARASITOLOGY. 1908.
Cambridge University Press, PO Box 92, London, NW1 2DB.
6, +   All aspects of the biology of parasites and their vectors.
Book reviews, monographic articles.
A, November, Yes, None.
June 1972, T.p. 187.   1400.
Per copy £3, per year £14.

577.1

BIOCHEMISTRY

1905 ANNALS OF CLINICAL BIOCHEMISTRY. 1969.
(Proceedings of the Association of Clinical Biochemists 1960-1968).
Association of Clinical Biochemists, 7 Warwick Court, London, WC1.
6, = ‡ + *   Clinical chemistry, chemical pathology and analytical biochemistry.
Book reviews, monographic articles.
A, Last Issue of volume, Yes, None.
T.p. 30, Ad.p. 11.
Free to members.

1906 THE BIOCHEMICAL JOURNAL. 1903.
The Biochemical Society (Publications), P.O. Box 32, Commerce Way, Whitehall Industrial Estate, Colchester, Essex, CO2 8HP.
24, ‡ + *   Scientific papers covering all aspects of biochemistry from contributors on original research.
Abstracts, monographic articles.
One per volume, after completion of volume. Yes, Every 25 volumes.
April 1972, T.p. 250.   c. 6100.
Per copy £2.25, per year £45, and Free to members.

1907 COMPARATIVE BIOCHEMISTRY AND PHYSIOLOGY. 1959.
Pergamon Press Ltd., Headington Hill Hall, Oxford, OX3 0BW.
12, = +   Biochemistry and physiology of animals and some plants.
Book reviews, monographic articles.
A, Last issue of volume, Yes, 10 year.
T.p. 60.
Per copy £4, per year £42.50 (each of 2 parts).

1908 HISTOCHEMICAL JOURNAL. 1968.
Chapman & Hall Ltd., 11 New Fetter Lane, London, EC4.
6, + ‡ =   Histochemistry and biochemistry.
Book reviews, letters, monographic articles.
A, November, No, None.
T.p. 90, Ad.p. 1.
Per copy £2.50, per year £12.

1909 THE INTERNATIONAL JOURNAL OF BIOCHEMISTRY. 1970.
Scientechnica (Publishers) Ltd., 42-44 Triangle West, Bristol, BS8 1EX.
6, ‡ + =   Forum for an international exchange of ideas and material, embracing all specialties, and providing the modern biochemist with a full and critical account of the most important developments in this field.
Monographic articles.
A, December, Yes, None.
February 1972, T.p. 124, Ad.p. 2.
Per copy £3, per year £15.

1910 THE JOURNAL OF STEROID BIOCHEMISTRY. 1969.
Pergamon Press Ltd., Headington Hill Hall, Oxford, OX3 0BW.
6, + =   Experimental and theoretical studies applied to steroid biochemistry.
Book reviews, monographic articles.
A, Last issue of volume, Yes, None.
Per copy £3.50, per year £18.

577.15

ENZYMES

1911 CYCLIC AMP. 1970
Biomedical Information Project, Dept. of Physiology, The University, Sheffield S10 2TN.
12, + ‡   All aspects subdivided by tissue. Includes

1912-1925

related enzymes and other related adenine nucleotides.
Current awareness service, titles, author's address, references.
No Index.
July 1972, T.p. 8.
Per copy 60p, per year £6.

1912 ENZYME REGULATION. 1971.
Biochemical Information Project, Dept. of Physiology, The University, Sheffield S10 2TN.
12, + ‡
Current awareness service, titles, authors address, references.
No Index.
June 1972, T.p. 6.
Per copy 60p, per year £6.

1913 RIBOSOMES. 1970.
Biochemical Information Project, Dept. of Physiology, The University, Sheffield S10 2TN.
12, + ‡ All aspects divided into animal, plants, yeasts, bacteria, viruses, E. coli.
Current awareness service, titles, author's address, references.
No Index.
July 1972, T.p. 10.
Per copy 60p, per year £6.

577.3

BIOPHYSICS

1914 BIOPHYSICS. Cover-to-cover translation of Biofizika. 1969.
Pergamon Press Ltd., Headington Hill Hall, Oxford OX3 0BW.
6, = + Application of physics to the investigation of processes in living organisms and the physics of these processes.
Monographic articles.
A, Last issue of volume, Yes, None.
Per copy £10.50, per year £60.

1915 QUARTERLY REVIEWS OF BIOPHYSICS: Official organ of the International Union for Pure and Applied Biophysics. 1968.
Cambridge University Press, PO Box 92, London, NW1 2DB.
4, + Biophysics and molecular biology.
Book reviews, monographic articles.
A, Last issue of volume, Yes, None.
February 1972, T.p. 161. 1200.
Per copy £2.50, per year £7.

577.4

**CONSERVATION
ECOLOGY
ENVIRONMENT**

1916 AMENITY: Bulletin of the Civic Trust for the North East. 1966.
Civic Trust for the North East, 34/35 Saddler Street, Durham.
3, * ‡ † Environment in the North East region.
Book notices, book reviews, legal notes, letters, articles, standards.
No Index.
April 1972, T.p. 8. 3500.
Free.

1918 BIOLOGICAL CONSERVATION. 1968.
Applied Science Publishers Ltd., Ripple Road, Barking, Essex.
4, + Original scientific and other papers dealing with the preservation of wildlife and the conservation of biological and allied natural resources throughout the world.
Book reviews, letters, monographic articles.
No Index.
January 1972, T.p. 80, Ad.p. 4. 1200.
Per year £8.

1919 BULLETIN OF ENVIRONMENTAL EDUCATION (BEE). 1971.
Town & Country Planning Association Environmental Education Unit, 17 Carlton House Terrace, London, SW1.
11, ○ = Theory and practice of environmental education with emphasis on the urban environment and general ecological issues. Colour coded resource pages.
Book notices, book reviews, commodity prices, letters, articles, new products.
No Index.
June 1972, T.p. 28. 3000.
Per copy 15p, per year £2.

1920 CHEMOSPHERE. 1972.
Pergamon Press Ltd., Headington Hill Hall, Oxford OX3 0BW.
6, † = Environmental affairs in the fields of chemistry, physics and biology.
Letters.
A, Last issue of volume, Yes, None.
Per copy £2.50, per year £14.

1921 CONSERVATION REVIEW. 1970.
Society for the Promotion of Nature Reserves, The Manor House, Alford, Lincs.
2, * ○ News sheet for members—brief articles and other matters of interest.
No Index.
Spring 1972, T.p. 8.
Free to members.

1922 CONTACT. 1966.
Civic Trust for the North West, 56 Oxford Street, Manchester M1 6EU.
4/6, * ○ Aims to maintain contact between the C.T.N.W. and a hundred or so civic societies in the north west, to stimulate activity and awareness of conservation matters.
Legal notes, brief articles.
No Index.
March 1972, T.p. 6. 5000.
Free.

1923 ENVIRONMENT. 1970.
17 Ridgmont Road, Bramhall, Cheshire.
12, =
No Index.
Per year £1.50.

1924 THE ENVIRONMENT THIS MONTH: The International Journal of Environmental Science. 1972.
Medical and Technical Publishing Co. Ltd., P.O. Box 55, St. Leonard's House, Lancaster.
12, ‡ + All aspects of environmental concern treated from the scientific viewpoint.
Book notices, book reviews, letters, monographic articles, new products, parliamentary reports, standards, tests.
6m, Dec./June, Yes, None.
July 1972, T.p. 112, Ad.p. 8. 7000.
Per copy £2, per year £18.

1925 ENVIRONMENTAL POLLUTION. 1970.
Applied Science Publishers Ltd., Ripple Road, Barking, Essex.
8, + Biological effects of pollution, and includes research papers on the ecological effects of all types of environmental pollution and pollution control.
Book reviews, monographic articles.
A, October, Yes, None.
April 1972, T.p. 81. 1500.
Per year £16.

1926 ENVIRONMENTAL POLLUTION MANAGEMENT. 1971.
The National Magazine Co. Ltd., 680 Garrett Lane, London, SW17.
12, + ‡   All matters relating to industrial pollution.
Book reviews, articles, reports, patents, standards, tests.
No Index.
June 1972, T.p. 18, Ad.p. 20.
Free, controlled circulation.

1927 EPOCH: to improve the quality of life. 1972.
Harvey Foundation, 2A Lebanon Road, Croydon, Surrey.
4, ○ ‡ =   All aspects of anti-pollution and environmental health.
Book notices, book reviews, letters, monographic articles, new products, reports, standards, tests.
A, Last issue of volume, Yes, None.
Per year £2.

1928 GRAPEVINE: Newletter of the Scottish Civic Trust. 1972.
Scottish Civic Trust, 24 George Square, Glasgow G2 1EF.
6, *   Matters concerning conservation, environment, with special appeal to members of civic and amenity societies in Scotland.
Book notices, book reviews, letters, articles.
No Index.
No. 1, 1972, T.p. 4.   1000.
Per copy 10p, per year 50p.

1929 INTERNATIONAL JOURNAL OF ENVIRONMENTAL STUDIES. 1970.
Gordon & Breach, 41/42 William 4th Street, London, WC2.
4, ○ ‡ +   Relationship between man and his environment. All aspects of the subjects, and appeals to social, natural, and applied scientists, as well as architects, town planners and other professional people.
Book notices, book reviews, legal notes, letters, monographic articles, new products, parliamentary reports, patents, standards, tests.
A, —, No, None.
Subscription on application.

1930 JOURNAL OF ENVIRONMENTAL PLANNING AND POLLUTION CONTROL. 1972.
Mercury House Business Publications Ltd., Waterloo Road, London, SE1 8UL.
4, = ‡ +   All aspects of environmental science.
Book notices, book reviews, letters, monographic articles.
A, —, Yes, None.
Per copy £2, per year £7.

1931 N.E.R.C. NEWS JOURNAL: Natural Environment Research Council. 1970.
Natural Environment Research Council, Alhambra House, 27-33 Charing Cross Road, London, WC2H 0AX.
4, + =   Research in the environmental sciences.
Book notices, letters, monographic articles, new products, obituaries, parliamentary reports, patents, standards, tests.
No Index.
No. 5, 1972, T.p. 16.
Free.

1932 OUTLOOK. 1971.
Bristol & West Building Society, P.O. Box 27, Broad Quay, Bristol. BS99 7AX.
4, ○   Housing and all aspects of conservation.
Articles.
2 yearly, Will be with every 8th issue, Yes, None.
Spring 1972, T.p. 20.   10000.
Per year 60p.

1933 RESEARCH BULLETIN. 1971.
School of Environmental Studies, University College London, Gower Street, London, WC1E 6BT.
1, +   A summary of all research currently being undertaken in the School of Environmental Studies.
No Index.
May 1971, T.p. 48.   700.
Free.

1934 SEED: Scottish Education for Environment and Development. 1972.
Geoffrey Hunt, Philosophy Dept., University, David Hume Tower, George Square, Edinburgh 8.
6, ○   Problems of environment and world economic development, including economic exploitation, racism and militarism, overpopulation, pollution and resource depletion.
Book reviews, letters, articles.
No Index.
May 1972, T.p. 24.   500.
Per copy 6p.

1935 STUDIES IN CONSERVATION. 1952.
International Institute for Conservation, 608 Grand Buildings, Trafalgar Square, London, WC2N 5HN.
4, ‡   Technical reports on aspects of the conservation and restoration of cultural property, particularly museum objects.
Book reviews, letters, monographic articles (occasional)
A, with No. 4 of Volume, Yes, None.
T.p. 48.   3000.
Per copy £1.75, per year £7.

578

MICROSCOPY

1936 FERRITIN: And other markers for electron microscopy. 1972.
(Ferritin 1970-1971)
Biomedical Information Project, Dept. of Physiology, The University, Sheffield S10 2TN.
12, + ‡   All aspects of ferritin and other markers e.g. horseradish, peroxidase, immunofluorescent tests.
Current awareness service, titles, authors' addresses, references.
No Index.
July 1972, T.p. 3.
Per copy 60p, per year £6.

1937 JOURNAL OF THE QUEKETT MICROSCOPICAL CLUB. 1868.
The Club, c/o Royal Society, Burlington House, London, W1.
4, ○ ‡ *   Book reviews, articles, new products.
3 year, —, Yes, None.
T.p. 30, Ad.p. 4.
Per year £1.50.

1939 MICROSCOPE. 1967.
(Microscope & Crystal Front 1937-1966)
Microscope Publications Ltd., 2 McGrove Mews, Belsize Lane, London, NW3.
4, ‡ = +   Original research in microscopy and their applications.
Book reviews, letters, monographic articles, new products.
A, 4th Quarter, Yes, None.
T.p. 85, Ad.p. 20.
Per copy £1.50, per year £5.

Key to reference symbols

○ popular   ‡ technical   = trade/professional

+ research   * society/institution   † house journal

1940-1952

1940 PERKIN-ELMER ELECTRON MICROSCOPY NEWS. 1972.
Perkin-Elmer Limited, Post Office Lane, Beaconsfield, Buckinghamshire HP9 1QA.
4, ‡ +   Book notices, book reviews, letters, monographic articles, new products, obituaries, patents, standards, tests.
No Index.
September 1972, T.p. 4.   1200.
Free.

581

BOTANY

1941 BSBI ABSTRACTS: Abstracts from literature relating to the vascular plants of the British Isles. 1971.
Botanical Society of the British Isles, c/o Department of Botany, British Museum (Natural History), London, SW7.
1, + *   Abstracts from the world literature relating to the floristics and taxonomy of vascular plants of the British Isles.
Abstracts.
No Index.
January 1972, T.p. 51, Ad.p. 2.
Per year £2.

1942 ANNALS OF BOTANY. 1888, New Series 1937.
Oxford University Press, Press Road, Neasden, London, NW10.
5, +   All fields of the plant sciences.
Book reviews, monographic articles.
A, —, Yes, None.
March 1972, T.p. 202, Ad.p. 4.   1500.
Per copy £2.25, per year £9.50.
Indexed in: IBZ.

1943 BOTANICAL JOURNAL OF THE LINNEAN SOCIETY. 1969.
(Proceedings of the Linnean Society 1838-1855; Journal of the Proceedings of the Linnean Society (Botany) 1857-1865)
Academic Press Inc. (London) Ltd., 24-28 Oval Road, London, NW1.
2 vols, each with 4 issues, * +   General field of experimental and descriptive biology, palaeontology and systematics as well as reports of ecological and conservation studies and expeditions, and papers of an historical nature.
6m, 2 per year sometime during following 6 months after completion of volume, Yes, None.
T.p. c. 100, Ad.p. 3.
Per vol. £10, including Index. Free to members.

1944 BULLETIN OF THE BRITISH MUSEUM (NATURAL HISTORY): BOTANY SERIES. 1951.
British Museum (Natural History), Cromwell Road, London, SW7 5BD.
Irregular, +   Taxonomic Botany.
Monographic articles.
Volume indexes are published.
500.
Subscription varies.

1945 CURTIS'S BOTANICAL MAGAZINE. 1787.
Bentham-Moxon Trust, Royal Botanic Gardens, Kew, Richmond, Surrey.
2, + ‡ ○   Contains coloured figures with descriptions and observations on the botany history and culture of choice plants.
2 year, At the end of each volume (4 parts), Yes, None.
Part III vol. 178 Dec. 1971, T.p. 38.   800.
Per copy £2.10.

1946 HOOKER'S ICONES PLANTARUM: Or Figures with descriptive characters and remarks of new and rare plants selected from the Kew Herbarium. 1867.
(Icones Plantarum, 1837-1854)
The Bentham-Moxon Trust, Royal Botanic Gardens, Kew, Richmond, Surrey TW9 3AB.
Irregular, +
Monographic articles.
At end of each Vol, —, Yes, None.
Subscription on application.

1947 JOURNAL OF EXPERIMENTAL BOTANY: An official Organ of the Society for Experimental Botany. 1950.
Oxford University Press, Press Road, Neasden, London, NW10.
4, +   Original research in the fields of plant physiology and bio-chemistry, bio-physics, experimental agronomy and related aspects of botanical science.
Book reviews, monographic articles.
A, —, Yes, None.
May 1972, T.p. 293, Ad.p. 4.   1600.
Per copy £4, per year, £13.
Indexed in: IBZ.

1948 KEW BULLETIN. 1946.
(Bulletin of Miscellaneous Information (Kew) 1887-1942)
HMSO, PO Box 569, London, SE1.
3, + =   Botanical research papers, particularly from the staff of the Royal Botanic Gardens, Kew and mainly taxonomic (revisionary or floristic), cytological or anatomical in character.
A, With last part of each volume, Yes, None.
April 1972, T.p. 233.
Per copy variable.

1949 RADIATION BOTANY.
Pergamon Press Ltd., Headington Hill Hall, Oxford OX3 0BW.
6, + =   All aspects of plant radiobilogy and the effects of ionizing radiation on plants and plant structures.
Book reviews, letters, monographic articles.
A, Last issue of volume, Yes, None.
Per copy £4, per year £18.

1950 TRANSACTIONS OF THE BOTANICAL SOCIETY OF EDINBURGH. 1970.
(Transactions & Proceedings of the Botanical Society of Edinburgh 1841-1969)
The Society, Royal Botanic Gardens, Edinburgh 3.
1, = + *   Research and field work on plant life especially in Scotland.
Monographic articles.
5 year, 1970, Yes, None.
T.p. 120.   670.
Per copy 75p.
Free to Fellows.
Indexed in: IBZ.

1951 WATSONIA: Journal and Proceedings of the Botanical Society of the British Isles. 1949.
(Report of the Botanical Society and Exchange Club of the British Isles 1880-1948).
Botanical Society of the British Isles, c/o British Museum (Natural History), London, SW7 5BD.
2, + *   Papers and records relating to the floristics and taxonomy of British and European vascular plants. Reports of the Society's activities, obituaries and book reviews.
Book reviews, monographic articles, obituaries, reports.
2 years, July 1972 et seq, Yes, None.
July 1972, T.p. 133, Ad.p. 4.
Per copy £2.

581.19

PHYTOCHEMISTRY

1952 THE NEW PHYTOLOGIST. 1902.
Blackwell Scientific Publications, Osney Mead, Oxford, OX2 0EL.

6, = † ‡ Plant biology.
Book reviews, monographic articles.
A, —, Yes, None.
May 1972, T.p. 136.
Per copy £4, per year £20.

1953 PHYTOCHEMISTRY. 1961.
Pergamon Press Ltd., Headington Hill Hall, Oxford, OX3 0BW.
12, = + Chemistry and biochemistry of plants.
Book reviews, monographic articles.
A, Last issue of volume, Yes, None.
T.p. 200.
Per copy £3, per year £34.

581.2

VIROLOGY

1954 JOURNAL OF GENERAL VIROLOGY. 1967.
Cambridge University Press, PO Box 92, London, NW1 2DB
12, + Study of plant and animal viruses.
Monographic articles.
Q, Last issue of each volume, Yes, None.
July 1972, T.p. 114, Ad.p. 1.   2150.
Per copy £4.50, per year £39.

1955 VIROLOGY ABSTRACTS. 1967.
Anthony G. Woolcott, Publisher, Information Retrieval Limited, 1 Falconberg Court, London, W1V 5FG.
12, + Abstracting and indexing services: covering agriculture, biological science and medical sciences.
Abstracts, book notices, book reviews, new products, patents.
A, 6-9 months after end of volume, No, None.
T.p. 120.   1000.
Per year £40 Europe: £67 Airmail.

582.26

ALGAE. PHYCOLOGY

1956 BRITISH PHYCOLOGICAL JOURNAL. 1969.
(British Phycological Bulletin, 1953-1968).
British Phycological Society, Dept. of Botany, University, Leeds, LS2 9JT.
2, * + All aspects of the study of algae.
Book reviews, monographic articles, obituaries,
A, October, No, None.
T.p. 144.   700.
Free to members.

582.28

MYCOLOGY

1957 BIBLIOGRAPHY OF SYSTEMATIC MYCOLOGY. 1943.
Commonwealth Mycological Institute, Ferry Lane, Kew, Richmond, Surrey, TW9 3AF.
2, ‡ Listing of papers and books on all aspects of the taxonomy of fungi.
6m, with part, Yes, None.
January 1972, T.p. 43.
Per year £1.

1958 BULLETIN OF THE BRITISH MYCOLOGICAL SOCIETY
The Society, c/o Dr. W. J. Byford, Broom's Barn Experimental Station, Higham, Bury St. Edmunds, Suffolk.
2, ○ ‡ * Mycology and plant pathology.
Book reviews, letters, monographic articles, obituaries, tests.
A, September, Yes, None.
Spring 1972, T.p. 4.   1400.
Per year £1.50.

1959 C.M.I./A.A.B. DESCRIPTIONS OF PLANT VIRUSES. 1970.
Commonwealth Mycological Institute/Association of Applied Biologists (CMI), Ferry Lane, Kew, Richmond, Surrey, TW9 3AF.
2, ‡ Standardised descriptions of plant viruses.
A, October, No, None,
October 1971, T.p. 80.
Per year £3.

1960 C.M.I. DESCRIPTIONS OF PATHOGENIC FUNGI AND BACTERIA. 1964.
Commonwealth Mycological Institute, Ferry Lane, Kew, Richmond, Surrey, TW9 3AF.
4, ‡ Standardised descriptions of pathogens.
2½ years, Not fixed, No, None.
April 1972, T.p. 20.
Per year £1.50.

1961 DISTRIBUTION MAPS OF PLANT DISEASES. 1942.
Commonwealth Mycological Institute, Ferry Lane, Kew, Richmond, Surrey, TW9 3AF.
2 sets, ‡ Maps giving world distribution of plant diseases, with supporting references.
3 year, Not fixed, No, None.
April 1972, T.p. 36.
Per year £1.25.

1962 INDEX OF FUNGI. 1940.
Commonwealth Mycological Institute, Ferry Lane, Kew, Richmond, Surrey, TW9 3AF.
2, ‡ A list, with full bibliographic citations, of the names of all new genera, species and varieties of fungi and lichens, new combinations and new names.
10 year, varies, Yes, None.
January 1972, T.p. 34.
Per year £1.

1963 REVIEW OF MEDICAL AND VETERINARY MYCOLOGY. 1951.
(Annotated Bibliography of Medical Mycology, 1943-1950),
Commonwealth Mycological Institute, Ferry Lane, Kew, Richmond, Surrey, TW9 3AF.
4, ‡ Fungal diseases of man and animals.
Abstracts, monographic articles.
A, —, Yes, None.
March 1972, T.p. 80, Ad.p. 2
Per year £10.

1964 REVIEW OF PLANT PATHOLOGY. 1970.
(Review of Applied Mycology, 1922-1969).
Commonwealth Mycological Institute, Ferry Lane, Kew, Richmond, Surrey, TW9 3AF.
12, ‡ All aspects of plant pathology.
Abstracts, monographic articles.
A, May, Yes, 40 year.
June 1972, T.p. 64, Ad.p. 4.
Per year £31.

1965 TRANSACTIONS OF THE BRITISH MYCOLOGICAL SOCIETY. 1896.
Cambridge University Press, PO Box 92, London, NW1 2DB.
6, + Biology of fungi and their relations with other plants.
Book reviews, monographic articles.
6m, June/December, Yes, None.
June 1972, T.p. 175.   2300.
Per copy £4, per year £18.

582.29

LICHENS

1966 BRITISH LICHEN SOCIETY BULLETIN. 1959.
(The British Lichen Society Circular, 1958)
British Lichen Society, c/o Department of Botany,

British Museum (Natural History), Cromwell Road, London, SW7 5BD.
2, ○ ‡ *   News of lichenological interest and recent literature on lichens.
Book notices, book reviews, letters, obituaries, tests.
10 year, November 1969, Yes, None.
April 1972, T.p. 15.   550.
Per copy 25p.

1967 THE LICHENOLOGIST. 1958.
Blackwell Scientific Publications (for the British Lichen Society), Osney Mead, Oxford OX2 0EL.
2, + = *   Systemic position of lichens within the classification of the Fungi on a modern basis; phytochemistry, including taxonomic status of chemical strains; dating of glacial movement and the use of lichens as indicators of atmospheric pollution.
Book reviews, monographic articles.
c. 2 years, 1968 et seq., Yes, None.
December 1970, T.p. 124, Ad.p. 2.   560.
Per copy £2, per year £3.

582.32

MOSSES

1968 TRANSACTIONS OF THE BRITISH BRYOLOGICAL SOCIETY. 1947.
Cambridge University Press, PO Box 92, London NW1.
1, +   Study of bryophytes especially in the UK and Commonwealth.
Book notices, book reviews, monographic articles, obituaries.
Irregular.
T.p. 220.   600.
Subscription varies.
Indexed in: IBZ.

582.35

FERNS

1969 BRITISH FERN GAZETTE. 1909.
British Pteridological Society, 46 Sedley Rise, Loughton, Essex.
1, * + ‡ =   All aspects of fern botany on a worldwide basis.
Book notices, book reviews, monographic articles.
A, 1st issue of each volume, No, None.
T.p. 53, Ad. p. 1.
Free to members.

591

ZOOLOGY

1970 ANIMALS: The International Wildlife Magazine. 1963.
Nigel Sitwell Ltd., 21-22 Great Castle St., London W1.
12, ○   Natural history, especially wildlife. Scientifically accurate, but popular writing. No domestic animals. Strong conservation theme. Whole animal kingdom.
Book reviews, letters, articles.
A, February, No, None.
February 1972, T.p. 40, Ad.p. 8.   35000.
Per copy 20p, per year £3.

1971 BULLETIN OF THE BRITISH MUSEUM (NATURAL HISTORY) ZOOLOGY SERIES. 1950.
British Museum (Natural History), Cromwell Road, London, SW7 5BD.
Irregular, +   Taxonomic zoology.
Monographic articles.
Volume indexes are published — Yes, None.
500.
Subscription varies.

1972 BULLETIN OF ZOOLOGICAL NOMENCLATURE. 1943.
International Trust for Zool.Nomen., 14 Belgrave Square, London, SW1X 8PS.
1, +.‡ *   Proposals on zoological nomenclature. Comments received from zoologists, geologists, etc. Decisions of the Commission on Zoological Nomenclature.
Letter, articles.
A, In last issue of volume, Yes, None.
Vol. 26, 1969-1970, T.p. 252.
Per year £9.

1973 CHESTER ZOO NEWS. 1962.
(Our Zoo News, 1937-1962).
The North of England Zoological Society, Zoological Gardens, Upton by Chester, Cheshire.
12, ○ *   News of events in collection i.e. births, arrivals; also notes on gardens new buildings, etc.
No Index.
May 1972, T.p. 15.   sold in Zoo and 800 (to members**,
Per copy 6p, per year 95p. ** Subscribers, Complimentary

1974 JOURNAL OF ZOOLOGY: Proceedings of the Zoological Society of London. 1965.
(Proceedings of the Zoological Society of London, 1830-1965).
Academic Press Inc. (London) Ltd. (for Zoological Society of London), 24-28 Oval Road, London NW1.
12, * +   General field of experimental and descriptive zoology and notices of the business transacted at the Scientific Meetings of the Society.
Monographic articles.
1 index per volume (i.e.) 3 per annum., With the first part of the succeeding volume, Yes, None.
C.T.p. 150.
Per year £28.35.
Indexed in: IBZ.

1975 ORYX: Journal of the Fauna Preservation Society. 1950.
(Journal of the Society for the Preservation of the Wild Fauna of the Empire, 1903-1921; Society for the Preservation of the Fauna of the Empire Journal. New series, 1921-1950).
The Fauna Preservation Society, c/o The Zoo, Regent's Park, London, NW1 4RY.
3, + * =   Conservation and status of endangered species, with emphasis on mammals.
News, General articles, book notices, book reviews.
2 year, —, Yes, None.
January 1972, T.p. 80. Ad.p.1.   3500.
Per copy 50p, per year £3.
Indexed in: IBZ.

1976 ZOOLOGICAL JOURNAL OF THE LINNEAN SOCIETY. 1969.
(Proceedings of the Linnean Society, 1835-1855;
Journal of the Proceedings of the Linnean Society Zoology 1857-65; Journal of Linnean Society (Zoology) 1868-1968).
Academic Press Inc. (London) Ltd., (for the Linnean Society), 24-28 Oval Road, London NW1.
2 vols each with 4 issues. * + =   General field of experimental and descriptive biology, palaeontology and systematics as well as reports of ecological and conservation studies and expeditions and papers of an historical nature.
6m, 2 per year sometime during following 6 months after completion of volume, Yes, None.
T.p. c. 100, Ad.p. 3.
Per vol £10. including index. Free to members.
Indexed in: IBZ.

1977 ZOO FEDERATION NEWS. 1971.
Federation of Zoological Gardens of Great Britain and Ireland, Zoological Gardens, Regent's Park, London NW1 4RY.
4, * †

Book notices, book reviews, letters, articles.
No Index.
May 1972, T.p. 12.
Per year 50p.

1978 ZOO MAGAZINE. 1959.
Young Zoologists' Club (XYZ Club), Zoological Society of London, Regent's Park, London, NW1 4RY.
3, ○ *   Popular material relating to animals and zoos, and details of the activities of the Zoological Society of London's Young Zoologists' Club.
Book reviews, articles.
No Index.
Easter 1972, T.p. 17.   4000.
Free to Young Zoologists' Club members.

591.3

EMBRYOLOGY

1979 JOURNAL OF EMBRYOLOGY AND EXPERIMENTAL MORPHOLOGY. 1953.
Cambridge University Press, PO Box 92, London, NW1 2DB.
6, +   Development processes in the lives of animals and plants. Descriptive and experimental embryology, biochemical and biophysical aspects of development.
Monographic articles.
6m, June/December, Yes, None.
June 1972, T.p. 140.   1550.
Per copy £4.50, per year £22.
Indexed in: IBZ.

1980 JOURNAL OF REPRODUCTION AND FERTILITY. 1960.
(Proceedings of the Society for the Study of Fertility, 1949-1954; Studies on Fertility, 1954-1959).
Blackwell Scientific Publications, Osney Mead, Oxford OX2 0EL.
12, +   Morphology, physiology, biochemistry and pathology of reproduction in man and other animals; the biological, medical and veterinary problems of fertility and lactation.
Monographic articles, obituaries.
Q, March, June, September, December, Yes, 10 year.
June 1972, T.p. 142, Ad.p. 6.
Per copy £3, per year £30.

591.5

ANIMAL ECOLOGY

1981 ANIMAL BEHAVIOUR. 1958.
(British Journal of Animal Behaviour, 1953-1957).
Bailliere, Tindall & Cassell Ltd. (for the Association for the Study of Animal Behaviour), 7-8 Henrietta Street, London, WC2E 8QE.
4, = +   All aspects of behaviour study.
Book reviews, monographic articles.
A, Last issue of year, Yes, None.
November 1971, T.p. 196, Ad.p. 3.
Per year £9, (Includes Animal Behaviour Monographs), Free to members.

1982 ANIMAL BEHAVIOUR MONOGRAPHS.
Bailliere, Tindall & Cassell Ltd., 7-8 Henrietta Street, London, WC2E 8QE.
3, = +
Monographic articles.
A, Last issue of year, Yes, None.
Pt. 3, 1971, T.p. 47.
Per year £4. Reduced subscription for subscribers to Animal Behaviour.

1983 THE JOURNAL OF ANIMAL ECOLOGY. 1932.
Blackwell Scientific Publications (for British Ecological Society), Osney Mead, Oxford, OX2 0EL.
3, + *   All aspects of the study of animals in relation to their environment.
Book reviews, monographic articles, reports, patents, standards, tests.
A, —, Yes, None.
June 1972, T.p. 256, Ad.p. 4.   2500.
Per year £14.
Indexed in: IBZ.

1984 THE JOURNAL OF APPLIED ECOLOGY. 1932.
Blackwell Scientific Publications (for the British Ecological Society), Osney Mead, Oxford, OX2 0EL.
3, = + *   Plant and animal ecology in its application to agriculture, forestry, horticulture, land-users, fisheries, pollution and conservation.
Book reviews, monographic articles,
A, November, Yes, None.
April 1972, T.p. 218, Ad.p. 6.   1500.
Per year £14.

1985 THE JOURNAL OF ECOLOGY. 1913.
Blackwell Scientific Publications (for the British Ecological Society), Osney Mead, Oxford, OX2 0EL.
3, + *   All aspects of ecology.
Book reviews, monographic articles.
A, November, Yes, Vols 1-20; 21-50.
March 1972, T.p. 319, Ad.p. 6.   2700.
Per year £14.

594

MOLLUSCS

1986 CONCHOLOGISTS' NEWSLETTER: Produced by the Conchological Society of Great Britain and Ireland. 1961.
C.S.G.B.& I, c/o P. E. Negus, 82 Chelsea Gardens, Chelsea Bridge Road, London SW1.
4, ○ ‡ *   Collecting and expedition notes, general and educational articles, offers and requests for exchanges, notes and queries.
Book notices, book reviews, letters, articles.
5 year, —, No, None.
March 1972, T.p. 10.   400.
Free to members only.

1987 JOURNAL OF THE CONCHOLOGICAL SOCIETY OF GREAT BRITAIN AND IRELAND. 1876.
(Quarterly Journal of Conchology, 1874-1875)
The Society, c/o 51 Wychwood Avenue, Luton, Beds., LU2 7HT.
2, * ‡ +   All facets of the subject of the mollusca, recent and fossil. Research papers, society proceedings.
Book notices, books reviews, monographic articles, obituaries.
5 year, —, Yes, None.
May 1971, T.p. 67.   500.
Per copy £2, per year £4. Free to members.
Indexed in: IBZ.

1988 PROCEEDINGS OF THE MALACOLOGICAL SOCIETY OF LONDON. 1893.
Blackwell Scientific Publications, Osney Mead, Oxford OX2 0EL.
3, + * =   All aspects of living molluscs including taxonomy, functional morphology, ecology, physiology, biochemistry and embryology. Papers are also included on fossil molluscs.
Book reviews, monographic articles.
2 year, December, Yes, None.
April 1972, T.p. 69, Ad.p. 2.   610.
Per copy £2, per year £5.

595.1

HELMINTHS

1989 HELMINTHOLOGICAL ABSTRACTS. Series A—Animal Helminthology. Series B—Plant Nematology. 1970.
(Previously Series A and B together 1932-1969).

1990 Commonwealth Agricultural Bureaux, Farnham Royal,
Slough, SL2 3BN.
4, = ‡ +
Abstracts.
A, —, Yes, None.
T.p. c. 125.
Per year £10 each to subscribers.

595.4

ARACHNOLOGY. SPIDERS

1990 BULLETIN OF THE BRITISH ARACHNOLOGICAL
SOCIETY. 1969.
c/o Peare Tree House, The Green, Blennerhasset,
Carlisle. CA5 3RE
3, * +   Research in arachnology: spiders, chelifers
and harvestmen.
Book notices, book reviews, letters, monographic articles, obituaries.
Three times annually, —, No, 2 year.
T.p. 24.
Per copy £1.50, per year £4. Free to members.

1991 NEWSLETTER OF THE BRITISH ARACHNOLOGICAL
SOCIETY. 1969.
c/o Peare Tree House, The Green, Blennerhasset,
Carlisle. CA5 3RE.
3, + *   Notices of events and reports of activities,
short articles, distribution records for British
species, study techniques etc.
No Index.
Free to members.

595.7

ENTOMOLOGY

1992 ANNUAL REPORT AND PROCEEDINGS OF THE
LANCASHIRE AND CHESHIRE ENTOMOLOGICAL
SOCIETY. 1877.
The Royal Institution, Colquitt St., Liverpool.
3 years, * = +   All orders of insects.
Monographic articles, tests.
3 years, —, Yes, None.
T.p. 111.   200.
Per copy £3. Free to members.

1993 THE BULLETIN OF THE AMATEUR ENTOMOLOGISTS' SOCIETY. 1941.
The Amateur Entomologists' Society, c/o 355 Hounslow
Road, Hanworth, Feltham, Middlesex.
4, + * =   Collecting and study of all orders of insects.
Reports of expeditions, making equipment, breeding
methods, field research.
Book reviews, letters, monographic articles.
A, —, No, None.
February 1972, T.p. 36, Ad.p. 4,   1200.
Per year £1.25.

1994 BULLETIN OF THE BRITISH MUSEUM (NATURAL
HISTORY): ENTOMOLOGY SERIES. 1950.
British Museum (Natural History), Cromwell Road,
London, SW7 5BD.
Irregular, +   Taxonomic entomology.
Monographic articles.
Volume indexes are published, —, Yes, None.
500.
Subscription Varies.

1995 BULLETIN OF ENTOMOLOGICAL RESEARCH. 1910.
Commonwealth Agricultural Bureaux, Farnham Road,
Slough, SL2 3BN.
4, ‡ = +   Original research concerning insects, mites
or ticks of economic importance in the agricultural,
medical or veterinary field, world wide.
Abstracts, book reviews,
A, Last part of volume, Yes, None.
T.p. 150.
Per year £7 to subscribers.
Indexed in: IBZ.

1996 THE ENTOMOLOGIST. Journal of the Society for
British Entomology. 1840.
British Trust for Entomology Ltd., 41 Queen's Gate,
London, SW7.
12, + = ‡   All aspects of entomology for the amateur
and professional.
Book reviews, letters, monographic articles, obituaries.
A, January/March, Yes, None.
T.p. 23.
Per copy 25p, per year £2. Reduced price to members.

1997 ENTOMOLOGISTS RECORD AND JOURNAL OF VARIATION. 1890.
F. W. Byers, 59 Gurney Court Road, St. Albans, Herts.
12, ‡ +   Lepidotera of the British Isles and other
forms of insect life.
Book reviews, letters, monographic articles.
A, —, No, None.
Per copy 25p, per year £3.

1998 ENTOMOLOGY ABSTRACTS. 1969.
Anthony G. Woolcott, Publisher, Information Retrieval
Limited, 1 Falconberg Court, London, W1V 5FG.
12, +   Abstracting and indexing services, covering
biological sciences and agriculture.
Abstracts, book notices, book reviews, new products.
A, 6-9 months after end of volume, No, None.
T.p. 150.   1000.
Per year £40 Europe, Airmail £67.

1999 INSECT BIOCHEMISTRY. 1971.
Scientechnica (Publishers) Ltd., 42-44 Triangle West,
Bristol, BS8 1EX.
4, +   Insect biochemistry and ideas on the biochemistry of all groups of arthropods.
Monographic articles.
A, —, Yes, None.
March 1972, T.p. 124, Ad.p. 4.   1750.
Per copy £4, per year £15.

2000 INTERNATIONAL JOURNAL OF INSECT MORPHOLOGY AND EMBRYOLOGY. 1971.
Pergamon Press Ltd., Headington Hill Hall, Oxford,
OX3 0BW.
4, = +
Book reviews, monographic articles.
A, Last issue of volume, Yes, None.
Per copy £3.50, per year £12.

2001 JOURNAL OF ENTOMOLOGY: A General Entomology.
B Taxonomic Entomology. 1971.
Royal Entomological Society, 41 Queen's Gate, London,
SW7.
2, = ‡ + *   General entomology.
Short articles.
A, —, Yes, None.
Per year £4 each part.

2002 JOURNAL OF INSECT PHYSIOLOGY. 1957.
Pergamon Press Ltd., Headington Hill Hall, Oxford,
OX3 0BW.
12, = +   Experimental and comparative insect
physiology.
Book reviews, monographic articles.
A, Last issue of volume, Yes, None.
T.p. 100.
Per copy £4, per year £44.

2003 PROCEEDINGS OF THE ROYAL ENTOMOLOGICAL
SOCIETY. 1926.
(Stylops 1932-1935).
Royal Entomological Society, 41 Queen's Gate, London
SW7.
1, = * +   Accounts of scientific meetings etc.
Monographic articles, obituaries, reports.

No Index.
T.p. 200.
Per year £1.20.

2004 REVIEW OF APPLIED ENTOMOLOGY. 1913.
Commonwealth Agricultural Bureaux, Farnham House, Farnham Royal, Slough, Bucks, SL2 3BN.
12, ‡ = + Every aspect of applied entomology. Series A—insect and other anthropod pests of culturated plants, trees etc. Series B—insects, ticks, mites etc. Conveying diseases to man and animals.
Abstracts.
A, Last part of each volume, Yes, None.
T.p. 42.
Per year Series A £10; B £4 to subscribers.

2005 TRANSACTIONS OF THE ROYAL ENTOMOLOGICAL SOCIETY. 1834.
Royal Entomological Society, 41 Queen's Gate, London, SW7.
4, = + * General and taxonomic entomology.
Book notices, monographic articles.
A, with last part of volume, Yes, None.
T.p. 120.
Per year £12.50.
Indexed in: IBZ.

597

FISH

2006 JOURNAL OF FISH BIOLOGY. 1969.
Academic Press Ltd., 24-28 Oval Road, London, NW1 7DX.
4, * + ‡ Of interest to fish biologists, fish pathologists, nutritionalists, geneticists, immunologists, parasitologists, environmental physiologists and behaviourists. Covers aspects of fish and fishing science, marine and freshwater.
Book notices, book reviews, monographic articles, obituaries, tests.
A, October, No, None.
January 1972, T.p. 192, Ad.p. 4. 1600.
Per year £9.

598.1

HERPETOLOGY. REPTILES

2007 BRITISH JOURNAL OF HERPETOLOGY. 1947.
British Herpetological Society, c/o Zoological Society of London, Regent's Park, London, NW1.
2, * ‡ + Zoology, natural history, biology, conservation of reptiles and amphibians.
Book notices, book reviews, letters, monographic articles, new products, obituaries.
6 years, 1973/4, No, None.
675.
Per copy 75p, per year £1.50.

598.2

BIRDS

2008 THE AVICULTURAL MAGAZINE: Journal of the Avicultural Society.
Taylor & Francis Ltd., 10-14 Macklin St., London, WC2B 5NF.
6, * Feeding, breeding and behaviour of bird species kept under captive conditions.
Book notices, book reviews, letters, monographic articles.
A, In last issue of volume, No, None.
March-April 1972, T.p. 36.
Per copy 53p, per year £3.
Indexed in: IBZ.

2009 BIRD LIFE: magazine of the Young Ornithologists Club.
Royal Society for the Protection of Birds, The Lodge, Sandy, Beds, SG19 2DL.
4, ○ Ornithology in general for the younger reader.
Book reviews, letters, monographic articles, news.
No Index.
January-March 1973, T.p. 37.
Free to members.

2010 BIRD STUDY: Incorporating Bird Migration. 1954.
British Trust for Ornithology, Beech Grove, Tring, Hertfordshire.
4, ‡ + † Reports on all types of ornithological studies, including numbers, distribution, behaviour, breeding success, migration and mortality.
Book reviews, letters, articles.
No Index.
June 1972, T.p. 59, Ad.p. 4.   c.6000.
(Members per copy 75p, per year £2.50). Subscribers per copy £1, per year £4.

2011 BIRDS. 1966.
(Bird Notes 1903).
Royal Society for the Protection of Birds, The Lodge, Sandy, Bedfordshire.
6, * Conservation of birds and other wildlife. Activities of The Royal Society for the Protection of Birds.
Book notices, book reviews, letters, articles.
Every two years, 1st January every alternate year, Yes, None.
May 1972, T.p. 28, Ad.p. 15.   110000.
Per copy 25p, per year £2. (includes membership of Soc.)

2012 BIRDS AND COUNTRY. 1948.
78 Surbiton Hill Park, Surbiton, Surrey.
4, = * ○ Wild life and the countryside in Britain and overseas.
Book notices, book reviews, articles.
No Index.
Winter 1971-2, T.p. 26, Ad.p. 1.
Per copy 15p, per year 90p.

2013 BULLETIN OF THE BRITISH ORNITHOLOGISTS CLUB.
c/o R.E.F. Peel, 24 Creighton Avenue, London, N10.
○
No Index.
Free to members.

2014 FOREIGN BIRDS.
c/o H.B. Wragg, 131 Berridge Road East, Nottingham, NG7 6HS.
○
No Index.
Subscription on application.

2015 THE IBIS: Journal of the British Ornithologists' Union. 1859.
Academic Press Inc. Ltd. (for British Ornithologists' Union), 22/24 Oval Road, London, NW1.
4, + Ornithology.
Abstracts, book notices, book reviews, letters, monographic articles, obituaries.
5 year, —, Yes, None.
T.p. 145, Ad.p. 4.
Per year £7. Free to members.
Indexed in: IBZ.

2016 INTERNATIONAL WILDFOWL RESEARCH BUREAU BULLETIN. 1969.
International Waterfowl Research Bureau, Slimbridge, Glos. GL2 7BX.
2, + Research—conservation involving waterfowl and wetlands.
Reports.
No Index.
December 1971, T.p. 84.
Per copy 50p. Free to delegates.

2017 JOURNAL OF R.A.F. ORNITHOLOGICAL SOCIETY.
110 Edinburgh Drive, Ickenham, Uxbridge, Middx.
○
No Index.
Subscription on application.

2018 KINGFISHER.
6 Gombards, St. Albans, Herts.
○
No Index.
Subscription on application.

2019 NEWSLETTER OF THE PERIVALE BIRD SANCTUARY.
c/o A. N. Tsuji, 3 Cambalt Road, London, SW15 6EL.
○
No Index.
Subscription on application.

2020 SCOTTISH BIRDS: The Journal of the Scottish Ornithologists' Club. 1958.
The Scottish Ornithologists' Club, 21 Regent Terrace, Edinburgh, EH7 5BT.
4, *○ = ‡   Papers and articles, including statistical information, on Scottish ornithology. Annual Scottish Bird Report Section of official Club notices.
Book notices, book reviews, monographic articles, obituaries.
2 year, March, Yes, None.
T.p. 60, Ad.p. 10.   2300.
Per copy 50p, per year £2.

2021 WATERFOWL. 1970.
(British Waterfowl Association Newsletter 1949-1969).
British Waterfowl Association, The High House, Epping, Essex.
4, *   Activities of duck and goose breeders—members plus information about waterfowl generally.
Book reviews, letters, articles.
No Index.
T.p. 48, Ad.p. 6.   1000.
Free to members.

2022 WILDFOWL. 1968.
(Wildfowl Trust Annual Report 1948-1967), Wildfowl Trust, Slimbridge, Glos. GL2 7BT.
1, + *   Biology and conservation of wildfowl, of their wetland habitat and of ecologically associated birds such as waders.
Book reviews, monographic articles.
No Index.
T.p. 172.   6000.
Free to members.

599

MAMMALS

2023 THE JOURNAL OF THE MAMMILLARIA SOCIETY.
c/o W. F. Maddams, 26 Glenfield Road, Banstead, Surrey.
○ +
No Index.
Subscription on application.

2024 MAMMAL REVIEW. 1970.
Blackwell Scientific Publs. Ltd. (for the Mammal Society), Osney Mead, Oxford, OX2 0EL.
4, ○ + =   All aspects of mammal biology.
Book notices, book reviews.
A, —, Yes, None.
June 1972, T.p. 42, Ad.p. 4.   c.850.
Per copy £1.50, per year £6.

599.735.3

DEER

2025 DEER: The Journal of The British Deer Society. 1966.
(Deer News. 1963-1966).
The British Deer Society, c/o The Deer Museum, Low Hay Bridge, Bouth by Ulverston, Lancs.
3, * + ○ =   All matters relating to deer in the U.K. and also articles, identification etc. of world deer from time to time. Research and management are important aspects.
Book notices, book reviews, legal notes, letters, monographic articles.
5 year, On completion of each volume, Yes, None.
March 1972, T.p. 57, Ad.p. 6.   2000.
Per year £4.

6

TECHNOLOGY

2026 ANNALS OF SCIENCE. 1936
Taylor & Francis Ltd., London, 10-14 Macklin St., WC2B 5NF.
4 ‡ +   History of science and technology since the Renaissance.
Book reviews, monographic articles.
A, In last issue of volume, Yes, None.
April 1972, T.p. 100.
Per copy £2.75, per year £10.
Indexed in: BHI, IBZ.

2027 BRITISH TECHNOLOGY INDEX: a current subject guide to articles in British technical journals. 1963.
The Library Association, 7 Ridgmount Street, London, WC1E 7AE.
12, + ‡   Indexes 320 technical periodicals
M, —, No, A.
April 1972, T.p. 87.   1508.
Per year £29.

2028 IRONBRIDGE QUARTERLY. 1972
Ironbridge Gorge Museum Trust, Church Hill, Ironbridge, Telford, Shropshire.
4, ○ ‡ + *   Development of the Ironbridge Gorge Museum, industrial archaeology, history of technology, museum and interpretive technique, industrial conservation.
Book reviews, monographic articles.
No Index.
April 1972, T.p. 4.   600
Per year 40p.

2029 JOURNAL OF MATERIALS SCIENCE. 1966.
Chapman & Hall Ltd., 11 New Letter Lane, London, EC4.
12, = ‡ +   Inter-disciplinary approach to the study of relationships between structure, properties and uses of materials.
Letters, monographic articles, book reviews.
A, December, Yes, None.
T.p. 88, Ad. p. 1.
Per copy £2.50, per year £12.
Indexed in: BTI.

2030 JOURNAL OF SYSTEMS ENGINEERING. 1969.
Department of Systems Engineering, University of Lancaster, Bailrigg, Lancaster.

2, ‡ + *   Developments in the application of systems concepts and a systematic approach to problem solving and systems design in industrial and public organisations. The emphasis is on papers describing practical projects which have been implemented.
Occasional book reviews, letters, monographic articles,
5 year, 1974, Yes, None.
Summer 1971, T.p. 98.   600
Per copy £2, per year £4.

2031 LASER. 1968.
26 Selwood Road, Addiscombe, Croydon, Surrey.
4, ○   Social, economic and political aspects of technological change.
Articles, letter, book reviews.
No Index.
No. 31, T.p. 47.
Per copy 25p.

2032 NEW TECHNOLOGY. 1967.
H.M.S.O., P.O. Box 569, London, SE1 9NH.
12 (issued as a supplement to Trade and Industry,)‡   Current technological developments with emphasis on contributions of government research establishments. Contains notes on forthcoming technical conferences.
Book notices, monographic articles, new products, standards, tests.
Indexed in quarterly indexes to Trade and Industry.—.
June 1972, T.p. 8.
Per copy 10p, per year £1.75, for the 12 issues of Trade and Industry containing New Technology.

2033 PROJECT. 1966.
H.M.S.O., PO. Box 569, London, SE1 9NH.
3, ‡   Engineering and science aimed at fifth and sixth formers, profusely illustrated. Aims to convey the scope for careers in engineering, and to demonstrate ways of becoming a chartered engineer.
Monographic articles.
No Index.
No 20, Autumn 1972, T.p. 36.
Per copy 32½p, per year £1.11. Free to schools and libraries.

2034 R & D ABSTRACTS: a journal of abstracts of science and technology reports. 1968.
Technology Reports Centre, Department of Trade and Industry, Orpington, Kent, BR5 3RF.
24 (2 vols each year)   Abstracts of scientific and technical papers received in the Centre from Government R & D establishments, Government supported R & D activities and other sources in the UK and abroad.
Abstracts of reports.
6m, Starting 1972 - 2 volumes per year, June and December each year, Yes, None.
1 April 1972, T.p. 133.   about 1000.
Per year £12.

2035 R & D MANAGEMENT. 1970.
Basil Blackwell & Mott Ltd., 5 Alfred Street, Oxford.
3, +   Presents the results of research aimed at identifying and systematically analyzing problems which are of importance to personnel managing resources for research.
Articles and reviews.
A, —, Yes, None.
Subscription on application.

2036 SCIENCE CHELSEA: journal of research at Chelsea. 1966.
Chelsea College Student Union, Manresa Road, London, SW3.
4, = + ‡   News and developments in scientific research.
Monographic articles.
No Index.
T.p. 34, Ad. p. 2.
Per copy 5p, per year 20p.

2037 TECHNOLOGY AND SOCIETY. 1967.
(The Technologist 1964)
Bath University Press, Claverton Down, Bath.
4, + = ‡   Aspects of inter-reactions and inter-dependence of technological and sociological advances.
Book notices, book reviews, monographic articles.
A, —, Yes, None.
T.p. 44, Ad. p. 3.
Per copy 40p, per year £2.

2038 TECHNOLOGY IRELAND. 1969.
Institute for Industrial Research and Standards, Ballyrum Road, Dublin, 9.
11, ‡   Applied science and technology.
Book notices, book reviews, letters, monographic articles, new products, obituaries, parliamentrary reports, standards.
A, May, No, None.
March 1972, T.p. 39, Ad. p. 9.   3200.
Per copy 17½p, per year £1.50.

2039 TRANSACTIONS OF THE NEWCOMEN SOCIETY. 1922.
The Newcomen Society, Science Museum, London, SW7.
1, ‡ * +   History of engineering and technology.
Book reviews, monographic articles.
A, —, Yes, 10 year.
Volumes 1 to 30 only-index issued in 1962.
T.p. 280.
Per year £4 and free to members.
Indexed in: BHI.

2040 UNDERCURRENTS IN SCIENCE AND TECHNOLOGY. 1972.
Undercurrents Partnership, 34 Cholmley Gds., Aldred Road, London, NW6.
4, ‡ +   Unorthodox scientific ideas and technological proposals that make possible a richer life-style for individuals and smaller communities in a decentralised ecologically-sound society. Alternative Society journal.
Book notices, book reviews, letters, articles, new products, obituaries, parliamentary reports, patents, tests.
A, —, Yes, None.
May 1972, T.p. 64.   2500.
Per copy 25p, per year £1.20.

608

PATENTS. TRADE MARKS

2041 CIPA; the journal, incorporating the Transactions, of the Chartered Institute of Patent Agents. 1971.
The Chartered Institute of Patent Agents, Staple Inn Buildings, High Holborn, London, WC1V 7PZ.
12, * ‡   Interests of the profession of patent agency.
Book reviews, legal notes, letters, articles, obituaries, parliamentary reports.
A, —, Yes, None.
April 1972, T.p. 43.
Free to members.

2042 DERWENT PUBLICATIONS.
Various national and subject and orientated publications covering patent literature.
Derwent Publications Ltd., Rochdale House, 128 Theobalds Road, London, WC1X 8RP.

2043 THE INVENTOR: journal of the Institute of Patentees and Inventors. 1961.
(IPI Newsletter, 1959—1961).

Key to reference symbols

○ popular   ‡ technical   = trade/professional

+ research   * society/institution   † house journal

Institute of Patentees and Inventors, 207-208 Abbey House, 2, Victoria Street, London, SW1H 0LD.
4, ‡ = + *   Patenting and invention, industrial innovation and technology.
Book notices, book reviews, legal notes, monographic articles, new products, obituaries, parliamentary reports, patents.
No Index.
March 1972, T.p. 26, Ad. p. 2.   2000.
Per copy 50p per year £2. Free to members.

2044 TRADE MARKET. 1971.
Brand Brokers Limited, P.O. 102, Normandy House, St. Helier, Jersey, Channel Islands.
4, =   Publication of trade marks for sale.
No Index.
April 1972, T.p. 39, Ad. p. 1.
Per year £25.

2045 TRADE MARKS JOURNAL. 1876.
Patent Office, St. Mary Cray, Orpington, Kent, BR5 3RD.
52, + = ‡   Applications etc. for trade marks.
A, —, Yes, None.
T.p. 39.
Per copy 35p, per year £18.20.

2046 OFFICIAL JOURNAL (PATENTS). 1884.
Patent office, St. Mary Cray, Orpington, Kent, BR5 3RD.
52, = + ‡   Applications, amendments for British patents and designs.
A, —, Yes, None.
T.p. 87.
Per copy 50p, per year £26.

61

MEDICAL SCIENCES

2047 AFRICAN JOURNAL OF MEDICAL SCIENCES. 1970.
Blackwell Scientific Publications, Osney Mead, Oxford, OX2 0EL.
4, + =   Provides a medium for international dissemination of information about medical sciences in Africa and elsewhere; publishes material from international conferences and aims to provide inter-regional co-operation in Africa.
Monographic articles.
A, October, Yes, None.
April 1972, T.p. 72, Ad. p. 4.   150.
Per copy £2.25, per year £8.

2048 BMA NEWS. 1966.
British Medical Association, BMA House, Tavistock Square, London, WC1H 9JP.
6, = *   Medico-political newsheet aimed to help all UK doctors keep in touch with B.M.A. HQ and provide information about the current medical scene.
No Index.
June 1972, T.p. 7, Ad. p. 1.   80 000.
Free.

2049 BRITISH JOURNAL OF HOSPITAL MEDICINE. 1968.
(Hospital Medicine—1966-1968)
Hospital Medicine Publications Ltd., (a subsidiary of TPL Magazines Ltd. (part of the Thomson Organization)), Northwood house, 93-99 Goswell Road, London, EC1V 7QA.
12, ‡ =   Provides technical review information to hospital doctors in an ethical professional journal on a strictly controlled circulation basis. The subject matter is wide and varied but is primarily devoted to mid-stream review articles contributed by eminent members of the medical profession.
Book reviews, letters, monographic articles, new products, parliamentary reports.
6m, January and July, Yes, None.
July 1972, T.p. 66, Ad. p. 54.   38064.
Per copy 37½p, per year £5. and Free. Controlled circulation.

2050 BRITISH JOURNAL OF MEDICAL EDUCATION: Journal of the Association for the Study of Medical Education. 1966.
British Medical Association, B.M.A. House, Tavistock Square, London, WC1H 9JR.
4, ‡ + = *   A medium for the interchange of information on medical education - undergraduate, postgraduate and continuing — throughout the world.
Book reviews, monographic articles, obituaries.
A, December, Yes, None.
March 1972, T.p. 78, Ad. p. 5.
Per year £5.

2051 BRITISH JOURNAL OF SPORTS MEDICINE. 1968.
(Bulletin of the British Association of Sport and Medicine).
The British Association of Sport and Medicine, c/o 39 Linkfield Rd., Mountsorrel, Nr. Loughborough, Leics.
4, ‡ + *   Medicine applied to exercise and sport. Exercise physiology, scientific basis of training. Proceedings of the British Association of Sport and Medicine.
Book reviews, letters, monographic articles, new products, obituaries, tests.
A, End of each volume, Yes, None.
April 1972, T.p. 50.   650.
Per copy 65p, per year £2.

2052 BRITISH MEDICAL BULLETIN. 1943.
Medical Department, The British Council, 97-99 Park Street, London, W1Y 4HQ.
3, + =   British achievements in spheres of medical research.
Book reviews, monographic articles.
A, September, Yes, None.
May 1972, T.p. 188, Ad.p. 13.   6500.
Per copy UK £2.25, per year £6.

2053 BRITISH MEDICAL JOURNAL. 1857.
British Medical Association, BMA House, Tavistock Square, London, WC1H 9JR.
52, ○ * = ‡   A comprehensive general medical journal, for every medical man or student who wishes to keep informed of research in medical science, of trends in clinical medicine, and of professional activities.
Book reviews, medico—legal notes, letters, monographic articles, obituaries, parliamentary reports.
Q, March, June, September and December, Yes, A.
8 July 1972, T.p. 96, Ad.p. 60.   84748.
Per copy 42p, per year £21.

2054 BRITISH MEDICINE: A Monthly Guide to Current Literature. 1972.
(British Medical Book List. 1950-1971; British Medical Index. 1967-1971).
Medical Department, The British Council, 65 Davies Street, London, W1Y 2AA.
12, ‡ + =   New medical books and periodicals. Forthcoming medical congresses and meetings. Lists of bibliographies and book lists. Principal contents of British medical journals.
A, End of year, No, None.
4000.
Per year £2.

2055 BULLETIN OF THE NATIONAL ASSOCIATION OF CLINICAL TUTORS. 1972.
Update Publications, 33 Alfred Place, London, WC1E 7DP.
4, * ‡   Official publication of an association of medical practitioners working in regional hospitals who have a part-time university post, charged to provide post-graduate education for doctors in the area served by these hospitals.
Articles.
No Index.
Free to members.

2056 CURRENT WORK IN THE HISTORY OF MEDICINE:
An International Bibliography. 1954.
The Wellcome Institute of the History of Medicine,
183 Euston Road, London, NW1.
4, ‡ +   Publications (periodical articles and books)
on the history of medicine and allied sciences
throughout the world. Arranged under subject headings, with index and addresses of authors.
No Index.
October-December 1971, T.p. 91.
Per copy Gratis.

2057 DOCTOR: The Newspaper for the General Practitioner.
1971.
Morgan-Sutton and Associates Ltd., 8 North Street,
Guildford, Surrey.
26, ‡ +   All matters affecting family doctors in the
practice of their profession as well as leisure
subjects of particular interest to them and their
families. Financial advice and other services,
including a special discount shopping scheme by
post are also provided.
Book notices, book reviews, letters, articles, new companies, new products.
No Index.
June 22, 1972, T.p. 16.   c. 25000.
Per copy 75p, per year £2.50. Free to all GP's.

2058 EMERGENCY MEDICINE. 1972.
40 Grays Inn Road, London, WC1.
26, =
No Index.
Free. Controlled circulation for GP's and junior hospital doctors.

2059 GENERAL PRACTITIONER.
Haymarket Publishing Co. Ltd., Gillow House, 5 Winsley
Street, London, W1A 2HP.
52, ‡ =   Medical newspaper.
Book notices, book reviews, commodity prices, legal
notes, letters, articles, new companies, new products,
obituaries, parliamentary reports, patents, standards,
tests.
No Index.
June 16, 1972, T.p. 10, Ad.p. 9.   28000.
Per copy 15p, per year £6.60.

2060 INTERNATIONAL JOURNAL OF EPIDEMIOLOGY.
1972.
Oxford University Press, Press Road, Neasden, London,
NW10.
4, +   To encourage persons in different countries to
express their approaches to epidemiological problems and to promote co-operation. Original articles and is also concerned with reviewing advances
in methods and the application of epidemiology
and teaching of the subject.
A, —, Yes, None.
Spring 1972, T.p. 82.
Per copy £2.50, per year £8.40.

2061 IRISH MEDICAL TIMES: The independent news weekly
for the Irish doctor. 1967.
Medical & Allied Publications Ltd., 24 Merchants Quay,
Dublin 8, Ireland.
52, ○ ‡ = + *
No Index.
June 16, 1972, T.p. 10, Ad.p. 4.   3600.
Per copy 5p, per year £2.50.

2062 JOURNAL OF INTERNATIONAL MEDICAL RESEARCH.
1972.
Cambridge Medical Publications Ltd., 435/437 Wellingborough Road, Northampton NN1.
6, = +
Book reviews, letters, monographic articles.
No Index.
Per year £8.

2063 JOURNAL OF THE IRISH MEDICAL ASSOCIATION.
I.M.A., 10 Fitzwilliam Place, Dublin 2.
12, = +
Book reviews, letters, monographic articles, parliamentary reports.
6m, January/July, Yes, None.
T.p. 40, Ad.p. 40.
Per copy 25p, Free to members.

2064 JOURNAL OF THE MEDICAL WOMEN'S FEDERATION.
1947.
(Medical Women's Federation Newsletter, 1919-1934;
MWF Quarterly Review, 1935-1946).
M.W.F., Tavistock House North, Tavistock Square,
London, WC1.
4, = ‡
Book reviews, letters, monographic articles.
No Index.
T.p. 40, Ad.p. 4.
Free to members.

2065 JOURNAL OF THE ROYAL COLLEGE OF GENERAL
PRACTITIONERS. 1967.
(College of General Practitioners Research Newsletter 1954-1957; Journal of the College of General
Practitioners 1958-1967).
The Longman Group Ltd., 33 Montgomery Street,
Edinburgh, EH7 5JX.
12, = + *   To improve standards of treatment and
increase the overall efficiency of the G.P.'s practice.
Book notices, book reviews, letters, monographic articles, tests.
6m, January/July, Yes, None.
T.p. 63, Ad.p. 15.   8000.
Per copy £1, per year £8. Free to members.

2066 JOURNAL OF THE ROYAL COLLEGE OF PHYSICIANS
OF LONDON. 1966.
Pitman Medical & Scientific Pub. Co. Ltd., 31 Fitzroy
Square, London, W1P 6BH.
4, = ‡   Integration of scientific disciplines in the
practice of medicine.
Book reviews, letters, monographic articles.
A, July, Yes, None.
T.p. 94, Ad.p. 22.
Per copy £1.50, per year £4.50. Free to members.

2067 JOURNAL OF THE ROYAL NAVAL MEDICAL SERVICE.
1915.
Institute of Naval Medicine, Alverstoke, Hants.
3, + = *   Medical, travel, personal experiences. News
of the Service.
Book reviews, letters, monographic articles, obituaries,
A, November, Yes, None.
Spring 1972, T.p. 70, Ad.p. 5.   1000.
Per copy 80p, per year £2.40.

2068 JOURNAL OF TROPICAL MEDICINE AND HYGIENE
1898.
Staples Ltd., 94 Wigmore Street, London, W1.
12, + ‡
Book reviews, articles, reports.
A, March, Yes, None.
T.p. 29, Ad.p. 5.   2500.
Per copy 30p, per year £3.50.

2069 THE LANCET. 1823.
The Lancet, Ltd., 7 Adam Street, London, WC2N 6AD.
52, = + ‡   Medicine and anything related to medicine.
Book notices, book reviews, legal notes, letters, monographic articles, obituaries, parliamentary reports.
6m, Early in following half year, Yes, None.
June 17, 1972, T.p. 54, Ad.p. 42.   c. 45000.
Per copy 25p, per year £8.

2070 MEDICAL & BIOLOGICAL ILLUSTRATION: The journal of the Institute of Medical and Biological Illustration. 1951.

British Medical Association, BMA House, Tavistock
   Square, London, WC1H 9JR.
4, ‡ = + *   Explores the rapidly expanding application
   of the arts and techniques of audio-visual communication to biomedical teaching and research.
Book reviews, monographic articles, obituaries.
A, October, Yes, None.
April 1972, T.p. 72, Ad.p. 5.
Per year £5.

2071 MEDICAL EQUIPMENT. 1969.
Milton Publishing Co. Ltd., 28 Craven Street, London, WC2N 5PD.
4, ‡ =   All types of medical equipment intended for hospitals and university departments of medicine.
Book reviews, new companies, new products.
No Index.
March 1972, T.p. 7, Ad.p. 5.   10054.
Per copy 75p, per year £3.

2072 MEDICAL HISTORY: A quarterly Journal devoted to the history and bibliography of medicine and the related sciences. 1957
Wellcome Institute of the History of Medicine, 183 Euston Road, London, NW1.
4, + * =   Official organ of the British Society for the History of Medicine. History of medical sciences; social history of medicine; medicine and literature; medicine and art.
Book notices, book reviews, monographic articles.
A, January, Yes, None.
April 1972, T.p. 105, Ad.p. 4.
Per copy £1.10, per year £4.

2073 MEDICAL NEWS-TRIBUNE. 1969.
(Medical News 1962-1969; Medical Tribune 1966-1969).
Medical Tribune Ltd., 37 New Bond Street, London, W1.
51, =
Book reviews, letters, articles.
No Index.
T.p. 20, Ad.p. Most.   6627.
Controlled circulation.

2074 THE MEDICAL TECHNICIAN. 1971.
A. E. Morgan Publications Ltd., 172 Kingston Road, Ewell, Epsom, Surrey.
12, ‡ =
Book notices, book reviews, letters, articles, new companies, new products, parliamentary reports, standards, tests.
No Index.
June 1972, T.p. 16.   13000.
Per year £2.50 and Free controlled circulation.

2075 MIMS IRELAND.
Medical & Allied Publications, 24 Merchants Quay, Dublin 8.
12, =
No Index.
Per year £3.

2076 MEDICAL WORLD. 1913.
MPU Publications Ltd., 55-56 Russell Square, London, WC1.
12, =   Clinical and medico-social topics, etc.
Book notices, book reviews, letters, monographic articles.
A, February/March, No, None.
T.p. 22, Ad.p. 6.   32000.
Per copy 17½p, Free, controlled circulation.

2077 MODERN MEDICINE. 1956.
Modern Medicine of Great Britain Ltd., Empire House, 414 High Road, London, W4.
12, ‡   All aspects of medicine, of interest to general practitioners, specialists and consultants.
Abstracts, book reviews, letters, monographic articles, new products.
A, February, Yes, None.
June 1972, T.p. 32, Ad.p. 29.   37034.
Per copy 35p, per year £4
Free, controlled circulation.

2078 MONTHLY INDEX OF MEDICAL SPECIALITIES. 1970.
Haymarket Publishing Ltd., Gillow House, 5 Winsley Street, London, W1A 2HG.
12, ‡   Ethical medical specialities available for prescription by doctors.
Commodity prices, new products.
No Index.
July 1972, T.p. 124, Ad.p. 66.   45000.
Per copy 50p, per year £6.

2079 ON-CALL: the junior doctors voice. 1967.
Junior Hospital Doctors Association Ltd., 136-139 Temple Chambers, Temple Avenue, London, EC4.
6, =   Medico-political.
Letters, monographic articles.
No Index.
T.p. 7, Ad.p. 5.   18000.
Free to junior doctors.

2081 POSTGRADUATE MEDICAL JOURNAL. 1925.
(Bulletin of the Fellowship of Medicine, 1919-1925).
Blackwell Scientific Publications, Osney Mead, Oxford, OX2 0EL.
12, + ○ =   International journal publishing original papers on subjects of current clinical importance, also review articles, current surveys and case reports. Several symposia are published devoted to a single specialist topic.
Book notices, book reviews, letters, monographic articles.
A, Early following year, Yes, None.
May 1972, T.p. 74, Ad.p. 6.   1600.
Per copy 90p, per year £8.

2082 THE PRACTITIONER. 1868.
Longman Group Ltd., Journals Division, 5 Bentinck Street, London, W1M 5RN.
12, = ‡   Provides in concise form a continuing course in post-graduate study presented by leading authorities at home and overseas.
Book reviews, letters, monographic articles.
6 m, —, Yes, None.
June 1972, T.p. 187, Ad.p. 102.   35000.
Per copy 30p, per year £4.

2083 PREVENT: the journal for all who would prevent disease. 1972.
Experts Publishers Ltd., 124 Upton Lane, London E7.
6, ‡ +   An international channel of communication through which medical, dental, veterinary and social workers and students in the field of prevention of disease can exchange information about research, clinical methods and ideas.
Book notices, book reviews, letters, monographic articles.
A, —, Yes, None.
T.p. 80.   3000.
Per year £10.

2084 PREVENTION: magazine for better health. 1956.
The Rodale Press, Berkhamsted, Herts.
12, ○ +   Advocates scientifically supported methods to combat diseases.
Book reviews, letters, articles, new products, standards, tests.
No Index.
July 1972, T.p. 70, Ad.p. 30.   60000.
Per copy 12½p, per year £1.90.

2085 PROCEEDINGS OF THE ROYAL SOCIETY OF MEDICINE. 1967.
(Medico-Chirurgical Transactions 1809-1907).
Royal Society of Medicine, 1 Wimpole Street, London W1.
12, + *   Reports of papers and discussions at meetings of the Society and of its 33 specialist sections.

Book notices, book reviews, monographic articles.
A, Approx. 6 months after end of volume, Yes, None.
July 1972, T.p. 76, Ad.p. 23.   16200.
Per copy £1.25, per year £15.   Free to members

2086 PSIONIC MEDICINE: journal of the Psionic Medical
Society. 1969.
Psionic Medical Society, c/o Sandy Balls Estate, Godshill, Fordingbridge, Hants.
2, ‡ * +   Concerning the use of medical dowsing to determine the constitutional causes of chronic disease in the individual and the means towards the removal of such causes usually through the use of homoeopathic medicines determined by the same techniques.
Book notices, book reviews, clinical cases, letters, monographic articles, obituaries.
No Index.
Winter/Spring 1970-71,
Per copy 30p, Free to members.

2087 PULSE: the doctor's newspaper. 1959.
Professional Projects Ltd., Ryde House, Chobham Road, Woking, Surrey.
52, =   General practice and hospital medicine.
No Index.
T.p. 15, Ad.p. 13.   39000.
Per copy 3p, per year £1.50.

2088 QUARTERLY JOURNAL OF MEDICINE: Official Organ of the Association of Physicians of Great Britain and Ireland. 1907, New Series 1932.
Oxford University Press, Press Road, Neasden, London, NW10.
4, +   Scientific basis of medical practice; deals with all aspects of general medicine.
Book reviews, monographic articles.
A, —, Yes, None.
April 1972, T.p. 121, Ad.p. 4.   3000.
Per copy £1.75, per year £5.

2089 REDBRIDGE MEDICAL JOURNAL. 1966.
London Borough of Redbridge Health and Welfare Dept., 17/23 Clements Rd., Ilford, Essex.
12, ‡ †   Medical or allied subjects, local comment and opinion. Local statistics and notices.
No Index.
June 1972, T.p. 25.   c. 600.
Free.

2090 RESUSCITATION. 1972.
The Middlesex Publishing Co. Ltd., 21 New Street, London, EC2M 4NT.
4, + * ‡   Medical research into various means and ways of resuscitation.
Book reviews, letters, monographic articles.
A, —, Yes, None.
March 1972, T.p. 84.
Per copy £2.50, per year £8.

2091 RURAL MEDICINE. 1969.
Rural Environment-Publications Ltd., Francis House, Kings Head Yard, Borough High Street, London, SE1 1NA.
4, ‡   For the country doctor about environmental health, including the occupational hazards of the agricultural industry.
Book reviews, letters, monographic articles.
No Index.
Spring 1972, T.p. 35, Ad.p. 6.   8500.
Per copy 53p, per year £2.10.

2092 SCIENTIFIC PROCEEDINGS OF THE CARDIFF MEDICAL SOCIETY. 1938.
The Cardiff Medical Society, c/o Royal Infirmary, Cardiff.
7, + =   Papers presented to the society.
No Index.
11 April 1972, T.p. 8.   c. 4000.
Free to members.

2093 SCOPE. 1969.
(British Medical Students Journal 1946-1969).
British Medical Students Association, B.M.A. House, Tavistock Sq., London, WC1.
5, * =   All matters of interest to medical students.
Book reviews, legal notes, letters, articles, obituaries, parliamentary reports.
No Index.
May 1972, T.p. 8, Ad.p. Most.   15000.
Free to members.

2094 SCOTTISH MEDICAL JOURNAL: journal of the Royal Medico-Chirurgical Society of Glasgow.
The Longman Group Ltd., 33 Montgomery Street, Edinburgh EH7 5JX.
12   All branches of medicine and historical subjects of medical interest.
Book reviews, letters, monographic articles.
A, Last issue of each volume, Yes, None.
April 1972, T.p. 44.
Per copy 50p, per year £4.   Free to members.

2095 SURGO: Glasgow University Medical Journal. 1933.
Glasgow University Medico-Chirurgical Society, The Union, University Avenue, Glasgow, W2.
3, + ‡ = *   General medical and paramedical interests.
Book reviews, letters, monographic articles, news, standards, tests.
No Index.
T.p. 18, Ad.p. 12.
Per copy 25p, per year 50p.

2096 TEACH-IN: The Journal for Junior Hospital Doctors and Senior Medical Students. 1972.
Update Publications Ltd., 33-34 Alfred Place, London, WC1E 7DP.
12, ‡ +   Final year medical students, junior hospital doctors up to the rank of registrar and to limited list of teachers, -consultants, senior registrars, staff of professional depts. and clinical tutors at postgraduate centres.
Letter, monographic articles.
A, December, Yes, None.
June 1972, T.p. 58, Ad.p. 21.
Per copy 60p, Per year £7, Students per copy 25p, per year £3, and Free, Controlled circulation.

2097 TROPICAL DOCTOR: a journal of modern medical practice. 1971.
Royal Society of Medicine, International Relations Office, Chandos House, 2 Queen Anne Street, London, W1M 0BR.
4, ‡   A practical medical journal aimed in particular at isolated doctors and other medical workers in developing countries remote from colleagues and from advanced medical centres.
Letters, monographic articles.
No Index.
April 1971, T.p. 48.   3770.
Per copy 75p, per year £3.

2098 ULSTER MEDICAL JOURNAL. 1928.
Ulster Medical Society, P.O. Box 222, Belfast City Hospital, Belfast, 9.
2, ‡ + =   General medical interest, reports of research work in the medical school, special lectures and addresses, historical items relating to medicine.
Book reviews, monographic articles.
No Index.
Winter 1972, T.p. 88, Ad.p. 4.   900.
Per copy 62½p, per year £1.25.

2099 UNIVERSITY COLLEGE HOSPITAL MAGAZINE. 1910.
R, Modley, 54 Grafton Way, London W1.
3, = +   General medical practice.
No Index.
T.p. 30, Ad.p. 16.

2100 UPDATE: the journal of postgraduate general practice. 1968.
Update Publications Ltd., 33-34 Alfred Place, London, WC1E 7DP.
24, ‡ +   All doctors in general practice in U.K., Northern Ireland and the Channel Islands.
Letters, monographic articles.
A, December 31, Yes, None.
June 1, 1972, T.p. 60, Ad.p. 60.   24000.
Per copy 50p, per year £12, Students per copy 21p, per year £5, and Free, controlled circulation.

2101 WELSH MEDICAL GAZETTE. 1970.
Welsh Medical Press Ltd., 22 Blenheim Rd., Cardiff.
4, ○ * + =   General medicine.
Book notices, book reviews, commodity prices, legal notes, letters, articles, new companies, new products, obituaries, parliamentary reports, standards, tests.
No Index.
Spring 1972, T.p. 14, Ad.p. 10.   c. 4000.
Free.

2102 WORLD MEDICINE. 1965.
New Medical Journals Ltd., Clareville House, 26/27 Oxendon Street, London, SW1Y 4EL.
27, ○ ‡ =   Clinical subjects and those of general interest to the doctor.
Book reviews, letters, articles, new products.
A, —, Yes, None.
14 June 1972, T.p. 120, Ad.p. 68.   45447
Per copy 25p, per year £6.72.

611

ANATOMY

2103 JOURNAL OF ANATOMY. 1916.
(Journal of Anatomy and Physiology 1866-1916).
Cambridge University Press (for Anatomical Society), PO Box 92, London, NW1 2DB.
9, +   Study of anatomy, embryology and histology.
Book reviews, monographic articles.
3 times yearly, Last issue of volume, Yes, None.
April 1972, T.p. 180.   1770.
Per copy £4, per year £27.

611.34

INTESTINES

2104 I.A.: quarterly journal of the Ileostomy Association of Great Britain and Ireland. 1957.
(I.A. Newsletter 1956).
Ileostomy Association of Great Britain and Ireland, 149 Harley Street, London, W1.
4, ○ ‡ = + *
Book reviews, letters, articles, new products.
A, January, Yes, None.
Spring 1972, T.p. 22, Ad.p. 26.
Per copy 12½p. Free to members.

2105 INTESTINAL ABSORPTION AND RELATED TOPICS. 1965.
Biomedical Information Project, Dept. of Physiology, University of Sheffield, Sheffield, S10 2TN.
12, + ‡   Absorption of all substances including drugs. Gut structure, enzymes, physiology, clinical, malabsorption techniques.
Abstracts, book notices.
6m, December, Yes, None.
May 1972, T.p. 12.   400-500.
Per copy 70p, per year £8.

612

PHYSIOLOGY

2108 JOURNAL OF PHYSIOLOGY. 1878.
Cambridge University Press, PO Box 92, London, NW1 2DB.
24, +   All branches of physiology.
Book reviews, monographic articles.
8 times a year, Last issue of volume, Yes, 2 year.
July 1972, T.p. 264.   3700.
Per copy £2.50, per year £48.
Indexed in: IBZ.

2109 MARINE BEHAVIOUR AND PHYSIOLOGY. 1972.
Gordon & Breach, 41/42 William 4th Street, London, WC2.
4, + ‡   Behaviour and its physiological bases as exhibited by marine organisms. Covers the whole range of phyla, invertebrate and vertebrate, and will include field observations as well as laboratory experiments in pertinent physiological aspects.
Book notices, book reviews, letters, monographic articles, new products, patents, standards, tests.
A, —, No, None.
Per year £14.10.

2110 NEUROPHYSIOLOGY. 1972.
Biomedical Information Project, Dept. of Physiology, The University, Sheffield, S10 2TN.
12, + ‡   Current awareness service, titles, authors' addresses, references.
No Index.
June 1972, T.p. 6.
Per copy 60p, per year £6.

2111 PHYSIOLOGY AND BEHAVIOUR.
Pergamon Press Ltd., Headington Hill Hall, Oxford, OX3 0BW.
12, + =
Monographic articles.
A, Last issue of volume, Yes, None.
Per copy £3.50, per year £40.

2112 PROCEEDINGS AND JOURNAL OF THE ELECTRO-PHYSIOLOGICAL TECHNOLOGISTS' ASSOCIATION. 1950.
The Electrophysiological Technologists' Association, Fleming Memorial Hospital, Newcastle upon Tyne, NE2 3AX.
3/4, ‡ = *   Brain wave recording technology and aplication to clinical problems in neurology, psychiatry, paediatrics and general medicine.
Book reviews, letters, monographic articles, obituaries.
A, With December issue of Journal, No, None.
April 1972, T.p. 58, Ad.p. 20.   500.
Per copy 50p, per year £2. Free to members.

2113 QUARTERLY JOURNAL OF EXPERIMENTAL PHYSIOLOGY. 1921.
The Longman Group Ltd., 33 Montgomery Street, Edinburgh, EH7 5JX.
4, ‡ =   All aspects of human and animal physiology.
Book reviews, letters, monographic articles.
A, Last issue of each volume, Yes, None.
April 1972, T.p. 156.
Per year £8.

612-012

VIVISECTION

2114 ANIMALS DEFENDER AND ANTI-VIVISECTION NEWS 1915.
(Zoophilist 1879-1915)
National Anti-Vivisection Society Ltd., 51 Harley Street, London, W1.
6, + *   Experiments on living animals.
Book notices, book reviews, letters, articles, obituaries, parliamentary reports.

A, December, No, None.
T.p. 36.
Per year 50p. Free to members.

2115 CONQUEST: Journal of the Research Defence Society. 1950.
(The Fight against Disease 1913-1949)
Research Defence Society, 11 Chandos Street, London, W1M 9DE.
1, + =   To make known the facts about experimental research involving the use of animals and conditions and regulations under which animal experiments are conducted in United Kingdom.
Book reviews, letters, articles.
No Index.
January 1972, T.p. 12.
Per year £1.05. Free to members.

2116 LABORATORY ANIMALS. 1967.
Laboratory Animals Limited, 7 Warwick Court, London, WC1R 5DP.
3, + =   All aspects of laboratory animal science, technique and education including work on the biology, pathology and nutrition of laboratory animals which is relevant to their use as experimental animals.
Book notices, book reviews, letters, monographic articles, obituaries.
A, September, Yes, None.
May 1972, T.p. 143, Ad.p. 28.   1206.
Per copy £2.25, per year £4.50.

612-3

NUTRITION

2117 BRITISH JOURNAL OF NUTRITION. 1947.
Cambridge University Press (for the Nutrition Society), PO Box 92, London, NW1 2DB.
6, +   All branches of nutrition covering clinical, experimental, agricultural and statistical aspects.
Monographic articles.
6m, Last issue of volume, Yes, None.
July 1972, T.p. 165, Ad.p. 2.   2300.
Per copy £4, per year £9.

2118 ECOLOGY OF FOOD AND NUTRITION. 1972.
Gordon & Breach, 41/42 William 4th Street, London, WC2.
4, ○ + ‡
Book reviews, legal notes, letters, monographic articles, new products, obituaries, standards, tests.
A, —, No, None.
Per year £5.

2119 NUTRITION: a bi-monthly review for dietitians and nutritionists. In association with the British Dietetic Association. 1936.
Newman Books Limited, 48 Poland Street, London, W1V 4PP.
6, ‡ =
Abstracts, book notices, book reviews, letters, monographic articles, new products, obituaries, tests.
A, With the last issue of year, No, None.
June 1972, T.p. 57, Ad.p. 2.   1790.
Per copy 75p, per year £4.

2120 NUTRITION ABSTRACTS AND REVIEWS. 1931.
Commonwealth Agricultural Bureaux, Farnham Royal, Slough, SL2 3BN.
4, = + ‡   Foods and feedingstuffs and the nutrition of man and of animals, wild and domesticated.
Abstracts.
A, —, Yes, None.
T.p. c. 125.
Per year £18 to subscribers.

2121 NUTRITION AND FOOD SCIENCE: in asscn. with British Nutrition Foundation. 1971.
(Review of Nutrition & Food Science, 1965).
Forbes Publications Ltd., Hartree House, Queensway, London, W2 4SH.
4, + = *   All aspects of nutrition: reports of research, school meals, obesity, book reviews, news items, reports of conferences, comments on legislation. Published in association with the British Nutrition Foundation.
Book reviews, articles, letters, parliamentary reports, standards, tests.
A, —, Yes, 7 year.
April 1972, T.p. 25.   3500.

2122 THE PROCEEDINGS OF THE NUTRITION SOCIETY. 1941.
Cambridge University Press, PO Box 92, London, NW1 2DB.
3, +   Human nutrition.
Abstracts (of communications), book reviews, monographic articles.
A, End of volume, Yes, None.
May 1972, T.p. 123.   2500.
Per copy £4, per year £9.

2123 SLIMMING AND NUTRITION. 1972.
(Slimming and Family Nutrition).
Slimming Magazine Ltd.,
6, ○   All aspects of slimming and nutrition.
Letters, articles, new companies, new products, standards, tests.
No Index.
135264.
Per copy 20p, per year £1.15.

612.015

METABOLISM

2124 CARBOHYDRATE METABOLISM ABSTRACTS. 1973.
A. G. Woolcott, Publisher Information Retrieval Limited, 1 Falconberg Court, London, W1V 5FG.
12, +   Covering the metabolism, functional aspects and structure of carbohydrates, the metabolism of compounds in cells and organisms; regulation and control of various metabolic processes, and studies in multi-cellular organisms, especially human diseases i.e. diabetes.
Abstracts, book notices.
A, monthly Author index, Annual Index, c. 9 months after end of volume, No, None.
T.p. c. 100.   c. 1000.
Per year £40.

2125 XENOBIOTICA. 1971
Taylor & Francis Ltd., 10-14 Macklin St., London WC2B 5NF.
6, ‡ = +   Drug metabolism and the metabolism of other foreign chemicals.
Book notices, book reviews, monographic articles.
A, in last issue of volume, Yes, None.
March 1972, T.p. 100.
Per copy £3, per year £15.

612.017

ALLERGY

2126 CLINICAL ALLERGY: Journal of the British Allergy Society. 1971.
Blackwell Scientific Publications, Osney Mead, Oxford, OX2 0EL.
4, + * =   Clinical and experimental observations in disease in all fields of medicine in which allergic hypersensitivity plays a part.
Letters, monographic articles.
A, December, Yes, None.
March 1972, T.p. 98, Ad.p. 6.
Per copy £2.25, per year £8.

612.46
KIDNEYS

2127 RENAL PHYSIOLOGY. 1970.
Biomedical Information Project, Dept. of Physiology, University of Sheffield, Sheffield, S10 2TN.
12, + ‡   Kidney structure, blood flow, filtration. Kidney tubule, enzymes. Excretion. Pharmacology including diuretics and hormones amphibian bladder and skin.
Current awareness service, titles, references, addresses.
No Index.
July 1972, T.p. 11.
Per copy 60p, per year £6.

2128 RENAL TRANSPLANTATION AND DIALYSIS. 1971.
Biomedical Information Project, Dept. of Physiology, The University, Sheffield, S10 2TN.
12, + ‡   Preservation immunology tissue typing, clinical, complications, dialysis and hemodialysis.
Current awareness service, titles, author's address, references.
No Index.
July 1972, T.p. 5.
Per copy 60p, per year £6.

612.6
FERTILITY. REPRODUCTION

2129 BIBLIOGRAPHY OF FAMILY PLANNING AND POPULATION. 1972.
Simon Population Trust, 141 Newmarket Road, Cambridge, CB5 8HA.
6 + 1 subject index, +   Serious studies on sex education, family planning and population; includes admin. reports, theses, congress, proceedings, census reports, books (and their chapters), as well as usual periodical literature, films.
A, June, Yes, None.
July 1972, T.p. 80.
Per copy £1, per year £6.

2130 BIRTH CONTROL CAMPAIGN BULLETIN. 1972.
Birth Control Compaign, 233 Tottenham Court Road, London, W1P 9AE.
4, †   All aspects of birth control field (contraception, sterilisation, abortion); details of members' activities.
Book notices, parliamentary reports, patents, standards, tests.
No Index.
Spring 1972, T.p. 4.
Free.

2131 FAMILY PLANNING. 1952.
Family Planning Association, 27/35 Mortimer St., London, W1A 4QW.
4, + * ‡   All aspects of family planning and sex education.
Book notices, book reviews, letters, articles, obituaries, parliamentary reports, standards, tests.
No Index.
July 1972, T.p. 24, Ad.p. ½.   8500.
Per copy 15p, per year 60p.

2132 IPPF MEDICAL BULLETIN. 1966.
International Planned Parenthood Federation, 18-20 Lower Regent Street, London, SW1Y 4PW.
6, ‡ =   New developments in family planning in its broadest sense, meant to give doctors throughout the world more interest in fertility control.
Book notices, book reviews, articles, new products, obituaries, standards, tests.
No Index.
June 1972, T.p. 4,   c. 2100.
Free on request.

2133 INTERNATIONAL PLANNED PARENTHOOD NEWS: Around the World News of Population and Birth Control. 1964.
(Around the World News of Population & Birth Control, 1952-1963).
IPPF, 18-20 Lower Regent Street, London SW1Y 4PW.
12, ○ * +   Birth control and general family planning information with particular reference to developing countries.
Book notices, book reviews, new products, obituaries.
One cumulative index 1952-1968 published in 1970.
April/May 1972, T.p. 8.   54640.
Per year 50p.

2134 RESEARCH IN REPRODUCTION. 1969.
International Planned Parenthood Federation, 18-20 Lower Regent Street, London SW1.
6, +   Advances in knowledge of reproductive physiology, and gives information on current events relevant to this field of study. Contents include reviews by particular scientists, summaries of certain areas of research, descriptions of places of unique interest
Book notices, book reviews, monographic articles.
No Index.
Jan. 1969, T.p. 4.   c. 18000.
Issued free by IPPF.

612.67
AGEING

2135 EXPERIMENTAL GERONTOLOGY. 1964.
Pergamon Press Ltd., Headington Hill Hall, Oxford, OX3 0BW.
6, = +   Biology of age processes in man and animals.
Monographic articles.
A, —, Yes, None.
Per copy £3.50, per year £20.

2136 GERONTOLOGY: occupational and social aspects of human ageing. 1970.
IPC Science & Technology Publications Ltd., 32 High Street, Guildford, Surrey.
4, + = ‡   Causes and effects of human ageing.
Book reviews, letters, monographic articles.
A, December, Yes, None.
T.p. 68, Ad.p. 1.
Per year £12.

612.78
SPEECH

2137 BRITISH JOURNAL OF DISORDERS OF COMMUNICATION. 1966.
(Speech, 1945-1957; Speech Pathology and Therapy, 1958-1965).
The Longman Group Ltd., 33 Montgomery Street, Edinburgh EH7 5JX.
2, = +   Receptive and expressive aspects of language, audiology, articulation and personal, social and environmental conditions relating to communication through spoken and written language.
Book reviews, letters, monographic articles, standards, tests.
No Index.
April 1972, T.p. 110, Ad.p. 3.   3000.
Per copy £1, per year £2.

612.82
NERVES

2138 NERVE CELL BIOLOGY. 1972.
Biomedical Information Project, Dept. of Physiology, The University, Sheffield S10 2TN.
12, + ‡
Current awareness service, titles, authors' addresses, references.

No Index.
June 1972, T.p. 9.
Per copy 60p, per year £6.

612.85

HEARING

2139 HEARING. 1963.
(Silent World 1946-1963)
Royal National Institute for the Deaf, 105 Gower Street, London, WC1E 6AH.
12, *   All matters affecting deafness and hearing impairments.
Book reviews, letters, monographic articles, new products, obituaries, parliamentary reports, tests.
No Index.
June 1972, T.p. 24, Ad.p. 8.   10000.
Per copy 8p, per year £1.

613

HEALTH. HYGIENE

2140 ABSTRACTS ON HYGIENE. 1968.
(Bulletin of Hygiene 1926-1967)
Bureau of Hygiene & Tropical Diseases, Keppel Street, London, WC1.
12, = +   All aspects of public health etc.
Abstracts, book reviews.
A, –, Yes, None.
T.p. 144.   2200.
Per year £13.

2141 HEALTH BULLETIN. 1941.
Her Majesty's Stationery Office, Bankhead Avenue, Sighthill, Edinburgh.
4, +
Book reviews, monographic articles, tests.
A, January, No, None.
June 1972, T.p. 64,   8500.
Free, controlled circulation and Per copy 20p.

2142 HEALTH PHYSICS.
Pergamon Press Ltd., Headington Hill Hall, Oxford, OX3 0BW.
12, +   Protection of man and his environment from unwarranted ionizing and non-ionizing radiation exposure.
Book reviews, monographic articles.
A, Last issue of volume, Yes, None.
Per copy £3, per year £28.

2143 HEALTH TRENDS. 1969.
Department of Health and Social Security, Ray House, 6/16 St. Andrew Street, London, EC4.
4, ‡ =   Management of medical work and development of NHS policies. Inform profession of medical activities of DHSS.
Book notices, monographic articles.
A, November, No, None.
T.p. 20.   58000.
Per copy 9p, per year 36p.

2144 JOURNAL OF HYGIENE. 1901.
Cambridge University Press, PO Box 92, London, NW1 2DB.
4, +   Bacterial and virus diseases of man and animals including epidemiology and immunology.
Monographic articles.
A, December, Yes, None.
March 1972, T.p. 202, Ad.p. 1.   1500.
Per copy £2, per year £7.
Indexed in: BTI, IBZ.

613.6

INDUSTRIAL MEDICINE

2145 BRITISH JOURNAL OF INDUSTRIAL MEDICINE. 1944.
British Medical Association, B.M.A. House, Tavistock Square, London, WC1H 9JR.
4, ‡   All aspects of occupational medicine e.g. the pneumonconioses, occupational cancers, industrial toxicology and psychology.
Book reviews, letters, monographic articles, obituaries.
A, October, Yes, None.
April 1972, T.p. 120, Ad.p. 8.
Per year £6.

2146 OCCUPATIONAL HEALTH. 1963
(Journal for Industrial Nurses)
Macmillan (Journals) Ltd., Brunel Road, Basingstoke, Hants.
6, = + ‡
Book reviews, monographic articles, new products, reports.
A, November/December, Yes, None.
T.p. 67, Ad.p. 5.
Per copy 30p, per year £2.

613.8

ADDICTION

2148 BRITISH JOURNAL OF ADDICTION. 1884.
Pergamon Press Ltd., (for Society for the Study of Addiction to Alcohol and other Drugs), Headington Hill Hall, Oxford OX3 0BW.
4, = +   Understanding and treatment of addiction and alcoholism.
Book notices, book reviews, monographic articles.
A, Last issue of volume, Yes, None.
T.p. 159, Ad.p. 4.
Per copy £2, per year £6.

613.81

ALCOHOLISM

2149 JOURNAL OF ALCOHOLISM: the journal of the Medical Council on Alcoholism.
(Bulletin of Alcoholism 1964-1967).
B. Edsall & Co. Ltd., 36 Eccleston Sq., London, SW1V 1PF.
4, ‡   Medico/social problems of alcoholism.
Book notices, book reviews, letters, monographic articles.
A, Last issue of volume, Yes, None.
Vol. 7, No. 1, T.p. 39, Ad.p. 1.   12000.
Per year £4.

613.86

MENTAL HEALTH

2150 BEACON HOUSE NEWS. 1962.
Northern Ireland Association for Mental Health, Beacon House, 84 University Street, Belfast BT7 1HE.
3, + = *   Mental health.
No Index.
March 1972, T.p. 16.   1200.
Free to members.

Key to reference symbols

○ popular   ‡ technical   = trade/professional

+ research   * society/institution   † house journal

613.89

MARRIAGE GUIDANCE

2151 MARRIAGE GUIDANCE.
National Marriage Guidance Council, 3 Gower Street, London, WC1E 6HA.
6, +   Counselling in the field of marriage and family life, sex education etc.
Book reviews, letters, monographic articles.
No Index.
March 1972, T.p. 30.
Per copy 22½, per year £1.

614

PUBLIC HEALTH

2152 COMMUNITY HEALTH: The Journal of the Royal Institute of Public Health & Hygiene. 1969.
John Wright & Sons Ltd., 42/44 Triangle West, Clifton, Bristol, BS8 1EX.
6, *   All aspects of public health and hygiene.
Book notices, book reviews, monographic articles, obituaries, tests.
A, May, Yes, None.
May/June 1972, T.p. 46, Ad.p. 4   3000.
Per copy 75p, per year £4.50.

2153 GOOD HEALTH: The Family Health Magazine. 1902.
The Stanborough Press Ltd., Alma Park, Grantham, Lincs.
6, ○   Health articles, gardening, knitting, recipes, stamps on medical themes, narcotics, home hints, nature notes, family articles, household hints, doctor's casebook, children's pages.
Book reviews, letters, articles, new products.
A, –, Yes, None.
Vol. 70, No. 2 1972, T.p. 52, Ad.p. 18.   30000.
Per copy 15p, per year £1.25.

2154 HEALTH. 1964.
(Health Horizon 1946-1963).
The Chest and Heart Association, Tavistock House North, Tavistock Square, London, WC1H 9JE.
4, ‡ +   Articles by specialists in health field with particular emphasis on community health.
Book notices, book reviews, articles.
No Index.
Per copy 35p, per year £1.20.

2155 JOURNAL OF THE ASSOCIATION OF PUBLIC ANALYSTS. 1963
Association of Public Analysts, 325 Kennington Road, London, SE11.
4, =
Book reviews, legal notes, letters, monographic articles, obituaries, standards, tests.
A, December, Yes, 10 year.
T.p. 35.
Per copy 75p, per year £2.50.

2156 JOURNAL OF THE INSTITUTE OF HEALTH EDUCATION. 1969.
Institute of Health Education, 35 Victoria Road, Sheffield, S10 2DJ.
4, = *   Practice of health education including content and methodology.
Book notices, book reviews, letters, monographic articles, new products.
A, –, Yes, None.
T.p. 26, Ad.p. 5.
Free to members.

2157 PUBLIC HEALTH. 1888.
Academic Press Inc (London) Ltd., 24-28 Oval Road, London, NW1.
6, =   Preventive medicine, social medicine, epidemiology and public health.
Book reviews, monographic articles, obituaries.
A, November, Yes, None.
T.p. 50.
Per year £3.

2158 ROYAL SOCIETY OF HEALTH JOURNAL. 1955.
(Journal of the Royal Sanitary Institute 1901-1955)
Royal Society for the Promotion of Health, 90 Buckingham Palace Road, London, SW1W 0SX.
6, = ‡   Public health.
Book notices, book reviews, legal notes, letters, monographic articles, new products, obituaries, parliamentary reports, patents, standards, tests.
A, February, Yes, None.
April 1972, T.p. 47, Ad.p. 16   28000.
Per copy 85p, per year £5.
Indexed in: BTI.

2159 SCOTTISH HEALTH STATISTICS. 1958.
HMSO, 13A Castle Street, Edinburgh, EH2 3AR.
1, ‡ +   Comprehensive selection of statistics derived from the range of N.H.S. activities in Scotland.
No Index.
T.p. 159.   200.
Per copy c. £5.50.

2160 YOUR ENVIRONMENT. 1969.
10 Roderick Road, London, NW3.
4, ○ ‡ + =   All aspects of conservation, pollution etc.
Book notices, book reviews, letters, monographic articles, news.
A, December, Yes, 10 year.
T.p. 32, Ad.p. 1.   2000.
Per year £1.50.

614.4

DISEASES

2161 TROPICAL DISEASES BULLETIN. 1912.
(Sleeping Sickness Bureau Bulletin 1908-1911).
Bureau of Hygiene & Tropical Diseases, Keppel Street, London, WC1.
12, + =   Tropical diseases and related subjects.
Abstracts, book reviews.
A, 18 months after December issue, Yes, None.
T.p. 127, Ad.p. 5.   1500.
Per copy 60p, per year £8 and Free, controlled circulation.

614.44

PREVENTIVE MEDICINE

2162 BRITISH JOURNAL OF PREVENTIVE & SOCIAL MEDICINE. 1947.
British Medical Association, BMA House, Tavistock Square, Lond, WC1H 9JR
4, = + ‡   Original work in the field, the emphasis on epidemiological methods in medical research.
Monographic articles, obituaries.
A, November, Yes, None.
May 1972, T.p. 66, Ad.p. 2.
Per year £5.50.

614.47

IMMUNOLOGY

2163 CLINICAL AND EXPERIMENTAL IMMUNOLOGY: An Official Journal of the British Society for Immunology. 1966.
Blackwell Scientific Publications, Oxford Osney Mead, Oxford, OX2 0EL.
12, + = *   Immunological phenomena in relation to disease. It publishes both papers that are clinical in character and also papers primarily concerned with animal experimentation, provided that the basic thesis is related to the immunological aspects of

disease or the application of immunological techniques to the study of disease.
Book reviews, monographic articles.
3 times year, April, August and December, Yes, None.
June 1972, T.p. 160, Ad.p. 4.   1400.
Per copy £3.25, per year £36.

2164 IMMUNOCHEMISTRY.
Pergamon Press Ltd., Headington Hill Hall, Oxford OX3 0BW.
12, = +   Chemical and physical aspects of immunology and related problems.
Book reviews, letters, monographic articles.
A, Last issue of volume, Yes, None.
Per copy £3, per year £28.

2165 IMMUNOLOGY: An Official Journal of the British Society for Immunology. 1958.
Blackwell Scientific Publications, Oxford Osney Mead, Oxford, OX2 0EL.
12, + * =   Immunological techniques are now being applied to a large number of biological problems, and are of importance to workers in many fields—pathology, microbiology, bacteriology, biochemistry, haematology, and biology in general.
Book reviews, monographic articles.
6m, June/December, Yes, None.
June 1972, T.p. 194, Ad.p. 4.   2486.
Per copy £2, per year £20.

614.6

BURIALS. CREMATION. FUNERALS

2166 FUNERAL SERVICE JOURNAL. 1946.
King & Hutchings (Westminster Press Ltd.), Blair House, Vine Steet, Uxbridge, Middx.
12, =   Funeral directors, suppliers and traders, and all in the funeral service industry, burial and cremation authorities, vehicle manufacturers to the trade.
Letters, articles, new products, obituaries, standards.
No Index
T.p. 24, Ad.p. 36.
Per year £1.72.

2167 PHAROS: Official journal of The Cremation Society and The International Cremation Federation. 1934.
The Pharos Press, 47 Nottingham Place, London, W1M 4BH.
4, ‡ = +   All subjects relevant to cremation and crematorium administration.
Legal notes, letters, articles, new companies, new products, obituaries, parliamentary reports, standards, tests.
No Index.
May 1972, T.p. 36, Ad.p. 11.   1500.
Per copy 25p, per year £1.

2168 RESURGAM: the journal of the Federation of British Cremation Authorities. 1947.
Federation of British Cremation Authorities, 50 Cannon Street, London, EC4N 6LA.
4, ‡   Cremation, crematoria, technical developments, law and regulations; matters of general interest to cremation authorities in U.K.
Book reviews, letters, monographic articles, tests.
No Index.
June 1972, T.p. 22, Ad.p. 87.   1000.
Per copy 50p. Free to members.

614.7

AIR POLLUTION

2169 ATMOSPHERIC ENVIRONMENT. 1967.
(Air Pollution 1958-1960; Air and Water Pollution 1961-1966)
Pergamon Press Ltd., Headington Hill Hall, Oxford OX3 0BW.
12, =   All aspects of air pollution research.
Book notices, book reviews, letters, monographic articles.
A, Last issue of volume, Yes, None.
T.p. 120.
Per copy £2.50, per year £26.

2170 CLEAN AIR. 1971
(Smokeless Air 1929-1970)
National Society for Clean Air, 136 North Street, Brighton, Sussex BNI lrg.
4, * +   Air pollution and allied matters.
Abstracts, book reviews, letters, monographic articles, new products, obituaries, standards, tests.
No Index.
Summer 1972, T.p. 38, Ad.p. 10.   c. 6000.
Per copy 30p, per year £1.10. Free to members.

614.8

ACCIDENTS. SAFETY

2171 ACCIDENT ANALYSIS AND PREVENTION. 1969
Pergamon Press Ltd., Headington Hill Hall, Oxford OX3 0BW.
4, = +   All aspects of transport and industrial safety.
Book reviews, monographic articles.
A, Last issue of volume, Yes, None.
T.p. 216.
Per copy £4.50, per year £16.

2172 ACCIDENTS: How they are caused and how to prevent them. 1949.
(Industrial Accidents 1933-1936; How Factory Accidents Happen 1937-1941)
H.M.S.O., PO Box 569, London, SE1.
4, ‡   Describes accidents which have happened and analyses the causes of them, also articles which give advice on accident prevention in specific industries or processes.
Monographic articles.
3 yrs, —, Yes, None.
April 1972, T.p. 38, Ad.p. 4.
Per copy 12½p, per year 60p.

2173 ARRIVE. 1970.
(The Pedestrian—1929-1969)
The Pedestrians Assn. for Road Safety, Suite 4, 166 Shaftesbury Avenue, London, WC2H 8JH.
3, + * †   All aspects of road safety with accent on pedestrian amenities.
Book notices, book reviews, legal notes, letters, obituaries, parliamentary reports.
No Index.
January 1972, T.p. 46.
Per copy 15p, per year 50p.

2174 CARE IN THE HOME. 1972.
Royal Society for Prevention of Accidents, 6 Buckingham Place, London, SW1E 6HR.
4, ○
No Index.
Per copy 25p.

2175 PROTECTION: Journal of Loss Prevention. 1963.
(Journal of the Institute of Industrial Safety Officers 1956-1962)
Alan Osborne and Associates (for the Institution of Industrial Safety Officers), 1/113 Blackheath Park, London, SE3.
11, = *   All aspects of accident, fire security prevention including health and environmental hazards.
Book notices, legal notes, letters, monographic articles, new products, standards, tests.
No Index.
May 1972, T.p. 18, Ad.p. 21.   7000.
Per copy 35p, per year £3.75.

2176 SAFETY & RESCUE. 1960
(Safe Times 1958-1959)
British Safety Council, Chancellor's Road, London, W6 9RS.
12, ‡ ○ =   All industrial safety affairs with additional coverage of home, road and water safety.
Legal notes, letters, new products, parliamentary reports.
No Index.
July 1972, T.p. 20, Ad.p. 8.
Per copy: 4p and Free to members.

2177 SCIATH: journal of the National Industrial Safety Organisation. 1968.
National Industrial Safety Organisation, Ansley House, Mespil Road, Dublin 4.
4, ‡ =
Per copy 10p.

614.84

FIRE PREVENTION

2178 CENTRE: Information and news about fire prevention activities. 1969.
(Activities Bulletin 1964-1966; FPA News 1967-1968)
Fire Protection Association, Aldermary House, Queen Street, London, EC4N 1TJ.
4, ○ ‡   News magazine for management, dealing with the techniques of industrial fire protection, particularly training, education, planning and propaganda.
Book notices, book reviews, legal notes, letters, monographic articles, new products, parliamentary reports, standards, tests.
No Index.
March 1972, T.p. 12.   11000.
Per copy 15p, per year 60p.

2179 FIRE: journal of the British Fire Services. 1908.
Universal Publications Ltd., Dudley Road, Tunbridge Wells, Kent.
12, = + ‡   Fire fighting, fire prevention etc.
Book reviews, letters, monographic articles, obituaries, parliamentary reports, patents, standards, tests.
A, August, Yes, None.
T.p. 26, Ad.p. 34.   5500.
Per copy 20p, per year £2.25.
Indexed in: BTI.

2180 FIRE INTERNATIONAL. 1963.
Unisaf Publications Ltd., Dudley Road, Tunbridge Wells, Kent.
4, = ‡ +   All aspects of fire and disaster protection, worldwide.
Book reviews, letters, monographic articles, new products, patents, standards, tests.
No Index.
T.p. 68, Ad.p. 40.
Per copy 50p, per year £2.

2181 FIRE PREVENTION: a guide for management. 1971.
(FPA Journal 1948)
Fire Protection Association, Aldermary House, Queen Street, London, EC4N 1TJ.
4, ‡   Technical articles, reports, statistics relating to fire losses and fire causes, deaths by fire: illustrated by diagrams, graphs, photographs. A special feature is the accounts of fires.
Book notices, book reviews, legal notes, letters, monographic articles, new products, obituaries, parliamentary reports, standards, tests.
No Index.
April 1972, T.p. 56.   12000.
Per copy £1, per year £3.

2182 FIRE PREVENTION SCIENCE AND TECHNOLOGY. 1972.
Fire Protection Association, Aldermary House, Queen Street, London, EC4N 1TJ.
4, ‡   Supplement to the FPA's quarterly journal FIRE PREVENTION providing information on new developments in fire protection for engineers and scientists in the UK and abroad.
Monographic articles.
No Index.
March 1972, T.p. 28.   2000 printed: circulation not yet stabilised.
Per copy 50p, per year £1.50.

2183 FIRE PROTECTION REVIEW: incorporating Emergency Services Review. 1938.
Benn Bros. Ltd., Lyon Tower, 125 High Street, Colliers Wood, London, SW19 2JN.
12, ‡ = *   Relating to the fire protection and fire fighting and fire engineering industry.
Letters, monographic articles, new companies, new products, parliamentary reports, patents, standards, tests.
A, December, Yes, None.
T.p. 27 average, Ad.p. 26 average.   4151.
Per copy 25p, per year £3.50.

2184 FIRE SURVEYOR: Journal for Fire Surveyors. 1972.
Victor Green Publications Ltd., (for Incorporated Association of Architects & Surveyors), 44 Bedford Row, London, WC1R 4LL.
6, ‡ = + *   All aspects of prevention, detection and fire fighting—reviews, and news of equipment and services—company information—informative and educational articles—case studies—close-up reports and surveys.
Book notices, book reviews, legal notes, letters, monographic articles, new companies, new products, obituaries, parliamentary reports, patents, standards, tests.
6m, −, No, None.
April 1972, T.p. 57, Ad.p. 37.   5000.
30p, per year £1.80p.

2185 INSTITUTION OF FIRE ENGINEERS QUARTERLY. 1941.
Institution of Fire Engineers, 148 New Walk, Leicester LEI 7QB.
4, ‡ * † =   Technical and educational aspects for all engaged in the fire engineering profession.
Book reviews, letters, monographic articles, obituaries, standards, tests.
2 yearly, −, Yes, None.
March 1972, T.p. 112, Ad.p. 8.   6000.
Per copy 75p, per year £2.75. Free to members.

2186 JOFRO. Joint Fire Research Organisation quarterly. 1968.
Joint Fire Research Organisation, Fire Research Station, Borehamwood, Herts.
4, ○ + ‡   News of events of the Fire Research Station and general articles of interest.
Abstracts, news, new products.
No Index.
T.p. 18.
Free.

2187 JOURNAL OF THE BRITISH FIRE SERVICES ASSOCIATION. 1949.
The Association, 86 London Road, Leicester LE2 5DJ.
3, ‡   Fire service matters in general.
Monographic articles, news.
No Index.
T.p. 46, Ad.p. 4.
Per year 50. Free to members.

2188 NU-SWIFT FIRE FIGHTING NEWS.
Nu-Swift International Ltd., Elland, Yorks, HX5 9DS.
= ‡ †
Letters, articles.
No Index.
No. 12, T.p. 4.
Free.

614.88

FIRST AID

2189 AMBULANCE: a journal for professional ambulance and first aid personnel. 1955.
(ICAP Journal 1947-1955)
Institute of Certified Ambulance Personnel, 5 Grove Terrace, London, NW5 1PH.
4,‡ =   Local authority ambulance personnel, factory first aid.
Articles, news.
No Index.
Spring 1972, T.p. 6, Ad.p. 1.   1500.
Per copy 15p, per year 80p.

2190 ST. JOHN REVIEW.
St. John Ambulance, 1 Grosvenor Crescent, London, SW1.
12, + * ‡ =   First aid and medical matters in general.
Book reviews, letters, monographic articles, new products.
No Index.
T.p. 21, Ad.p. 4.   7000.
Per copy 10p, per year £2.

615.1

PHARMACY

2191 ADVERSE DRUG REACTION BULLETIN. 1966.
Newcastle Regional Hospital Board, Editorial Office, Shotley Bridge General Hospital, Consett, Co. Durham.
6, ‡   Reviews of adverse drug reactions reported in the medical literature.
A, December, No, None.
T.p. 4.   9500.
Subscription: On application.

2192 AFRICAN MIMS: incorporating African Medical Practitioner. 1969.
NC Magazines Ltd., 172-174 Kingston Road, Ewell, Surrey.
6, = ‡   Index to ethical pharmaceutical preparations.
No Index.
T.p. 76, Ad.p. 16.
Free, controlled circulation.

2193 BIOCHEMICAL PHARMACOLOGY. 1958.
Pergamon Press Ltd., Headington Hill Hall, Oxford OX3 0BW.
26, = +   Research into the developments of biologically active substances and their mode of action at the biochemical and sub-cellular level.
Book notices, book reviews, monographic articles.
A, Last issue of volume, Yes, None.
T.p. 208.
Per copy £2.50, per year £56.
Indexed in: IBZ.

2194 BRITISH JOURNAL OF MUSIC THERAPY. 1968.
(Bulletin of the Society for Music Therapy 1958-1968)
British Society for Music Therapy, 48 Lanchester Road, London, N6 4TA.
3, = + *   Study and research in music therapy, medical and educational aspects.
Book notices, book reviews, monographic articles.
A, —, No, None.
Spring 1972, T.p. 40.   600.
Per year £2 and Free to members.

2195 BRITISH JOURNAL OF PHARMACOLOGY: Journal of the British Pharmacological Society. 1968.
(British Journal of Pharmacology & Chemotherapy 1946-1947)
Macmillan (Journals) Ltd., Brunel Road, Basingstoke, Hants.
9, * ‡ + =   Pharmacology in Britain and research worldwide.
Monographic articles, obituaries.
A, Last issue in each volume, No, None.
T.p. 217, Ad.p. 6.
Per copy £5.50, per year £16.

2196 CHEMIST & DRUGGIST.
Benn Brothers Limited, 25 New Street Square, London, EC4A 3JA.
51, =   Pharmaceutical retailers, wholesalers and manufacturers.
Book notices, book reviews, commodity prices, legal notes, letters, monographic articles, new companies, new products, obituaries, parliamentary reports, patents, standards, tests.
6m, —, Yes, None.
July 15 1972, T.p. 18, Ad.p. 14.   15167.
Per copy 30p, per year £8.

2197 COMPARATIVE AND GENERAL PHARMACOLOGY. 1970.
Scientechnica (Publishers) Limited, 42-44 Triangle West, Bristol BS8 1EX.
4, ‡ + =   All general aspects of the subject, although special consideration is given to those dealing with more than one species from a comparative point of view. Offers a focal point for the dissemination of knowledge and ideas for the modern pharmacologist.
Monographic articles.
A, December, Yes, None.
March 1972, T.p. 124, Ad.p. 2.
Per copy £4, per year £15.

2198 DRUG & THERAPEUTICS BULLETIN. 1962.
Consumers' Association, 14 Buckingham Street, London, WC2N 6DS.
26, = ‡   Appraises new or widely promoted drugs, examining critically the claims made for them in advertising, and also comparing them with established drugs used for the same conditions.
Commodity prices, new products, standards, tests.
No Index.
T.p. 4.   c.6000.
Per copy 15p, per year £3.75.

2199 FOLIO PHARMACEUTICA. 1965.
Pharmaceutical Promotion Ltd., 41 Parker Street, London, WC2B 5NX
6, ‡ =   Concise presentation of essential data about new and current pharmaceutical preparations for all prescribing doctors.
New products.
No Index.
25000.
Free, controlled circulation.

2200 GEN. The newspaper of Fisons Pharmaceutical Division. 1972.
Fisons Ltd., Loughborough, Leics.
= †   Articles, news.
No Index.
October/November 1972, T.p. 8.
Free.

2201 GRACE. 1960.
Gerard House (1965) Ltd., 736B Christchurch Road, Bournemouth.
4, ○   For those interested in keeping in good health without the aid of drugs.
Book notices, book reviews, letters, articles, new products.
No Index.
T.p. 48, Ad.p. 8.   12000.
Per copy 10p, per year 50p.

2202 HEALTH FOR ALL. 1927.
Health for all Publishing Co., 3B Bedford Park, Croydon, CR9 2AT.
12, ○ =   Health, drugless healing, diet, exercise, organic gardening.
Book reviews, letters, articles, new products.

A, September, Yes, None.
June 1972, T.p. 37, Ad.p. 46.   18295.
Per copy 16½p, per year £1.97.

2203 HEALTH FROM HERBS. 1965.
(Herb Doctor 1910-1920; Medical Herbalist 1920-1960; Fitness 1960-1965).
100 Portland Road, Worthing, Sussex.
6, = ○   Herbal remedies in prevention of disease and maintenance of health.
Book reviews, letters, articles, news, parliamentary reports.
No Index.
T.p. 19, Ad.p. 2.
Per copy 10p.

2204 HEALTHY LIVING. 1966.
Foremost Press Ltd., PO Box 1, Wirral, Cheshire.
12, ○   Health matters mainly in relation to diet and physical fitness.
Book reviews, articles, new products, obituaries.
A, —, Yes, None.
June 1972, T.p. 36, Ad.p. 14.   12000.
Per copy 4p, per year 90p.

2205 HERBAL PRACTITIONER. 1945.
National Institute of Medical Herbalists Ltd., 169 Norfolk Street, Sheffield.
2, ‡ =   Herbal remedies.
Book reviews, monographic articles, tests.
No Index.
T.p. 26, Ad.p. 30.
Free to members.

2206 JOURNAL OF HOSPITAL PHARMACY: official organ of the Guild of Hospital Pharmacists. 1963.
(Public Pharmacist 1950-1962).
Alchemist Publications, (Division of Thos. Waide & Sons Ltd.), 25 Oxford St., London, W1.
12, ‡ + *   Developments of interest to hospital pharmacists.
Book reviews, letters, monographic articles, tests.
No Index.
No. 6, 1972, T.p. 16, Ad.p. 15.   2500.
Per copy 25p, per year £3.

2207 JOURNAL OF PHARMACY AND PHARMACOLOGY. 1949.
(Quarterly Journal of Pharmacy and Pharmacology 1928-1948).
Pharmaceutical Society of Great Britain, 17 Bloomsbury Square, London, WC1.
12, +   Development and evolution of medicinal substances.
Book reviews, letters, monographic articles.
A, March/April, Yes, None.
T.p. 71, Ad.p. 5.
Per copy £1, per year £9.
Indexed in: IBZ.

2208 PHARMACEUTICAL JOURNAL. 1841.
Pharmaceutical Society of Great Britain, 17 Bloomsbury Square, London, WC1.
52, * = + ‡   All aspects of pharmacy.
Book notices, book reviews, commodity prices, legal notes, letters, monographic articles, new products, obituaries, parliamentary reports, tests.
2 year, —, Yes, None.
T.p. 31, Ad.p. 16.   32000.
Free to members.
Indexed in: IBZ.

2209 PHARMACY MANAGEMENT: a journal for the progressive pharmacist. 1961.
Pharmaceutical Business Analysis Service, 27 Park View, Hatch End, Pinner, Middx., HA5 4LL.
4, + * =   Pharmaceutical economics, statistics, market research surveys and socio-economic investigations. Business methods and reviews of overseas pharmaceutical conditions. Journal of the Institute of Pharmacy Management.
Legal notes, monographic articles.
None, No index.
June 1972, T.p. 28.   1250.
Per year £4.

2210 PRESCRIBERS' JOURNAL. 1960.
Department of Health and Social Security, Ray House, 6/16 St. Andrew's Street, London, EC4.
6, ‡   Pharmacology and therapeutic procedures—reviews of current practice in medicine.
Monographic articles, new products.
A, December, Yes, None.
T.p. 24.   80000.
Per copy 10p, per year 50p.

2211 THE SCOTTISH PHARMACIST. 1950.
The Scottish Pharmacist, 5 Loudoun Street, Mauchline KA5 5BD, Ayrshire.
12, = ‡   Deals with the social and recreational activities of pharmacists in Scotland, together with news and views of all pharmaceutical affairs.
Book notices, book reviews, letters, new products, obituaries.
No Index.
May 1972, T.p. 16.   2000.
Per copy 10p, per year £1.

2212 SCRIP—Health Services and Industry News. 1972.
Deltakos Division of J. Walter Thompson Company Ltd., 40 Berkeley Square, London, W1X 6AD.
50, = ‡ + *   News on the international pharmaceutical scene and the health care market, finance, new legislation, share prices, new products and equipment, people, patents and conferences with country surveys and in-depth feature coverage of product markets, companies and topical events.
Book notices, book reviews, legal notes, letters, articles, new companies, new products, obituaries, parliamentary reports, patents, standards, tests.
No Index.
June 15, 1971, T.p. 20.
Per year £47.50.

2213 YOU AND YOUR HEALTH. 1972.
Leyden Publishing Co. Ltd., 5-7 Carnaby Street, London, W1A 4XT.
4, ○ =   Self medication and the maintenance of positive good health in everyday life.
Book reviews, letters, articles.
No Index.
Autumn 1972, T.p. 30, Ad.p. 10.
Per copy 15p.

615.78

NEURO PHARMACOLOGY

2214 NEURO PHARMACOLOGY. 1962.
Pergamon Press Ltd., Headington Hill Hall, Oxford, OX3 0BW.
6, = +   Mechanisms of drug actions.
Book reviews, monographic articles.
A, Last issue of volume, Yes, None.
Per copy £4, per year £22.

615.8

PHYSIOTHERAPY

2215 BRAILLE JOURNAL OF PHYSIOTHERAPY [in Braille and on tape]
Association of Blind Chartered Physiotherapists, 204 Great Portland Street, London, W1.
12, =
No Index.
Free to members.

2216 BRAILLE PHYSIOTHERAPISTS QUARTERLY [in Braille and on tape]
Association of Blind Chartered Physiotherapists, 204 Great Portland Street, London, W1.
4, =
No Index.
Free to members.

2217 BRITISH NATUROPATHIC JOURNAL AND OSTEOPATHIC REVIEW. 1961.
(British Naturopathic Association News).
British Naturopathic and Osteopathic Association, 6 Netherhall Gardens, London, NW3.
4, ‡ =   Health, nutrition, osteopathy.
Book reviews, letters, monographic articles, obituaries, reports.
No Index.
Spring 1972, T.p. 21, Ad.p. 10.   500.
Per copy 24p, per year 95p.

2218 PHYSIOTHERAPY. 1915.
Chartered Society of Physiotherapy, 14 Bedford Row, London, WC1.
12, =
Book reviews, letters, monographic articles, news, parliamentary reports.
A, January, No, None.
T.p. 43, Ad.p. 36.   15000.
Per copy 25p, per year £2.50.

615.83

NUDISM

2219 BRITISH NATURISM: official journal of the Central Council for British Naturism. 1964.
The Council, Sheepcote, Orpington, Kent, BR5 4ET.
4, * ○
Letters, new products, obituaries, standards.
No Index.
T.p. 28, Ad.p. 4.
Free to members.

615.849

RADIOLOGY

2220 BRITISH JOURNAL OF RADIOLOGY. 1924.
(Archives of Skiagraphy 1896-1897; Archives of the Roentgen Ray 1897-1915; Journal of the Röntgen Society 1904-1924).
The British Institute of radiology: diagnostic, Street, London, W1M 7PG.
12, ‡ + =   All aspects of radiology: diagnostic, radiotherapy, radiological physics, nuclear medicine, radiation protection, radiobiology, medical ultrasonics, radiological equipment.
Abstracts, book reviews, letters, monographic articles, obituaries.
A, December, Yes, None.
June 1972, T.p. 130, Ad.p. 50.   4552.
Per copy £1.20, per year £12.
Indexed in: IBZ

2221 CLINICAL RADIOLOGY: journal of the Faculty of Radiologists. 1960.
(Journal of the Faculty of Radiologists 1949-1959).
The Longman Group Ltd., 33 Montgomery Street, Edinburgh, EH7 5JX.
4, = ‡   Diagnostic radiology and radiotherapy with the main emphasis on clincial aspects of radiology.
Book reviews, monographic articles, obituaries.
A, October, Yes, None.
T.p. 112, Ad.p. 18.   3600.
Per copy £1.75, per year £6.50.

2222 INTERNATIONAL JOURNAL OF RADIATION BIOLOGY. 1960.
Taylor & Francis Ltd., 10-14 Macklin St., London, WC2B 5NF.
12, ‡ = +   Research papers on all aspects of radiation effects in biological and chemical systems.
Book notices, book reviews, monographic articles.
6 m, in last issue of volume (2 per year), Yes, None.
July 1972, T.p. 101, Ad.p. 2.
Per copy £3, per year £32.50.

2223 RADIOGRAPHY: journal of the Society of Radiographers. 1935.
The Society of Radiographers, 14 Upper Wimpole St., London, W1M 8BN.
12, ‡ *   Radiography and allied subjects.
Book notices, book reviews, legal notes, letters, monographic articles, new products, obituaries, parliamentary reports, standards, tests.
A, December, Yes, None.
June 1972, T.p. 29, Ad.p. 26.   7000.
Per copy 25p, per year £4. Free to members.

2224 RADIOIMMUNOASSAY. 1970.
Biomedical Information Project, Dept. of Physiology, The University, Sheffield, S10 2TN.
12, + ‡
Current awareness service, titles, authors' addresses, references.
No Index.
July 1972, T.p. 6.
Per copy 60p, per year £6.

2225 X-RAY FOCUS: an international publication on medical radiology and radiography. 1955.
Ilford Limited, Ilford, Essex.
3, ‡ † =   Latest developments in medical radiology and radiography.
Monographic articles.
No Index.
No. 3, 1972, T.p. 23.
Free.

615.851

PSYCHOTHERAPY

2226 GROUP ANALYSIS. 1967.
Pergamon Press (for Institute of Group Analysis), Headington Hill Hall, Oxford, OX3 0BW.
3, = ○   Method, techniques and applications of group analysis.
Book notices, book reviews, letters, articles.
A, With No. 1 of each volume, No, None.
T.p. 68.
Subscription on application.

2227 QUARTERLY JOURNAL OF THE SLEEP-LEARNING ASSOCIATION. 1964.
The Sleep-Learning Association, 14 Belsize Crescent, London, NW3 5QU.
4, ‡ + *   All aspects of hypnoopaedia, in the British Isles and abroad, largely translations of foreign reports and articles. It is also a vehicle for exchange of information between members.
Abstracts, book notices, book reviews, letters, monographic articles.
No Index.
Winter/Spring 1968, T.p. 48, T.p. 48.   3000.
Per copy 75p, per year £2.

615.9

TOXICOLOGY

2228 FOOD AND COSMETICS TOXICOLOGY. 1963.
Pergamon Press Ltd. (for the British Industrial Biological Research Assocn.), Headington Hill Hall, Oxford, OX3 0BW.

6, = + Toxicology of food additives, cosmetics, agricultural, industrial and environmental chemicals and natural products.
Book reviews, monographic articles.
A, Last issue of volume, Yes, None.
T.p. 150.
Per copy £5, per year £28.

2229 TOXICOLOGICAL AND ENVIRONMENTAL CHEMISTRY REVIEWS. [in preparation].
Gordon & Breach, 41/42 William 4th Street, London, WC2.
4, + ‡ Fundamental aspects of analysis, metabolism, and general chemistry and biochemistry of xenobiotic compounds and natural toxins as related to the environment and human health. Are considered: pesticides, air and water pollutants, food additives, drugs, toxic natural and industrial products, and compounds with long-term biological effects.
Book notices, book reviews, letters, monographic articles, new products, tests.
A, —, No, None.
Subscription on application.

2230 TOXICON.
Pergamon Press Ltd., Headington Hill Hall, Oxford, OX3 0BW.
6, + = Poison derived from the tissues of animals and plants.
Book reviews, monographic articles.
A, Last issue of volume, Yes, None.
Per copy £3.50, per year £18.

616

CLINICAL PRACTICE. PATHOLOGY. SURGERY

2231 ANNALS OF TROPICAL MEDICINE AND PARASITOLOGY 1907.
Liverpool University Press, 123 Grove Street, Liverpool, L7 7AF.
4, + = Tropical medicine and parasitology. Recent published articles have dealt with clinical, epidemiological, parasitological, and aspects of communicable diseases, the taxonomy of parasites, and the problems of nutrition and environment.
Monographic articles.
A, December, Yes, None.
June 1972, T.p. 128, Ad.p. 4.   850.
Per copy £3.25, per year £12.

2232 BIO-MEDICAL ENGINEERING. 1965.
United Trade Press Ltd., 9 Gough Square, London, EC4.
12, † ‡ = Developments in the applications of technology to clinical medicine.
Book notices, book reviews, letters, monographic articles, new companies, new products, standards, tests.
A, January, Yes, None.
T.p. 43, Ad.p. 26.   5900.
Per year £3.

2233 THE BRITISH JOURNAL OF CLINICAL PRACTICE. 1956.
(Medical Bookman & Historian 1946-1949; Medicine Illustrated 1949-1955).
Harvey & Blythe Ltd., Lloyds Banks Chambers, 216 Church Road, Hove, Sussex.
12, ‡ + Ethical medical journal for the medical profession, hospitals, universities—world wide.
Book reviews, monographic articles.
A, January, Yes, None.
June 1972, T.p. 67, Ad.p. 22.   10900.
Per copy 50p, per year £3.15.

2234 BRITISH JOURNAL OF EXPERIMENTAL PATHOLOGY. 1920.
H.K. Lewis & Co. Ltd., 136 Gower Street, London, WC1E 6BS.

6, + Experimental research into causation, diagnosis and cure of disease in man.
Monographic articles.
A, December, Yes, None.
April 1972, T.p. 145.
Per copy £1.75, per year £9.

2236 CLINICAL SCIENCE. 1934.
(HEART (1909-1933)).
Blackwell Scientific Publications, Osney Mead, Oxford, OX2 0EL.
12, + * = Clinical investigation in the broadest sense.
Letters, monographic articles.
6m, June/December, Yes, None.
June 1972, T.p. 134, Ad.p. 2.   c. 2000.
Per copy £2, per year £20.
Indexed in: IBZ.

2237 INJURY: The British Journal of Accident Surgery. 1969.
John Wright & Sons Ltd., 42-44 Triangle West, Bristol, BS8 1EX.
4, ‡ Orthopaedic, accident & traumatic surgery.
Book reviews, letters, monographic articles, tests.
A, April, Yes, None.
T.p. 80, Ad.p. 16.
Per year £6.50.

2238 JOURNAL OF CLINICAL PATHOLOGY: The Journal of the Association of Clinical Pathologists. 1947.
British Medical Association, BMA House, Tavistock Square, London, WC1H 9JR.
12, ‡ + = * Each branch of pathology, with prominence given to its clinical application. Technical methods, notes on new or improved apparatus.
Book reviews, letters, monographic articles, obituaries.
A, December, Yes, None.
May 1972, T.p. 88, Ad.p. 24.
Per year £12.

2239 JOURNAL OF PATHOLOGY: Journal of the Pathological Society of Great Britain and Ireland. 1969.
(Journal of Pathology and Bacteriology).
Longman Group Limited, 43/49 Annandale Street, Edinburgh, EH7 4AT.
12, † Experimental pathology, morbid anatomy and comparative pathology.
Book notices, book reviews, monographic articles, obituaries.
4m, —, Yes, None.
March 1972, T.p. 76.   3250.
Per copy £2.

2240 JOURNAL OF THE ROYAL COLLEGE OF SURGEONS OF EDINBURGH. 1955.
Royal College of Surgeons, 18 Nicolson Street, Edinburgh, EH8 9DW.
6, + * General surgery and the specialties—orthopaedic surgery, urology, neurosurgery, thoracic surgery, radiology, otolaryngology etc.; original articles on matters of topical interest.
Book reviews, monographic articles.
A, November, Yes, 5 year.
July 1970, T.p. 72.   7000.
Per copy £1, per year £5.

2241 LIFE SCIENCES. Pt. 1—Physiology and pharmacology. Pt. 2—Biochemistry, general and molecular biology.
Pergamon Press Ltd., Headington Hill Hall, Oxford, OX3 0BW.
26, = + Bio-medical science.
Book reviews, monographic articles.
A, Last issue of volume, Yes, None.
Per copy £1, per year £40 Pts. 1 & 2.

2242 PHYSICS IN MEDICINE AND BIOLOGY: the official journal of the Hospital Physicists Association. 1955.

The Institute of Physics, London and Bristol, Netherton
House, Marsh Street, Bristol, BS1 4BT.
Bi-monthly, + ‡   Applications of theoretical and practical physics to medicine, physiology, biology. Publishes original papers, review articles, abstracts.
Abstracts, book notices, book reviews, letters, monographic articles.
A, —, Yes, None.
March 1972, T.p. 173.
Per copy £4, per year £24.

616—002.5

TUBERCULOSIS

2243 BTTA REVIEW: Supplement to Tubercle, the journal of the British Thoracic and Tuberculosis Association. 1971.
E. & S. Livingstone Ltd., 5 Bentinck Street, London, W1M 5RN.
4, = ‡   All aspects of tuberculosis and related infections.
Articles.
No Index.
March 1972, T.p. 21.
With Tubercle.

2244 TUBERCLE: Journal of the British Thoracic and Tuberculosis Association.
Longman Group Ltd., 33 Montgomery Street, Edinburgh, EH7 5JX.
4, Medical   Tuberculosis in all its aspects—clinical bacteriological and epidemiological.
Book reviews, letters, monographic articles.
A, 1st. issue of each volume, Yes, 10 year.
March 1972, T.p. 56.
Per year £6.

616-002.73

LEPROSY

2245 LEPROSY REVIEW. 1930.
Academic Press Inc. (London) Ltd., (for British Leprosy Relief Association), 24-28 Oval Road, London, NW1.
4, ‡   Leprosy—field-work, research, administration.
Abstracts, book notices, book reviews, letters, monographic articles, obituaries, standards, tests.
A, With last Quarterly issue, No, None.
No. 1, 1969, T.p. 40.   1200.
Per year £3.

2246 PROJECT: The Leprosy Mission's Youth Magazine. 1972
(Into Orbit).
The Leprosy Mission, 50 Portland Place, London, W1N 3DG.
3, *   To inform young people of what The Leprosy Mission and other societies and govts. are doing for leprosy sufferers in 34 countries.
No Index.
May 1972, T.p. 8.   c. 10360.
Free.

616—006.6

CANCER

2247 BRITISH JOURNAL OF CANCER. 1947.
H. K. Lewis & Co. Ltd., 136 Gower Street, London, WC1E 6BS.
6, +   Clinical epidemiological, pathological or molecular aspects of oncology.
Book notices, letters, monographic articles.
A, December, Yes, None.
April, 1972 T.p. 70, Ad.p. 5.
Per copy £2, per year £10.
Indexed in: IBZ.

2248 EUROPEAN JOURNAL OF CANCER. 1964.
Pergamon Press Ltd., Headington Hill Hall, Oxford, OX3 0BW.
6, = ‡ +   All aspects of cancer.
Book reviews, letters, monographic articles.
A, —, Yes, None.
Per copy £5, per year £27.

616—053.2

PAEDIATRICS

2249 ARCHIVES OF DISEASE IN CHILDHOOD. 1926.
British Medical Association, B.M.A. House, Tavistock Square, London, WC1H 9JR.
12, = ‡ +   Child health and disease, with emphasis on clinical paediatrics.
Book reviews, letters, monographic articles, obituaries.
A, December, Yes, None.
June 1972, T.p. 150, Ad.p. 16.
Per year £12.

616—053.9

GERIATRICS

2250 AGE AND AGEING: Official Journal of the British Geriatrics Society and of the British Society for Research in Ageing. 1972.
Bailliere, Tindall & Cassell Ltd., 7-8 Henrietta Street, London, WC2 8QE.
4, = +   Gerontology and geriatrics, including research on ageing and the clinical, epidemiological and psychological aspects of medicine in old age.
Book notices, book reviews, letters, monographic articles.
A, —, Yes, None.
May 1972, T.p. 63, Ad.p. 10.
Per year £8.

2251 MODERN GERIATRICS: Devoted to the diseases of middle age and beyond. 1970.
Modern Medicine of Great Britain Ltd., Empire House, 414 High Road, London W4.
6, ‡   All aspects of geriatrics, of interest to general practitioners and geriatric physicians.
Abstracts, book reviews, letters, monographic articles, new products.
A, —, Yes, None.
May 1972, T.p. 33, Ad. p. 30.   26509.
Per copy 35p, per year £2. Free, controlled circulation.

616—074

LABORATORY TECHNOLOGY

2252 MEDICAL LABORATORY TECHNOLOGY. 1971.
(Laboratory Journal 1913-1950; Journal of Medical Laboratory Technology, 1951-1970).
Academic Press Inc. (London) Ltd., 24-28 Oval Road, London, NW1.
4, * ‡ +   Procedures, research and development in medical laboratory technology.
Book notices, book reviews, monographic articles, standards, tests.
A, October, Yes, None.
April 1972, T.p. 123, Ad. p. 40.   12000.
Per year £5.60.

Key to reference symbols

○ popular   ‡ technical   = trade/professional

+ research   * society/institution   † house journal

616—083
NURSING

2253 DISTRICT NURSING. 1958.
(Queen's Nurses' Magazine 1904-1958).
Queen's Institute of District Nursing, 57 Lower Belgrave Street, London, SW1W OLR.
12, ‡   Care of the patient in the community.
Book notices, book reviews, letters, new products, obituaries.
A, Integral part of March issue, No, None.
June 1972, T.p. 20, Ad. p. 9.   2300.
Per copy 12½p, per year £1.50.

2254 HEALTH VISITOR: The journal of the Health Visitors' Association. 1962.
(Woman Health Officer 1926-1961).
B. Edsall & Co. Ltd., 36 Eccleston, Square, London, SW1V 1PF.
12, * =   Medico/social nursing in the community
Book notices, book reviews, letters, monographic articles, obituaries, parliamentary reports.
A, December, Yes, None.
June 1972, T.p. 40, Ad. p. 18.   6381.
Per copy 15p, per year £1.50.

2255 INTERNATIONAL JOURNAL OF NURSING STUDIES. 1964.
Pergamon Press Ltd., Headington Hill Hall, Oxford, OX3 0BW.
4, = + ‡   All aspects of nursing.
Book reviews, monographic articles.
A, Last issue of volume, Yes, None.
T.p. 70.
Per copy £3.50, per year £12.

2256 JOURNAL OF THE INSTITUTE OF HOME HELP ORGANISERS. 1956.
The Institute, 15 Blackheath Road, Greenwich, London, SE10.
4, =
Letters, new companies, new products, obituaries, parliamentary reports, patents, standards, tests.
No Index.
T.p. 19.
Free to members.

2257 MIDWIFE AND HEALTH VISITOR. 1965.
Recorder Press Ltd., Recorder House, Church Street, London, N16.
12, =
Book notices, book reviews, letters, monographic articles, tests.
A, December, No, None.
T.p. 21, Ad. p. 22.
Free, controlled circulation.

2258 NATNEWS. 1965
National Association of Theatre Nurses, 6 Gordon Road, Windsor, Berks.
4, = *   Theatre nursing and allied medical topics.
Book reviews, letters, monographic articles, news, obituaries, reports, standards, tests.
No Index.
T.p. 18, Ad. p. 20.   3750.
Free to members.

2259 NURSING BIBLIOGRAPHY. 1972.
Royal College of Nursing, Henrietta Place, Cavendish Square, London, W1M 0AB.
12, =
No Index.
Per year £3.20.

2260 NURSING MIRROR. 1888.
IPC Business Press Ltd., Dorset House, Stamford Street, London, SE1.
52, ○ ‡   All nursing matters.
Book reviews, legal notes, letters, new products, obituaries, parliamentary reports.
6m, January/June, Yes, None.
T.p. c. 37, Ad.p. c. 160.   61000
Per copy 5p, per year £4.60.

2261 WORLD OF IRISH NURSING: Official journal of the Irish Nurses Organisation. 1972.
(Irish Nurses' Journal; Irish Nurse; Irish Nurses' Magazine.)
Maxwell Publicity Ltd., 49 Wainsfort Park, Dublin 6.
12, =
Book notices, book reviews, letters, articles, obituaries, No Index.
April 1972, T.p. 13.   5000.
Free to members

616—089.5
ANAESTHESIA

2262 ANAESTHESIA: official journal of the Association of Anaesthetists of Great Britain and Ireland. 1946.
Blackwell Scientific Publications, Osney Mead, Oxford.
6, ‡ + *   Anaesthetic techniques, equipment and drugs.
Book reviews, letters, monographic articles, new products, standards, tests.
A, January, Yes, None.
T.p. 100, Ad. p. 36.   5200.
Per year £6.

2263 ANAESTHESIA AND ANALGESIA. 1971.
A. E. Morgan Pub. Co. Ltd., 172 Kingston Road, Ewell, Epsom, Surrey.
4, = ‡
Book reviews, letters, monographic articles,
A, —, Yes, None.
Subscription on application.

2264 BRITISH JOURNAL OF ANAESTHESIA. 1923.
The St. Ann's Press, Park Road, Altrincham, Cheshire WA14 5QQ.
12, ‡ +   All branches of anaesthesia, including the application of basic sciences. 2 issues each year deal mainly with material of educational value. Anaesthetists, anesthesiologists and depts. of anaesthesia in hospitals and universities, dentists, vet. surgeons, pharmacologists and physiologists.
Abstracts, book notices, book reviews, letters, monographic articles, new products,
A, —, Yes, None.
1, 1971, T.p. 108.   6300.
Per year £6.50.

616.12
CARDIOLOGY

2265 BRITISH HEART JOURNAL: The official Journal of the British Cardiac Society. 1939.
British Medical Association, B.M.A. House, Tavistock Square, London WC1H 9JR.
12, * = + ‡   Original work on the heart and circulation—anatomical, physiological and pathological
Monographic articles, obituaries,
A, December, Yes, None.
June 1972, T.p. 104, Ad. p. 12.
Per year £12. Inland £12; Overseas £13 or £18 combined with Cardiovascular Research
Indexed in: IBZ.

2266 CARDIOVASCULAR RESEARCH: Published in association with the British Cardiac Society. 1967.
British Medical Association, BMA House, Tavistock Square, London WC1H 9JR.
6, = ‡ + *   Basic research in physiological, pathological, pharmacological, biochemical, biophysical, haemodynamic, surgical and similar advances in the study of the heart and circulation.

Book reviews, monographic articles, obituaries.
A, November, Yes, None.
May 1972, T.p. 102, Ad. p. 9.
Per year £8, or £18 combined with British Heart Journal.

2267 HEART: Journal of the British Heart Foundation. 1963.
British Heart Foundation, 57 Gloucester Place, London W1H 4DH.
3, ○ +   Research projects which are sponsored and financed by the Foundation. Articles are written to appeal to a lay as well as medical audience.
Letters, monographic articles.
No Index.
Summer 1972, T.p. 16.
Free to members

2268 HOPE: A magazine of Optimism. 1967.
(Cardiac Newsletter 1960-1967)
The Chest and Heart Association, Tavistock House North, Tavistock Square, London, WC1H 9JE.
4, ○   Articles written by doctors and members of para-medical services, as well as patients themselves. Of special interest to chest, heart and 'stroke' patients.
Book notices, book reviews, letters, articles.
No Index, None.
Per copy 25p, Per year £1.

2269 JOURNAL OF MOLECULAR AND CELLULAR CARDIOLOGY. 1970.
Academic Press Inc (London) Ltd., 24-28 Oval Road, London NW1.
6, ‡ +   Fundamental aspects of cardiology and the cardiovascular system at the cellular, sub-cellular and molecular levels etc.
Monographic articles.
A, End of each volume, Yes, None.
June 1972, T.p. 106.
Per copy £1.67, per year £10

616.15

HAEMATOLOGY

2270 BRITISH JOURNAL OF HAEMATOLOGY. 1955.
Blackwell Scientific Publications, Osney Mead, Oxford OX2 0EL
12, +   Original research in clinical, laboratory and experimental haematology.
Book notices, book reviews, letters, monographic articles,
6m, June/December, Yes, None.
June 1972, T.p. 146, Ad. p. 6.
Per copy £1.50, per year £15.
Indexed in: IBZ.

2271 CLINICS IN HAEMATOLOGY. 1972.
WB Saunders Company Limited, 12 Dyott Street, London, WC1A 1DB.
3, =   Concise, detailed descriptions and sound evaluations of established new methods of diagnosis and treatment, new advances in knowledge of the basic sciences, new drugs and new techniques in haematology.
Monographic articles.
Each issue, –, Yes, None.
T.p. c. 225
Per copy £4.50, per year £9.

616.2

DISEASES OF THE CHEST

2272 BRITISH JOURNAL OF DISEASES OF THE CHEST. 1959.
(Britsh Journal of Tuberculosis 1906-1958)
Bailliere, Tindall & Cassell Ltd., 7-8 Henrietta Street, Covent Garden, London WC2E 8QE.

4, = +   All aspects of diseases of the chest, their causes and treatment.
Book reviews, monographic articles, reports.
A, October, Yes, None.
October 1971, T.p. 67, Ad. p. 16.
Per copy £1.25, per year £4.

2273 THE JOURNAL OF LARYNGOLOGY AND OTOLOGY. 1887.
Headley Brothers Ltd., The Invicta Press, Ashford, Kent.
12, ‡ +   The science and practice of laryngology, otology and rhinology.
Monographic articles,
A, December, Yes, None.
January 1972, T.p. 104, Ad. p. 12.   c. 2200.
Per copy £1, per year £8.
Indexed in: IBZ

2274 THORAX: official journal of the Thorax Society. 1946.
British Medical Association, BMA House, Tavistock Square, London WC1H 9JR.
6, ‡ * + =   Original work on the anatomy, physiology and pathology of the chest and heart. Descriptions of techniques and apparatus used in modern cardiac surgery.
Monographic articles, obituaries.
A, November, Yes, None.
May 1972, T.p. 122, Ad. p. 9.
Per year £8.
Indexed in IBZ

616.3

GASTROENTEROLOGY

2275 CLINICS IN GASTROENTEROLOGY. 1972.
WB Saunders Company Limited, 12 Dyott Street, London WC1A 1DB.
3, =   Concise, detailed descriptions and sound evaluations of established new methods of diagnosis and treatment, new advances in knowledge of the basic sciences, new drugs and new techniques in gastroenterology.
Monographic articles.
Each issue, –, Yes, None.
T.p. c. 225.
Per copy £4.50, per year £9.

2276 GUT: Journal of the British Society of Gastroenterology. 1960.
British Medical Association, BMA House, Tavistock Square, London WC1H 9JR.
12, * ‡ + =   All aspects of gastroenterology.
Book reviews, monographic articles, obituaries.
A, December, Yes, other.
May 1972, T.p. 82, Ad. p. 10.
Per year £12.

616.314

DENTISTRY

2277 ARCHIVES OF ORAL BIOLOGY. 1956.
Pergamon Press Ltd., Headington Hill Hall, Oxford OX3 0BW.
12, = +   All aspects of investigation and action on oral and dental tissues and bone; their environment and functions.
Monographic articles.
A, Last issue of volume, Yes, None.
T.p. 120.
Per copy £4, per year £46.

2278 BRITISH DENTAL JOURNAL: journal of the British Dental Association. 1903.
(Monthly Review of Dental Surgery 1872-1879; journal of the British Dental Association 1880-1902)
The Association, 64 Wimpole Street, London W1M 8AL.

24, * + ‡ =   Dentistry in general.
Book notices, book reviews, letters, monographic articles, new products, obituaries, parliamentary reports, standards.
6m, August/February, Yes, None.
T.p. 45, Ad. p. 50.
Free to members.

2279 THE BRITISH DENTAL SURGERY ASSISTANT. 1957.
Association of British Dental Surgery Assistants, Bank Chambers, 3 Market Place, Poulton, Blackpool, Lancs.
11, * =
Letters and news.
No Index.
June 1972, T.p. 10, Ad. p. 5.   3000.
Per copy 15p, per year £1.50.

2280 BRITISH JOURNAL OF ORAL SURGERY. 1963.
The Longman Group Ltd., 33 Montgomery Street, Edinburgh EH7 5JX.
3, ‡ =   Oral surgery and oral pathology. Less specialised articles of value to general dental practitioners.
Book reviews, letters, articles,
No Index.
March 1972, T.p. 100, Ad. p. 12
Per year £4.50.

2281 DENTAL PRACTICE. 1969.
(Dental News 1962-1969)
A. E. Morgan Publications Ltd., 172, Kingston Road, Ewell, Epsom, Surrey.
12, ‡ =   Modern techniques, equipment and materials.
Book reviews, letters, articles, new products.
No Index.
T.p. 28, Ad. p. 11.   14200.
Per copy 25p, Per year £2.50 and Free, controlled circulation.

2282 DENTAL PRACTITIONER AND DENTAL RECORD. 1950.
John Wright & Sons Ltd., 42/44, Triangle West, Clifton, Bristol, BS8 1EX.
12, ‡ =   All aspects of dental treatment.
Book reviews, monographic articles, obituaries, tests.
A, August, Yes, None.
January 1972, T.p. 40, Ad. p. 14.   2000.
Per copy 45p, per year £4.50.

2283 THE DENTAL TECHNICIAN. 1948.
The Dental Technician Ltd., 203 Kings Cross Road, London, WC1X 9DB.
12, ‡ =   All aspects of dental technology.
Articles.
No Index.
June 1972, T.p. 8, Ad. p. 17.   3000.
Per copy 10p, per year £1.20.

2284 GLASGOW DENTAL JOURNAL. 1970.
University of Glasgow, Dental Hospital and School, 378 Sauchiehall Street, Glasgow C3.
2, = ‡
No Index.
Subscription on application.

2285 JOURNAL OF THE BRITISH ENDODONTIC SOCIETY. 1966.
Henry Evan & Co. Ltd., 53 Paddington St. London W1
4, =   Study and advance of endodontics.
Book reviews, letters, new products.
No Index.
T.p. 16, Ad. p. 8.
Per copy 25p, per year £1.

2286 JOURNAL OF THE IRISH DENTAL ASSOCIATION. 1956.
The Association, 29 Kenilworth Square, Dublin 6.
6, =
Book reviews, letters, monographic articles, news.

A, —, Yes, None.
T.p. 34, Ad. p. 18.
Free to members.

2287 THE PROBE: Journal of the General Dental Practitioners' Association. 1964.
Bouverie Publishing Co. Ltd. 2/3 Salisbury Court, Fleet Street, London EC4Y 8AB.
12, ‡ = + *   Dentistry as it affects the general dental practitioner: new ideas, review of equipment, dento/politics, books, letters, etc.
Book reviews, legal notes, letters, articles, new products, obituaries, standards, tests.
A, June, Yes, None.
May 1972, T.p. 27, Ad. p. 29.   14500.
Per copy £2.

616.4

ENDOCRINOLOGY

2288 CLINICAL ENDOCRINOLOGY. 1972.
Blackwell Scientific Publications, Osney Mead, Oxford OX2 0EL.
4, + =   Human endocrine disorder, its pathogenesis, diagnosis and treatment.
Book reviews, monographic articles,
A, October, Yes, None.
April 1972, T.p. 92, Ad. p. 4.
Per copy £2.25, per year £8.

2289 CLINICS IN ENDOCRINOLOGY AND METABOLISM. 1972.
WB Saunders Company Limited, 12 Dyott Street, London, WC1A 1DB.
3, =   Concise, detailed descriptions and sound evaluations of established new methods of diagnosis and treatment, new advances in knowledge of the basic sciences, new drugs and new techniques in endocrinology and metabolism.
Monographic articles.
Each issue, —, Yes, None.
T.p.c. 225.
Per copy £4.50, per year £9.

2290 JOURNAL OF ENDOCRINOLOGY. 1939.
Society of Endocrinology, Biochemical Society (Publications), P.O. Box No. 32, Commerce Way, Whitehall Industrial Estate, Colchester, Essex.
12, ‡ + *   Scientific papers on results of research in endocrinology and allied subjects.
Book reviews, monographic articles.
Q, at end of each volume (4 per year), Yes, Every 20 volumes.
June 1972, T.p. 171.
Per copy £3, per year £32 and free to members.
Indexed in: IBZ.

616.5

DERMATOLOGY

2291 TRANSACTIONS OF THE ST. JOHN'S HOSPITAL DERMATOLOGICAL SOCIETY.
St. John's Hospital Dermatological Society, 5, Lisle Street, London WC2H 7BJ.
2, *‡ +   Dermatology and related subjects.
Book reviews, monographic articles.
A, 2nd issue of year, Yes, None.
T.p. 123, Ad. p. 10
Per year £2.50.

616.594

TRICHOLOGY

2292 THE TRICHOLOGIST.
Institute of Trichologists, 228 Stockwell Road, Brixton, London SW9.

3/4 +
Book notices, book reviews, letters, articles, news.
No Index.
T.p. 17.   500.
Free to members.

616.6
UROLOGY

2293 BRITISH JOURNAL OF UROLOGY: official journal of the British Association of Urological Surgeons. 1928.
The Longman Group Ltd., 33 Montgomery Street, Edinburgh EH7 5JX.
6, †, =   All aspects of urology.
Book reviews, letters, monographic articles.
A, December, Yes, 10 year.
June 1972, T.p. 128, Ad. p. 23.   4000.
Per copy £1, per year £6.
Indexed in: IBZ.

616.72
RHEUMATIC DISEASES

2294 ARC: Magazine of the Arthritis and Rheumatism Council for Research. 1965.
Arthritis & Rheumatism Council, 8 Charing Cross Rd, London WC2.
3, ○   Items of general interest regarding arthritis and rheumatism with special reference to progress in research.
Monographic articles.
No Index.
Summer 1972, T.p. 20.   15000.
Per copy 5p, Free to members.

2295 ANNALS OF THE RHEUMATIC DISEASES: A journal of clinical rheumatology and connective tissue research. 1939.
British Medical Association, B.M.A. House, Tavistock Square, London WC1H 9JR.
6, ‡ + =   Every manifestation of the rheumatic diseases.
Book notices, book reviews, letters, monographic articles, obituaries.
A, November, Yes, None.
May 1972, T.p. 75, Ad. p. 15.
Per year £8.
Indexed in: IBZ.

2296 BRA REVIEW. 1950.
British Rheumatism & Arthritis Association, 1 Devonshire Place, London W1N 2BD.
4, * =
Book reviews, commodity prices, letters, articles, new products, obituaries, parliamentary reports.
2 yearly, –, Yes, None.
Spring 1972, T.p. 32, Ad. p. 4.   20000.
Per copy 15p, Free to members.

2297 RHEUMATOLOGY AND PHYSICAL MEDICINE. 1970.
(Annals of Physical Medicine 1951-1970)
Bailliere, Tindall & Cassell Ltd, 7-8, Henrietta Street, London WC2E 8QE.
4, = +   Rheumatic diseases in general.
Book reviews, monographic articles.
A, Last issue of year, Yes, None.
May 1972, T.p. 59, Ad. p. 10
Per copy £1.25, per year £3.75.

616.74
MUSCULAR DYSTROPHY

2298 MUSCULAR DYSTROPHY JOURNAL. 1957.
Muscular Dystrophy Group of Great Britain, 26 Borough High St. London, SE1 9QG.

4, ○ + *   Covers all aspects of Group activities, fund raising, research etc., includes articles of interest to sufferers, physically handicapped. Provides news of products and aids for physically handicapped.
Book reviews, letters, articles, new products, obituaries, parliamentary reports.
No Index.
T.p. 12, Ad. p. 3.   12000.
Free to members and others.

616.8
NEUROLOGY

2299 BRAIN. 1869.
Macmillan (Journals) Ltd, Brunel Road, Basingstoke, Hants.
4, + =   All aspects of neurology.
Book notices, book reviews, monographic articles.
A, December, Yes, None.
T.p. 232, Ad. p. 10
Per copy £1.25, per year £5.
Indexed in: IBZ.

2300 DEVELOPMENTAL MEDICINE AND CHILD NEUROLOGY. 1962.
(Cerebral Palsy Bulletin - 1958-1961)
Spastics International Medical Publications, 20-22 Mortimer Street, London W.1.
6, + =   Paediatrics and child neurology: covers all aspects of normal and abnormal child development.
Abstracts, book reviews, letters, monographic articles,
A, February, Yes, None.
T.p. 145, Ad. p. 1.   2500.
Per copy 50p, per year £6.30.

2301 INTERNATIONAL JOURNAL OF NEUROSCIENCE. 1970.
Gordon & Breach, 41/42 William 4th Street, London, WC2.
6, + ‡   Problems of nervous tissue, the nervous system, and behaviour, and all related and impinging areas of the subject, both theoretical and experimental.
Book notices, book reviews, letters, monographic articles, new products, tests.
No Index.
Subscription on application.

2302 JOURNAL OF NEUROCHEMISTRY. 1955.
Pergamon Press Ltd., Headington Hill Hall, Oxford, OX3 0BW.
12, = +   Metabolism and function of the nervous system.
Book notices, monographic articles.
A, Last issue of volume, Yes, None.
T.p. 125.
Per copy £3, per year £34.

2303 JOURNAL OF NEUROLOGY, NEUROSURGERY AND PSYCHIATRY. 1944.
British Medical Association, BMA House, Tavistock Square, London, WC1H 9JR.
6, + ‡ =   Current research, throwing light on practice in neurology, neurosurgery and psychiatry.
Book reviews, monographic articles, obituaries.
A, December, Yes, None.
June 1972, T.p. 134, Ad.p. 18.
Per year £8.
Indexed in: IBZ.

2304 NEUROPSYCHOLOGIA. 1963.
Pergamon Press Ltd., Headington Hill Hall, Oxford, OX3 0BW.
4, = +   Study and explanation of human behaviour from the neurological standpoint.
Book reviews, monographic articles.
A, Last issue of volume, Yes, None.
Per copy £4.50, per year £16.

616.832

PARAPLEGIA

2305 PARAPLEGIA. 1963.
The Longman Group Ltd., 33 Montgomery Street, Edinburgh, EH7 5JX.
4, ‡ = +   Concerning injuries and diseases of the spinal cord.
Book reviews, letters, monographic articles.
A, Last issue of each volume, No, None.
Per year £5.25.

616.853

EPILEPSY

2306 THE CANDLE: British Epilepsy Association. 1965.
(The Journal 1955-1965).
British Epilepsy Association, 3/6 Alfred Place, London, WC1 7ED.
2, ○ ‡ + *
Book notices, book reviews, letters, articles.
3 year, —, Yes, None.
Spring 1972, T.p. 47.   5000.
Free to members.

616.857

MIGRAINE

2307 HEMICRANIA: Journal of the Migraine Trust. 1969.
The Migraine Trust, 23 Queen Square, London, WC1N 3AY.
4, +   Reports on research findings and discussion of various aspects of migraine and its treatment.
Abstracts, monographic articles.
A, With first issue of next volume, No, None.
Vol. 1, No. 4 1972, T.p. 13, Ad.p. 2.   17500.
Free to members.

2308 MIGRAINE NEWS. 1967.
The Migraine Trust, 23 Queen Square, London, WC1N 3AY.
4, *   News of research, membership activities, profiles of personalities and bodies associated with the Migraine Trust, discussion of and suggestions on aspects of migraine.
Book notices, book reviews, monographic articles, obituaries.
No Index.
June 1972, T.p. 4.   10000.
Per year 25p.

616.89

MENTAL DISORDERS. PSYCHIATRY

2309 BRITISH JOURNAL OF MEDICAL PSYCHOLOGY. 1922.
(British Journal of Psychology, Medical Section 1920-1922).
Cambridge University Press (for the British Psychological Society), PO Box 92, London, NW1 2DB.
4, +   Psychology and mental illness and physical diseases having psychological components.
Book reviews, monographic articles.
A, December, Yes, None.
June 1972, T.p. 99, Ad.p. 4.   2050.
Per copy £2.25, per year £6.50.
Indexed in: IBZ.

2310 BRITISH JOURNAL OF PSYCHIATRY: The Journal of Mental Science. 1963.
(Journal of Mental Science? 1856).
Headley Brothers Ltd., (for the Royal College of Psychiatrists), The Invicta Press, Ashford, Kent.
12, + *   Includes work done in every psychiatric field and to reflect every school of thought within the specialty. Contributions on psychology, sociology, anthropology and other related subjects are welcome insofar as they have relevance to clinical psychiatry.
Book notices, book reviews, letters, monographic articles, parliamentary reports.
6m, Bound in June and Dec. issues, Yes, None.
June 1972, T.p. 116, Ad.p. 22.   7000.
Per copy £1.50, per year £15.

2311 BRITISH JOURNAL OF SOCIAL PSYCHIATRY AND COMMUNITY HEALTH. 1967.
Avenue Publishing Co., 18 Park Avenue, London, NW11.
4, ‡ + =   Psychiatry, sociology, psychology, social work, nursing, educational, general medical practice.
Book notices, book reviews, letters, monographic articles, obituaries, parliamentary reports, tests.
No Index.
T.p. 70, Ad.p. 4.   2000.
Per year £3.

2312 COMMENTS ON CONTEMPORARY PSYCHIATRY. 1971.
Gordon & Breach, 41/42 William 4th Street, London, WC2.
6, ○ +   Psychiatry and clinical psychology.
Book notices, book reviews, letters, monographic articles, tests.
No Index.
Subscription on application.

2313 ENERGY AND CHARACTER: The Journal of Bioenergetic Research. 1970.
Abbotsbury Publications, Abbotsbury, Weymouth, Dorset.
3, +   The study of emotional health as a biological energy process, the understanding of self-expression in bodily movements and social behaviour.
Book notices, book reviews, monographic articles, obituaries, tests.
Occasional, —, Yes, None.
January 1972, T.p. 82, Ad.p. 1.   800.
Per copy 75p, per year £2.

2314 INTERNATIONAL JOURNAL OF SOCIAL PSYCHIATRY. 1957.
Avenue Publishing Co., 18 Park Avenue, London, NW11.
4, ‡ + =   Psychiatry, sociology, psychology, social work, nursing, educational, general medical practice.
Book notices, book reviews, letters, monographic articles, obituaries, parliamentary reports, tests.
No Index.
T.p. 70, Ad.p. 4.   2000.
Per year £3.

2315 JOURNAL OF BEHAVIOUR THERAPY AND EXPERIMENTAL PSYCHIATRY. 1970.
Pergamon Press Ltd., Headington Hill Hall, Oxford, OX3 0BW.
4, = +
Book notices, book reviews, monographic articles.
A, Last issue of volume, Yes, None.
Per copy £4.50, per year £16.

2316 JOURNAL OF MENTAL DEFICIENCY RESEARCH. 1957.
National Society for Mentally Handicapped Children, 86 Newman Street, London, W1.
4, + = *   Biochemistry, cytogenetics, neuropathology, paediatric and psychology of mental deficiency.
Book reviews, monographic articles.
A, —, Yes, None.
December, 1971, T.p. 80, Ad.p. 12.
Per copy 75p, per year £4.60.
Indexed in: IBZ.

2317 JOURNAL OF MENTAL SUBNORMALITY. 1954.
Midland Society for the Study of Mental Subnormality, Monyhull Hospital, Birmingham, 30.
2, * + =   Practical aspects of the work.

Book reviews, letters, monographic articles.
A, —, Yes, None.
T.p. 50, Ad.p. 4.
Subscription on application.

2318 **JOURNAL OF PSYCHIATRIC RESEARCH.** 1963.
Pergamon Press Ltd., Headington Hill Hall, Oxford, OX3 0BW.
4, = +   Psychiatry and cognate subjects.
Book reviews, monographic articles.
A, Last issue of volume, Yes, None.
Per copy £5, per year £16.

2319 JOURNAL OF PSYCHOSOMATIC RESEARCH. 1956.
Pergamon Press Ltd., Headington Hill Hall, Oxford, OX3 0BW.
6, + =   Psychosomatic medicine.
Book reviews, monographic articles.
A, Last issue of volume, Yes, None.
T.p. 100.
Per copy £4, per year £18.

2320 MENTAL HEALTH. 1940.
National Association for Mental Health, 39 Queen Anne Street, London, W1.
4, * = ○
Book reviews, monographic articles, news.
No Index.
T.p. 43, Ad.p. 5.
Free to members.

2321 MIND AND MENTAL HEALTH MAGAZINE. 1971.
(Mental Health magazine).
National Association for Mental Health, 39 Queen Anne Street, London W1 AOJ.
4, ‡ + * =   Problems of stress and human relations. Reports on trends in the promotion of mental health and in the care of the emotionally ill.
Book notices, book reviews, letters, monographic articles.
No Index.
Spring 1972, T.p. 48, Ad.p. 2.   6500.
Per copy 20p, per year 80p.

2322 PSYCHOLOGICAL MEDICINE: A Journal for research in psychiatry and the allied sciences. 1970.
British Medical Association, BMA House, Tavistock Square, London, WC1H 9JR.
4, ‡   Original research in clinical psychiatry and the basic sciences related to it.
Book reviews, monographic articles, obituaries.
A, November, Yes, None.
May 1972, T.p. 106, Ad.p. 10.
Per year £6.

616.97

VENEREAL DISEASES

2323 BRITISH JOURNAL OF VENEREAL DISEASES: The Journal of the Medical Society for the Study of Venereal Diseases. 1925.
British Medical Association, BMA House, Tavistock Square, London WC1H 9JR.
6, * = ‡ +   Designed to disseminate, exchange and increase knowledge among consultants, practitioners, research workers, teachers and others concerned with the problem of venereal diseases.
Book reviews, monographic articles, obituaries.
A, December, Yes, None.
April 1972, T.p. 70, Ad.p. 4.
Per year £8.
Indexed in: IBZ.

616.995

HELMINTHOLOGY

2324 JOURNAL OF HELMINTHOLOGY. 1923.
London School of Hygiene & Tropical Medicine, Keppel Street, London, WC1.
4, * = + ‡   All aspects of helminthology.
Monographic articles.
A, Last issue of year, Yes, None.
T.p. 129.
Per year £3.50.

617

SURGERY

2325 ANNALS OF THE ROYAL COLLEGE OF SURGEONS OF ENGLAND. 1947.
The Royal College of Surgeons of England, 35/43 Lincoln's Inn Fields, London, WC2A 3PN.
12, ‡ = + *   Surgical, dental surgery, anaesthetic and research topics.
Monographic articles, obituaries, tests.
6m, —, Yes, A.
January 1972, T.p. 52, Ad.p. 14.   10500.
Per copy 50p, per year £7.

2326 BRITISH JOURNAL OF PLASTIC SURGERY. 1947.
The Longman Group Ltd., 33 Montgomery Street, Edinburgh EH7 5JX.
4, =
Book reviews, monographic articles.
A, October, Yes, 10 year.
T.p. 100, Ad.p. 5.   3000.
Per copy £1.25p, per year £5.

2327 BRITISH JOURNAL OF SURGERY. 1913.
John Wright & Sons Ltd., 42/44, Triangle West, Clifton, Bristol. BS8 1EX.
12, ‡ = +   Surgery & surgical research.
Book reviews, monographic articles, obituaries, tests.
A, December, Yes, 10 year.
April, 1972, T.p. 84, Ad.p. 24.   6500.
Per copy £1, per year £10.

617.3

ORTHOPAEDICS

2328 JOURNAL OF BONE AND JOINT SURGERY. 1918.
The Longman Group Ltd., 33 Montgomery Street, Edinburgh EH7 5JX.
4, ‡ + =   Treatment of injuries of bone, muscles, nerves or skin.
Book reviews, monographic articles.
A, November, Yes, None.
T.p. 226, Ad.p. 46.   20000.
Per year £3.10.

617.5

HANDS

2329 THE HAND: Journal of the British Society for Surgery of The Hand. 1969.
Longman's Group, 33 Montgomery St., Edinburgh, EH7 5JX.
3, = ‡   For surgeons and practitioners in other disciplines with a particular interest in surgery of the hand.
Book reviews, monographic articles, new products, obituaries.
5 year, 1974, Yes, None.
June 1972, T.p. 100, Ad.p. 11.   1500.
Per copy £2, per year £6.

617.7

OPHTHALMOLOGY

2330 BRITISH JOURNAL OF OPHTHALMOLOGY. 1917.
British Medical Association, B.M.A. House, Tavistock Square, London, WC1H 9JR.
12, ‡ = +   Designed for the clinician and research worker and includes original articles, case notes, information on new appliances, book reviews.
Book reviews, monographic articles, obituaries.
A, December, Yes, 10 year.
April 1972, T.p. 64, Ad.p. 25.
Per year £12 or £21 combined with Ophthalmic Literature.
Indexed in: IBZ.

2331 BRITISH JOURNAL OF PHYSIOLOGICAL OPTICS. 1925.
British Optical Association, 65 Brook Street, London, W1Y 2DT.
Irregular, *   Visual optics and related subjects.
Abstracts, book notices, book reviews, monographic articles.
A, First issue of next volume, No, None.
T.p. 72.   5000.
Free to members.
Indexed in: IBZ.

2332 BRITISH ORTHOPTIC JOURNAL. 1938.
British Orthoptic Society, Tavistock House (North), Tavistock Square, London, WC1.
1, * =   Diagnosis and treatment of defects of binocular vision.
Book notices, book reviews, commodity prices, monographic articles, new products, obituaries, standards, tests.
5 year, 1972, Yes, None.
1969, T.p. 148, Ad.p. 18.   2000.
Per copy £1.05.

2333 THE CONTACT LENS. 1966.
O.S. & S. Ltd., 14 Peterborough Rd., Harrow, Middx.
4, ‡ =   For all concerned with contact lenses, practising, fitting, researching, manufacturing: but not for the layman.
Book notices, book reviews, letters, monographic articles, new products, reports, standards, tests.
A, Last issue of volume, Yes, None.
Subscription on application.

2334 THE DISPENSING OPTICIAN. 1935.
The Association of Dispensing Opticians, 22 Nottingham Place, London, W1M 4AT.
8, = ‡ *   Practice and science of optical dispensing.
Abstracts, book notices, book reviews, letters, monographic articles, new products, obituaries, parliamentary reports.
No Index.
May/June 1972, T.p. 37, Ad.p. 38.   3500.
Per copy 15p, per year £1.25.

2335 EXPERIMENTAL EYE RESEARCH. 1961.
Academic Press Inc.(London) Ltd., 28-28 Oval Road, London, NW1.
6, +   Original research on the anatomy, physiology, biochemistry, and biophysics of the eye.
Book reviews, monographic articles.
A, October, Yes, None.
July 1972, T.p. 85, Ad.p. 2.   1000.
Per year £22.

2336 MANUFACTURING OPTICS INTERNATIONAL. 1969.
(Manufacturing Optician 1947-1966; Manufacturing Optician International 1967-1968).
Hatton Press Ltd., 69 Aldwych, London, WC2.
12, = + ‡   Current developments in optics.
Book notices, book reviews, letters, monographic articles, new companies, new products.
A, July, Yes, None.
T.p. 33, Ad.p. 34.
Free, controlled circulation.

2337 OPHTHALMIC LITERATURE. 1947.
British Medical Association, B.M.A. House, Tavistock Square, London, WC1H 9JR.
6, ‡   Abstracts of articles on the wide field of ophthalmology published throughout the world. Each volume contains some 5,000 abstracts—covering one year.
Abstracts.
A, June, No, None.
March 1972, T.p. 83, Ad.p. 2.
Per year £12, or £21 Combined with British Journal of Ophthalmology.

2338 THE OPHTHALMIC OPTICIAN. 1960.
British Optical Association and Association of Optical Practitioners, 65 Brook Street, London W1Y 2DT.
25, + * =   Reporting the clinical and news developments of British ophthalmic optics.
Book reviews, legal notes, letters, articles, new products.
A, —, Yes, None.
June 10, 1972, T.p. 16, Ad.p. 35.   7595.
Per copy 15p, per year £4.50.

2339 OPTICS TECHNOLOGY. 1968.
IPC & Technology Publications Ltd., 32 High Street, Guildford, Surrey.
4, = + ‡   Optical methods and their applications in Science and industry.
Book reviews, letters, monographic articles, new products.
A, February, Yes, None.
T.p. 47, Ad.p. 8.   900.
Per copy £1.50, per year £6.

2340 THE SCOTTISH OPTICIAN. 1951.
The Scottish National Committee of Ophthalmic Opticians, 38 Chalmers Street, Dunfermline.
12, ‡ = *   Ophthalmic optical matters, and reports on optical matters generally.
Book reviews, legal notes, letters, articles, new products, obituaries, parliamentary reports, patents, standards, tests.
No Index.
June 1972, T.p. 19, Ad.p. 12.   1000.
Per copy 10p, per year £1.36.

2341 TRANSACTIONS OF THE OPHTHALMOLOGICAL SOCIETIES OF THE UNITED KINGDOM. 1962.
(Transactions of the Ophthalmological Society of the United Kingdom 1880-1961).
Churchill/Livingstone, 104 Gloucester Place, London, W1.
1, ‡ * =   Papers read at the Annual Congress of the Ophthalmological Society of the United Kingdom, the Oxford Ophthalmological Congress and at meetings of the Societies affiliated to the O.S.U.K.
A, February, No, 10 year.
1971, T.p. 956.   c. 1700.
Per copy £5.
Free to Members.

618

GYNAECOLOGY

2342 THE JOURNAL OF OBSTETRICS AND GYNAECOLOGY OF THE BRITISH COMMONWEALTH. 1961.
(The Journal of Obstetrics and Gynaecology of the British Empire. 1902-1960.)
The Royal College of Obstetricians and Gynaecologists, 27 Sussex Place, Regent's Park, London, NW1.
12, ‡ +   Obstetrics and gynaecology, and any related science.
Book reviews, monographic articles.

A, January of succeeding year, Yes, None.
6, 1972, T.p. 96, Ad.p. 28.   Over 5000.
Per copy 75p, per year £6.50.

618.2

OBSTETRICS

2343 MIDWIVES CHRONICLE: Official Journal of the Royal College of Midwives.
(Nursing Notes 1887).
Nursing Notes Ltd., 98 Belsize Lane, London, NW3 5BB.
12, ‡ =   Midwifery and allied subjects.
Book notices, book reviews, letters, monographic articles, obituaries, parliamentary reports.
A, December, Yes, None.
June 1972, T.p. 17, Ad.p. 22.   19000.
Per copy 6p, per year £1.05.

619

VETERINARY SCIENCE

2344 BRITISH VETERINARY JOURNAL. 1949.
(Veterinary Journal 1875-1948).
Bailliere Tindall & Cassell Ltd., 7-8 Henrietta Street, Covent Garden, London, WC2E 8QE.
12, = +   Study & practice of veterinary medicine and recording scientific progress in the field.
Book notices, book reviews, monographic articles.
A, December, Yes, None.
February 1972, T.p. 55, Ad.p. 4.
Per copy £1, per year £8.
Indexed in: IBZ.

2345 EQUINE VETERINARY JOURNAL: Official Journal of the British Equine Veterinary Association. 1968.
Henderson Group One, 1 Roberts Mews, Lowndes Place, London SW1X 8DA.
4, ‡   Devoted exclusively to equine veterinary surgery; containing papers on original clinical observations in all aspects of equine veterinary surgery and medicine; abstracts of papers in overseas journals.
Abstracts, book reviews, articles.
A, October, Yes, None.
April 1972, T.p. 61, Ad.p. 6.   1500.
Per copy £2.50, per year £9.

2346 INDEX OF VETERINARY SPECIALITIES. 1960.
NC Magazines, 172 Kingston Road, Ewell, Surrey.
6, = + ‡   Index listing ethical veterinary preparations in the U.K.
New products.
No Index.
T.p. 61, Ad.p. 26.
Subscription on application.

2347 INDEX VETERINARIUS. 1933
Commonwealth Agricultural Bureaux, Farnham Road, Slough, SL2 3BN.
12, = + ‡   Index of 16000 titles of veterinary literature and of related literature such as medicine, physiology and bacteriology.
Q, —, Yes, A.
Per year £11.25 to subscribers.

2348 JOURNAL OF COMPARATIVE PATHOLOGY. 1965.
(Journal of Comparative Pathology and Therapeutics 1888-1964).
Liverpool University Press, 123 Grove Street, Liverpool, L7 7AF.
4, + =   Original research over the whole field of veterinary science-pathology, microbiology, parasitology, immunology, and biochemistry-and the animal species dealt with include domestic, laboratory, and wild animals.
Monographic articles.
A, October, Yes, None.
April 1972, T.p. 124, Ad.p. 2.   850.
Per copy £2.50, per year £10.
Indexed in: IBZ.

2349 JOURNAL OF SMALL ANIMAL PRACTICE: An International Journal sponsored by the British Small Animal Veterinary Association. 1960.
Blackwell Scientific Publications, Osney Mead, Oxford, OX2 0EL.
12, ○ +   Original research papers and clinical reports having a direct bearing on small animal veterinary practice throughout the world. Also the official publication of the World Small Animal Veterinary Association.
Book reviews, letters, monographic articles.
A, December, Yes, None.
May 1972, T.p. 72, Ad.p. 8.   2200.
£1.75, per year £18.

2350 RESEARCH IN VETERINARY SCIENCE: a journal of the British Veterinary Association. 1960.
Blackwell Scientific Publications, Osney Mead, Oxford, OX2 0EL.
6, + * =   Contributions to the knowledge on the health and disease of animals including studies in comparative medicine.
Letters, monographic articles.
A, November, No, None.
May 1972, T.p. 102, Ad.p. 4.   1000.
Per copy £2.25, per year £11.

2351 TROPICAL ANIMAL HEALTH AND PRODUCTION. 1969.
The Longman Group Ltd., (for Centre for Tropical Veterinary Medicine), 33 Montgomery Street, Edinburgh, EH7 5JX.
4, = ‡ *   Veterinary medicine and animal production, and the utilisation of animal resources.
Book reviews, letters, monographic articles.
A, Last issue of year, Yes, None.
May 1972, T.p. 44.   1000.
Per year £6.

2352 VETERINARY NEWS: newspaper for the Veterinary Surgeon. 1965.
NC Magazines Ltd., 172 Kingston Road, Ewell, Surrey.
12, =
Book reviews, articles, new companies, new products, parliamentary reports, tests.
No Index.
T.p. 6, Ad.p. 6.
Per copy 5p, per year 75p.

2353 THE VETERINARY RECORD: Journal of the British Veterinary Association. 1888.
British Veterinary Association, 7 Mansfield Street, London, W1M 0AT.
52, + =   Scientific and clinical matters of veterinary and allied subjects such as agriculture.
Book reviews, letters, monographic articles, obituaries, parliamentary reports.
6m, —, Yes, None.
April 15, 1972, T.p. 34, Ad.p. 36.   7500.
Per copy 35p, per year £15. Free to members.

2354 VETERINARY SCIENCE. 1931.
Commonwealth Agricultural Bureaux, Farnham Royal, Slough, SL2 3BN.
12, = + ‡   Veterinary and related sciences.
Abstracts.
A, —, Yes, None.
T.p. c.42.
Per year £14 to subscribers.

Key to reference symbols

○ popular   ‡ technical   = trade/professional

+ research   * society/institution   † house journal

62

ENGINEERING

2355 APEX: The technical journal of Amalgamated Power Engineering Ltd. 1969.
(Allen Engineering Review: 1939-1968 (also Crossley Chronicles)).
Amalgamated Power Engineering Limited, Bedford.
3, ‡ † +   Technical features, developments, and application of the products of APE member companies.
Monographic articles, new products.
No Index.
March 1972, T.p. 34.   10000.
Free.

2356 BEMA BULLETIN. 1945.
BEMA Ltd., Royal London House, Queen Charlotte St., Bristol, BS1 4EZ.
12, ○ = ‡ *   Trade association magazine covering members' products, capacities, and employees, especially in the West of England.
Book reviews, letters, articles, new companies, new products, obituaries, standards.
No Index.
June 1972, T.p. 15, Ad.p. 25.   1100.
Free.

2357 BLUEPRINT. 1970.
Engineering ITB, St. Martin's House, 140 Tottenham Court Road, London, W1P 9LN.
4, ‡ =   News and policies about systematic training in the engineering industry.
Legal notes, letters, articles, parliamentary reports.
5 year, —, No, None.
June 1972, T.p. 8.
Free.

2358 BRITISH ENGINE TECHNICAL REPORT. 1952.
Longridge House, Manchester, M60 4DT.
1, ‡   Reports on investigation into causes of failure of engineering components in service. Specialist articles on related subjects, non-destructive testing, fatigue, corrosion, etc.
Monographic articles.
10 year, 1971, Yes, None.
1971, Vol. 10, T.p. 84.   10000.
Per copy £1.

2359 BRITISH ENGINEER: Journal of the Institution of British Engineers. 1928.
Henry Publications Ltd., 3 Marlborough Place, Brighton, Sussex.
6, * = ‡   Current engineering topics of all kinds, with special emphasis on new ideas, techniques and developments available, inventiveness and manpower that will lead to greater efficiency, productivity and reliability.
Book notices, book reviews, legal notes, letters, monographic articles, new products, obituaries, patents, standards.
A, March, No, None.
May 1972, T.p. 27, Ad.p. 17.   7911.
Per copy 20p, per year £1.20 and Free to members.

2360 THE CONSULTING ENGINEER. 1946.
Construction Publications Ltd. (an associate company of Northwood Publications Ltd., part of The Thomson Organisation Ltd.), Elm House, 10-16 Elm Street, London, WC1X 0BP.
12, ‡ =   Engineers' function in the concept, design, supervision and construction of capital projects including heating, ventilating and electrical installations plus management, economics and politics affecting the running of a consultancy.
Book notices, book reviews, legal notes, letters, articles, new companies, new products, parliamentary reports, patents, standards, tests.
A, December, Yes, None.
June 1972, T.p. 33, Ad.p. 71.   5152.
Per year £3.

2362 DESIGN AND COMPONENTS IN ENGINEERING. 1961.
Engineering, Chemical & Marine Press Ltd., Bowling Green Lane, London, EC4.
22, + ‡ =   News of design ingenuity from world sources. Production techniques.
Book notices, book reviews, letters, new products, tests.
No Index.
T.p. 38, Ad.p. 38.   19000.
Free, controlled circulation

2363 DESIGN ENGINEERING: The ideas journal for design engineers. 1964
Morgan Grampian (Publishers) Limited, Morgan-Grampian House, Calderwood Street, London, SE18 6QH.
12, ‡   Design developments in all fields of mechanical, hydraulic, electrical, electronic and materials engineering.
Book reviews, legal notes, letters, monographic articles, new products, patents, standards, tests.
No Index.
June 1972, T.p. 78, Ad.p. 150.   20254.
Per copy £1, per year £10 and Free, controlled circulation.

2364 DISPOSABLES AND NONWOVENS. 1970.
Brooklands Press Ltd., 44 Hatton Garden, London, EC1N 8AE.
4, ‡ =   All aspects of the disposable industry, raw materials, process machinery, making-up and marketing.
Book reviews, articles, new products, patents, standards, tests.
No Index.
Free, controlled circulation.

2365 THE ENGINEER: The Weekly for Engineering Management. 1856.
Morgan-Grampian Ltd., Morgan-Grampian House, Calderwood St., London, SE18 6QH.
52, = ‡ +   Authoritative news and feature coverage for engineers who hold executive positions in manufacturing industry. Editorial content presents a balanced view of engineering technology and engineering management, with particular emphasis on specific areas—design, production, factory management, and research and development—in the context of manufacturing activity as a whole.
Book reviews, letters, monographic articles, new products.
None now, but 100 year index published.
13-7-1972, T.p. 41, Ad.p. 41.   28718.
Per copy 50p, per year £20, and Free, controlled circulation.
Indexed in: BTI, IBZ.

2366 ENGINEERING DESIGNER. 1955.
F. P. Kennett, 1 Earls Lane, South Mimms, Potters Bar, Herts.
12, = +
Book notices, book reviews, letters, monographic articles, new products, standards.
5 year, January, No, None.
T.p. 24, Ad.p. 2.   7700.
Per copy $12\frac{1}{2}$p, per year £1.50.
Free to members.
Indexed in: BTI.

2367 ENGINEERING FRACTURE MECHANICS.
Pergamon Press Ltd., Headington Hill Hall, Oxford, OX3 0BW.
4, = +   Research and advanced applications of fracture mechanics.
Book reviews, monographic articles.
A, Last issue of volume, Yes, None.
Per copy £6.50, per year £24.

2368 ENGINEERING IN MEDICINE. 1971.
Medical Engineering Working Party, The Institution of Mechanical Engineers, 1 Birdcage Walk, London, SW1H 9JJ.
4, ‡ +   Covers subjects from instrumentation, equipment, hospital services and orthopaedics to aids to diagnosis, etc., with technical and general interest articles plus hospital, overseas and general news.
Book notices, book reviews, monographic articles, new products.
A, October, Yes, None.
T.p. 24, Ad.p. 8.   600.
Per copy 65p, per year £2.50.

2369 ENGINEERING MATERIALS AND DESIGN. 1958
IPC Industrial Press Ltd., 33-39 Bowling Green Lane, London, EC1.
12, ‡   Design engineering in all aspects.
Book notices, book reviews, legal notes, letters, monographic articles, new products, patents, standards, tests.
A, January, Yes, None.
T.p. 30, Ad.p. 70.   27000.
Per copy £1, per year £12.
Indexed in: BTI.

2370 ENGINEERING PRODUCTION. 1970.
IPC Industrial Press Ltd., 33-39 Bowling Green Lane, London, EC1.
22, ‡   Production methods and processes.
Book notices, book reviews, commodity prices, legal notes, letters, monographic articles, new companies, new products, obituaries, patents, standards, tests.
A, —, Yes, None.
T.p. 30, Ad.p. 70.   1500.
Per copy £2, per year £1.

2371 ENGINEERS DIGEST. 1940.
Engineers Digest Ltd., 120 Wigmore Street, London, W1.
12, + ‡   International review of design and production, research and development.
Book notices, book reviews, letters, abstracts, articles.
A, February, Yes, None.
T.p. 63, Ad.p. 57.   8000.
Per copy 30p, per year £3.50.
Indexed in: BTI.

2372 ENVIRONMENTAL ENGINEERING: journal of the Society of Environmental Engineers. 1962.
Policy Journals Ltd., 13-14 Homewell, Havant, Hants.
6, * = +   All aspects of environmental engineering; stock, vibration, climatic, contamination.
Book notices, book reviews, letters, monographic articles, new companies, new products, obituaries, standards, tests.
A, January, No, None.
T.p. 20, Ad.p. 6.
Per copy 37½p, per year £4.25.
Indexed in: BTI.

2373 THE HOUSE JOURNAL OF KENNEDY AND DONKIN. 1950.
Kennedy & Donkin, Consulting Engineers, Premier House, Percy Street, Woking, Surrey.
2, †   Technical articles associated with specific projects and more general subjects connected with the work of the firm. News items concerning work progress, branch offices, staff and social activities.
No Index.
Free.

2374 THE HOYT NOTCHED INGOT. 1929.
The Hoyt Metal Co of London Ltd., Deodar Road, Putney, London, SW15 2NX.
3, ○ ‡ †   An engineering review and miscellany.
Book reviews, monographic articles, new products.
No Index.
March 1972, T.p. 36.
Free.

2375 HUNTING GROUP REVIEW. 1951.
Hunting Group Ltd., 4 Dunraven Street, Park Lane, London, W1Y 4HN.
4, †   Covering the Hunting Group's interests in: shipping, oil, aviation, survey, industrial, engineering.
Articles, new companies, new products, reports, patents, standards, tests.
No Index.
Summer 1972, T.p. 24.   13000.
Free.

2376 INTERNATIONAL JOURNAL OF ENGINEERING SCIENCE. 1963.
Pergamon Press Ltd., Headington Hill Hall, Oxford, OX3 0BW.
12, = +   Applications of physics, chemistry and mathematical sciences to engineering.
Monographic articles.
A, In last issue of volume, Yes, None.
T.p. 100.
Per copy £3.50, per year £40.

2377 JOURNAL OF THE INSTITUTE OF ENGINEERS AND TECHNICIANS LTD. 1968.
Swifts (Luton) Ltd., Stewart St., Luton, Beds.
4, † ‡   Engineering interests in general, including management.
Book reviews, letters, articles, new products, obituaries, patents, standards, tests.
No Index.
Summer 1972, T.p. 19, Ad.p. 1.   3000.
Per copy 25p, per year £1.
Free to members.

2378 THE JOURNAL OF THE INSTITUTION OF MUNICIPAL ENGINEERS. 1965.
(1873-1878 Papers presented at meetings were collected and printed. Volume I of the Institution's Proceedings started.
1878-1913 Proceedings of the Institution.
1913-1962 The Journal of the Institution of Municipal and County Engineers.
1962-1965 The Chartered Municipal Engineer.)
The Institution of Municipal Engineers, 25 Eccleston Square, London, SW1V 1NX.
12, ‡ + *
Book notices, legal notes, letters, monographic articles, obituaries, parliamentary reports, patents, standards, tests.
A, January following year of publication, Yes, None.
May 1972, T.p. 24, Ad.p. 17.   11145.
Per copy 50p, per year £6.
Indexed in: BTI.

2379 JOURNAL OF THE JUNIOR INSTITUTION OF ENGINEERS. 1891.
(Junior Engineering Society Transactions 1884-1890).
The Institution, 33 Ovington Square, London, SW3.
12, * = ‡ +   All disciplines of engineering and related sciences.
Book reviews, letters, monographic articles, new products.
A, September, Yes, 5 year.
T.p. 36, Ad.p. 6.   3500.
Per copy 25p, per year £3. Free to members.

2380 JOURNAL OF THE LONDON ASSOCIATION OF ENGINEERS.
The Association, 12 St. Martin's Drive, Eynsford, Dartford, Kent.
4, * = ‡
Articles, news.
No Index.
T.p. 28, Ad.p. 5.
Free to members.

2381 THE MANCHESTER ENGINEER. 1892.
(Manchester Association of Engineers Transactions)
The Manchester Association of Engineers, c/o The

M.T.A. Office, U.M.I.S.T., Sackville Street, Manchester.
1, ‡ Various problems, aspects etc. in the engineering field.
No Index.
Per year £1.

2382 THE MATRIX AND TENSOR QUARTERLY. 1950.
The Tensor Society of Gt. Britain, 66 South Terrace, Surbiton, Surrey.
4, ‡ + * Devoted to the application of determinants, matrices, vectors, dyadics and tensors to the engineering and physical sciences.
Book reviews, letters, monographic articles, obituaries, standards, tests.
No Index.
June 1972, T.p. 48.   500.
Per year £2.

2383 NEWS LETTER. 1948.
Renold Limited, Renold House, Wythenshawe, Manchester, M22 5WL.
5, † ‡ Devoted mainly to articles covering usage of the company's products. There are from time to time, announcements of new products, new premises and other company news of a major nature.
Articles, new products.
No Index.
T.p. 14.   40000.
Free to customers.

2384 PROCEEDINGS OF THE SOUTH WALES INSTITUTE OF ENGINEERS. 1857.
The Institute, Park Place, Cardiff.
3, ‡ * All aspects of engineering.
Articles.
A, 3rd part of volume, Yes, None.
T.p. 17, Ad.p. 7.
Per copy 50p.

2385 THE PROFESSIONAL ENGINEER: journal of the Engineers' Guild. 1946.
Engineers' Guild, 400/403 Abbey House, 2 Victoria Street, London, SW1.
4, * =
Book reviews, letters, monographic articles, news, obituaries.
No Index.
T.p. 17, Ad.p. 3.
Free to members.

2386 RUSSIAN ENGINEERING JOURNAL. Cover-to-cover translation of 'Vestnik Mashinostroeniya'. 1959.
Production Engineering Research Association, Melton Mowbray, Leicestershire.
12, ‡ + Recent developments in all fields of engineering in Russia.
Book notices, book reviews, monographic articles, patents.
A, January, No, None.
T.p. 100.   370.
Per copy £2.60, per year £20.70.

2387 SKILL. 1969.
Engineering ITB, St. Martin's House, 140 Tottenham Court Road, London, W1P 9LN.
3/4, ‡ = Systematic training in small to medium engineering firms, and Group Training Schemes.
Legal notes, letters, articles, parliamentary reports.
No Index.
Dec. 1971, T.p. 10.
Free.

2388 SOCIETY OF ENGINEERS JOURNAL. 1854.
Society of Engineers Inc., Abbey House, Victoria Street, Westminster, London, SW1H 0ND.
4, ‡ = * All branches of engineering and their interrelationships.
Book reviews, monographic articles.
A, No. 4 of year, Yes, 1910-1970.
October/December 1971, T.p. 39.
Per copy 30p. Free to members.

2389 WOMAN ENGINEER. 1919.
The Women's Engineering Society, 25 Foubert's Place, London, W1V 2AL.
4, ‡ * Events relevant to the Society's activities—items of technical and sociological interest to members and other readers.
Abstracts, book notices, book reviews, letters, monographic articles, obituaries.
No Index.
Spring 1972, T.p. 14, Ad.p. 4.   450-500.
Per copy 30p, per year £1.25.

2390 WORKS ENGINEERING. 1906.
Fuel & Metallurgical Journals Ltd., 17-19 John Adam Street, London, WC2.
12, ‡ = Stream, power, maintenance and industrial services for the works engineer.
Book notices, book reviews, letters, articles.
No Index.
Subscription on application.

620.1

TESTING MATERIALS

2391 BRITISH JOURNAL OF NON-DESTRUCTIVE TESTING. 1962.
Non-Destructive Testing Society of Great Britain, 700 London Road, Westcliff-on-Sea, Essex.
4, ‡ Non destructive testing techniques and developments.
Book reviews, letters, new products, standards.
A, December, Yes, None.
T.p. 40, Ad.p. 26.   2000.
Free to members. Per year £1.
Indexed in: BTI.

2392 INTERNATIONAL JOURNAL OF NONDESTRUCTIVE TESTING. 1969.
Gordon & Breach, 41/42 William 4th Street, London, WC2.
4, + ‡ Original research and development dealing with discoveries relating material properties to measurable physical phenomena. Special emphasis is given to new methods and techniques resulting from current theoretical and laboratory investigations.
Book notices, book reviews, letters, monographic articles, new products, tests.
No Index.
Subscription on application.

2393 JOURNAL OF STRAIN ANALYSIS. 1965.
The Institution of Mechanical Engineers, 1 Birdcage Walk, London, SW1H 9JJ.
4, ‡ + Stress and strain in materials.
Letters, monographic articles.
A, October, Yes, None.
July 1969, T.p. 80, Ad.p. 4.   1000.
Per copy £2.10, per year £8.
Indexed in: BTI.

2394 NON-DESTRUCTIVE TESTING. 1967.
IPC Science & Technology Publications Ltd., 32 High Street, Guildford, Surrey.
4, ‡ + Economics of NDT and best methods of installing and maintaining systems.
Book reviews, monographic articles, new products, patents.
A, February, Yes, None.
T.p. 65, Ad.p. 24.   1400.
Per copy £1.50, per year £6.

2395 NDT INFO. 1968.
IPC Science and Technology Publications Ltd., 32 High Street, Guildford, Surrey.
12, = + ‡   Current awareness service in nondestructive testing.
A, March, No, None.
T.p.18.   250.
Per year £6.

2396 RUSSIAN ULTRASONICS. 1971.
Multi Science Publishing Co. Ltd., 28 Greville St., London, EC1.
4, ‡ + *   Full translations of Russian papers on all aspects of ultrasonics, selected from a range of Russian journals.
Monographic articles.
No Index.
January 1972, T.p. 55.
Per copy £5, per year £20.

2397 STRAIN: journal of the British Society for Strain Measurement. 1964.
The Society, 281 Heaton Road, Newcastle on Tyne NE6 5BB.
4, * + ‡ =   Strain measurement and associated topics.
Book notices, book reviews, letters, monographic articles, standards, tests.
A, January, No, None.
T.p. 43, Ad.p. 7.   1000.
Free to members.
Indexed in: BTI.

2398 SURFACE WAVE ABSTRACTS. 1971.
Multi Science Publishing Co. Ltd., 28 Greville Street, London, EC1.
4, ‡ + *   Ultrasonic surface elastic waves. Generation and technological applications.
Abstracts, book notices, book reviews.
A, Running author sources and journal index. Yes, None.
December 1971, T.p. 40.
Per year £24.

2399 ULTRASONICS. 1963.
IPC Science & Technology Publications Ltd., 32 High Street, Guildford, Surrey.
4, +   Uses of ultrasound in industry.
Book reviews, letters, monographic articles, new products, patents.
A, January, Yes, None.
T.p. 63, Ad.p. 3.   2000.
Per copy £1.50, per year £6.
Indexed in: BTI.

620.193

CORROSION

2400 ANTI-CORROSION, METHODS AND MATERIALS. 1966. (Corrosion Technology 1954-1965).
Sawell Publications Ltd., 4 Ludgate Circus, London, EC4.
2, = + ‡   Corrosion prevention and control.
Book notices, book reviews, letters, monographic articles, new products, patents, standards, tests.
A, December, No, None.
T.p. 25, Ad.p. 7.   3500.
Per copy 40p, per year £5.
Indexed in: BTI.

2401 BRITISH CORROSION JOURNAL. 1965.
British Joint Corrosion Group, 14 Belgrave Square, London, SW1X 8PS.
6, + ‡ =   Metallurgical, chemical, electrochemical and physical theory and practice as they affect corrosion and its prevention.
Book notices, book reviews, letters, monographic articles, new products, (obituaries).
A, November, Yes, 5 year.
March 1972, T.p. 48.   >1000.
Per copy £2, per year £10 (Members of BJCG £3 per annum).
Indexed in: BTI.

2402 CORROSION CONTROL ABSTRACTS: English translation of Referativnyy zhurnal Korroziya i Zashchita ot Korrozii. No. 1, 1966.
Scientific Information Consultants Ltd., 661 Finchley Road, London, NW2 2HN.
12, ‡ +   English translation of about 6000 bibliogr. entries and abstracts per year from the Soviet abstracting journal on corrosion, which covers: corrosion theory, corrosion of metals and alloys under operating condition, protective metal coatings and chemical surface treatment, non-metallic corrosion-resistant materials and coatings, corr. inhibitors, etc.
Abstracts, book notices, book reviews, patents, tests.
A, —, No, None.
12, 1970, T.p. 60.
Per year £32.

2403 CORROSION PREVENTION AND CONTROL. 1954.
Scientific Surveys Ltd., 11a Gloucester Road, London, SW7.
6, + =   Chemical, atmospheric, marine corrosion.
Book reviews, articles, news, new products.
No Index.
T.p. 40, Ad.p. 30.
Per year £2.50.
Indexed in: BTI.

2404 CORROSION SCIENCE. 1961.
Pergamon Press Ltd., Headington Hill Hall, Oxford, OX3 0BW.
12, = +   Corrosion science and technology.
Book reviews, letters, monographic articles.
A, Last issue of volume, Yes, None.
T.p. 75.
Per copy £3, per year £30.
Indexed in: BTI.

621

MECHANICAL ENGINEERING

2405 ABSTRACTS FROM TECHNICAL & PATENT PUBLICATIONS. 1949.
The British Internal Combustion Engine Research Institute Limited, 111-112 Buckingham Avenue, Slough, Bucks, SL1 4PH.
51, ‡ = +   Mechanical engineering, particularly problems relating to vibration, noise, stress, thermodynamics, gas flow, high pressure hydraulics, in internal combustion engines and similar structures, instrumentation, fuels and lubricants.
Abstracts, new products, reports, patents, standards.
No Index.
T.p. 15.   c. 120
Per year £30.

2406 BULLETIN OF MECHANICAL ENGINEERING EDUCATION. 1962.
Pergamon Press Ltd., Headington Hill Hall, Oxford, OX3 0BW.
4, =   Teaching methods, syllabuses and aids, laboratory instruments, computational methods.
Book reviews, monographic articles.
A, Last issue of year, Yes, None.
Per copy £4, per year £14.
Indexed in: BTI.

2407 CHARTERED MECHANICAL ENGINEER. 1953.
The Institution of Mechanical Engineers, 1 Birdcage Walk, London, SW1H 9JJ.
11, ‡ * + =   Theoretical and practical developments in the various disciplines of mechanical engineering.

Abstracts, book notices, book reviews, letters, monographic articles, new products, obituaries, standards, tests.
A, January, No, None.
T.p. 50, Ad.p. 70.   74000.
Per copy £1.20, per year £12.
Indexed in: BTI.

2408 CURRENT AWARENESS BULLETIN FOR MECHANICAL ENGINEERING. 1970.
University of Surrey Library, Guildford, Surrey.
26, +   References to periodical articles on mechanical engineering of interest to University of Surrey academic staff.
No Index.
14th June 1972, T.p. 9.   91.
Per year £10.

2409 INTERNATIONAL JOURNAL OF MECHANICAL SCIENCES. 1960.
Pergamon Press Ltd., Headington Hill Hall, Oxford, OX3 0BW.
12, = +   Mechanical and civil engineering.
Book reviews, letters, monographic articles.
A, Last issue of volume, Yes, None.
T p. 100.
Per copy £3, per year £32.
Indexed in: BTI.

2410 JOURNAL OF MECHANICAL ENGINEERING SCIENCE. 1958.
The Institution of Mechanical Engineering, 1 Birdcage Walk, London, SW1H 9JJ.
6, + ‡   Various aspects of the broad field of mechanical engineering.
Abstracts, letters, monographic articles.
A, December, Yes, None.
T.p. 68.   1500.
Per copy £2.10, per year £12.
Indexed in: BTI.

2411 JOURNAL OF MECHANISMS.
Pergamon Press Ltd., Headington Hill Hall, Oxford, OX3 0BW.
4, = +   Theory and practical application of mechanical movement.
Book reviews, monographic articles.
A, Last issue of volume, Yes, None.
Per copy £6.50, per year £24.

2412 MACHINERY MARKET: Machinery & Engineering Materials Gazette. 1879.
The Machinery Market Limited, 146a Queen Victoria Street, London, EC4V 5AR.
52, = ‡   Makers, factors and merchants of industrial engineering products, and users of machinery, equipment and materials in a wide range of industries in the UK and overseas.
Book reviews, commodity prices, legal notes, letters, articles, new companies, new products, obituaries, patents, standards, tests.
A, —, Yes, None.
8th June, 1972, T.p. 31, Ad.p. 85.   c.9750.
Per copy 10p, per year £5.20.

2413 MACHINES AND TOOLING: Cover-to-cover translation of 'Stanki i Instrument'. 1959.
Production Engineering Research Association, Melton Mowbray, Leicestershire.
12, ‡ +   Reports developments in various branches of Russian mechanical engineering, particularly production technology.
Book notices, monographic articles, new products, patents, standards, tests.
A, January, No, None.
T.p. 74.   450.
Per copy £2.20, per year £17.30.

2414 MECHANICAL SCIENCES ABSTRACTS: (Akademiya nauk SSSR, Mashinovedeniye) No. 1-3, 1965.
(Machine Science Abstracts).
Scientific Information Consultants Ltd., 661 Finchley Road, London, NW2 2HN.
6, ‡ +   English digest of the bimonthly journal of the Academy of Sciences USSR, covering analysis and synthesis of mechanisms, dynamics of machinery, theories of transmission and machines, of automatic machines, accuracy and reliability of machines and mechanisms, computer application in machine design, etc.
Condensed translations.
No Index.
4-6, 1970, T.p. 104.
Per year £16.

2415 RESALE WEEKLY: journal of used plant and machinery. 1964.
Croft Publishing Co. Ltd., Unit 4, Sewell Street Industrial Estate, Plaistow, London, E13.
52, = ‡
No Index.
Ad.p. 45.
Per year £3.50.

621-039
NUCLEAR ENERGY

2416 BRITISH NUCLEAR ENERGY SOCIETY JOURNAL. 1962.
(British Nuclear Energy Conference 1956-1961).
The Institution of Civil Engineers, 1-7 Great George Street, Westminster, London, SW1P 3AA.
4, ‡ + = *   Original papers and discussion on a wide variety of subjects; also information and authoritative scientific and technological comments on developments in nuclear energy throughout the world. Contains bibliographies, lists of references, background information on selected topics, reports of meetings and international conferences arranged by the Society.
Book reviews, letters, monographic articles, new products, obituaries. tests.
A, January, No, None.
April 1972, T.p. 196.   2500.
Per copy £2.75, per year £6 members, per copy £2.75, per year £11 non-members.

2417 JOURNAL OF THE INSTITUTION OF NUCLEAR ENGINEERS. 1971.
(Nuclear Energy 1962-1970).
Institution of Nuclear Engineers, 24 Holwood Road, Bromley, Kent.
6, * + †   Research and all levels of the study of nuclear technology.
Book reviews, letters, monographic articles, obituaries, patents, standards, tests.
A, January/February, Yes, None.
November/December 1971, T.p. 32.   2500.
Per copy £1, per year £6.

2418 NUCLEAR ENGINEERING INTERNATIONAL: Incorporating Nuclear Power. 1956.
IPC Electrical Electronic Press Ltd., Dorset House, Stamford St., London, SE1 9LU.
12, ‡ = +   All aspects of the peaceful uses of nuclear energy—research, development, design and construction of nuclear power plant, operation of nuclear power plant, economics of nuclear power, nuclear fuel cycle from uranium supply to radioactive waste treatment.
Book reviews, letters, monographic articles, new companies, new products, obituaries, parliamentary reports.
A, —, Yes, None.
August 1972, T.p. 44, Ad.p. 36.   5600.
Per copy £1.25, per year £10.

621-186.2
VACUUM TECHNOLOGY

2419 VACUUM. 1951.
Pergamon Press Ltd. (for the British Vacuum Council), Headington Hill Hall, Oxford, OX3 0BW.
12, + = ‡   Whole field of vacuum science, technology, and applications.
Monographic articles, letters, book reviews.
A, Last issue of volume, Yes, None.
Per copy £2, per year £20.

621-27
SPRINGS

2420 THE SPRING JOURNAL. 1945.
The Spring Research Association, Henry Street, Sheffield, S3 7EQ, Yorks.
4, ‡ +   Technical and managerial appeal, reports of technical meetings, notes and news of the work of the Association, summaries of research reports, abstracts of current literature, advertisements.
Abstracts, book notices, book reviews, letters, monographic articles, new products, obituaries, patents, standards, tests.
7 years, 1967, Yes, None.
June 1972, T.p. 50, Ad.p. 2.   Members only.

621-426
WIRE

2421 WIRE INDUSTRY: the international monthly journal. 1934.
Wire Industry Ltd., 157 Station Road East, Oxted, RH8 0QE, Surrey.
12, =   Every aspect of the manufacture and working of wire, rod, bar and tube, reviews of machinery equipment and processes etc.
Book notices, book reviews, monographic articles, new companies, new products, patents, standards, tests.
A, December, Yes, None.
June 1972, T.p. 31, Ad.p. 45.   5079.
Per copy 60p, per year £4.60.
Indexed in: BTI.

621-52
AUTOMATION

2422 AUTOMATICA.
Pergamon Press Ltd., Headington Hill Hall, Oxford, OX3 0BW.
6, = +   Control systems including all facets of automatic control.
Book reviews, monographic articles.
A, Last issue of volume, Yes, None.
Per copy £3.50, per year £20.

2423 AUTOMATION. 1966.
ED Publications Ltd., 120 Wigmore Street, London, W1.
12, = + ‡   Automation systems and components.
Book notices, book reviews, monographic articles, new companies, new products, standards, tests.
No Index.
T.p. 31, Ad.p. 29.   15000.
Per year £3.50 and Free, controlled circulation.

2424 CONTROL & INSTRUMENTATION. 1969.
(Control 1958-69, Instrument Review 1958-68, Measurement & Instrument Review 1968).
Morgan Grampian (Publishers) Ltd., Calderwood St., London, SE18 9QH.
11, ‡ +   Industrial and scientific technology from basic instruments to computer controlled systems.
Book reviews, letters, monographic articles, new companies, new products.
A, January, Yes, None.
June 1972, T.p. 32, Ad.p. 43.   15304.
Per copy £1, per year £7, Free, controlled circulation
Indexed in: BTI.

2425 KYBERNETES: Int. Journal of Cybernetics and General Systems. 1972.
Gordon & Breach, 41/42 William 4th Street, London, WC2.
4, +   Philosophy of cybernetics, artificial intelligence, nature and validation of general systems, cybernetics modelling, engineering cybernetics, computer simulation, bio and neurocybernetics, economic and social systems, and dynamics, ecosystems, adaptive systems and computer sciences.
Book notices, book reviews, letters, monographic articles, new companies, tests.
A, —, No, None.
Per year £15.50.

621-76
SEALS

2426 FLUID SEALING ABSTRACTS. 1969.
(Current Information Guide on Fluid Sealing 1966-1968).
British Hydromechanics Research Association, Cranfield, Bedford.
6, ‡ +   World literature on static seals, dynamic seals and sealing materials. Some 400 abstracts are produced annually.
Abstracts, patents.
6m, —, No, A.
January/February 1972, T.p. 14, Ad.p. 1.   250.
Per year £20.

621.1
STEAM ENGINEERING

2427 LIGHT STEAM POWER. 1949.
Kirk Michael, Isle of Man.
6, ‡ = + ○   Steam power for cars, boats and small stationary units—modern, vintage and veteran.
Book reviews, letters, articles, new products, patents.
A, November/December, Yes, None.
T.p. 49, Ad.p. 4.
Per copy 33p, per year £2.
Indexed in: BTI.

2428 STEAM MAN: The magazine devoted to all forms of steam engine. 1971.
Steam Man Publications, Stag House, Lowlands Crescent, Great Kingshill, High Wycombe, Bucks.
2, ‡ *   Working and preserving steam engines, particularly stationary engines.
Book notices, book reviews, letters, monographic articles, new products.
No Index.
Autumn 1971, T.p. 20, Ad.p. 1.   1000.
Per copy 34p, for 4 issues £1.35p.

2429 FLUID POWER ABSTRACTS. 1970.
BHRA Fluid Engineering, Cranfield, Bedford.
12, ‡ + =   All aspects of oil hydraulics and pneumatics, including equipment, systems, applications, fluids, contamination, transmission.
Abstracts, book notices, book reviews, new companies, new products, patents, standards.
6m, July/January, No, None.
January, 1972, T.p. 22.   300.
Per year £20.

621.22

HYDRAULIC POWER ENGINEERING

2430 **FLUID POWER INTERNATIONAL.** 1935.
Morgan-Grampian Ltd., Calderwood Street, London, SE18 6QH
12, = ‡   Fluid power industry.
Articles, news, new products, patents.
A, −, Yes, None.
T.p. 40, Ad.p. 60.   6900.
Per copy 50p, per year £6, and Free, controlled circulation.
Indexed in: BTI.

2431 **HYDRAULIC PNEUMATIC POWER.** 1955.
Trade & Technical Press Ltd., Crown House, Morden, Surrey.
12, +   Hydraulic equipment.
Monographic articles, news, new products.
No Index.
T.p. 31, Ad.p. 40.   2100.
Per year £3.60.
Indexed in: BTI.

2432 **BEHAVIOURAL TECHNOLOGY.** 1970.
William Clowes & Sons Ltd., Hawkins Road, The Hythe, Colchester, Essex.
6, = ‡
Articles.
No Index.
May 1972, T.p. 16.
Per year £1.75.   Free to Schools.

2433 **BROOK MAGAZINE.** 1937.
Publicity Department, Brook Motors Ltd., (A Hawker-Siddeley Company), Empress Works, Huddersfield, HD1 3LJ.
4, † ‡ =   Brook electric motors and control gear installed in industry.
Articles, new products, standards.
No Index.
Vol. 34, No. 137, T.p. 28.   20000.
Free.

2434 **CIRCUIT NEWS.** 1968.
The Electricity Council, Trafalgar Buildings, 1 Charing Cross, London, SW1A 2DS.
12, †   Marketing activities of the electricity supply industry.
No Index.
June 1972, T.p. 16, Ad.p. 7.   83000.
Free.

2435 **CONTACT.** 1969.
(Electron).
Electrical Electronic & Telecommunications Union, Hayes Court, West Common Road, Hayes, Bromley, Kent.
4, * = ‡
Book notices, book reviews, commodity prices, legal notes, letters, articles, new companies, new products, obituaries, parliamentary reports, standards.
No Index.
T.p. 16.   380000.
Per copy 2½p, per year 16p.

2436 **CONTROL & SCIENCE RECORD.** Including Automation, Education and Management. 1966.
(Science & General Quarterly 1963, Science & General Record, 1964-65).
Institution of Electrical Engineers, Savoy Place, London, WC2R 0BL.
4, + ‡   Contains papers covering the fields of control and automation and electrical science, education and management taken from the three previous issues of Proceeding IEE.
Letters, monographic articles.
A, December, Yes, None.
June 1972, T.p. 84.   2400.
Per copy £4.60, per year £16.50.

2437 **CURRENT PAPERS IN ELECTRICAL & ELECTRONIC ENGINEERING.** 1969.
(Current Papers in Electrotechnology 1964-1968).
INSPEC, The Institution of Electrical Engineers, Savoy Place, London, WC2R 0BL.
12, + =   Current awareness tool for dissemination within laboratories and development organisations, providing the title, authors, and bibliographic reference for every entry published in its companion Abstracts Journal, using the same classification system.
Current titles.
No Index.
Per copy £1.40, per year £14.

2438 **DOMESTIC ELECTRICAL APPLIANCE INDUSTRY STATISTICS.** 1970.
BEAMA, 8 Leicester Street, Leicester Square, London, WC2.
12, =
No Index.
Per year £15.

2439 **ERA ABSTRACTS.** 193 .
Electrical Research Association, Cleeve Road, Leatherhead, Surrey.
52, ‡ +   Electrical engineering, electronics, and allied areas.
Abstracts.
No Index.
10.6.72, T.p. 12.
Per year £5, to members.   £12 to non-members.

2440 **ELECTRIC TECHNOLOGY USSR.** Translation of selected articles from Elektrichestvo. 1969.
Pergamon Press Ltd., Headington Hill Hall, Oxford, OX3 0BW.
4, ‡ +   Technical and economic aspects of power supply systems, design and application of electrical machines.
Monographic articles.
No Index.
Per copy £13, per year £48.

2441 **ELECTRICAL & ELECTRONICS ABSTRACTS.** 1966.
(Electrical Engineering Abstracts 1898-1966).
INSPEC, The Institution of Electrical Engineers, Savoy Place, London, WC2R 0BL.
12, + ‡ =   c. 200 classified subject codes embracing both heavy electrical and electronics engineering aspects. The subject index has about 900 alphabetical subject headings under which relevant entries are listed. In excess of 40,000 items per year included.
Abstracts.
6m, −, No, 4 years.
Per copy £10, per year £105.   Journals available in either paper or microfiche editions. Comb. sub to paper and microfiche £157.50.

2442 **ELECTRICAL AND ELECTRONICS TECHNICIAN ENGINEER:** journal of the Institution of Electrical & Electronics Technician Engineers. 1966.
The Institution, 2 Savoy Hill, London, WC2.
6, * + ‡ =   Manufacture, operation and maintenance, development and research in the electrical and electronic engineering industries.
Book notices, book reviews, letters, monographic articles, new companies, news, new products, standards, tests.
No Index.
T.p. 30, Ad.p. 5.   11600.
Per copy 50p, per year £2.50.

2443 ELECTRICAL COMMUNICATION. 1922.
International Telephone & Telegraph Corp., 190 Strand, London, WC2R 1DU.
4, ‡ + † =
New products, patents, standards, tests.
A, —, No, None.
T.p. varies. 15000.
Per copy 45p, per year £1.70.

2444 ELECTRICAL CONTRACTOR AND RETAILER. 1903.
Electrical Contractors Association, 55 Catherine Place, London, SW1.
12, = +
Book notices, book reviews, letters, articles, new products, obituaries, parliamentary reports, standards, tests.
No Index.
T.p. 21, Ad.p. 42.
Per copy 15p, per year £1.50.

2445 ELECTRICAL AND ELECTRONICS MANUFACTURER.
Trade News Ltd., 203/9 North Gower Street, London, NW1.
12, =
No Index.
Per copy 22½p, per year £2.50. Free, controlled circulation.

2446 ELECTRICAL EQUIPMENT. 1961.
Shaw Publishing Co., Ltd., 180 Fleet Street, London, EC4.
12, = + ‡   Theory and practice of electrical engineering.
Book notices, book reviews, commodity prices, letters, monographic articles, new companies, new products, obituaries, standards.
No Index.
T.p. 34, Ad.p. 48. 14000.
Per copy 50p, per year £5. Free, controlled circulation

2447 ELECTRICAL EXPORT REVIEW. 1962.
IPC Electrical-Electronic Press Ltd., Dorset House, Stamford Street, London, SE1 9LU.
4, ‡   All branches of electrical, electronic and allied industries: manufacturing, sales and distribution of all types of electrical and electronic equipment and appliances; electricity supply, inc. generation, transmission, distribution and contracting; installation and maintenance of equipment.
Monographic articles, new companies, new products.
A, —, Yes, None.
July-September 1972, T.p. 24, Ad.p. 28. 8779.
Per copy 50p, per year £2.

2448 ELECTRICAL POWER ENGINEER. 1918.
Electrical Power Engineers Association, 15 Newgate Street, London, EC1.
12, ‡
Articles, news.
A, —, Yes, None.
T.p. 12. 29000.
Per copy 75p.
Indexed in: BTI.

2449 ELECTRICAL REVIEW. 1892.
(The Telegraphic Journal and Electrical Review 1872-1891.).
IPC Electrical-Electronic Press Ltd., Dorset House, Stamford Street, London, SE1.
5, ‡ =   All branches of electrical, electronic and allied industries: manufacturing sales and distribution of all types of electrical and electronic equipment and appliances; electricity supply, including generation, transmission, distribution and contracting; installation and maintenance of elec. equipment.
Book notices, book reviews, letters, articles, new companies, new products, patents.
6m, January and July, No, None.

30 June 1972, T.p. 35, Ad.p. 39. 11353.
Per copy 12½p, per year £10.75.
Indexed in: BTI, IBZ.

2450 ELECTRICAL SUPERVISOR incorporating The Executive Engineer. 1931.
(Contact 1914-1930).
Association of Supervisory and Executive Engineers, Wix Hill House, West Horsley, Surrey.
10, ‡ *   Engineering and engineering management. Association news and developments.
Book reviews, letters, articles, new companies, new products, obituaries, patents, standards, tests.
No Index.
March 1972, T.p. 26, Ad.p. 32. 8000.
Per copy 30p, per year £3.
Indexed in: BTI

2451 ELECTRICAL TIMES. 1902.
(Lightning 1891-1901).
IPC Electrical-Electronic Press Ltd., Dorset House, Stamford Street, London SE1.
51, ‡ =   Electrical engineering other than telecommunications, computer science and electronics; especially in electricity supply, electrical installation contracting, manufacturing and applications in user industries. Related commercial information.
Book notices, book reviews, commodity prices, letters, monographic articles, new companies, new products, obituaries, parliamentary reports, standards.
6m, Variable, Yes, None.
29th June, 1972, T.p. 43, Ad.p. 39. 8231.
Per copy 12½p, per year £10.75.
Indexed in: BTI.

2452 ELECTRICAL WHOLESALER: Journal of the Electrical Wholesalers Federation. 1962.
Batiste Publications Ltd., 203/209 North Gower Street, London, NW1.
12, = *   Marketing and use of electrical goods.
Articles, news, new products.
No Index.
T.p. 36, Ad.p. 46. 4300.
Per year £2.25.

2453 ENERGY CONVERSION.
Pergamon Press Ltd., Headington Hill Hall, Oxford, OX3 0BW.
4, = +   All aspects of energy conversion.
Book reviews, monographic articles.
A, Last issue of volume, Yes, None.
Per copy £5.50, per year £20.

2454 IEE NEWS: for the professional electrical, electronics and control systems engineer. 1964.
The Institution of Electrical Engineers, Publishing Department, PO Box 8, Southgate House, Stevenage, Herts., SG1 1HQ.
22, ‡ *   News of the electrical and electronics industry and the engineering profession; the main communication link between the IEE and its members.
Letters, articles, new companies, new products, obituaries.
No Index.
29th June 1972, T.p. 5, Ad.p. 3. 62000.
Per copy 10p, per year £2.

2455 INTERNATIONAL JOURNAL OF ELECTRICAL ENGINEERING EDUCATION. 1963.
Pergamon Press Ltd., Headington Hill Hall, Oxford, OX3 0BW.
4, + ‡   Teaching of electrical engineering subjects.
Book reviews, letters, monographic articles.

Key to reference symbols

○ popular   ‡ technical   = trade/professional

+ research   * society/institution   † house journal

A,—,Yes,None.
Per copy £3.50, per year £12.
Indexed in: BTI.

2456 NEWSLETTER: ECONOMIC DEVELOPMENT COMMITTEE FOR ELECTRICAL ENGINEERING. 1966.
National Economic Development Office, Millbank, London, SW1P 40X.
‡
No Index.

2457 POWER RECORD. 1964.
(Power Quarterly 1963).
Institution of Electrical Engineers, Savoy Place, London, WC2R 0BL.
4, + ‡ = * Contains papers covering the field of power engineering taken from the three previous issues of proceedings IEE.
Letters, monographic articles.
A, December, Yes, None.
March 1972, T.p. 336, Ad.p. 1. 7000.
Per copy £4.60, per year £16.50.

2458 PRIVATE WIRE: A private communication for the interest of customers and associates of British Driver-Harris Co., Ltd. 1954.
Stocker Hocknell Limited, 4, Market Square, Amersham, Buckinghamshire.
4, ‡ = † A running commentary of the electricity using world generally, with emphasis on resistance materials, bimetal and cables.
No Index.
March 1972, T.p. 16. 2300.
Free.

2459 PROCEEDINGS OF THE INSTITUTION OF ELECTRICAL ENGINEERS. 1/49.
(J. Soc. Telegraph Eng. 1871-1880, J. Soc. Telegraph Eng. & Electricians 1881-88, J. IEE 1889-1948).
Institution of Electrical Engineers, Savoy Place, London, WC2R 0BL.
12 + IEE Reviews, + ‡ = * Important and fundamental work in the general field of electrical, electronic and control engineering.
Letters, monographic articles.
6m, June, December, Yes, 10 year.
July 1972, T.p. 143, Ad.p. 2. 6500.
Per copy £4.60, per year £46.
Indexed in: BTI, IBZ.

2460 SEABOARD: South Eastern Electricity Board Magazine. 1948.
South Eastern Electricity Board, Queen's Gardens, Hove, Sussex, BN3 2LS.
6, ○ ‡ † Recording the activities and interests of Seeboard and its people in distributing electricity throughout the South East of England, together with stories and pictures of interests allied to uses of electricity everywhere.
Book reviews, legal notes, letters, monographic articles, new products, obituaries, parliamentary reports, standards, tests.
A, Spring, No, None.
April-May 1972, T.p. 53. 11000.
Free.

621.3.024

DIRECT CURRENT

2461 DIRECT CURRENT. 1969.
Pergamon Press Ltd., Headington Hill Hall, Oxford, OX3 0BW.
4, ‡ All aspects of DC technology.
Book reviews, monographic articles.
No Index.
Per copy £1.50, per year £6.

621.319.1

FERROELECTRICS

2462 FERROELECTRICS. 1970.
Gordon & Breach, 41/42 William 4th Street, London, WC2.
4, + ‡ Forum for people working in ferroelectrics and related materials such as ferroelastics, ferroelectric-ferromagnetic, electrooptics, piezoelectrics, pyroelectrics, nonlinear dielectrics, and liquid crystals.
Book notices, book reviews, letters, monographic articles, new products, tests.
A, —, No, None.
Subscription on application.

621.33

ELECTRIC TRACTION

2463 NEWSSHEET, ELECTRIC TRANSPORT DEVELOPMENT SOCIETY. 1960.
The Society, 101 Woodwater Lane, Exeter, EX2 5NP.
6, * + = The British transport scene and reports from abroad.
Book notices, book reviews, news.
No Index.
Free to members.

621.38

ELECTRONICS

2464 AERIAL. 1953.
GEC-Marconi Electronics Limited, Marconi House, Chelmsford, CM1 1PL.
4, ○ ‡ † Short, illustrated articles on products, contracts, developments, installations and activities generally of the member companies of GEC-Marconi Electronics Limited.
No Index.
T.p. 21, Ad.p. 6. 15000.
Free, controlled circulation.

2465 COMPONENTS STANDARD: quarterly product review of ITT Components Group Europe. 1967.
ITT Components Group Europe, Edinburgh Way, Harlow, Essex.
‡ = Review of new electronic products and developments from ITT, for designers, buyers, scientists and engineers in the electronic and electrical fields.
Monographic articles, new products.
No Index.
April 72, T.p. 13, Ad.p. 2. 35000.
Free, controlled circulation.

2466 ELECTRON: The journal for engineers and managers in electronics. 1972.
IPC Electrical-Electronic Press, Dorset House Stamford Street, London, SE1.
24, ‡ All technically biased aspects of electronics, with special emphasis on products and their application.
Commodity prices, letters, monographic articles, new companies, new products, reports, patents, standards, tests.
No Index.
15 June 1972, T.p. 29, Ad.p. 24. 24500.
Per copy 25p, per year £6, and Free, controlled circulation.

2467 ELECTRONIC COMPONENTS. 1966.
(Radio and Electronic Components 1959-1965).
United Trade Press, 9 Gough Square, London, EC4.
12, = + ‡ Manufacture and application of components.
Book notices, book reviews, letters, monographic articles, obituaries, tests.
A, January, Yes, None.

T.p. 56, Ad.p. 107.   20000.
Per copy 50p, per year £7.
Indexed in: BTI

2468 ELECTRONIC ENGINEERING. 1941.
Morgan Grampian (Publishers) Ltd., Calderwood Street, London, SE18 6QH.
12, = ‡
Book reviews, news, articles, new products.
A, –, Yes, None.
T.p.c. 70, Ad. p.c. 200   20000.
Per year £5, and Free, controlled circulation.
Indexed in: BTI.

2469 ELECTRONICS AND COMMUNICATIONS ABSTRACTS. 1961.
Multi-Science Publishing Company Ltd., 28 Greville Street, London EC1.
12, ‡ + *   All aspects of electronics and communication science and its application.
Abstracts, book notices, book reviews.
6m, –, Yes, None.
February 1972, T.p. 108.
Per copy £1.50, per year £17.50.

2470 ELECTRONICS & POWER: The Journal of the Institution of Electrical Engineers. 1964.
(Journal of the IEE, 1955-1963).
The Institution of Electrical Engineers Publishing Department, PO Box 8, Southgate House, Stevenage, Herts. SG1 1HQ.
22, ‡ *   Advances in electrical and electronic sciences and technology and their impact on the professional engineer and management.
Book notices, book reviews, letters, monographic articles, new companies, new products, obituaries, standard.
A, December, Yes, None.
July 1972, T.p. 42, Ad.p. 36.   62000.
Per copy £1.35, per year £13.50.
Indexed in: BTI

2471 ELECTRONICS LETTERS. 1965.
Institution of Electrical Engineers, Savoy Place, London, WC2R 0BL.
26, +   Provides speedy dissemination of research and development results in electronic science and engineering, control and allied fields.
Research letters.
A, with last issue of year, Yes, 10 years.
13 July 1972, T.p. 23.   2600.
Per copy £2.75, per year £27.50.

2472 ELECTRONICS RECORD. 1964.
(Electronics Quarterly 1963).
Institution of Electrical Engineers, Savoy Place, London, WC2R 0Bl.
4, + ‡   Contains papers covering the field of electronics taken from the three previous issues of proceedings IEE.
Letters, monographic articles.
A, December, Yes, None.
June 1972, T.p. 80.   3250.
Per copy £4.60, per year £16.50.

2473 ELECTRONICS TODAY INTERNATIONAL. 1972.
Whitehall Press Limited, Wrotham Place, Wrotham, Sevenoaks, Kent.
12, ‡ ○   All aspects of electronics in manner designed to appeal to the knowledgeable layman as well as the technician.
Book reviews, letters, monographic articles, new companies, new products, patents, standards, tests.
A, –, No, None.
July 1972, T.p. 8, Ad.p. 74.   64500.
Per copy 20p, per year £3.

2474 ELECTRONICS WEEKLY: the technical and business newspaper of electronics and communications. 1960.
IPC Electrical-Electronic Press Ltd., (a member of IPC Business Press Ltd.), Dorset House, Stamford Street, London, SE1 9LU.
51, ‡ =   News and technical features for engineers and others professionally engaged in electronics manufacture, marketing or use.
Book notices, book reviews, commodity prices, letters, monographic articles, new companies, new products, obituaries, parliamentary reports.
No Index.
21.6.72, T.p. 14, Ad.p. 10.   17583.
Per copy 4p, per year £2.25.
Indexed in: BTI

2475 EVERYDAY ELECTRONICS. 1971.
IPC Magazines Ltd., Fleetway House, Farringdon St., London, EC4.
12, ○ ‡   Simple electronic designs for the home constructor, aimed chiefly at the beginner and those with only an elementary knowledge of the subject. Easy to follow articles on construction and theory.
A, Jan.-Mar, Yes, None.
October 1972, T.p. 34, Ad.p. 25.
Per copy 15p, per year £2.35.

2476 INTERNATIONAL JOURNAL OF CONTROL. 1965.
(Journal of Electronics and Control 1955-1964).
Taylor & Francis Ltd., 10-14 Macklin Street, London, WC2B 5NF.
12, ‡ = +   The theory of process control and automation.
Monographic articles.
6m, in last issue of volume (2 per year), Yes, None.
July 1972, T.p. 207.
Per copy £4, per year £45.
Indexed in: BTI

2477 INTERNATIONAL JOURNAL OF ELECTRONICS. 1965.
Taylor & Francis Ltd., 10-14 Macklin St., London, WC2B 5NF.
12, ‡ = +   Describes new researches in the field of active electronic components and systems containing active components.
Monographic articles.
6m, in last volume (2 per year), Yes, None.
July 1972, T.p. 119.
Per copy £3, per year £33.
Indexed in: BTI, IBZ.

2478 MARCONI REVIEW. 1928.
GEC-Marconi Electronics Ltd., Baddow Research Laboratories, West Hanningfield Road, Great Baddow, Essex.
4, † *   Electronic and mechanical research covering the fields of radar and communication.
Monographic articles.
A, March, Yes, None.
July 1972, T.p. 96.   c. 3000.
Per copy 75p, per year £3.

2479 MEDICAL ELECTRONICS AND COMMUNICATIONS ABSTRACTS. 1966.
Multi Science Publishing Co., Ltd., 28 Greville St., London, EC1.
4, ‡ + *   Medical electronics, as applied to measurement, display, computer diagnostics, prosthetics. Communication includes speech and learning, neurological networks and modelling.
Abstracts, book notices, book reviews.
A, –, Yes, None.
October 1971, T.p. 44.
Per copy £4.50, per year £17.50.

2480 MICROELECTRONICS AND RELIABILITY. 1962.
Pergamon Press Ltd., Headington Hill Hall, Oxford, OX3 0BW.
6, + =   Advanced techniques in microelectronics.
Book reviews, letters, monographic articles.
A, last issue of volume, Yes, None.
Per copy £4.50, per year £24.

2481 NEW ELECTRONICS: incorporating Electronics Today. 1968.
Juniper Journals Ltd., (part of the Thomson Organisation Ltd.), 49-50 Hatton Garden, London EC1N 8XS.
24, ‡
New companies, articles, new products, and other applications.
No Index.
18.7.72, T.p. 20, Ad.p. 20.   23500.
Per copy 50p, per year £10, and Free, controlled circulation.

2482 PRACTICAL ELECTRONICS. 1964.
IPC Magazines Ltd., Fleetway House, Farringdon St., London, EC4.
12, ○ ‡   Electronic designs of all types for the home constructor, with supporting articles dealing with circuit theory, new advances in the technology, and industrial news.
A, Jan/Mar, Yes, None.
October 1972, T.p. 42, Ad.p. 58.   95000.
Per copy 20p, per year £2.65.

621.39

TELECOMMUNICATIONS

2484 GEC TELECOMMUNICATIONS. 1946.
(The Magnet Telephone Society Resumes—up to 1930; Current Comments—1930-1939).
GEC Telecommunications Ltd., PO Box 53, Telephone Works, Coventry, Warks.
1, ‡   Research, development and manufacture of a comprehensive range of telecommunications equipment and systems.
Monographic articles, new products.
5 year, 1967 et seq., Yes, Irregular.
No. 39, 1972, T.p. 48.   4500.
Free

2485 INTERCOM: Journal of the Home Office Directorate of Telecommunications. 1972.
Home Office, 60 Rochester Row, London, SW1.
2, ‡ + †   The work in current engineering and research of the Directorate for its members and members of its customer services such as police and fire services.
Letters, monographic articles.
No Index.
June 1972, T.p. 64.   3500.
Free

2486 NEW QUARTERLY JOURNAL. 1966.
Institution of Post Office Electrical Engineers, CT/ETW 15 Post Office Tower, Howland Street, London, WC1.
4, = + ‡ *
Letters, articles, news, new products, reports, tests.
No Index.
T.p. 30, Ad.p. 3.   4500.
Free to members.

2487 POINT TO POINT COMMUNICATIONS. 1970.
(Point to Point Telecommunications 1956-1969).
Marconi Communication Systems Limited, Marconi House, Chelmsford, Essex.
3, ‡ +   Professional communication enquiries.
A, —, Yes, None.
Per copy 50p, per year £1.50.

2488 THE POST OFFICE ELECTRICAL ENGINEERS' JOURNAL. 1908.
POEE Journal, 2-12 Gresham St, London, EC2V 7AG.
4, ‡   Current developments in telecommunications engineering.
Abstracts, book notices, book reviews, letters, monographic articles.
A, January, Yes, None.
April 1972, T.p. 65, Ad.p. 25.
Per copy 21p, per year £1.24.

2489 POST OFFICE TELECOMMUNICATIONS JOURNAL. 1948.
The Post Office, 23 Howland Street, London, W1P 6HQ.
4, ‡ †   Operation and management of telecommunications.
Book reviews, monographic articles, new products.
A, December, Yes, None.
Spring 1972, T.p. 33, Ad.p. 27.   42500.
Per copy 9p, per year 50p.

2490 THE POST OFFICE ENGINEER: journal of the Society of Post Office Engineers. 1909.
Society, 14 King Street, London EC2.
12, * ‡   Trade Union and Post Office developments.
Letters, news, obituaries.
A, December, No, None.
T.p. 26.
Free to members.

2491 POST OFFICE ENGINEERING UNION JOURNAL. 1919.
Post Office Engineering Union, Greystoke House, Hanger Lane, London, W5.
12, * ‡   Union affairs.
Book reviews, letters, news, parliamentary reports.
A, —, Yes, None.
T.p. 18, Ad.p. 6.
Free to members.

2492 SYSTEMS TECHNOLOGY. 1967.
The Plessey Company Limited, Ilford, Essex.
3, † ‡ =   Telecommunications and electronic systems and equipment.
Monographic articles, new products.
2 year, —, No, None.
December 1971, T.p. 36.   9000.
Free.

621.395.63

PUBLIC ADDRESS SYSTEMS

2493 PUBLIC ADDRESS: Journal of the Association of Public Address Engineers. 1972.
(Public Address Engineers Journal 1949-1971).
Asscn. of Public Address Engineers Ltd., 6 Conduit St. London, W1R 9TG.
12, = + *   Public address industry and its allied services.
Book notices, book reviews, legal notes, letters, monographic articles, new companies, new products, obituaries, patents, standards, tests.
A, December, Yes, None.
May 1972, T.p. 11, Ad.p. 15.   600.
Per copy 25p, per year £3.

621.396

RADIO

2494 AIRADIO NEWS. 1967.
Airadio Division, Marconi-Elliott Avionic Systems Limited, Christopher Martin Road, Basildon, Essex.
4, ‡ =   Covers commercial and technical activities of the Airadio Division, Marconi-Elliott Avionics, in the civil and military avionics field.
New products.
No Index.
May 1972, T.p. 4.   4200.
Free.

2495 ELECTRICAL & RADIO TRADING. 1945.
(Electricity 1890-1929; Broadcaster 1923-1937; Radio Marketing 1937-1939; Electrical Trading and Radio Marketing 1939-1945).

IPC Electrical-Electronic Press Ltd., Dorset House, Stamford Street, London, SE1.
51, = ‡   Retailers, wholesalers installers, suppliers and manufacturers of electrical appliances and accessories, T.V., radio and audio goods, aerials and other associated equipment, electrical installation constructing firms.
Book reviews, commodity prices, legal notes, letters, articles, new companies, new products, obituaries, parliamentary reports, standards, tests.
A, December, Yes, None.
29.6.1972, T.p. 21, Ad.p. 35.   13085.
Per copy 12½p, per year £5.55.

2496 I.P.R.E. REVIEW: official journal of Incorporated Practitioners in Radio and Electronics Ltd. 1950.
(The Practical Radio Engineer 1936-1949).
Incorporated Practitioners in Radio and Electronics, (I.P.R.E.) Ltd., 32 Kidmore Road, Caversham, Reading, RG4 7LU.
3, ‡ * =
Book notices, book reviews, letters, monographic articles, obituaries, tests.
No Index.
No. 11, 1972, T.p. 24.   750.
Per year £1.25.
Free to members.

2497 MARCONI COMMUNICATION SYSTEMS. 1969.
(Marconi Telecommunication News, 1969).
Marconi Communication Systems Limited, Marconi House, Chelmsford, CM1 1PL.
6, ‡   New systems and equipments, interesting contracts and market and company news to the Company's customers and other interested in radio and line communications and broadcasting.
No Index.
T.p. 4.   16000.
Free, controlled circulation.

2498 MARINER. 1963.
(Marconi Mariner 1947-1963).
The Marconi International Marine Co., Ltd., Elettra House, Westway, Chelmsford, Essex.
6, †   Produced to maintain a link between the company's head office, its seagoing radio officers and technical and other staff at depots and service agencies throughout the world.
Book reviews, letters, monographic articles, new companies, new products, obituaries.
Bi-annually, May/June, Yes, None.
May/June 1972, T.p. 48.   4500.
Per copy 8p, per year 75p.

2499 PRACTICAL WIRELESS. 1932.
IPC Magazines Limited (Magazine Division), Fleetway House, Farringdon Street, London, EC4 4AD.
12, ‡ ○ =   Gives circuits and constructional details for a variety of electronic projects: Radio, Hi-Fi, Amplifier, Test Gear and ancilliary equipment. Also includes theoretical articles. Aimed at the D-I-Y electronic enthusiast.
Regular features: news and comment, amateur bands, short wave and broadcast bands, medium wave column. Special feature articles and supplements throughout the year.
A, June/July, Yes, None.
November 1972, T.p. 47, Ad.p. 68.   102509.
Per copy 20p, per year £2.65.

2500 RACAL REVIEW.
Racal Group Services Limited, 26 Broad Street, Wokingham, Berkshire.
4, ‡ = †   Radio communications equipment, electronic test equipment, data transmission equipment, computer peripherals.
Monographic articles, new products, standards, tests.
No Index.
February 1972, T.p. 26.
Free.

2501 RADIO & ELECTRICAL RETAILING. 1945.
Trade Papers (London) Ltd.,/Turret Press (Holdings) Ltd., 157 Hagden Land, Watford, WD1 8LW.
12, ‡ =
Book reviews, letters, articles.
No Index.
June 1972, T.p. 38, Ad.p. 38.
Per year £3.50.

2502 THE RADIO AND ELECTRONIC ENGINEER: Journal of the Institution of Electronic and Radio Engineers. 1962.
(Journal of the British Institution of Radio Engineers 1939-1961).
Institution of Electronic and Radio Engineers, 8-9, Bedford Square, London, WC1B 5RG.
12, = ‡ *   Electronics and radio engineering and kindred subjects, education and management.
Abstracts, book notices, book reviews, letters, monographic articles, new products, obituaries.
A, February, Yes, Subject index with abstracts, 5-8 years.
May 1972, T.p. 60, Ad.p. 16.   15390.
Per copy £1, per year £11.

2503 THE RADIO & ELECTRONICS CONSTRUCTOR. Incorporating the Radio Amateur. 1947.
Data Publications Ltd., 57 Maida Vale, London, W9 1SN.
12, ○ ‡   Radio, Television, Hi-Fidelity and Audio, Radio Control, Short Wave News, Electronic Projects.
Book reviews, articles, new products, obituaries, tests.
A, July, No, None.
June 1972, T.P. 50, Ad.p. 18.   25000.
Per copy 20p, per year £2.70.

2504 RADIO COMMUNICATION: incorporating RSGB Bulletin. 1968.
(RSGB Bulletin 1925-1967),
Radio Society of Great Britain, 35 Doughty Street, London, WC1.
12, = + ‡ *   All aspects of communication between 1.8 MHz and 21 GHz, including teletype, television and satellite communication. Covers technical and operating aspects.
Book notices, book reviews, letters, monographic articles, new products, obituaries, tests.
A, December, Yes, None.
T.p. 61, Ad.p. 18.   17000.
Per copy 20p, per year £2.50. Free to members.

2505 SCRIPT. 1972.
London Region Free Radio Campaign, 35 Glenmore Road, London, NW3.
6, ○   News of unofficial radio stations.
No Index.
Per copy 10p.

2506 THE SIGNAL: journal of the Radio and Electronic Officers Union. 1921.
(The Radiograph-1920).
Radio and Electronic Officers' Union, 4-6 Branfill Road, Upminster, Essex, RM14 2XX.
6, =   Trade Union news, Reports on International Maritime Regulatory Bodies Meetings (IMCO, ITU, ILO, etc.), latest marine radio and electronic equipment and up-to-date news from the marine radio companies.
Book reviews, letters, articles, new products, obituaries.
No Index.
March/April 1972, T.p. 28, Ad.p. 7.   3700.
Per copy 25p, per year £1.50.

2507 WIRELESS WORLD: Electronics, television, radio, audio. 1913.
(The Marconigraph 1911).
IPC Electrical-Electronic Press Ltd., Dorset House, Stamford Street, London, SE1 9LU.

12, ‡ Written for the individual engineer or technician, endeavours to cover all the advances in circuit ideas and new techniques. Also includes details of constructional projects such as amplifiers, tuners and test instruments.
Book notices, book reviews, letters, monographic articles, new products, obituaries, standards, tests.
A, −, No, None.
May 1972, T.p. 53, Ad.p. 119.   57082.
Per copy 20p, per year £4.35.
Indexed in: BTI, IBZ

2508 ZODIAC: Quarterly magazine of the Cable and Wireless Group of Companies. 1972.
The Zodiac (1906-1972).
The Zodiac Publishing Co. Ltd., (associated with Cable and Wireless Ltd.), Mercury House, Theobalds Road, London, WC1X 8RX.
4, ○ = ‡ * General interest material with some relevance to telecommunications and the Cable and Wireless Group in particular. Designed to appeal to non-Group readers worldwide.
Letters, articles.
No Index.
No. 1, T.p. 17, Ad.p. 7.   15000.
Free.

621.396.96

RADAR

2509 RRE JOURNAL. 1954.
(TRE Journal 1944-1953).
Royal Radar Establishment, Malvern, Worcs.
Irregular, + Research in radar and electronics and associated fields carried out at the Royal Radar Establishment.
Monographic articles.
No Index.
Subscription on application.

2510 RADAR AND ELECTRONICS. 1946.
Radar and Electronics Association, 43 Grove Park Road, Chiswick, London, W.4.
4, = + ‡ * Aspects of radar and related fields of electronics.
Letters, articles.
No Index.
T.p. 18, Ad.p. 6.
Per year £2. Free to members.

2511 RADAR SYSTEMS INTERNATIONAL. 1970.
Marconi Radar Systems Limited, Crompton Works, Chelmsford, Essex.
4, ‡ Civil aviation, airport and air line authorities.
No Index.
T.p. 4.   4000.
Free, controlled circulation.

621.397

TELEVISION

2512 BULLETIN OF THE ROYAL TELEVISION SOCIETY
Royal Television Society, 166 Shaftesbury Avenue, London, WC2.
4, =
No Index.
Free to members only.

2513 JOURNAL OF THE SOCIETY OF FILM AND TELEVISION ARTS. 1959,
(British Film Academy Journal 1954-1959)
Society of Film and Television Arts Ltd., 80 Great Portland Street, London, W1N 6JJ.
4, = Subjects connected with film and television production (non-technical). Each issue confined to one subject.
Book notices, book reviews, articles.

No Index.
Autumn 1971, T.p. 20.
Per copy 25p, per year £1 and Free to members.

2514 LOOK AND LISTEN. 1959.
Hansom Books, Artillery Mansions, 75 Victoria Street, London, SW1Z 0HZ.
12, ○ World radio and television programmes.
Book notices, book reviews, letters, articles, obituaries.
No Index.
Per copy 30p, per year £4.05.

2515 RELAY ASSOCIATION JOURNAL. 1935.
(Radio Relay Review 1932-1936)
Relay Services Association of Great Britain, 75 Cannon Street, London, EC4.
6, = ‡ TV relay and rental affairs.
Book reviews, legal notes, letters, new companies, news, new products, obituaries, parliamentary reports, standards.
No Index.
T.p. 19, Ad.p. 2.
Free to members.

2516 THE RELAY ENGINEER: Journal of the Society of Relay Engineers. 1971.
(Proceedings of Society of Relay Engineers, 1946-1970.)
Society of Relay Engineers, 10 Avenue Road, Dorridge, Solihull, Warwickshire.
2, ‡ * Engineering in the television relay (Cable-TV) industry.
Book reviews, letters, monographic articles, new products, obituaries.
6 year, −, Yes, None.
January 1972, T.p. 64,
Per copy 50p, per year £1. Free to members.

2517 SOUND AND VISION BROADCASTING. 1960.
Marconi Communication Systems Limited, Marconi House, Chelmsford, Essex.
3, ‡ + Television and braodcasting.
No Index.
T.p. 48, Ad.p. 12.   7000.
Per copy 75p, per year £2.25.

2518 TELEVISION: Servicing, construction colour developments. 1970.
(Practical Television, 1950-1970)
IPC Magazines Ltd. (Magazine Division), Fleetway House, Farringdon Street, London, EC4 4AD.
12, ‡ + = Television constructional colour and monochrome projects, test equipment, aerials etc., servicing, trade news and technical information. TV theory, TV transmission and studio technology.
Regular features: Servicing, TV-DX, TV Trade Information, problems solved, book reviews.
A, October/November, Yes, None.
August 1972, T.p. 39, Ad.p. 13.   32539.
Per copy 20p, per year £2.65.

621.56

REFRIGERATION

2519 FREEZE. 1972.
Hereford Press Ltd., 117 Cheyne Walk, London, SW10.
4, ○ = Home freezing-advising the housewife on freezers, frozen food, cooking and bulk buying.
Book reviews, commodity prices, letters, articles, new companies, new products.
No Index.
April-June 1972, T.p. 39, Ad.p. 35.
Per copy 20p, per year £1.

2520 JOURNAL OF REFRIGERATION. 1958.
Journal of Refrigeration Ltd., 19 Harcourt Street, London, W1.

12, = ‡   All aspects of refrigeration technology.
Book reviews, articles, new products, patents.
    patents.
A, —, Yes, None.
T.p. 19, Ad.p. 3
Per copy 20p, per year £2.50.
Indexed in: BTI.

2521 THE PROCEEDINGS OF THE INSTITUTE OF REFRIGERATION. 1900.
The Institute of Refrigeration, 272 London Road, Wallington, Surrey.
1, ‡ † *   Refrigeration in all its applications.
Monographic articles.
No Index.
T.p. 75.   2000.
Per copy £2.

2522 REFRIGERATION AND AIR CONDITIONING. 1898.
MacLaren Publishers Ltd., P.O. Box 109, 69/77 Davis House, High Street, Croydon, CR9 1QH.
12, ‡ =   Application of refrigeration and air conditioning equipment to environmental control in factory, office and home; and in the storage and transportation of perishables, in industrial manufacturing processes and science and medicine.
Book notices, book reviews, commodity prices, legal notes, monographic articles, new companies, new products, parliamentary reports, patents, standards.
A, —, Yes, None.
June 1972, T.p. 40, Ad.p. 75.   4786.
Per copy 30p, per year £3.50.

2523 WORLD REFRIGERATION AND AIR CONDITIONING.
World Refrigeration, 11A, Gloucester Road, London, SW7.
6, = ‡   Articles, news, new products.
No Index.
Per year £2.25.
Indexed in: BTI.

621.6
FLUID CONVEYING

2524 FLUIDRIVE NEWS. 1938.
(Hydynamic Newsletter, 1936-1938), Fluidrive Engineering Co. Ltd., Fluidrive Works, Worton Road, Isleworth, Middlesex.
4/6, †   Industrial external house journal, describing for Sales promotion, installations and applications of the Company's product, fluid couplings.
Occasional.
April 1972, T.p. 6.   10000.
Gratis.

621.65
PUMPS

2525 PUMPS: official organ of the European Committee of Pump Manufacturers.
Trade & Technical Press Ltd., Crown House, Morden, Surrey,
11, ‡
Monographic articles, news, new products.
No Index.
T.p. 33, Ad.p. 12.
Per year £3.50.
Indexed in: BTI.

2526 PUMPS AND OTHER FLUIDS MACHINERY ABSTRACTS. 1971.
BHRA Fluid Engineering, Cranfield, Bedford.
6, ‡ = +   Industrial pumps (rotodynamic, positive-displacement, and other types) and similar fluids machines such as fans, blowers, and compressors; jet pumps and ejectors; hydraulic turbines; marine propellers. Pumping systems and other related topics.
Abstracts, book notices, patents, standards.
6m, July and January (approx.), Yes, A.
January/February 1972, T.p. 39.
Per year £20.

621.7 : 744
DRAWING OFFICE PRACTICE

2527 TASS JOURNAL. 1972.
(Data Journal)
Technical & Supervisory Section of the Amalgamated Union of Engineering Workers, Onslow Hall, Little Green, Richmond, Surrey.
12, ○ ‡ =
Book reviews, letters, articles, obituaries, parliamentary reports.
No Index.
May 1972, T.p. 26, Ad.p. 6.
Free to members.

621.72
DIECASTING. PATTERN MAKING

2528 BRITISH MASTER PATTERNMAKER. 1962.
National Society of Master Patternmakers, 12 Cherry Street, Birmingham 2.
4, = ‡ * +   Review of current activities and latest techniques in the patternmaking industry.
Book reviews, letters, monographic articles, new companies, new products, obituaries, standards, tests.
A, January, No, None.
April 1972, T.p. 16, Ad.p. 8.
Free to members.

2529 CAST for economic production. 1972.
IPC Industrial Press Ltd., 33-39 Bowling Green Lane, London, EC1.
4, ‡   To provide production and design engineers in UK industry with information on diecasting and other foundry services available.
No Index.
T.p. 30, Ad.p. 70.   1500.
Per copy £2, per year £8.

621.74
FOUNDRY PRACTICE

2530 BCIRA JOURNAL. 1960.
(BCIRA Journal of Research and Development 1945-1959)
British Cast Iron Research Association, Alvechurch, Birmingham B48 7QB.
6, ‡ +   Reports on BCIRA investigations and articles of interest to ironfoundry technologists. Abstracts from world foundry literature.
Abstracts, book notices, book reviews, monographic articles, patents, standards, tests.
A, March, Yes, None.
July 1972, T.p. 88.   2200.
Free to BCIRA members only.

2531 ASSOCIATION OF BRONZE AND BRASS FOUNDERS BULLETIN. 1946.
Association, 69 Harborne Road, Birmingham 15.
4, = ‡   All matters affecting the industry.
Commodity prices, articles, news, standards, statistics.
No Index.
T.p. 24.
Free to members.

2532 THE BRITISH FOUNDRYMAN. 1957.
(Proceedings of the Institute of British Foundrymen 1904-1956).
All Institute, 137/139 Euston Road, London, NW1.
12, = ‡   Science and practice of founding.
Monographic articles.
A, December, No, None.
T.p. 83, Ad.p. 40.   11000.
Per copy £1, per year £10.
Indexed in: BTI.

2533 FOUNDRY TRADE JOURNAL. 1902.
(Iron and Steel Trades Journal c. 1860-1901)
Fuel and Metallurgical Journals, John Adam House, John Adam Street, London, WC2N 6JH.
51, ‡ =   World's foundry industry, diecasting and investment-casting.
Book notices, book reviews, commodity prices, letters, articles, new companies, new products, parliamentary reports, patents.
6m, c. 3m after completion of volume, Yes, None
T.p. 45, Ad.p. 29,   4825.
Per copy 15p, per year £8.80.
Indexed in: BTI.

2534 RUSSIAN CASTINGS PRODUCTION: Cover to cover translation of Liteinoe Proizvodstvo. 1961.
British Cast Iron Research Association, Alvechurch, Birmingham, B48 7QB.
12, ‡ +   Foundry technology, metallurgy, foundry plant and engineering. Reports of research and of practical experience.
Book notices, book reviews, monographic articles, obituaries, standards, tests.
A, April, Yes, None.
March 1971, T.p. 48.
Per copy £2, per year £15

621.74.04

DIECASTING

2535 DIECASTING & METAL MOULDING.
Brooklands Press Ltd., 44 Hatton Garden, London, EC1N 8AE.
6, ‡ =   Diecasting technology and uses of cast components.
Book reviews, articles, new companies, new products, reports, patents, standards, tests.
No Index.
January/February 1970, T.p. 18, Ad.p. 22.   5500.
Per copy 30p, per year £3 and Free, controlled circulation.

621.762

POWDER METALLURGY

2536 POWDER METALLURGY.
Institute of Metals, 17 Belgrave Square, London, SW1.
2, * = ‡ +   Powder metallurgy and technology.
Monographic articles.
A, Autumn, Yes, None.
T.p. 351, Ad.p. 18.
Per copy £2, per year £5 (non members)
Indexed in: BTI

621.791

WELDING

2537 METAL CONSTRUCTION & The British Welding Journal. 1969.
(The British Welding Journal, 1938-1968)
British Fuel & Metallurgical Journals Ltd., 17-19 John Adam Street, London, WC2N 6JH.
12, ‡ = + *   Welding technology in general.
Book notices, book reviews, letters, monographic articles, new companies, new products, obituaries, patents, standards.
A, February, Yes, None.
June 1972, T.p. 38, Ad.p. 17.   7200.
Per copy £1.20, per year £12.

2538 WELDING AND METAL FABRICATION. 1933,
IPC Technical Press Ltd., 33-40 Bowling Green Lane, London, EC1.
12, ‡
Book reviews, new products, news.
A, —, Yes, None.
T.p. 60, Ad.p. 60.   6000.
Per copy 40p, per year £5.20.
Indexed in: BTI.

2539 WELDING IN THE WORLD/LE SOUDAGE DANS LE MONDE. 1962.
General Secretariat, International Institute of Welding, 54 Princes Gate, Exhibition Road, London, SW7.
6, ‡   Welding and allied processes.
Book notices, book reviews, monographic articles, obituaries.
A, November/December, Yes, None.
T.p. 73,   1000.
Per copy £1.25, per year £7.50.

2540 WELDING RESEARCH INTERNATIONAL. 1972.
(Welding International Research & Development. 1971).
The Welding Institute, Abington Hall, Abington, Cambridge, CB1 6AL.
4, ‡ + =   All aspects of welding technology.
Book notices, monographic articles.
A, December, Yes, None.
No. 1, 1972, T.p. 92.
Per copy £12, per year £42. (Non-members); £16 per year to research members of W.I.

621.793

METAL FINISHING

2541 CANNING JOURNAL: Electroplating & Polishing News. 1960.
W. Canning & Company Limited, Great Hampton Street, Birmingham, B18 6AS.
1, ‡ †   Recent developments in metal finishing processes and equipment in particular developments in electroplating and in polishing.
New products.
No Index.
1972, T.p. 32.   20000.
Free.

2542 ELECTROPLATING & METAL FINISHING. 1947.
Wheatland Journals Ltd. (Part of Turret Press (Holdings) Ltd.), 157 Hagden Lane, Watford, Herts.
12, ‡   Whole field of metal finishing.
Book notices, book reviews, letters, monographic articles, new companies, new products, obituaries, patents, standards, tests.
No Index.
May 1972, T.p. 24, Ad.p. 31.   3278.
Per copy 49p, per year £5.95.

2543 METAL FINISHING ABSTRACTS. 1959.
Finishing Publications Ltd., 17 Cranmer Road, Hampton Hill, Middlesex.
6, ‡ +   Abstracts all literature published throughout the world on metal finishing including papers and articles, patents, books, standard specifications, translations, reports, etc.
Abstracts, book notices, book reviews.
A, November/December, No, None.
March 1972, T.p. 64.   c. 950.
Per copy £4.66, per year £28.

2544 METAL FINISHING JOURNAL. 1955.
Fuel & Metallurgical Journals Ltd., John Adam House, John Adam Street, London, WC2N 6JH.
12, = ‡   Science and technology of paint application, electro deposition, vitreous enamelling, galvanizing, anodising, metal spraying and all metal finishing processes.
Monographic articles, new products, reports, tests.
No Index.
T.p. 31, Ad.p. 25.   1710.
Per copy 30p, per year £3.60.
Indexed in: BTI.

2545 METAL FINISHING PLANT & PROCESSES. 1969.
Finishing Publications Ltd., 17 Cranmer Road, Hampton Hill, Middlesex.
6, ‡ =   Presents in abbreviated form as complete a survey as possible of all new products and processes, plant and chemicals for finishing on an international scale, classified into 20 sections.
New products.
A, incl. Trade and Company Names. —, No, None.
March 1972, T.p. 31, Ad.p. 5.   c. 3000.
Per copy £2.30, per year £14.

621.798

PACKAGING

2546 CONVERTER. 1964.
Factory Publications Ltd., (Mercury House Group), 103-119 Waterloo Road, London, SE1.
12, = ‡ +   Paper, board, film and foil converting technology.
Book reviews, letters, monographic articles, news, new products, patents, tests.
A, —, Yes, None.
T.p. 23, Ad.p. 36.   4000.
Per copy 50p, per year £5 and Free, controlled circulation.

2547 CONVERTING INDUSTRY. 1968.
(Paper Box and Bag Maker, 1958-1967)
S.C. Philips & Co. Ltd., 50 Fetter Lane, London, EC4.
12, † ‡   Conversion of paper, paperboard, film and foil.
No Index.
T.p. 24, Ad.p. 12.   3000.
Per copy 30p, per year £3 and Free, controlled circulation.

2548 FOODPACK. 1965.
(Produce Packaging, 1955-1964).
BPS Exhibitions Ltd., 6 London Street, London, W2.
4, ‡   Food and allied packaging industry.
Book reviews, letters, news.
No Index.
T.p. 20, Ad.p. 22.   6000.
Free, controlled circulation.

2549 MODERN PURCHASING. 1966.
Maclean-Hunter Ltd., 30 Old Burlington Street, London, W1X 2AE.
12, ‡ =
Book notices, book reviews, commodity prices, legal notes, letters, articles, new companies, new products, parliamentary reports, patents, standards, tests.
No Index.
T.p. 30, Ad.p. 52.   17500.
Free, Controlled circulation.

2550 PIRA MARKETING ABSTRACTS. 1972.
PIRA, Randalls Road, Leatherhead, Surrey.
12, ‡   Marketing and marketing techniques in the paper and board, printing and packaging industries.
Abstracts, book notices.
A, —, Yes, None.
£25 (£17.50 to PIRA members).

2551 PIRA PACKAGING JOURNAL.
PIRA, Randalls Road, Leatherhead, Surrey.
2, ‡ = +   Research projects.
Monographic articles.
No Index.
Free to members.

2552 PACKAGING. 1930.
The Tudor Press Ltd., 75 Carter Lane, London, EC4V 5ET.
12, = ‡   Reports new materials, machines and methods as applied to the packaging industry.
Monographic articles, new companies, new products.
A, January, Yes, None.
May 1972, T.p. 36, Ad.p. 40.   9037.
Per copy 30p, per year £3.50.
Indexed in: BTI.

2553 PACKAGING ABSTRACTS. 1944.
PIRA, Randalls Road, Leatherhead, Surrey.
12, ‡   Digest of articles on packaging, including materials, containers, machinery, and packaging of special products.
Abstracts, book notices.
A, —, Yes, None.
Per year £17.50.

2554 PACKAGING NEWS. 1954.
Maclean-Hunter Ltd., 30 Old Burlington Street, London, W1.
12, ‡ = +   All aspects of packaging technology.
Book reviews, letters, monographic articles, new companies, new products, standards, tests, news.
No Index.
T.p. 24, Ad.p. 24.   16000.
Free, controlled circulation.

2555 PACKAGING TECHNOLOGY. 1968.
(Institute of Packaging Journal, 1948-1967).
Institute of Packaging, Malcolm House, Empire Way, Wembley, Middx.
6, = ‡ +   Packaging technology.
Book notices, book reviews, letters, monographic articles, new products, standards, tests.
No index.
T.p. 23, Ad.p. 23.
Free to members.

2556 PACKAGING WEEK. 1969.
Magazines for Industry Inc., 59 Fleet Street, London, EC4.
26, =   All aspects of packing industry.
No Index.
T.p. 8, Ad.p. 7.
Free, Controlled circulation.

2557 PAPERBOARD PACKAGING INTERNATIONAL. 1964.
Magazines for Industry Inc., 59 Fleet Street, London, EC4.
4, =
Commodity prices, monographic articles, new companies, new products, patents.
No Index.
Free, controlled circulation.

2558 PROSPECT.
Tupperware Co. Ltd., 43 Upper Grosvenor Street, London, SW1.
6, = †
News.
No Index.
Free to dealers.

Key to reference symbols

○ popular   ‡ technical   = trade/professional

+ research   * society/institution   † house journal

621.822.7

BALL BEARINGS

2559 BALL BEARING JOURNAL: a quarterly review of rolling bearing engineering. 1926.
Skefko Ball Bearing Company Limited, Leagrave Road, Luton, Bedfordshire.
4, ‡ ○ + † Covers all aspects of ball and roller bearing engineering, including spherical plain bearings. Features theoretical articles giving bearing load calculations, new developments (e.g. hydrostatic bearings), and general engineering applications.
Monographic articles, new products.
A, —, Yes, None.
No. 170, T.p. 32.   c. 16000.
Free.

621.86

MATERIALS HANDLING

2560 CJ INTERNATIONAL GUIDE TO USED PLANT AND EQUIPMENT. 1972.
IPC Contract Journals Ltd., Tower House, Southampton Street, London, WC2E 9QX.
52, = ‡
No Index.

2561 CONSTRUCTION PLANT & EQUIPMENT incorporating Muck Shifter & Cranes. 1972.
Morgan Grampian (Professional Press) Ltd., 30 Calderwood Street, Woolwich, London, SE18 6QH.
12, ‡ All activities connected with the plant line industry.
Commodity prices, legal notes, letters, articles, new companies, new products, tests.
No Index.
12000.
Free, controlled circulation.

2562 CONSTRUCTION PLANT HIRE. 1967.
(Plant Hire, Contractors equipment and materials, 1962-1966),
Plant and Equipment Publications Ltd., The Adelphi, John Adam Street, London, WC2N 6AY.
12, ‡ A specialist journal for the plant-hire industry.
Articles, new companies, new products, obituaries, patents, standards, tests.
No Index.
June 1972, T.p. 16, Ad.p. 24.
Per year £1.75 and Free, controlled circulation.

2563 CONTAINERISATION INTERNATIONAL. 1967.
The National Magazine Co. Ltd., 680 Garrett Lane, London, SW17.
12, = All matters relating to container freight throughout the world.
Letters, articles, new companies, new products, parliamentary reports, patents, standards, tests.
No Index.
June 1972, T.p. 33, Ad.p. 50.   24534.
Free, controlled circulation.

2564 CONVEYANCER NEWS. 1972.
(Conveyancer Quarterly News),
Conveyancer Ltd., PO Box 24, Warrington, WA5 1QT
3, = †
Monographic articles, new products.
No Index.
Spring 1972, T.p. 24.
Free.

2565 CONVEYOR JOURNAL: House Journal of Manufacturers Equipment Company Limited, Hull. 1958.
Group Publicity, J.H. Fenner & Co. Ltd., Marfleet, Hull.
3, † Latest Rapistan Installations and new products.
Short articles.
3 yearly, —, Yes, None.
May 1972, T.p. 15.   6000.
Free.

2566 COPE IN SCOTLAND. 1971.
Virginia House, 62 Virginia Street, Glasgow, G1 1PX.
26, = Materials handling and transport industries in Scotland.
No Index.
Free.

2567 FREIGHT MANAGEMENT. 1966.
Temple Press Ltd., 40 Bowling Green Lane, London, EC1.
12, = ‡ Economic movement of freight by all means, and ancillary services.
Book notices, book reviews, legal notes, letters, monographic articles, news, new products, parliamentary reports, standards, tests.
A, —, Yes, None.
T.p. 39, Ad.p. 55.   20000.
Free, controlled circulation.

2568 INTERNATIONAL CONTAINER DIRECTORY.
Magazine for Industry Inc., 56 Fleet Street, London, EC4Y 1JU.
2, =
No Index.
Subscription on application.

2569 MATERIALS HANDLING & MANAGEMENT. 1968.
(IMH Journal)
Turnmill Press Ltd. (for Institute of Materials Handling), 65/66 Turnmill Street, London, EC1.
6, * + ‡ = All aspects of materials and other handling.
Book reviews, letters, monographic articles, news, new products, obituaries.
No Index.
T.p. 25, Ad. p. 25.   5200.
Per copy 50p, per year £2.50, Free to members.

2570 MATERIALS HANDLING NEWS. 1955.
IPC Technical Press, 33-40 Bowling Green Lane, London, EC1.
12, ‡ = Production, packaging, storage and distribution containers.
Book notices, book reviews, monographic articles, new companies, new products, tests.
No Index.
T.p. 50, Ad.p. 50.   18000.
Free, controlled circulation.

2571 MECHANICAL HANDLING. 1891.
IPC Technical Press, 33-40 Bowling Green Lane, London, EC1.
12, = ‡
Book reviews, articles, news, new products, patents.
A, —, Yes, None.
T.p. 60, Ad.p. 180.   7000.
Per copy 40p, per year £5.50.
Indexed in: BTI.

2572 STORAGE HANDLING DISTRIBUTION: journal of Materials Management. 1957.
(Industrial Trucks & Storage Equipment News)
Turret Press Ltd./Turret Press (Holdings) Ltd., 157 Hagden Lane, Watford, WD1 8LW.
12, = ‡
Letters, Book reviews, articles.
No Index.
May 1972, T.p. 52, Ad.p. 52.
Per year £5.85.

2573 TRANSPORT AND MATERIALS HANDLING. 1972.
Irish Publishing Co., 39 Lower Leeson Street, Dublin 2.
= ‡
No Index.
5000.
Controlled circulation.

621.89
LUBRICATION

2574 PROSPECTS.
Acheson Colloids Co., Plymouth, PL4 0SP.
3, ‡ †   Case histories to illustrate the successful use of Acheson lubricants and coatings. News of new Acheson products. Technical and research articles.
Monographic articles, new companies, new products, standards, tests.
No Index.
10000.
Free.

2575 TRIBOLOGY. 1968.
IPC Science & Technology Publications Ltd., 32 High Street, Guildford, Surrey.
4, + ‡   Science and technology of function, lubrication and news.
Book reviews, letters, monographic articles, news, new products, patents, standards.
A, February, Yes, None.
T.p. 53, Ad.p. 1.   c. 1000.
Per copy £2, per year £7.

2576 TRIBOS: Tribology Abstracts. 1968.
British Hydromechanics Research Association, Cranfield, Bedford.
12, ‡ + =   Friction, wear, lubrication, bearings, and associated subjects, drawn from world literature. About 1600 abstracts p.a. currently.
Abstracts.
6m, July/January, No, A.
January 1972, T.p. 30, Ad.p. 1.   250.
Per year £20.

621.9
MACHINE TOOLS

2577 INTERNATIONAL JOURNAL OF MACHINE TOOL DESIGN AND RESEARCH. 1961.
Pergamon Press Ltd., Headington Hill Hall, Oxford, OX3 0BW.
4, = +   Advanced machine tool design and research.
Book reviews, letters, monographic articles.
A, Last issue of volume, Yes, None.
T.p. c. 300.
Per copy £4.50, per year £16.

2578 MACHINE TOOL ENGINEERING. 1966.
(British Machine Tool Engineering, 1920-1965)
Associated British Machine Tool Makers Ltd., 17 Grosvenor Gardens, London, SW1.
4, ‡ = +
Book reviews, letters, articles, news, new products, standards, tests.
A, January, Yes, None.
T.p. 28, Ad.p. 24.
Free, controlled circulation.
Indexed in: BTI.

2579 MACHINE TOOL RESEARCH.
Machine Tool Industry Research Association, Hulley Road, Hurdsfield, Macclesfield, Cheshire.
‡ +
Private circulation to members only.

2580 MACHINE TOOLS & TOOLING.
Hanover Press, 4 Mill Street, London, W1.
6, ‡ =   Postal fact-finder service on developments in the industry.
No Index.
Ad.p. 22.   20000.
Free, controlled circulation.

2581 MACHINERY & PRODUCTION ENGINEERING. 1965.
(Machinery, 1912-1965).
The Machinery Publishing Co. Ltd., New England House, New England Street, Brighton, BN1 4HN.
52, ‡ =   Current technical developments in the metal-working industry (U.K. and Abroad), with particular reference to manufacturing methods and equipment, machine tools, design, tooling and management techniques, largely written by own editorial staff of trained engineers.
Abstracts, book notices, book reviews, letters, monographic articles, new companies, new products, obituaries, standards, tests,
6m, 6-9 months after end of half year, No, None.
19/7/72, T.p. 41, Ad.p. 89.   10148 (8172 paid)
Per copy 10p, per year £5.20.
Indexed in: BTI.

2582 MACHINERY LLOYD. 1929.
Engineering, Chemical & Marine Press Ltd., 20-23 Greville Street, London, EC1.
12, ‡ =   Review of engineering equipment.
Book notices, book reviews, monographic articles, new products, tests.
No Index.
T.p. 30, Ad.p. 67.
Free, controlled circulation.

2583 PRODUCTION TECHNOLOGY: Abstracts and Reports from Eastern Europe. 1969.
(Russian Machine Tools 1963-1968).
Machine Tool Industry Research Assoc., Hulley Road, Hurdsfield, Macclesfield, Cheshire.
4, ‡ +   Complete guide to technical articles and books on production technology originating in Eastern Europe and USSR, and gives a comprehensive picture of the development of production engineering methods and machine tool design in USSR, Czechoslovakia, Poland, Hungary, Rumania, and Yugoslavia, and occasionally from Japan and India.
Abstracts, book notices.
No Index.
March, 1972, T.p. 31.   c. 500.
Per year £15.

2584 TOOLING. 1948.
Sawell Publications, 4 Ludgate Circus, London, EC4.
12, = ‡   Gauge and tool industry, precision engineering.
Articles, news, new products, patents.
A, —, Yes, None.
T.p. 45, Ad.p. 35.   3500.
Per copy 20p, per year £2.
Indexed in: BTI.

622
MINING

2585 COAL NEWS: newspaper of Britain's mining industry. 1961.
(Coal Magazine, 1947-1961).
National Coal Board, Hobart House, Grosvenor Place, London, SW1X 7AE.
12, †   Published in 17 separate coalfield editions, this tabloid newspaper fully reports the coal industry's challenges and achievements for mineworkers, their families, staff and management.
Book reviews, letters, articles, new products, obituaries, parliamentary reports, patents, tests.
No Index.
June 1972, T.p. 13, Ad.p. 3.   c. 200000.
Per copy 5p, per year 60p, 17 editions per set 33p, per year £5.60.

2586 COLLIERY GUARDIAN. 1858.
(Steel and Coal; The Iron and Coal Trades Review)
Fuel & Metallurgical Journals Ltd., John Adam House, 17-19 John Adam St., London, WC2N 6JH.

12, ‡ = +   Technical development of all aspects of coal mining throughout the world.
Book notices, book reviews, letters, monographic articles, new products, obituaries, parliamentary reports, patents, standards, tests.
A, March for preceding year, No, None.
June 1972, T.p. 38, Ad.p. 38.
Per copy 60p, per year £7.80.
Indexed in: BTI.

2587 IMM ABSTRACTS. 1950.
Institute of Mining & Metallurgy, 44 Portland Place, London, W1N 4BR.
6, * = ‡ +   Geology, mining and processing of minerals (except coal).
Abstracts,
No Index.
T.p. 32.   1000.
Per year £3.

2588 INDUSTRIAL MINERALS. 1967.
Metal Bulletin Ltd., 46 Wigmore Street, London, W1H 0BJ.
12, =   Commercial intelligence on non-metallic minerals.
Book reviews, commodity prices, letters, news, new products, obituaries,
6m, January/July, No, None.
T.p. 31, Ad.p. 19.   2150.
Per copy 50p, per year £6.

2589 INTERNATIONAL MINING EQUIPMENT. 1950.
Rhodes Industrial Services Ltd., 54-55 Wilton Road, London, SW1.
6, ‡   Mining engineering.
Book reviews, news, new companies, articles.
No Index.
T.p. 18, Ad.p. 2
Per year £2.50.
Indexed in: BTI.

2590 MINE AND QUARRY. 1972.
(Mining and Minerals Engineering 1968-1971; Colliery Engineering 1924; Mine and Quarry Engineering 1936)
Ashire Publishing Ltd., 42 Grays Inn Road, London, WC1X 8LR.
12, = ‡ +   Locating, extraction and processing of all minerals.
Book notices, letters, monographic articles, new products.
No Index.
T.p. 40, Ad.p. 28.   8000.
Per year £3.50.
Indexed in: BTI.

2592 THE MINING ENGINEER. 1960.
(Transactions, Institution of Mining Engineers, 1889-1960)
3 Grosvenor Crescent, London, SW1X 7EG.
12, * = ‡   Practice and theory of mining technology.
Book notices, book reviews, commodity prices, legal notes, letters, monographic articles, new companies, new products, obituaries, parliamentary reports, patents, standards, tests,
A, September, No, 10 year, viz. 1949-1959, 1959-1969.
October-September 1972, T.p. 64, Ad.p. 10.   5000.
Per copy £1.05, per year £12.50. Free to members.
Indexed in: BTI.

2593 MINING JOURNAL. 1835,
Mining Journal Ltd., 15 Wilson Street, London, EC2.
52, = + ‡   Mining in 130 countries.
Commodity prices, news.
6m, March/September, No, None.
T.p. 19, Ad.p. most.   6000.
Per year £8.50.

2594 MINING MAGAZINE. 1909.
Mining Journal Ltd., 15 Wilson Street, London, EC2.
12, = ‡ †   Techniques, processes, equipment and management methods.
Monographic articles, new products.
6m, March/September, Yes, None.
T.p. 79, Ad.p. most.   6000.
Per copy 35p, per year £4.20.
Indexed in: BTI.

2595 MINING RESEARCH AND DEVELOPMENT REVIEW. 1970.
(Bretby Broadsheet 1961-1969).
National Coal Board, Mining Research and Development Establishment, Ashby Road, Stanhope Bretby, Burton-on-Trent, Staffs. DE15 0QD.
3, ‡ + =   Research, development and testing in aid of the mining of coal and its preparation for the market. (Circulation largely with in NCB itself, to keep a large and geographically dispersed industry informed on this work.)
Monographic articles.
No Index.
November. 1970, T.p. 16.
Free.

2596 MINING TECHNOLOGY. 1969.
(AIMME Journal)
Association of Mining, Electrical & Mechanical Engineers, c/o 34 Great James Street, London, WC1.
12, * = ‡   Practice and theory in coal, mineral and metalliferous mining, opencast and quarry work.
Book reviews, letters, monographic articles, new companies, new products, parliamentary reports, patents, standards, tests.
A, August, Yes, None.
T.p. 24, Ad.p. 20.   5000.
Per copy 40p, per year £3.50. Free to members.

2597 NATIONAL NEWSLETTER OF THE BRITISH ASSOCIATION OF COLLIERY MANAGEMENT. 1947.
BACM, 317 Nottingham Road, Basford, Nottingham.
3, =   Trade union affairs.
Book reviews, letters, articles, news, parliamentary reports.
No Index.
T.p. 34, Ad.p. 6. Free to members.

2598 SAFETY IN MINES ABSTRACTS. 1969.
(Abstracts of Current Publications, 1952-1968)
Safety in Mines Research Establishment, Red Hill, off Broad Lane, Sheffield. S3 7HQ.
6, +   Subject coverage reflects the Establishments' current interests in health and safety in mines and quarries, and the use of electrical equipment in hazardous areas in other industries.
Each issue (2m), —, No, A.
Subscription on application.

622.35

QUARRYING

2599 QUARRY MANAGERS JOURNAL. 1917.
Quarry Managers Journal Ltd., 62-64 Baker Street, London, W1M 2BN.
12, = ‡   All asepcts of surface minerals.
Book notices, book reviews, legal notes, letters, monographic articles, new products, standards, tests.
A, February/March, Yes, None.
T.p. 40, Ad.p. 80.
Per copy 20p, per year £2.25.
Indexed in: BTI.

623.4
GUNS

2600 AFV/WEAPONS PROFILE. 1969.
Profile Publications Limited, Coburg House, Sheet Street, Windsor, Berks.
12-15, ○ ‡   International AFV's of popular and specialist interest.
Monographic articles,
A, —, Yes, None.
46, T.p. 20.   c. 10000.
Per copy 40p, per year £4.80.

2601 JOURNAL OF THE ARMS AND ARMOUR SOCIETY. 1953.
The Arms & Armour Society, c/o 17 St Charles Square, London, W10 6EF.
2, ‡ + *   The history of arms and armour of all periods and countries, excluding only completely modern arms.
Book and article notices, monographic articles.
3 yearly, on the completion of a volume, Yes, None.
September 1970, T.p. 68, Ad.p. 2.   c.850.
Per year £1.25.

2602 SMALL ARMS IN PROFILE. 1971.
Profile Publications Limited, Coburg House, Sheet Street, Windsor, Berks.
12, ○ ‡   International weapons of popular or specialist interest.
Monographic articles.
A, —, Yes, None.
No. 10, T.p. 20.
Per copy 40p, per year £4.80.

623.8
NAVAL ENGINEERING

2604 NAVAL RECORD. 1966.
Monitor (Naval Publications) Ltd., The Secretary, 4 Vicarage Road, Eastbourne, Sussex.
6, ‡ =   International coverage of current naval construction.
Book reviews, letters, monographic articles, new products, standards, tests.
No Index.
November 1971, T.p. 24, Ad.p. 8.   2200.
Per copy 37½p, per year £2.50.

2605 WARSHIP PROFILE. 1970.
Profile Publications Limited, Coburg House, Sheet Street, Windsor, Berks.
14, ○ ‡   International warships since 1900 of popular or technical interest.
A, Included in Annual Bound Volume, Yes, None.
No. 20, T.p. 24.   c.10000.
Per copy 50p, per year £6.

624
CIVIL ENGINEERING

2606 ACE: Articles in Civil Engineering. 1969.
University of Bradford Library, Richmond Road, Bradford, BD7 1DP.
12, + ‡ =   Current awareness service for whole field of civil engineering and construction industry; includes engineering geology, power generation, public health, water supply, pollution, urban planning and traffic engineering. Covers mainly English-language periodical and report literature.
Subject grouping for easy scanning; item numbering for personal index compilation.
No Index.
January 1972, T.p. 28.
Per year £7.

2607 ARUP JOURNAL. 1966.
Ove Arup Partnership, 13 Fitzroy Street, London, W1P 6BQ.
4, ‡ † =   Architecture, structural, civil and services engineering.
Monographic articles.
A, March, No, None.
September 1971, T.p. 23.
Free.

2608 CIVIL ENGINEERING AND PUBLIC WORKS REVIEW. 1906.
Lomax, Erskine & Co. Ltd., 8 Buckingham Street, London, WC2.
12, = ‡
Book notices, book reviews, commodity prices, legal notes, letters, monographic articles, new products, obituaries, standards.
A, December, No, None.
T.p. 50, Ad.p. 69.
Per copy 25p, per year £3.
Indexed in: BTI.

2609 CIVIL ENGINEERING TECHNICIAN: Journal of the Society of Civil Engineering Technicians. 1968.
Institution of Civil Engineers for S.C.E T., 1-7 Great George Street, Westminster, London, SW1P 3AA.
4, ‡ * =
Commodity prices, letters, monographic articles, obituaries, parliamentary reports, tests.
No Index.
August 1971, T.p. 28, Ad.p. 5.
Per copy 50p, per year £2.

2610 CONSTRUCTION: official journal of the Construction Industry Federation. 1972.
The Federation, 36 Morehampton Road, Dublin, 4.
12, ‡ =

2611 CONSTRUCTION TECHNOLOGY: Building and architecture in Scotland. 1966.
(Scottish Public Services 1963-66).
Forth Publishing Group, 45 Moray Place, Edinburgh, EH3 6DD.
12, = ‡   Architects, surveyors, civil engineers and local authorities in Scotland, interested in new construction and maintenance.
Book notices, book reviews, monographic articles, new products, tests.
No Index.
July 1972, T.p. 36, Ad.p. 36.
Per copy 25p, per year £3 and Free, controlled circulation.

2612 CONTRACTORS' PLANT REVIEW: Official Journal of the Contractors' Mechanical Plant Engineers. 1962.
Wheatland Journals Ltd., 157 Hagden Lane, Watford, Herts.
12, * ‡
Book reviews, legal notes, letters, articles, new companies, new products, obituaries, patents, tests.
No Index.
June 1972, T.p. 32, Ad.p. 36.   8250.
Per year £4.95.

2613 DOE CONSTRUCTION. 1972.
Directorate General of Development (Housing and Construction), Department of the Environment, Thames House South, Millbank, London, SW1P 4QH.
4, ‡ †   Technical and management information covering all aspects of construction. Through the feedback of information it helps those concerned with design, economics, construction and maintenance to share each others' experience.
Abstracts, book notices, legal notes, letters, monographic articles, new products, standards, tests.
Q, Cumulative index in each issue, Yes, None.
March 1972, T.p. 48, Ad.p. 16.   12500.
Per copy 50p, per year £1.80.

2614 EARTH AND SKY: Magazine of Howard Farrow Construction Ltd. 1954.
Stocker Hocknell Limited, 4, Market Square, Amersham.
4, ‡ †   Cumulative record of Farrow contribution to building and civil engineering world and of projects completed, with studies of developing construction and management techniques.
No Index.
March 1972, T.p. 16.   2000.
Free.

2615 EUROPEAN CIVIL ENGINEERING ABSTRACTS. 1972.
CITIS (Construction Industry Translation and Information Services), 130 Foxrock Park, Foxrock, Dublin, Ireland and 30 Baker St., London, W1M 2DS.
6, ‡ + =   Abstracts, up to 200 words each, in English, of articles appearing in all the main European civil engineering journals (incl. British).
Abstracts, book notices.
A, December, Yes, None.
March 1972, T.p. 50.
Subscription on application.

2616 HIGHWAYS DESIGN AND CONSTRUCTION.
IPC Building & Contract Journals Ltd., 40 Bowling Green Lane, London, EC1.
12, = ‡   Latest developments, worldwide, in highway planning, design and construction.
Letters, monographic articles.
No Index.
Per year £3.

2617 INSTITUTION OF CIVIL ENGINEERS. PROCEEDINGS: Part 1: Design and Construction. Part 2: Research and Theory.
(Minutes of Proceedings 1837-1935; Journal 1936-1951; Proceedings (Parts 1, 2, 3) 1952-1956; Proceedings (Monthly) 1957-1972).
The Institution of Civil Engineers, 1-7 Great George Street, Westminster, London, SW1P 3AA.
Part 1: (Feb, May, Aug and Nov.); Part 2: (Mar, June, Sept, Dec.), ‡ + *   Intended as an essential reference for practising civil engineers, this contains formal and original technical papers which record the construction and planning of civil engineering works, describes new research and methods of analysis, outlines new techniques for construction and maintenance and reviews present-day technology. Part 1: (Design and Construction) contains papers on the practice of civil engineering. Part 2: (Research and Theory) deals with the experimental, mathematical and theoretical aspects.
Monographic articles.
A, —, Yes, None, but details of PROCEEDINGS are contained in the 5-yearly bound index to all ICE publications.
May, 1972, T.p. 93, Ad.p. 1. June 1972, T.p. 125.   (Part 1: 20000), Part 2: 9000).
ICE Members, per copy 40p, per year £1. Non-members, per copy £1.25, per year £4.
Indexed in: BTI.

2618 INTERNATIONAL CONSTRUCTION. 1962.
IPC Building & Contract Journals Ltd., 32, Southwark Bridge Road, London, SE1.
12, ‡   Civil engineering and construction including roads, dams, power stations, harbours, airports, industrial building, etc. on a worldwide basis.
Abstracts, monographic articles, new products, patents, standards.
A, January, No, None.
June 1972, T.p. 35, Ad.p. 35.   20327.
Per year £6 and Free, controlled circulation.

2619 JOURNAL OF TERRAMECHANICS. 1964.
Pergamon Press Ltd. (for the International Society for Terrain Vehicle Systems), Headington Hill Hall, Oxford, OX3 0BW.
4, + =   Research and development on vehicle systems for off-road operations.
Book reviews, monographic articles.
A, Last issue of volume, Yes, None.
T.p. 80, Ad.p. 4.
Per copy £6, per year £22.

2620 JOURNAL OF WILLIAM MALLINSON & DENNY MOTT LTD. 1970.
(The Journal of William Mallinson & Sons Ltd. 1950-1969).
William Mallinson & Denny Mott Ltd., 130 Hackney Road, London, E27 QR.
4, †   All members (employees) of Group in UK. Eire; Netherlands; Belgium; Australia; Thailand.
Articles, new products, obituaries, tests, staff news.
No Index.
Jan. 1972, T.p. 40.
Free.

2621 NEW CIVIL ENGINEER: magazine of the Institution of Civil Engineers. 1972.
Institution of Civil Engineers, 1-7 Great George Street, Westminster, London, SW1P 3AA.
52, ‡ = *   All aspects of civil engineering.
Book reviews, letters, monographic articles, new products.
A, —, Yes, None.
June 1972, T.p. 64, Ad.p. 64.   46000.
Per copy 50p, per year £3.50 and Free to members.

2622 PROJECT SCOTLAND. 1972.
62 Virginia Street, Glasgow, G1 1PX.
52, =   Plant, building and construction.
No Index.
Free, controlled circulation.

2623 STRUCTURAL ENGINEER. 1923.
Institution of Structural Engineers, 203-9 North Gower Street, London, NW1.
12, = ‡
Book reviews, articles, news.
No Index.
14500.
Per year £4.50.
Indexed in: BTI.

2624 SURVEYOR: Local Government Technology. 1892.
Building & Contract Journals Ltd., Dorset House, Stamford Street, London, SE1 9LU.
52, ‡   Roads, street lighting, transportation. water supply, main drainage and sewage treatment, town and country planning, public cleansing, parks and recreation, civic building of all kinds.
Book notices, book reviews, legal notes, letters, monographic articles, new products, obituaries, parliamentary reports, standards.
6m, —, Yes, None.
30-6-1972, T.p. 25, Ad.p. 25.   6742.
Per copy 15p, per year £7.80.
Indexed in: BTI.

2625 TAYWOOD NEWS: The House Magazine of the Taylor Woodrow Group of Companies. 1947.
Taylor Woodrow Services Ltd., 345 Ruislip Road, Southall, Middlesex.
6, †   Describes construction projects carried out by Taylor Woodrow and Associated Companies throughout the world, together with sports and social activities of T.W. employees; appointments, etc.
No Index.
March/April 1972, T.p. 60.   9500.
Free.

2626 TECHNICAL NOTES. 1943.
CIBA-GEIGY (UK) Limited, Plastics Division, Duxford, Cambs, CB24QA.
12, ‡ ○ †   CIBA-GEIGY synthetic resins, adhesives and ancillary products. Reports case histories of industrial, professional and general interest.
Monographic articles.
5 year, December 1968, No, None.
4/1972, T.p. 8.   25000.
Free.

624.01

STRUCTURAL MATERIALS

2627 COMPOSITES: the technology of composite materials. 1969.
IPC Science & Technology Publications Ltd., 32 High Street, Guildford, Surrey.
4, + ‡ All materials comprising a reinforcement in a matrix in addition to structures such as honeycombs, laminates etc.
Book reviews, letters, monographic articles, new products, patents.
A, January, Yes, None.
T.p. 60, Ad.p. 3.
Per copy £2.50, per year £10.

2628 CONSTRUCTION STEELWORK METALS AND MATERIALS: the journal of metals and materials in building and construction. 1968.
Portal Press Limited, 72 London Road, Croydon, CR0 2TB.
11, ‡ Application of metals in building and construction, with emphasis on structural steelwork.
Book notices, book reviews, letters, monographic articles, new companies, new products, obituaries, reports, patents, standards, tests.
No Index.
April/May 1972, T.p. 38, Ad.p. 20. 8350.
Per copy 25p, per year £2.75 and Free, controlled circulation.

624.131

SOIL MECHANICS

2629 GÉOTECHNIQUE.
The Institution of Civil Engineers, 1-7 Great George Street, Westminster, London, SW1P 3AA.
4, ‡ + * Theory and practice of all aspects of soil mechanics.
Book reviews, letters, monographic articles, new products, obituaries, standards, tests.
A, December, Yes, None.
March 1972, T.p. 192, Ad.p. 13. 4000.
Per copy £1.25, per year £4.50 members. Per copy £1.75, per year £6.50 non-members.
Indexed in: BTI.

624.19

TUNNELS AND TUNNELLING

2630 TUNNELS AND TUNNELLING. 1969.
Wilton Publications Ltd., 8 Buckingham Street, London, WC2.
6, + ‡ = International research, design and construction techniques for road, rail, sewers etc. in addition to planning, maintenance and operation.
Book notices, book reviews, letters, monographic articles, new companies, new products, patents, standards, tests.
A, November/December, No, None.
T.p. 32, Ad.p. 28. 5000.
Per copy 25p, per year £1.50.
Indexed in: BTI.

625.1

RAILWAY ENGINEERING

2631 BRANCH LINE NEWS. 1971.
(Branch Line News Sheet 1964-1970; Branch Line News 1955-1964).
Branch Line Society, 18 Higher Drive, Purley, Surrey.
26, * Current developments in the railway network of the British Isles—especially branch and minor lines. Details of activities by the society and other bodies.
Book and record reviews, articles.
A, February, No, None.
12/7/72, T.p. 10. 500.
Per year £1.50.

2632 DEVELOPMENT REPORT. 1952.
Railway Development Association, 3 Hall Way, Purley, Surrey.
4, * Work of the association, advocating modernising and development or railways.
No Index.
Autumn 1971, T.p. 6.
Per year £1.
Free to members.

2633 FESTINIOG RAILWAY MAGAZINE: Journal of the Festiniog Railway Society. 1958.
(Newsletter 1955-1958)
Festiniog Railway Society Limited, 17 Tynymaes, Ffestiniog, Blaenau Ffestiniog, Merioneth.
4, * † News and opinion of the Festiniog Railway; anything related thereto.
Book notices, letters, monographic articles, new products, obituaries, tests.
Cumulated index to 1966.
Autumn 1971, T.p. 36, Ad.p. 2. 5500.
Free to members.

2634 FIVE FOOT THREE. 1966.
Railway Preservation Society of Ireland, 416 Lisburn Road, Belfast 9.
2, * ‡ ○ Irish steam railway locos, past and present.
Book notices, book reviews, letters, articles, news.
5 year probably, —, No, None.
T.p. 28.
Free to members.

2635 GREAT NORTH REVIEW. 1964.
Great North of Scotland Railway Assocn., 14 Gordon Road, Bridge of Don, Aberdeen, AB2 8PT.
4, † All aspects of the former GNSR and its constituents and successors.
Book notices, book reviews, legal notes, letters, monographic articles, obituaries.
5 year, May 1969, No, None.
February 1972, T.p. 17, Ad.p. 2.
Per year £1.

2636 GREAT WESTERN ECHO: journal of the Great Western Society. 1963.
Great Western Society Ltd., 196 Norwood Road, Southall, Middx.
4, * ‡ + Matters of interest to the Society and the study of the achievements of the ex-Great Western Railway.
Book reviews, letters, monographic articles.
No Index.
Spring 1972, T.p. 16, Ad.p. 1. 4500.
Per copy 12½p, per year 50p.

2637 HMRS JOURNAL. 1951.
Historical Model Railway Society, c/o 81 Sylvia Avenue, Hatch End, Pinner, Middx.
4, * Drawings, articles and photographs relating to the railways of Great Britain and models thereof.
Book reviews, monographic articles, obituaries.
3 year, Last issue of volume (every 3 years), No, None.
T.p. 24. 600.
Free to members.

2638 INDUSTRIAL LOCOMOTIVE SOCIETY JOURNAL. 1947.
Industrial Locomotive Society, 'Channings', Kettlewell Hill, Woking, Surrey.
* Railways connected with industry.
Book notices, book reviews, letters, monographic articles.
No Index.
T.p. 28.
Per copy £1. Free to members.

2639 JOURNAL OF THE RAILWAY AND CANAL HISTORICAL SOCIETY. 1955.
Railway & Canal Historical Society, 34, Manor Avenue, Caterham, Surrey, CR3 6AN.
4, + *   Articles and historical data relating to railways and canals, including technical, economic and social aspects of the history of these two forms of transport.
Book notices, book reviews, letters, monographic articles, obituaries.
A, January, No, None.
April 1970, T.p. 32.   500.
Supplied only to members of the Society and to University and Public Libraries.

2640 JOURNAL OF THE STEPHENSON LOCOMOTIVE SOCIETY. 1909.
Stephenson Locomotive Society, 49, Acfold Road, Handsworth Wood, Birmingham, B20 1HG.
12, ○ +   Society announcements and general articles on railway matters.
Book notices, book reviews, letters.
A, March, No, None.
6, 1972, T.p. 32, Ad.p. 3.   2200.
Per year £2. Free to members.

2641 LIVE RAIL. 1972.
Southern Electric Group, 28 Hill View Road, Orpington, Kent.
4, ○
No Index.
Per copy 12p.

2642 LLANFAIR RAILWAY JOURNAL. 1968.
(The Earl 1959-1967)
Welshpool & Llanfair Light Railway Preservation Co. Ltd., 20 The Terraces, Morda, Oswestry, Salop.
4, * †   News of events on the Welshpool and Llanfair Light Railway; reports of policy decisions; relevant articles; and references to important events on associated railways.
Book notices, book reviews, letters, monographic articles, obituaries.
No Index.
July 1972, T.p. 24, Ad.p. 1.   1400.
Per copy 13p. Free to members.

2643 THE LOCOMOTIVE JOURNAL: Official Organ of the Associated Society of Locomotive Engineers and Firemen. 1880.
ASLEF, 9 Arkwright Rd., London, N.W.3.
12, * = ‡   TU journal—covers matters of domestic and general industrial interest, plus political material, women's page, games article, etc.
No Index.
June 1972, T.p. 11, Ad.p. 1.   30000.
Per copy 2p, per year 40p.

2644 LOCOMOTIVES IN PROFILE. 1970.
Profile Publications Limited, Coburg House, Sheet Street, Windsor, Berks.
12, ‡   International steam locomotives of historical or technical interest.
Monographic articles.
No Index.
24, T.p. 24.
Per copy 45p, per year £5.40.

2645 MODEL RAILWAY CONSTRUCTOR. 1934.
Ian Allan Ltd., Terminal House, Shepperton, Middlesex, TW17 8AS.
12, ○ ‡   All scales and gauges of model railways 2 mm scale—10 mm scale (Gauges N-1). Illustrated articles on model railway layouts, construction of locomotives, rolling stock and all accessories.
Book reviews, commodity prices, letters, new products, obituaries, tests.
A, December, No, None.
July 1972, T.p. 40, Ad.p. 12.   27500.
Per copy 20p, per year £2.75.

2646 MODERN RAILWAYS. 1961.
(Trains Illustrated 1945-Locomotive Magazine 1897-)
Ian Allan Ltd., Terminal House, Shepperton, Middx.
12, ○ ‡ = *   Railways of today and the future in Britain and overseas. Descriptions of new equipment, traffic handling, operating methods, new techniques. Main line, suburban, rapid transit, guided hovercraft etc.
Book reviews, letters, monographic articles, new products, parliamentary reports, standards, tests.
A, December, No, None.
July 1972, T.p. 40, Ad.p. 8.   21000.
Per copy 20, per year £2.75.

2647 THE NARROW GAUGE. 1953.
Narrow Gauge Railway Society, 47 Birchington Avenue, Birchencliffe, Huddersfield, HD3 3RD.
4, *   Narrow gauge railways in all parts of the world, locomotives, modelling and related subjects.
Letters, monographic articles.
Q, Each issue, Cumulative index in preparation, No.
Spring 1972, T.p. 43, Ad.p. 9.   1000.
Free to members.

2648 NARROW GAUGE NEWS. 1957.
Narrow Gauge Railway Society, 47 Birchington Avenue, Birchencliffe, Huddersfield, HD3 3RD.
6, *   Current developments on narrow gauge railways in all parts of the world. Reports of Society activities.
Book reviews, notes.
(Index for 1957-1965 in preparation.)
June 1972, T.p. 18.   650.
Free to members.

2649 NARROW GAUGE TELEGRAPH. 1969.
(Talyllyn Telegraph 1965 Festiniog Railway News 1968)
Talyllyn Rly./Great Little Trains of Wales, Wharf Station, Towyn, Merioneths.
1, ○   Holiday making public for information and historical/technical details on various railways participating in its editorial content.
Book reviews, commodity prices, articles, new products, obituaries.
No Index.
1972, T.p. 12, Ad.p. 1.
Per copy 4p.

2650 PROCEEDINGS OF THE INSTITUTION OF RAILWAY SIGNAL ENGINEERS. 1912.
The Institution of Railway Signal Engineers, 21, Avalon Road, Earley, Reading.
1, ‡ *   Modern developments in the field of railway signal engineering.
Technical papers. Institution announcements etc., obituaries.
No Index.
1970/71, T.p. 198, Ad.p. 12.
Per copy £2.10. Free to members.

2651 PUSH & PULL. 1965.
Keighley & Worth Valley Railway Preservation Society, Haworth Station, Haworth, Keighley, Yorks.
4, * ○   Steam railway preservation.
Book notices, book reviews, letters, monographic articles, new products, reports, tests.
No Index.
Summer 1972, T.p. 33, Ad.p. 3.   3000.
Per copy 15p, per year 75p.

2652 RAILPOWER. 1963.
Railway Industry Association, 30/34 Buckingham Gate, London, SW1E 6LH.
3, ‡ =   British railway supply industry.
No Index.

2653 RAILWAY ENGINEERING JOURNAL. 1972.
(Railway Division Journal 1970-1971).
The Institution of Mechanical Engineers, (Railway Division), 1 Birdcage Walk, London, SW1H 9JJ.
6, ‡ + *   Latest developments in various aspects of railway engineering.
Book reviews, letters, monographic articles, new products.
A, −, Yes, None.
T.p. 56, Ad. p. 10.   2800.
Per copy 60p, per year £6.

2654 THE RAILWAY ENTHUSIASTS AND HISTORIANS GUIDE TO THEIR LITERATURE. 1972.
Bryan Jackson, Maple Cottage, Ashburnham Avenue, Harrow-on-the-Hill.
4, ○   Railway books, old and new, UK and abroad.
No Index.
Per year 80p.

2655 RAILWAY FORUM. 1962.
(Railway Preservation Society Newsletter).
Haraton Ltd., 31 Old Croft Road, Walton-on-the-Hill, Stafford.
4, * ‡ + ○   Records, with photographs and text, the activities of railway preservation societies in Great Britain.
Book notices, book reviews, letters, news, obituaries.
No Index.
T.p. 29.
Free, controlled circulation.

2656 RAILWAY GAZETTE. 1905.
(Various titles dating back to 1835 when it was titled Railway Magazine).
IPC Business Press Ltd., 22 Greville Street, London, SE1.
27, = ‡ +   Management, operations, engineering of railways.
Book notices, book reviews, letters, monographic articles, new companies, new products, parliamentary reports, patents, standards, tests.
No Index.
T.p. 40, Ad.p. 52.
Per copy 20p, per year £4.80.

2657 RAILWAY INVIGORATION SOCIETY PROGRESS REPORT. 1964.
Railway Invigoration Society, BM-RIS, London, WC1.
4, *   The R.I.S. fights for the retention and improvement of Britain's railway services. Its progress report is designed to further these aims by giving views on matters affecting the railways and by providing reports on the Society's activities.
Book reviews, letters, articles, parliamentary reports.
No Index.
June 1972, T.P. 16.   350.
Free to members.

2658 RAILWAY MAGAZINE. 1897.
Temple Press Ltd., 40 Bowling Green Lane, London, EC1.
12, ‡ +   Current railway practice and development.
Book notices, book reviews, letters, monographic articles, news.
A, February, Yes, None.
T.p. 58, Ad.p. 13.   37000.
Per copy 20p, per year £2.40.
Indexed in: BTI.

2659 RAILWAY OBSERVER. 1929.
Railway Correspondence & Travel Society, 82 Naval Road, London, N11.
12, * ‡ =   Railway preservation, mechanism etc.
Book reviews, news.
A, February, Yes, None.
T.p. 35, Ad.p. 1.
Free to members.

2660 RAILWAY REVIEW: official journal of the National Union of Railwaymen. 1880.
King's Cross Publishing Co. Ltd., 205 Euston Road, London, NW1.
52, = ‡   News of railway practice and development. Union affairs.
No Index.
T.p. 12.
Per copy 2½p.

2661 RAILWAY WORLD. 1952.
(Railways 1939-1952)
Ian Allan Ltd., Terminal House, Shepperton, Middx.
12, ○ *   Railways, historical, in Britain and overseas. All aspects are covered but today's events are dealt with briefly since they are covered by the Groups other magazine, Modern Railways.
Book reviews, letters, monographic articles.
A, December, No, None.
July 1972, T.p. 48, Ad.p. 8.   36000.
Per copy 20p, per year £2.75.

2662 TALYLLYN NEWS: Journal of the Talyllyn Railway Preservation Society. 1953.
Talyllyn Railway Preservation Society, c/o 14 Castello Avenue, London SW15 6EA.
4, * †   Matters relating to the activities of the Talyllyn Railway Preservation Society and the Talyllyn Railway.
Book reviews, letters, monographic articles, obituaries.
No Index.
June 1972, T.p. 36, Ad.p. 3.   c. 3000.
Free to members.

2663 TRAINS ILLUSTRATED. 1946.
Ian Allan Ltd., Terminal House, Shepperton, Middx. TW17 8AS.
4, ○   Largely pictorial presentation of steam railways past and present.
No Index.
Summer 1972, T.p. 48.
Per copy 50p, per year £2.25.

625.5

ROPEWAYS

2664 ELEVATOR LIFT & ROPEWAY ENGINEERING: LIFT. 1972.
(International Ropeway Review. 1959-1971)
Welmar Publications Limited, 8 Marwell, Westerham, Kent.
6, ‡   Equipment, accessories, developments, installations and news covering the closely-related fields of vertical lifts and elevators, aerial ropeways and cableways, whether for passenger or industrial uses.
Book notices, book reviews, letters, monographic articles, new products, obituaries, patents, standards, tests.
A, November/December, No, None.
May/June 1972, T.p. 39, Ad.p. 8.
Per year £3.

625.7

HIGHWAY ENGINEERING

2665 HIGHWAY STATISTICS. 1963.
(Road Motor Vehicles 1957-1962.)
Her Majesty's Stationary Office (for the Department of the Environment), P.O. Box 569, London, SE1.

Key to reference symbols

○ popular   ‡ technical   = trade/professional

+ research   * society/institution   † house journal

1, ○ Statistics of road vehicles, vehicle mileage performed, road mileage, road expenditure, passenger and goods transport, road transport taxation and expenditure, car ownership and driving licences.
No Index.
1970, T.p. 82.
Per year 85p.

2666 JOURNAL OF THE INSTITUTION OF HIGHWAY ENGINEERS. 1948.
(The Highway Engineer, 1930-1933; Institution Jnl. 1934-1936; Bulletin 1936-1947)
Industrial Newspapers Ltd., John Adam House, 17-19 John Adam Street, London, WC2.
12, ‡ * All aspects of highway engineering, design, construction, materials, plant, traffic engineering etc.
Book reviews, letters, new products, obituaries.
A, January, No, None.
April 1972, T.p. 40, Ad.p. 8.
Per copy 60p, per year £7.20.
Indexed in: BT1.

2667 ROADS & ROAD CONSTRUCTION. 1923.
Carriers Publishing Co. Ltd., Blenheim House, Battersea High Street, London, SW11.
12, ‡ Book notices, book reviews, letters, monographic articles, news, new products, obituaries, standards, tests.
A, January, Yes, None.
T.p. 32, Ad. p. 20.
Per copy 20p, per year £2.
Indexed in: BT1.

626

HYDRAULIC ENGINEERING

2668 WATER POWER: The International journal for hydroelectric development. 1949.
IPC Electrical-Electronic Press Ltd., Dorset House, Stamford Street, London, SE1 9LU.
12, ‡ = + All aspects of international hydroelectric development.
Abstracts, book reviews, letters, monographic articles, new products, reports, tests.
A, February, Yes, None.
July 1972, T.p. 41, Ad.p. 28.   2305.
Per copy 62½p, per year £8.
Indexed in: BTI, IBZ.

626.073

AIR CARGO

2669 AIR CARGO: handbook of U.K. information. 1972.
Hereford Press Ltd., 117 Cheyne Walk, London, SW10.
2, = Airports, agencies, charter airlines in the U.K.
No Index.

627.2

MARINE ENGINEERING

2670 HYDROSPACE. 1967.
Spearhead Publications Ltd., Kinnaird Lodge, Kinnaird Avenue, Bromley, Kent.
6, = ‡ + Marine technology, dredging, coastal engineering etc.
Book notices, book reviews, letters, monographic articles, new companies, news, new products, tests.
No Index.
3000.
Per year £5.

627.9

COASTGUARDS

2672 THE COASTGUARD: official journal of H.M. Coastguard. 1946.
(Coastguard News Letter)
Information Division, Department of Trade and Industry, 1 Victoria Street, London, SW1H 0ET.
4, † = Activities, techniques, equipment and history of H.M. Coastguard. Also other aspects of marine safety and life-saving activity.
Book reviews, letters, monographic articles, tests.
No Index.
July 1972, T.p. 40.   8500.
Free of charge to members of H.M. Coastguard.

628.1

WATER SUPPLY

2673 BRITISH WATER SUPPLY. 1969.
(The Journal, British Waterworks Association)
British Waterworks Association, 34 Park Street, London, W1.
12, ‡ = * Water supply industry, pollution, water treatment and amenity uses.
Book reviews, letters, monographic articles.
A, —, Yes, None.
July 1970, T.p. 48, Ad.p. 4.
Per copy 25p, per year £1.50.
Free to members.

2674 EFFLUENT & WATER TREATMENT JOURNAL. 1961.
Thunderbird Enterprises Ltd., 102 College Road, Harrow, Middx HA1 1BQ.
12, ‡ = + * Treatment and disposal of trade and municipal wastes. Treatment of industrial water and its re-use. Desalination.
Book reviews, legal notes, letters, monographic articles, new companies, new products, parliamentary reports, patents, tests.
A, December, Yes, None.
May 1972, T.p. 28, Ad.p. 32.   4950.
Per copy 60p, per year £7.
Indexed in: BTI.

2675 JOURNAL OF THE INSTITUTION OF WATER ENGINEERS. 1947.
Institution of Water Engineers, 6-8 Sackville Street, London, W1X 1DD.
8, ‡ * All aspects of the science of water engineering.
Book notices, book reviews, letters, monographic articles, obituaries, parliamentary reports, standards.
A, December, Yes, 5 year.
T.p. 58, Ad.p. 41.   3900.
Per copy 75p, per year £6. Free to members.
Indexed in: BTI.

2676 LIBRARY LIST.
The Water Research Association, Ferry Lane, Medmenham, Marlow, Bucks SL7 2HO.
12, ‡ + Whole field of water supply. Marginal coverage of effluent disposal.
No Index.

2677 NOTES ON WATER POLLUTION. 1958.
Department of the Environment, Water Pollution Research Laboratory, Elder Way, Stevenage, Herts. SG1 1TH.
4, ‡ = + Effects of pollution of natural waters and methods for water pollution control.
Short articles.
No Index.
June 1972, T.p. 4.   7000.
Free.

2678 WRA DIGEST. 1961.
The Water Research Association, Ferry Lane, Medmenham, Marlow, Bucks SL7 2HO.
Irregular, ‡ Engineers and scientists engaged at technical level in water supply.
Research and technical innovation.
Occasional.

2679 WATER AND WASTE TREATMENT. 1950.
D. R. Publications Ltd., 103 Brigstock Road, Thornton Heath, Surrey.
12, ‡ Water supply and sewage disposal. Pollution of water and air.
Book reviews, monographic articles, new companies, new products, parliamentary reports.
A, December, Yes, None.
May 1972, T.p. 32, Ad.p. 11.   9000.
Free, controlled circulation.
Indexed in: BTI, IBZ.

2680 WATER & WATER ENGINEERING.
Fuel & Metallurgical Journal Ltd., 17/19 John Adam Street, London, WC2 N6JH.
‡ = All aspects of the water cycle, including resources, location and exploitation.
Book notices, book reviews, legal notes, letters, monographic articles, new companies, new products, obituaries, parliamentary reports, patents, standards, tests.
A, —, Yes, None.
T.p. 45, Ad.p. 43.   2761.
Per copy 50p, per year £6.
Indexed in: BTI.

2681 WATER POLLUTION ABSTRACTS. 1949.
(WPR Summary of Current Literature 1927-1948)
HMSO, P.O. Box 569, London, SE1.
12, = ‡ + Conservation of water resources, treatment of sewage etc.
Abstracts.
A, —, Yes, None.
T.p. 48.
Per copy 25p, per year £3.50.

2682 WATER POLLUTION CONTROL. 1967.
(Journal & Proceedings of the Institute of Sewage Purification 1908-1966)
Institute of Water Pollution Control, Ledson House, 53 London Road, Maidstone, Kent.
6, = + ‡ All aspects of sewage and its treatment, pollution, effluents etc.
Monographic articles, news, tests.
A, December, Yes, None.
T.p. 110, Ad.p. 24.   3000.
Per copy £1.50, per year £10.
Indexed in: BTI.

2683 WATER RESEARCH: journal of the International Association of Water Pollution Research. 1967.
Pergamon Press Ltd., Headington Hill Hall, Oxford OX3 0BW.
12, = + * All aspects of development in water pollution control.
Book reviews, monographic articles.
A, Last issue of volume, Yes, None.
T.p. 100.
Per copy £3.50, per year £40.

2684 WATER RESEARCH NEWSHEET. 1967.
The Water Research Association, Ferry Lane, Medmenham, Marlow, Bucks SL7 2HD.
3/4, ‡ + Illustrated topics of practical value to the water supply industry.
No Index.
T.p. 8.
Free.

2685 WATER TREATMENT AND EXAMINATION: The Journal of the Society for Water Treatment and Examination. 1968.
(Proceedings of the Society for Water Treatment and Examination 1952-1967)
S.W.T.E., North Derbyshire Water Board, West Street, Chesterfield, Derbyshire, S40 4TZ.
4, ‡ + * = All aspects of science of water treatment and examination.
Book notices, book reviews, letters, monographic articles, obituaries, parliamentary reports, patents, standards, tests.
A, December, Yes, None.
Part 2, 1972, T.p. 104, Ad.p. 17.   1000.
Per copy £1.25, per year £5. Free to members.

628.5
POLLUTION

2686 POLLUTION: environmental news bulletin. 1971.
Microinfo Ltd., 4 High Street, Alton, Hampshire.
12, ‡ = Details of national and international planning, progress and legislation; new products and anti-pollution processes; exhibition, conference news; new technical reports and publications. Abstracts of world literature on motor cars and the environment provided from the computer.
Abstracts, book notices, book reviews, legal notes, letters, new products, parliamentary reports, patents, standards, tests.
No Index.
June 1972, T.p. 16.
Per year £13.

2687 POLLUTION MONITOR. 1971.
Wealden Press Ltd., Quarry Hill Parade, Tonbridge, Kent.
6, ‡ = To advise industry and public authority what machinery, equipment, systems and services are available to measure or control pollution of the air, water and urban areas.
Book reviews, letters, articles, new companies, new products, tests.
No Index.
April/May 1972, T.p. 25, Ad.p. 7.
Per year £6.

628.54
WASTE TREATMENT

2688 INDUSTRIAL RECOVERY. 1969.
(Industrial Salvage 1942-1969)
National Industrial Materials Recovery Association, Carolyn House, Dingwall Road, Croydon CR9 2YU.
12, = + ‡ Reclamation and re-cycling of waste and by-products of industry.
Letters, monographic articles, news, new products.
No Index.
T.p. 18, Ad.p. 30.   4000.
Per year £5. Free to members.

2689 MATERIALS RECLAMATION WEEKLY. 1968.
(Waste Trade World 1912-1968)
Maclaren Publishers Ltd., P.O. Box 109, 69/77 Davis House, High Street, Croydon CR9 1QH.
52, = ‡ Whole field of raw materials reclamation, but particularly metals, paper, textiles, plastics, rubber and chemicals.
Commodity prices, legal notes, articles, new companies, new products, parliamentary reports, tests.
No Index.
June 17th 1972, T.p. 35, Ad.p. 31.   5618.
Per copy 10p, per year £5.

2690 WASTE DISPOSAL. 1968.
Ernest Rhodes (Promotions) Ltd., 276/282 Corn Exchange, Fennel Street, Manchester M4 3HF.
6, + ‡ All aspects of waste disposal including reclamation of derelict land.
Monographic articles, news.

628.9

ILLUMINATING ENGINEERING

2691 LIGHT & LIGHTING and Environmental Design. 1908.
The Illuminating Engineering Society, York House,
199 Westminster Bridge Road, London, SE1 7UN.
○ ‡ *   All aspects of light sources and application, interior and exterior; international coverage.
Book reviews, letters, monographic articles, new products, obituaries.
A, December, Yes, None.
June 1972, T.p. 30, Ad.p. 5.   6500.
Per copy 35p, per year £4.20. Free to members.
Indexed in: BTI, IBZ.

2692 LIGHTING EQUIPMENT NEWS. 1967.
Equipment News Ltd., 35 Red Lion Square, London, WC1.
12, ‡ =   All aspects of lighting.
Book notices, book reviews, commodity prices, letters, monographic articles, new companies, new products, obituaries, standards, tests.
No Index.
T.p. 34, Ad. p. 29.   13500.
Free, controlled circulation.

2693 LIGHTING JOURNAL. 1968.
British Lighting Industries Ltd., 52 Lawrence Road, London, N15.
=
No Index.
Subscription on application.

2694 LIGHTING RESEARCH & TECHNOLOGY. 1969.
The Illuminating Engineering Society, York House, Westminster Bridge Road, London, SE1 7UN.
4, ‡ + *   Research on light sources and vision and materials used in lighting equipment and their application.
Abstracts, letters, monographic articles.
A, with last issue of year, No, None.
Vol. 4, No. 2, 1972, T.p. 58.
Per copy £2, per year £7.50. Reduction for members.

2695 PUBLIC LIGHTING. 1935.
Association of Public Lighting Engineers, 78 Buckingham Gate, London, SW1E 6PF.
4, ‡ = *   Research, production, design, maintenance of public lighting, qualifications of public lighting engineers etc.
Book notices, book reviews, commodity prices, legal notes, letters, monographic articles, new companies, new products, obituaries, parliamentary reports, patents, standards, tests.
No Index.
December 1971, T.p. 102, Ad.p. 22.   1900.
Per copy 40p, per year £1.85.
Indexed in: BTI.

629.11.012.5

TYRES

2696 GOODYEAR NEWS. Winter 1947 (New series). 1925 (First series).
Goodyear Tyre & Rubber Co. (GB) Ltd., Stafford Road, Wolverhampton.
4, ‡ = †   Tyre trade with particular emphasis on the part played by the Goodyear company.
Commodity prices, articles, new companies, new products, obituaries, standards, tests.
No Index.
Spring 1972, T.p. 20.
Free.
A, January/February, No, None.
T.p. 26, Ad.p. 9.   1500.
Per copy 25p. Free to members.

2697 TAB—Tyres Accessories Batteries: official journal of the National Tyre Distributors Association. 1965.
(Tyre Distributor. 1963-65)
Northwood Publications Ltd. (Thomson Organisation Ltd)., Northwood House, 93-99 Goswell Road, London, EC1V 7QA.
6, = ‡ †   Tyre manufacturing and distributive trade.
Letters, articles, new companies, new products, obituaries.
No Index.
June/July 1972, T.p. 21, Ad.p. 29.   3179.
Per copy 17½p, per year £1.

629.111.4

PRAMS

2698 PRAM & NURSERY TRADER.
(Pram World & Nursery Times International).
Wheatland Journals Ltd.,/Turret Press (Holdings) Ltd., 157 Hagden Lane, Watford, WD1 8LW.
12, =
Book reviews, articles, letters.
No Index.
May 1972, T.p. 14, Ad.p. 14.
Per year £2.75.

2699 PRAM RETAILER. 1965.
Blandford-Hyde Publishing Co. Ltd., 167 High Holborn, London, WC1V 6PH.
4, =   All facets of the industry.
Letters, articles, new companies, new products, patents, standards, tests.
No Index.
January 1972, T.p. 7, Ad.p. 13.   5180.
Per year £1 and Free, controlled circulation.

629.113

AUTOMOBILE ENGINEERING

2700 AM. 1948.
Aston Martin Owners Club, 47 Linchen Road, London, W13.
4, ○
Book notices, book reviews, letters, monographic articles.
A, February, Yes, None.
T.p. 37, Ad.p. 16.   1200.
Free to members.

2701 THE ABSTAINING DRIVER. 1966.
Abstaining Motorists' Association, 40 Waterloo Road, Bramhall, SK7 2NX Cheshire.
2, * =   News of the Society. Articles of technical interest to Motorists. Articles dealing with the alcohol problems in relation to motorists.
Book notices, book reviews, letters, articles, new products, reports, patents, standards, tests.
No Index.
Winter 1972, T.p. 16.   250.
Per year £1.50.

2702 ACCESSORY AND GARAGE EQUIPMENT. 1956.
H.I. Thompson Press Ltd., 2 Ellis Street, Sloane Square, London, SW1.
12, = ‡   Garage equipment and planning.
Book notices, book reviews, commodity prices, legal notes, monographic articles, new companies, new products, standards, tests.
No Index.
T.p. 32, Ad.p. 48.   38500.
Controlled circulation.

2703 AUTO ACCESSORY INTERNATIONAL. 1969.
D. Dansie/B. Harvey, 5 King Harry Lane, St. Albans, Herts.
4, = ‡ Means of communication between all levels of automotive parts and accessory trades and EEC and high car level owning countries throughout the world.
Book reviews, commodity prices, legal notes, letters, monographic articles, new companies, new products, obituaries, tests.
No Index.
T.p. 29, Ad.p. 19. c. 10000.
Free, controlled circulation.

2704 AUTO ACCESSORY RETAILER: speed shop review. 1969.
(Auto Accessory International).
B. Harvey/D. Dansie, 5 King Harry Lane, St. Albans, Herts.
12, ‡ = All aspects of the UK automotive parts and accessory industry from manufacturer through distributor to retailer.
Book reviews, commodity prices, legal notes, letters, articles, new companies, new products, obituaries, patents, standards, tests.
No Index.
Mid-May 1972, T.p. 68, Ad.p. Most. 10000.
Per year £2.10 and Free, controlled circulation.

2705 AUTOCAR. 1895.
Iliffe Transport Publications Ltd., Dorset House, Stamford Street, London SE1.
52, ‡ ○ All aspects of motoring.
Book reviews, articles, news, new products.
6m, —, Yes, None.
T.p. 50, Ad.p. 100. 108000.
Per copy 12½p, per year £8.75.
Indexed in: BTI.

2707 AUTOMOTIVE DESIGN ENGINEERING. 1962.
Business Pubs., Mercury House, Waterloo Road, London, SE1.
12, = ‡ + Designers and development engineers in the automotive industry both U.K. and Common Market Areas.
Book notices, book reviews, legal notes, monographic articles, new companies, new products, patents, standards, tests.
A, January, Yes, None.
June 1972, T.p. 25, Ad.p. 25. 6500.
Per copy £1, per year £12 and Free, controlled circulation.
Indexed in: BTI.

2708 AUTOMOTIVE ENGINEERING. 1970.
Institution of Mechanical Engineers, 1 Birdcage Walk, Westminster, London, SW1.
11, * = + ‡ Automobile engineering in general.
Book notices, book reviews, letters, monographic articles, new companies, new products.
A, —, Yes, 5 year.
5500.
Free to members.

2709 AUTOWORLD. 1966.
(Ici Renault 1960-66).
PSL Publications Ltd., 9 Ely Place, London, EC1N 6SQ.
6, ○ ‡ Published on behalf of Renault Ltd and of particular interest to Renault owners. Regular features of general appeal to all family motorists, including touring, road tests, food and drink, do-it-yourself maintenance, etc.
Book reviews, letters, articles, new products, tests.
No Index.
June 1972, T.p. 31, Ad.p. 1. 35000.
Per copy 20p, per year £1.20.

2710 BODY. 1964.
(Journal of the VBRA 1919-1963).
Vehicle Builders & Repairers Association, 13/14 Park Place, Leeds, 1.
12, * = ‡.
Legal notes, letters, new companies, new products, obituaries, parliamentary reports.
No Index.
T.p. 20, Ad.p. 20. 2550.
Free to members.

2711 CAMDA NEWS: Journal of the Car & Motorcycle Drivers Association. 1958.
The Car & Motorcycle Drivers' Association Ltd., 110 Bridge Road, Litherland, Liverpool, L21 6PU.
4, * Association news letter covering driver education, road safety, advanced driving techniques, sporting, safety and social events.
Book reviews, letters, new products, obituaries.
No Index.
March 1972, T.p. 7, Ad.p. 1. 1600.
Free to members.

2712 CAR incorporating Cars Competition News. 1965.
(Small Car 1962-1964).
The National Magazine Co., Ltd., Chestergate House, Vauxhall Bridge Road, London, SW1V 1HF.
12, ‡ ○ Car people, car driving and cars in general.
Book reviews, prices, letters, articles, new companies, new products, tests.
No Index.
June 1972, T.p. 52, Ad.p. 44. 55251.
Per copy 20p, per year £3.25.

2713 CAR ADVERTISER. 1959.
Brittain Press Ltd., Classified House, New Bridge Street, London, EC4.
52, ○ New and used cars.
No Index.
T.p. 40, Ad.p. 40.
Per copy 2½p.

2714 CAR FINDER.
(Motoring Weekly Advertiser).
Haymarket Publishing Limited, Gillow House, 5 Winsley Street, London, W1.
52, ○ Motor trade advertising medium, with used car prices guide.
No Index.
T.p. 4, Ad.p. 84. 20000.
Per copy 5p, per year £2.60.

2715 CAR MECHANICS. 1958.
Mercury House Publications Ltd., Waterloo Road, London, SE1.
12, ○ ‡ Do-it-yourself motor repairs.
Book reviews, commodity prices, letters, monographic articles, news, new products, tests.
No Index.
T.p. 47, Ad.p. 83. 264000.
Per copy 12½p, per year £2.

2716 CARS AND CAR CONVERSIONS. 1965.
Link House Publications Ltd., Link House, Dingwall Avenue, Croydon, Surrey CR9 2TA.
12, ○ For motoring enthusiasts who appreciate extra performance. Rallying, autocross and other sporting aspects.
Book reviews, commodity prices, letters, articles, new products, tests.
No Index.
T.p. 47, Ad.p. 74. 92000.
Per copy 20p.

2717 CARS IN PROFILE. 1972.
(Classic Cars in Profile).
Profile Publications Limited, Coburg House, Sheet Street, Windsor, Berks.
12, ○ ‡ International cars of popular and specialist interest:- veteran, vintage, or modern.

A, Included in Annual Bound Volume of 12 Profiles, Yes, None.
No. 1, T.p. 24.
Per copy 50p, per year £6.

2718 CHASSIS: The journal of ERF Limited. 1962.
ERF Ltd., Sun Works, Sandbach, Cheshire.
2, ‡ =   Mailed direct to all companies who have purchased ERF vehicles. Aimed at furthering relations between manufacturer and end user. Also includes technical data of interest to operators.
Articles, tests.
No Index.
Spring 1972, T.p. 32.   8000.
Free.

2719 CIVIL SERVICE MOTORING. 1967.
(CSMA Gazette 1927-1967).
Civil Service Motoring Association Ltd., 4 Norris Street, Haymarket, London, SW1.
12, ‡ *   All aspects of motoring.
Book reviews, legal notes, letters, monographic articles, news, new products, obituaries, standards, tests.
No Index.
T.p. 30, Ad.p. 8.   167000.
Free to members.

2720 CUSTOM CAR. 1970.
Link House Publications Ltd., Link House, Dingwall Avenue, Croydon, Surrey CR9 2TA.
12, ○   For the brighter, younger motorist who likes his motoring to have an individual flavour. Deals with customising cars, reports on drag racing, hot rodding, stock car racing, new models, exotic old cars and performance conversions.
Book reviews, letters, articles, new products, tests.
No Index.
Per copy 15p.

2721 DRIVE: AA Motorist's Magazine. 1967.
Drive Publications Ltd., Berkeley Square House, Berkeley Square, London, W1.
4, ○ ‡   Regular features on AA services, car maintenance, road tests etc., plus articles on road safety, consumer protection as it affects the motorist and car travel in Britain and abroad.
Book notices, commodity prices, legal notes, letters, monographic articles, tests.
No Index.
Summer 1972, T.p. 90, Ad.p. 37.   4500000.
Per copy 15p. (Free to AA members.)

2722 FODEN NEWS.
Fodens Limited, Elworth House, Elworth Works, Sandbach, Cheshire.
4, ○ = ‡   Coverage of new Foden products, corporate information, interest articles on customers and their businesses.
Letters, articles, new products, obituaries.
No Index.
April 1972, T.p. 22.   6500.
Free.

2723 FORD TIMES. 1912.
Ford Motor Co. Ltd., Warley, Brentwood, Essex.
12, ‡ = ○   Car mechanics and travel.
Book notices, book reviews, commodity prices, legal notes, letters, monographic articles, news, new products.
No Index.
T.p. 20, Ad.p. Most.
Per copy 2½p, per year 50p.

2724 GARAGE. 1963.
(Journal of Motor Trade Management).
Ridgway Publications, 62 Doughty Street, London, WC1.
52, =   All aspects of the motor trade.
Legal notes, letters, monographic articles, new companies, new products, obituaries, tests.

No Index.
T.p. 22, Ad.p. 40.   c. 14000.
Free, controlled circulation.

2725 GARAGE AND TRANSPORT EQUIPMENT. 1955.
Hulton Publications Ltd., Audrey House, Ely Place, London, EC1.
12, ‡ =   Review of new equipment, components accessories and services applicable to the garage trade, and transport management.
New products.
No Index.
June 1972, T.p. 25, Ad.p. 50.   31059.
Free, controlled circulation.

2726 GOOD MOTORING. 1935.
H. I. Thompson Press Ltd., 2 Ellis Street, Sloane Street, London, SW1X 9AN.
12, ○   All motoring matters of interest to members of the Company of Veteran Motorists with an emphasis on road safety and courtesy.
Book reviews, legal notes, letters, articles, new products, tests.
No Index.
June 1972, T.p. 22, Ad.p. 18.   108000.
Per year £1.65.

2727 HIGH ROAD. 1969.
British Leyland Motor Corporation Ltd., PO Box 33, Coventry, CV4 9DB.
12, = + ‡   Travel, technical, legal, insurance etc.
Book notices, book reviews, commodity prices, legal notes, letters, articles, new companies, new products, tests.
No Index.
T.p. 40, Ad.p. 26.   132000.
Per copy 15p, per year £1.80.
Controlled circulation.

2728 INSITE: The magazine for BP dealers. 1971.
(B.P. Progress 1955-1971).
Sonostrips Ltd., 49B Station Road, Edgware, Middx. MA8 7HX (for Shell-Mex and B.P. Ltd.)
6, = †   BP Dealers. Concerned with matters of the garage trade.
Articles, new products.
No Index.
January 1972, T.p. 24.   5000.
Free.

2729 IRISH MOTOR TRADER. 1923.
Graphic Publications Ltd., 47 Dawson Street, Dublin 2.
12, ‡ = ○ +   Irish motoring industry, garages, car sales, petrol stations, tractors, etc.
Book reviews, commodity prices, legal notes, letters, new companies, patents, standards, tests.
No Index.
T.p. 15, Ad.p. 14.   3500
Per copy 10p, per year £1.

2730 JOURNAL OF AUTOMOTIVE ENGINEERING. 1970.
The Institution of Mechanical Engineers, 1 Birdcage Walk, London, SW1H 9JJ.
11, ‡ + †   Industrial and technical aspects of the automobile industry and field, plus news of the activities and personalities of the Automobile Division, I Mech E.
Book notices, book reviews, monographic articles, new companies, new products, obituaries, standards, tests.
On request.
T.p. 32, Ad.p. 10.   5000.
Per copy 60p, per year £6.

2731 MIRA ABSTRACTS: A monthly survey of automobile research and development. 1972.
(MIRA Abstracts 1946-54; MIRA Monthly Summary 1955-1967; Automobile Abstracts 1968-71).
Motor Industry R.A., Lindley, Nr. Nuneaton, Warks.

12, ‡ + All aspects of motor-vehicle research, incl. noise, air pollution, safety. Fuels, lubricants, etc. for motor vehicles. Motor-vehicle materials. Test methods for vehicles and vehicle components. Abstracts, literature surveys.
M, During first half of following year, Yes, A.
June 1972, T.p. 40.   750.
Per year £25.

2732 THE M.S.A. NEWS. 1972.
(The MSA Journal 1963-1972).
The Motor Schools Association of Great Britain, Atherton House, 12 Tilton Street, London, SW6 7LR.
6, = † Human interest stories, changes in motoring laws and driver instructor registration rules, safety matters, matters of professional interest, research in driver education, the economics of operation etc. etc.
Book reviews, commodity prices, legal notes, letters, new products, obituaries, parliamentary reports, standards, tests.
No Index.
T.p. 4.   10000.
Free.

2733 THE MOTOR. 1903.
Temple Press Ltd., 40 Bowling Green Lane, London, EC1.
52, ○ ‡ New models, sporting cars.
Book reviews, articles, news, new products.
6m, −, Yes, None.
T.p. 50, Ad.p. 100.   102000.
Per copy 12½p, per year £8.75.
Indexed in: BTI.

2734 MOTOR BUSINESS. 1954.
The Economist Intelligence Unit Ltd., Spencer House, 27 St. James's Place, London, SW1A 1NT.
4, ‡ = + Detailed coverage of the international automotive industries and markets and analyses of both present conditions and future prospects.
No Index.
T.p. 50.
Per copy £15, per year £50.

2735 MOTOR INDUSTRY: Incorporating Motor Service and Automobile Electricity. 1948.
(Motor Commerce 1919-1947).
Collins & French Ltd., 45 South Street, Chichester, Sussex.
12, = ‡ Developments and future trends of the industry.
Legal notes, letters, new products, obituaries, tests.
No Index.
May 1972, T.p. 32, Ad.p. 12.   6500.
Per copy 35p, per year £4.

2736 MOTOR MANAGEMENT: journal of the Institute of the Motor Industry. 1970.
(Journal of the Institute of the Motor Industry c. 1964-1969).
Institute of the Motor Industry, 'Fanshaws', Brickendon, Hertford.
6, * ‡ = Manufacture, distribution, sales service.
Book reviews, letters, monographic articles, new products.
No Index.
May 1972, T.p. 23, Ad.p. 1.   13500.
Per copy 25p, per year £1.50.
Free to members.

2737 MOTOR MARKET NEWS. 1970.
Press Features International for British Car Auctions (Publications) Ltd., 187 Wollaton Street, Nottingham.
12, =.
Commodity prices, legal notes, letters, articles, new products, standards, tests.
No Index.
June 1972, T.p. 10, Ad.p. 2.   25000.
Free.

2738 MOTOR TRADE EXECUTIVE. 1960.
The Motor Agents Assoc., 201 Great Portland Street, London, W1N 6AB.
12, = All aspects of the motor trade and industry.
Book reviews, legal notes, letters, articles, new companies, new products, patents, standards, tests.
A, January, Yes, None.
June 1972, T.p. 26, Ad.p. 24.   20000.
Members 18p per copy, £2.10p per year. Non members 25p per copy, £3 per year.

2739 MOTORING LIFE. 1949.
Motoring Life, 39 Lower Ormond Quay, Dublin 1.
12, ‡ Automobile engineering in general.
Letters, articles, news, tests.
No Index.
T.p. 21, Ad.p. 17.
Per copy 10p, per year £1.25.

2740 MOTORISTS GUIDE TO NEW & USED CAR PRICES. 1962.
Blackfriars Press Periodicals Ltd., P.O. Box 80, Smith Dorrien Road, Leicester.
12, ○ List prices and extras on 7000 new and used cars.
Book reviews, commodity prices, articles, new companies, new products, standards, tests.
No Index.
June 1972, T.p. 168, Ad.p. 7.   60000.
Per copy 25p, per year £3.

2741 MOTOR TRADE EQUIPMENT MONITOR. 1968.
New Media Ltd., 5/6 Argyll Street, London, W1.
4, = Garages.
New Products.
No Index.
25000.
Controlled circulation.

2742 POPULAR MOTORING. 1962.
Mercury House Publications Ltd., Waterloo Road, London, SE1.
12, = ‡ ○ Practical do-it-yourself motoring etc.
Book reviews, legal notes, letters, articles, news, new products, tests.
No Index.
T.p. 40, Ad.p. 52.   115000.
Per copy 12½p, per year £2.

2743 PRACTICAL MOTORIST. 1954.
(Practical Motorist & Motor Cyclist 1934-1940).
General Magazines Group, IPC Magazines Ltd., Fleetway House, Farringdon St., London, EC4A 4AD.
12, ○ ‡ Use, maintenance and overhaul of motor cars; camping and caravanning; road tests; related features.
Letters, articles, new products, tests.
A, November, No, None.
October, 1972, T.p. 54, Ad.p. 77.   193846.
Per copy 18p, per year £3.10.

2744 SAFER MOTORING. 1961.
RFWW Publications Ltd., Lloyds Bank Chambers, Cirencester, Glos.
12, ○ All Volkswagen enthusiasts.
Book notices, book reviews, commodity prices, legal notes, letters, new companies, news, new products, obituaries, tests.
No Index.
T.p. 34, Ad.p. 30.
Per copy 12½p, per year £1.80.

2745 SEDDON ATKINSON MAGAZINE. 1971.
(Rangeability 1963-1966; The Atkinson 1967-1971).
Atkinson Vehicles Ltd., Walton-le-Dale, Preston, PR5 4AS.
4, = † Features and news of interest to owners of Atkinson and Seddon trucks and buses.
Book notices, book reviews, articles, new products.

No Index.
Winter 1971, T.p. 30.   5000.
Free.

2746 SERVICE STATION. 1925.
Penton Publishing Co. Ltd., 26/28 Addiscombe Road, Croydon CR9 5BH.
12, =   Modern garage operation.
Book reviews, legal notes, letters, news, new products.
No Index.
T.p. 32, Ad.p. 83.   16000.
Per copy 12½p, per year £1.80.
Controlled circulation.

2747 TRIUMPH NEWS. 1970.
(Standard-Triumph News—1958).
The Triumph Motor Co. Ltd., Canley, Coventry.
12, †   House journal covering interests of company and employees.
Letters, articles, new companies, new products, obituaries.
No Index.
Jan. 1972, T.p. 8.   17000.
Free.

2748 VETERAN CAR. 1938.
Veteran Car Club of Great Britain, 36 New England Road, Haywards Heath, Sussex.
4, ‡ = ○   All aspects of motoring history.
A, —, No, None.
T.p. 50, Ad.p. 2.   2200.
Free to members.

629.118

MOTOR CYCLES

2749 MOTOR CYCLE & CYCLE TRADER. 1895.
Wheatland Journals Ltd/Turret Press (Holdings) Ltd., 157 Hagden Lane, Watford WD1 8LW.
28, ○ ‡ =
New products, news, articles.
No Index.
13 June 1972, T.p. 22, Ad.p. 22.
Per year £4.20.

2750 TWO WHEELER DEALER. 1970.
(N.A. Journal c. 1930-1969).
East Midland Allied Press Ltd., 117 Park Rd., Peterborough.
12, =   Cycle and motor cycle trade includes also scooters, mopeds and 3 wheel cars.
Commodity prices, legal notes, letters, articles, new companies, new products, obituaries, tests.
No Index.
May 1972, T.p. 12, Ad.p. 28.   6400.
Per year £2.10.

629.12

SHIPBUILDING

2751 CHANDLER AND BOATBUILDER: the Boat Trade Journal. 1965.
Hudson Publications Ltd., 300, Ashley Rd., Parkstone, Poole, Dorset.
12, =   All aspects connected with the yacht and small boat trades.
Book notices, book reviews, commodity prices, legal notes, letters, articles, new companies, new products, obituaries.
A, January, Yes, None.
June 1972, T.p. 28, Ad.p. 28.   2850 (controlled).
Free to U.K. Trade.

2752 THE FUNNEL: The Journal of the Steam Boat Association of Great Britain. Feb. 1972.
The Steam Boat Association of Great Britain, 72 Marlborough Rd., Ashford, Middx. TW15 3PW.
3/4, * ‡   Historical and Technical information about steam launches and steam yachts.
Letters, monographic articles, new products, book reviews.
No Index.
T.p. 14, Ad.p. ½.   200.
Free to members.

2753 JOURNAL OF ABSTRACTS. 1968.
(Journal of The British Ship R.A.—1962/1968. Journal of The British Shipbuilding R.A./1946-1962).
British Ship Research Association, Wallsend Research Station, Wallsend, Northumberland.
12, ‡ +   Technical material of interest to shipbuilders, marine engineers and shipowners.
Abstracts.
A, —, No, None.
February 1972, T.p. 75.   1500.
Per year £15. Free to members

2754 MARINE ENGINEERING AND SHIPBUILDING ABSTRACTS. 1971.
The Institute of Marine Engineers, 76 Mark Lane, London, EC3R 7JN.
4, ‡ = † *   Full length illustrated abstracts from the world's marine technical press classified under over 100 groups.
Abstracts, patents, standards, tests.
A, January, No, None.
Pt. 4 1971, T.p. 48.
Per copy £1, per year £4.

2755 MARINE ENGINEERS REVIEW. 1971.
The Institute of Marine Engineers, 76 Mark Lane, London, EC3R 7JN.
12, ‡ = + *   Internationally based marine technology for marine engineers and others interested in or connected with marine engineering.
Book notices, book reviews, letters, monographic articles, new companies, new products, obituaries, patents, standards, tests.
A, January, Yes, None.
June 1972, T p. 48, Ad.p. 36.   19400.
Per copy 50p, per year £6.

2756 MARINE PRODUCT GUIDE. 1972.
Marine Publications, 55, High West Street, Dorchester, Dorset.
12, = ‡ ○   Boatings and yachting—an international digest of new sail boats, yachts, power boats and materials, equipment and fittings as they become available.
No Index.
Subscription on application.

2757 THE MOTOR SHIP. 1920.
IPC Industrial Press Ltd., 33-39 Bowling Green Lane, London, EC1.
12, ‡   Shipbuilding and shipping industry in general.
Letters, monographic articles, new companies, new products, obituaries, patents, standards, tests.
A, May, Yes, None.
T.p. 40, Ad.p. 80.   8500.
Per year £6.
Indexed in: BTI, IBZ.

2758 MULTIHULL INTERNATIONAL. 1968.
(Catamaran and Trimaran International News 1964-1967).
Marine Publications, 55 High West Street, Dorchester, Dorset.
12, = ‡ ○   Catamarans and trimarans—sail and power—10 ft. to 300 ft.
Book notices, book reviews, commodity prices, letters, articles, new products, tests.
A, January, Yes, None.
T.p. 23, Ad.p. 9.   6000.
Per copy 20p, per year £3.

2759 THE NAVAL ARCHITECT: Journal of the Royal Institution of Naval Architects. 1971.
(Transactions of the RINA 1860-1971).
Royal Institution of Naval Architects, 10 Upper Belgrave Street, London, SW1X 8BQ.
4, ‡ = + *   Design of ships and all sea-going craft, maritime research work, Institution Technical Papers with discussion, on shipbuilding and shipping.
Book notices, book reviews, letters, monographic articles, new companies, new products, obituaries, patents, standards, tests.
A, October, No, None.
April 1972, T.p. 99, Ad.p. 6.   6100.
Per copy £3.50, per year £12
Indexed in: BTI, IBZ.

2760 REED'S MARINE EQUIPMENT NEWS and Marine Engineering Digest. 1957.
Thomas Reed Publications Ltd., Saracen's Head Buildings, 36-37 Cock Lane, London, EC1A 9BY.
12, ‡ =   New marine equipment in digest form so that it can be quickly read and assimilated.
Book notices, new products.
No Index.
May 1972, T.p. 15, Ad.p. 13.   12500.
Per year £3.

2761 SHIP AND BOAT INTERNATIONAL: incorporating International Tug and Workboat. 1969.
(Ship and Boat Builder—June 1947 first issue (various names in interim period, all similar))
Thomas Reed Publications Ltd., Saracen's Head Buildings, 36-37 Cock Lane, London, EC1A 9BY.
12, ‡ =   Design, construction, operation and maintenance of ferries, coasters, barges, lightships, tugs, dredgers, fishing vessels, harbour craft and all specialised small ships, and pleasure craft design and construction.
Book reviews, letters, new products, reports.
No Index.
January 1972, T.p. 30, Ad.p. 22.   7000.
Per year £7.
Indexed in: BTI.

2762 SHIPBUILDING AND MARINE ENGINEERING INTERNATIONAL. 1972.
(Shipbuilding International 1958-1972 Marine Engineering and Naval Architect 1879-1972.)
Whitehall Press Limited, Wrotham Place, Wrotham, Sevenoaks, Kent.
12, ‡   Comprehensive technical coverage of international shipbuilding and marine engineering.
Book notices, book reviews, legal notes, letters, monographic articles, new companies, new products, patents, standards, tests.
A,—, No, None.
July 1972, T.p. 45, Ad.p. 55.   17000.
Per year £4.50 and Free, controlled circulation.

2763 SHIPBUILDING AND SHIPPING RECORD. 1913.
IPC Industrial Press Ltd., 33-39, Bowling Green Lane, London, EC1.
52, ‡   International shipbuilding and shipbuilding Industry.
Commodity prices, legal notes, letters, monographic articles, new products, obituaries, parliamentary reports, patents, standards, tests.
A, February, Yes, None.
T.p. 30, Ad.p. 70.   4500.
Per year £8.50.
Indexed in: BTI, IBZ.

2764 TANKER AND BULK CARRIER. 1965.
(Tanker Times 1958-1964).
Terminus Publications Ltd., Speedway House, Quarry Hill Parade, Tonbridge, Kent.
12, = ‡   Tankers, containerships, bulk carriers etc.
Book reviews, letters, monographic articles, news, new products.
A, May, No, None.
T.p. 20, Ad.p. 26   4000.
Per year £2.25.
Indexed in: BTI.

2765 TRANSACTIONS: Institute of Marine Engineers. 1889.
The Institute of Marine Engineers, 76, Mark Lane, London, EC3R 7JN.
8/16, ‡ = + *   All aspects of ship building, operation and handling and related topics.
Monographic articles.
A, January, Yes, None.
Pt. 5, Vol. 84, T.p. 12, Ad.p. 2.   c.3250.
Per copy £1, per year £12.50. Free to members.
Indexed in: BTI.

2766 TRANSACTIONS OF THE NORTH EAST COAST INSTITUTION OF ENGINEERS AND SHIPBUILDERS. 1884.
North East Coast Institution of Engineers and Shipbuilders, Bolbec Hall, Newcastle upon Tyne, NE1 1TB.
6, ‡ +   Maritime sciences, naval architecture, shipbuilding, marine engineering, mechanical engineering, ship operation.
Book reviews, monographic articles, obituaries.
A, July, Yes, None.
May, 1972, T.p. 40, Ad.p. 6.
Per copy £1, per year £6. Free to members.
Indexed in BTI, IBZ.

2767 TRANSACTIONS OF THE INSTITUTION OF ENGINEERS AND SHIPBUILDERS IN SCOTLAND. 1871.
The Institution, 183 Bath Street, Glasgow, C2.
7, * ‡ + =   All aspects of shipbuilding.
Book notices, book reviews, monographic articles.
A, July, Yes, 10 year.
T.p. 97, Ad.p. 6.
Per year £4.20. Free to members.

629.125.5

LIFEBOATS

2768 THE LIFE-BOAT: Journal of the Royal National Life-Boat Institution. 1852.
Royal National Life-Boat Institution, 42 Grosvenor Gardens, London, SW1.
4, ○ * †   A record of the work of the RNLI in the U.K, world's other life-boat services, general articles associated with life-saving at sea, section aimed to interest yachtsmen and get their support.
Book reviews, letters, new life-saving products, obituaries.
Q,—, Yes, None.
April, 1972, T.p. 35, Ad.p. 15.   40000.
Per copy 15p, per year 82p.

629.13

AERONAUTICS

2769 THE AERONAUTICAL JOURNAL. 1897.
(Journal of the Royal Aeronautical Society 1923-1968).
The Royal Aeronautical Society, 4 Hamilton Plane, London, W1V 0BQ.
12, ‡ + * =   A permanent record of aeronautical development, proceedings of Society, papers from all over the world, reviews, summaries from aeronautical research establishments, lectures of Sections and Groups within the Society.
Book notices, book reviews, legal notes, letters, monographic articles, obituaries.

Key to reference symbols

○ popular   ‡ technical   = trade/professional

+ research   * society/institution   † house journal

A, December, No, None.
May 1972, T.p. 67.   c.14000.
Per copy £1.75, per year £20. Free to members.
Indexed in: BTI, IBZ.

2770 THE AERONAUTICAL QUARTERLY. 1949.
The Royal Aeronautical Society, 4 Hamilton Place, London, W1V 0BQ.
4, ‡ = +   Aeronautics and allied sciences.
Monographic articles.
A, November, Yes, None.
T.p. 100.
Per copy £1.25, per year £5. Free to members.
Indexed in: BTI, IBZ.

2771 AEROSPACE: the monthly newspaper of the Royal Aeronautical Society. 1969.
The Royal Aeronautical Society, 4 Hamilton Place, London, W1V 0BQ.
12, ○ ‡ = + *   Monthly newspaper of the RAeS containing current news in aeronautics, reviews, features and notices.
Book notices, book reviews, letters, monographic articles, new companies, new products, obituaries, tests.
No Index.
June 1972, T.p. 8.   27000.
Free to members.

2772 AIR-BRITAIN DIGEST. 1972.
Air-Britain (Historians) Ltd., Stove Cottage, Great Sampford, Saffron Walden, Essex.
6, ○
Per copy 20p.

2773 AIR-BRITAIN NEWS.
Air-Britain (Historians) Ltd., Stove Cottage, Gt. Sampford, Saffron Walden, Essex.
12, ○
Subscription on application.

2774 AIR ENTHUSIAST. 1971.
FineScroll Limited, De Worde House, 283 Lonsdale Road, London, SW13 9QW.
12, ‡   Aviation—covers aeronautical history, also reports and interprets movements in the whole world industry and the developments of design and policies. Written specifically for the discerning, international air-minded fraternity which demands accurate facts.
6m, July/January, Yes, 2 year.
July 1972, T.p. 51, Ad.p. 7.   68300.
Per copy 30p, per year £4.

2775 AIR PICTORIAL: journal of the Air League. 1950.
Seymour Press (for the Air League), 334, Brixton Road, London, SW9.
12, = ‡ ○   Aviation, past and present. To promote all aspects of British aviation.
Book notices, book reviews, letters, monographic articles, news, new products, parliamentary reports.
A, January, Yes, None.
T.p. 33, Ad.p. 10.   40000.
Per copy 15p, per year £2.50.

2776 AIRCRAFT ENGINEERING. 1929.
Bunhill Publications Ltd., 4 Ludgate Circus, London, EC4.
12, ‡   Practical aircraft engineering and construction.
Book reviews, new companies, new products.
A, January, No, None.
T.p. 28, Ad.p. 8.   2273.
Per copy 40p, per year £4.50.
Indexed in: BTI, IBZ.

2777 AIRCRAFT ILLUSTRATED. 1968.
Ian Allan Ltd., Terminal House, Shepperton, Middlesex, TW17 8AS.
12, ○   Powered aircraft (NOT missiles, space vehicles). Historical to modern, aircraft modelling, service and civil flying, air aces, news. NOT aero engines and accessories.
Book reviews, letters, monographic articles, new companies, new products.
For 1968-1970 only.
July 1972, T.p. 42, Ad.p. 6.   33500.
Per copy 20p, per year £2.75.

2778 AIRCRAFT IN PROFILE. 1965.
Profile Publications Limited, Coburg House, Sheet Street, Windsor, Berks.
12-15, ○ ‡   International aircraft of popular and specialist appeal.
Monographic articles.
A, Included in annual bound volume, Yes, None.
No. 238, T.p. 24.   c.12500.
Per copy 40p, per year £4.80.

2779 AVIATION REVIEW. 1955.
Smiths Industries, Aviation Division, Kelvin House, Wembley Park Drive, Wembley, Middx. HA9 0NH.
4, † = ‡ +   Aviation, aeronautics, systems and avionics.
Book reviews, articles, new products, obituaries, standards, tests.
No Index.
March 1972, T.p. 20.   4500.
Free.

2780 FLIGHT INTERNATIONAL. 1967.
(Flight 1909).
IPC Business Press, Dorset House, Stamford Street, London, SE1.
52, ○ ‡ =   Aerospace in all its forms:- regular news and comment (air transport, defence, spaceflight, private flying, light commercial, world news); special features; technical descriptions and drawings; directories; gazetteers etc; photos and articles of historical interest.
Book notices, book reviews, monographic articles, new products, tests.
6m, —, Yes, None.
20-7-72, T.p. 37, Ad.p. 27.   40000.
Per copy 18p, per year £12.
Indexed in: BTI.

2781 FLYING REVIEW INTERNATIONAL. 1968.
Haymarket Publishing Group, Gillow House, 5 Winsley Street, London, W1N 8AP.
12, = ‡   Review of current trends in military and commercial aircraft design and operation.
Book reviews, letters, monographic articles, new companies, news, new products.
A, December, Yes, None.
T.p. 52, Ad.p. 20.   53000.
Per copy 20p, per year £3.50.

2782 HELICOPTER WORLD. 1958.
Air Age Publications Ltd., 1 Temple Chambers, London, EC4.
12, ‡   World helicopter industry.
No Index.
T.p. 30, Ad.p. 5.
Per year £1.50.
Indexed in: BTI.

2783 HOVER CLUB NEWS. 1970.
Hover Club of Great Britain, 128 Queens Road, Portsmouth, Hants, PO2 7NE.
12, ○   Technical advice on building, safety and use of amateur hovercraft both sporting and pleasure.
Book notices, book reviews, legal notes, letters, articles, new companies, new products, standards, tests.
No Index.
May/June 1972, T.p. 10, Ad.p. 1.   350.
Per copy 15p, per year £1.80.

2784 HOVERING CRAFT AND HYDROFOIL. 1961.
Kalerghi Publications, 51 Welbeck Street, London, W1.
12, = +   Design development, building, maintenance, performance and operating costs, power plants and components of hovercraft, hydrofoils, heavy load carrying systems, air cushion landing systems,

tracked air cushion vehicles, air cushion applicators, conveyors, pallets and other industrial developments of the air cushion principle. Also deals with other new developments in past transportation.
Monographic articles, new companies, new products, parliamentary reports, patents.
No Index.
5, 1972, T.p. 32, Ad.p. varies.
Per year £15.
Indexed in: BTI.

2785 JOURNAL OF THE GUILD OF AIR PILOTS AND AIR NAVIGATORS. 1972.
c/o Royal Aeronautical Society, 251 Regent Street, London, W1.
4, = ‡
No Index.
T.p. 21.
Free to members.

2786 LIGHT AVIATION: journal of the Royal Aero Club. 1966.
(Royal Aero Club Gazette 1946-1965).
Park Lane Publications Ltd., 54/55 Wilton Road, London, SW1.
12, * = + ‡   General aviation.
Book reviews, legal notes, letters, monographic articles, new companies, news, new products, obituaries, parliamentary reports, patents, standards, tests.
No Index.
T.p. 15, Ad.p. 5.   3500.
Free to members.

2787 REED'S AIRCRAFT AND EQUIPMENT NEWS: Airports and Avionics. 1959.
Thomas Reed Publications Ltd., 36/7 Cock Lane, London, EC1A 9BY.
4, ‡ = +   Presents in digest form latest information on aircraft equipment, production and services for operation and maintenance including airport requirements.
New companies, new products, standards, tests.
No Index.
April 1972, T.p. 16, Ad.p. 10.   8100.
Per copy 25p, per year £1.

2788 TECH AIR: Journal of the Society of Licensed Aircraft Engineers and Technologists. January 1966.
(Technical Instructor of the SLAE. 1945-1951; Journal of the S.L.A.E. 1952-1965).
Society of Licensed Aircraft Engineers & Technologists, Grey Tiles, Kingston Hill, Kingston upon Thames, Surrey, KT2 7LW.
12, * ‡ =   Technical information relating to aircraft maintenance.
Book reviews, letters, monographic articles, new products, obituaries.
A, December, Yes, None.
June 1972, T.p. 20, Ad.p. 3.
Per copy 30p, per year £3.75.
Indexed in: BTI.

629.19

SPACEFLIGHT

2789 ASTRONAUTICA ACTA.
Pergamon Press Ltd., Headington Hill Hall, Oxford, OX3 0BW.
6, = +   All aspects of astronautics.
Book reviews, monographic articles.
A, Last issue of volume, Yes, None.
Per copy £4.50, per year £24.

2790 BUFORA JOURNAL. 1964.
(BUFOA Journal 1963).
British Unidentified Flying Object Research Association, 15 Freshwater Court, Crawford Street, London, W1H 1HS.

4, * +   Material relating to UFO reports, their investigation and evaluation and Association news and business; theories etc. Scientific investigation and research.
Book notices, book reviews, letters, articles, obituaries.
No Index.
Spring 1972, T.p. 36.   600.
Free to members only.

2791 FLYING SAUCER REVIEW. 1954.
Flying Saucer Service Ltd., 21 Cecil Court, London, WC2.
6, ○ ‡
Book reviews, articles, news.
No Index.
T.p. 30.
Per copy 25p, per year £1.50.

2792 SPACEFLIGHT. 1956.
British Interplanetary Society, 12 Bessborough Gardens, London, SW1V 2JJ.
12, ○   News and current events in space research and technology.
Book reviews, letters, monographic articles.
A, December, Yes, None.
July 1972, T.p. 40, Ad.p. 2.   5000.
Per copy £4.50.   Free to members.

2793 SPACELINK. 1964.
Lionel Beer, 15 Freshwater Court, Crawford Street, London, W1H 1HS.
1, ○   UFO reports, flying saucer scene, and related topics including strange phenomena and space.
Book notices, book reviews, letters, articles, obituaries.
No Index.
April 1971, T.p. 30.   2000.
Per copy 20p.

2794 SPACEWISE. 1969.
Martec Publishing Group Ltd., 61 Berners Street, London, W1P 3AE.
12, ‡ + ○   Space in the widest sense.
No Index.
T.p. 60, Ad.p. 3.   100000.
Per copy 25p, per year £3.50.

63

AGRICULTURE

2795 AGTEC: Fisons Agricultural Technical Information.
Fisons Ltd., Fertilizer Division, Harvest House, Felixstowe, Suffolk, IP11 7LP.
= ‡
No Index.
Spring 1972, T.p. 43.
Free.

2796 AGRICULTURAL CO-OPERATIVE BULLETIN. 1959.
International Co-operative Alliance, 11 Upper Grosvenor Street, London, W1X 9PA.
12, = + *   Reports on activities of agricultural Co-operatives.
Book notices, commodity prices, legal notes, letters, articles, new companies, new products, obituaries, patents, standards, tests.
A, December, Yes, None.
T.p. 11.
Subscription on application.

2797 AGRICULTURAL AND VETERINARY CHEMICALS AND AGRICULTURAL ENGINEERING. 1959.
Chandler Publications Ltd., Ivy Hatch, Sevenoaks, Kent.
6, ‡ +   Research and field trials on agricultural and veterinary theories.
Book notices, book reviews, letters, monographic articles, new companies, new products, standards, tests.
No Index.
T.p. 18, Ad.p. 6.   4150.
Per copy 50p, per year £3.

2798 AGRICULTURAL HISTORY REVIEW. 1953.
The British Agricultural History Society, Museum of English Rural Life, The University, Whiteknights, Reading, RG6 2AG.
2, * + =   Study of the history of agriculture and rural economy.
Book notices, book reviews, letters, monographic articles, obituaries.
5 year, 1969, et seq, Yes, None.
T.p. 96, Ad.p. 6.   c.850.
Per copy £1.50, per year £3.
Indexed in: BHI.

2799 AGRICULTURAL MERCHANT. 1970.
58 Mark Lane, London, EC3R 7NP.
12, =
No Index.
Per year £4.

2800 AGRICULTURAL PROGRESS. 1924.
Agricultural Education Association, Cliftonfield, Shipton Road, York.
1, + ‡   Education and research in agriculture.
Book reviews, monographic articles.
No Index.
T.p. 197.
Free to members.

2801 AGRICULTURAL STATISTICS SCOTLAND. 1913.
HMSO, Sighthill, Edinburgh, EH2 3AR.
1, ‡ = +   Section I contains the results of the twice yearly Scottish Agricultural Censuses and gives comprehensive details of cropping, stocking and farm labour together with other detailed statistics and structural analysis. Section 2 mainly comprises agricultural produce prices data.
No Index.
Subscription on application.

2802 AGRICULTURAL SUPPLY INDUSTRY. 1971.
Magazines for Industry Inc., 59 Fleet Street, London, EC4Y 1JU.
52, ○ ‡ = +   The UK agricultural supply industry agricultural merchants.
Commodity prices, legal notes, new companies, new products, parliamentary reports, tests.
A, January, No, None.
T.p. 4, Ad.p. 4.   1853.
Per year £5.

2803 AGRICULTURE. 1955.
(Agricultural Journal 1894).
HMSO, PO Box 569, London, SE1.
12, * = ‡ +   Agriculture and horticulture in all aspects.
Book reviews, letters, articles.
A, January, Yes, None.
T.p. 48, Ad.p. 14.
Per copy 6p, per year £1.5.
Indexed in: BTI, IBZ.

2804 ASSOCIATION OF AGRICULTURE JOURNAL. 1963.
Association of Agriculture, 78 Buckingham Gate, London, SW1E 6PE.
2, ‡ †   Agriculture for the informed layman; statistics on agriculture England and abroad.
Book reviews, legal notes, articles.
No Index.
January 1972, T.p. 24.
Per year 50p.

2805 COMMONWEALTH PRODUCER. 1952.
(Production & Export 1916; Empire Production & Export 1923; Empire Producer 1935).
Commonwealth Producers' Organisation, 25 Victoria Street, London, SW1.
6, * =   Marketing etc concerning agriculture worldwide.
Book reviews, commodity prices, legal notes, monographic articles, news, new products, parliamentary reports.
No Index.
T.p. 17, Ad.p. 7.
Per copy 12½p, per year 75p. Free to members.

2806 EXPERIMENTAL AGRICULTURE. 1965.
(Empire Journal of Experimental Agriculture 1933-1964).
Cambridge University Press, PO Box 92, London, NW1 2DB.
4, +   Results of experimental work in animal and crop husbandry with an emphasis on research carried out in tropical areas.
Book reviews, monographic articles, tests.
A, October, Yes, None.
October 1971, T.p. 95, Ad.p. 4.   1000.
Per copy £2, per year £7.

2807 INTERNATIONAL JOURNAL OF AGRARIAN AFFAIRS:
Produced by the University of Oxford Institute of Agrarian Affairs in conjunction with the International Association of Agricultural Economists. 1939.
Oxford University Press, Press Road, Neasden, London, NW10.
Irregular (each volume comprises six issues and appears over a period of about three years), ‡ +   Agricultural economics or rural welfare.
No Index.
April 1970, T.p. 58.   250.
Per copy 53p, per year £3.15.

2808 JOURNAL OF AGRICULTURAL ECONOMICS. 1928.
(Journal and Proceedings of the Agricultural Economics Society 1930-1955).
Agricultural Economics Society, Department of Agricultural Economics and Management, The University, Reading, RG6 2AR.
2, * = +   History, statistics, economics and sociology of the agricultural and food industries.
Book reviews, monographic articles.
A, September, No, None.
T.p. 169, Ad.p. 5.
Per year £3.50. Free to members.

2809 JOURNAL OF AGRICULTURAL SCIENCE. 1905.
Cambridge University Press, P.O. Box 92, London, NW1 2DB.
6, +   Research in pure and applied sciences relating to agricultural problems. Covers a wide range of topics in soil science, crop research and research on farm animals.
Monographic articles.
6m, June/December, Yes, 10 year.
June 1972, T.p. 166.   1500.
Per copy £4, per year £18.
Indexed in: IBZ.

2810 JOURNAL OF THE NATIONAL INSTITUTE OF AGRICULTURAL BOTANY. 1922.
The Institute, Huntingdon Road, Cambridge.
1, ‡ +   Crop variety improvement, seeds.
Monographic articles.
3 year, End of each volume, Yes, None.
T.p. 242.   5750.
Per year £1. Free to members.

2811 NAAS QUARTERLY REVIEW. 1948.
HMSO, PO Box 569, London, SE1.
4, ‡   Current technical and scientific aspects of farming.
Monographic articles.
3 year, —, No, None.
T.p. 45.
Free to members.

2812 OUTLOOK ON AGRICULTURE. 1956.
Plant Protection Ltd/ICI, Jealott's Hill Research Station, Bracknell, Berkshire, RG12 6EY.

c. 3, ‡ +   Reviews progress in agriculture and agricultural sciences, with particular emphasis on crop production and crop protection, and with some attention to future developments. The coverage of agriculture is worldwide.
Book notices, book reviews, monographic articles.
c. 2 year, c. Every 6 issues, Yes, None.
No. 5, 1971, T.p. 46.   7000.
Per copy £2, per year £4.

2813 OXFORD AGRARIAN STUDIES. 1972.
University of Oxford, Institute of Agricultural Economics, Dartington House, Little Clarendon Street, Oxford OX1 2HP.
2, + ‡ =
Book reviews, monographic articles.
A, —, Yes, None.
T.p. 80.
Per year £1.50.

2814 PLANT VARIETIES AND SEED GAZETTE. 1965.
HMSO, PO Box 569, London, SE1.
12, = ‡   Communication medium for matters covered by the Plant Varieties and Seeds Act 1964.
News, obituaries, parliamentary reports.
No Index.
T.p. 10.
Per copy 10p, per year £1.50.

2815 SCOTTISH AGRICULTURE: The Journal of the Department of Agriculture and Fisheries for Scotland. 1946.
(Scottish Journal of Agriculture, 1918-1946).
Her Majesty's Stationery Office, Atlantic House, Holborn Viaduct, London, EC1P 1BN.
4, + ‡ =   All aspects of farming and agriculture. Aim is to keep farmers and growers up-to-date with the results.
Book notices, book reviews, monographic articles.
A, —, Yes, None.
T.p. 56, Ad.p. 8.   3300.
Per copy 15p, per year 78p. (Subject to change).

2816 TROPICAL AGRICULTURE: Journal of the Imperial College of Tropical Agriculture. 1925.
Butterworth & Co. Ltd., 88 Kingsway, London, WC2.
4, = ‡ +
Book notices, book reviews, monographic articles, obituaries.
A, —, Yes, None.
T.p. 88, Ad.p. 8.
Per copy £1.20, per year £4.50.

2817 TROPICAL PRODUCTS QUARTERLY. 1959.
Commonwealth Secretariat, Marlborough House, Pall Mall, London, SW1Y 5HX.
4, = +   Production and trade statistics.
Commodity prices.
A, March, Yes, None.
June 1972, T.p. 110.
Per year £6.

2818 TROPICAL SCIENCE: Quarterly journal of the Tropical Products Institute. 1959.
(Colonial Plant and Animal Products 1950-56, Bulletin of the Imperial Institute 1903-48).
HMSO, Atlantic House, Holborn Viaduct, London, EC1P 1BN.
4, ‡ *   Plant and animal products of tropical and sub-tropical countries. Especially post-harvest aspects of these products including technological and economic problems arising in their handling, processing, preservation, storage, quality control, marketing and utilization, and including industries based on these products.
Book notices, book reviews, monographic articles, new products, obituaries, etc. etc.
A, April, Yes, None.
April 1972, T.p. 99.   2300.
Per copy 65p, per year £2.81.

2819 WORLD AGRICULTURAL ECONOMICS AND RURAL SOCIOLOGY ABSTRACTS. 1959.
Commonwealth Agricultural Bureaux, Farnham Royal, Slough, SL2 3BN.
4, = + ‡   Agricultural economics and rural sociology.
Abstracts.
A, —, Yes, None.
T.p. c. 125.
Per year £9 to subscribers.

2820 WORLD CROPS. 1949.
Morgan Grampian (Publishers) Ltd., 28 Essex Street, Strand, London, WC2.
6, ‡   Technology, political economic and social aspects of agriculture particularly where these have relevance in more than one country. There is a bias towards the interests of the developing countries. Plantation, estate and peasant farming are equally covered.
Book reviews, monographic articles.
A, Nov/Dec, Yes, None.
March/April 1972, T.p. 49, Ad.p. 11.   3500.
Per copy £1, per year £4.

2821 Y TIR (The Land) and Welsh Farmer: Journal of the Farmer Union of Wales. 1958.
Farmers' Union of Wales, Llys Amaeth, Queens Square, Aberystwyth.
6, = *   Union affairs and Welsh agriculture.
Book reviews, commodity prices, legal notes, letters, articles, new products, obituaries, parliamentary reports.
No Index.
March/April 1972, T.p. 24.   15034.
Per copy 7½p, per year 50p.

631

FARMING

2822 ARABLE FARMER AND VEGETABLE GROWER. 1966.
Farming Press Ltd., Fenton House, Wharfedale Road, Ipswich.
12, ‡   All aspects of the growing, harvesting and marketing of cereals, potatoes, sugarbeet and field-scale vegetables.
Commodity prices, letters, new products.
No Index.
T.p. 35, Ad.p. 37.   13500.
Per copy 10p, per year £1.80.

2823 BRITISH FARMER: Journal of the National Farmers Union. 1948.
(NFU Record).
N.F.U., Agriculture House, Knightsbridge, London, SW1.
18, * = ‡
Book reviews, legal notes, letters, monographic articles, news, new products, obituaries, parliamentary reports.
No Index.
T.p. 66, Ad.p. Most.   170000.
Per copy 10p.

2824 EURO-FARM BUSINESS. 1972.
Farm Business Ltd., 2 Church Street, Warwick.
4, ‡ = †   Business management and technical aspects of farming and agriculturally allied industries. Particular emphasis placed upon the changes in British agriculture as a result of EEC entry.
Monographic articles, new products, parliamentary reports, standards.
No Index.
June 1972, T.p. 36, Ad.p. 3.   2000.
Per year £5.

2826 FARM BUILDING R & D INDEX. 1970.
The Scottish Farm Buildings Investigation Unit, Craibstone, Bucksburn, Aberdeen.

1, ‡ +   Lists current research projects and recent publications of organisations in Europe undertaking research and development work relating to farm buildings.
A, With annual issue in September, No, None.
1971, T.p. 36.   150.
Per copy 50p.

2827 FARM BUILDING R & D STUDIES. 1071.
The Scottish Farm Buildings Investigation Unit, Craibstone, Bucksburn, Aberdeen.
2, ‡ +   Reviews and reports of research and development work on farm buildings, particularly work carried out at The Scottish Farm Buildings Investigation Unit.
Monographic articles.
No Index.
May 1971, T.p. 28.   750.
Per copy 50p, per year £1.

2828 FARM BUILDING PROGRESS. 1965.
The Scottish Farm Buildings Investigation Unit, Craibstone, Bucksburn, Aberdeen.
4, ‡ + †   Farm developments and farm building research, development, design, construction and costs.
Book reviews, letters, monographic articles.
A, January, No, None.
April 1972, T.p. 36.   960.
Per copy 50p, per year £1.

2829 FARM BUILDINGS DIGEST. 1967.
Farm Buildings Centre, National Agricultural Centre, Kenilworth, Warwickshire.
4, ○ ‡ =   Farm buildings and associated fixed and mechanical equipment.
Abstracts, legal notes, monographic articles, new products, parliamentary reports.
A, 1 April, No, None.
Autumn 1972, T.p. 29, Ad.p. 10.   3000.
Per year £2 and Free, controlled circulation.

2830 FARMERS GUARDIAN.
United Newspapers Publications Ltd., 127 Fishergate, Preston, PR1 2DN.
52, = ‡   Farming news.
Commodity prices, letters, new products, parliamentary reports.
No Index.
T.p. 22, Ad.p. Most.   23500.
Per copy 5p.

2831 FARMING IN THE EAST MIDLANDS. 1952.
Department of Agriculture and Horticulture, University of Nottingham, School of Agriculture, Sutton Bonington, Loughborough, Leics., LE12 5RD.
1, + =   Analysis of financial results of farms in the East Midlands over one year.
No Index.
1970-71, T.p. 51.
Per copy 50p.

2832 FARMING LEADER.
National Farmers' Union of Scotland, 17 Grosvenor Crescent, Edinburgh, EH12 5EN.
12, =
No Index.
Per year 50p, and Free to members.

2833 FARM WEEK: Incorporating Irish Stockbreeder and Ulster Agriculture. 1961.
Morton Newspaper Group, Windsor Avenue, Lurgan.
52, ‡ =   General farming.
Commodity prices, letters, new companies, new products, obituaries, parliamentary reports, patents, standards, tests.
No Index.
27.6.1972. T.p. 24, Ad.p. Most.   17500.
Per copy 5p.

2834 INTERNATIONAL JOURNAL OF FARM BUILDING RESEARCH. 1966.
International Commission of Agricultural Engineering, 53 Upper Ground, London, SE1.
2, = ‡ +
Monographic articles, news.
No Index.
T.p. 32.   200.
Per copy £1.50.

2835 IRISH FARMERS' JOURNAL. 1948.
The Agricultural Trust, The Irish Farm Centre, Naas Road, Dublin 12.
52, ‡   Technical newspaper bought and closely read by the better farmers. Also a farm home section appeal for wives etc.
No Index.
1-7-1972, T.p. 44, Ad.p. Most.   69063.
Per copy 6p, per year £4.42.

2836 IRISH FARMING NEWS: Official organ of the Irish Creamery Milk Suppliers Association. 1969.
Irish Creamery Milk Suppliers Assocn., John Feely House, 15 Upper Mallow Street, Limerick, Ireland.
4, =   Milk production, equipment, care of herds; milk products of all kinds, processing and marketing. Farm building grants and payments. Economics of the farm methods. Advisory services etc.
Commodity prices, articles, new products, standards, tests.
No Index.
Summer 1972, T.p. 14, Ad.p. Most.
Per copy 10p, and Free to members.

2837 JOURNAL OF THE FARM BUILDINGS ASSOCIATION. 1957.
Farm Buildings Association, The Estate Office, Bratton, Clovelly, Okehampton, Devon, EX20 4LB.
1, ‡ + †
Book notices, book reviews, legal notes, monographic articles, new products, obituaries.
A, −, Yes, None.
1000+.
Per copy £1.

2838 MODERN GRASSLAND FARMING. 1968.
Imperial Chemical Industries Ltd. (Agricultural Division), PO Box 1, Billingham, Teesside, TS23 1LB.
Occasional, ‡   Business techniques of grassland farming.
Letters, articles, new products, obituaries, patents.
No Index.
Spring 1968, T p. 33, Ad.p. 6.   180000.
Free.

2839 NOTTINGHAMSHIRE FARMERS' JOURNAL. 1950.
(N.F.U. Record).
Nottinghamshire National Farmers' Union, 7 The Ropewalk, Nottingham, NG1 1BR.
12, =   All farming and National Farmers' Union topics.
Abstracts, book notices, book reviews, commodity prices, legal notes, letters, monographic articles, obituaries, parliamentary reports, standards, tests.
No Index.
5/1972, T.p. 8-15, Ad.p. 8-15.   2300.
Free to members.

2840 SCOTTISH FARMER. 1961.
Scottish Agricultural Journals Co. Ltd., 39 York Street, Glasgow, C2.
52, = ‡ +   Scottish agriculture.
Book reviews, commodity prices, legal notes, letters, news, new products, parliamentary reports, tests.
No Index.
T.p. 20, Ad.p. 28.   24500.
Per copy 5p, per year £3.50.

2841 SOUTH LINCOLNSHIRE FARMER. 1964.
(The Record 1923-1964).
National Farmers' Union, Springfield, Spalding, Lincs.
12, =
Commodity prices, legal notes, new products, tests, news.
No Index.
T.p. 10, Ad.p. 8.   3200.
Free to members.

2842 SOUTHERN FARMER. 1947.
J.J. Black (Publishers) Ltd., Somerset Farm, Cranleigh, Surrey.
12, =
Articles, news.
No Index.
T.p. 8, Ad.p. Most.
Per copy 2p, per year 30p.

631.1

FARM MANAGEMENT

2843 BIG FARM MANAGEMENT. 1971.
(Farm & Country 1957-1970; Sport & Country 1941-1957; Illustrated Sporting & Dramatic News).
Northwood Publications Limited, (trade and technical publishing division of The Thomson Organisation Limited), Northwood House, 93-99 Goswell Road, London, EC1V 7QA.
12/16, ‡ =   Produced for the man who plans, controls and finances the big farm (especially 300 acres and over). Covers overall management, finance, marketing, large-scale arable production, management and feeding of the big herd.
Book reviews, legal notes, letters, monographic articles, new products, parliamentary reports, standards, tests.
A, On request, from February, No, None.
June 1 1972, T.p. 22, Ad.p. 29.   18348.
Per copy 25p, per year £4.

2844 FARM MANAGEMENT: The Journal of the Farm Management Association. 1967.
Farm Management Association, National Agricultural Centre, Kenilworth, Warwickshire.
3, * ‡ =   All aspects of management whether in production, marketing or agricultural merchandising.
Abstracts, monographic articles.
4 yearly, Autumn 1971 (1st index), No, None.
Spring 1972, T.p. 51, Ad.p. None.   2200.
Per copy 50p, per year £1.50.

2845 FARM MANAGEMENT REVIEW. 1972.
North of Scotland College of Agriculture, School of Agriculture, Aberdeen.
= ‡
No Index.

631.3

FARM MACHINERY

2846 AGRICULTURAL AND GARDEN MACHINERY SERVICE: official journal of the British Agricultural & Garden Machinery Association.
(AMTDA Journal).
BAGMA, Penn Place, Rickmansworth, Herts.
12, ‡ = *
Book reviews, letters, articles.
No Index.
September 1972, T.p. 52.
Per copy 30p, per year £3.60 and Free to members.

2847 AGRICULTURAL MACHINERY JOURNAL. 1946.
Agricultural Press Ltd., 161 Fleet Street, London EC4.
12, ‡ =   Farm mechanisation and new machinery.

Book reviews, letters, articles, new products.
No Index.
Per copy 15p, per year £2.30.

2848 FARM. 1950.
Ford Motor Co. Ltd., Public Relations Dept., Basildon, Essex.
6, = ‡ +   Progress on farm mechanisation.
Book notices, book reviews, letters, new companies, new products, patents, standards, tests, news.
No Index.
T.p. 18, Ad.p. 14.
Per copy 5p, per year 40p.

2849 FARM ENGINEERING INDUSTRY. 1969.
Farm Engineering Industry Publications Ltd., 64a Lansdowne Road, South Woodford, London, E18.
12, = ‡ +   All aspects of farm machinery.
Book notices, book reviews, commodity prices, letters, articles, new companies, new products, obituaries, patents, standards, tests, news.
A, January, No, None.
T.p. 22, Ad.p. 21.   3000.
Per copy 15p, per year £1.50.

2850 INTERNATIONAL HARVESTER REVIEW. 1967.
International Harvester Company of Great Britain Limited, PO Box 25, 259 City Road, London, EC1P 1AD.
6, †   News of tractors, farm equipment, construction equipment and industrial equipment for company employees and others.
Company affairs, new products, obituaries.
No Index.
Free.

2851 JOURNAL OF AGRICULTURAL ENGINEERING RESEARCH. 1956.
Academic Press Inc. (London) Ltd., 24-28 Oval Road, London, NW1.
4, + ‡ =   Theoretical and practical aspects of mechanics in agriculture.
Book reviews, monographic articles.
A, February, Yes, None.
Per year £6.

2852 RED MACHINERY GUIDE. 1960.
Red Machinery Guide Ltd., 15 North Audley Street, London, W1.
12, =   Specifications and prices for new and used agricultural machinery.
Commodity prices, legal notes, new products.
No Index.
T.p. 103, Ad.p. 2.   1000.
Controlled circulation.

631.4

SOIL SCIENCE

2853 HDRA NEWSLETTER. 1958.
Henry Doubleday Research Association, 20 Convent Lane, Bocking, Braintree, Essex.
4, =   Organic farming and horticulture with emphasis on use of Russian Comfrey.
No Index.
T.p. 35.
Free to members.

2854 JOURNAL OF THE SOIL ASSOCIATION. 1968.
(Mother Earth. 1946-1967).
New Bells Press, Walnut Tree Manor, Haughley, Stowmarket, Suffolk, IP14 3RS.
4, ‡ + = *   Agriculture, land use and the countryside, pollution, food, health.
Book notices, book reviews, letters, monographic articles.
No Index.
January 1972, T.p. 52, Ad.p. 10.   6000.
Free to members.

2855 JOURNAL OF SOIL SCIENCE: Sponsored by the
British Society of Soil Science. 1949.
Oxford University Press, Press Road, Neasden, London, NW10.
4, +   Research over the whole field of pure and applied soil science.
Book reviews, monographic articles.
A, −, Yes, None.
March 1972, T.p. 117.   2000.
Per copy £1.75, per year £6.
Indexed in: OBZ

2856 SOIL BIOLOGY AND BIOCHEMISTRY. 1969.
Pergamon Press Ltd., Headington Hill Hall, Oxford, OX3 0BW.
4, + =   Research on soil organisms, their biochemical activities and their influence on plant growth.
Short-articles.
A, Last issue of volume, Yes, None.
Per copy £4, per year £14.

2857 SOILS AND FERTILIZERS. 1937.
Commonwealth Agricultural Bureaux, Farnham Royal, Slough, Bucks, SL2 3BN.
6, + = ‡   Soil and fertilizer science.
Abstracts.
A, −, Yes, None.
T.p. c. 83.
Per year £14 to subscribers.

2858 SPAN (Soil-Plant-Animal-maN). 1967.
New Bells Press, Walnut Tree Manor, Haughley, Nr. Stowmarket, Suffolk.
12, ○   Nutrition, farming, conservation and the countryside.
Book notices, book reviews, legal notes, letters, articles, new products, obituaries, parliamentary reports.
No Index.
May 1972, T.p. 8.   c. 6000.
Per copy 5p, and Free to members.

631.5

CULTIVATION

2859 CURRENT ADVANCES IN PLANT SCIENCE. 1972.
R. Maxwell Ltd., Headington Hall, Oxford, OX3 0PJ.
12, = ‡ +   Book reviews, letters, monographic articles.
A, −, Yes, None.
Per year £20.

2860 NURSERYMAN AND GARDEN CENTRE: incorporating Nurseryman Seedsman & Glasshouse Grower; Garden Centre Trading; Amenity Horticulture 1965.
(Nurseryman & Seedsman 1894-1964).
Benn Brothers Limited, 25 New Street Square, London, EC4 3JA.
52, ‡ = +   Horticulture, glasshouse growers, nurserymen, garden centres, pet stores, florists, out-door living and leisure gardening supplies, amenity horticulture.
Book reviews, commodity prices, legal notes, letters, articles, new products, obituaries.
6m, Last issue June and December, Yes, None.
15.6.1972, T.p. 16, Ad.p. 12.   4950.
Per year £5.

2861 PLANT BREEDING ABSTRACTS. 1930.
Commonwealth Agricultural Bureaux, Farnham Royal, Slough, Bucks, SL2 3BN.
4, = + ‡   Genetics, cytology, breeding and varietal trials of all the principal agricultural crops.
Abstracts.
A, −, Yes, None.
T.p. c. 500.
Per year £14 to contributing countries.

631.51

PLOUGHING

2862 BULLETIN OF NEWS AND INFORMATION. 1958.
World Ploughing Organisation, Alfred Hall, Foulsyke, Loweswater, Cockermouth, Cumb.
2/3, ○ = + ‡   Ploughing competitions, tillage, machinery etc.
No Index.
August 1971, T.p. 8.
Free to members.

631.8

FERTILIZERS

2863 FEED & FARM SUPPLIES. 1970.
(World Feeds & Protein News; Fertilizer Feed & Pesticide Journal 1919-1970; Feed & Farming Stuffs Supplies).
Turret Press Ltd./Turret Press (Holdings) Ltd., 157 Hagden Lane, Watford, WD1 8LW.
12, ‡ = +   Marketing and distribution of feed, seed, fertilizers, pesticides and veterinary chemicals.
Articles, new companies, new products, news, reports.
No Index.
June 1972, T.p. 22, Ad.p. 18.
Per year £8.25 including yearly 'International Milling & Feed Manual'.

2864 FERTILIZER INTERNATIONAL. 1969.
(The World of NPKS 1968-1969; The NPKS Bulletin 1962-1967).
The British Sulphur Corp. Ltd., Parnell House, 25 Wilton Rd., London, SW1V 1NH, England.
12, = ‡   The fertilizer industry, worldwide, as news items. Special sections for international marketing, news of the world, fertilizer market place, company news, plant and equipment, etc.
Book notices, book reviews, commodity prices, new companies, new products, tests.
No Index.
June 1972, T.p. 8.
Per copy £1, per year £12.

2865 STATISTICAL SUPPLEMENT: Raw Materials Supply; Fertilizer Trade. 1970.
British Sulphur Corporation Ltd., Parnell House, 25 Wilton Road, London, SW1V 1NH.
2, ‡ = + *   Production and trade in fertilizer raw materials for the world analysed on a country basis. Supplement to Sulphur, Nitrogen and Phosphorus and Potassium.
No Index.

632

PEST CONTROL

2866 INTERNATIONAL PEST CONTROL. 1963.
(Pest Technology 1958).
Rhodes Industrial Magazines Ltd., 54/55 Wilton Road, London, SW1.
6, + ‡ =
Book notices, book reviews, letters, monographic articles, new companies, news, new products, patents, standards, tests.
A, January, No, None.
T.p. 31, Ad.p. 11.   5000.
Per copy 50p, per year £2.50.

2867 PESTICIDE SCIENCE: A Journal of International Research and Technology on Crop Protection and Pest Control. 1970.
Academic Press (for Society of Chemical Industry), 24-28 Oval Road, London, NW1 7DX.

6, ‡ + = Insecticides, herbicides, fungicides, etc., their effectiveness, harmful effects, residues in food and agricultural products, how they act, relation of activity with chemical structure.
New products, Calendar of Meetings.
A, December, Yes, None.
April 1972, T.p. 143. 600.
Per copy £2, per year £10.

2868 PHYSIOLOGICAL PLANT PATHOLOGY: An International Journal of Experimental Plant Pathology. 1970.
Academic Press Inc. (London) Ltd. 24-28 Oval Road, London, NW1.
4, + = Work on physiological, biochemical, ultrastructural, genetical or molecular aspects of host-parasite interactions, on environmental effects on such relationships and on modifications of host metabolism induced by pathogens.
Book reviews.
A, April, Yes, None.
2(2), T.p. 100, Ad.p. 1. 650.
Per copy £2.50, per year £10.

2869 PLANT PATHOLOGY: a record of current work on plant diseases and pests. 1952.
HMSO, PO Box 569, London, SE1.
4, = ‡ + Plant diseases, plant pests, rodent and bird damage etc.
Monographic articles.
A, December, No, None.
T.p. 48, Ad.p. 2.
Per copy 50p, per year £2.

632.5

WEEDS

2870 WEED ABSTRACTS. 1954.
Commonwealth Agricultural Bureaux, Farnham Royal, Slough, Bucks, SL2 3BN.
6, + = ‡ Weeds, weed control and allied subjects.
Abstracts.
A, —, Yes, None.
T.p. c. 83.
Per year £8 to contributing countries.

2871 WEED RESEARCH: Official Journal of the European Weed Research Council. 1961.
Blackwell Scientific Publications, Osney Mead, Oxford, OX2 0EL.
4, + * = Study of weeds and their control and related topics. Reviews of technical conferences and symposia, and news items.
Monographic articles.
A, December, Yes, None.
June 1972, T.p. 92, Ad.p. 4. 980.
Per copy £2.50, per year £8.

633

FIELD CROPS

2872 FIELD CROP ABSTRACTS. 1948.
Commonwealth Agricultural Bureaux, Farnham Royal, Slough, SL2 3BN, Bucks.
4, = + ‡ Annual field crops, temperate and tropical.
Abstracts.
A, —, Yes, None.
T.p. c. 125.
Per year £10 to subscribers.

2873 HERBAGE ABSTRACTS. 1931.
Commonwealth Agricultural Bureaux, Farnham Royal, Slough, SL2 3BN.
4, = + ‡ Sown and natural grasslands, pasture plants and fodder crops.
Abstracts.
A, —, Yes, None.
T.p. c. 125.
Per year £8 to subscribers.

2874 PLANTATION CROPS. 1948.
Commonwealth Secretariat, Marlborough House, Pall Mall, London, SW1Y 5HX.
1/2, ‡ = + Review of production, trade, consumption and prices relating to coffee; cocoa, tea, sugar, spices, tobacco and rubber.
No Index.
No. 13, T.p. 298.
Per copy £2.

2875 VEGETABLE OILS & OILSEEDS. 1948.
Commonwealth Secretariat, Marlborough House, Pall Mall, London, SW1Y 5HX.
1, ‡ = + Review of production, trade, utilisation and prices relating to groundnuts, soya beans, sunflower seed, rapeseed, copra, oil palm products, linseed and other major oilseeds and oils.
No Index.
No. 20, T.p. 198.
Per copy £2.

633.1

CEREALS

2876 GRAIN BULLETIN. 1954.
Commonwealth Secretariat, Marlborough House, Pall Pall, London, SW1Y 5HX.
12, = + Production statistics and freight rates etc.
Commodity prices.
A, January, Yes, None.
June 1972, T.p. 47.
Per year £6.

2877 GRAIN CROPS. 1950.
Commonwealth Secretariat, Marlborough House, Pall Mall, London, SW1Y 5HX.
1/2, ‡ = + Review of production, trade, consumption and prices relating to wheat, wheat flour, maize, barley, oats, rye and rice.
No Index.
No. 14, T.p. 203.
Per copy £2.

2878 THE LONDON CORN CIRCULAR. 1842.
The London Corn Circular Ltd., 52 Mark Lane, London, EC3.
52, = Corn and agricultural trades.
Commodity prices, letters, new companies, new prodicts, obituaries, parliamentary reports, patents.
No Index.
T.p. 18, Ad.p. 2. 1500.
Per year £5.25.

633.18

RICE

2879 RICE BULLETIN. 1954.
Commonwealth Secretariat, Marlborough House, Pall Mall, London, SW1Y 5HX.
12, = Production and trade statistics.
Commodity prices.
A, January, Yes, None.
June 1972, T.p. 25.
Per year £3.

Key to reference symbols

○ popular   ‡ technical   = trade/professional

+ research   * society/institution   † house journal

633.2

GRASSLAND

2880 JOURNAL OF THE BRITISH GRASSLAND SOCIETY. 1946.
The Society, c/o Grassland Research Institute, Horley, Maidenhead, Berks.
4, * = + ‡
Book reviews, letters, monographic articles, tests.
A, December, Yes, None.
T.p. 88, Ad.p. 2.   2000.
Per copy £3, per year £4. Free to members.

2881 NORGRASS: The journal of the North of Scotland Grassland Society. 1962.
North of Scotland Grassland Society, c/o 581 King Street, Aberdeen.
1, ‡ *   All aspects of grassland husbandry and its relationship to agriculture in general.
Monographic articles, obituaries.
No Index.
No. 12, T.p. 40.   500.
Free to Members and press only.

633.491

POTATOES

2882 POTATO QUARTERLY. 1972.
(Potato Post' 1950's-1971).
Potato Marketing Board, 50 Hans Crescent, Knightsbridge, London, SW1X 0NB.
4, =   The main objectives are to keep potato producers and other sections of the potato trade informed of the Board's policies and activities together with the latest research developments.
Book reviews, legal notes, letters, articles.
No Index.
May 1972, T.p. 27, Ad.p. 13.   45000.
Per year 50p. Free to charge to all registered potato producers and licensed potato merchants.

2883 THE SEED POTATO: journal of the National Association of Seed Potato Merchants. 1961.
National Association of Seed Potato Merchants, 11a High Street, Chippenham, Wilts.
4, ‡ = +   Breeding, tuber diseases, planting methods, trial grounds—seed, storage, varieties and their uses, export, processing etc.
Commodity prices, legal notes, letters, monographic articles, new products, obituaries, parliamentary reports, standards, tests.
Q, Seasonally, Yes, None.
Spring 1972, T.p. 18, Ad.p. 10.   1000.
Per copy 25p, per year £1. Free to members.

633.51

COTTON

2884 COTTON GROWING REVIEW. 1967.
(The Empire Cotton Growing Review, 1924-1966).
Cotton Research Corporation, 14 Grosvenor Place, London, SW1X 7JL.
4, = +   Aspects of agricultural research bearing on cotton production.
Abstracts, book notices, book reviews, letters, monographic articles, obituaries.
A, October, Yes, None.
April 1972, T.p. 106.   1000.
Per copy 75p, per year £3.

634.0

FORESTRY

2885 ARBORICULTURAL ASSOCIATION JOURNAL. 1964.
Friary Press, Dorchester, Dorset.
2, * † ‡   Arboriculture in all its manifestations—selection, propagation, cultivation, maintenance, and replacement of amenity trees and woodlands. Also covers the role of trees in conservation and amenity terms and ancillary matters of interest to a profesionally-based organisation.
Abstracts, book reviews, letters, monographic articles, obituaries.
6 yr, 1971, Yes, None.
February 1972, T.p. 32.   725.
Per copy 15p.

2886 COMMONWEALTH FORESTRY REVIEW. 1946.
(Empire Forestry Journal 1921-1945).
Commonwealth Forestry Association, 18 Northumberland Avenue, London, WC2.
4, ‡   All matters pertaining to Commonwealth forestry.
Book reviews, letters, monographic articles, new products, obituaries.
A, With first issue of subsequent year, Yes, None.
March 1972, T.p. 90, Ad.p. 10.   1700.
Per copy £1.25, per year £5. Free to members.

2887 ELM NEWSLETTER. 1972.
Forestry Commission, 25 Savile Row, London, W1X 2AY.
4, = ‡
No Index.

2888 FORESTRY: The Journal of the Society of Foresters of Great Britain. 1927.
Oxford University Press, Press Road, Neasden, London, NW10.
2, + ‡   Practice and research in both growing of timber and its utilization. Includes basic sciences of forest physiology and ecology, forest soils, wood structure and timber physics, and allied sciences such as forest entomology and forest mycology.
Book reviews, monographic articles.
A, —, Yes, None.
No. 1, 1972, T.p. 127, Ad.p. 10.   1300.
Per copy £1.50, per year £4.

2889 FORESTRY ABSTRACTS. 1939.
Commonwealth Agricultural Bureaux, Farnham Royal, Slough, SL2 3BN.
4, = + ‡   Forestry in all aspects.
Abstracts.
A, —, Yes, None.
T.p. c. 125.
Per year £16 to subscribers.

2890 FORESTRY AND HOME GROWN TIMBER. 1972.
Benn Brothers Ltd., 74 Drymen Road, Bearsden, Glasgow.
6, ‡ + =   All aspects of Britain's forest industries and needs of growers; news and technical articles for home timber merchants. Production and marketing of British timber, and harvesting and extraction techniques.
Book notices, book reviews, letters, monographic articles, new products, reports, standards, tests.
No Index.
February 1972, T.p. 32, Ad.p. 31.   4000.
Per copy 50p, per year £2.

2891 FORESTRY COMMISSION LIBRARY REVIEW. 1965.
Library, Forestry Commission, Forest Research Station, Alice Holt Lodge, Wrecclesham, Farnham, Surrey.
3, ‡ +   Lists additions of new books, periodicals, bibliographies and translations in the Forestry Commission library, together with publications by staff. Contains articles of interest on aspects of information and library work.
Book notices.
No Index.
April 1972, T.p. 23.
Free.

2892 OXFORD UNIVERSITY FOREST SOCIETY JOURNAL. 1920.
Oxford University Forest Society, Department of Forestry, South Parks Road, Oxford, OX1 3RB.
1, * =   General forestry interest. Also Society notes etc.
Monographic articles.
None regular, 4-8 yearly.
1972, T.p. 103, Ad.p. 5.   c. 300.
Per copy 40p.

2893 QUARTERLY JOURNAL OF FORESTRY. 1906.
(Transactions of the English Arboricultural Society—1885-1905).
Royal Forestry Society of England, Wales and Northern Ireland, 102 High Street, Tring, Herts.
4, ‡ * Mainly forestry and arboriculture; but considerable coverage of wildlife, woodland ecology, forestry education, reports of overseas forestry tours; book reviews, correspondence columns and internal Society communications.
Book notices, book reviews, letters, monographic articles, obituaries.
A, January, Yes, None.
April 1972, T.p. 95, Ad.p. 25.   5000.
Per copy 50p, per year £2.

2894 SCOTTISH FORESTRY: Journal of the Royal Scottish Forestry Society. 1947.
(Journal of the Royal Scottish Arboricultural Society 1854-1946).
Royal Scottish Forestry Society, 26 Rutland Square, Edinburgh, EH1 2BU.
4, ‡ + * All aspects of forestry and allied subjects.
Book reviews, notes, letters, monographic articles, new products.
A, October, Yes, None.
January 1972, T.p. 94, Ad.p. 26.   2000+.
Per copy 50p, per year £2.

2895 SCOTTISH WOODLAND OWNERS ASSOCIATION NEWSLETTER. 1967.
Scottish Woodland Owners Association, 6 Chester Street, Edinburgh, EH3 7RD.
4, ‡ *   Private forestry.
Book notices, book reviews, commodity prices, legal notes, letters, new products, parliamentary reports.
No Index.
Spring 1972, T.p. 4.   2000.
Free to members.

2896 TIMBER GROWER: Quarterly publication of the Timber Growers' Organisation Ltd. 1962.
(News Sheet 1961).
Timber Growers' Organisation Ltd., National Agriculture Centre, Kenilworth, Warwickshire, CV8 2LG.
4, * =   Forestry, especially from the viewpoint of the private woodland owner, associated matters such as timber based industry, recreation etc.
Book notices, book reviews, commodity prices, letters, monographic articles, new products.
No Index.
May 1972, T.p. 52, Ad.p. 25.
Per copy 37½p, per year £1.50.

2897 TREES: Journal of the Men of the Trees.
Men of the Trees, Crawley Down, Crawley, Sussex.
3, *   Tree preservation.
Articles, news.
No Index.
Spring 1972, T.p. 76, Ad.p. 4.
Per copy 30p, per year 80p. Free to members.

634.1

FRUIT

2898 FRUIT. 1948.
Commonwealth Secretariat, Marlborough House, Pall Mall, London, SW1Y 5HX.
1, ‡ = +   Review of production and trade relating to fresh, canned, frozen and dried fruit, fruit juices and wine.
No Index.
No. 18, T.p. 358.
Per copy £2.

2899 FRUIT INTELLIGENCE. 1950.
Commonwealth Secretariat, Marlborough House, Pall Mall, SW1Y 5HX.
12, =   Statistics.
Commodity prices.
A, January, Yes, None.
May 1972, T.p. 59.
Per year £12.

2900 RETAIL FRUIT TRADE REVIEW. 1953.
Retail Fruit Trade Federation Ltd., Russell Chambers, Covent Garden, London, WC2.
12, =
Book reviews, legal notes, letters, news, parliamentary reports.
A, —, No, None.
T.p. 13, Ad.p. 14.   32000.
Free to members.

2901 WEEKLY FRUIT SUPPLIES. 1951.
Commonwealth Secretariat, Marlborough House, Pall Mall, London, SW1Y 5HX
52, =   Statistics.
Commodity prices.
No Index.
27-6-1972, T.p. 4.
Per year £10.

635

HORTICULTURE

2902 AMATEUR GARDENING. 1884.
General Magazines Division, IPC Magazines, Fleetway House, Farringdon Street, London, EC4A 4AD.
52, ○ =   Plant growing, garden design, house plants, flower arranging etc.
Letters, articles, new products.
No Index.
15-7-1972, T.p. 17, Ad.p. 17.   180000.
Per copy 6p, per year £6.

2903 COMMERCIAL GROWER: Fruit grower, market gardener and glasshouse nurseryman.
Benn Bros. Ltd., 25 New Street Square, London, EC4.
52, ‡   Commercial horticulture.
Book reviews, commodity prices, letters, articles, new products, obituaries.
6m, June/December, Yes, None.
T.p. 15, Ad.p. 28.   8750.
Per copy 10p, per year £5.

2904 GARDEN NEWS. 1958.
East Midland Allied Press Ltd., 117 Park Rd., Peterborough.
52, ○   Gardening for the home-owner.
Book reviews, letters, articles, new products.
No Index.
May 26th, 1972, T.p. 17, Ad.p. 14.   91799.
Per copy 6p, per year £4.94.

2905 GARDEN SUPPLIES RETAILER.
Sawell Publications Ltd., 4 Ludgate Circus, London, EC4.
6, =   Domestic garden supplies.
Commodity prices, letters, new companies, news, new products, obituaries, tests.
No Index.
T.p. 16, Ad.p. 13.   21000.
Controlled circulation.

2906 GARDENERS CHRONICLE/THE HORTICULTURAL
TRADE JOURNAL. 1969.
(Gardeners Chronicle 1841; Horticultural Trade Journal 1897-1969).
Haymarket Publishing Limited, Gillow House, 5 Winsley Street, London, W1.
52, ○ =   Horticultural trade in U.K. and amenity horticulture.
Book notices, book reviews, commodity prices, legal notes, letters, articles, new companies, new products, tests.
6m, −, Yes, None.
11086.
Per copy 12½p, per year £7.

2907 THE GROWER: Glasshouse, Fruit, Vegetables and Ornamentals Grower. 1965.
(Grower & Prepacker 1957-1965).
Grower Publications Ltd., 49 Doughty St., London, WC1N 2LP.
51, + = ‡   Surveys the whole field of commercial horticultural production, packing and selling.
Book notices, commodity prices, legal notes, letters, articles, new companies, new products, obituaries, parliamentary reports.
6m, last week June and Dec, Yes, None.
May 20, 1972, T.p. 45, Ad.p. 26.   c. 11200.
Per copy 10p, per year £5.

2908 HORTICULTURAL ABSTRACTS. 1931.
Commonwealth Agricultural Bureaux, Farnham Royal, Slough, SL2 3BN.
4, = + ‡   Horticultural and plantation crops, both temperate and tropical.
Abstracts.
A, −, Yes, 5 year.
T.p.c. 125.
Per year £14 to contributors.

2909 JOURNAL OF HORTICULTURAL SCIENCE. 1948.
(Journal of Pomology 1919-1921; Journal of Pomology and Horticultural Science 1922-1947).
East Malling Research Station, Maidstone, Kent.
4, +   All aspects of horticultural science relating to the production and storage of temperate and tropical fruits, vegetables and flowers, e.g. nutrition, pathology, propagation, breeding, storage physiology, etc.
Book reviews, monographic articles.
A, January, Yes, None.
April 1972, T.p. 136.   c. 1000.
Per copy £2.50, per year £8.

2910 JOURNAL OF THE ROYAL HORTICULTURAL SOCIETY. 1866.
(Proceedings of the R.H.S. 1838-1843; Journal (First Series) 1846-1855; Proceedings R.H.S. 1859-1865).
The Royal Horticultural Society, Vincent Square, London, SW1P 2PE.
12, ○ * =   Gardening.
Book notices, book reviews, letters, monographic articles, obituaries.
A, December, Yes, 10 year.
June 1972, T.p. 44, Ad.p. 23.   65000.
Per copy 25p, per year £3.

2911 NORTHERN GARDENER.
Northern Horticultural Society, Harlow Car Gardens, Harrogate, Yorks.
6, ○ =.
No Index.
Free to members.

2912 ROSE BULLETIN. 1971.
Royal National Rose Society, Bore Hill, Chiswell Green Lane, St. Albans, Herts.
4, ○ =.
No Index.
Free to members.

2913 SCIENTIFIC HORTICULTURE: journal of the Horticultural Education Association. 1932
Horticultural Education Association, c/o The Elvy & Gibbs Partnership, 11 Best Lane, Canterbury, Kent.
1, + ‡ =   Horticultural research.
Book reviews, monographic articles, new products, reports, standards, tests.
No Index.
1972, T.p. 172, Ad.p. 2.   2500.
Per copy £1.75.

635.8

MUSHROOMS

2914 MGA BULLETIN: Monthly Journal of the Mushroom Growers' Assoc. 1945.
Mushroom Growers' Association, Agriculture House, Knightsbridge, London, SW1X 7NJ.
12, = +   All aspects of mushroom growing, practical as well as scientific.
Book reviews, commodity prices, letters, articles, new products, obituaries, reports.
3 yearly, irregular, Yes, 25 years.
July 1971, T.p. 28, Ad.p. 20.   1000.
Per copy 50p. Confidential to members.

635.9

FLOWERS

2915 BRITISH FLOWER INDUSTRY ASSOCIATION JOURNAL.
The Association, 35 Wellington Street, Covent Garden, London, WC2.
12, =   Flower growing, wholesaling and retailing.
Book reviews, legal notes, letters, news, new products, obituaries, parliamentary reports, standards, tests.
No Index.
T.p. 23, Ad.p. 17.   10000.
Free to members.

2916 BRITISH IRIS SOCIETY NEWSLETTER. c. 1954
British Iris Society, 72 South Hill Park, London, NW3 2SN.
3, ○ ‡ =   Irises, iridaceae generally and all matters pertaining thereto. News and Society information.
Book reviews, articles, news.
No Index.
January 1972, T.p. 19.
Free to members.

2917 BULLETIN OF THE AFRICAN SUCCULENT PLANT SOCIETY. 1966.
The African Succulent Plant Society, 54 Fishponds Road, Hitchin, Herts. SG5 1NS.
6, ○ ‡ + *   Study of all the succulent plants with the exception of the cacti. Supply of seeds and plants of rare and uncommon species.
Book notices, book reviews, letters, monographic articles, new products, obituaries.
A, With first issue of the following year, Yes, None.
T.p. 40, Ad.p. 8.   1000.
Per year £1.50.

2918 BULLETIN OF THE NATIONAL SWEET PEA SOCIETY. 1900.
The Society, 33 Priory Road, Rustington, Littlehampton, Sussex.
2, = ○.
News.
No Index.
T.p. 12.
Free to members.

2919 ESSEX SUCCULENT REVIEW. 1963.
The Editor, 33 Bridge Avenue, Upminster, Essex.
4, ‡ * =   Cultivation of succulent plants (including cacti). Growers' experiences within Society and of

growing. News of local Branches of Cactus Societies.
Book notices, book reviews, letters, articles, obituaries, reports, tests.
None issued at moment (10 year in prep.).
June 1972, T.p. 24, Ad.p. 2.   150.
Per copy 10p, per year 35p.

2920 THE FLORIST. 1947.
Lonsdale Publications Ltd., 120 Lower Ham Road, Kingston on Thames, Surrey.
12, = +   New techniques, aids to selling, Latest materials, forthcoming events, stop press news.
Book notices, book reviews, commodity prices, letters, new companies, new products, obituaries, patents, standards, tests.
No Index.
June 1972, T.p. 15, Ad.p. 21.
Per year £1.50.

2921 THE FLOWER ARRANGER: The official publication of the National Association of Flower Arrangement Societies. 1961.
National Association of Flower Arrangement Societies, Lye End Link, St John's, Woking, Surrey.
4, * ○ =   Styles of arrangement, growing plants for arranging, photographs of exhibitions and festivals and internal news and organisation.
Book reviews, monographic articles, obituaries, tests.
A, Spring, No, None.
T.p. 48, Ad.p. 24.   27000.
Per copy 15p, per year £1.

2922 INTERNATIONAL CAMELLIA JOURNAL. 1952.
International Camellia Society, Bodnant Garden, Tal-y-cafn, Colwyn Bay, Denbighshire, N. Wales.
1, * +   All aspects of camellia culture throughout the world. Botanical and horticultural study of camellias.
Book notices, book reviews, letters, monographic articles, new products, obituaries, patents, standards, tests.
No Index.
March 1970, T.p. 96, Ad.p. 4.   2000.
Per copy £1.

2923 THE JOURNAL OF THE SCOTTISH ROCK GARDEN CLUB.
c/o J. B. Duff, Hon. Publications Manager, Langfauld, Glenfarg, Perth.
○ =
No Index.
Free to members.

2924 NATIONAL BEGONIA SOCIETY BULLETIN.
The Society, c/o 50 Woodlands Farm Road, Erdington, Birmingham 24.
3/4, ○   Cultivation of begonias.
Letters, news.
No Index.
T.p. 12.
Free to members.

2925 NATIONAL CACTUS & SUCCULENT SOCIETY JOURNAL. 1946.
(Yorkshire Cactus Journal 1946).
National Cactus & Succulent Society, 19 Crabtree Road, Botley, Oxford OX2 9DU.
4, * + ○   Cactus and succulent plant cultivation, botany, ecology, plant conservation.
Book reviews, letters, monographic articles.
A, June, No, None.
June 1972, T.p. 37, Ad.p. 11.   5200.
£1.50. Free to members.

2926 PELARGONIUM NEWS. 1954.
British Pelargonium & Geranium Society, 129 Aylesford Ave., Beckenham, Kent, BR3 3RX.
3, * + ‡   Worldwide topics of this specialist subject 'Geraniaceae'.
Breeding, cultivation, research, taxonomy, book reviews, letters.
No Index.
August 1971, T.p. 20, Ad.p. 4.   1800.
Per year £1.

2927 QUARTERLY BULLETIN OF THE ALPINE GARDEN SOCIETY. 1930.
Alpine Garden Society, Lye End Link, St. John's, Woking, Surrey.
4, *   Rock and alpine plants in cultivation and in the wild. Descriptions of new plants, details of new locations etc.
Book reviews, monographic articles, obituaries.
A, December, Yes, 10 year.
March 1972, T.p. 84, Ad.p. 16.   6500.
Per copy 75p, per year £2.50.

636

ANIMALS

2928 THE ANIMALS FRIEND MAGAZINE. 1894
National Council for Animals Welfare, 126 Royal College St., London, NW1.
4, ○ =   All aspects of animal work especially the encouragement of a humane attitude towards animals and birds.
Legal notes, letters, articles, obituaries, parliamentary reports.
No Index.
Spring 1972, T.p. 20.
Per copy 8p. Free to members.

2929 ANIMALS MAGAZINE: Journal of the PDSA. 1943.
Peoples' Dispensary for Sick Animals, PDSA. 1943. South Street, Dorking, Surrey.
12, ○.
News.
No Index.
T.p. 20.
Per copy 5p, per year 50p.

2930 FUR AND FEATHER. 1891.
(Rabbit Keeper & Show Reporter 1888, Small Pets 1889). Watmoughs Limited, Idle, Bradford, Yorks.
26, =   Care of animals—Details of shows.
Book notices, book reviews, commodity prices, letters, articles.
No Index.
29.6.1972, T.p. 30, Ad.p. 17.
Per copy 15p, per year £4.75.

2931 PET PRODUCT MARKETING AND GARDEN SUPPLIES. 1970.
(Pet Trade Journal & Garden Supplies 1955-1969).
Knighton Publications, 5 Knighton Close, South Croydon CR2 6DP.
12, =   Pet and garden products.
Book notices, book reviews, commodity prices, legal notes, letters, new companies, news, new products, obituaries.
No Index.
T.p. 24, Ad.p. most.
To trade only.

636.08

STOCK BREEDING

2932 ANIMAL BREEDING ABSTRACTS. 1933.
Commonwealth Agricultural Bureaux, Farnham Royal, Slough SL2 3BN.
4, = + ‡   Animal breeding in general.
Abstracts.
A, —, Yes, None.
T.p. c. 125.
Per year £12 to subscribers.

2933 ANIMAL PRODUCTION: Journal of the British Society of Animal Production. 1959.
(Proceedings of the British Society of Animal Production 1944-1958).
Longman Group Limited, 43/45 Annandale Street, Edinburgh, EH7 4AT.
6, + = ‡ Research findings in any scientific field related to animal production, including breeding and genetics, nutrition, physiology, biochemistry, animal behaviour.
Monographic articles.
A, November, Yes, 10 year.
April 1972, T.p.124, Ad.p.4. 2250.
Per copy £1.75, per year £9.

636.083.1

STABLE MANAGEMENT

2934 STABLE MANAGEMENT: incorporating Riding School & Stable Management. 1964.
Riding School & Stable Management Ltd., 1 Tahoma Lodge, Lubbock Road, Chislehurst, Kent.
6, ‡ = Devoted to the administrative, business, supply and equipment interests of those who own and manage riding schools, livery stables and riding stables.
Book notices, book reviews, commodity prices, letters, articles, new companies, new products, standards, tests.
No Index.
June/July 1972, T.p. 26, Ad.p. 4. 5500.
Per year £1.50.

636.1

HORSES

2935 ARAB HORSE SOCIETY NEWS. 1955.
Arab Horse Society, Sackville Lodge, Lye Green, Nr. Crowborough, Sussex.
2, ○ = * All aspects of breeding, general information, etc.
Book notices, book reviews, letters, articles, obituaries, tests.
6m, May/November, Yes, 5 year.
Autumn 1971, T.p. 86, Ad.p. 82. 3000.
Per copy 40p, per year 75p.

2936 THE SHETLAND PONY STUD-BOOK SOCIETY MAGAZINE. 1968.
Shetland Pony Stud-Book Society, 8 Whinfield Road, Montrose, Angus.
2, ‡ * = Information of interest and use to Shetland pony breeders, together with technical articles of the same nature.
Book notices, book reviews, commodity prices, legal notes, letters, articles, new companies, new products, obituaries, tests.
No Index.
Spring 1972, T.p. 35, Ad.p. 43. 1300.
Per copy, 25p, per year 50p.

2937 WELSH PONY & COB SOCIETY JOURNAL. 1962.
Charles Clarke Ltd., 19/23 Boltro Road, Haywards Heath, Sussex.
1, ○ ‡ * Instructive articles, also news and views on Welsh ponies and cobs throughout the world. Designed to bring members of the society closer together, wherever they live.
Book reviews, commodity prices, monographic articles, new products, obituaries, tests.
No Index.
1972, T.p.117, Ad.p. 225 of studs. 5000.
Per copy 50p.

636.2

CATTLE

2938 THE ABERDEEN-ANGUS REVIEW: official Journal of the Aberdeen-Angus Cattle Society. 1919.
The Aberdeen-Angus Cattle Society, 6 King's Place, Perth.
1, = * . Details of breed achievements in various shows and sales throughout Britain and Ireland during the year. Features on personalities and herds, matters of interest to, and useful to, the breed.
Commodity prices, letters, articles, news.
No Index.
January 1972, T.p. 63, Ad.p. 70. 3000.
Per copy 50p.

2939 AYRSHIRE CATTLE SOCIETY'S JOURNAL. 1929.
Ayrshire Cattle Society, 1 Racecourse Road, Ayr.
4, = + Matters of interest to Ayrshire breeders at home and overseas.
No Index.
Summer 1972, T.p. 50, Ad.p. 50. 4800.
Per year £1.

2940 BRITISH FRIESIAN JOURNAL. 1919.
(Milk 1919).
The British Friesian Cattle Society, Scotsbridge House, Rickmansworth, Herts. WD3 3BB.
6, * ‡ = Any matters pertaining to the breed, milk production and allied subjects.
No Index.
T.p. 61, Ad.p. 59. 15000.
Free to members.

2941 DAIRY SHORTHORN JOURNAL. 1932.
Shorthorn Society of the UK & GB & Ireland, Green Lodge, Great Bowden, Market Harborough, Leics.
12, = Dairy Shorthorn breed and other agricultural news.
Articles, news.
No Index.
T.p.12, Ad.p. 8. 2000.
Per copy 20p, per year £2.

2942 GALLOWAY JOURNAL. 1952.
Galloway Cattle Society, Normandale, Castle-Douglas.
1, * ‡ Galloway breed of cattle.
Commodity prices, letters, monographic articles, news, obituaries, standards, tests.
No Index.
T.p. 111, Ad.p. 82.
Free to members.

2943 GUERNSEY BREEDERS' JOURNAL. 1947.
The English Guernsey Cattle Society, Giggs Hill Green, Thames Ditton, Surrey.
2, * Dedicated to the improvement of the Guernsey breed of cattle, records developments within the breed and provides stimulus for existing and potential breeders of Guernsey cattle.
Letters, monographic articles, obituaries, standards.
No Index.
No. 1. 1972, T.p. 26, Ad.p. 36. 2000.
Per copy 5p (Members), 15p (Non-members), per year 10p (Members), 30p (Non-members).

2944 HEREFORD BREED JOURNAL. 1963.
Hereford Herd Book Society, Hereford House, Hereford.
1, = Pedigrees and commercial Hereford cattle breeding.
Monographic articles, news, tests.
No Index.
T.p. 140, Ad.p. 174. 6000.
Free to members.

2945 INTERNATIONAL MARKET SURVEY: Cattle-sheep-pigs. 1968/69.
Meat and Livestock Commission, Economic Information Service, Queensway House, Bletchley, Bucks.
4, =   Summarises the meat production situation in European countries and those of the Commonwealth, and North and South America. Foreign exchange rates and metric conversion are given.
Commodity prices, new products.
No Index.
Summer 1972, T.p. 71.
Per copy Free.

2946 JERSEY AT HOME: official publication of the Royal Jersey Agricultural & Horticultural Society.
The Society, Springfield, St. Helier, Jersey CI.
3, * = ‡ ○   Dairy industry, Jersey cattle breeders.
Articles, news.
No Index.
T.p. 29, Ad.p. 17.
Free to members.

2947 THE JERSEY. 1970.
(The Jersey Cow 1920-1970).
Jersey Cattle Society of the U.K., 154 Castle Hill, Reading, Berks.
2, + *   The Jersey Breed in the United Kingdom, appertaining to breeding, research and Jersey affairs in general.
Prices, legal notes, letters, articles, tests.
No Index.
Summer 1972, T.p. 25, Ad.p. 25.   3000.
Per year £1. and Free to Members of Society.

2948 LIVESTOCK FARMING. 1970.
(Beef and Sheep Farming 1964-1969).
Alan Exley Ltd., P.O. Box 1, Battle, Sussex.
12, ‡ = +   Information calculated to improve the profitability of the larger dairy, beef, and sheep farms of the U.K.
Monographic articles, new products.
No Index.
T.p. 25, Ad.p. 27.   25000.
Per copy 12p, per year £2. and Free, controlled circulation.

2949 MARKET SURVEY: Cattle-sheep-pigs. 1968/69.
Meat and Livestock Commission, Economic Information Service, Queensway House, Bletchley, Bucks.
4, =   Details of fatstock slaughtering and meat production for cattle, sheep and pigs. Imports and export figures, supplies, costs of feedstuffs and prices for the United Kingdom are all given.
Commodity prices.
No Index.
Summer 1972, T.p. 35.
Per copy Free.

636.3
SHEEP

2950 BLACKFACE SHEEP BREEDERS' ASSOCIATION JOURNAL. 1948.
The Blackface Sheep Breeders' Association, 24 Beresford Terrace, Ayr, KA7 2EL.
1, *   Countryside and farming as a whole, and the sheep industry in particular. It also gives details of the Association's Council and district office bearers.
Commodity prices, letters, monographic articles.
No Index.
1972, T.p. 22, Ad.p. 22.   c.1500.
Free to members.

636.39
GOATS

2951 BRITISH GOAT SOCIETY MONTHLY JOURNAL. 1909.
The Society, Rougham, Bury St. Edmunds, Suffolk.
11, * = ‡ +   All aspects of goat breeding etc.
Book reviews, letters, articles, news.
A, December, Yes, None.
T.p. 29, Ad.p. 3.
Free to members.

636.4
PIGS

2952 THE BRITISH LANDRACE PIG JOURNAL. 1961.
The British Landrace Pig Society, 18 Yorkersgate, Malton, Yorkshire, YO17 0AL.
2, * =   Matters pertaining to the British Landrace Breed in particular, and the pig industry in general.
No Index.
Spring 1972, T.p. 16, Ad.p. 20.
Free to members.

2953 INTERNATIONAL MARKET SURVEY: Pigs. 1969.
Meat and Livestock Commission, Economic Information Service, Queensway House, Bletchley, Buckinghamshire.
2, =   Details of numbers of pigs produced, slaughtered etc. in European countries. Prices of bacon, pigs are quoted. Details of exchange rates and metric conversion are given.
Commodity prices, new products.
No Index.
Winter 1971, T.p. 39.
Free.

2954 PIG BREEDERS GAZETTE. 1927.
National Pig Breeders Association, 51a Clarendon Road, Watford, Herts, WD1 1HT.
2, =   Pig breeding.
Book notices, book reviews, commodity prices, articles, tests.
No Index.
January 1972, T.p. 52, Ad.p. 23.   5800.
Per copy 25p, per year 50p.

636.5
POULTRY

2955 BRITISH CHICKEN ASSOCIATION GROWERS BULLETIN.
The Association, High Holborn House, 52/54 High Holborn, London, WC1.
6, ‡ =
Commodity prices, news.
No Index.
T.p. 4.
Free to members.

2956 BRITISH POULTRY SCIENCE. 1960.
Longman Group Limited, 43/45 Annandale Street, Edinburgh, EH7 4AT.
6, + =   Physiology, biochemistry, genetics of poultry.
Monographic articles.
No Index.
July 1972, T.p. 92, Ad.p. 2.   900.
Per copy £2, per year £7.

2957 NATIONAL ASSOCIATION OF POULTRY PACKERS LTD. MARKET PRICE REPORT.
The Association, High Holborn House, 52/54 High Holborn, London, WC1.
52, =
Commodity prices.
No Index.
T.p. 2.
Free to members.

2958 NATIONAL ASSOCIATION OF POULTRY PACKERS LTD. WEEKLY INDUSTRY.
The Association, 52/54 High Holborn, London, WC1.
52, = ‡
Commodity prices, legal notes, news, parliamentary reports.
No Index.
T.p. 3.
Free to members.

2959 POULTRY INDUSTRY. 1935.
Agricultural Press Ltd., 161 Fleet Street, London, EC4.
12, =   Poultry breeding and industry.
Articles, news.
No Index.
T.p. 25, Ad.p. 20.   6500.
Free, controlled circulation.

2960 POULTRY WORLD. 1874.
Agricultural Press Ltd., 161-166 Fleet Street, London, EC4P 4AA.
52, ‡ =   Commercial poultry and eggs. Breeding, production and marketing. All aspects of the industry are included in news and market reports plus feature articles.
Book notices, book reviews, commodity prices, legal notes, letters, articles, new companies, new products, obituaries, parliamentary reports, standards, tests.
No Index.
8/6/72, T.p. 20, Ad.p. 20.   14529.
Per copy 10p, per year £7.50.

636.596

PIGEONS

2961 PIGEONS AND PIGEON WORLD. 1951.
(Pigeons and Bantams 1947-1951).
Fancy Press Ltd., 'Overdale' 55 Langham Road, Bowdon, Altrincham, Cheshire.
12, ○   Pigeons; news, varieties, shows, racing etc.
Book reviews, letters, articles, news, obituaries, standards, tests.
No Index.
T.p. 25, Ad.p. 7.
Per copy 15p, per year £1.80.

636.7

DOGS

2962 DOG NEWS: official journal of the National Dog Owners Association. 1966.
Kemp's Printing & Publishing Co. Ltd., 299 Grays Inn Road, London, WC1.
12, * =   Breeding, training etc.
Book reviews, letters, articles, obituaries, standards.
No Index.
T.p. 22.   10000.
Free to members.

2963 DOG WORLD. 1928.
Dog World Ltd., Press House, Wotton Road, Ashford, Kent.
52, ○ = ‡   News of shows, breeds, etc.
No Index.
16 June 1972, T.p. 54, Ad.p. 3.
Per copy 17p, per year £10.

2964 DOG'S LIFE. 1965.
Burlington Publishing Co. (1942) Ltd., Cordwallis Estate, Clivemont Road, Maidenhead, Berks.
12, ○
Book reviews, letters, news, new products.
No Index.
T.p. 29, Ad.p. 16.   13800.
Per copy 15p, per year £2.50.

2965 KENNEL GAZETTE. 1893.
The Kennel Club, 1-4, Clarges Street, Piccadilly, London, W1Y 8AB.
12, †   Official journal of the Kennel Club, information on all shows and trials held in G.B., Kennel Index, articles of interest to the canine world.
Book reviews, letters, obituaries.
No Index.
June 1972, T.p. 32, Ad.p. 6.   5500.
Per copy 20p, per year £2.40.

2966 OUR DOGS. 1895.
Our Dogs Publishing Co. Ltd., 5 Oxford Rd., Station Approach, Manchester, M60 1SY.
52, =   Canine matters—mainly show news.
No Index.
June 9, 1972. T.p. 54, Ad.p. 10.
Per copy 15p, per year £11.50.

636.8

CATS

2967 FELINE ADVISORY BUREAU NEWS BULLETIN. 1959.
Feline Advisory Bureau, The Barn Cottage, Tytherington, Walton-under-Edge, Glos.
4, * = ‡   All aspects of feline science including veterinary topics.
Book notices, book reviews, legal notes, letters, news, new products, obituaries, parliamentary reports.
No Index.
T.p. 30, Ad.p. 4.   700.
Per copy 50p, per year £1.50.

636.9

HAMSTERS

2968 NATIONAL HAMSTER COUNCIL JOURNAL. 1954.
The Council, c/o Crantock, Goatacre Lane, Medstead, Alton, Hants.
12, ○
News.
No Index.
T.p. 16.
Free to members.

636.92

RABBITS

2969 QUARTERLY NEWSLETTER. 1967.
Commercial Rabbit Association. Tyning House, Shurdington, Cheltenham, Glos.
4, = *   All subjects of interest to commercial rabbit producers and others engaged in the industry.
Commodity prices, legal notes, letters, articles, new products, obituaries, standards, tests.
No Index.
Spring 1972, T.p. 21.
Free to members.

637.1

DAIRYING. MILK INDUSTRY

2970 DAIRY EDUCATION. 1964.
National Milk Publicity Council Inc., John Princes Street, London, W1M 0AP.
3, =   Educational establishments in England and Wales only.
Book reviews, letters, articles.
No Index.
Spring 1972, T.p. 4.
Free.

2971 DAIRY FARMER and dairy beef producer. 1929.
Farming Press Ltd., Fenton House, Wharfedale Road, Ipswich, IP1 4LG.
12, ‡   Feature articles and items of practical value to commercial milk producers.
Abstracts, book reviews, commodity prices, letters, monographic articles, new companies, new products, tests.
No Index.
April 1972, T.p. 124, Ad.p. 67.   15000.
Per copy 15p, per year £2.25.

2972 DAIRY INDUSTRIES incorporating Dairy engineering. 1936.
United Trade Press Ltd., 9 Gough Square, Fleet Street, London, EC4.
12, = ‡ +   Milk processing, bulk delivery and processing of dairy products.
Book reviews, monographic articles, new companies, news, new products, obituaries, patents.
A, December, No, None.
T.p. 35, Ad.p. 33.
Per copy 25p, per year £5.
Indexed in: BTI.

2973 DAIRY PRODUCE. 1948.
Commonwealth Secretariat, Marlborough House, Pall Mall, London, SW1Y 5HX.
1/2, ‡ = +   Review of production, trade, consumption and prices relating to butter, cheese, condensed milk, milk powder, casein, eggs, and egg products.
No Index.
No. 20, T.p. 128.
Per copy £2.

2974 DAIRY SCIENCE ABSTRACTS. 1939.
Commonwealth Agricultural Bureaux, Farnham Royal, Slough, SL2 3BN.
12, = + ‡   Science and technology of dairying in all aspects.
Abstracts.
A, –, Yes, None.
T.p.c. 42.
Per year £12 to subscribers.

2975 DAIRYING. 1970.
(Royal Association of British Dairy Farmers Journal– 1969).
The Association, 17 Devonshire Street, London, W1N 2BQ.
3, * =   Dairy farming and the dairy industry.
Legal notes, articles, news, new products, standards.
No Index.
T.p. 29, Ad.p. 14.
Free to members.

2976 JOURNAL OF DAIRY RESEARCH. 1929.
Cambridge University Press (for the National Institute for Research in Dairying and the Hannah Dairy Research Institute), P.O. Box 92, London, NW1 2DB.
3, +   All aspects of dairy science—the welfare of the cow, milk yields, foodstuffs, analysis of milk, manufacture of cheese, butter etc., uses of skim milk, milk preservatives etc.
Monographic articles.
A, October, Yes, Vols. 1-10.
February 1972, T.p. 182.   1140.
Per copy £4.50, per year £10.

2977 JOURNAL OF THE SOCIETY OF DAIRY TECHNOLOGY. 1947.
Society of Dairy Technology, 172A Ealing Road, Wembley, Middlesex, HA0 4QD.
4, = ‡ + *   New technical developments in the industry.
Book notices, book reviews, letters, monographic articles, obituaries, standards.
A, January, Yes, None.
19/6/1972, T.p. 54, Ad.p. 8.   2742.
Free to members.

2978 THE MILK INDUSTRY. 1920.
National Dairymen's Association, 37 Queen's Gate, London, SW7.
12, + = ‡   Milk distribution, processing and manufacture; dairy science and technology dairy sales; promotion and economics; plant equipment and transport.
Book notices, book reviews, letters, monographic articles, new companies, new products, obituaries, parliamentary reports, standards, tests.
A, January, Yes, None.
5, 1972, T.p. 40, Ad.p. 20.   7000.
Per copy 25p, per year £2.50.

2979 MILK NEWS. 1959.
Aberdeen & District Milk Marketing Board, Twin Spires, Bucksburn, Aberdeen, AB2 9NR.
12, ‡ =   Milk News contains news, comment, and articles of local, national and international importance to milk producers in the Aberdeen and District MMB's area of Aberdeen, Banff & Kincardine.
Commodity prices, articles, new companies, new products, obituaries, standards, tests.
No Index.
6, 1972, T.p. 16/20, Ad.p. Variable.
Free.

2980 MILK PRODUCER: journal of the Milk Marketing Board. 1954.
(Home Farmer 1934-1953).
Milk Marketing Board, Thames Ditton, Surrey.
12, ‡
Book reviews, commodity prices, legal notes, articles, new companies, news, new products.
Index available irregularly—details on application.
T.p. 14, Ad.p. 18.   95000.
Free to producers.

2981 SMMB BULLETIN. 1959.
(News Bulletin 1954-1958).
Scottish Milk Marketing Board, Underwood Road, Paisley, Renfrew.
12, ‡ = +   All aspects of dairy farming.
Commodity prices, articles, new products, standards, tests.
A, –, No, None.
T.p. 14, Ad.p. 10.
Free to producers.

2982 UNIGATE NEWS. 1966.
(U.D. Notebook 1920-1965, Milkmade 1951-1965).
Unigate Ltd., 34 Palace Court, London, W2 4HX.
6, †
Letters, monographic articles, new companies, new products, obituaries.
No Index.
May 1972, T.p. 24.   30000.
Free.

2983 WEEKLY DAIRY PRODUCE SUPPLIES. 1955.
Commonwealth Secretariat, Marlborough House, Pall Mall, London, SW1Y 5HX.
52, =   Production/import statistics.
Commodity prices.
No Index.
26.6.1972, T.p. 2.
Per year £3.

Key to reference symbols

○ popular   ‡ technical   = trade/professional

+ research   * society/institution   † house journal

637.14
ICE CREAM

2984 ICE CREAM AND FROZEN CONFECTIONERY: official journal of the Ice Cream Alliance.
(Ice Cream Journal, 1949-1954).
Ice Cream Alliance Ltd., 90/94 Gray's Inn Road, London, WC1.
12, ‡ = +   Ice cream trade in general.
Book reviews, legal notes, letters, new companies, new products, obituaries, parliamentary reports, patents, standards, tests.
No Index.
May 1972, T.p. 25, Ad.p. 55.   3500.
Per copy 15p, per year £2.50.

637.4
EGGS

2985 BRITISH EGG ASSOCIATION NEWSLETTER. 1969.
(BEA Information Sheet).
The Association, High Holborn House, 52/54 High Holborn, London, WC1.
12, + =
Commodity prices, news, statistics, parliamentary reports.
No Index.
T.p. 10.
Free to members.

2986 MARKET REPORT: Journal of the National Egg Producer Retailers' Association. 1969.
(Quality Egg 1967-1968).
Miles Media Ltd., High Street, Gillingham, Dorset.
52, = ‡   Commercial egg industry price and supply information. Technical news of interest to producers.
Commodity prices, news, new products.
No Index.
T.p. 8, Ad.p. 12.
Per copy 10p, per year £1.20 and Free controlled circulation.

2987 MARKET REVIEW: Situation and Outlook Report. 1968.
International Egg Commission, Room 434, Agriculture House, Knightsbridge, London, SW1.
2, ‡ = + *   Egg statistics from countries worldwide.
No Index.
31.13.1971, T.p. 28.   c. 275.
Issued free to members and others interested.

2988 SIX-MONTHLY STATISTICAL BULLETIN. 1966.
International Egg Commission, Room 434, Agriculture House, Knightsbridge, London, SW1.
2, ‡ = + *   Egg statistics from some 28 countries throughout the world.
No Index.
30.9.1971, T.p. 28.   c. 325.
Issued free to members and others interested.

637.5
MEAT

2989 MEAT. 1948.
Commonwealth Secretariat, Marlborough House, Pall Mall, London, SW1Y 5HX.
1/2, ‡ = +   Review of production, trade, consumption and prices relating to beef and veal, mutton and lamb, pig-meat, poultry meat, offals, canned meat.
No Index.
No. 18, T.p. 143.
Per copy £1.50.

2990 MEAT: marketing, management, manufacturing. 1971.
(Meat Industry 1969-1971; Meat Marketing, 1930-1968)
IPC Consumer Industries Press, 161/166 Fleet St., London, EC4P 4AA.
10, =
Book reviews, commodity prices, letters, articles, new companies, new products, obituaries, parliamentary reports, standards, tests.
No Index.
May 1972, T.p. 17, Ad.p. 42.   10000.
Per copy 15p, per year £2 and Free controlled circulation.

2991 MEAT AND DAIRY PRODUCE BULLETIN. 1947.
Commonwealth Secretariat, Marlborough House, Pall Mall, London, SW1Y 5HX.
12, = +   Trade statistics.
Commodity prices.
A, January, Yes, None.
June 1972, T.p. 52.
Per year £12.

2992 MEAT TRADER. 1966.
National Federation of Meat Traders Associations, 29 Linkfield Lane, Redhill, Surrey.
10, =   All aspects of meat retailing, particularly from the consumer angle.
Legal notes, letters, articles, news, parliamentary reports.
No Index.
T.p. 26, Ad.p. 5.   11400.
Free to members.

2993 MEAT TRADES JOURNAL. 1888.
5 Charterhouse Square, London, EC1.
52, =   Livestock and cattle and dead meat trades.
No Index.
T.p. 40, Ad.p. 40.   24000.
Per copy 5p, per year £3.

637.56
FISH TRADE

2994 FISH FRIERS REVIEW. 1925.
Fish Friers Review Ltd., Federation House, 289 Dewsbury Road, Leeds, LS11 5HW.
12, = †   Developments in fried fish trade; news of National Federation of Fish Friers, commodities; legislation; equipment.
Book reviews, commodity prices, legal notes, letters, articles, new companies, new products, obituaries, parliamentary reports, standards, tests.
No Index.
June 1972, T.p. 29, Ad.p. 35.   6000.
Subscription on application.

2995 FISH TRADES GAZETTE. 1883.
Retail Journals Ltd., 17/19 John Adam Street, London, WC2.
52, =   Retailing and marketing aspects.
Book notices, book reviews, commodity prices, legal notes, letters, monographic articles, new companies, new products, obituaries, parliamentary reports, standards, tests.
No Index.
T.p. 25, Ad.p. 52.
Per copy 5p, per year £2.60.

637.6
HIDES SKINS

2996 HIDES AND SKINS QUARTERLY. 1960.
Commonwealth Secretariat, Marlborough House, Pall Mall, London, SW1Y 5HX.
4, = +   Trade statistics.
Commodity prices.
No Index.
March 1972, T.p. 44.
Per year £3.

638.1

BEEKEEPING

2997 APICULTURAL ABSTRACTS. 1950.
Bee Research Association, Hill House, Chalfont St. Peter, Gerrards Cross, Bucks, SL9 0NR.
4, ‡ +   A survey in English of scientific literature in all the world's languages, on bees, beekeeping, bee forage, hive products and pollination. A complete subject and author information retrieval system is available through index cards and computer print-outs.
Abstracts, patents, standards,
A, No. 4, No, complete author and subject index available on computer.
No. 1 1972, T.p. 55, Ad.p. 1.
Per year £9.50 to non-members, special inclusive subscriptions for members.

2998 BEE WORLD. 1919.
Bee Research Association, Hill House, Chalfont St. Peter, Gerrards Cross, Bucks, SL9 0NR.
4, ‡ †   Official organ of the Association, which includes reports of the Association's activities. Provides news about recent developments in practical and scientific work on bees for beekeepers and scientists.
Book notices, book reviews, monographic articles, new products, obituaries, tests.
A, No. 4 each year, No, None.
No. 2, 1972, T.p. 44, Ad.p. 2.
Per year £2.50 for members, £4 for non-members.

2999 BEEKEEPING. 1935.
Devon Beekeepers Association, Wobernia, Seaton, Devon.
8, * = ‡   Hobby and semi commercial interests.
Book notices, book reviews, letters, news, obituaries, standards, tests.
2 year, —, No, None.
T.p. 16, Ad.p. 4.   1200.
Free to members.

3000 JOURNAL OF APICULTURAL RESEARCH. 1962.
Bee Research Association, Hill House, Chalfont St. Peter, Gerrards Cross, SL9 0NR.
3, ‡ +   Original research papers on apiculture from all parts of the world to meet the needs of scientists for such a journal in the English language.
A, in No. 3 each year, No, None.
No. 1, 1972, T.p. 62, Ad.p. 2.
Per year £5.50 to non-members, special inclusive subscription for members.

639.1.04

GAMEKEEPING

3001 BULLETIN OF THE GAME CONSERVANCY. 1969.
Game Conservancy, Fordingbridge, Hants.
1, ‡ + *   Gamekeeping and allied subjects.
Book reviews, articles.
No Index.
Subscription on application.

3002 GAME CONSERVANCY ANNUAL REVIEW. 1969.
The Game Conservancy, Fordingbridge, Hampshire.
1, ‡ + *   A review of the year's work undertaken by The Game Conservancy.
Monographic articles.
No Index.
T.p. 91.   3000.
Per copy 50p.

3003 GAMEKEEPER AND COUNTRYSIDE: for people interested in field sports and natural history. 1897.
c/o Gilbertson & Page Ltd., Tamworth Road, Hertford, Herts.
12, ○ ‡ + =   Field sports (not games); natural history; rural occupations.
Book reviews, legal notes, letters, articles, obituaries, tests.
No Index.
June 1972, T.p. 25, Ad.p. 9.   9500.
Per copy 15p, per year £1.80.

3004 GAMEKEEPERS GAZETTE. 1908.
Gamekeepers Association of the U.K., Pentridge, Salisbury, Wilts.
6, * =   Gamekeeping and country pursuits.
Book reviews, legal notes, letters, articles, news, obituaries.
No Index.
T.p. 12, Ad.p. 7.   1000.
Free to members.

639.2

FISHING INDUSTRY

3005 FISH INDUSTRY REVIEW: Quarterly journal of the White Fish Authority. 1970.
(Fishery Economics Research Unit Quarterly Bulletin).
White Fish Authority, Lincoln's Inn Chambers, 2/3 Cursitor Street, London, EC4A 1NQ.
4, + ‡ † =   All aspects of fishing and fishing industry.
Abstracts, book notices, book reviews, commodity prices, monographic articles, new products, tests.
A, —, No, None.
No. 2, 1972, T.p. 40.   2000.
Per copy 75p, per year £3. Free to senior management in the industry.

3006 FISHING NEWS. 1913.
A. J. H. Publications Ltd., 110 Fleet Street, London, EC4A 2JL.
52, ‡ = +   All aspects of the commercial fishing industry; catching, processing, distribution, research. Provides news of, and comment on, all activities in and affecting the industry and publishes regular features on new boats and equipment.
No Index.
T.p. 7, Ad.p. 5.   10886.
Per copy 8p, per year £5.

3007 FISHING NEWS INTERNATIONAL. 1961.
Arthur J. Heighway Publications Ltd., Ludgate House, 110 Fleet St., London, EC4 2JL.
12, ‡ =   The world-wide commercial fisheries. Fishermen, vessel owners, processors, distributors, marine scientists and administrators in the fishing industries of 150 countries and territories.
Book reviews,
Letters, monographic articles, new products, reports.
No Index.
June 1972, T.p. 40, Ad.p. 40.   5500.
Per copy 40p, per year £5.50.

3008 IRISH SKIPPER: journal of the Fishing Industry. 1964.
Irish Maritime Press Ltd., 7, Crampton Quay, Dublin, 2.
12, =
No Index.
Per copy 6p.

3009 SCOTTISH FISHERIES BULLETIN.
HMSO, Bankhead Avenue, Sighthill, Edinburgh.
4, =   Notes on the Scottish fishing industry.
No Index.
Free to Fishermen and the industry.

3010 SCOTTISH SEA FISHERIES STATISTICAL TABLES. 1951.
(1809—Report by the Commission for Herring Fisheries. 1878—Herring Fisheries of Scotland Report. 1882—Annual Report of the Fishery Board for Scotland. 1920—Report on the Fisheries of Scotland.)
Her Majesty's Stationery Office, Sighthill, Edinburgh.

1, = + Quantity and value of each species of fish landed in Scotland by British and foreign vessels according to areas and methods of fishing; treatment of catch and number of vessels and fishermen. Commodity prices.
No Index.
Subscription on application.

3011 TOILERS OF THE DEEP. 1886.
Royal National Mission to Deep Sea Fishermen, 43 Nottingham Place, London, W1M 4BX.
4,* = Evangelical welfare to fishermen and their families.
Letters, news, obituaries, parliamentary reports.
No Index.
T.p. 26.   40000.
Free to members.

3012 WORLD FISHING. 1952.
Morgan Grampian Ltd., Commercial Exhibitions & Publications Ltd., Riverside House, Hough Street, Woolwich, London, SE18 6LR.
12,‡ = + All aspects of the commercial fishing industry, world wide. New vessels, fishing methods, research reports, new gear and equipment for fishing vessels of all types from inshore to distant water.
Book reviews, letters, monographic articles, new companies, new products, parliamentary reports, patents, standards, tests.
No Index.
May 1972, T.p. 31, Ad.p. 49.   6300.
Per copy 38p, per year £4.
Indexed in: BTI

639.93
AQUARIA

3013 THE AQUARIST & PONDKEEPER incorporating the Reptilian Review. Late 1920's.
(The Amateur Aquarist 1924)
Buckley Press Ltd., The Butts, Half Acre, Brentford, Middx.
12,○ + ‡ Keeping of freshwater temperate and tropical fish, saltwater fish and aquatic life forms as well as amphibians and reptiles, under aquarium and vivarium conditions. Caters for hobbyists and serious students of ichthyology.
Book notices, book reviews, commodity prices, letters, monographic articles, new products, tests.
A, —, Yes, None.
June 1972, T.p. 32-36, Ad.p. 48-50.   26000.
Per copy 26½p, per year £3.06.

3014 PET FISH MONTHLY: the practical fishkeeping magazine. 1966.
PF Publications, 554 Garratt Lane, London SW17 0NY.
12,○ ‡ = All aspects of keeping fish in ponds and aquaria.
Book notices, book reviews, letters, articles, new products, obituaries, tests.
A, —, No, None.
June 1972, T.p. 24, Ad.p. 24.
Per copy 15p, per year £2.46.

64
CATERING. DOMESTIC SCIENCE

3015 BRIDES AND SETTING UP HOME. 1964.
(Brides 1955-1964).
Condé Nast Publications Ltd., Vogue House, Hanover Square, London, W1.
6,○ All aspects of weddings and bridal activities and interests.
No Index.
T.p. 73, Ad.p. 76.   74000.
Per copy 20p, per year £1.50.

3016 CATERING & HOTEL MANAGEMENT. 1970.
(Hotel & Restaurant Management 1934-1970)
Blandford Group, 167 High Holborn, London WC1.
12, = Hotels, restaurants, canteens, schools, hospitals, civic and institutional catering.
Book notices, book reviews, legal notes, letters, articles, new products.
A, —, No, None.
May 1972, T.p. 35, Ad.p. 35.   44900.
Free, Controlled circulation and Per year £1.50.

3017 CATERING TIMES. 1967.
(Hotel and Catering Times 1963-1966).
Northwood Publications, Elm House, Elm Street, London, WC1.
52, = ‡ All aspects of hotel and catering industry.
Book reviews, commodity prices, legal notes, letters, news, new products, obituaries, parliamentary reports.
No Index.
T.p. 27, Ad.p. 5.   25000.
Per copy 2½p, per year £1.30.

3018 FAMILY CIRCLE. 1963.
Standbrook Publications Ltd., Elm House, Elm Street, London, WC1.
12,○ General matters of domestic interest, especially cookery.
No Index.
T.p. 51, Ad.p. 37.   1155276.
Per copy 10p.

3019 GOOD HOUSEKEEPING: incorporating Nashs Pall Mall, House Beautiful & G. H. Factfinder. 1922.
The National Magazine Co., Ltd., Chestergate House, Vauxhall Bridge Road, London, SW1V 2HF.
12,○ Topics of interest to intelligent women. Domestic subjects in general.
No Index.
June 1972, T.p. 80, Ad.p. 124.   199184.
Per copy 20p, per year £3.25.

3020 HOME ECONOMICS. 1950.
Forbes Publications Ltd., Hartree House, Queensway, London, W2 4SH.
12,○ Educational in home economics field.
Book reviews, letters, articles, new products, parliamentary reports, standards, tests.
A, December, Yes, None.
July 1972, T.p. 24, Ad.p. 23.   15000.
Per year £3.25.

3021 HOME SEWING & KNITTING. 1972.
(Woman's Realm Home Sewing & Knitting 1966-1972).
I.P.C. Magazines, Ltd., 189 High Holborn, London, WC1V 7BA.
10, ‡ ○ Practical homemaking and fashion features of a do-it-yourself nature, i.e. knitting, crafts, furnishing, dressmaking, woodwork, general sewing, home ideas, toys, hobbies.
Articles.
No Index.
June 1972. T.p. 55, Ad.p. 11.   172000.
Per copy 15p, per year £2.05.

3022 HOMES AND GARDENS. 1919.
IPC Women's Group Magazines, Tower House, Southampton Street, London WC2E 9QX.
12,○ New/converted/town/country houses; gardens, gardening, garden plans; general interest; non-fiction book extracts; furnishing, household, fashion, cookery, wine; motoring, travel, books, fiction, antiques, furnishing/household supplement.
Book reviews, legal notes, letters, articles, new products, standards, tests.

No Index.
T.p. 100, Ad.p. 108.   199000.
Per copy 25p, per year £4.25.

3023 HOUSEWIVES TODAY: A journal for home-makers. 1947.
The Eveleen Bloomfield Association Ltd., 49 Birchwood Avenue, Sidcup, Kent.
11,†   To provide British housewives with an effective voice in all matters concerning the welfare of themselves and their families. To show that overcontrol by the State is not in the interests of a free and happy home life in the Christian tradition.
Book notices, book reviews, commodity prices, legal notes, letters, articles, new companies, new products, obituaries, parliamentary reports.
No Index.
June 1972, T.p. 12.
Per copy 15p, per year £2.

3024 IDEAL HOME and Gardening: incorporating Housewife. 1920.
IPC Magazines Ltd., 189 High Holborn, London, WC1V 7BA.
12,○   The home—that is, the structure, the surroundings and the contents.
Book notices, book reviews, commodity prices, letters, articles, new companies, new products, standards, tests.
No Index.
May 1972, T.p. 96, Ad.p. 107.
Per copy 20p, per year £3.75.

3025 INSTANT COOKERY. 1971.
Bird Publications Ltd., 27 Albemarle Street, London, W1X 3FA.
12, = ○
No Index.
Per copy 15p.

3026 IRISH CATERING REVIEW. 1970.
Jemma Publications, Richardson House, Main Street, Blackrock, Co. Dublin.
6, =
No Index.

3027 LIVING. 1967.
Standbrook Publications Ltd., Elm House, Elm Street, London, WC1.
12,○   General matters of domestic interest.
Letters, articles, new products.
No Index.
T.p. 98, Ad.p. 32.   475000.
Per copy 6p, per year 75p.

3028 LONDON BRIDE. 1969.
Dominion Press Ltd., Grand Building, Trafalgar Square, London, WC2.
4,○   Advice for couples to be married in the London area.
No Index.
15000.
Per copy 12½p.

3029 MARINE AND AIR CATERING: Airport Catering and Duty-Free Shops. 1968.
(The Chief Steward).
Benn Brothers Ltd., Lyon Tower, 125 High Street, Colliers Wood, London, SW19 2JN.
12, =   Marine and air catering in general.
Book reviews, letters, monographic articles, new products, obituaries, standards, tests.
No Index.
T.p. 144, Ad.p. 58.   1750.
Per year £3.25.

3030 SHOPPING AND HOMES GAZETTE. 1966.
Priory Press Ltd., Priory House, Royston, Herts.
12,○ =   Advertising throughout North Herts, North Essex and South Cambridgeshire.
Book reviews, letters, new products.
No Index.
T.p. 12, Ad.p. Most.
Free, controlled circulation.

3031 WOMAN AND HOME. 1926.
IPC Magazines Ltd., Fleetway House, Farringdon Street, London, EC4.
12,○   All matters of domestic interest.
Book reviews, letters, articles, new products.
No Index.
T.p. 120, Ad.p. 61.   700000.
Per copy 12½p, per year £2.50.

3032 WOMAN, BRIDE AND HOME. 1968.
IPC Magazines Ltd., 189 High Holborn, London, WC1.
6,○   Features of interest to engaged girls and young wives.
Letters, new products.
No Index.
T.p. 60, Ad.p. 60.   173000.
Per copy 15p, per year £1.30.

3033 WOMAN'S JOURNAL. 1927.
IPC Magazines, Tower House, Southampton Street, London, WC2E 9QX.
12,○   All women's interests: beauty, cookery, decoration, fashion, fiction, general features, travel, home, features on topical subjects treated in depth, profiles.
Book reviews, letters, articles.
T.p. 45, Ad.p. 40.   165000.
Per copy 20p, per year £3.50.

3034 WOMAN'S OWN. 1934.
IPC Magazines Ltd., Tower House, Southampton Street, London WC2.
52,○   All subjects with feminine angle, behind-the-headline features, medical, psychological, miscellaneous personalities, fiction, practical housekeeping, emotional human interest, service.
Book notices, book reviews, commodity prices, letters, articles, new products, standards, tests.
No Index.
2000000.
Per copy 10p, per year £3.50.

64.024.1

HOTELS

3035 BRITISH HOTELIER & RESTAURATEUR. 1968.
(BHRA Journal 1907-1968).
British Hotels, Restaurants & Caterers Association. 20 Upper Brook St., London, W1Y 2BH.
12, = *   News of association activities, legal and fiscal matters, articles of practical value to hotel-businessmen in the running of their businesses.
Book reviews, legal notes, letters, articles, new products, obituaries, parliamentary reports, standards, tests.
No Index.
June 1972, T.p. 17, Ad.p. 15.   15000.
Available only to members.

3036 HOTEL CATERING AND INSTITUTIONAL MANAGEMENT ASSOCIATION JOURNAL. 1972.
(Institutional Hotel and Catering Management 1971; H.C.I. Journal 1952-1971; Institutional Management 1950-1971).
HCIMA, 191 Trinity Road, London SW17 7HN.
12, * =   Hotel and catering and allied fields.
Book notices, book reviews, legal notes, letters, monographic articles, obituaries.
No Index.
June 1972, T.p. 19, Ad.p. 20.   c. 20000.
Per copy 35p, per year £4.

64.024.4
BARS

3037 THE BARTENDER: official journal of the United
Kingdom Bartender's Guild. 1934.
Pall Mall Ltd., South Bank House, Black Prince Road,
Lambeth, London SE11.
12, =
No Index.
T.p. 21, Ad.p. 13.   2500.
Free to members.

64.027
VILLAGE LIFE

3038 RURAL LIFE. 1957.
Institute of Rural Life at Home & Overseas, 27 Northumberland Road, New Barnet, Herts.
4, ○ *   Aspects of community development in rural
areas throughout the world, as education, agriculture,
health and housing.
Book notices, book reviews, letters, monographic
articles, new products.
No Index.
Vol. 17, No. 1, 1972, T.p. 33; Ad.p. 1.   1000.
Free to members.

3039 VILLAGE LIFE.
National Federation of Village Produce Associations,
Northam, North Road, Berkhamsted, Herts.
4, *   Country and rural activities.
Letters, articles, news.
No Index.
T.p. 32, Ad.p. 4.
Per copy 5p.

641.3
GROCERY TRADE

3040 CO-OPERATIVE GROCER. 1963.
Co-operative Marketing Services Ltd., Borough
Chambers, High Street, Stockport, Cheshire.
12, ‡ = +   Co-operative grocery trade dealing with
all aspects of grocery retailing (new products)
market research, etc.
No Index.
5, 1972, T.p. 25, Ad.p. 25.   3000.
Per copy 20p, per year £2.40.

3041 EUROPEAN GROCERY LETTER. 1957.
Mr. Colin Scott, 1 Saint Paul's Close, Clitheroe,
Lancashire, BB7 2NB.
3, = +   A forum for the discussion of developments
in senior grocery management throughout Britain
and all Europe.
Book notices, book reviews, letters, articles, new
products.
No Index.
Free, controlled circulation

3042 THE GROCER and Grocery Marketing. 1861.
William Reed Ltd., 19 Eastcheap, London, EC3.
52, =   All engaged in the food trade, retail, wholesale, manufacturer. Everything to do with
running their businesses.
Book notices, book reviews, commodity prices, legal
notes, letters, new companies, new products,
obituaries, parliamentary reports, patents,
standards, tests.
No Index.
July 1st 1972, T.p. 42, Ad.p. 82.   53002.
Per copy 5p, per year £5.

3043 GROCERY DISTRIBUTION. 1972.
(Way Ahead 1968-1971).
Institute of Grocery Distribution, Grange Lane, Letchmore Heath, Watford, WD2 8DQ.
12, = †   Coming events within the Institute. Reports
of conferences and seminars of interest to food
manufacturers, retailers and distributors.
Reviews of the Institute's publications and reports
by working party.
Book notices, book reviews, legal notes, articles,
standards,
No Index.
June 1972, T.p. 9.
Free to members.

3044 GROCERS GAZETTE. 1881.
1 Pudding Lane, London, EC3.
52, =   Retail Trade.
Articles, news, new products.
No Index.
T.p. 50, Ad.p. 35.   21500.
Per copy 4p, per year £3.

3045 THE IRISH GROCERY WORLD. 1892.
Irish Grocery World, 114 Somerton Road, Belfast,
BT15 4DG.
26, =
No Index.
T.p. 4, Ad.p. 4.
Per year 75p.

3046 SHAWS PRICE GUIDE. 1938.
Shaw's Price Guides Limited, 4 The Broadway,
London, N8 9SP.
12, = +   Grocery and allied trades.
Commodity prices.
No Index.
June 1972, T.p. 72.   80000.
Per copy 25p, per year £2.

3047 THE WHOLESALE GROCER. 1950.
National Federation of Wholesale Grocers & Provision Merchants, 18 Fleet Street, London EC4.
12, = ‡   Topics of interest to wholesale grocers
including transport, warehousing, marketing etc.
Book reviews, legal notes, letters, articles, news,
new products, obituaries, parliamentary reports.
No Index.
T.p. 19, Ad.p. 8.   1600.
Per copy 7½p, per year 90p.

641.56
VEGETARIANISM

3048 THE JEWISH VEGETARIAN. 1964.
The Jewish Vegetarian & Natural Health Society,
'Bet Tev', 855, Finchley Road, London, NW11.
○ +   Natural health, compassion for all living
creatures in conformity with the original bible
teachings. Anti-battery farming and indiscriminate
use of chemicals.
Book notices, book reviews, letters, monographic
articles, new products.
No Index.
Spring 1972, T.p. 38, Ad.p. 10.   c. 700.
Per copy 10p, per year £1.

3049 THE VEGETARIAN. 1971.
(Vegetarian 1952; Vegetarian Messenger 1847;
British Vegetarian 1959).
The Vegetarian Society (UK) Limited, Parkdale,
Dunham Road, Altrincham, Cheshire.
12, ○ = +   Vegetarianism—economics, health—
nutrition, research—ethics—cookery.
Abstracts, book notices, book reviews, letters,
monographic articles, new products.
No Index.
Per copy 15p. Free to members.

643.7
DO-IT-YOURSELF HOUSEHOLD REPAIRS

3050 DIY TRADE. 1960.
Whitehall Press Limited, Wrotham Place, Wrotham, Sevenoaks, Kent.
12, =   Trade journal for retailers selling do-it-yourself products and equipment.
Book reviews, commodity prices, legal notes, letters, monographic articles, new companies, new products, obituaries, parliamentary reports.
No Index.
June 1971, T.p. 27, Ad.p. 38.   8000.
Per copy 25p, per year £2.75.

3051 DO IT YOURSELF. 1957.
Link House Publications Ltd., Link House, Dingwall Avenue, Croydon, Surrey, CR9 2TA.
12, ○   Largely concerned with home decorations and improvements, conversions, extensions etc. Also the garden, the car, plumbing, electrical work, wine making and handicrafts.
Book reviews, commodity prices, legal notes, letters, articles, new products, tests.
A, January, Yes, None.
T.p. 50, Ad.p. 86.   212000.
Per copy 10p, per year £1.75.

3052 THE ELECTRICAL AGE. 1926.
Electrical Association for Women, 26 Foubert's Place, London, W1V 2AL.
4, * ○   Electricity in the home and related subjects.
New products, reports.
No Index.
T.p. 28, Ad.p. 6.
Per copy 5p, per year 30p.

3053 HOMECARE. 1966.
British Hardware Promotion Council Ltd., 19-21 Hatton Garden, London, EC2.
6, = + ○   All aspects of home care including do-it-yourself.
Letters, news, new products, tests.
No Index.
T.p. 12, Ad.p. Most.   250000.
Free via hardware retailers.

3054 HOMEMAKER: The his and her do-it-yourself magazine. 1969.
IPC Magazines Ltd., 189 High Holborn, London, WC1V 7BA.
12, ○   Do-it-yourself magazine of equal appeal to both men and women. As well as giving instruction in do-it-yourself techniques, it puts great emphasis on ideas and colour and home furnishing advice.
Letters, articles, new products.
No Index.
August 1972, T.p. 40, Ad.p. 52.   141000.
Per copy 15p, per year £2.75.

3055 PRACTICAL HOUSEHOLDER: Incorporating Practical Home Building and Decorating. 1955.
IPC Magazines Ltd., Fleetway House, Farringdon Street, London, EC4.
12, ○ ‡   Home improvements, structural, constructional and maintenance, from simple to ambitious projects. Free reader advisory service. Occasional free supplements covering wide variety of subjects—bathrooms, kitchens, heating, etc.
Regular features on products recently introduced to consumer market, letters, readers' hints, answers to current home maintenance and decor problems, etc., special features in colour.
A, Spring, Yes, None.
October 1972, T.p. 46 + 24p, Ad.p. 103.   198684.
Per copy 15p, per year £2.70.

645.1
FLOOR COVERINGS

3056 CARPET & FLOOR COVERING NEWS. 1971.
(Published as supplement to Cabinet Maker and Retail Furnisher).
Benn Brothers, Ltd., 25 New Street Square, London, EC4A 3JA.
10, = ‡   The carpet industry, both manufacturing and retail in all departments, including manufacturers' suppliers, and wholesalers. All subjects of trade interest are covered.
Book notices, book reviews, commodity prices, legal notes, letters, articles, new companies, new products, parliamentary reports, standards, tests.
No Index.
23.6.72, T.p. 27, Ad.p. 16.   9700.
Per copy 20p, per year £1.75.

3057 CARPETS & TEXTILES. 1965.
IPC Consumer Industries Press, 40 Bowling Green Lane, London, EC1.
10, =   New lines and developments in the carpet and household textile trades. How to display and how to make the most of new merchandise.
Letters, articles, new companies, new products.
No Index.
T.p. 30, Ad.p. 35.   4500.
Per copy 25p, per year £2.50.

3058 FLOORING JOURNAL. 1972.
(Floors & Contract Carpeting 1971).
A4 Publications Ltd., Press House, 25 High Street, Edenbridge, Kent.
12, ‡ =   Flooring industry covering all aspects of interest to manufacturer, contractor, specifier etc.
No Index.
Per year £3.

645.31
BLINDS

3059 BLINDS & SHUTTERS: official journal of the British Blind and Shutter Association. 1972.
(Blindmaker 1952-1972).
Wheatland Journals Ltd., 157 Hagden Lane, Watford, Herts.
4, ‡ = *   Making and using window blinds and shutters.
Commodity prices, articles, new companies, new products, obituaries, patents.
No Index.
April 1972, T.p. 21, Ad.p. 27.   4000.
Per copy $12\frac{1}{2}$p, per year 50p.

646.72
HAIRDRESSING

3060 HAIR & BEAUTY. 1866.
(Hairdressers Chronicle).
Park Lane Publications Ltd., 54/55 Wilton Road, London, SW1.
12, = ‡   Hair dressing and fashion, salon design and maintenance.
Articles, news, new products, patents, standards, tests.
No Index.
T.p. 38, Ad.p. 10.   13000.
Per copy 20p, per year £2.50.

3061 HAIRDRESSERS JOURNAL. 1882.
IPC Consumer Industries Press Ltd., 40 Bowling Green Lane, London EC1.
52, =   Men's and women's hairdressing.
Book notices, legal notes, letters, new companies, new products, obituaries, parliamentary reports.
No Index.
T.p. 56, Ad.p. 33.   27000.
Per copy $12\frac{1}{2}$p, per year £8.50.

648

CLEANING. LAUNDERING

3062 ABLC JOURNAL. 1919.
(IBL Journal).
Association of British Launderers & Cleaners Ltd., 22 Lancaster Gate, London, W2.
12, = *
Articles, news, new products.
A, January, Yes, None.
T.p. 24, Ad.p. 15.
Free to members.

3063 LAUNDRY AND CLEANING. 1961.
(Laundry Journal and Laundry Record 1885-1960).
IPC Consumer Industries Press Ltd., 40 Bowling Green Lane, London, EC1.
26, ‡ =   Laundry, dry cleaning and allied trades.
Supplement: Laundry and Cleaning International 6 p.a.
Letters, monographic articles, new companies, new products.
No Index.
T.p. 15, Ad.p. 5.   10000.
Per year £4.

3064 POWER LAUNDRY & CLEANING NEWS. 1903.
Practical Press Ltd., 1 Dorset Buildings, London EC4.
26, =   Laundering in general.
Articles, new products.
No Index.
T.p. 60, Ad.p. 40.
Per copy 10p, per year £3.75.

648.53

WINDOW CLEANING

3065 WINDOW TALK. 1964.
National Federation of Master Window Cleaners, 104 Hathersage Road, Chorlton-on-Medlock, Manchester, Lancashire, M13 0HX.
4, =   Trade magazine for Master Window Cleaners in the United Kingdom.
Letters, articles, new products, standards, tests.
No Index.
Per copy 5p. Free to members.

649

CHILDCARE

3066 EARLY CHILD DEVELOPMENT AND CARE. 1971.
Gordon & Breach, 41/42 William 4th Street, London, WC2.
4, ○ +   All aspects of early child development and care: social, educational, and preventive medical programs for young children; experimental and observational studies; critical reviews.
Book notices, book reviews, letters, monographic articles, tests.
No Index.
Subscription on application.

3067 INTERNATIONAL JOURNAL OF EARLY CHILDHOOD. c.1969.
Irish University Press, 81 Merrion Square, Dublin 2.
4, = +
Book reviews, letters, monographic articles.
A, –, Yes, None.
Per year £5.50.

3068 MOTHER. 1936.
IPC Magazines Ltd., 189 High Holborn, London, WC1.
12, ○   All subjects of interest to parents.
Book reviews, letters, articles, news, new products.
No Index.
T.p. 62, Ad.p. 62.   114000.
Per copy 15p, per year £2.50.

3069 MOTHER & BABY. 1956.
The Illustrated Publications Co. Ltd., 12-18 Paul Street, London EC2A 4JS.
12, ○   Authoritative information on every aspect of pregnancy and babycare by doctors, psychologists, nurses, educationalists, and other specialists. Also free knitting and sewing patterns; Q and A; competition; recipes etc.
Abstracts, book notices, book reviews, commodity prices, legal notes, letters, monographic articles, new companies, new products, obituaries, parliamentary reports, patents, standards, tests.
A, December, No, None.
July 1972, T.p. 41, Ad.p. 14.   30000.
Per copy 15p, per year £2.

3070 MOTHER AND CHILD. 1922.
Victoria Vernon (Publications) Ltd., 54/55 Wilton Road, London, SW1.
6, ‡ ○ =   Maternal and child welfare and social services.
Book reviews, articles.
No Index.
May/June 1972, T.p. 20, Ad.p. 2.   2108.
pe
Per year £1.63.

3071 NURSERY WORLD. 1925.
(All About Children 1965-1967).
Bouverie Publishing Co., Ltd., 2 Salisbury Court, Fleet Street, London, EC47 8AB.
52, ○ =   Care of babies and young children; medical, educational, psychological articles; general interests: cookery, knitting, crochet, craft; personal stories from parents, child care workers; nursery nursing; questions and answers on above subjects. Also ante and post-natal subjects, and stories for children.
Book reviews, letters, articles, new products.
No Index.
T.p. 28, Ad.p. 8.
Per copy 10p, per year £5.

65

BUSINESS

3072 BUSINESS ADMINISTRATION: Journal of profit improvement. 1968.
Morgan-Grampian (Professional Press) Ltd., Morgan-Grampian House, 30 Calderwood Street, London, SE18 6QH.
12, ‡ =   Deals with all aspects of operational management, mainly through case-histories and interviews with practical businessmen.
Book notices, book reviews, legal notes, letters, monographic articles, new products.
No Index.
June 1972, T.p. 34, Ad.p. 54.   30000.
Per copy £1, per year £10 and Free, Controlled circulation.

3073 BUSINESS ARCHIVES. c.1954.
Business Archives Council, 63 Queen Victoria Street, London, EC4.
2, * = ‡
Book notices, book reviews, monographic articles, news, obituaries, standards, tests.
No Index.
T.p. 60, Ad.p. 5.
Per year £5.50. Free to members.
Indexed in: BHI.

3074 BUSINESS HISTORY. 1959.
Frank Cass & Co. Ltd., 67 Great Russell Street, London, WC1B 3BT.

2, = + ‡   Business history, industrial management, commercial enterprise and cognate areas of economic development.
Book notices, book reviews, monographic articles.
A, July, Yes, None.
January 1972, T.p. 100, Ad.p. 5.
Per copy £1.75, per year £3.50.
Indexed in: BHI.

3075 BUSINESS MANAGEMENT. 1967.
(Business 1928),
Business Publications, Mercury House, Waterloo Road, London, SE1.
12, + ‡ =   Industrial management, financial and research.
Book reviews, commodity prices, letters, monographic articles, new companies.
No Index.
T.p. 36, Ad.p. 36.   17000.
Per copy 37½p, per year £4.50.

3076 CENTRE FOR BUSINESS RESEARCH NEWSLETTER. 1971.
Centre for Business Research (in association with Manchester Business School), Manchester Business School, Booth Street West, Manchester M15 6PB.
4, +   On-going research and course activities at Manchester Business School; current economic/ management etc., trends of interest to people in research and/or business.
Book notices, internal publications, monographic articles.
No Index.
Spring 1972, T.p. 16.
Gratis.

3077 CO-OPERATIVE MANAGEMENT AND MARKETING. 1968.
(Agenda; Co-operative Official).
Co-operative Press Ltd., 418 Chester Road, Manchester 16.
12, ‡ + =   Management and marketing for co-operative officials.
Book reviews, monographic articles, new products.
No Index.
T.p. 35, Ad.p. 33.   12100.
Free, Controlled circulation.

3078 EUROPEAN INTELLIGENCE. 1969.
(Opera Mundi-Europe 1964-1969).
European Intelligence Ltd., Agroup House, 16 Lonsdale Gardens, Tunbridge Wells, Kent.
26, ‡ =   Digest of some 150-200 business moves in West Europe (mergers, expansion etc), plus economic and industrial trends sections, plus articles by named experts.
New companies.
6m, —, Yes, 5 year.
22.6.1972, T.p. 28.
Per year £75.

3079 NANTIS NEWS. 1971.
Nottingham and Nottinghamshire Technical Information Service, Central Library, South Sherwood Street, Nottingham, NG1 4DA.
12, ‡   Reviews and assesses new and existing sources of business, scientific and technical information for all who provide a service to commerce and industry.
Book notices, book reviews, articles.
No Index.
June 1972, T.p. 8.
Per year £1. Free to members.

3080 SCOTLAND. 1947.
Scottish Council (Development & Industry), 1 Castle Street, Edinburgh, EH2 3AJ.
12, =   All aspects of Scottish business, commercial and industrial life.
Articles.

No Index.
June 1972, T.p. 36, Ad.p. 36.
Per copy 20p, per year £2.50.

651

OFFICE MANAGEMENT

3081 MEMO: The Pitman Magazine. 1970.
(Pitman Shorthand News; Office Training 1938-1970).
Pitman Periodicals Ltd., 33 Warwick Square, London, SW1V 2AN.
52, ‡ ○ =   Teaching aid for Pitman shorthand, Pitman script and training in all duties of a shorthand/typist/and secs.
Book notices, book reviews, commodity prices, legal notes, letters, articles, new products, obituaries, patents, standards, tests.
No Index.
T.p. c. 40, Ad.p. 18.   95000.
Per year £5.

3082 NEW DAWN: journal of the Union of Shop, Distributive and Allied Trades. 1921.
Union of Shop, Distributive and Allied Workers, 188 Wilmslow Road, Fallowfield, Manchester M14 6LJ.
12, *   Reports of negotiations covering wages and working conditions in the trades for which the Union caters, reports of conferences and local events, legal matters affecting members, and items of general and political interest.
Book reviews, legal notes, letters, monographic articles, obituaries, parliamentary reports.
A, January, No, None.
6, 1972, T.p. 30.   22000.
Free to members.

3083 OFFICE MANAGEMENT: journal of the Institute of Administrative Management. 1952.
(Office Management Association Bulletin 1947-1951).
The Institute of Administrative Management, 205 High Street, Beckenham, Kent, BR3 1BA.
4, ‡ + *   Administrative management including all aspects of management techniques.
Book reviews, legal notes, letters, monographic articles.
No Index.
Spring 1972, T.p. 48, Ad.p. 6.   8000.
Per copy £1.

3084 OFFICE SKILLS FOR THE TEACHER. 1971.
(Memo Key).
Pitman Periodicals Ltd., 33 Warwick Square, London, SW1V 2AH.
12, ‡ + ○ =   All aspects of office training—shorthand, Pitman script, bookkeeping (elementary) filing etc.
Book notices, book reviews, legal notes, letters, new products, patents, standards, tests.
No Index.
T.p. 24, Ad.p. 8.   15000.
Per year £1.80.

651.2

OFFICE EQUIPMENT

3085 BUSINESS EQUIPMENT DIGEST. 1961.
BED Business Journals Ltd., Park House, Park Street, Croydon CR9 1UA.
12, ‡ =   Selection and purchasing of business equipment or services.
Book notices, book reviews, legal notes, letters, articles, new companies, new products, standards, tests.

Key to reference symbols

○ popular   ‡ technical   = trade/professional

+ research   * society/institution   † house journal

No Index.
June 1972, T.p. 42, Ad.p. 42. 50219.
Free, controlled circulation.

3086 BUSINESS EQUIPMENT GUIDE. 1970.
(Business Equipment Buyers Guide 1962-1970).
B.E.D. Business Books Ltd., Park House, Park Street, Croydon, CR9 1UA.
2, ‡
Commodity prices.
No Index.
July 1972, T.p. 370. 2000.
Per copy £6, per year £5.

3087 BUSINESS SYSTEMS AND EQUIPMENT. 1964.
(Scope 1954).
Maclean-Hunter Ltd., 30 Old Burlington Street, London, W1.
12, = ‡   Current management techniques.
Book notices, book reviews, letters, monographic articles, news, new products.
A, –, Yes, None.
T.p. 25, Ad.p. 25. 27000.
Per year £3 and Free, Controlled circulation.

3088 INDEX TO OFFICE EQUIPMENT AND SUPPLIES. 1967.
Maclaren Group, 69/77 High Street, Croydon, CR9 1QH.
12, = ‡   Office Products, Machinery and Systems.
Book reviews, letters, new products, patents.
No Index.
May 1972, T.p. 72, Ad.p. Most. 60000.
Per copy 30p, per year £3.60.

3089 INSIGHT: a new viewpoint on business methods. 1959.
Kalamazoo Limited, Northfield, Birmingham, B31 2RW.
4, ‡ =   Office equipment.
No Index.
No. 63, T.p. 4. 11000.
Free.

653

SHORTHAND

3090 IPS JOURNAL & REPORTERS MAGAZINE. 1956.
(IPS Journal 1898-1956).
Incorporated Phonographic Society, 2-12 Wilson Street, London, EC1.
4, * =   Shorthand and typewriting.
Book notices, book reviews, letters, tests.
No Index.
T.p. 27, Ad.p. 1.
Free to members.

654.1

TELEGRAPHY

3091 INTERNATIONAL BROADCAST ENGINEER. 1964.
(International TV Technical Review; International Sound Engineer).
Television Mail Ltd., 31 St. George Street, London, W1.
12, = ‡   Broadcasting in general.
Book reviews, letters, monographic articles, news, new products, patents.
No Index.
T.p. 28, Ad.p. 11.
Per copy 25p, per year £3.75.
Indexed in: BTI

655

PRINTING

3092 BOOK TOKENS NEWS. 1972.
Bookseller, 152 Buckingham Palace Road, London, SW1.

Irreg., =
No Index.
Free.

3093 BRITISH PRINTER. 1888.
Maclean-Hunter Ltd., 30 Old Burlington Street, London, W1.
12, = ‡   Mainly type design and printing.
Book reviews, monographic articles, new companies, news, new products.
A, December, Yes, None.
T.p. 55, Ad.p. 111. 10351.
Per copy 25p, per year £3.50.
Indexed in: BTI.

3094 DIXON'S PAPER CIRCULAR.
L. S. Dixon & Co. Ltd., Sir Thomas Street, Liverpool, L1 6BR.
12, † =   News relating to the printing industry in general and L. S. Dixon Group in particular, including humorous items and items of general interest which may be irrelevant to the industry.
Book notices, commodity prices, letters, new products, obituaries.
No Index.
June 1972, T.p. 4. 10000.
Free.

3095 FLOWERS FROM THE PRINTSHOP. 1966.
(Ember Press Publications 1953-1955; Friday Market 1956-1961).
A. L. Shearn, 11 Ember Gardens, Thames Ditton, Surrey.
c. 3, ○   Techniques in writing and letterpress printing, publishing from small presses, fleurons and patterning. Non-commercial.
Articles.
No Index.
May 1972, T.p. 10. c. 250.
Per copy varies.

3096 IN-PLANT PRINTER AND ART MATERIALS BUYER. 1961.
In-Plant Printer Ltd., 58 Parker Street, London, WC2.
12, =   Printing and allied industries.
News, new products.
No Index.
T.p. 64, Ad.p. Most. 9740.
Per copy 20p, per year £2.40.

3097 INKLINGS. 1948.
Coates Bros. Inks Ltd., Easton Street, London, WC1X 0DP.
4, ‡ =   Technical journal covering subjects of interest to all levels of the printing trade. Materials, techniques and processes discussed, with a bias towards the printing ink usage and, in particular, new developments.
Monographic articles.
No Index.
No. 81, T.p. 8. 14000.
Free

3098 JOURNAL OF THE PRINTING HISTORICAL SOCIETY. 1965.
Printing Historical Society, St Bride Institute, Bride Lane, Fleet Street, London, EC4.
1, ‡ + *   Original contributions on the history of printing and related trades, with particular (though not exclusive) emphasis on technical developments since 1800.
Monographic articles.
No Index.
No. 6, 1970, T.p. 110, Ad.p. 10. c. 950.
Per year £2.10.

3099 MANAGEMENT IN PRINTING. 1971.
Institute of Management in Printing, 55 Temple Chambers, London, EC4.

6, =
No Index.
Per year £2.

3100 MANAGING PRINTER. 1916.
Printing Management Association, 55 Temple Chambers, London, EC4.
12, =
No Index.
Free to members.

3101 MEMBERS CIRCULAR. 1901.
British Federation of Master Printers, 11 Bedford Row, London, WC1R 4DX.
12, * =   Issued to member firms of the BFMP and containing news and information concerning the printing industry on industrial relations, legal and taxation, conferences and meetings, economics and marketing, technical, safety, education
Book reviews, new products, obituaries, parliamentary reports, patents, standards.
A, January, Yes, None.
February 1972, T.p. 30, Ad.p. 22.   6050.
Controlled circulation to member firms of the BFMP.

3102 MODERN IRISH PRINTER. 1957.
Graphic Publications Ltd., 47 Dawson Street, Dublin, 2.
12, = ‡ +   Graphic arts including, printing, publishing, advertising and packaging.
Book reviews, articles, new companies.
No Index.
April/May 1972, T.p. 14, Ad.p. 6.
Per copy 15p, per year £1.80.

3103 MONOTYPE BULLETIN.
Monotype Corporation Ltd., 43 Fetter Lane, London, EC4.
4, ‡ =
No Index.
Subscription on application.

3104 MONOTYPE RECORDER.
Monotype Corporation, 43 Fetter Lane, London, EC4.
12, = ‡ +   Developments in type design.
Book reviews, monographic articles, news, new products.
No Index.
Subscription on application.

3105 PIRA NEWS.
PIRA, Randalls Road, Leatherhead, Surrey.
‡ + *   News of current activities of the Research Association.
No Index.
Free to members only.

3106 PRINT. 1968.
(Graphical Journal 1963).
National Graphical Association, 63/67 Bromham Road, Bedford.
12, =   Printing craft trade union news.
Book reviews, letters, monographic articles, news, new products, parliamentary reports.
No Index.
106500.
Per copy 3p, per year 40p.

3107 PRINT BUYER. 1966.
Print Buyer Magazine Ltd., 58 Parker Street, London, WC2.
12, = ‡   Purchasing of print, paper etc.
Book reviews, letters, monographic articles, new companies, news, new products, standards, tests.
A, October, No, None.
T.p. 47, Ad.p. 89.   10400.
Per copy 25p, per year £3.

3108 PRINT ROOM. 1969.
(Small Offset Supplies 1966-1968).
Northwood Publications Ltd., 16 Elm Street, London, WC1.

12, = ‡   Reprography in general.
Book reviews, letters, monographic articles, news, new products.
No Index.
T.p. 21, Ad.p. 18.   10000.
Free, controlled circulation.

3109 PRINTING ABSTRACTS. 1946.
PIRA, Randalls Road, Leatherhead, Surrey.
12, ‡   Digest of articles on printing, plate-making, composing, newspaper production, bookbinding, inks, etc.
Abstracts, book notices.
A, —, Yes, None.
Per year £17.50.

3110 PRINTING AND BOOKBINDING TRADE REVIEW. 1958.
George L. Howe Press Service Limited, 85 Elmhurst Drive, Hornchurch, Essex, RM11 1PB.
12, = ‡ +   Machinery, equipment, materials and production in printing, bookbinding, book publishing and production, print finishing, platemaking, newspaper production and papermaking.
Book notices, book reviews, new products.
No Index.
May 1972, T.p. 20, Ad.p. 20.
Per copy 10p, per year £1.
Indexed in: BTI.

3111 THE PRINTING ART. 1973.
Stellar Press, Huggins Lane, Welham Green, Hatfield, Herts.
4, = ‡
No Index.
Per year £3.

3112 PRINTING EQUIPMENT AND MATERIALS. 1964.
Northwood Publications Ltd., 10-16 Elm Street, London, WC1.
12, =
No Index.
Free, controlled circulation.

3113 PRINTING JOURNAL.
PIRA, Randalls Road, Leatherhead, Surrey.
2, = ‡ +   Research projects carried out by the Association.
Monographic articles.
No Index.
Free to members.

3114 PRINTING TRADES JOURNAL. 1963.
(Sales and Wants Advertiser, 1887-1962).
Benn Brothers Ltd., 25 New Street Square, London, EC4A 3JA.
12, ‡ =   Emphasis on new equipment and processes, and business management. Includes sales and wants advertiser.
Book reviews, commodity prices, monographic articles, new companies, new products, obituaries, parliamentary reports, patents, tests.
No Index.
March 1972, T.p. 47, Ad.p. 69.   8049.
Per copy 35p, per year £4.50.

3115 PRINTING WORLD. 1954.
(British and Colonial Printer 1878-1954)
Benn Brothers Ltd., Lyon Tower, Colliers Wood, London, SW19.
= ‡   All aspects of the printing industry.
Book notices, book reviews, legal notes, letters, articles, new companies, new products, obituaries, patents, standards, tests.
No Index.
19.7.1972, T.p. 20, Ad.p. 12.   5000.
Per copy 12p, per year £7.

3116 PRIVATE PRINTER AND PRIVATE PRESS. 1968.
P. Hoy, 97 Holywell Street, Oxford.
Irregular, =   Little and private presses.

Book reviews, monographic articles.
No Index.
T.p. 70.
Subscription on application.

3117 PROFESSIONAL PRINTER: incorporating Printing Technology. Proceedings of the Institute of Printing. 1973.
(Printing Technology 1957-1972).
Institute of Printing, 10/11 Bedford Row, London, WC1R 4DZ.
6, ‡ *   Technology, management design, education and training, together with items of interest to members: proceeds of council, members correspondence, etc.
Digests, book reviews, letters, monographic articles, obituaries.
No Index.
T.p. 24, Ad.p. 8.   2000.
Per year £7.

3118 REPRODUCTION: Small Offset User. 1964.
BED Business Journals Ltd., Park House, Park Street, Croydon, CR9 1UA.
12, ‡ = *   Selection or/and purchasing of reprographic equipment, materials and services.
Book notices, book reviews, letters, articles, new companies, new products, standards, tests.
No Index.
June 1972, T.p. 42, Ad.p. 42.   15213.
Free, controlled circulation.

3119 SCOTTISH TYPOGRAPHICAL JOURNAL. 1857.
136 West Regent Street, Glasgow, C2.
12, =
No Index.

3120 SMALL PRINTER. 1965.
(ISPA News).
British Printing Society, BM/ISPA, Mono House, London, WC1.
12, * =   Small business and hobby printing, letterpress and lithographic etc.
Book reviews, letters, articles, new products.
A, January, No, None.
T.p. 29, Ad.p. 2.
Free to members.

3121 SOGAT JOURNAL. 1967.
Society of Graphical and Allied Trades, 13-16 Borough Road, London, SE1.
12, = *   Trade union affairs.
Book notices, book reviews, letters, articles, news, obituaries, parliamentary reports.
No Index.
T.p. 42, Ad.p. 5.
Per copy 2½p.

3122 TIN-PRINTER AND BOX MAKER. 1924.
Canning Publications, 28 Monument Street, London, EC3.
12, = ‡ +   Printing on tinplate and the manufacture of metal boxes.
Book notices, book reviews, commodity prices, monographic articles, new companies, news, new products, patents, standards, tests.
No Index.
T.p. 16, Ad.p. 8.
Per copy 10p, per year £1.
Indexed in: BTI.

655.3

PRINTING PROCESSES

3123 LITHOPRINTER. 1958.
Haymarket Publishing Limited, Gillow House, 5 Winsley Street, London, W1.
12, ‡ =   Lithoprinting industry in all its aspects.
New companies, articles, new products, personality.

No Index.
July 1972, T.p. 38, Ad.p. 69.   6653.
Per copy 25p, per year £4.
Indexed in: BTI

3124 SCREEN PRINTING & POINT OF SALE NEWS. 1951.
Batiste Publications Ltd., 203-9 North Gower Street, London, NW1.
12, =   Screen printing industry, typography, display.
No Index.
T.p. 45, Ad.p. 35.   5235.
Per year £2.50.

3125 SMALL OFFSET PRINTING. 1969.
Maclean-Hunter Ltd., 30 Old Burlington Street, London, W1X 2AE.
12, =   Plant, equipment, supplies and services.
Articles, new companies, news, new products.
No Index.
T.p. 56, Ad.p. Most.   12397.
Per year £3. Free, controlled circulation.

655.5

BOOK PUBLISHING. BOOK SELLING

3126 BOOK COLLECTING & LIBRARY MONTHLY. 1968.
42 Trafalgar St., Brighton, Sussex.
12, ○ = + *   Bibliography and antiquarian books.
Book notices, book reviews, letters, monographic articles.
6m, —, No, A.
Per copy 20p, per year £2.

3127 THE BOOK EXCHANGE: The International Medium for books wanted and for sale. 1948.
Fudge & Co. Ltd., Sardinia House, Sardinia St., London, WC2A 3NW.
12, =
No Index.
June 1972, T.p. 25, Ad.p. 7.
Per year £1.50.

3128 THE BOOK MARKET: The books for sale weekly. 1951.
The Clique Ltd., 170 Finchley Road, London, NW3.
50, =   Antiquarian and out of print books for sale.
No Index.
December 2, 1971, Ad.p. 16.
Per year £4.

3129 BOOK TRADE. 1971.
(The Publisher 1837-1970).
Whitehall Press Ltd., Wrotham Place, Wrotham, Sevenoaks, Kent.
12, =
No Index.
Subscription on application.

3130 THE BOOKDEALER: the trade weekly for books wanted and for sale. 1971.
Fudge & Co. Ltd., Sardinia House, Sardinia St., London, WC2A 3NW.
51, =   Books wanted and for sale by the antiquarian and second-hand book trade (trade only).
No Index.
14th June 1972, T.p. 1, Ad.p. 63.   1000.
Per year £3.10.

3131 THE BOOKSELLER: The Organ of the book trade. 1858.
(Publisher & Bookseller 1928-1932, Bent's Literary Advertiser 1802-1858).
J. Whitaker & Sons, Ltd., 13 Bedford Square, London, WC1B 3JE.
52, = +   Contains each week full list of books published in U.K. that week, with news of current and forthcoming books and publishers announcements.
Book notices, book reviews, letters, articles, new companies, new products, parliamentary reports.

No Index.
10.6.1972, T.p. 35, Ad.p. 35.   14500.
Per copy 10p, per year £6.20.

3132 THE CLIQUE: The Antiquarian Booksellers Medium. 1890.
The Clique Ltd., 170 Finchley Road, NW3.
50, =   Books wanted by trade only.
No Index.
June 10, 1972, Ad.p. 48.
Per year £4.

3134 THE GEE REPORT: Confidential information for Publishers, Booksellers, Lit. Agents, Press and Authors. 1971.
Gee Report, 110 Goldhurst Terrace, London, NW6.
26, ‡   Forthcoming book projects, high level appointments, trends in publishing.
No Index.
23.6.1972, T.p. 4, Ad.p. 2.   200.
Per year £25.

3135 NATIONAL NEWSAGENT: incorporating Sweet and Tobacco Retailing. 1902.
Haymarket Publishing Limited, Gillow House, 5 Winsley Street, London, W1.
52, =   Trade newspaper for newsagents and allied trades.
Book notices, book reviews, commodity prices, legal notes, letters, articles, new companies, new products, obituaries, parliamentary reports.
No Index.
T.p. 32, Ad.p. 13.   20000.
Per copy 12p, per year £7.

3136 NEW STATIONER.
British Stationery and Office Equipment Association, 6 Wimpole Street, London, W1.
12, =
No Index.
Free to members.

3137 PAPERBACKS IN PRINT. 1960.
J. Whitaker & Sons Ltd., 13 Bedford Square, London, WC1B 3JE.
2, =   A reference catalogue of paperbacks available in Great Britain, classified in 52 categories and with author and title indexes.
No Index.
Per copy £3.50.

3138 PENGUIN NEWS. 1972.
Penguin Books, Harmondsworth, Middx.
12, =
Book news.
No Index.
Per year 30p.

3139 PENGUINS IN PRINT. 1967.
Penguin Books Ltd. (Longman/Penguin), Harmondsworth, Middlesex.
3, ○   Includes all Penguin books that are in print and 3 months forthcoming books.
Commodity prices, new products.
No Index.
May/August, 1972, T.p. 50.   225000.
Per year 30p.

3140 THE PUBLISHER. 1837.
(British Books; Publishers Circular).
Publishers Circular Ltd., 79 Limpsfield Road, South Croydon, Surrey, CR2 97E.
6, =   Publishing and allied trades.
No Index.
T.p. 26, Ad.p. 17.
Per copy 37½p, per year £3.15.

3141 PUFFIN POST. 1967.
Penguin Books (Longman/Penguin), Bath Road, Harmondsworth, Middx.

4, ○   A magazine for young readers (members of the Puffin Club) to tell them about books, authors and artists and give young people a chance to see their own writing in print.
Book notices, book reviews, commodity prices, letters, articles.
No Index.
Vol. 6, No. 1, T.p. 32.   40000.
Per year 50 p. Different rates for school groups—families etc.

3142 REPRINT REVIEW.
Reprint Review, 47 Museum Street, London, WC1.
Irregular, =   Reprints, re-issues and new editions of publications.
No Index.
T.p. 4.
Free, controlled circulation.

3143 RETAIL NEWSAGENT. 1970.
(Retail Newsagent, Bookseller & Stationer; News & Book Trade Review & Stationers Gazette 1889-1969).
News & Book Trade Review, & Stationers Gazette Ltd., 15 Charterhouse Street, London, EC1N 6RL.
52, =   Newsagency interests and activities of publishing distributive industry, UK and Eire.
On above trading interests generally.
No Index.
15.7.1972, T.p. 26, Ad.p. 10.   c. 19000.
Per copy 9p, per year £6.

3144 SMITH'S TRADE NEWS. 1952.
(Smith's Trade Circular 1926).
W. H. Smith & Son, Strand House, Portugal Street, London, WC2A 2HS.
52, =   Events in magazine, newspaper and book trades.
No Index.
T.p. 20, Ad.p. 20.   17250.
Per year £3.90.

3145 STATIONERY TRADE REVIEW. 1932.
Whitehall Press Limited, Wrotham Place, Wrotham, Sevenoaks, Kent.
12, =   Trade journal for stationery, office equipment and associated trades.
Book notices, book reviews, commodity prices, legal notes, letters, monographic articles, new companies, new products, obituaries, parliamentary reports.
No Index.
March 1972, T.p. 36, Ad.p. 80.   6200.
Per copy 25p, per year £2.85.

3146 WHITAKER'S BOOKS OF THE MONTH & BOOKS TO COME: incorporating Current Literature. 1970.
(Current Literature 1858-1969).
J. Whitaker & Sons Ltd., 13 Bedford Square, London, WC1B 3JE.
12, =   Contains a list of books published during the months of issue, and also of books announced for publication in the next two months.
No Index.
July 1972, T.p. 92.   4000.
Per year £7.20.

656

TRANSPORT

3147 SALVESEN NEWS. 1963.
Christian Salvesen Ltd., 50 East Fettes Avenue, Edinburgh, EH4 1EQ.
1, † =   Handling and storage of food.
Articles, new products, obituaries.
A, —, No, None.
No. 7, 1971, T.p. 76.
Free.

3148 TRANSPORTATION NEWS.
The Goodyear Tyre & Rubber Co. (G.B.) Ltd.,
Wolverhampton.
4, ‡ =   General interest in the haulage business.
New products, parliamentary reports, standards, tests.
A, –, Yes, None.
T.p. 7, Ad.p. 1.   25000.
Free.

3149 TRANSPORTATION RESEARCH.
Pergamon Press Ltd., Headington Hill Hall, Oxford,
OX3 0BW.
4, + =   Design and operation of transportation
systems.
Book reviews, letters, notes and queries, monographic
articles.
A, Last issue of volume, Yes, None.
Per copy £5.50, per year £20.

656.03

TICKETS

3150 JOURNAL OF THE TRANSPORT TICKET SOCIETY.
1964.
(Ticket & Fare Collection Society Newsletter 1946-
1963).
Transport Ticket Society, 18 Villa Road, Luton,
LU2 7NT.
12, * ○   Current and historical practice in fare col-
lection methods and tickets, British and overseas.
Book notices, book reviews, letters, monographic
articles.
A, January, No, None.
June 1972, T.p. 38.   500.
Free to members.

656.073

FREIGHT

3151 FREIGHT: journal of the Freight Transport Associ-
ation Ltd. 1969.
Industrial Road Transport, Freight Transport Associ-
ation, Sunley House, Bedford Park, Croydon, Surrey,
CR9 1XU.
12, ‡ = +   All matters affecting the movement of
freight.
Book reviews, legal notes, letters, new products,
obituaries, parliamentary reports, standards, tests.
No Index.
May 1972, T.p. 26, Ad.p. 29.   17000.
Free to members.

3152 FREIGHT NEWS WEEKLY. 1969.
(Freight News International. 1954-1969).
Blandford Publications Ltd., 167 High Holborn, London,
WC1.
52, =   Every aspect of the freight industry.
Book notices, book reviews, legal notes, letters,
articles, new companies, new products, obituaries,
parliamentary reports, tests.
No Index.
23/6/72, T.p. 12, Ad.p. 12.   29927.
Per copy 20p, per year £5.

3153 FREIGHTWAY: Journal of the National Freight
Corporation. 1970.
National Freight Corporation, Argosy House, 215
Great Portland Street, London, W1N 6BD.
4, †   All aspects of freight and its conveyance.
Book reviews, monographic articles, new companies,
new products.
No Index.
May 1972, T.p. 25.   5000.
Free.

3154 ICHCA MONTHLY JOURNAL: International Cargo
Handling Co-ordination Association. 1967.
(ICHCA Quarterly Journal 1963-1966).
Trade News Ltd., 203/209 North Gower Street,
London, NW1.
12, = +   All aspects of transport by road, rail, sea
and handling of loads.
Book notices, book reviews, monographic articles,
news, new products.
A, –, Yes, 3 year.
T.p. 28, Ad.p. 11.
Free to members.

656.56

PIPES. PIPELINES

3155 THE PIPELINE INDUSTRIES GUILD BULLETIN.
1960.
The Guild, 7 Iddesleigh House, Caston Street, London,
SW1.
4, = ‡ +
Book notices, book reviews, letters, news, new
products.
No Index.
Free to members.

3156 PIPES & PIPELINES INTERNATIONAL. 1956.
Scientific Surveys Ltd., 11a Gloucester Road, London,
SW7.
12, +   Piping, chemicals, plumbing, pipes and pipe-
lines, fabrication, transportation and conveyance
of fluids.
No Index.
Per copy 35p, per year £4.
Indexed in: BTI.

656.8

POST

3157 COURIER: the Post Office staff newspaper. 1966.
(Post Offices Magazines 1934-1966).
Post Office, St. Martin's-le-Grand, London, EC1.
12, =   News and features to interest staff of the
Post Office and their families.
No Index.
T.p. 12, Ad.p. 1.   224000.
Per copy 2p.

3158 SUB-POSTMASTER.
National Federation of Sub-Postmasters, 22 Windlesham
Gardens, Shoreham-by-Sea, Sussex.
4, =
No Index.
Free to members.

656.835

PHILATELY

3159 AIR MAIL NEWS. 1958.
British Air Mail Society, c/o Hon. Secretary, T.C.
Marvin, 3 Lankton Close, Beckenham, Kent, BR3 2DZ.
4, * +   News and information to members of the
Society. Articles covering aerophilately.
No Index.
January 1972, T.p. 20, Ad.p. 3.   c.165.
Free to members only.

3160 BRITISH POST MARK SOCIETY. QUARTERLY
BULLETIN. 1958.
British Postmark Society, 42 Corrance Road, London,
SW2.
4, *   All types of British postal markings, particularly
those of the present century.
Book reviews, monographic articles.
A, April, No, None.
T.p. 32.
Available to members only.

3161 DF NEWSLETTER: house journal of David Feldman Ltd., Dublin. 1968.
David Feldman Ltd., 102 Leinster Road, Dublin 6.
4, † ○   All aspects of stamp collecting.
Prices.
No Index.
Autumn 1971, T.p.16.
Per year £1.

3162 THE G.B. JOURNAL. 1956.
Great Britain Philatelic Society, 14 Medway Crescent, Leigh-on-Sea, Essex, SS9 2UY.
6, + *   The adhesive stamps, postal stationery, postmarks and postal history of Great Britain, including Ireland prior to 1925.
Book notices, book reviews, letters, monographic articles.
A, At end of each volume (November each year), No, None.
May 1972, T.p.20, Ad.p.7.   850.
Per year £3.

3163 HOVER COVER. 1971.
Hovermail Collector's Club, c/o 30 Milverton Road, Winchester, Hants.
4, * +   Wide selection of articles and features on Hovermails, i.e. philatelic covers carried on hovercraft, stamps and postmarks depicting hovercraft, etc., plus articles and features on the history and development of hovercraft.
A, May, No, None.
May 1972, T.p.36, Ad.p.2.   150.
Per copy 25p, per year £1.

3164 THE LOG BOOK. 1971.
The Ship Stamp Society, 33a Ridgeway Road, Timperley, Cheshire.
4, ○
No Index.
Per year £1.68.

3165 PHILATELIC BULLETIN. 1963.
The British Post Office, Postal Headquarters, St. Martin's-le-Grand, London, EC1A 1HQ
12, ○   Book reviews, commodity prices, letters, articles, new products.
A, —, Yes, None.
June 1972, T.p.16.
Per year 50p.

3166 PHILATELIC EXPORTER. 1945.
Philatelic Exporter Ltd., PO Box 4, Edgware, Middx.
12, =   Wholesale stamp trade.
No Index.
T.p.5, Ad.p.25.
Per year £1.50.

3167 PHILATELIC MAGAZINE. 1911.
Harris Publications, 16 John Adam Street, London, WC2.
26, =   All aspects of philately.
Book notices, book reviews, letters, new companies, news, new products, obituaries.
No Index.
T.p.4, Ad.p.35.   20000.
Per copy 10p, per year £2.75.

3168 PHILATELIC TRADER. 1899.
Harris Publications, 16 John Adam Street, London, WC2.
26, =
Book notices, book reviews, new companies, news, new products, obituaries.
No Index.
Ad.p.26.   3000.
Per year £1.50.

3169 PTS JOURNAL. 1947.
Philatelic Traders Society Ltd., 27 John Adam Street, London, WC2.
6, * =   Trade magazine for the Society members only.
No Index.
T.p.9, Ad.p.15.
Free to members only.

3170 PHILATELY: journal of the British Philatelic Association Ltd. 1945.
British Philatelic Association, 446 Strand, London, WC2R 0RA
4, ○ * †   Various aspects of philately. Association news. Reports from affiliated societies at home and overseas.
Book notices, book reviews, letters, articles.
2 yearly, in last issue in odd-numbered years, No, None.
June 1972, T.p.12, Ad.p.4.   1500.
Per copy 7½p, per year £1.20. Free to members.

3171 RAILWAY PHILATELY: journal of the Railway Philatelic Group. 1966.
The Railway Philatelic Group, 59a Hartley Road, Kirkby-in-Ashfield, Nottingham, NG17 8DS.
4, ‡ = +   Philatelists interested in railways and railway postal activities and postal history connected with railways.
Book notices, book reviews, commodity prices, letters, monographic articles.
A, December, Yes, None.
December 1971, T.p.34, Ad.p.2.   350.
Per copy 40p, per year £1.50.

3172 SCOTTISH STAMP NEWS: The Magazine of the Alba Stamp Group. 1971.
(Philatelic Phanfare 1946; Stamp News 1947/49).
Stanley K. Hunter, 34 Gray Street, Glasgow, Scotland, G3 7TY.
12, ○ *   To encourage the collection of stamps and allied material connected with Scotland.
Book notices, book reviews, commodity prices, letters, monographic articles.
A, December, No, None.
T.p.10, Ad.p.1.   100.
Per copy 10p, per year 75p.

3173 STAMP COLLECTING. 1913.
Stamp Collecting Ltd., 42 Maiden Lane, London, WC2E 7LL.
52, ○   All aspects of stamp collecting and postal history: philatelic news, book reviews and society reports.
Book reviews, articles, reports.
6m, Paged in last number of each vol. (March and Sept.), No, None.
29 June 1972, T.p.12, Ad.p.32.   30000.
Per copy 7½p, per year £4.50.

3174 STAMP LOVER: including Index to Current Philatelic Literature. 1908.
National Philatelic Society, 44 Fleet Street, London, EC4.
6, ○ *
Book notices, book reviews, letters, monographic articles.
A, January, Yes, None.
T.p.22, Ad.p.8.
Free to members.

3175 THE STAMP MAGAZINE. 1934.
Link House Publications Ltd., Link House, Dingwall Avenue, Croydon, Surrey, CR9 2TA.
12, ○   Provides in depth, philatelic coverage for both collectors and investors. Covers new issues, charges and histories.
Book reviews, commodity prices, letters, monographic articles, new products.
A, December, No, 10 year.
T.p.30, Ad.p.78.   49000.
Per copy 15p, per year £2.

3176 STAMP MONTHLY. 1970.
(Gibbons Stamp Monthly 1927-1970).
Stanley Gibbons Magazines Ltd., Drury House, Russell Street, London, WC2B 5HD.
12,○ =   General interest stamp collecting magazine, for all ages. Stamp news, stamp market, designs and exhibitions, features. All new stamps listed in Stanley Gibbons catalogue supplement. Regular full-colour part-work included.
Book reviews, commodity prices, letters, monographic articles, new products, obituaries.
A, May, No, None.
June 1972, T. p. 40, Ad. p. 32.   53000.
Per copy 15p, per year £2.50.

3177 STAMP WEEKLY. 1967.
Link House, Dingwall Avenue, Croydon, Surrey.
52,○   Stamp news and general articles and tips.
Book reviews, commodity prices, legal notes, letters, monographic articles, news, new products, parliamentary reports.
No Index.
T. p. 13, Ad. p. 7.   26300.
Per copy 10p, per year £4.50.

3178 STAMPS OF IRELAND. 1965.
David Feldman Ltd., 102 Leinster Road, Dublin 6.
1,○
Prices.
No Index.
March 1972, T. p. 44.
Per copy 25p.

656.96

REMOVAL SERVICES

3179 REMOVALS & STORAGE: official journal of the Furniture Removal Industry. 1924.
British Association of Removers, 279 Grays Inn Road, London, WC1X 8SY.
12, =   Matters of interest to the removal industry and affairs relating to the British Association of Removers.
Letters, articles, new products, obituaries, parliamentary reports.
A, December, Yes, None.
June 1972, T. p. 96, Ad. p. 68.   1800.
Per copy 16p, per year £2. Free to members.

657

ACCOUNTANCY. BOOK-KEEPING

3180 ACCOUNTANCY. 1920.
(Incorporated Accountant's Journal 1889-1919).
Inst. of Chartered Accountants in England & Wales. 56/66 Goswell Road, London, EC1M 7AB.
12, ‡ * =   Accounting, investment, tax, banking, auditing, law, EDP, finance, cost analysis, management, estate duty, business machines.
Book notices, book reviews, legal notes, letters, monographic articles, new products, obituaries, parliamentary reports.
A, January, Yes, None.
April 1972, T. p. 80, Ad. p. 56.   38000.
Per copy 25p, per year £3.75.

3181 ACCOUNTANCY AGE. 1969.
Haymarket Publishing Ltd., Gillow House, 5 Winsley Street, London, W1.
52, ‡ *   All technical and news matter relevant to qualified accountants in UK.
Book notices, legal notes, letters, monographic articles, new companies, new products, parliamentary reports.
No Index.
14. 7. 72, T. p. 18, Ad. p. 14.   67000.
Per copy 20p, per year £6, (free to qualified circulation).

3182 ACCOUNTANCY IRELAND: The Journal of the Institute of Chartered Accountants in Ireland. 1969.
The Institute of Chartered Accountants in Ireland, 7 Fitzwilliam Place, Dublin 2.
6, ‡ = *   News items relating to economic and business affairs and to the accountancy profession in general.
Book reviews, letters, monographic articles.
A, Approx. March, No, None.
August 1972, T. p. 37, Ad. p. 9.   45000.
Per copy 20p, per year £1.20.

3183 THE ACCOUNTANT. 1874.
Gee & Co. (Publishers) Ltd., 151 Strand, London, WC2R 1JJ.
52, ‡ =   Accountancy profession throughout the world. Besides covering the profession's activities, it carries a wide range of comment on every aspect of the work of both practising and industrial accountants. Regular features include: Current Affairs, Finance and Commerce; Management Information; Computer Commentary; Equipment Notes and News; The Accounting World; Taxation Cases; Current Law; Correspondence; Book Reviews; Students' pages.
Book reviews, legal notes, letters, monographic articles, new products, obituaries, parliamentary reports, standards.
6m, −, Yes, None.
June 15th 1972, T. p. 40, Ad. p. 36.   17500.
Per copy 17p, per year £10.50.

3184 THE ACCOUNTANT'S MAGAZINE: Journal of The Institute of Chartered Accountants of Scotland. 1897.
The Accountants' Publishing Co. Ltd., 27 Queen Street, Edinburgh EH2 1LA.
12, ‡ + *   Accounting, law, economics, auditing, EDP, management accounting, business topics, taxation, investment, students' topics, company accounts, current reading.
Book notices, book reviews, legal notes, letters, monographic articles, obituaries, standards.
A, January, Yes, None.
July 1972, T. p. 52, Ad. p. 28.   11600.
Per copy 25p, per year £3.

3185 ACCOUNTANTS WEEKLY. 1972.
(Accountants Week 1970-1972).
Morgan-Grampian Co. Ltd., Calderwood Street, Woolwich, London, SE18.
52, =   Professional activities, economic trends, investment, taxation, general management techniques etc.
Book reviews, legal notes, letters, articles.
No Index.
20 October 1972, T. p. 12, Ad. p. 8.   55000.
Per copy 10p, per year £4 and Free to qualified accountants.

3186 ACCOUNTING AND BUSINESS RESEARCH. 1970.
(Accounting Research, 1947-1958).
Institute of Chartered Accountants in England and Wales, 56-66 Goswell Road, London, EC1M 7AB.
4, + ‡   Aims to provide a bridge between the accountant in industry or practice and the research which is going on in the academic world.
Book reviews, letters, articles.
A, −, Yes, None.
Spring 1972, T. p. 74, Ad. p. 1.   2400.
Per copy £1.25, per year £5.

3187 ACCOUNTING + DATA PROCESSING ABSTRACTS. 1971.
(Part of Anbar Management Services, previously included in Anbar Management Services Abstracts, 1961-1971).
Anbar Publications Ltd., (* see below) PO Box 23, Wembley, HA9 8DJ.
8, ‡ = + * Abstracts from British and overseas publications of articles of interest to accountants and managers responsible for the use of computers.
Abstracts, book notices, new products.
6m, After 4th and 8th issues, Yes, A binder is included, A.
31 May 1972, T. p. 32, Ad. p. 3.
£20 per year. * In association with the Institute of Chartered Accountants in England and Wales.

3188 BOOK-KEEPERS JOURNAL: journal of the Institute of Book-keepers. 1920.
Institute of Book-Keepers & Related Data Processing, 418-422 Strand, London, WC2.
4, = ‡ * Book-keeping, accounting and general business practice.
Book notices, book reviews, letters, monographic articles, new products.
2 yearly, —, Yes, None.
Spring 1972, T. p. 23.
Free to members.

3189 CERTIFIED ACCOUNTANT. 1972.
(Certified Accountants Journal 1905-1971).
Association of Certified Accountants, 22 Bedford Square, London, WC1B 3HS.
11, * Taxation, economics, finance and law.
Book reviews, legal notes, letters, monographic articles.
A, February, Yes, None.
June 1972, T. p. 37, Ad. p. 23.
Per copy 20p, per year £3.

3190 THE COMMERCIAL ACCOUNTANT. 1947.
Society of Commercial Accountants, 40 Tyndalls Park Road, Bristol 8.
4, ‡ * = Accounting, business finance, management, data processing; taxation, company and commercial law.
Book notices, book reviews, legal notes, monographic articles.
No Index.
January 1972, T. p. 82, Ad. p. 4.   7000.
Per year £1.50.

3191 COMPANY ACCOUNTANT: the journal for all accountants engaged in industry, banking and commerce. 1931.
Institute of Company Accountants, 11 Portland Road, Edgbaston, Birmingham, B16 9HW.
6, *
Book notices, book reviews, legal notes, letters, monographic articles, new companies, obituaries, parliamentary reports.
No Index.
May/June 1972, T. p. 20.   8000.
Per copy 20p, per year £1.80. Free to members.

3192 THE COST ENGINEER: journal of the Association of Cost Engineers. 1962.
Association of Cost Engineers, 33 Ovington Square, London, SW3.
6, ‡ * = Theory and practice of cost engineering.
Abstracts, book notices, book reviews, letters, monographic articles, obituaries.
No Index.
July 1971, T. p. 12, Ad. p. Now offering to members and non-members 700
Per copy 50p, per year £3. Free to members.

3193 THE EXECUTIVE ACCOUNTANT. 1950.
Association of Industrial & Commercial Executive Accountants Ltd., 4-9 Wood Street, London, EC2.
3, =
Book reviews, letters, articles.
A, —, Yes, None.
T. p. 36, Ad. p. 1.   300.
Free to members.

3194 HOTEL ACCOUNTANT. 1969.
British Association of Hotel Accountants, c/o 13 Southampton Place, London, WC1A 2AR.
4, * Accountancy relevant to hotel industry.
Letters, articles, news items.
No Index.
Nov. 1971, T. p. 12.   150.
Free to members.

3195 THE INTERNATIONAL ACCOUNTANT. 1966.
(International Accountants Journal 1932-1965).
Association of International Accountants, Temple Chambers, Temple Avenue, London, EC4.
4, = Professional, commercial and management accounting worldwide.
Book notices, book reviews, legal notes, letters, monographic articles, news, new companies, parliamentary reports.
A, March, No, None.
T. p. 32, Ad. p. 5.
Free to members.

3196 MANAGEMENT ACCOUNTING: journal of the Institute of Cost and Management Accountants. 1965.
(Cost Accountant 1921-1965).
Institute of Cost and Management Accountants, 63 Portland Place, London, W1N 4AB.
11, ‡ * Current developments in cost and management accountancy and related fields such as computers, operational research and economics.
Abstracts, book notices, book reviews, legal notes, letters, monographic articles, obituaries.
A, January, Yes, None.
6, 1972, T. p. 30, Ad. p. 20.   38029.
Per copy 22p, per year £2.45.

3197 THE REGISTERED ACCOUNTANT. 1960.
British Association of Accountants & Auditors, 2/4 Chiswick High Road, London, W4.
4, =
Book notices, book reviews, letters, articles, news, obituaries, parliamentary reports.
No Index.
T. p. 23, Ad. p. 1.
Free to members.

657.47

COSTING

3198 COSTING: cost and industrial accounting review. 1950.
Incorporated Association of Cost & Industrial Accountants Ltd., 60a Station Road, Upminster, Essex.
4, * = Cost accounting.
Book notices, book reviews, legal notes, monographic articles, new companies.
No Index.
2800.
Free to members.

Key to reference symbols

○ popular   ‡ technical   = trade/professional

+ research   * society/institution   † house journal

658

BUSINESS AND INDUSTRIAL MANAGEMENT

3199 ANBAR MANAGEMENT SERVICES BIBLIOGRAPHY.
Anbar Publications Ltd., P.O. Box 23, Wembley, HA9 8DJ.
3, ‡ = + *   Classified list, with author index, of books noted in journals abstracted for Anbar Management Services, with bibliographical details and references to reviews.
Part of Anbar Management Services. Issued free to subscribers to one or more of the abstracting journals together with index. Also available separately.
Book notices.
No Index.
September 1971-April 1972, T. p. 65.
Per year £20 for full service. Apply for others.

3200 ASTMS GAINS. 1968.
Association of Scientific Technical & Managerial Staffs, 15 Half Moon Street, London, W1.
12, *   Association affairs.
No Index.
T. p. 4, Ad. p. 1.
Free to members.

3201 ASTMS JOURNAL. 1968.
Association of Scientific, Technical and Managerial Staffs, 15 Half Moon Street, London, W1.
6, *   Association affairs.
No Index.
T. p. 18, Ad. p. 6.
Free to members.

3202 CURRENT CONTENTS IN MANAGEMENT.
Library, Manchester Business School, Booth Street West, Manchester.
52, =
No Index.
Per year £6.72.

3203 THE DIRECTOR. 1947.
Institute of Directors, 10 Belgrave Square, London, SW1.
12, = *   General management, industrial and financial news and developments.
Book reviews, letters, monographic articles, new products.
No Index.
T. p. 80, Ad. p. 120.   43000.
Per year £10.

3204 FACTORY: The journal of engineering management 1972.
Morgan-Grampian (Publishers) Ltd., Calderwood St., Woolwich, London, SE18.
12, ‡ =   Works engineers dealing specifically with environmental control (heat, light, ventilation; power); maintenance and welfare; safety; handling and storage; cleaning.
Book notices, commodity prices, letters, articles, new products, parliamentary reports, patents, standards, tests.
A, —, Yes, None.
13250.
Per year £5.

3205 FACTORY MANAGEMENT. 1934.
Northwood Publications Ltd., Elm House, 10-16 Elm Street, London, WC1.
12, =   Industrial management, with bias to automation.
No Index.
13700.
Free, controlled circulation.

3206 INDUSTRIAL MANAGEMENT. 1971.
Business Publications Ltd., Waterloo Road, London, SE1.
12, =
Book reviews, letters, articles.
No Index.
Per copy 50p.

3207 INTERNATIONAL MANAGEMENT. (English language edition). 1946.
McGraw-Hill International Publications, McGraw-Hill House, Maidenhead, SL6 QL, Berkshire.
12, =   Reviews management techniques and ideas from around the world through case studies, company reviews, personal interviews with senior business reports from own international correspondents.
Book notices, book reviews, letters, monographic articles, tests.
A, —, Yes, None.
May 1972, T. p. 20, Ad. p. 48.   100000.
Per copy £1, per year £10.

3208 INTERNATIONAL MANAGEMENT. (Spanish language Edition). 1946.
McGraw-Hill International Publications Co. Ltd., McGraw-Hill House, Maidenhead, SL6 QL, Berkshire.
6, =   Reviews management techniques and ideas from around the world through case studies, company reviews, personal interviews with senior business reports from own international correspondents.
Book notices, book reviews, letters, monographic articles, tests.
A, —, Yes, None.
March/April 1972, T. p. 50, Ad. p. 22.   30000.
Per copy £1, per year £5.

3209 JOURNAL OF COMPARATIVE ADMINISTRATION. 1969.
Sage Publications Ltd., 44 Hatton Garden, London, EC1.
4, =   Treats the central analytic questions of public organisations, presenting intra- or inter-systems comparisons, and studying administrative bureaucracies as agents of change.
Monographic articles.
A, —, Yes, None.
August 1971, T. p. 125.
Per year £8.

3210 JOURNAL OF MANAGEMENT STUDIES. 1964.
Basil Blackwell & Mott Ltd., 5 Alfred Street, Oxford, OX1 4HB.
3, = +   The advance of all branches of knowledge directly related to the practice of management.
Articles and Reviews.
A, —, Yes, None.
T. p. 146, Ad. p. 6.   1500.
Per copy £1, per year £3.

3211 LIGHT PRODUCTION ENGINEERING. 1963.
Factory Publications Ltd., 180 Fleet Street, London, EC4.
12, = ‡ +   Materials, machining and assembly techniques, processes and management systems.
Book reviews, letters, monographic articles, new companies, news, new products, patents, standards, tests.
No Index.
T. p. 27, Ad. p. 40.   125000.
Per copy 50p, per year £5 and Free, controlled circulation.

3212 LONG RANGE PLANNING.
Pergamon Press Ltd., Headington Hill Hall, Oxford, OX3 0BW.
4, = +   Concepts and techniques involved in the development of strategy and generation of long range plans.
Monographic articles.
A, Last issue of volume, Yes, None.
Per copy £3, per year £10.

3213 MANAGEMENT ABSTRACTS: Digests and Reviews.
British Institute of Management, Management House, Parker Street, London, WC2B 5PT.
4, ○ + Management research and reviews of new films.
Abstracts, book notices, book reviews, new products.
A, —, No, None.
No. 1, 1972, T.p. 30, Ad.p. 1.   59000.
Per year £3.

3214 MANAGEMENT BY OBJECTIVES. 1971.
Classified Media Ltd., 101 Hatton Garden, London, EC1.
4, = Management by objectives and related methods of improving management performance in business and non-profit organizations, including management development, organization development, corporate planning, and application of the behavioural sciences.
Book reviews, letters, monographic articles.
A, April, Yes, None.
October 1971, T.p. 56.
Per year £10.

3215 MANAGEMENT DECISION: the Bradford review of management technology. 1966.
(Institute of Scientific Business 1962-1966).
MCB (Management Decision) Ltd., 200 Keighley Road, Bradford, Yorkshire BD9 4JZ.
3, = New experience and techniques for management, covering marketing, finance, personnel, corporate planning etc.
Book reviews, monographic articles.
A, Spring, Yes, None.
Summer 1971, T.p. 95.   2000.
Per copy £3.95, per year £13.95.

3216 MANAGEMENT IN ACTION. 1969.
(Office Magazine 1954-1964; Office Methods & Machines 1964-1969).
MIA Publishing Ltd., 9 Victoria Road, Coulsdon, CR3 2NN, Surrey.
12, = Middle managers in commerce and industry local and national government, particularly those concerned with business systems and management techniques.
Book notices, book reviews, legal notes, letters, monographic articles, new products.
A, December, Yes, None.
T.p. 40, Ad.p. 20.   7500.
Per copy 45p, per year £5.40.

3217 MANAGEMENT TODAY: Journal of the British Institute of Management. 1966.
(The Manager 1933-1936).
Management Publications Ltd., Gillow House, 5 Winsley Street, London W1A 2HG.
12, ‡ = * Case histories of companies in Britain, the US, Europe and elsewhere. Management theory and techniques: economic forecasts; studies in key areas of business management and national policy, etc.
Book reviews, letters, monographic articles.
6m, July/January, No, None.
T.p. 95, Ad.p. 93.   63000.
Per copy 50p, per year £8. Free to members.

3218 MASS PRODUCTION. 1924.
Sawell Publications Ltd., 4 Ludgate Circus, London, EC4.
12, = ‡
News, new products.
A, —, Yes, None.
T.p. 70, Ad.p. 60.   4000.
Per copy 15p, per year £2.

3219 MIDLAND INDUSTRIALIST. 1965.
Peterson Publishing Co. Ltd., Peterson House, Livery Street, Birmingham 3.
6, = ‡ +
Articles, news.
No Index.
T.p. 48.
Subscription on application.

3220 NORTHERN INDUSTRY: Management Journal for the Northern region. 1970.
Paull & Goode Publishing Ltd., Midland Bank Chambers, St. Thomas St., Sunderland.
12, = Management in Northern England at senior and middle management levels.
Book reviews, letters, articles, new companies, new products, obituaries, parliamentary reports, standards, tests.
No Index.
June 1972, T.p. 21, Ad.p. 18.   3400.
Per copy 20p, per year £2.95.

3221 PRODUCTION ENGINEER. 1953.
(Journal of the Institution of Production Engineers 1922-1952).
The Institution, 10 Chesterfield Street, London, W1X 8DE.
12, * = All aspects of production technology and production management.
Book reviews, letters, monographic articles, news, new products.
A, December, No, None.
T.p. 51, Ad.p. 48.   18000.
Per copy 75p, per year £10. Free to members.
Indexed in: BTI.

3222 PUBLIC ENTERPRISE: journal of the Public Enterprise Group. 1971.
Public Enterprise Group, 15a Sanderstead Hill, South Croydon, Surrey.
3, * Information concerning activities and performance of public enterprise. Analysis of and comment upon its present and future role of public sector and its constituent parts and enterprises within the economy.
Book reviews, letters, monographic articles, parliamentary reports.
No Index.
No. 1, 1971, T.p. 25.
Per copy 68p, per year £2.

3223 TOP MANAGEMENT ABSTRACTS. 1971.
(Part of Anbar Management Services. Previously included in Anbar Management Services Abstracts, 1961-1971).
Anbar Publications Ltd., P.O. Box 23, Wembly, HA9 8DJ.
8, ‡ = + * Abstracts from British and overseas publications of articles of interest to top management.
Abstracts, book notices.
6m, After 4th and 8th issues, Yes, A binder is included, A.
29 February 1972, T.p. 24.
Per year £20 for full service. Apply for others.

3224 UNI ROPA. 1972.
K. Edwards, Broadstairs, Kent.
= Executive newsletter.
No Index.
Subscription on application.

3225 WORKS MANAGEMENT. 1949.
Institution of Works Managers, 34 Bloomsbury Way, London, WC1A 2SB.
11, ‡ * Works management in the widest sense e.g. anything from computers to tea breaks.
Abstracts, book notices, book reviews, letters, monographic articles, new products, obituaries.
No Index.
June 1972, T.p. 26, Ad.p. 8.   15280.
Per copy 50p, per year £5.50.
Indexed in: BTI.

658.013

INDUSTRIAL PSYCHOLOGY

3226 NIIP BULLETIN. 1966.
National Institute of Industrial Psychology, 14 Welbeck Street, London, W1M 8DR.
2/3, ○ ‡ = +   Reports on work in the fields of occupational and industrial psychology for practitioners.
Book notices, book reviews, legal notes, letters, monographic articles, new products, obituaries, standards, tests.
No Index.
Spring 1971, T.p. 31.
Free to members.

3227 OCCUPATIONAL PSYCHOLOGY. 1938.
(Journal of the National Institute of Industrial Psychology. 1922-31; The Human Factor. 1932-37.).
National Institute of Industrial Psychology, 14 Welbeck Street, London, W1M 8DR.
4, ‡ + *   Applications of psychology and other social sciences in industry, commerce and professional work. Reports on research, surveys, trends, developments. Of interest to practitioners and interested laymen.
Book notices, book reviews, letters, monographic articles, new products, obituaries, tests.
A, In last issue of each volume, Yes, 1938-1953 published 1954; 1938-1969 published 1969.
No. 1, 1972, T.p. 52, Ad.p. 4.   3000.
Per year £6.

658.15

FINANCIAL MANAGEMENT

3228 BUSINESS AND FINANCE. 1964.
Business & Finance Ltd., PO Box 320, Botanic Road, Glasnevin, Dublin 9.
51, =   Irish industry, commerce, finance, economics and politics.
Book reviews, commodity prices, letters, articles, new companies, news, new products, parliamentary reports, patents, standards, tests.
No Index.
T.p. 30, Ad.p. 18.   9000.
Per copy 10p.

3229 HOSPITAL SERVICE FINANCE: The Official Journal of the Association of Hospital Treasurers. 1950.
The Association, c/o Sherwood Hospital, Hucknall Road, Nottingham, NG5 1PD.
6, ‡ + =   Minutes of meetings: reports of Conference and Week-End School; professional notes and correspondence appertaining to Hospital Service financial management.
Letters, news, articles, obituaries, parliamentary reports, standards, tests.
No Index.
March 1972, T.p. 22.
Free to members.
Per copy 17½p, per year £1.05. Free to members.

658.2

PLANT EQUIPMENT

3230 INDUSTRIAL EQUIPMENT NEWS. 1951.
IPC Industrial Press Ltd., 33-39 Bowling Green Lane, London, EC1R 0NE
24, ‡ =   All kinds of new and previously unpublished products, for use in British manufacturing industry.
Book reviews, new products, regular supplements on specific industries.
No Index.
Mid-April 1972, T.p. 104, Ad.p. 66.   33600.
Free, controlled circulation.

3231 WHAT'S NEW: The Industrial Products & Equipment Guide. 1971.
Morgan-Grampian (Publishers) Ltd., Morgan-Grampian House, 30 Calderwood Street, Woolwich, London, SE18 6QH.
12, ‡   Significant new advances in products and equipment for industrial and factory use.
Book notices, book reviews, new products.
No Index.
T.p.c. 100, Ad.p. 60.   30000.
Free, controlled circulation.

658.3

PERSONNEL MANAGEMENT

3232 IPM DIGEST. 1965.
Institute of Personnel Management, 5 Winsley Street, London, W1N 7AQ.
12, =   Institute work, policy and publications in personnel management.
No Index.
T.p. 8, Ad.p. 16.   10300.
Free to members.

3233 PERSONNEL + TRAINING ABSTRACTS. 1971.
(Part of Anbar Management Services, previously included in Anbar Management Services Abstracts, 1961-1971).
Anbar Publications Ltd., P.O. Box 23, Wembley, HA9 8DJ.
8, ‡ = + *   Abstracts from British and overseas publications of articles of interest to personnel managers and training officers.
Abstracts, book notices.
6m, After 4th and 8th issues, Yes, A binder is included, A.
31 May 1972, T.p. 35.
Per year £20 for full service. Apply for others.

3234 PERSONNEL MANAGEMENT. 1969.
(Personnel & Training Management 1967-1968; Personnel Management & Methods 1920-1966).
Business Publications Ltd., Mercury House, Waterloo Road, London, SE1.
12, =   Personnel management in general. Industrial training.
Book reviews, legal notes, letters, monographic articles, news, new products.
A, January, No, None.
T.p. 35, Ad.p. 29.   23000.
Free to members.

3235 PERSONNEL REVIEW. 1971.
Gower Press (in conjunction with Institute of Personnel Management), Epping, Essex.
4, = + *   New developments in the research, theory and practice of personnel management.
Abstracts, book notices, book reviews, letters, monographic articles.
A, December, No, None.
Autumn 1971, T.p. 80, Ad.p. 10.   2000.
Per copy £1.50, per year £6. I.P.M. members rate per copy £1.13, per year £4.50.

3236 THE SUPERVISOR: journal of the Institute of Industrial Supervisors. 1949.
Pergamon Press Ltd., Headington Hill Hall, Oxford, OX3 0BW.
12, =
No Index.
11500.
Free to members.

3237 SUPERVISORY MANAGEMENT: journal of the Institute of Supervisory Management. 1949.
Institute of Supervisory Management, 22 Bore Street, Lichfield, Staffs.
4, = *   All aspects of supervising work.
Book reviews, monographic articles.
A, −, Yes, None.
Spring 1972, T.p. 48.
Per copy 75p, per year £3. Free to members.

658.5
PRODUCTION MANAGEMENT

3238 ANNALS OF THE C.I.R.P. 1952.
Pergamon Press Ltd., Headington Hill Hall, Oxford, OX3 0BW.
4, = ‡   Scientific research and study of the mechanical processing of all solid materials. Quality control etc.
A, Last issue of volume, Yes, None.
Per copy £4.50, per year £16.

3239 INTERNATIONAL JOURNAL OF PRODUCTION RESEARCH. 1971.
Taylor & Francis Ltd., (for the Institution of Production Engineers), 10-14 Macklin St., London WC2B 5NF.
4, ‡ = +   Research into the various aspects of the efficient utilisation of productive resources.
Book notices, book reviews, monographic articles.
A, in last issue of volume, Yes, None.
July 1972, T.p. 98, Ad. p. 4.
Per copy £3, per year £10.
Indexed in: BTI.

3240 PERA BULLETIN. 1947.
The Production Engineering Research Assoc., Melton Mowbray, Leicestershire.
5, ‡ +   All aspects of production engineering, including metal forming, metal cutting, inspection, management, materials, mechanical handling, plastics, foundry practice etc.
Abstracts, book reviews.
No Index.
T.p. 13.
Free, confidential to members.

3241 PRODUCTION EQUIPMENT DIGEST. 1954.
Hulton Publications Ltd., Audrey House, Ely Place, London, EC1.
12, ‡ = +   Review of new industrial equipment components, materials and services.
New products.
No Index.
June 1972, T.p. 25, Ad.p. 50.   26301.
Free, controlled circulation.

658.542
WORK STUDY

3242 O&M BULLETIN: The Journal of Government Management Services. 1945.
Civil Service Department, Management Services, Whitehall, London, SW1A 2AZ.
4, ‡ +   Management services field, including O&M, computers, operational research and personnel management, and are of particular interest to persons engaged in this field. Case studies.
Book notices, book reviews, letters, monographic articles, Office equip't, new products.
A, Usually with November edition, Yes, None.
May 1972, T.p. 50.   4700.
Per year £1.

3243 WORK STUDY. 1946.
Sawell Publications Ltd., 4 Ludgate Circus, London, EC4.
12, = ‡
No Index.
5100.
Per copy 25p, per year £1.80.
Indexed in: BTI.

3244 WORK STUDY AND MANAGEMENT SERVICE. 1968.
(Work Study & Industrial Engineering 1857-1962; Work Study & Management 1863-1967).
Institute of Work Study Practitioners, 9/10 River Front, Enfield, Middx.
12, * = ‡ +
Book notices, book reviews, letters, monographic articles, news, new products, obituaries.
A, −, Yes, None.
T.p. 30, Ad.p. 48.   16500.
Free to members.

658.562
QUALITY CONTROL

3245 QUALITY ENGINEER. 1935.
Institution of Engineering Inspection, 616 Grand Buildings, London, WC2.
6, = ‡   Standards of inspection and quality control in engineering and allied industries.
No Index.
Per copy 20p, per year £1.50.
Indexed in: BTI.

3246 QUALITY MATTERS. 1972.
National Council for Quality and Reliability, 1 Birdcage Walk, London, SW1H 9JJ.
Irreg., =
No Index.
Free to members.

658.57
ERGONOMICS

3247 APPLIED ERGONOMICS. 1969.
Iliffe Science & Technology Publications Ltd., 32 High Street, Guildford.
4, = + ‡   Inter-relations between people and their occupations, equipment, environment and work systems.
Book reviews, letters, monographic articles.
A, December, Yes, None.
T.p. 68.
Per copy £2.50, per year £10.

3248 ERGONOMICS. 1957.
Taylor & Francis Ltd., (for the Ergonomics Research Society), 10-14 Macklin St., London, WC2B 5NF.
6, ‡ = + *   Deals with human factors in work, machine control and equipment design.
Abstracts, book notices, book reviews, monographic articles.
A, In last issue of volume, Yes, None.
March 1972, T.p. 115.
Per copy £2.75, per year £14.
Indexed in: BTI.

3249 ERGONOMICS ABSTRACTS. 1969.
Taylor & Francis Ltd., 10-14 Macklin St., London, WC2B 5NF.
4, ‡ = +   Abstracts of current literature in psychology, physiology, bio-mechanics and engineering relevant to work.
Abstracts.
A, In last issue of volume, Yes, None.
No. 1, 1972, T.p. 91.
Per copy £4.50, per year £16.

658.58

MAINTENANCE ENGINEERING

3250 CLEANING & MAINTENANCE: building maintenance, restoration, renovation, cleaning, sanitation, hygiene. 1952.
Turret Press Ltd/Turret Press (Holdings) Ltd., 157 Hagden Lane, Watford, WD1 8LW.
12, ‡ =
Book reviews, articles.
No Index.
May 1972, T.p. 26, Ad.p. 26.
Per copy 43p, per year £6.15.

3251 MAINTENANCE ENGINEERING. 1962.
(Plant and Factory Maintenance Engineering 1961; Plant and Factory Maintenance 1956-1960).
Factory Publications Ltd., 89 Blackfriars Road, London, SE1.
12, = ‡ Electrical and mechanical engineering, pneumatics, fluidics, hydraulics etc.
Book reviews, legal notes, letters, monographic articles, news, new products, patents, standards, tests.
A, December, Yes, None.
T.p. 30, Ad.p. 44.   19000.
Per copy 50p, per year £5.
Free, controlled circulation.

658.7

PURCHASING

3252 PURCHASING JOURNAL. 1954.
Institute of Purchasing & Supply, York House, Westminster Bridge Road, London, SE1.
12, = Purchasing, materials management, storage control etc.
Book reviews, commodity prices, legal notes, letters, new products, standards.
A, January, No, None.
T.p. 40, Ad.p. 50.   11500.
Free to members.

658.8

MARKETING

3253 EUROMONITOR REVIEW. 1968.
Euromonitor Publications Limited, 125 Pall Mall, London, SW1.
6, + Marketing conditions, prospects and consumer behaviour in Europe as a whole, with a special focus on comparative data in the main economic blocks and throughout various countries.
Commodity prices, monographic articles, new companies, new products, obituaries, reports.
No Index.
October 1971, T.p. 43.
Per copy £4, per year £30.

3254 EUROPEAN JOURNAL OF MARKETING: reporting current research, theory and practice. 1971.
(British Journal of Marketing 1968-71).
Mercury House Business Publications Ltd., Mercury House, Waterloo Road, London, SE1 8UL.
4, + = Original research in marketing. For the formally educated in marketing, provides the opportunity for continued refreshment of knowledge required in study. For those whose education in marketing was provided primarily by experience, the journal affords the framework for the further interpretation and development of that experience.
Book notices, book reviews, monographic articles.
A, Issue No. 4 each volume, Yes, 5 year.
Spring 1972, T.p. 68.
Per copy £2, per year £7.

3255 EUROPEAN MARKETING DATA AND STATISTICS. 1961.
Euromonitor Publications Limited, 125 Pall Mall, London, SE1.
1, + Data on geographic demographic, industrial production, consumption and trade conditions of all Western European countries in a standardised and comparative format.
Commodity prices, monographic articles, new companies, new products, obituaries.
No Index.
T.p. 130.
Per copy £20.

3256 EXPORT TIMES: the independent journal of international marketing. 1970.
Cobb-Thornton Publishing Ltd., 60 Fleet Street, London, EC4.
12, =
Book reviews, commodity prices, legal notes, letters, articles, new companies, new products, parliamentary reports.
No Index.
May 1972, T.p. 32, Ad.p. Most.
Per year £5 and Free, controlled circulation.

3257 HAVERING CONSUMER GROUP MAGAZINE.
The Group, c/o 97 Woodfield Drive, Romford, Essex.
4, ○
News.
No Index.
T.p. 15.
Free to members.

3258 INCENTIVE MARKETING. 1961.
Maclaren Publishers Ltd., PO Box 109, 69/77 Davis House, High Street, Croydon, CR9 1QH.
12, ‡ = Latest premium offers, competitions, manufacturers' coupon schemes, trading stamps, and retail and dealer premiums and incentives. An annual Buyer's Guide and Directory lists premium suppliers, promotion consultants and ancillary services.
Book notices, book reviews, commodity prices, legal notes, letters, articles, new companies, new products, obituaries, parliamentary reports.
No Index.
June 1972, T.p. 16, Ad.p. 19.   3802.
Per copy 25p, per year £2.50.

3259 INTERNATIONAL JOURNAL OF PHYSICAL DISTRIBUTION. 1970.
MCB (Physical Distribution Management) Limited, 200 Keighley Road, Bradford, BD9 4J2.
6, ‡ + New developments in the pattern of management of marketing logistics and distribution systems; retailing and wholesaling.
Book reviews, Register of Research, monographic articles.
A, –, Yes, 5 year.
T.p. 104, Ad.p. 5.   1500.
Per copy £3.95, per year £13.95.

3260 INTERNATIONAL TAX-FREE TRADER AND DUTY-FREE WORLD. 1972.
International Trade Publications Ltd., John Adam House, 17/19 John Adam Street, London, WC2.
4, = Every international airport and ship's shop; every airline—whether scheduled or charter—having an in-flight shop; all major shops in tax-free areas of the world. Also ship terminals.
Book notices, book reviews, commodity prices, legal notes, letters, articles, new companies, new products, obituaries, patents, standards, tests.
No Index.
No. 1, 1972, T.p. 37, Ad.p. 28.   3500.
Per copy £1, per year £4.

3261 MARKETING: Monthly Journal of the Institute of Marketing. 1924.
Haymarket Press Ltd.(for Institute of Marketing), Gillow House, 5 Winsley Street, London, W1N 8AP.
12, ‡ = + *   Principles and practice of marketing. Features on techniques including advertising, market research, selling, within the framework of marketing as a total business concept.
Book notices, book reviews, letters, monographic articles, new products, obituaries, standards.
A, January, Yes, None.
June 1972, T.p. 32, Ad.p. 32.   20000.
Per copy 37½p, per year £5.
Free to members.

3262 MARKETING AND DISTRIBUTION ABSTRACTS. 1971.
(Part of Anbar Management Services, previously included in Anbar Management Services Abstracts, 1961-1971).
Anbar Publications Ltd., P.O. Box 23, Wembley, HA9 8DJ, (in association with the Institute of Marketing).
8, ‡ = + *   Abstracts from British and overseas publications of articles of interest to marketing and distribution managers.
Abstracts, book notices.
6m, After 4th and 8th issues, Yes, A binder is included, A.
31 May 1972, T.p. 23.
Per year £20.
For fuller service apply for others.

3263 MARKETING IN EUROPE. 1962.
The Economist Intelligence Unit Ltd., Spencer House, 27 St. James's Place, London, SW1A 1NT.
12, ‡ = +   Similar in purpose, scope and appeal to Retail Business, but covers markets in the major European countries.
A, Approx. June, Yes, None.
T.p. 50.
Per copy £9, per year £60.

3264 MINTEL: Market Intelligence. 1972.
Maclaren Publishers Ltd., P.O. Box 109, Davis House, 69/77 High Street, Croydon CR9 1QH.
12, ‡ +   Market reports on five areas of consumer marketing and a new product review. The markets covered include food, drink and tobacco, cosmetics, household and automotive products, and consumer durables.
Monographic articles.
No Index.
June 1972, T.p. 48.
Per copy £6, per year £60.

3265 NIELSEN RESEARCHER. 1960.
A.C. Nielsen Company Limited, Nielsen House, Headington, Oxford, OX3 9RX.
6, ‡ = +   Brief comments on aspects of marketing and marketing research.
A, December, No, None.
May-June 1972, T.p. 8.   5500.
Free.

3266 SALES ENGINEERING: Journal of the Institution of Sales Engineers. 1971.
(Sales Engineer 1969-1972).
ISE Publications Ltd., Queensway, Royal Leamington Spa, Warwicks.
12, * =   Industrial selling and marketing matters; proceedings of the Institution of Sales Engineers.
Book notices, book reviews, legal notes, letters, monographic articles, new companies, new products, obituaries, standards, tests.
No Index.
June 1972, T.p. 25, Ad.p. 6.   12000.
Per copy 25p, per year £3.
Free to members.

3267 SELLING. 1955.
Stuart Thomson Ltd., 1 Tahara Lodge, Lubbock Road, Chislehurst, Kent.
12, =   Industrial sales techniques and methods.
Book reviews, articles, news, new products.
No Index.
T.p. 6, Ad.p. 2.
Per copy 15p, per year £1.80.

3268 SELLING TODAY. 1968.
(On the Road 1883-1967).
United Commercial Travellers Association, Bexton Lane, Knutsford, Cheshire, WA16 9DA.
12, * =   Salesmanship in practice.
Book notices, book reviews, legal notes, letters, articles, new products, obituaries, parliamentary reports, patents, standards, tests.
No Index.
July 1972, T.p. 30, Ad.p. 6.   28000.
Per year £2, and Free to members.

658.87

RETAIL MARKETING

3269 DO IT YOURSELF RETAILING. 1961.
Link House Publications Ltd., Link House, Dingwall Avenue, Croydon, Surrey, CR9 2TA.
12, =   The do-it-yourself magazine for the do-it-yourself retail trade. Regular news of new products.
Book reviews, commodity prices, letters, articles.
No Index.
T.p. 24, Ad.p. 24.   11500.
Free, controlled circulation.

3270 INSIGHT. 1972.
Housewives Trust, 4th Floor, Bedford Chambers, Covent Garden, London WC2E 8HA.
6, ○ =   Information on price-changes, packaging, cost and comparisons, new products and new marketing methods.
No Index.

3271 THE INSPECTOR. 1938.
Institute of Shops Acts Administration, Shops and Other Acts Dept., Guildhall, London, EC2.
12, ‡ =   Safety, health, welfare, working conditions.
Book reviews, legal notes, letters, articles, obituaries, parliamentary reports, standards, tests.
A, January, Yes, None.
March 1970, T.p. 14.   380.
Per year £2.50

3272 INTERNATIONAL VENDING TIMES: Food Service News. 1970.
(Vending Times 1967-1969).
Weald of Kent Publications (Tonbridge) Ltd., 3 Castle Street, Tonbridge, Kent.
12, =   All types of automatic merchandising machinery, vendible products, ingredients, and allied equipment including disposables. Methods of operating, marketing and servicing machines. Food, and methods of food preparation for automatic and manual canteen service.
Book reviews, letters, new products.
No Index.
7500.
Per copy 30p, per year £3.50.

3273 RETAIL BUSINESS. 1958.
The Economist Intelligence Unit Ltd., Spencer House, 27 St. James's Place, London, SW1A 1NT.
12, ‡ = +   Covers the UK market for consumer goods. Special reports provide detailed profiles of consumer goods markets. A Retail Trade Review discusses the year's development in a specific retail outlet type.

A, Approx. June, Yes, None.
T.p. 55.
Per copy £7, per year £55.

3274 SELF SERVICE TIMES AND MODERN MARKETING. 1957.
Arthur Heighway Publications Ltd., 110 Fleet Street, London, EC4.
12, = ‡   Grocery and allied trades in self service and supermarket field.
Book reviews, letters, articles, new companies, news, new products.
No Index.
T.p. 15, Ad.p. 12.   11178.
Per copy 15p, per year £2.25.
Free, controlled circulation.

3275 THE TRADER: Incorporating Credit Trader, Small Trader and Wholesaler, Shopkeeper and Retail Trader, Surplus Stocks Advertiser, The Retailer, Small Trader and Shopkeeper, Wholesalers Gazette, Management and Buying, Export Record, Retail Credit, Consumer Credit. 1969.
(Small Trader and Wholesaler 1932-1969).
City Magazines, Aldwych House, 81 Aldwych, London WC2B 4HL.
12, =   Retailers of all types including market traders and factory agents, wholesalers of consumer goods and importers, mail order firms, manufacturers.
Commodity prices, legal notes, letters, new companies, new products, patents, standards.
No Index.
July 1972, T.p. 200, Ad.p. 194.   20000.
Per copy 10p, per year £2.40.

3276 VENDING. 1958.
NC Magazines Ltd., 172 Kingston Road, Ewell, Surrey.
12, =   Automatic vending.
No Index.
T.p. 20, Ad.p. 10.   9500.
Free, controlled circulation.

658.883

CREDIT MANAGEMENT

3277 CREDIT MANAGEMENT: Journal of the Institute of Credit Management. 1964.
(Transactions 1950-1964).
Institute of Credit Management, 3 Berners Street, London, W1.
6, * =   All matters dealing with the work of the Credit Executive and the Institute in general.
Book reviews, letters, monographic articles.
No Index.
June/July 1972, T.p. 24, Ad.p. 6.   2000.
Per copy 12½p, per year 75p and Free to members.

659

PUBLICITY

3278 THE COMMUNICATOR OF TECHNICAL INFORMATION: The Communicator. 1968.
(the Bulletin of The Institute of Technical Publicity & Publications', 1965-1968).
The Institute of Technical Publicity and Publications Ltd., c/o 17 Bluebridge Avenue, Brookmans Park, Hatfield, Herts.
4, *   Technical publications and/or publicity departments in engineering and other manufacturing firms, scientific research and development departments, Government technological departments and establishments, educational establishments.
Abstracts, book notices, book reviews, legal notes, letters, monographic articles, new products, standards, tests.
No Index.
May, 1972, T.p. 12, Ad.p. 1.   1600.
Free to members and Per copy 50p, per year £2.

659.1

ADVERTISING

3279 ADMAP. 1964.
ADMAP Publications Limited, 273a Kings Road, London, SW3.
11, ‡ = +   Advertising, market and media research people working in advertising agencies, advertiser companies and market research companies.
Book notices, book reviews, letters, monographic articles, new products, tests.
None.
May 1972, T.p. 24, Ad.p. 14.   4693.
Per copy £1, per year £5.

3280 ADVERTISEMENT PARADE: Facts through ads. 1955.
(AP International Research 1958-1968).
Visual Publications Ltd., 32 Liverpool Road, Worthing, Sussex.
11, = +   Reproductions (reduced 4:1) of advertisements from some 40 countries, classified by product groups. Also photographs of posters, also on an international basis.
No Index.
11.7.72, T.p. 72.
Per copy £4.50, per year £36.

3281 ADVERTISERS WEEKLY. 1913.
Admark Publishing Co. Ltd., Mercury House, 103/119 Waterloo Road, London, SE1.
52, = ‡ +   Advertising and marketing.
Book reviews, legal notes, letters, new companies, news, new products, parliamentary reports, standards.
No Index.
T.p. 30, Ad.p. 38.   13500.
Per copy 15p, per year £8.

3282 ADVERTISING AND MARKETING. 1967.
Business Expansion Ltd., 54 The Grove, London, W5.
6, = ‡ +   Case histories in advertising and marketing.
No Index.
T.p. 40, Ad.p. 15.   5000.
Per year £2. Free, controlled circulation.

3283 ADVERTISING AND MARKETING MANAGEMENT: official journal of the Incorporated Advertising Managers' Association. 1964.
Advertising Management Ltd., 348 Grays Inn Road, London WC1.
12, =   Marketing and communications.
Monographic articles, news.
No Index.
T.p. 20, Ad.p. 12.   4500.
Per copy 50p, per year £4. Free, controlled circulation.

3284 ADVERTISING QUARTERLY. 1964.
Advertising Association, 1 Bell Yard, London, WC2.
4, = ‡ +   Advertising in all respects.
Book notices, book reviews, monographic articles, parliamentary reports.
No Index.
T.p. 50, Ad.p. 10.
Per copy 75p, per year £2.50.

3285 ADVERTISING STATISTICAL REVIEW. 1968.
(Statistical Review 1932-1968).
Legion Publishing Co. Ltd., 25 Breams Buildings, London, EC4.
12, = ‡   Statistics from 200 product groups.
New products.
No Index.
T.p. 50.
Subscription on application.

3286 BRITISH DIRECT MAIL ADVERTISING ASSOCIATION NEWSLETTER. 1971.
110 St. Martins Lane, London, WC2.
12, =
No Index.
Free to members.

3287 BRITISH RATE AND DATA. 1954.
Maclean-Hunter Ltd., 30 Old Burlington Street, London, W1X 2AE.
12, =   Facts and figures for the advertising industry.
No Index.
T.p. 444, Ad.p. Most.   4509.
Per copy £4, per year £14.

3288 EXCHANGE & MART. 1868.
Link House Publications Ltd., PO Box 154, Pembroke House, Wellesley Road, Croydon, CR9 2BX.
52, ○ ‡ =   Classified and mail order advertising.
No Index.
22-28 June 1972, Ad.p. 160.   341507.
Per copy 5p, per year £6.76.

3289 INDUSTRIAL ADVERTISING AND MARKETING. 1964.
Admark Publishing Co. Ltd., Mercury House, Waterloo Road, London, SE1.
12, = ‡
Book reviews, letters, monographic articles, news, parliamentary reports.
No Index.
T.p. 29, Ad.p. 21.   3600.
Per copy 52½p, per year £5.

3290 MEAL MONTHLY DIGEST. 1967.
Media Expenditure Analysis Ltd., 66 Dean Street, London, W1.
12, +   Advertising expenditure details in press and TV for approx. 10,000 products.
No Index.

3291 PERISCOPE: a look around the world of publicity in the North East. 1964.
North East Publicity Association, c/o Repro Services Ltd., 17 Portland Terrace, Newcastle upon Tyne, NE2 1SJ.
4, * =   Publicity and advertising.
Book notices, book reviews, letters, articles, new products, parliamentary reports.
No Index.
Autumn 1971, T.p. 22, Ad.p. 10.   1500.
Free.

659.113.2

MARKET RESEARCH

3293 EVAF NEWSLETTER. 1966.
EVAF Secretariat, 39/40 St. James's Place, London, SW1.
c. 5, *   Announcements and reports of events and courses run by EVAF and its component Divisions. Membership news and amendments. News of events organised by other bodies of interest to market researchers.
No Index.

3294 HANDYMAN WHICH? 1971.
Consumers' Association, 14 Buckingham Street, London, WC2N 6DS.
4, + = ○   All tools, print, laminated plastics, wood and basic supplies such as screws.
Commodity prices, articles, new companies, new products, tests.
A, —, No, None.
May 1972, T.p. 60.   2000.
Per copy 60p, per year £4.

3295 INDUSTRIAL MARKETING RESEARCH ABSTRACTS. 1969.
Industrial Marketing Research Association, Leomansley House, Lichfield, Staffs.
2, = +
Abstracts.
A, —, Yes, None.
T.p. 50.
£3 members £5 non-members.

3296 IMRA JOURNAL. 1963.
Industrial Marketing Research Association, Leomansley House, Lichfield, Staffs.
4, = ‡ +
Book reviews, monographic articles.
No Index.
T.p. 50.   1000.
Per copy 50p, per year £1.50.
Free to members.

3297 JOURNAL OF THE MARKET RESEARCH SOCIETY. 1969.
(Commentary 1959-1968).
Market Research Society, 51 Charles Street, London, W1X 7PA.
4, + ‡ = *   Technical advances and practical applications, appraisals of specific problem areas and correspondence, news items and reviews in the broad field of market and social research.
Book notices, book reviews, letters, monographical articles.
A, January, Yes, None.
April 1972, T.p. 54, Ad.p. 2.   3100.
£3 per year and Free to members.

3298 MARKET RESEARCH ABSTRACTS. 1964.
Market Research Society, 51 Charles Street, London, W1X 7PA.
2, + ‡ = *   Research, statistics, psychology and sociology, economics, marketing advertising and business management. Sections comprise: survey techniques; statistics modelling and forecasting; attitude and behaviour research; psychology; communication; applications of research; general applications.
Abstracts.
6m, With each issue, No, None.
250.
£5. £2.50 to members of MRS.

3299 MARKET RESEARCH GERMANY/ITALY/BENELUX. 1971.
Euromonitor Publications Ltd., 125 Pall Mall, London, SW1.
6, +   During the year every important aspect of consumer markets in each of these three journals is examined in detail, providing vital information not elsewhere available.
Commodity prices, monographic articles, new companies, new products, obituaries, reports.
No Index.
T.p. 35.
Per copy £2.50, per year £15 per country.

3300 MARKET RESEARCH GREAT BRITAIN. 1961.
Euromonitor Publications Limited, 125 Pall Mall, London, SE1.
12, +   Covers full range of consumer markets in Great Britain exclusively.
Commodity prices, monographic articles, new companies, new products, obituaries, reports.
No Index.
T.p. 35.
Per copy £3, per year £20.

Key to reference symbols

○ popular   ‡ technical   = trade/professional

+ research   * society/institution   † house journal

3301 MONEY WHICH? 1968.
Consumers' Association, 14 Buckingham Street, London, WC2N 6DS.
4, + = Covers saving and investments, insurance, taxation, borrowing and money services. It aims to produce a magazine which will make financial subjects clear to the layman.
Commodity prices, legal notes.
A, —, No, None.
December. 1971, 60.   408000.
Per copy 60p, per year £4.

3302 MOTORING WHICH? 1962.
Consumers' Association, 14 Buckingham Street, London, WC2N 6DS.
4, + = Testing the performance of cars.
Commodity prices, new products, standards, tests.
A, —, No, None.
January 1972, T.P. 60.   306000.
Per copy 60p, per year £4.

3303 THE NEWSLETTER OF CARDIFF AND DISTRICT CONSUMER GROUP. 1970.
Cardiff and District Consumer Group, c/o Chairman, 7 Bryngwyn Road, Cyncoed, Cardiff.
6, * ○ Any topic of interest to consumers.
No Index.
March/April 1972, T.p. 3.
Free to members.

3304 OXFORD CONSUMER. 1962.
Oxford Consumers' Group, 11 Cooper Place, Headington Quarry, Oxford, OX3 8JW.
4, ○ Shops and consumer services in Oxford, Abingdon, Witney and surrounding districts.
Reports of surveys, projects, etc.
No Index.
June 1972, T.p. 26.   c. 1200.
Per year £1.

3305 SHEFFIELD CONSUMER. 1963.
Sheffield Consumer Group, 548 Loxley Road, Loxley, Sheffield, S6 6RT.
3, ○ + Projects on consumer items, e.g. food shop hygiene, TV rentals, Deep freezers etc.
Commodity prices, letters, tests.
No Index.
c. 200.
Per year 60p.

3306 TARGET. 1968.
Winchester Consumer Group, Secretary, Mrs. S. Cope, 10 Hubert Road, Winchester, Hants.
4, ○ * Items of consumer interest, with particular reference to local conditions.
Commodity prices, letters, new products, standards, tests.
No Index.
January 1971, T.p. 20.   250.
Per copy 15p, per year £1 (inc. membership of Group)

3307 VALUE: Southend-on-Sea Consumer Group News. 1967.
(Southend-on-Sea Consumer Group News. 1963-1967).
Southend-on-Sea Consumer Group, 501 Sutton Road, Southend-on-Sea, SS2 5PR.
4/5, + = Surveys of local services, amenities, shops etc. Consumer complaints. Reports of meetings. Shopping advice. Articles of consumer education.
Commodity prices, legal notes, letters, articles.
When possible, usually December or January, No, None.
No. 1, 1972, T.p. 6.
Per year 80p.

3308 WHICH? 1957.
Consumers' Association, 14 Buckingham Street, London, WC2N 6DS.
12, + * ○ Testing of consumer durables and some consumer services.
Commodity prices, new products, tests.
A, —, No, None.
March 1972, T.p. 30.   600000.
Per copy 30p, per year £2.50.

659.15

DISPLAYS. EXHIBITIONS

3309 BDS NEWS: British Display Society. 1969.
(News Sheet).
British Display Society, Alderman House, 37 Soho Square, London, W1Y 5DG.
2/4, = * ‡ Display and related subjects; items of general interest to professional display designers.
Book notices, book reviews, letters, articles, new products, obituaries.
No Index.
T.p. 5.   2000.
Free to members.

3310 CONFERENCES AND EXHIBITIONS AND EXECUTIVE TRAVEL. 1954.
TTG Publications Ltd., Adelphi, John Adam Street, London, WC2.
12, =
No Index.
Per year £1.50.

3311 DISPLAY INTERNATIONAL: Journal of commercial presentation. 1970.
(Display 1919-1970)
Blandford Publications Ltd, 167 High Holborn, London, WC1V 6PH.
12, = New products and installation in the field of display and commercial decor. Coverage includes all aspects of window display, merchandising, point of sale and exhibition presentation.
Book notices, book reviews, letters, articles, new companies, new products, obituaries.
No Index.
May 1972, T.p. 10, Ad.p. 10.   18824.
Per copy 20p, per year £3.50.

3312 EXHIBITION BULLETIN. 1949.
The London Bureau, 266-272 Kirkdale, Sydenham, London, SE26 4RZ.
12, = + * Exhibition listings on a world geographical basis, giving dates, title, venue and organisers' addresses with cross-reference via classified index. Advance information up to four years.
No Index.
June 1972, T.p. 63, Ad.p. 13.   3523.
Per copy £1, per year £4.25.

66

INDUSTRIAL CHEMISTRY

3313 BULLETIN OF THE INSTITUTE OF SCIENCE TECHNOLOGY. 1954.
Institute of Science Technology, 66 Seggart Terrace, Aberdeen, AB1 5UD.
12, ‡ * Institute news, courses, etc.
No Index.
T.p. 10, Ad.p. 6.   4500.
Free to members.

3314 CHEMICAL AGE INTERNATIONAL. The International Chemical News Weekly. 1972.
(Chemical Age 1919-1972).
Benn Brothers Limited, 25 New Street Square, London, EC4A 3JA.
51, ○ ‡ Up-to-date news coverage of the international chemical manufacturing and marketing industries: chemical plant contracting and chemical engineering.
Book notices, book reviews, commodity prices, legal notes, letters, articles, new companies, new products,

obituaries, parliamentary reports, patents, standards.
No Index.
July 21, 1972, T.p.17, Ad.p.6.   5216.
Per copy 25p, per year £13.
Indexed in: BTI.

3315 CHEMICAL COMMUNICATIONS. 1965.
Chemical Society, Burlington House, Piccadilly, London, W1V 0BN.
26, ‡ =
No Index.
6666.
Per year £2.50.

3316 CHEMICAL INSIGHT: Mike Hyde's Perspective on the International Chemical Industry. 1972.
M. C. Hyde, 44 The Keep, London, SE3 0AF.
24, = ‡ +   For those who need to know the thinking behind decisions, to know how events may affect profits or an independent analysis of trends and developments.
News, short articles.
A, —, Yes, None.
T.p. 8.
Per year £75.

3317 CHEMICAL PROCESSING. 1954.
Engineering Chemical & Marine Press Ltd., 33-39 Bowling Green Lane, London, EC1.
12, ‡   Chemistry in the chemical and processing industries.
Book notices, book reviews, letters, monographic articles, new products.
No Index.
T.p. 40, Ad.p. 40.   16000.
Free, controlled circulation.
Indexed in: BTI.

3318 CHEMISTRY & INDUSTRY. 1923.
(Journal of the Society of Chemical Industry, 1881-1923).
Society of Chemical Industry, 14 Belgrave Square, London, SW1X 8PS.
24, ‡ = + *   The Society's news journal, covering the broader aspects of the chemical industry. Includes original papers and communications, statistical and commercial surveys, notes on new laboratory methods and apparatus.
Book notices, book reviews, letters, monographic articles, new companies, new products, obituaries, parliamentary reports, patents, standards, tests.
A, December, Yes, None.
1-1-1972, T.p.44, Ad.p. 22.   9713.
Per copy 50p, per year £12. and Free to members.
Indexed in: BTI.

3319 EUROPEAN CHEMICAL NEWS. 1962.
Engineering Chemical & Marine Press Ltd., 33-39 Bowling Green Lane, London, EC1.
52, = ‡ +   Chemical industry and Europe.
Book reviews, commodity prices, monographic articles, new companies, news, new products, obituaries, patents, standards.
Q, Month after end of quarter, Yes, None.
T.p. 22, Ad.p. 26.   7681.
Per copy 22½p, per year £12.

3320 JACB. 1970.
(Journal of Applied Chemistry 1950-70.)
Academic Press Ltd. (for Society of Chemical Industry), 14 Belgrave Square, London, SW1.
12, + ‡ *   Research papers on subjects and techniques of interest to applied chemists, chemical and process engineers and manufacturers of microbiological products.
Abstracts, book notices, book reviews, monographic articles.
A, —, No, None.
March 1972, T.p.148, Ad.p. 1.   2300.
Per year £20.

3321 JOURNAL OF APPLIED CHEMISTRY AND BIO-TECHNOLOGY. 1971.
(Journal of Applied Chemistry, 1951-1970)
Society of Chemical Industry (by Academic Press), 14 Belgrave Square, London, SW1X 8PS.
12, ‡ = +   Chemical and allied industries including fermentation technology, enzymic and other biochemical processes.
Monographic articles, new products, patents, standards, tests.
A, December, Yes, None.
May 1972, T.p. 94, Ad.p. 1.   2600.
Per year £20.

3322 JOURNAL OF THE RAMSAY SOCIETY OF CHEMICAL ENGINEERS (University College, London. 1953.
Ramsay Society of Chemical Engineers, University College, Gower Street, London, WC1.
1, * = ‡ +
Monographic articles, news, obituaries, tests.
No Index.
T.p. 61, Ad.p. 12.
Free to members.

3323 MANUFACTURING CHEMIST & AEROSOL NEWS. 1964.
(Manufacturing Chemist 1930-1963, Chemical Products & Aerosol News 1962-1963, Chemical Products 1938-1962).
Morgan-Grampian Publishers) Ltd., Morgan-Grampian House, Calderwood St, London SE18 6QH.
12, ‡ =   Technical and marketing information for manufacturers of pharmaceuticals, cosmetics and toiletries, soaps and detergents, polishes, household chemicals (bleaches, disinfectants, etc), pesticides, fungicides, herbicides, veterinary products, automotive chemical products, fine chemicals and intermediates.
Book notices, book reviews, letters, monographic articles, new products, obituaries.
No Index.
June 1972, T.p. 32, Ad.p. 42.   4000+.
Per copy £1, per year £6 UK.

66.01

CHEMICAL ENGINEERING

3324 CHEMICAL ENGINEER AND TRANSACTIONS OF THE INSTITUTION OF CHEMICAL ENGINEERS. 1964.
(Transactions of the Institution of Chemical Engineers, 1923-1963).
The Institution, 16 Belgrave Square, London, SW1.
10, * ‡ + =   Chemical engineering in general.
Book reviews, legal notes, letters, monographic articles, news, new products, obituaries, standards, tests.
A, December, Yes, None.
T.p. 80, Ad.p. 15.   10200.
Free to members.
Indexed in: BTI.

3325 CHEMICAL ENGINEERING COMMUNICATIONS. 1972.
Gordon & Breach, 41/42 William 4th Street, London, WC2.
6, + ‡   Chemical engineering, applied chemistry and related fields.
Monographic articles.
A, —, No, None.
Subscription on application.

3326 CHEMICAL ENGINEERING JOURNAL: the journal of Loughborough University of Technology Chemical Engineering Dept. 1965.
Dept. Chemical Engineering, University of Technology, Loughborough, Leics.
1, ‡ + = †   Research on chemical engineering and associated topics with the university dept. (includes process control and particle technology.)
Monographic articles.

3327   CHEMICAL ENGINEERING SCIENCE. 1951.
Pergamon Press Ltd., Headington Hill Hall, Oxford, OX3 0BW.
12, = +   Scientific aspects of chemical engineering.
Book reviews, letters, monographic articles.
A, Last issue of volume, Yes, None.
T.p. 125,
Per copy £4.50, per year £48.
Indexed in: BTI.

3328   PROCESS ENGINEERING incorporating Chemical and Process Engineering.
Morgan Grampian Ltd., Calderwood Street, London, SE16 6QH.
12, ‡ = +   Chemical and allied industries, food, drink, tobacco, soaps, paint, plastics, rubber, coal, petroleum etc.
Book reviews, letters, monographic articles, new companies, new products, tests.
No Index.
June 1972, T.p. 66, Ad.p. 66.   17250.
Per copy £1, per year £10 and Free, controlled circulation,
Indexed in: BTI.

3329   PROCESS TECHNOLOGY INTERNATIONAL. 1972.
(British Chemical Engineering, 1956-1972).
IPC Industrial Press Ltd., 33 Bowling Green Lane, London, EC1R 0NE.
12, = ‡ +   Techniques of chemical engineering as applied to industry.
Book reviews, monographic articles.
A, —, Yes, None.
Per copy 50p, per year £4.50.
Indexed in: BTI.

3330   THEORETICAL CHEMICAL ENGINEERING ABSTRACTS. 1964.
Theoretical Chemical Engineering Abstracts, PO Box No. 146, Liverpool, L69 2BL.
6, ‡ + *   Current abstracts of world-wide published scientific and technical literature in chemical engineering and subsidiary subjects.
Abstracts, book notices.
A, February of year following completion of volume, Yes, None.
May/June 1971, T.p. 36.
Subscription on application.

66.046

THERMAL PROCESSES

3331   INDUSTRIAL AND PROCESS HEATING. 1961.
Factory Publications, 89 Blackfriars Road, London, SE1.
12, ‡ + =   Process heating of metal, plastics, brick and tile, cement and lime, glass, new methods and equipment.
Book reviews, monographic articles, news, new products.
No Index.
T.p. 42, Ad.p. most.   10500.
Per copy 50p, per year £5.
Free, controlled circulation.

66.083

PRESSURE VESSELS

3332   PRESSURE VESSELS AND PIPING. 1973.
Applied Science Publishers Ltd., Ripple Road, Barking, Essex.

4, +   Presents current developments in all aspects of the technologies associated with the design, manufacture, inspection, operations and maintenance of pressure vessels and similar components, and of related topics as applied to gas containers, piping and pipelines.
Book reviews, monographic articles.
A, January, Yes, None.
Subscription on application.

661.21

SULPHUR

3339   ORGANIC COMPOUNDS OF SULPHUR, SELENIUM, AND TELLURIUM (Specialist Periodical Reports). 1971.
The Chemical Society, Burlington House, London, W1V 0BN.
2 year, +   A biennial critical review of the literature on the subject.
Monographic articles.
2 year, —, Yes, None.
1970, T.p. 494.
Per copy £11.

3340   SULPHUR: incorporating Journal of World Sulphur. 1953.
British Sulphur Corporation, Parnell House, 25 Wilton Road, London, SW1.
6, ‡ =   Sulphur and sulphuric acid production, consumption, trade, transportation, technical developments, prices and industry outlook.
Book reviews, commodity prices, legal notes, monographic articles, new companies, new products, patents, standards, tests.
A, mid-year, Yes, None.
Jan/Feb 1972, T.p. 45, Ad.p. 15.
Per copy £7, per year £42.

661.63

PHOSPHORUS

3341   ORGANOPHOSPHORUS CHEMISTRY: (specialist Periodical Reports). 1970.
The Chemical Society, Burlington House, London, W1V 0BN.
1, +   An annual critical review of the literature on organophosphorus compounds and their derivatives.
Monographic articles.
A, —, Yes, None.
1971, T.p. 303.
Per copy £7.

3342   PHOSPHORUS & POTASSIUM.
British Sulphur Corp., 25 Wilton Road, London, SW1V 1NH.
6, = ‡   Worldwide manufacture and distribution of phosphate and potash fertilizers, chemicals and raw materials.
Book reviews, commodity prices, monographic articles, new companies, new products.
A, Varies, Yes, None.
T.p. 44, Ad.p. 10.
Per year £42.

661.938

NITROGEN

3343   NITROGEN. 1959.
British Sulphur Corp., 25 Wilton Road, London, SW1.
6, ‡ = +   All aspects of the nitrogen fertilizer industry, including technical products. Regular sections appear covering production, usage and trade, supported by comments on the international developments of price trends, manufacture and freight rates.

Book reviews, commodity prices, monographic articles, new companies, new products, patents, standards, tests.
A, Mid year, Yes, None.
T.p. 38, Ad.p. 14.
Per year £42.

662.536

MATCH BOXES

3344 B.P.S. MAGAZINE.
(Phillumatch 1964-1970).
British Phillumatic Society, 16 Santley House, Baylis Road, London, SE1 7RD.
6, *   Matchcover collecting, B.P.S. Magazine is general; 'aich' is specially for collectors of Hilton Hotel matchcovers; 'Lantern' is specially for Holiday Inn matchcover collectors. 'Target' for 'County Seat' matchcover collectors.
News and brief notes.
No Index.
July/August 1972, T.p. 8.
Free to members.

662.6

FUEL TECHNOLOGY

3345 C.U.C. NEWS. 1956.
Coal Utilisation Council, 19 Rochester Row, London, SW1P 1LD.
6, ‡ = + * †   Solid fuel domestic heating, giving information about Head Office, Regional and allied activities. Articles on technical training and information are included.
Book reviews, legal notes, letters, articles, new companies, new products, obituaries, parliamentary reports, standards, tests.
No Index.
February 1972, T.p. 4.   21250.
Free.

3346 COKE AND CHEMISTRY U.S.S.R.: organ of the Ministry of Ferrous Metallurgy of the USSR and the Central Board of the Scientific-Technical Society of Ferrous Metallurgy. 1959, No. 8.
Coal Tar Research Association, Oxford Road, Gomersal, Clekheaton, Yorks. BD19 4HH
12, ‡ + =   Coal carbonisation and the recovery and refining of the by-products of coking. Current advances in Russian coking technology. Translation of Koks i Khimiya.
Abstracts, book notices, book reviews, commodity prices, letters, monographic articles, new products, obituaries, patents, standards, tests.
A, With No. 12 of each year, Yes, None.
No. 11, 1971, T.p. 59.
Per copy £2.60, per year £20.70.

3347 COKE REVIEW: A quarterly guide to published material of interest to the coking industry. 1952.
British Coke Research Association, Chesterfield, Derbyshire, S42 6JS.
4, ‡   Preparation, properties, testing and uses of solid fuels, particularly metallurgical coke; by-products of carbonisation; carbon science.
Abstracts.
A, bound with issue no. 4, Yes, None.
July-Sept. 1971, T.p. 54.   c. 600.
Per copy 50p, per year £2.

3348 COMBUSTION & FLAME. 1957.
Butterworth & Co. Ltd., 88 Kingsway, London, WC2.
6, = ‡
Abstracts, book notices, book reviews, commodity prices, legal notes, letters, monographic articles, new companies, new products, obituaries, parliamentary reports, patents, standards, tests.
A, —, Yes, None.
Per year £9.
Indexed in: BTI.

3349 COMBUSTION SCIENCE AND TECHNOLOGY. 1969.
Gordon & Breach, 41/42 William 4th Street, London, WC2.
6, ‡ +   Flame and fire research, flame radiation, chemical fuels and propellants, reacting flows, thermochemistry, atmospheric chemistry and combustion phenomena related to aircraft gas turbines, chemical rockets, ramjets, automotive engines, furnaces and environmental studies.
Book notices, book reviews, letters, monographic articles, new products, tests.
6m, At close of each volume, No, c. 2 year.
Subscription on application.

3350 ENERGY DIGEST. 1972.
(The Journal of Fuel and Heat Technology 1952-1972; Fuel Efficiency).
Turret Press Ltd., Turret Press (Holdings) Ltd., 157 Hagden Lane, Watford, WD1 8LW.
6, ‡ +
Book notices, book reviews, new products, patents, standards, tests.
No Index.
Per year £7.

3351 FUEL: a journal of fuel science. 1948.
(Fuel in Science & Practice 1922-1947).
Iliffe Science & Technology Publications Ltd., 32 High Street, Guildford.
4, = ‡   Fuel science including materials—relates to fuels and combustion in general.
Book notices, book reviews, letters, monographic articles, news, obituaries, patents, standards, tests.
A, October, No, None.
T.p. 96, Ad.p. 3.
Per year £10.
Indexed in: BTI, IBZ.

3352 FUEL ABSTRACTS AND CURRENT TITLES. 1960.
(Fuel Abstracts 1947-1958).
Institute of Fuel, 18 Devonshire Street, London, W1N 2AV.
12, ‡ +   All aspects of fuel technology.
Abstracts.
A, Mid year, Yes, None.
T.p. 136.
Per year £22.

3353 JOURNAL OF FUEL & HEAT TECHNOLOGY. 1952.
Turret Press Ltd., 65-66 Turnmill Street, London, WC1.
6, ‡ +
No Index.
Per year £6.
Indexed in: BTI.

3354 JOURNAL OF THE INSTITUTE OF FUEL. 1926.
Institute of Fuel, 18 Devonshire Street, London, W1.
12, * ‡ +   Fuel technology in general.
Monographic articles, news, book reviews.
A, —, Yes, None.
T.p. 35, Ad.p. 40.   7370.
Per copy £1, per year £10.50.
Free to members.
Indexed in: BTI.

3355 NEW DOMESTIC APPLIANCES. 1967.
Coal Utilisation Council, 19 Rochester Row, London, SW1P 1LD.
6, = ‡   Advice on new equipment and correct fuel.
New companies, new products, patents, standards, tests.
No Index.
January 1968, T.p. 4.   21250.
Free.

662.62

COAL TECHNOLOGY

3356 SOLID FUEL incorporating Coal Merchant and Shipper. 1966.
(O'Connels Coal and Iron 1890; Coal and Appliances Digest 1951-1965).
Harper Trade Journals Ltd., South Bank House, Black Prince Road, London, SE1.
26, ‡ =   All aspects of solid fuel distributive trade.
New products, parliamentary reports, news, articles.
No Index.
T.p. 19, Ad.p. 13.
Per copy 15p, per year £2.50.

662.76

GAS TECHNOLOGY

3357 DOMESTIC GAS. 1972.
(Gas Showroom 1954-1971).
Benn Brothers Limited, 25 New Street Square, London, EC4A 3JA.
12, ‡   Devoted to the promotion of sales and services of all gas appliances used in the home. Also the official medium of the Confederation for the Registration of Gas Installers.
Book notices, book reviews, legal notes, letters, articles, new companies, new products, obituaries, parliamentary reports, patents, standards, tests.
A, –, No, None.
July 1972, T.p. 24, Ad.p. 20.   9300.
Per copy 20p, per year £3.

3358 GAS IN INDUSTRY. 1958.
W. King Ltd., 100 Grays Inn Road, London, WC1.
12, ‡   Promotion of use of gas in industrial processes.
No Index.
5600.

3359 GAS MARKETING AND DOMESTIC GAS.
(Gas Marketing).
Benn Bros. Ltd., Lyon Tower, 125 High Street, Colliers Wood, London, SW19.
12, = ‡   Household gas appliances in industry and trade.
Commodity prices, articles, new products.
No Index.
T.p. 55p.
Per copy 20p, per year £2.

3360 GAS SERVICE. 1922.
W. King Ltd., 100 Grays Inn Road, London, WC1.
12, = ‡   Gas sales, domestic and commercial. Gas engineering.
No Index.
4168.

3361 GAS WORLD.
Benn Brothers Limited, 25 New Street Square, London, EC4A 3JA.
51, ‡   News coverage of the world's gas industry. Fuel policy, new techniques, development and research and covers the whole technological field of gas supply and manufacture.
Book reviews, letters, articles, new companies, new products, obituaries, patents.
6m, July/January, No, None.
15 July 1972, T.p. 15, Ad.p. 9.   2850.
Per copy 15p, per year £7.50.
Indexed in: BTI, IBZ.

3362 INDUSTRIAL & COMMERCIAL GAS. 1928.
Benn Brothers Ltd., 25 New Street Square, London, EC4A 3JA.
12, ‡   Research and development in the industrial and commercial gas field.
Book notices, book reviews, letters, monographic articles, new companies, new products, obituaries, standards, tests.
6m, January/June, Yes, None.
July 1972, T.p. 17, Ad.p. 17.   7250.
Per year £1.50.
Indexed in: BTI.

3363 JOURNAL OF THE INSTITUTION OF GAS ENGINEERS. 1960.
(Transactions of the Institution of Gas Engineers 1863-1959).
The Institution of Gas Engineers, 17 Grosvenor Crescent, London, SW1.
12, * ‡ + =   Engineering as applied to the gas industry
Book notices, monographic articles, new products, obituaries, patents, standards, tests.
A, December, Yes, None.
5500.
Per copy 50p, per year £6.
Indexed in: BTI.

3364 NATURAL GAS & LPG. 1967.
Scientific Surveys Ltd., 11A Gloucester Road, London, SW7.
6, = ‡
No Index.
5200.
Per year £2.50.
Free, controlled circulation.

3365 SCOPE. 1967.
(Commentary 1945-1966).
Women's Gas Federation, 29 Great Peter Street, London, SW1.
4, ○ *   Use of gas in the home.
Book reviews, letters, news, new products, obituaries.
No Index.
T.p. 40, Ad.p. 6.   17500.
Per copy 9p, per year 35p.

663.1

ALCOHOLIC BEVERAGES

3366 FREE TRADE REVIEW AND CLUB MANAGEMENT. 1959.
Independent Trade Press Ltd., Wheatsheaf House, Carmelite Street, London, EC4.
10, =   Free licensed catering trade.
No Index.
T.p. 24, Ad.p. Most.   12000.
Per year £1.
Free, controlled circulation.

3367 IRISH LICENSING WORLD.
Jemma Publications Ltd., Richardson House, Main Street, Blackrock, Co. Dublin.
No Index.
Per copy 12½p.

3368 THE LICENSED VINTNER: official journal of the Irish Licensed Trade. 1934.
L.V.A. Centre, Anglesea Road, Ballsbridge, Dublin, 4.
9, = *   Licensing trade in Ireland.
Commodity prices, legal notes, letters, articles, new companies, new products.
No Index.
May 1972, T.p. 10, Ad.p. 10.   5598.
Per year £1.50.

3369 LICENSEE. 1966.
The Morning Advertiser, 18-20 St. Andrew Street, London, EC4.
12, =   News Sheet of the licensing trade.
No Index.
June 1972, T.p. 9, Ad.p. 3.   35000.
Per copy 5p, per year 80p.

3370 LONDON PUBS. 1971.
8 Charing Cross Road, London, WC2.

12, ○
No Index.
Per copy 20p.

3371 NATIONAL GUARDIAN. Scotland's top selling licensed trade weekly. 1881.
Munro Barr Publications, 94 Hope Street, Glasgow C2.
52, = Aspects of the licensing trade wherever applicable.
Legal notes, articles, new companies, new products.
No Index.
T.p. 14, Ad.p. 7.   4000.
Per copy 2½p, per year £1.75.

3372 OFF-LICENCE JOURNAL. 1921.
1 Dorset Buildings, London, EC4.
12, = Trade news, sales techniques, window display.
No Index.
7000.
Per year £1.

3373 OFF LICENCE NEWS. 1970.
(Wine & Spirit Trade Review 1863-1969).
William Reed Ltd., 19 Eastcheap, London, EC3.
52, = Weekly newspaper for off license holders covering all aspects of the drink trade.
Book notices, commodity prices, legal notes, letters, new companies, new products, obituaries, parliamentary reports, patents, standards, tests.
No Index.
June 29 1972, T.p. 12, Ad.p. 3.   18243.
Per copy 5p, per year £3.

3374 SCOTTISH LICENSED TRADE NEWS. 1964.
IPC Consumer Industries Press Ltd., Dorset Buildings, Salisbury Sq., London, EC4.
51, =
Book notices, legal notes, letters, articles, new companies, new products, obituaries, standards.
No Index.
June 16, 1972, T.p. 16, Ad.p. Most.   10544.
Free, controlled circulation.

663.2

WINES

3375 ABOUT WINE. 1971.
36-38 Southampton Street, London, WC2E 7HE.
12, ○ =
No Index.
Per year £1.80.

3376 HARPERS WINE AND SPIRIT GAZETTE. 1885.
Harper Trade Journals, Black Prince Road, London, SE1.
52, = Wine and spirit news.
Book reviews, letters, articles, new companies, new products.
No Index.
T.p. 16, Ad.p. 40.   3500.
Per year £8.

3377 RIDLEYS WINE & SPIRIT TRADE CIRCULAR. 1848.
Ridleys Ltd., Wheatsheaf House, Carmelite Street, London, EC4.
12, = All aspects of wine and spirit production and distribution and allied trades.
Book reviews, commodity prices, legal notes, letters, articles, new companies, news, new products, obituaries, patents.
No Index.
T.p. 37, Ad.p. 35.   3650.
Per year £3.15.

3378 WINE AND FOOD. 1933.
Wine & Food Publications Ltd., 1 Hanover Square, London, W1.
6, = ○

Book notices, book reviews, monographic articles.
No Index.
T.p. 56, Ad.p. 26.
Per copy 17½p, per year £1.50.

3379 WINE AND SPIRIT TRADE INTERNATIONAL. 1972.
(Wine and Spirit Trade Record 1874-1972).
Haymarket Publishing Limited, Gillow House, 5 Winsley Street, London, W1.
12, = All aspects of the wine and spirit trade.
Book reviews, commodity prices, letters, articles, new companies, new products, obituaries, tests.
No Index.
July 1972, T.p. 53, Ad.p. 43.
Per copy 50p, per year £3.50.

3380 WINE-BUTLER. 1955.
Harper Trade Journals Ltd., 22 Cousin Lane, London, EC4.
12, = Wines and their service.
No Index.

3381 WINE MAGAZINE. 1958.
Wines & Spirit Publications Ltd., Victoria House, Southampton Row, London, WC2.
6, = ○ Growing and drinking wine.
A, —, Yes, None.
Per copy 15p, per year £1.10.

3382 WINE MINE. 1959.
Peter Dominic Ltd., 12 York Gate, London, NW1.
2, = ○ Wines, wine tasting and making.
No Index.
T.p. 140, Ad.p. 20.   150000.
Per copy 10p.
Free from Dominic wine shops.

663.4

BREWING

3383 THE BEERMAT MAGAZINE. 1960.
The British Beer-mat Collectors Society, 142 Leicester Street, Wolverhampton, Staffs, WV6 0PS.
12, * ○ Brewery history, take-overs, closures, etc. Details of new mat printings. Illustrations of old mats. Tips for collectors. Formation of local groups. News from such groups.
Commodity prices, letters, articles, new products.
No Index.
June 1972, T.p. 26, Ad.p. 2.   600.
Per copy 5p, per year 60p.
Non-members 90p per year.

3384 THE BREWER. 1971.
(Brewers' Guild Journal 1950-1970, Journal of Incorporated Brewers' Guild 1930-1949, Journal of the Operative Brewers' Guild 1914-1929).
Brewers' Guild Publications Ltd., 8 Ely Place, London, EC1N 6SD.
12, ‡ * = Science of brewing.
Abstracts, book notices, book reviews, legal notes, letters, monographic articles, new companies, new products, obituaries.
A, January, Yes, None.
February 1972, T.p. 39, Ad.p. 27.
Per copy 35p, per year £4.

3385 BREWERS' GUARDIAN. Incorporating International Brewer and Distiller. 1871.
Northwood Publications Ltd., (Thomson Organisation Ltd.), Northwood House, 93-99 Goswell Road, London, EC1V 7QA.
12, ‡ = Latest scientific and technical advances in brewing and malting, together with market information appointments and new plant and materials.
Book reviews, legal notes, letters, monographic articles, new companies, new products, obituaries.

A, December, No, None.
June 1972, T.p. 34, Ad.p. 54.   3000.
Per copy 25p, per year £3.

3386 BREWING REVIEW: official journal of the Brewers Society. 1972.
(Brewing Trade Review 1886-1972).
Brewing Publications Ltd., 19 Briset Street, London, EC1.
12, = + ‡ *   Brewing and allied trades.
Book reviews, legal notes, letters, articles, new companies, new products, patents, standards, tests.
A, January, Yes, None.
T.p. 96, Ad.p. 40.
Per copy 20p, per year £2.50.

3387 BULLETIN OF CURRENT LITERATURE. 1952.
Brewing Industry Research Foundation, Nutfield, Redhill, Surrey.
12, = ‡ +   Literature on malting, brewing and allied fields.
Book notices, new products, patents, standards.
No Index.
Free to members.

3388 INTERNATIONAL BREWING & DISTILLLNG. 1971.
(Brewers Journal 1865-1966, International Brewers Journal 1967-1970).
William Reed Ltd., 19 Eastcheap, London, EC3.
12, ‡ =   A technical paper for all the brewery and distilling trade. Head Brewer Distiller. Transport etc. all aspects of brewing and distilling.
Abstracts, letters, monographic articles, new companies, new products, obituaries, parliamentary reports, patents, standards, tests.
No Index.
June 1972, T.p. 29, Ad.p. 27.   5500.
Per copy 25p, per year £3.

3389 JOURNAL OF THE INSTITUTE OF BREWING. 1901.
(Journal Federated Institute of Brewing 1896-1900; Transactions of the Institute of Brewing 1891-1895; Transactions of the Laboratory Club 1887-1890).
The Institute of Brewing, 33 Clargos Street, London, W1.
6, ‡ +   Scientific background to malting and brewing, with emphasis on raw materials and their transformation.
Abstracts, book notices, book reviews, letters, monographic articles, obituaries.
A, February, No, 10 year.
March/April 1972, T.p. 112, Ad.p. 36.   3500.
Per copy £2, per year £15.
Indexed in: BTI.

663.6

SOFT DRINKS

3390 SOFT DRINKS TRADE JOURNAL. 1947.
(Mineral Water Trade Journal-1888-1946).
National Association of Soft Drinks Manufacturers Ltd., The Gatehouse, 2 Holly Road, Twickenham, TW1 4EF.
12, =   Soft drinks topics—at home and abroad—details of new plant and machinery.
Book reviews, legal notes, letters, articles, new products, obituaries, parliamentary reports.
No Index.
June 1972, T.p. 28, Ad.p. 39.   3000.
Per copy 25p, per year £3.

663.91

COCOA

3391 ALLIANCE JOURNAL: Journal of the Cocoa, Chocolate and Confectionery Alliance. 1948.
The Cocoa, Chocolate and Confectionery Alliance, 11 Green Street, London, W1Y 3RF.
12, =   Interests of Alliance members in the field of sales. Emphasis on statistical information.
Commodity prices, legal notes, monographic articles, obituaries, parliamentary reports.
A, January, No, None.
May 1972, T.p. 12, Ad.p. 2.   1200.
Free to members.

3392 COCOA GROWERS' BULLETIN. 1963.
Cadbury Limited, Bournville, Worcs.
2, ‡ =   All aspects of cocoa growing and research from field to market. Brief surveys of production and consumption.
Abstracts, book reviews, letters, monographic articles.
2 yearly, —, Yes, None.
September 1971, T.p. 44.
Free.

663.93

COFFEE

3393 COFFEE NEWS. 1950.
Coffee Promotion Council Ltd., 10 Eastcheap, London, EC3.
3/4, * =   Coffee prices and import statistics.
Articles, news, new products, obituaries, tests.
No Index.
Free, controlled circulation.

663.97

TOBACCO

3394 TOBACCO. 1881.
International Trade Publications Limited, John Adam House, 17-19 John Adam Street, London, WC2N 6JH.
12, =   All matters relating to the UK tobacco industry.
Book notices, book reviews, commodity prices, legal notes, letters, monographic articles, new companies, new products, obituaries, parliamentary reports, patents, standards, tests.
No Index.
January 1972, T.p. 37, Ad.p. 51.   6097.
Per copy 25p, per year £3, (includes copy of Tobacco Year Book and Smokers' Handbook).

3395 TOBACCO INTELLIGENCE. 1948.
Commonwealth Secretariat, Marlborough House, Pall Mall, London, SW1Y 5HX.
12, = +   Statistics of exports, production etc.
Commodity prices.
A, January, Yes, None.
June 1972, T.p. 23.
Per year £6.

3396 WORLD TOBACCO. 1963.
International Trade Publications Ltd., John Adam House, 17-19 John Adam Street, London, WC2N 6JH.
4, = ‡   All matters relating to tobacco manufacture and distribution on an international level, including marketing of tobacco leaf and machinery.
Book notices, book reviews, commodity prices, legal notes, letters, monographic articles, new companies, new products, obituaries, patents, standards, tests.
No Index.
Dec. 1971/Jan. 1972, T.p. 47, Ad.p. 79.   3359.
Per copy £1.30, per year £5.20.

664

FOOD TECHNOLOGY

3397 BFMIRA ABSTRACTS. 1947.
The British Food Manufacturing Industries, Research Association, Randalls Road, Leatherhead, Surrey.

12, + ‡ = * Abstracts are taken from current scientific and technical literature of interest to the food manufacturing industry, including technological developments in: food processing, analytical and microbiological quality control, packaging and storage, plant and machinery, and effluent treatment.
Abstracts, patents.
A, January/February, No, None.
June 1972, T.p. 83.   1200.
Per year £50.

3398 FMF REVIEW; incorporating Food World: Official journal to the Food Manufacturers' Federation. 1972.
Turrett Press Ltd., 65/66 Turnmill Street, London, EC1M 5RA.
12, = * Reports the activities of the Food Manufacturers' Federation, —work of committees together with exclusive technical and general features.
Abstracts, book reviews, legal notes, letters, monographic articles, new companies, obituaries, parliamentary reports, patents, standards, tests.
No Index.
May 1972, T.p. 16, Ad.p. 16.
Per year £4.90.

3399 BRITISH FOOD JOURNAL. 1898.
Peterson Publishing Co. Ltd., Peterson House, Livery Street, Birmingham 3.
6, = + ‡ Food quality control, hygiene, and food technology in general.
Book notices, book reviews, legal notes, letters, articles, new companies, news, new products, parliamentary reports, patents, standards, tests.
A, November/December, Yes, None.
T.p. 29, Ad.p. 2.
Per copy 50p, per year £2.75.

3400 FOOD AND DRINK WEEKLY.
Maclaren Publishers, P.O. Box 109, 69/77 Davis House, High Street, Croydon, CR9 1QH.
52, = Provides directors, operational managers and executives with news of product research and development, quality control, production and distribution, marketing, plant maintenance in the food, soft drink, brewing and spirit distilling manufacturing and processing industries.
Book notices, commodity prices, legal notes, articles, new companies, new products, obituaries, parliamentary reports, patents.
No Index.
June 23rd 1972, T.p. 12, Ad.p. 3.   10139.
Per year £3.50, and Free, controlled circulation.

3401 FOOD MANUFACTURE. 1927.
Morgan-Grampian Ltd., 28 Essex Street, London, WC2.
12, ‡ Technical developments in processing and handling of food.
Book notices, book reviews, letters, monographic articles, new companies, new products, obituaries, patents, standards, tests.
No Index.
June 1972, T.p. 42, Ad.p. 42.   5000.
Per copy £1, per year £10 and free, controlled circulation.
Indexed in: BTI, IBZ.

3402 FOOD SCIENCE AND TECHNOLOGY ABSTRACTS. 1969.
International Food Information Service, Farnham Royal, Slough, Bucks, SC2 3BN.
12, + = ‡ World food science and related literature.
Abstracts.
M, —, Yes, A.
T.p. c. 40.
Per year £100.

3403 FOOD TRADE REVIEW. 1939.
(Food Industries Review—1933-1939; Food Canning Preserving & Selling 1931-1938).
Food Trade Review Ltd., 7 Garrick Street, London, WC2E 9AT.
12, = Food manufacturing, processing and food packing.
Book notices, book reviews, letters, articles, new companies, new products, obituaries, patents, standards, tests.
A, December, No, None.
June 1972, T.p. 43, Ad.p. 49.   4767.
Per copy 60p, per year £5.
Indexed in: BTI.

3404 JOURNAL OF FOOD TECHNOLOGY: Institute of Food Science and Technology (U.K.). 1966.
Blackwell Scientific Publications, Osney Mead, Oxford, OX2 0EL.
4, + * = ‡ Pure research in the various sciences associated with food to practical experiments designed to improve technical processes. Reviews of specialized sections of food science or technology also included.
Book reviews, monographic articles.
A, December, Yes, None.
March 1972, T.p. 109, Ad.p. 3.   2160.
Per copy £2.50, per year £9.

3405 JOURNAL OF THE SCIENCE OF FOOD AND AGRICULTURE. 1950.
(Part of Journal of the Society of Chemical Industry, 1881-1950).
Academic Press (for Society of Chemical Industry), 24-28 Oval Road, London, NW1 7DX.
12, ‡ + = Food including chemistry, flavour, nutritive value, keeping quality, preparation etc. Agriculture including crops, fertilisers, annual husbandry, feeding stuffs, soils.
A, December, Yes, None.
May 1972, T.p. 130.   2330.
Per copy £2, per year £20.
Indexed in: BTI.

3406 SEED. 1972.
8A All Saints Road, London, W11.
○ For those interested in food eaten and the environment.
No Index.

664.1

SUGAR

3407 INTERNATIONAL SUGAR JOURNAL. 1899.
(The Sugar Cane 1869-1898).
The International Sugar Journal Ltd., 23A Easton Street, High Wycombe, Bucks.
12, ‡ + = Agriculture, chemistry and engineering of sugar production from beet and cane, raw sugar refining and by-products utilization as well as some background economic information on sugar as a commodity.
Book reviews, letters, new products, obituaries, patents, tests.
A, December, Yes, None.
June 1972, T.p. 32, Ad.p. 25.   3300.
Per copy 40p, per year £3.
Indexed in: BTI, IBZ.

3408 SUGAR REVIEW.
C. Czarmikow Ltd., Sugar Production Brokers, Plantation House, Mincing Lane, London, EC3.
=
No Index.

Key to reference symbols

○ popular   ‡ technical   = trade/professional

+ research   * society/institution   † house journal

664.14

CONFECTIONERY

3409 CONFECTIONERY AND TOBACCO NEWS. 1962.
(Confectionery News 1937-1961).
IPC Consumer Industries Press Ltd., 33-39 Green Lane, London, EC1.
26, =   Retailing of confectionery and tobacco.
Book reviews, legal notes, letters, new companies, news, new products, obituaries, parliamentary reports.
No Index.
T.p. 8, Ad.p. 8.   15280.
Per copy 5p, per year £1.50.

3410 RETAIL CONFECTIONER. 1927.
Retail Confectioners Association Publications & Exhibitions Ltd., 53 Christchurch Avenue, London, N12.
12, =
No Index.
Per copy 7½p, per year £1.10.

3411 THE TRIPLE TRADER: Confectioner, tobacconist, stationer.
Maclaren Publishers, P.O. Box 109, 69/77 Davis House, High Street, Croydon CR9 1QH.
24, =   Case studies of how traders have improved turnover and profitability by modernisation and the use of modern business methods. It includes trade news and describes new products, promotions and campaigns.
Commodity prices, legal notes, articles, new companies, new products, obituaries, parliamentary reports.
No Index.
June 15th 1972, T.p. 15, Ad.p. 10.   25948.
Per year £2.

3412 WHOLESALE CONFECTIONER. 1952.
Aldridge Press Ltd., 7 Queen Square, Brighton.
12, =
No Index.
Per copy 12½p, per year £2.

664.6

BAKERY

3413 BAKERS' REVIEW. 1956.
(National Association Review 1887-1955).
National Association of Master Bakers, Queen's House, Holly Road, Twickenham, Middx.
51, = ‡ +   Baking industry in general.
No Index.
T.p. 19, Ad.p. 25.   6700.
Per copy 6p.

3414 BAKERY MANAGEMENT: incorporating The Baker. 1971.
(The Baker 1877-1970).
Retail Journals Ltd., John Adam House, 17/19 John Adam Street, London, WC2N 6JH.
12, ‡ = + *   Bakery managers and owners of craft bakery businesses; manufacturers of raw ingredients; suppliers of equipment and machinery; educational centres; (teachers); makers of packaging materials and machinery; transport services, etc.
Book notices, book reviews, commodity prices, legal notes, letters, monographic articles, new companies, new products, obituaries, parliamentary reports, standards, tests.
No Index.
June 1972, T.p. 20, Ad.p. 20.
Per copy 25p, per year £2.50.

3415 BAKING INDUSTRIES JOURNAL: incorporating Biscuit Maker and Plant Baker. 1968.
Maclaren Publishers Ltd., P.O. Box 109, 69/77 Davis House, High Street, Croydon CR9 1QH.
12, ‡ = *   Information on new machines, processing techniques and materials, product marketing and promotions, technical conferences, packaging innovations, city and commodity news.
Book notices, commodity prices, legal notes, monographic articles, new companies, new products, obituaries, parliamentary reports.
A, January, No, None.
June 1972, T.p. 29, Ad.p. 32.   2317.
Per copy 30p, per year £3.50.

3416 THE BRITISH BAKER. 1887.
Maclaren Publishers, P.O. Box 109, 69/77 Davis House, High Street, Croydon CR9 1QH.
52, =   New processes, ingredients, equipment, current trade prices, tax matters, marketing techniques and the activities of bakery trade associations and research establishments.
Commodity prices, legal notes, letters, articles, new companies, new products, obituaries, parliamentary reports, patents, standards, tests.
No Index.
June 23rd 1972, T.p. 25, Ad.p. 39.   11596.
Per copy 6p, per year £3.50.

3417 MASTER BAKER. 1908.
114 Somerton Road, Belfast, BT15 4DG.
12, =   Bakery and confectionery in Ireland.
No Index.
T.p. 5, Ad.p. 5.
Per year 50p.

3418 WHEAT FLOUR BREAD. 1968.
The Flour Advisory Bureau, 21 Arlington Street, London, SW1A 1RN.
2, ○ ‡   Flour and its use in broadest context.
Receipes, articles, news.
No Index.
Spring 1972, T.p. 12.
Free

664.7

MILLING

3419 FLOUR MILLING AND BAKING RESEARCH ASSOCIATION ABSTRACTS. 1967.
(British Baking Industries Research Association Abstracts. 1948-1966).
Flour Milling and Baking Research Association, Chorleywood, Rickmansworth, Herts, WD3 5SH.
6, ‡ = +   Literature on flourmilling, baking and allied trades: indicative abstracts.
Abstracts.
A, January, No, None.
T.p. 53.   c. 1600.
Per year £15.75.

3420 FLOUR MILLING & BAKING RESEARCH ASSOCIATION BULLETIN. 1967.
(Research Association of British Flour-Millers Bulletin 1924-1947; British Baking Industries Research Association Bulletin 1948-1966).
Flour Milling & Baking Research Assoc., Chorleywood, Rickmansworth, Herts, WD3 5SH.
6, ‡ = +   Reports news and results of the Research Association's research work on flour-milling and baking, to members of the R.A.
Book notices, legal notes, letters, articles, new products, obituaries, parliamentary reports, patents, standards, tests.
A, December, No, None.
T.p. 32.   c. 1800.
Free to members only.

3421 THE GAZETTE. 1963.
Flour Milling and Baking Research Assn., Chorleywood, Rickmansworth, Herts, WD3 5SH.
12, ‡ +   Review of current literature on flour-
milling and allied topics.
Book reviews, abstracts, commodity prices, legal
notes, letters, new products, obituaries, parliamentary reports, patents, standards, tests.
A, January, No, 5 year.
T.p. 4.   500.
Per year £15.75.

3422 MILLING: international journal of the flour and feed
industries. 1891.
(Milling Flour & Feed).
Turret Press Ltd/Turret Press (Holdings) Ltd., 157
Hagden Lane, Watford, WD1 8LW.
12, =   Flour milling, feeding stuffs and compound
manufacturing industries.
Book reviews, letters, articles.
No Index.
June 1972, T.p. 28, Ad.p. 28.
Per year £9 including yearly International Milling &
Feed Manual.

664.8

PRESERVATION TECHNOLOGY

3423 CANNING AND PACKING. 1953.
(Canning Industry and Packing Trades Gazette 1931-
1952).
Canning Publications, 28 Monument Street, London,
EC3.
6, = + ‡   Canning, processing and packing of food
products. History of food preservation.
Book notices, book reviews, commodity prices, letters,
monographic articles, new companies, news, new
products, standards, tests.
No Index.
T.p. 13, Ad.p. 3.
Per copy 17½p, per year £1.
Indexed in: BTI.

3424 FOOD PROCESSING INDUSTRY. 1969.
(Food Processing & Marketing 1964-1969).
IPC Consumer Industrial Press Ltd., 40 Bowling
Green Lane, London, EC1.
12, ‡   Processing of edible foods in U.K.
Book reviews, letters, articles.
No Index.
T.p. 30, Ad.p. 40.   7000.
Per year £6.
Indexed in: BTI.

3425 FROZEN FOODS: monthly journal of the frozen and
allied food industries. 1948.
(Quick Freezing).
Retail Journals Ltd., (Industrial Newspapers Group),
17/19 John Adam Street, London, WC2.
12, = + ‡   Production, wholesaling and distribution
of frozen foods and allied subjects.
Book notices, book reviews, commodity prices, legal
notes, letters, monographic articles, new companies,
news, new products, parliamentary reports, patents,
standards, tests.
No Index.
T.p. 20, Ad.p. 32.
Per copy 20p, per year £2.50. Controlled circulation.
Indexed in: BTI.

3426 JOURNAL OF STORED PRODUCTS RESEARCH.
1965.
Pergamon Press Ltd., Headington Hill Hall, Oxford,
OX3 0BW.
4, + =   Laboratory and field studies on pests of
stored products.
Book reviews, monographic articles.
A, Last issue of volume, Yes, None.
T.p. 100, Ad.p. 4.
Per copy £4, per year £15.

665.5

PETROLEUM TECHNOLOGY

3427 AD MAGAZINE. 1961.
Sono Strips Ltd., (For Shell-Mex and B.P. Ltd.).,
49B Station Road, Edgware HA8 7HX, Middx.
4, ○ ‡ = †   Oil and oil products.
Book reviews, letters, monographic articles, obituaries.
No Index.
Spring 1972, T.p. 20.   4000.
Free.

3428 THE BULLETIN: quarterly Journal of the Association
for Petroleum Acts Administration. 1965.
c/o Teeside Fire Brigade Headquarters, Park Road
South, Middlesbrough, Teesside, TS5 6LG.
4, ‡ =   All aspects concerning conveyance, storage
and safe handling of petroleum spirit and all substances coming within the scope of the Petroleum
(Consolidation) Act 1928 and its associated legislation. Articles and information are published from
members of the oil industry and those concerned
with enforcement of safety legislation.
Legal notes, letters, monographic articles, new products, obituaries, parliamentary reports, patents,
standards, tests.
A, January, No, None.
April 1972, T.p. 40.   1000.
Per year £1.50 and Free to members.

3429 INSTITUTE OF PETROLEUM ABSTRACTS. 1969.
(Formerly incorporated with Journal of the Institute
of Petroleum).
Institute of Petroleum, 61 New Cavendish Street,
London, W1M 8AR.
4, ‡   Abstracts of petroleum literature worldwide.
Abstracts.
A, —, Yes, None.
March 1972, T.p. 85.   3500.
Per year £4.

3430 JOURNAL OF THE INSTITUTE OF PETROLEUM.
1938.
(Journal of the Institution of Petroleum Technologists,
1914-1937).
Institute of Petroleum, 61 New Cavendish Street,
London, W1M 8AR.
6, ‡ +   Petroleum science and technology.
Book notices, book reviews, letters, monographic
articles, obituaries, standards, tests.
A, —, Yes, None.
May 1972, T.p. 56.   7000.
Per copy 75p, per year £3.50.
Indexed in: BTI.

3431 OIL AND PETROCHEMICAL EQUIPMENT NEWS.
1963.
(British Petroleum Equipment News 1959-1962).
Council of British Manufacturers of Petroleum
Equipment, 118 Southwark Street, London, SE1.
4, ‡ =   Equipment manufactured in UK and other
developments.
Book notices, book reviews, articles, new products,
obituaries, parliamentary reports, patents,
standards, tests.
No Index.
T.p. 36, Ad.p. 36.   2850.
Free to members.
Indexed in: BTI.

3432 PETROLEUM CHEMISTRY USSR [Selected paper
from 'Neftekhimiya']. 1969.
Pergamon Press Ltd., Headington Hill Hall, Oxford,
OX3 0BW.

4, = + ‡   Chemistry of petroleum fractions and the use of petroleum as a base for the manufacture of industrial chemicals.
Monographic articles.
A, Last issue of volume, Yes, None.
Per copy £15, per year £56.

3433 PETROLEUM REVIEW. 1968.
(Institute of Petroleum Review, 1946-1967).
Institute of Petroleum, 61 New Cavendish Street, London W1M 8AR.
12, ○ ‡ * †   News and features relating to the petroleum industry in general.
Book notices, book reviews, letters, monographic articles, new products.
A, —, Yes, None.
May 1972, T.p. 42, Ad.p. 22.   7250.
Per copy 30p, per year £3.
Indexed in: BTI, IBZ.

3434 PETROLEUM TIMES. 1899.
Engineering Chemical & Marine Press Ltd., 33-39 Bowling Green Lane, London, EC1.
26, ‡   International petroleum industry.
No Index.
7300.
Per copy 27½p, per year £7.
Indexed in: BTI.

666.1

GLASS TECHNOLOGY

3435 GLASS. 1923.
Fuel & Metallurgical Journals Ltd., John Adam House, 17-19 John Adam Street, London, WC2.
12, = ‡ +
Monographic articles, news, new products, patents.
A, —, Yes, None.
T.p. 14, Ad.p. 16.
Per copy 25p, per year £3.
Indexed in: BTI.

3436 GLASS AGE: architectural, application, design, construction. 1958.
Blandford Press Ltd., 167 High Holborn, London, WC1V 6PH.
4, = ‡   Architectural application of modern flat glass construction, its framing, fixing, mastic, sealant and gasket techniques. Decorative glass. Trade and association news and products.
Book reviews, letters, monographic articles, new companies, new products, obituaries.
No Index.
May 1972, T.p. 26, Ad.p. 32.   5080.
Per copy 25p, per year £1.25.

3437 THE GLASS CIRCLE. 1972.
Oriel Press Ltd., 32 Redley Place, Newcastle-on-Tyne, NE1 8LH.
= ○ ‡   Papers from meetings of the Circle of Glass Collectors.
Per copy £2.25.

3438 GLASS JOURNAL.
Fuel & Metallurgical Journals Ltd., John Adam House, 17/19 John Adam Street, London, WC2N 6JH.
12, = ‡   All new developments, processes and products in the industry.
Book reviews, commodity prices, new products, patents.
No Index.
2000.
Per copy 30p, per year £3.60.

3438A GLASS TECHNOLOGY. 1960.
(Journal of the Society of Glass Technology 1917-1959).
Society of Glass Technology, Thornton, Hallam Gate Road, Sheffield, S10 5BT.
6, ‡ *   All aspects of the technology of the making of glass and the production of glass wear, and news of the Society.
Abstracts, book notices, book reviews, letters, monographic articles, obituaries, patents, standards, tests.
A, December, Yes, None.
December 1971, T.p. 36, Ad.p. 24.   2251.
Per copy £2.25, per year £12.50. Joint Subscription with Physics & Chemistry of Glasses £20.

3438B JOURNAL OF THE BRITISH SOCIETY OF SCIENTIFIC GLASSBLOWERS. 1964.
British Society of Scientific Glassblowers, c/o 53a Kennel Ride, Ascot, Berks.
4, ‡ + = † *
Book notices, book reviews, letters, monographic articles, new products, obituaries, tests.
4 year, —, No, None.
T.p. 35, Ad.p. 14.   700.
Per copy 50p, per year £1.80.

3438C PHYSICS & CHEMISTRY OF GLASSES. 1960.
(Journal of the Society of Glass Technology 1917-1959).
Society of Glass Technology, Thornton, Hallam Gate Road, Sheffield, S10 5BT.
6, + *   Original studies of the physics and chemistry of glasses both experimental and theoretical.
Abstracts, book notices, book reviews, letters, monographic articles, patents, standards, tests.
A, December, Yes, None.
December 1971, T.p. 44.   2143.
Per copy £2.25, per year £12.50. Joint subscription with Glass Technology £20.

666.25

STAINED GLASS

3439 JOURNAL OF THE BRITISH SOCIETY OF MASTER GLASS PAINTERS. 1929.
The Society, 6 Queen Square, London, WC1.
1, = *   Activities of members and subjects likely to interest same.
Book notices, book reviews, legal notes, letters, monographic articles, obituaries.
No Index.
T.p. 40.   250.
Per copy 80p. Free to members.

666.3

CERAMICS

3440 BRITISH CERAMIC REVIEW. 1966.
British Ceramic Plant & Machinery Manufacturers Association, PO Box 9, Sunbury, Middx.
2, = + ‡   New British products and manufacturing techniques for all types of ceramic products.
Letters, articles, news, new products, tests.
A, May, Yes, None.
T.p. 15, Ad.p. 29.   6500.
Free, controlled circulation.

3441 THE BRITISH CLAYWORKER: journal of the heavy clay refractory and ceramic industries. 1892.
Turret Press, 65 Turnmill Street, London, EC1.
12, + ‡ =
Book reviews, articles.
No Index.
May 1972, T.p. 20, Ad.p. 20.
Per copy 47p, per year £6.60 includes yearly 'International Ceramic Industries Manual'.
Indexed in: BTI.

3442 CERAMIC REVIEW: The Magazine of the Craftsmen Potters Association of Great Britain. 1970.
Craftsmen Potters Association of Great Britain, William Blake House, Marshall Street, London, W1.
6, ‡ * ○   Techniques used today by the craft potter today in this country and abroad. Exhibitions of pottery and related books are reviewed. Archeological and historical articles, also the teaching of pottery.
Book reviews, letters, articles, new products, standards tests.
2 yearly, March 1972, No, None.
March-April 1972, T.p. 24, Ad.p. 3.   3000.
Per copy 30p, per year £2.

3443 CERAMICS: official journal of The British Pottery Managers' Association. 1949.
Turret Press Ltd/Turret Press (Holdings) Ltd., 157 Hagden Lane, Watford, WD1 8LW.
12, ‡ =   Pottery, heavy clay, glass, refractory and silicote industries.
Articles, news, abstracts.
No Index.
May 1972, T.p. 16, Ad.p. 16.
Per year £6.20 including yearly 'International Ceramic Industries Manual'.
Indexed in: BTI, IBZ.

3444 CLAY CRAFTS & STRUCTURAL CERAMICS: Journal of the Institute of Clay Technology. 1927.
London & Sheffield Publishing Co., 65-66 Turnmill Street, London, EC1.
12, = ‡   Manufacture of bricks, tiles, pipes, etc.
No Index.
Per copy 27½p, per year £3.
Indexed in: BTI.

3445 CLAY MINERALS: journal of the Clay Minerals Group of the Mineralogical Society. 1962.
Blackwell Scientific Publications, Osney Mead, Oxford, OX2 0EL.
2, ‡ =   Clay minerals and allied substances.
Book reviews, monographic articles.
A, —, Yes, None.
December 1971, T.p. 108.
Per copy £2.50, per year £4.

3446 CLAYS AND CLAY MINERALS. c. 1950.
Pergamon Press Ltd., Headington Hill Hall, Oxford, OX3 0BW.
6, = +   Research on the science and technology of clays.
Book reviews, monographic articles.
A, Last issue of volume, Yes, None.
Per copy £4, per year £20.

3447 IN FACT. 1954.
British Ceramic Research Association, Queens Road, Penkhull, Stoke-on-Trent.
4, †   Current activities of B.Ceram.R.A.
Book notices, book reviews, monographic articles, new companies, new products, obituaries.
A classified list of titles of articles has been issued once. (1968).
June 1969, T.p. 20.
Free to members and other selected organizations only.

3448 TABLEWARE INTERNATIONAL: incorporating Pottery Gazette. 1970.
(Pottery Gazette & Glass Trade Review 1877-1970).
International Trade Publications Ltd., 17-19 John Adam St., London, WC2.
12, = ‡   Glass, tableware, pottery and allied products.
Book reviews, letters, monographic articles, new products, obituaries.
No Index.
July 1972, T.p. 40, Ad.p. 60.   5000.
Per copy 25p, per year £3.50.

3449 REFRACTORIES JOURNAL. 1925.
London & Sheffield Publishing Co., 65-66 Turnmill Street, London, EC1.
12, ‡
No Index.
Per copy 29p, per year £3.25.
Indexed in: BTI.

3450 TRANSACTIONS & JOURNAL OF THE BRITISH CERAMIC SOCIETY incorporating British Ceramic Abstracts. 1971.
(Transactions of the British Ceramic Soc. 1900-1970; Journal of the British Ceramic Society).
The British Ceramic Society, Shelton, House, Stoke Road, Shelton, Stoke-on-Trent, ST4 2DR.
8, ‡ + = *   Research and practice on pottery, refractories and structural ceramics industries, special ceramics, raw materials and ancilliary industries: cement: plaster: ceramic colours and glazes: kilns and firing.
Abstracts, book notices, book reviews, monographic articles, new products, obituaries, patents, standards, tests.
A, As soon after year end as practicable, Yes, None.
21.6.72, T.p. 49, Ad.p. 21.   2100.
Per copy £2.50, per year £16.
Indexed in: BTI, IBZ.

3451 WEDGWOOD REVIEW. 1957.
Josiah Wedgwood & Sons Limited, Barlaston, Stoke-on-Trent, Staffs.
4, †   To promulgate information about the company, its products and employees and to maintain contact with staff members working away from the factory and as a link between the firm and its customers and to keep informed the members of Wedgwood Societies, lecturers, collectors, historians, etc.
Book reviews, new products, obituaries.
No Index.
T.p. 16.
Free.

666.924

WHITING

3452 WELWYN NEWSLETTER. 1971.
(Welwyn Newsletter 1964-1968; Welwyn Digest 1969-1970).
Welwyn Hall Research Association, Church St., Welwyn, Herts.
6, †   News of activities from research and Library. New books. Exhibitions etc. Diary. Members' news. Statistics. New products and equipment. Subject area:— Lime, Whiting, Calcium, Silicate, Bricks and related.
Abstracts, also issued separately on cards, book notices, book reviews, new products, patents, standards.
No Index.
Mar./April 1972, T.p. 21.   200.
Free, restricted circulation.

666.94

CEMENT

3453 CEMENT AND CONCRETE RESEARCH.
Pergamon Press Ltd., Headington Hill Hall, Oxford, OX3 0BW.
6, = +   Theoretical and experimental studies in the physics and chemistry of cement etc.
Book reviews, monographic articles.
A, Last issue of volume, Yes, None.
Per copy £2.50, per year £12.

3454 CEMENT, LIME & GRAVEL. 1926.
Quarry Managers Journal Ltd., 62-4 Baker Street, London, W1M 2BN.

12, ‡ Cement, lime, gravel, chalk, ready-mixed concrete and concrete products.
Articles, news, new products.
No Index.
T.p. 29, Ad.p. 42.
Per copy 15p, per year £1.75.
Indexed in: BTI.

3455 CEMENT TECHNOLOGY. 1970.
(Cement and Lime Manufacture, 1928-1969).
Cement and Concrete Association, 52 Grosvenor Gardens, London, SW1W 0AQ.
6, ‡ +   All aspects of cement manufacture from the winning of the raw materials to the final transportation of the cement.
Book notices, book reviews, letters, monographic articles, new products, standards, tests.
A, December, Yes, None.
May/June 1972, T.p. 36, Ad.p. 12.   2000.
Per copy 50p, per year £3.
Indexed in: BTI.

666.97

CONCRETE

3456 CONCRETE: The journal of The Concrete Society. 1966.
(Concrete & Constructional Engineering 1906-1965).
Cement and Concrete Association, 52 Grosvenor Gardens, London, SW1W 0AQ.
12, ‡ = + * †   Concrete in building and civil engineering.
Book notices, book reviews, letters, monographic articles, new products, obituaries, parliamentary reports, patents, standards, tests.
A, approx. December, No, None.
May 1972, T.p. 33, Ad.p. 43.   11000.
Per copy 25p, per year £3.

3457 MAGAZINE OF CONCRETE RESEARCH. 1947.
Cement and Concrete Association, Wexham Springs, Slough.
4, ‡ +
No Index.
Per year £1.
Indexed in: BTI, IBZ.

3458 PRECAST CONCRETE. 1970.
(Concrete Building and Concrete Products 1926-1969).
Cement & Concrete Association, 52 Grosvenor Gardens, London, SW1 W0AQ.
12, + = * ○ ‡   Serves management in the international precast concrete manufacturing industry. Deals with every aspect of the operation starting with the beginning of the material through every phase to the marketing of the finished product.
Book notices, book reviews, commodity prices, legal notes, letters, monographic articles, new companies, new products, obituaries, parliamentary reports, patents, standards, tests.
A, End of December or begining of January, Yes, None.
June 1972, T.p. 22, Ad.p. 35.   2272.
Per copy 25p, per year £3.

3459 STRATA: magazine of the Ready Mixed Concrete Ltd. Group of Companies. 1947.
Ready Mixed Concrete Ltd. Group of Companies, RMC House, High Street, Feltham, Middx.
2, †   Articles, products.
No Index.
Winter, 1971, T.p. 32.   16000.
Free.

3460 SUBSTRATA: journal of the Ready Mixed Concrete Ltd. Group of Companies. 1947.
Ready Mixed Concrete Ltd. Group of Companies, RMC House, High Street, Feltham, Middx.
6, †
Letters, articles, new companies, new products, obituaries, tests.
No Index.
April 1972, T.p. 8.   16000.
Free.

667.2

DYEING

3461 INTERNATIONAL DYER TEXTILE PRINTER, BLEACHER AND FINISHER. 1959.
(The Dyer, Textile Printer, Bleacher & Finisher 1879-1958).
IPC Business Press, Dorset House, Stamford St., SE1.
24, ‡ =   Dyeing and finishing sections of the textile industry.
Book notices, book reviews, articles, new companies, new products.
6m, January/July, Yes, None.
7 July 1972, T.p. 32, Ad.p. 36.   2885.
Per year £4.

3462 JOURNAL OF THE SOCIETY OF DYERS AND COLOURISTS. 1884.
Society of Dyers and Colourists, P.O. Box 244, 82 Grattan Road, Bradford, BD1 2JB.
12, ‡ + * =   All aspects of the science and technology of colour and coloration, as applied in particular to the textile industry but also in other colour-using industries, e.g. paints, inks, plastics, photography.
Abstracts, book notices, book reviews, letters, monographic articles, new products, obituaries, patents, standards, tests.
A, March, Yes, None.
May 1972, T.p. 32, Ad.p. 20.   4800.
Per year £14*
*including Annual 'Review of Progress in Coloration and Related Topics' and 'SDC News'.
Indexed in: BTI, IBZ.

3463 SDC NEWS. 1969.
Society of Dyers and Colourists, P.O. Box 244, 82 Grattan Road, Bradford, BD1 2JB.
12, ‡ *   News-sheet covering activities of Society of Dyers and Colourists, e.g. reports on symposia, lectures, promotions, appointments and industrial news.
New companies, new products, obituaries.
No Index.
June 1972, T.p. 6.   4800.
Issued free with Journal of Society of Dyers and Colourists.

667.6

PAINT. SURFACE COATINGS

3464 INDUSTRIAL FINISHING AND SURFACE COATINGS incorporating Corrosion. 1970.
(Industrial Finishing 1948-1970).
Wheatland Journals Ltd. (part of Turret Press (Holdings) Ltd.), 157 Hagden Lane, Watford, WD1 8LW, Herts.
12, ‡ =   All aspects of finishing products and processes including plating, painting, anodising, cleaning, pretreatment, powder coating etc.
Book notices, book reviews, letters, monographic articles, new companies, new products, obituaries, patents, standards, tests.
No Index.
May 1972, T.p. 31, Ad.p. 45.   6850.
Per year £5.
Indexed in: BTI.

3465 JOURNAL OF THE OIL AND COLOUR CHEMISTS'
ASSOCIATION. 1918.
Oil and Colour Chemists' Association, Wax Chandlers'
Hall, Gresham Street, London, EC2V 7AB.
12, ‡ *   Scientific and technological papers of high
standard of ability and originality, covering aspects
of the industries served. The technical and social
activities of the Association and its sections.
Book reviews, letters, monographic articles, new companies, new products, obituaries, tests.
A, December, Yes, 10 year.
6, 1972, T.p. 89, Ad.p. 28.   5479.
Per copy £1, per year £10.
Indexed in: BTI.

3466 PAINT MANUFACTURE: Pigments, resins, varnishes,
inks, powder coatings. 1930.
Morgan-Grampian (Publishers) Ltd., Calderwood Street,
Woolwich, London, SE18.
12, ‡ = +
Book notices, book reviews, letters, monographic
articles, new companies, new products, obituaries,
patents, standards, tests.
A, —, No, None.
March 1972, T.p. 25, Ad.p. 36.   2962.
Per copy £1, per year UK £6, Overseas £10.

3467 PAINT TECHNOLOGY. 1936.
Sawell Publications Ltd., 4 Ludgate Circus, London,
EC4.
12, ‡   Chemistry and technology of paint, printing
inks and allied coatings.
Book reviews, letters, monographic articles, news,
new products, obituaries, patents, standards, tests.
A, December, No, None.
T.p. 39, Ad.p. 23.   2300.
Per copy 37½p, per year £3.
Indexed in: BTI.

3468 POLYMERS, PAINT & COLOUR JOURNAL. 1971.
(Oil and Colourmen's Journal 1879-1949; Paint Oil &
Colour Journal 1950-1971).
Fuel & Metallurgical Journals Ltd., 17/19 John Adam
St., London, WC2N 6JH.
26, ‡ =   Raw materials and additives for the paint,
plastics, printing ink, adhesives, and allied industries.
Commodity prices, letters, articles, new products,
reports.
6m, July and January, Yes, None.
T.p. 20, Ad.p. 27.   2400.
Per copy 30p, per year £7.80.

3469 PRODUCT FINISHING. 1948.
Sawell Publications Ltd., 4 Ludgate Circus, London,
EC4.
12, = ‡ +   Finishes and their application.
Book notices, book reviews, letters, monographic
articles, new companies, news, new products, obituaries, patents, standards, tests.
A, December, No, None.
T.p. 50, Ad.p. 50.
Per copy 37½p, per year £3.
Indexed in: BTI.

3470 SURFACE COATINGS: industrial finishes and their
applications. 1965.
(Paint Journal 1953-1964).
Office Publications Ltd., Mercury House, Waterloo
Road, London, SE1.
10, ‡   Coatings, pretreatment, anti-corrosion techniques etc.
Book notices, book reviews, letters, monographic
articles, new companies, news, new products,
obituaries, standards, tests.
A, January, No, None.
T.p. 32, Ad.p. 20.   6450.
Per copy 50p, per year £5.
Indexed in: BTI.

3471 TRANSACTIONS OF THE INSTITUTE OF METAL
FINISHING. 1959.
(Journal of the Electrodepositors Society 1937-1958).
Institute, 178 Goswell Road, London, EC1.
4, * = + ‡   New aspects of research, applications and
processes, including printed circuitry and organic
finishing.
Book reviews, letters, monographic articles, news,
new products, obituaries, standards, tests.
A, December, Yes, 5 year.
T.p. 101, Ad.p. 25.   2000.
Per copy £1.50, per year £7.50, Free to members.

3472 WORLD SURFACE COATINGS ABSTRACTS. 1969.
(Review of Current Literature on the Paint & Allied
Industries 1928-1968).
The Paint Research Association, Waldegrave Road,
Teddington, Middx., TW11 8LD.
12, + ‡   Current abstracts of world coatings literature including journals, patents, standards, specifications, conference papers, books, etc. covering
all aspects of the science and technology of paints,
printing inks and related materials.
Abstracts, book notices, book reviews, legal notes,
patents, standards, tests.
A, July, Yes, None.
March 1972, T.p. 128, Ad.p. 4.   1100.
Per copy £3.33, per year £40.

668.5

COSMETICS. PERFUMES

3473 BEAUTY THERAPY JOURNAL. 1966.
Association of Beauty Therapists, 4 Berkeley Mews,
Portman Square, London, W1.
Irreg., * =   Notes of general interest to members
of the beauty therapy profession.
Book reviews, letters, articles, new products, obituaries.
No Index.
No. 2, 1971, T.p. 20.
Free to members.

3474 INTERNATIONAL PERFUMER: Essential Oils, Aromatics, Spices & Flavours. 1950.
(Essential Oils & Aromatics Monthly Reporter 1935-
1949).
H. B. Squire, International Perfumer, 12a KC.,
East Molesey, Surrey, KT8 9HL.
12, ○ ‡ = +   The international news magazine of the
perfumery and cosmetic industry. A fragrances
and flavours digest for all those whose work involves the senses of smell and taste.
General news, book notices, book reviews, commodity
prices, articles, new companies, new products.
No Index.
April/May 1972, T.p. 24, Ad.p. Most.
Per year £2.50.

3475 JOURNAL OF THE SOCIETY OF COSMETIC
CHEMISTS. 1950.
Blackwell Scientific Publications (for Society of Cosmetic Chemists of Great Britain), Osney Mead,
Oxford, OX2 0EL.
13, + = *   Cosmetics in general.
Book reviews, monographic articles.
A, Last issue of volume, Yes, None.
1 April 1972, T.p. 61, Ad.p. 10.
Per copy £2.10, per year £14, Free to members.

3476 SOAP, PERFUMERY & COSMETICS. 1928.
United Trade Press Ltd., 9 Gough Square, London, EC4.
12, = ‡   Cosmetics, perfumery, detergent and allied
industries.
Book reviews, articles, new companies, news.
A, —, Yes, None.
T.p. 22, Ad.p. 39.
Per copy 35p, per year £4.

668.7

COAL TAR

3477 REVIEW OF COAL TAR TECHNOLOGY. 1949.
Coal Tar Research Association, Oxford Road, Gomersal, Cleckheaton, Yorks, BD19 4HH.
2, ‡ + =   Review of world developments in the chemistry and utilization of coal tar, light oils, middle oils, pitch, and tar acids and bases.
New products, patents, standards, tests.
6m, Issued with each part, Yes, None.
July-December 1971, T.p. 97.
Per copy £2, per year £4, Free to members.

3478 ROAD TAR. 1945.
British Tar Industry Association, 132-135 Sloane Street, London, SW1X 9BB.
3, ‡ =   Users of road tar and allied binders.
Book reviews, letters, monographic articles, obituaries, standards, tests.
No Index.
Spring 1972, T.p. 13, Ad.p. 5.   6000.
Per year 60p.

669

METALLURGY

3479 ACTA METALLURGICA.
Pergamon Press Ltd., Headington Hill Hall, Oxford, OX3 0BW.
12, = +   Theoretical and experimental studies contributing to the understanding of the properties and behaviour of solids.
Book reviews, letters, monographic articles.
A, Last issue of volume, Yes, None.
Per copy £3, per year £34.

3480 DROP FORGING BULLETIN. 1966.
(Technical Bulletin 1949).
(i) National Association of Drop Forgers and Stampers and (ii) Drop Forging Research Assn., (i) 245 Grove Lane, Handsworth, Birmingham, 20 2HB, (ii) Shepherd Street, Sheffield, S3 7BA.
‡ + †   Abstracts of technical articles published in various journals: details of Patents affecting industry: details of draft specifications issued by British Standards Institution: List of books contained in N.A.D.F.S. and D.F.R.A. Libraries.
Abstracts, new products, patents, standards.
No Index.
March 1972, T.p. App. 28.   c. 500.
Free to members.

3481 FULMER RESEARCH INSTITUTE NEWSLETTER. 1968.
Fulmer Research Institute Ltd., Stoke Poges, Slough, Bucks.
4, + †   News of research work carried out at the Institute on contract for sponsors. Fields cover material science especially metallurgy.
No Index.
June 1972, T.p. 2.   23000.
Free.

3482 JOURNAL OF PHYSICS F: Metal Physics. 1971.
The Institute of Physics, London and Bristol, Netherton House, Marsh Street, Bristol, BS1 4BT.
12, ‡ +   Electronic band structure, Fermi surfaces, electronic transport in metals, optical properties, x-ray spectra superconductivity, alloys and alloying behaviour including Kondo alloys, magnetic properties of metals and alloys where specific to these systems as well as phonons in metals.
Book notices, book reviews, letters, monographic articles.
A, December, Yes, None.
January 1972, T.p. 208.
Per copy £2.50, per year £28.

3483 JOURNAL OF THE INSTITUTE OF METALS. 1967.
(Journal of the Institute of Metals with Bulletin and Metallurgical Abstracts 1909-1966).
Metals & Metallurgy Trust, 17 Belgrave Square, London, SW1.
12, * = + ‡   All aspects of metallurgy of non-ferrous metals.
Monographic articles.
A, —, Yes, None.
T.p. 32.   5100.
Free to members.
Indexed in: BTI, IBZ.

3484 METAL BULLETIN: World Steel & Metal News. 1915.
Metal Bulletin Limited, 46 Wigmore St., London, W1H 0BJ.
100, = ‡   Provides international market intelligence and trade news covering the steel and non-ferrous metal industries.
Book notices, book reviews, commodity prices, letters, articles, new products, obituaries, parliamentary reports, patents, standards, tests.
6m, January and July, No, None.
May 16th 1972, T.p. 18, Ad.p. 24.   c. 8700.
Per copy 23p, per year £23.

3485 METALLURGIA. 1929.
Kennedy Press Ltd, 31 King Street, Manchester, 3.
12, ‡ +   Metal technology.
6m, —, Yes, None.
Per copy 20p, per year £2.50.
Indexed in: BTI.

3486 METALLURGICAL JOURNAL.
University of Strathclyde, Glasgow.
4, ‡ +
Monographic articles.
No Index.
Subscription on application.

3487 METALS ABSTRACTS. 1968.
(Metallurgical Abstracts, 1908-1967; Review of Metal Literature, 1924-1967).
The Institute of Metals, 17 Belgrave Square, London, SW1. American Society for Metals.
12, ‡ = *   Properties of metals and alloys and processes which affect these properties.
Abstracts.
M, Middle of each month, Yes, A.
May 1972, T.p. 192.
Per copy £4.25, per year £10 for members. Apply for rates for libraries and organisations.

3488 METALS AND MATERIALS.
Institute of Metals, 17 Belgrave Square, London, SW1.
12, ‡ +
No Index.
12645.
Free to members.
Indexed in: BTI.

3489 METALWORKING PRODUCTION. 1955.
(The Machinist 1900-1955).
McGraw-Hill Publishing Co., Shoppenhangers Road, Maidenhead, Berks.
52, ‡ = +
Letters, monographic articles, news, new products, parliamentary reports, standards.
A, February, Yes, None.
T.p. 31, Ad.p. 50.   10215.
Per year £3.
Indexed in: BTI, IBZ.

3490 METALWORKING PRODUCTION INTERNATIONAL. 1968.
Morgan Grampian (Publishers) Ltd., Calderwood Street, London, SE18 6QH.

6, = ‡ +   Production engineering technology and development including metalcutting, metal forming, management aspects.
Letters, monographic articles, new products.
No Index.
T.p. 20, Ad.p. 30.   8015.
Free, controlled circulation.

3491 THE PHYSICS OF METALS AND METALLOGRAPHY.
[Cover-to-cover translation of Fizika Metallov i Metallovedenie]. 1958.
Pergamon Press Ltd., Headington Hill Hall, Oxford, OX3 0BW.
12, + =   Theoretical problems and experimental investigations into physical properties of metals and alloys.
Book reviews, monographic articles.
A, Last issue of volume, Yes, None.
Per copy £5.50, per year £60.

3492 RUSSIAN METALLURGY: English translation of Izvestiya Akademii Nauk SSSR 'Metally' No. 1. 1962.
(Russian Metallurgy and Mining).
Scientific Information Consultants Ltd., 661 Finchley Road, London, NW2 2HN.
6, ‡ +   Ferrous and non-ferrous metallurgy, incl. ore benefiation, extraction and refining, mechanical properties at ordinary and elevated temperatures, alloy compositions and structures effects of impurities and methods of purification, methods of testing, new properties.
Monographic articles, tests.
A, —, No, None.
4, 1970, T.p. 164.
Per year £45.

3493 SCRIPTA METALLURGICA.
Pergamon Press Ltd., Headington Hill Hall, Oxford, OX3 0BW.
12, = + ‡   Letters journal describing theoretical and experimental studies contributing to the understanding of the properties and behaviour of solids in terms of fundamental particles, forces and energies.
A, Last issue of volume, Yes, None.
Per copy £2, per year £20.

669.1

IRON. STEEL

3494 BRITISH STEEL. 1968.
British Steel Corporation, 33 Grosvenor Place, London, SW1.
4, ○ ‡ = + †   Covering the problems, personalities, and progress of the British steel industry in its social, economic and political context.
Book reviews, monographic articles, new products, parliamentary reports, standards, tests.
2 yearly, —, Yes, None.
April 1972, T.p. 36.   17000.
Free to restricted circulation.

3495 BRITISH STEELMAKER. 1935.
British Steelmaker Ltd., Stamford House, Turnmill Street, London, EC1.
12, ‡   Iron and steel production in general.
Book notices, book reviews, letters, monographic articles, new companies, news, new products, obituaries, standards, tests.
No Index.
T.p. 27, Ad.p. 23.   2418.
Per copy 17½p, per year £2.25.
Indexed in: BTI.

3496 IRON AND STEEL. 1941.
(Iron & Steel Industry 1927-1940).
Iliffe Science & Technology Publications Ltd., 32 High Street, Guildford.
6, ‡   Steelmaking, ironmaking, iron and steel founding, organization and management.
Book reviews, monographic articles, news, new products, patents, standards, tests.
A, December, Yes, None.
T.p. 60, Ad.p. 55.   2969.
Per copy 75p, per year £5.50.
Indexed in: BTI, IBZ.

3497 JOURNAL OF THE IRON AND STEEL INSTITUTE. 1869.
Iron & Steel Institute, 4 Grosvenor Gardens, London, SW1.
12, = ‡ + *
Abstracts, book reviews, monographic articles.
A, —, Yes, None.
Per year £25.
Indexed in: BTI, IBZ.

3498 JOURNAL OF RESEARCH OF THE STEEL CASTINGS RESEARCH AND TRADE ASSOCIATION. 1968.
(Journal of the British Steel Castings Research Association 1951-1968).
The Association, East Bank Road, Sheffield, S2 3PT.
4, ‡ +   Steel castings research.
No Index.
Confidential to members only.

3499 MAN AND METAL: Journal of the Iron & Steel Trades Confederation. 1923.
(Journal of the Iron and Steel Trades Confederation 1917-1923).
Swinton House, 324 Gray's Inn Road, London, WC1X 8DD.
12, ○ = * +   Union and subject interests in the fields of metallurgy.
Book notices, book reviews, legal notes, letters, articles, new companies, new products, obituaries, parliamentary reports.
No Index.
Junt 1972, T.p. 28, Ad.p. 4.   20000.
Per year 60p and Free to members.

3500 SCRATA JOURNAL OF RESEARCH. 1968.
(B.S.F.A. Journal of Research & Development 1951-1952; B.S.C.R.A. Journal 1953-1968).
Steel Castings Research & Trade Association, East Bank Road, Sheffield, S2 3PT.
4, +   Research & Development on Steel Castings
CONFIDENTIAL JOURNAL—Available only to SCRATA member firms.
Letters, monographic articles, tests.
A, December, Yes, None.

3501 SPECIAL STEELS REVIEW. 1969.
(ESC Review, 1965-1968).
British Steel Corporation, Special Steels Division, The Mount, PO Box 64, Broomhill, Sheffield, S10 2PZ, Yorkshire.
3, ‡ =   Uses and potential uses of BSC Special Steels Divisions products.
Monographic articles.
No Index.
Spring 1971, T.p. 32.   3000.
Free, controlled circulation.

3502 STAINLESS STEEL: Journal of the Stainless Steel Development Association. 1967.
Stainless Steel Development Association, 65 Vincent Square, London, SW1P 2NY.

Key to reference symbols

○ popular   ‡ technical   = trade/professional

+ research   * society/institution   † house journal

4,‡ =   Applications of stainless steel.
Book notices, articles, new products, standards.
3 yearly, Autumn 1969, Yes, None.
Spring 1972, T.p. 24.   15000.
Free in U.K. £1 per year overseas.

3503 STEEL CASTINGS ABSTRACTS. 1968.
(B.S.F.A. Abstracts 1951-1952; B.S.C.R.A. Abstracts 1953-1968).
Steel Castings Research and Trade Association, East Bank Road, Sheffield, S2 3PT.
6,‡ +   Steel founding industry and allied subjects.
Abstracts.
A, March (Subject Index) November (Name Index), Yes, None.
Nov/Dec. 1971, T.p. 57.
Per year £10.

3504 STEEL IN THE USSR. Selection of translated articles from Stal. 1971.
Iron & Steel Institute, 4 Grosvenor Gardens, London, SW1.
12, = ‡ +   Metallurgy, especially ferrous.
Book reviews, monographic articles.
No Index.
Subscription on application.

3505 STEEL TIMES. 1964.
(Iron Trade Review 1866-1869; Iron & Coal Trades Review 1869-1962; Steel & Coal 1962-1963).
Fuel & Metallurgical Journals Ltd., 17/19 John Adam St., London, WC2N 6JH.
‡ =   Iron and steel industry in general.
Book notices, book reviews, letters, articles, new companies, new products, obituaries, parliamentary reports, patents, standards, tests.
A, January, No, None.
2450.
Per copy 60p, per year £7.80.
Indexed in: BTI, IBZ.

3506 STEEL USER NEWS. 1970.
Corporate Laboratories, British Steel Corporation, Hoyle Street, Sheffield, S3 7EY.
4,‡   Technical information on steel products, processes, investigations, specifications etc.
Book notices, letters, monographic articles, new products, standards, tests.
No Index.
June 1972, T.p. 4.   500.
Free.

669.2

NON-FERROUS METALS

3507 BNF ABSTRACTS: summarising published information on non-ferrous metallurgy and technology. 1970.
(BNF Bulletin, 1920-1969).
BNFMRA (The British Non-Ferrous Metals Research Association), Euston Street, London, NW1 2EU.
12,‡ + =   Current awareness of various aspects of technology, research and development and production in the non-ferrous metals industry. Contains approximately 400 abstracts per month which are prepared from 250 technical journals and the lastest British Patent specs.
Abstracts, book notices, book reviews, patents, standards.
A, —, Yes, None.
March 1972, T.p. 67.
Per year £15. Free to members.

669.24

NICKEL

3508 WIGGIN NICKEL ALLOYS. 1948.
Henry Wiggin & Company Limited, Holmer Road, Hereford, HR4 9SL.
3/4,‡ †   Uses of high-nickel alloys to resist corrosion and high temperature or provide some other physical property such as electrical resistance or low thermal expansion in all industries.
Monographic articles.
No Index.
December 1971, T.p. 16.
Free.

669.25

COBALT

3509 COBALT. 1958.
Cobalt Information Centre, 7 Rolls Buildings, Fetter Lane, London, EC4.
4,‡ +   Metallurgical applications, research and development of cobalt and its alloys.
Monographic articles, abstracts.
A, March, Yes, None.
T.p. 56.
Free, controlled circulation.

669.3

COPPER

3510 COPPER ABSTRACTS: Selected abstracts of recent literature on copper and copper alloys. 1959.
Distributed by Copper Development Association, Orchard House, Mutton Lane, Potters Bar, Herts.
6,‡ =   Abstracts of articles relating to the casting, fabrication, joining, properties and applications of copper and copper alloys.
Abstracts.
A, December, No, None.
No. 6, 1971, T.p. 26.   c. 6000.
Free.

669.4

LEAD

3511 LEAD ABSTRACTS. 1958.
Lead Development Association, 34 Berkeley Square, London, W1X 6A5.
6,‡ + * =   An extensive review of current world literature on the uses of lead and its products.
Abstracts, book notices, patents, standards, tests.
A, March, Yes, None.
May 1972, T.p. 24.   8000.
Gratis.

669.5

ZINC

3512 ZINC ABSTRACTS. 1943.
Zinc Development Association, 34 Berkeley Square, London, W1X 6A5.
6,‡ + * =   An extensive review of current world literature on the uses of zinc, cadmium and other products.
Abstracts, book notices, patents, standards, tests.
A, March, Yes, None.
June 1972, T.p. 48.   10000.
Gratis.

669.6

TIN

3513 MONTHLY STATISTICAL BULLETIN.
International Tin Council, 28 Haymarket, London, SW1.
12, = ‡   Tables dealing with production, consumption, imports, exports, trade etc.
No Index.
T.p. 72.
Per copy 50p, per year £5.

3514 TIN AND ITS USES: quarterly review of the Tin Research Institute. 1939.
Tin Research Institute, Frazer Road, Perivale, Greenford, Middx.
4, ‡ + *   Scientific and general coverage of all aspects of the usage of tin; its alloys and chemical applications.
Book reviews, monographic articles, new products, obituaries, patents, standards, tests.
No Index.
No. 92, 1972, T.p. 16.   40000.
Free.
Indexed in: BTI.

3515 TIN INTERNATIONAL: incorporating Tin Printer and Box Maker and Canning and Packing. 1928.
Tin Publications Ltd., 7 High Road, London, W4 2NE.
12 =   All aspects of tin production and consumption, including mining, smelting, refining, tin-using industry, related equipment and services, trading and marketing, with supporting statistical section.
Abstracts, book notices, book reviews, commodity prices, letters, new companies, new products, obituaries, patents, standards, tests.
A, January, No, None.
May 1972, T.p. 24, Ad.p. 16.   4600.
Per copy 50p, per year £4.50.
Indexed in: BTI.

669.71

ALUMINIUM

3516 ALUMINIUM FOR SCHOOLS. 1964.
Aluminium Federation, Broadway House, Catthorpe Road, Five Ways, Birmingham, B15 1TN.
3, ○   Uses of aluminium in industry, the home and in school. Sent to school teachers on the Federation's mailing list, as a newsletter.
No Index.
Summer 1972, T.p. 8.   7000.
Free.

671

JEWELLERY

3517 BRITANNIA. 1963.
(British Jeweller Overseas—1940-1962).
British Jewellery & Giftware Fed., Ltd., St. Dunstan's House, Carey Lane, London, EC2.
4, =   Official export journal for the jewellery, silverware and horological trades.
Book notices, book reviews, commodity prices, legal notes, letters, monographic articles, new companies, new products, obituaries, parliamentary reports, patents, standards, tests.
No Index.
T.p. 14, Ad.p. 28.   c. 4000.
Per year £1.20.

3518 BRITISH JEWELLER & WATCH BUYER. 1971.
(British Jeweller—1933-1970).
British Jewellery & Giftware Fed. Ltd., St. Dunstan's House, Carey Lane, London, EC2.
12, =   Jewellery, silver-ware, cutlery, giftware and horological trades.
Book notices, book reviews, commodity prices, legal notes, letters, monographic articles, new companies, new products, obituaries, parliamentary reports, patents, standards, tests.
No Index.
6000.
Per copy 18p, per year £1.75.

3519 BUYERS GUIDE.
British Jewellery & Giftware Federation Ltd., St. Dunstan's House, Carey Lane, London, EC2.
2 yearly, =   British jewellery, silverware and horological trades.
No Index.
6000.
Per copy £1.

3520 GEMS: The British Lapidary Magazine. 1969.
R.F. Lambert, Lapidary Publications, 29 Ludgate Hill, London, EC4.
8, = ‡
Book notices, book reviews, commodity prices, letters, monographic articles, new products, standards, tests.
No Index.
July/Aug. 1972, T.p. 31, Ad.p. 36.   7000.
Per copy 21p, per year £1.60.

3521 JEWELLER: Official journal of the British Watch & Clockmakers Guild. 1873-1972.
(Jeweller & Metalworker 1873-1972).
Wheatland Journals Ltd., 157 Hagden Lane, Watford, Herts.
24, ‡ = *   Precious metals, jewellery and horological trades.
Commodity prices, legal notes, letters, articles, new companies, new products, obituaries, patents.
No Index.
June 1, 1972, T.p. 24, Ad.p. 8.   4000.
Per copy 12p, per year £2.90.

3522 RETAIL JEWELLER: Incorporating The Gemmologist & Horological Review. 1963.
NAG Press Ltd./Northwood Publications Ltd., 93/99 Goswell Road, London, EC1V 7QA.
26, =   Retail and wholesale jewellery.
Book reviews, commodity prices, legal notes, letters, new companies, new products, obituaries, parliamentary reports, standards.
No Index.
7 June 1972, T.p. 10, Ad.p. Most.   9186.
Per copy 11p, per year £2.75.

672.3

METAL WORKING

3523 METAL FORMING: incorporating Drop Forger. 1966.
Fuel & Metallurgical Journals Ltd., 17-19 John Adam Street, London, WC2.
12, ‡   Forging, extruding and rolling.
Monographic articles.
A, —, Yes, None.
T.p. 22, Ad.p. 23.   2629.
Per copy 25p, per year £3.
Indexed in: BTI.

3524 SHEET METAL INDUSTRIES. 1927.
Fuel & Metallurgical Journals Ltd., 17/19 John Adam St., London, WC2N 6JH.
12, = ‡   Deals with the technologies of production, pressings, fabrication, welding and finishing of ferrous and non-ferrous sheet metals. Also coverage of stockholders.
Monographic articles, new companies, new products.
A, January, No, None.
5200.
Per copy 60p, per year £7.20.
Indexed in: BTI, IBZ.

674

CARPENTRY. TIMBER TECHNOLOGY. WOOD

3525 BOARD MANUFACTURE. 1966.
(Board 1958-1965).
Press Media Ltd., Ivy Hatch, Sevenoaks, Kent.
12, ‡ Manufacture of building boards and allied materials.
Book notices, book reviews, letters, monographic articles, new companies, news, new products, standards, tests.
No Index.
T.p. 15, Ad.p. 9.   4500.
Per copy 32½p, per year £2.

3526 DIY AND WOODWORKING INFORMATION. 1972.
Westwood Publishing Group Ltd., Morden, Surrey.
12, = For manufacturers and suppliers.
No Index.

3527 JOURNAL OF THE INCORPORATED BRITISH INSTITUTE OF CERTIFIED CARPENTERS. 1900.
The Institute, 37 Soho Square, London, W1.
4, = ‡ + Timber trade in general.
Book reviews, letters, articles, news, new products.
No Index.
T.p. 34, Ad.p. 3.
Free to members.

3528 JOURNAL OF THE INSTITUTE OF WOOD SCIENCE. 1958.
Institute, 62 Oxford Street, London, W1.
3, * = + ‡
Book notices, book reviews, monographic articles.
2 year, —, Yes, None.
T.p. 59.
Free to members.

3529 PRACTICAL WOODWORKING. 1966.
IPC Magazines Ltd., Fleetway House, Farringdon Street, EC4 4AD.
12, ○ ‡ = All aspects of working with wood and related products by hand or machine—constructional furniture and cabinet making, hobbies, handicrafts, teaching etc.—with account on home improvement and DIY.
Book reviews, commodity prices, letters, articles, new products, tests.
A, March, Yes, None.
May 1972, T.p. 21, Ad.p. 23.   60000.
Per copy 25p, per year £3.80.

3530 TIMBER & PLYWOOD incorporating Board News. 1885.
The Middlesex Publishing Co., Ltd., 21 New Street, London, EC2M 4NT.
52, = Timber and allied trades, UK and overseas.
Letters, new companies, new products, obituaries, parliamentary reports, standards, tests.
No Index.
14.6.72, T.p. 19, Ad.p. 29.
Per copy 16p, per year £8.50.

3531 TIMBER TRADES JOURNAL and Woodworking Machinery. 1873.
Benn Brothers Ltd., 25 New Street Square, London, EC4A 3JA.
52, = Timber importing, merchanting, and distributing operations of the U.K. with special focus on market trends (statistical analyses of imports, consumption and stocks), sources of supply (shippers) and sawmilling and processing.
Book notices, book reviews, commodity prices, legal notes, letters, articles, new companies, new products, obituaries, parliamentary reports, standards, tests.
No Index.
24th June 1972, T.p. 45, Ad.p. 51.   7927.
Per copy 15p, per year £8.

3532 WOOD. 1936.
Benn Bros. Ltd., 154 Fleet Street, London, EC4.
10, = ‡ + All constructional and industrial applications of timber and timber-derived products.
Book notices, book reviews, commodity prices, letters, monographic articles, new companies, news, new products, obituaries, patents, standards, tests.
A, January, Yes, None.
T.p. 32, Ad.p. 16.   6000.
Per copy 30p, per year £3.75.
Indexed in: BTI.

3533 WOOD & EQUIPMENT NEWS. 1968.
Westbourne Journals Ltd., Crown House, Morden, Surrey.
12, = Product information and new developments, woodworking equipment and materials.
Book reviews, letters, news, new products.
No Index.
13000.
Free, controlled circulation.

3534 WOODWORKER. WOOD—METAL—PLASTICS. 1968.
(The Woodworker 1901-1967).
Evans Bros. Ltd., Montague House, Russell Square, London, WC1.
12, = ○ Wood, metal, plastics and glass fibre, also antiques, timbers, techniques, plastics, design.
Book reviews, commodity prices, letters, monographic articles, news, new products.
A, December, Yes, None.
T.p. 32, Ad.p. 11.   26400.
Per copy 15p, per year £2.15.

3535 WOODWORKING INDUSTRY. 1945.
Trade Chronicles Ltd., Mercury House, Waterloo Road, London, SE1.
12, = ‡ + Seasoning, processing and finishing of timber products.
Book notices, book reviews, commodity prices, legal notes, letters, articles, new companies, news, new products, parliamentary reports, patents, standards, tests.
No Index.
T.p. 42, Ad.p. 50.   3359.
Per copy 37½p, per year £4.
Indexed in: BTI.

676

PAPER TECHNOLOGY

3536 EUROPEAN BOARD MARKETS. 1965.
Magazines for Industry Inc., 59 Fleet Street, London, EC4Y 1JU.
52, = European pulp, paper and board markets and manufacturers. Machinery for board making.
Commodity prices, new companies, new products.
No Index.
T.p. 4, Ad.p. 4.   1600.
Per year £7.

3537 PAPER: incorporating World's Paper Trade Review and The Paper Maker. 1972.
(World's Paper Trade Review 1879-1972; The Paper Maker 1891-1972).
Benn Brothers Ltd., Lyon Tower, Colliers Wood, London, SW19 2JN.
24, = Pulp and paper manufacture.
Book reviews, commodity prices, letters, monographic articles, new companies, new products, obituaries, patents, standards, tests.
A, January, Yes, None.
June 7, 1972, T.p. 35, Ad.p. 41.   4500.
Per copy 30p, per year £7.50.

3538 PAPER & BOARD ABSTRACTS. 1968.
(Kenley Abstracts 1965-1967).
PIRA, Randalls Road, Leatherhead, Surrey.

12,‡ Digest of articles on paper and board making, processes, machines, testing and products.
Abstracts, book notices.
A, −, Yes, None.
Per year £15.

3539 PAPER AND PACKAGING BULLETIN. 1972.
(Paper Bulletin 1955-1971).
The Economist Intelligence Unit Ltd., Spencer House, 27 St. James's Place, London, SW1A 1NT.
4,‡ = + Provides a service of concise and reliable analyses of trends in paper, its raw materials and plastic packaging products for consumers and producers.
No Index.
T.p. 50.
Per copy £15, per year £50.

3540 PAPER FACTS & FIGURES. 1961.
Northwood Publications Ltd., (The Thomson Organisation Ltd.), Northwood House, 93-99 Goswell Road, London, EC1V 7QA.
6, = Manual of the paper trade in the UK for printing and writing paper and boards. Carries details of branded lines—UK produced and imported—including up-to-date prices.
Index to branded lines (approx 900) each issue.
June-July 1972, T.p. 220, Ad.p. 40.   4250.
Per year £6.

3541 PAPER TECHNOLOGY. 1960.
(Transactions of the Technical Section of BPBMA).
British Paper & Board Makers Association, 3 Plough Place, Fetter Lane, London, EC4.
6,‡ + = New plant, mills, processes, research in papermaking and manufacturing and finished products.
Book notices, book reviews, letters, monographic articles, news, new products, obituaries, reports, standards, tests.
A, December, Yes, None.
T.p. 49, Ad.p. 30.
Free to members.
Indexed in: BTI.

3542 PAPER TRAINING NEWS. 1971.
Paper & Paper Products Industry Training Board, Star House, Potters Bar, Herts.
4, =
No Index.
Free.

676.813
POSTCARDS

3543 INTERNATIONAL POSTCARD MARKET. 1968.
96 Idmiston Road, West Norwood, London, SE27 9HL.
4, ○ Collection of old picture postcards in GB, USA, Europe.
Book notices, book reviews, letters.
No Index.
May 1972, T.p. 9, Ad.p. 4.   1200.
Per copy £1.

677
TEXTILES

3544 THE AMBASSADOR. 1946.
Ambassador Publishing Co., Ltd., 49 Park Lane, London, W1.
12, = All merchandise available in departmental stores, including clothing and textiles.
Articles, news, new products.
No Index.
T.p. 37, Ad.p. 63.
Per year £4.

3545 INDUSTRIAL FIBRES. 1948.
Commonwealth Secretariat, Marlborough House, Pall Mall, London, SW1Y 5HX.
1/2,‡ = + Review of production, trade and consumption relating to wool, cotton, man-made fibres, silk, flax, jute, hard fibres and other hemps, mohair, and coir.
No Index.
No. 19, T.p. 254.
Per copy £2.

3546 JOURNAL OF THE TEXTILE INSTITUTE. 1910.
The Textile Institute, 10 Blackfriars Street, Manchester M3 5DR.
12, + * Scientific and technological papers relating to textiles and embracing all fibres and all processes.
Letters, monographic articles.
A, Cumulative, December, Yes, None.
6, 1972, T.p. 62.   4000.
Per year £25 with, 'Textile Progress' and 'The Textile Institute and Industry'.

3547 THE NEWS REEL: House Journal of the Coats Patons Group of Companies. 1965.
(The News Reel—House Journal of J. & P. Coats, Limited 1948-1965).
Coats Patons Limited, 155 St. Vincent Street, Glasgow, G2 5PA.
4, † To provide news of and information on Coats Patons people and companies throughout the world in the field of textiles.
Letters, monograhic articles, new companies, new products, obituaries, patents, standards, tests.
No Index.
Spring 1972, T.p. 36.   15000.
Per copy 2½p, per year 10p.

3548 TEXTILE HISTORY. 1968.
David & Charles, South Devon House, Newton Abbot, Devon.
1, + Economic history of the textile industries. History of art and design in this field.
Book reviews, monographic articles.
No Index.
T.p. 128.
Per year £1.20.

3549 TEXTILE INSTITUTE AND INDUSTRY.
Textile Institute, 10 Blackfriars Street, Manchester, M3 5DR.
12, = ‡
No Index.
8500.
Free to members.
Indexed in: BTI.

3550 TEXTILE MANUFACTURER. 1875.
11 Albert Square, Manchester, M2 5HD.
12, = ‡ All aspects of textile manufacture, fibres, spinning, weaving, knitting, dyeing, bleaching, finishing, printing, stitch-bonding, laminating, etc. Production, materials, processes and management.
Book notices, book reviews, legal notes, letters, monographic articles, new companies, new products, obituaries, patents, standards, tests.
A, March, Yes, None.
June 1972, T.p. 44, Ad.p. 20.   4500.
Per copy 50p, per year £6.
Indexed in: BTI.

3551 TEXTILE MONTH.
Textile Business Press Ltd., Stratham House, Talbot Road, Stretford, Manchester, M32 0EP.
12, = ‡ + Every aspect of international textiles.
Book reviews, commodity prices, letters, new products, obituaries, standards, tests.
No Index.

T.p. 41, Ad.p. 95.
Free, controlled circulation.
Indexed in: BTI.

3552 TEXTILE NEWS. 1969.
Textile Business Press Ltd., Statham House, Talbot Road, Stretford, Manchester, M32 0EP.
26, =
No Index.
3500.
Per copy 12½p, per year £3.25.

3553 TEXTILE PRODUCTION. 1969.
Haymarket Publishing Group, Gillow House, Winsley Street, London, W1.
12, = ‡
No Index.
8000.
Per year £3.

3554 TEXTILE PROGRESS: A Critical Appreciation of Recent Developments. 1969.
The Textile Institute, 10 Blackfriars Street, Manchester M3 5DR.
4, + * =   Critical reviews of recent developments in textile science and technology, each issue being concerned with one or two main subjects.
Q, In each issue (name and subject), No, None.
T.p. Variable.   2000.
Per copy £5, per year £25 with J. Textile Institute and The Textile Institute and Industry.

3555 TEXTILES. 1972.
(Shirley Link).
Shirley Institute, Manchester, M20 8RX, England.
3, ○ ‡ =   Production and properties of fibres, yarns and fabrics. Performance and end uses. Domestic and industrial textiles. Technical developments. Basic technology.
Monographic articles, new products.
A, October (no. 3 issue of each vol), No, None.
February 1972, T.p. 28.   1500.
Per copy £1.25, per year £3.50.

3556 TEXTILES OF IRELAND AND LINEN TRADE CIRCULAR. 1852.
Granite Publications, 29 Craigowen Road, Carrickfergus, NI.
12, =
No Index.
Per year £3.

3557 WORLD TEXTILE ABSTRACTS. 1969.
(Shirley Institute Summary of Current Literature 1921-1968; Journal of the Textile Institute Abstracts Section 1922-1965; Textile Abstracts 1966-1968/69).
Shirley Institute, Manchester, M20 8RX.
24, ‡ = +   Comprehensive survey in English of world literature on textiles: periodical articles; British and United States patents; British, American and international standards; books, pamphlets, and theses.
Abstracts
A, also 'Monthly Subject indexes at special rates, 6-7 months after volume completion, Yes, None.
15 June 1972, T.p. 73.
Per year £29.

677.1

FLAX. JUTE. LINEN ETC.

3558 BULLETIN OF THE SCOTTISH TEXTILE RESEARCH ASSOCIATION. 1970.
(Bulletin of the British Jute Trade Research Association to 1969).
The Association, Kinnoull Road, Kingsway West, Dundee.
3, ‡ +   Spinning, weaving, dyeing and finishing of jute and allied fibres. Carpet manufacture etc.
Abstracts, book notices.
2 year, —, Yes, 10 year.
Free to members only.

3559 CORDAGE, CANVAS & JUTE WORLD Natural and Synthetic Fibres. 1919.
Wheatland Journals Limited, 157 Hagden Lane, Watford, Herts.
12, = ‡ +   All industries concerned with the buying and selling of the cordage, canvas, jute, twine, cord and textile industries.
Commodity prices, monographic articles, new companies, new products, obituaries, patents, standards.
No Index.
May 1972, T.p. 23, Ad.p. 5.   2000.
Per year £6.05.

3560 JUTE & SYNTHETICS REVIEW.
(Jute & Canvas Review 1939).
Hughes, Sanders & Howard Ltd., 222 Strand, London, WC2.
12, =
No Index.
Per year £3.

3561 LAMBEG RESEARCH REVIEW. 1966.
(Linen Research 1940-1966).
Lambeg Industrial Research Association, Lambeg, Lisburn, Co. Antrim, N. Ireland.
4, ‡ +   Review of new ideas, processes and machinery arising from research at LIRA or elsewhere.
Book notices, book reviews, monographic articles, new products, obituaries, patents, standards, tests.
No Index.
T.p. 8.
Free to LIRA members only.

3562 PRICES CURRENT (Jute & Linen). 1953.
(Dundee Prices Current (Jute & Linen) 1851-1952).
J. W. Warden & Co., 12 Panmure Street, Dundee.
50, ‡ =   Worldwide textile trade and makers, from raw material to finished yarn and cloth.
Commodity prices, legal notes, letters, new companies, new products, obituaries, parliamentary reports, patents, standards, tests.
No Index.
T.p. 4, Ad.p. 4.
Per year £6.

3563 WORLD FIBRE NEWS: a weekly summary of textile fibre news. 1972.
(Jute Makers & Prices 1946-1971).
Hughes, Saunders & Howard Ltd., 222 Strand, London, WC2R 1BA.
52, =
No Index.
15 September 1972, T.p. 8.
Per year £7.50.

677.2

COTTON

3564 COTTON OUTLOOK. 1972.
(Cotton and General Economic Review 1923-1972).
Liverpool Cotton Services Ltd., Cotton Exchange Building, Liverpool, 3.
52, =   International raw cotton marketing and allied subjects.
Commodity prices.
No Index.
6.2.1970, T.p. 22, Ad.p. 4.
Per year £30.

677.3

WOOL

3566 WIRA NEWS. 1968.
Wira, Headingley Lane, Leeds, LS6 1BW.
6, ‡ = +   All stages of textile processing, mainly wool textiles, from raw material to finished garment. All matters relating to the technological advance of the industry, emanating either from Wira or elsewhere. Services for the industry.
New products, standards, tests, technical and other developments, conference reports.
No Index.
May 1972, T.p. 8.   3000.
Free.

3567 WIRASCAN. 1967.
Wira, Headingley Lane, Leeds, LS6 1BW.
52, ‡ = +   Current awareness service alerting subscribers, mostly in the wool textile and allied industries, of technical publications and current developments in their field.
Abstracts, book notices, new products, patents, standards.
Spasmodic, —, No, None.
5 June 1972, T.p. 2.   250.
Per year £10.

3568 WIRASCAN FOR CLOTHIERS. 1972.
Wira, Headingley Lane, Leeds, LS6 1BW.
12, ‡ = +   Current awareness service alerting subscribers, mostly in the clothing industry of technical publications and current developments in their fields deriving from wool.
Abstracts, book notices, new products.
No Index.
June 1972, T.p. 4.   50.
Per year £10.

3569 WOOL INTELLIGENCE: including Fibres Supplement. 1947.
Commonwealth Secretariat, Marlborough House, Pall Mall, London, SW1Y 5HX.
12, = +   Trade statistics.
Commodity prices.
A, January, Yes, None.
May 1972, T.p. 76.
Per year £12.

3570 WOOL RECORD & TEXTILE WORLD. 1900.
Textile Business Press Ltd., 91 Kirkgate, Bradford.
52, =   International trade news.
No Index.
Per year £5.
Indexed in: BTI.

3571 WOOL SCIENCE REVIEW. 1948.
International Wool Secretariat, Research and Development Department, Carlton Gardens, London, SW1Y 5AE.
3/4, ‡ =   Authoritative discussion of recent advances in wool science and technology.
Articles.
Every 10 issues, irregularly, No, None.
April 1972, T.p. 60.   7000.
Free.
Indexed in: BTI.

678

PLASTICS. RUBBER

3572 BRITISH PLASTICS. 1929.
Engineering, Chemical & Marine Press Ltd., 33-40 Bowling Green Lane, London, EC1.
12, ‡
No Index.

13500.
Per copy $37\frac{1}{2}$p, per year £5.50.
Indexed in: BTI.

3573 BRITISH POLYMER JOURNAL. 1969.
Society of Chemical Industry (by Academic Press), 14 Belgrave Square, London, SW1X 8PS.
6, ‡ = +   The latest developments in international polymer research and papers from symposia and international conferences.
Book reviews, monographic articles, new products, patents, standards, tests, calendar of meetings.
A, November, Yes, None.
March 1972, T.p. 81, Ad.p. 3.   500.
Per year £10.
Indexed in: BTI.

3574 INTERNATIONAL RUBBER DIGEST. c.1947.
International Rubber Study Group, Brettenham House, 5/6 Lancaster Place, London, WC2E 7ET.
12, =   News and statistics.
No Index.
T.p. 7.
Per year £2.

3575 JOURNAL OF THE IRI. 1967.
(Institution of the Rubber Industry Transactions and Proceedings 1925-1966).
Rubber & Technical Press Ltd., Tenterden, Kent.
6, * = +   Official publication of the Institution of the Rubber Industry carrying news and technical articles of high calibre. Devoted entirely to rubber.
Book reviews, monographic articles, obituaries, patents, standards, tests.
A, February issue insert, No, 5 year.
June 1972, T.p. 30, Ad.p. 17.   c. 5530.
Per copy £1.50, per year £9.
Indexed in: BTI.

3576 NR TECHNOLOGY: Rubber Developments Supplement. 1970.
Natural Rubber Producers' Research Association, 56 Tewin Road, Welwyn Garden City, Herts.
4, ‡ +   Specialized accounts of NRPRA technological research.
Reports, tests.
A, with Rubber Developments, No, None.
Part 1 1972, T.p. 36.   17000.
Free.

3577 NEW TRADE NAMES IN THE RUBBER AND PLASTICS INDUSTRIES. 1962.
Rubber and Plastics Research Association of Great Britain, Shawbury, Shrewsbury SY4 4NR.
1, ‡ + =   New trade names in the rubber and plastics industries for the previous year from date of publication. Each issue contains approx 5000 new trade names and a short abstract.
Abstracts.
No Index.
1970.   500.
Per copy £3. (RAPRA Members £2).

3578 PRT POLYMER AGE. 1970.
(Rubber & Plastics Age 1920-1969).
Rubber & Technical Press Ltd., Tenterden, Kent.
12, ‡ = +   Marketing developments; case histories; cost effectiveness comparisons; process and materials selection; technology of monomers, polymers, chemicals, fibre, machinery and instruments in the adhesive, building, packaging, clothing, engineering, footwear, furniture, medical, transport industries, etc.
Book reviews, letters, monographic articles, new companies, new products, obituaries, standards, tests.
A, March, on request only, No, 2 year.
May 1972, T.p. 23, Ad.p. 32.   c. 4229.
Per copy 85p, per year £10.
Indexed in: BTI.

3579 PLASTICS & POLYMERS: The journal of the Plastics
Institute. 1968.
(Transactions and Journal of the Plastics Institute
1931-1967).
Plastics Institute, 11 Hobart Place, London, SW1W 0HL.
6, ‡ + =   All areas of the plastics industry and
academic establishments concerned with plastics.
Original papers, conference papers and general
news.
Book notices, book reviews, letters, monographic
articles, obituaries.
A, June, Yes, 5 year.
June 1972, T.p. 64, Ad.p. 12.   6945.
Per copy £2, per year £12.
Indexed in: BTI.

3580 PLASTICS & RUBBER WEEKLY. 1963.
(Rubber & Plastics Weekly; Rubber Journal & International Plastics; India Rubber Journal).
Maclaren Publishers Ltd., P.O.Box 109, Davis House,
69/77 High Street, Croydon CR9 1QH.
52, ‡   Plastics, rubber, consumer durable, capital
equipment and vehicle manufacturing. Discusses
new materials, equipment, processes and applications; and interprets the latest advances in polymer
technology.
Book notices, book reviews, commodity prices,
legal notes, letters, articles, new companies,
new products, obituaries, parliamentary
reports, patents.
No Index.
June 23rd 1972, T.p. 24, Ad.p. 17.   28855.
Per year £4.

3581 PLASTICS, RUBBERS, TEXTILES. 1970.
(Rubber & Plastics Age 1920-1969).
Rubber & Technical Press Ltd., 25 Lloyd Baker Street,
London, WC1.
12, = ‡ +   Marketing of plastic, rubber and synthetic
fibre materials, etc.
Book notices, book reviews, letters, monographic
articles, new companies, news, new products.
A, 1st issue of next volume, No, None.
T.p. 19, Ad.p. 18.   5000.
Per year £8.
Indexed in: BTI

3582 POLYMER SCIENCE USSR [cover-to-cover translation of Vysokomolekulyarnye Soyedineniya]. 1969.
Pergamon Press Ltd., Headington Hill Hall, Oxford,
OX3 0BW.
12, = +   Polymer chemistry and physics.
Monographic articles.
A, Last issue of volume, Yes, None.
Per copy £6, per year £66.

3583 QUARTERLY LIST OF PUBLICATIONS. 1967.
Natural Rubber Producers' Research Association,
56 Tewin Road, Welwyn Garden City, Herts.
4, +   Abstracts of NRPRA scientific and technical
papers. Intended for circulation to institutions
or individuals engaged in polymer research.
Abstracts, book notices.
Index of Publications, 1938-1969.
October/December 1971, T.p. 9.   600.
Free.

3584 QUARTERLY RUBBER STATISTICAL NEWS SHEET.
c.1969.
International Rubber Study Group, Brettenham House,
5/6 Lancaster Place, London, WC2E 7ET.
4, =
No Index.
T.p. 12.
Per year 65p.

3585 RAPRA ABSTRACTS. 1968.
(Plastics RAPRA Abstracts, Rubber RAPRA Abstracts
etc back to 1920).
Rubber and Plastics Research Association of Great
Britain, Shawbury, Shrewsbury SY4 4NR
52, ‡ + =   Abstracts from the world's polymer
literature and British and US patents. Coverage
350 journals. Total abstracts per year approx
25,000—50% to literature and 50% to patents.
Literature section available on computer readable
tape.
Abstracts, book notices, book reviews, commodity
prices, legal notes, new products, parliamentary
reports, patents, standards, tests.
6m, July-December, Yes, None.
5.6.1972.   2000.
Per year £60. Free to RAPRA members.

3586 REINFORCED PLASTICS. 1956.
Craftsman Publications, 87 Lambs Conduit St.,
London, WC1N 3NA.
12, ‡   Polyester/glass-fibre and similar mouldings.
Book notices, monographic articles, new products.
A, September/October, Yes, None.
T.p. 18, Ad.p. 12.   3800.
Per copy 25p, per year £4.
Indexed in: BTI.

3587 RUBBER DEVELOPMENTS. 1947.
Natural Rubber Producers' Research Association,
56 Tewin Road, Welwyn Garden City, Herts.
4, ‡   A review of developments in natural rubber
research, technology and use.
Book notices, book reviews, monographic articles, new
products, obituaries, standards, tests.
A, first part, subsequent volume, Yes, None.
Part 1 1972, T.p. 32.   17000.
Free.

3588 RUBBER JOURNAL. 1964.
(Various back to 1884).
Maclaren Publishers Ltd., P.O. Box 109, 69/77 Davis
House, High Street, Croydon CR9 1QH.
12, = ‡   Reports of immediate commercial value on
applied rubber technology, marketing and management. Covers new chemicals, rubbers, machinery
and processes, and case histories of successful
new products.
Commodity prices, legal notes, letters, articles, new
companies, new products, obituaries, parliamentary
reports, patents, standards, tests.
No Index.
June 1972, T.p. 31, Ad.p. 38.   3394.
Per copy 25p, per year £2.65.
Indexed in: BTI.

3589 RUBBER STATISTICAL BULLETIN. c.1945.
International Rubber Study Group, Brettenham House,
5/6 Lancaster Place, London, WC2E 7ET.
12, =   Statistics only.
No Index.
T.p. 44.
Per year £5.

3590 RUBBER TRENDS. 1958.
The Economist Intelligence Unit Ltd., Spencer House,
27 St. James's Place, London, SW1A 1NT.
4, ‡ = +   Emphasises the study of long-term trends.
In addition to information on production and world
trade, each issue analyses the outlook of the main
consuming countries and reports on trends in important rubber-using industries.
No Index.
T.p. 40.
Per copy £15, per year £50.

3591 SOVIET PLASTICS: RAPRA translation of Plasticheskie Massy. 1960.
Rubber and Plastics Research Association, Shawbury,
Shrewsbury, SY4 4NR.
12, = ‡ +
Monographic articles, new products, obituaries,
standards, tests.

No Index.
No. 1, 1972, T.p. 86.   300.
Per copy £4.35, per year £34.50.

3592 SOVIET RUBBER TECHNOLOGY: RAPRA translation of Kauchuk i Rezina. 1959.
Rubber and Plastics Research Association, Shawbury, Shrewsbury, SY4 4NR, England.
12, + = ‡
Book notices, book reviews, monographic articles, new products, obituaries, standards, tests.
No Index.
No. 1, 1971, T.p. 50.   250.
Per copy £4.05, per year £32.70.

679.89

DIAMONDS

3593 INDUSTRIAL DIAMOND REVIEW incorporating Industrial Diamond Abstracts. 1944.
Industrial Diamond Information Bureau, 7 Rolls Buildings, Fetter Lane, London, EC4A 1HZ.
12, ‡ =   Properties of diamonds (whole stone, grit, powder); manufacture of diamond tools; all applications in mechanical and civil engineering, glass, stone, ceramics, plastics, mining etc. industries.
Abstracts, book notices, book reviews, letters, monographic articles, new companies, new products, obituaries, patents, standards, tests.
A, Varies—usually June/July, Yes, Vol. 1-30 (photostat) on special request.
June 1972, T.p. 26, Ad.p. 24.   3760.
Per copy 20p, per year £2.40.
Indexed in: BTI.

681.11

HOROLOGY

3594 ANTIQUARIAN HOROLOGY: proceedings of the Antiquarian Horological Society. 1953.
The Antiquarian Horological Society, 28 Welbeck Street, London, W1M 7PG.
4, ‡ + *   Work of clockmakers of the past and the background and beginnings of horology, and of the meetings and proceedings of the A.H.S.
Book notices, book reviews, letters, monographic articles, obituaries.
2 years, December, Yes, None.
March 1972, T.p. 60, Ad.p. 44.   2250.
£3.50 (London members) £2.50 (others).

3595 HOROLOGICAL JOURNAL: official journal of the British Horological Institute. 1858.
Brant Wright Associates Ltd., Box No. 22, Ashford, Kent.
12, ‡ =   Horology in general.
Book notices, book reviews, legal notes, letters, monographic articles, new companies, new products, obituaries, standards, tests.
A, July, No, None.
May 1972, T.p. 22, Ad.p. 14.   51500.
Per copy 25p, per year £3.25.

3596 WATCHMAKER, JEWELLER & SILVERSMITH: official journal of the National Association of Goldsmiths. 1875.
IPC Consumer Industries Press Ltd., 33/39 Bowling Green Lane, London, EC1.
12, = ‡   Business needs of retail jewellers.
Book reviews, legal notes, letters, monographic articles, new companies, news, new products, obituaries, standards, tests.
No Index.
T.p. 42, Ad.p. 60.   6018.
Per copy 17½p, per year £2.10.

681.14

COMPUTERS. DATA PROCESSING

3597 COMPUTER & CONTROL ABSTRACTS. 1969.
(Control Abstracts 1966-1969).
INSPEC, The Institution of Electrical Engineers, Savoy Place, London, WC2R 0BL.
12, + ‡   Consists of 4 main sections: Systems and Control Theory, Control Technology, Computer Programing and Applications, and Computer Systems and Equipment. Each section has about 50 classified subject codes. Subject index has about 700 alpha. subject headings. Approx 24,000 items per year currently included.
Abstracts.
6m, —, No, 2 year.
Per copy £5, per year £55*
* Journals available in either paper or microfiche editions. Combined sub. to paper and microfiche editions £82.50 pa.

3598 THE COMPUTER BULLETIN. 1957.
The British Computer Society, 29 Portland Place, London, W1N 4AP.
12, * ‡ =   Computer applications of all kinds and on their social and human implications. Official society journal.
Book notices, book reviews, commodity prices, letters, monographic articles, new companies, new products, tests.
A, March, Yes, None.
20000.
Per copy 50p, per year £4.50. Free to members.
Indexed in: BTI.

3599 COMPUTER COMMENTARY.
Computer Consultants Ltd., GPO Box 8, Llandudno.
12, =
No Index.
Per year £3.

3600 COMPUTER EDUCATION.
Schools Council Publications, c/o College of Technology, Stafford.
4, = ‡   Book reviews.
No Index.
T.p. 8.
Free to members.

3601 COMPUTER EXECUTIVE: Journal of the Visible Record Society. 1972.
(Journal of the Visible Record Society).
MSOR Ltd., 288 High Street, Croydon, Surrey, CR0 1NG.
12, = ‡   For the small-scale computer industry and its ancillaries.
T.p. 12.
Per copy 40p, per year £3.60.
Free to members.

3602 COMPUTER INTERNATIONAL.
International Computers Ltd., ICL House, Putney, London, SW15.
Irregular, = ‡   News of the computer industry and its applications.
No index.
T.p. 8.
Free.

3603 THE COMPUTER JOURNAL. 1957.
The British Computer Society, 29 Portland Place, London, W1N 4AP.
4, ‡ * =   Scientific business and commercial subjects relating to computers and allied computer field.

Key to reference symbols

○ popular   ‡ technical   = trade/professional

+ research   * society/institution   † house journal

Book notices, book reviews, letters, monographic articles.
A, May, Yes, None.
14000.
Per copy £2, per year £8. Free to members.
Indexed in: BTI.

3604 COMPUTER MANAGEMENT. 1970.
(Mechanised Accounting & Computer Management—1966-1969).
Special Interest Publications Ltd., 196 Shaftesbury Avenue, London, WC2.
12, ‡ =   For data processing management, senior accountants and general management in industry, commerce and government covering new hardware and software developments and advanced techniques in the management and use of computer installations.
Book notices, book reviews, letters, monographic articles, new companies, new products, standards.
No index.
20000.
Per year £7.50.

3605 COMPUTER SURVEY.
United Trade Press Ltd., 9 Gough Square, London, EC4.
6, = ‡
No Index.
3665.
Per year £5.

3606 COMPUTER WEEKLY. 1966.
IPC Electrical Electronic Press Ltd., Dorset House, Stamford Street, London, SE1.
51, ‡ =   Newspaper of the computer industry and as such is directed at computer users and manufacturers. It aims to provide news and informed comment about computer developments in the UK and throughout the world.
Book notices, book reviews, letters, monographic articles, new companies, new products, parliamentary reports, standards.
No Index.
15.6.1972, T.p.6, Ad.p.9.   45500.
Per copy 10p, per year £8.

3607 COMPUTERS AND STRUCTURES. 1971.
Pergamon Press Ltd, Headington Hill Hall, Oxford, OX3 OBW.
6, = +   Application of computers (digital, analog and hybrid) to the solution of scientific and engineering problems related to hydrospace, aerospace and terrestrial structures.
Book reviews, monographic articles.
A, Last issue of volume, Yes, None.
Per copy £4.50, per year £24.

3608 COMPUTERS IN BIOLOGY AND MEDICINE.
Pergamon Press Ltd., Headington Hill Hall, Oxford, OX3 OBW.
4, = +
Book reviews, monographic articles.
A, Last issue of volume, Yes, None.
Per copy £3, per year £10.

3609 CURRENT PAPERS ON COMPUTERS & CONTROL. 1969.
(Current Papers on Control 1966-1968).
INSPEC, The Institution of Electrical Engineers, Savoy Place, London, WC2R OBL.
12, + ‡ =   Current awareness tool for dissemination within laboratories and development organisations.
No Index.
Per copy £1.20, per year £12.

3610 DATA PROCESSING. 1959.
IPC Electrical-Electronic Press Ltd., Dorset House, Stamford St., London, SE1.
6, ‡ + = *   Across the board coverage of all aspects of computing techniques including descriptions of hardware, software and computer-based applications and management techniques.
Book notices, book reviews, letters, monographic articles, new companies, new products, standards, tests.
A, Jan-Feb, Yes, None.
July/August 1972, T.p.60, Ad.p.20.   4399.
Per copy £1.50, per year £8.
Indexed in: BTI.

3611 DATA PROCESSING PRACTITIONER. 1967.
Institute of Data Processing, 418-422 Strand, London, WC2.
4, = + *   Data processing and business computing.
Book reviews, letters, monographic articles, new products.
2 yearly, —, Yes, None.
Spring 1972, T.p.25.
Free to members.

3612 DATA SYSTEMS. 1958.
Business Publications Ltd., Mercury House, Waterloo Road, London, SE1.
12, ‡
No Index.
7676
Per copy 60p, per year £6.
Indexed in: BTI.

3613 DATASCENE. 1969
BED Group, Park House, Park Street, Croydon, CR9 1VA.
12, =
No Index.
15000
Free, controlled circulation.

3614 DATAWEEK. 1967.
Business Publications Ltd., Mercury House, Waterloo Road, London, SE1.
52, =
No Index
40000
Free, controlled circulation.

3615 FORMAT: Computer Laboratory Newsletter. 1970.
University College, Dublin Computer Laboratory, Belfield, Dublin 4.
2, = ‡

3616 THE HONEYWELL COMPUTER JOURNAL. 1967.
Honeywell Information Systems Ltd., Honeywell House, Great West Road, Brentford, Middx.
4, = ‡ +
Per year £4.40.

3617 INTERNATIONAL JOURNAL FOR NUMERICAL METHODS IN ENGINEERING. 1969.
John Wiley & Sons Limited, Baffins Lane, Chichester, Sussex.
4, +   Structural analysis, heat transfer, fluid mechanics and other subjects influenced by computer-aided design.
Book reviews, letters, monographic articles.
A, —, Yes, None.
May-June 1972, T.p.145.
Per year £15.

3618 INTERNATIONAL JOURNAL OF BIO-MEDICAL COMPUTING. 1970.
Applied Science Publishers Ltd., Ripple Road, Barking, Essex.
4, +   Original papers, interpretative reviews and discussion of fundamental research and new developments in the application of computers to medicine in particular and the biosciences in general.
Book reviews, letters, monographic articles.
A, October, Yes, None.
April 1972, T.p.79.   450.
Per year £12.

3619 INTERNATIONAL JOURNAL OF COMPUTER MATHEMATICS. 1967.
Gordon & Breach, 41/42 William 4th Street, London, WC2.
4, ‡ +   Theory of programming languages and their translators, and work concerning mathematical techniques which are of interest to computer users in the fields of numerical analysis operations research, econometrics and applied mathematics in general.
Book notices, book reviews, letters, monographic articles, new companies, tests.
No Index.
Subscription on application.

3620 JOURNAL OF THE INSTITUTION OF COMPUTER SCIENCES. 1970.
Institution of Computer Sciences, 37-39 London End, Beaconsfield, Bucks.
4, * + =   Research and applications in the fields of computer sciences, including such subjects as automation, data retrieval, systems analysis and design, electronic data processing, artificial intelligence, all various forms of computer programming, cybernetics, the study of adaptive systems, theory of automata and the application and use of all these methods in all aspects of the use of computers.
Book notices, book reviews, letters, monographic articles, new products, standards, tests.
A, March, Yes, None.
No. 1, 1972, T.p. 25, Ad.p. 3.   1000.
Per copy 53p, per year £2.10 and Free to members.

3621 JOURNAL OF STATISTICAL COMPUTATION AND SIMULATION. 1972.
Gordon & Breach, 41/42 William 4th Street, London, WC2.
4, + ‡   Relationship between statistics and the computer, publishing original and significant works in areas of statistics which are related to or are dependent upon the computer; for example, computer algorithms related to probability or statistics, studies in statistical interference by means of simulation techniques and implementation of interactive statistical systems.
Book notices, book reviews, letters, monographic articles, new companies, tests.
A, –, No, None.
Per year £15.50.

3622 PAGE: Bulletin of the Computer Arts Society. 1969.
Computer Arts Society, c/o A. Sutcliffe, ICL, Lovelace Road, Bracknell, Berks.
8, * =   The creative uses of computers and other electronics and technology in graphics, sculpture, music, dance, theatre, writing, and other arts; including descriptions of projects and discussion of implications: society activities.
Book notices, book reviews, articles, new products.
No Index.
April 1972, T.p. 6.
Free to members.

3623 REALTIME. 1968.
Computers For People, c/o 10 Mornington Crescent, London, NW1.
12, ‡ ○
Interrelationships of computers and allied fields and society.
Book reviews, letters, articles, new products, cartoons.
No Index.
Spring 1972, T.p. 14.   1000.
60p per six issues.

3624 SOFTWARE PRACTICE AND EXPERIENCE. 1971.
John Wiley & Sons Limited, Baffins Lane, Chichester, Sussex.
4, +   Means of communication of results of practical experience for the benefit of the computing community.
Book reviews, monographic articles.
A, –, Yes, None.
April-June 1972, T.p. 89.
Per year £8.50.

3625 SOFTWARE WORLD. 1969.
AP Publications Ltd., Morley House, Holborn Viaduct, London, EC1.
4, =
No Index.
5000.
Per year £8.50.

3626 TIME SALE. 1972.
Media Promotion Ltd., 1 Chester Close, Chester Street, London, SW1X 7BG.
6, = ‡   Computer industry.
No Index.

681.2

INSTRUMENTATION

3627 AUTOMATIC MONITORING AND MEASURING. 1965.
(English translation of Avtometriya)
Plenum Publishing Co. Ltd., Antvar House, London Road, Wembley, Middx.
6, ‡ +   Sensing and processing of metered information; analog and digital metering instruments and converters; methods and systems for processing metered data by means of specialized computers; peripherals; man-machine systems; metering information and adaptive systems; components.
Monographic articles, new products, tests.
No Index.
Subscription on application.

3628 CONTACT. 1967.
Marconi Instruments Limited, Longacres, St. Albans, Herts.
6, †   An international news bulletin for customers and contacts of Marconi Instruments Limited, manufacturers of electronic measuring instruments.
Abstracts, monographic articles, new products, and news items.
No Index.
Issue 24, T.p. 4.   Controlled 45000.

3629 INSTRUMENT PRACTICE incorporating Process Control and Automation. 1946.
United Trade Press Ltd., 9 Gough Square, Fleet Street, London, EC4.
12, = + ‡   Instrument and process control technology in general.
Book notices, book reviews, commodity prices, letters, monographic articles, new companies, news, new products, obituaries, patents, standards, tests.
A, December, Yes, None.
T.p. 48, Ad.p. 35.   7900.
Per copy 35p, per year £3.50.
Indexed in: BTI.

3630 JOURNAL OF PHYSICS E: Scientific Instruments. 1968.
(Journal of Scientific Instruments 1923-1969)
The Institute of Physics, London and Bristol, Netherton House, Marsh Street, Bristol BS1 4BT.
12, ‡ * =   Deals with instrumentation and measurement, describes modifications to, or new applications of, scientific instruments. Experimental projects in instrument physics and classified lists of manufacturers and their products and where possible the results of user surveys.
Book notices, book reviews, letters, monographic articles.
A, December, Yes, None.
March 1972, T.p. 103, Ad.p. 8.   4682.
Per copy £1.50, per year £18.

3631 MARCONI INSTRUMENTATION. 1947.
Marconi Instruments Limited, Longacres, St. Albans, Herts.
4/3,‡   A technical information bulletin for the telecommunications industry.
Monographic articles, new products, standards, tests.
2 year, in last issue of volume, No, None.
May 1972, T.p. 24.   Controlled 46000.

3632 MEASUREMENT AND CONTROL: Journal of the Institute of Measurement and Control. 1968.
(Transactions of the Society of Instrument Technology. 1947)
Institute of Measurement and Control, 20 Peel Street, London, W8.
12,‡ + * =   All aspects of the measurement and control industry.
Book notices, book reviews, letters, monographic articles, new companies, new products, standards, tests.
A, as available, Yes, None.
May 1972, T.p. 36, Ad.p. 17.   6267.
Per copy £1, per year £12.
Free to members.
Indexed in: BTI.

3633 METRON. Measurement, control, automation. 1969.
(Instrument Abstracts 1946)
SIRA, Chislehurst, Kent.
12, + = ‡   Measurement and control techniques and instrument performance, design, manufacture and markets.
Abstracts, book reviews, news.
M, −, Yes, A.
T.p. 48, Ad.p. 12.
Subscription on application and Free to members.

3634 PERKIN-ELMER INSTRUMENT NEWS. 1950.
Perkin-Elmer Limited, Post Office Lane, Beaconsfield, Buckinghamshire HP9 1QA.
4,‡ =   Book notices, book reviews, letters, monographic articles, new products, obituaries, patents, standards, tests.
No Index.
August 1972, T.p. 12.   42500.
Free.

681.84

SOUND RECORDING AND REPRODUCTION

3635 AUDIO. 1972.
IPC Magazines Ltd., Fleetway House, Farringdon Street, London, EC4.
12, ○ ‡ =   All aspects of the Hi Fi musical scene by well known personalities, equipment reviews in layman terms, comprehensive record reviews, in depth profiles of personalities in the musical world, projects on building Hi Fi equipment.
A, −, Yes, None.
Per copy 20p, per year £3.80.

3636 AUDIO RECORD REVIEW: incorporating the Gramophone Record. 1933.
Heathcock Press Ltd., Pembroke House, Wellesley Road, Croydon.
12, ‡ + =   Record reviews, classical, pop, folk.
No Index.
Per copy 12½p, per year £2.

3637 AUDIO VISUAL: incorporating Film User and Industrial Screen. 1972.
(Film User 1946-1971)
Maclaren Publishers, P.O. Box 109, 69/77 Davis House, High Street, Croydon CR9 1QH.
12, ‡ + *   Solely devoted to audio visual communication, provides advice on optimum use of existing equipment, and where to obtain the most suitable new hardware. Also reviews the latest films and other software.
Book notices, commodity prices, legal notes, articles, new companies, new products, parliamentary reports, tests.
No Index.
June 1972, T.p. 22, Ad.p. 21.   c. 20000.
Per copy 25p, per year £3.25 and Free, controlled circulation.

3638 BUDGET PRICE RECORDS. 1966.
Francis Antony Ltd., 20 East Hill, St. Austell, Cornwall.
4, ○   Complete and cumulative catalogue of all records currently available at less than £1.
No Index.
March, 1972, T.p. 79.
Per copy 25p.

3639 CTV REPORT: Incorporating CTV News. 1971.
Insight, 306a Fulham Road, London, SW10.
12, ‡ = +   Non-broadcast television with particular emphasis on cassette televisual equipment, programmes and marketing.
Book notices, articles, new companies, new products, standards, tests.
6m, October/March, Yes, A.
April 1972, T.p. 10.
Per year £23.

3640 DISC. 1972.
(Disc and Music Echo, 1966; Disc Weekly, 1958)
IPC Specialist & Professional Press, 161-166 Fleet Street, London, EC4 P4AA.
52, ○ =   Popular music encompassing Pop, Rock, Folk, Soul.
No Index.
June 24, 1972, T.p. 28, Ad.p. Most.   74000.
Per copy 6p, per year £5.

3641 EASY LISTENING. 1972.
Telltime Ltd., 7 Carnaby Street, London, W1.
12, ○   Middle of the road music: TV, theatre, film, record, tape.
No Index.

3642 GOOD LISTENING AND RECORD COLLECTOR. 1972.
(Record Collector)
Spotlight Publications Ltd., 12 Sutton Row, London, W1V 5FH.
12, ○ =
No Index.
Per copy 10p.

3643 THE GRAMOPHONE. 1923.
General Gramophone Publications Ltd., 177-179 Kenton Road, Kenton, Harrow, Middx WA3 0HA.
12, = ‡ ○   Reviews of all UK released classical records plus selective popular recordings. Articles on personalities etc.
Book reviews, letters, news, obituaries, tests.
A, July, No, None.
T.p. 40, Ad.p. 120.   70700.
Per copy 15p.

3644 HI-FI ANSWERS. 1972.
Haymarket Publishing Co., Gillow House, 5 Winsley Street, London, W1.
12, ○
Per copy 20p.

3645 HI-FI FOR PLEASURE. 1973.
Blakeham Productions Ltd., 23 Denmark Street, London, WC2H 8NA.
12, ○ ‡   Equipment, mostly for the layman.
Book reviews, articles, new products.
No Index.
Per copy 20p.

3646 HI-FI NEWS AND RECORD REVIEW. 1957.
  Link House Publications Ltd., Link House, Dingwall
    Avenue, Croydon, Surrey CR9 2TA.
  12, ○ Reviews and discussions of Hi-Fi equipment
    in the interests of achieving highest quality sound
    reproduction. Reviews and grades recordings
    under classical, light, 'pop' and Jazz.
  Book reviews, letters, new products, tests.
  A, December, No, None.
  T.p. 36, Ad.p. 71.   40000.
  Per copy 15p, per year £2.50.

3647 HI FI SOUND incorporating Amateur Tape Recording.
    1967.
  Haymarket Publishing Limited, Gillow House, 5
    Winsley Street, London, W1.
  12, ○ ‡ Consumer coverage of Hi Fi equipment and
    techniques.
  Book reviews, commodity prices, letters, articles,
    new products, tests.
  No Index.
  41572.
  Per copy 20p, per year £3.44.

3648 THE HILLANDALE NEWS. 1959.
  City of London Phonograph and Gramophone Society,
  10 South Street, Caversham, Reading, Berkshire.
  6, ‡ * The history of all aspects of sound recording,
    reproduction in particular the era of vertical-cut
    recordings.
  Book notices, book reviews, commodity prices, legal
    notes, letters, articles, new companies, new products,
    obituaries, patents, standards, tests.
  A, —, No, None.
  1000
  Per year £1.25.

3649 THE MUSIC BOX: Journal of The Musical Box Society
    of Great Britain. 1962/3.
  The Musical Box Society of G.B., Bylands, Crockham
    Hill, Edenbridge, Kent.
  4, * ○ All forms of period mechanical music.
  Book notices, book reviews, letters, monographic
    articles, obituaries, patents, etc.
  2 yearly, Each 8 issues, Yes, None.
  Spring 1972, T.p. 39, Ad.p. 3.   c. 420.
  Per year £3.

3650 MUSIC WEEK: Incorporating Record & Tape Retailer.
    1972.
  (Record & Tape Retailer).
  Billboard Publications, 7 Carnaby Street, London, W1.
  52, = All aspects of the music industry and record/
    tape retail trade.
  Commodity prices, letters, new companies, new pro-
    ducts, tests.
  No Index.
  June 24, 1972, T.p. 24, Ad.p. Most.   8000.
  Per copy 20p, £8.50 per year.

3651 THE NEW CASSETTES (& Cartridges). 1970.
  Francis Antony Ltd., 20 East Hill, St. Austell, Cornwall.
  12, ○ Listing new releases monthly.
  No Index.
  5, 1972, T.p. 14, Ad.p. 2.
  Per copy 5p.

3652 NEW CONSENSUS AND REVIEW. 1972.
  Record Specialities, 9 Dean Street, London, W1.
  12, ○ Record collecting.
  No Index.
  Per copy 25p, per year £3.

3653 NEW MUSICAL EXPRESS. 1952.
  (Musical Express 1946-1951).
  IPC Magazines Ltd., 112 Strand, London, WC2R 0AN.
  52, ○ Pop record industry.
  No Index.
  T.p. 20, Ad.p, Most.   215000.
  Per copy 5p.

3654 THE NEW RECORDS. 1952.
  Francis Antony Ltd., 20 East Hill, St. Austell, Cornwall.
  12, ○ Listing of all new L.P. releases.
  No Index.
  5, 1972, T.p. 14, Ad.p. 2.
  Per copy 5p.

3655 POPULAR HI FI. 1971.
  Haymarket Publishing Limited, Gillow House, 5 Winsley
    Street, London, W1.
  12, ○ Consumer magazine for Hi Fi enthusiasts.
  Letters, articles, new companies, new products, tests.
  No Index.
  43762.
  Per copy 20p, per year £3.56.

3656 THE RECORD COLLECTOR: a magazine for collec-
    tors of Recorded Vocal Art. 1947.
  (Record Collectors' Bulletin 1946).
  James Dennis, 61 Fore Street, Ipswich, IP4 1JL.
  12, ○ = Each issue gives photo, biography and dis-
    cography of a famous classical vocalist plus other
    articles of interest to collectors of historical vocal
    records. Artists' active careers always finished,
    so issues are permanent reference works.
  Book reviews, letters articles, obituaries.
  A, as last 2 pp. each completed Vol., Yes, None.
  July 1971, T.p. 47, Ad.p. 2.   850.
  Per year £2.

3657 RECORD COLLECTOR FOR GOOD LISTENING. 1971.
  (Record Bargains).
  Spotlight Publications Ltd., 12 Sutton Row, London,
    W1V 5FH.
  12, ○ All popular and light classical music especially
    record releases.
  Book reviews, letters.
  No Index.
  June 1972, T.p. 30, Ad.p. 10.   50000.
  Per copy 10p.

3658 RECORDED SOUND. 1961.
  (Bulletin of the British Institute of Recorded Sound
    19?-1960.
  British Institute of Recorded Sound, 29 Exhibition Road,
    London, SW7.
  4, + * Music; literature; drama; bio-acoustics; oral
    history and all aspects of recorded sound except
    technical matters; discographies; lecture texts;
    book reviews; illustrated.
  Book reviews, monographic articles.
  Last one Oct. 1971 cumulative from 1955.
  October 1971, T.p. 45, Ad.p. 9.
  Per copy 60p, per year £2.

3659 RECORDS AND RECORDING. 1957.
  Hansom Books, Artillery Mansions, 75 Victoria Street,
    London, SW1 0HZ.
  12, ○ Mainly classical records, cassettes, tapes and
    audio equipment.
  Book notices, book reviews, commodity prices, letters,
    monographic articles, new products, obituaries,
    standards, tests.
  No Index.
  August 1972, T.p. 96, Ad.p. 20.
  Per copy 25p, per year £3.60.

3660 RECORDS OF THE MONTH.
  Trade Papers (London) Ltd./Turret Press (Holdings)
    Ltd., 157 Hagden Lane, Watford, WD1 8LW.
  12, ○
  No Index.
  May 1972, T.p. 16.
  Per year £2.

3661 SCREEN 'N' HEARD. 1972.
  Little John Publications, 15-21 Wilton Way, Hackney,
    London, E8.

12, ○ Film and record reviews.
No Index.
Per copy 25p.

3662 SHOUT. 1968.
(Soul Music 1967-1968).
Clive Richardson, 46 Slades Drive, Chislehurst, Kent, BR7 6JX.
12, + ○ Discographical and biographical research in the field of Rhythm & Blues music, including recording artists' session discographies, detailed biographies, label listings, record and book reviews and ephemerical data.
Book reviews, articles, obituaries, see above.
A, January, No, None.
May 1972, T.p. 1. c. 1000.
Per copy 15p, per year £1.75.

3663 SOUND & PICTURE TAPE RECORDING. 1971.
(Tape Recording Magazine 1957).
Anglia Echo Newspapers Ltd., 2-6 High Street, Haverhill, Suffolk.
12, ○ = All domestic and non-professional studio uses of tape recording and associated equipment.
Book reviews, letters, monographic articles, new products, parliamentary reports, patents, standards, tests.
No Index.
July 1972, T.p. 31, Ad.p. 20. 12000.
Per copy 15p, per year £2.50.

3664 STUDIO SOUND.
Link House Publications Ltd., Link House, Dingwall Avenue, Croydon, Surrey, CR9 2TA.
12, ‡ The technicalities of tape recorders and recording; reviews of equipment and professional recording studios.
Book reviews, commodity prices, letters, articles, new products.
A, December, No, None.
T.p. 23, Ad.p. 16.
Per copy 15p, per year £2.

682.1

FARRIERY

3665 FARRIERS' JOURNAL: for the Farrier, Blacksmith and Agricultural Engineer. 1894.
Farriers' Journal Publishing Co. Ltd., 48 Spencer Place, Leeds, LS7 4BR.
12, ‡ = + * Material of interest to members of the National Master Farriers' Blacksmiths' & Agricultural Engineers' Association other members of the trade, apprentices and interested parties.
Book notices, book reviews, commodity prices, letters, articles, new companies, new products, obituaries, standards, tests.
No Index.
June 1972, T.p. 12, Ad.p. 12. 2000.
Per copy 5p, per year 60p.

683

HARDWARE

3666 HARDWARE MERCHANDISER. 1968.
(Ironmonger 1859-1967).
Morgan-Grampian Ltd., Calderwood Street, London, SE16 6QH.
12, = Management in the hardware trade.
Book reviews, commodity prices, legal notes, letters, new products.
No Index.
T.p. 67, Ad.p. 68. 9500.
Per copy 17½p, per year £2.50.

3667 HARDWARE REVIEW. 1969.
(Hardware Trades Review, 1968).
Indcom Publications Ltd., Faversham House, 103 Brigstock Road, Thorton Heath, Croydon, Surrey.
12, = Product information for hardware buyers. Advice on retailing.
New products.
No Index.
June 1972, T.p. 16, Ad.p. Most. 22214.
Free, controlled circulation.

3668 HARDWARE TRADE JOURNAL. 1874.
Benn Brothers Ltd., 154 Fleet Street, London, EC4.
52, = Events and trends in the trade, reviews of new products, promotions etc.
Book notices, book reviews, commodity prices, legal notes, letters, articles, new companies, new products.
No Index.
T.p. 31, Ad.p. 46. 14500.
Per copy 15p, per year £5.

684

FURNITURE

3669 CABINET MAKER & RETAIL FURNISHER: incorporating Furnishing World. 1880.
Benn Brothers Ltd., 25 New Street Square, London, EC4A 3JA.
52, = ‡ All aspects of the furnishing and allied trades, wholesale, manufacturing and retail. Covers furniture, bedding, upholstery, carpets, raw materials, machinery, textiles, and all subjects of trade interest.
Book reviews, legal notes, letters, monographic articles, new products, obituaries, parliamentary reports.
No Index.
14.7.72, T.p. 18, Ad.p. 17. 11350.
Per copy 15p, per year £7.50.

3670 DECOR AND CONTRACT FURNISHING. 1970.
(Commercial Decor and Contract Furnishing Digest 1964-1969).
Westbourne Journals Ltd., Crown House, Morden, Surrey.
12, = New products and developments in the contract furnishing field.
Book notices, book reviews, letters, news, new products.
No Index.
Per copy 17½p, per year £2.10.
Free, controlled circulation.

3671 FURNISHING IRELAND. 1972.
Jemma Publications Ltd., Richardson House, Main Street, Blackrock, Co. Dublin.
6, =

3672 FURNISHING REVIEW. 1964.
Northwood Publications Ltd., Elm House, 10-16 Elm Street, London, WC1.
12, =
No Index.
10600.
Free, controlled circulation.

3673 FURNISHING WORLD. 1931.
Trade Chronicles Ltd., Mercury House, 103-119 Waterloo Road, London, SE1.
26, = Retail furnishing trade, furniture and carpet manufacturers etc.
No Index.
T.p. 11, Ad.p. 5. 10500.
Per copy 5p, per year £2.

3674 FURNITURE AND BEDDING PRODUCTION: the manufacturers' journal. 1964.
Magnum Publications Ltd., 157 Station Road East, Oxted, RH8 0QE, Surrey.

12, =   Latest processes, materials, machinery and equipment used in the industries.
Book notices, book reviews, monographic articles, new companies, new products, patents, standards, tests.
A, December, Yes, None.
June 1972, T.p. 20, Ad.p. 36.   4020.
Per copy 50p, per year £2.80.

3675 FURNITURE HISTORY: The Journal of the Furniture History Society. 1965.
Furniture History Society, c/o Victoria & Albert Museum, London, SW7.
1, + *   Furniture of all periods and countries, but in practice mainly English, mainly 16th-19th cents.
Book reviews, monographic articles.
No Index.
1971, T.p. 140.   750.
Per year £3.15.

3676 MONTHLY BULLETIN. 1948.
Association of Master Upholsterers, 4 Sutherland Avenue, London, W9.
11, = ‡   All matters of interest in the field of upholstery.
Letters, news, new products, standards, tests.
No Index.
T.p. 10, Ad.p. 8.
Free to members.

3677 WEEKLY CIRCULAR OF THE CHAIR FRAME MANUFACTURERS ASSOCIATION. 1945.
The Association, 4 Sutherland Avenue, London, W9.
52, = ‡   Craft of chair making.
Letters, news, new products.
No Index.
T.p. 3.
Free to members.

685

LEATHER. SHOE TRADE

3678 BLMRA JOURNAL. 1958.
(British Leather Manufacturers' Research Association Monthly Digest 1943-1957).
BLMRA, Milton Park, Egham, Surrey, TW20 9UQ.
12, + =   Applied research on all aspects of leather manufacture, behaviour and use. Treatment of industrial wastes and effluents.
Abstracts, book reviews.
A, —, No, None.
Confidential to Association members.

3679 FOOTWEAR DIGEST. 1972.
(Shoemaking Progress 1971).
Shoe & Allied Trades Research Association, SATRA House, Rockingham Road, Kettering.
6, ‡ = +   A world digest of current developments in the footwear industry and allied trades covering fashion; technology; materials; equipment; retailing.
Abstracts, book notices, book reviews, new companies, new products, patents, standards, tests.
2 monthly, —, Yes, None.
March/April 1972, T.p. 34.   1050.
Per year £12.

3680 FOOTWEAR WEEKLY. 1963.
(Footwear Organiser 1919-1945; Footwear 1946-1962).
IPC Consumer Industries Press Ltd., 33-39 Bowling Green Lane, London, EC1.
51, = ‡ +   Shoe business, retailing, styling and production.
Book notices, book reviews, commodity prices, legal notes, letters, articles, new companies, news, new products, parliamentary reports, patents, standards, tests.
No Index.
T.p. 12, Ad.p. 8.   10500.
Per copy 4p, per year £2.

3681 INTERNATIONAL LEATHERGOODS BUYER incorporating Glove Buyer. 1966.
Leathergoods Association of Buyers & Retailers, 9 St. Thomas Street, London, SE1.
4, =   Fashion trends and merchandising of all types of leather goods.
New products.
No Index.
T.p. 44, Ad.p. Most.   16000.
Free, controlled circulation.

3682 JOURNAL OF THE BRITISH BOOT AND SHOE INSTITUTION. 1936.
Rubber and Technical Press Ltd. (for British Boot & Shoe Institution), Tenterden, Kent.
6, ‡ = +   Technical information to the footwear industry on machinery, materials, components, processes, marketing from student to managing director level.
Book notices, book reviews, letters, monographic articles, obituaries.
A, —, No, None.
July-August 1972, T.p. 30, Ad.p. 5.   4000.
Per copy £2, per year £12, Free to members.
Indexed in: BTI.

3683 JOURNAL OF THE SOCIETY OF LEATHER TRADES' CHEMISTS. 1917.
The Society, 52 Crouch Hall Lane, Redbourn, Herts.
12, = ‡ +
Book reviews, monographic articles, patents.
A, January, Yes, None.
T.p. 40, Ad.p. 16.   1600.
Per copy 50p, per year £6, Free to members.
Indexed in: BTI.

3684 LEATHER, INTERNATIONAL JOURNAL OF THE INDUSTRY: incorporating Leather Trades Review. 1867.
Benn Brothers Ltd., 25 New Street Square, London, EC4A 3JA.
12, = ‡   Provides tanners and suppliers with a comprehensive service. Includes regular features such as raw material reviews; scientific and technical aspects of leather production; fashion trends and monthly reports from the major leather producing countries.
Articles, news.
No Index.
T.p. 32, Ad.p. 100.   3121.
Per copy 50p, per year £6.

3685 LEATHERGOODS. 1917.
Benn Bros. Ltd., 25 New Street Square, London, EC4.
12, =   Luggage, leathergoods, handbag, umbrella and allied trades.
Book reviews, commodity prices, letters, articles, new companies, new products.
No Index.
T.p. 39, Ad.p. 109.   4500.
Per year £4.

3686 SATRA BULLETIN. 1935.
Shoe and Allied Trades Research Association, Satra House, Rockingham Road, Kettering.
12, = ‡ +   A review of research and other work carried out by, and services available from SATRA.
Legal notes, letters, articles, new products, obituaries, patents, standards, tests.
A, —, No, None.
T.p. 20.
Free available only to SATRA members.

3687 SHOE & LEATHER NEWS incorporating Shoe & Leather Record. 1916.
New Century Publishing Co. Ltd., 84-88 Great Eastern Street, London, EC2.

51, ‡ = News events in the shoe and leather trades. Fashion marketing, financial, retailing, staff training, and technology as they affect shoe manufacturing and distribution.
Book reviews, commodity prices, legal notes, letters, new companies, new products, obituaries, parliamentary reports, patents.
No Index.
May 25, 1972, T.p. 27, Ad.p. 37.   8000.
Per copy 10p, per year £6.50.

3688 SHOEBIZ. 1969.
BSC Footwear Ltd., Sunningdale Road, Leicester, LE3 1UR.
4, † Circulated to the staff of BSC's shoe shops throughout the UK—Lilley & Skinner, Saxone, Dolcis, True-Form, Manfield, Freeman Hardy Willis, Curtess—the shoe factories in the Midlands and Scotland and Ulster and the distribution centre at Leicester.
No Index.
Summer 1972, T.p. 8.   27000.
Free.

3689 SHOE MANUFACTURER'S MONTHLY. 1895.
Halford Publishing Co. Ltd., Spencer Chambers, 4 Market Place, Leicester.
12, = Manufacturing trade news.
No Index.
Per year 60p.

3690 SHOE MATERIALS PROGRESS. 1971.
(Poromerics Progress 1968-1971).
Shoe & Allied Trades Research Association, SATRA House, Rockingham Road, Kettering.
6, ‡ = + Technical scientific and economic aspects of developments in footwear materials and components.
Abstracts, book notices, book reviews, monographic articles, new products, patents, standards, tests.
2 monthly, —, Yes, None.
April 1972, T.p. 68.   250.
Free.

685.8

SPORTS EQUIPMENT

3691 HARPERS SPORTS & GAMES. 1946.
(Harpers Sports & Games Distributor 1931; Harpers Sports & Games Weekly 1938).
Harper Trade Journals Ltd., 22 Cousin Lane, London, EC4.
26, = News for manufacturers, wholesalers and retailers of sports and games equipment worldwide.
No Index.
T.p. 12, Ad.p. 15.   1500.
Per year £1.50.

3692 SPORTS AND RECREATION EQUIPMENT. 1971.
(Sports Equipment News 1965-1970).
Benn Bros. Ltd., 25 New Street Square, London, EC4A 3JA.
3, = Sports equipment in general, both recreational and educational.
Book reviews, new products.
No Index.
Free, controlled circulation.

3693 SPORTS TRADER: incorporating Sports Dealer. 1907.
Benn Brothers Ltd., 125 High Street, London, SW19.
12, = Development in design, availability and marketing of sports merchandise produced in the U.K. and principal world countries and distributed through retail outlets.
Book reviews, legal notes, letters, new companies, new products, obituaries, parliamentary reports, patents, standards, tests.

No Index.
T.p. 31, Ad.p. 31.   4000.
Per copy 40p, per year £4.

687

CLOTHING INDUSTRY

3694 BEAUTY COUNTER: Fashion & beauty. 1963.
JMP Services Ltd., Amberley House, Norfolk Street, London, WC2.
= Retail beauty trade.
Book reviews, commodity prices, letters, monographic articles, new companies, news, new products.
No Index.
T.p. 20, Ad.p. 16.   10240.
Free, controlled circulation.

3695 BRITISH CLOTHING MANUFACTURER. 1965.
Textile Trade Publications Ltd., 20 Soho Square, London, W1.
12, ‡ = + Men's and women's outerwear, women's and children's dresses and underwear.
Articles, new products.
No Index.
T.p. 22, Ad.p. 66.
Per copy 25p, per year £4.

3696 CLOTHING INSTITUTE JOURNAL. 1951.
Clothing Institute, 17/18 Henrietta Street, London, WC2E 8QN.
6, = + * ‡ All aspects of the clothing industry.
Abstracts, book reviews, letters, monographic articles.
No Index.
T.p. 62, Ad.p. 20.
Free to members.

3697 CLOTHING RESEARCH JOURNAL. 1973.
Clothing Institute, Hillview Gardens, London, NW4 2JS.
3, =
A, —, Yes, None.
Per year £6.

3698 DRAPERS' RECORD. 1887.
Textile Trade Publications Ltd., (Part of the Thomson Organisation), 20 Soho Square, London, W1.
52, = News and views of women's and children's fashion and textile trades, domestic textiles, furnishing fabrics, apparel, wholesale, manufacturing and especially retail trades.
No Index.
June 17, 1972, T.p. 54, Ad.p. 50.
Per copy 10p.

3699 DRAPERY AND FASHION WEEKLY. 1959.
IPC Consumer Industries Press Ltd., 40 Bowling Green Lane, London, EC1.
51, = Fibres, fabrics, fashions and accessories for women's wear, childrens wear and household textile trade buyers—the merchandising newspaper of the industry.
Book reviews, legal notes, letters, new companies, new products, obituaries.
No Index.
June 16, 1972, T.p. 24, Ad.p. Most.
Per copy 6p, per year £4.

3700 FMT NEWS. 1969.
Federation of Merchant Tailors, 19 Hanover Square, London, W1R 9DA.
4, * = ‡ Bespoke tailoring.
Letters, news.
No Index.
T.p. 4.   350.
Free to members.

3701 FABRIC FORECAST.
Benjamin Dent Publications Ltd., 40 New Oxford Street, London, WC1.

2, = Fabric ranges for the women's fashion industry one year ahead of the consumer market.
Book notices, book reviews, letters, articles, new companies, news, new products, standards, tests.
No Index.
T.p.133, Ad.p.Most.
Free, controlled circulation.

3702 FASHION FORECAST. 1946.
Benjamin Dent Publications Ltd., 40 New Oxford Street, London, WC1.
6, = Women's ready-to-wear industry—domestic and for export—about 6-9 months ahead of the season.
Book notices, book reviews, letters, new companies, news, new products, standards, tests.
No Index.
T.p. 62, Ad.p. Most.   10000.
Free, controlled circulation.

3703 FUR AND LEATHER REVIEW. 1963.
Fur Review Ltd., 27 Garlick Hill, London, EC4V 2BA.
11, = Every aspect of fur throughout the world.
Book notices, book reviews, commodity prices, legal notes, letters, economic articles, new companies, new products, obituaries, parliamentary reports, patents, standards, tests.
No Index.
June 1972, T.p. 50, Ad.p. 13.   c.1500.
Per year £3.50.

3704 FUR WEEKLY NEWS. 1933.
Fur Weekly News Ltd., 87/93 Lambs Conduit St., London, WC1.
52, = Trade news and auction prices.
Book notices, book reviews, letters, new products, obituaries.
No Index.
T.p.12, Ad.p. Most.
Per copy 10p, per year £3.50.

3705 GARMENT WORKER. 1931.
National Union of Tailors & Garment Workers, 14 Kensington Square, London, W8.
12, = Union news.
No Index.
T.p.17.   18500.
Free to members.

3706 JUNIOR AGE: official organ of the National Children's Wear Association. 1948.
(Children's Outfitter 1936-1947).
Blandford-Hyde Publishing Co., Ltd., 167 High Holborn, London, WC1V 0PII.
12, = Childrens wear speciality, retail shops and departmental stores, buyers in wholesale houses, multiple retail houses and catalogue overseas: Board of Trade departments and retail outlets.
Book notices, book reviews, letters, articles, new companies, new products, standards, tests.
No Index.
June 1972, T.p. 20, Ad.p. 36.   6500.
Per copy 20p, per year £3.

3707 MODE MAGAZINE. 1972.
Sigford Ltd., 52 Hagley Road, Stourbridge, Worcs.
4, = Advertising medium for fashion and dressmaking.
No Index.
Per copy 25p.

3708 WEAR: The Leather Fashion Magazine. 1971.
Leather Institute, 9 St. Thomas St., London, SE1.
2, = Devoted entirely to leatherwear and fashion. Advance style information. Manufacturing and retail developments.
No Index.
April 1972, T.p. 120, Ad.p. 81.   10000.
Per copy 50p, per year £1.

687.2
UNDERWEAR

3709 CORSETRY & UNDERWEAR. 1935.
Circle Publications Ltd., 47 Hertford Street, London, W1.
12, = Promotion of interests of corsetry, underwear, swimwear etc.
Book reviews, commodity prices, letters, new companies, news, new products, standards, tests.
No Index.
T.p. 16, Ad.p. 52.   8900.
Free, controlled circulation.

3710 KAYSER NEWS. 1965.
(Flair 1959-1964)
Kayser Bondor Ltd., Baldock, Herts.
2, = Promotional newspaper directed to buyers and store assistants throughout U.K. and abroad.
New products.
No Index.
Spring 1972, T.p. 8.   8800.
Free.

687.3
HOSIERY. KNITWEAR

3711 BRITISH HOSIERY & KNITWEAR: official magazine of the British Hosiery & Knitwear Export Group. 1949.
Ambassador Publishing Services Ltd., 49 Park Lane, London, W1.
3, =
New products.
No Index.
T.p. 16, Ad.p. 28.
Per year £1.

3712 BRITISH HOSIERY JOURNAL. 1953.
British Hosiery Journal, 53 Regent Road, Leicester.
12, =
No Index.
Per copy 15p, per year £2.

3713 BRITISH KNITTING INDUSTRY: Formerly Hosiery Times. 1970.
(Hosiery Times 1929-1970).
Textile Mercury Ltd., 1 Ford Lane, Salford, Lancs. M6 6PX.
12, ‡ = + The knitting industry (hosiery, knitwear etc.) and associate industries, i.e. yarns, fibres, dyeing and finishing, garment manufacture. Fashion and fabrics, design, marketing and other management matters including factory organisation.
Book notices, book reviews, letters, articles, new companies, new products, obituaries, patents, standards, tests.
No Index.
April 1972, T.p. 59, Ad.p. 61.
Per copy 15p, per year £2.75.
Indexed in: BTI.

3714 BUTTONS. 1957.
HW Bradwick, 22 Cross Street, London, N1.
12, =
No Index.
Per copy 17½p, per year £2.50.

3715 HOSIERY ABSTRACTS. 1949.
Hosiery & Allied Trades Research Association, 7 Gregory Blvd., Nottingham, NG7 6LD.
12, ‡ = † Abstracts on knitting, clothing and related textile topics.
Abstracts, book notices, new products, patents, standards.
No Index.
T.p. 23.   1500.
Per year £7.50.

Key to reference symbols

○ popular   ‡ technical   = trade/professional

+ research   * society/institution   † house journal

3716 THE HOSIERY TRADE JOURNAL. 1900.
(Knitters Circular and Monthly Record 1894-1899).
The Hosiery Trade Journal Ltd., 11 Millstone Lane,
  Leicester (Ferry Pickering Group Ltd., Coventry
  Road, Hinckley, Leics).
12, ‡ = All aspects of production and marketing of
  knitted fabrics and garments, includes yarns,
  machinery and production developments, plus dye-
  ing and finishing techniques, markets and fashion
  trends in stockings, socks, jersey fabrics and knit-
  ted outerwear.
Book notices, book reviews, letters, new companies,
  new products, obituaries, patents, standards, tests.
No Index.
June 1972, T.p. 84, Ad.p. 110.
Per copy 50p, per year £6.
Indexed in: BTI.

3717 JERSEY FABRICS INTERNATIONAL. 1972.
(Jersey 1962-1971).
The Hosiery Trade Journal Ltd., 11 Millstone Lane,
  Leicester.
6, = Fibre, fabric and fashion news for garment-
  makers. Largely pictorial with fabric illustrations
  and with live fabric samples.
No Index.
Jan/Feb. 1972, T.p. 50, Ad.p. 44.
Per copy £1, per year £5.

3718 KNITTING & HABERDASHERY REVIEW. 1967.
(Knitting Wool Review 1958-1967).
AS Damery, Chesterfield House, Bloomsbury Way,
  London, WC1.
10, =
Letters, new companies, news, new products, standards,
  tests.
No Index.
T.p. 28, Ad.p. 24.
Per year £1.50.

3719 KNITTING NEWS. 1969.
The Hosiery Trade Journal Ltd., 11 Millstone Lane,
  Leicester. (Ferry Pickering Group Ltd., Coventry
  Rd., Hinckley, Leics).
12, = Supplement to the hosiery trade journal.
No Index.
Free with Hosiery Trade Journal.

3720 KNITWEAR & STOCKINGS. 1953.
(Underwear & Stockings 1947).
Circle Publications Ltd., 47 Hertford Street, London,
  W1.
12, = Specialised trade service.
Book reviews, commodity prices, letters, monographic
  articles, new companies, news, new products,
  obituaries, patents, standards, tests.
No Index.
T.p. 23, Ad.p. 29.   8757.
Free, controlled circulation.

3721 MERIDIAN NEWS. 1929.
Meridian Limited, Haydn Road, Nottingham.
4, † News for employees.
No Index.
Spring 1972, T.p. 4.
Free.

687.4

MILLINERY

3722 MILLINERY AND BOUTIQUE.
H. W. Bradnick, 22 Cross Street, London, N1.
12, =
No Index.
Per copy 32½p, per year £3.25.

687.54

CHIROPODY

3723 BRITISH JOURNAL OF CHIROPODY. 1965.
(British Chiropody Journal: 1933-1965).
The Durlacher Press, 258 Altrincham Road, Manchester
  M22 4AA.
12, ‡ + = Chiropody and all aspects of footcare.
  Reviews the medical literature for material aper-
  taining to the foot. Cover both private practice and
  National Health Service.
Book notices, book reviews, commodity prices, legal
  notes, letters, monographic articles, new companies,
  new products, obituaries, parliamentary reports,
  patents, standards, tests.
No Index.
June 1972, T.p. 16, Ad.p. 11.
Per copy 20p, per year £1.50.

3724 THE CHIROPODIST: journal of the Society of
  Chiropodists. 1914.
The Society of Chiropodists, 8 Wimpole Street, London,
  W1M 8BX.
12, ‡ * Articles of professional interest to prac-
  ticing chiropodists, comments on public affairs of
  interest to chiropodists, news of Society and Branch
  activities of interest to members.
Book notices, book reviews, letters, monographic
  articles, new products, obituaries, parliamentary
  reports, tests.
A, March/April, No, None.
June 1972, T.p. 46, Ad.p. 18.   5000.
Per copy 20p, per year £2.40.

687.9

BRUSHES

3725 BRUSHES: journal of the world's brush industry.
(Brushes & Toilet Goods).
Wheatland Journals Ltd.(Turret Press/Holdings/Ltd.)
  157 Hagden Lane, Watford, WD1 8LW.
12, = ‡ All aspects of manufacture, sale and use of
  brushes.
Book notices, commodity prices, legal notes, new com-
  panies, new products, obituaries, patents, standards,
  tests.
No Index.
May 1972, T.p. 25, Ad.p. 31.
Per year £6.10 including directory issue.

3726 BRUSHES INTERNATIONAL: journal of the World's
  Brush Industry. 1972.
(Brushes; Brushes and Toilet Goods; Brushmaking).
Wheatland Journals Ltd., 157 Hagden Lane, Watford,
  WD1 8LW.
12, = ‡ All matters of interest to the brush indus-
  try and its suppliers of materials and machinery.
Book notices, book reviews, letters, new companies,
  new products, obituaries, patents, standards, tests.
No Index.
T.p. 44, Ad.p. Varies.
Per copy 50p, per year £6.10.

688

GIFTS

3727 THE GIFT BUYER INTERNATIONAL. 1964.
Ralph Sadgrove, 33 Gamage Building, Holborn, London,
  EC1N 2NA.
12, = Tableware, glass, china, stainless steel, leathergoods, gifts novelties, paintings and prints, occasional furniture, lighting, decor, jewellery and
  fancy goods.
Abstracts, book notices, book reviews, commodity
  prices, legal notes, letters, monographic articles,

new companies, new products, obituaries, parliamentary reports, patents, standards, tests.
No Index.
June 1972, T.p. 44, Ad.p. 44.   4750.
Per year £5.

3728 GIFTS. 1968.
(Gifts & Fancy Goods 1951-1968).
Benn Bros., Ltd., Lyon Tower, 125 High St., Colliers Wood, London, SW19.
12, =   Wholesale and retail gift trade.
Legal notes, letters, articles, new companies, new products, obituaries.
No Index.
July 1972, T.p. 55, Ad.p. 75.   5500.
Per copy 40p, per year £5.

688.7
TOYS

3729 BRITISH GO JOURNAL. 1967.
British Go Association, 60 Wantage Road, Reading, Berkshire. RG3 2SF.
4, *   News of recent and forthcoming events in Britain and abroad of interest to Go players, and instruction in all phases of the game.
Book notices, book reviews, letters, monographic articles.
No Index.
March 1972, T.p. 16.   600.
Free to members.

3730 BRITISH TOYS. 1954.
British Toy Manufacturers Association Ltd., Regent House, 89 Kingsway, London, WC2B 6RS.
12, =   News of the industry especially for the manufacturing and retail and export sections.
Book reviews, commodity prices, legal notes, letters, new companies, new products, obituaries, standards, tests.
No Index.
May 1972, T.p. 24, Ad.p. Most.   18839.
Per copy 10p, per year £1.25.

3731 THE BULLETIN: The British Model Soldier Society. 1935.
The British Model Soldier Society, 16 Charlton Road, Kenton, Harrow, Middx.
6, ○ +   Military modelling, uniforms.
Book reviews, letters, articles.
No Index.
April 1972, T.p. 33, Ad.p. 15.   1400.
Per year £2. Members only

3732 GAMES & PUZZLES. 1972.
Edu-Games (U.K.) Ltd., P.O. Box 4, London, N6 4DF.
12, ○   The only consumer magazine that comprehensively covers all types of games, puzzles and competitions. It is directed at all age groups and covers board, group, educational, war, word etc. games.
Book notices, book reviews, commodity prices, letters, articles, new products, standards, tests.
No Index.
July 1972, T.p. 36, Ad.p. 2.
Per copy 20p, per year £2.40.

3733 GAMES & TOYS. 1914.
H. Richard Simmons Ltd., 30/31 Knightrider St., St. Paul's Churchyard, London, EC4.
12, =   Toy trade both at home and abroad.
Book reviews, legal notes, letters, new companies, new products, obituaries, patents.
No Index.
June 1972, T.p. 18, Ad.p. 18.
Per copy 25p, per year £2.50.

3734 HOW TO BUY TOYS. 1972.
Toy Publications (for James Galt), 7c Carlton Drive, London, SW15.
2, ○ =   Kinds of toys and their appropriate age groups.
No Index.
Per copy 30p.

3735 PUZZLER. 1972.
16 Ellerdale Road, London, NW3.
12, ○   Recreational puzzles.
No Index.
Per copy 20p.

3736 TOY TRADER: official journal of the National Association of Toy Retailers. 1908.
Wheatland Journals Ltd., 157 Hagden Lane, Watford, WD1 8LW.
12, = *   Voice opinions on all aspects of the toy trade, reflecting the latest merchandizing trends. Plus full coverage of new products and information and coverage of various international toy fairs.
Book reviews, letters, articles, new companies, new products, obituaries, patents, standards, tests.
A, January, Yes, None.
June 1972, T.p. 24, Ad.p. 20.   10000.
Per year £4.05.

3737 TOYS INTERNATIONAL. 1962.
Trade News Ltd., 203-9 North Gower Street, London, NW1.
6, =
No Index.
4282.
Free, controlled circulation.

688.72
MODELMAKING

3738 AEROMODELLER: incorporating Model Aircraft. 1935.
Model & Allied Publications Ltd., 13-35 Bridge Street, Hemel Hempstead, Herts.
12, ○ ‡
Letters, articles, new products, obituaries, tests.
A, January, No, None.
April 1972, T.p. 35, Ad.p. 22.   30990.
Per copy 15p, per year £2.35.

3739 AIRFIX MAGAZINE: for plastic modellers. 1960.
PSL Publications Ltd., 9 Ely Place, London, EC1N 6SQ.
12, ○ = ‡ +   All aspects of constructing and converting plastic model construction kits, including aircraft, military figures and vehicles, ships and railways. Regular new product reviews.
Book reviews, letters, articles, new products.
No Index.
June 1972, T.p. 36, Ad.p. 19.   40762.
Per copy 15p, per year £2.52.

3740 MILITARY MODELLING MAGAZINE. 1971.
Model & Allied Publications Limited, 13/35 Bridge Street, Hemel Hempstead, Herts.
12, ‡   All matters of militaria in miniature; model soldiers, tanks and artillery, warships and war time aircraft. Periods of interest from 1000 BC to present day.
Book notices, book reviews, commodity prices, letters, monographic articles, new companies, new products, obituaries, tests.
A, January, Yes, None.
July 1972, T.p. 37, Ad.p. 25.   40000.
Per copy 15p, per year £2.35.

3741 MINIATURE WARFARE & MODEL SOLDIERS. 1969.
John Tunstill, 36 Kennington Road, London, SE1.
12, ○   War games and model soldiers. Uniforms, weapons and tactics from 2000 BC to 2000 AD.

Book reviews, letters, articles, new products.
No Index.
May 1972, T.p. 20, Ad.p. 5.   8000.
Per copy 22½p, per year £3.15.

3742 MODEL CARS: incorporating Miniature Auto. 1964.
(Model Cars, 1946-1964)
Model & Allied Publication Limited, 13/35 Bridge Street, Hemel Hempstead, Herts.
12, ‡   Covers all subjects relating to models of automobiles and related subjects; electric slot racers, radio control racing cars, miniature die cast collecting, Dinky toys etc.
Book notices, book reviews, commodity prices, letters, monographic articles, new companies, new products, obituaries, tests.
A, January, Yes, None.
July 1972, T.p. 30, Ad.p. 18.   11000.
Per copy 15p, per year £2.35.

3743 MODEL ENGINEER. 1898.
Model & Allied Publications (MAP) Ltd., 13-35 Bridge Street, Hemel Hempstead, Herts.
24, = ○ ‡   Live steam-model locomotives, traction engines and allied subjects.
Book reviews, letters, monographic articles, news, new products, obituaries, reports, patents, standards, tests.
A, –, No, None.
T.p. 40, Ad.p. 9.   25160.
Per copy 15p, per year £4.50.

3744 MODEL MAKER & MODEL BOATS. 1964.
Model & Allied Publications Ltd., 13-35 Bridge Street, Hemel Hempstead, Herts.
12, = ○ ‡   Model power boat and yacht design, construction, operation and allied subjects.
Book reviews, letters, monographic articles, news, new products, obituaries, standards, tests.
A, February, No, None.
Per copy 12½p, per year £1.75.

3745 MODEL SHIPWRIGHT. 1972.
Conway Maritime Press Ltd., 7 Nelson Road, Greenwich, London, SE10.
4, ○ ‡   For all interested in ships and ship models— model makers, collectors, photographers and historians. Club news, book reviews, queries etc.
Book notices, book reviews, letters, monographic articles.
A, –, Yes, None.
T.p. 96, Ad.p. 6.   2000.
Per year £3.50.

3746 RADIO CONTROL MODELS & ELECTRONICS. 1960.
Model & Allied Publications Limited, 13-35 Bridge Street, Hemel Hempstead, Herts.
12, ‡   Radio controlled aspects of aeromodelling, small section on radio controlled cars and boats.
Book reviews, commodity prices, letters, articles, new products, obituaries, tests.
A, January, No, None.
May 1972, T.p. 43, Ad.p. 29.   22345.
Per copy 20p, per year £3.

3747 RAILWAY MODELLER. 1949.
Reco Publications & Publicity Ltd., Pecoway House, 7/9 Harbour Road, Seaton, Devon, EX12 2LU.
12, ○   All aspects of railway modelling.
Book reviews, letters, monographic articles, new products, obituaries.
A, Approximately February each year, Yes, None.
July 1972, T.p. 35, Ad.p. 28.   51854.
Per copy 18p, per year £2.94.

3748 SCALE MODELS. 1969.
Argus Press Ltd., 12/18 Paul Street, London, EC2.
12, ‡   Scale models of all types but particularly aircraft.

Book reviews, commodity prices, letters, articles, new companies, new products, obituaries, reports, tests.
A, January/February, Yes, None.
July 1972, T.p. 35, Ad.p. 16.   26163.
Per copy 15p, per year £2.35.

689
HOBBIES

3749 COMPETITORS JOURNAL & MONEY MATTERS. 1950.
City Magazines Ltd., Aldwych House, Aldwych, London, WC2.
52, ○   Competition news, advice and general features.
Book reviews, letters, news, new products.
No Index.
T.p. 12, Ad.p. 4.   68000.
Per copy 5p, per year £2.50.

69
BUILDING

3750 BUILD INTERNATIONAL. 1968.
Applied Science Publishers Ltd., Ripple Road, Barking, Essex.
6, ‡   Original and up-to-date information on building research and development by specialists in building research stations, industry, universities, technological institutes and professional practices.
Book notices, book reviews, letters, monographic articles, new products.
A, January, Yes, None.
January/February 1972, T.p. 64.   1000.
Per year £10.

3751 BUILDING: the newspaper of the Design and Construction team. 1966.
(The Builder 1842-1966).
The Builder Group, 4 Catherine Street, London, WC2B 5JN.
52, ‡ =
Book reviews, letters, monographic articles, new products.
6m, Last issue in June, last issue in December, No, None.
T.p. 66, Ad.p. 128.
Per copy 10p, per year £5.20.
Indexed in: BTI, IBZ.

3752 BUILDING AND CONTRACT JOURNAL. 1972.
Irish Publishing Co. Ltd., 39 Lower Leeson Street, Dublin, 2.
12, =
No Index.
Per copy 15p.

3753 BUILDING & HEATING PRODUCTS GUIDE. 1965.
New Property Press, 5 St. Peter's Street, London, N1.
2, = ‡   Advertising entries only.
No Index.

3754 BUILDING DESIGN: the weekly newspaper for the building team. 1970.
Morgan-Grampian (Publishers) Ltd., Morgan-Grampian House, Calderwood St., London, SE18 6QH.
52, ○ ‡ = +   Architects, quantity surveyors, municipal engineers, housing managers, consulting engineers, interior designers and building contractors.
Book notices, book reviews, legal notes, letters, monographic articles, new companies, new products, obituaries, parliamentary reports, patents, standards, tests.
Unpublished for office use only.
23.6.72, T.p. 24.   27543.
Per copy 10p, per year £5. Controlled—free within publisher's terms.

3755 BUILDING MAINTENANCE. 1967.
Factory Publications Ltd., Mercury House, Waterloo Road, London, SE1.
12, = ‡ +   Building maintenance market industry, commerce and local government.
Book reviews, monographic articles, news, new products, parliamentary reports, standards, tests.
No Index.
8790.
Free, controlled circulation.

3756 BUILDING SCIENCE. 1965.
Pergamon Press Ltd., Headington Hill Hall, Oxford, OX3 0BW.
4, = +   Application of scientific principles to problems in design, construction and use of buildings.
Book reviews, letters, monographic articles.
A, Last issue of volume, Yes, None.
T.p. 250.
Per copy £5, per year £16.

3757 BUILDING SCIENCE ABSTRACTS. 1928.
HMSO, PO Box 569, London, SE1.
12, = + ‡   Building science in all aspects.
Abstracts.
A, —, No, None.
Per year £3.50.

3758 BUILDING SPECIFICATION. 1970.
Industrial Publications Ltd., 42 High Street, Croydon, CR0 1NA, Surrey.
12, = ‡   Building specification and designing.
Book notices, book reviews, commodity prices, letters, monographic articles, new products, patents, standards, tests.
No Index.
May 1972, T.p. 59, Ad.p. 59.   30119.
Per copy 60p, and Free, controlled circulation.

3759 BUILDING TECHNOLOGY AND MANAGEMENT: Journal of the Institute of Building. 1963.
(Journal of the Institute of Builders).
The Institute of Building, Englemere, Kings Ride, Ascot. Berks.
12, ‡ * +   Management of building companies and technical subjects; also education and training for building.
Book notices, book reviews, legal notes, letters, monographic articles, obituaries.
No Index.
June 1972, T.p, 18, Ad.p. 12.   20500.
Per copy 38p, per year £3.50.
Indexed in: BTI.

3760 BUILDING WORKER. 1947.
Amalgamated Union of Building Trade Workers, Crescent Lane, Clapham, London, SW4.
12, =
Book reviews, letters, monographic articles, news.
A, —, Yes, None.
13000.
Per copy 2½p, per year 30p.

3761 BUILT ENVIRONMENT. 1972.
(Official Architecture and Planning 1937-1972).
Architectural & Planning Publications Ltd., 4 Catherine St., Aldwych, London, WC2B 5JN.
12, ‡ =   All with an interest in planning, designing and building. Selected aspects of the built environment (e.g. urban motorways, primary schools) are studied in detail each month.
Book reviews, letters, monographic articles.
A, December, Yes, None.
June 1972, T.p. 44, Ad.p. 24.   8100.
Per copy 35p, per year £3.60.

3762 CONTRACT JOURNAL: incorporating Building Industry News and British Constructional Engineer.
IPC Building & Contract Journals Ltd., (member of the IPC Business Press Group), 32 Southwark Bridge Road, London, SE1.
52, ‡ =   Up to the minute news items on important events in the construction industry: management articles: technical articles on important projects, new equipment and techniques: interviews with prominent personalities: economic comment: people in the news: plant and equipment data: materials and components data: contracts awarded: contracts open: projects.
Book reviews, commodity prices, legal notes, letters, articles, new companies, new products, obituaries, parliamentary reports, standards, tests.
No Index.
20. 7. 1972, T.p. 62, Ad.p. 62.   13776.
Per copy 20p, per year £9.50p.

3763 CUBITTS MAGAZINE. 1962.
Holland, Hannen & Cubitts Limited, 1 Queen Anne's Gate, London, SW1H 9BT.
2, ‡ † =   Trade and technical appeal contributed from outside and within the organisation. Company news.
Monographic articles, new companies, new products.
No Index.
Autumn 1971, T.p. 20.
Free.

3764 THE FACULTY OF BUILDING REVIEW.
The Faculty of Building, The Secretariat, 10 Manor Way, Boreham Wood, Hertfordshire, WD6 1QQ.
4, ‡ *   Architects, engineers, surveyors, building and civil engineering contractors, and allied professions and trades.
Monographic articles, tests.
No Index.
Winter 1970, T.p. 40.   3000.
Per copy 25p, per year £1.50.

3765 IRISH CONTRACTS WEEKLY. 1953.
Irish Contracts Weekly, 6 Berkeley Street, Dublin, 7.
52, ‡ =   All aspects of building and engineering industries in Ireland.
Book reviews, commodity prices, new companies, new products.
No Index.
Per year £4.20.

3766 MASTER BUILDERS JOURNAL: official Journal of the Federation of Master Builders. 1955.
Trade Press (FMB) Ltd., 33 John Street, London, WC1.
12, = ‡   Trade and technical information, industrial relations, industry legislation.
Book notices, book reviews, legal notes, letters, articles, news, new products, parliamentary reports, standards, tests.
No Index.
T.p. 27, Ad.p. 25.   20100.
Free to members.
Indexed in: BTI.

3767 NATIONAL BUILDER and sub-contractor. 1971.
(The National Builder 1920-1921)
Federated Employers Press Ltd., 82 New Cavendish Street, London, W1M 8AD.
12, ‡ = *   NFBTE affairs, legislation affecting the building industry, costs, labour statistics, etc.
Book reviews, commodity prices, legal notes, letters, monographic articles, new products, obituaries, parliamentary reports.
A, February, Yes, None.
June 1972, T.p. 23, Ad.p. 52.   16000.
Per copy 30p, per year £3.40.
Indexed in: BTI.

3768 NEW BUILDING. 1961.
(Speculative Builder 1960)
New Property Press, 5 St. Peter's Street, London, N1.
10, = ‡   Coverage of new building projects and developments. Information about new products and materials.
Book notices, book reviews, articles, new products.
No Index.
January 1972, T.p. 18, Ad.p. 25.   18000.
Per copy 17p, per year £2.50 and Free, controlled circulation.

69—024
ROOFING

3769 THE ROOFING CONTRACTOR: Journal of the National Federation of Roofing Contractors. 1943.
(Slate Trade Gazette 1902-1942).
The Federation, West Bar Chambers, 38 Boar Lane, Leeds, LS1 5DE.
6, = ‡
Book notices, book reviews, legal notes, letters, articles, news, new products, obituaries, parliamentary reports, standards, tests.
No Index.
T.p. 19, Ad.p. 21.
Free to members.

69.003.12
QUANTITIES

3770 THE QUANTITY SURVEYOR: the Journal of the Institute of Quantity Surveyors. 1944.
The Institute of Quantity Surveyors, 98 Gloucester Place, London, W1H 4AT.
6, ‡ + = *   Building and civil engineering industries in UK and abroad, Institute and Branch news.
Book reviews, legal notes, letters, monographic articles, new products, obituaries.
2 year, June of even numbered years, No, None.
May/June 1972, T.p. 23, Ad.p. 8.
7100.
Per copy 50p, per year £3. Free to members.

691
BUILDING MATERIALS

3771 BRICK BULLETIN. 1963.
Brick Development Association, 3-5 Bedford Row, London, WC1R 4BU.
4, =
No Index.
Free.

3772 BUILDERS' MERCHANTS JOURNAL: Inc. Builders Merchants Review. 1920.
Benn Brothers Limited, 25 New Street Sq., London, EC4A 3JA.
12, =
Book reviews, letters, articles, new products, obituaries, parliamentary reports, standards.
No Index.
5211.
Per copy 25p, per year £2.

3773 BUILDING EQUIPMENT & MATERIALS: Incorporating Plastics Applications. 1972.
(Building Equipment News-1955)
IPC Building & Contract Journals Ltd., 32 Southwark Bridge Road, London, SE1 9EX.
12, ‡ =   New building products, monthly feature reviewing new products in a particular field, which have appeared during the last twelve months. Product reports of major U.K. and European building exhibitions.
Book reviews, new products, standards.
No Index
June 1972, T.p. 40, Ad.p. 20.   27000.
Per copy 35p, per year £5 and Free, controlled circulation.

3774 BUILDING MATERIALS: the journal of evaluation and specification. 1940.
A4 Publications Ltd., PO Box 7, Church Road, Woldingham, Surrey.
12, = ‡   Evaluation and specification of building materials and associated subjects.
Book notices, book reviews, commodity prices, letters, monographic articles, new companies, news, new products, reports, patents, standards, tests.
A, January, Yes, None.
T.p. 44, Ad.p. 34.   5500.
Free, controlled circulation.
Indexed in: BTI. IBZ.

3757 DEVELOPMENT AND MATERIALS BULLETIN. 1967.
Greater London Council, GLC Bookshop, County Hall, London, SE1 7PB.
10, ‡ = +   Critical appraisals of building materials, and methods of construction.
New products, standards, tests.
Nos. 1-46, July 1971, Yes, None.
Per copy 50p, per year £5.

3776 LBC REVIEW: the house journal of London Brick Co. Ltd. 1971.
(Phorpres News.)
London Brick Company Limited, Stewartby, Bedford.
6, †   Company news.
Letters, articles, new companies, new products, obituaries.
No Index.
May/June 1972, T.p. 40.   3500.
Per copy 2½p.

3777 MARLEY NEWS. 1953.
Marley Ltd., Sevenoaks, Kent.
4, ‡ = †   Deals with the application and use of Company's products, both at home and overseas. Articles of interest to architects, building contractors, plumbers etc.
Articles, new products, tests.
No Index
Winter 1972, T.p. 12.
Free.

3778 MODERN PLASTERING. 1967.
Federated Employers Press, 82 New Cavendish St., London W1M 8AD
4, ‡ =   Plaster work and dry lining for contractors, architects and surveyors.
Legal notes, letters, articles, new products, standards, tests.
No Index.
Spring 1972, T.p. 12, Ad.p. 8.   3210.
Per copy 18p, per year 70p.

3779 NEWSDAY. 1971.
British Gypsum Limited, Ferguson House, 15-17 Marylebone Road, London, NW1 5JE.
4, =   News for specifiers and users in the building industry.
Articles, new products, tests.
No Index.
April 1972, T.p. 8.
Free.

696
PLUMBING

3780 PLUMBING. 1970.
(Journal of the Registered Plumbers Association).
Institute of Plumbing, North Street, Hornchurch, Essex.

4, = ‡ +
Book notices, book reviews, legal notes, letters, articles, news, new products, obituaries, parliamentary reports, patents, standards, tests.
No Index.
T.p. 22, Ad.p. 28.   27000.
Free to members.

3781 PLUMBING EQUIPMENT NEWS AND HEATING ENGINEER. 1963.
Peterson Publishing Co. Ltd., Peterson House, Livery Street, Birmingham 3.
12, ‡ + =   Plumbing and domestic heating.
Book reviews, letters, monographic articles, new companies, news, new products, patents, standards, tests.
No Index.
21700.
Free, controlled circulation.

3782 PLUMBING & HEATING ENGINEER. 1879.
Dale Reynolds & Co. Ltd., 121 Kingsway, London, WC2.
12, = ‡
No Index.
6000.
Per copy 10p, per year £1.50.

3783 PLUMBING & HEATING JOURNAL. 1969.
(Plumbing Trade Journal & Heating Review, 1963-1969; Plumbing Trade Journal 1921-1962).
Plumbing Trade Journal Co. Ltd., 30 Princes Street, Southport, Lancs.
12, = ‡
Book reviews, legal notes, letters, monographic articles, news, new products, obituaries, standards, tests.
No Index.
T.p. 28, Ad.p. 19.   8000.
Per copy 10p, per year £1.50.

3784 SCOTTISH PLUMBERS JOURNAL. 1923.
B. W. Parker, 30 George Square, Glasgow, C2
6, =
No Index.
1698.
Per copy 5p, per year 30p.

3785 SCOTTISH PLUMBING AND HEATING MONTHLY. 1969.
(Scottish Master Plumber 1952-1968).
SP Technical Publications Ltd., 2 Walker Street, Edinburgh.
12, = ‡   All aspects of plumbing and allied trades.
Commodity prices, legal notes, letters, news, new products, patents.
No Index.
T.p. 19, Ad.p. 18.   1690.
Per copy 5p, per year 70p.

697

AIR CONDITIONING. HEATING. VENTILATING

3786 DISTRICT HEATING ASSOCIATION JOURNAL. 1970.
(Newsletter)
District Heating Association, Derbyshire House, St. Chad's Street, London, WC1.
4, ‡ = *   District heating and total energy: social welfare and environment; energy economics, fuel policies; central heating; group heating; institutional services; industrial process heating/total energy; steam raising/power generation; underground mains.
Book notices, book reviews, commodity prices, legal notes, letters, monographic articles, new companies, new products, obituaries, parliamentary reports, patents, standards, tests.
No Index.
Third Quarter 1971, T.p. 27, Ad.p. 15.   3000.
Per copy £1, Free to members.

3787 DOMESTIC HEATING AND AIR CONDITIONING: Journal of the Domestic Heating Society. 1965.
The Domestic Heating Society, 23 Northaw Road, Cuffley, Herts.
4, ‡ = + *   Domestic heating appliance and ancillary manufacturers, merchant distributors, fuel interests, architects and consultants. All who wish to be informed on trends and technicalities in domestic comfort making.
Book reviews, letters, monographic articles, new products, obituaries, standards, tests.
No Index.
March 1972, T.p. 15, Ad.p. 6.   850.
Per copy 25p, per year £1.

3788 DOMESTIC HEATING ENGINEER: Journal of the Institute of Domestic Heating Engineers. 1966.
(IDHE News 1965-1966)
E. E. Farrow, Rowan Wood, Southwell Road, Benfleet, Essex.
6, * = ‡   Domestic heating and allied technologies.
Book reviews, letters, monographic articles, news, new products, obituaries, standards, tests.
No Index.
T.p. 32, Ad.p. 6.
Free to members.

3789 DOMESTIC HEATING NEWS. 1961.
Equipment News Ltd., 35 Red Lion Square, London, WC1.
12, = ‡   Heating, plumbing, insulation, ventilation.
Book notices, book reviews, commodity prices, letters, monographic articles, new companies, news, new products, obituaries, standards, tests.
No Index.
T.p. 39, Ad.p. 43.   17607.
Free, controlled circulation.

3790 HVRA NEWSLETTER. 1965.
Heating & Ventilating Research Association, Old Bracknell Lane, Bracknell, Berks.
6, ‡ = +   HVRA Research and services.
No Index.
April 1972, T.p. 6.   1800.
Free to members.

3791 THE HEATING & VENTILATING ENGINEER and Journal of Air Conditioning. 1927.
Technitrade Journals Limited, 11-13 Southampton Row, London, WC1.
12, ‡ = +   Heating, ventilating and air-conditioning.
Book notices, book reviews, legal notes, letters, monographic articles, new companies, new products, obituaries, parliamentary reports, patents, standards, tests.
A, July, Yes, None.
June 1972, T.p. 53, Ad.p. 65.
Per copy 25p, per year £4.
Indexed in: BTI.

3792 HEATING AND VENTILATING REVIEW. 1960.
Heating & Ventilating Publications Ltd., 103 Brigstock Road, Thornton Heath, Surrey.
12, = ‡   New methods and products for industry, public buildings, and the home.
Monographic articles, new companies, news, new products, patents, standards.
No Index.
T.p. 64, Ad.p. most.   21429.
Free, controlled circulation.

3793 HEATING VENTILATING AND AIR CONDITIONING NEWS. 1971.
(Heating & Ventilating News).
Brookland Press Ltd., 44 Hatton Garden, London, EC1N 8AE.
12, ‡ =   Heating, ventilating and air conditioning.
Book notices, articles, new companies, new products, parliamentary reports, standards, tests.
No Index.
Free, controlled circulation.

3794 IHVE JOURNAL: Journal of the Institution of Heating and Ventilating Engineers. 1969.
(Journal of the IHVE 1933-1969; Proceedings of the IHVE 1899-1933)
Batiste Publications Ltd., 203-209 Gower Street, London, NW1.
12, * ‡ + =   Heating, ventilating, air-conditioning, water supply etc.
Book notices, book reviews, letters, monographic articles, news, new products, obituaries, standards, tests.
A, May, Yes, 5 year.
T.p. 40, Ad.p. 60.   5692.
Per year £6, Free to members.

3795 JOURNAL OF THERMAL ANALYSIS. 1969.
Heyden & Son Limited, Spectrum House, Alderton Crescent, London, NW4 3XX.
4, ‡ + =   Communications on thermal investigations. The main subjects covered are: Thermo-gravimetry, derivate-thermogravimetry, differential thermal analysis, derivatography, thermodilatometry, thermometry, thermal gas-analysis. etc.
Book reviews, monographic articles, new products, obituaries.
A, —, Yes, None.
No. 1, 1970, T.p. 105, Ad.p. 4.
Per year £7.50.

3796 LPG: the magazine for LPG dealers. 1964.
Sonostrips Ltd. (for Shell-Mex and B.P. Ltd.) 49b Station Road, Edgware, London, HA8 7HX.
4, = †
Legal notes, letters, articles, new products, obituaries, patents, standards, tests.
No Index.
Spring 1972, T.p. 20, Ad.p. 4.   4800.
Free.

3797 OIL AND GAS FIRING: The Journal of the British Oil and Gas Firing Equipment Manufacturers Association. 1966.
(Oil Firing 1958-1966).
Oil Firing Publications Ltd., The Fernery, Market Place, Midhurst, Sussex.
11, ‡   Information on technical developments in equipment burning oil or gas. Comment on fuel policy. News of companies and personalities in the industry. News bulletins from the British Oil and Gas Firing Equipment Manufacturers Association.
Abstracts, book notices, book reviews, legal notes, letters, monographic articles, new companies, new products, obituaries, standards, tests.
No Index.
March 1972, T.p. 23, Ad.p. 8.   3004.
Per copy 20p, per year £2.75.
Indexed in: BTI.

3798 SPIRAX TOPICS. Technical information for the Works Engineer and Manager. 1940.
Stocker Hocknell Limited, 4 Market Square, Amersham, Buckinghamshire.
6, ‡ = †   Propagation of the best techniques in handling process steam, hot water, and compressed air in commerce and industry throughout the world.
No Index.
No. 2, 1972, T.p. 8.   30000
Free.

3799 THE STEAM AND HEATING ENGINEER: Environmental services for industrial, commercial and public buildings. 1963.
(The Steam Engineer. 1931-1963)
Troup Publications Limited, 76 Oxford Street, London, W1N 0HH.
12, ‡ =   Management, design, specification, purchase, installation, operation and maintenance of plant, materials and equipment for mechanical and electrical engineering services for industrial, commercial and public buildings.
Book reviews, letters, monographic articles, new companies, new products, obituaries, parliamentary reports, patents, standards, tests.
No Index.
April 1972.   15974
Free, controlled circulation.
Indexed in: BTI.

3800 THERMAL ABSTRACTS. 1964.
(HVRA Library Bulletin 1960-1965).
Heating and Ventilating Research Association, Old Bracknell Lane, Bracknell, Berks.
6, ‡ + =   Heating, ventilating air conditioning and the mechanical services of buildings generally.
Abstracts, translations, standards.
A, December, No, 5 year.
No. 1, 1972, T.p. 25.   1700.
Per year £16.

3801 THERMAL ENGINEERING [Cover-to-Cover translation of Teploenergetika]. 1964.
Pergamon Press Ltd., Headington Hill Hall, Oxford, OX3 0BW.
12, + = ‡   Research and practice in the power industry, including district heating.
Monographic articles.
A, Last issue of volume, Yes, None.
T.p. 138.
Per copy £4, per year £32.

3802 WARM AIR HEATING AND ENVIRONMENTAL ENGINEERING. 1968.
Peterson Publishing Co. Ltd., Peterson House, Livery Street, Birmingham, 3.
12, = ‡ +   Environmental engineering including heating, ventilating, lighting etc.
Book notices, book reviews, letters, monographic articles, new companies, news, new products, obituaries, patents, standards, tests.
No Index.
Free, controlled circulation.

697.98

DUST CONTROL

3803 FILTRATION AND SEPARATION: Incorporating Dust Control and Air Cleaning. 1965.
(Filtration 1964).
Uplands Press Ltd., 1 Katharine Street, Croydon, CR9 1LB, Surrey.
6, ‡ =   All aspects of filtration, separation, clarification, dust control, air cleaning and related processes, together with the equipment, plant, installations and products required to operate them. It thus serves users of filtration, separation, dust control and air cleaning equipment for every application in all industries.
Abstracts, book notices, book reviews, monographic articles, new products, obituaries, patents, standards, tests.
A, Nov/Dec, No, None.
January/February 1972, T.p. 70, Ad.p. 54.   4058.
Per copy 75p, per year £4.

698

PAINTING AND DECORATING

3804 BUILDER AND DECORATOR. 1972.
Strode Publications Ltd., MAP House, 243 Caledonian Road, London, N1 1ED.
12, ‡ =   Building and decorating especially for the smaller firm.
Book notices, book reviews, legal notes, letters, monographic articles, new products, obituaries, standards, tests.

No Index.
October 1972, T.p. 8, Ad.p. 8.   30000.
Per copy 10p, per year £1.60.

3805 DECORATING CONTRACTOR incorporating The Decorator. 1902.
Strode Publications Ltd., MAP House, 243 Caledonian Road, London, N1 1ED.
12, ‡ =   Specialist painting and contracting.
Book notices, book reviews, legal notes, letters, monographic articles, new products, obituaries, standards, tests.
No Index.
September 1972, T.p. 23, Ad.p. 16.   3300.
Per copy 25p, per year £2.40.

3806 MASTERPAINTER AND DECORATOR: The Journal of the National Federation of Master Painters and Decorators. 1971.
(National Master Painter, 1930-1969; Masterpainter 1969-1971).
National Federation of Master Painters and Decorators, 6 Haywra Street, Harrogate, Yorkshire, HG1 5BL.
11, = †   All matters and subjects of interest to the painting and decorating trade.
Book reviews, commodity prices, legal notes, letters, monographic articles, new products, obituaries, standards, tests.
No Index.
April 1972, T.p. 20, Ad.p. 8.   2750.
Free to members.

3807 PAINTING AND DECORATING JOURNAL. 1969.
(Journal of Decorative Art and British Decorator 1881-1954; Painting and Decorating 1954-1968).
Sutherland Publishing Co. Ltd., 30 Princes Street, Southport, Lancs.
12, = ‡   Painting and decorating, new materials etc.
Book reviews, legal notes, articles, news, new products, obituaries, standards, tests.
No Index.
T.p. 31, Ad.p. 18.   4592.
Per copy 15p, per year £1.50.
Indexed in: BTI.

3808 SCOTTISH DECORATORS QUARTERLY REVIEW. 1922.
Scottish Decorators Federation, 14 Craigleith Hill Avenue, Edinburgh, EH4 2JA.
4, =
News, new products.
No Index.
T.p. 48, Ad.p. 23.
Free to members.

3809 WALLPAPER PAINT AND WALLCOVERING: Journal of the Wallpaper Paint and Wallcoverings Association of G.B. 1965.
(Wallpaper and Paint Retailers Journal 1955-1964).
20 Huntingdon House, 220 Cromwell Rd., London, SW5 05W.
12, =   For retailers, merchants and suppliers of wallcoverings, paints and allied decorative products for home users and sale via retail shops.
Book reviews, legal notes, letters, articles, new products, obituaries, standards.
No Index.
April 1971, T.p. 18, Ad.p. 10.   12000.
Per copy 17p, per year £2.

699.8

INSULATION

3810 INSULATION: thermal, acoustic, vibration. 1956.
Lomax, Erskine & Co. Ltd., 8 Buckingham Street, London, WC2.
6, = ‡   All aspects of insulation of houses, factories and industrial buildings.
Book reviews, commodity prices, letters, monographic articles, new companies, news, new products, obituaries, standards.
No Index.
T.p. 23, Ad.p. 28.   4403.
Per copy 15p, per year £1.50.
Indexed in: BTI.

7
THE ARTS

3811 AHEAD IN YORKSHIRE. 1971.
Yorkshire Arts Association, Glyde House, Glydegate, Bradford, 5.
4, ○
No Index.
Subscription on application.

3812 AIRMAIL: Information on information sources relevant to artists. 1972.
(Catalyst 1969-1971).
Art Information Registry Ltd., Burlington House, Piccadilly, London, W1V 9AG.
2, =
No Index.
March 1972, T.p. 22.

3813 APOLLO. 1925.
Financial Times, Bracken House, 10 Cannon St., London, EC4.
12, ○ = *   Art and antiques.
Book notices, book reviews, letters, monographic articles.
6m, –, Yes, None.
T.p. 86, Ad p. 120.
Per copy £1, per year £12.
Indexed in: BHI, IBZ.

3814 ARK. 1951.
Royal College of Art, Exhibition Road, London, SW7 2RJ.
3, ○   Art and design, painting, photography.
Index of issues 1-48, published autumn 1971.
Spring 1972, T.p. 90.   1500.
Per copy 55p, per year £1.65.

3815 ART AND ARTISTS. 1966.
Hansom Books, Artillery Mansions, 75 Victoria Street, London, SW1H 0H2.
12, ○   Painting and sculpture, modern and classical.
Book notices, book reviews, commodity prices, legal notes, letters, monographic articles, new companies, new products, obituaries, tests.

Key to reference symbols

○ popular   ‡ technical   = trade/professional

+ research   * society/institution   † house journal

No Index.
August 1972, T.p. 52, Ad.p. 10.
Per copy 50p, per year £6.60.

3816 THE ART SALES INDEX: The Picture Dealers' Handbook. 1972.
(Connoisseur Art Sales Index 1968-1972).
Art Sales Index Ltd., Pond House, Weybridge, Surrey.
10, ○ = +   Computer produced. World wide art auction results listed monthly in sequence of artist giving full details. Builds up to 20,000 pictures a year. Current prices of 7,000 artist plus investment guide
No Index.
T.p. 650, Ad p. 20.   1500.
Per year U.K. £35.

3817 THE ARTIST. 1890.
Artist Publishing Co. Ltd., 46 Charlotte Street, London, W1.
12, = ‡   Painting, sculpture and the graphic arts.
Book reviews, letters, news, new products.
No Index.
T.p. 28, Ad.p. 12.
Per copy 25p, per year £3.25.

3818 ARTS NORTH.
Northern Arts, 31 New Bridge Street, Newcastle upon Tyne, NE1 8JY.
12, ○   Monthly diary of arts events in Northumberland, Durham, Cumberland, Westmorland, North Yorkshire.
No Index.
June 1972, T.p. 8.
Free.

3819 ARTS REVIEW. 1961.
(Art News and Review 1949-1961).
Richard Gainsborough Periodicals Ltd., 8 Wyndham Place, London, W1H 2AY.
26, ○ = *   Visual art, painting, sculpture, graphics, art gallery guide, art auction and price information, art book reviews, features on artists and exhibitions.
Book notices, book reviews, commodity prices, letters, monographic articles.
A, January, No, None.
17 June, 1972, T.p. 22, Ad.p. 10.   10000.
Per copy 25p, per year £6.25.

3820 BURLINGTON MAGAZINE. 1903.
Burlington Magazine, 258-268 Grays Inn Road, London, WC1.
12, = ‡ ○   Art history and criticism for the Connoisseur.
Monographic articles, works of art on the market.
A, March, Yes, None.
T.p. 74, Ad.p. 60.
Per copy 75p, per year £8.
Indexed in: BHI, IBZ.

3821 CATALYST.
Arts Information Registry, 71 Stepney Green, London, E1.
5, ○   Information media between artists in all fields.
No Index.
Per year 50p.

3822 THE CONNOISSEUR. 1901.
The National Mag. Co. Ltd., Chestergate House, Vauxhall Bridge Road, London, SW1V 2HF.
12, +   All subjects of interest to art collectors.
Book notices, book reviews, prices, monographic articles.
6m, —, Yes, 2 year.
June 1972, T.p. 88, Ad.p. 198.   15316.
Per copy £1, per year £12.
Indexed in: BHI.

3823 THE DESIGNER: Journal of the Society of Industrial Artists and Designers. 1966.
(Journal of the Society of Industrial Artists 1948-1966)
Society of Industrial Artists & Designers, 12 Carlton House Terrace, London, SW1.
11, ‡ * †   Besides dealing with professional matters, the major part of every issue is given over to a special area of design—interiors, pubs, hotels, exhibitions, industrial design, consumer products, glass, ceramics, furniture, fashion, textiles, packaging, illustration, graphics, photography—besides general articles on visual environment and economics of design.
Book notices, book reviews, legal notes, letters, articles, new products, obituaries, standards.
No Index.
June 1972, T.p. 18, Ad.p. 8.   7000
Per copy 20p, per year £2.50.

3824 EASTWORD. 1972.
Eastern Arts Association, 30 Station Rd., Cambridge.
12, *   A diary of events of all the major arts events in the eastern counties, together with articles on the arts.
Book notices, book reviews, articles, new products, parliamentary.
No Index.
June 1972, T.p. 8.   17500.
Per year £2.

3825 FORM. 1966.
Philip Steadman, 85 Norwich Street, Cambridge.
3, = ‡   Research in the plastic arts, literature, photography, the cinema. Special interest in history of the modern movement, construction, structuralism, kinetic art, concrete poetry.
No Index.
T.p. 36.
Per copy 25p, per year £1.

3826 GREATER LONDON ARTS. 1971.
Greater London Arts Association, 27 Southampton Street, London, WC2.
12, *   Amateur and professional arts in the region.
No Index.
6, 1972, T.p. 4.
Per copy 5p.

3827 THE IMAGE. 1972.
The Baroque Press, 28 James Street, London, W1M 5HS.
12, =   Graphics in general.
No Index.
Per year £6.

3828 INTERNATIONAL AUCTION RECORDS: engravings, drawings, watercolours paintings and sculpture. 1968.
(International Yearbook of Sales 1967).
Hilmarton Manor Press, Calne, Wilts.
1, =   International guide to auction prices of paintings, watercolours, drawings, engravings and sculpture.
Prices.
A, —, No, None.
1972/73, T.p. 880, Ad.p. 45.   2000.
Per copy £11.50.

3829 JOURNAL OF CONNOISSEURSHIP AND ART TECHNOLOGY. 1970.
Gordon & Breach Ltd., 12 Bloomsbury Way, London, WC1.
○ = ‡
A, —, Yes, None.
Per year £7.50.

3830 THE JOURNAL OF THE ROYAL SOCIETY FOR THE ENCOURAGEMENT OF ARTS, MANUFACTURES AND COMMERCE. JOURNAL OF THE ROYAL SOCIETY OF ARTS. 1852.
(Journal of the Society of Arts until 1907).
George Bell & Sons Limited, York House, Portugal Street, London, WC2.

12, * ‡ +   Arts, manufactures and commerce, particularly industrial design, and including the Commonwealth; the application of science to industry.
Book reviews, letters, monographic articles, obituaries.
A, Summer, Yes, 10 year.
T.p. 72, Ad.p. 2.   10250.
Per copy 35p, per year £4.74.
Indexed in: BHI, BIT, IBZ.

3831 JOURNAL OF THE WARBURG AND COURTAULD INSTITUTES. 1937-38.
Warburg Institute, Woburn Square, London, WC1H 0AB.
= +   Classics and the arts.
Monographic articles.
A, with volume, Yes, None.
Vol. 34, 1971, T.p. 415.
Per year £6.

3832 LAURELS: the magazine of the East Midlands Arts Association. 1972.
East Midlands Arts Association, 1 Frederick Street, Loughborough, Leics, LE11 3BH.
4, * =   Articles on subjects of interest to people interested in the arts in the E. Midlands.
No Index.
February 1972, T.p. 32.
Per copy 10p, Free to members.

3833 LEONARDO. 1968.
Pergamon Press Ltd., Headington Hill Hall, Oxford, OX3 0BW.
4, = +   Visual or plastic fine arts.
Book reviews, monographic articles.
A, Last issue of volume, Yes, None.
T.p. 125, Ad.p. 10.
Per copy £3, per year £10.

3834 THE MONTH IN YORKSHIRE: (Different title monthly) 1970.
Yorkshire Arts Association, Glyde House, Bradford, 5.
11, ○   Arts events in Yorkshire compiled as poster/diary with lively articles to stimulate more interest in all art forms.
Book reviews, letters, articles.
No Index.

3835 ORIENTAL ART. 1948.
Oriental Art Magazine Ltd., 12 Ennerdale Road, Richmond, Surrey.
4, = ‡
A, December, Yes, None.
T.p. 100, Ad.p. 38.
Per year £3.50.

3836 POPULAR ARTS REVIEW. 1972.
8 Laneside Avenue, Rutherglen, Glasgow.
2, ○
Per copy 30p.

3837 REALITÉS. 1972 (in English).
195 Sloane Street, London, SW1X 9RE.
12, ○ =
Book reviews, monographic articles.
No Index.
Per year £7.

3838 SOUTHERN ARTS.
Southern Arts Association, 78 High Street, Winchester.
12, ○

3839 STUDIO INTERNATIONAL: Journal of modern art. 1963.
(Studio 1893-1962).
Cory Adams & Mackay, 37 Museum Street, London, WC1.
11, = ○
Book reviews, letters, news.
No Index
T.p. 54, Ad.p. 21.   12500.
Per copy 70p, per year £6.50.
Indexed in: BHI, IBZ.

3840 TRENDS AND TOPICS: Journal of the Association of Arts Centres in Scotland. 1971.
Association of Arts Centres in Scotland, 21b Strathearn Road, Edinburgh, EH9 2AB.
2, =   All aspects of the arts in Scotland: development of arts centres.
Book reviews, letters, monographic articles, parliamentary reports, standards, tests.
5 year, —, Yes, None.
T.p. 24.   400.
Per copy 15p and Free to members.

3841 UMBRELLA. 1972.
Demarco Gallery, 8 Melville Cres., Edinburgh, EH3 7NB.
12, ○ = †   Deals with all the arts, on an international basis, with particular reference to Scotland.
Brief articles, news.
No Index.
May 1972, T.p. 12.   4000.
Per copy 10p, per year £1.50. (£1. for member of 'Friends of Demarco Gallery')

711

TOWN AND COUNTRY PLANNING

3842 BURISA NEWSLETTER. 1972.
British Urban & Regional Information Systems, County Planning Dept., Alpha House, 120 Kings Road, Reading, RG1 3DN, Berks.
6, =
No Index.
Per year £1. Institutions £4.

3843 COCKBURN ASSOCIATION NEWSLETTER: Edinburgh Civic Trust Newsletter. 1972.
(Cockburn Association Annual Reports 1875-1971).
The Cockburn Association, 41, Castle Street, Edinburgh, EH2 3BG.
4, * =   Past and future activities, all aspects of planning and conservation, with particular reference to Edinburgh and the surrounding area. Summaries of the Association's submissions to the local authority about planning matters.
Short articles, news.
A, probably, —, No, None.
July 1972, T.p. 24.   2000.
Per copy 10p, per year 50p.

3844 ENVIRONMENT AND PLANNING: international journal of urban and regional research. 1969.
Pion Limited, 207, Brondesbury Park, London, NW2 5JN.
6, + *   Economic, social, and spatial structure of cities and regions. Mathematical models, statistical techniques, applied to transport, urban planning, pollution, policy formulation. Contributions from geographers, sociologists, economists, political scientists.
Abstracts, book reviews, letters, monographic articles, editorial.
A, Last issue of each volume, Yes, None.
T.p. 120.
Per copy £3.50, per year £10 inland.

3845 FORMA: Journal of the Student Planners Association. 1972.
Dept. of Town Planning, Oxford Polytechnic, Gipsy Lane, Headington, Oxford.
=

3846 HOUSING AND PLANNING REVIEW. 1964.
(Housing and Planning News Bulletin 1942-1947; British Housing and Planning Review 1948-1963).
National Housing & Town Planning Council, 11 Green Street, London, W1Y 4ES.
6, = ‡ +   All matters relating to housing and planning.
Book notices, book reviews, letters, monographic articles, news, obituaries, parliamentary reports.

No Index.
T.p. 25, Ad.p. 7.
Per copy 20p.

3847 JOURNAL OF THE ROYAL TOWN PLANNING INSTITUTE. 1971.
(Journal of the Town Planning Institute 1925-1971).
Royal Town Planning Institute, 26, Portland Place, London, W1N 4BE.
10, ‡ + * †   Broad planning field—all aspects. Special issues devoted to Education for Planning, Planning in Developing Countries etc. Transportation.
Book notices, book reviews, legal notes, letters, monographic articles, obituaries, parliamentary reports, standards.
A, early January, Yes, None.
March 1972, T.p. 53, Ad.p. 4.   10250.
Per copy 37p, per year £4.
Indexed in: BHI.

3848 NEW TOWNS BULLETIN. 1972.
The New Towns Association, Glen House, Stag Place, London, SW1E 5AJ.
12, ‡ +   References to parliamentary, legal, technical and professional information relevant to the New Towns.
Abstracts, parliamentary reports.
A,—, Yes, None.
T.p. 4.   600.
Per year £3.75.

3849 PLANNING AND TRANSPORTATION ABSTRACTS. 1969.
(Planning Abstracts, 1969).
Greater London Council, Research Library, The County Hall, London, SE1 7PB.
12, + =   Abstracts of periodical articles, reports, conference papers, pamphlets, government publications and books on local government, statistics, population, urban and regional planning, transportation, social services, architecture and civic design, housing, employment.
Abstracts.
Occasional cumulative indexes.
May 1972, T.p. 47.   600.

3850 REGIONAL STUDIES: Journal of the Regional Studies Association. 1967.
Pergamon Press Ltd., Headington Hill Hall, Oxford, OX3 0BW.
4, = +   Regional planning from all points.
Book notices, book reviews, monographic articles.
A, Last issue of volume, Yes, None.
Per copy £3, per year £10.

3851 TOWN AND COUNTRY PLANNING. 1904.
Town & Country Planning Association, 28 King Street, London, WC2.
12, = ‡
Book reviews, monographic articles.
No Index.
T.p. 83.   5592.
Per copy 15p, per year £2.

3852 TOWN PLANNING REVIEW. 1910.
Liverpool University Press, 123, Grove Street, Liverpool, L7 7AF.
4, + =   Town and regional planning, civic design, landscape design, transport, new town, land use, urban renewal, and economic and sociological subjects.
Book notices, book reviews, monographic articles.
A, October, Yes, None.
April 1972, T.p. 91, Ad.p. 3.   1800.
Per copy £1.25, per year £4.
Indexed in: BHI, BTI.

3853 URBAN AFFAIRS QUARTERLY. 1966.
Sage Publications Ltd., St. George's House, 44 Hatton Garden, London, EC1N 8ER.

4, =
Monographic articles.
A,—, Yes, None.
June 1971, T.p. 110.
Per year £7. Individual £4.70.

3854 URBAN DESIGN BULLETIN. 1970.
Greater London Council, GLC Bookshop, County Hall, London, SE1 7PB.
Infrequent, ‡ +   Technical documents summarising problems and practice derived from, and related to, urban design in London.
No Index.
T.p. varies.
Subscription fixed individually.

3855 URBAN STUDIES. 1964.
Longman Group Ltd., 43/49 Annandale Street, Edinburgh, EH7 4AT.
3, ○ = +   All aspects of community life and development.
Book notices, book reviews, monographic articles.
A, Last issue of year, Yes, None.
June 1972, T.p. 110, Ad.p. 4.   1800.
Per copy £1.75, per year £4.50.
Indexed in: BHI.

3856 ZOO. 1969.
Environmental Design Group Edinburgh, Dept. of Town & Country Planning, Heriot-Watt University, 39 Palmerston Place, Edinburgh.
1/2, ‡ + *   Each issue contains articles relating to one aspect of town and country planning of interest to students, professionals and interested laymen.
Book reviews, letters, monographic articles.
No Index.
No. 5, T.p. 36, Ad p. 3.   750.
Per copy 20p.

712

LANDSCAPING

3857 THE GROUNDSMAN: Official Journal of the Institute of Groundsmanship. 1947.
TTG Publications Ltd., The Adelphi, John Adam Street, London, WC2.
12, ‡ =   Groundsmanship in public and private service in the UK.
Book reviews, letters, articles, new companies, news, new products, obituaries, tests.
No Index.
T.p. 23, Ad.p. 18.   3800.
Free to members.

3858 THE JOURNAL OF THE SPORTS TURF RESEARCH INSTITUTE. 1951.
(The Journal of The Board of Greenkeeping Research 1929-1951).
The Sports Turf Research Institute, Bingley, Yorkshire, BD16 1AU.
1, ○ ‡ + † =   Sports and amenity turf (e.g. sports clubs, local authorities, schools, etc.)
Abstracts, book notices, book reviews, letters, monographic articles.
No Index.
1971, T.p. 155, Ad.p. 52.   4250.
£2.50 (including Sports Turf Bulletin). Free to members.

3859 LANDSCAPE DESIGN: Journal of the Institute of Landscape Architects. 1970.
(Journal of the Institute of Landscape Architects, 1945-1969).
Institute of Landscape Architects, 12, Carlton House Terrace, London, SW1.
4, ‡ * =   The art and science of landscape architecture.

Book notices, book reviews, letters, monographic articles, new firms, new products, obituaries, parliamentary reports, standards.
Irregular, May 1971 (1966-70), No, None.
May 1972, T.p. 35, Ad.p. 20.   2500.
Per copy 40p, per year £1.25.

3860 PARKS AND RECREATION: the Official Journal of the Institute of Park and Recreation Administration.
(Journal of Park Administration 1936-1969).
Journal of Park Administration Ltd., The Adelphi, John Adam Street, London, WC2N 6AY.
12, * = ‡   Park and recreation administration, horticulture and equipment.
Book reviews, letters, monographic articles, new companies, new products, obituaries.
No Index.
May 1972, T.p. 24, Ad.p. 32.
Free to members.

3861 PARKS AND SPORTS GROUNDS—GOLF COURSES. 1935.
Clarke and Hunter (London) Ltd., Armour House, Bridge Street, Guildford, Surrey.
12, ‡ = +   All aspects of turf maintenance and provision of outdoor sports, recreation facilities; parks, playing fields, sports grounds, golf courses.
Book notices, book reviews, letters, articles, new companies, new products, obituaries, standards, tests.
None regularly.
T.p. 30, Ad p. 70.
Per copy 20p, per year £2.40.

3862 PLAYING FIELDS: Journal of the National Playing Fields Association.
The National Playing Fields Assn., 57B Catherine Place, London, S.W.1.
4, + ‡   Recreation, sport and associated interests.
Book notices, book reviews, legal notes, letters, articles, new products, obituaries, parliamentary reports.
No Index.
January/March 1970, T.p. 46, Ad.p. 14.
Per copy 10p.

3863 SPORTS TURF BULLETIN. 1951.
The Sports Turf Research Institute, Bingley, Yorkshire, BD16 1AU.
4, ○ † = +   Sports and amenity turf (e.g. sports clubs, local authorities, schools, etc.)
Articles, news.
No Index.
April-June 1972, T.p. 11.   4250.
Per year £2.50 but supplied only with annual Journal at above subscription. Free to members.

719
RURAL LIFE

3864 THE FIELD: incorporating Land and Water and The County Gentleman. 1853.
Harmsworth Press Ltd., 8, Stratton Street, London, W1X 6AT.
52, ○ ‡ +   All sporting, natural and political aspects concerning the countryside.
Book reviews, letters, articles, obituaries.
6m, but not published.
1 June 1972, T.p. 37, Ad.p. 42.   30000.
Per copy 15p, per year £9.85.

72
ARCHITECTURE

3865 APIS BULLETIN. 1971.
Architecture & Planning Information Service, Science Library, The Queen's University of Belfast, Belfast, BT9 5EQ.

48, =   Current awareness service for architects and planners in teaching, research and practice. Lists publications and contents of periodicals received at the University Library. Intended for weekly scanning, not a retrospective searching.
Book notices, standards.
No Index.
16 June 1972, T.p. 7.   100.
Per year £7.

3866 ARSE: Architectural Radicals, Students & Educators. 1969.
Architectural Radicals, Students & Educators Group, c/o David Wild, 20 Chalcot Rd., London, NW1 8LL.
Irreg. ○ * +   Radical critique of current architectural orthodoxy and its impoverished 'ideology' of 'professionalism'.
Abstracts, book notices, book reviews, letters, monographic articles, obituaries.
No Index.
16.6.72, T.p. 20.   3000.
Per copy 15p, per year 30p.

3867 ARCHIGRAM. 1961.
59, Aberdare Gardens, London, NW6.
Irreg. +   Experiment in architecture, urban design, architectural education, art.
Articles, new products.
Yearly, No, No.
1971, T.p. 40.   6000.
Per copy 30p.

3868 THE ARCHITECT.
IPC Building & Contract Journals Ltd., 40, Bowling Green Lane, London, EC1
12, = ‡   Forum for architectural ideas and opinion.
Book reviews, letters, monographic articles.
No Index.
Per year £6 and Free, controlled circulation.

3869 ARCHITECT AND BUILDING NEWS. 1854.
Building & Contract Journals Ltd., 32, Southwark Bridge Road, London, SE1.
26, ‡   New buildings, with costings.
Book reviews, letters, articles.
No Index.
16200.
Free, controlled circulation.

3870 ARCHITECT AND SURVEYOR. 1958.
(The Parthenon 1926-1958).
Incorporated Association of Architects & Surveyors, 29, Belgrave Square, London, SW1.
6, = * ‡   All aspects of architecture and surveying.
Book reviews, legal notes, letters, articles, new products.
No Index.
T.p. 34, Ad.p. 2.   4200.
Free to members.
Indexed in: BTI.

3871 THE ARCHITECTS' JOURNAL. 1895.
Architectural Press Ltd., 9-13, Queen Anne's Gate, London, SW1H 9BY.
52, ‡ = +   Architecture, building design and related professions.
Book notices, book reviews, letters, monographic articles, new products, obituaries, parliamentary reports, tests.
6m, Varies, Yes, None.
5.7.1972, T.p. 54, Ad.p. 116.   21183.
Per copy 15p, per year £8.
Indexed in: BHI, BTI, IBZ.

3872 ARCHITECTURAL HISTORY. Journal of the Society of Architectural Historians of Great Britain. 1958.
Society, 8, Belmount Avenue, Melton Park, Newcastle-on-Tyne, NE3 5QD.
1, + *
Monographic articles.

A, With volume, Yes, None.
T.p. 80.
Per copy £2.10. Non members £3.15.
Indexed in: BHI.

3873 THE ARCHITECTURAL REVIEW. 1896.
Architectural Press Ltd., 9-13, Queen Anne's Gate, London, SW1H 9BY.
12, ‡ = +   An international review of the finest and the most significant buildings and their interiors.
Art reviews, book reviews, letters, monographic articles, obituaries, etc.
6m, Feb or March and Aug or Sept, Yes, None.
May 1972, T.p. 67, Ad.p. 30.   12503.
Per copy, 37p, per year £4.50.
Indexed in: BHI, BTI, IBZ.

3874 ARCHITECTURE EAST MIDLANDS. 1965.
Lincolnshire Standard Group Ltd., Chronicle Building, Waterside North, Lincoln.
6, = ‡   Architecture and allied trades in the area.
No Index.
T.p. 24, Ad.p. 36.   2000.
Per copy 25p.

3875 BIG A: magazine of the Department of Architecture and Planning, Queen's Belfast. 1971.
Architectural Society, Queen's University of Belfast, Department of Architecture, Queen's University of Belfast, Belfast, BT7 1NN.
1, † ‡   Educational concerns in the Department; local architectural issues; forum for student and staff opinion; Readers intended to be members of the Department, students and local architectural practitioners.
News items, short articles, critical reviews of architectural prospects.
No Index.
No. 2, 1972, T.p. 12, Ad.p. 2.
Per copy 5p.

3876 ERA: Journal of the Eastern Region of the RIBA. 1968.
JMP Services Ltd., Amberley House, Norfolk Street, London, WC2.
6, = ‡   Architectural activity in East Anglia.
Book notices, book reviews, letters, monographic articles, obituaries.
No Index.
T.p. 20, Ad.p. 13.   2500.
Free to members.

3877 NORTHERN PERSPECTIVE. 1968.
(Northern Architect 1962-1968).
Paull & Goode Publishing Ltd., Midland Bank Chambers, St. Thomas Street, Sunderland.
6, ‡ * =   Architectural practices throughout four Northern Counties of England.
Book reviews, legal notes, letters, articles, new companies, new products.
No Index.
May/June 1972, T.p. 22, Ad p. 18.   2250.
Per copy 15p, per year £1.50.

3878 PORTICO: Journal of the Faculty of Architects and Surveyors. 1929.
(Journal of the Faculty of Architects and Surveyors 1926-1928).
The Faculty of Architects & Surveyors, 68, Gloucester Place, London, W1H 3HL.
4, = * ‡   Matters of interest to the architectural and surveying professions.
Book reviews, legal notes, letters, articles, new products, obituaries, parliamentary reports, standards, tests
No Index
June 1972, T.p. 30, Ad.p. 4.   c. 2500.
Per copy 50p, per year £2.

3879 RIBA ANNUAL REVIEW OF PERIODICAL ARTICLES. 1965.
Royal Institute of British Architects, 66, Portland Place, London, W1N 4AD.
1, ‡   Architecture, building, town and country planning and other allied subjects.
Abstracts, book notices, commodity prices, legal notes, letters.
No Index.
Vol. 5, 1969-70, T.p. 113.
Per year £5 members, £7 non-members.

3880 RIBA JOURNAL. 1879.
Royal Institute of British Architects, 66, Portland Place, London, W1N 4AD.
12, * = ‡   Work, views and policies of the RIBA and its members.
Book reviews, legal notes, letters, monographic articles, news, obituaries.
A, December, Yes, 2 year.
T.p. 45, Ad.p. 65.   31000.
Per copy 25p, per year £3. Free to members.
Indexed in: BHI.

3881 RIBA LIBRARY BULLETIN. 1946.
Royal Institute of British Architects, 66, Portland Place, London, W1N 4AD.
4, ‡   Architecture, building, town and country planning and other allied subjects.
Abstracts, book notices.
No Index.
No. 1, 1972, T.p. 33.
Per year £2 members, £4 non-members.

3882 TRANSACTIONS OF THE ANCIENT MONUMENTS SOCIETY. 1953.
Ancient Monuments Society, 33, Ladbroke Square, London, W11 5NT.
1, ‡ * +   Architectural, archaeological and historical papers and drawings.
Book reviews, monographic articles, parliamentary reports on town and country planning matters.
10 year, 1962, Yes, None.
1969, T.p. 41.   2500.
Per copy £1.20.
Indexed in: BHI.

3883 VERNACULAR ARCHITECTURE. 1970.
Oriel Press, 32, Ridley Place, Newcastle-upon-Tyne, NE1 8LH.
1, + *   All aspects of the study of vernacular architecture.
Book reviews, letters, articles.
No Index.
1971, T.p. 24.   500.
Per copy £1.25, per year £1.25.

3884 YORKSHIRE ARCHITECT: Journal of the R.I.B.A. Yorkshire Region. 1968.
(Perspective East Yorkshire).
Paull & Goode Publishing Ltd., Midland Bank Chambers, St. Thomas Street, Sunderland.
6, = * ‡   Architectural practices in Yorkshire.
Book reviews, legal notes, letters, articles, new companies, obituaries.
No Index.
May/June 1972, T.p. 22, Ad.p. 17.   2250.
Per copy 17p, per year £1.50.

72.011

DESIGN

3885 DESIGN. 1949.
Design Council, 28, Haymarket, London, SW1Y 4SU.
12, ‡ = +   All aspects of product, graphic and interior design and the environment.
Book notices, book reviews, commodity prices, letters, monographic articles, new companies, new products,

obituaries, parliamentary reports, patents, standards, tests.
A, March, Yes, None.
April 1972, T.p. 60, Ad.p. 40.   19845.
Per copy 35p, per year £5.10.

3886 SIMULATION AND GAMES: an international journal of theory, design and research.
Sage Publications Ltd., St. George's House, 44, Hatton Garden, London, EC1N 8ER.
4, = ‡   Theoretical and empirical problems related to man, man-machine and machine simulations of social processes.
Abstracts, book notices, book reviews, commodity prices, legal notes, letters, monographic articles, new companies, new products, obituaries, parliamentary reports, patents, standards, tests.
A,—, Yes, None.
June, 1971, T.p. 120.
Per year £8, individual £5.40.

725.21
SHOPFITTING

3887 SHOP EQUIPMENT AND SHOPFITTING NEWS. 1957.
Westbourne Publications Ltd., Crown House, Morden, Surrey.
12, =
Book notices, book reviews, news, new products.
No Index.
14500.
Free, controlled circulation.

3888 SHOPFITTING AND EQUIPMENT MONITOR. 1967.
Westbourne Publications Ltd., Crown House, Morden, Surrey.
4, =
No Index.
14000.
Free, controlled circulation.

3889 SHOP FITTING INTERNATIONAL. 1969.
(Shop and Shopfitting Review 1955-1968).
Blandford Publications Ltd., 167, High Holborn, London, WC1V 6PH.
12, =   New developments and installations in shop equipment and decor, including the fitting of stores, shops, supermarkets, banks, building societies, hotels, restaurants, public houses and all public commercial premises.
Book reviews, letters, articles, new companies, new products, obituaries.
No Index.
May 1972, T.p. 14, Ad.p. 14.   19146.
Per copy 20p, per year £3.50.

725.74
SWIMMING BATHS

3890 SWIMMING POOL REVIEW. 1960.
Clarke and Hunter (London) Ltd., Armour House, Bridge St., Guildford, Surrey.
4, ‡ = +   All aspects of design, construction and maintenance of private school, sports clubs and local authority pools, including water treatment.
Book notices, book reviews, letters, articles, new companies, new products, obituaries, standards, tests.
5 year, 1970, Yes, None.
T.p. 57, Ad.p. 90.
Per copy 20p, per year 80p.

726
CHURCH BUILDINGS

3891 CHURCHBUILDING. 1962.
(Church Buildings Today 1960-1961).
John Catt Ltd., 116 High Street, Billericay, Essex.
3, = ‡
Book notices, book reviews, letters, monographic articles.
No Index.
T.p. 24, Ad.p. 4.
Per copy 25p, per year 75p.

726.8
PYRAMIDS

3892 PYRAMIDOLOGY MAGAZINE. 1952.
(Pyramidology, 1941-1951).
Institute of Pyramidology, 31, Station Road, Harpenden, Hertfordshire.
4, +   Pyramidology in all its branches.
Book notices, book reviews, monographic articles, obituaries.
A,—, Yes, None.
2nd Quarter 1972, T.p. 16, Ad.p. 4.
Per year 75p.

728.76
CARAVANS

3893 CARAVAN. 1933.
Link House Publications Ltd., Link House, Dingwall Avenue, Croydon, Surrey, CR9 2TA.
12, O ‡   Caravanning from the family leisure and the sporting points of view. Many test reports on towcars, caravans and equipment. Touring areas.
Commodity prices, letters, articles, new products, tests.
No Index.
T.p. 40, Ad.p. 49.
Per copy 12½p, per year £2.

3894 EN ROUTE. 1963.
Caravan Club Ltd., 65, South Molton Street, London, W1Y 2AB.
12, * O   Touring, caravanning in UK and overseas.
Letters, monographic articles, news, new products, tests.
No Index.
T.p. 29, Ad.p. 3.   80000.
Free to members.

3895 MOBILE HOME. 1960.
Heathcock Press Ltd., 44, Wellesley Road, West Croydon, CR9 2DY.
6, = O   The caravan as home.
Letters, news, new products, tests.
No Index.
T.p. 31, Ad.p. 21.
Per copy 15p, per year £1.20.

3896 MODERN CARAVAN. 1950.
Link House Publications Ltd., Link House, Dingwall Avenue, Croydon, CR9 2TA.
12, O   How to get the most out of family caravanning for weekends, holidays, and touring. New vans and equipment regularly reviewed.
Commodity prices, letters, articles, new products, tests.
No Index.
T.p. 65, Ad p. 141.
Per copy 10p, per year £2.

3897 NCC MEMBERS NEWSLETTER: official publication of the National Caravan Council. 1971.
(NCC News 1950-1970).

Bromley Office Supplies & Printing Co. Ltd., 39-41, East Street, Bromley, Kent.
12, =   Caravanning.
No Index.
Free to members.

3898 PRACTICAL CARAVAN incorporating Caravan Life. 1969.
Haymarket Publishing Limited, Gillow House, 5 Winsley Street, London, W.1.
12, ○   Practical touring caravanning covering every aspect of buying, maintaining and using a caravan.
Prices, letters, articles, new products, tests.
No Index.
July 1972, T.p. 42, Ad.p. 70.   40000.
Per copy 17½p, per year £3.12.

729

ARCHITECTURAL DESIGN

3899 ARCHITECTURAL DESIGN. 1948.
(Architectural Design and Construction 1930-1948).
Standard Catalogue Co. Ltd., 26, Bloomsbury Way, London, WC1A 2SS.
12, ‡ =   Architectural and environmental subjects.
Book reviews, letters, monographic articles, new products.
A, January, Yes, None.
June 1972, T.p. 59, Ad.p. 3.   13000.
Per copy 40p, per year £4.80.
Indexed in: BTI.

3900 BULLETIN OF COMPUTER AIDED ARCHITECTURAL DESIGN. 1969.
University of Strathclyde, ABACUS, School of Architecture, Univ. of Strathclyde, Glasgow, G1 0NG.
4, ‡ +   All building applications of computers.
Book notices, book reviews, commodity prices, letters, articles, new products.
No Index.
None.
January 1972, T.p. 19.   300.
Per year £1.

736

STONEMASONRY

3901 STONE INDUSTRIES. 1966.
Park Lane Publications Ltd., 70 Chiswick High Rd., London, W4.
6, ‡   Architects, stonemasons, church authorities, quarry owners and other users and suppliers of stone, marble, slate, etc. in English-speaking countries.
Book notices, book reviews, letters, monographic articles, new companies, new products, standards, tests.
A, January-February, Yes, None.
c. 5000.
Per year £2.50. Free, controlled circulation.

737

NUMISMATICS

3902 THE BRITISH NUMISMATIC JOURNAL, including the proceedings of the British Numismatic Society for the year. 1916.
(The British Numismatic Journal and proceedings of the British Numismatic Society 1905-1914).
British Numismatic Society, Warburg Institute, Woburn Square, London, WC1H 0AB.
1, + *   Coins and currency, medals, and tokens (etc.) of Great Britain and Ireland, the Commonwealth, and the English-speaking world, from the earliest times.
Book notices, book reviews, monographic articles, obituaries.
A, —, Yes, 10 year.
Vol 39, 1970, T.p. 224.   c. 465.
Per copy £4.20.

3903 COIN COLLECTING WEEKLY. 1972.
Independent Magazines Ltd., 181 Queen Victoria Street, London, EC4.
52, ○
No Index.
Per copy 10p.

3904 COIN MONTHLY. 1966.
Numismatic Publishing Co., Sovereign House, High Street, Brentwood, Essex.
12, = ○   All branches of numismatics from coins and medals to tokens and banknotes.
Book reviews, commodity prices, letters, monographic articles, new companies, new products.
4 yearly, November 1970 (last issue), No, None.
August 1972, T.p. 77, Ad.p. 55.   26253.
Per copy 20p, per year £3.10.

3905 COINS. 1970.
(Coins & Medals 1964-1970).
Link House Publications Ltd., Link House, Dingwall Avenue, Croydon, Surrey, CR9 2TA.
12, ○   All aspects of numismatics from the points of view of both coin collectors and investors.
Book reviews, commodity prices, letters, articles.
A, December, No, None.
T.p. 30, Ad.p. 54.   27000.
Per copy 15p, per year £2.

3906 COINS, MEDALS & CURRENCY DIGEST. 1969.
Morland Lee Ltd., 2 Arundel Street, London, WC2.
12, = ‡   Numismatics in general.
Book notices, book reviews, commodity prices, letters, monographic articles, news, new products, obituaries.
No Index.
T.p. 128, Ad.p. 34.   43000.
Per copy 20p, per year £2.40.

3907 COINS, MEDALS & CURRENCY WEEKLY. 1968.
(Coins, Medals and Currency, 1967-1968).
Morland Lee Ltd., 2 Arundel Street, London, WC2.
52, = ‡ ○   Numismatics in general.
Book notices, book reviews, commodity prices, letters, monographic articles, news, new products.
A, —, Yes, None.
T.p. 16, Ad.p. 5.   15000.
Per copy 10p, per year £4.50.

3908 CUNOBELIN. 1963.
British Association of Numismatic Societies, 6 Handside Close, Welwyn Garden City, Herts.
1, * =   Numismatics.
Book notices, book reviews, monographic articles, obituaries.
No Index.
T.p, 65, Ad.p. 8.
Controlled circulation.

739.1

SILVER

3909 SILVER BULLETIN: collecting and investing. 1969.
Morland Lee Ltd., 2 Arundel Street, London, WC2.
12, = ‡   Primarily antiques.
Commodity prices, monographic articles.
No Index.
T.p. 12.
Per year £3.

739.8
ANTIQUES

3910 ANTIQUE COLLECTING: journal of the Antique Collectors Club. 1966.
The Club, Clapton, Woodbridge, Suffolk.
12, ○ ‡
Book reviews, commodity prices, letters, articles.
No Index.
T.p. 41, Ad.p. 1.
Free to members.

3911 ANTIQUE COLLECTOR. 1930.
Antique Collector Ltd., Victoria Chambers, 16 Strutton Ground, Victoria Street, London, SW1.
6, ○ =   Antiques, including all aspects of furniture, glass, ceramics, paintings, silver and oriental items. Coverage of current exhibitions.
Book notices, book reviews, letters, monographic articles, obituaries.
A, —, Yes, None.
T.p. 45, Ad.p. 35.
Per copy 50p, per year £3.

3912 ANTIQUE DEALER AND COLLECTORS GUIDE. 1946.
City Magazines, Aldwych House, Aldwych, London, WC2 4BHL.
= ‡ ○   Antiques for antique dealers and collectors. Covers all aspects of antique collecting.
Book notices, book reviews, commodity prices, letters, monographic articles.
No Index.
July 1972, T.p. 44, Ad.p. 62.   30000.
Per copy 40p, per year £6.25.

3913 ANTIQUE FINDER. 1961.
Antique Finder Ltd., 34/40 Ludgate Hill, London, EC4.
12, = ‡
Book notices, book reviews, commodity prices, legal notes, monographic articles, news, reports.
No Index.
T.p. 41, Ad.p. 23.
Per year £4 (Trade only).

3914 ANTIQUES. 1963.
Antique & General Advertising Ltd., The Old Town House, High Street, Wendover, Bucks.
6, ○ =   Regional surveys of antiques sources with guides to current trends.
Book reviews, reports.
A, —, Yes, None.
Per copy 25p, per year £1.25.

3915 ANTIQUES IN BRITAIN. 1964.
Antique & General Advertising Ltd., The Old Town House, High Street, Wendover, Bucks.
1, ○ =   Comprehensive survey of the antiques trade in Britain with detailed reviews of sources and complete directory to provincial antique dealers.

3916 ANTIQUES TRADE GAZETTE. 1971.
Metropress Ltd., 1 Newport House, 15/18 Great Newport Street, London, WC2.
52, =
No Index.
Per year £7.

3917 ANTIQUES WORLD. 1969.
Antique & General Advertising Ltd., High Street, Wendover, Bucks.
12, =   International antique trade.
Book reviews, commodity prices, legal notes, letters, new companies, news, new products, obituaries.
No Index.
T.p. 8.   5000.
Free, controlled circulation.

3918 ART & ANTIQUES WEEKLY. 1968.
Morland Lee Ltd., 2 Arundel Street, London, WC2.
52, = ‡   Antiques, paintings and sculpture, emphasis on collecting.
Book notices, book reviews, commodity prices, legal notes, letters, monographic articles, news, obituaries.
A, —, Yes, None.
T.p. 20, Ad.p. 7.   21000.
Per copy 10p, per year £5.25.

746
LACE. NEEDLEWORK

3919 CREATIVE NEEDLECRAFT. 1968.
Forbes Publications Ltd., Hartree House, Queensway, London, W2 4SH.
3, ○   Educational in needlecraft field.
Book reviews, articles, new products.
No Index.
April 1972, T.p. 23, Ad.p. 13.   5500.
Per year 90p.

3920 EMBROIDERY. 1932
Embroiderers Guild, 73 Wimpole Street, London, W1M 8AX.
4, * = ‡ +   All types of embroidery, including, lace, macrame, smocking, collage etc.
Book reviews, letters, articles.
A, December. Yes, None.
T.p. 23, Ad.p. 11.   9273.
Per copy 20p, per year £1.

3921 LACEMAKING: the newsletter of the Lace Society of Wales. 1968.
Lace Society of Wales, c/o 57 Annefield Park, Gresford, Wrexham, Denbighshire, LL12 8NR.
6, * =   Craft of pillow, or bobbin, lace making or collecting and associated skills.
Book notices, book reviews, commodity prices, letters, articles, new products, obituaries.
No Index.
October 1971, T.p. 6.
Free to members only.

3922 NEEDLEWOMAN AND NEEDLECRAFT. 1939.
(Needlecraft Practical Journal 1900-1938).
Needlecraft Ltd., School Street, Bromley Cross, Bolton, Lancs.
4, ○   General needlework and tapestry, knitting and crochet.
No Index.
T.p. 24, Ad.p. 4.   38000.
Per copy 20p, per year 90p.

3923 STITCHCRAFT. 1932.
Condé Nast Publications Ltd, Belmont Road, Chiswick, London, W4.
12, ○   Knitting, crochet, needlework, tapestry, rugmaking.
Book notices, book reviews, articles, new products.
No Index.
March 1972, T.p. 35, Ad.p. 5.   143586.
Per copy 15p, per year £2.10.

747
INTERIOR DESIGN

3924 INTERIOR DESIGN. 1969.
(Interior Design & Contract Furnishing 1957-1968).
Crown House Publications Ltd., Crown House, Morden, Surrey.

Key to reference symbols

○ popular   ‡ technical   = trade/professional

+ research   * society/institution   † house journal

12, =   Interior design in the contract field.
Book reviews, letters, monographic articles, news, new products.
No Index.
6000.
Per copy 25p, per year £3.

75
ART

3925 LEISURE PAINTER. 1967.
Reeves & Sons Ltd., Lincoln Road, Enfield, Middx.
4, ○
No Index.
June 1972, T.p. 42, Ad.p. 6.   11200.
Per copy 85p.

77
PHOTOGRAPHY

3926 AMATEUR PHOTOGRAPHER. 1884.
IPC Specialist & Professional Press, 161-166 Fleet Street, London, EC4.
52, ○ ‡ = +   To provide the serious amateur with the most complete coverage of every aspect of photography, with contributions by specialists in various fields, examples in colour and monochrome work, impartial reports on new cameras and a regular cine section.
Book reviews, commodity prices, letters, monographic articles, new companies, new products, tests.
6m, —, Yes, None.
14.6.1972, T.p. 40, Ad.p. 80.   c. 76000.
Per copy $12\frac{1}{2}$p, per year £10.

3927 THE BRITISH JOURNAL OF PHOTOGRAPHY. 1859.
Henry Greenwood & Co. Ltd., 24 Wellington Street, Strand, London, WC2.
52, ‡ = +   Photography in all its aspects.
Abstracts, book notices, book reviews, commodity prices, legal notes, letters, new products, parliamentary, tests.
A, —, Yes, None.
T.p. 26, Ad.p. 26.   13000.
Per copy 10p, per year £6.
Indexed in: BTI.

3928 CREATIVE CAMERA. 1967.
(Camera owner 1964-1966)
Coo Press Ltd., 19 Doughty Street, London.
12, =   Photographic art.
Book reviews, letters, news, new products.
No Index.
T.p. 32, Ad.p. 3.   10080.
Per copy 20p, per year £2.50.

3929 DREAM. 1972.
Gresham Publishing Group, 1 Great James Street, London, WC1.
12, ○   Stories in photographs.
No Index.
T.p. 48.
Per copy $12\frac{1}{2}$p.

3930 FORENSIC PHOTOGRAPHY. 1972.
Forensic Publishing Company, P.O. Box 18, Bognor Regis, PO22 7AA.
4, ‡ +   All aspects of photography as it concerns the prevention and detection of crime and the use of photography for the purposes of the Law.
Book notices, legal notes, letters, monographic articles.
A, February, Yes, None.
3000.
Per year £1.

3931 INDUSTRIAL AND COMMERCIAL PHOTOGRAPHER. 1960.
Maclaren Publishers Ltd., P.O. Box 109, 69/77 Davis House, High Street, Croydon CR9 1QH.
12, ‡ =   Industrial and commercial photographer reports on the modern techniques used by professional photographers in industry, commerce, advertising, portraiture, science, medicine and graphic arts.
Commodity prices, legal notes, monographic articles, new companies, new products, obituaries.
A, —, Yes, None.
June 1972, T.p. 67, Ad.p. 72.   5793
Per copy 25p, per year £3.25

3932 JOURNAL OF PHOTOGRAPHIC SCIENCE. 1953.
(Section B of The Photographic Journal: 1945-1952).
The Royal Photographic Society, 14 South Audley Street, London, W1Y 5DP.
6, ‡ +   Covers highly specialized aspects of photographic science and technology.
Abstracts, book notices, book reviews, monographic articles, new products, obituaries, patents, standards, tests.
A, with the November/December issue, Yes, None.
Jan-Feb. 1972, T.p. 36.   4700.
Per copy £1.25, per year £7.
Free to members and bona fide orgs.
Indexed in: BTI, IBZ

3933 MASTER PHOTOGRAPHER. 1960.
Master Photographers Association, 80 Rochester Row, London, SW1.
4, ‡ = *   Professional photography.
Book reviews, letters, articles, new products.
No Index.
Spring 1972, T.p. 12, Ad.p. 1.
Free to members.

3934 MODERN PHOTOGRAPHER. 1968
NC Magazines Ltd. (for the Photographic Dealers Association), 172-4 Kingston Road, Ewell, Surrey.
6, = ○
No Index.
Per copy 5p.

3935 PHOTO FINISHER. 1929.
Wholesale Photo Finishers Association, 50 Great Russell Street, London, WC1.
12, * =   Developments in photographic processing.
Monographic articles, news, new products.
No Index.
T.p. 31, Ad.p. 21.
Free to members.

3936 PHOTOGRAPHIC ABSTRACTS. 1921.
Scientific and Technical Group of the Royal Photographic Society, 14 South Audley Street, London, W1Y 5DP.
6, + ‡ =   Abstracts of technical articles and patents published on photographic science and technology.
Abstracts.
A, As soon as possible after close of year, Yes, 10 year.
No. 6, 1971. T.p. 64.   850.
Per copy £3.50, per year £20.

3937 PHOTOGRAPHIC JOURNAL. 1853.
The Royal Photographic Society, 14 South Audley Street, London, W1Y 5DP.
12, ○ ‡ *   All aspects of photography, including the work of The RPS.
Letters, monographic articles, obituaries.
A, early the following year, Yes, None.
May 1972, T.p. 48, Ad.p. 12 inc. cover.   5500.
Per copy 30p, per year £3.50. Free to members.
Indexed in: BTI.

3938 PHOTOGRAPHIC PROCESSOR: journal of the Association of Photographic Laboratories. 1970.
(Photo Finisher).

Henry Greenwood & Co. Ltd.. 24 Wellington St., London, WC2E 7DH.
12, ‡ =   Material of interest to photographic processing houses plus domestic news particular to the A.P.L.
Book reviews, commodity prices, legal notes, letters, monographic articles, new companies, new products, obituaries.
A, December, Yes, None.
May 1972, T.p. 23, Ad.p. 13.
Per copy 30p, and Free to members.

3939 PHOTOGRAPHY. 1932.
(Good Photography; Colour Photography).
Fountain Press Ltd., 46-7 Chancery Lane, London, WC2.
12, =
No Index.
Per copy 20p, per year £3.

3940 PHOTOGRAPHY INDEX FOR AMATEURS. 1969.
Marjan Press, Bedwell Community Centre, Bedwell Crescent, Stevenage, Herts.
4, = ‡
No Index.
Per year £1.

3941 PHOTOSCENE: Ireland's only photographic magazine. 1972.
Boyne Valley Publishing Co., 30 James Street, Drogheda, Co. Louth.
12, = ○
No Index.
Per year £2.50.

3942 PRACTICAL PHOTOGRAPHY. 1959.
(Popular Photography 1954-1959).
East Midland Allied Press Ltd., 117 Park Rd., Peterborough.
12, ○   Practical aspects of photography.
Book rewiews, legal notes, letters, articles, new products, tests.
No Index.
May 1972, T.p. 33, Ad.p. 23.   38960.
Per copy 17½p, per year £3.

771.3

CAMERAS

3943 SLR CAMERA. 1967.
(Camera Magazine 1964-1966)
Haymarket Publishing Limited, Gillow House, 5 Winsley Street, London, W1.
12, ○ ‡   Selection and use of single-lens reflex equipment.
Prices, letters, articles, new products, tests.
No Index.
July 1972, T.p. 51, Ad.p. 48.   35374
Per copy 20p, per year £3.12.

778.1

REPROGRAPHY

3944 MICRODOC: Journal of the Microfilm Association of Great Britain. 1962.
Microfilm Association of Great Britain, c/o Science Library, Queens University of Belfast, Chlorine Gardens, Belfast 9.
4, + ‡ * =   Microfilm, microtexts, micropublishing, photocopying, computer output microfilm (COM), computer input microfilm, application of microfilm to all fields, standards for microfilm.
Abstracts, book notices, book reviews, letters, monographic articles, new products, obituaries, patents, standards, tests.
A, December, Yes, 4 year.
No. 2, 1972, T.p. 35, Ad.p. 2.
Per vol. £4.

3945 MICROINFO: micrographics news bulletin. 1970.
Microinfo Ltd., 4 High Street, Alton, Hampshire.
12, ‡ =   International coverage of new products, processes and applications across the whole field of microfilm and microfilm/computer technology. News of developments in business systems, drawing office applications, library usage, micropublishing and systems based on the use of computer-generated microfilm.
Book notices, book reviews, letters, patents, standards, tests.
No Index.
May 1972, T.p. 12.
Per year £15.

3946 REPRO: journal of the Institute of Reprographic Technology, 52-55 Carnaby Street, London W1V 1PF. 1963.
In 'Reproduction' the material being provided by the Institute.
B.E.D. Business Journals, Park House, Park Street, Croydon.
12, * = ‡   Institute news, correspondence, some technical information on reprography.
Book notices, book reviews, letters, monographic articles, new products, obituaries, parliamentary reports, tests.
No Index.

3947 RUMA: Report of University Microfilms Activity. 1970.
University Microfilms Ltd. (A Xerox Company), Tylers Green, High Wycombe, Bucks.
6, + =   All aspects of University Microfilms' activity reported. New products, projects announced. Existing ones explained. Articles included to make better know the techniques and problems of micropublishing.
Book notices, commodity prices, new products.
A, With No. 6, No, None.
January/February 1973, T.p. 4,   c. 1800.
Free.

778.5

CINEMATOGRAPHY

3948 BRITISH KINEMATOGRAPHY SOUND AND TELEVISION. 1966.
(British Kinematography Journal 1933-1965).
British Kinematography, Sound & Television Society, 40A Chagford Street, London, NW1.
12, ‡ ○ =   Cinema, sound recording and television equipment and techniques.
Monographic articles, news.
A, December, Yes, None.
T.p. 25, Ad.p. 20.
Per copy 50p, per year £4.20. Free, controlled circulation.
Indexed in: BTI.

3949 8 mm MAGAZINE. 1962.
Haymarket Press, Gillow House, 5 Winsley Street, London, W1.
12, ○ ‡   All items of interest to 8mm cine enthusiasts.
Letters, monographic articles, news, new products, standards, tests.
No Index.
T.p. 52, Ad.p. 18.   22000.
Per copy 17½p, per year £2.40.

3950 MOVIE MAKER incorporating Amateur Cine World and 8mm Movie Maker. 1967.
Fountain Press (Model and Allied Publications), 46 Chancery Lane, London, WC2.
12, ‡   Film technique and film equipment. Aimed at movie makers in general and the amateur in particular.

78

MUSIC

3951 ANTIQUE RECORDS. 1972.
Sir John Hall, 29, Embercourt Road, Thames Ditton, Surrey, KT7 0LH.
○   Aimed at collectors of all kinds of serious music (ie as antiques).
No Index

3952 THE BRITISH CATALOGUE OF MUSIC. 1957.
The Council of the British National Bibliography Ltd., 7 Rathbone Street, London, W1P 2AL.
3, ‡ = *   A record of music and books about music recently published in Great Britain, based upon material deposited at the Copyright Receipt Office of the British Museum, arranged according to a system of classification with an alphabetical index under composers, titles, arrangers, instruments etc.
A,—, Yes, 5 year.
2nd interim issue 1971, T.p. 46.   900.
Per year £6.

3953 COMPOSER. 1958.
Composers Guild of Great Britain, 10 Stratford Place, London, W1N 9AE.
4, * ○   Musical composition and analysis of music; interviews with composers; guide to writing for particular instruments; music in education; book reviews; premieres and commissions; area reports of the musical scene.
Book reviews, articles.
Irregular.
Spring 1972, T.p. 34, Ad.p. 6.   1200.
Per copy 30p, per year £1.20.
Indexed in: BHI.

3954 IN TUNE: the magazine of the Friends of the Scottish National Orchestra. 1972.
150 Hope Street, Glasgow, G2 2TH.
2, ○
No Index
Per copy 20p.

3955 LE GRAND BATON: Journal of the Sir Thomas Beecham Society. 1964.
The Sir Thomas Beecham Society, 46 Wellington Avenue, Westcliff-on-Sea, Essex.
4, ○ *   Articles; discographies; biographical notes on great conductors and musical performers.
No Index.
Free to members

3956 LIVING MUSIC. 1963.
Musical Instrument Promotion Association, 44 Berners Street, London, W1P 3AB.
4, = ‡ *   Public relations service to education. Articles and pictures on school music, music making.
News, new products.
No Index.
T.p. 30, Ad.p. 14.
Per copy 10p, per year 50p.

3957 LONDON COLLEGE OF MUSIC MAGAZINE. 1956.
The College, 47 Great Marlborough Street, London, W1.
3, * =   College activities and music and musicians in general.
Book reviews, letters, monographic articles, news.
No Index.
T.p. 30, Ad.p. 6.
Per copy 25p.

3958 MAKING MUSIC. 1946.
Rural Music Schools Assn., Little Benslow Hills, Hitchin, Herts, SG4 9RD.
3, ‡   General interest to amateur musicians and their teachers, reviews of books and music, lists of music weekend and holiday courses organised by many different bodies, notes on music activities in the counties.
Book notices, book reviews, letters, articles, obituaries.
No Index.
Summer 1972, T.p. 28, Ad.p. 10.   c.700.
Per copy 15p, per year 55p.

3959 MUSIC AND LETTERS. 1920.
Oxford University Press, Press Road, Neasden, London, NW10.
4, +   Musical studies in general.
Book reviews, letters, articles.
A,—, Yes, None.
April 1972, T.p. 119, Ad p.19.   1600.
Per copy 60p, per year £2.
Indexed in: BHI, IBZ.

3960 MUSIC AND MUSICIANS. 1952.
Hansom Books, Artillery Mansions, 75 Victoria Street, London, SW1H 0H2.
12, ○   World coverage of classical music, composers and artists.
Book notices, book reviews, letters, monographic articles, obituaries.
No Index.
August 1972, T p. 64, Ad.p. 10.   9000.
Per copy 35p, per year £4.65.
Indexed in: BHI.

3961 MUSIC BUSINESS WEEKLY. 1969.
Longacre Press Ltd., 161 Fleet Street, London, EC4.
52, = ‡   All record and musical instrument retail and wholesale outlets, manufacturers, artists and agents.
Book reviews, commodity prices, legal notes, letters, articles, new companies, news, new products.
No Index.
T.p. 28, Ad.p. 9.   20000.
Per copy 15p, per year £5.50.

3962 MUSIC INDUSTRY. 1964.
Tofts & Woolf (Publishers) Ltd., 64A Lansdowne Road, South Woodford, London, E18.
=   Musical instrument and sheet music trade throughout the world.
Book reviews, legal notes, letters, monographic articles, new companies, news, new products.
No Index
T.p. 33, Ad p. 49.   2921.
Free, controlled circulation.

3963 MUSICAL OPINION. 1877.
Musical Opinion Ltd., 87 Wellington Street, Luton.
12, ○   Includes brass bands, military music, church music and instruments. Reviews of records and new music.
Book reviews, letters.
No Index.
T.p. 31, Ad p. 24.
Per copy 12½p, per year £1.70.
Indexed in: BHI.

3964 THE MUSICAL TIMES. 1844.
Novello & Co. Ltd., 27 Soho Square, London, W1V 6BR.
12, ○ ‡   For the amateur or professional musician; contains scholarly and topical musical articles, reviews of concerts, records, books, music, church and organ music section, monthly diary of musical events in London, music supplement.
Book notices, book reviews, letters, monographic articles, obituaries.
A, December, Yes, None.

June 1972, T.p. 60, Ad.p. 49.   12000 approx.
Per copy 20p, per year £3.
Indexed in: BHI.

3965 OLD TIME MUSIC. 1971
33 Brunswick Gardens, London, W8.
4, ○
No Index.
Per copy 25p.

3966 PROCEEDINGS OF THE ROYAL MUSICAL ASSOCIATION. 1944
(Proceedings of the Musical Association 1874-1944).
The Association, 44 Philip Victor Road, Handsworth, Birmingham 21.
1, * †   History and art of music.
Monographic articles.
Occasional, Vols. 1-90.
T.p. 110, Ad.p. 13.
Free to members.
Indexed in: BHI.

3967 ROYAL COLLEGE OF MUSIC MAGAZINE: A Journal for Past and Present Students of the R.C.M., and Official Journal of the RCM Union.
Royal College of Music, Prince Consort Road, London, S.W.7.
3, =
Book notices, book reviews, letters, monographic articles, obituaries.
No Index.
T.p. 35.   1800.
Per copy 25p, per year 75p.
Indexed in: BHI.

3968 RMA RESEARCH CHRONICLE. 1961.
Royal Musical Association, 44 Philip Victor Road, Handsworth, Birmingham 21.
1, +   Musicologically 'raw material': lists indices, catalogues, calendars, bibliographical studies, etc.
Letters, monographic articles.
No Index.
T.p. 110, Ad.p. 2.
Per year £1 (75p to members).
Indexed in: BHI.

3969 SIR THOMAS BEECHAM SOCIETY NEWS-LETTER. 1966.
The Sir Thomas Beecham Society, 46 Wellington Avenue, Westcliff-on-Sea, Essex, SS0 9XB.
6, * ○   Reports of meetings; record reviews; any items of historical interest re Sir Thomas Beecham.
No Index.
Free to members.

3970 SOUNDINGS. A Music Journal. 1970.
Department of Music, University College, Cardiff.
1, +   All periods of musical history, with a balance between extended, scholarly essays and less detailed lighter pieces.
Book notices, book reviews, monographic articles.
No Index.
1971/72, T.p. 90, Ad p. 4.   c.250.
Per copy £1.

3971 TEMPO: a quarterly journal of modern music. 1939.
Boosey and Hawkes Music Publishers Ltd., 295 Regent St., London, W1.
4, ‡   20th Century music.
Book reviews, letters, monographic articles.
4 year, —, No, None.
T.p. 27, Ad.p. 5.
Per copy 15, per year £1.
Indexed in: BHI.

3972 WELSH MUSIC. 1959.
Guild for the Promotion of Welsh Music, 4 Southville Road, Newport, Mon.
4, * + =   Music in Wales, especially present day effort and achievement.

Book reviews, letters, monographic articles, music reviews, record reviews.
No Index
T.p. 73, Ad.p. 8.
Free to members.

78.071

COMPOSERS

3973 DELIUS SOCIETY NEWSLETTER. 1962.
The Society, c/o 45 Redhill Drive, Edgware, Middx.
○ *   Life and work of Delius and his music.
Book notices, book reviews, articles, news.
No Index.
T.p. 11.   250.
Free to members.

3974 TRITSCH-TRATSCH: the magazine of the Johann Strauss Society of Great Britain. 1966.
Johann Strauss Society of Great Britain, 301A Harrow Road, Wembley, Middx.
3, *   Music of the Viennese Strauss Family and their contempories.
Book notices, book reviews, letters, monographic articles, record reviews.
No Index.
August 1969, T.p. 16, Ad.p. 1.   300.
Per year 40p.

782

OPERA

3975 ABOUT THE HOUSE: the magazine of the Friends of Covent Garden. 1962.
Friends of Covent Garden, Royal Opera House, London, WC2.
3, ○ †   Opera, ballet music and the history of the Lyric theatre.
Letters, monographic articles, obituaries.
No Index.
Christmas 1971, T.p. 70, Ad.p. 6.
Free to members.

3976 GILBERT AND SULLIVAN JOURNAL. 1925.
The Gilbert and Sullivan Society, c/o 23 Burnside, Sawbridgeworth, Herts.
3, * +   All aspects of the lives and achievements of W.S. Gilbert and Arthur Sullivan and their joint and separate works.
Book reviews, letters, monographic articles, news.
5 year, 1970, Yes, None.
T.p. 14, Ad.p. 4.
Free to members.

3977 NODA BULLETIN: official magazine of the National Operatic and Dramatic Association. 1935.
National Operatic & Dramatic Ass., 1 Crestfield Street, London, WC1H 8AV.
3, *   Amateur theatre.
Book reviews, legal notes, letters, articles, obituaries.
No Index.
October 1971, T.p. 50, Ad.p. 30.   4250.
Per year £1. and Free to members.

3978 OPERA. 1950.
Seymour Press Ltd., 334 Brixton Road, London, SW9.
12, ○   Reviews of international operas, records.
A, —, Yes, None.
T.p. 78, Ad.p. 4.   11600.
Per copy 20p, per year £3.
Indexed in: BHI.

3979 SAVOYARD. 1963.
D'Oyly Carte Opera Trust Ltd., 1 Savoy Hill, London, WC2.
3, ○   News of Gilbert and Sullivan operas.

Articles.
No Index.
Per year £1.

783

CHURCH MUSIC

3980 CHURCH MUSIC. 1958.
Church Music Association of Great Britain, 28 Ashley Place, London, SW1.
6, * ‡ + =   All aspects of church music in the UK and abroad.
Book notices, book reviews, commodity prices, letters, articles, news, new products, obituaries.
No Index.
T.p. 28, Ad.p. 4.   3000.
Free to members.

3981 METHODIST CHURCH MUSIC SOCIETY BULLETIN. 1970.
M.C.M.S., 5 Leyton Villas, Redland, Bristol, BS6 6JF.
3, ○   Every aspect of hymnology
Book notices, book reviews, letters, monographic articles, obituaries.
No Index, None.
T.p. 14 or 18.   1000.
Per copy 17½p. Free to members.

785.12

BRASS BANDS

3982 BRASS BAND NEWS. 1881-1958, 1969-
Wright & Round Limited, Parliament Street, Gloucester.
12, ○ =   Activities of brass and military bands, technical, and instructional articles personality features. Adjudicators, professional cards. etc..
No Index.
June 1972, T.p. 10.
Per copy 7½p.

3983 BRITISH BANDSMAN. 1887.
Bandsman's Press Ltd., 210 Strand, London, WC2.
52, = ○   All matter relative to the brass band scene at home and abroad.
Book reviews, commodity prices, letters, news, new products, obituaries.
No Index.
T.p. 8, Ad.p. Most.
Per copy 5p, per year £2.50.

3984 FANFARE: Journal of the Royal Military School of Music, Kneller Hall. 1968.
John Pope Esq (for the School.)
R: Military Sch. of Music, Kneller Hall, Twickenham, Middx TW2 7DU.
1, =   Military music, bands, bandsmen. Annual calendar of band concerts, events. News of R. Mil. School of Music.
Book reviews, letters, articles, obituaries.
Index will eventually be compiled.
1972, T.p. 30, Ad.p. 4.   3000.
Per copy 20p.

3985 SOUNDING BRASS: incorporating The Conductor; official organ of the National Association of Brass Band Conductors. 1972.
Novello & Co. Ltd., 27 Soho Square, London, W1.
4, ‡ + *   Brass instrumentalists, teachers, brass band conductors, composers of brass music, brass band enthusiasts, school bands.
Book reviews, commodity prices, letters, monographic articles, new products, obituaries, tests.
No Index.
April 1972, T.p. 20, Ad.p. 12.   5000
Per copy 15p, per year 74p.

785.16

JAZZ

3986 JAZZ JOURNAL. 1948.
Novello & Co. Ltd., Borough Green, Kent.
12, = ○   All aspects of jazz; record reviews, biographies, photography.
Book notices, book reviews, commodity prices, letters, news, obituaries.
A, January, No, None.
T.p. 34, Ad.p. 6.   10100.
Per copy 15p, per year £2.

3987 JAZZ TIMES. 1964.
British Jazz Society, 10 Southfield Gardens, Twickenham, Middx.
12, * ○   All aspects of New Orleans jazz etc.
No Index.
T.p. 10, Ad.p. 7.   7800.
Per copy 5p, per year £1.

786/789

INSTRUMENTS

3988 BEAT INSTRUMENTAL AND INTERNATIONAL RECORDING STUDIO.
Beat Instrumental, 58 Parker Street, London, WC2B 5QB.
12, ○   For all players of guitars, drums, keyboard instruments.
No Index.
Per copy 25p.

3989 GALPIN SOCIETY JOURNAL. 1947.
Galpin Society, c/o Rose Cottage, Bois Lane, Chesham Bois, Amersham, Bucks.
1, + *   History of musical instruments.
Book notices, book reviews, letters, monographic articles, obituaries.
A, —, Yes, 5 year.
T.p. 210, Ad p. 6.
Free to members.
Indexed in: BHI.

786

KEYBOARD INSTRUMENTS

3990 KEYBOARD. 1969.
Tofts & Woolf (Publishers) Ltd., 64A Lansdowne Road, South Woodford, London, E18.
6, ○   Keyboard instrumentation, principally the organ, piano, accordion, harpsichord from the amateur's viewpoint.
Book reviews, letters, news, new products.
No Index.
T.p. 44, Ad.p. 11.   5000.
Per copy 30p, per year £2.50.

786.2

PIANO

3991 PIANO WORLD AND MUSIC TRADES REVIEW. 1972.
(Pianomaker; Music and Radio Retailer; Piano World and Music Trades International 1969-1971; Music Trades Review).
Trade Papers (London) Ltd/Turret Press (Holdings) Ltd., 157 Hagden Lane, Watford, WD1 8LW.
12, =
Book reviews, letters, articles, sheet music, equipment.
No Index.
June 1972, T.p. 24, Ad.p. 24.
Per year £2.70 including yearbook.

786.6

ORGAN

3992 **KEY FRAME.**
Fair Organ Preservation Society, 65 Market Road, Thrapston, Northants.
4, ○
No Index.
Per copy 12½p. Free to members.

3993 **THE ORGAN.** 1921.
Musical Opinion Ltd., 87 Wellington Street, Luton, Beds.
4, ‡ = +   New and old instruments. International historical material on organs and their builders.
Book reviews, letters, monographic articles.
A, April, Yes, None.
T.p. 44, Ad.p. 4.   2500.
Per copy 30p, per year £1.50.
Indexed in: BHI.

3994 **THE ORGAN CLUB JOURNAL.**
The Organ Club, c/o Graham R. Bamber, 93 Lynton Road, Acton, London, W3 9HL.
6, * ○   All matters relating to pipe organs, primarily of the church or concert-hall variety. Cinema organs officially included but actually ignored. Some coverage of electronic organs, but this is subsidiary.
Book and record reviews, letters, monographic articles, obituaries, specifications.
A, Printed as part of No. 6 issue, No, None.
No. 3-1972, T.p. 14.   c.850.
Available to Club members only. Membership, town £2, country £1.50.

3995 **ORGANISTS REVIEW.**
Incorporated Association of Organists, 9 Hill View, Milton, Stoke-on-Trent, ST2 7AR.
4, ○
No Index.
Per year 50p.

786.8

ACCORDION

3996 **Accordion Times and Modern Musician.** 1936.
(Harmonica News).
J. J. Black (Publishers) Ltd., Somerset House, Cranleigh, Surrey.
12, = + ○   Accordion, harmonica and concertina.
Book reviews, letters.
No Index.
Per copy 5p, per year 70p.

787

STRING INSTRUMENTS

3997 **CHELYS:** The Journal of the Viola da Gamba Society. 1969.
Viola da Gamba Society, 123 Russell Lane, London, N.20.
1, + *   Matter related to viols—the instruments, their makers; the music, its sources, the composers.
Book reviews, letters, monographic articles, obituaries.
None yet issued, probably to be 5 yrly.
T.p. 56, Ad.p. 6.   c.300.
Per copy £2.10.

3998 **JOURNAL OF THE LUTE SOCIETY.**
Lute Society, 5 Wilton Square, London, N1.
4, ○
No Index.
Free to members.

3999 **THE STRAD.** 1890.
Lavender Publications Ltd., Borough Green, Kent.
12, = ○   All stringed instruments played with the bow.
No Index.
T.p. 29, Ad.p. 20.
Per copy 10p, per year £1.50.
Indexed in: BHI.

788.1

TRUMPET

4000 **THE TRUMPETER.** 1954.
The National School Brass Band Association, c/o 2, Gray's Close, Barton-le-Clay, Bedford.
3, * ○ ‡ +   Reports on activities of the National School Brass Band Association (formed in 1952) and individual school brass bands. Band music reviews. General articles on teaching, arranging for brass groups etc.
5 year, Spring Term 1971, No, None.
Summer 1972, T.p. 20.   400.
Free to members.

788.9

PIPES

4001 **THE PIPE BAND:** official organ of the Scottish Pipe Band Association. 1949.
(Piping, Drumming and Highland Dancing).
The Scottish Pipe Band Association, 45 Washington Street, Glasgow, G3 8AZ.
6, ○ *   All pipe bands throughout the world plus pipe band enthusiasts and Highland dancing—worldwide.
Book notices, book reviews, commodity prices, letters, new companies, new products, obituaries.
No Index.
2/1972, T.p. 28-32, Ad.p. approx 14.   2000 +.
Per copy 10p, per year 75p.

789.5

BELLRINGING

4002 **THE RINGING WORLD:** official journal of the Central Council of Church Bell Ringers. 1911.
The Council, c/o Seven Corners Press Ltd., Onslow Street, Guildford, Surrey.
52, ‡ ○   Change ringing and campanology in general.
Book notices, book reviews, letters, monographic articles, news, obituaries.
A, –, No, None.
T.p. 20, Ad.p. 4.   5850.
Free to members.

791.4

CINEMA

4003 **BRITISH NATIONAL FILM CATALOGUE.** 1963.
British Industrial & Scientific Film Association, 193/7 Regent Street, London, W1.
4, ‡ + =   Complete list of short films available in the UK since 1963.
Q, March, June, September, October, No, A.
T.p. 36, Ad.p. 8.
Per copy £4.50, per year £8.50.

4004 **CINEMA AND T.V. TODAY.** 1971.
(Today's Cinema, Kine Weekly 1907).
British and American Film Holdings, Film House, 142 Wardour Street, London, W1V 4BR.
52, + =   Trade paper for the film and T.V. industry.
Commodity prices, articles.
No Index.
17.6.1972, T.p. 14, Ad.p. 14.   5000.
Per copy 20p, per year £9.40.

4005 CINEMA RISING. 1972.
Cinema Rising Ltd., 12/13 Little Newport Street, London, WC2.
12, ○
No Index.
Per copy 15p.

4006 CONTINENTAL FILM REVIEW. 1952.
Eurap Publishing Co. (London) Ltd., 71 Oldhill Street, London, N16 6LX.
12, ○   Film reviews and features.
No Index.
June 1972, T.p. 35.
Per copy 15p, per year £2.20.

4007 FILM: The Magazine of the British Federation of Film Societies. 1954.
British Federation of Film Societies, 81 Dean Street, London.
4, * ○   Films—festivals, current, national, historical, film-makers.
Book notices, book reviews, letters, articles, reports.
No Index.
Spring 1972, T.p. 35, Ad.p. 1.   7500.
Per copy 15p, per year 65p.

4008 FILM AND SOCIETY. 1971.
E.L.I. Communications Ltd., 4a Albany Terrace, Regents Park, London, NW1 4DS.
4, =
No Index.
Per year £1.

4009 FILM REVIEW. 1972.
(ABC Film Review 1951-1972).
EMI Cinemas & Leisure Ltd., 30/31 Golden Square, London, W1.
12, ○   Coverage of films on release and in production by means of reviews, articles, interviews, lavish picture spreads, etc. Occasional retrospective articles. At present sold to patrons of 260 ABC cinemas, but expected to expand.
No Index.
July 1972, T.p. 64.
Per copy 10p.

4010 FILMS AND FILMING. 1954.
Hansom Books, Artillery Mansions, 75 Victoria Street, London, SW1H 0H2.
12, ○   World cinema.
Book notices, book reviews, letters, monographic articles, obituaries.
No Index.
July 1972, T.p. 80, Ad.p. 10.   35000.
Per copy 35p, per year £4.65.

4011 FILMS ILLUSTRATED. 1971.
(Films in London 1969-1970; Films Fortnightly 1970-1971)
Films in London Publications, 59 Temple Chambers, 3 Temple Avenue, London, EC4Y 0ET.
12, ○   Features, interviews and reviews connected with the current cinema scene.
Book reviews, letters.
No Index.
June 1972, T.p. 40, Ad.p. 4.   12030.
Per copy 25p, per year £3.80.

4012 L'INCROYABLE CINEMA: The Film magazine of fantasy & imagination. 1969.
Orion Press, 81 Marlborough Road, Salford, Manchester M8 7DT.
2, ○ ‡   Coverage of films of science fiction and fantasy content with special interest in the technical effects and behind the scenes work involved in producing such films.
Book notices, book reviews, interviews, letters, monographic articles, new products, obituaries, film reviews.
No Index.
Autumn 1971, T.p. 60, Ad.p. 4.   1500
Per copy 25p, per year 60p.

4013 MONOGRAM. 1971.
(Brighton Film Review 1968-1970)
Monogram Publications, 63 Old Compton Street, London, W1V 5PN.
4, ○ +   Cinema: film-reviews, film-literature, articles on directors, genres, general aesthetic problems connected with film.
Book notices, book reviews, articles.
No Index.
March 1972, T.p. 44, Ad.p. 2.   2500.
Per copy 30p, per year £1.

4014 PHOTOPLAY. 1950.
Argus Press Ltd., 12-18 Paul Street, London, EC2.
12, ○   Articles and features from all aspects of the film world.
No Index.
T.p. 64.   78230.
Per copy 10p, per year £1.50.

4015 SIGHT AND SOUND. 1932.
British Film Institute, 81 Dean Street, London, W1.
4, ○   Film productions, past and present.
No Index.
28400.
Per copy 25p, per year £1.50.
Indexed in: BHI.

791.5

PUPPETS

4016 PUPPET POST: Official journal of the Educational Puppetry Association. 1943.
The E.P.A., 23A Southampton Place, London, WC1A 2BP.
2, * ‡ =   Educational aspects of puppetry.
Book notices, book reviews, letters, monographic articles.
No Index.
T.p. 32.   c. 200.
Per year £1.25.

791.7

CIRCUS

4017 THE WORLD'S FAIR. 1904.
The World's Fair Ltd., P.O. Box 57, Union Street, Oldham, OL1 1DY.
52, =   National trade weekly for travelling showmen, market traders, and operators and manufacturers of coin operated amusement machines. It also covers the steam traction engine preservation movement, rallies and allied events.
No Index.
17/6/72, T.p. 27, Ad.p. 31.   26000.
Per copy 5p, per year £5.50.

792

THEATRE

4018 AMATEUR STAGE. 1946.
Stacey Publications, 1 Hawthorndene Road, Hayes, Bromley, Kent.
12, ○ ‡   All aspects of amateur dramatic and musical productions.
Book reviews, letters, articles, new products.
A, December, Yes, None.
June 1972, T.p. 50, Ad.p. 18.   8000.
Per copy 15p, per year £2.

4019 ARDÁN: Iris an Chomhairle Náisiúnta Drámaíochta. 1963.
An Chomhairle Náisiúnta Drámaíochta, 6 Sráid Fhearchair, Dublin, 2.
3, + = *   Drama in the Irish language. Distributed and sold to groups producing plays in Irish and to Festival Committees organising festivals for such groups and to those who patronise plays in the Irish language.
Book notices, book reviews, monographic articles, obituaries.
No Index.
Summer 1972, T.p. 20, Ad.p. 4.   1000.
Per copy 10p.

4020 CALL BOY: Journal of the British Music Hall Society. 1963.
The Society, 1 King Henry Street, London, N16.
4, * = + ○   Light entertainment past and present.
Book notices, book reviews, letters, news, new products, obituaries.
No Index.
T.p. 23, Ad.p. 1.   1000.
Free to members only.

4021 CREATIVE DRAMA. 1950.
Educational Drama Association, Drama Centre, Rea Street South, Birmingham 5.
2, ‡   To foster the knowledge and application of creative and child drama in schools; also with mentally handicapped persons.
Book reviews.
Approx. 2 years, Separately, Yes, approx. 5 years.
No. 3, 1971, T.p. 32, Ad.p. 2.   2500
Per copy 15p, per year 40p.

4022 DRAMA: Quarterly Theatre Review. 1919.
British Drama League, 9/10 Fitzroy Square, London, W1P 6AE.
4, = ○   General matters of theatre interest.
Book notices, book reviews, articles, obituaries.
A, Winter issue (December), Yes, None.
Summer 1972, T.p. 64, Ad.p. 20.   c. 7500.
Per copy 25p, per year £1.20.
Indexed in: BHI.

4023 FORUM. 1969.
London Borough of Newham, Education Offices, Broadway, Stratford, London, E15.
1, ○ =   News of events in the field of drama in Newham schools.
No Index.
No. 1, T.p. 43.   500.
Free.

4024 GAMBIT: International Theatre Review. 1963.
Calder & Boyars Ltd., 18 Brewer Street, London, W1.
4, ‡   Intellectual theatre magazine. Colleges, theatres, theatre groups, individual subscribers.
Book reviews, letters, monographic articles.
No Index.
June 1972, T.p. 128, Ad.p. 4.   1200.
Per copy 75p, per year £2.65.

4025 LLWYFAN: Cylchgrawn Theatr Cymru. 1968.
Welsh Theatre Association, Waterloo Street, Bangor, Caernarvonshire.
2, ○ *   Journal of the Welsh Theatre Association dealing entirely in Welsh with indigenous professional and amateur theatre—contemporary and historical—and aspects of international, particularly European, theatre.
Book notices, book reviews, articles, new products.
No Index.
No. 6, 1971, T.p. 30.   2500.
Per copy 25p, per year 50p.

4026 MARLOVIAN CHRONICLE. 1957.
The Marlowe Society, 193 White Horse Hill, Chislehurst, Kent.
Irregular, ○ + *   Elizabethan period of history with particular reference to Christopher Marlowe and his plays and poems and the Elizabethan theatre.
Book notices, book reviews, news items, letters, monographic articles, obituaries.
Irregular, —, No, None.
May 1972, T.p. 4.   200.
Per copy 3p, Free to members.

4027 PLAYS AND PLAYERS. 1953.
Hansom Books, Artillery Mansions, 75 Victoria Street, London, SW1H 0HZ.
12, ○   World theatre, full text of new London production every month.
Book notices, book reviews, letters, monographic articles, obituaries.
No Index.
August 1972, T.p. 56, Ad.p. 10.   16000.
Per copy 35p, per year £4.65.

4028 SCOTTISH THEATRE: Scotland's magazine of the stage. 1969.
Scottish Theatre Publications, Thornfield House, Kirknewton, Midlothian, Scotland.
6, ○   A complete review of theatre in Scotland, both professional and amateur, with emphasis on the promotion of a vigorous native drama. Coverage of current productions.
Book reviews, letters, obituaries.
No Index.
May-June 1972, T.p. 24, Ad.p. 4.   1000.
Per copy 25p, per year £1.50.

4029 SPOTLIGHT CASTING DIRECTORY. 1927.
The Spotlight, 43 Cranbourn Street, London, WC2H 7AP.
2, =   Casting directory for stage, television, films, radio.
No Index.
T.p. 3100.
Trade only £4.

4030 SPOTLIGHT CONTACTS. 1946.
The Spotlight, 43 Cranbourn Street, London, WC2H 7AP.
2, ○ =   Reference work containing names and addresses of theatrical agents, managers, T.V. companies etc.
No Index.
T.p. 104.   c. 7000.
Per copy 35p.

4031 STAGE AND TELEVISION TODAY. 1959.
(The Stage 1880-1958)
Carson & Comerford Ltd., 19-21 Tavistock Street, London, WC2.
52, =   Professional newspaper for all persons engaged in the entertainment world.
Book reviews, letters, monographic articles, news, obituaries, parliamentary reports.
No Index.
T.p. 13, Ad.p. 7.   30572.
Per copy 5p, per year £3.50.

4032 THEATRE NIGHTS. 1970.
Bill Freedman Ltd., 33 Henrietta Street, London, WC2.
6, ○   News and information about the theatrical scene.
No Index.
May 1972, T.p. 14.
Free.

4033 THEATRE NOTEBOOK. 1945.
I. K. Fletcher, 22 Buckingham Gate, London, SW1.
4, = ○   Theatre history.
Book notices, book reviews, articles.
A, —, Yes, None.
T.p. 39.
Free to members of the Society for Theatre Research.

Key to reference symbols

○ popular   ‡ technical   = trade/professional

+ research   * society/institution   † house journal

4034 THEATRE QUARTERLY. 1971.
 Eyre Methuen—A.B.P. Ltd., 39 Goodge Street, London, W1P 1FD.
 4, ○ + ‡ Serious but lively magazine examining all aspects of the theatre, past and present, in Britain and throughout the world.
 Book notices, book reviews, letters, monographic articles.
 A, —, No, None.
 Jul Sep. 1972, T.p. 106, Ad.p. 10.   5000.
 Per copy 80p, per year £3.50.

792.8
BALLET

4035 DANCE AND DANCERS. 1950.
 Hansom Books, Artillery Mansions, 75 Victoria Street, London, SW1H 0H2.
 12, ○ Ballet, classical and modern stage and film dancing.
 Book notices, book reviews, letters, monographic articles, obituaries.
 No Index.
 July 1972, T.p. 48, Ad.p. 10.
 Per copy 35p, per year £4.65.

4036 POINTE. 1972.
 Scottish Theatre Publications, Thornfield House, Kirknewton, Midlothian.
 4, ○ = Ballet in Scotland.
 No Index.
 Per copy 25p.

793.3
DANCING

4037 BALLROOM DANCING TIMES. 1956.
 Dancing Times Ltd., 18 Hand Court, High Holborn, London, WC1.
 12, ○ ‡ Classical, old time and modern dancing etc.
 Book notices, book reviews, letters, obituaries.
 No Index.
 T.p. 32, Ad.p. 16.   7500.
 Per copy 12½p, per year £1.80.

4038 DANCE NEWS.
 Dance News Ltd., 22 Shaftesbury Avenue, London, W1V 8AP.
 52, ○
 No Index.
 Per copy 5p, per year £3.50.

4039 THE DANCING TIMES.
 Dancing Times Ltd., 18 Hand Court, High Holborn, London, WC1.
 12, ○ ‡ Ballet and all forms of theatrical dancing.
 Book notices, book reviews, letters, obituaries.
 5 year, 1970, Yes, None.
 T.p. 28, Ad.p. 28.   12000
 Per copy 25p, per year £3.30.

4040 ENGLISH DANCE AND SONG. 1936.
 The English Folk Dance and Song Society, Cecil Sharp House, 2 Regents Park Road, London, NW1 7AY.
 4, ○ + * † Popular and scholarly coverage of all types of folk music (song, dance, instrumental) plus some folklore and crafts. Each issue includes 16 page inset 'EFDSS News' which is the house journal of the English Folk Dance and Song Society.
 Book reviews, letters, articles, obituaries.
 No Index.
 Summer 1972, T.p. 24, Ad.p. 16.   12000.
 Per copy 20p, per year 80p.

4041 SCOTTISH DANCE ARCHIVES. 1972.
 Scottish Dance Archives, 50 Wicks Crescent, Formby, Liverpool.
 2, ○
 Per year 40p.

793.31
FOLK DANCES

4042 FOLK MUSIC JOURNAL. 1965.
 (Journal of the English Folk Dance & Song Society 1932-64; Journal of the English Folk Dance Society 1914-1922; Folk Music Journal 1899-1931).
 English Folk Dance and Song Society, Cecil Sharp House, 2 Regents Park Road, London, NW1.
 1, ○ + * Folk song, folk dances and customs connected with either.
 Book notices, book reviews, letters, monographic articles, obituaries.
 5 year, 1969, Yes, None.
 1966, T.p. 50.   7000.
 Per year £3, Free to members.

4043 JOURNAL OF THE INTERNATIONAL FOLK MUSIC COUNCIL. 1949.
 W. Heffer Ltd., Cambridge.
 1, ○ Folk music and dance research in English, French or German.
 No Index.
 Per year £1.
 Indexed in: BHI.

793.8
CONJURING

4044 ABRACADABRA
 Goodliffe the Magician, Arden Forest Industrial Estate, Alcester, Warks.
 ○
 No Index.
 Per year £4.25.

4045 THE MAGIC CIRCULAR. 1906.
 Magic Circle, 84 Chenies Mews, London, WC1.
 11, * ○ New tricks, illusions, historical items.
 Book reviews, letters, articles, news, obituaries.
 A, November, No, None.
 1300.
 Free to members.

794.1
CHESS

4046 BRITISH CHESS MAGAZINE. 1881.
 British Chess Magazine Ltd., 9 Market Street, St. Leonards-on-Sea, Sussex.
 12, ○ Devoted exclusively to the game of chess. Tournament reports, championships, articles, news and problems.
 Book notices, book reviews, letters, articles.
 A, —, Yes, None.
 June 1972, T.p. 44.
 Per copy 25p, per year £3.

4047 THE CHESS PLAYER. 1971.
 The Chess Player, 12 Burton Avenue, Carlton, Nottingham NG4 1PT.
 12, ○
 No Index.
 Per year £6.

4048 CORRESPONDENCE CHESS: Quarterly Journal of the B.C.C.A. 1963.
 (B.C.C.A. Magazine 1949-1963)
 British Correspondence Chess Association, c/o D.J. Rogers, 90 Park Drive, London, W3 8NB.
 4, * Correspondence chess in general.
 Book reviews, letters, articles.
 A, Spring (openings only), Yes, None.
 Spring 1972, T.p. 32, Ad.p. 2.   1000.
 Per copy 15p, per year 60p (Free to members)

794.7

BILLIARDS

4049 BILLIARD AND SNOOKER JOURNAL. 1972.
P. Fenelon, 1 Ennafort Grove, Raheny, Dublin 5.
12, ○
No Index.
Per year £1.20.

795

BOOKMAKERS

4050 THE BRITISH BOOKMAKER: The Official Journal of the National Association of Bookmakers. 1964.
National Association of Bookmakers Ltd., Sabian House, 26-27 Cowcross Street, London, EC1.
12, =   Racing and betting.
Book notices, book reviews, legal notes, letters, articles, new products, obituaries, parliamentary reports.
No Index.
June 1972, T.p. 8, Ad.p. Most.
Per year £1.

4051 THE LICENSED BOOKMAKER AND BETTING OFFICE PROPRIETOR. 1962.
City Magazines Ltd., Aldwych House, 81 Aldwych, London, WC2.
12, =   Covers all aspects—legal, political, commercial—concerning the operation of betting shops, news, views, pictures, equipment, services, with special attention to shop design and security.
Book reviews, legal notes, letters, articles, new companies, new products, obituaries, parliamentary reports, tests.
No Index.
June 1972, T.p. 36, Ad.p. 19.   6500.
Per year £2.

795.41

BRIDGE

4052 BRIDGE MAGAZINE. 1926.
John Waddington Ltd., Wakefield Road, Leeds, 10.
12, ‡   Theory of bridge; reports on bridge events; humorous articles on bridge; problems and competitions.
Book notices, book reviews, letters, obituaries.
6m, Private circulation, No, None.
June 1972, T.p. 62, Ad.p. 2.
Per copy 30p, per year £3.

796

ATHLETICS

4053 ATHLETICS ARENA INTERNATIONAL. 1963.
Arena Publications, 325 Streatham High Road, London, SW16.
12, ○   Track and field athletics in Britain and abroad.
Book reviews, letters, articles.
A, —, Yes, 6 year.
T.p. 10, Ad.p. 2.
Per copy 20p, per year £2.

4054 ATHLETICS WEEKLY. 1950.
(Athletics 1945-1950).
World Athletics & Sporting Publications Ltd., 344 High Street, Rochester, Kent.
52, ○   All aspects of athletics in Britain and throughout the world. Results, ranking lists, coaching/technique articles. Official news etc.
Book reviews, articles.
No Index.
June 17 1972, T.p. 36, Ad.p. 6.   12000.
Per copy 10p, per year £6.50.

4055 SPORTSWORLD: official magazine of the British Olympic Association. 1972.
(World Sports 1937-1971).
Country & Sporting Publications, 23-27 Tudor Street, London, EC4.
12, ○   All sporting activity.
Book reviews, letters, articles.
No Index.
T.p. 50, Ad.p. 14.   39500.
Per copy 20p.

796.27

CROQUET

4056 THE CROQUET GAZETTE: official organ of the Croquet Association. 1970.
(The Croquet Association Gazette 1904-1969).
The Croquet Association, c/o The Hurlingham Club, London, SW6.
5, ○*   To report results and give accounts of tournaments, to publish letters and articles relating to croquet and to publish official notices relating to the sport.
No Index.
July 1971, T.p. 20, Ad.p. 1.   750.
Per year £1.50 and Free to members.

796.28

CURLING

4057 THE SCOTTISH CURLER. 1954.
R.W. Welsh, 2 Coates Crescent, Edinburgh, 3.
9, ○   Reports and comment on the game of curling in Scotland and 14 countries.
No Index.
T.p. 18, Ad.p. 14.
Per copy 10p, per year £1.

796.281

BOWLS

4058 WORLD BOWLS incorporating British Bowls. 1958.
C.M. Jones, 'Lowlands', Wenhaston, Halesworth, Suffolk, IP19 9DY.
12, ○ =   News and views of the British bowls scene.
Book reviews, letters, articles.
No Index.
July 1972, T.p. 17, Ad.p. 5.
Per copy 10p, per year £1.30

796.31

TABLE TENNIS

4059 TABLE TENNIS NEWS: Official Journal of the English Table Tennis Association. 1966.
(Table Tennis 1966).
Wallace (Printers) Ltd., 44 Crook St., Bolton, Lancs.
8, *   Home and international coverage of all important competitive events. Coaching articles and schools' events of a national character. Postbag feature.
No Index.
April 1972, T.p. 28, Ad.p. 8.   3000.
Per copy 10p, per year £1.

796.32

BASKETBALL. NETBALL

4060 BASKETBALL: Official Journal of the Amateur Basket Ball Association. 1960.
Amateur Basket Ball Association, PO Box I.W.3., Leeds, 16.

4, ○ Provides the opportunity for players, officials coaches and enthusiasts to read about the game in all aspects.
Book reviews, commodity prices, letters, monographic articles, new products, standards.
No Index.
Summer 1972, T.p. 33, Ad.p. 11. 2500.
Per copy 12p, per year 60p.

4061 NETBALL.
The Official Magazine of the All England Netball Association.
All England Netball Association, 26 Park Crescent, London, W1N 4ER.
4, ‡ * Supplied to netball clubs, colleges and schools as well as to interested individuals in UK and other Commonwealth countries and South Africa.
Book notices, book reviews, letters, monographic articles, standards, tests.
No Index.
March-May 1972, T.p. 40, Ad.p. 7. 2300.
Per copy 12½p, per year 50p.

796.332

FOOTBALL

4062 FOOTBALL ACADEMY. 1972.
Sports Academy Ltd., Walmar House, 288 Regent Street, London, W1R 5HF.
12, ○ Football coaching directed at young players and those responsible for the coaching of youngsters. Incorporates the GOLD STAR Award scheme, approved by the F.A.
Articles.
No Index.
No. 6, 1972, T.p. 28. 65000.
Per copy 20p, per year £2.75.

4063 FOOTBALL MONTHLY. 1951.
Longacre Press Ltd., 161-6 Fleet Street, London, EC4.
12, ○ No Index.
220000.
Per copy 15p, per year £2.50.

4064 FOOTBALL PICTORIAL. 1970.
(Football Supporter 1969).
Mercury House Publications Ltd., Mercury House, Waterloo Road, London, SE1.
12, = ○ ‡ Every aspect of professional soccer.
Book reviews, letters, articles, news, new products.
A, April, Yes, None.
T.p. 41, Ad.p. 5.
Per copy 12½p per year £2.

4065 LEAGUE FOOTBALL. 1972.
(Football League Review 1966-1972; Soccer Review 1965-1966).
The Football League Ltd., Clifton Drive South, Lytham St. Annes, FY8 1JG, Lancs.
40, ○ As part of match-day programme at most Football League Club grounds, and on subscription. Official statements and interpretations of the current soccer scene.
No Index.
T.p. 17, Ad.p. 7. c. 325000.
Per copy 5p, per year £2.
Free in club programmes.

4066 MONTHLY SOCCER. 1969.
Martec Publishing Group Ltd., 61 Berners Street, London, W1.
12, ○
No Index.
50000.
Per copy 15p.

4067 RACING & FOOTBALL OUTLOOK. 1900.
Websters Publications Ltd., 79 Temple Chambers, Temple Avenue, London, EC4.
52, ○ Racing and football information.
No Index.
Per copy 5p.

4068 THE SKY BLUE. 1967.
Coventry City Football Club, Coventry.
24/26, ○ Activities of the Club.
No Index.
T.p. 20, Ad.p. 4.
Per copy 5p.

4069 SOCCER STAR. 1952.
Websters Publications Ltd., 79 Temple Chambers, London, EC4.
52, ○ Football news and comment.
No Index.
T.p. 29, Ad.p. 1.
Per copy 10p, per year £5.50.

4070 WORLD SOCCER. 1960.
Websters Publications Ltd., 79 Temple Chambers, London, EC4.
12, ○
No Index.
Per copy 15p, per year £2.50.

796.333

RUGBY

4071 RUGBY LEAGUER. 1947.
South Lancashire Newspapers Ltd., 164 College Street St. Helens, Lancs.
40/42, ○ Rugby football,
Letters, news.
No Index.
T.p. 4. 12500.
Per copy 5p, per year £2.50.

4072 RUGBY WORLD.
Longacre Press Ltd., 161-166 Fleet Street, London, EC4.
12, ○
No Index.
14400.
Per copy 15p.

4073 WELSH RUGBY. 1961.
Western Sporting Press Ltd., 28 Church Rd., Whitchurch, Cardiff.
12, ○ Welsh Rugby.
Book reviews, letters, articles.
No Index.
T.p. 30, Ad.p. 22. 13000.
Per copy 15p, per year £1.80.

796.34

BADMINTON. SQUASH

4074 BADMINTON GAZETTE: Official organ of the Badminton Association of England. 1907.
The Association, 24 The Charter Road, Woodford Green, Essex.
6, ○ Articles of topical interest, reports and reviews etc.
No Index.
T.p. 22, Ad.p. 9. 5000.
Free to members.

4075 THE SQUASH PLAYER. 1971.
A.C.M. Webb (Publishing) Ltd., 60 Fleet Street, London, EC4.
12, ○

Book reviews, letters, articles.
No Index.
Per year £4.20.

796.342

TENNIS

4076 LAWN TENNIS: Official journal of the Lawn Tennis Association
(Lawn Tennis and Badminton 1893; British Lawn Tennis 1939).
British Lawn Tennis Ltd., 'Lowlands' Wenhaston, Suffolk, 1P19 9DY.
○ =   News and views of the British tennis scene.
Book reviews, letters, articles.
No Index.
June 1972, T.p. 25, Ad.p. 13.
Per copy 17p, per year £2.

796.344

LACROSSE

4077 LACROSSE: Official Magazine of All England Women's Lacrosse Association. 1949.
Langhams, Langham Herald Press, Farnham.
5, *   News and match reports on all aspects of lacrosse.
No Index.
March 1972, T.p. 31, Ad.p. 1.
Free to members.

796.352

GOLF

4078 BRITISH GOLF GREENKEEPER. 1912.
British Golf Greenkeepers Association, Addington Court Golf Club, Addington, Croydon.
12, = ‡   News and interest articles for greenkeepers, green committees, golf clubs & allied trades
No Index.
T.p. 11, Ad.p. 5.
Per copy 5p, per year 80p.

4079 GOLF COURSE & CLUB HOUSE MANAGEMENT. 1935.
184 Fleet Street, London, EC4.
6, =
No Index.
Subscription on application.

4080 GOLF FIXTURES: monthly calendar. 1946.
English Golf Union, 12A Denmark Street, Wokingham, Berks.
12, ○   Open golf tournaments for current and following year.
No Index.
T.p. 17, Ad.p. 2.
Free to golf clubs and societies.

4081 GOLF INTERNATIONAL. 1971.
Park Street Publishing Co., Kennington Oval, London, SE11.
52, ○
No Index.
Per copy 10p.

4082 GOLF MONTHLY. 1911.
Munro Barr Publications, 94 Hope Street, Glasgow, C2.
12, ○   International golf and personalities. Some instructional material.
Book reviews, letters, new products, obituaries.
No Index.
T.p. 48, Ad.p. 20.   32500.
Per copy 20p, per year £2.40.

4083 GOLF TRADE JOURNAL: Official journal of the Professional Golfers Association. 1969.
Golf World Ltd., South Road, Brighton.
12, =   Golf professionals and the trade.
No Index.
2650.
Per year £2.

4084 GOLF WEEKLY. 1969.
Atlas Publishing Ltd., 10 Kennington Park Place, London, SE11.
52, ○
No Index.
T.p. 16, Ad.p. 5.   32000.
Per copy 10p, per year £4.

4085 GOLF WORLD incorporating Golfing. 1970.
Golf World Ltd., South Road, Brighton.
12, ○   All aspects of golf for the amateur and professional.
No Index.
60000.
Per copy 20p, per year £2.50.

796.353

POLO

4086 BI-POLO NEWS: Official news-sheet of the Bicycle Polo Association of Great Britain.
The Association, c/o 2 Crossways, Tatsfield, Westerham, Kent.
4, ○
No Index.
T.p. 17.
Free to members.

796.358

CRICKET

4087 CRICKETER. 1920.
Mercury House Publications Ltd., Waterloo Road, London, EC1.
12, ○
Book notices, book reviews, letters, news, obituaries.
No Index.
T.p. 30, Ad.p. 6.
Per copy 15p.

4088 PLAYFAIR CRICKET MONTHLY. 1960.
Dickens Press Ltd., 161 Queen Victoria Street, London, EC4.
12, ○   International cricket scene all the year round.
Book reviews, letters, articles, news.
No Index.
T.p. 30, Ad.p. 2.   17500.
Per copy 15p, per year £2.50.

796.4

GYMNASTICS

4089 HEALTH AND STRENGTH. 1892.
Health & Strength Publishing Co. Ltd., Halton House, 20/23 Holborn, London, EC1.
12, ○   Physical culture, weight training, body building, health.
Book notices, letters, articles, news.
No Index.
T.p. 48, Ad.p. 10.   15500.
Per copy 15p, per year £2.50.

4090 REMEDIAL GYMNASTICS & RECREATIONAL THERAPY: Journal of the Society of Remedial Gymnasts. 1964.
(Remedial Gymnast 1948-1964).
R.A. Slinn Ltd., 52 Kettering Road, Northampton.

4, * =   Book notices, book reviews, letters, monographic articles, obituaries, parliamentary reports.
No Index.
August 1971, T.p. 24, Ad.p. 4.   500.
Per copy 23p, per year £1.25.

796.47
ACROBATICS

4091 ACROBATICS: Official journal of the Association of Acrobats. 1954.
Association of Acrobats, 27 Bridge Way, Twickenham, TW2 7JL.
12, ○ ‡ =   Circus, theatre, cabaret, dance studios, technical, news and instruction features.
Book notices, book reviews, articles.
No Index.
May 1972, T.p. 16, Ad.p. 2.   1000.
Per copy 15p, per year £1.80.

796.51
RAMBLING

4092 HEEL AND TOE: bulletin of the Scottish Area of the Ramblers' Association. 1965.
(Scottish Area of the Ramblers Association).
S.A.R.A., 173 Braidcroft Road, Glasgow, SW3.
4, * ○   Rambling in Scotland, footpaths and rights of way.
News and notes, book notices, book reviews, short articles.
No Index.
Spring 1972, T.p. 9.
Free to members.

4093 LAKELAND RAMBLER. 1939.
Ramblers' Association (Lake District Area), 62 Loop Road North, Whitehaven.
1, ○
Book reviews, articles, news.
No Index.
T.p. 122, Ad.p. 10.
Free to members.

4094 RUCKSACK: Magazine of the Ramblers' Assn. 1960.
(Ramblers News 1952-60).
Ramblers' Association, 1/4 Crawford Mews, London, W1H 1PT.
4, ‡ *   News and features for all who walk in the countryside. Ramblers' Assn policy and activities. Matters concerning access and public paths.
Book reviews, legal notes, letters, articles, obituaries, parliamentary reports.
No Index.
Spring 1972, T.p. 32, Ad.p. 8.   23000.
Per copy 5p, per year 30p.

796.52
MOUNTAINEERING

4095 THE ALPINE JOURNAL: A record of mountain adventure and scientific observation. 1863.
The Alpine Club, 74 South Audley St., London, W1Y 5FF.
1, ‡ *   All aspects of mountains and mountaineering in all parts of the world.
Book reviews, monographic articles, obituaries.
A, —, No, 15 year.
T.p. 430, Ad.p. 20.   3500.
Subscription on application.

4096 CLIMBER AND RAMBLER. 1969.
(The Climber 1962-1968).
George Outram & Co. Ltd., 146 King Street, Castle Douglas, Kirkcudbright, Scotland.
12, = ○ ‡   Mountaineering, rambling, camping and allied pursuits.
Book notices, book reviews, commodity prices, letters, articles, news, new products, standards, tests.
No Index.
9894.
Per copy 12½p, per year £2.

4097 THE JOURNAL OF THE LADIES' ALPINE CLUB. 1907.
Ladies' Alpine Club, c/o Bishop's Lodge, 10 Springfield Rd., Leicester, LE2 3BD.
1, *   Mountaineering.
Book reviews, articles, obituaries.
No Index.
1972, T.p. 61.   160.
Per copy 60p, per year 60p.

4098 MOUNTAIN. 1969.
(Mountain Craft 1950-1968).
Mountain Magazines Ltd., 102A Westbourne Grove, London, W2.
6, = ‡ +   Mountaineering and craft.
Book reviews, commodity prices, letters, articles, news, new products, obituaries.
No Index.
T.p. 24, Ad.p. 12.   7000.
Per copy 20p, per year £1.50.

4099 MOUNTAIN LIFE. 1972.
(Mountaineering 1947-1971).
British Mountaineering Council, 26 Park Crescent, London, W1N 4EE.
6, ‡ ○   National mountaineering affairs.
Book notices, book reviews, letters, monographic articles, new products, standards, tests.
No Index.
June 1972, T.p. 38, Ad.p. 2.   7000.
Per copy 25p, per year £1.90.

4100 ROCKSPORT. 1968.
Rocksport, 14 Warser Gate, Nottingham.
6, ‡ ○   Rockclimbing and mountaineering in the British Isles.
Book notices, book reviews, commodity prices, letters, articles, new products, obituaries, standards, tests.
No Index.
April/May 1972, T.p. 32, Ad.p. 10.   4000.
Per copy 20p, per year £1.50.

796.54
CAMPING

4101 CSE NEWS: incorporating Camping Equipment Trader, The Camp Site Operator. 1969.
Camping & Sports Equipment Limited, 4 Spring Street, London, W2 3RB.
12, =   Camping, caravanning and sports equipment.
Commodity prices, letters, articles, new products.
No Index.
November 1969, T.p. 36, Ad.p. Most.   5,760.
Per year £4.

4102 CAMPING. 1970.
(Popular Camping 1961-1969).
Link House Publications, Link House, Dingwall Avenue, Croydon, CR9 2TA.
12, ○   Helpful practical approach to all aspects of camping; new equipment and techniques; camping sites and holiday areas in Britain and abroad.
Book reviews, commodity prices, letters, articles, new products, tests.
No Index.
T.p. 42, Ad.p. 54.
Per copy 15p, per year £1.50.

4103 CAMPING & CARAVANNING. 1971.
(Camping & Outdoor Life 1907-1970).
Camping Club of Great Britain & Ireland, 11 Lower Grosvenor Place, London, SW1.
12, * ○   All aspects of camping, caravanning, motor caravans, trailer tents, touring at home and abroad and all outdoor activities.
Book reviews, letters, articles, new products.
No Index.
June 1972, T.p. 33, Ad.p. 58.   60000.
Free to members.

4104 LIGHTWEIGHT CAMPER.
Youth Camping Association, The Office, Upper Flat, 14 East Road, Enfield, Middx.
○
No Index.

4105 PRACTICAL CAMPER. 1967.
(The Camper—1961-1967)
Haymarket Publishing Limited, Gillow House, 5 Winsley Street, London, W1.
12, ○   How to camp, where to camp, practical illustrated features on camping, equipment and touring at home and abroad.
Commodity prices, letters, articles, new products, tests.
No Index.
July 1972, T.p. 44, Ad.p. 62.   35000.
Per copy 17p, per year £2.62.

796.6

CYCLING

4106 CYCLETOURING: the CTC magazine. 1963.
(The CTC Gazette 1878-1963)
Cyclists' Touring Club, Cotterell House, 69 Meadrow, Godalming, Surrey.
6, *   Recreational and pleasure cycling, touring, holiday travel and countryside; CTC national and local activities.
Book reviews, letters, articles.
A, Incorporated in Oct. issue, No, None.
April/May 1972, T.p. 23, Ad.p. 9.   18000.
Per year £1.

4107 CYCLING. 1969.
(Cycling and Sporting Cyclist 1891-1869).
Longacre Press Ltd., 161 Fleet Street, London, EC4.
52, ○   All aspects of cycling.
Book notices, book reviews, commodity prices, legal notes, letters, new companies, news, new products, obituaries, standards, tests.
No Index.
T.p. 29, Ad.p. 2.   18147.
Per copy 10p, per year £6.50.

796.6.1

KARTING

4108 KARTING. 1960.
(Go-Karter 1959).
Karting Magazine Ltd., Bank House, Summerhill, Chislehurst, Kent.
12, ○   Everything to do with karts and kart racing.
Book reviews, commodity prices, letters, articles, new companies, new products, tests.
No Index.
July 1972, T.p. 20, Ad.p. 8.   14000.
Per copy 18p.

796.7

MOTOR RACING

4109 AUTOSPORT. 1950.
Haymarket Publishing Limited, Gillow House, 5 Winsley Street, London, W1.
52, ○ ‡   Specialised coverage of all motor sporting events at home and abroad.
Letters, articles, tests, personality features, technical articles.
No Index.
July 13, 1972, T.p. 51, Ad.p. 45.   35113.
Per copy 15p, per year £10.10.

4110 B.A.R.C. NEWS. 1967.
(Junior Car Club Gazette 1922-1950; BARC Gazette 1950-1967).
Sutherland House, 5-6 Argyll Street, London, W1.
12, * ○   News on the Club's past and future events, details of facilities for members, features, etc.
Book reviews, letters, articles, new products, obituaries.
No Index.
June 1972, T.p. 8, Ad.p. 1.   10000.
Free to members.

4111 BRITISH RACING NEWS: A British Racing & Sports Car Club Publication. 1970.
British Racing & Sports Car Club, Empire House, Chiswick High Road, London, W4 5TW.
12, * ○   International motor sport.
Book reviews, letters, new products, obituaries, tests.
No Index.
June 1972, T.p. 8, Ad.p. 2.   7500.
Free to BRSCC members only.

4112 CARS AND CAR CONVERSIONS.
Link House Publications, Link House, Dingwall Avenue, Croydon CR9 2TA.
12, ○ =   Motoring for the enthusiast. Racing, rallying, modification of cars and engines. Road/track tests.
Book notices, commodity prices, letters, articles, new products, tests.
No Index.
June 1972, T.p. 47, Ad.p. 74.
Per copy 20p.

4113 DRAG RACING & HOT ROD MAGAZINE: official Journal of the British Drag Racing & Hot Rod Association. 1966.
(Drag Racing Magazine 1965).
Whitelane Publications Ltd., 52 Whitehorse Lane, South Norwood, London, SE25.
12, ○ ‡   Drag racing in general.
Letters, articles, news, new products, tests.
No Index.
T.p. 20, Ad.p. 3.   6500.
Per copy 15p, per year £2.
Free to members.

4114 HOT CAR.
Mercury House Publications Ltd., Mercury House, Waterloo Road, London, SE1.
12, ○   Hot rod and 'specials' enthusiasts.
Letters, articles, news, tests.
No Index.
103000.
Per copy 15p.

4115 MOTOR SPORT: Incorporating Speed and Brooklands Gazette. 1924.
Teesdale Publishing Co. Ltd., Standard House, Bonhill Street, London, EC2.
12, ○ ‡ = +   Motor sporting field; Formula One, Two and Three, sports cars etc. Also new cars, tuning cars, rallying, veteran, Edwardian and vintage cars, special features, news from Continent of Europe and America.
Book notices, book reviews, letters, monographic articles, new products, obituaries, standards, tests.
A, January, Yes, None.
June 1972, T.p. 48, Ad.p. 91.   160000.
Per copy 15p, per year £2.60.

4116 R.A.C. MOTOR SPORT NEWS. 1964.
Lodgemark Press Ltd., Bank House, Summerhill, Chislehurst, Kent.

4117-4132

4, ‡ Covers all new regulations and news on motor sport.
Book reviews, letters, articles, new companies, new products, obituaries, patents, tests.
No Index.
Spring 1972, T.p. 3, Ad.p. 1.
Per year £1.

796.72

MOTOR CYCLING

4117 BIKE. 1971.
National Magazine Co. Ltd., 680 Garrett Lane, London, SW17.
5, ○ Motor cycle, driving tests, personalities.
No Index.
May 1972, T.p. 54, Ad.p. 18.   65000.
Per copy 30p.

4118 MOTOR CYCLE. 1903.
IPC Specialist & Professional Press, 161-166 Fleet Street, London, EC4.
52, ○ ‡ To cater for the keen motor cyclist (and those who ride scooters or drive sidecar outfits or three wheelers) with practical features on maintenance and riding, road-tests, technical descriptions, sports reports, sports topics and design studies.
Commodity prices, articles, new products, tests.
No Index.
12.7.1972, T.p. 20, Ad.p. 10.   86000.
Per copy 7p, per year £5.50.

4119 MOTOR CYCLE MECHANICS. 1972.
(Motorcycle Scooter and 3-wheeler mechanics 1959-1972)
Mercury House Consumer Publications Ltd., 109 Waterloo Road, London, SE1.
12, ‡ ○
Book notices, legal notes, letters, articles, standards, tests.
No Index.
T.p. 34, Ad.p. 33.
Per copy 15p.

4120 MOTOR CYCLE NEWS. 1957.
East Midland Allied Press Ltd., 117 Park Road, Peterborough.
52, ○ Caters for motor cyclists from a practical point of view, in addition supplying up to date reports from all branches of the sport.
Book reviews, letters, new products, tests.
No Index.
14th June 1972, T.p. 22, Ad.p. 22.   115239.
Per copy 7p, per year £5.70.

4121 MOTORCYCLE RIDER: Incorporating Unity.
(Unity 1964-1972)
British Motorcyclists Federation Ltd., 225 Coventry Road, Ilford, Essex.
6, * ○ ‡
Club news.
No Index.
June/July 1972, T.p. 18, Ad.p. 12.   2750.
Per copy 10p.

4122 MOTORCYCLE SPORT. 1959.
Teesdale Publishing Co. Ltd., Standard House, Bonhill Street, London, EC2.
12, ○ ‡ = + Book notices, book reviews, commodity prices, letters, monographic articles, new products, obituaries, standards, tests.
A, January, Yes, None.
July 1972, T.p. 29, Ad.p. 13.   30000.
Per copy 13p, per year £2.

4123 MOTOR CYCLIST ILLUSTRATED. 1958.
City Magazines Ltd., Aldwych House, 81 Aldwych, London, WC2.
12, = ‡ ○ Motor cycle sports, including technical features.
No Index.
T.p. 42, Ad.p. 13.   29200.
Per copy 20p, per year £3.

796.83

BOXING. JUDO. WRESTLING.

4125 BOXING NEWS. 1909.
City Magazines Ltd., Aldwych House, 81 Aldwych, London, WC2.
52, ○
No Index.
Per copy 5p.

4126 BOXING WORLD. 1971.
17 Shaftesbury Avenue, London, W1.
52, ○
No Index.
Per copy 8p

4127 JUDO: martial arts magazine. 1956.
Judo Ltd., 91 Wellesley Road, Croydon, Surrey.
12, ○ Book notices, book reviews, letters, monographic articles, obituaries.
No Index.
April 1972, T.p. 36, Ad.p. 4.   6000.
Per copy 20p, per year £2.40.

4128 RINGSPORT. 1960.
Ringsport Publications, 5 Stockland Street, Caerphilly, Glam CF8 1GD.
12, ○ = British boxing and wrestling.
Articles.
No Index.
No. 142, T.p. 12.
Per year £1.50.

4129 THE WRESTLER. 1961.
The Wrestler Ltd., Caxton House, Ham Road, Shoreham-by-Sea, Sussex BN4 6QD.
12, ○ Wrestling and wrestlers.
Book notices, book reviews, articles, letters.
No Index.
June 1972, T.p. 34.
Per copy 25p, per year £3.36.

796.91

SKATING. SKIING

4130 SCOTTISH SKI CLUB JOURNAL. 1909.
Scottish Ski Club, 17 Elmbank Street, Glasgow C2.
1, ○ All facets of skiing.
Book reviews, letters, articles, news, new products, obituaries, standards.
A, December, No, None.
T.p. 54, Ad.p. 26.   2200.
Free to members.

4131 SKATING WORLD. 1936.
Cyril Beastall, 92 Westbrook Avenue, Margate, Kent.
9, ○ All competitive activities in ice and roller skating internationally, including speed, dance and figure skating, news re trends, new rinks, personalities, instructive articles, book reviews, obituaries.
Book reviews, letters, articles, tests.
No Index.
June 1971, T.p. 20, Ad.p. 6.
Per copy 10p, per year £1.25.

4132 SKI SURVEY. 1972.
(British Ski Year Book; Ski Notes and Queries, Alpine Ski Club Annual)

Ski Club of Great Britain, 118 Eaton Square, London, SW1 W9AF.
3, ○ =   Broadest possible coverage of skiing by all grades of skiers. Permanent record of world's main ski events. Reports on equipment, fashions, travel and ski developments in many countries.
Book reviews, monographic articles.
No Index.
T.p. 64.   12800
Per copy 25p, per year 75p.

4133 THE SKIER. 1959.
G. Outram & Co. Ltd., Castle Douglas, Kirkcudbright, Scotland.
12, ○
No Index.
Per copy 12½p.

797.1
BOATING

4134 BOAT NEWS. 1973.
East Midlands Allied Press, Oundle Road, Peterborough PE2 9QR.
52, ○ =
Book notices, letters, articles, new products.
No Index.
Per copy 10p.

4135 CRUISING ASSOCIATION BULLETIN. 1910.
Cruising Association, Chiltern Court, Baker Street, London, NW1.
2, * =   Information, accounts, stories on matters relating to cruising (mainly European waters) and covering actual cruises, ports and harbours, boats and equipment. Also news about Association activities.
Book reviews, letters, articles, new products.
No Index.
June 1972, T.p. 70, Ad.p. 4.   c. 2500.
Free to members.

4136 INTERNATIONAL BOAT INDUSTRY. 1970.
(International Boating 1968-1970)
IPC Transport Press, Dorset House, Stamford Street, London, SE1.
6, =   Pleasure boating and related industries.
Commodity prices, legal notes, letters, articles, new companies, new products, obituaries, parliamentary reports, patents, standards, tests.
December.
April 1972, T.p. 35, Ad.p. 41.   9300.
Free, controlled circulation.

4137 MOTOR BOAT AND YACHTING. 1904.
Temple Press Ltd., 40 Bowling Green Lane, London, EC1
26, ○
No Index.
29005.
Per copy 15p, per year £5.50.
Indexed in: BTI.

4138 PRACTICAL BOAT OWNER. 1967.
IPC Magazines Ltd., 69-76 Long Acre, London, WC1.
12, ○ ‡
No Index.
46613.
Per copy 20p, per year £3.50.

4139 SMALL BOAT. 1951.
Link House Publications Ltd., Link House, Dingwall Avenue, Croydon, Surrey CR9 2TA.
12, ○   Handling and maintaining all manner of waterborne craft up to approximately 25 ft. long—sailing dinghys, canoes, motor-cruisers, outboards for racing and cruising.
Book reviews, commodity prices, letters, articles, new products, tests.
No Index.
T.p. 40, Ad.p. 40.   23000.
Per copy 15p, per year £2.

797.12
CANOEING. ROWING

4140 CANOE—CAMPER. 1948.
Canoe-Camping Club, 15 Whalley Road, Hale, Altrincham.
4, ○
Book reviews, articles, news.
No Index.
T.p. 28, Ad.p. 3.
Free to members.

4141 CANOEING IN BRITAIN: the magazine of the British Canoe Union. 1950.
British Canoe Union, 36 St. Marys Place, Newcastle 1.
4, *   Articles of interest to sport and environment.
Book notices, book reviews, commodity prices, legal notes, letters, articles, new companies, new products, obituaries, patents, standards, tests.
No Index.
June 1972, T.p. 14, Ad.p. 14.   7500.
Per copy 20p, per year 80p.

4142 ROWING. 1949.
Amateur Rowing Association, Embankment, London, SW15.
9, ○
No Index.
Per copy 15p, per year £1.50.

797.14
YACHTING

4143 A.Y.R.S. AIRS. 1971.
Amateur Yacht Research Society, Hermitage, Newbury, Berkshire.
4, * +   Developments and ideas for yachts, mainly sail.
Book reviews, letters, articles, new products, tests.
No Index.
April 1972.
T.p 56.
Free to members.

4144 DINGHY SAILING. 1972.
Prenbourne Publishing Co. Ltd., 3 Heathcock Court, Strand, London, WC2.
12, ○
Book reviews, letters, monographic articles, new products.
No Index.
Per year £3.

4145 R.Y.A. MAGAZINE. 1968.
Royal Yachting Association, 5 Buckingham Gate, London, SW1.
2, ○
No Index.
Free to members.

4146 ROYAL NAVAL SAILING ASSOCIATION JOURNAL. 1936.
R.N.S.A., c/o R.N. Club, Pembroke Road, Portsmouth, Hants.

Key to reference symbols

○ popular   ‡ technical   = trade/professional

+ research   * society/institution   † house journal

2, ○ House journal covering Association activities, with articles by members about their own voyages etc. Book reviews.
Book reviews, letters, articles, obituaries.
No Index.
Spring 1972, T.p.100, Ad.p.20.   5000.
Free to members.

4147 SAIL: Annual Report of the Sail Training Association. 1956.
The Sail Training Association, Bosham, Chichester, Sussex.
1, ○ = * † Annual report and descriptions of the Association's work.
A, −, Yes, None.
2250.
Free to members and supporters.

4148 YACHTING & BOATING WEEKLY. 1965.
Illustrated Newspapers Ltd., Elm House, Elm Street, London, WC1.
52, = ○ New boats, gear and equipment. Navigation, fishing etc.
Book notices, book reviews, legal notes, letters, monographic articles, new companies, news, new products, obituaries, parliamentary reports, patents, standards, tests.
No Index.
T.p. 18, Ad.p. 10.   23500.
Per copy 10p, per year £3.50.

4149 YACHTING MONTHLY. 1906.
IPC Magazines Ltd., 69-76 Long Acre, London, WC2.
12, ○
No Index.
23700.
Per copy 20p, per year £3.50.

4150 YACHTING WORLD. 1894.
Temple Press Ltd., 40 Bowling Green Lane, London, EC1.
12, ○
No Index.
36700.
Per copy 20p, per year £3.

4151 YACHTS AND YACHTING. 1947.
Yachting Press Ltd., 196 Eastern Esplanade, Southend-on-Sea, SS1 3AA.
26, = ○ ‡ All aspects of yachting and technical development in the sport.
Book reviews, articles, news, new products, tests.
6m, January/July, Yes, A.
T.p. 41, Ad.p. 46.
Per copy 15p, per year £5.

797.2
SWIMMING

4152 BATHS SERVICE: Journal of the Institute of Baths Management.
The Institute of Baths Management, Giffard House, 36/38 Sherrard Street, Melton Mowbray, Leics, LE13 1XJ.
12, ‡ = * Covering swimming pools and allied recreational activities. Of interest to architects and engineers concerned with the design and construction of swimming pools and sports centres.
Book notices, book reviews, legal notes, letters, monographic articles, new companies, new products, obituaries, standards, tests.
A, January, Yes, None.
July 1972, T.p. 32, Ad.p. 28.   2500.
Per copy 40p, per year £2.80.

4153 THE SCOTTISH DIVER: Magazine of the Scottish Sub-Aqua Club. 1960.
The Scottish Sub-Aqua Club, 1 Windmill Road, Hamilton, Scotland, ML3 6LX

6, ○ * Broadly, diving in Scotland, In particular items of interest and information to members of the Scottish Sub Aqua Club based on 16 Royal Crescent, Glasgow, C3.
Book notices, book reviews, commodity prices, legal notes, letters, articles, new products, tests.
5 year, May 1970, No, None.
May/June 1972, T.p. 17. Ad.p. 11.   1000.
Per copy 6p, per year 51p.

4154 SWIMMING TIMES. 1925.
(Waddon Swimming News 1923).
Swimming Times Ltd., 2 George Street, Croydon, Surrey.
12, ○ Swimming, diving and water polo.
Book notices, book reviews, letters, articles, news, obituaries, reports, tests.
No Index.
T.p. 33, Ad.p. 15.
Per copy 15p, per year £1.50.

4155 TRITON: Journal of the British Sub Aqua Club. 1955.
(Neptune 1953-1954).
Eaton/Williams Publications, 40 Grays Inn Road, London, WC1.
6, ○ Magazine for the amateur sports diver.
Letters, articles, new products.
No Index.
May/June 1972, T.p. 25, Ad.p. 25.   15000.
Per copy 20p, per year £1.40.

797.5
PARACHUTING

4156 SPORT PARACHUTIST. 1964.
British Parachute Association Ltd., Artillery Mansions, 75 Victoria Street, London, SW1H 0HW.
6, * ○ General information on sport parachuting, including safety, training and competitions.
Letters, monographic articles, new products, standards, tests.
No Index.
April 1972, T.p. 25, Ad.p. 5.   4000.
Per copy 23p, per year £1.30.

797.55
FLYING. GLIDING

4157 PILOT: Flying for business and pleasure. 1972.
(Pilot and Light Aeroplane 1967-1971).
The White House, Church Road, Claygate, Surrey.
○ ‡ All aspects of light aviation.
Book reviews, commodity prices, letters, articles, new products.
No Index.
T.p. 34.
Per copy 25p.

4158 POPULAR FLYING: Journal of the Popular Flying Association. 1957.
Popular Flying Association, 2 Waldens Park Road, Horsell, Woking, Surrey.
6, ○ ‡ † Light aviation (non commercial) all aspects.
Book reviews, letters, monographic articles, new products, obituaries.
No Index.
May/June 1972, T.p. 28, Ad.p. 4.   2000.
Per copy 20p, per year £1.50.

4159 SAILPLANE AND GLIDING. 1950.
British Gliding Association, 75 Victoria Street, London, SW1.
6, ○ ‡
A, −, Yes, None.
T.p. 40, Ad.p. 20.
Per copy 25p, per year £2.

798.1

EQUESTRIANISM

4160 THE BRITISH RACEHORSE. 1949.
Turf Newspapers Ltd., 55 Curzon Street, London, W1.
5, ‡ =   Racing and breeding industry. Comprehensive coverage of stud farms and training establishments in British Isles. Also, expanding readership among overseas buyers of British bloodstock
Book notices, book reviews, commodity prices, letters monographic articles, obituaries, tests.
A, December, Yes, None.
Summer 1972, T.p. 80, Ad.p. 10.
Per copy £1, per year £5.

4161 HORSE AND HOUND. 1884.
IPC Magazines Ltd., Tower House, Southampton Street, London, WC2E 9QX.
52, ○   Up-to-the-minute news and authoritative features on all aspects of the horse world, both at home and abroad, covering racing, hunting, show jumping, bloodstock sales and all the major shows and events.
Letters, articles.
No Index.
61995.
Per year £8.

4162 HORSE & PONY. 1971.
Scottish Farmer Publications Ltd., 39 York St., Glasgow, G2 8JL.
12, ○   Equestrian sports.
Book notices, book reviews, letters, articles, new products.
No Index.
June 1972, T.p. 29, Ad.p. 17.
Per copy 16p.

4163 HORSE WORLD: The official organ of the Association of British Riding Schools.
Alan Exley Ltd., PO Box 1, Battle, Sussex.
12, ○ *
Book reviews, letters, articles, new products.
No Index.
June 1972, T.p. 38, Ad.p. 6.
Per copy 15p, Free to members.

4164 LIGHT HORSE. 1951.
(Show Jumping, 1950).
D.J. Murphy (Publishers) Ltd., 19 Charing Cross Road, London, WC2H 0EY.
12, ‡ ○ = *   Showing, show jumping, hunting, point-to-pointing, horse trials, polo, dressage, driving and all aspects of the equestrian world.
Book reviews, commodity prices, letters, articles, new products, obituaries.
A, —, Yes, None.
June 1972, T.p. 44, Ad.p. 18.   18500.
Per copy 15p, per year £2.25.

4165 PONY: The magazine for the young rider. 1949.
D.J. Murphy (Publishers) Ltd., 19 Charing Cross Road, London, WC2H 0EY.
12, ‡ ○ = *   All horse lovers, pony breeders, riders.
Book reviews, commodity prices, letters, articles, new products, obituaries.
A, —, Yes, None.
June 1972, T.p. 44, Ad.p. 18.   35000.
Per copy 15p, per year £2.25.

4166 RIDING: The official journal of the Riding Clubs Movement. 1936.
IPC Magazines Ltd., Tower House, Southampton Street, London, WC2E 9QZ.
12, ○   The horselover's magazine. Expert advice month by month on every aspect of horsemanship. Reports of major event, articles on famous horses, riders, studs and breeds. Special section for young riders.
Book reviews, letters, articles.
No Index.
T.p. 24, Ad.p. 15.   31050.
Per year £2.75.

4167 THE STATISTICAL ABSTRACT. 1920.
Thoroughbred Breeders Association, 26 Bloomsbury Way, London, WC1A 2SP.
2, ‡ ○   Horseracing statistics classified under various headings e.g. sires, sires of dams etc.
No Index.
T.p. 248.
Free to members.

4168 STUD & STABLE. 1961.
Stud & Stable Ltd., 149 Fleet Street, London, EC4A 2BU.
12, ‡ =   Horse racing and breeding (thoroughbreds only), with emphasis on the international aspects of the sport.
A, January, No, None.
January 1972, T.p. 56, Ad.p. 68.
Per copy 50p, per year £7.

799.1

ANGLING. FISHING

4169 ANGLERS MAIL.
IPC Magazines Ltd., 69-76 Long Acre, London, WC2.
52, ○
No Index.
Per copy 5p, per year £3.50.

4170 ANGLING: incorporating Creel and Anglers World. 1954.
(Creel 1967, Anglers World 1969).
City Magazines Ltd., Aldwych House, 81 Aldwych, London, WC2.
12, ○   Coarse, soft water and game fishing.
Book reviews, letters, articles, new products.
No Index.
T.p. 60, Ad.p. 20.   30300.
Per copy $17\frac{1}{2}$p, per year £2.50.

4171 ANGLING TIMES. 1953.
East Midland Allied Press Ltd., 117 Park Rd. Peterborough.
52, ○ ‡   All aspects of the sport.
Book reviews, commodity prices, letters, articles, new products.
No Index.
June 15, 1972, T.p. 29, Ad.p. 15.   158040.
Per copy 6p, per year £5.46.

4172 FLYFISHERS JOURNAL. 1911.
Flyfishers Club, 71 Pall Mall, London, SW1.
4, * ○   Fly fishing with special relevance to salmon and trout, with both wet and dry fly.
Book reviews, letters, articles, news, obituaries, tests.
A, Spring, Yes, None.
T.p. 48, Ad.p. 5.   1200.
Free to members.

4173 ROD AND LINE. 1962.
D. Macleod Ltd., 45-49 Cowgate, Kirkintilloch.
12, ○
No Index.
5400.
Per copy 10p.

4174 THE SALMON AND TROUT MAGAZINE: Journal of the Salmon and Trout Association. 1910.
The Salmon and Trout Association, Fishmongers' Hall, London, EC4R 9EL.
3, ‡ + * ○   U.K. and international fisheries: scientific, administrative, legislative matters discussed. Some popular articles on angling technique and practice at home and abroad. River conservation, pollution.

Book reviews, legal notes, letters, monographic articles, obituaries,
After 24 issues, –, No, None.
November 1971, T.p. 69, Ad.p. 18.   5000.
Per copy 75p, Free to members.

4175 TACKLE & GUNS. 1970.
(Fishing Tackle Dealer, 1956-1970).
East Midland Allied Press Ltd., 117 Park Road, Peterborough.
12, =   Intensive coverage of the fishing tackle and gun trade.
Book reviews, commodity prices, legal notes, letters, articles, new companies, new products, obituaries, parliamentary reports, patents, tests.
No Index.
June 1972, T.p. 17, Ad.p. 42.
Per year £2.

4176 TROUT & SALMON. 1955.
East Midland Allied Press Ltd., 117, Park Road, Peterborough.
12, ○   Aspects of game fishing.
Letters, articles, news, new products.
No Index.
June 1972, T.p. 47, Ad.p. 45.   33131.
Per copy 20p, per year £3.12.

799.2

FALCONRY

4177 THE FALCONER.
British Falconers Club, c/o 94 High Street, Saxilby, Lincoln, LN1 2HG.
1, ○   Practical falconry.
Book reviews, letters, articles.
No Index.
Free to members only.

799.3

SHOOTING

4178 BLACK POWDER: The official journal of the Muzzle Loaders Association of Great Britain. 1952.
The Muzzle Loaders Association of Great Britain, The Old Manor House, Radcliffe-on-Trent, Notts.
10, *   Covers all aspects of shooting and collecting antique muzzleloading firearms.
Book notices, book reviews, letters, monographic articles, new products, tests.

No Index.
Feb/Mar 1972, T.p. 16, Ad.p. 2.   900.
Membership Subscription: £2 per annum.

4179 GUNS REVIEW. 1960.
Ravenhill Publishing Co. Ltd., Standard House, Bonhill Street, London, EC2.
12, ○ ‡ =   All aspects of guns and shooting antique, modern, target, sporting, rough, clay, Bisley and auctions.
Book reviews, commodity prices, legal notes, letters, monographic articles, new companies, new products, obituaries, patents, standards, tests.
A, January, Yes, None.
July 1972, T.p. 24, Ad.p. 20.   12500.
Per copy 25p, per year £3.75.

4180 NATIONAL RIFLE ASSOCIATION JOURNAL. 1860.
The Association, Bisley Camp, Brookwood, Woking, Surrey.
4, ○   Aspects of rifle and pistol shooting.
Book notices, book reviews, commodity prices, letters, monographic articles, news, obituaries, reports, tests.
A, Winter, Yes, None.
T.p. 32, Ad.p. 8.
Free to members.

4181 WAGBI MAGAZINE. 1971.
(Wildfowler & Rough Shooter, 1967-1970).
Wildflowers Association of Great Britain and Ireland, 104 Watergate Street, Chester.
2, *   Sports of wildfowling and rough shooting and the affairs of the Association.
Book reviews, commodity prices, legal notes, letters, articles, parliamentary reports, tests.
No Index.
Spring 1972, T.p. 30, Ad.p. 12.
Free to members.

799.32

ARCHERY

4182 JOURNAL OF THE SOCIETY OF ARCHER-ANTIQUARIES. 1958.
The Society of Archer-Antiquaries, 'Ascham', 14 Grove Road, Barnes, London, SW13 0HQ.
1, + ○ ‡   All aspects of the history and development of the bow and arrow from earliest times to the present day.
Book reviews, articles.
No Index.
Vol. 14, 1971, T.p. 36.   c. 370.
Free to members, £1.25 to non-members.

8

LITERATURE

4183 ADAM: International Review. 1942.
Frank Cass & Co. Ltd. Woburn Press, 67 Great Russell Street, London, WC1B 3BT.
4, + =   Literature and arts, printed mainly in English, partly in French.
Book notices, articles.
No Index.
Nos. 349-351, 1971, T.p. 80, Ad.p. 2.
Per copy 75p, per year £3.

4184 AMBIT: A quarterly of poems, short stories, drawings and criticism. 1959.
Ambit, 17 Priory Gdns, London, N6.
○

Book notices, book reviews.
No Index.
No. 51, 1972, T.p. 52.
Per copy 25p, per year 75p.

4185 APPROACH MAGAZINE: A journal of inter-disciplinary research. 1967.
Approach Magazine Publishing Co., St. Peter's College, Oxford.
3, ‡   Literary and philisophic journal primarily concerned with methods in the different academic subjects and the broad issue of objectivity in literature and the social science.

Book notices, book reviews, letters, articles.
No Index.
T.p. 36, Ad.p. 3.
Per copy 15p, per year £1.

4186 CHAPMAN. 1972.
(The Chapman, 1970-1971).
10 Spottiswoode Road, Edinburgh, EH9 1BQ.
4, ○   The arts and philosophy, poetry, music, etc.
Book notices, book reviews, articles.
No Index.
Summer 1972, T.p. 59, Ad.p. 1.   2000.
Per copy 30p, per year £1.10.

4187 CRITICAL QUARTERLY. 1959.
Oxford University Press, Press Road, Neasden, London, NW10.
4, ○ +   Presents lively, perceptive and lucid critical comment on drama, poetry, the novel, journalism, and all forms of the written and spoken word. Special but not exclusive interest in the twentieth century.
Book reviews, letters.
No Index.
Summer 1971, T.p. 87, Ad.p. 17.   4500.
Per copy 38p, per year £1.50.

4188 FETTER LANE REVIEW. 1968.
82 Fetter Lane, London, EC4.
Irregular, ○   Literature in general.
No Index.
Per copy 40p.

4189 JOURNAL OF COMMONWEALTH LITERATURE:
Published for the University of Leeds. 1966.
Oxford University Press, Press Road, Neasden, London, NW10.
2, +   Scholarly and critical articles and reviews of recent books. Includes an Annual Bibliography of Commonwealth Literature which is arranged according to regions and includes South Africa. Each area bibliography lists all imaginative writings; bibliographies, articles, and reviews on them; selective non-fiction.
No Index.
June 1971, T.p. 138, Ad.p. 2.   1000.
Per copy 90p, per year £1.80.

4190 JOURNAL OF EUROPEAN STUDIES. 1971.
Seminar Press/Academic Press, 24-28 Oval Rd., London, NW1 7DD.
4, +   All aspects of European literature, history and thought. Comparative and interdisciplinary. Middle Ages to the present.
Book notices, book reviews, monographic articles.
A, March, Yes, None.
Subscription on application.

4191 LITTACK.
Ember Press, 27 Brook Road, Epping, Essex.
Irregular, ○   Literary work.
Book notices, book reviews, letters, articles.
No Index.
No. 1, T.p. 90.   500.
Per copy 40p, per year £1 for 3 issues.

4192 MODERN LANGUAGE REVIEW. 1905.
Modern Humanities Research Association, Honorary Secretary, Bedford College, Regent's Park, London, NW1 4NS.
4, + * =   Academic research in modern and medieval European literature and languages, including English.
Book notices, book reviews, monographic articles.
A, October, Yes, 10 year.
1971, T.p. 972.   2500.
Per year £7.

4193 OASIS, Incorporating Expression Magazine. 1969.
Oasis Books, 12 Stevenage Road, London, SW6 6ES.
3, ○   A magazine devoted to literature and art. Fiction, poetry, graphics, articles on the arts, occasional reviews and comment. Material not restricted to GB. Translations are a regular feature, both prose and poetry.
Book notices, book reviews, articles, parliamentary.
Occasional, Approx. every four issues, No, None.
No. 6, May 1972, T.p. 91, Ad.p. 1.   500.
Per copy 18p, per year 60p.

4194 PHALANX. 1969.
Raymond Donovan, St. Cuthbert's Society, University, Durham.
2/3, ○   Literature and the arts in general, poetry, prose, drawings, art work.
No Index.
T.p. 38, Ad.p. 4.   1000.
Per copy 15p.

4195 PLANET. 1970.
Planet, Llangeitho, Tregaron, Cardiganshire, Wales.
6, ○   Literature, literary topics, and current affairs with special reference to Wales.
Book notices, book reviews, monographic articles.
No Index.
May 1972, T.p. 96,   2000.
Per copy 30p, per year £2.

4196 RESURGENCE.
24 Abercorn Place, London, NW8.
6, ○   International review of literature and the arts.
No Index.
Per copy 15p, per year £1.

4197 SHADOW: Fantasy literature review. 1968.
D. A. Sutton, 194 Station Rd., Birmingham, B14 7TE.
4, + ○   Reviews current horror, supernatural and fantasy fiction. Biographies of authors, bibliographies. Surveys of aspects of the genre. Poetry, fiction, news, letters, artwork.
No Index.
27.6.72, T.p. 35, Ad.p. 1.   200.
Per copy 20p, per year 80p.

4198 TRIVIUM: An interdisciplinary journal of interest to all concerned with humane studies. 1966.
Univ. of Wales Press, Merthyr House, James Street, Cardiff CF1 6EU.
1, + =   Interdisciplinary articles and notes related to: classics, English, French, geography, German, history, philosophy, theology, and Welsh. (No science). Also book notices and reviews in same subjects.
Book notices, book reviews, articles.
10 year, −, Yes, None.
1972, T.p. 150, Ad.p. 4.   300.
Libraries: £1.75. Individuals: £1.50.

8–1

POETRY

4199 AGENDA. 1959.
5 Cranbourne Court, Albert Bridge Road, London, SW11 4PE.
4, ○   Poetry and criticism.
Book notices, book reviews.
No Index.
Autumn/Winter 1971/2, T.p. 149.
Per copy 45p, per year £2.

4200 AKROS. 1965.
Akros Publications, 14 Parklands Avenue, Penwortham, Preston, Lancs.
3, ○   Scottish poetry and literary criticism, with reviews (of Scottish poetry mainly).
Book notices, book reviews, letters, monographic articles, poetry.

No Index.
August 1971, T.p. 74, Ad.p. 4.   750.
Per copy £1 per 4 issues.

4201 ALL IN. 1968.
Nina Steane, 31 Headlands, Kettering, Northants.
2/3, ○   Poetry, posters, sometimes to be folded or cut in small booklets, illustrated in black and white, often one colour added. Poets so far have included MacBeth, Hughes, Patten, Horovitz.
No Index.
No. 15.   Limited circulation.
Per copy 15-20p, per year £1.

4202 APPRENTICE: Oxford and Cambridge poetry. 1971.
c/o Magdalene College, Cambridge.
Irregular, ○
No Index.
Subscription on application.

4203 BB BKS BOOK ISSUES. 1967.
(Poetmeat 1963-1967).
BB Bks, 1 Spring Bank, Salesbury, Blackburn, Lancs, BB1 9EU.
3, ○   Experimental, avant-garde, underground, counter-culture poetry and creative prose. Psycho-experimental research and oriental mysticism. Veganism. Anarcho-pacifist theoretics. Mainly a specialist literary press and largely poetry.
No Index.
Per copy 25p, per year £1.

4204 BLACK EGGS: Poetry review. 1971.
Blue Dog Publications, Basement, 37 Andover Road, Winchester, Hants.
4, ○   Current poetry, short stories, articles, drawings new, mostly young, usually unpublished, writers English and American.
No Index.
Autumn 1971, T.p. 32.   1000.
Per copy 20p, per year £1.

4205 CANDELABRUM. 1970.
Red Candle Publications, 19 South Hill Park, London, NW3.
2, ○   Contemporary poetry.
3 year, —, No, None.
T.p. 32.   700.
Per copy 17½p.

4206 CARCANET. 1962.
Parchment (Oxford) Ltd., 100 Bullingdon Road, Oxford,
3, ○   New poetry and reviews of current poetry.
Book notices, book reviews, letters.
3 year, —, Yes, None.
T.p. 40, Ad.p. 4.
Subscription on application.

4207 CARET: Poetry magazine. 1972.
T. McMahon, 31 Marlborough Park Central, Belfast, BT9 6HN.
3, ○
No Index.
T.p. 39.
Per copy 15p.

4208 CONTRASTS. 1972.
R. Pemberton, 76 Rosedale Ave., Gt. Crosby, Liverpool, LZ23 0UQ.
Irregular, ○   Poetry of all types, by well known and less less known authors; occasional pictures; review of poetry books.
No Index.
No. 9, 32.
Per copy 15p, 60p for 4 issues.

4209 CRABGRASS: Poetical sonatas. 1969.
Crabgrass Productions, 7 Rugby Road., Belfast, 7.
1, ○   Poetry and graphics.

No Index.
No. 5, 1972, T.p. 40, Ad.p. 1.   1200.
Per copy 15p.

4210 THE CROYDON SEPARATIST. 1972.
Good Elf Publications, c/o 18 Clairview Road, Streatham, London, SE16.
3/4, ○   Poetry, articles, humour. Cartoons etc will be used in an attempt to complete the more serious intentions behind the sister magazine GOOD ELF.
Book notices, book reviews, notes, letters, obituaries.
No Index.
August 1972, T.p. 14, Ad.p. 1.   500.
Per copy 5p.

4211 DATR. 1971.
Smoothie Publications, 67 Vere Rd., Brighton.
2/3
Poetry and prose. Emphasis on modern previously unpublished material.
Book notices, book reviews, letters.
No Index.
No. 2, 1972, T.p. 20, Ad.p. 2.   300.
Per copy 15p, 45p for 3 issues.

4212 DELTA: A Literary Review. 1953.
Delta, 9 Sharrow View, Sheffield S7 1ND.
3, ○   Poetry, prose fiction, criticism, reviews, literary criticism. Fine arts generally.
Book notices, book reviews, monographic articles, fiction, poetry.
5 year, —, No, None.
Spring 1972, T.p. 48.
Per copy 25p, per year 75p.

4213 ENVOI: A quarterly review of new poetry. 1956.
J C Meredith Scott, Ed Lagan nam Bann, Ballachulish, Argyll, Scotland.
3, ○   Poetry, traditional not barred; non-political; not noticeably erotic.
Book reviews.
No Index.
No. 18, T.p. 20.   600.
Per copy 33p, per year £1.

4214 ER: Oxford local poetry magazine. 1972.
Circle Books, 16 Davenant Road, Oxford, OX2 8BX.
Irregular, ○   A broadsheet for local poets/artists.
Book notices, book reviews, poetry.
No Index.
T.p. 2.   200.
Per copy 3p.

4215 EXIT. 1966.
22 Bostocks Lane, Risley, Derbys.
2, ○ ‡ =   Poetry, prose and illustrations mainly avant-garde/experimental.
Book notices.
No Index.
500.
Price varies.

4216 FISHPASTE. 1967.
Peter Hoy, 97 Holywell Street, Oxford.
Irregular, ○   Poetry.
No Index.
T.p. 2.

4217 FORMAT. 1968.
Alan & Joan Tucker, The Bookshop, Station Road, Stroud, Glos.
1,   Poetry only.
No Index.
T.p. 28.   100+.
£1.50.

4218 GOOD ELF. 1970.
Good Elf Publications, Lawrence Upton, 18 Clairview Road, Streatham, London, SW16.

3/4, ○   Poetry and prose by living writers throughout the world; reviews; information; articles on literary matters. It attempts to make people who have ignored serious writing aware of the use of poetry to them.
No Index.
5/6, T.p. 40, Ad.p. 3.   1000.
Per copy 16p.

4219   HALLAMSHIRE & OSGOLDCROSS POETRY EXPRESS H.O.P.E. 1972.
Headland Poetry, 745 Abbeydale Road, Sheffield, S7 2B9.
3/5, ○ ‡ = +   All aspects of poetry and related arts.
Book notices, book reviews, letters, articles, obituaries.
No Index.
July 1972, T.p. 6.   1000.
£2 Life subscription.

4220   INFORMER: International poetry magazine. 1966.
Circle Books, 16 Davenant Road, Oxford, OX2 8BX.
Irregular, ○   Poetry, short stories, literary articles, artwork, photos, parts of plays, etc.
No Index.
July 1971, T.p. 64, Ad.p. 3.   1000.
Per copy 25p, per year £1.

4221   IN PARTICULAR. 1967.
Peter Hoy, 97 Holywell Street, Oxford.
Irregular, = +   Original poetry and translations of poetry, critical essays.
No Index.
T.p. 160, Ad.p. 1.
Subscription on request.

4222   THE LACE CURTAIN: A magazine of poetry and criticism. 1968.
New Writers' Press, 19 Warrenmount Place, Dublin, 8.
2, ○   Poetry and criticism.
No Index.
Summer 1971, T.p. 95.
Per copy 40p.

4223   LAISSEZ FAIRE: The spirit of competition. 1971.
Ember Press, 27 Brook Road, Epping, Essex.
4, ○   Review of the 'little mag' scene in poetry.
Book reviews.
No Index.
No. 2, T.p. 3.   250.
Per copy 10p, per year 40p.

4224   LUDD'S MILL. 1971.
Ludd's Mill Poetry Publishing Co-operative, 4 Novell Road, Almondbury, Huddersfield, Yorks.
5, ○   Poetry, limited book and record reviews.
No Index.
Per copy 10p, per year 50p.
Free to members.

4225   MAC.
c/o 42 Ladyland Road, Maybole, Ayr.
○   Poetry.
No Index.
Subscription on application.

4226   MEDIUM.
20 Morningside Place, Norris Green, Liverpool, 11.
○   Poetry.
No Index.
Subscription on application.

4227   MERLIN, 1972.
(No address on copy—but of University origin).
Irregular, ○   Arts review with a bias towards poetry.
No Index.
No. 1, 1972, T.p. 42.

4228   MUSE MAGAZINE. 1971.
Birmingham Poetry Centre, Birmingham & Midland Institute, Margaret Street, Birmingham 3.
2, ○   Midlands poetry and writing, mainly previously unpublished work.
Book reviews, letters, articles.
No Index.
T.p. 60.   500.
Per copy 15p.

4229   NEW DEPARTURES. 1959.
New Departures, Piedmont, Bisley, Stroud, Glos., GL6 7BU.
Irregular, ○   Popular arts subjects, especially poetry.
Book notices, book reviews, poems.
No Index.
5000.
£1 per 3 issues.

4230   NEW POETRY. 1971.
Atlantic Press, 122 Grand Buildings, Trafalgar Square, London, WC2N 5EP.
2, ○   New poetry by new writers.
Book notices, book reviews, letters.
No Index.
3/4, T.p. 140.
Per copy £1, per year £2.

4231   NORTHERN HOUSE PAMPHLET POETS.
Northern House, 58 Queen's Road, Newcastle on Tyne, NE2 2PR.
Irregular, ○   Small collections by new or established poets. Each issue contains 10-16 poems, often on a single theme.
No Index.
No. 14, T.p. varies.
60p per 4 issues.

4232   NOTEBOOKS OF PIERRE MENARD. 1969.
Peter Hoy, 97 Holywell Street, Oxford.
12, = +   Translation work in progress.
Book reviews, poetry.
No Index.
T.p. 14.
Subscription on request.

4233   OPENINGS. 1964.
Openings Press, Rooksmoor House, Woodchester, Glos.
Irregular, ○   Concrete, visual, experimental poetry, generally on single cards, wall-sheets etc.
No Index.

4234   ORBIS: The official quarterly of the International Poetry Society. 1969.
Hub Publications Ltd., Youlgrave, Bakewell, Derbyshire, England.
4, *   Articles, poems, literary criticism, mainly by Members and Fellows of the International Poetry Society; keeps a watchful eye on the arts generally. Reviews.
Book notices, book reviews, letters.
Biennial, –, No, None.
Nos. 10/11, T.p. 52.   2-3000.
Per copy 30p, per year £1.20 (£1 p.a. to I.P.S. members.)

4235   OSTRICH. 1971.
Erdesdun Pomes, 10 Greenhaugh Road, South Wellfield, Whitley Bay, Northumberland.
4, ○   A compilation of new poems by British poets.
Poetry.
No Index.
June 1972, T.p. 10.   200.
Per copy 10p, per year 50p.

4236   OUTPOSTS. 1944.
Outposts Publications, 72 Burwood Road, Walton on Thames, Surrey.
4, ○   Poetry (contemporary).
Poetry, articles and book reviews.

No Index.
Summer 1972, T.p. 35.
Per copy 20p, per year 80p.

4237 POET. 1972.
Derek Maggs, 36 Sherard Road, London, SE9 6EP.
4, ○
No Index.
Per copy 25p.

4238 POETRY OF THE CIRCLE IN THE SQUARE. 1966.
Bill Pickard, Director of Literature, Bristol Arts Centre, King Square, Bristol, 2.
2, ○   Poetry of all kinds written by members of Bristol Arts Centre.
No Index.
February 1972, T.p. 20.   500.
Per copy 5p, per year 20p.

4239 POETRY REVIEW. 1913.
(Poetical Gazette 1909-1912).
The Poetry Society, 21 Earls Court Square, London, SW5.
4, *   Largely works by contemporary poets. Critical articles on poetry, news.
A, March. Yes, None.
Spring 1972, T.p. 100.   2000.
Per copy 40p, Free to members.

4240 POETRY SUPPLEMENT. 1957.
The Poetry Book Society, 105 Piccadilly, London, W1V 0AU.
1, ○ *   Poems by contemporary poets, and brief biographical details of the poets.
A, —, Yes, None.
1971, T.p. 18.
Free to members.

4241 POETRY WALES: Cylchgrawn cenedlaethol o farddoniaeth newydd. March 1965.
Christopher Daviss Ltd., (Llyfrau'r Dryw), Llandybie, Ammanford, Carmarthenshire.
4, ○ =   Poems, mainly in English but some in Welsh, by Welsh poets and on Welsh themes, articles on Welsh and Anglo-Welsh literature, reviews of new poetry from Wales and abroad.
No Index.
Autumn 1971, T.p. 100, Ad.p. 5.   500.
Per copy 38p, per year £1.52p.

4242 RAM. 1972.
J. Hilton, 1 Frondirion, Glanrafon Hill, Bangor, N. Wales.
4, ○   Poetry.
No Index.
Subscription on application.

4243 THE REVIEW.
Ian Hamilton, 72 Westbourne Terrace, London, W2.
4, ○   Poetry and criticism.
No Index.
T.p. 68.
Per copy 25p, per year £1.
Indexed in: BHI.

4244 SAMPHIRE: New Poetry. 1968.
Kemble Williams, South Bank, Spring Road, Ipswich, Suffolk.
4, ○   Poetry, reviews, criticisms, prose, letters.
Book notices, book reviews, letters.
No Index.
July 1972, T.p. 32.   600.
Per copy 15p, per year 60p.

4245 SECOND AEON. 1966.
Second Aeon Publications, 3 Maplewood Court, Maplewood Ave., Llandaff North, Cardiff, CF4 2NB.
3, ○   Modern poetry and related subjects. Translations, traditional works, concrete and visual poetries, plus a large round up of other small press activity in each issue.

Book notices, book reviews, letters, articles.
No Index.
No. 14, T.p. 132, Per copy 20p, 90p for 4 issues.

4246 STAND: A quarterly of the arts. 1952
Stand, 58 Queens Road, Newcastle on Tyne, NE2 2PR.
4, ○   Covers new unpublished poetry, fiction, drama, criticism of literature, theatre, music, art.
Book reviews.
Irregular, —, No, 10 years.
No. 4, 1969, T.p. 73, Ad.p. 9.   4200.
Per copy 37p, per year £1.25.

4247 STEREO HEADPHONES: An occasional review of the new poetries.
Nicholas Zurbrugg, Church Steps, Kersey, Nr. Ipswich, Suffolk.
Irregular, + ○   International experimental and avant garde poetry plus manifestos and critical writings and reviews.
Book reviews, articles, poems.
No Index.
Issue 5, T.p. 56.   500.
Per copy 40p.

4248 STREETWORD.
M. Dobbie Esq., 8 Findham Ave., Hayes, Middx.
Irregular, ○   Poetry.
No Index.
Per copy 10p.

4249 SUZANNE. 1972.
J. Harrison, 28 Okehampton Road, Exeter.
Irregular.   Poetry.
No Index.
Per copy 10p.

4250 VIEWPOINTS. 1958.
VP Press, 20 Droylsden Road, Newton Heath, Manchester, M10 6HB.
6, ○   All forms of poetry and creative writings.
No Index.
T.p. 19.
Per copy $12\frac{1}{2}$, per year £1.

4251 VOLE. 1972.
C. M. Pickles, The Red House, Whitehill Road, Hitchin, Herts.
6, ○   Poems and stories.
No Index.
Per year 60p.

4252 WORKSHOP NEW POETRY. 1971.
(Writers Workshop 1967; Workshop 1967-1971; Workshop Poetry Magazine 1971).
Workshop Press Ltd., 2 Culham Court, Granville Road, London, N4 4JB.
6, ○   Contemporary poetry.
No Index.
No. 15, T.p. 36, Ad.p. 2.   2000
Per copy 25p, per year £1.50.

4253 WRITER'S FORUM (various titles).
Writer's Forum, 262 Randolph Avenue, London, W9.
c.12, ○ +   New developments in poetry—young writers, experiment, sound and visual poetry and other on-going areas of poetry.
No Index.
Sept. 1971, T.p. 32.   500.
Per copy 25p.

4254 YORK POETRY: being an anthology of poems offered to the York Poetry Society. 1971.
York Poetry Society, c/o Manor Cottage, Museum Gardens, York, YO1 2DR.
2, ○
No Index.
Per copy 20p.

4255 ZERONE. 1972.
Good Elf Publications & Zerone Publications, 18 Clairview Rd., London, SW16.
3/4, ○ ‡ † *   Magazine of *The Bec Poets* intended to provide a platform for unknown poets and to interest the public in the work of the group which is readings and 'poetry workshop' meetings.
No Index.
August 1972, T.p. 20.   200.
Per copy 10p.

8.03

TRANSLATION

4256 THE JOURNALS OF PIERRE MENARD. 1969.
Peter Hoy, 97 Holywell Street, Oxford.
4, = +   Theory and practice of translation into and from most European languages, each issue devoted to one translation.
Book reviews, monographic articles.
No Index.
T.p. 50.
Subscription on request.

8.08

AUTHORSHIP

4257 THE AUTHOR: journal of the Society of Authors. 1890.
The Society of Authors, 84 Drayton Gardens, London, SW10 9SD.
4, ‡ = *   Problems of authorship as a business and a profession.
Book reviews, legal notes, letters, articles.
None published. For consultation only at above address.
Summer 1972, T.p. 37, Ad.p. 12.   4500.
Per copy 25p, per year £1.

4258 THE WRITER: How to write and sell. 1920.
Bond Street Publishers, 124 New Bond Street, London, W1A 4LJ.
12, ‡   All subjects of interest to writers, both freelance and professional.
Book notices, book reviews, letters, monographic articles.
No Index.
June 1972, T.p. 44, Ad.p. 4.
Per copy 25p, per year £3.

4259 YOUNG WRITER. 1969.
Young Writer Group (sponsored by The Ashford Community), 2A Chertsey Road, Ashford Common, Middx.
12, ○   Aimed at adolescents of fifth and sixth years: but membership of the group is open to any literate child.
Book notices, book reviews, letters, articles.
No Index.
October 1969, T.p. 10.
Free to members.

820

ENGLISH

4261 ANDURIL. 1971.
The Tolkein Society, 31 Great Dell, Welwyn Garden City, Herts.
4, ○   Magazine of fantasy.
Articles, reviews.
No Index.
No. 2, 1972, T.p. 40.
Per year £1.

4262 THE ANGLO WELSH REVIEW: A National Review in English of Welsh Arts and Letters. 1957.
(Dock Leaves, 1949-1957).
The Anglo/Welsh Review and Dock Leaves, Ty Newydd, Lodge Hill, Caerleon, Newport, Mon. NP6 1DA.
3, ○ =   The arts, music, literature, poetry, stories, criticism, book reviews. About Wales or by people living in Wales or born in Wales—any connection with Wales.
Book notices, book reviews, letters, monographic articles.
No Index.
45, T.p. 283, Ad.p. 3.   1800.
Per copy 50p, per year £1.25.

4263 ANTACUS. 1970.
Villiers Publications, Ingestre Road, Tufnell Park, London, NW5.
4, ○
No Index.
Subscription on application.

4264 APEX ONE. 1971.
Inca Books, 36 Ashmead Road, London, SE8.
2, ○   Miscellany of unpublished creative and critical literature.
No Index.
2000.
Per year £4.

4265 BIBLIOGRAPHICAL BULLETIN OF THE INTERNATIONAL ARTHURIAN SOCIETY. 1949.
Professor Lewis Thorpe, Editor, The University, Nottingham.
1, +   Complete listing with critical analyses, of all books and articles published in the world during the previous calendar year on Arthurian literature in all languages. It includes a list of members, with addresses.
Abstracts, monographic articles, obituaries.
A, Integral with issue.
Vol. XXII, 1971, T.p. 216.   c. 1000.
Per copy £1.50. Non members £5.

4266 BRITISH SOCIETY FOR EIGHTEENTH-CENTURY STUDIES NEWSLETTER. 1972.
The Society, c/o Dept. of English, University College, Gower Street, London, WC1.
2, ○ =
Book notices, book reviews, letters, articles.
No Index.
No. 1, 1972, T.p. 9.
Per year £2. (50p Research Students).

4267 BROWNING SOCIETY NOTES. 1970.
Browning Society of London, c/o Prof. A. N. Kincaid, 29 Southmoor Road, Oxford, OX2 6RF.
3, + =   Life and works of Robert and Elizabeth Browning. Slant slightly more biographical than critical. Publication of original letters, family documents; talks given to Browning Society; reviews of books, performances, readings; research notes and queries; reports on work in progress, on Browning sites, and London Browning Society activities.
Book notices, book reviews, letters, monographic articles.
No Index.
March 1972, T.p. 34.   c.250.
Per copy 50p, per year £1.25.

4268 CORNHILL MAGAZINE. 1860.
John Murray Publishers Ltd., 50 Albemarle Street, London, W1X 4BD.
4, ○ =   Started by Thackeray, it is an illustrated magazine that provides for its readers the first publication of a lively variety of fiction and non-fiction from the best, and from the most promising, writers.

Key to reference symbols

○ popular   ‡ technical   = trade/professional

+ research   * society/institution   † house journal

Poetry, short stories, literary criticisms.
No Index.
Spring 1972, T.p. 194, Ad.p. 5.
Per copy 30p, per year £1.50.
Indexed in: BHI, IBZ.

4269 CYPHER. 1970.
James Goddard and Mike Sandow, Woodlands Lodge, Woodlands, Southampton, Hants.
4, ○   Review and discussion of science fiction, interviews with prominent writers.
Book reviews, letters, articles, obituaries.
No Index.
May 1972, T.p. 66.   c.300.
Per copy 20p, per year 60p.

4271 THE DICKENSIAN. 1905.
The Dickens Fellowship, The Dickens House, 48 Doughty Street, London, WC1 2LF.
3, = + *   Articles of special interest to students and researchers (as well as to Dickens lovers) of biographical and critical value.
Book notices, book reviews, monographic articles, obituaries.
A, January, 1905-1934/1935-1964/under review.
January 1972, T.p. 70, Ad.p. 5.   2000.
Per copy 10p, per year £1.50. Free to members.

4272 ENGLISH: literature, criticism, teaching. 1936.
Oxford University Press (for the English Association), Press Road, Neasden, London, NW10.
3, * + =   Reviews, articles, poetry, reprints etc.
A, —, No, None.
T.p. 42, Ad.p. 9.
Free to members.

4273 ESSAYS IN CRITICISM: a quarterly journal of literary criticism. 1951.
The Editors, Temple House, Brill, Aylesbury, Bucks.
4, + =   English, American and European literature.
Book reviews, letters, articles.
A, January, Yes, 10 year.
T.p. 110, Ad.p. 10.   c.2550.
Per copy 50p, per year £2.
Indexed in: BHI, IBZ.

4274 FORGE: A Literary Periodical from Wolverhampton Polytechnic. 1970.
Arts Department, The Polytechnic, Wolverhampton.
1/2, ○   To consider critically the central achievements in English literature, holding in mind especially the student in college or university.
Monographic articles.
No Index.
No. 1, 1972, T.p. 44.
Per copy 20p.

4275 THE GISSING NEWSLETTER. 1965.
C.C. Kohler, 141 High Street, Dorking, Surrey.
4, +   Detail of Gissing scholarship and tracings of works and sales of same.
Book notices, book reviews, letters, brief articles.
No Index.
January 1972, T.p. 20.   200.
£1.25.

4276 JABBERWOCKY. The Lewis Carroll Society Magazine. c.1970.
Lewis Carroll Society, Room 16, South Block, County Hall, London, SE1 7PB.
4, ○   Book notices, book reviews, letters, articles.
No Index.
Summer 1972, T.p. 30.
Free to members.

4277 JOURNAL OF THE H.G. WELLS SOCITEY: incorporating Bulletin and Wellsian. 1972.
(Bulletin and Wellsian) 1960-1971.
H.G. Wells Society, 125 Markyate Road, Dagenham, Essex.
2/3, + * ○   Promotion of an active interest in and an appreciation of the life, work and thought of H.G. Wells.
Book notices, book reviews, legal notes, letters, monographic articles, obituaries, parliamentary reports.
10 year, —, Yes, None.
Spring 1972, T.p. 8.   300.
£2 per year (individuals £1 per year).

4278 THE KIPLING JOURNAL. 1927.
The Kipling Society, 18 Northumberland Avenue, London, WC2.
4, * ○   Works of, and writings by, Kipling.
Book notices, book reviews, letters, monographic articles, obituaries.
No Index.
c.900.
Per year £1.75.

4279 THE LONDON REVIEW. 1966.
The London Review, 60 The Priory, Priory Park, London, SE3 9UZ.
2, +   Literary research, with particular emphasis on study in depth of single works.
Monographic articles.
No Index.
Winter 1971/72, T.p. 37, Ad.p. 1.
Per copy 20p.

4280 THE MALLORN: The Official Journal of the Tolkein Society. 1970.
The Tolkein Society, c/o 31 Great Dell, Welwyn Garden City, Herts.
4, *   Appreciation and criticism of the Works of Dr. Prof. John Ronald Reuel Tolkein. Comparison with and Influences on other authors in the field of fantasy.
Book notices, book reviews, letters, articles, obituaries.
5 year, 1975, Yes, None.
No. 5, T.p. 26.   130.
Per copy 30p, per year £1.

4281 THE NEW RAMBLER: Journal of The Johnson Society of London. 1942.
The Johnson Society of London, Broadmead, Eynsford Road, Farningham, Kent, DA4 0BQ.
2, + *   Dr. Johnson and his circle and literature, life and thought of the eighteenth century.
Book notices, book reviews, letters, monographic articles, obituaries.
No Index.
Autumn 1971, T.p. 52, Ad.p. 2.   350.
Per year £1.20 to non-members. Free to members.

4282 REVIEW OF ENGLISH LITERATURE. 1960.
Longmans Green & Co. Ltd., 48 Grosvenor Street, London, W1.
4, =
Monographic articles,
A, —, Yes, None.
T.p. 94, Ad p. 8.
Per copy 20p, per year 80p.

4283 SCOTTISH INTERNATIONAL REVIEW. 1968.
Scottish International Review Ltd., 23 George Square, Edinburgh, EH8 9LD.
10, ○   Arts, literature, contemporary social topics, politics, social history.
Book notices, book reviews, letters, monographic articles.
5 year, Still to be issued, No, None.
May 1972, T.p. 34, Ad.p. 4.   2500.
Per copy 15p, per year £1.50.

4284 SCOTTISH LITERARY NEWS: The Newsletter of the Association for Scottish Literary Studies. 1970.
Association for Scottish Literary Studies, c/o Department of English Literature, University of Aberdeen, Taylor Building, Old Aberdeen, Scotland.

4, + * Information, critical articles on Scottish literature, bibliography, reviews and brief notices, occasional creative writing—e.g., poems.
No Index.
August 1971, T.p. 52, Ad.p. 1.   500.
Per copy 25p, per year £2.50.

4285 SHAKESPEARE SURVEY. 1948.
Cambridge University Press, Bentley House, 200 Euston Road, London, NW1.
1, = +   Shakespeare; life, times, works and criticism.
A,—, Yes, 10 year.
T.p. 180.

4286 SHAKESPEAREAN AUTHORSHIP REVIEW. 1959.
(Shakespeare Fellowship News-Letter 1941-1958).
The Shakespearean Authorship Society, 25 Montagu Square, London, W1H 1RE.
2, + *   The problem of the authorship of the plays and poems attributed to William Shakespeare, etc.
Book reviews, letters, monographic articles, obituaries.
No Index.
Autumn 1971, T.p. 24.   c.200.
Per year £1.

4287 SHAVIAN: the journal of the Shaw Society. 1946.
(Bulletin 1941-1952).
Shaw Society, 125 Markyate Road, Dagenham, Essex.
2/3, ○ + *   A wider interest in and a deeper understanding of the life work and thought of George Bernard Shaw.
Book notices, book reviews, legal notes, letters, monographic articles, obituaries, parliamentary reports.
5 year,—, Yes, 10 year.
Spring 1972, T.p. 32, Ad.p. 4.   600.
Per year £1.

4288 SIGNAL: Approaches to children's books. 1970.
The Thimble Press, Weaver's, Amberley, Glos. GL5 5BA.
3, *   Critical essays about children's literature, biographical studies of children's authors, reprints of 19th century articles about children's reading.
Book reviews, monographic articles.
A, September, Yes, None.
September 1971, T.p. 48.   600.
Per copy 40p, per year £1.

4289 TALIESIN. 1961.
Yr Academi Gymreig (The Welsh Academy of Letters), c/o The Secretary, The Welsh Academy, St. David's College, Lampeter, Cards.
2, =   A literary review for Welsh language authors. It contains poems, short stories, essays, book reviews, interviews, articles on non-literary arts, translations of short literary works in Welsh, etc.
Book reviews, monographic articles, obituaries.
No Index.
December 1971, T.p. 150, Ad.p. 3.   750.
Per copy 80p.

4290 TENNYSON RESEARCH BULLETIN. 1967.
The Tennyson Society, City Library, Free School Lane, Lincoln.
1, +   Covers all aspects of international research on the life and work of Alfred Lord Tennyson. Contributions include shorter articles, details of specific research, reviews, notices, notes and queries etc.
Book notices, book reviews, letters, monographic articles.
5 year, Summer, Yes, None.
1971, T.p. 28, Ad.p. 1.   500.
Per copy £1.50 personal £2. institutional.

4291 TRANSACTIONS OF THE BRONTË SOCIETY. 1895.
Bronte Society, Old Parsonage, Howarth, Keighley, Yorks.
1, = + ○   Life, times and work of the Bronte family.
Monographic articles.
No Index.
Free to members.
Indexed in: BHI.

4292 TRANSATLANTIC REVIEW. 1959.
33 Ennismore Gardens, London, SW7 1AE,
4, = ○   Poetry, fiction, interviews with theatrical and film people, drawings.
No Index.
No. 41, 1972, T.p. 180.   2500.
Per copy 25p, per year 85p.

4293 A WAKE NEWSLITTER: studies of James Joyce's Finnegans Wake. 1962.
Clive Hart, Department of Literature, University of Essex, Wivenhoe Park, Colchester, Essex.
6, +   Explication and criticism of Finnegans Wake, with occasional notes and articles on Joyce's other works.
Book notices, book reviews, letters, monographic articles, obituaries.
10 year, February 1972, No, None.
December 1971, T.p. 12.   500.
Per copy 25p, per year £1.25.

830

GERMAN

4294 GERMAN LIFE AND LETTERS. 1936.
Basil Blackwell & Mott Ltd., 5 Alfred Street, Oxford, OX1 4HB.
4, +   All aspects of German literature and criticism, both in mediaeval and modern periods.
Book reviews, monographic articles.
A, No. 4 of each volume, Yes, None.
T.p. 79, Ad.p. 4.   1000.
Per year £3.50.
Indexed in: BHI, IBZ.

4295 OXFORD GERMAN STUDIES. 1966.
Oxford University Press, Press Road, Neasden, London, NW10.
1, +   German literary history, and related subjects such as philosophy, art, and social history.
Book reviews, monographic articles.
A,—, Yes, None.
No. 6, 1971-2, T.p. 174.   200.
Per year £1.50.

839.5

SCANDINAVIA

4296 SCANDINAVICA: An International Journal of Scandinavian Studies. 1962.
Academic Press Inc. (London) Ltd., 24-28 Oval Road, London, NW1.
2, +   Scholarly articles on Scandinavian literature and history. Book reviews. Bibliographies (covering books and articles in periodicals). Contributions printed in English, German or French.
Book notices, book reviews, monographic articles.
A, November, Yes, 10 year.
T.p. 88.
Per year £3.

840

FRENCH

4297 FRENCH NOTES AND QUERIES. 1968.
Peter Hoy, 97 Holywell Street, Oxford.
4, +   Aspects of contemporary French literature.
Book reviews, monographic articles.
No Index.
T.p. 64.
Subscription on request.

4298 NOTTINGHAM FRENCH STUDIES. 1962.
The Editor, Nottingham French Studies, The University, Nottingham.
2, + = Literature of France from c. 1500 to today—in English or French.
Monographic articles.
No Index.
October 1971, T.p. 43   500.
Per copy 50p, per year £1.
Indexed in: BHI.

875
GREEK

4299 PROCEEDINGS OF THE VIRGIL SOCIETY. 1962.
Waldens & Co. Ltd., 18 Station Approach, London, SW11.
1, * + Virgil studies.
Book reviews, monographic articles.
No Index.
1969-1970, T.p. 114.
Subscription on application.

883
UKRAINIAN

4300 UKRAINIAN REVIEW. 1954.
The Association of Ukrainians in GB, 49 Linden Gardens, London, W2 4HG.
4, + Political and literary research and study of Ukraine.
Abstracts, book notices, book reviews, letters, monographic articles.
No Index.
Summer 1972, T.p. 112, Ad.p. 1.   1500.
Per copy 50p, per year £2

891.65
WELSH

4301 YTRAETHODYDD (the Essayist). CYLCHGRANN CHWARTEROL (Quarterly Journal). 1845.
Methodist Book Centre, Caernarvon, St. Davids Rd., Caernarfon.
4, = + Mostly literary material—but with theological and philosophical contributions.
Book reviews, monographic articles.
No Index.
T.p. 86, Ad.p. 4.   700.
Per copy 20p, per year 80p.

892.4
HEBREW. JEWISH.

4302 JOURNAL OF JEWISH STUDIES. 1948.
Frank Cass & Co. Ltd., (for Jewish Chronicle Publications), 67 Great Russell Street, London, WC1B 3BT.
2, + Devoted to the comprehensive study of Jewish history and civilization.
Book notices, book reviews, monographic articles.
A, last issue of each volume (autumn), No, None.
Spring 1972, T.p. 100, Ad.p. 4.
Per copy £1.50, per year £2.50.
Indexed in: BHI, IBZ.

9
GEOGRAPHY. HISTORY

4303 ANNUAL BULLETIN OF HISTORICAL LITERATURE. 1911.
Historical Association, 59a Kennington Park Road, London, SE11 4JH.
1, + ‡
Book notices.
A, —, Yes, None.
1969, T.p. 190, Ad.p. 4.
Per copy £1.

4305 BULLETIN, BURNHAM ON CROUCH LOCAL HISTORY SOCIETY. 1972.
The Society, 12 Granville Terrace, Burnham-on-Crouch, Essex.
4, = ○
No Index.
Per copy 7½p.

4306 BULLETIN OF THE GROUP FOR THE STUDY OF IRISH HISTORIC SETTLEMENT. 1970.
Group for the Study of Irish Historic Settlement, Dept. of Geography, Queen's University Belfast, Northern Ireland.
1, + Settlement and economy of Ireland in medieval and post-medieval periods.
Book notices, book reviews, monographic articles.
No Index.
250.
Per copy 25p. Free to members.

4307 BULLETIN OF THE INSTITUTE OF HISTORICAL RESEARCH. 1923.
Institute of Historical Research, Senate House, London, WC1E 7HU.
2, + * Medieval and modern history; notes and documents; historical news; accessions and migrations of historical manuscripts; corrections to *Dictionary of National Biography*.
Monographic articles.
A, November, Yes, None.
May 1972, T.p. 153, Ad.p. 12.   1360.
Per copy £1.80, per year £3.55.
Indexed in: BHI, IBZ.

4308 BULLETIN OF THE JOHN RYLANDS LIBRARY. 1903.
The John Rylands Library, Deansgate, Manchester, M3 3EH.
2, + Articles dealing with the Library's rare MSS. and books; the Library's annual lectures; monographs by English, American and Continental scholars embodying the results of research in the fields of the humanities and the arts.
No Index.
Per year £2.75.
Indexed in: BHI, IBZ.

4309 BULLETIN OF THE SCOTTISH GEORGIAN SOCIETY. 1972.
Scottish Georgian Society, 41 Castle Street, Edinburgh, EH2 3BH.
1, ○
No Index.
Per year 60p.

4310 CAKE AND COCKHORSE: The Magazine of the Banbury Historical Society. 1959.
Banbury Historical Society, c/o Banbury Museum, Marlborough Road, Banbury, Oxon.

3, + * History of the town of Banbury and the neighbouring parts of Oxfordshire, Northamptonshire and Warwickshire.
Book notices, book reviews, letters, monographic articles, obituaries.
3 year,—, Yes, None.
Summer 1972, T.p. 16.   500.
Per copy 20p, per year 60p. Free to members

4311 CHESHIRE HISTORY NEWSLETTER. 1971
c/o Watergate House, Watergate Street, Chester, CH1 2LW
2, =
No Index.
T.p. 22.
Per year £1.

4312 EAST LONDON PAPERS: A Journal of History, Social Studies and the Arts. 1958.
East London Papers Charitable Trust, History Dept. Queen Mary College, Mile End Road, London, E1 4NS.
2, ○ * +   All aspects of the life of East London, past, present and future.
Book reviews, monographic articles.
5 year, 1962, 1967, No, None.
Winter 1970-1971, T.p. 54.
Per copy 60p.

4313 ENGLISH HISTORICAL REVIEW. 1886.
Longmans Group Ltd., 5 Bentinck Street, London, W1.
4, +   World history, especially medieval.
Book reviews, monographic articles.
A, October, Yes, None.
T.p. 224, Ad.p. 16.
Per copy £1.05, per year £4.50.
Indexed in: BHI, IBZ.

4314 GATESHEAD AND DISTRICT LOCAL HISTORY SOCIETY. BULLETIN. 1969.
Gateshead and District Local History Society, Central Library, Prince Consort Road, Gateshead, NE8 4LN.
2, ○ *   All aspects of the local history of Gateshead and the immediate surrounding area.
Articles.
No Index.
January 1972, T.p. 18. c.120.
Free.

4315 THE HISTORICAL JOURNAL. 1957.
(Cambridge Historical Journal 1923-1956).
Cambridge University Press (for Cambridge Historical Society), PO Box 92, London, NW1 2DB.
4, +   History from fifteenth century to the present.
Book reviews, monographic articles.
A, December, Yes, None.
June 1972, T.p. 189, Ad.p. 11.   1600.
Per copy £1.50, per year £5.
Indexed in: BHI, IBZ.

4316 HISTORY: the journal of the Historical Association. 1912.
Historical Association, 59a Kennington Park Road, London, SE11.
3, ‡ + *   For the professional historian containing reviews of recent historical works.
Book reviews, monographic articles.
A,—, Yes, None.
February 1972, T.p. 167, Ad.p. 22.
Per year £2.50. Free to members
Indexed in: BHI, IBZ.

4317 HISTORY TODAY. 1951.
Financial Times Ltd., 388-9 Strand, London, WC2R 0LT.
12, ○ =   World history from ancient times to modern.
Book reviews, letters, monographic articles, obituaries.
A, December, Yes, None.
June 1972, T.p. 74, Ad.p. 6.   33000.
Per copy 30p, per year £3.50.
Indexed in: BHI.

4318 INTERNATIONAL HISTORY MAGAZINE. 1973. *
Subscription Department, 75-79 Farringdon Street, London, EC4A 4BJ.
12, ○
Book reviews, monographic articles.
No Index.
Per copy 50p, per year £5.

4319 JOURNAL OF CONTEMPORARY HISTORY. 1966.
Sage Publications Ltd., St. George's House, 44 Hatton Garden, London, EC1N 8ER.
4, +   Study and discussion of 20th C. history, especially European.
Monographic articles.
A,—, No, None.
No. 3, 1971, T.p. 196.
Per copy £1.05, per year £6. £4 individual.
Indexed in: BHI.

4320 JOURNAL OF IMPERIAL AND COMMONWEALTH HISTORY. 1972.
Frank Cass & Co. Ltd., 67 Great Russell Street, London, WC1B 3BT.
3, + =   History of the British Empire and the emergence of the Commonwealth of Nations; main emphasis on matters of a broad Commonwealth nature, with particular attention being focused on British imperial policy, colonial rule and local response.
Book notices, book reviews, monographic articles.
A,—, Yes, None.
Per copy £2, per year £6.

4321 JOURNAL OF THE OLD ATHLONE SOCIETY. 1969.
Old Athlone Society, Athlone, County Westneath, Ireland.
2 issues every 3 years, *   Athlone local material i.e. covering an area about 25 miles radius from the town, being archaeology, local history, genealogy, folklore and similar relevant subjects.
Legal notes, letters, monographic articles.
Index and title page will only be supplied at end of each volume, vol. I should be completed about 1975 with No. 4.
No. 1, T.p. 65.   500.
Per copy 75p.

4322 JOURNAL OF THE WATFORD AND DISTRICT INDUSTRIAL HISTORY SOCIETY. 1971.
Watford & District I.H.S., 49 Longcroft Rd., Maple Cross, Rickmansworth, Herts.
1, *   Local history/technology.
Articles.
No Index.
Per copy 15p.

4323 THE LEICESTERSHIRE HISTORIAN. 1967.
Leicestershire Local History Council, c/o County Record Office, 57 New Walk, Leicester.
2, * ○
Book notices, book reviews, monographic articles.
No Index.
Winter-Spring 1971-1972, T.p. 32.
Per copy 20p.

4324 THE LOCAL HISTORIAN: quarterly journal of the Standing Conference for Local History. 1968.
(Amateur Historian 1952).
National Council of Social Service for the Standing Conference for Local History, 26 Bedford Square, London.
4, ○ +   Local historians:-covers general background material, sources and research methods.
Book notices, book reviews, letters.
2 yearly,—, No, None.
No. 2, 1972, T.p. 54, Ad.p. 6.   1800.
Per copy 25p, per year £1.05.
Indexed in: BHI.

4325 LOCAL HISTORY BULLETIN.
Gloucestershire Community Council, Community House, College Green, Gloucester.
2, ○   Amateur history in the Cotswolds.
Book notices, book reviews, letters, monographic articles, obituaries, parliamentary reports.
Full index under preparation, 2 year.
Spring 1972, T.p. 16.   300.
Per copy 20p.

4326 LOCAL HISTORY BULLETIN FOR SOUTH-EAST SCOTLAND. 1970.
University of Edinburgh, Dept. of Educational Studies, 11 Buccleuch Place, Edinburgh, EH8 9JT.
Irreg. =
No Index.
Subscription on application.

4327 LOCAL HISTORY RECORDS. 1962.
The Bourne Society, 52 Buxton Lane, Caterham, Surrey.
1, ○ +   Covers all aspects of local history—archaeology, documents, transport, crafts. Memories—in readable articles and fine drawings and maps.
Monographic articles, obituaries.
A, November, No, 10 year.
1972, Vol. XI, T.p. 40, Ad.p. 6.   5000.
Per copy 15p.

4328 MEDIUM AEVUM. 1932.
Basil Blackwell & Mott Ltd., 5 Alfred Street, Oxford, OX1 4HB.
3, +   Entire field of mediaeval studies, from the Romanesque period to the early sixteenth century.
Articles and reviews.
A, —, Yes, None.
Subscription on application.

4329 MIDLAND HISTORY. 1971.
Phillimore (for University of Birmingham School of History).   Shopwyke Hall, Chichester, Sussex.
2, † ○   Scholarly local history and allied subjects
Book notices, book reviews, monographic articles.
No Index.
Autumn 1971, T.p. 61, Ad.p. 6.
Per year £2.

4330 NORTHERN SCOTLAND. 1972.
Centre for Scottish Studies, King's College, University, Aberdeen, AB9 2UB.
1, ○   Academic historical journal.
No Index.
Per year £1.25.

4331 NOTTINGHAM MEDIAEVAL STUDIES. 1957.
The Editor, Nottingham Mediaeval Studies, The University, Nottingham.
1, + =   The languages, literatures, history and general culture, including music, painting, architecture of mediaeval Europe.
Monographic articles.
A, Integral with issue.
Vol. XX, 1971, T.p. 95.   500.
Per copy 75p.

4332 PAST AND PRESENT: a journal of historical studies. 1952.
Titus Wilson & Son Ltd., 28 Highgate, Kendal, Westmorland.
4, ○ ‡ + *
Book reviews, articles.
A, November, Yes, 10 year.
May 1972, T.p. 160, Ad.p. 20.   c.5000.
Per copy £1, per year £3.

4333 THE PEMBROKESHIRE HISTORIAN: Journal of the Pembrokeshire Local History Society. 1959.
The Society, 4 Victoria Place, Herefordwest.
2, + *   History of Pembrokeshire.
Book notices, book reviews, monographic articles.
No Index.
T.p. 80.   1000.
Per copy 50p.

4334 RENAISSANCE AND MODERN STUDIES. 1957.
University of Nottingham, University Park, Nottingham.
1, +
Monographic articles.
No Index.
T.p. 119, Ad.p. 4.
Per year £1.
Indexed in: BHI.

4335 RESEARCH IN PROGRESS IN ENGLISH AND HISTORICAL STUDIES IN THE UNIVERSITIES OF THE BRITISH ISLES. 1971.
St. James Press Ltd., 1a Montagu Mews North, London, W.1.
2 yearly, + =   Description of research in progress in English and History faculties in U.K. and Irish universities.
2 yearly, —, No, None.
1971, T.p. 109.
Subscription on application.

4336 THE RICARDIAN: Journal of the Richard III Society. 1961.
Richard III Society, 72 Heathfield Rd., Croydon, Surrey.
4, ○   Deals with the period of 1400-1500 in British history, mainly covering the reign of Richard III 1483-1485.
Book notices, book reviews, letters, monographic articles.
Only one issued to date, included in September 1969 issue.
June 1972, T.p. 30, Ad.p. 1.   1000.
Per copy 25p, per year £1.

4337 THE RICKMANSWORTH HISTORIAN. 1961.
The Rickmansworth Historical Society, c/o 18 Pheasants Way, Rickmansworth, Herts.
2, ○ * ‡   Local historical and archaeological interests in general.
Book notices, book reviews, letters, monographic articles, obituaries.
5 year, In an issue following every 10 copies. No, None.
Spring 1972, T.p. 17, Ad.p. 7.
Per copy 8p and Free to members.

4338 ROMFORD RECORD. 1968.
Romford and District Historical Society, Central Library, St. Edward's Way, Romford, RM1 3AR, Essex.
1, * ○   Local history of the London Borough of Havering (Romford, Hornchurch, Upminster, Rainham, Collier Row, Havering-atte-Bowes).
Letters, monographic articles, obituaries.
No Index.
3, 1970, T.p. 66.   650.
Per copy 23p.

4339 ROYAL STUART PAPERS. 1972.
Royal Stuart Society, 8 Lakeside Avenue, Redbridge, Ilford, Essex.
Irreg. +   History of the Royal House of Stuart.
Monographic articles.
Occasional, —, No, None.
May 1972, T.p. 19.
Per copy 15p.

4340 ROYALIST VIEWPOINT 1968.
(Royinform 1962-1968).
The Royal Stuart Society, 8 Lakeside Avenue, Redbridge, Ilford, Essex.
6, + *   Stuart dynasty and European royalty.
Book notices, book reviews, letters, articles.
No Index.
June 1972, T.p. 12.
Per copy £2.

4341 SCOTTISH HISTORICAL REVIEW. 1903.
The Aberdeen University Press Ltd., Farmers Hall, Aberdeen, Scotland, AB9 2XT.
2, +   Scottish history.
Book reviews, monographic articles.
A, With second of the year's issues, Yes, None.
April 1972, T.p. 88, Ad.p. 6.
Per copy £1.30, per year £2.50.

4342 SEVERN AND WYE REVIEW: A journal for the Lower Wye Valley and Severnside. 1970.
Phillimore & Co. Ltd., Shopwyke Hall, Chichester, Sussex.
2, ○   Local history, archaeology and allied subjects.
Book notices, book reviews, letters, monographic articles, obituaries.
No Index.
Winter 1971-72, T.p. 32.
Per copy 30p, per year £1.

4343 STAINES LOCAL HISTORY SOCIETY JOURNAL. 1967.
Editor, 413 Stroude Road, Virginia Water, Surrey.
1/2, + *   Research into history of Staines, Ashford (M'sex), Stanwell and Laleham by members of the Society—a preliminary to ultimate publication of History of Ancient Parishes of Staines.
Abstracts, monographic articles.
Every 6 Issues, February 1972 (with No. 6), No, None.
February 1972, T.p. 17, Ad.p. Nil.   150.
Per copy 12½p. (By post 16½p).

4344 TRANSACTIONS OF THE HISTORIC SOCIETY OF LANCASHIRE AND CHESHIRE. 1849.
Council of the Historic Society of Lancs. and Chesh.
c/o Dr. M. J. Power (Editor), School of History, The University, Liverpool.
1, + *   History and archaeology of Lancashire and Cheshire, from pre-historic times to the twentieth century.
Book reviews, monographic articles.
A, —, Yes, None.
1971, T.p. 180.   c.550.
Per year £2.

4345 TRANSACTIONS OF THE ROYAL HISTORICAL SOCIETY. 1869.
The Society, c/o Cheyne Walk, London, SW10.
1, + *   British history.
Monographic articles.
No Index.
Subscription on application.
Indexed in: BHI, IBZ.

4346 VIATOR: Medieval and Renaissance studies. 1970.
University of California Press, 2-4 Brook Street, London, W1.
1, + =   Embraces all aspects of medieval and renaissance studies between late antiquity and A.D. 1600, particularly, but not exclusively, stressing intercultural research.
Monographic articles.
No Index.
1971, T.p. 396.
Per copy £5.75.

4347 WARWICKSHIRE HISTORY. 1969.
Warwickshire Local History Society, 47 Newbold Terrace, Leamington Spa, Warwickshire.
2, * +   Research work on aspects of Warwickshire local history such as parish records, social customs, architecture and topography.
Book reviews, monographic articles.
2 year, —, Yes, None.
Autumn, 1971, T.p. 36.   500.
Per copy 40p, per year £1.

4348 WELSH HISTORY REVIEW. 1960.
University of Wales Press, Merthyr House, James Street, Cardiff, CF1 6EU.
2, ‡ +
Book notices, book reviews, monographic articles, parliamentary reports, standards, tests.
2 years, with 4th issue, Yes, None.
Subscription on application.

4349 THE WIENER LIBRARY BULLETIN. 1945.
Institute of Contemporary History, 4 Devonshire Street, London, W.1.
4, = +   Modern Jewish history and impact of totalitarian structures like Nazism and fascism.
Monographic articles.
No Index.
No. 3/4, 1972, T.p. 45.
Per copy 38p, per year £1.50.
Indexed in: BHI.

91

GEOGRAPHY

4350 AREA. 1969.
Institute of British Geographers, 1 Kensington Gore, London, SW7 2AR.
4, ‡ + =   Geography in general.
Letters, articles, news.
None as yet but will be 5 yr. cumulative + annual supplements.
No. 1, 1972, T.p. 76.   2500.
Per year £3. Free to members.

4351 THE EAST MIDLAND GEOGRAPHER. 1954.
Department of Geography, The University, Nottingham.
2, + =   Research articles and notes on the geography of the East Midland region of England.
Book reviews, monographic articles.
Every 4 years, —, Yes, None.
June 1972, T.p. 50.   650
Per copy 60p, per year £1.20.

4352 GEO ABSTRACTS. 1972.
Part A = Landforms & Quaternary
B = Biogeography & Climatology
C = Economic Geography
D = Social Geography
E = Sedimentology
F = Regional & Community Planning.
(Geographic Abstracts Parts A-D 1966-1971).
Geo Abstracts, University of East Anglia, Norwich, NOR 88C.
Each Part 6 issues per year, + =   All aspects of fields as shown by subtitles.
Abstracts.
A each part, following year, No, 5 year each part.
1972, T.p. varies by part.   A 1800; B 1200; C 1200; D 1200; E 650; F 600.
Per copy 61p, per year £3.65 per part.

4353 GEOGRAPHICAL JOURNAL. 1893.
Royal Geographical Society, London, SW7.
4, * + =   World geography with scientific accounts of recent explorations and travels.
Book reviews, monographic articles, news, obituaries.
A, Last issue of year, Yes, None.
T.p. 153, Ad.p. 13.
Per copy £1, per year £4.50. Free to members.
Indexed in: BHI, IBZ.

4354 GEOGRAPHICAL MAGAZINE. 1935.
IPC Magazines Ltd., 128 Long Acre, London, WC2E 9QH.
12, ○ = + ‡   Modern geographical thought and research in every aspect for the general reader.
Monographic articles, news, book reviews.
A, —, Yes, None.
T.p. 67, Ad.p. 16.   63572.
Per year £4.50.
Indexed in: BHI, IBZ.

4355 GEOGRAPHY. 1927.
(Geographical Teacher 1901-1926).
Geographical Association, 343 Fulwood Road, Sheffield, S10 3BP.
4, * +   All aspects of geography, including teaching.
Book reviews, legal notes, monographic articles, obituaries.
A, November, Yes, None.
April 1972, T.p. 96, Ad.p. 16.   9500.
Per copy 80p, per year £3.
Indexed in: BHI, IBZ.

4356 INSTITUTE OF BRITISH GEOGRAPHERS. TRANSACTIONS. 1965.
(Transactions and Papers 1933-1965).
Institute of British Geographers, 1 Kensington Gore, London, SW7 2AR.
3, ‡ + =   Research papers on geography contributed by members.
Monographic articles, obituaries.
5 year, last 1967 next 1972, Yes, None.
March 1972, T.p. 180.   2300.
Per year £8.

4357 IRISH GEOGRAPHY. 1947.
(Bulletin Geographical Society of Ireland 1944-46).
Geographical Society of Ireland, University College, Dublin, 4.
1, +   Geographical research papers related to Ireland.
Book notices, book reviews, articles.
5 year, 1968, Yes, None.
1971, T.p. 130.   c 600.
Per copy £1.

4358 NEW GEOGRAPHICAL LITERATURE AND MAPS. 1951.
Royal Geographical Society, 1 Kensington Gore, London, SW7 2AR.
2, + *   Brief abstracts of all accessions (during the period concerned) to the Royal Geographical Society Library and Map Room.
Abstracts.
No Index.
December 1971, T.p. 105.   750.
Per copy £2, per year £4.

4359 READING GEOGRAPHER. 1970.
Dept. of Geography, Reading University, Whiteknights, Reading, RG6 2AF.
1, + =   Current research in both human and physical geography and geographical methodology.
Book reviews, letters, monographic articles.
None yet issued.
March 1972, T.p. 77, Ad.p. 11.   250.
Per copy 20p.

4360 SCOTTISH GEOGRAPHICAL MAGAZINE. 1885.
Royal Scottish Geographical Society, 10 Randolph Crescent, Edinburgh, 3.
3, ‡ + *   Geographical science.
Book reviews, monographic articles.
2 yearly, Indexed in December issue of year 2, Yes, None.
April 1972, T.p. 72.   4000.
Per year £1.50.
Indexed in: BHI, IBZ.

912

MAPS

4361 THE ORIENTEER: The Magazine of the British Orienteering Federation. 1968.
British Orienteering Federation, 18 Doneraile St., London, SW6 3EN.
6, *   Sport of orienteering (and allied subjects), its development and techniques. The official organ of the sport in U.K.
Book notices, book reviews, letters, articles, new products, obituaries, tests.
No Index.
May 1972, T.p. 22, Ad.p. 3.   2700.
Per copy 12p, per year 80p.

929.1

GENEALOGY

4362 FAMILY HISTORY: Journal of the Institute of Heraldic and Genealogical Studies. 1962.
Institute of Heraldic and Geneological Studies, Northgate, Canterbury, Kent.
6, = ‡ *
Book notices, book reviews, monographic articles, obituaries.
2 year, —, Yes, None.
April 1972, T.p. 32.
Per copy 25p, per year £2. Free to members.
Indexed in: BHI.

4363 THE GENEALOGICAL QUARTERLY. 1932.
Fudge & Co. Ltd., Sardinia House, Sardinia St., London, WC2A 3NW.
4, ○ +   For everyone interested in family history.
Book notices, book reviews, articles.
No Index.
Summer 1972, T.p. 46, Ad.p. 2.   1000.
Per copy 70p, per year £2.25.

4364 GENEALOGISTS' MAGAZINE: Journal of the Society of Genealogists. 1925.
Phillimore & Co. Ltd. (for the Society), Shopwyke Hall, Chichester, Sussex.
4, + ‡   Genealogy and related subjects.
Book notices, book reviews, letters, monographic articles, obituaries.
3 year, December, Yes, None.
March 1971, T.p. 60, Ad.p. 7.
Per year £2. Free to members.
Indexed in: BHI.

4365 IRISH ANCESTOR. 1969.
The Irish Ancestor, Pirton House, Sydenham Villas, Dundrum, Dublin 14, Ireland.
2, + ○   Irish genealogy, family history, social history (architecture, domestic inventories, furniture, clothes, paintings, etc), biography and all aspects of domestic life in Ireland, principally during the last 300 years.
Abstracts, book notices, book reviews, monographic articles.
No Index.
No. 2, 1971, T.p. 58-70, Ad.p. Usually none.   550-850.
Membership £2.10.

4366 IRISH GENEALOGIST: Official organ of the Irish Genealogical Research Society. 1937.
The Society, 82 Eaton Square, London, SW1.
1, * + ○   Book reviews, monographic articles, news.
A, with volume, No, 10 year.
T.p. 90.
Free to members.

4367 JOURNAL OF BUTLER SOCIETY. 1968.
Dolmen Press, Dublin.
1, +   The history of the Butler family during the past eight centuries, its dispersion through Europe and America.
Book notices, book reviews, letters, articles, obituaries.
No Index.
Journal I. 1968, T.p. 72, Ad.p. 10.   1000.
Per copy 62p.

4368 NORTH CHESHIRE FAMILY HISTORIAN. 1972
N. Hawkin, Family History Society of Cheshire, 89 Dalebrook Road, Sale, Cheshire.
4, = ○
No Index.
Subscription on application.

4369 THE SCOTTISH GENEALOGIST: Quarterly journal of
the Scottish Genealogy Society. 1954.
The Society, 16 Charlotte Square, Edinburgh, 2.
4, ○ +   Research into Scottish family history.
Book reviews, letters, monographic articles, obituaries.
A, Last issue, Yes, None.
March 1972, T.p. 28.   460.
Per copy 25p, per year £1.
Free to members.
Indexed in: BHI.

929.6

HERALDRY

4370 THE COAT OF ARMS. 1950.
The Heraldry Society, 28 Museum Street, London, WC1A
  1LH.
4, *   Heraldry.
Book notices, book reviews, letters, monographic articles.
Per volume, varies, Yes, None.
January 1971, T.p. 50, Ad.p. 6.   c 2000.
Per copy 40p, per year £1.60.

930.26

ARCHAEOLOGY

4371 G.S.I.A. JOURNAL. 1971
(G.S.I.A. Newsletter, 1964-1971)
Gloucestershire Society for Industrial Archaeology,
  c/o 6/7 Montpellier Street, Cheltenham, Glos.
1, ○ ‡ + *   Industrial archaeology mainly relevant to
  Gloucestershire—History of industry, transport,
  mines and manufactures.
Book reviews, letters, monographic articles.
Autumn 1971, T.p. 99.
Per year 75p. Free to members

4372 ANATOLIAN STUDIES. 1951.
British Institute of Archaeology at Ankara, 140
  Cromwell Road, London, SW7.
1, * +   Archaeology and art of Turkey in all periods.
Monographic articles. 10 year, Yes, None.
T.p. 175   700.
Per year £3.
Indexed in: BHI

4373 ANTIQUARIES JOURNAL: The Journal of the Society
  of Antiquaries of London. 1921.
Oxford University Press, Press Road, Neasden,
  London, NW10.
2, +   Archaeological and antiquarian subjects, notes,
  book reviews, proceedings of the Society of
  Antiquaries, a classified bibliography of recent
  publications and a list of articles in British and
  foreign periodical literature dealing with archae-
  ology, etc.
Book reviews, letters, monographic articles.
A, —, Yes, None.
Prt 1, 1971, T.p. 166.   460.
Per copy £2.50, per year £5.
Indexed in: BHI, IBZ.

4374 ANTIQUITY: a quality review of archaeology. 1927.
W. Heffer & Sons Ltd., 104 Hills Road, Cambridge.
4, + = ○ =   Archaeology worldwide.
Book notices, book reviews, monographic articles.
A, December, Yes, vols 1-25.
T.p. 79, Ad.p. 4.
Per copy 75p, per year £2.50.
Indexed in: BHI, IB2.

4375 THE ARCHAEOLOGICAL JOURNAL. 1884.
Royal Archaeological Institute, c/o London Museum,
  Kensington Palace, London, W8.
1, + *   Archaeology and antiquities, mainly British.
Book reviews, monographic articles.
No Index.
Free to members.
Indexed in: BHI, IBZ

4376 ARCHAEOLOGY ABROAD. 1972.
Archaeology Abroad Service, 31-4 Gordon Square,
  London, WC1H 0PY.
2/3, =   Opportunities for archaeological work in
  other countries.
No Index.
Free.

4377 ARCHAEOMETRY: Bulletin of the Oxford University
  Research Laboratory for Archaeology. 1958.
Cambridge University Press, PO Box 92, London,
  NW1 2DB.
2, + =   Applications of the natural sciences to
  archaeology.
Monographic articles.
A, —, Yes, None.
T.p. 182, Ad.p. 4.   400.
Per year £4.50.

4378 BRITANNIA. 1970.
Society for the Promotion of Roman Studies, 31-4
  Gordon Square, London, WC1.
1, * + =   Romano—British and corrected studies
  including a survey of Romano—British excavations.
Monographic articles.
No Index.
Per copy £3. £4 to members.

4379 CURRENT ARCHAEOLOGY. 1967.
Andrew and Wendy Selkirk, 9 Nassington Road,
  London, NW3 2TX.
6, ○   Bridges the gap between amateur and professional in archaeology: it gives the latest news
  of archaeological excavations in Britian.
Book notices, book reviews, letters, monographic
  articles.
2 year, November 1970, Yes, None.
March 1972, T.p. 32.   5000.
Per year £1.50.

4380 INDUSTRIAL ARCHAEOLOGY: Journal of the history
  of industry and technology. 1966.
(The Journal of Industrial Archaeology 1964-1965)
David & Charles (Publishers) Ltd., South Devon House,
  Newton Abbot, Devon.
4, + ○   History of industry and technology.
Book reviews, monographic articles.
A, November, Yes, None.
Per copy 65p, per year £2.50.
Indexed in: BHI.

4381 INTERNATIONAL JOURNAL OF NAUTICAL
  ARCHAEOLOGY AND UNDERWATER EXPLORA-
  TION. 1972.
Seminar Press (Harcourt, Brace, Jovanovich), 24-28
  Oval Road, London, NW1
1, ○ ‡ + *   World coverage of all aspects of underwater archaeology; excavation of land sites of
  nautical significance; relevant aspects of geology,
  ecology, oceanography, numismatics, ballistics,
  maritime law, photo-recording, data-processing,
  conservation.
Book notices, book reviews, letters, monographic
  articles.
2 years—, Yes, None.
March 1972, T.p. 248, Ad.p. 3
Per copy £2.50.

Key to reference symbols

○ popular   ‡ technical   = trade/professional

+ research   * society/institution   † house journal

4382 JOURNAL OF EGYPTIAN ARCHAEOLOGY. 1914.
Egypt Exploration Society, 2-3 Doughty Mews, London, WC1
1, =   Archaeology of Egypt to the end of the Roman period.
Book notices, book reviews, letters, monographic articles, news, obituaries.
No index.
T.p. 244.
Free to members.
Indexed in: BHI, IBZ.

4383 JOURNAL OF ROMAN STUDIES. 1911.
Society for the Promotion of Roman Studies, 31-34 Gordon Square, London, WC1.
1, * = +   Archaeology, art, literature and history of Italy and Roman Empire down to c A.D 700.
Book reviews, monographic articles.
A, −, Yes, 20 year.
T.p. 332, Ad.p. 11.   2400.
Per copy £3. (£4 to non-members).
Indexed in: BHI, IBZ

4384 LEVANT: Journal of the British School of Archaeology in Jerusalem. 1969.
British School of Archaeology in Jerusalem, 2, Hinde Mews, Marylebone Lane, London, W1M 5 RH.
1, +   The archaeology of Palestine and neighbouring countries from earliest times to about 1800 A.D.
Monographic articles, obituaries.
No Index.
IV (1972), T.p. 159, Ad.p. 2.   500.
Per copy £4. 20.

4385 MEDIEVAL ARCHAEOLOGY. 1957.
Society for Medieval Archaeology, c/o University College, Gower Street, London, WC1.
1, * + =   Post-Roman archaeology in Europe.
Book reviews, monographic articles.
5 years, −, Yes, None.
1400.
Per copy £3 personal, £4 institutional.
Indexed in: BHI.

4386 MILLNOTES. 1970.
J. Kenneth Major, 2 Eldon Road, Reading, RG1 4DH.
3, ‡   All aspects of the study of wind and watermills, their history, technology and preservation.
Book notices, book reviews, letters, monographic articles, reports.
No Index.
May 1972, T.p. 15.
Subscription on application.

4387 THE NEW DIFFUSIONIST: A Study of Inter-relationships in Cultural Anthropology. 1970.
G. Kraus. 39, West Street, Great Gransden, Sandy Beds.
4, + *   Ancient civilization as revealed through archaeology and ethnography and studied from angle of Diffusionist School. Controversial and analytical.
Book notices, book reviews, letters, monographic articles, obituaries.
A, October, Yes, None.
April 1972, T.p. 46.   20.
Per copy 20p, per year £1.

4388 NEWSLETTER OF THE SCOTTISH SOCIETY FOR INDUSTRIAL ARCHAEOLOGY. 1969.
S.S.I.A. c/o Dept. of Technology, Royal Scottish Museum, Edinburgh.
2, ○ ‡
No Index.
Free to members.

4389 PROCEEDINGS OF THE PREHISTORIC SOCIETY. 1935.
(Proceedings of the Prehistoric Society of East Anglia 1908-1935).
The Prehistoric Society, Dept of Archaelogy, Cambridge.
1/2, * = +   Aspects of prehistory throughout the World; main areas covered: British Isles, continental Europe, Africa, Australia, India.
Book reviews, monographic articles.
No Index.
1971, T.p. 672.   2000.
Per year £3.
Indexed in: BHI.

4390 WORLD ARCHAEOLOGY. 1969.
Routledge and Kegan Paul, 68-74 Carter Lane, London, EV4V 5EL.
3, ‡ +
Reviews and articles.
A, −, Yes, None.
June 1972.
Per copy £1.90, per year £4.50.

930.26[1]

SCOTLAND

4391 AYRSHIRE ARCHAEOLOGICAL AND NATURAL HISTORY SOCIETY COLLECTIONS. 1950.
(Archaeological collections of Ayrshire and Galloway; Archaeological collections of Ayr and Wigton)
c/o Ayr Public Library, 12 Main Street, Ayr.
2 yearly. + *   History, archaeology, and natural history of Ayrshire and adjoining areas.
Book notices, book reviews, monographic articles, obituaries.
In each vol.
T.p. 170.   1,000.
£2. Free to members.

4392 PROCEEDINGS OF THE SOCIETY OF ANTIQUARIES OF SCOTLAND. 1851.
The Society of Antiquaries of Scotland, National Museum of Antiquities, Queen Street, Edinburgh 1.
1, + * =   The prehistory and history of Scotland with an emphasis on archaeology.
Monographic articles, obituaries.
A, In each vol., Yes, Vols. 1-24, 25-48, 49-81.
T.p. c 200.   2000.
Per copy £3.
Indexed in: BHI, IBZ.

4393 TRANSACTIONS OF THE GLASGOW ARCHAEOLOGICAL SOCIETY.
Oliver & Boyd Ltd., Tweeddale Court, 14, High Street, Edinburgh 1.
4, * + =
Monographic articles.
No Index.
T.p. 60.
Subcription on application.

930.26[2]

IRELAND

4394 JOURNAL OF COUNTY KILDARE ARCHAEOLOGICAL SOCIETY. 1891.
Co. Kildare Arch. Society., Tullig, Dublin Rd., Naas.
1, + ‡   Archaeology, history, folk of Kildare and adjacent counties.
Book reviews, monographic articles.
6 year, At end of each vol., Yes, None.
No 3, 1968, T.p. 40.
Per copy £1.
Free to members.

4395 JOURNAL OF THE KERRY ARCHAEOLOGICAL AND HISTORICAL SOCIETY. 1968.
Society, Kerry County Library, Tralee, Co. Derry.

1, *   Archaeology, history and folklore, with particular reference to County Kerry.
Monographic articles.
A, −, Yes, None.
No. 5. 1972, T.p. 174.
Per copy £2.
Family Membership £3. Student 50p.

4396 ULSTER JOURNAL OF ARCHAEOLOGY. 1853.
Ulster Archaeological Society, 7 Sans Souci Park, Belfast 9.
1, = +   Local archaeology.
Monographic articles.
No Index.
Subscription on application.

930.26[3]
ENGLAND

4397 ARCHAEOLOGIA AELIANA. 1852.
Society of Antiquaries of Newcastle upon Tyne, Black Gate, Newcastle upon Tyne, 1.
1, + *   Antiquities and archaeology. Particularly relating to N.E. England.
Book reviews, monographic articles.
A, With volume, Yes, None.
T.p. c. 360.
Per year £3.15
Free to members.
Indexed in: BHI, IBZ.

4398 ARCHAEOLOGIA CANTIANA. 1858.
Kent Archaeological Society, The Museum, Maidstone, Kent.
1, * = +   History and archaeology of Kent.
Book notices, book reviews, monographic articles, obituaries.
A, with each volume, Yes, 5 year.
1971, T.p. 261.   c. 1200.
Per year £2.50.
Indexed in: BHI.

4399 BERKSHIRE ARCHAEOLOGICAL JOURNAL. 1930.
(Berks, Bucks and Oxon Archaeological Journal 1878-1930),
The Society, c/o 'Turstins' High St., Upton, Didcot, Berks.
1, ‡ + *   Antiquities and history of Berkshire.
Book reviews, monographic articles, obituaries, reports.
A, −, Yes, 25 years.
1969, T.p. 64.   c. 450.
Per Copy £1.50.
Indexed in: BHI, IBZ.

4400 BI-ANNUAL BULLETIN OF THE WILTSHIRE ARCHAEOLOGICAL AND NATURAL HISTORY SOCIETY. 1966.
(Bulletin: Wiltshire Archeological and Natural History Magazine 1960-1962),
The Society, 41 Long Street, Devizes, Wilts.
2, * ○   Local history, natural history of the county of Wiltshire.
Book notices, book reviews, monographic articles.
No Index.
T.p. 20.
Free to members.

4401 BRADFORD ANTIQUARY. 1881.
Bradford Historical & Antiquarian Society, Mechanics Institute, Bridge Street, Bradford, 1.
Irregular, * + ○
Monographic articles, news.
No Index.
T.p. 80.
Per copy £1.

4402 BRITISH ARCHAEOLOGICAL ABSTRACTS. 1968.
Council for British Archaeology, 8 St. Andrew's Place, London, NW1 4LB.
2, +   Archaeology of Gt. Britain and Ireland from Palaeolithic to about A.D. 1500; some coverage of later periods, and also some coverage of relevant Continental publications.
Abstracts.
A, October, Yes, 5 year.
April 1972, T.p. 98.   c. 650.
Per year £5 for instns., £2.50 for indivs.

4403 CAMERTONIA. 1947.
Bath & Camerton Archaeological Society, 61 Pulteney Street, Bath.
= ‡ +
No Index.
Free to members.

4404 COMMITTEE FOR NAUTICAL ARCHAEOLOGY: NEWSLETTER.
Institute of Archaeology, 31-4 Gordon Square, London, WC1.
4, ○ +
No Index.
Free to members.

4405 CORNISH ARCHAEOLOGY. 1962.
(Proceedings of the West Cornwall Field Club, 1954-1961).
Cornwall Archaeological Society, c/o Institute of Cornish Studies, Trevenson House, Pool, Redruth, Cornwall.
1, ○ ‡ +   Entire field of past, Cornwall and Scilly—includes industrial and settlement archaeology, conventional prehistory and protohistory, some local history.
Book reviews, monographic articles.
Prob. 10 yearly.
1970, T.p. 150, Ad.p. 1.   c. 600-650.
£2 members, £2.50 non-members.

4406 DERBYSHIRE ARCHAEOLOGICAL JOURNAL. 1961.
(Journal of the Derbyshire Archaeological & Natural History Society 1879-1960).
The Society, 35 St. Mary's Gate, Derby.
1, * + =   Archaeology and history of Derbyshire.
Book notices, book reviews, monographic articles, news.
A, −, No, 10 year.
Free to members.
Indexed in: BHI.

4407 DERBYSHIRE MISCELLANY: local history bulletin of the Derbyshire Archaeological Society. 1956.
The Society, 35 St. Mary's Gate, Derby.
2, * + = ○   Any Derbyshire history paper not suited to the main Society journal.
Book notices, book reviews, letters, monographic articles, news.
2 year, −, No, None.
T.p. 70.   300.
Per copy 60p.

4408 DEVON ARCHAEOLOGICAL SOCIETY: PROCEEDINGS. 1929.
The Society, c/o Royal Albert Museum, Queen Street, Exeter.
1, * +
Monographic articles.
5 year, −, No, None.
T.p. 36.
Free to members.
Indexed in: BHI.

4409 EAST HERTS ARCHAEOLOGICAL SOCIETY NEWSLETTER. 1949.
The Society, 27 West Street, Hertford.
2, =   Archaeological activities, discoveries, news in the county.

No Index.
T.p. 4.
Free to members.
Indexed in: BHI.

4410 HERTFORDSHIRE ARCHAEOLOGY. 1968.
(East Herts Archaeological Society Transactions 1899-1967).
East Herts Archaeological Society & St. Albans & Herts Archaeological & Architectural Society, 27 West Street, Hertford.
2 yearly, = +   Excavations, research and documentary studies.
Monographic articles.
No Index.
T.p. 150.
Free to members.

4411 JOURNAL OF THE CHESTER ARCHAEOLOGICAL SOCIETY. 1967.
(Journal of the Chester & North Wales Architectural, Archaeological & Historic Society 1850-1966).
The Society, c/o John Sherratt & Son Ltd., St. Ann's Press, Park Rd., Altrincham.
1, + *   Archaeology, history and architecture of Chester, Cheshire and N. Wales.
Monographic articles, obituaries.
No Index.
£2.50 p.a. for individual members, £4 p.a. for libraries and institutions.

4412 LINCOLNSHIRE HISTORY AND ARCHAEOLOGY. 1966.
(Lincolnshire Architectural and Archeological Society Transactions 1850-1964; Lincolnshire Historian 1947-1965).
Lincolnshire Local History Society, 86 Newland, Lincoln.
1, * +   All aspects of archaeology and history of the county including architecture, literature, biography.
Book notices, monographic articles.
No Index.
Free to members.

4413 THE LONDON ARCHAEOLOGIST. 1968.
The London Archaeologist Publishing Committee, 7 Coalecroft Road, London, SW15.
4, ○ +   Provides up-to-date news on London's archeology through reports of recent excavations, articles on important topics by research workers, notes on special projects, details of current excavations.
Book reviews, letters, monographic articles.
No Index.
Spring 1972, T.p. 25, Ad.p. 2.   1800.
Per copy 15p, per year 60p.

4414 NORFOLK ARCHAEOLOGY. 1846.
Norfolk & Norwich Archaeological Society, Garsett House, St. Andrew's Hall Plain, Norwich, NOR 16J.
1, * = ‡ +   Archaeology of Norfolk.
Monographic articles, obituaries.
4 year, —, Yes, 40 years.
T.p. 120.
Free to members.
Indexed in: BHI.

4415 NORTHAMPTONSHIRE ARCHAEOLOGY: Bulletin of the Northamptonshire Federation of Archaeological Societies. 1973.
(Bulletin of the N.F.A.S. 1966).
Northamptonshire Federation of Archaeological Societies, c/o Department of Adult Education, The University, Leicester.
1, + ○   Reports of archaeological fieldwork/interim notes on excavations/short archaeological notes/all on matters within Northants or close to the county's borders.
Monographic articles.

No Index.
April 1970, T.p. 64.
Per copy 40p.

4416 NORTHERN NOTES. 1967.
'Northern Notes', 2 Whinway, Washington, Co. Durham.
4, ○ +   Historical and bibliographic material relating to Northumbria published for record purposes, incl. transcripts of documents, architectural and archaeological drawings, etc.
Letters, monographic articles.
Occasional, Proposed 1973, No, None.
Vol. 3, 1970, T.p. 4.   250.
Per copy 15p, per year 60p.

4417 OLD CORNWALL. 1925.
Federation of Old Cornwall Societies, 'Pengarth' Trewirgie Hill, Redruth, Cornwall.
2, ○ +   Folklore, antiquities, language, dialect, history, genealogy etc. of Cornwall.
Book notices, book reviews, monographic articles, obituaries.
6 year, After completion of vol. 12, No, None.
Spring 1972, T.p. 43.   1200.
Per copy 20p, per year 40p.

4418 PROCEEDINGS OF THE CAMBRIDGE ANTIQUARIAN SOCIETY. 1893.
(Reports & Communications of the Cambridge Antiquarian Society 1859-1892).
Imray Laurie Norie & Wilson Ltd., Wych House, St. Ives, Huntingdon.
1, +   Archaeology and local history of the Hunts and Cambridge region.
Monographic articles.
App. 40 yrs, —, Yes, None.
Vol. LXIII, 1971, T.p. 89.   c. 300.
Per copy £3.
Indexed in: BHI.

4419 PROCEEDINGS OF THE SUFFOLK INSTITUTE OF ARCHAEOLOGY. 1848.
The Institute, Bury St. Edmunds, Suffolk.
1, * + = ○   County archaeology and history.
Book reviews, monographic articles.
3 year, —, Yes, None.
T.p. 100.
Free to members.
Indexed in: BHI.

4420 THE RYEDALE HISTORIAN: A Periodical Publication by the Helmsley & District Group of the Yorkshire Archaeological Society. 1965.
Helmsley & District Arch. Soc., c/o 22 Station Road, Helmsley, York.
2 yearly, ○ + *   Local history and archaeology of southern half of North Yorks. Moors National Park, and western Vale of Pickering.
Book reviews, monographic articles.
No Index.
No. 6, 1972, T.p. 68.   500.
Per copy 35p.

4421 SHOPSHIRE NEWSLETTER. 1957.
Shropshire Archaeological Society, 20 Garmston Road, Shrewsbury.
2, ○ + *   Current news on archaeological, local historical and architectural activity in Shropshire together with brief research items.
Book notices, book reviews, monographic articles, obituaries.
None, No Index.
May 1972, T.p. 24.   400.
Per copy 25p, per year 50p.

4422 SOMERSET ARCHAEOLOGY AND NATURAL HISTORY PROCEEDINGS. 1961.
(Proceedings of the Somerset Archaeological & Natural History Society 1849-1967).
The Society, Taunton Castle, Taunton.

1, * +   Archaeology, natural history, local history.
Book notices, book reviews, monographic articles,
  obituaries.
A, –, Yes, None.
T.p. 132.
Free to members.
Indexed in: BHI.

4423 SUSSEX ARCHAEOLOGICAL SOCIETY NEWSLETTER. 1970.
Sussex Archaeological Society, Barbican House, Lewes, Sussex.
4, *   Notices about Society business and activities; interim reports on archaeological excavations, and notes on current research and publications in local history relating to the county of Sussex.
Book notices, book reviews, obituaries.
No Index.
June 1972, T.p. 4.   1600.
(Available only as part of Society subscription of £2.50).

4424 SUSSEX INDUSTRIAL HISTORY: Journal of the Sussex Industrial Archaeology Study Group. 1971.
Phillimore & Co. Ltd., Shopwyke Hall, Chichester, Sussex.
2, ○   Industrial history and archaeology and local history
Book notices, book reviews.
No Index.
Winter 1971/72, T.p. 32.
Per copy 40p, per year 75p.

4425 TRANSACTIONS OF THE ARCHITECTURAL AND ARCHAEOLOGICAL SOCIETY OF DURHAM & NORTHUMBERLAND. 1968.
Oriel Press Ltd. (for the Society), 32 Ridley Place, Newcastle upon Tyne, NE1 8LH.
Occasional, ‡ *   Antiquities and history of the counties of Durham and Northumberland.
Abstracts, monographic articles.
Occasional, –, No, None.
Vol. 2, 1970, T.p. 119.
Per copy £2.
Indexed in: BHI.

4426 TRANSACTIONS OF THE BIRMINGHAM & WARWICKSHIRE ARCHAEOLOGICAL SOCIETY. 1971.
(Trans. Birmingham Archaeological Society 1899-1970, Birmingham & Midland Institute, Archaeological Section Transactions 1870-1898).
Birmingham & Warwickshire Archaeological Society, Birmingham & Midland Institute, Margaret St., Birmingham.
1, + *   Archaeological activity in Warwickshire and the West Midlands and aspects of local history.
Book reviews, monographic articles.
Vols. 1-69 indexed in 1954, separately, –, None.
Vol. 79, T.p. 122.
Free to members only.

4427 TRANSACTIONS OF THE BRISTOL & GLOUCESTERSHIRE ARCHAEOLOGICAL SOCIETY. 1876.
The Bristol & Glos. Arch. Society, 45a Henley Grove, Henleaze, Bristol, BS9 4EQ.
‡ +   Excavations, history, heraldry, biography.
Book notices, book reviews, monographic articles, obituaries.
A, –, Yes, 10 year.
1972, T.p. 255.   1000.
Per copy £2, per year £1.05, Free to members.
Indexed in: BHI.

4428 TRANSACTIONS OF THE CUMBERLAND AND WESTMORLAND ANTIQUARIAN AND ARCHEOLOGICAL SOCIETY. 1866.
Titus Wilson & Son Ltd., 28 Highgate, Kendal.
1, = +   Archaeology, history, geneology, etc.
Book reviews, letters, monographic articles.
No Index.
T.p. 250.
Free to members.
Indexed in: BHI.

4429 TRANSACTIONS OF THE LANCASHIRE AND CHESHIRE ANTIQUARIAN SOCIETY. 1883.
The Society, c/o The Portico Library, 57 Mosley Street, Manchester, 2.
1, * + =   Local history including social, economic, political, antiquarian etc, history and folk lore.
Book notices, book reviews, letters, monographic articles, obituaries.
A, with volume, Yes, 10 year.
T.p. 160.   450.
Free to members.
Indexed in: BHI.

4430 TRANSACTIONS OF THE LEICESTERSHIRE ARCHAEOLOGICAL & HISTORICAL SOCIETY. 1866.
The Society, Guildhall, Leicester.
1, * +
Monographic articles.
A, with volume, Yes, None.
Free to members.
Indexed in: BHI.

4431 TRANSACTIONS OF THE LONDON & MIDDLESEX ARCHAEOLOGICAL SOCIETY. 1855.
The Society, Bishopsgate Institute, 230 Bishopsgate, London, EC2.
1, + = *   History, topography and archaeology of Greater London.
Book notices, monographic articles, obituaries.
3 year, with last part of volume, Yes, None.
1971, T.p. 100.   600.
Per copy £2.10.
Indexed in: BHI.

4432 TRANSACTIONS OF THE SHROPSHIRE ARCHAEOLOGICAL SOCIETY (with which is incorporated the Shropshire Parish Register Society). 1878.
Shropshire Archeological Society, Attingham Park, Shrewsbury.
1, * + =   Archaeology, local history and architectural history of Shropshire.
Book reviews, monographic articles, obituaries.
3 years, –, Yes, None.
T.p. 60.   400.
Per copy £2.10.
Indexed in: BHI.

4433 TRANSACTIONS OF THE SOUTH STAFFORDSHIRE ARCHAEOLOGICAL AND HISTORICAL SOCIETY. 1969.
(Transactions Lichfield Archaeological and Historical Society 1961-1962, Transactions Lichfield and South Staffordshire Archaeological and Historical Society 1963-1968).
South Staffs. Archaeological and Historical Society, c/o 58 Wednesbury Road, Walsall, WS1 3RS.
1, * + = ○   Archaeological and historical subjects relating to South Staffordshire.
Monographic articles, obituaries.
No Index.
T.p. 74.
Per year £1.10.
Free to members.
Indexed in: BHI.

4434 TRANSACTIONS OF THE THOROTON SOCIETY OF NOTTINGHAMSHIRE. 1897.
Thoroton Society of Nottinghamshire, c/o The Honorary Secretary, 21 Mapperley Hall Drive, Nottingham, NG3 5EY.
1, * =   Expert articles on archaeological, historic and antiquarian subjects in Nottinghamshire.
A, –, Yes, None.

1970, T.p. 116.   c. 800.
Free to members only.
Indexed in: BHI.

4435 WILTSHIRE ARCHAEOLOGICAL AND NATURAL HISTORY MAGAZINE. 1854.
The Society, 41 Long Street, Devizes, Wilts.
1, * + ‡ = ○   Archaeology, local and natural history.
Book notices, book reviews, letters, monographic articles, obituaries.
A, with volume, Yes, None.
T.p. 199.
Free to members.
Indexed in: BHI.

4436 WILTSHIRE INDUSTRIAL ARCHAEOLOGY. 1969.
Salisbury & South Wilts Industrial Archaeological Society, The Secretary, 34 Countess Road, Amesbury, Wilts.
1, *   Any aspect of industrial archaeology in South Wiltshire.
Monographic articles.
No Index.
Oct. 1971, T.p. 31.   c. 350+.
Per copy 30p.

4437 WORCESTERSHIRE ARCHAEOLOGY NEWSLETTER. 1967.
Worcester City Museum, Foregate St., Worcester, WR1 1DT.
2, ○ + *   All current archaeological research; fieldwork, excavation, and documentary—in the county of Worcester.
Book notices, articles.
No Index.
December 1971, T.p. 19.
Free.

4438 YORKSHIRE ARCHAEOLOGICAL JOURNAL. 1893.
(Yorkshire Archaeological and Topographical Journal 1869-1892).
Yorkshire Archaeological Society, Claremont, Clarendon Rd., Leeds, LS2 9NZ.
1, + *   All aspects of the history and archaeology of Yorkshire, with occasional articles covering a wider area in the North of England.
Book reviews, monographic articles, obituaries.
4 yearly, 1971, Yes, None.
1971, T.p. 199.   1100.
Per year £2.50.
Indexed in: BHI, IBZ.

930.26[4]

WALES

4439 ARCHAEOLOGIA CAMBRENSIS: The Journal of the Cambrian Archaeological Association. 1846.
Cambrian Archaeological Association, c/o Edleston House, Queen's Road, Aberystwyth, Cards.
1, *   Archaeology and history of Wales and the Marches.
Book notices, book reviews, monographic articles, obituaries.
A, with issue 1846-1900; 1901-1950 in 1973, other.
1971, T.p. 144.   c. 1000.
Per copy £3.50.
Indexed in: BHI.

4440 CEREDIGION: journal of the Cardiganshire Antiquarian Society. 1950.
(Transactions of the Cardiganshire Antiquarian Society 1909-1940).
The Society, 26 Alban Square, Aberavon.
1, * + =
Monographic articles.
4 year, Last of period (1 vol = 4 years), Yes, None.
T.p. 147.
Free to members.
Indexed in: BHI.

4441 TRANSACTIONS OF THE ANGLESEY ANTIQUARIAN SOCIETY AND FIELD CLUB. 1913.
Hon. Secretary, c/o 22 Lon Ganol, Menai Bridge.
1, + *   History, literature and archaeology of Anglesey.
Book reviews, monographic articles, obituaries.
No Index.
T.p. c. 200.   1000.
Per year £1.

4442 TRANSACTIONS OF THE RADNORSHIRE SOCIETY. 1931.
The Radnorshire Society, c/o Radnorshire County Library HQ., Cefnllys Road, Llandrindod Wells, Radnorshire, Wales.
1, * =   Historical and antiquarian interest, including record material, relating to Radnorshire.
Book notices, book reviews, monographic articles, obituaries.
A, —, Yes, Vols. 1-26, 1956.
1971, T.p. 80.
Per copy 75p.
Free to members.
Indexed in: BHI.

938

GREECE

4443 GREECE AND ROME: Published for the Classical Association. 1931, New Series 1954.
Oxford University Press, Press Road, Neasden, London, NW10.
2, ○ +   Greek and Roman literary, historical and archaeological interest.
Book reviews, monographic articles.
A, —, Yes, None.
April 1972, T.p. 116, Ad.p. 8.   1800.
Per copy £1.25, per year £2.
Indexed in: BHI, IBZ.

941

SCOTLAND

4444 BORDER LIFE. 1966.
Border Life Publications Ltd., 27 Channel Street, Galashiels, Selkirk.
12, ○   Life in the seven Scottish border counties, social and historical.
Book reviews, letters, articles, new companies.
No Index.
T.p. 34, Ad.p. 14.
Per copy 15p, per year £2.50.

4445 ELGIN SOCIETY NEWSLETTER. 1971.
The Society, 80 Duncan Drive, Elgin, IV30 2NH.
○
No Index.
Per copy 5p.

4446 INVERNESS PICTORIAL. 1972.
(Northern Counties Magazine).
Ecceslitho, North Church Place, Inverness.
12, ○   Local news and views about people and places in the north.
Book notices, book reviews, commodity prices, letters, articles, new products, obituaries, patents, standards, tests.
No Index.
June 1972, T.p. 29, Ad.p. 11.   3050.
Per copy 15p.

4447 THE NEW SHETLANDER. 1947.
Shetland Council of Social Service, 4b Market St., Lerwick, Shetland.
4, * ○   Poetry, short stories, articles on all aspects of life and which help keep alive the Shetland dialect.
Book reviews, letters, articles.
No Index.
No. 99, 1972, T.p. 25, Ad.p. 11.   3000.
Per copy 15p.

4448 NORTH 7: A journal about development in the Highlands and Islands. 1967.
Highlands & Islands Development Board, Bridge House, 27 Bank Street, Inverness, IV1 1QR
4, = + ○   Current development in the Highlands and Islands. One issue per annum a precis of the HIDB Annual Report.
Book notices, book reviews, new companies, new products.
No Index.
May 1972, T.p. 26, Ad.p. 2.   7000.
Per copy 5p, per year 20p.

4449 THE PATRIOT. 1950.
The Scottish Patriots, 31 Howard Place, Edinburgh, E5 5JY.
6, ○   Current Scottish interests.
Articles, news.
No Index.
June/July 1972, T.p. 4.
Per copy 4p, per year 35p.

4450 SCOTIA REVIEW. 1972.
33a Huddart Street, Wick, Caithness.
3, ○
No Index.
Per copy 25p.

4451 SCOTS INDEPENDENT. 1926.
Scots Independent (Newpapers) Ltd., 16 Upper Bridge St., Stirling, FK8 1ER.
12, ○   Scottish political scene; Scottish culture, art, history.
No Index.
June 1972, T.p. 13, Ad.p. 1.
Per copy 10p, per year £1.50.

4452 SCOTTISH FIELD. 1903.
George Outram & Co. Ltd., 70 Mitchell Street, Glasgow, C1.
12, ○   Scottish scene—historical, topographical, social.
Book reviews, letters, articles, news.
No Index.
T.p. 40, Ad.p. 26.   52600.
Per copy 12p, per year £3.

4453 SCOTTISH STUDIES: journal of the School of Scottish Studies, University of Edinburgh. 1957.
University of Edinburgh, School of Scottish Studies, 27 George Square, Edinburgh.
2, * + =   Research into Scottish traditional life, including first-hand reports on fieldwork, tape recordings etc.
Book notices, book reviews, monographic articles, obituaries.
2 year, —, Yes, 10 year.
T.p. 96.
Per copy £1.25, per year £2.
Indexed in: BH1.

4454 TRAVEL TRADE GUIDE, SCOTLAND. 1969.
Scottish Tourist Board, 2 Rutland Place, Edinburgh.
1, =   Information on car hire, coach tours, a diary of events, handling agents, hotels paying commission, inclusive tours and information centres in Scotland and means of transport to Scotland
No Index.
1972, T.p. 88.   6000.
Free.

941.5

IRELAND

4455 ULSTER COMMENTARY.
N. Ireland Information Service, Stormont Castle, Belfast, 4.
12, ○   Topical articles on all aspects of N. Ireland life.
No Index.
May 1972, T.p. 16.   80000.
Free.

942

ENGLAND

4456 C.P.R.W. NEWSLETTER.
Welshpool Printing Company. Severn Street, Welshpool, (for Council for the Protection of Rural Wales).
3, * ‡   To keep members of the above society adequately informed regarding matters which affect the amenity and development in the countryside of Wales.
Book reviews, legal notes, letters, reports.
No Index.
T.p. 12.
Free to members.

4457 BEDFORDSHIRE MAGAZINE. 1947.
White Crescent Press Ltd., Crescent Road, Luton, Beds
4, + = ○   Bedfordshire life and history.
Book notices, book reviews, letters, articles.
2 year, Summer, Yes, None.
T.p. 44, Ad.p. 15.   4000.
Per copy 15p, per year £1.

4458 THE BLACKCOUNTRYMAN. 1968.
The Black Country Society, 49 Victoria Rd., Tipton, Staffs.
4, +   All aspects of Black Country life with special reference to industrial history, archaeology, folk lore and culture.
Book reviews, articles.
No Index.
Winter 1972, T.p. 72.   4000.
Per copy 17p.
Free to members.

4459 BRADFORD BYSTANDER. 1964.
Ilustrated County Magazine Group Ltd., 19 Piccadilly, Bradford 1.
12, ○   Social, sporting and industrial life.
Book reviews, letters, articles.
A, —, Yes, None.
Per copy 15p, per year £2.50.

4460 BUCKS LIFE AND THAMES VALLEY COUNTRYSIDE. 1960.
(Thames Valley Countryside).
Letchworth Printers Ltd., Norton Way North, Letchworth, Herts.
12, ○   County interest, industrial, social, historical and economic.
Book reviews, letters, articles.
None.
June 1972, T.p. 30, Ad.p. 10.   3500.
Per copy 15p, per year £2.25.

4461 CAMBRIDGESHIRE, HUNTINGDON AND PETERBOROUGH LIFE. 1966.
Cambridgeshire Life Limited, 2 Crown Yard, St. Ives, Huntingdonshire.
12, ○   Social life and popular topography.
Articles, news.
No Index.
T.p. 43, Ad.p. 21.
Per copy 20p, per year £2.50.

4462 CANTIUM: a magazine of Kent local history. 1969.
Phillimore and Co,(for Kent Council of Social Service) Phillimore and Co, Shopwyke Hall, Chichester, Sussex.
4, ○ +   Local history in Kent; emphasis on source material. Notes and queries and news of local history societies in Kent.
Book notices, book reviews, letters, monographic articles.
No Index.
Spring 1972, T.p. 23, Ad.p. 2.   400.
Per copy 27½p, per year £1.05.

4463 CHESHIRE AND NORTH WALES. DEESIDER.
Cheshire and North Wales Newspaper Co. Ltd., 8 Bridge Street, Chester.
12, ○   Popular history and topography.
Monographic articles.
No Index.
T.p. 29, Ad.p. 12.
Per copy 15p.

4464 CHESHIRE LIFE. 1934.
Whitethorn Press Ltd., (a member of the Thomson Organisation) Thomson House, Withy Grove, Manchester, M60 4BL.
12, ○/*   County of Cheshire in all aspects, both modern, historical and topographical.
Book reviews, legal notes, letters, articles, new companies.
No Index.
June 1972, T.p. 37, Ad.p. 63.   13006.
Per copy 20p, per year £3.

4465 COMMONWEALTH: Journal of the Royal Commonwealth Society. 1970.
(Commonweath Journal 1961-1969)
The Society, 18 Northumberland Avenue, London WC2.
6, * + = ○   Commonwealth affairs world wide.
Book notices, book reviews, letters, monographic articles, news.
A, —, Yes, None.
T.p. 43, Ad.p. 14.
Per copy 20p,
Free to members.

4466 COTSWOLD LIFE. 1967.
Roy Faiers Ltd, 8A St Davids Hill, Exeter.
12, ○   Topical, historical, geographical interest.
Book reviews, letters, articles, news.
No Index.
T.p. 68, Ad.p. 24.
Per copy 15p, per year £2.50.

4467 COUNTRY QUEST. 1960.
North Wales Newspapers Ltd. Caxton Press, Oswestry, Salop.
12, ○   Country subjects related to Wales and the border counties.
Book notices, book reviews, letters, monographic articles.
A, September or October issues, No, None.
June 1972, T.p. 41, Ad.p. 25.   9000.
Per copy 25p, per year £2.34.

4468 THE DALESMAN. 1939.
Dalesman Publishing Co. Ltd., Clapham, Via Lancaster.
12, ○   Yorkshire history and topography.
Book reviews, letters, articles, news.
No Index.
T.p. 55, Ad.p. 36.
Per copy 15p, per year £1.50.

4469 DEFEND KENT. 1967.
Wildlife and Country Photos Ltd., Orcombe, Peckham Bush, Tonbridge, Kent.
1, ○   Conservation in Kent, with some reference to the wider issues.
Book notices, book reviews, letters, articles.
No Index.
Oct. 1971, T.p. 41, Ad.p. 6.   5000.
Per copy 15p, per year 15p.

4470 DERBYSHIRE LIFE AND COUNTRYSIDE. 1964.
(The Derbyshire Countryside—1931-1964)
Derbyshire Countryside Ltd., Lodge Lane, Derby DE1 3HE.
12, ○   Reflects every facet of life in Derbyshire from personalities and social events to local history and nature notes etc.
Book reviews, letters, articles, new companies, new products, obituaries.
No Index.
June 1972, T.p. 36, Ad.p. 47.   14000.
Per copy 15p, per year £2.40.

4471 DEVON LIFE. 1965.
Roy Faiers Ltd., 8A St Davids Hill, Exeter.
12, ○   County magazine including articles of topical, geographical and historic interest.
Book reviews, letters, monographic articles, news.
No Index.
T.p. 68, Ad.p. 24.
Per copy 15p, per year £2.50.

4472 DORSET: the county magazine. 1967.
Dorset Publishing Co., Milborne Port, Sherborne, Dorset.
6, ○ +   Historical and countryside magazine devoted entirely to the county of Dorset and with a news section dealing with conservation, the environment and pollution problems, local history studies.
Book notices, book reviews, letters, monographic articles.
No Index.
4, 1972, T.p. 60, Ad.p. 15.   10500.
Per copy 20p, per year £1.60.

4473 EAST ANGLIAN MAGAZINE. 1935.
East Anglian Magazine Ltd., 6 Great Colman Street, Ipswich 1P4 2AE.
12, ○   All aspects of East Anglia, including its history, geography, humour and present day developments.
Book reviews, letters, articles.
A, November, Yes, None.
July 1972, T.p. 40, Ad.p. 20   10000.
Per copy 18p, per year £2.80.

4474 EAST COAST DIGEST AND GREENWICH TIMES. 1972.
Conway Maritime Press Ltd., 7 Nelson Road, London, SE10.
4, ○   All matters of interest on the East Coast area: historical, topographical, social, industrial.
Book notices, book reviews, letters, monographic articles.
A, December, Yes, None.
Summer 1972, T.p. 96, Ad.p. 6.   2000.
Per copy 50p, per year £2.

4475 EAST COAST MARINER. 1970.
(Norfolk Sailer)
Norfolk Nautical Society, Opie House, Castle Meadow, Norwich NOR O3D.
+ *   Maritime history with particular reference to Norfolk and Suffolk.
Book notices, book reviews, letters, monographic articles.
No Index.
No 19, 1971, T.p. 32.
Per copy 15p, per year 75p.
Free to members.

4476 EAST RIDING BYSTANDER. 1970.
(Beverley Bystander, 1968-1969).
Treharne Publications (Hull) Ltd., Midland Bank Chambers, 9, Lairgate, Beverley, Yorkshire.

12, * ○ Cultural, social and county life of region. Also carries features on various aspects of the region such as residential and/or industrial developments.
Book reviews, commodity prices, letters, articles, new products, tests.
A, —, Yes, None.
April 1972, T.p. 36, Ad.p. 20.
Per copy 15p, per year £2.50.

4477 ESSEX COUNTRYSIDE. 1952.
Letchworth Printers Ltd., Norton Way North, Letchworth, Herts.
12, ○ County interest, industrial, social, historical and economic.
Book reviews, letters, articles.
No Index.
July 1972, T.p. 40, Ad.p. 50. 30000.
Per copy 18p, per year £2.70.

4478 ESSEX JOURNAL. 1966.
Phillimore & Co. Ltd., (for the Essex Archaeological & Historical Congress) Shopwyke Hall, Chichester, Sussex.
4, + * Articles on the local history and archaeology of the County of Essex (including London Boroughs formerly in Essex); reports of the Congress, local societies, country and local authorities on planning, development conservation, etc.
Book notices, book reviews, letters, monographic articles.
A, January, No, None.
Summer 1972, T.p. 28, Ad.p. 3. 1000.
Per copy 25p, per year £1.

4479 GUILDFORD AND DISTRICT OUTLOOK incorporating West Surrey Outlook and Going Places. 1923.
Woking Review Ltd., 1 Duke Street, Woking, Surrey.
12, ○ Local, topical, newsmagazine with family appeal.
No Index.
May 1972, T.p. 24, Ad.p. Most.
Per copy 4p.

4480 HAMPSHIRE: The County Magazine. 1960.
Paul Cave Publications Ltd., 39 Above Bar, Southampton, Hampshire.
12, ○ Dealing with the major problems confronting the inhabitants of the county and also dealing with the county's historic tradition.
Books notices, book reviews, commodity prices, letters, articles, new companies, new products, obituaries, patents, standards, tests.
No Index.
June 1972, T.p. 40, Ad.p. 40. 11376.
Per copy 15p, per year £2.40p.

4481 HERTFORDSHIRE COUNTRYSIDE. 1945.
Letchworth Printers Ltd., Norton Way North, Letchworth, Herts.
12, ○ County interest, industrial, social, historical and economic.
Book reviews, letters, articles.
No Index.
July 1972, T.p. 49, Ad.p. 25. 12000.
Per copy 15p, per year £2.25.

4482 ILLUSTRATED BRISTOL NEWS. 1959.
Illustrated County Magazine Group Ltd., The Radcliffe Press, Hogg Lane, Radcliffe on Trent, Nottingham.
12, ○ = Covers the social, industrial and sport of Bristol, Bath, Weston-Super-Mare and surrounding counties.
Book reviews, articles.
No Index.
May 1972, T.p. 44, Ad.p. 32. 9247.
Per copy 20p, per year £2.80.

4483 IN BRITAIN: Coming Events. 1964.
(Coming Events in Britain—1930-1964)
British Tourist Authority, 64 St. James's Street, London, SW1A 1NF.
12, ○ Articles of general tourist interests. Numerous photographic and other illustrations in colour and black and white. Coming events, shows, tournaments, royal occasions, festivals etc.
Book reviews, letters.
A, Indexes issued at irregular intervals, No, None.
July 1972, T.p. 40, Ad.p. 19. 153755.
Per copy 20p, per year £2.50.

4484 JERSEY LIFE.
Jersey Life Ltd., Grosvenor Street, St. Helier, Jersey. CI.
12, ○ Social and topographical.
Book notices, book reviews.
No Index.
T.p. 48, Ad.p. 40.
Per copy 15p, per year £2.50.

4485 JOURNAL OF THE LONDON SOCIETY. 1913.
The Society, 4 Carmelite Street, London, EC4
3/4, * To stimulate a wider concern for the City and its preservation from all points of view.
Book reviews on London, letters.
No Index.
T.p. 11.
Free to members.

4486 KENT: Journal of the Association of Men of Kent and Kentish Men. 1902.
Association of Men of Kent and Kentish Men, Cornwallis House, Pudding Lane, Maidstone.
4, * History and topography of Kent.
Book reviews, legal notes, articles, reports.
No Index.
Spring 1972, T.p. 20, Ad.p. 2. 5600.
Per copy 6p.
Free to members.

4487 KENT LIFE. 1962.
Kent Messenger Group, 123 Week Street, Maidstone, Kent.
12, ○ Local history and topography.
Book reviews, letters, articles, news.
No Index.
T.p. 44, Ad.p. 60. 12000.
Per copy 15p, per year £2.50.

4488 KNOW BRITAIN. 1952.
Educational Publications Ltd., East Ardsley, Wakefield.
2, ○
Book notices, book reviews.
No Index.
T.p. 96.
On request.

4489 LANCASHIRE LIFE. 1947.
Whitethorn Press Ltd., (a member of the Thomson Organisation.) Thomson House, Withy Grove, Manchester, M60 4BL.
12, ○ * Reflecting the activities of the County with specific emphasis on its social, scholastic and town life.
Book reviews, letters, articles, new companies.
No Index.
June 1972, T.p. 34, Ad.p. 58. 16807.
Per copy 20p, per year £3.

4490 LEEDS AND WEST RIDING TOPIC.
(Leeds and Harrogate Topic 1967-1971)
John Ball Publications Ltd., Topic House, 389 Alfred Street North, Nottingham. NG3 1AA.

Key to reference symbols

○ popular   ‡ technical   = trade/professional

+ research   * society/institution   † house journal

12, ○   Social, commercial industrial life of the area.
Book reviews, articles, new products.
No Index.
May 1972, T.p. 41, Ad.p. 41.
Per copy 15p, per year £2.25.

4491 LEEDS GRAPHIC. 1958.
Illustrated County Magazine Group Ltd., Carr Crofts,
 Armley, Leeds, LS12 3HA
12, ○   Social, sporting and business life of Leeds and
 surrounding areas.
Book reviews, monographic articles.
No Index.
Per copy 15p, per year £3.

4492 LEICESTER AND RUTLAND TOPIC.
John Ball Publications Ltd., Topic House, 398 Alfred
 Street North, Nottingham, NG3 1AA.
12, ○   Social, commercial and industrial life of
 the area.
Book reviews, articles, new products.
No Index.
December 1971, T.p. 53, Ad.p. 53.
Per copy 15p, per year £3.

4493 LEICESTER GRAPHIC. 1955.
58 Granby Street, Leicester.
12, ○   Local history and topography.
Book reviews, letters, articles, news.
No Index.
Per copy 20p, per year £3.

4494 LIBRARY NOTES. 1972.
Royal Commonwealth Society, Northumberland
 Avenue, London WC2N 5BJ.
10, =
No Index.
Per year £1.

4495 LINCOLNSHIRE LIFE. 1961.
Lincolnshire Life Ltd., Barclay's Bank Chambers,
 Victoria Street, Grimsby.
12, ○   County lore, tradition, history etc.
Book reviews, letters.
No Index.
T.p. 46, Ad.p. 26.   15747.
Per copy 20p, per year £2.50.

4496 LONDON SOCIETY JOURNAL. 1913.
The Society, 3 Dean's Yard, London SW1.
3/4, * + = ○   History, archaeology, architecture and
 current developments.
Book reviews, monographic articles,
No Index.
T.p. 16.
Free to members.

4497 THE MANCHESTER REVIEW. 1936.
The Manchester Cultural Committee, The Central
 Library, St. Peter's Square, Manchester M2 5PD.
2, ○ *   Articles of local (i.e. Manchester and
 district) interest and on bibliographical, literary
 and cultural topics; and on services provided by
 the Cultural Committee.
Occasional book notices and book reviews,
 monographic articles.
3 yearly, –, Yes, None.
Spring 1972, T.p. 32.   400.
Per year 25p.

4498 MANCHESTER SKETCH. 1966.
Illustrated County Magazine Group Ltd., Hogg Lane,
 Radcliffe-on-Trent, Nottingham.
12, ○   Social, sporting and industrial life of Manchester
 and district.
Book reviews, articles.
No Index.
Per copy 15p, per year £2.50.

4499 NATIONAL TRUST NEWS. 1972.
(National Trust and Newsletter 1868-1971)
The National Trust, 42 Queen Annes Gate, London, SW1.
3, ○ *   Preservation and presentation of historic
 building and unspoilt countryside, specially those
 owned by the National Trust.
Book notices, book reviews, letters, articles, obituaries.
No Index.
June 1972. T.p. 13, Ad.p. 6.   280000.
Free to members.

4500 NORFOLK FAIR. 1967.
Roy Faiers Ltd., Cucumber Lane, Brandall, Norfolk.
12, ○   County interest, history.
Letters, monographic articles.
No Index.
T.p. 42, Ad.p. 26.   7000.
Per copy 15p, per year £2.50.

4501 NORTH MAGAZINE. 1971.
North Magazine, 49 Stonegate, York.
12, ○   All aspects of life from history to sport, archi-
 tecture to cookery, in Northumberland, Durham and
 North Yorkshire.
Book notices, book reviews, letters, articles, new
 products, obituaries.
No Index.
May 1972, T.p. 33, Ad.p. 7.   5000.
Per copy 24p, per year £2.94.

4502 NORTHAMPTON AND COUNTY INDEPENDENT. 1905.
Northampton Independent Ltd., (part of United News-
 papers Ltd.) The Parade, Northampton.
12, ○   Popular history and topography.
No Index.
June 1972, T.p. 32, Ad.p. 32.   5700.
Per copy 10p.

4503 NORTHAMPTONSHIRE AND BEDFORDSHIRE LIFE.
 1969.
Cambridgeshire Life Limited, 2 Crown Yard, St. Ives,
 Huntingdonshire.
6, ○   Local history and topography.
No Index.
T.p. 44, Ad.p. 22.
Per copy 20p.

4504 NORTHAMPTONSHIRE PAST AND PRESENT: Journal
 of the Northamptonshire Record Society. 1948.
Northamptonshire Record Society, Delapre Abbey,
 Northampton.
1, + *   Northamptonshire history.
Book notices, book reviews, monographic articles,
 obituaries.
After end of each volume (6 issues), Yes, None.
1971/72, T.p. 67, Ad.p. 5.   c.4000.
Per year 15p, and Free to members.

4505 THE NORTHUMBRIAN. 1971.
The Northumbrian Publishing Co., 36 St. Marys Place,
 Newcastle upon Tyne, 1.
6, ○ *   Country news, local history, tourism and
 outdoor pursuits.
Book reviews, commodity prices, letters, articles,
 obituaries, tests.
No Index.
June/July 1972, T.p. 12, Ad.p. 4.   18000.
Per copy 12p, per year 85p.

4506 NOTTINGHAM TOPIC.
John Ball Publications Ltd., Topic House, 389 Alfred
 Street North, Nottingham, NG3 1AA.
12, ○   Social, commercial and industrial life of the
 area.
Book reviews, articles, new products.
No Index.
March 1972, T.p. 50, Ad p. 50.
Per copy 15p, per year £2.50.

4507 OMMA: Here in Cornwall. 1971.
Kernow Branch of Celtic League, c/o Lodener Press,
14/16 Market St., Padstow, Cornwall.
1, * ○   Cornish affairs and Inter Celtic relations.
Book notices, book reviews, letters, monographic articles, obituaries
A,—, No, 2 year.
20/6/1972, T.p. 22.   500.
Per copy 20p.

4508 PROGRESS WALES. 1970.
(Industrial Wales 1946-1969).
Development Corporation for Wales, 15 Park Place, Cardiff.
4, + = ‡   General survey and news of industry for executives, personnel managers etc.
Articles, new companies, news, new products.
No Index.
3000.
Free to members.

4509 PUBLICATIONS OF THE THORESBY SOCIETY. 1889.
The Society, 23 Clarendon Road, Leeds, LS8 9NZ.
1, ○ *   History of Leeds and neighbourhood.
Articles, obituaries.
No Index.
T.p. 114.
Per year £1.50. Free to members.
Indexed in: BHI.

4510 THE REVIEW for Addlestone, Byfleet, Chertsey, New Haw, Weybridge: Incorporating Byfleet Review. 1935.
Woking Review Ltd., 1 Duke Street, Woking, Surrey.
12, ○   Local, topical, newsmagazine with family appeal.
No Index.
June 1972, T.p. 24, Ad.p. Most.
Per copy Free.

4511 SHEFFIELD SPECTATOR. 1965.
Illustrated County Magazine Group Ltd., 22 Collegiate Crescent, Sheffield 10.
12, * ○   Social, sporting and industrial life of Sheffield.
Book reviews, articles, new companies, news, new products.
No Index.
T.p. 65, Ad.p. 27.
Per copy 15p, per year £2.50.

4513 STAFFORDSHIRE MAGAZINE: Incorporating Six Towns Magazine. 1972.
(Six Towns Magazine 1963-1971)
33 Albion Street, Hanley, Stoke-on-Trent, Staffs.
12, ○   History and topography of the locality.
Book reviews, letters, articles, new products, obituaries, tests.
No Index.
T.p. 46.
Per copy 17½, per year £2.50.

4514 SUSSEX LIFE. 1965.
Kent Messenger Group, 123 Week Street, Maidstone, Kent.
12, ○   Local history and topography.
Book reviews, letters, articles, news.
No Index.
T.p. 44, Ad.p. 60.   14318.
Per copy 15p, per year £2.40.

4515 THIS ENGLAND: A quarterly reflection of English life. 1968.
This England Ltd., PO Box 52, Cheltenham, Glos.
4, ○   Illustrated articles on England's famous people and places, history, folklore, crafts, etc.
Book notices, book reviews, letters, articles.
No Index.
Summer 1972, T.p. 70, Ad.p. 6.   52000.
Per copy 55p, per year £2.20.

4516 TOPICAL DATES AND FACTS NEWSLETTER. 1950.
Writers Publishing Association, BCM Buildings, London, WC1.
12, ○   Advance news of events, festivals, old customs, anniversaries etc of interest to writers, journalists.
No Index.
Per year £2.75 private; £4.20 newspapers; £6.30 libraries.

4517 TRANSACTIONS: Chigwell Local History Society. 1970.
Chigwell Local History Society, 3 Parndon House, Valley Hill, Loughton, Essex.
1, * +
Articles.
Infrequent,—, Yes, None.
No. 1, 1970, T.p. 38.   1000.
Per copy 40p.

4518 TRANSACTIONS OF THE HONOURABLE SOCIETY OF CYMMRODORION. 1892.
The Society, 118 Newgate Street, St. Pauls, London, EC1.
1, +   Encouragement of literature, science and art in Wales, Welsh history.
Monographic articles,
Irregular,—, No, None.
T.p. 141.
Subscription on application.

4519 WESSEX LIFE: Incorporating Somerset Life and Wiltshire Life. 1969.
(Somerset Life 1966).
R. Faiers Ltd., 8A St. David's Hill, Exeter.
12, ○   Topographical, geographical, historical items of interest to county residents.
Book reviews, letters, monographic articles, news.
No Index.
T.p. 68, Ad.p. 16.
Per copy 15p, per year £2.10.

4520 WOKING REVIEW. 1935.
(Woking Offers 1933-1935).
Woking Review Ltd., 1 Duke Street, Woking, Surrey.
12, ○   Local, topical news magazine with family appeal.
No Index.
May 1972, T.p. 32, Ad.p. Most.
Per copy Free.

4521 YORKSHIRE LIFE. 1964.
(Yorkshire Life Illustrated—1953/Yorkshire Illustrated—Yorkshire Life. Amalgamated August 1953).
Whitethorn Press Ltd., (a member of the Thomson Organisation,) Thomson House, Withy Grove, Manchester, M60 4BL.
12, ○   Events of general interest, historical and topographical.
Book reviews, letters, articles, obituaries.
No Index.
June 1972, T.p. 34, Ad.p. 46.   14545.
Per copy 20p, per year £3.

4522 YORKSHIRE RIDINGS MAGAZINE. 1969.
(The Ridings 1964, The Yorkshire Ridings, 1966).
The Ridings Publishing Company, 33 Beverley Road, Driffield, Yorkshire.
12, ○   A general Yorkshire magazine mixing topicality with articles of a wider county interest (historical, topographical).
Book reviews, articles, letters.
No Index
June 1972, T.p. 30, Ad.p. 22.   9000.
Per copy 15p, per year £2.25 (inc postage).

942.9

WALES

4523 FFLINT. 1968.
Gwasg Gwenffrwd, Talwrn Glas, Afonwen, Caerwys, Flintshire, CH7 5UB.

2, ○ +   All topics of relevance to Flintshire. (Bilingual).
Book notices, book reviews, letters, monographic articles, obituaries.
5 year, —, No, None.
Per copy 50p, per year £1.

943.9

EASTERN EUROPE

4524 THE SLAVONIC AND EAST EUROPEAN REVIEW. 1970.
(The Slavonic Review 1922-1969).
Cambridge University Press, PO Box 92, London, NW1 2DB.
4, +   All aspects of Eastern Europe and the USSR.
Book reviews, monographic articles.
A, last issue of volume, Yes, None.
July 1972, T.p. 156, Ad.p. 1.   1380.
Per copy £1.30, per year £4.
Indexed in: BHI, IBZ.

944

FRANCE

4525 BRITAIN—FRANCE: Journal of the Franco-British Society.
Franco-British Society, 1 Old Burlington Street, London, W1X 1LA.
3, * †   Franco-British affairs.
Abstracts, book notices, book reviews, monographic articles.
No Index.
Spring 1972, T.p. 14, Ad.p. 2.
Per year 20p. Free to members.

946

SPAIN

4526 ANGLO-SPANISH SOCIETY QUARTERLY REVIEW. 1957.
Anglo-Spanish League of Friendship, Anglo-Spanish Society, 5 Cavendish Square, London, W1M 9HA.
4, *
Book notices, book reviews, articles, obituaries.
No Index.
Spring 1972, T.p. 24, Ad.p. 7.   900.
Per copy 10p. Free to members.

4527 IBERIAN STUDIES: Journal of the Iberian Social Studies Association. 1972.
University of Keele. Managing Editor: Dr. J. Naylon, Department of Geography, University of Keele, Newcastle, Staffs., ST5 5BG.
2, + *   Iberian anthropology, economics, geography, history, politics and sociology. Mainly metropolitan Spain and Portugal, but also the modern overseas provinces.
Book notices, book reviews, letters, monographic articles.
With each issue, Spring/Autumn, Yes, A.
Spring 1972, T.p. 41.   300.
Per copy £2.

4528 REPORT ON SPAIN. 1971.
(Spain Today 1964-1971).
Curzon-Grantham Ltd., 31 St. James's Place, London, S.W.1.
4, ○ = *   Reflects political, economic, social, commercial and holiday events in Spain.
Articles.
No Index
Spring 1972, T.p. 12.   3000.
Free.

947

USSR

4529 F.C.I.—FEATURES AND NEWS FROM BEHIND THE IRON CURTAIN. 1951.
(Information Service of Free Czechoslovakia 1949-1951).
Free Czechoslovak Press Ltd., 4 Holland Rd., London, W14 8AZ.
48/50, +   Political, economic, military, cultural news and information about the Soviet orbit.
Book notices, book reviews, obituaries, parliamentary reports.
For internal use only.
12.7.1972, T.p. 4.   600.
Per year £5 individuals, £12 organisations and press.

4530 ABSEES: Soviet and East European Abstracts Series. 1970.
(Information Supplement to Soviet Studies 1964-1970).
University of Glasgow, 9 Southpark Terrace, Glasgow, W.2.
4, +   Abstracts from Soviet and East European books and press/Albania, Bulgaria, Czechoslovakia, East Germany, Hungary, Poland, Romania, USSR, Yugoslavia/; bibliographies; newsletter about Soviet studies in the U.K.
Abstracts, book notices, book reviews.
A, July, No, None.
April 1972, T.p. 278, Ad p. 16.   1000.
Per copy £1.75, per year £6.

4531 BRITISH-SOVIET FRIENDSHIP. 1956.
(Russia Today).
British Soviet Friendship Society, 36 St. Johns Square, London, EC1.
12, *   British-Soviet relations.
No Index.
T.p. 8.
Free to members, per year 90p.

4532 THE JOURNAL OF BYELORUSSIAN STUDIES. 1965.
The Anglo-Byelorussian Society, 230 Strand, London, W.C.2.
1, +   Byelorussian history, art, culture, ethnography, geography and all similar subjects.
Chronicle, book reviews, monographic articles, obituaries, reports.
A, —, Yes, 4 year.
1970, T.p. 120.   600.
Per copy 75p.

4533 SOVIET STUDIES. 1949.
University of Glasgow, Glasgow, W2.
4, + =
Book notices, book reviews, letters, monographic articles.
A, —, Yes, None.
T.p. 120.
Per copy £1, per year £3.50.
Indexed in: BHI, IBZ.

947.7

UKRAINE

4534 UKRAINIAN THOUGHT.
The Ukrainian Review, 49 Linden Gardens, Notting Hill Gate, London, W2.
4, +
Book reviews, letters, articles.
No Index.
T.p. 110.
Per copy 50p, per year £2.

948
SCANDINAVIA

4535 SAGA BOOK OF THE VIKING SOCIETY. 1908.
Viking Society for Northern Research University College London, Gower St., London, WC1.
1, * +   Scandinavian studies.
Book reviews, monographic articles.
A,—, Yes, 4 year.
1971-1, T.p. 219.   650.
Per copy £2.50.

948.9
DENMARK

4536 DENMARK: A quarterly review of Anglo-Danish relations. 1946.
(Anglo-Danish Review 1924-39).
Anglo-Danish Society, 7 St. Helen's Place, London, EC3.
4, * ○   Political, economic, social and cultural.
Book notices, book reviews, articles, obituaries.
No Index.
Spring 1972, T.p. 12, Ad.p. 8.   1000.
Per copy 12½p, per year 50p.

949.5
GREECE

4537 THE JOURNAL OF HELLENIC STUDIES. 1880.
Society for the Promotion of Hellenic Studies, 31-34 Gordon Square, London, WC1H 0PP.
1, * + =   Greek language, literature, history and art in the ancient, byzantine and modern periods.
Book notices, book reviews, monographic articles.
Vols. 9-42, published 1923, No.
1971, T.p. 240, Ad.p. 12.   2800.
Members £3, Non-members £4.
Indexed in: BHI, IBZ.

4538 KRIKOS: International Greek Review. 1950.
Krikos Ltd., 33 Mapesbury Road, London, NW2.
10, ○   Portrays life and activities of Greeks throughout the world. Contains general articles on Greek culture, history, economy and shipping.
Book notices, book reviews, letters, monographic articles, new products, obituaries.
No Index.
March 1972, T.p. 48, Ad p. 14.   7000.
Per year £4.

950
ASIA

4539 ASIA MAJOR: A British journal of Far Eastern studies. 1924.
Percy Lund, Humphries & Co. Ltd., Bradford.
2, +   General studies of the Far East.
Book notices, book reviews, monographic articles.
A,—, Yes, None.
T.p. 139, Ad p. 9.
Per year £5.
Indexed in: BHI, IBZ.

4540 ASIAN AFFAIRS: Journal of the Royal Central Asian Society. 1970.
(Proceedings of the Central Asian Society: 1903-1913
Journal of the Central Asian Society: 1914-1930
Journal of the Royal Central Asian Society 1931-1969)
Royal Central Asian Society, 42 Devonshire St., London, W1N 1LN.
3, * +
Book notices, book reviews, letters, monographic articles, obituaries.
A, October, Yes, None.
February 1972, T.p. 126.
Free to members.
Indexed in: BHI.

4541 BULLETIN OF THE SCHOOL OF ORIENTAL AND AFRICAN STUDIES, UNIVERSITY OF LONDON. 1940.
(Bulletin of the School of Oriental Studies, University of London, 1917-1940).
School of Oriental and African Studies, University of London, WC1.
3, +   Asian and African studies, with special reference to language, history, culture, and civilization.
Book notices, book reviews, articles, obituaries.
No Index.
June 1972, T.p. 230, Ad.p. 11.
Per copy £4, per year £12

4542 EASTERN WORLD. 1947.
Foreign Correspondents Ltd., 58 Paddington Street, London, W1.
12, = + *   Political and economic developments in Asia.
Book reviews.
A, December, Yes, None.
T.p. varies, Ad.p. varies.   6000.
Per year £2.

4543 JOURNAL OF CONTEMPORARY ASIA. 1970.
c/o 37 Macaulay Court, London, SW4 0QU.
4, +   Current political and economic developments in Asia.
Book notices, book reviews, monographic articles.
No Index.
Vol. 2, No. 2, 1972, T p. 96, Ad.p. 7.   725.
Per copy 95p, per year £3.

4544 JOURNAL OF THE ROYAL ASIATIC SOCIETY OF GREAT BRITAIN AND IRELAND. 1834.
(Transactions, 1827-1833).
The Royal Asiatic Society, 56 Queen Anne Street, London, W1M 9LA.
2, + * =   Investigation and encouragement of science, literature and the arts in relation to Asia.
Book reviews, letters, monographic articles, obituaries.
No Index.
T.p. 100, Ad.p. 10.   c. 1450.
Per copy £2.10, per year £4 20.
Indexed in: BHI.

4545 MODERN ASIAN STUDIES 1967.
Cambridge University Press, PO Box 92, London, NW1 2DB.
4, +   History, geography, politics, sociology, literature, economics and social anthropology of South Asia, South-East Asia, China and Japan.
Book reviews, monographic articles.
A, October, Yes, None.
3-4 October 1971, T.p. 120, Ad.p. 4.   1300.
Per copy £1.50, per year £5.

4546 SOUTH ASIAN REVIEW: Journal of the Royal Society for India, Pakistan and Ceylon. October, 1969.
(Asian Review 1967-1969).
Royal Society for India, Pakistan and Ceylon, 3 Temple Chambers, Temple Avenue, London, EC4Y 0HB.
4, + *   Politics, economics, sociology, religions, art and letters, and interpreting current events, in India, Pakistan and Ceylon. Large book section including review articles.
Book reviews, letters, monographic articles.
A, October, No, None.
April 1972, T.p. 90.   c. 1500.
Per copy 62½p, per year £2.50.
Indexed in: BHI, IBZ.

4547 USSR AND THIRD WORLD: A survey of Soviet and Chinese relations with Africa, Asia and Latin America. 1971.

Central Asian Research Centre, 1b Parkfield Street, London, N1 0PR.
8, + = All aspects of Soviet and Chinese relations with Third World countries—political, military, economic etc.—are covered. Material is drawn from newspapers, radio broadcasts and journals of many countries.
Notes.
No Index.
January 1972, T.p. 75.   400.
Per copy £1.50, per year £15.

951
CHINA

4548 BROADSHEET: China Policy Study Group. 1963.
China Policy Study Group, 62 Parliament Hill, London, NW3.
12, + * Politics and current affairs news relating to China.
Book reviews, articles.
No Index.
April 1972, T p. 4.
Per copy 4p, per year 80p.

951.5
TIBET

4549 SHAMBHALA: Occasional papers of the Institute of Tibetan Studies. 1971.
The Institute, 36 King Street, Tring, Herts.
Irregular, =
No Index.
T.p. 48.
Per copy 45p.

953
ARABIA

4550 THE ARAB WORLD: Journal of the Anglo-Arab Association. 1963.
Anglo-Arab Association, West End House, Hills Place, London, W1R 1AG.
4, + Modern developments in the Arab regions, archaeological discoveries, social changes and news of Arab and British people in London associated with the Middle East
News, articles.
No Index.
Winter 1971, T.p. 28, Ad p. 8   1000.
Per copy 20p, per year 90p.
Indexed in: BHI.

954.9
BANGLADESH

4551 BANGLADESH NEWSLETTER. 1971.
F. S. Jafri, 391 Kingston Road, London, SW20.
○
No Index.
Subscription on application.

956
MIDDLE EAST

4552 INTERNATIONAL JOURNAL OF MIDDLE EAST STUDIES. 1970.
Cambridge University Press, PO Box 92, London, NW1 2DB.
4, + Research into the social and cultural history of the Middle East from the seventh century to the present.
Book reviews, monographic articles.
A, October, Yes, None.
July 1972, T.p. 143. Ad.p. 5.   1600.
Per copy £2.50, per year £7.

4553 MIDDLE EAST INTERNATIONAL. 1971.
Middle East International Publishers Ltd., 4 Vincent Square, London, SW1.
12, ○ + Middle East current affairs
Book notices, book reviews, letters, articles, parliamentary reports.
No Index.
March 1972, T.p. 39, Ad.p. 4.   3500
Per copy 25p, per year £3.

4554 MIDDLE EASTERN STUDIES. 1964.
Frank Cass & Co Ltd, 67 Great Russell Street, London, WC1B 3BT.
3, + = Contemporary Middle East and its recent past.
Book notices, book reviews, monographic articles.
A, October, Yes, None.
January 1972, T.p. 136, Ad.p. 5.
Per copy £2, per year £6.
Indexed in: BHI.

4555 PALESTINE EXPLORATION QUARTERLY: Embodying the Quarterly Statement of the Palestine Exploration Fund. 1869.
Palestine Exploration Fund, 2, Hinde Mews, Marylebone Lane, London, W1.
2, + * To obtain and disseminate non-political information respecting ancient and modern Syria... (i.e. Syria, Lebanon, Jordan and Israel).
Book notices, book reviews, monographic articles, obituaries.
2 yearly, Last issue of year concerned 1911-1963, Yes.
July-December 1971, T.p. 144.
Per year £1.25.
Indexed in: BHI, IBZ.

959
INDOCHINA. VIETNAM

4556 INDOCHINA. 1970.
(Vietnam, 1969-1970).
Vietnam Solidarity Campaign, 182 Pentonville Road, London, N1.
9, ○ Current events in Indochina, U.S. war policy, British complicity, and international anti-war movements.
Book reviews, letters, articles, obituaries, parliamentary reports.
No Index.
Mar/June 1972, T.p. 7, Ad.p. 1.   1600
Per copy 6p, per year 60p.

960
AFRICA

4557 AFRICA: An International business, economic and political monthly. 1971.
Africa Journal Ltd., 28 Great Queen Street, London, WC2.
12, ○ + * Business, economic and political aspects of events in Africa, covering at least one country in depth in each issue.
Book notices, book reviews, letters, monographic articles.
A, January, Yes, None.
June 1972, T.p. 70, Ad.p. 30.   34500.
Per copy 25p, per year £2.50.
Indexed in: BHI, IBZ.

4558 AFRICA CONTEMPORARY RECORD. 1969.
Rex Collings Ltd., 6 Paddington St., London, W1.

1, +, =, *   Part one—Original essays on African affairs, Part Two—country by country survey (of every African Country), Part Three reprints of original documents concerning politics, religion, economics, finance, industry, education etc.
A, —, Yes, None.
1972, T.p. 1200, Ad.p. 3.   2500.
Per copy £12.50.

4559 AFRICA DIGEST. 1954.
(Information Digest 1952).
Africa Publications Trust, 48 Grafton Way, London, W1 5LB.
6, +   Political and economic matters affecting the African continent.
Book notices, book reviews, parliamentary reports.
Every 2 years, —, No, None.
Feb. 1972, T.p. 24.   2250.
Per year £2.

4560 AFRICA RESEARCH BULLETIN: (a) Political, Social & Cultural Series; (b) Economic, Financial & Technical Series. 1964.
Africa Research Limited, 1 Parliament St., Exeter, EX4 3DZ.
12 issues each in Series (a) and (b), +   Account of every significant development throughout Africa, information categorized under subject headings within the two series of the Bulletin.
6m, March and August, No, A.
June 15, 1972, T.p. 30.
Per year (a) £20, (b) £33.50, Combined £46.

4561 AFRICAN AFFAIRS: The Journal of The Royal African Society. 1901.
Oxford University Press, Press Road, Neasden, London, NW10.
4, +   A review of topics of current interest throughout the African continent, mainly in the fields of economics, politics, administration and recent history; reflecting a wide variety of professional and political views from both inside and outside Africa.
Book reviews, lectures, conference obituaries, papers.
A, —, Yes, None.
April 1972, T.p. 107, Ad.p. 6.   1000
Per copy £1, per year £3.50.
Indexed in: BHI, IBZ.

4562 THE AFRICAN COMMUNIST: Quarterly Journal of the South African Communist Party. 1959.
Inkululeko Publications, 39 Goodge Street, London, W1.
4, O *   Published 'in the interests of African solidarity and as a forum for Marxist-Leninist thought throughout our Continent', the journal features critical reviews of developments in African countries.
Book notices, book reviews, letters, monographic articles, obituaries.
A, —, Yes, None.
2nd Quarter 1972, T.p. 120.
Per copy 15p, per year 60p.

4563 BULLETIN OF THE AFRICAN STUDIES ASSOCIATION OF THE UNITED KINGDOM. 1964.
African Studies Association of the U.K. c/o Centre of West African Studies, PO Box 363, University of Birmingham B15 2SD
3, +, =   Progress of African studies in UK and other parts of world, including research in progress, review of publications etc.
Book notices, letters, articles, obituaries.
No Index.
April 1972, T.p. 34.
Per copy 40p and Free to members.

4564 GUERRILHEIRO. 1970.
Committee for Freedom in Mozambique, Angola & Guiné, 531 Caledonian Road, London, N7.

6, O   The liberation struggle in the Portuguese colonies, the situation in Portugal, Britain's role, foreign economic involvement, etc.
Book notices, book reviews, articles, new companies.
No Index.
March/April 72, T.p. 12.   1400.
Per copy 5p, per year 40p.

4565 INTERNATIONAL AFRICAN BIBLIOGRAPHY. 1971.
International African Institute, 10-11 Fetter Lane, London EC4A 1BJ.
4, =
No Index.
Per year £2.25.

4566 THE JOURNAL OF AFRICAN HISTORY. 1960.
Cambridge University Press, PO Box 92, London, NW1 2DB.
4, +   History of the whole African Continent from earlier times to the present.
Book reviews, monographic articles
A, October, Yes, None.
May 1972, T.p. 175, Ad.p. 4.   2500.
Per copy £1.50, per year £5.
Indexed in: BHI.

4567 NEW AFRICA. Africa Trade & Development. 1963.
(Africa Trade & Development 1959-1962).
Foreign Correspondents Ltd., 58 Paddington Street, London, W.1.
12, = +   Political and economic developments in Africa.
Book reviews.
A, December, Yes, None.
T.p. varies, Ad.p. varies.   6000.
Per year £2.

4568 SECHABA: Official Organ of the African National Congress, South Africa. 1967.
Sechaba Publications, 49 Rathbone Street, London, W1A-4NL.
12, +   Covers the political and economic situation in South Africa.
Book notices, book reviews, monographic articles.
No Index.
May 1972, T.p. 24.   20000.
Per year £1.50.

4569 SOUTH AFRICAN STUDIES. 1972.
Sechaba Publications, 49 Rathbone St., London, W1A-4NL.
4, +   Documents and discussion material on South Africa published by African National Congress of South Africa.
Monographic articles.
No Index.
No. 3. T.p. 96.   10000.
Per year 60p.

4570 ZAIRE AFRICA: A monthly digest of news and opinion. 1972.
E. D. O'Brien Organisation, 2 Old Burlington Street, London, W1X 2LH.
12, O
No Index.
T.p. 4.
Subscription on application.

963

ETHIOPIA

4571 ETHIOPIA OBSERVER: Journal of independent opinion, economics and the arts. 1957.
Mrs F. Holmans, 57 Carter Lane, London, EC4.
4, +
Monographic articles.
No Index.

973

U.S.A.

4572 AFRO-AMERICAN STUDIES. 1971.
Gordon & Breach, 41/42 William 4th Street, London, WC2.
4, ○ +   History, sociology, economics, psychology, and education, and includes information about their interdisciplinary aspects as well as centering its attention on the development of relevant interdisciplinary programs.
Book notices, book reviews, legal notes, letters, monographic articles, tests.
None.
Subscription on application.

4573 JOURNAL OF AMERICAN STUDIES. 1967.
Cambridge University Press, PO Box 92, London, NW1 2DB.
3, +   History, society, government, economics, politics, geography and literature of the USA.
Book reviews, monographic articles.
A, September, Yes, None.
April 1972, T.p. 128, Ad.p. 4.   1500.
Per copy £2, per year £4.
Indexed in: BHI.

4574 JOURNAL OF THE CONFEDERATE HISTORICAL SOCIETY. 1962.
Mr. M. A. Rich, Editor., 'Laceys', Berry Lane, Chorleywood, Herts.
4, *   Devoted to all aspects of the study of the American Civil War, with particular emphasis on the Confederate States of America.
Abstracts, book notices, book reviews, letters, monographic articles.
No Index.
Autumn 1971, T.p. 40.   300 approx.
Per year £1.50. Free to members.

4575 NEW WORLD ANTIQUITY. 1953.
Markham House Press, Ltd., 58 West Street, Brighton.
6, +   Antiquities of North and South America and their relationship to early history.
Book reviews, articles.
A, Middle of following year, Yes, None.
Jan/Feb. 1972, T.p. 24.   500.
Per year £2.

4576 NEWSLETTER: CONFEDERATE HISTORICAL SOCIETY. 1966.
The Society, c/o 'Laceys', Berry Lane, Chorleywood, Herts.
4, + = ○   Study of the American Civil War 1861-5.
Articles, news, letters.
No Index.
T.p. 12.
Free to members.

980

SUMATRA

4577 BERITA KADJIAN SUMATERA. 1971.
(Sumatra Research Bulletin).
The Sumatra Research Council, c/o Centre for South-East Asian Studies, The University of Hull, Hull, HU6 7RX.
2, = * +   Sumatra society, culture, economics, literature and development or change in all these spheres. Information about current research, recent publications, higher degree theses.
Book notices, book reviews, monographic articles, research notes and news.

T.p. 90.
Per copy 50p, per year £2.
Indexed in: BHI.

No Index.
May 1972, T.p. 59.   500.
Per copy 50p, per year £1.

981

BRAZIL

4578 BRAZIL JOURNAL. 1943.
Brazilian Chamber of Commerce in Great Britain, 35 Dover Street, London, W1X 3RA.
4, =   Trade and other affairs related to the two countries.
Book notices, book reviews, legal notes, letters, new companies, new products, patents, standards, tests.
No Index.
October/December 1971, T.p. 20, Ad.p. 15.   600.
Per year £1.50.

4579 NEWSLETTER OF THE LUSO-BRAZILIAN SECTION, ASSOCIATION OF BRITISH HISPANISTS. 1971.
Dr. R. C. Willis, Department of Spanish and Portuguese Studies, The University, Manchester, M13 9PL.
1, *   Cultural calendar and review of Luso-Brazilian affairs affecting British academics; notices of prizes, scholarships and assistantships; index of theses and research work in progress.
Book notices, letters.
A, —, No. None.
T.p. 20.   120.
Private distribution without subscription.

983

CHILE

4580 CHILEAN NEWS: Organ of the Anglo-Chilean Society. 1945.
The Society, 3 Hamilton Place, London, W1.
3, *   News from Chile particularly related to the UK, news of social events in Great Britain.
Book reviews, letters, articles, news, obituaries.
No Index.
T.p. 6.   500.
Free to members.

990

CARIBBEAN

4581 JOURNAL OF CARIBBEAN HISTORY. 1970.
Caribbean Universities Press (part of Xerox Group of the USA), (Order to Ginn & Co. Ltd., 18 Bedford Row, London, WC1R 4EJ).
2, +   Social, economic and constitutional history of the Caribbean and in related aspects of British, U.S. and Latin American history.
Monographic articles.
None.
Nov. 1970, T.p. 88, Ad.p. 4.
Per copy 88p, per year £1.50.

991

INDONESIA

4582 INDONESIAN NEWS.
Embassy of Republic of Indonesia, 38 Grosvenor Square, London W1.
○
Subscription on application.

993.1

NEW ZEALAND

4583 NEW ZEALAND NEWS. 1927.
The Tweeddale Press Ltd., 90 Marygate, Berwick-upon-Tweed, Northumberland.

52, ○ ‡ = *   Aiming to foster relationship between U.K., New Zealand and the Commonwealth.
Book notices, book reviews, commodity prices, legal notes, letters, articles, new companies, new products, obituaries, parliamentary reports, standards, tests.
No Index.
June, 1972, T.p. 17, Ad.p. 3.   9000.
Per copy 7½p, per year £3.75.

998
ARCTIC. ANTARCTIC

4584 BRITISH ANTARCTIC SURVEY BULLETIN. 1963.
British Antarctic Survey, 30, Gillingham Street, London, SW1 1HY.

3, + ‡ =   Monographic articles.
Every 5 issues, —, With list of contents and index for every 5 issues, None.
January 1972, T.p. 144.   c. 500.
Per copy £1.50, per year £4.50.

4585 POLAR RECORD. 1931.
Scott Polar Research Institute Cambridge CB2 1ER.
3, + * ‡   Historical and general interest related to the north and south polar and subpolar regions; field notes; obituaries of polar personalities; and a bibliography of recent polar literature.
Book notices, book reviews, letters, monographic articles, obituaries.
2 years, —, No, None.
January 1972, T.p. 195.   1250.
Per copy £1.25, per year £3.75.

LATE ENTRIES

0
GENERAL

02
LIBRARIES. LIBRARIANSHIP.

4586 NLL ANNOUNCEMENT BULLETIN: a guide to British reports, translations and theses. 1970.
National Lending Library for Science and Technology, Boston Spa, Yorkshire.
12, = ‡ +   Literature produces by British Government organisation, industry, universities and learned institutions.
No Index.
March 1973, T.p. 73.
Free.

4587 NLL REVIEW. 1971.
HMSO, PO Box. 569, London, SE1.
4, = ‡ +   News of activities, progress and research carried out by, or sponsored by, the National Lending Library for Science and Technology.
Book notices, book reviews, monographic articles, news, new products.
No Index.
October 1972, T.p. 32.
Per copy 50p, per year £2.18.

4588 STRESS.
Library Association, Yorkshire Branch, c/o Dept. of Librarianship, Polytechnic, Leeds.
=   Information on the changes in all kinds of public library in Yorkshire.
No Index.

4588A VINE. 1972.
Mrs. C. M. Overton, Information Officer, OSTI Library Automation Project, University Library, University Road, Southampton.
3/4, = ‡ +   Up to date picture of the activities of the projects and other automation work of special interest not reported elsewhere.
Articles, news.
No Index.
March 1973, T.p. 11.
Free to librarians, systems staff and lecturers.

028
READING

4589 GOOD READING. 1972.
United Writers Publications, Trevail Mill, Zennor, St. Ives.
2, ○ =
No Index.
T.p. 106.
Per copy 50p.

05
GENERAL PERIODICALS

4590 THE BILLINGHAM POST. 1952.
Imperial Chemical Industries Ltd., Agricultural Division, PO Box 1, Billingham, Teesside, TS23 1LB.
26, †   Information about the Agricultural Division of ICI and the people in it.
Articles, new products, standards, tests.
No Index.
16 June 1972, T.p. 8.   10300.
Free.

4591 BLACK OUTCRY. 1972.
E. Sparks, Norwood Technical College, Knights Hill, London, SE27.
○   Progressive black students and teachers.
No Index.
Per copy 5p.

4592 FURTHER ADVENTURES. 1972.
IA Publications, 14 Ridgeway, Putnoe, Bedford.
6, ○
No Index.
Per copy 7p.

4593 FUSS—Forum for University Staff and Students. 1968.
The University of Kent, The Editor, FUSS, Room 150, The Registry, University of Kent.
6, †   Provides a regular forum for discussion between staff, students and friends of the University... all matters relating to the University and to the world of education in general... Also has articles from educational specialists (e.g. MP's for Higher Education).
Book notices, book reviews, letters, monographic articles, new products, obituaries, reports, standards, tests.
No Index.
February 1973, T.p. 32, Ad.p. 2.   2900.
Free.

4594 THE GLASGOW REVIEW: Scotland's magazine of the arts. 1964.
Joseph Mulholland, editor, 43 Westbourne Gdns, Glasgow, G12 9XQ.
12, ○ +   Fiction, poetry, drama, criticism, reviews, comment, film, fine art, photography, planning, law notes, sociology, politics, ballet, opera, music.
Book notices, book reviews, legal notes, letters, monographic articles.
No Index.
Jan-March 1973, T.p. 41, Ad.p. 9.   4000.
Per copy 20p.

4595 HERE NOW.
22 Torquay Parade, Hebburn, Co. Durham.
○.   Fringe magazine.
No Index.

4596 IMPERIAL REVIEW.
Imperial Tobacco Group Ltd. Imperial House, 1 Grosvenor Place, London, SW1X 7HB.
4, †
No Index.
Free.

4597 MAD.
Thorpe and Porter Ltd., 135/141 Wardour Street, London, W1V 4AP.
12, ○
No Index.
Per copy 12½p.

4598 MOLE EXPRESS. 1969.
7 Summer Terrace, Manchester, 14.
12, ○
No Index.
Per copy 10p.

4599 MOVEMENT. 1973.
14 Hanley Road, London, N4
12, ○   'Underground' information publication, publications lists and abstracts.
No Index.
Per copy 5p.

4600 ONE.
D. Chaloner, 8 Granville Road, Cheadle Hulme, Cheshire, SK8 SQL.
○   'Fringe' magazine.
No Index.

4601 QUORUM.
GM Publications, 515 Finchley Road, London, NW3.
12, ○   'Magazine of the gay world'.
No Index.
Per year 75p.

4602 RED RAG.
96 Grove Road, London, N12.
○   By a Marxist Collective in the Women's liberation movement.
No Index.
Per copy 10p.

4603 SAD TRAFFIC.
12 Regent Street South, Barnsley, Yorks.
○   Fringe magazine.
No Index.

4604 UNIVERSITY OF LONDON BULLETIN. 1972.
University of London, 24 Russell Square, London, WC1.
6 each session, ○
No Index.

1
PHILOSOPHY

168
SYSTEMATIZATION

4605 BIOCHEMICAL SYSTEMATICS. 1973.
Pergamon Press Ltd., Headington Hill Hall, Oxford, OX3 0BW.
4, = ‡
Book reviews, monographic articles.
A, –, Yes, None.
Per year £12.

2
RELIGION. THEOLOGY

4606 RELIGION: Journal of religion and religions. 1971.
Routledge and Kegan Paul Ltd., 68 Carter Lane, Ludgate Hill, London, EC4.
2, +   Religion in all aspects including political.
Book notices, book reviews, monographic articles
6m, –, Yes, None.
Autumn 1972, T.p. 86, Ad.p. 7.   500.
Per copy £2, per year £3.

4607 RELIGION IN COMMUNIST COUNTRIES. 1973.
=   Religion in East Europe, Russia and China.
No Index.
(New journal: No further details on going to press).

22
BIBLE. CHRISTIAN RELIGION

4608 AWAKE.
Watch Tower Bible and Tract Society, Watch Tower House, The Ridgeway, London, NW7 1RN.
6, ○
No Index.
Per year 65p.

4609 THE WATCHTOWER. 1879.
Watch Tower Bible & Tract Society, Watch Tower House, The Ridgeway, London, NW7 1RN.
6, ○
No Index
Per year 65p.

282
ROMAN CATHOLIC CHURCH

4610 CATHOLIC COMMUNICATIONS INSTITUTE OF IRELAND. ABSTRACT OF PERIODICALS. 1973.
The Institute, Pranstown House, Booterstown Avenue, Co. Dublin.
12, =
No Index.
Subscription on application.

4611 CATHOLIC COMMUNICATIONS INSTITUTE OF IRELAND WEEKLY NEWS INDEX. 1973.
The Institute, Pranstown House, Booterstown Avenue, Co. Dublin.
52, =
No Index.
Per year £7.

285
PRESBYTERIAN. CHURCHES.

4612 MODERN FREE CHURCHMAN.
Union of Modern Free Churchmen, c/o 79 Friern Watch Avenue, London, N12.
2, ○
No Index.
Per copy 25p.

289.6
SOCIETY OF FRIENDS (QUAKERS)

4613 IRISH YOUNG FRIEND. 1972.
Religious Society of Friends, 6 Eustace Street, Dublin, 2.
12, O =
No Index.
Per copy 6p.

3
SOCIAL SCIENCES

32
CURRENT AFFAIRS. POLITICS

4614 CANDOUR.
Candour Publishing Co., Forest House, Liss, Hants.
O   National Front matters.
No Index.

4615 THE INTERNATIONALIST. 1970.
Voluntary Committee on Overseas Aid and Development, Parnell House, 25 Wilton Road, London, SW1.
12, =   International social issues.
Book reviews, articles.
No Index.
Subscription on application

4616 IRISH DEMOCRAT.
Connolly Publications, 283 Grays Inn Road, London, WC1.
12, =
No Index.

4617 NEW INTERNATIONALIST. 1973.
Oxfam, 74A High Street, Wallingford, Berks.
12, O
No Index.
Per year £3.

4618 SPEARHEAD.
Albion Press, 50 Pawsons Road, Croydon, CR0 2QF.
12, O   Contemporary British Nationalist opinion.
Letters, articles, news.
No Index.
November 1972, T.p. 20.
Per copy 10p, per year £1.50.

328
PARLIAMENTS

4619 REVIEW OF PARLIAMENT.
Parliamentary Digest Ltd., 171 Queen Victoria Street, London, EC4.
52   Comprehensive summary of proceedings in both Houses including progress of legislation, statements, white papers, question time.
(Cumulative), —, No, A.
Subscription on application.

329.14
SOCIALISM

4620 ARCHITECTS FOR A REALLY SOCIALIST ENVIRONMENT. 1971.
D. Wild, 20 Chalcot Road, London, NW1 8LL.
O
No Index.
Subscription on application.

331.88
TRADE UNIONS

4621 NALGO ACTION NEWS. 1972.
42 Southwood Avenue, London, N6.
= O
No Index.
Per copy 2p.

332
BANKING. FINANCIAL ECONOMICS

4622 FINANCIAL EUROPEAN. 1973.
Stockmark Publications, Suite 13, St. Martin's House, 29 Ludgate Hill, London, EC4M 7BD.
12, =
No Index.
Per year £10.

4623 MONEYSAVERS: Official newsletter of the Moneysavers Association. 1972.
The Association, Tower Suite, 1 Whitehall Place, London, SW1.
12, O
No Index
Per year £6.50.

4624 STOCK MARKET RESEARCH REVIEWS.
Professor C. W J. Granger, Dept. of Mathematics, University, Nottingham.
3, =   Research in the behaviour of capital markets, including the use of statistical techniques and databanks for storing and analysing the movement of stock prices and other financial information, portfolio selection, effects of mergers etc.
Monographic articles.
No Index.
Per year £4 for libraries, £8.50 for firms.

332.6
INVESTMENT FINANCE

4625 INVESTORS BULLETIN. 1972.
Suite 491, Park West, Marble Arch, London, W2.
12, =   Share predictions.
No Index.

332.7
CREDIT

4626 NEWSLETTER: Irish League of Credit Unions.
Irish League of Credit Unions, 9 Appion Way, Dublin, 6.
12, =
No Index.

333
LAND. PROPERTY

4627 HOUSING AND CONSTRUCTION STATISTICS. 1972.
(Housing Statistics: Monthly Bulletin of Construction Statistics).
HMSO, PO Box 569, London, SE1.
4, =
No Index.
T.p. 84.
Per copy 75p.

4628 PARKER'S PROPERTY PRICE GUIDE.
Parker's Price Guides, 52 Parker Street, London, WC2B 5QB.
12, ○ =
No Index.
Per year £3.50.

4629 PROPERTY NEWS. 1973.
Creation Group Ltd., PO Box 320, Creation House, Botanic Road, Dublin, 9.
○
No Index.
Per copy 5p.

338.7
COMPANIES

4630 STREET RESEARCH. 1972.
32 Birchdale Street, Moss Side, Manchester, M14 4JD.
Irregular
No Index.
T.p. 50.
Per copy 12p.

34
LAW

4631 LAG BULLETIN. 1972.
Legal Action Group, Nuffield Lodge, Regents Park, London, NW1.
12, =
No Index.
Per year £10.

343
CRIMINAL LAW

4632 JOURNAL OF CRIMINAL JUSTICE. 1973.
Pergamon Press, Headington Hill Hall, Oxford, OX3 0BW.
4, =
A,—, Yes, None.
Per year £14.

347.7
BUSINESS LAW

4633 NEW SECRETARY. 1972
Dominion Press, 530 Grand Buildings, Trafalgar Square, London, WC2N 5BR.
12, =
No Index.
Per copy 15p.

352
LOCAL GOVERNMENT

4634 FOCUS ON LOCAL GOVERNMENT. 1972.
(Councillor; Focus on Correction).
Conservative Central Office, 32 Smith Square, London, SW1.
4, =
No Index.
T.p. 24.
Per copy 10p.

355.1
ARMY

4635 ARMIES AND WEAPONS. 1972.
Ian Allan Ltd., Terminus House, Shepperton, Middx. TW17 8AJ.
12, ○ ‡
No Index.
Per year 75p.

4636 THE 1745 ASSOCIATION AND MILITARY HISTORY SOCIETY QUARTERLY NOTES.
Miss B. Fairweather, Invercoe House, Glencoe, Argyll.
4, ○
No Index.

361
SOCIAL WORK

4637 NEEDLE.
27 Pearman Street, London, SE1.
8/9   Hospital ancillary work, health and social work etc. Politics.
No Index.

362.4
WELFARE SERVICES TO THE PHYSICALLY HANDI-CAPPED

4638 CCD BULLETIN. 1972.
Central Council for the Disabled, 34 Eccleston Square, London, SW1.
○
No Index.

362.5
WELFARE SERVICES TO THE POOR

4639 THE CYRENIAN. 1972.
National Campaign for the Homeless and Roofless, 7 Sole Street, Crundale, Canterbury.
2, =
No Index.
T.p. 4.
Per copy 5p.

362.7
CHILD WELFARE

4640 CONCERN. 1972.
National Children's Bureau.
4, = ○
No Index.

37
EDUCATION

4641 ITV EDUCATION.
Independent Broadcasting Authority, 70 Brompton Road, London, SW3 1EY.
12, ○ =   News of ITV School programmes.
No Index.
January 1973, T.p. 4.
Free.

4642 LIBERTARIAN TEACHER.
Libertarian Education Group, 180 Melbourne Road, Leicester.
5, = ○
No Index.
Per copy 10p.

371.9

EDUCATION OF SPECIAL CLASSES

4643 DYSLEXIA REVIEW. 1972.
North Survey Dyslexia Society, c/o Mrs V. M. Fisher, Cambridge Cottage, Broadway, Laleham, Staines, Middx, TW18 1SB.
= ‡
No Index.
Free to members.

4644 TEACHER OF THE DEAF. c. 1900.
Royal School for the Deaf, 50 Topsham Road, Exeter, EX2 4NF.
6, = ‡
No Index.
Per year £2.90.

381

CHAMBERS OF COMMERCE

4645 FLASHPOINT. 1972
Junior Chamber Dublin, 34 Upper Gardiner Street, Dublin.
12, =
No Index.

382

INTERNATIONAL TRADE

4646 MOODIES JAPANESE REVIEW. 1972.
Moodies Services Ltd., 6 Bonhill Street, London, EC2.
=
No Index.
Per year £10.

386

CANALS. INLAND WATERWAYS

4647 NAVVIES.
Waterway Recovery Group, c/o 4 Wentworth Court, Wentworth Avenue, Finchley, London, N3 1YD.
‡ ○
No Index.
Per year 25p.

4648 SCOTTISH INLAND WATERWAYS ASSOCIATION NEWSLETTER. 1972.
The Association, c/o House of Premnay, Insch, Aberdeen.
12, ○ = ‡
No Index.

396

WOMEN

4649 WOMEN'S LIBERATION REVIEW. 1972.
Women's Literature Collective, 27 Deeds Grove, High Wycombe, Bucks.
Irregular, ○   All aspects of interest to the movement, including some fiction, poetry and articles.
No Index.
2000.
Per copy 30p.

4650 WOMEN'S STUDIES. 1972.
Gordon and Breach, 12 Bloomsbury Way, London, WC1.
2, =
Monographic articles.
No Index.
T.p. 161.
Per year £2.65.

397

GYPSIES

4651 O GLASO ROMANO. 1972.
Gypsy Council, 14 Princes Avenue, London, N3.
4, ○ =
No Index.
Per copy 12½p.

4652 ROMANO DROM.
Gypsy Council, 61 Blenheim Crescent, London, W11.
3/4, ○   Gypsy life in England and abroad.
Book reviews, letters.
No Index.
December 1972, T.p. 7, Ad.p. 1.   2000.
Per 4 issues—50p.

4
LANGUAGES. PHILOLOGY

4653 ONWARDS. 1970.
Schools Council Modern Languages Project, University, York.
=
No Index.

414

PHONETICS

4654 JOURNAL OF PHONETICS. 1973.
Seminar Press, 24-28 Oval Road, London, NW1.
4, =
No Index.
Per year £8.60.

5
SCIENCE

4655 SCIENCE, MEDICINE AND MAN. 1973.
Pergamon Press Ltd., Headington Hill Hall, Oxford, OX3 0BW.
4, = ‡ +
A, —, Yes, None.
Per year £12.

532
FLUID MECHANICS

4656 COMPUTERS AND FLUIDS. 1973.
Pergamon Press Ltd., Headington Hill Hall, Oxford, OX3 0BW.
4, = ‡
Book reviews, monographic articles.
A, —, Yes, None.
Per year £24.

537.5
RADIATION

4657 RADIOLOGICAL PROTECTION BULLETIN. 1972.
National Radiological Protection Board, Clifton Avenue, Belmont, Sutton, Surrey.
4, = ‡
No Index.
Free.

55
GEOLOGY

4658 PROCEEDINGS OF THE GEOLOGICAL SOCIETY OF GLASGOW. 1966.
University of Glasgow, Dept. of Extra-Mural Education, 57-9 Oakfield Avenue, Glasgow, G12 8LE.
1, = ‡ +
Monographic articles.
No Index.
Subscription on request.

4659 WELSH GEOLOGICAL QUARTERLY. 1965.
Geologists Association (South Wales Group), Cardiff.
4, = ‡
No Index.
Free to members.

574
BIOLOGY

4660 BIOLOGICAL MEMBRANE ABSTRACTS. 1973.
Information Retrieval Ltd., 1 Falconberg Court, London, W1V 5FG.
12, + ‡
Abstracts.
A, —, Yes, None.

4661 INTERNATIONAL JOURNAL OF NUCLEAR MEDICINE AND BIOLOGY. 1973.
Pergamon Press, Ltd., Headington Hill Hall, Oxford, OX3 0BW.
4, = ‡ +
A, —, Yes, None.
Per year £12.

591.5
ANIMAL ECOLOGY

4662 BEHAVIOURAL BIOLOGY ABSTRACTS A—ANIMAL BEHAVIOUR. 1973.
Information Retrieval Ltd., 1 Falconberg Court, London, W1V 5FG.
4, = ‡ +
Abstracts.
A, —, Yes, None.

6
TECHNOLOGY

61
MEDICAL SCIENCES

4663 JOURNAL OF ULTRASOUND IN MEDICINE AND BIOLOGY. 1973.
Pergamon Press, Headington Hill Hall, Oxford, OX3 0BW.
4, = ‡
Book reviews, letters, monographic articles.
A, —, Yes, None.
Per year £16.

614
PUBLIC HEALTH

4664 CURRENT LITERATURE ON COMMUNITY HEALTH AND PERSONAL SOCIAL SERVICES.
Dept. of Health and Social Security Library, Alexander Fleming House, Elephant and Castle, London, SE1.
12, =
No Index.

4665 HEALTH AND SOCIAL SERVICE JOURNAL: incorporating Community Medicine 1908-1973.
(British Hospitals Journal),
Whitefriars Press.
= Health services and care professions.
No Index.

614.7
AIR POLLUTION

4666 AIR POLLUTION ABSTRACTS. 1972.
Dept. of Trade & Industry, Warren Spring Laboratory, PO Box 20, Gunners Wood Road, Stevenage, Herts. SG1 2BX.
= ‡ +
Abstracts.
A, —, Yes, None.
Subscription on application.

615.851
PSYCHOTHERAPY

4667 ART PSYCHOTHERAPY. 1973.
Pergamon Press Ltd., Headington Hill Hall, Oxford, OX3 0BW.
4, = ‡
Book reviews, monographic articles.
A, —, Yes, None.
Per year £12.

616.314
DENTISTRY

4668 JOURNAL OF DENTISTRY. 1972.
J. Wright & Sons Ltd., 42-44 Triangle West, Bristol, BS8 1EX.
6, = ‡
Book reviews, letters, monographic articles.
No Index.
Per copy £1.

616.89
MENTAL DISORDERS. PSYCHIATRY

4669 NEWSLETTER: MENTAL HEALTH ASSOCIATION OF IRELAND. 1973.
The Association, 7 Upper Pembroke Street, Dublin 2.
4, =
No Index

62
ENGINEERING

4670 DESIGN ENGINEERING—Product Information. 1973.
Morgan-Grampian Co., 30 Calderwood Street, Woolwich, London, SE18.
12, = ‡   Card ordering service.
No Index.
Subscription on application.

4671 LETTERS IN APPLIED AND ENGINEERING SCIENCES. 1973.
Pergamon Press, Headington Hill Hall, Oxford, OX3 0BW.
6, = ‡ +
No Index.
Per year £16.

4672 MECHANICAL SCIENCES RESEARCH COMMUNICATIONS. 1973.
Pergamon Press, Headington Hill Hall, Oxford, OX3 0BW.
12, = ‡ +
No Index.
Per year £14.

621
MECHANICAL ENGINEERING

4673 MECHANICAL ENGINEERING NEWS. 1973.
Institution of Mechanical Engineers, 1 Birdcage Walk, London, SW1H 9JJ.
12, = ‡ +
Book reviews, letters, articles.
No Index.
Free to members.

621-186
PRESSURE VESSELS

4674 INTERNATIONAL JOURNAL OF PRESSURE VESSELS AND PIPING. 1973.
Applied Science Publishers Ltd., Ripple Road, Barking, Essex.
‡ + =
Book reviews, letters, monographic articles,
A, —, Yes, None.
Per year £14.

621.3
ELECTRICAL ENGINEERING

4675 COMPUTERS AND ELECTRICAL ENGINEERING. 1973.
Pergamon Press Ltd., Headington Hill Hall, Oxford, OX3 0BW.
4, = ‡
Monographic articles.
A, —, Yes, None.
Per year £24.

4676 ECA BULLETIN. 1972.
Electrical Contractors Association, 55 Catherine Place, London, SW1E 6ET.
4, = ‡ * †
No Index.
Free to members.

4677 ELECTROTECHNOLOGY. 1973.
(Electrical & Electronics Technical Engineer, 1966-1972).
Institution of Electrical & Electronics Technician Engineers, 2 Savoy Hill, London WC2R 0BS.
= ‡   Manufacture, operation, maintenance, R and D in the electrical and electronic industries.
Book notices, book reviews, letters, monographic articles, new companies, news, new products, standards, tests.
No Index.
T.p. 30, Ad.p. 5.   11600.
Per year £2.

4678 INTERNATIONAL JOURNAL OF CIRCUIT THEORY AND APPLICATIONS. 1973.
John Wiley & Sons, Baffins Lane, Chichester, Sussex.
= ‡ +
A, —, Yes, None.
Per year £13.

621.38
ELECTRONICS

4679 NATIONAL ELECTRONICS REVIEW. 1965.
National Electronics Council, Abell House, John Islip Street, London, SW1P 4LN.
6, = ‡
No Index.
Per year £2.75.

622
MINING

4679A CAMBORNE SCHOOL OF MINES JOURNAL. 1972.
(Camborne School of Mines Magazine 1900-1971).
Camborne School of Mines, Camborne, Cornwall.
1, ‡ + =
Monographic articles.
No Index.
Vol. 72, 1972, T.p. 72p.
Free to past students etc.

624
CIVIL ENGINEERING

4680 NEW CIVIL ENGINEER. 1972.
Institution of Civil Engineers, Great George Street, London, SW1.
12, = ‡ +
Book reviews, letters, monographic articles.
No Index.
Free to members.

627.2
MARINE ENGINEERING

4681 ESTUARINE AND COASTAL MARINE SCIENCE. 1973.
Academic Press Inc. (London) Ltd., 24-28 Oval Road, London, NW1.
4, = ‡ +
Book reviews, monographic articles.
A, —, No, None.
Per year £10.60.

4682 OFFSHORE SERVICES: incorporating Dredging and Coastal Engineering. 1972.
(Hydrospace).
Spearhead Publications Ltd., 2 Fife Road, Kingston-on-Thames, Surrey.
6, ‡ = +   Marine technology in all aspects.
No Index.
Per copy £1, per year £5.

629.113
AUTOMOBILE ENGINEERING

4683 PARKER'S CAR PRICE GUIDE.
Parker's Price Guides, 58 Parker Street, London WC2B 5QB.
12, ‡ =
No Index.
Per year £3.50.

629.13
AERONAUTICS

4684 AIR CUSHION AND HYDROFOIL SYSTEMS BIBLIOGRAPHY SERVICE. 1972.
R. Trillo Ltd., Broadlands, Brockenhurst, Hants.
6, = ‡ +
A, with Part 6, Yes, None.
Per year £3.50.

634.1
FRUIT

4685 EUROFRUIT. 1973.
Lockwood Press Ltd., 6-7 Gough Square, Fleet Street, London, EC4A 3DL.
=   Simultaneous publication in English, French and German.
No Index.
Subscription on application.

635.9
FLOWERS

4686 OFFSETS.
National Auricula & Primula Society, 67 Warnham Court Road, Carshalton Beeches, Surrey.
4, ○
No Index.
Free to members.

64.024.1
HOTELS

4687 HOTEL TARIFF STUDY OF GREAT BRITAIN.
Cornwell, Greene, Bertram, Smith & Co., 20 Kingsway, London, WC2B 6LH.
2, =
No Index.

65
BUSINESS

4688 MULTINATIONAL BUSINESS. 1972.
Economist Intelligence Unit Ltd., 27 St. James's Place, London, SW1.
4, =
No Index.
Subscription on application.

655
PRINTING

4689 THE CAXTONIAN: House journal of Mardon Son & Hall Ltd. 1948.
Mardon Son & Hall Limited, Carton Printers, Temple Street, Bristol, BS99 7PB.
2, †   Printing.
Articles, new products, obituaries.
Every eight numbers. Next index 1974.
Winter 1971, T.p. 67.
Free.

4690 THE PRINTING ART. 1973.
The Stellar Press, Welham Green, Hatfield, Herts.
4, = ‡
No Index.
Per year £3.

656.073
FREIGHT

4691 FREIGHT TRANSPORT-SERVICES. 1972.
Morgan-Grampian Ltd., 30 Calderwood Street, London, SE18.
= ‡
No Index.
Per copy £1.

4692 FREIGHT TRANSPORT EQUIPMENT. 1972.
Morgan-Grampian Ltd., 30 Calderwood Street, London, SE18.
= ‡
No Index.
Per copy £1.

658
BUSINESS AND INDUSTRIAL MANAGEMENT

4693 JOURNAL OF ENVIRONMENTAL MANAGEMENT. 1973.
Academic Press, 24-28 Oval Road, London, NW1.
4, =
Book reviews, letters, monographic articles.
A, —, Yes, None.
Per year £6.60.

Key to reference symbols

○ popular   ‡ technical   = trade/professional

+ research   * society/institution   † house journal

4694 OMEGA: the international journal of management science. 1973.
Pergamon Press Ltd., Headington Hill Hall, Oxford, OX3 0BW
6, =
Book reviews, monographic articles.
A, –, Yes, None.
Per year £18.

663.2
WINES

4695 AMATEUR WINEMAKER. 1957.
CJJ and MF Barry, North Croye, The Avenue, Andover, Hants.
12, ○
No Index.
Per copy 10p.

664
FOOD TECHNOLOGY

4696 FOOD PROGRESS. 1972.
Institute of Industrial Research, Ballymun Road, Dublin 9.
= ‡
No Index.
Subscription on application.

681.14
COMPUTERS. DATA PROCESSING

4697 COMPUTER DIGEST. 1972.
Special Interest Publications, 196 Shaftesbury Avenue, London, WC2.
52, = ‡
No Index.
Subscription on application.

4698 COMPUTERS AND ALGORITHMS. 1973.
Pergamon Press Ltd., Headington Hill Hall, Oxford, OX3 0BW.
4, = ‡
Book reviews, monographic articles.
A, –, Yes, None.
Per year £20.

4699 COMPUTERS AND GRAPHICS. 1973.
Pergamon Press Ltd., Headington Hill Hall, Oxford, OX3 0BW.
4, = ‡
Book reviews, monographic articles.
No Index.
Per year £20.

4700 COMPUTERS AND MATHEMATICS. 1973.
Pergamon Press Ltd., Headington Hill Hall, Oxford, OX3 0BW.
4, = ‡
Book reviews, monographic articles.
A, –, Yes, None.
Per year £20.

4701 COMPUTING. 1973.
Haymarket Publishing Co., Craven House, Fouberts Place, London, W1.
= ‡
No Index.
Subscription on application

4702 IRISH COMPUTER SOCIETY BULLETIN. 1973.
The Society, 90 St. Stephen's Green, Dublin 2.
4, = ‡
No Index.

681.84
SOUND RECORDING AND REPRODUCTION

4703 THE MONTHLY LETTER: EMG.
EMG Gramophones Ltd., 26 Soho Square, London, W1V 6BB.
12, ○ =
No Index.
Per year £1.75.

687
CLOTHING INDUSTRY

4704 MANUFACTURING CLOTHIER: incorporating Tailor and Cutter. 1973.
United Trade Press Ltd., 42-43 Gerrard Street, London, W1V 7LP.
12, =
No Index.
Subscription on application.

7
THE ARTS

711
TOWN AND COUNTRY PLANNING

4705 NORTHERN LIGHT. 1972.
North East Scotland Development Authority, 15 Union Terrace, Aberdeen, AB1 1NJ.
=
No Index.

8
LITERATURE

820
ENGLISH

4705A THE BYRON JOURNAL. 1973.
6 Gertrude Street, London, SW10 0JN.
5, = + ○ Life, art and achievements of Lord Byron and his influence on his contemporaries and successors.
Book reviews, letters, monographic articles.
No Index.
Per copy 50p, per year £2.

9
GEOGRAPHY. HISTORY

950
ASIA
4706 RONIN.

P. Billingsley, 24 Riglett Crescent, London, W12.
Left wing view of Asian affairs.
No Index.
Per copy 15p.

APPENDIX 1

JOURNALS CARRYING ABSTRACTS

Numbers refer to entries in main sequence.

ABSEES: Soviet and East European Abstracts Series   4530
Abstracts from Technical and Parent Publications (British Internal Combustion Engine Research Institute Ltd)   2405
Abstracts on Hygiene   2140
Accounting and Data Processing Abstracts   3187
Acoustics Abstracts   1645
Advances in Applied Probability   1583
Air Pollution Abstracts   4666
Amino Acids, Peptide and Protein Abstracts   1853
Analytical Abstracts   1747
Animal Breeding Abstracts   2932
Apicultural Abstracts   2997
Applied Ergonomics   3247
Aquatic Sciences and Fisheries Abstracts   1855
Atomic Absorption and Flame Emission Spectroscopy Abstracts   1655

BCIRA Journal   2530
BFMIRA Abstracts   3397
BLMRA Journal   3678
BNF Abstracts   3507
BSBI Abstracts   1941
Behavioural Biology Abstracts   1856
Biological Membrane Abstracts   1858
Biological Rhythms   1860
British Archaeological Abstracts   4402
British Geological Literature   1792
British Journal of Photography   3927
British Journal of Physical Education   1249
British Journal of Physiological Optics   2331
British Journal of Radiology   2220
British Journal of Urology   2293
Building Science Abstracts   3757
Bulletin of Entomological Research   1995
Bulletin of the Scottish Institute of Missionary Studies   465

Calcified Tissue Abstracts   1863
Carbohydrate Metabolism Abstracts   2124
Cell Membranes   1887
Ceramics   3443
Chartered Mechanical Engineer   2407
Chemoreception Abstracts   1864
Clean Air   2170
Clothing Institute Journal   3696
Cocoa Growers Bulletin   3392
Coke and Chemistry USSR   3346
Coke Review   3347
Computer and Control Abstracts   3597
Contact Lens   2333
Copper Abstracts   3510
Corrosion Control Abstracts   2402
Cost Engineer   3192
Cotton Growing Review   2884
Cybernetics Abstracts   1585
Cyclic Amp   1911

Czechoslovak Science and Technology Digest   1505

Dairy Science Abstracts   2974
Deep-Sea Research and Oceanographic Abstracts   1835
Developmental Medicine and Child Neurology   2300
Drop Forging Bulletin   3480

ERA Abstracts   2439
Electrical and Electronics Abstracts   2441
Electronics and Communications Abstracts   2469
Electrostatics Abstracts   1675
Engineers Digest   2371
Entomology Abstracts   1998
Environment and Planning   3844
Enzyme Regulation   1912
Equine Veterinary Journal   2345
Ergonomics   3248
Ergonomics Abstracts   3249
European Civil Engineering Abstracts   2615

Farm Buildings Digest   2829
Farm Management   2844
Ferritin   1936
Field Crop Abstracts   2872
Filtration and Separation   3803
Fish Industry Review   3005
Flour Milling and Baking Research Association Abstracts   3419
Fluid Power Abstracts   2429
Fluid Sealing Abstracts   2426
Fluidics Feedback   1639
Food Science and Technology Abstracts   3402
Footwear Digest   3679
Forestry Abstracts   2889
Fuel Abstracts and Current Titles   3352

Gas and Liquid Chromatography Abstracts   1752
Gas-Chromatography—Mass Spectrometry Abstracts   1753
The Gazette (Flour Milling and Baking Research Association)   3421
Genetics Abstracts   1883
Geo Abstracts   4352
Glass Technology   3438A

Heat and Fluid Flow   1640
Helminthological Abstracts   1989
Hemicrania   2307
Herbage Abstracts   2873
High Temperatures—High-Pressures   1673
Horticultural Abstracts   2908
Hosiery Abstracts   3715
Hospital Abstracts   1041

IMM Abstracts   2587
Ibis   2015
Industrial Diamond Review   3593
Industrial Marketing Research Abstracts   3295
Institute of Petroleum Abstracts   3429

International Brewing and Distilling   3388
International Political Science Abstracts   669
Intestinal Absorption and Related Topics   2105

JACB   3320
J. P. Weekly Law Digest   955
Journal of Abstracts of the British Ship Research Association   2753
Journal of Glaciology   1825
Journal of Mechanical Engineering Science   2410
Journal of the Institute of Brewing   3389
Journal of the Iron and Steel Institute   3497
Journal of the Society of Dyers and Colourists   3462
Journal of the Sports Turf Research Institute   3858

Language Teaching Abstracts   1192
Laser-Raman Spectroscopy Abstracts   1658
Law Societys' Gazette   910
Lead Abstracts   3511
Leprosy Review   2245
Library and Information Bulletin   19
Library and Information Science Abstracts   52
Library Bulletin (D.O.E.)   194
Lighting Research and Technology   2694
LOGA—Local Government Annotations Service   984

MIRA Abstracts   2731
Man: Research Abstracts   390
Management Abstracts   3213
Marine Engineering and Shipbuilding Abstract   2754
Market Research Abstracts   3298
Marketing and Distribution Abstracts   3262
Mass Spectrometry Bulletin   1661
Mechanical Sciences Abstracts   2414
Medical Electronics and Communications Abstracts   2479
Metal Finishing Abstracts   2543
Metals Abstracts   3487
Microbiology Abstracts   1900
Microdoc   3944
Mineralogical Abstracts   1788
Modern Geriatrics   2251
Modern Medicine   2077

Nerve Cell Biology   2138
Neurophysiology   2110
Neutron Activation Analysis Abstracts   1694
New Geographical Literature and Maps   4358
New Towns Bulletin   3848
New Trade Names in the Rubber and Plastics Industries   3577
Noise and Vibration Bulletin   1648
Nuclear Magnetic Resonance Spectrometry Abstracts   1663
Nucleic Acids Abstracts   1875

APPENDIX 1

Nutrition 2119
Nutrition Abstracts and Reviews 2120

Ophthalmic Literature 2337

PERA Bulletin 3240
PIRA Marketing Abstracts 2550
Packaging Abstracts 2553
Paper and Board Abstracts 3538
Particulate Information 1636
Personnel and Training Abstracts 3233
Personnel Review 3235
Photographic Abstracts 3936
Physics Abstracts 1623
Physics and Chemistry of Glasses 3438C
Physics in Medicine and Biology 2242
Planning and Transportation Abstracts 3849
Plant Breeding Abstracts 2861
Pollution 2686
Poverty and Human Resources Abstracts 608
Printing Abstracts 3109
Production Technology: Abstracts and Reports from Eastern Europe 2583
Programmed Learning and Educational Technology 1163
Pumps and other Fluids Machinery Abstracts 2526

Quarterly Bulletin of the Intelligence Unit, Greater London Council 995

R and D Abstracts 2034
R.A.P.R.A. Abstracts 3585
RIBA Annual Review of Periodical Articles 3879
RIBA Library Bulletin 3801
Race Relations Abstracts 706
Radio and Electronic Engineer 2502
Radioimmunoassay 2224
Renal Physiology 2127
Renal Transplantation and Dialysis 2128
Repro 3946
Research in Librarianship 64
Research in Special Education 1254
Research Into Higher Education Abstracts 1289
Review of Applied Entomology 2004
Review of Medical and Veterinary Mycology 1963
Review of Plant Pathology 1964
Rheology Abstracts 1705
Ribosomes 1913

SATIS 1498
Shoe Materials Progress 3690
Sociology of Education Abstracts 1174
Solid-liquid flow abstracts 1643
Soviet Jewish Affairs 578
Speleological Abstracts 1832
Spring Journal 2420

Steel Castings Abstracts 3503
Surface Wave Abstracts 2398

Technical Education Abstracts 1269
Theoretical Chemical Engineering Abstracts 3330
Thermal Abstracts 3800
Thin-Layer Chromatography Abstracts 1755
Top Management Abstracts 3223
Transactions and Journal of the British Ceramic Society 3450
Tribos 2576

Virology Abstracts 1955

Water Pollution Abstracts 2681
Water Power 2668
Weed Abstracts 2870
Welwyn Newsletter 3452
Wire Industry 2421
World Agricultural Economics and Rural Sociology Abstracts 2819
World Surface Coatings Abstracts 3472
World Textile Abstracts 3557

X-Ray Fluorescence Spectrometry Abstracts 1668

Zinc Abstracts 3512

APPENDIX 2

DISCONTINUED JOURNALS

Titles for which definite information of cessation has been received

* = Notification received after going to print.

A.E.C. Gazette
A.E.I. Journal of Telecommunications
A.T.G. Bulletin
Abstracts of World Medicine
Action
Aerospace Review
African Abstracts
Aim
Air Cushion Vehicles
Album
Alcan Magazine
Allied Star
Aluminium Courier
Amateur Artist
Ambience
Anbar Management Services Abstracts
Anglia Speed Sport
Applied Plastics and Reinforced Plastics
Arepo
Artifex
Arts Bulletin
Arts Lab Newsletter
Aspect
Astronomy
Automobile Connoisseur
Automobile Engineer

Baby Pictorial
BACIE Memoranda
BCURA Gazette
BCURA Monthly Bulletin
Ballet Today
Batchelor's Magazine
Benham Review
Bibliographical Bulletin for Welding and Allied Processes
Birds Eye Views
Bournville Works Magazine
Bradley's Magazine
Breakthrough
Briefing
British Journal of Dermatology
British Medical Abstracts and Therapeutic Progress
Bucks Safety Management Aid
Building Equipment News
Building Industries
Bulletin: British Road Federation
Bulletin of the Department of Education, Queens University, Belfast
Bulletin of the Robert Owen Bicentenary Association
By the Way

*Canning and Packing
Canterbury Consumer
Capital and Scimitar News
Catalyst
Caterers Association Bulletin
Catering Management
Central Africa Research Bulletin
Central Committee on English Bulletin
Centre News
Chemical and Process Engineering
Chest and Heart
Child Care
Clarion
Club

Coin-op Launderette and Unit Cleaner
Colour
Commercial Studies Teacher
Commercial Vehicles
Component Technology
Computer Aided Design
Concrete Materials, Technology and Construction Abstracts
Confectionery Manufacture and Marketing
Congregational Monthly
Cosmos
Counter Scene
Crossword

Dadd
Data Management
Digest of Scottish Statistics
Display Storefitting Decor
Diving Review
Duckett's Register

East Anglian Motorist
Econtel Research Memorandum
Educational Electronic Equipment
Enfield Borough Bulletin
Enfield Consumer
Export Service Bulletin
Export Management
Expression
Eye
Eye for Technology

Faber Music News
Factual News Information
Fair Isle Bird Observatory Bulletin
Fairway and Hazard
Farm Building Circular
Farm Machine Design Engineering
Farm Management Notes
Fashion and Knitting Patterns
Festivals
Flair
Flame
Flight Safety
Focus on Education
Food and Drink Weekly
Footwear Manufacturers Journal
Form
Formula
Formwork Abstracts
Forward

G.P.
Gibbs Magazine
Goldsmith's Today
Greek Observer
Greenbat Review
Greenbat Topics
Ground Engineering

Harrodian Gazette
Hawker Siddeley Review
Hawker Siddeley Technical Review
Health Culturist
Health Information Digest
Health Overseas
Hotel and Restaurant Management
Huddersfield Consumer

I.T.F. Documentation
I.T.F. Technical Bulletin
Imagery
Impact
Inside Story
Institute of Education Bulletin
Instrument and Control Engineering
Interludes
Intermedica
International Abstracts
International Bulletin for the Printing and Allied Trades
International Hotel Review
*Into Orbit
Investment Special
Iron Ore and Alloying Metals

Jazz Monthly
Jewson Newsheet
Journal of Electronics and Control
Journal of Psychophysical Research

Kenning Car Mart Courier
Kett

Laboratory Electronic Equipment
Laboratory Equipment
Laser Review
Leather Wear
Letters on Librarianship and Kindred Topics
Leyland Journal
Light Engineering
Lightweight Aggregate and Lightweight Concrete Abstracts
Link
Lintas Review
Logos
London Bulletin
Low Cost Automation Review

MIRA Bulletin
Machine Design and Control
Man About
Mash Tun
*Maternal and Child Care
Maternelle
Meat Processor and Packer
Methodist Magazine
Minerals Quarterly
*Model Cars
Modern Hairdressing News
Modern Home Buyer
*Money Management
Monthly Bulletin of Construction Statistics

N.C.L. Newsletter
N.C.R. Factory Post
New Doctor
New Epoch
New Product Newsletter
New Student
Newcastle Medical Journal
Newcastle Papers in Architecture and Building Science
Newsletter of the British Computer Society
Northlott Magazine
Northern Ireland Libraries

APPENDIX 2

Occasion
Optical News
Orbit
Oriel

P.I.R.A. Paper and Board Journal
P.I.R.A. Patent Abstracts
Papers in Psychology
Perspective
Pictorial Science
Pig Progress
Pilot and Light Aeroplane
Plastics in Building
Plastics in Engineering
Plessey Electronics
Plessey International News
Politiks
Pollution Control
Powerboat and Watersport
Practical Home Building and Decorating
Precast Concrete Abstracts
Precision
Presbyterian Outlook
Prestressed Concrete Abstracts
Priapus
Priestman Bulletin
Priestman News International
Product Design Engineering

Quad
Quarterly Review
Reaction
Ready Mixed Concrete Abstracts
Reconciliation
Recording Right Journal
*Records of the Month
Refreshment

Report on Overseas Trade
Reprint Review
Research in Physical Education
Research Review
Resources
Rink Report
Rolls Royce News
Rural Pharmacists News

SPD Magazine
S.Q.J.—Students Quarterly Journal
Science Bulletin
Science and General Record
Scientology
Scope
Scotnews
Scottish Country Bulletin
Scottish Economic Review
Scrap and Waste Reclamation and Disposal
Share Catalogue
Shepherd News
Shop Equipment Selector
Skill
Social Justice
Somethings
*Span
Stave
Stramit Advertiser
Structural Concrete Abstracts
Student Technologist
Sunday Companion
Survey (Schools Council)
System

Tailor and Cutter
Talking Shop

Target
Tawny Owl
Teacher Education in New Countries
Teaching
Technology in Agriculture
Templetonian
Third Rail
*Tin Printer and Box Maker
Tomorrow's Teacher
Top Jobs
Torque
Toys and Gifts
Trace
Tracks
Transport

U.F.O. Chronicle
University Television Newsletter

Veterinary Digest
Veterinary Doctor
Vickers Magazine
View

WandS
Welsh Dominion
Welsh Schoolmaster
West Country Homefinder
Westminster Abbey—One
West's Magazine
Wills Magazine
Women in Council
World Business
World Studies Education Service

Young Teacher Newsletter

APPENDIX 3

SOCIETIES AND THEIR PUBLICATIONS

Numbers refer to entries in the main sequence.

ABERDEEN-ANGUS CATTLE
SOCIETY
   Aberdeen-Angus Review   2938
ADDITIONAL CURATES SOCIETY
   Home Mission News   520
ADVERTISING ASSOCIATION
   Advertising Quarterly   3284
AFRICAN STUDIES ASSOCIATION OF
THE UNITED KINGDOM
   Bulletin of the African Studies
   Association of the United Kingdom
   4563
AFRICAN SUCCULENT PLANT
SOCIETY
   Bulletin of the African Succulent
   Plant Society   2917
AGRICULTURAL ECONOMICS
SOCIETY
   Journal of Agricultural Economics
   2808
AGRICULTURAL EDUCATION
ASSOCIATION
   Agricultural Progress   2800
ALL ENGLAND NETBALL
ASSOCIATION
   Netball   4061
ALL ENGLAND WOMENS LACROSSE
ASSOCIATION
   Lacrosse   4077
ALPINE GARDEN SOCIETY
   Quarterly Bulletin of the Alpine
   Garden Society   2927
AMALGAMATED UNION OF BUILDING
TRADE WORKERS
   Building Worker   3760
AMALGAMATED UNION OF
ENGINEERING WORKERS
   Tass Journal   2527
AMATEUR BASKET BALL
ASSOCIATION
   Basketball   4060
AMATEUR ENTOMOLOGISTS
SOCIETY
   Bulletin of the Amateur Entomo-
   logists Society   1993
AMATEUR ROWING ASSOCIATION
   Rowing   4142
AMATEUR YACHT RESEARCH
SOCIETY
   A.Y.R.S. Airs   4143
ANATOMICAL SOCIETY
   Journal of Anatomy   2103
ANCIENT MONUMENTS SOCIETY
   Transactions of the Ancient Monu-
   ments Society   3882
ANCIENT ORDER OF FORESTERS
   Foresters' Miscellany   1074
ANDERSONIAN NATURALISTS OF
GLASGOW
   Glasgow Naturalist   1531
ANGLESEY ANTIQUARIAN SOCIETY
& FIELD CLUB
   Transactions of the Anglesey
   Antiquarian Society and Field Club
   4441
ANGLO-ARAB ASSOCIATION
   Arab World   4550
ANGLO-BYELORUSSIAN SOCIETY
   Journal of Byelorussian Studies
   4532
ANGLO-CHILEAN SOCIETY
   Chilean News   4580

ANGLO-DANISH SOCIETY
   Denmark   4536
ANGLO-SPANISH SOCIETY
   Anglo-Spanish Society Quarterly
   Review   4526
ANTHROPOSOPHICAL SOCIETY IN
GREAT BRITAIN.
   Anthroposophical Quarterly   378
ANTIQUARIAN HOROLOGICAL
SOCIETY
   Antiquarian Horology   3594
ARAB HORSE SOCIETY
   Arab Horse Society News   2935
ARBORICULTURAL ASSOCIATION
   Arboricultural Association Journal
   2885
ARCHITECTURAL & ARCHAEO-
LOGICAL SOCIETY OF DURHAM &
NORTHUMBERLAND
   Transactions of the Architectural
   and Archaeological Society of
   Durham & Northumberland   4425
ARCHITECTURAL SOCIETY, QUEEN'S
UNIVERSITY OF BELFAST
   Big A   3875
ARMS & ARMOUR SOCIETY
   Journal of the Arms and Armour
   Society   2601
ARMY CADET FORCE ASSOCIATION
   Cadet Journal and Gazette   1002
ART LIBRARIES SOCIETY
   ARLIS Newsletter   26
ASLIB
   Aslib Book List   4
   Aslib Information   27
   Aslib Proceedings   28
   Aslib Transport and Planning Group
   Newsletter   29
   Forthcoming International
   Scientific and Technical Conferen
   ces   333
   Journal of Documentation   2
   Program   63
ASSOCIATED SOCIETY OF LOCO-
MOTIVE ENGINEERS AND FIREMEN
   Locomotive Journal   2643
ASSOCIATION FOR PETROLEUM
ACTS ADMINISTRATION
   Bulletin   3428
ASSOCIATION FOR PROGRAMMED
LEARNING & EDUCATIONAL
TECHNOLOGY
   Programmed Learning and Educa-
   tional Technology   1163
ASSOCIATION FOR PROMOTING
RETREATS
   Vision   427
ASSOCIATION FOR SCIENCE
EDUCATION
   Education in Science   1203
   School Science Review   1204
ASSOCIATION FOR SCOTTISH
LITERARY STUDIES
   Scottish Literary News   4284
ASSOCIATION FOR SPECIAL
EDUCATION
   Research in Special Education
   1254
   Special Education   1255
ASSOCIATION FOR THE EDUCATION
OF PUPILS FROM OVERSEAS
   Multiracial School   1199

ASSOCIATION FOR THE STUDY OF
ANIMAL BEHAVIOUR
   Animal Behaviour   1981
   Animal Behaviour Monographs   1982
ASSOCIATION FOR THE STUDY OF
MEDICAL EDUCATION
   British Journal of Medical
   Education   2050
ASSOCIATION OF ACROBATICS
   Acrobatics   4091
ASSOCIATION OF AGRICULTURE
   Association of Agriculture Journal
   2804
ASSOCIATION OF ANAESTHETISTS
OF GREAT BRITAIN AND IRELAND
   Anaesthesia   2262
ASSOCIATION OF APPLIED
BIOLOGISTS
   Annals of Applied Biology   1854
ASSOCIATION OF ARTS CENTRES IN
SCOTLAND
   Trends & Topics   3840
ASSOCIATION OF ASSISTANT
LIBRARIANS
   Assistant Librarian   30
   Open Access   59
   Outpost   61
ASSOCIATION OF BEAUTY
THERAPISTS
   Beauty Therapy Journal   3473
ASSOCIATION OF BLIND CHARTERED
PHYSIOTHERAPISTS
   Braille Journal of Physiotherapy
   2215
   Braille Physiotherapists Quarterly
   2216
ASSOCIATION OF BRITISH ADOPTION
AGENCIES
   Child Adoption   1063
ASSOCIATION OF BRITISH DENTAL
SURGERY ASSISTANTS
   British Dental Surgery Assistant
   2279
ASSOCIATION OF BRITISH HAIR-
DRESSERS AND CLEANERS LTD
   A B L C Journal   3062
ASSOCIATION OF BRITISH
HISPANISTS LUSO-BRAZILIAN
SECTION
   Newsletter of the Luso-Brazilian
   Section, Association of British
   Hispanists   4579
ASSOCIATION OF BRITISH RIDING
SCHOOLS
   Horse World   4163
ASSOCIATION OF BRONZE AND
BRASS FOUNDERS
   Association of Bronze and Brass
   Founders Bulletin   2531
ASSOCIATION OF BURGLARY
INSURANCE SURVEYORS
   Security Surveyor   981
ASSOCIATION OF CASHIERS
   Cashier   806
ASSOCIATION OF CERTIFIED
ACCOUNTANTS
   Certified Accountant   3189
ASSOCIATION OF CHILD
PSYCHOLOGY AND PSYCHIATRY
   Journal of Child Psychology and
   Psychiatry and Allied Disciplines
   396

APPENDIX 3

ASSOCIATION OF CHRISTIAN TEACHERS
    Spectrum   1175
ASSOCIATION OF CLINICAL BIOCHEMISTS
    Annals of Clinical Biochemistry   1905
ASSOCIATION OF CLINICAL PATHOLOGISTS
    Journal of Clinical Pathology   2238
ASSOCIATION OF COMMONWEALTH UNIVERSITIES
    Bulletin of Current Documentation   1
ASSOCIATION OF COST ENGINEERS
    Cost Engineer   3192
ASSOCIATION OF DISPENSING OPTICIANS
    Dispensing Optician   2334
ASSOCIATION OF EDUCATION COMMITTEES
    Education   1122
ASSOCIATION OF HOSPITAL & WELFARE ADMINISTRATIONS
    Bulletin   1039
ASSOCIATION OF HOSPITAL TREASURERS
    Hospital Service Finance   3229
ASSOCIATION OF INDUSTRIAL & COMMERCIAL EXECUTIVE ACCOUNTANTS
    Executive Accountant   3193
ASSOCIATION OF INTERNATIONAL ACCOUNTANTS
    International Accountant   3195
ASSOCIATION OF JEWISH REFUGEES IN GREAT BRITAIN
    AJR Information   81
ASSOCIATION OF INDUSTRIAL MEDICAL OFFICERS
    Transactions of the Society of Occupational Medicine   796
ASSOCIATION OF MASTER UPHOLSTERERS
    Monthly Bulletin   3676
ASSOCIATION OF MEDICAL RECORDS OFFICERS
    Medical Record   1036
ASSOCIATION OF MEDICAL SECRETARIES
    Medical Secretary   952
ASSOCIATION OF MEN OF KENT & KENTISH MEN
    Kent   4486
ASSOCIATION OF MINING, ELECTRICAL & MECHANICAL ENGINEERS
    Mining Technology   2596
ASSOCIATION OF MUNICIPAL CORPORATIONS
    Municipal Review   990
ASSOCIATION OF PHOTOGRAPHIC LABORATORIES
    Photographic Processor   3938
ASSOCIATION OF PHYSICIANS OF GREAT BRITAIN AND IRELAND
    Quarterly Journal of Medicine   2088
ASSOCIATION OF POLISH MERCHANTS AND INDUSTRIALISTS
    Wiadomosci Gospodareze   326
ASSOCIATION OF PSYCHIATRIC SOCIAL WORKERS
    British Journal of Psychiatric Social Work   1017
ASSOCIATION OF PUBLIC ADDRESS ENGINEERS LTD.
    Public Address   2493

ASSOCIATION OF PUBLIC ANALYSTS
    Journal of the Association of Public Analysts   2155
ASSOCIATION OF PUBLIC HEALTH INSPECTORS
    Environmental Health   982
ASSOCIATION OF PUBLIC LIGHTING ENGINEERS
    Public Lighting   2695
ASSOCIATION OF PUBLIC PASSENGER TRANSPORT OPERATORS
    APPTO   1420
ASSOCIATION OF RECOGNISED ENGLISH LANGUAGE SCHOOLS
    ARELS Journal   1194
ASSOCIATION OF SCHOOL NATURAL HISTORY SOCIETIES
    Starfish   1554
ASSOCIATION OF SCIENTIFIC, TECHNICAL MANAGERIAL STAFFS
    ASTMS Gains   3200
    ASTMS Journal   3201
ASSOCIATION OF SUPERVISORY AND EXECUTIVE ENGINEERS
    Electrical Supervisor   2450
ASSOCIATION OF TEACHERS IN COLLEGES AND DEPARTMENT OF EDUCATION
    Education for Teaching   1126
ASSOCIATION OF TEACHERS IN TECHNICAL INSTITUTIONS
    Technical Journal   1270
ASSOCIATION OF TEACHERS OF DOMESTIC SCIENCE
    Housecraft   1267
ASSOCIATION OF TEACHERS OF GEOLOGY
    Geology   1212
ASSOCIATION OF TEACHERS OF GERMAN
    Treffpunkt   1201
ASSOCIATION OF TEACHERS OF MANAGEMENT
    Management Education & Development   1216
ASSOCIATION OF TEACHERS OF MATHEMATICS
    Mathematics Teaching   1209
ASSOCIATION OF TEACHERS OF PRINTING AND ALLIED SUBJECTS
    ATPAS Bulletin   1215
ASSOCIATION OF TEACHERS OF RUSSIAN
    Journal of Russian Studies   1202
ASSOCIATION OF UKRAINIANS IN GREAT BRITAIN
    Ukrainian Review   4300
ASSOCIATION OF UNIVERSITY TEACHERS
    AUT Bulletin   1280
ATLANTIC EDUCATION TRUST
    Correspondents World Wide   655
AUDIO-VISUAL LANGUAGE ASSOCIATION
    Audio-Visual Language Journal   1459
AUTOMOBILE ASSOCIATION
    Drive   2721
AVICULTURAL SOCIETY
    Avicultural Magazine   2008
AYRSHIRE ARCHAEOLOGICAL & NATURAL HISTORY SOCIETY
    Ayrshire Archaeological & Natural History Society Collections   4391
AYRSHIRE CATTLE SOCIETY
    Ayrshire Cattle Society's Journal   2939

BADMINTON ASSOCIATION OF ENGLAND
    Badminton Gazette   4074
BALINT SOCIETY
    Journal of the Balint Society   389
BANBURY HISTORICAL SOCIETY
    Cake and Cockhorse   4310
BAPTIST HISTORICAL SOCIETY
    Baptist Quarterly   542
BAPTIST MISSIONARY SOCIETY
    Quest   546
BATH & CAMERTON ARCHAEOLOGICAL SOCIETY
    Camertonia   4403
BEE RESEARCH ASSOCIATION
    Apicultural Abstracts   2997
    Bee World   2998
    Journal of Apicultural Research   3000
BEHAVIOURAL ENGINEERING ASSOCIATION
    Behavioural Engineering Association Conference Proceedings   380
BELFAST NATURAL HISTORY AND PHILOSOPHICAL SOCIETY
    Proceedings & Reports: Belfast Natural History and Philosophical Society   1546
BERKSHIRE ARCHAEOLOGICAL SOCIETY
    Berkshire Archaeological Journal   4399
BIBLE CHURCHMEN'S MISSIONARY SOCIETY
    Mission   470
BIBLIOGRAPHICAL SOCIETY
    Library   18
BICYCLE POLO ASSOCIATION OF GREAT BRITAIN
    Bi-Polo News   4086
BIOCHEMICAL SOCIETY
    Biochemical Journal   1906
BIRMINGHAM & WARWICKSHIRE ARCHAEOLOGICAL SOCIETY
    Transactions of the Birmingham & Warwickshire Archaeological Society   4426
BLACK COUNTRY SOCIETY
    Blackcountryman   4458
BLACKFACE SHEEP BREEDERS' ASSOCIATION
    Blackface Sheep Breeders' Association Journal   2950
BOTANICAL SOCIETY OF EDINBURGH
    Transactions of the Botanical Society of Edinburgh   1950
BOTANICAL SOCIETY OF THE BRITISH ISLES
    BSBI Abstracts   1941
    Watsonia   1951
BOUME SOCIETY
    Local History Records   4329
BOY'S BRIGADE
    Boy's Brigade Gazette   1100
BRADFORD HISTORICAL & ANTIQUARIAN SOCIETY
    Bradford Antiquary   4401
BRANCH LINE SOCIETY
    Branch Line News   2631
BREWERS SOCIETY
    Brewing Review   3386
BRICK DEVELOPMENT ASSOCIATION
    Brick Bulletin   3771
BRISTOL & GLOUCESTERSHIRE ARCHAEOLOGICAL SOCIETY
    Transactions of the Bristol & Gloucestershire Archaeological Society   4427

BRISTOL NATURALISTS SOCIETY
  Proceedings of the Bristol
  Naturalists Society 1547
BRITISH ACTORS' EQUITY ASSOCIATION (Incorporating the Variety Artistes' Federation)
  Equity 800
BRITISH AGRICULTURAL AND GARDEN MACHINERY ASSOCIATION
  Agricultural and Garden Machinery Service 2846
BRITISH AGRICULTURAL HISTORY SOCIETY
  Agricultural History Review 2798
BRITISH AIR MAIL SOCIETY
  Air Mail News 3159
BRITISH ALLERGY SOCIETY
  Clinical Allergy 2126
BRITISH AND FOREIGN BIBLE SOCIETY
  Word in Action 437
BRITISH AND IRISH ASSOCIATION OF LAW LIBRARIANS
  Law Librarian 47
BRITISH ARACHNOLOGICAL SOCIETY
  Bulletin of the British Arachnological Society 1990
  Newsletter of the British Arachnological Society 1991
BRITISH ASSOCIATION FOR COMMERCIAL AND INDUSTRIAL EDUCATION
  Bacie Journal 1281
  Bacie News 1282
BRITISH ASSOCIATION FOR THE ADVANCEMENT OF SCIENCE
  BA Record 1493
BRITISH ASSOCIATION OF ACCOUNTANTS & AUDITORS
  Registered Accountant 3197
BRITISH ASSOCIATION OF BLIND ESPERANTISTS
  Ĉe Ni 1471
BRITISH ASSOCIATION OF COLLIERY MANAGEMENT
  National Newsletter of the British Association of Colliery Management 2597
BRITISH ASSOCIATION OF HOTEL ACCOUNTANTS
  Hotel Accountant 3194
BRITISH ASSOCIATION OF INDUSTRIAL EDITORS
  Communication 350
BRITISH ASSOCIATION OF NUMISMATIC SOCIETIES
  Cunobelin 3908
BRITISH ASSOCIATION OF ORGANISERS AND LECTURERS IN PHYSICAL EDUCATION
  Bulletin of Physical Education 1250
BRITISH ASSOCIATION OF REMOVERS
  Removals & Storage 3179
BRITISH ASSOCIATION OF RETIRED PERSONS
  British Association of Retired Persons: Members' Quarterly Bulletin 1016
BRITISH ASSOCIATION OF SOCIAL WORKERS
  British Journal of Social Work 1018
  Parliament and Social Work 1026
  Social Work Today 1030
BRITISH ASSOCIATION OF SPORT AND MEDICINE
  British Journal of Sports Medicine 2051

BRITISH ASSOCIATION OF UROLOGICAL SURGEONS
  British Journal of Urology 2293
BRITISH BEER-MAT COLLECTORS SOCIETY
  Beermat Magazine 3383
BRITISH BLIND AND SHUTTER ASSOCIATION
  Blinds & Shutters 3054
BRITISH BOOT AND SHOE INSTITUTION
  Journal of the British Boot and Shoe Institution 3682
BRITISH BRYOLOGICAL SOCIETY
  Transactions of the British Bryological Society 1968
BRITISH CARDIAC SOCIETY
  British Heart Journal 2265
  Cardiovascular Research 2266
BRITISH CARTOGRAPHIC SOCIETY
  Cartographic Journal 1602
BRITISH CERAMIC PLANT & MACHINERY MANUFACTURERS ASSOCIATION
  British Ceramic Review 3440
BRITISH CERAMIC SOCIETY
  Transactions and Journal of the British Ceramic Society 3450
BRITISH CHICKEN GROWERS ASSOCIATION
  British Chicken Growers Association Bulletin 2955
BRITISH COKE RESEARCH ASSOCIATION
  Coke Review 3347
BRITISH COMPUTER SOCIETY
  Computer Bulletin 3598
  Computer Journal 3603
BRITISH CORRESPONDENCE CHESS ASSOCIATION
  Correspondence Chess 4048
BRITISH DEER SOCIETY
  Deer 2025
BRITISH DENTAL ASSOCIATION
  British Dental Journal 2278
BRITISH DISPLAY SOCIETY
  BDS News 3309
BRITISH DRAG RACING & HOT ROD ASSOCIATION
  Drag Racing & Hot Rod Magazine 4113
BRITISH ECOLOGICAL SOCIETY
  Journal of Applied Ecology 1984
  Journal of Ecology 1985
BRITISH ECOLOGY SOCIETY
  Journal of Animal Ecology 1983
BRITISH EGG ASSOCIATION
  British Egg Association Newsletter 2985
BRITISH ENDODONTIC SOCIETY
  Journal of the British Endodontic Society 2285
BRITISH EPILEPSY ASSOCIATION
  Candle 2306
BRITISH EQUINE VETERINARY ASSOCIATION
  Equine Veterinary Journal 2345
BRITISH ESPERANTO ASSOCIATION
  British Esperantist 1470
BRITISH FEDERATION OF FILM SOCIETIES
  Film 4007
BRITISH FIRE SERVICES ASSOCIATION
  Journal of the British Fire Services Association 2187
BRITISH FLOWER INDUSTRY ASSOCIATION
  British Flower Industry Association Journal 2915

BRITISH FOOD MANUFACTURING INDUSTRIES RESEARCH ASSOCIATION
  BFMIRA Abstracts 3397
BRITISH FRIESIAN CATTLE SOCIETY
  British Friesian Journal 2940
BRITISH GERIATRICS SOCIETY
  Age and Ageing 2250
BRITISH GLIDING ASSOCIATION
  Sailplane & Gliding 4159
BRITISH GO ASSOCIATION
  British Go Journal 3729
BRITISH GOAT SOCIETY
  British Goat Society Monthly Journal 2951
BRITISH GOLF GREENKEEPERS ASSOCIATION
  British Golf Greenkeeper 4078
BRITISH GRASSLAND SOCIETY
  Journal of the British Grassland Society 2880
BRITISH HERPETOLOGICAL SOCIETY
  British Journal of Herpetology 2007
BRITISH HOROLOGICAL INSTITUTE
  Horological Journal 3595
BRITISH HOSIERY AND KNITWEAR EXPORT GROUP
  British Hosiery and Knitwear 3711
BRITISH HOTELS, RESTAURANTS AND CATERERS ASSOCIATION
  British Hotelier and Restaurants 3035
BRITISH INDUSTRIAL & SCIENTIFIC FILM ASSOCIATION
  British National Film Catalogue 4003
BRITISH INDUSTRIAL BIOLOGICAL RESEARCH ASSOCIATION
  Food and Cosmetics Toxicology 2228
BRITISH INSTITUTE OF INTERNATIONAL AND COMPARATIVE LAW
  International and Comparative Law Quarterly 923
BRITISH INSTITUTE OF RADIOLOGY
  British Journal of Radiology 2220
BRITISH INSTITUTE OF RECORDED SOUND
  Recorded Sound 3658
BRITISH INTERPLANETARY SOCIETY
  Journal of the British Interplanetary Society 1598
  Spaceflight 2792
BRITISH IRIS SOCIETY
  British Iris Society Newsletter 2916
BRITISH JAZZ SOCIETY
  Jazz Times 3987
BRITISH JEWELLERY AND GIFTWARE FEDERATION LTD
  Britannia 3517
  British Jeweller and Watch Buyer 3518
  Buyers Guide 3519
BRITISH JOINT CORROSION GROUP
  British Corrosion Journal 2401
BRITISH KINEMATOGRAPHY SOUND & TELEVISION SOCIETY
  British Kinematography Sound and Television 3948
BRITISH LANDRACE PIG SOCIETY
  British Landrace Pig Journal 2952
BRITISH LEPROSY RELIEF ASSOCIATION
  Leprosy Review 2245

APPENDIX 3

BRITISH LICHEN SOCIETY
   British Lichen Society Bulletin 1966
   Lichenologist 1967

BRITISH MEDICAL ASSOCIATION
   Annals of the Rheumatic Diseases 2295
   Archives of Disease in Childhood 2249
   British Journal of Industrial Medicine 2145
   British Journal of Preventive and Social Medicine 2162
   Journal of Medical Genetics 1885
   Journal of Neurology, Neurosurgery & Psychiatry 2303

BRITISH MEDICAL STUDENTS ASSOCIATION
   Scope 2093

BRITISH MODEL SOLDIER SOCIETY
   Bulletin 3731

BRITISH MUSEUM SOCIETY
   British Museum Society Bulletin 337

BRITISH MUSIC HALL SOCIETY
   Call Boy 4020

BRITISH MYCOLOGICAL SOCIETY
   Bulletin of the British Mycological Society 1958
   Transactions of the British Mycological society 165

BRITISH NATURALISTS ASSOCIATION
   Country-side 1527

BRITISH NATUROPATHIC AND OSTEOPATHIC ASSOCIATION
   British Naturopathic Journal and Osteopathic Review 2217

BRITISH NUCLEAR ENERGY SOCIETY
   British Nuclear Energy Society Journal 2416

BRITISH NUMISMATIC SOCIETY
   British Numismatic Journal 3902

BRITISH OCCUPATIONAL HYGIENE SOCIETY
   Annals of Occupational Hygiene 792

BRITISH OIL AND GAS FIRING EQUIPMENT MANUFACTURERS ASSOCIATION
   Oil and Gas Firing 3797

BRITISH OLYMPIC ASSOCIATION
   Sportsworld 4055

BRITISH OPTICAL ASSOCIATION
   British Journal of Physiological Optics 2331

BRITISH OPTICAL ASSOCIATION AND ASSOCIATION OF OPTICAL PRACTITIONERS
   Ophthalmic Optician 2338

BRITISH ORIENTEERING FEDERATION
   Orienteer 4361

BRITISH ORNITHOLOGISTS CLUB
   Bulletin of the British Ornithologists Club 2013

BRITISH ORNITHOLOGISTS UNION
   Ibis 2015

BRITISH ORTHOPTIC SOCIETY
   British Orthoptic Journal 2332

BRITISH PAPER AND BOARD MAKERS ASSOCIATION
   Paper Technology 3541

BRITISH PARACHUTE ASSOCIATION
   Sport Parachutist 4156

BRITISH PELARGONIUM AND GERMANIUM SOCIETY
   Pelargonium News 2926

BRITISH PHARMACOLOGICAL SOCIETY
   British Journal of Pharmacology 2195

BRITISH PHILLUMATIC SOCIETY
   B.P.S. Magazine 3344

BRITISH PHYCOLOGICAL SOCIETY
   British Phycological Journal 1956

BRITISH POST MARK SOCIETY
   British Post Mark Society Quarterly Bulletin 3160

BRITISH POTTERY MANAGERS' ASSOCIATION
   Ceramics 3443

BRITISH PRINTING SOCIETY
   Small Printer 3120

BRITISH PSYCHOLOGICAL SOCIETY
   British Journal of Psychology, Medical Section 382
   British Journal of Social and Clinical Psychology 383
   British Journal of Psychology 382

BRITISH PTERIDOLOGICAL SOCIETY
   British Fern Gazette 1969

BRITISH RECORDS ASSOCIATION
   Archives 355

BRITISH RED CROSS SOCIETY
   Crosstalk 1034
   Junior Journal 1035

BRITISH RHEUMATISM AND ARTHRITIS ASSOCIATION
   BRA Review 2296

BRITISH SHIP RESEARCH ASSOCIATION
   Journal of Abstracts 2753

BRITISH SMALL ANIMAL VETERINARY ASSOCIATION
   Journal of Small Animal Practice 2349

BRITISH SOCIETY FOR EIGHTEENTH CENTURY STUDIES
   British Society for Eighteenth Century Studies Newsletter 4266

BRITISH SOCIETY FOR IMMUNOLOGY
   Immunology 2165
   Clinical and Experimental Immunology 2163

BRITISH SOCIETY FOR MUSIC THERAPY
   British Journal of Music Therapy 2194

BRITISH SOCIETY FOR PHENOMENOLOGY
   Journal of the British Society for Phenomenology 405

BRITISH SOCIETY FOR SOCIAL RESPONSIBILITY IN SCIENCE
   Bulletin of the British Society for Social Responsibility in Science 1504
   Science for People 1515

BRITISH SOCIETY FOR STRAIN MEASUREMENT
   Strain 2397

BRITISH SOCIETY FOR SURGERY OF THE HAND
   Hand 2329

BRITISH SOCIETY FOR THE PHILOSOPHY OF SCIENCE
   British Journal for the Philosophy of Science 1503

BRITISH SOCIETY OF AESTHETICS
   British Journal of Aesthetics 413

BRITISH SOCIETY OF ANIMAL PRODUCTION
   Animal Production 2933

BRITISH SOCIETY OF DOWSERS
   Journal of the British Society of Dowsers 1822

BRITISH SOCIETY OF GASTROENTEROLOGY

BRITISH SOCIETY OF RHEOLOGY
   Rheology Abstracts 1705
   Bulletin of the British Society of Rheology 1704

BRITISH SOCIETY OF SCIENTIFIC GLASSBLOWERS
   Journal of the British Society of Scientific Glassblowers 3438B

SOCIETY OF GLASS TECHNOLOGY
   Physics and Chemistry of Glasses 3438C

BRITISH SOCIETY OF SOIL SCIENCE
   Journal of Soil Science 2855

BRITISH SOCIOLOGICAL ASSOCIATION
   Sociology 616

BRITISH-SOVIET FRIENDSHIP SOCIETY
   British-Soviet Friendship 4531

BRITISH SPELEOLOGICAL ASSOCIATION
   Bulletin of the British Speleological Association 1826
   Journal of the British Speleological Association 1828
   Proceedings of the British Speleological Association 1831
   Speleological Abstracts 1832

BRITISH SPELEOLOGICAL ASSOCIATION

BRITISH STANDARDS INSTITUTION
   BSI News 1442
   Quarterly Bulletin of the British Standards Institution 1443

BRITISH STATIONERY AND OFFICE EQUIPMENT ASSOCIATION
   New Stationer 3136

BRITISH TAR INDUSTRY ASSOCIATION
   Road Tar 3478

BRITISH THORACIC AND TUBERCULOSIS ASSOCIATION
   BTTA Review 2243
   Tubercle 2244

BRITISH TOY MANUFACTURERS ASSOCIATION
   British Toys 3730

BRITISH UNIDENTIFIED FLYING OBJECT RESEARCH ASSOCIATION
   Bufora Journal 2790

BRITISH VETERINARY ASSOCIATION
   Veterinary Record 2353
   Research in Veterinary Science 2350

BRITISH WATCH AND CLOCKMAKERS GUILD
   Jeweller 3521

BRITISH WATERFOWL ASSOCIATION
   Waterfowl 2021

BRITISH WATERWORKS ASSOCIATION
   British Water Supply 2673

BRONTË SOCIETY
   Transactions of the Brontë Society 4291

BROWNING SOCIETY OF LONDON
   Browning Society Notes 4267

BUDDHIST SOCIETY
   Middle Way 561

BURNHAM-ON-CROUCH LOCAL HISTORY SOCIETY
   Bulletin, Burnham-on-Crouch Local History Society 4305

CAMBORNE-REDRUTH NATURAL HISTORY SOCIETY
   Journal of the Camborne-Redruth Natural History Society 1537

CAMBRIDGE ANTIQUARIAN SOCIETY
    Proceedings of the Cambridge Antiquarian Society   4418
CAMBRIAN ARCHAEOLOGICAL ASSOCIATION
    Archaeologia Cambrensis   4439
CAMBRIDGE BIBLIOGRAPHICAL SOCIETY
    Transactions   23
CAMBRIDGE HISTORICAL SOCIETY
    Historical Journal   4315
CAMBRIDGE PHILOSOPHICAL SOCIETY
    Biological Reviews of the Cambridge Philosophical Society   1859
    Proceedings of the Cambridge Philosophical Society   1575
CAR AND MOTORCYCLE DRIVERS' ASSOCIATION
    CAMDA News   2711
CARDIFF MEDICAL SOCIETY
    Scientific Proceedings of the Cardiff Medical Society   2092
CARDIFF NATURALISTS SOCIETY
    Cardiff Naturalists Society Reports & Transactions   1525
    Transactions of the Cardiff Naturalists' Society   1556
CARDIGANSHIRE ANTIQUARIAN SOCIETY
    Ceredigion   4440
CATENIAN ASSOCIATION
    Catena   446
CATHOLIC BIBLICAL ASSOCIATION OF GREAT BRITAIN
    Scripture Bulletin   436
CATHOLIC COMMUNICATIONS INSTITUTE OF IRELAND
    Catholic Communications Institute of Ireland. Abstract of Periodicals   4610
    Catholic Communications Institute of Ireland. Weekly News Index   4611
CAVE DIVING GROUP OF GREAT BRITAIN
    Cave Diving Group Newsletter   1827
CAVE RESEARCH GROUP
    Newsletter of the Cave Research Group of Great Britain   1830
    Transactions of the Cave Research Group of Great Britain   1834
CELTIC LEAGUE
    A'bhrarach Ur   1068
CENTRAL COUNCIL FOR BRITISH NATURISM
    British Naturism
CERTIFIED BAILIFF'S ASSOCIATION OF ENGLAND & WALES
    Bailiff Journal   961
CHAIR FRAME MANUFACTURERS ASSOCIATION
    Weekly Circular of the Chair Frame Manufacturers Association   3677
CHARTERED INSTITUTE OF TRANSPORT
    Chartered Institute of Transport Journal   1373
CHARTERED INSURANCE INSTITUTE
    Journal of the Chartered Insurance Institute   1090
CHARTERED SOCIETY OF PHYSIOTHERAPY
    Physiotherapy   2218
CHEMICAL SOCIETY
    Aliphatic Alicyclic and Saturated Heterocyclic Chemistry   1707
    Alkaloids   1783
    Amino Acids Peptides and Proteins   1853
    Annual Reports on the Progress of Chemistry   1709
    Aromatic and Heteroaromatic Chemistry   1780
    Biosynthesis   1745
    Carbohydrate Chemistry   1778
    Chemical Communications   3315
    Chemical Society Reviews   1711
    Chemical Thermodynamics   1727
    Chemistry in Britain   1712
    Dialectric and Related Molecular Processes   1785
    Education in Chemistry   1211
    Electrochemistry   1730
    Electron Spin Resonance   1656
    Electronic Structure and Magnetism of Inorganic Compounds   1758
    Fluorocarbon and Related Chemistry   1768
    General Discussions of the Faraday Society   1722
    Index of Reviews in Organic Chemistry   1769
    Inorganic Chemistry of the Transition Elements   1760
    Inorganic Reaction Mechanisms   1761
    Journal of the Chemical Society   1714
    Journal of the Chemical Society: Dalton Transactions   1762
    Journal of the Chemical Society: Faraday Transactions I   1723
    Journal of the Chemical Society: Faraday Transactions II   1724
    Journal of the Chemical Society: Perkin Transactions I   1771
    Journal of the Chemical Society: Perkin Transactions II   1772
    Mass Spectrometry   1660
    Nuclear Magnetic Resonance   1662
    Organic Compounds of Sulphur, Selenium and Tellurium (Specialist Periodical Reports)   3339
    Organometalic Chemistry   1174
    Organophosphorus Chemistry (Specialist Periodical Reports)   3341
    Photochemistry   1732
    Russian Chemical Reviews   1719
    Russian Journal of Inorganic Chemistry   1704
    Russian Journal of Physical Chemistry   1725
    Spectroscopic Properties of Inorganic and Organometallic Compounds   1667
    Surface and Defect Properties of Solids   1775
    Symposia of the Faraday Society   1726
    Terpenoids and Steroids   1781
CHEST AND HEART ASSOCIATION
    Health   2154
CHESTER ARCHAEOLOGICAL SOCIETY
    Journal of the Chester Archaeological Society   4411
CHIGWELL LOCAL HISTORY SOCIETY
    Transactions: Chigwell Local History Society   4517
CHURCH LADS BRIGADE
    Brigade   1101
CHURCH MISSIONARY SOCIETY
    CMS Magazine   466
    In   469
    Pacemaker   471
    Swift   473
CHURCH MUSIC ASSOCIATION OF GREAT BRITAIN
    Church Music   3980
CHURCH OF ENGLAND CHILDRENS SOCIETY
    Gateway   1064
CITY OF LONDON PHONOGRAPH AND GRAMOPHONE SOCIETY
    Hillandale News   3648
CIVIL SERVICE MOTORING ASSOCIATION
    Civil Service Motoring   2719
CLASSICAL ASSOCIATION
    Classical Quarterly   1484
    Greece and Rome   4443
    Proceedings of the Classical Association   1486
CLOTHING INSTITUTE
    Clothing Institute Journal   3696
    Clothing Research Journal   3697
COAL TAR RESEARCH ASSOCIATION
    Coke and Chemistry U.S.S.R.   3346
COCKBURN ASSOCIATION
    Cockburn Association Newsletter   3843
COMMERCIAL RABBIT ASSOCIATION
    Quarterly Newsletter   2969
COMMONWEALTH FORESTRY ASSOCIATION
    Commonwealth Forestry Review   2886
COMMONWEALTH PARLIAMENTARY ASSOCIATION
    Parliamentarian   713
COMMONWEALTH SOCIETY
    Commonwealth   4465
COMMUNE MOVEMENT
    Communes   598
COMMUNICATIONS GUILD LTD
    Contemporary Communications   128
COMPUTER ARTS SOCIETY
    Page   3622
CONCHOLOGICAL SOCIETY OF GREAT BRITAIN & IRELAND
    Conchologist's Newsletter   1986
    Journal of the Conchological Society of Great Britain and Ireland   1987
CONCRETE SOCIETY
    Concrete   3456
CONFEDERATE HISTORICAL SOCIETY
    Journal of the Confederate Historical Society   4574
    Newsletter: Confederate Historical Society   4576
CONSTRUCTION INDUSTRY FEDERATION
    Construction   2610
CONSTRUCTION INDUSTRY INFORMATION GROUP
    CIIG Bulletin   36
CONSTRUCTION SURVEYORS INSTITUTE
    Construction Surveyor   1604
CONSUMERS ASSOCIATION
    Drug & Therapeutics Bulletin   2198
    Handyman Which?   3294
    Money Which?   3301
    Motoring Which?   3302
    Which?   3308
CORNISH METHODIST HISTORICAL ASSOCIATION
    Journal of the Cornish Methodist Historical Association   551
CORNWALL ARCHAEOLOGICAL SOCIETY
    Cornish Archaeology   4405

COSTUME SOCIETY
   Costume   1445
COTTESWOLD NATURALISTS' FIELD CLUB
   Proceedings of the Cotteswold Naturalists Field Club   1548
COUNCIL FOR THE PROTECTION OF RURAL WALES
   C.P.R.W. Newsletter   4456
COUNTRY GENTLEMENS ASSOCIATION
   Country Gentlemen's Magazine   832
COUNTRY LANDOWNERS ASSOCIATION
   Country Landowner   833
COUNTY COUNCILS ASSOCIATION
   County Councils Gazette   983
COUNTY KILDARE ARCHAEOLOGICAL SOCIETY
   Journal of County Kildare Archaeological Society   4394
CRAFTSMEN POTTERS ASSOCIATION OF GREAT BRITAIN
   Ceramic Review   3442
CRAVEN POTHOLE CLUB
   Journal of the Craven Pothole Club   1829
CREMATION SOCIETY AND INTERNATIONAL CREMATION FEDERATION
   Pharos   2167
CROQUET ASSOCIATION
   Croquet Gazette   4056
CROYDON NATURAL HISTORY AND SCIENTIFIC SOCIETY LTD.
   Bulletin of the Croydon Natural History and Scientific Society   1524
   Croydon Bibliographies for Regional Survey   1528
   Proceedings of the Croydon Natural History and Scientific Society   1549
CRUISING ASSOCIATION
   Cruising Association Bulletin   4135
CUMBERLAND & WESTMORLAND ANTIQUARIAN & ARCHAEOLOGICAL SOCIETY
   Transactions of the Cumberland & Westmorland Antiquarian & Archaeological Society   4428
CUMBERLAND GEOLOGICAL SOCIETY
   Proceedings of the Cumberland Geological Society   1807

DELIUS SOCIETY
   Delius Society Newsletter   3973
DERBYSHIRE ARCHAEOLOGICAL SOCIETY
   Derbyshire Archaeological Journal   4406
   Derbyshire Miscellany   4407
DEVON ARCHAEOLOGICAL SOCIETY
   Devon Archaeological Society: Proceedings   4408
DEVON BEEKEEPERS ASSOCIATION
   Beekeeping   2999
DICKENS FELLOWSHIP
   Dickensian   4271
DINER'S CLUB OF GREAT BRITAIN
   Signature   277
DOMESTIC HEATING SOCIETY
   Domestic Heating and Air Conditioning   3787
DORSET NATURAL HISTORY AND ARCHAEOLOGICAL SOCIETY
   Proceedings of the Dorset Natural History and Archaeological Society   1550

EAST AFRICAN WILD LIFE SOCIETY
   East African Wildlife Journal   1529

EAST HERTS ARCHAEOLOGICAL SOCIETY
   East Herts Archaeological Society Newsletter   4409
   Hertfordshire Archaeology   4410
EAST MIDLANDS ARTS ASSOCIATION
   Laurels   3832
EAST MIDLANDS GEOLOGICAL SOCIETY
   Mercian Geologist   1804
EASTERN ARTS ASSOCIATION
   Eastword   3824
ECONOMICS ASSOCIATION
   Economics   763
EDINBURGH MATHEMATICAL SOCIETY
   Proceedings of the Edinburgh Mathematical Society   1576
EDINBURGH MEDICAL MISSIONARY SOCIETY
   Healing Hand   468
EDUCATIONAL DRAMA ASSOCIATION
   Creative Drama   4021
EDUCATIONAL PUPPETRY ASSOCIATION
   Puppet Post   4016
EGYPT EXPLORATION SOCIETY
   Journal of Egyptian Archaeology   4382
ELECTORAL REFORM SOCIETY
   Representation   934
ELECTRIC TRANSPORT DEVELOPMENT SOCIETY
   News Sheet, Electric Transport Development Society   2463
ELECTRICAL ASSOCIATION FOR WOMEN
   Electrical Age   3052
ELECTRICAL CONTRACTORS ASSOCIATION
   ECA Bulletin   4676
   Electrical Contractor and Retailer   2444
ELECTRICAL POWER ENGINEERS ASSOCIATION
   Electrical Power Engineer   2448
ELECTRICAL WHOLESALERS FEDERATION
   Electrical Wholesaler   2452
ELECTROPHYSIOLOGICAL TECHNOLOGISTS ASSOCIATION
   Proceedings and Journal of the Electrophysiological Technologists Association   2112
ELGIN SOCIETY
   Elgin Society Newsletter   4445
ENGINEER SURVEYOR'S ASSOCIATION
   Engineer Surveyor   1605
ENGINEERS GUILD
   Professional Engineer   2385
ENGLISH ASSOCIATION
   English   4272
ENGLISH FOLK DANCE AND SONG SOCIETY
   English Dance and Song   4040
   Folk Music Journal   4042
ENGLISH GUERNSEY CATTLE SOCIETY
   Guernsey Breeders' Journal   2943
ENGLISH PLACE-NAME SOCIETY
   Journal of the English Place-Name Society   1476
ENGLISH-SPEAKING UNION
   Concord   654
ENGLISH TABLE TENNIS ASSOCIATION
   Table Tennis News   4059

ERGONOMICS RESEARCH SOCIETY
   Ergonomics   3248
ESPERANTO TEACHERS ASSOCIATION
   Esperanto Teacher   1474
ESSEX NATURALISTS' TRUST
   Essex Naturalist's Trust Bulletin   1530
EUROPEAN COMMITTEE OF PUMP MANUFACTURERS
   Pumps   2525
EUROPEAN PHYSICAL SOCIETY
   Europhysics News   1614
EUROPEAN PROPERTY OWNERS ASSOCIATION
   Europroperty Magazine   836
EUROPEAN WEED RESEARCH COUNCIL
   Weed Research   2871

FABIAN SOCIETY
   Third World   1061
   Venture   745
FACULTY OF RADIOLOGISTS
   Clinical Radiology   2221
FACULTY OF TEACHERS IN COMMERCE LTD.
   Teacher in Commerce   1190
FAIR ORGAN PRESERVATION SOCIETY
   Key Frame   3992
FAMILY HISTORY SOCIETY OF CHESHIRE
   North Cheshire Family Historian   4368
FAMILY PLANNING ASSOCIATION
   Family Planning   2131
FARADAY SOCIETY
   General Discussion of the Faraday Society   1722
   Journal of the Chemical Society: Faraday Transactions I   1723
   Journal of the Chemical Society: Faraday Transactions II   1724
   Symposia of the Faraday Society   1726
FARM BUILDINGS ASSOCIATION
   Journal of the Farm Buildings Association   2837
FARM MANAGEMENT ASSOCIATION
   Farm Management   2844
FAUNA PRESERVATION SOCIETY
   Oryx   1975
FEDERATION OF MASTER BUILDERS
   Master Builder's Journal   3766
FEDERATION OF MERCHANT TAILORS
   FMT News   3700
FEDERATION OF OLD CORNWALL SOCIETIES
   Old Cornwall   4417
FEDERATION OF SYNAGOGUES
   Hamaor   567
FESTINIOG RAILWAY SOCIETY
   Festiniog Railway Magazine   2633
FIRE PROTECTION ASSOCIATION
   Centre   2178
   Fire Prevention   2181
   Fire Prevention Science and Technology   2182
FLOUR MILLING AND BAKING RESEARCH ASSOCIATION
   Flour Milling and Baking Research Association Abstracts   3419
   Flour Milling and Baking Research Association Bulletin   3420
   Gazette   3421

FOLKLORE SOCIETY
  Folklore   1452
FOOD MANUFACTURERS' FEDERATION
  FMF Review   3398
FORENSIC SCIENCE SOCIETY
  Journal of the Forensic Science Society   921
FRANKLIN INSTITUTE
  Journal of the Franklin Institute   1619
FRANCO-BRITISH SOCIETY
  Britain—France   4525
FREIGHT TRANSPORT ASSOCIATION
  Freight   3151
FRESHWATER BIOLOGICAL ASSOCIATION
  Freshwater Biology   1867
FRIENDS HISTORICAL SOCIETY
  Journal of the Friends Historical Societies   559
FRIENDS OF COVENT GARDEN
  About the House   3975
FRIENDS OF THE LIBRARY (Trinity College, Dublin)
  Long Room   21
FRIENDS OF THE SCOTTISH NATIONAL ORCHESTRA
  In Tune   3954
FURNITURE HISTORY SOCIETY
  Furniture History   3675

GALLOWAY CATTLE SOCIETY
  Galloway Journal   2942
GALPIN SOCIETY
  Galpin Society Journal   3989
GALTON FOUNDATION
  Journal of Biosocial Science   1870
GAMEKEEPERS ASSOCIATION OF THE UK
  Gamekeepers Gazette   3004
GATESHEAD AND DISTRICT LOCAL HISTORY SOCIETY
  Gateshead and District Local History Society, Bulletin   4314
GEMMOLOGICAL ASSOCIATION OF GREAT BRITAIN
  Journal of Gemmology and Proceedings of the Gemmological Association of Great Britain   1790
GENERAL DENTAL PRACTITIONER'S ASSOCIATION
  Probe   2287
GENERAL STUDIES ASSOCIATION
  Bulletin of the General Studies Association   1113
GENETICAL SOCIETY OF GREAT BRITAIN
  Heredity   1884
GEOGRAPHICAL ASSOCIATION
  Geography   4355
GEOGRAPHICAL SOCIETY OF IRELAND
  Irish Geography   4357
GEOLOGICAL SOCIETY
  Geological Society Special Reports   1799
  Journal of the Geological Society   1801
  Memoirs of the Geological Society   1803
  Quarterly Journal of Engineering Geology   1810
GEOLOGICAL SOCIETY OF GLASGOW
  Proceedings of the Geological Society of Glasgow   1808, 4658
GEOLOGISTS' ASSOCIATION
  Proceedings of the Geologists Association   1809

GEOLOGISTS ASSOCIATION (South Wales Group)
  Welsh Geological Quarterly   4659
GILBERT & SULLIVAN SOCIETY
  Gilbert & Sullivan Journal   3976
GIRL GUIDES ASSOCIATION
  Brownie   1102
  Guider   1104
  Ranger   1105
  Today's Guide   1107
GLASGOW UNIVERSITY MEDICO-CHIRUGICAL SOCIETY
  Surgo   2095
GLOUCESTERSHIRE SOCIETY FOR INDUSTRIAL ARCHAEOLOGY
  G.S.I.A. Journal   4371
GOSHEN FELLOWSHIP
  Zion's Herald   460
GRADUATE'S FELLOWSHIP
  Christian Graduate   447
GREAT BRITAIN PHILATELIC SOCIETY
  G.B. Journal   3162
GREAT NORTH OF SCOTLAND RAILWAY ASSOCIATION
  Great North Review   2635
GREAT OUSE RESTORATION SOCIETY
  Lock Gate   1388
GREAT WESTERN SOCIETY
  Great Western Echo   2636
GREATER LONDON ARTS ASSOCIATION
  Greater London Arts   3826
GREATER LONDON ASSOCIATION FOR THE DISABLED
  Glad News   1054
GUILD FOR THE PROMOTION OF WELSH MUSIC
  Welsh Music   3972
GUILD OF FREEMEN OF THE CITY OF LONDON
  Freeman   158
GUILD OF HOSPITAL PHARMACISTS
  Journal of Hospital Pharmacy   2206
GUILD OF SURVEYORS
  Survey   1606
GUILD OF TEACHERS OF BACKWARD CHILDREN
  Guild of Teachers of Backward Children   1253
GYPSY LORE SOCIETY
  Journal of the Gypsy Lore Society   1449

H.G. WELLS SOCIETY
  Journal of the H.G. Wells Society   4277
HAMPSHIRE FIELD CLUB
  Hampshire Field Club Proceedings   1534
HANSARD SOCIETY
  Parliamentary Affairs   714
HARKER GEOLOGICAL SOCIETY
  Journal of the Harker Geological Society   1802
HEALTH VISITORS ASSOCIATION
  Health Visitor   2254
HEARTS OF OAK BENEFIT SOCIETY
  Hearts of Oak Journal   1023
HERALDRY SOCIETY
  Coat of Arms   4370
HEREFORD HERD BOOK SOCIETY
  Hereford Breed Journal   2944
HISTORIC SOCIETY OF LANCASHIRE & CHESHIRE
  Transactions of the Historic Society of Lancashire and Cheshire   4344

HISTORICAL ASSOCIATION
  Annual Bulletin of Historical Literature   4303
  History   4316
  History Teachers Newsletter   1224
  Teaching History   1225
HISTORICAL MODEL RAILWAY SOCIETY
  HMRS Journal   2637
HISTORICAL SOCIETY OF THE METHODIST CHURCH IN WALES
  BathaFarn   549
HISTORICAL SOCIETY OF THE PRESBYTERIAN CHURCH OF WALES
  Journal of the Historical Society of the Presbyterian Church of Wales   537
HISTORY OF EDUCATION SOCIETY
  History of Education Society Bulletin   1141
HONOURABLE SOCIETY OF CYMM RODORION
  Transactions of the Honourable Society of Cymm Rodorion   4518
HORTICULTURAL EDUCATION ASSOCIATION
  Scientific Horticulture   2913
HOSPITAL PHYSICISTS ASSOCIATION
  Physics in Medicine and Biology   2242
HOTEL CATERING AND INSTITUTIONAL MANAGEMENT ASSOCIATION
  Hotel Catering and Institutional Management Association Journal   3036
HOWARD LEAGUE FOR PENAL REFORM
  Howard Journal of Penology and Crime Prevention   947
HOWEY FOUNDATION
  Epoch   1927
HUGUENOT SOCIETY OF LONDON
  Proceedings of the Huguenot Society of London   534
  Huguenot Society of London Quarto Series   533

IBERIAN SOCIAL STUDIES ASSOCIATION
  Iberian Studies   4527
ILEOSTOMY ASSOCIATION OF GREAT BRITAIN AND IRELAND
  IA   2104
ILLUMINATING ENGINEERING SOCIETY
  Light and Lighting   2691
IMPERIAL SOCIETY OF TEACHERS OF DANCING
  Dance   1222
INCORPORATED ADVERTISING MANAGERS' ASSOCIATION
  Advertising & Marketing Management   3283
INCORPORATED ASSOCIATION OF ARCHITECTS & SURVEYORS
  Architect and Surveyor   3870
  Fire Surveyor   2184
INCORPORATED ASSOCIATION OF ASSISTANT MASTERS IN SECONDARY SCHOOLS
  AMA   1266
INCORPORATED ASSOCIATION OF COST & INDUSTRIAL ACCOUNTANTS
  Costing   3198
INCORPORATED ASSOCIATION OF ORGANISTS
  Organists Review   3995

APPENDIX 3

INCORPORATED BRITISH INSTITUTE OF CERTIFIED CARPENTERS
   Journal of the Incorporated British Institute of Certified Carpenters 3527
INCORPORATED PHONOGRAPHIC SOCIETY
   IPS Journal and Reporters Magazine 3090
INCORPORATED PRACTITIONERS IN RADIO AND ELECTRONICS LTD
   IPRE Review 2496
INCORPORATED SOCIETY OF VALUERS AND AUCTIONEERS
   Valuer 972
INDEPENDENT SCHOOLS ASSOCIATION
   Independent School 1144
INDIAN ASSOCIATION
   Mancunian Indian 702
INDUSTRIAL LAW SOCIETY
   Industrial Law Journal 949
INDUSTRIAL LOCOMOTIVE SOCIETY
   Industrial Locomotive Society Journal 2638
INDUSTRIAL MARKETING RESEARCH ASSOCIATION
   IMRA Journal 3296
   Industrial Marketing Research Abstracts 3295
INDUSTRIAL POLICE AND SECURITY ASSOCIATION
   Security and Protection 979
INLAND WATERWAYS ASSOCIATION
   Bulletin of the Inland Waterways Association 1387
INNER LONDON TEACHERS ASSOCIATION
   Centre Point 1226
INTERNATIONAL SOCIETY FOR THE EVANGELIZATION OF THE JEWS
   Herald 568
INSTITUTE FOR THE COMPARATIVE STUDY OF HISTORY, PHILOSOPHY AND THE SCIENCES
   Systematics 409
INSTITUTE FOR THE STUDY OF CONFLICT
   Conflict Studies 709
INSTITUTE OF ACTUARIES
   Journal of the Institute of Actuaries 1091
INSTITUTE OF ARCHAEOLOGY
   Committee for Nautical Archaeology: Newsletter 4404
INSTITUTE OF BANKERS
   Journal of the Institute of Bankers 811
INSTITUTE OF BATHS MANAGEMENT
   Baths Service 4152
INSTITUTE OF BIOLOGY
   Biologist 1861
   Journal of Biological Education 1213
INSTITUTE OF BOOK-KEEPERS
   Book-keepers Journal 3188
INSTITUTE OF BREWING
   Journal of the Institute of Brewing 3389
INSTITUTE OF BRITISH FOUNDRYMEN
   British Foundrymen 2532
INSTITUTE OF BRITISH GEOGRAPHERS
   Area 4350
   Institute of British Geographers, Transactions 4356

INSTITUTE OF CAREERS OFFICERS
   Careers Quarterly 1240
INSTITUTE OF CERTIFIED AMBULANCE PERSONNEL
   Ambulance 2189
INSTITUTE OF CHARTERED ACCOUNTANTS IN ENGLAND AND WALES
   Accountancy 3180
   Accounting and Business Research 3186
   Accounting & Data Processing Abstracts 3187
INSTITUTE OF CHARTERED ACCOUNTANTS IN IRELAND
   Accountancy Ireland 3182
INSTITUTE OF CHARTERED ACCOUNTANTS OF SCOTLAND
   Accountant's Magazine 3184
INSTITUTE OF CLAY TECHNOLOGY
   Clay Crafts & Structural Ceramics 3444
INSTITUTE OF COMPANY ACCOUNTANTS
   Company Accountants 3191
INSTITUTE OF CONTEMPORARY HISTORY
   Wiener Library Bulletin 4349
INSTITUTE OF COST AND MANAGEMENT ACCOUNTANTS
   Management Accounting 3196
INSTITUTE OF CRAFT EDUCATION
   Practical Education 1162
INSTITUTE OF CREDIT MANAGEMENT
   Credit Management 3277
INSTITUTE OF DATA PROCESSING
   Data Processing Practitioner 3611
INSTITUTE OF DIRECTORS
   Director 3203
INSTITUTE OF FUEL
   Fuel Abstracts and Current Titles 3352
   Journal of the Institute of Fuel 3354
INSTITUTE OF GROUNDSMANSHIP
   Groundsman 3857
INSTITUTE OF GROUP ANALYSIS
   Group Analysis 2226
INSTITUTE OF HEALTH EDUCATION
   Journal of the Institute of Health Education 2156
INSTITUTE OF HEALTH SERVICE ADMINISTRATORS
   Hospital and Health Services Review 1043
   Hospital and Health Services Purchasing
INSTITUTE OF HERALDIC AND GENEALOGICAL STUDIES
   Family History 4362
INSTITUTE OF HISTORICAL RESEARCH
   Bulletin of the Institute of Historical Research 4307
INSTITUTE OF HOME HELP ORGANISERS
   Journal of the Institute of Home Help Organisers 2256
INSTITUTE OF HOUSING MANAGERS
   Housing 841
INSTITUTE OF INDUSTRIAL RESEARCH
   Food Progress 4696
INSTITUTE OF INDUSTRIAL SUPERVISORS
   Supervisor 3236

INSTITUTE OF JEWISH AFFAIRS
   Christian Attitudes on Jews and Judaism 565
   Patterns of Prejudice 575
   Soviet Jewish Affairs 578
INSTITUTE OF LANDSCAPE ARCHITECTS
   Landscape Design 3859
INSTITUTE OF MARINE ENGINEERS
   Marine Engineering and Shipbuilding Abstracts 2754
   Marine Engineers Review 2755
   Transactions: Institute of Marine Engineers 2765
INSTITUTE OF MARKETING
   Marketing 3261
INSTITUTE OF MATERIALS HANDLING
   Materials Handling and Management 2569
INSTITUTE OF MATHEMATICS AND ITS APPLICATIONS
   Journal of the Institute of Mathematics and its Applications 1567
INSTITUTE OF MEASUREMENT AND CONTROL
   Measurement and Control 3632
INSTITUTE OF MEDICAL AND BIOLOGICAL ILLUSTRATION
   Medical and Biological Illustration 2070
INSTITUTE OF METAL FINISHING
   Transactions of the Institute of Metal Finishing 3471
INSTITUTE OF METALS
   Journal of the Institute of Metals 3483
   Metals Abstracts 3487
   Metals and Materials 3488
   Powder Metallurgy 2536
INSTITUTE OF MINING AND METALLURGY
   IMM Abstracts 2587
INSTITUTE OF MUNICIPAL TREASURERS AND ACCOUNTANTS
   Local Government Finance 986
INSTITUTE OF NAVIGATION
   Journal of Navigation 1610
INSTITUTE OF PACKAGING
   Packaging Technology 2555
INSTITUTE OF PARK & RECREATION ADMINISTRATION
   Parks and Recreation 3860
INSTITUTE OF PERSONNEL MANAGEMENT
   IPM Digest 3232
   Personnel Review 3235
INSTITUTE OF PETROLEUM
   Institute of Petroleum Abstracts 3429
   Journal of the Institute of Petroleum 3430
   Petroleum Review 3433
INSTITUTE OF PHYSICS
   Journal of Physics 1615, 1616, 1693, 1701, 3482, 3630
   Metal Physics 1620
   Physics Bulletin 1624
   Physics Education 1210
   Reports on Progress in Physics 1626
   Review of Physics in Technology 1627
INSTITUTE OF PLUMBING
   Plumbing 3780
INSTITUTE OF POPULATION REGISTRATION
   Population Registration 640
INSTITUTE OF PRINTING
   Professional Printer 3117

INSTITUTE OF PSYCHO-ANALYSIS
   International Journal of Psycho-
   analysis 404
INSTITUTE OF PSYCHOLOGY
   Man 390
INSTITUTE OF PSYCHOPHYSICAL
RESEARCH
   Proceedings of the Institute of
   Psychophysical Research 391
INSTITUTE OF PURCHASING &
SUPPLY
   Purchasing Journal 3252
INSTITUTE OF PYRAMIDOLOGY
   Pyramidology Magazine 3892
INSTITUTE OF QUANTITY
SURVEYORS
   Quantity Surveyor 3770
INSTITUTE OF RACE RELATIONS
   Race 704
   Race Relations Abstracts 706
   Race Today 708
INSTITUTE OF REFRIGERATION
   Proceedings of the Institute of
   Refrigeration 2521
INSTITUTE OF REPROGRAPHIC
TECHNOLOGY
   Repro 3946
INSTITUTE OF ROAD TRANSPORT
ENGINEERS
   Transport Engineer 1418
INSTITUTE OF SCIENCE
TECHNOLOGY
   Bulletin of the Institute of Science
   Technology 3313
INSTITUTE OF SHOPS ACTS
ADMINISTRATION
   Inspector 3271
INSTITUTE OF SOCIAL ANTHRO-
   POLOGY
   Journal of the Anthropological
   Society of Oxford 1852
INSTITUTE OF STATISTICIANS
   Statistician 635
INSTITUTE OF SUPERVISORY
MANAGEMENT
   Supervisory Management 3237
INSTITUTE OF TECHNICAL PUB-
LICITY AND PUBLICATIONS
   Communicator of Technical
   Information 3278
INSTITUTE OF THE MOTOR IN-
DUSTRY
   Motor Management 2736
INSTITUTE OF TRAINING OFFICERS
   Training Officer 1179
INSTITUTE OF TRICHOLOGISTS
   Trichologist 2292
INSTITUTE OF WATER POLLUTION
CONTROL
   Water Pollution Control 2682
INSTITUTE OF WEIGHTS AND
MEASURES ADMINISTRATION
   Monthly Review of the Institute
   of Weights and Measures Adminis-
   tration 1436
INSTITUTE OF WELFARE OFFICERS
   Welfare Officer 1033
INSTITUTE OF WOOD SCIENCE
   Journal of the Institute of Wood
   Science 3528
INSTITUTE OF WORK STUDY PRAC-
   TITIONERS
   Work Study and Management Ser-
   vice 3244
INSTITUTION OF BRITISH
ENGINEERS
   British Engineer 2359

INSTITUTION OF CHEMICAL
ENGINEERS
   Chemical Engineer and Transactions
   of the Institution of Chemical
   Engineers 3324
INSTITUTION OF CIVIL ENGINEERS
   Control and Science Record 2436
   Geotechnique 2629
   Institution of Civil Engineers
   Proceedings 2617
   New Civil Engineer 2621
   New Civil Engineer 4680
INSTITUTION OF COMPUTER
SCIENCES
   Journal of the Institution of Com-
   puter Sciences 3620
INSTITUTION OF ELECTRICAL AND
ELECTRONICS TECHNICIAN
ENGINEERS
   Electrical and Electronics Tech-
   nician Engineer 2442
   Electro Technology 4677
INSTITUTION OF ELECTRICAL
ENGINEERS
   IEE News 2454
   Electronics and Power 2470
   Electronics Letters 2471
   Electronics Record 2472
   Power Record 2457
   Proceedings of the Institution of
   Electrical Engineers 2617
INSTITUTION OF ELECTRONIC AND
RADIO ENGINEERS
   Radio and Electronic Engineer
   2502
INSTITUTION OF ENGINEERING
INSPECTION
   Quality Engineer 3245
INSTITUTION OF ENGINEERS AND
SHIPBUILDERS IN SCOTLAND
   Transactions of the Institution of
   Engineers & Shipbuilders in Scot-
   land 2767
INSTITUTION OF FIRE ENGINEERS
   Institution of Fire Engineers
   Quarterly 2185
INSTITUTION OF GAS ENGINEERS
   Journal of the Institution of Gas
   Engineers 3363
INSTITUTION OF HEATING &
VENTILATING ENGINEERS
   IHVE Journal 3794
INSTITUTION OF HIGHWAY
ENGINEERS
   Journal of the Institution of High-
   way Engineers 2666
INSTITUTION OF INDUSTRIAL SAFETY
OFFICERS
   Protection 2175
INSTITUTION OF MECHANICAL
ENGINEERS
   Automotive Engineering 2708
   Chartered Mechanical Engineer
   2407
   Engineering in Medicine 2368
   Heat and Fluid Flow 1640
   Journal of Automotive Engineering
   2730
   Journal of Mechanical Engineering
   Science 2410
   Journal of Strain Analysis 2393
   Mechanical Engineering News
   4673
   Railway Engineering Journal 2653
INSTITUTION OF MINING AND
METALLURGY
   Transactions of the Institution of
   Mining and Metallurgy 1812

INSTITUTION OF MINING ENGINEERS
   Mining Engineer 2592
INSTITUTION OF MUNICIPAL
ENGINEERS
   Journal of the Institution of
   Municipal Engineers 2378
INSTITUTION OF NUCLEAR
ENGINEERS
   Journal of the Institution of Nu-
   clear Engineers 2417
INSTITUTION OF POST OFFICE
ELECTRICAL ENGINEERS
   New Quarterly Journal 2486
INSTITUTION OF PRODUCTION
ENGINEERS
   International Journal of Production
   Research 3239
   Production Engineer 3221
INSTITUTION OF RAILWAY SIGNAL
ENGINEERS
   Proceedings of the Institution of
   Railway Signal Engineers 2650
INSTITUTION OF STRUCTURAL
ENGINEERS
   Structural Engineer 2623
INSTITUTION OF THE RUBBER
INDUSTRY
   Journal of the IRI 3575
INSTITUTION OF WATER ENGINEERS
   Journal of the Institution of Water
   Engineers 2675
INSTITUTION OF WORKS MANAGERS
   Works Management 3225
INSURANCE INSTITUTE OF LONDON
   Journal of the Insurance Institute
   of London 1092
INTERNATIONAL ARTHURIAN
SOCIETY
   Bibliographical Bulletin of the
   International Arthurian Society
   4265
INTERNATIONAL ASSOCIATION FOR
EARTHQUAKE ENGINEERING
   International Journal of Earthquake
   Engineering and Structural Dyna-
   mics 1819
INTERNATIONAL ASSOCIATION OF
AGRICULTURAL ECONOMISTS
   International Journal of Agrarian
   Affairs 2807
INTERNATIONAL ASSOCIATION OF
APPLIED PSYCHOLOGY
   International Review of Applied
   Psychology 386
INTERNATIONAL ASSOCIATION OF
HYDROLOGICAL SCIENCE
   Hydrological Sciences Bulletin
   1839
INTERNATIONAL ASSOCIATION OF
INDIVIDUAL PSYCHOLOGY
   Individual Psychology News Letter
   384
INTERNATIONAL ASSOCIATION OF
MUSIC LIBRARIES
   Brio 34
INTERNATIONAL ASSOCIATION OF
SEDIMENTOLOGISTS
   Sedimentology 1823
INTERNATIONAL ASSOCIATION OF
WATER POLLUTION RESEARCH
   Water Research 2683
INTERNATIONAL BAR ASSOCIATION
   International Bar Journal 902
INTERNATIONAL CAMELLIA
SOCIETY
   International Camellia Journal
   2922
INTERNATIONAL CARGO HANDLING
CO-ORDINATION ASSOCIATION
   ICHCA Monthly Journal 3154

APPENDIX 3

INTERNATIONAL CIVIL AIRPORT ASSOCIATION
 Airports International 1433
INTERNATIONAL DANCE TEACHERS ASSOCIATION
 Dance Teacher 1223
INTERNATIONAL EGG COMMISSION
 Market Review 2987
 Six Monthly Statistical Bulletin 2988
INTERNATIONAL GLACIOLOGICAL SOCIETY
 Ice 1824
 Journal of Glaciology 1825
INTERNATIONAL INSTITUTE FOR CONSERVATION OF HISTORIC AND ARTISTIC WORKS
 Studies in Conservation 346
INTERNATIONAL INSTITUTE OF WELDING
 Welding in the World 2539
INTERNATIONAL LANGUAGE [IDO] SOCIETY OF GREAT BRITAIN
 Ido-Letro 1469
INTERNATIONAL MEDICAL SOCIETY OF PARAPLEGIA
 Paraplegia 2305
INTERNATIONAL ORDER OF GOOD TEMPLARS
 English Templar Youth 1073
 Good Templar Watchword 1075
 Juvenile Templar 1077
INTERNATIONAL PHONETIC ASSOCIATION
 Journal of the International Phonetic Association 1477
INTERNATIONAL POETRY SOCIETY
 Orbis 4234
INTERNATIONAL SOCIETY FOR KRISHNA CONSCIOUSNESS
 Back to Godhead 414
INTERNATIONAL SOCIETY FOR TERRAIN VEHICLE SYSTEMS
 Journal of Terramechanics 2619
INTERNATIONAL STUDY GROUP FOR MATHEMATICS LEARNING
 Journal of Structural Learning 1566
INTERNATIONAL TEMPERANCE ASSOCIATION
 Alert 411
INTERNATIONAL TRANSPORT WORKERS FEDERATION
 ITF Journal 1376
 ITF Newsletter 1377
INTERNATIONAL UNION FOR PURE AND APPLIED BIOPHYSICS
 Quarterly Reviews of Biophysics 1915
INTERNATIONAL UNION OF PURE AND APPLIED CHEMISTRY
 IUPAC Information Bulletin 1713
 Pure and Applied Chemistry 1717
IRISH COMPUTER SOCIETY
 Irish Computer Society Bulletin 4702
IRISH CREAMERY MILK SUPPLIERS ASSOCIATION
 Irish Farming News 2836
IRISH DENTAL ASSOCIATION
 Journal of the Irish Dental Association 2286
IRISH GENEALOGICAL RESEARCH SOCIETY
 Irish Genealogist 4366
IRISH MEDICAL ASSOCIATION
 Journal of the Irish Medical Association 2063
IRISH NURSES ORGANISATION
 World of Irish Nursing 2261

IRISH SCIENCE TEACHERS ASSOCIATION
 Science 1205
IRISH SOCIETY FOR ARCHIVES
 Irish Archives Bulletin 357
IRON AND STEEL INSTITUTE
 Journal of the Iron and Steel Institute 3497
 Steel in the USSR 3504
IRON AND STEEL TRADES CONFEDERATION
 Man and Metal 3499

JERSEY CATTLE SOCIETY OF THE U.K.
 The Jersey 2947
JEWISH VEGETARIAN & NATURAL HEALTH SOCIETY
 Jewish Vegetarian 3048
JOHANN STRAUSS SOCIETY OF GREAT BRITAIN
 Tritsch-Tratsch 3974
JOHNSON SOCIETY OF LONDON
 New Rambler 4281
JOINT ASSOCIATION OF CLASSICAL TEACHERS
 Didaskalos 1228
JOSEPHINE BUTLER SOCIETY
 Shield 591
JUNIOR ASTRONOMICAL SOCIETY
 Hermes 1588
JUNIOR HOSPITAL DOCTORS ASSOCIATION
 On-Call 2079
JUNIOR INSTITUTION OF ENGINEERS
 Journal of the Junior Institution of Engineers 2379
JUSTICES' CLERKS' SOCIETY
 Justices' Clerk 958

KEIGHLEY & WORTH VALLEY RAILWAY PRESERVATION SOCIETY
 Push and Pull 2651
KENT ARCHAELOGICAL SOCIETY
 Archaeologia Cautiana 4398
KENT COUNCIL OF SOCIAL SERVICE
 Cantium 4462
KIPLING SOCIETY
 Kipling Journal 4278

LACE SOCIETY OF WALES
 Lacemaking 3921
LANCASHIRE AND CHESHIRE ANTIQUARIAN SOCIETY
 Transactions of the Lancashire and Cheshire Antiquarian Society 4429
LANCASHIRE & CHESHIRE ENTOMOLOGICAL SOCIETY
 Annual Report and Proceedings of the Lancashire & Cheshire Entomological Society 1992
LANCASHIRE AND CHESHIRE FAUNA SOCIETY
 Proceedings of the Lancashire and Cheshire Fauna Society 1551
LANCASHIRE DIALECT SOCIETY
 Journal of the Lancashire Dialect Society 1467
LAW SOCIETY
 Law Society's Gazette 910
LAW SOCIETY OF SCOTLAND
 Journal of the Law Society of Scotland 904
LAWN TENNIS ASSOCIATION
 Lawn Tennis 4076
LEATHER INSTITUTE
 Wear 3708

LEATHERGOODS ASSOCIATION OF BUYERS & RETAILERS
 International Leathergoods Buyer 3681
LEEDS GEOLOGICAL ASSOCIATION
 Journal of Earth Sciences 1800
LEICESTERSHIRE ARCHAEOLOGICAL & HISTORICAL SOCIETY
 Transactions of the Leicestershire Archaeological & Historical Society 4430
LEWIS CARROLL SOCIETY
 Jabberwocky 4276
LIBRARY ACTION GROUP
 Library Action 50
LIBRARY ASSOCIATION
 Bibliotheck 5
 Book Trolley 32
 British Humanities Index 3
 Catalogue and Index 72
 County Newsletter 37
 East Midlands Bibliography 13
 Easterner 39
 Focus on International and Comparative Librarianship 41
 Journal of Librarianship 44
 Kent Newsletter 45
 Leg News 46
 Library and Information Bulletin 19
 Library and Information Science Abstracts 52
 Library Association Record 51
 Library History 53
 Medical Section of the Library Association Bulletin 56
 North Western Newsletter 57
 YLG News 69
 Yorkshire Librarian 71
LIBRARY ASSOCIATION, YORKSHIRE BRANCH
 Stress 4588
LIBRARY ASSOCIATION OF IRELAND
 An Leabharlaun 25
 Northern Ireland Libraries 25
LIGHT RAILWAY TRANSPORT LEAGUE
 Modern Tramway 1425
 Tramway Review 1427
LIGUE DES BIBLIOTHEQUES EUROPEENNES DE RECHERCHE
 Liber Bulletin 48
LINCOLNSHIRE LOCAL HISTORY SOCIETY
 Lincolnshire History and Archaeology 4412
LINCOLNSHIRE NATURALISTS UNION
 Transactions of the Lincolnshire Naturalists' Union 1557
LINNEAN SOCIETY
 Botanical Journal of the Linnean Society 1943
 Zoological Journal of the Linnean Society 1976
LIVERPOOL GEOLOGICAL SOCIETY
 Amateur Geologist 1791
LONDON & MIDDLESEX ARCHAEOLOGICAL SOCIETY
 Transactions of the London & Middlesex Archaeological Society 4431
LONDON ASSOCIATION OF ENGINEERS
 Journal of the London Association of Engineers 2380
LONDON MATHEMATICAL SOCIETY
 Bulletin of the London Mathematical Society 1563

Journal of the London Mathematical Society 1568
Proceedings of the London Mathematical Society 1577
LONDON RECUSANT SOCIETY
London Recusant 504
LONDON SOCIETY
Journal of the London Society 4485
LONDON SOCIETY
London Society Journal 4496
LORD'S DAY OBSERVANCE SOCIETY
Joy and Light 462
LUTE SOCIETY
Journal of the Lute Society 3998

MAGISTRATES' ASSOCIATION
Magistrate 954
MALACOLOGICAL SOCIETY OF LONDON
Proceedings of the Malacological Society of London 1988
MAMMAL SOCIETY
Mammal Review 2024
MAMMILLARIA SOCIETY
Journal of the Mammillaria Society 2023
MANCHESTER ASSOCIATION OF ENGINEERS
Manchester Engineer 2381
MANCHESTER LITERARY AND PHILOSOPHICAL SOCIETY
Memoirs and Proceedings 1508
MANCHESTER TRANSPORT MUSEUM SOCIETY
765 Journal 354
MARKET RESEARCH SOCIETY
Journal of the Market Research Society 3297
Market Research Abstracts 3298
MARLOWE SOCIETY
Marlovian Chronicle 4026
MARRIED WOMEN'S ASSOCIATION
Married Women's Association Bulletin 1079
MASTER PHOTOGRAPHER'S ASSOCIATION
Master Photographer 3933
MATHEMATICAL ASSOCIATION
Mathematical Gazette 1570
Mathematics in School 1573
MEDICAL SOCIETY FOR THE STUDY OF VENEREAL DISEASES
British Journal of Venereal Diseases 2323
MEDICAL WOMENS' FEDERATION
Journal of the Medical Women's Federation 2064
MEDICO-LEGAL SOCIETY
Medico-Legal Journal 922
MENTAL HEALTH ASSOCIATION OF IRELAND
Newsletter Mental Health Association of Ireland 4669
MERCHANT NAVY & AIRLINE OFFICERS' ASSOCIATION
Telegraph 1413
METHODIST CHURCH MUSIC SOCIETY
Methodist Church Music Society Bulletin 3981
METHODIST MISSIONARY SOCIETY
New 553
MICROFILM ASSOCIATION OF GREAT BRITAIN
Microdoc 3944
MIDLAND SOCIETY FOR THE STUDY OF MENTAL SUBNORMALITY
Journal of Mental Subnormality 2317

MINERALOGICAL SOCIETY
Clay Minerals 3445
Mineralogical Magazine 1788, 1789
Mineralogical Abstracts 1788
MODERN HUMANITIES RESEARCH ASSOCIATION
Modern Language Review 1465
MODERN LANGUAGE ASSOCIATION
Modern Languages 1193
MONARCHIST LEAGUE
Monarchist 928
MONEYSAVERS ASSOCIATION
Moneysavers 4623
MOTOR AGENTS ASSOCIATION
Motor Trade Executive 2738
MOTOR INDUSTRY RESEARCH ASSOCIATION
Mira Abstracts 2731
MOTOR SCHOOLS ASSOCIATION OF GREAT BRITAIN
MSA News 2732
MUSCULAR DYSTROPHY GROUP OF GREAT BRITAIN
Muscular Dystrophy Journal 2298
MUSEUMS ASSOCIATION
Monthly Bulletin 341
Museums Calendar 342
Museums Journal 343
MUSHROOM GROWERS' ASSOCIATION
MGA Bulletin 2914
MUSIC BOX SOCIETY OF GREAT BRITAIN
Music Box 3649
MUSICAL INSTRUMENT PROMOTION ASSOCIATION
Living Music 3956
MUZZLE LOADERS ASSOCIATION OF GREAT BRITAIN
Black Powder 4178

N.S.P.C.C.
Child's Guardian 412
NAMES SOCIETY
Viz 1475
NARROW GAUGE RAILWAY SOCIETY
Narrow Gauge 2647
Narrow Gauge News 2648
NATIONAL ANTI-VIVISECTION SOCIETY
Animals Defender and Anti-Vivisection News 2114
NATIONAL ASSOCIATION FOR MENTAL HEALTH
Mental Health 2320
Mind 2321
NATIONAL ASSOCIATION FOR THE CARE AND RESETTLEMENT OF OFFENDERS
NACRO Information Bulletin 1024
NATIONAL ASSOCIATION FOR REMEDIAL EDUCATION
Remedial Education 1167
NATIONAL ASSOCIATION FOR THE TEACHING OF ENGLISH
English in Education 1196
NATIONAL ASSOCIATION OF ALMSHOUSES
Almshouses Gazette 1060
NATIONAL ASSOCIATION OF BOOKMAKERS
British Bookmaker 4050
NATIONAL ASSOCIATION OF BRASS BAND CONDUCTORS
Sounding Brass 3985
NATIONAL ASSOCIATION OF CLINICAL TUTORS
Bulletin of the National Association of Clinical Tutors 2055

NATIONAL ASSOCIATION OF DROP FORGERS AND STAMPERS
Drop Forging Bulletin 3480
NATIONAL ASSOCIATION OF FLOWER ARRANGEMENT SOCIETIES
Flower Arranger 2921
NATIONAL ASSOCIATION OF GOLDSMITHS
Watchmaker, Jeweller and Silversmith 3596
NATIONAL ASSOCIATION OF LADIES CIRCLES
Ladies Circle Magazine 1078
NATIONAL ASSOCIATION OF MASTER BAKERS
Bakers' Review 3413
NATIONAL ASSOCIATION OF PARISH COUNCILS
Parish Council's Review 993
NATIONAL ASSOCIATION OF POULTRY PACKERS LTD
National Association of Poultry Packers Ltd. Weekly Industry 2958
NATIONAL ASSOCIATION OF PROBATION OFFICERS
Probation 943
NATIONAL ASSOCIATION OF ROUND TABLES OF GREAT BRITAIN AND IRELAND
News and Views 1080
NATIONAL ASSOCIATION OF SCHOOLMASTERS
New Schoolmaster 1229
NATIONAL ASSOCIATION OF SEED POTATO MERCHANTS
Seed Potato 2883
NATIONAL ASSOCIATION OF SOFT DRINKS MANUFACTURERS LTD
Soft Drinks Trade Journal 3390
NATIONAL ASSOCIATION OF TEACHERS OF THE MENTALLY HANDICAPPED
Teaching and Training 1258
NATIONAL ASSOCIATION OF THEATRE NURSES
Natnews 2258
NATIONAL ASSOCIATION OF TOY RETAILERS
Toy Trader 3736
NATIONAL AURICULA AND PRIMULA SOCIETY
Offsets 4686
NATIONAL BEGONIA SOCIETY
National Begonia Society Bulletin 2924
NATIONAL BOOK LEAGUE
Books 75
NATIONAL CACTUS AND SUCCULENT SOCIETY
National Cactus and Succulent Society Journal 2925
NATIONAL CARAVAN COUNCIL
NCC Members Newsletter 3897
NATIONAL CHILDRENS WEAR ASSOCIATION
Junior Age 3706
NATIONAL COUNCIL FOR ANIMALS WELFARE
Animals' Friend Magazine 2928
NATIONAL COUNCIL FOR EDUCATIONAL TECHNOLOGY
British Journal of Educational Technology 1111
NATIONAL COUNCIL FOR QUALITY AND RELIABILITY
Quality Matters 3246

APPENDIX 3

NATIONAL COUNCIL FOR THE SUPPLY AND TRAINING OF TEACHERS OVERSEAS
    Overseas Challenge   1230

NATIONAL DAIRYMEN'S ASSOCIATION
    Milk Industry   2978

NATIONAL DOG OWNERS ASSOCIATION
    Dog News   2962

NATIONAL EGG PRODUCER RETAILERS' ASSOCIATION
    Market Report   2986

NATIONAL FARMERS UNION
    British Farmer   2823

NATIONAL FEDERATION OF BUSINESS AND PROFESSIONAL WOMEN'S CLUBS OF GREAT BRITAIN AND N. IRELAND
    Business and Professional Woman   1069

NATIONAL FEDERATION OF MASTER PAINTERS AND DECORATORS
    Masterpainter and Decorator   3806

NATIONAL FEDERATION OF MEAT TRADERS ASSOCIATIONS
    Meat Trader   2992

NATIONAL FEDERATION OF OLD AGE PENSIONS ASSOCIATIONS
    Pensioners Voice   1056

NATIONAL FEDERATION OF PARENT-TEACHER ASSOCIATIONS
    Parent-Teacher   1231

NATIONAL FEDERATION OF ROOFING CONTRACTORS
    Roofing Contractor   3769

NATIONAL FEDERATION OF SUB-POSTMASTERS
    Sub-Postmaster   3158

NATIONAL FEDERATION OF VILLAGE PRODUCE ASSOCIATIONS
    Village Life   3039

NATIONAL FEDERATION OF WOMEN'S INSTITUTES
    Home & Country   1076

NATIONAL FROEBEL FOUNDATION
    Froebel Journal   1263

NATIONAL GRAPHICAL ASSOCIATION
    Print   3106

NATIONAL INDUSTRIAL MATERIALS RECOVERY ASSOCIATION
    Industrial Recovery   2688

NATIONAL INSTITUTE FOR ADULT EDUCATION
    Adult Education   1272
    Teaching Adults   1278

NATIONAL INSTITUTE OF AGRICULTURAL BOTANY
    Journal of the National Institute of Agricultural Botany   2810

NATIONAL INSTITUTE OF INDUSTRIAL PSYCHOLOGY
    NIIP Bulletin   3226
    Occupational Psychology   3227

NATIONAL INSTITUTE OF MEDICAL HERBALISTS
    Herbal Practitioner   2205

NATIONAL OPERATIC & DRAMATIC ASSOCIATION
    NODA Bulletin   3977

NATIONAL PHILATELIC SOCIETY
    Stamp Lover   3174

NATIONAL PIG BREEDERS ASSOCIATION
    Pig Breeders Gazette   2954

NATIONAL PLAYING FIELDS ASSOCIATION
    Playing Fields   3862

NATIONAL RIFLE ASSOCIATION
    National Rifle Association Journal   4180

NATIONAL SCHOOL BRASS BAND ASSOCIATION
    Trumpeter   4000

NATIONAL SOCIETY FOR CLEAN AIR
    Clean Air   2170

NATIONAL SOCIETY FOR MENTALLY HANDICAPPED CHILDREN
    Journal of Mental Deficiency Research   2316

NATIONAL SOCIETY OF CHILDREN'S NURSERIES
    Nursery Journal   1264

NATIONAL SOCIETY OF MASTER PATTERNMAKERS
    British Master Patternmaker   2528

NATIONAL SOCIETY OF OPERATIVE PRINTERS GRAPHICAL AND MEDIA PERSONNEL
    Journal and Graphic Review   186

NATIONAL TROLLEYBUS ASSOCIATION
    Trolleybus Magazine   1428

NATIONAL UNION OF RAILWAYMEN
    Railway Review   2660

NATIONAL UNION OF SEAMEN
    Seaman   1408

NATIONAL UNION OF TAILORS AND GARMENT WORKERS
    Garment Worker   3705

NATIONAL UNION OF TEACHERS
    Higher Education Journal   1290
    Secondary Education   1290
    Teacher   1237

NATIONAL SWEET PEA SOCIETY
    Bulletin of the National Sweet Pea Society   2918

NATURAL HISTORY AND ANTIQUARIAN SOCIETY OF MID-ARGYLL
    Kist   1539

NATURAL HISTORY SOCIETY OF NORTHUMBERLAND, DURHAM & NEWCASTLE-ON-TYNE
    Transactions of the Natural History Society of Northumberland, Durham & Newcastle-on-Tyne   1559

NEW TOWNS ASSOCIATION
    New Towns Bulletin   3848

NEWCOMEN SOCIETY
    Transactions of the Newcomen Society   2039

NEWSPAPER SOCIETY
    Production Journal   352

NON-DESTRUCTIVE TESTING SOCIETY OF GREAT BRITAIN
    British Journal of Non-Destructive Testing   2391

NORFOLK & NORWICH ARCHAEOLOGICAL SOCIETY
    Norfolk Archaeology   4414

NORFOLK AND NORWICH NATURALISTS SOCIETY
    Transactions of the Norfolk and Norwich Naturalists Society   1558

NORFOLK NAUTICAL SOCIETY
    East Coast Mariner   4475

NORTH EAST COAST INSTITUTION OF ENGINEERS & SHIPBUILDERS
    Transactions of the North East Coast Institution of Engineers & Shipbuilders   2766

NORTH EAST PUBLICITY ASSOCIATION
    Periscope   3291

NORTH OF ENGLAND ZOOLOGICAL SOCIETY
    Chester Zoo News   1973

NORTH OF SCOTLAND GRASSLAND SOCIETY
    Norgrass   2881

NORTH SURREY DYSLEXIA SOCIETY
    Dyslexia Review   4643

NORTHAMPTONSHIRE FEDERATION OF ARCHAEOLOGICAL SOCIETIES
    Northamptonshire Archaeology   4415

NORTHAMPTONSHIRE RECORD SOCIETY
    Northamptonshire Past & Present   4504

NORTHERN HORTICULTURAL SOCIETY
    Northern Gardener   2911

NORTHERN IRELAND ASSOCIATION FOR MENTAL HEALTH
    Beacon House News   2150

NUTRITION SOCIETY
    British Journal of Nutrition   2117
    Proceedings of the Nutrition Society   2122

OIL AND COLOUR CHEMISTS ASSOCIATION
    Journal of the Oil and Colour Chemists Association   3465

OLD ATHLONE SOCIETY
    Journal of the Old Athlone Society   4321

OPHTHALMOLOGICAL SOCIETIES OF THE UNITED KINGDOM
    Transactions of the Ophthalmological Societies of the United Kingdom   2341

ORGAN CLUB
    Organ Club Journal   3994

OXFORD INSTITUTE OF AGRARIAN AFFAIRS
    International Journal of Agrarian Affairs   2807

OXFORD SOCIETY FOR SOCIAL RESPONSIBILITY IN SCIENCE
    Fulcrum   160

OXFORD UNIVERSITY FOREST SOCIETY
    Oxford University Forest Society Journal   2892

OXFORD UNIVERSITY INSTITUTE OF ECONOMICS AND STATISTICS
    Bulletin of the Oxford University Institute of Economics and Statistics   624

OXFORD UNIVERSITY LIBERAL SOCIETY
    Fringe   723

PALAEONTOLOGICAL ASSOCIATION
    Palaeontology   1850
    Special Papers in Palaeontology   1851

PARENTS' NATIONAL EDUCATIONAL UNION
    PNEU   1161

PATHOLOGICAL SOCIETY OF GREAT BRITAIN AND IRELAND
    Journal of Pathology   2239

PEDESTRIANS' ASSOCIATION FOR ROAD SAFETY
    Arrive   2173

PEMBROKESHIRE LOCAL HISTORY SOCIETY
    Pembrokeshire Historian   4333

PEOPLES' DISPENSARY FOR SICK ANIMALS
    Animals Magazine   2929

APPENDIX 3

PERSONAL RIGHTS ASSOCIATION
   Individualist   666
PHARMACEUTICAL SOCIETY OF GREAT BRITAIN
   Journal of Pharmacy and Pharmacology   2207
   Pharmaceutical Journal   2208
PHILATELIC TRADERS SOCIETY
   PTS Journal   3169
PHILOLOGICAL SOCIETY
   Transactions of the Philological Society   1466
PHOTOGRAMMETRIC SOCIETY
   Photogrammetric Record   1609
PHOTOGRAPHIC DEALERS' ASSOCIATION
   Modern Photographer   3934
PHYSICAL EDUCATION ASSOCIATION OF GREAT BRITAIN AND NORTHERN IRELAND
   British Journal of Physical Education   1249
   Outdoors   1252
PLASTICS INSTITUTE
   Plastics and Polymers   3579
POETRY BOOK SOCIETY
   Poetry Supplement   4240
POETRY SOCIETY
   Poetry Review   4239
POLITICAL STUDIES ASSOCIATION OF THE UNITED KINGDOM
   Political Studies   683
POLITICS ASSOCIATION
   Teaching Politics   1188
POPULAR FLYING ASSOCIATION
   Popular Flying   4158
POST OFFICE ENGINEERING UNION
   Post Office Engineering Union Journal   2491
PREHISTORIC SOCIETY
   Proceedings of the Prehistoric Society   4389
PRESBYTERIAN HISTORICAL SOCIETY OF ENGLAND
   Journal of the Presbyterian Historical Society of England   538
PRINTING HSITORICAL SOCIETY
   Journal of the Printing Historical Society   3098
PRINTING MANAGEMENT ASSOCIATION
   Managing Printer   3100
PRISON OFFICERS ASSOCIATION
   Prison Officers Magazine   941
PRIVATE LIBRARIES ASSOCIATION
   Private Library   62
PROFESSIONAL GOLFERS ASSOCIATION
   Golf Trade Journal   4083
PSIONIC MEDICAL SOCIETY
   Psionic Medicine   2086
PSYCHOLOGICAL SOCIETY OF IRELAND
   Irish Journal of Psychology   387
PUBLIC ROAD TRANSPORT ASSOCIATION
   Public Road Transport Association Journal   1426

QUEKETT MICROSCOPICAL CLUB
   Journal of the Quekett Microscopical Club   1937

RAF ORNITHOLOGICAL SOCIETY
   Journal of the RAF Ornithological Society   2017
RADAR AND ELECTRONICS ASSOCIATION
   Radar and Electronics   2510
RADICAL PHILOSOPHY GROUP
   Radical Philosophy   372
RADIO AND ELECTRONIC OFFICERS UNION
   Signal   2506
RADIO SOCIETY OF GREAT BRITAIN
   Radio Communication   2504
RADNORSHIRE SOCIETY
   Transactions of the Radnorshire Society   4442
RAILWAY AND CANAL HISTORICAL SOCIETY
   Journal of the Railway and Canal Historical Society   2639
RAILWAY CORRESPONDENCE & TRAVEL SOCIETY
   Railway Observer   2659
RAILWAY DEVELOPMENT ASSOCIATION
   Development Report   2632
RAILWAY INDUSTRY ASSOCIATION
   Railpower   2652
RAILWAY INVIGORATION SOCIETY
   Railway Invigoration Society Progress Report   2657
BRITISH PHILATELIC ASSOCIATION
   Philately   3170
RAILWAY PHILATELIC GROUP
   Railway Philately   3171
RAILWAY PRESERVATION SOCIETY
   Railway Forum   2655
RAILWAY PRESERVATION SOCIETY OF IRELAND
   Five Foot Three   2634
RAMBLERS ASSOCIATION
   Rucksack   4094
RAMBLERS ASSOCIATION (Lake District Area)
   Lakeland Rambler   4093
RAMBLERS ASSOCIATION (Scottish Area)
   Heel and Toe   4092
RAMSAY SOCIETY OF CHEMICAL ENGINEERS
   Journal of the Ramsay Society of Chemical Engineers   3322
REGIONAL STUDIES ASSOCIATION
   Regional Studies   3850
RELAY SERVICES ASSOCIATION OF GREAT BRITAIN
   Relay Association Journal   2515
RELIGIOUS SOCIETY OF FRIENDS
   Irish Young Friend   4613
RESEARCH DEFENCE SOCIETY
   Conquest   2115
RETAIL CONFECTIONER'S ASSOCIATION
   Retail Confectioner   3410
RICHARD III SOCIETY
   Ricardian   4336
RICKMANSWORTH HISTORICAL SOCIETY
   Rickmansworth Historian   4337
ROAD HAULAGE ASSOCIATION
   Roadway   1415
ROMFORD & DISTRICT HISTORICAL SOCIETY
   Romford Record   4338
ROTARY INTERNATIONAL IN GREAT BRITAIN & IRELAND
   Rotary   1081
ROYAL AERONAUTICAL SOCIETY
   Journal of the Guild of Air Pilots and Air Navigators   2785
   Aerospace   2771
   Aeronautical Quarterly   2770
   Aeronautical Journal   2769
ROYAL AFRICAN SOCIETY
   African Affairs   4561
ROYAL ARCHAEOLOGICAL INSTITUTE
   Archaeological Journal   4375
ROYAL ASIATIC SOCIETY OF GREAT BRITAIN & IRELAND
   Journal of the Royal Asiatic Society of Great Britain & Ireland   4544
ROYAL ASSOCIATION OF BRITISH DAIRY FARMERS
   Dairying   2975
ROYAL ASTRONOMICAL SOCIETY
   Geophysical Journal of the Royal Astronomical Society   1816
   Monthly Notices of the Royal Astronomical Society   1589
   Quarterly Journal of the Royal Astronomical Society   1591
ROYAL CENTRAL ASIAN SOCIETY
   Asian Affairs   4540
ROYAL COLLEGE OF GENERAL PRACTITIONERS
   Journal of the Royal College of General Practitioners   2065
ROYAL COLLEGE OF NURSING
   Nursing Bibliography   2259
ROYAL COLLEGE OF PHYSICIANS OF LONDON
   Journal of the Royal College of Physicians of London   2066
ROYAL COLLEGE OF PSYCHIATRISTS
   British Journal of Psychiatry   2310
ROYAL COLLEGE OF SURGEONS OF EDINBURGH
   Journal of the Royal College of Surgeons of Edinburgh   2240
ROYAL COMMONWEALTH SOCIETY
   Library Notes   4494
ROYAL ECONOMIC SOCIETY
   Economic Journal   757
ROYAL ENTOMOLOGICAL SOCIETY
   Journal of Entomology   2001
   Proceedings of the Royal Entomological Society   2003
   Transactions of the Royal Entomological Society   2005
ROYAL FORESTRY SOCIETY OF ENGLAND, WALES AND NORTHERN IRELAND
   Quarterly Journal of Forestry   2893
ROYAL GEOGRAPHICAL SOCIETY
   Geographical Journal   4353
   New Geographical Literature and Maps   4358
ROYAL GEOLOGICAL SOCIETY OF CORNWALL
   Transactions of the Royal Geological Society of Cornwall   1813
ROYAL HISTORICAL SOCIETY
   Transactions of the Royal Historical Society   4345
ROYAL HORTICULTURAL SOCIETY
   Journal of the Royal Horticultural Society   2910
ROYAL INSTITUTE OF BRITISH ARCHITECTS
   RIBA Annual Review of Periodical Articles   3879
   RIBA Journal   3880
   RIBA Library Bulletin   3881
ROYAL INSTITUTE OF BRITISH ARCHITECTS (Eastern Region)
   Ero   3876
ROYAL INSTITUTE OF BRITISH ARCHITECTS (Yorkshire Region)
   Yorkshire Architect   3884
ROYAL INSTITUTE OF INTERNATIONAL AFFAIRS
   International Affairs   667
   World Today   695

APPENDIX 3

ROYAL INSTITUTE OF PHILOSOPHY
    Philosophy   371
ROYAL INSTITUTE OF PUBLIC
HEALTH AND HYGIENE
    Community Health   2152
ROYAL INSTITUTION OF CHARTERED
SURVEYORS
    Chartered Surveyor   1603
ROYAL INSTITUTION OF NAVAL
ARCHITECTS
    Naval Architect   2759
ROYAL JERSEY AGRICULTURAL
& HORTICULTURAL SOCIETY
    Jersey at Home   2946
ROYAL MEDICO-CHIRURGICAL
SOCIETY OF GLASGOW
    Scottish Medical Journal   2094
ROYAL METEOROLOGICAL SOCIETY
    Quarterly Journal of the Royal
    Meteorological Society   1845
    Weather   1846
ROYAL MICROSCOPICAL SOCIETY
    Journal of Microscopy   1670
    Royal Microscopical Society
    Proceedings   1671
ROYAL MUSICAL ASSOCIATION
    RMA Research Chronicle   3968
    Proceedings of the Royal Musical
    Association   3966
ROYAL NATIONAL LIFE-BOAT
INSTITUTION
    Life-Boat   2768
ROYAL NATIONAL ROSE SOCIETY
    Rose Bulletin   2912
ROYAL NAVAL SAILING ASSOCIATION
    Royal Naval Sailing Association
    Journal   4146
ROYAL PHOTOGRAPHIC SOCIETY
    Journal of Photographic Science
    3932
    Photographic Abstracts   3936
    Photographic Journal   3937
ROYAL SCOTTISH FORESTRY
SOCIETY
    Scottish Forestry   2894
ROYAL SCOTTISH GEOGRAPHICAL
SOCIETY
    Scottish Geographical Magazine
    4360
ROYAL SOCIETY
    Biographical Memoirs of Fellows
    of the Royal Society   1501
    Notes and Records of the Royal
    Society   1511
    Philosophical Transactions of the
    Royal Society   1574
    Proceedings of the Royal Society
    1578
ROYAL SOCIETY FOR INDIA,
PAKISTAN & CEYLON
    South Asian Review   4546
ROYAL SOCIETY FOR THE PREVEN-
TION OF ACCIDENTS
    British Journal of Occupational
    Safety   793
    Care in the Home   2171
ROYAL SOCIETY FOR THE ENCOUR-
AGEMENT OF ARTS, MANUFACTURES
AND COMMERCE
    Journal of the Royal Society for
    the Encouragement of Arts,
    Manufactures and Commerce,
    Journal of the Royal Society of
    Arts   3830
ROYAL SOCIETY FOR THE PRO-
MOTION OF HEALTH
    Royal Society of Health Journal
    2158

ROYAL SOCIETY FOR THE PRO-
TECTION OF BIRDS
    Birds   2011
ROYAL SOCIETY OF EDINBURGH
    Proceedings of the Royal Society
    of Edinburgh   1514
    Transactions of the Royal Society
    of Edinburgh   1521
ROYAL SOCIETY OF MEDICINE
    Proceedings of the Royal Society
    of Medicine   2085
    Tropical Doctor   2097
ROYAL STATISTICAL SOCIETY
    Journal of the Royal Statistical
    Society   628
ROYAL STUART SOCIETY
    Royal Stewart Papers   4339
    Royalist Viewpoint   4340
ROYAL TELEVISION SOCIETY
    Bulletin of the Royal Television
    Society   2512
ROYAL TOWN PLANNING INSTITUTE
    Journal of the Royal Town Plan-
    ning Institute   3847
ROYAL YACHTING ASSOCIATION
    RYA Magazine   4145
RURAL DISTRICT COUNCILS
ASSOCIATION
    Rural District Review   996
RURAL MUSIC SCHOOLS
ASSOCIATION
    Making Music   3958

SAIL TRAINING ASSOCIATION
    Sail   4147
ST CUTHBERT'S SOCIETY University
of Durham
    Phalanx   4194
ST. JOHN'S HOSPITAL DERMATO-
LOGICAL SOCIETY
    Transactions of the St. John's
    Hospital Dermatological Society
    2291
ST. SYMEON'S FELLOWSHIP
    Aion   83
SALISBURY & SOUTH WILTS INDUS-
TRIAL ARCHAEOLOGICAL SOCIETY
    Wiltshire Industrial Archaeology
    4436
SALMON AND TROUT ASSOCIATION
    Salmon and Trout Magazine   4174
SCHOOL LIBRARY ASSOCIATION
    School Librarian   66
SCOTS PHILOSOPHICAL CLUB
    Philosophical Quarterly   370
SCOTTISH CATHOLIC HISTORIES
ASSOCIATION
    Innes Review   501
SCOTTISH DECORATORS
FEDERATION
    Scottish Decorators Quarterly
    Review   3808
SCOTTISH ESPERANTO
FEDERATION
    Esperanto en Skotlando   1473
SCOTTISH GENEALOGY SOCIETY
    Scottish Genealogist   4369
SCOTTISH GEORGIAN SOCIETY
    Bulletin of the Scottish Georgian
    Society   4309
SCOTTISH INLAND WATERWAYS
ASSOCIATION
    Scottish Inland Waterways
    Association Newsletter   4648
SCOTTISH INSTITUTE OF MISSIONARY
STUDIES
    Bulletin of the Scottish Institute of
    Missionary Studies   465
SCOTTISH LANGUAGE SOCIETY
    Crann-Tara   1492

SCOTTISH LIBRARY
ASSOCIATION
    SLA News   65
SCOTTISH ORNITHOLOGISTS' CLUB
    Scottish Birds   2020
SCOTTISH PIPE BAND ASSOCIATION
    Pipe Band   4001
SCOTTISH SCHOOLMASTERS
ASSOCIATION
    Scottish Schoolmaster   1236
SCOTTISH SECONDARY TEACHERS
ASSOCIATION
    Scottish Secondary Teachers'
    Association Bulletin   1268
SCOTTISH SOCIETY FOR INDUSTRIAL
ARCHAEOLOGY
    Newsletter of the Scottish Society
    for Industrial Archaeology   4388
SCOTTISH TARTANS SOCIETY
    Proceedings of the Scottish Tartans
    Society   1446
SCOTTISH WOMEN'S RURAL
INSTITUTES
    Scottish Home and Country   1082
SCOTTISH WOODLAND OWNERS
ASSOCIATION
    Scottish Woodland Owners
    Association Newsletter   2895
SCOUT ASSOCIATION
    Scouter   1106
SCUNTHORPE MUSEUM SOCIETY
    Journal of the Scunthorpe Museum
    Society   340
SELBOURNE SOCIETY
    Selbourne Magazine   1553
THE 1745 ASSOCIATION AND
MILITARY HISTORY SOCIETY
    The 1745 Association and Military
    History Society Quarterly Notes
    4636
SHAKESPEAREAN AUTHORSHIP
SOCIETY
    Shakespearean Authorship Review
    4286
SHAW SOCIETY
    Shavian   4287
SHETLAND PONY STUD-BOOK
SOCIETY
    Shetland Pony Stud-Book Society
    Magazine   2936
SHIP STAMP SOCIETY
    Log Book   3164
SHORTHORN SOCIETY OF THE U.K.
& G.B.& IRELAND
    Dairy Shorthorn Journal   2941
SHROPSHIRE ARCHAEOLOGICAL
SOCIETY
    Shropshire Newsletter   4421
    Transactions of the Shropshire
    Archaeological Society   4432
SIR THOMAS BEECHAM SOCIETY
    Le Grand Baton   3955
    Sir Thomas Beecham Society
    Newsletter   3969
SLEEP-LEARNING ASSOCIATION
    Quarterly Journal of the Sleep-
    Learning Association   2227
SOCIETY FOR AFRICAN CHURCH
HISTORY
    Bulletin of the Society for African
    Church History   479
SOCIETY FOR ANALYTICAL
CHEMISTRY
    Proceedings of the Society for
    Analytical Chemistry: Analytical
    Division, Chemical Society   1749
    Analyst   1746

SOCIETY FOR ARMY HISTORICAL
RESEARCH
    Journal of the Society for Army
    Historical Research   1006
SOCIETY FOR BRITISH ENTOMOLOGY
    Entomologist   1996
SOCIETY FOR CO-OPERATIVE
STUDIES
    Bulletin   848
SOCIETY FOR EDUCATION IN FILM
AND TELEVISION
    Screen   1247
SOCIETY FOR EDUCATION
THROUGH ART
    Athene   1217
SOCIETY FOR EXPERIMENTAL
BOTANY
    Journal of Experimental Botany
    1947
SOCIETY FOR MEDIEVAL
ARCHAEOLOGY
    Medieval Archaeology   4385
SOCIETY FOR PROCLAIMING
BRITAIN IS ISRAEL
    Bible Impact   429
    Brith   431
SOCIETY FOR PSYCHICAL RESEARCH
    Journal of the Society for
    Psychical Research   400
    Proceedings of the Society for
    Psychical Research   403
SOCIETY FOR RESEARCH INTO
HIGHER EDUCATION
    Research into Higher Education
    Abstracts   1289
SOCIETY FOR THE BIBLIOGRAPHY
OF NATURAL HISTORY
    Journal of the Society for the
    Bibliography of Natural History
    1538
SOCIETY FOR THE PROMOTION OF
HELLENIC STUDIES
    Journal of Hellenic Studies   4537
SOCIETY FOR THE PROMOTION OF
NATURE RESERVES
    Conservation Review   1921
SOCIETY FOR THE PROMOTION OF
ROMAN STUDIES
    Britannia   4378
    Journal of Roman Studies   4383
SOCIETY FOR THE STUDY OF
ADDICTION TO ALCOHOL AND
OTHER DRUGS
    British Journal of Addiction   2148
SOCIETY FOR THE STUDY OF
ALCHEMY AND EARLY CHEMISTRY
    Ambix   1708
SOCIETY FOR THE STUDY OF
FERTILITY
    Journal of Reproduction and
    Fertility   1980
SOCIETY FOR THE STUDY OF
LABOUR HISTORY
    Society for the Study of Labour
    History Bulletin   613
SOCIETY FOR THEATRE RESEARCH
    Theatre Notebook   4033
SOCIETY FOR WATER TREATMENT
AND EXAMINATION
    Water Treatment and Examination
    2685
SOCIETY OF ANALYTICAL
PSYCHOLOGY LTD
    Journal of Analytical Psychology
    388
SOCIETY OF ANTIQUARIES OF
LONDON
    Antiquaries Journal   4373
SOCIETY OF ANTIQUARIES OF
NEWCASTLE-UPON-TYNE
    Archaeologia Aeliana   4397
SOCIETY OF ANTIQUARIES OF
SCOTLAND
    Proceedings of the Society of
    Antiquaries of Scotland   4392
SOCIETY OF ARCHER-ANTIQUITIES
    Journal of the Society of Archer-
    Antiquities   4182
SOCIETY OF ARCHITECTURAL
HISTORIANS OF GREAT BRITAIN
    Architectural History   3872
SOCIETY OF ARCHIVISTS
    Journal of the Society of Archivists
    358
SOCIETY OF ASSISTANTS TEACHING
IN PREPARATORY SCHOOLS
    News and Views   1158
SOCIETY OF AUTHORS
    Author   4257
SOCIETY OF CHEMICAL INDUSTRY
    Chemistry & Industry   3318
    J A C B   3320
    Journal of Applied Chemistry and
    Biotechnology   3321
    Journal of the Science of Food and
    Agriculture   3405
    Pesticide Science   2867
SOCIETY OF CHIROPODISTS
    Chiropodist   3724
SOCIETY OF CIVIL ENGINEERING
TECHNICIANS
    Civil Engineering Technician
    2609
SOCIETY OF CIVIL SERVANTS
    Civil Service Opinion   966
SOCIETY OF COMMERCIAL
ACCOUNTANTS
    Commercial Accountant   3190
SOCIETY OF COSMETIC CHEMISTS
OF GREAT BRITAIN
    Journal of the Society of Cosmetic
    Chemists   3475
SOCIETY OF DAIRY TECHNOLOGY
    Journal of the Society of Dairy
    Technology   2977
SOCIETY OF DYERS AND
COLOURISTS
    Journal of the Society of Dyers and
    Colourists   3462
    SDC News   3463
SOCIETY OF ENDOCRINOLOGY
    Journal of Endocrinology   2290
SOCIETY OF ENGINEERS
    Society of Engineers Journal   2388
SOCIETY OF ENVIRONMENTAL
ENGINEERS
    Environmental Engineering   2372
SOCIETY OF FILM AND TELE-
VISION ARTS LTD
    Journal of the Society of Film and
    Television Arts   2513
SOCIETY OF FORESTERS OF GREAT
BRITAIN
    Forestry   2888
SOCIETY OF GENEALOGISTS
    Genealogists' Magazine   4364
SOCIETY OF GLASS TECHNOLOGY
    Glass Technology   3438A
    Physics & Chemistry of Glasses
    3438C
SOCIETY OF GRAPHICAL AND
ALLIED TRADES
    SOGAT Journal   3121
SOCIETY OF INDEXERS
    Indexer   73
SOCIETY OF INDUSTRIAL ARTISTS
AND DESIGNERS
    Designer   3823
SOCIETY OF INVESTMENT
ANALYSTS
    Investment Analyst   824
SOCIETY OF LEATHER TRADES
CHEMISTS
    Journal of the Society of Leather
    Trades Chemists   3683
SOCIETY OF LICENSED AIRCRAFT
ENGINEERS & TECHNOLOGISTS
    Tech Air   2788
SOCIETY OF MASTER GLASS
PAINTERS
    Journal of the British Society of
    Master Glass Painters   3439
SOCIETY OF OCCUPATIONAL
MEDICINE
    Transactions of the Society of
    Occupational Medicine   796
SOCIETY OF POST OFFICE ENGIN-
EERS
    Post Office Engineer   2490
SOCIETY OF RADIOGRAPHERS
    Radiography   2223
SOCIETY OF RELAY ENGINEERS
    Relay Engineer   2516
SOCIETY OF REMEDIAL GYMNASTS
    Remedial Gymnastics and
    Recreational Therapy   4090
SOCIETY OF ST. JOHN CHRYSOSTOM
    Chrysostom   495
SOCIETY OF TEACHERS OF SPEECH
AND DRAMA
    Speech and Drama   1221
SOCIETY OF UNIVERSITY CARTO-
GRAPHERS
    SUC Bulletin   1601
SOIL ASSOCIATION
    Journal of the Soil Association
    2854
SOMERSET ARCHAEOLOGICAL
& NATURAL HISTORY SOCIETY
    Somerset Archaeology and Natural
    History Proceedings   4422
SOUTH PLACE ETHICAL SOCIETY
    Ethical Record   410
SOUTH STAFFORDSHIRE ARCHAE-
OLOGICAL & HISTORICAL SOCIETY
    Transactions of the South Stafford-
    shire Archaeological & Historical
    Society   4433
SOUTH WALES INSTITUTE OF
ENGINEERS
    Proceedings of the South Wales
    Institute of Engineers   2384
SOUTHERN ARTS ASSOCIATION
    Southern Arts   3838
SOUTHERN ELECTRIC GROUP
    Live Rail   2641
SPASTICS SOCIETY
    Special Education   1255
SPORTS TURF RESEARCH
INSTITUTE
    Journal of the Sports Turf Research
    Institute   3838
    Sports Turf Bulletin   3863
STAINES LOCAL HISTORY SOCIETY
    Staines Local History Society
    Journal   4343
STAINLESS STEEL DEVELOPMENT
ASSOCIATION
    Stainless Steel   3502
STANDING CONFERENCE FOR LOCAL
HISTORY
    Local Historian   4324
STEAM BOAT ASSOCIATION OF
GREAT BRITAIN
    Funnel   2752
STEPHENSON LOCOMOTIVE SOCIETY
    Journal of the Stephenson Loco-
    motive Society   2640

APPENDIX 3

STUDENT PLANNERS ASSOCIATION
    Forma   3845
STUDENT PSYCHOLOGICAL SOCIETY, UNIVERSITY COLLEGE, DUBLIN
    Thornfield Journal   395
SUFFOLK INSTITUTE OF ARCHAEOLOGY
    Proceedings of the Suffolk Institute of Archaeology   4419
SURREY NATURALISTS TRUST
    Newsletter of the Surrey Naturalists Trust   1544
    Surrey Naturalist   1555
SUSSEX ARCHAEOLOGICAL SOCIETY
    Sussex Archaeological Society Newsletter   4423
SUSSEX INDUSTRIAL ARCHAEOLOGY STUDY GROUP
    Sussex Industrial History   4424

TALYLLYN RAILWAY PRESERVATION SOCIETY
    Narrow Gauge Telegraph   2649
    Talyllyn News   2662
TENNYSON SOCIETY
    Tennyson Research Bulletin   4290
TENSOR SOCIETY OF GREAT BRITAIN
    Matrix and Tensor Quarterly   2382
TEXTILE INSTITUTE
    Journal of the Textile Institute   3546
    Textile Institute and Industry   3549
    Textile Progress   3554
THEOLOGICAL STUDENTS FELLOWSHIP
    TSF Bulletin   422
THEOSOPHICAL SOCIETY IN ENGLAND
    Theosophical Journal   377
THORACIC SOCIETY
    Thorax   2274
THORESBY SOCIETY
    Publications of the Thoresby Society   4509
THOROTON SOCIETY OF NOTTINGHAM
    Transactions of the Thoroton Society of Nottinghamshire   4434
THOROUGHBRED BREEDERS ASSOCIATION
    Statistical Abstract   4167
TIMBER GROWERS' ORGANISATION LTD
    Timber Grower   2896
TOLKIEN SOCIETY
    Anduril   4261
    Mallorn   4280
TOWN AND COUNTRY PLANNING ASSOCIATION
    Bulletin of Environmental Education   1919
    Town and Country Planning   3851
TRAMWAY & LIGHT RAILWAY SOCIETY
    Bulletin of the Tramway & Light Railway Society   1421
TRAMWAY MUSEUM SOCIETY
    Journal of the Tramway Museum Society   1424
TRANSPORT TICKET SOCIETY
    Journal of the Transport Ticket Society   3150
TROPICAL PRODUCTS INSTITUTE
    Tropical Science   2818

ULSTER ARCHAEOLOGICAL SOCIETY
    Ulster Journal of Archaeology   4396
ULSTER MEDICAL SOCIETY
    Ulster Medical Journal   2098
UNITARIAN HISTORICAL SOCIETY
    Transactions of the Unitarian Historical Society   555
UNITED COMMERCIAL TRAVELLERS ASSOCIATION
    Selling Today   3268
UNITED KINGDOM READING ASSOCIATION
    Reading   77
UNIVERSITY OF EDINBURGH GRADUATES ASSOCIATION
    University of Edinburgh Journal   311
UNIVERSITY OF LOUGHBOROUGH, SOCIAL SCIENCE SOCIETY
    Feedback   586

VEGETARIAN SOCIETY (UK) LTD
    Vegetarian   3049
VEHICLE BUILDERS AND REPAIRERS ASSOCIATION
    Body   2710
VIKING SOCIETY FOR NORTHERN RESEARCH
    Saga Book of the Viking Society   4535
VIOLA DA GAMBA SOCIETY
    Chelys   3997
VIRGIL SOCIETY
    Proceedings of the Virgil Society   4299
VISIBLE RECORD SOCIETY
    Computer Executive   3601

WALLPAPER, PAINT AND WALLCOVERINGS ASSOCIATION OF GREAT BRITAIN
    Wallpaper, Paint and Wallcovering   3809
WARWICKSHIRE LOCAL HISTORY SOCIETY
    Warwickshire History   4347
WATCHTOWER BIBLES AND TRACT SOCIETY
    Awake   4608
    Watchtower   4609
WATFORD & DISTRICT INDUSTRIAL HISTORY SOCIETY
    Journal of the Watford and District Industrial History Society   4322
WEBB SOCIETY
    Webb Society Quarterly Journal   1594
WELDING INSTITUTE
    Welding Research International   2540
WELSH BIBLIOGRAPHICAL SOCIETY
    Journal of the Welsh Bibliographical Society   16
WELSH LIBRARY ASSOCIATION
    Y Ddolen   70
WELSH PONY AND COB SOCIETY
    Welsh Pony and Cob Society Journal   2937
WELSH THEATRE ASSOCIATION
    Llwyfan   4025
WELSHPOOL AND LLANFAIR LIGHT RAILWAY PRESERVATION CO. LTD
    Llanfair Railway Journal   2642

WESLEY HISTORICAL SOCIETY
    Proceedings of the Wesley Historical Society   554
WESLEY HISTORICAL SOCIETY LANCASHIRE & CHESHIRE BRANCH
    Journal of the Wesley Historical Society, Lancashire & Cheshire Branch   552
WHITEHALL MUSICAL AND DRAMATIC SOCIETY
    Anthos   86
WHOLESALE PHOTO FINISHER'S ASSOCIATION
    Photo Finisher   3938
WILDFOWLERS ASSOCIATION OF GREAT BRITAIN & IRELAND
    WAGBI Magazine   4181
WILTSHIRE ARCHAEOLOGICAL & NATURAL HISTORY SOCIETY
    Bi-Annual Bulletin of the Wiltshire Archaeological & Natural History Society   4400
    Wiltshire Archaeological & Natural History Magazine   4435
WOMEN'S ENGINEERING SOCIETY
    Woman Engineer   2389
WOOLHOPE NATURALISTS FIELD CLUB
    Transactions of the Woolhope Naturalists Field Club   1560
WORCESTERSHIRE NATURALISTS CLUB
    Worcestershire Naturalists Club Newsletter   1561
WORKERS' EDUCATIONAL ASSOCIATION
    WEA News   1182
WORLD EXPEDITIONARY ASSOCIATION
    Expedition News   1375
WRITERS PUBLISHING ASSOCIATION
    Topical Dates & Facts Newsletter   4516

YORK POETRY SOCIETY
    York Poetry   4254
YORKSHIRE ARCHAEOLOGICAL SOCIETY
    Yorkshire Archaeological Journal   4438
YORKSHIRE ARCHAEOLOGICAL SOCIETY (HEMSLEY & DISTRICT GROUP)
    Ryedale Historian   4420
YORKSHIRE ARTS ASSOCIATION
    Month in Yorkshire   3834
YORKSHIRE DIALECT SOCIETY
    Transactions of the Yorkshire Dialect Society   1468
YOUNG ORNITHOLOGISTS CLUB
    Bird Life   2009
YOUNG SOCIALISTS
    Keep Left   731
    Left   733
YOUNG ZOOLOGISTS CLUB
    Zoo Magazine   1978
YOUTH CAMPING ASSOCIATION
    Lightweight Camper   4104
YOUTH HOSTELS ASSOCIATION
    Hostelling News   1066

ZOOLOGICAL SOCIETY OF LONDON
    Journal of Zoology   1974
ZULULAND SWAZILAND ASSOCIATION
    Net   523

INDEX

Numbers refer

(a) *to* titles in specific *subject* fields (italics)

(b) *to* titles in *current* use.

(c) *from superseded* title/s to that in current use.

All titles follow presentation of title page—no inversions are employed.

ABC Air Cargo Guide   1429
ABC Airways   1431
ABC Film Review   4009
ABC Goods Transport Guide   1370
ABC Guide to International Travel   1371
ABC Rail Guide   1386
ABC World Airways Guide   1431
ABLC Journal   3062
ACE   2606
ACU Bulletin of Current Documentation   1
AD Magazine   3427
AFU/Weapons Profile   2600
AIMME Journal   2596
AJR Information   81
AM   2700
AMA   1266
AMTDA Journal   2846
AP International Research   3280
APIS Bulletin   3865
APPTO   1420
ARC   2294
ARELS Journal   1194
ARLIS Newsletter   26
ASTMS Gains   3200
ASTMS Journal   3201
ATM Bulletin   1216
ATPAS Bulletin   1215
AUT Bulletin   1280
AWRE News   82
AYRS Airs   4143
A'Bhratach Ur   1068
Aberdeen-Angus Review   2938
Aberdeen Chamber of Commerce Journal   1325
About the House   3975
About Wine   3375
Abracadabra   4044
Absees   4530
Abstaining Driver   2701
Abstracts from Technical and Patent Publications   2405
Abstracts of Current Publications   2598
Abstracts on Hygiene   2140
Accessory and Garage Equipment   2702
Accident Analysis and Prevention   2171
Accidents   *2171-2177*
Accidents   2172
Accordion   *3996*
Accordion Times and Modern Musician   3996
Accountancy   *3180-3197*
Accountancy   3180
Accountancy Age   3181
Accountancy Ireland   3182
Accountant   3183
Accountant's Magazine   3184
Accountants Week   3185
Accountants Weekly   3185
Accounting and Business Research   3186
Accounting & Data Processing Abstracts   3187

Accounting Research   3186
Accounts Relating to Trade and Navigation of the United Kingdom   1357
Achievement   1296
Acoustics   *1645-1648*
Acoustics Abstracts   1645
Acrobatics   *4091*
Acrobatics   4091
Acta Metallurgica   3479
Activities Bulletin   2178
Adam   4183
Addiction   *2148*
Adhesion   *1706*
Admap   3279
Adult Education   *1272-1278*
Adult Education   1272
Advance   443
Advance   1499
Advancement of Science   1500
Advances in Applied Probability   1583
Advances in Physics   1611
Advent Witness   441
Adverse Drug Reaction Bulletin   2191
Advertisement Parade   3280
Advertisers Weekly   3281
Advertising   *3279-3291*
Advertising & Marketing   3282
Advertising & Marketing Management   3283
Advertising Quarterly   3284
Advertising Statistical Review   3285
Aerial   2464
Aerodynamics   *1644*
Aeromodeller   3738
Aeronautical Journal   2769
Aeronautical Quarterly   2770
Aeronautics   *2769-2788, 4684*
Aerosols   *1734*
Aerospace   2771
Aesthetics   *413*
Africa   4557
Africa Comtemporary Record   4558
Africa, History   *4557-4570*
   Language   *1487-1489*
Africa Digest   4559
Africa Research Bulletin   4560
Africa Trade & Development   *4567*
African Affairs   4561
African Communist   4562
African Development   1348
African Journal of Medical Sciences   2047
African Language Studies   1488
African Language Review   1487
African Mims   2192
African Social Research   596
Afro-American Studies   4572
Age and Ageing   2250
Ageing   *2135-2136*
Agenda   3077
Agenda   4199
Agriculture   *2795-2821*
Agriculture Co-operative Bulletin   2796
Agricultural and Garden Machinery Service   2846

Agricultural and Veterinary Chemicals and Agricultural Engineering   2797
Agricultural History Review   2798
Agricultural Journal   2803
Agricultural Machinery Journal   2847
Agricultural Merchant   2799
Agricultural Progress   2800
Agricultural Statistics Scotland   2801
Agricultural Supply Industry   2802
Agriculture   2803
Agtec   2795
Ahead in Yorkshire   3811
Ahimsa Communities   598
Aion   83
Air and Travel Training World   1432
Air and Water Pollution   2169
Air-Britain Digest   2772
Air-Britain News   2773
Air Cargo   *2669*
Air Cargo   2669
Air Conditioning   *3786-3802*
   Pollution   *2169-2170, 4666*
   Transport   *1429-1435*
Air-Cushion and Hydrofoil Systems Bibliography Service   4684
Air Enthusiast   2774
Air Mail News   3159
Air Pictorial   2775
Air Pollution   2169
Air Pollution Abstracts   4666
Airadio News   2494
Aircraft Engineering   2776
Aircraft Illustrated   2777
Aircraft in Profile   2778
Airfix Magazine   3739
Airmail   3812
Airport and Ground Services   1433
Airports International   1433
Akademiya Nauk SSSR, Mashinovedeniye   2414
Akros   4200
Alcoholic Beverages   *3366-3374*
Alcoholism   *2149*
Alert   411
Algae   *1956*
Algebra   *1581*
Aliphatic Alicyclic and Saturated Heterocyclic Chemistry   1707
Alkaloids   *1783*
Alkaloids   1783
All about Children   3071
All England Law Reports   888
All In   4201
Allen Engineering Review   2355
Allergy   *2126*
Alliance   645
Alliance Bulletin   645
Alliance Journal   3391
Almshouses Gazette   1060
Alpine Journal   4095
Alpine Ski Club Annual   4132
Alternative   646
Aluminium   *3516*
Aluminium for Schools   3516
Amateur Aquarist   3013
Amateur Architecture   287

INDEX

Amateur Ciné World 3950
Amateur Gardening 2902
Amateur Geologist 1791
Amateur Historian 4324
Amateur Photographer 3926
Amateur Stage 4018
Amateur Tape Recording 3647
Amateur Winemaker 4695
Ambassador 3544
Ambit 4184
Ambix 1708
Ambulance 2189
Amenity 1916
Amenity Horticulture 2860
American Behavioural Scientist 580
American Philosophical Quarterly 359
Amgueddfa 334
Amino Acids 1779
Amino Acids, Peptide and Protein Abstracts 1853
Amino-acids Peptides and Proteins 1779
Ampleforth Diary 84
Ampleforth Journal 84
An Bratach 1068
An Cosantóir 999
An Deo-Greine 285
An Gaidheal 285
An Leabharlaun 25
Anaesthesia 2262-2264
Anaesthesia 2262
Anaesthesia and Analgesia 2263
Analysis 408
Analysis 360
Analyst 1746
Analytical Abstracts 1747
Analytical Chemistry 1746-1750
Anarchism 860
Anarchy 860
Anatolian Studies 4372
Anatomy 2103
Anbar Management Services Abstracts 3187, 3223, 3233, 3262
Anbar Management Services Bibliography 3199
Anduril 4261
Anglers Mail 4169
Anglers World 4170
Anglican Church 514-526
Angling 4169-4176
Angling 4170
Angling Times 4171
Anglo-American Law Review 889
Anglo-American Trade News 1349
Anglo-Danish Review 4536
Anglo-Spanish Society Quarterly Review 4526
Anglo Welsh Review 4262
Animal Behaviour 1981
Animal Behaviour Monographs 1982
Animal Breeding Abstracts 2932
*Animal Ecology 1981-1985, 4662
    Welfare 938-940*
Animal Production 2933
Animal World 938
Animals 2928-2931
Animals 1970
Animals Defender and Anti-Vivisection News 2114
Animals' Friend Magazine 2928
Animals Magazine 2929
Annabel 85
Annals of Applied Biology 1854
Annals of Botany 1942
Annals of Clinical Biochemistry 1905
Annals of Eugenics 1879
Annals of Human Genetics 1879
Annals of Occupational Hygiene 792

Annals of Physical Medicine 2297
Annals of Science 2026
Annals of the Andersonian Naturalists Society 1531
Annals of the CIRP 3238
Annals of the Rheumatic Diseases 2295
Annals of the Royal College of Surgeons of England 2325
Annals of Tropical Medicine and Parasitology 2231
Annotated Bibliography of Medical Mycology 1963
Annual Bulletin of Historical Literature 4303
Annual Estimates of the Population of Scotland 636
Annual Report and Bulletin of the Walker Art Gallery, Liverpool 335
Annual Report and Proceedings of the Lancashire and Cheshire Entomological Society 1992
Annual Report of the Fishery Board for Scotland 3010
Annual Report of the Registrar General for Scotland 637
Annual Reports on the Progress of Chemistry 1709
Antacus 4263
Antarctic, History 4584-4585
Anthos 86
Anthropology 1852
Anthroposophical Quarterly 378
Anti-Apartheid News 696
Anti-Corrosion Methods and Materials 2400
Antiquarian Horology 3594
Antiquaries Journal 4373
Antique Collecting 3910
Antique Collector 3911
Antique Dealer and Collectors Guide 3912
Antique Finder 3913
Antique Records 3951
Antiques 3910-3918
Antiques 3914
Antiques in Britain 3915
Antiques Trade Gazette 3916
Antiques World 3917
Antiquity 4374
Anvil 1334
Apex 2355
Apex One 4264
Apicultural Abstracts 2997
Apollo 3813
Apostolic Herald 444
Applicable Analysis 408
Applied Acoustics 1646
Applied Electrical Phenomena 1731
Applied Ergonomics 3247
Apprentice 4202
Approach Magazine 4185
Approaches 497
Appropriation Accounts 802
Appropriation Accounts 962
Aquaria 3013-3014
Aquarist and Pondkeeper 3013
Aquarius 87
Aquatic Biology Abstracts 1855
Aquatic Sciences and Fisheries Abstracts 1855
Arab Horse Society News 2935
Arab Report and Record 647
Arab World 4550
Arabia, History 4550
Arable Farmer 2822
Arachnology 1990-1991
Arboricultural Association Journal 2885

Archaeologia Aeliana 4397
Archaeologia Cambrensis 4439
Archaeologia Cantiana 4398
Archaeological Collections of Ayr & Wigton 4391
Archaeological Collections of Ayrshire & Galloway 4391
Archaeological Journal 4375
*Archaeology 4371-4390
    See also: England, Greece, Ireland, Scotland, Wales*
Archaeology Abroad 4376
Archaeometry 4377
Archer 88
Archery 4182
Archigram 3867
Architect 3868
Architect & Building News 3869
Architect and Surveyor 3870
Architects for a Really Socialist Environment 4620
Architects Journal 3871
Architectural Design 3899-3900
Architectural Design 3899
Architectural Design and Construction 3899
Architectural History 3872
Architectural Review 3873
Architecture 3865-3884
Architecture East Midlands 3874
Archives 355-358
Archives 355
Archives of Disease in Childhood 2249
Archives of Oral Biology 2277
Archives of Skiagraphy 2220
Archives of the Roentgen Ray 2220
Archivum Linguisticum 1458
Arctic, History 4584-4585
Ardán 4019
Area 4350
Ark 3814
Armies and Weapons 4635
Arms Control 925
Army 999-1007, 4635-4636
Army Orders 1000
Army Quarterly and Defence Journal 1001
Aromatic and Heteroaromatic Chemistry 1780
Aromatic Chemistry 1780
Around the World News of Population and Birth Control 2133
Arrive 2173
ARSE 3866
Art 3925
    Education 1217-1218
Art and Antiques Weekly 3918
Art and Artists 3815
Art and Craft in Education 1259
Art News and Review 3819
Art Psychotherapy 4667
Art Sales Index 3816
Artificial Languages 1469
Artist 3817
Arts 3811-3841
Arts North 3818
Arts Review 3819
Arup Journal 2607
Asia, History 4539-4547, 4706
Asia Major 4539
Asian Affairs 4540
Asian Review 4546
Aslib Book List 4
Aslib Information 27
Aslib Proceedings 28
Aslib Transport and Planning Group Newsletter 29
Aspect 241
Aspects of Education 1108

Assistant Librarian 30
Association of Agriculture Journal 2804
Association of Bronze and Brass Founders Bulletin 2531
Association of Teachers of Russian Journal 1202
Associations 1068-1082
Assurance Magazine 1091
Assurance Magazine and Journal of the Institute of Actuaries 1091
Astronautica Acta 2789
Astronomy 1587-1594
Astronomy and Space 1587
Astrophysical Letters 1595
Astrophysics 1595-1597
Athene 1217
Atkinson 2745
Athletics 4053-4055
Athletics 4054
Athletics Arena International 4053
Athletics Weekly 4054
Atmospheric Environment 2169
Atom News 89
Atomic Absorption and Flame Emission Spectroscopy Abstracts 1655
Auctioneer 835
Audio 3635
Audio Record Review 3636
Audio Visual 3637
Audio-Visual Language Journal 1459
Auditor 929
Author 4257
Authorship 4257-4259
Auto Accessory International 2703
Auto Accessory International 2704
Auto Accessory Retailer 2704
Autocar 2705
Automatic Monitoring and Measuring 3627
Automatica 2422
Automation 2422-2425
Automation 2423
Automobile Abstracts 2731
Automobile Electricity 2735
Automobile Engineering 2700-2748, 4683
Automobile Design Engineering 2707
Automotive Engineering 2708
Autosport 4109
Autoworld 2709
Aviation Review 2779
Avicultural Magazine 2008
Avtometriya 3627
Awake 4608
Ayrshire Archaeological & Natural History Society Collections 4391
Ayrshire Cattle Society's Journal 2939
Azania Combat 697

BA News 90
BA Record 1493
BACIE Bulletin 1281
BACIE Journal 1281
BACIE Memorandum 1282
BACIE News 1282
BARC Gazette 4110
BARC News 4110
BASRA Journal 1494
BB Bks Book Issues 4203
BCIRA Journal 2530
BCIRA Journal of Research and Development 2530
BDS News 3309
BEA Information Sheet 2985
BEA Magazine 91
BEE 1919
BEMA Bulletin 2356
BFMIRA Abstracts 3397
BHRA Journal 3035
BLMRA Journal 3678
BLMRA Monthly Digest 3678
BMA News 2048
BNF Abstracts 3507
BNF Bulletin 3507
BOAC News 92
BP Progress 2728
BPS Magazine 3344
BRA Review 2296
BSBI Abstracts 1941
BSCRA Abstracts 3503
BSCRA Journal 3500
BSFA Abstracts 3503
BSFA Journal of Research and Development 3500
BSI News 1442
BSSRS Newsheet 1515
BTTA Review 2243
BUFOA Journal 2790
BUFORA Journal 2790
BURISA Newsletter 3842
Back to Godhead 414
Badminton 4074-4075
Badminton Gazette 4074
Bailiff Journal 961
Bailiffs 961
Baker 3414
Bakers' Review 3413
Bakery 3413-3418
Bakery Management 3414
Baking Industries Journal 3415
Ball Bearing Journal 2559
Ball Bearings 2559
Ballet 4035-4036
Ballroom Dancing Times 4037
Balthus 1450
Baltic Exchange Magazine 1391
Bangladesh, History 4551
Bangladesh Newsletter 4551
Bank of England Quarterly Bulletin 1297
Bank of England Statistical Abstract 803
Banker 804
Bankers' Magazine 805
Banking 802-821, 4622-4624
Baptist 543
Baptist Churches 542-548
Baptist Quarterly 542
Baptist Times 543
Barclaycard Magazine 93
Barclay's Bank Review 1300
Barclays International Quarterly 1298
Barclay's International Review 1299
Barclays Overseas Review 1299
Barclays Review 1300
Barnsley 1326
Bars 3037
Bartender 3037
Basketball 4060-4061
Basketball 4060
BathoFarn 549
Baths Service 4152
Beacon 361
Beacon 1055
Beacon House News 2150
Beat Instrumental and International Recording Studio 3988
Beauty Counter 3694
Beauty Therapy Journal 3473
Bedfordshire Magazine 4457
Bee World 2998
Beef and Sheep Farming 2948
Beekeeping 2997-3000
Beekeeping 2999
Beermat Magazine 3383
Behavior Genetics 1880
Behaviour Research and Therapy 379
Behavioural Biology Abstracts 1856
Behavioural Biology Abstracts A-Animal Behaviour 4662
Behavioural Engineering Association Conference Proceedings 380
Behavioural Technology 2432
Bellringing 4002
Belmont Standard 94
Benefits International 1015
Bent's Literary Advertiser 3131
Berita Kadjian Sumatera 4577
Berks, Bucks & Oxon Archaeological Journal 4398
Berkshire Archaeological Journal 4399
Beverley Bystander 4476
Bi-Annual Bulletin of the Wiltshire Archaeological and National History Society 4400
Bi-Polo News 4086
Bible 429-437, 4608-4609
Bible Impact 429
Bible Society News 437
Bible Translator 430
Bibliographical Bulletin of the International Arthurian Society 4265
Bibliographical Studies 508
Bibliography 4-24
Bibliographies of Chemists 1710
Bibliography of Family Planning & Population 2129
Bibliography of Seismology 1817
Bibliography of Systematic Mycology 1957
Bibliotheck 5
Big A 3875
Big Farm Management 2843
Bike 4117
Billiard and Snooker Journal 4049
Billiards 4049
Billingham Post 4590
Biochemical Journal 1906
Biochemical Pharmacology 2193
Biochemical Systematics 4605
Biochemistry 1905-1910
Biodeterioration Research Titles 1894
Biofizika 1914
Biographical Memoirs of Fellows of the Royal Society 1501
Biological Conservation 1918
Biological Journal of the Linnean Society 1857
Biological Membrane Abstracts 1858, 4660
Biological Reviews and Biological Proceedings of the Cambridge Philosophical Society 1859
Biological Reviews of the Cambridge Philosophical Society 1859
Biological Rhythms 1860
Biologist 1861
Biology 1835-1878, 4660-4661
Biology and Human Affairs 1881
Biology Teaching 1213
Biomedical Engineering 2232
Biophysics 1914-1915
Biophysics 1914
Biotheology 1703
Biosynthesis 1745
Bird Life 2009
Bird Migration 2010
Bird Notes 2011
Bird Study 2010
Birds 2008-2022
Birds 2011

INDEX

Birds and Country 2012
Birmingham & Midland Institute, Archaeological Section, Transactions 4426
Birmingham Chamber of Commerce Journal 1343
Birth Control Campaign Bulletin 2130
Biscuit Maker and Plant Baker 3415
Bitman 95
Black Dwarf 263
Black Eggs 4204
Black Flag 96
Black Outcry 4591
Black Powder 4178
Black Voice 97
Blackcountrymen 4458
Blackface Sheep Breeders' Association Journal 2950
Blackfriars 482
Blackwood's Magazine 98
Blesmag 1051
Blindmaker 3054
Blinds 3059
Blinds & Shutters 3054
Blue Rat 99
Blueprint 2357
Board 3525
Board Manufacture 3825
Board News 3530
Board of Trade Journal 1319
Board of Trade Labour Gazette 778
Boat News 4134
Boating 4134-4139
Bodleian Library Record 31
Bodleian Quarterly Record 31
Body 2710
Bondholder's Register 948
Bonds 948
Bonus 1083
Book Collecting and Library Monthly 3126
Book Collector 6
Book Exchange 3127
Book Keeping 3180-3197
Book Market 3128
Book of Job 100
Book Publishing 3126-3146
Book Reviews 75-78
Book Selling 3126-3146
Book Tokens News 3092
Book Trade 3129
Book Trolley 32
Bookdealer 3130
Book-Keepers Journal 3188
Bookmakers 4050-4051
Books 75
Books and Bookmen 33
Books For Your Children 7
Bookseller 3131
Boots News 101
Border Life 4444
Botanical Journal of the Linnean Society 1943
Botany 1941-1951
Bournville Reporter 102
Bournville Works Magazine 102
Bowls 4058
Bowmaker Magazine 103
Boxing 4125-4129
Boxing News 4125
Boxing World 4126
Boy's Brigade Gazette 1100
Bradford Antiquary 4401
Bradford Bystander 4459
Braille Journal of Physiotherapy 2215
Braille Physiotherapists Quarterly 2216

Brain 2299
Branch Line News 2631
Brass Band News 3982
Brass Bands 3982-3985
Brazil, History 4578-4579
Brazil Journal 4578
Brazilian Bulletin 1350
Bretby Broadsheet 2595
Breton News 648
Brewer 3384
Brewer's Guardian 3385
Brewer's Guild Journal 3384
Brewers Journal 3388
Brewing 3383-3389
Brewing Review 3386
Brewing Trade Review 3386
Brick Bulletin 3771
Brides 3015
Brides & Setting Up Home 3015
Bridge 4052
Bridge Magazine 4052
Brig 104
Brigade 1101
Brighton Film Review 4013
Brighton Folk Diary 105
Brio 34
Bristol Ports Journal 1392
Britain and Israel 649
Britain and Overseas 1351
Britain—France 4525
Britannia 3517
Britannia 4378
Britannic Magazine 106
Brith 431
British Aid 623
British Aid Statistics 623
British and Colonial Printer 3115
British Antarctic Survey Bulletin 4584
British Archaeological Abstracts 4402
British Association of Retired Parsons: Members' Quarterly Bulletin 1016
British Baker 3416
British Baking Industries Research Association Abstracts
British Baking Industries Research Association Bulletin 3420
British Bandsman 3983
British Book News 76
British Bookmaker 4050
British Books 3140
British Bowls 4058
British Bulletin of Publications on Latin America, the West Indies, Portugal and Spain 8
British Catalogue of Music 3592
British Ceramic Abstracts 3450
British Ceramic Review 3440
British Chemical Engineering 3329
British Chess Magazine 4046
British Chicken Growers Association Bulletin 2955
British Chiropody Journal 3723
British Clayworker 3441
British Clothing Manufacturer 3695
British Constructional Engineer 3762
British Corrosion Journal 2401
British Deaf News 1052
British Dental Journal 2278
British Dental Surgery Assistant 2279
British Direct Mail Advertising Association Newsletter 3286
British Economy Survey 750
British Education Index 1109
British Egg Association Newsletter 2985

British Engine Technical Report 2358
British Engineer 2359
British Esperantist 1470
British Export Gazette 1364
British Farmer 2823
British Fern Gazette 1969
British Film Academy Journal 2513
British Fleet News 107
British Flower Industry Association Journal 2915
British Food Journal 3399
British Foundryman 2532
British Friesian Journal 2940
British Geological Literature 1792
British Go Journal 3729
British Goat Society Monthly Journal 2951
British Golf Greenkeeper 4078
British Heart Journal 2265
British Hosiery and Knitwear 3711
British Hosiery Journal 3712
British Hospital Equipment Directory 1037
British Hospital Journal 1038
British Hospitals Journal 4665
British Hotelier and Restaurateur 3035
British Housing & Planning Review 3846
British Humanities Index 3
British Iris Society Newsletter 2916
British Israel Quarterly 574
British Jeweller 3518
British Jeweller and Watch Buyer 3518
British Jeweller Overseas 3517
British Journal for the History of Science 1502
British Journal for the Philosophy of Science 1503
British Journal of Addiction 2148
British Journal of Administrative Law 918
British Journal of Aesthetics 413
British Journal of Anaesthesia 2264
British Journal of Animal Behaviour 1981
British Journal of Applied Physics 1616
British Journal of Audiology 1053
British Journal of Cancer 2247
British Journal of Chiropody 3723
British Journal of Clinical Practice 2233
British Journal of Criminology 944
British Journal of Delinquency 944
British Journal of Diseases of the Chest 2272
British Journal of Disorders of Communication 2137
British Journal of Educational Studies 1110
British Journal of Educational Technology 1111
British Journal of Experimental Biology 1871
British Journal of Experimental Pathology 2234
British Journal of Haematology 2270
British Journal of Herpetology 2007
British Journal of Hospital Medicine 2049
British Journal of Industrial Medicine 2145
British Journal of Industrial Relations 783
British Journal of Industrial Safety 793
British Journal of Marketing 3254

INDEX

British Journal of Mathematical and Statistical Psychology   381
British Journal of Medical Education   2050
British Journal of Medical Psychology   2309
British Journal of Music Therapy   2194
British Journal of Non-Destructive Testing   2391
British Journal of Nutrition   2117
British Journal of Occupational Safety   793
British Journal of Ophthalmology   2330
British Journal of Oral Surgery   2280
British Journal of Pharmacology   2195
British Journal of Photography   3927
British Journal of Physical Education   1249
British Journal of Physiological Optics   2331
British Journal of Plastic Surgery   2326
British Journal of Political Science   650
British Journal of Preventive and Social Medicine   2162
British Journal of Psychiatric Social Work   1017
British Journal of Psychiatry   2310
British Journal of Psychology   382
British Journal of Radiology   2220
British Journal of Social and Clinical Psychology   383
British Journal of Social Psychiatry and Community Health   2311
British Journal of Social Work   1018
British Journal of Sociology   597
British Journal of Sports Medicine   2051
British Journal of Surgery   2327
British Journal of Tuberculosis   2272
British Journal of Urology   2293
British Journal of Venereal Diseases   2323
British Kinematography Journal   3948
British Kinematography Sound and Television   3948
British Knitting Industry   3713
British Landrace Pig Journal   2952
British Lawn Tennis   4076
British Lichen Society Bulletin   1966
British Machine Tool Engineering   2578
British Master Patternmaker   2528
British Medical Book List   2054
British Medical Bulletin   2052
British Medical Index   2054
British Medical Journal   2053
British Medical Students Journal   2093
British Medicine   2054
British Mensa Activities Bulletin   1112
British Museum Quarterly   336
British Museum Society Bulletin   337
British National Bibliography   9
British National Film Catalogue   4003
British Naturism   2219
British Naturopathic Association News   2217
British Naturopathic Journal and Osteopathic Review   2217
British Nuclear Energy Conference   2416
British Nuclear Energy Society Journal   2416

British Numismatic Journal   3902
British Numismatic Journal and Proceedings of the British Numismatic Society   3902
British Orthoptic Journal   2332
British Petroleum Equipment News   3431
British Phycological Bulletin   1956
British Phycological Journal   1956
British Plastics   3572
British Polymer Journal   3573
British Post Mark Society Quarterly Bulletin   3160
British Poultry Science   2956
British Printer   3093
British Racehorse   4160
British Racing News   4111
British Rate & Data   3287
British Ski Year Book   4132
British Society For Eighteenth-Century Studies Newsletter   4266
British Soviet Friendship   4531
British Steel   3494
British Steelmaker   3495
British Survey   694
British Tax Review   861
British Technology Index   2027
British Toys   3730
British Trade Journal and Export World   1365
British Union Catalogue of Periodicals   10
British Vegetarian   3049
British Veterinary Journal   2344
British Water Supply   2673
British Waterfowl Association Newsletter   2021
British Welding Journal   2537
British YMCA Review   475
Broadcaster   2495
Broadsheet   445
Broadsheet   4548
Brook Magazine   2433
Brook '72   108
Brooklands Gazette   4115
Brownie   1102
Browning Society Notes   4267
Brown's Geological Information Bulletin   1793
Brushes   3725-3726
Brushes   3725
Brushes and Toilet Goods   3725
Brushes International   3726
Bucks Life and Thames Valley Countryside   4460
Buddhism   560-562
Buddhism in England   561
Budger Price Records   3838
Budger Price Records   3638
Build International   3750
Builder   3751
Builder and Decorator   3804
Builders Merchants Journal   3772
Builders Merchants Review   3772
Building   3750-3768
  Materials   3771-3779
  Societies   854-859
Building   3751
Building and Contract Journal   3752
Building and Heating Products Guide   3753
Building Design   3754
Building Equipment and Materials   3773
Building Equipment News   3773
Building Industry News   3762
Building Maintenance   3755
Building Materials   3774
Building Science   3756
Building Science Abstracts   3757

Building Societies Institute Quarterly   854
Building Society Affairs   855
Building Societies Statistics   856
Building Specification   3758
Building Surveyor   1604
Building Technology and Management   3759
Building Worker   3760
Built Environment   3761
Bulletin   958
Bulletin   1039
Bulletin   3428
Bulletin & Wellsian   4277
Bulletin of Alcoholism   2149
Bulletin of Computer Aided Architectural Design   3900
Bulletin of Current Documentation   1
Bulletin of Current Literature   3387
Bulletin of Economic Research   751
Bulletin of Entomological Research   1995
Bulletin of Environmental Education   1919
Bulletin of Hispanic Studies   1483
Bulletin of Hygiene   2140
Bulletin of International Association of Applied Psychology   386
Bulletin of Mechanical Engineering Education   2406
Bulletin of Miscellaneous Information (Kew)   1948
Bulletin of News and Information   2862
Bulletin of North East Group For The Study of Labour History   784
Bulletin of Physical Education   1250
Bulletin of the African Studies Association of the United Kingdom   4563
Bulletin of the African Succulent Plant Society   2917
Bulletin of the Amateur Entomologists Society   1993
Bulletin of the Board of Celtic Studies   1490
Bulletin of the British Arachnological Society   1990
Bulletin of the British Association of Sport and Medicine   2051
Bulletin of the British Institute of Recorded Sound   3658
Bulletin of the British Jute Trade Research Association   3558
Bulletin: British Model Soldier Society   3731
Bulletin of the British Museum (Natural History) [varies series]   1523, 1787, 1794, 1944, 1971, 1994
Bulletin of the British Mycological Society   1958
Bulletin of the British Ornithologists Club   2013
Bulletin of the British Society for Social Responsibility in Science   1504
Bulletin, British Society of Rheology   1704, 1705
Bulletin of the British Speleological Association   1826
Bulletin, Burnham-on-Crouch Local History Society   4305
Bulletin of the Croydon Natural History and Scientific Society   1524
Bulletin of the Fellowship of Medicine   2081
Bulletin of the Game Conservancy   3001
Bulletin of the General Studies Association   1113

INDEX

Bulletin, Geographical Society of Ireland 4357
Bulletin of the Geological Survey of Great Britain 1795
Bulletin of the Group for the Study of Irish Historic Settlement 4306
Bulletin of the Imperial Institute 2818
Bulletin of the Industrial Law Society 949
Bulletin of the Inland Waterways Association 1387
Bulletin of the Institute of Historical Research 4307
Bulletin of the Institute of Physics and the Physical Society 1624
Bulletin of the Institute of Science Technology 3313
Bulletin of the Institute of Technical Publicity and Publications 3278
Bulletin of the International Seismological Centre 1818
Bulletin of the John Rylands Library 4308
Bulletin of the London Mathematical Society 1563
Bulletin of the National Association of Clinical Tutors 2055
Bulletin of the Natural Sweet Pea Society 2918
Bulletin of the Oxford Universory Institute of Economics and Statistics 624
Bulletin, Public Schools Appointments Bureau 1243
Bulletin of the Royal Television Society 2512
Bulletin of the School of Oriental and African Studies, University of London 4541
Bulletin of the School of Oriental Studies, University of London 4541
Bulletin of the Scottish Georgian Society 4309
Bulletin of the Scottish Institute of Missionary Studies 465
Bulletin of the Scottish Textile Research Association 3558
Bulletin of the Shaw Society 4287
Bulletin of the Society for African Church History 479
Bulletin [of the] Society for Co-operative Studies 848
Bulletin of the Society for Music Therapy 2194
Bulletin of the Society of Local Archivists 358
Bulletin of the Standing Conference of Societies Registered for Adoption 1063
Bulletin of the Tramway & Light Railway Society 1421
Bulletin: Wiltshire Archaeological & Natural History Magazine 4399
Bulletin of Zoological Nomenclature 1972
Bulletin on Soviet and East European Jewish Affairs 578
Burials 2166-2168
Burlington Magazine 3820
Burslem Bulletin 290
Buses 1422
Buses Illustrated 1422
Business 3072-3080, 4688
  Law 949-953, 4633
  and Industrial Management 3199-3225, 4693-4694
Business 3075
Business Administration 3072

Business and Finance 3228
Business and Professional Woman 1069
Business Archives 3073
Business Credit 828
Business Economist 752
Business Equipment Buyers Guide 3086
Business Equipment Digest 3085
Business Equipment Guide 3086
Business Forecast 753
Business History 3074
Business Management 3075
Business Monitor 1301
Business Systems and Equipment 3087
Business Travel 1372
Business Travel World 1372
Buttons 3714
Buyer's Guide 3519
Buzz 469
Byfleet Review 4510
Byron Journal 4705A

C & T: Luton Commerce & Trade Journal 1327
CADIG Newsletter 35
CAFD Newsletter 930
CAMDA News 2711
CB Magazine 141
CBI Education and Training Bulletin 1114
CBI Industrial Relations Bulletin 785
CBI Industrial Trends Survey 874
CBI Members Bulletin 875
CBI Metrication Bulletin 1437
CBI Review 876
CBI Smaller Firms Bulletin 877
CCD Bulletin 4638
CETO News 1131
CIIG Bulletin 36
CIPA 2041
CITE Newsletter 1200
CJ: International Guide to used Plant and Equipment 2560
CMI/AAB Descriptions of Plant Viruses 1959
CMI Descriptions of Pathogenic Fungi and Bacteria 1960
CMS Magazine 466
CPRW Newsletter 4456
CSE News 4101
CSMA Gazette 2719
CTC Gazette 4106
CTV News 3639
CTV Report 3639
CUC News 3345
Cabinet Maker and Retail Furnisher 3056
Cabinet Maker and Retail Furnisher 3669
Cadet Journal and Gazette 1002
Caernarvonshire Record Office Bulletin 356
Cake and Cockhorse 4310
Calcified Tissue Abstracts 1863
Caliban 109
Call Boy 4020
Camborne School of Mines Journal 4679A
Camborne School of Mines Magazine 4679A
Cambrian Law Review 890
Cambridge Historical Journal 4315
Cambridgeshire, Huntingdon & Peterborough Life 4461
Cambridge Journal of Education 1115
Cambridge Law Journal 891

Cambridge Quarterly 110
Cambridge Review 111
Camden Journal 112
Camera Magazine 3943
Camera Owner 3928
Cameras 3943
Camertonia 4403
Camp Site Operator 4101
Campaign 349
Camper 4105
Camping 4101-4105
Camping 4102
Camping and Caravanning 4103
Camping & Outdoor Life 4103
Camping Equipment Trader 4101
Canals 1387-1390, 4647-4648
Cancer 2247-2248
Candelabrum 4205
Candida 113
Candle 2306
Candour 4614
Canning and Packing 3423
Canning and Packing 3515
Canning Industry and Packing Trades Gazette 3423
Canning Journal 2541
Canning Quarterly News 114
Canoe-Camper 4140
Canoeing 4140-4142
Canoeing in Britain 4141
Canterbury Cathdral Chronicle 514
Cantium 4462
Cape Magazine 115
Cape News 115
Capella 116
Car 2712
Car Advertiser 2713
Car Finder 2714
Car Mechanics 2715
Cara 117
Caravan 3893
Caravan Life 3898
Caravans 3893-3898
Carbohydrate Chemistry 1778
Carbohydrate Metabolism Abstracts 2124
Carbohydrates 1778
Carbon 1767-1768
Carbon 1767
Carcanet 4206
Cardiac Newsletter 2268
Cardiff Naturalists' Society Reports and Transaction 1525, 1556
Cardiology 2265-2269
Cardiovascular Research 2266
Care in the Home 2174
Career 1239
Career Scotland 1241
Careers 1239-1246
Careers Quarterly 1240
Caret 4207
Caribbean History 4581
Carpentry 3525-3535
Carpet and Floor Covering News 3056
Carpets & Textiles 3057
Carrier Free 1677
Cars and Car Conversions 2716
Cars and Car Conversions 4112
Car's Competition News 2712
Cars in Profile 2717
Carthusian 118
Cartographic Journal 1602
Cartography 1601-1602
Case Con 1019
Cashier 806
Cast 2529
Catalogue and Index 72
Catalyst 3812
Catalyst 3821

Catamaran and Trimaran International News 2758
Catena 446
Catering 3015-3034
Catering and Hotel Management 3016
Catering Times 3017
Catholic Church 497-513, 4610-4611
  Education 1187
Catholic Citizen 498
Catholic Communications Institute of Ireland Abstract of Periodicals 4610
Catholic Communications Institute of Ireland Weekly News Index 4611
Catholic Education Today 1187
Catholic Fireside 499
Catholic Herald 300
Catholic Teachers Journal 1187
Cars 2967
Cattle 2938-2949
Cave Diving Group Newsletter 1827
Cave Science 1828
Caves 1826-1834
Caxtonian 4689
Ĉe Ni 1471
Cell and Tissue Kinetics 1886
Cell Membranes 1887
Celtic Languages 1490-1491
Celtic News 651
Cement 3453-3455
Cement and Concrete Research 3453
Cement and Lime Manufacture 3455
Cement, Lime and Gravel 3454
Cement Technology 3455
Central Government 998
Centre 2178
Centre For Business Research Newsletter 3076
Centre Point 1226
Ceramic Review 3442
Ceramics 3440-3451
Ceramics 3443
Cereals 2876-2878
Cerebral Palsy Bulletin 2300
Ceredigion 4440
Ceres 119
Certified Accountant 3189
Certified Accountants Journal 3189
Chambers of Commerce 1325-1346, 4645
Chandler & Boatbuilder 2751
Change 415
Changes in Rates of Wages and Hours of Work 777
Channel 1638
Chapman 4186
Character and Energy 120
Charrilock 121
Chartered Institute of Transport Journal 1373
Chartered Mechanical Engineer 2407
Chartered Municipal Engineer 2378
Chartered Secretary 953
Chartered Surveyor 1603
Chassis 2718
Chelys 3997
Chemical Age 3314
Chemical Age International 3314
Chemical and Process Engineering 3328
Chemical Communications 3315
Chemical Engineer & Transactions of the Institution of Chemical Engineers 3324
Chemical Engineering 3324-3330
Chemical Engineering Communications 3325
Chemical Engineering Journal 3326
Chemical Engineering Science 3327

Chemical Insight 3316
Chemical Processing 3317
Chemical Products 3323
Chemical Products & Aerosol News 3323
Chemical Society Reviews 1711
Chemical Thermodynamics 1727
Chemist & Druggist 2196
Chemistry 1707-1721
  Teaching 1211
  See also
  Analytical Chemistry
  Biochemistry
  Electrochemistry
  Geochemistry
  Inorganic Chemistry
  Organic Chemistry
  Physio Chemistry
  Thermochemistry etc
Chemistry and Industry 3318
Chemistry in Britain 1712
Chemoreception Abstracts 1864
Chemosphere 1920
CHEMSCAN-Radiation and Photochemistry 1684
Chemscan-Steroids 1782
Cheshire and North Wales Deesider 4463
Cheshire History Newsletter 4311
Cheshire Life 4464
Cheshire Smile 1020
Chess 4046-4048
Chess Player 4047
Chest Diseases 2272-2274
Chester Zoo News 1973
Chief Steward 3029
Child Adoption 1063
Child and Man 1116
Child Care 3066-3071
  Psychology 396
  Welfare 1063-1065, 4640
Child Education 1260
Child Education Quarterly 1261
Childrens Book Review 11
Children's Literature in Education 1117
Children's Outfitter 3706
Children's Rights 122
Child's Guardian 412
Chile, History 4580
Chilean News 4580
China, History 4548
China Trade and Economic Newsletter 1352
Chiropodist 3724
Chiropody 3723-3724
Chowanna 1118
Chrism 515
Christian Action 432
Christian Attitudes on Jews and Judaism 565
Christian Church 443-460
  History 479-480
Christian Churches and Sects 483-493
  See also under names of religions eg. Anglican
Christian Endeavour 443
Christian Graduate 447
Christian Pacifist 456
Christian Record 516
Christian Religion 429-437, 4608-4609
Christian Socialist 652
Christian Words 550
Christianity 443-460
Chromatographia 1751
Chronicle of the West India Committee 1362
Christus Rex Journal 612

Chromatography 1751-1757
Chrysostom 495
Church and Educational Equipment Digest 1130
Church and School Equipment News 442
Church Army 474
  Buildings 3891
  Furnishing 442
  In Wales 529-532
  Music 3980-3981
  of Scotland 527-528
Church Army Review 474
Church Buildings Today 3891
Church Music 3980
Church News 483
Church of England Newspaper 517
Church Quarterly 484
Church Quarterly Review 484
Church Teacher 525
Church Times 518
Churchbuilding 3891
Cinema 4003-4015
Cinema and TV Today 4004
Cinema Rising 4005
Cinematography 3948-3950
Circadian Rhythms 1860
Circuit Magazine 123
Circuit News 2434
Circulator 124
Circus 4017
Cistercian Studies 481
Civil Appropriation Accounts 802
Civil Defence 1010
  Engineering 2606-2626
  Service 966-969
Civil Defence 1010
Civil Engineering & Public Works Review 2608
Civil Engineering Technician 2609
Civil Estimates 1316
Civil Judicial Statistics 625
Civil Judicial Statistics (Scotland) 892
Civil Liberty 932
Civil Service Motoring 2719
Civil Service Opinion 966
Civil Service Statistics 967
Clare Market Review 125
Classic Cars in Profile 2717
Classical Languages 1484-1486
Classical Quarterly 1484
Classical Review 1485
Clay Crafts & Structural Ceramics 3444
Clay Minerals 3445
Claymore 1021
Clays and Clay Minerals 3446
Clean Air 2170
Cleaning 3062-3064
Cleaning & Maintenance 3250
Climber 4096
Climber and Rambler 4096
Clinical Allergy 2126
Clinical and Experimental Immunology 2163
Clinical Endocrinology 2288
Clinical Practice 2231-2242
Clinical Radiology 2221
Clinical Science 2236
Clinics in Endocrinology and Metabolism 2289
Clinics in Gastroenterology 2275
Clinics in Haematology 2271
Clique 3132
Clothing Industry 3694-3708 4704
Clothing Institute Journal 3696
Clothing Research Journal 3697
Club & Institute Journal 1070
Club Committee 1071

INDEX

Club Mirror   1072
Coaching Journal and Bus Review   1423
Coach and Appliances Digest   3356
Coal Magazine   2585
Coal Merchant and Shipper   3356
Coal News   2585
Coal Tar   *3477-3478*
Coal Technology   *3356*
Coastguard   2672
Coastguard News Letter   2672
Coastguards   *2672*
Coat of Arms   4370
Cobalt   *3509*
Cobalt   3509
Cockburn Association Annual Reports   3843
Cockburn Association Newsletter   3843
Cocoa   *3391-3392*
Cocoa Growers' Bulletin   3392
Coffee   *3393*
Coffee News   3393
Coil Collecting Weekly   3903
Coin Monthly   3904
Coins   3905
Coins & Medals   3905
Coins, Medals and Currency   3907
Coins, Medals and Currency Digest   3906
Coins, Medals and Currency Weekly   3907
Coke and Chemistry USSR   3346
Coke Review   3347
Collective Phenomena   1739
College of General Practitioners Research Newsletter   2065
Colliery Engineering   2590
Colliery Guardian   2586
Colonial Plant and Animal Products   2818
Colour Photography   3939
Colour Review   1218
Combustion & Flame   3348
Combustion Science and Technology   3349
Coming Alive   445
Coming Events in Britain   4483
Commentary   3297
Commentary   3365
Comments on Astrophysics and Space Physics   1596
Comments on Atomic and Molecular Physics   1690
Comments on Contemporary Psychiatry   2312
Comments on Earth Sciences: Geophysics   1814
Comments on Plasma Physics & Controlled Fusion   1691
Comments on Solid State Physics   1699
Commerce   *1296-1323*
Commercial Accountant   3190
Commercial Decor and Contract Furnishing Digest   3670
Commercial Education   *1190*
Commercial Grower   2903
Commercial Teacher   1119
Commercial Training   *1271*
Committee For Natutical Archaeology: Newsletter   4404
Common Crier   126
Common Market   *870-873*
Common Market Law Reports   870
Common Market Law Review   893
Common Market Newsletter   871
Commonwealth   4465
Commonwealth Forestry Review   2886

Commonwealth Journal   4465
Commonwealth Producer   2805
Commonwealth Survey   691
Commonwealth Trade   1353
Communes   598
Communication   350
Communications   *1370-1384*
Communicator of Technical Information   3278
Communism   *747-749*
Community   620
Community Development Journal   621
Community Forum   622
Community Health   2152
Community Medicine   4665
Companies   4630
Company Accountant   3191
Company Information   1303
Comparative and General Pharmacology   2197
Comparative Biochemistry and Physiology   1907
Comparative Group Studies   581
Comparative Political Studies   653
Comparative Studies in Society and History   582
Competitors Journal and Money Matters   3749
Components Standard   2465
Composer   3953
Composers   *3973-3974*
Composites   2627
Comprehensive Education   1120
Compulsory Military Service and the Objector   1008
Computer and Control Abstracts   3597
Computer Bulletin   3598
Computer Commentary   3599
Computer Digest   4697
Computer Education   3600
Computer Executive   3601
Computer International   3602
Computer Journal   3603
Computer Management   3604
Computer Survey   3605
Computer Weekly   3606
Computers   *3597-3626, 4697-4702*
Computers and Algorithms   4698
Computers and Electrical Engineering   4675
Computers and Fluids   4656
Computers and Graphics   4699
Computers and Mathematics   4700
Computers and Structures   3607
Computers in Biology and Medicine   3608
Computing   4701
Concern   4640
Conchologist's Newsletter   1986
Concord   654
Concrete   *3456-3460*
Concrete   3456
Concrete and Constructional Engineering   3456
Concrete Building and Concrete Products   3458
Conductor   3985
Confectionery   *3409-4312*
Confectionery and Tobacco News   3409
Confectionery News   3409
Conferences   *333*
Conferences and Exhibitions and Executive Travel   3310
Conflict   709
Conflict Studies   709
Congregational Monthly   540
Conjuring   *4044-4045*
Connective Tissue Research   1888
Connoisseur   3822

Connoisseur Art Sales Index   3816
Conquest   2115
Conservation   *1916-1935*
Conservation Review   1921
Construction   2610
Construction Plant and Equipment   2561
Construction Plant Hire   2562
Construction Steelwork   2628
Construction Surveyor   1604
Construction Technology   2611
Consuls   *926-927*
Consulting Engineer   2360
Consumer Affairs Bulletin   849
Contact   127
Contact   489
Contact   789
Contact   1922
Contact   2435
Contact   2450
Contact   3628
Contact Lens   2333
Containerisation International   2563
Contemporary Communications   128
Contemporary Physics   1612
Contemporary Review   129
Contents of Recent Economics Journals   754
Continental Film Review   4006
Contract Journal   3762
Contractors Plant Review   2612
Contracts   *948*
Contrasts   4208
Contributions to Atmospheric Physics   1840
Control   2424
Control Abstracts   3597
Control and Instrumentation   2424
Control and Science Record   2436
Converter   2546
Converting Industry   2547
Conveyancer and Property Lawyer   894
Conveyancer News   2564
Conveyancer Quarterly News   2564
Conveyor Journal   2565
Cook's Continental Time-table   1374
Co-operative Grocer   3040
Co-operative Management and Marketing   3077
Co-operative News Service   850
Co-operative Official   3077
Co-operative Review   851
Co-operative Societies   848-853
Co-Partners Magazine   294
Co-Partnership   786
Cope in Scotland   2566
Copper   *3510*
Copper Abstracts   3510
Cordage & Canvas and Jute World   3559
Cormorant   1003
Cornhill Magazine   4268
Cornish Archaeology   4405
Correspondence Chess   4048
Correspondents World Wide   655
Corrosion   *2400-2404*
Corrosion   3464
Corrosion Control Abstracts   2402
Corrosion Prevention and Control   2403
Corrosion Science   2404
Corrosion Technology   2400
Corsetry and Underwear   3709
Cosmetics   *3473-3476*
Cosmic Physics   *1685*
Cosmopolitan   130
Cost Accountant   3196
Cost Engineer   3192
Costing   *3198*

INDEX

Costing 3198
Costume 1445-1446
Costume 1445
Cotswold Life 4466
Cotton 2884, 3365
Cotton and General Economic Review 3564
Cotton Growing Review 2884
Cotton Outlook 3564
Cottsman 131
Councillor 4634
Countdown 289
Countertalk 132
Country Gentleman 3864
Country Gentlemen's Magazine 832
Country Landowner 833
Country Life 1526
Country Quest 4467
Country-Side 1527
Country Standard 799
County Councils Association Gazette 983
County Councils Gazette 983
County Newsletter 37
Courier 3157
Covenanter 1004
Coventry Chamber of Commerce Journal 1328
Coventry Commerce 1328
Cover 1084
Crabgrass 4209
Craft Teacher News 1227
Craftwork 878
Cranes 2561
Crann-Tara 1492
Creative Camera 3928
Creative Drama 4021
Creative Needlecraft 3919
Crèche News 1264
Credit 828-831 4626
  Management 3277
Credit 829
Credit Management 3277
Credit Retailer 830
Creel 4170
Cremation 2166-2168
Cricket 4087-4088
Cricketer 4087
Crime & Detection 945
Criminal Appeal Reports 935
Criminal Law 935-937 4632
Criminal Law Review 936
Criminal Statistics Scotland 937
Criminologist 945
Criminology 944-947
Criminology 946
Crisis Paper 656
Critical Quarterly 1478
Critical Quarterly 4187
Croner's Export Digest 1366
Croquet 4056
Croquet Association Gazette 4056
Croquet Gazette 4056
Crossbow 657
Crossby Chronicles 2355
Crosslink 133
Crosstalk 1034
Croydon Bibliographies for Regional Survey 1528
Croydon Separatist 4210
Crucible 416
Cruel Sports 939
Cruelty to Children 412
Cruising Association Bulletin 4135
Crusade Magazine 485
Crynhoad & Ystadegau Cymru 627
Cryogenics 1674
Crystal Lattice Defects 1786
Crystallography 1786
Cubitts Magazine 3763

Cultivation 2859-2861
Cultural Anthropology 1444
Cunard Trafalgar 134
Cunobelin 3908
Curling 4057
Currency 823
Current 135
Current Advances in Plant Science 2859
Current Affairs 645-695 4614-4618
Current Archaeology
Current Awareness Bulletin: Human Sciences and Management 583
Current Awareness Bulletin for Technical Engineering 2408
Current Bibliography of Published Material Relating to North Staffordshire and South Cheshire 12
Current Comments 2484
Current Contents in Management 3202
Current Information Guide on Fluid Sealing 2426
Current Law 895
Current Literature 3146
Current Literature on Community Health and Personal Social Services 4664
Current Paper in Electrical and Electronics Engineering 2437
Current Papers in Electrotechnology 2437
Current Papers in Physics 1613
Current Papers on Computers and Control 3609
Current Papers on Control 3609
Current Work in The History of Medicine 2056
Curtis's Botanical Magazine 1945
Custom Car 2720
Customs 869
CWM 265
Cybernetics Abstracts 1585
Cycletouring 4106
Cyclic Amp 1911
Cycling 4106-4107
Cycling 4107
Cycling & Sporting Cyclist 4107
Cylchgrawn Llyfrgell Genedlaethol Cymru 38
Cypher 4269
Cyrenian 4639
Cytobios 1889
Cytology 1886-1893
Czechoslovak Science and Technology Digest 1505

'D' Trooper Monthly 1103
DACAAL 61
DATA Journal 2527
DCO Quarterly 1298
DF Newsletter 3161
DIY and Woodworking Information 3526
DIY Trade 3050
DJNN and Writers World 330
DOE Construction 2613
DOE World 139
Dairy Education 2970
Dairy Engineering 2972
Dairy Farmer 2971
Dairy Industries 2972
Dairy Produce 2973
Dairy Science Abstracts 2974
Dairy Shorthorn Journal 2941
Dairying 2970-2983
Dairying 2975
Dalesman 4468
Dalton's Weekly 834
Dance 1222

Dance and Dancers 4035
Dance Journal 1222
Dance News 4038
Dance Teacher 1223
Dancing 4037-4041
  Teaching 1222-1223
Dancing Times 4039
Dark Horse 136
Data Processing 3597-3626, 4697-4702
Data Processing 3610
Data Processing Practitioner 3611
Datascene 3613
Data Systems 3612
Dataweek 3614
Datr 4211
David Brown Tractor News 137
Day by Day 658
Day Nursery Journal 1264
Deaf News 1052
Deaf Quarterly Times 1052
Debate 711
Decimal Currency News 1440
Decor and Contract Furnishing 3670
Decorating Contractor 3805
Decorator 3805
Deep-Sea Research and Oceanographic Abstracts 1835
Deer 2025
Deer 2025
Defend Kent 4469
Delius Society Newsletter 3973
Delta 4212
Demography 636-644
Denmark, History 4536
Denmark 4536
Dental News 2281
Dental Practice 2281
Dental Practitioner and Dental Record 2282
Dental Technician 2283
Dentistry 2277-2287, 4668
Department of Employment Gazette 778
Derbyshire Archaeological Journal 4406
Derbyshire Countryside 4470
Derbyshire Life and Countryside 4470
Derbyshire Miscellany 4407
Dermatology 2291
Derwent Publications 2042
Design 3885-3886
  See also Architectural Design Interior Design
Design 3885
Design and Components in Engineering 2362
Design Engineering 2363
Design Engineering—Product Information 4670
Designer 3823
Development and Materials Bulletin 3775
Development News Digest 659
Developmental Medicine and Child Neurology 2300
Development Report 2632
Devon, Archaeological Society Proceedings 4408
Devon Life 4471
Dhi Fonetik Titcer 1477
Dialectric and Related Molecular Processes 1785
Dialects 1467-1468
Dialogue 448
Diamonds 3593
Diary of Entertainments and Events 991
Dickensian 4271

INDEX

Dickinson News 138
Dictionaries 79
Didaskalos 1228
Diecasting 2528-2529, 2535
Diecasting and Metal Moulding 2535
Digest of Scottish Statistics 633
Digest of Statistics, Northern Ireland 626
Digest of Welsh Statistics 627
Diner's Club Magazine 277
Dinghy Sailing 4144
Diocesan Magazine of William Wykeham 109
Diplomatic Bookshelf 926
Direct Current 2461
Direct Current 2461
Direction 453
Director 3203
Disarmament 925
Disc 3640
Disc and Music Echo 3640
Disc Weekly 3640
Diseases 2161
   See also under specific subjects e.g. Chest Diseases
Diseases of the Chest 2272-2274
Dispensing Optician 2334
Display 3311
Display International 3311
Displays 3309-3312
Disposables and Nonwovens 2364
Distribution Maps of Plant Diseases 1961
District Heating Association Journal 3786
District Nursing 2253
Divine Light 467
Dixon's Paper Circular 3094
Do-It-Yourself 3050-3055
Do it Yourself 3051
Do it Yourself Retailing 3269
Dock Leaves 4262
Doctor 2057
Documentation 1-2
Dog News 2962
Dog World 2963
Dogs 2962-2966
Dog's Life 2964
Domestic Electrical Appliance Industry Statistics 2438
Domestic Gas 3357
Domestic Heating and Air Conditioning 3787
Domestic Heating Engineer 3788
Domestic Heating News 3789
Domestic Science 3015-3034
Dominicans 482
Doomlore 140
Dorset 4472
Dowsing 1822
Drag Racing—Hot Rod Magazine 4113
Drag Racing Magazine 4113
Drama 4022
Drama Education 1221
Drapers' Record 3698
Drapery and Fashion Weekly 3699
Drawdown 141
Drawing Office Practice 2527
Dream 3929
Dreamer 142
Dredging & Coastal Engineering 4682
Drive 2721
Drop Forger 3523
Drop Forgin' Bulletin 3480
Drug & Therapeutics Bulletin 2198
Dundee Chamber of Commerce Journal 1329
Durham Research Review 1121
Durham University Journal 143

Dust Control 3803
Dundee Prices Current 3562
Dust Control and Air Cleaning 3803
Dyeing 3461-3463
Dyer, Textile Printer, Bleaches and Finisher 3461
Dyslexia 4643
Dyslexia Review 4643

ECA Bulletin 4676
EEC Supplement 872
EMGAS 144
ERA Abstracts 2439
ERHB Magazine 1040
ESC Review 3501
ESSRA Magazine 585
EUAF Newsletter 3293
Earl 2642
Early Child Development and Care 3066
Earth and Extra-terrestrial Sciences 1597
Earth and Sky 2614
Earthquakes 1817-1820
East African Wildlife Journal 1529
East Anglian Magazine 4473
East Coast Digest 4474
East Coast Mariner 4475
East Herts Archaeological Society Newsletter 4409
East Herts Archaeological Society Transactions 4409
East Kent Omnibus 145
East London Papers 4312
East Midland Geographer 4351
East Midlands Bibliography 13
East Riding Bystander 4476
East-West Digest 660
Eastern Churches 495-496
   Europe, History 4524
Eastern Churches Review 496
Eastern Europe 1330
Eastern World 4542
Easterner 39
Eastword 3824
Easy Listening 3641
Echograms 146
Echoing Times 146
Ecology 1916-1935
Ecology of Food and Nutrition 2118
Economic Age 755
Economic and Social Review 756
Economic Journal 757
Economic Planning 886-887
Economic Progress Report 758
Economic Review 759
Economic Selections 760
Economic Trends 761
Economica 762
Economics 750-775
   See also Financial Economics, Labour Economics etc.
Economics 763
Economist 764
Economy and Society 584
Edinburgh Chamber of Commerce and Manufacturers Quarterly Journal 1331
Edinburgh Gazette 147
Education 1108-1184, 4641-4642
   see also Adult Education, Elementary Education, Higher Education of Special Classes etc.
Education 1122
Education and Community Relations 698
Education and Training 1283
Education and Urban Society 1123
Education Equipment 1124
Education For Development 1125

Education For Teaching 1126
Education in Chemistry 1211
Education in Science 1203
Education in the North 1127
Education Libraries Bulkhn 40
Education of Special Classes 1253-1258, 4643-4644
Education 3-13 1128
Education Today 1129
Educational and Church Equipment 1130
Educational Broadcasting International 1131
Educational Media International 1132
Educational Research 1133
Educational Television International 1131
Educational Times 1129
Effluent and Water Treatment Journal 2674
Efrydiau Athron Yddol 362
Eggs 2985-2988
8 mm Magazine 3949
8 mm Movie Maker 3950
Electoral Law 934
Electric Technology USSR 2440
Electric Traction 2463
Electrical Age 3052
Electrical and Electronics Abstracts 2441
Electrical and Electronics Manufacturer 2445
Electrical and Electronics Technician Engineer 2442
Electrical & Radio Trading 2495
Electrical Communication 2443
Electrical Contractor and Retailer 2444
Electrical Engineering 2432-2460, 4675-4678
Electrical Engineering Abstracts 2441
Electrical Equipment 2446
Electrical Export Review 2447
Electrical Power Engineer 2448
Electrical Review 2449
Electrical Supervisor 2450
Electrical Times 2451
Electrical Trading and Radio Marketing 2495
Electrical Wholesaler 2452
Electrical & Electronics Technical Engineer 4677
Electricity 1676
Electricity 2495
Electro Optics 1649
Electro Technology 4677
Electrochemistry 1729-1731
Electrochemistry 1730
Electrochemistry in Industrial Processing and Biology 1731
Electrochimica Acta 1729
Electron 798
Electron 2435
Electron 2466
Electron Spin Resonance 1656
Electronic Components 2467
Electronic Engineering 2468
Electronic Structure and Magnetism of Inorganic Compounds 1758
Electronics 2464-2483, 4679
Electronics and Communications Abstracts 2469
Electronics and Power 2470
Electronics Letters 2471
Electronics Record 2472
Electronics Quarterly 2472
Electronics Today 2481
Electronics Today International 2473

Electronics Weekly   2474
Electroplating and Metal Finishing   2542
Electrostatics   1675
Electrostatics Abstracts   1675
Elektrichestvo   2440
Elementary Education   1259-1265
Elevator Lift and Ropeway Engineering   2664
Elgin Society Newsletter   4445
Elim Evangel   486
Elizabethan   148
Elm Newsletter   2887
Embassy   968
Ember Press Publications   3095
Embroidery   3920
Embryology   1979-1980
Emergency Medicine   2058
Emergency Post   449
Emergency Services Review   2183
Empire   745
Empire Cotton Growing Review   2884
Empire Forestry Journal   2886
Empire Journal of Experimental Agriculture   2806
Empire Producer   2805
Empire Production and Export   2805
Empire Survey Review   1607
Employment and Productivity Gazette   779
En Route   3894
Encounter   149
Endeavour   1506
Endocrinology   2288-2290
Energy and Character   2313
Energy Conversion   2453
Energy Digest   3350
Engineer   2365
Engineer Surveyor   1605
Engineering   2355-2390, 4670-4672
   See also Automobile Engineering, Civil Engineering, Electrical Engineering, Highway Engineering, Hydraulic Power Engineering, Illuminating Engineering, Maintenance Engineering, Marine Engineering, Mechanical Engineering, Railway Engineering, Steam Engineering.
Engineering Designer   2366
Engineering Frictive Mechanics   2367
Engineering in Medicine   2368
Engineering Materials and Design   2369
Engineering Production   2370
Engineers Digest   2371
England, Archaeology   4397-4438
   History   4456-4522
   Language   1478-1481
   Literature   4261-4293
   Teaching   1194-1200
English   1195
English   4272
English Dance and Song   4040
English for Immigrants   1199
English Historical Review   4313
English in Education   1196
English Language Teaching   1197
English-Speaking World   654
English-Teaching Abstracts   1192
English Templar Youth   1073
Ensign   150
Entaco News   150
Enterprise   540
Entomologist   1996
Entomologists Record   1997
Entomology   1992-2005

Entomology Abstracts   1998
Environment   1916-1935
Environment   1923
Environment and Behavior   600
Environment & Planning   3844
Environment this Month   1924
Environment Biology and Medicine   1865
Environmental Engineering   2372
Environmental Health   982
Environmental Pollution   1925
Environmental Pollution Management   1926
Envoi   4213
Enzyme Regulation   1912
Enzymes   1911-1913
Epilepsy   2306
Epoch   1927
Equestrianism   4160-4168
Equine Veterinary Journal   2345
Equity   800
Equity Letter   800
Er   4214
Era   3876
Ergonomics   3247-3249
Ergonomics   3248
Ergonomics Abstracts   3249
Esperantist   1470
Esperantist Teacher   1474
Esperanto   1470-1474
Esperanto Contact   1472
Esperanto en Skotlando   1473
Esperanto Teacher   1474
Essays in Criticism   4273
Essential Oils and Aromatics Monthly Reporter   3474
Essex Countryside   4477
Essex Education   1134
Essex Journal   4478
Essex Naturalists' Trust Bulletin   1530
Essex Succulent Review   2919
Estates Gazette   835
Estates Journal   835
Estimated Soil Moisture Deficit and Potential Evapotranspiration over Great Britain   1841
Estuarine and Coastal Marine Science   4681
Ethical Record   410
Ethics   410
Ethiopia, History   4571
Ethiopia Observer   4571
Etoniana   151
Euro-Farm Business   2824
EuroFruit   4685
Eurolaw Commercial Intelligence   896
Euromoney   807
Euromonitor Review   3253
European—Atlantic Review   1354
European Baptist   544
European Board Markets   3536
European Chemical News   3319
European Civil Engineering Abstracts   2615
European Grocery Letter   3041
European Intelligence   3078
European Journal of Cancer   2248
European Journal of Marketing   3254
European Judaism   566
European Law Digest   897
European Marketing Data & Statistics   3255
European Parliament Digest   712
European Polymer Journal   1735
European Reviews   1354
European Studies Teachers Series   1135

European Training   1136
European Trends   872
Europhysics News   1614
Europroperty Magazine   836
Evangelical Presbyterian   535
Evangelical Quarterly   450
Evangelism   438-440
Every-day Electronics   2475
Everyman   87
Exchange & Mart   3288
Excise   869
Executive Accountant   3193
Exeter Museums Bulletin   338
Exhibition Bulletin   3312
Exhibitions   3309-3312
Exit   4215
Expedition News   1375
Experimental Agriculture   2806
Experimental Chemistry   1739
Experimental Eye Research   2335
Experimental Gerontology   2135
Export Courier   1367
Export Direction   1368
Export News   152
Export Times   3256
Export Trade   1364-1369
Expository Times   433
Expression   153
Expression   4193

FCI Features and News from behind the Iron Curtain   4529
FMF Review   3398
FMT News   3700
FPA Journal   2181
FT Abstracts in Science and Technology   1495
Fabric Forecast   3701
Fabulous 208   154
Factory   3204
Factory Management   3205
Faculty of Building Review   3764
Fairplay International Shipping Journal   1393
Falconer   4177
Falconry   4177
Family Circle   3018
Family Expenditure Survey   780
Family History   4362
Family Law   898
Family Planning   2131
Fanfare   3984
Fanfare for Britain   879
Far East Trade and Development   1355
Farm   2848
Farm and Country   2843
Farm Building Progress   2828
Farm Building R & D Index   2826
Farm Building R & D Studies   2827
Farm Buildings Digest   2829
Farm Engineering Industry   2849
Farm Machinery   2846-2852
   Management   2843-2845
Farm Management   2844
Farm Management Review   2845
Farm Week   2833
Farmers Guardian   2830
Farming   2822-2842
Farming in the East Midlands   2831
Farming Leader   2832
Farmer's Journal   3665
Farriery   3665
Fashion Forecast   3702
Fastener News   155
Fate and Horoscope   375
Federation of Insurance Institutes of Great Britain & Ireland, Journal   1090
Feed and Farm Supplies   2863

INDEX

387

INDEX

Feed and Farming Stuffs Supplies 2863
Feedback 586
Feline Advisory Bureau News Bulletin 2967
Ferns 1969
Ferritin 1936
Ferroelectrics 2462
Ferroelectrics 2462
Fertility 2129-2134
Fertilizer Feed and Pesticide Journal 2863
Fertilizer International 2864
Fertilizers 2863-2865
Festiniog Railway Magazine 2633
Festiniog Railway News 2649
Fetter Lane Review 4188
Fflint 4523
Fibre Science and Technology 1687
Fibres Post 1507
Field 3864
Field Crop Abstracts 2872
Field Crops 2872-2875
Fields and Quanta 1700
Fight Against Disease 2115
Film 4007
Film and Society 4008
Film Review 4009
Film User 3637
Films (Chemistry) 1784
Films and Filming 4010
Films Fortnightly 4011
Films Illustrated 4011
Films in London 4011
Filtration 1744
Filtration 3803
Filtration and Separation 3803
Financial Circular 986
Financial Economics 802-821, 4622-4624
    Management 3228-3229
    See also Economics
Financial European 4622
Financial Statement and Budget Report 808
Financial Times-European Law Newsletter 899
Fire 2179
Fire International 2180
Fire Prevention 2178-2188
Fire Prevention 2181
Fire Prevention Science and Technology 2182
Fire Protection Review 2183
Fire Surveyor 2184
First Aid 2189-2190
First Employment of University Graduates 1284
Fish 2006
    Trade 2994-2995
Fish Friers Review 2994
Fish Industry Review 3005
Fish Trades Gazette 2995
Fishing 4169-4176
    Industry 3005-3012
Fishing News 3006
Fishing News International 3007
Fishing Tackle Dealer 4175
Fishpaste 4216
Fitness 2203
Five Foot Three 2634
Fizika Metallov i Metallovedenie 3491
Flair 3710
Flambeau 156
Flashpoint 4645
Flax 3558-3563
Fleet Street Letter 661
Flight 2780
Flight Deck 1011

Flight International 2780
Floor Coverings 3056-3058
Flooring Journal 3058
Floors and Contract Carpeting 3058
Florist 2920
Flour Milling and Baking Research Association Abstracts 3419
Flour Milling & Baking Research Association Bulletin 3420
Flower Arranger 2921
Flowers 2915-2927, 4686
Flowers From the Printshop 3095
Fluid Conveying 2524
Fluid Mechanics 1637-1643, 4656
Fluid Power Abstracts 2429
Fluid Sealing Abstracts 2426
Fluid Power International 2430
Fluidics Feedback 1639
Fluidrive News 2524
Fluorocarbon and Related Chemistry 1768
Flyfisher's Journal 4172
Flying 4157-4159
Flying Angel News 1394
Flying Review International 2781
Flying Saucer Review 2791
Focus 662
Focus on Education 4634
Focus on Industry and Commerce 1304
Focus on International and Comparative Librarianship 41
Focus on Local Government 4634
Focus on Social Work and Service in Scotland 1022
Foden News 2722
Folio Pharmaceutica 2199
Folk and Country 1451
Folk Dances 4042-4043
Folk Music Journal 4042
Folk-Record 1452
Folk Review 1451
Folklore 1450-1455
Folklore 1452
Folk-Lore Journal 1452
Food and Cosmetics Toxicology 2228
Food and Drink Weekly 3400
Food Canning, Preserving and Selling 3403
Food Industries Review 3403
Food Manufacture 3401
Food Processing & Marketing 3424
Food Processing Industry 3424
Food Progress 4696
Food Science and Technology Abstracts 3402
Food Technology 3397-3406, 4696
Food Trade Review 3403
Foodpack 2548
Foot World 3398
Football 4062-4070
Football Academy 4062
Football League Review 4065
Football Monthly 4063
Football Pictorial 4064
Football Supporter 4064
Footwear 3680
Footwear Digest 3679
Footwear Organiser 3680
Footwear Weekly 3680
Ford Times 2723
Foreign Birds 2014
Forensic Medicine 921-922
Forensic Photography 3930
Forester's Miscellany 1074
Forestry 2885-2897
Forestry 2888
Forestry Abstracts 2889
Forestry and Home Grown Timber 2890

Forestry Commission Library Review 2891
Forge 4274
Form 3825
Forma 3845
Forma et Functio 1866
Format 3615
Format 4217
Forthcoming International Scientific and Technical Conferences 333
Fortnight 663
Fortnightly 129
Forum 601
Forum 1332
Forum 4023
Forum for the Discussion of New Trends in Education 1137
Foundry Practice 2530-2534
Foundry Trade Journal 2533
France, History 4525
    Language 1482
    Literature 4297-4298
Free Church Chronicle 536
Free Form 157
Free Trade 870-873
Free Trade Review and Club Management 3366
Freedom 931
Freeman 158
Freeman 543
Freemasons 1067
Freemasons Magazine 1067
Freethinker 428
Freethinking 428
Freeze 2519
Freight 3151-3154 4691-4692
Freight 3151
Freight Management 2567
Freight News International 3152
Freight News Weekly 3152
Freight Transport Equipment 4692
Freight Transport Services 4691
Freightway 3153
French Notes and Queries 4297
French Studies 1482
Frendz 159
Freshwater Biology 1867
Friday Market 3095
Friend 557
Friends 159
Friends Quarterly 558
Friends Quarterly Examiner 558
Fringe 723
Froebel Bulletin 1263
Froebel Journal 1263
Frozen Foods 3425
Fruit 2898-2901, 4685
Fruit 2898
Fruit Intelligence 2899
Fuel 3351
Fuel Abstracts 3352
Fuel Abstracts and Current Titles 3352
Fuel in Science and Practice 3351
Fuel Technology 3345-3355
Fulcrum 160
Fulmer Research Institute Newsletter 3481
Fundamentals of Cosmic Physics 1685
Funeral Service Journal 2166
Funerals 2166-2168
Funnel 2752
Fur and Feather 2930
Fur and Leather Review 3703
Fur Weekly News 3704
Furnishing Ireland 3671
Furnishing Review 3672
Furnishing World 3669
Furnishing World 3673

Furniture 3669-3677
Furniture and Bedding Production 3674
Furniture History 3675
Further Adventures 4592
Further Education 1285
Further Left 727
Fuss 4593
Futures 886

GB Journal 3162
GEC Journal of Science and Technology 1496
GEC Telecommunications 2484
GSIA Journal 4371
GSIA Newsletter 4371
Gaelic Languages 1492
Galloway Journal 2942
Galpin Society Journal 3989
Gambit 4024
Game Conservancy Annual Review 3002
Gamekeeper and Countryside 3003
Gamekeepers Gazette 3004
Gamekeeping 3001-3004
Games and Puzzles 3732
Games and Toys 3733
Garage 2724
Garage and Transport Equipment 2725
Garavi Gujarat 699
Garden Centre Trading 2860
Garden News 2904
Garden Supplies Retailer 2905
Gardeners Chronicle 2906
Garment Worker 3705
Gas and Liquid Chromatography Abstracts 1752
Gas-Chromatography Mass-Spectrometry Abstracts 1753
Gas in Industry 3358
Gas Marketing 3359
Gas Marketing and Domestic Gas 3359
Gas Service 3360
Gas Showroom 3357
Gas Technology 3357-3365
Gas World 3361
Gastroenterology 2275-2276
Gateshead and District Local History Society Bulletin 4314
Gateway 1064
Gazette 3421
Gazette of the Institute of Medical Laboratory Technology 1740
Gee Report 3134
Geirladur Prifysgol Cymru 79
Gemmologist 3522
Gemmology 1790
Gems 3520
Gen 1085
Gen 2200
Genealogical Quarterly 4363
Genealogists' Magazine 4364
Genealogy 4362-4369
General Discussions of the Faraday Society 1722
General Education 1138
General Periodicals 81-332, 4590-4604
General Practitioner 2059
General Weekly Shipping List 1397
Generalities 1086
General's Review 1087
Genetical Research 1882
Genetics Abstracts 1883
Geo Abstracts 4352
Geochemistry 1821
Geochimica et Cosmochimica Acta 1821

Geoforum 1796
Geographical Abstracts 4352
Geographical Journal 4353
Geographical Magazine 4354
Geographical Teacher 4355
Geography 4350-4360
Geography 4355
Geological Journal 1797
Geological Magazine 1798
Geological Society Special Reports 1799
Geology 1791-1813, 4658-4659
Geology 1212
Geology Teaching 1212
Geophysical Fluid Dynamics 1815
Geophysical Journal of the Royal Astronomical Society 1816
Geophysics 1814-1816
Geotechnique 2629
Geriatrics 2250-2251
German Language 1201
  Literature 4294-4295
German Life & Letters 4294
Gerontology 2136
Gibbons' Stamp Monthly 3176
Gift Buyer International 3727
Gifts 3727-3728
Gifts 3728
Gifts and Fancy Goods 3728
Gilbert & Sullivan Journal 3976
Girl About Town 161
Girl Guide Gazette 1104
Giroscope 162
Gissing Newsletter 4275
Glaciology 1824-1825
Glad News 1054
Glasgow Chamber of Commerce Journal 1337
Glasgow Dental Journal 2284
Glasgow Naturalist 1531
Glasgow Review 4594
Glass 3435
Glass Age 3436
Glass Circle 3437
Glass Journal 3438
Glass Technology 3435-3438C
  See also Stained Glass
Glass Technology 3438A
Gliding 4157-4159
Global Tapestry Journal and Vegan Action 163
Glove Buyer 3681
Go-Karter 4108
Goats 2951
Going Metric 1438
Going Places 4479
Golf 4078-4085
Golf Course & Clubhouse Management 4079
Golf Fixtures 4080
Golf International 4081
Golf Monthly 4082
Golf Trade Journal 4083
Golf Weekly 4084
Gold World 4085
Golfing 4085
Gongster 164
Good Elf 4218
Good Health 2153
Good Housekeeping 3019
Good Housekeeping Fact Finder 3019
Good Listening and Record Collector 3642
Good Motoring 2726
Good Photography 3939
Good Reading 4589
Good Templar Watchword 1075
Goodwill 165
Goodyear News 2696
Government and Opposition 664

Government expenditure below the line 812
Grace 2201
Grain Bulletin 2876
Grain Crops 2877
Gramophone 3643
Gramophone Record 3636
Granta 166
Grapevine 1928
Graphic Journal 3106
Grassland 2880-2881
Great Newspapers Reprinted 351
Great North Review 2635
Great Western Echo 2636
Greater London Arts 3826
Grebe 1532
Greece, History 4537-4538
  Literature 4299
Greece and Rome 4443
Greenwich Observatories 1592/3
Greenwich Time Report 1441
Griffin 1139
Grocer 3042
Grocers Gazette 3044
Grocery Distribution 3043
Grocery Trade 3040-3047
Groundsman 3857
Group Analysis 2226
Grower 2907
Grower and Prepacker 2907
Growing Point 14
Guernsey Breeders' Journal 2943
Guerrilheiro 4564
Guide 1107
Guide to Payments Risks and Import Regulations Abroad 1322
Guideposts 451
Guides 1104
Guild of Teachers of Backward Children 1253
Guildford & District Outlook 4479
Guns 2600-2602
Guns Review 4179
Gut 2276
Gymnastics 4089-4090
Gynaecology 2342
Gypsies 1449, 4651-4652

HCI Journal 3036
HDRA Newsletter 2853
HMRS Journal 2637
H. R. Owen Ltd. Reports 168
HVRA Library Bulletin 3800
HVRA Newsletter 3790
Habitat 1533
Haematology 2270-2271
Hair and Beauty 3060
Hairdressers Chronicle 3060
Hairdressers Journal 3061
Hairdressing 3060-3061
Half Yearly Bulletin 1471
Hallamshire & Osgoldeross Poetry Express 4219
Hamaor 567
Hampshire 4480
Hampshire Field Club Proceedings 1534
Hamsters 2968
Hand 2329
Hands 2329
Handy Shopping Guide 1395
Handyman Which? 3294
Hanes Gweithwyr Cymru 710
Hardware 3666-3668
Hardware Merchandiser 3666
Hardware Review 3667
Hardware Trade Journal 3668
Hardware Trades Review 3667
Harlequin 167
Harmonica News 3996

INDEX

Harpers Bazaar 169
Harpers Sports and Games 3691
Harpers Sports and Games Distributor 3691
Harpers Sports and Games Weekly 3691
Harpers Wine and Spirit Gazette 3376
Harvester 452
Havering Consumer Group Magazine 3257
Headquarters Gazette 1106
Healing Hand 468
Health 2140-2144
   See also Mental Health, Public Health etc.
Health 2154
Health and Social Service Journal 4665
Health and Strength 4089
Health Bulletin 2141
Health Education 1214
Health Education Journal 1214
Health for All 2202
Health from Herbs 2203
Health Physics 2142
Health Trends 2143
Health Visitor 2254
Healthy Living 2204
Hearing 2139
Hearing 2139
Heart 2236
Heart 2267
Hearts of Oak Journal 1023
Heat and Fluid Flow 1640
Heat Transfer 1672
Heating 3786-3802
Heating and Ventilating Engineer 3791
Heating & Ventilating News 3793
Heating and Ventilating Review 3792
Heating, Ventilating & Air Conditioning news 3793
Hebrew Literature 4302
Heel and Toe 4092
Helicopter World 2782
Helminthological Abstracts 1989
Helminthology 2324
Helminths 1989
Hemicrania 2307
Her Majesty's Consuls List 927
Herald 568
Heraldry 4370
Heralds of Sunrise 440
Herb Doctor 2203
Herbage Abstracts 2873
Herbal Practitioner 2205
Here Now 4595
Heredity 1879-1885
Heredity 1884
Hereford Breed Journal 2944,
Hermathena 363
Hermes 1588
Herpetology 2007
Herring Fisheries of Scotland Report 3010
Hers 170
Hertfordshire Archaeology 4410
Hertfordshire Countryside 4481
Hi-Fi Answers 3644
Hi-Fi For Pleasure 3645
Hi-Fi News and Record Review 3646
Hi-Fi Sound 3647
Hibernia 171
Hides 2996
Hides and Skins Quarterly 2996
High Road 2727
High Temperature Physics 1673
High Temperatures—High Pressures 1673

Higher Education 1280-1295
Higher Education Bulletin 1286
Higher Education Journal 1290
Higher Education Review 1288
Highlights 529
Highway Engineer 2666
Highway Engineering 2665-2667
Highway Statistics 2665
Highways Design and Construction 2616
Hillandale News 3648
Hire Purchase Journal 828
Hire Trading 831
Histochemical Journal 1908
Historical Journal 4315
History 4303-4349
   See also: under names of various countries, i.e., Brazil, France, Indonesia etc.
History Teaching 1224-1225
History 4316
History of Economic Thought Newsletter 765
History of Education 1140
History of Education Society Bulletin 1141
History Teachers Newsletter 1224
History Today 4317
Hobbies 3749
Home & Country 1076
Home & Economic Affairs Newsletter 1333
Home & Family 519
Home Economics 3020
Home Farmer 2980
Home Mission Field 520
Home Mission News 520
Home Owner 838
Home Sewing and Knitting 3021
Home Study 1274
Home Words 521
Homecare 3053
Homefinder 837
Homemaker 3054
Homes and Gardens 3022
Homes Overseas 839
Honey 172
Honeywell Computer Journal 3616
Hooker's Icones Plantarum 1946
Hoover News 173
Hope 2268
Horological Journal 3595
Horological Review 3522
Horology 3594-3596
Horse and Hound 4161
Horse & Pony 4162
Horses 2935-2937
Horse World 4163
Horticultural Abstracts 2908
Horticultural Trade Journal 2906
Horticulture 2902-2913
Hosiery 3711-3721
Hosiery Abstracts 3715
Hosiery Times 3713
Hosiery Trade Journal 3716
Hospital 1043
Hospital Abstracts 1041
Hospital & Health Management 1044
Hospital & Health Services Purchasing 1042
Hospital and Health Services Review 1043
Hospital & Nursing Home Management 1044
Hospital and Social Service Journal 1038
Hospital Career 1242
Hospital Gazette 1043
Hospital Management 1044
Hospital Medicine 2049

Hospital Service Finance 3229
Hospitals Purchasing 1042
Hospital Purchasing Guide 1042
Hospitals 1037-1048
Hostelling News 1066
Hot Car 4114
Hotel 174
Hotel Accountant 3194
Hotel and Catering Times 3017
Hotel and Restaurant Management 3016
Hotel Catering & Institutional Management Association Journal 3036
Hotel Tariff Study of Great Britain 4687
Hotels 3035-3036, 4687
Hotline 175
House Beautiful 3019
House Journal of Kennedy and Donkin 2373
Housebuyer 840
Housecraft 1267
Household Repairs 3050-3055
Houses and Estates 840
Housewife 3024
Housewives Today 3023
Housing 841
Housing and Construction Statistics 4627
Housing & Planning News Bulletin 3846
Housing and Planning Review 3846
Housing Centre Review 843
Housing Return for Scotland 842
Housing Review 843
Housing Special 847
Housing Statistics 4627
Hover Club News 2783
Hover Cover 3163
Hovering Craft and Hydrofoil 2784
How to Buy Toys 3734
Howard Journal 947
Howard Journal of Penology and Crime Prevention 947
How Factory Accidents Happen 2172
Hoyt Notched Ingot 2374
Hob 1334
Huguenot Society of London Quarto Series 533
Huguenots 533-534
Human Context 364
Human Factor 3227
Human Relations 602
Human Rights 929-933
Human World 176
Humanist 406
Humanities 3
Humberside Export News 1369
Hunting Fleet Magazine 177
Hunting Fleet Newsletter 177
Hunting Group Review 2375
Hydrogen 178
Hyde Park Socialist 728
Hydraulic Engineering 2668
   Power Engineering 2429-2431
Hydraulic Pneumatic Power 2431
Hydrological Sciences Bulletin 1839
Hydrology 1839
Hydrospace 2670
Hydrospace 4682
Hydynamic Newsletter 2524
Hygiene 2140-2144
   See also Industrial Hygiene & Safety

IA 2104
IA Newsletter 2104
IBBRIS 1894
IBL Journal 3062

ICAP Journal 2189
ICHCA Monthly Journal 3154
ICHCA Quarterly Journal 3154
ICI Magazine 1497
IDHE News 3788
IEE News 2454
IHVE Journal 3794
IMH Journal 2569
IMM Abstracts 2587
IMRA Journal 3296
IPI Newsletter 2043
IPM Digest 3232
IPPF Medical Bulletin 2132
IPRE Review 2496
IPS Journal 3090
IPS Journal and Reporters Magazine 3090
ISGML Bulletin 1566
ISPA News 940
ISPA News 3120
ITB News 1432
ITF Journal 1376
ITF Newsletter 1377
ITV Education 4641
ITV Education News 1142
IUPAC Information Bulletin 1713
Iberian Studies 4527
IBIS 2015
Ice 1824-1825
Ice 1824
Ice Cream 2984
Ice Cream and Frozen Confectionery 2984
Ice Cream Journal 2984
Ici Renault 2709
Icones Plantarum 1946
Ideal Home 3024
Ideas 1143
Idler 179
Ido-Letro 1469
Illuminating Engineering 2691-2695
Illustrated Bristol News 4482
Illustrated London News 180
Illustrated Sporting and Dramatic News 2843
Image 3827
Images 181
Immunochemistry 2164
Immunology 2163-2165
Immunology 2165
Impact 530
Impact 665
Imperial Review 4596
Import 1363
Import Trade 1363
In 469
In Britain 4483
In Fact 3447
In Particular 4221
In Plant Printer and Art Materials Buyer 3096
In Print 182
In Tune 3954
Incentive Marketing 3258
Incomes Data Reports 790
Incomes Data Studies 791
Incorporated Accountants' Journal 3180
Incorporated Linquist 1460
Incorporated Secretaries Journal 953
Incorporated Statistician 635
Independent School 1144
Index 3088
Index of Fungi 1962
Index of Reviews in Organic Chemistry 1769
Index of Veterinary Specialities 2346
Index to Forthcoming Russian Books 15
Index Veterinarius 2347

Indexer 73
Indexing 72-74
India Rubber Journal 3580
Individual Psychology News Letter 384
Individualist 666
Indochina, History 4556
Indochina 4556
Indonesia, History 4582
Indonesian News 4582
Industrial Accidents 2172
Industrial Advertising & Marketing 3289
Industrial Aerodynamics Abstracts 1644
Industrial and Commercial Gas 3362
Industrial and Commercial Photographer 3931
Industrial and Commercial Training 1271
Industrial and Process Heating 3331
Industrial Archaeology 4380
Industrial Chemistry 3313-3323
  Economics 874-885
  Hygiene & Safety 792-797
  Medicine 2145-2147
  Psychology 3226-3227
  Relations 783-789
Industrial Diamond Abstracts 3593
Industrial Diamond Review 3593
Industrial Equipment News 3230
Industrial Fibres 3545
Industrial Finishing and Surface Coatings 3464
Industrial Law Journal 949
Industrial Locomotive Society Journal 2638
Industrial Management 3206
Industrial Marketing Research Abstracts 3295
Industrial Minerals 2588
Industrial Nottingham 1335
Industrial Participation 786
Industrial Recovery 2688
Industrial Relations Bulletin 787
Industrial Relations Law Reports 901
Industrial Relations Review and Report 788
Industrial Safety 794
Industrial Salvage 2688
Industrial Screen 3637
Industrial Society 789
Industrial Trucks and Storage Equipment News 2572
Industrial Tyneside 1330
Industrial Wales 4508
Industrial Welfare 789
Industry 874-885
Information Digest 4559
Information Service of Free Czechoslovakia 4529
Information Storage and Retrieval 74
Information Supplement to Soviet Studies 4530
Informer 157
Informer 4220
Infra-red Physics 1654
Infrared Physics 1654
Injury 2237
Inklings 3097
Inland Revenue Statistics 862
Inland Waterways 1387-1390, 4647-4648
Innes Review 501
Inorganic and Nuclear Chemistry Letters 1759
Inorganic Chemistry 1758-1764
Inorganic Chemistry of the Trinsition Elements 1760
Inorganic Reaction Mechanisms 1761

Insect Biochemistry 1999
Insigh 3089
Insight 3270
Insight Magazine 399
Insite 2728
Inspector 3271
Instant Cookery 3025
Institute of British Geographers: Transactions 4356
Institute of British Geographers, Transactions and Papers 4356
Institute of Packaging Journal 2555
Institute of Petroleum Abstracts 3429
Institute of Petroleum Review 3433
Institute of Scientific Business 3215
Institute of Transport Journal 1373
Institution of Civil Engineers Proceedings 2617
Institution of Fire Engineers Quarterly 2185
Institution of the Rubber Industry, Transactions and Proceedings 3575
Institutional Hotel and Catering Management 3036
Institutional Management 3036
Instrument Abstracts 3633
Instrument Practice 3629
Instrument Review 2424
Instrumentation 3627-3634
Instruments 3988-3989
Insulation 3810
Insulation 3810
Insurance 1083-1099
Insurance Broker's Monthly 1088
Insurance Institute of Great Britain and Ireland, Journal 1090
Insurance Record 1089
Intelligence 1154
Inter-City ABC 1378
Intercom 2485
Interior Design 3924
Interior Design 3924
Interior Design and Contract Furnishing 3924
International Abstracts of Biological Sciences 1868
International Accountant 3195
International Accountants Journal 3195
International Affairs 667
International African Bibliography 4565
International and Comparative Law Quarterly 923
International Auction Records 3828
International Yearbook of Sales 3828
International Bank Note Society 823
International Bar Journal 902
International Bar News 902
International Biodeterioration Bulletin 1895
International Biodeterioration Bulletin Reference Index Supplement 1894
International Boat Industry 4136
International Boating 4136
International Brewer and Distiller 3385
International Brewers Journal 3388
International Brewing & Distilling 3388
International Broadcast Engineer 3091
International Camellia Journal 2922
International Cataloguing 42
International Construction 2618
International Container Directory 2568

INDEX

International Co-operative Bulletin 852
International Currency Review 809
International Defence and Aid Fund Information Service Manual 700
International Democratic Review 668
International Dyer, Textile Printer, Bleacher and Finisher 3461
International Financial Bulletin 810
International Harvester Review 2850
International History Magazine 4318
International Journal for Numerical Methods in Engineering 3617
International Journal for Parasitology 1896
International Journal for Radiation Physics and Chemistry 1678
International Journal of Agrwian Affairs 2807
International Journal of Applied Radiation and Isotopes 1679
International Journal of Biochemistry 1909
International Journal of Bio-medical computing 3618
International Journal of Circuit Theory and Applications 4678
International Journal of Computer Mathematics 3619
International Journal of Control 2476
International Journal of Early Childhood 3067
International Journal of Earthquake Engineering and Structural Dynamics 1819
International Journal of Electrical Engineering Education 2455
International Journal of Electronics 2477
International Journal of Engineering Science 2376
International Journal of Environmental Analytical Chemistry 1748
International Journal of Environmental Studies 1929
International Journal of Epidemiology 2060
International Journal of Farm Building Research 2834
International Journal of Heat and Mass Transfer 1672
International Journal of Insect Morphology and Embryology 2000
International Journal of Machine Tool Design and Research 2577
International Journal of Magnetism 1686
International Journal of Man-Machine Studies 781
International Journal of Mathematical Education in Science and Technology 1208
International Journal of Mechanical Sciences 2409
International Journal of Middle East Studies 4552
International Journal of Nautical Archaeology and Underwater Exploration 4381
International Journal of Neuroscience 2301
International Journal of Non-Destructive Testing 2392
International Journal of Non-Linear Mechanics 1628
International Journal of Nuclear Medicine and Biology 4661
International Journal of Nursing Studies 2255

International Journal of Physical Distribution 3259
International Journal of Polymeric Materials 1736
International Journal of Pressure Vessels and Piping 4674
International Journal of Production Research 3239
International Journal of Psycho-analysis 404
International Journal of Psychology 385
International Journal of Radiation Biology 2222
International Journal of Rock Mechanics and Mining Sciences 1848
International Journal of Social Psychiatry 2314
International Journal of Solids and Structures 1629
International Journal of Sulfur Chemistry 1766
International Journal of Systems Science 1565
International Law 923
International Leathergoods Buyer 3681
International Library Review 43
International Licensing 880
International Management (English language Edition) 3207
International Management (Spanish Language Edition) 3208
International Market Survey 2945
International Market Survey 2953
International Marxist 729
International Mining Equipment 2589
International Perfumer 3474
International Pest Control 2866
International Planned Parenthood News 2133
International Political Science Abstracts 699
International Postcard Market 3543
International Review of Applied Linguistics in Language Teaching 1191
International Review of Applied Psychology 386
International Ropeway Review 2664
International Rubber Digest 3574
International Seismological Summary 1818
International Socialism 730
International Sound Engineer 3091
International Studies Quarterly 670
International Sugar Journal 3407
International TV Technical Review 3091
International Tax-Free Trader & Duty-Free World 3260
International Tourism Quarterly 1379
International Trade 1348-1362 4646
International Travel Requirements 1371
International Tug and Workboat 2761
International Vending Times 3272
International Wildfowl Research Bureau Bulletin 2016
Internationalist 671
Internationalist 4615
Interviewing 80
Intestinal Absorption and Related Topics 2105
Intestines 2104-2105
Into Orbit 2246
Intra-Science Chemistry Reports 1770
Inventor 2043

Inverness Pictorial 4446
Investment Analyst 824
Investment Finance 824-827 4625
Investors Bulletin 4625
Investors Guardian 825
Ireland, Archaeology 4344 4396, *History* 4455
Irish Ancestor 4365
Irish Archives Bulletin 357
Irish Baptist Historical Society Journal 545
Irish Catering Review 3026
Irish Communist 747
Irish Computer Society Bulletin 4702
Irish Contracts Weekly 3765
Irish Democrat 672
Irish Democrat 4616
Irish Evangelical 535
Irish Farmers' Journal 2835
Irish Farming News 2836
Irish Freedom 672
Irish Genealogist 4366
Irish Geography 4357
Irish Grocery World 3045
Irish Industry 881
Irish Journal of Education 1145
Irish Journal of Psychology 387
Irish Law Times and Solicitors Journal 903
Irish Liberation Press 746
Irish Library 25
Irish Licensing World 3367
Irish Medical Times 2061
Irish Messenger 502
Irish Motor Trader 2729
Irish Nurse 2261
Irish Nurses' Journal 2261
Irish Nurses' Magazine 2261
Irish Post 183
Irish Presbyterian 539
Irish Skipper 3008
Irish Sword 1009
Irish Young Friend 4613
Iron 3494-3506
Iron and Coal Trades Review 2586
Iron and Coal Trades Review 3505
Iron and Steel 3496
Iron and Steel Industry 3496
Iron and Steel Trades Journal 2533
Iron Trade Review 3505
Ironmonger 3666
Ironbridge Quarterly 2028
Isis 184
Itch 322
Izvestiya, Akademii Nauk SSR, 'Metally' 3492

JACB 3320
JOFRO 2186
JP Supplement 935
JP Weekly Law Digest 955
Jabberwocky 4276
Jamaica & West Indian Review 1361
Jamaican Weekly Gleaner 185
Japan News 438
Jazz 3986-3987
Jazz Journal 3986
Jazz Times 3987
Jersey 2947
Jersey 3717
Jersey at Home 2946
Jersey Cow 2947
Jersey Fabrics International 3717
Jersey Life 4484
Jetline Schedules 1434
Jeweller 3521
Jeweller and Metalworker 3521
Jeweller 3517-3522
Jewish Gazette 569

Jewish Literature 4302
Jewish Missionary Herald 568
Jewish Quarterly 570
Jewish Telegraph 571
Jewish Tribune 572
Jewish Vegetarian 3048
John Peel Jottings 1535
Jordans' Daily Register 1303
Journal (First Series) 2910
Journal and Graphic Review 186
Journal and Proceedings of the IRTE 1418
Journal and Proceedings of the Agricultural Economics Society 2808
Journal and Proceedings of the Institute of Sewage Purification 2682
Journal for Industrial Nurses 2146
Journal for the Theory of Social Behaviour 603
Journal of Abstracts 2753
Journal of Adhesion 1706
Journal of Administration Overseas 998
Journal of Aerosol Science 1734
Journal of African Administration 998
Journal of African History 4566
Journal of Agricultural Economics 2808
Journal of Agricultural Engineering Research 2851
Journal of Agricultural Science 2809
Journal of Alcoholism 2149
Journal of American Studies 4573
Journal of Analytical Psychology 388
Journal of Anatomy 2103
Journal of Anatomy and Physiology 2103
Journal of Animal Ecology 1983
Journal of Agricultural Research 3000
Journal of Applied Bacteriology 1897
Journal of Applied Chemistry 3320
Journal of Applied Chemistry 3321
Journal of Applied Chemistry and Biotechnology 3321
Journal of Applied Ecology 1984
Journal of Applied Mathematics and Mechanics 1630
Journal of Applied Probability 1584
Journal of Atmospheric and Terrestrial Physics 1842
Journal of Automotive Engineering 2730
Journal of Behaviour Therapy and Experimental Psychiatry 2315
Journal of Biological Education 1213
Journal of Biomechanics 1631
Journal of Biosocial Science 1870
Journal of Black Studies 701
Journal of Bone and Joint Surgery 2328
Journal of Business Law 950
Journal of Byelorussian Studies 4532
Journal of Caribbean History 4581
Journal of Cell Science 1890
Journal of the Central Asian Society 4540
Journal of Chemical Thermodynamics 1728
Journal of Child Psychology and Psychiatry and Allied Disciplines 396
Journal of Clinical Pathology 2238
Journal of Colour and Appearance 1715
Journal of Commerce 1305

Journal of Commerce and Shipping Telegraph 1305
Journal of Common Market Studies 873
Journal of Commonwealth Literature 4189
Journal of Commonwealth Political Studies 673
Journal of Comparative Administration 3209
Journal of Comparative Pathology 2348
Journal of Comparative Pathology and Therapeutics 2348
Journal of Connoisseurship and Art Technology 3829
Journal of Contemporary Asia 4543
Journal of Contemporary History 4319
Journal of Coordination Chemistry 1716
Journal of Criminal Justice 4632
Journal of Curiculum Studies 1146
Journal of Dairy Research 2976
Journal of Decorative Art & British Decorator 3807
Journal of Dentistry 4668
Journal of Development Studies 604
Journal of Documentation 2
Journal of Earth Sciences 1800
Journal of Ecclesiastical History 480
Journal of Ecology 1985
Journal of Educational Administration and History 1147
Journal of Educational Technology 1111
Journal of Egyptian Archaeology 4382
Journal of Electronics and Control 2476
Journal of Embryology and Experimental Morphology 1979
Journal of Endocrinology 2290
Journal of Entomology 2001
Journal of Environmental Management 4693
Journal of Environmental Planning and Pollution Control 1930
Journal of European Studies 4190
Journal of Experimental Biology 1871
Journal of Experimental Botany 1947
Journal of Fish Biology 2006
Journal of Fluid Mechanics 1641
Journal of Food Technology 3404
Journal of Fuel and Heat Technology 3353
Journal of Fuel and Heat Technology 3350
Journal of Gemmology and Proceedings of the Gemmological Association of Great Britain 1790
Journal of General Microbiology 1898
Journal of General Virology 1954
Journal of Glaciology 1825
Journal of Hellenic Studies 4537
Journal of Helminthology 2324
Journal of Horticultural Science 2909
Journal of Hospital Pharmacy 2206
Journal of Hygiene 2144
Journal of Imperial and Commonwealth History 4320
Journal of Industrial Archaeology 4380
Journal of Industrial Economics 882
Journal of Inorganic and Nuclear Chemistry 1763
Journal of Insect Physiology 2002
Journal of InterAmerican Studies and World Affairs 674

Journal of International Medical Research 2062
Journal of Jewish Studies 4302
Journal of Laryngology and Otology 2273
Journal of Latin American Studies 587
Journal of Librarianship 44
Journal of Linquistics 1416
Journal of Local Administration Overseas 998
Journal of Management Studies 3210
Journal of Materials Science 2029
Journal of Mathematical Sociology 605
Journal of Mechanical Engineering Science 2410
Journal of Mechanisms 2411
Journal of Mechanochemistry and Cell Mobility 1891
Journal of Medical Genetics 1885
Journal of Medical Laboratory Technology 2252
Journal of Medical Microbiology 1899
Journal of Mental Deficiency Research 2316
Journal of Mental Subnormality 2317
Journal of Microscopy 1670
Journal of Modern African Studies 675
Journal of Molecular and Cellular Cardiology 2269
Journal of Molecular Biology 1873
Journal of Moral Education 1149
Journal of Motor Trade Management 2724
Journal of Natural History 1536
Journal of Navigation 1610
Journal of Neurochemistry 2302
Journal of Neurocytology 1892
Journal of Neurology, Neurosurgery & Psychiatry 2303
Journal of Mental Science 2310
Journal of Non Metals 1642
Journal of Nuclear Energy 1692
Journal of Obstetrics and Gynaecology of the British Commonwealth 2342
Journal of Obstetrics and Gynaecology of the British Empire 2342
Journal of Park Administration 3860
Journal of Pathology 2239
Journal of Pathology and Bacteriology 1899
Journal of Petrology 1849
Journal of Pharmacy and Pharmacology 2207
Journal of Philosophical Studies 371
Journal of Phonetics 4654
Journal of Photographic Science 3932
Journal of Physical Education 1249
Journal of Physiology 2108
Journal of Planning and Property Law 905
Journal of Plasma Physics 1618
Journal of Physics 1615, 1616, 1693, 1701, 3482, 3630
Journal of Physics and Chemistry of Solids 1617
Journal of Pomology 2909
Journal of Pomology and Horticultural Science 2909
Journal of Psychiatric Research 2318
Journal of Psychosomatic Research 2319
Journal of Public Administration 963
Journal of Quantitative Spectroscopy

INDEX

and Radiative Transfer 1657
Journal of Refrigeration 2520
Journal of Reproduction and Fertility 1980
Journal of Research of the Steel Castings Research and Trade Association 3498
Journal of Roman Studies 4383
Journal of Russian Studies 1202
Journal of School Hygiene and Physical Education 1249
Journal of Scientific Instruments 3630
Journal of Scientific Physical Training 1249
Journal of Semitic Studies 573
Journal of Small Animal Practice 2349
Journal of Social Policy 606
Journal of Soil Science 2855
Journal of Sound and Vibration 1647
Journal of Statistical Computation and Simulation 3621
Journal of Stored Products Research 3426
Journal of Steroid Biochemistry 1910
Journal of Strain Analysis 2393
Journal of Structural Learning 397
Journal of Structural Learning 1566
Journal of Systems Engineering 2030
Journal of Terramechanics 2619
Journal of the Anthropological Society of Oxford 1852
Journal of the Arms and Armour Society 2601
Journal of the Association of Public Analysts 2155
Journal of the Association of Law Teachers 1189
Journal of the Balint Society 389
Journal of the Board of Greenkeeping Research 3858
Journal of the British Boot and Shoe Institution 3682
Journal of the British Ceramic Society 3450
Journal of the British Dental Association 2278
Journal of the British Endodontic Society 2285
Journal of the British Fire Services Association 2187
Journal of the British Grassland Society 2880
Journal of the British Institution of Radio Engineers 2502
Journal of the British Interplanetary Society 1598
Journal of the British Ship Research Association 2753
Journal of the British Shipbuilding Research Association 2753
Journal of the British Society for Phenomenology 405
Journal of the British Society of Dowsers 1822
Journal of the British Society of Master Glass Painters 3439
Journal of the British Society of Scientific Glassblowers 3438B
Journal of the British Speleological Association 1828
Journal of the British Steel Castings Research Association 3498
Journal, British Waterworks Association 2673
Journal of The Butler Society 4367
Journal of the Camborne-Redruth Natural History Society 1537

Journal of the Central Landowners' Association 833
Journal of the Chartered Insurance Institute 1090
Journal of the Chartered Surveyors Institution 1603
Journal of the Chemical Society 1714
Journal of the Chemical Society: Section A 1762
Journal of the Chemical Society: Section B 1772
Journal of the Chemical Society: Section C 1771
Journal of the Chemical Society: Section D 1714
Journal of the Chemical Society: Dalton Transactions 1762
Journal of the Chemical Society: Faraday Transactions I 1723
Journal of the Chemical Society: Faraday Transactions II 1724
Journal of the Chemical Society: Perkin Transactions I 1771
Journal of the Chemical Society: Perkin Transactions II 1772
Journal of the Chester & North Wales Architectural, Archaeological & Historic Society 4410
Journal of the Chester Archaeological Society 4411
Journal of the College of General Practitioners 2065
Journal of the Conchological Society of Great Britain and Ireland 1987
Journal of the Confederate Historical Society 4574
Journal of the Cornish Methodist Historical Association 551
Journal of County Kildare Archaeological Society 4394
Journal of the Craven Pothole Club 1829
Journal of the Derbyshire Archaeological & Natural History Society 4405
Journal of the Electro-depositors Society 3471
Journal of the English Folk Dance & Song Society 4042
Journal of the English Folk Dance Society 4042
Journal of the English Place-Name Society 1476
Journal of the Faculty of Architects and Surveyors 3878
Journal of the Faculty of Radiologists 2221
Journal of the Farm Buildings Association 2837
Journal, Federated Institute of Brewing 3389
Journal of the Forensic Science Society 921
Journal of the Franklin Institute 1619
Journal of the Friends Historical Society 559
Journal of the Geological Society 1801
Journal: Glasgow Chamber of Commerce 1337
Journal of the Guild of Air Pilots and Air Navigators 2785
Journal of the Gypsy Lore Society 1449
Journal of the H.G. Wells Society 4277
Journal of the Harker Geological Society 1802
Journal of the Historical Society of the Presbyterian Church of Wales 537

Journal of the IHVE 3794
Journal of the IRI 3575
Journal of Incorporated Brewers' Guild 3384
Journal of the Incorporated British Institute of Certified Carpenters 3527
Journal of the Institute of Actuaries 1091
Journal of the Institute of Bankers 811
Journal of the Institute of Biology 1861
Journal of the Institute of Brewing 3389
Journal of the Institute of Builders 3759
Journal of the Institute of Civil Defence 1010
Journal of the Institute of Engineers and Technicians Ltd 2377
Journal of the Institute of Fuel 3354
Journal of the Institute of Health Education 2156
Journal of the Institute of Home Help Organisers 2256
Journal of the Institute of Industrial Safety Officers 2175
Journal of the Institute of Landscape Architects 3859
Journal of the Institute of Mathematics and its Applications 1567
Journal of the Institute of Metals 3483
Journal of the Institute of Navigation 1610
Journal of the Institute of Petroleum 3429
Journal of the Institute of Petroleum 3430
Journal of the Institute of the Motor Industry 2736
Journal of the Institute of Transport 1373
Journal of the Institute of Wood Science 3528
Journal of the Institute of Education of Durham and Newcastle Universities 1148
Journal of the Institution of Civil Engineers 2617
Journal of the Institution of Computer Sciences 3620
Journal of the Insitution of Electrical Engineers 2470
Journal of the Institution of Gas Engineers 3363
Journal of the Institution of Highway Engineers 2666
Journal of the Institution of Municipal Engineers 2378
Journal of the Institution of Municipal and County Engineers 2378
Journal of the Institution of Nuclear Engineers 2417
Journal of the Institution of Petroleum Technologists 3430
Journal of the Institution of Production Engineers 3221
Journal of the Institution of Water Engineers 2675
Journal of the Insurance Institute of London 1092
Journal of the International Folk Music Council 4043
Journal of the International Phonetic Association 1477
Journal of the Irish Dental Association 2286

Journal of the Irish Medical Association 2063
Journal of the Iron and Steel Institute 3497
Journal of the Iron and Steel Trades Confederation 3499
Journal of the Junior Institution of Engineers 2379
Journal of the Kerry Archaeological and Historical Society 4395
Journal of the Ladies' Alpine Club 4097
Journal of the Lancashire and Cheshire Branch of the Wesley Historical Society 552
Journal of the Lancashire Dialect Society 1467
Journal of the Law Society of Scotland 904
Journal of the Leicester and County Chamber of Commerce and Industry 1338
Journal of the Linnean Society 1976
Journal of the London Association of Engineers 2380
Journal of the London Mathematical Society 1568
Journal of the London Society 4485
Journal of the Lute Society 3998
Journal of the Mammillaria Society 2023
Journal of the Manx Museum 339
Journal of the Marine Biological Association of the United Kingdom 1872
Journal of the Market Research Society 3297
Journal of the Mechanics and Physics of Solids 1632
Journal of the Medical Women's Federation 2064
Journal of the National Institute of Agricultural Botany 2810
Journal of the National Institute of Industrial Psychology 3227
Journal of the Oil and Colour Chemists' Association 3465
Journal of the Old Athlone Society 4321
Journal of Operative Brewers' Guild 3384
Journal of the Presbyterian Historical Society of England 538
Journal of the Printing Historical Society 3098
Journal of the Proceedings of the Linnean Society 1943
Journal of the Queen's Regiment 1005
Journal of the Quekett Microscopical Club 1937
Journal of the RAF Ornithological Society 2017
Journal of the Railway and Canal Historical Society 2639
Journal of the Ramsay Society of Chemical Engineers 3322
Journal of the Registered Plumbers Association 3780
Journal of the Röntgen Society 2220
Journal of the Royal Aeronautical Society 2769
Journal of the Royal Asiatic Society of Great Britain & Ireland 4544
Journal of the Royal Central Asian Society 4540
Journal of the Royal College of General Practitioners 2065
Journal of the Royal College of Physicians of London 2066
Journal of the Royal College of Surgeons of Edinburgh 2240
Journal of the Royal Horticultural Society 2910
Journal of the Royal Institution of Chartered Surveyors 1603
Journal of the Royal Microscopical Society 1670
Journal of the Royal Naval Medical Service 2067
Journal of the Royal Sanitary Institute 2158
Journal of the Royal Scottish Arboricultural Society 2894
Journal of the Royal Society for the Encouragement of Arts, Manufactures & Commerce. Journal of the Royal Society of Arts 3830
Journal of the Royal Statistical Society 628
Journal of the Royal Town Planning Institute 3847
Journal of the Science of Food and Agriculture 3405
Journal of the Scottish Rock Garden Club 2923
Journal of the Scunthorpe Museum Society 340
Journal of the Society for Army Historical Research 1006
Journal of the Society for Psychical Research 400
Journal of the Society for the Bibliography of Natural History 1538
Journal of the Society for the Preservation of the Wild Fauna of the Empire 1975
Journal of the Society of Archer-Antiquities 4182
Journal of the Society of Archivists 358
Journal of the Society of Arts 3830
Journal of the Society of Chemical Industry 3318
Journal of the Society of Chemical Industry 3405
Journal of the Society of Comparative Legislation 923
Journal of the Society of Cosmetic Chemists 3475
Journal of the Society of Dairy Technology 2977
Journal of the Society of Dyers and Colourists 3462
Journal of the Society of Film and Television Arts 2513
Journal of the Society of Glass Technology 3438A/C
Journal of the Society of Industrial Artists 3823
Journal of the Society of Leather Trades Chemists 3683
Journal of the Society of Licensed Aircraft Engineers & Technologists 2788
Journal of the Society of Telegraph Engineers 2459
Journal of the Soil Association 2854
Journal of the Sports Turf Research Institute 3858
Journal of the Stephenson Locomotive Society 2640
Journal of the Surveyors' Institution 1603
Journal of the Textile Institute 3546
Journal of the Town Planning Institute 3847
Journal of the Tramway Museum Society 1424
Journal of the Transport Ticket Society 3150
Journal of the VBRA 2710
Journal of the Visible Record Society 3601
Journal of the Warburg and Courtauld Institutes 3831
Journal of the Watford & District Industrial History Society 4322
Journal of the Welsh Bibliographical Society 16
Journal of the William Morris Society 187
Journal of the World Financial Community 809
Journal of Theological Studies 417
Journal of Theoretical Biology 1874
Journal of Thermal Analysis 3795
Journal of Transport Economics and Policy 1380
Journal of Transport History 1381
Journal of Tropical Medicine and Hygiene 2068
Journal of Ultrasound in Medicine and Biology 4663
Journal of Verbal Learning and Verbal Behaviour 1150
Journal of West African Languages 1489
Journal of William Mallinson & Denny Mott Ltd 2620
Journal of World Sulphur 3340
Journal of World Trade Law 951
Journal of Zoology 1974
Journalism 349-354
Journals of Pierre Menard 4256
Joy and Light 462
Judaism 565-579
Judicial Statistics, Scotland 937
Judo 4125-4129
Judo 4127
Junior Age 3706
Junior Astronomer 1588
Junior Bookshelf 17
Junior Car Club Gazette 4110
Junior Education Equipment 1151
Junior Engineering Society Transactions 2379
Junior Journal 1035
Juridicial Review 906
Justice of the Peace 956
Justice of the Peace and Local Government Review 956, 960
Justice of the Peace Reports 957
Justices' Clerk 958
Jute 3558-3563
Jute and Canvas Review 3560
Jute and Synthetics Review 3560
Jute Markets and Prices 3563
Juvenile Missionary Herald 548
Juvenile Templar 1077

KWA News 188
Karting 4108
Karting 4108
Kauchuk i Rezina 3592
Kayser News 3710
Keep Left 731
Kelvin Magazine 268
Kenley Abstracts 3538
Kennel Gazette 2965
Kent 4486
Kent Education Gazette 1152
Kent Life 4487
Kent Newsletter 45
Kew Bulletin 1948
Key Frame 3992
Keyboard 3990
Keyboard Instruments 3990
Kidneys 2127-2128

INDEX

Kine Weekly 4004
King 211
Kingfisher 2018
Kingdom Overseas 553
Kingdom Voice 439
Kipling Journal 4278
Kist 1539
Knights Industrial Reports 1306
Knights Official Advertiser of Local Management in England and Wales 985
Knitters Circular and Monthly Record 3716
Knitting and Haberdashery Review 3718
Knitting News 3719
Knitting Wool Review 3718
Knitwear 3711-3721
Knitwear and Stockings 3720
Know Britain 1382
Know Britain 4488
Kraftsman 189
Krikos 4538
Kybernetes 2425

LAG Bulletin 4631
LBC Review 3776
LEG News 46
LIBER Bulletin 48
LOGA 984
LPG 3796
LSE 766
LUT Chemical Engineering Particle Abstracts 1636
Lab 1741
Laban Art of Movement Guild Magazine 1251
Laboratory Animals 2116
Laboratory Chemistry 1740-1743
Laboratory Equipment Digest 1742
Laboratory Journal 2252
Laboratory Practice 1743
Laboratory Technology 2252
Labour Economics 777-782
Labour Gazette 778
Labour Weekly 732
Labour Worker 741
Lace 3919-3923
Lace Curtain 4222
Lacemaking 3921
Lacrosse 4077
Lacrosse 4077
Ladies Circle Magazine 1078
Laissez Faire 4223
Lakeland Rambler 4093
Lambeg Research Review 3561
Lambeth Local 190
Lancashire Life 4489
Lancet 2069
Land 832-847, 4627-4629
Land and Liberty 863
Land and Water 3864
Land values 863
Landscape Design 3859
Landscaping 3857-3863
Language and Speech 1462
Language in Society 1463
Language-Teaching Abstracts 1192
Languages 1458-1466, 4653
  Teaching 1191-1193
  See also under type e.g. *Esperanto* and/or *Country.*
Lapis Industrial Opportunities 884
Laser 2031
Laser-Raman Spectroscopy Abstracts 1658
Laundering 3062-3064
Laundry and Cleaning 3063

Laundry Journal and Laundry Record 3063
Lawels 3832
Law 888-920, 4631
  See also Business Law, Criminal Law, Electoral Law, International Law, Legal Personnel
Law Journal 913
Law Librarian 47
Law Notes 907
Law Quarterly Review 908
Law Reports 909
Law Society's Gazette 910
Law Teacher 1189
Law Times Reports 888
Lawn Tennis 4076
Lawn Tennis & Badminton 4076
Le Grand Baton 3955
Le Maitre Phonetique 1477
Lead 3511
Lead Abstracts 3571
League Doings 939
League Football 4065
Learning 397
Learning for Living 1185
Leather 3678-3690
Leather 3684
Leather Trades Review 3684
Leathergoods 3685
Leeds & Harrogate Topic 4490
Leeds & West Riding Topic 4490
Leeds Graphic 4491
Leeds Journal 1339
Leeds Local 191
Leeds Student 192
Left 733
Legal and General Gazette 1093
Legal Education 1189
Legal Executive 959
Legal Personnel 955-960
Leicester and Rutland Topic 4492
Leicester Graphic 4493
Leicestershire Historian 4323
Leisure Painter 3925
Lensbury Club News 193
Leonardo 3833
Leprosy 2245-2246
Leprosy Review 2245
Letters in Applied and Engineering Sciences 4671
Levant 4384
Liaison 51
Liberal Catholic 503
Liberal News 724
Liberal News Commentary 724
Liberals 723-726
Libertarian Teacher 4642
Librarians for Social Change 49
Librarianship 25-71
Libraries 25-71, 4586-4588
Library 18
Library Action 50
Library and Information Bulletin 19
Library and Information Science Abstracts 52
Library Assistant 30
Library Association Record 51
Library Bulletin 194
Library History 53
Library List (WRA) 2676
Library Notes 4494
Library Review 54
Library Science Abstracts 52
Library World 55
Licensed Bookmaker and Betting Office Proprietor 4051
Licensed Vintner 3368
Licensee 3369
Lichenologist 1967
Lichens 1966-1967

Life and Work 527
Life and Worship 487
Life-boat 2768
Lifeboats 2768
Life of the Spirit 482
Life Sciences 2241
Light 401
Light and Lighting 2691
Light Aviation 2786
Light Horse 4164
Light Production Engineering 3211
Light Steam Power 2427
Lighting Equipment News 2692
Lighting Journal 2693
Lighting Research and Technology 2694
Lightning 2451
Lightweight Camper 4104
Lincolnshire Architectural and Archaeological Society Transactions 4411
Lincolnshire Historian 4411
Lincolnshire History and Archaeology 4412
Lincolnshire Life 4495
Linear and Multilinear Algebra 1581
Linen 3558-3563
Linen Research 3561
Ling Association Leaflet 1249
Linguists' Review 1460
Link 251
Link 1275
Link 1340
Listener 195
Liteinoe Proizvodstvo 2534
Literary Guide 406
Literary Repository 20
Literature 4183-4198
  See also: England, France, Germany etc.
Lithoprinter 3123
Littack 4191
Liturgical Studies 463
Liturgy 463-464
Liturgy 487
Liturgy Bulletin 464
Live Rail 2641
Liverpool and Manchester Geological Journal 1797
Liverpool Bulletin and Walker Art Gallery, Annual Report 335
Livestock Farming 2948
Living 3027
Living Music 3956
Llanfair Railway Journal 2642
Llen Cymru 196
Lloyds Bank Monthly 1307
Lloyds Bank Monthly Financial Report 1307
Lloyds Bank Review 1307
Lloyds List 1396
Lloyd's Loading List 1397
Lloyd's Log 1398
LlwyFan 4025
Llyfrau Newydd 197
Loans From The Consolidated Fund 812
Loans From The National Loans Fund 812
Local Financial Returns (Scotland) 864
Local Government 983-997, 4634
Local Government Chronicle 985
Local Government Finance 986
Local Government Officer 994
Local Government Review 960
Local Government Service 994
Local Government Studies 987
Local Historian 4324

INDEX

Local History Bulletin   4325
Local History Bulletin for South-East Scotland   4326
Local History Records   4329
Local Population Studies   638
Local Taxation Returns (Scotland)   864
Lock Gate   1388
Locke Newsletter   365
Locomotive Journal   2643
Locomotive Magazine   2646
Locomotives in Profile   2644
Log Book   3164
London   988
London Archaeologist   4413
London Bride   3028
London Bulletin   742
London College, of Music Magazine   3957
London Corn Circular   2878
London Educational Review   1153
London Gazette   198
London Magazine   199
London Oz   243
London Pubs   3370
London Quarterly & Holborn Review   484
London Recusant   504
London Review   4279
London Shell   200
London Society Journal   4496
London Teacher & Schools Review   1226
London Weekly Diary of Social Events   201
Long Range Planning   3212
Long Room   21
Look and Listen   2514
Look Now   202
Lord's Day Magazine   462
Lore and Language   1453
Love Affair   203
Loving   204
Low Temperature Physics   1674
Loyalist Links   522
Lubrication   2574-2576
Lucas Reflections   205
Ludd's Mill   4224
Lyons Mail   206

MACE Bulletin   210
MACE Forum   210
MEAL Monthly Digest   3290
MEB News   207
MGA Bulletin   2914
MIMS Ireland   2075
MIRA Abstracts   2731
MIRA Monthly Summary   2731
MLQ   734
MPTA Journal   1420
MRA Information Service   461
MSA Journal   2732
MSA News   2732
MWF Quarterly Review   2064
Mabon   208
Mac   4225
Mac Matters   209
Machine Science Abstracts   2414
Machine Tool Engineering   2578
Machine Tool Research   2579
Machine Tools   2577-2584
Machine Tools and Tooling   2580
Machinery   2581
Machinery and Production Engineering   2581
Machinery Lloyd   2582
Machinery Market   2412
Machines and Tooling   2413

Machinist   3489
Mad   4597
Madonna   453
Magazine of Concrete Research   3457
Magazine of the Japan Evangelistic Band   438
Magazine of the Sunrise Band   440
Magic Circular   4045
Magistrate   954
Magistrates   954
Magnetic Resonance Review   1659
Magnetism   1686
Maintenance Engineering   3250-3251
Maintenance Engineering   3251
Making Music   3958
Mallorn   4280
Mammal Review   2024
Mammals   2023-2024
Man   390
Man and Metal   3499
Management Education   1216
   See under Business Management, Credit Management, Farm Management, Financial Management, Industrial Management, Office Management, Personnel Management, Production Management, Stable Management
Management Abstracts   3213
Management Accounting   3196
Management by Objectives   3214
Management Decision   3215
Management Education & Development   1216
Management in Action   3216
Management in Printing   3099
Management Today   3217
Manager   3217
Managing Printer   3100
Manchester Association of Engineers Transactions   2381
Manchester Engineer   2381
Manchester Review   4497
Manchester School of Economic & Social Studies   767
Manchester Sketch   4498
Mancunian Indian   702
Mandate Chips   307
Manifold   1569
Manufacturers' Agent   883
Manufacturing Chemist   3323
Manufacturing Chemist & Aerosol News   3323
Manufacturing Clothier   4704
Manufacturing Optician   2336
Manufacturing Optician International   2336
Manufacturing Optics International   2336
Maps   4361
Marconi Communication Systems   2497
Marconi Instrumentation   3631
Marconi Mariner   2498
Marconi Review   2478
Marconi Telecommunication News   2497
Marconigraph   2507
Marine and Air Catering   3029
Marine Behaviour and Physiology   2109
Marine Engineering   2670, 4681-4682
Marine Engineering & Naval Architect   2762
Marine Engineering and Shipbuilding Abstracts   2754
Marine Engineers Review   2755
Marine Observer   1843
Marine Product Guide   2756

Mariner   2498
Mariner's Mirror   1012
Maritime History   1399
Market Place   1308
Market Report   2986
Market Research   3293-3308
Market Research/Germany/Italy/Benelux   3299
Market Research/Great Britain   3300
Market Research Abstracts   3298
Market Review   2987
Market Survey   2949
Marketing   3253-3268
   See also Retail Marketing
Marketing   3261
Marketing & Distribution Abstracts   3262
Marketing in Europe   3263
Marley News   3777
Marlovian Chronicle   4026
Marriage Guidance   2151
Marriage Guidance   2151
Married Women's Association Bulletin   1079
Masonic Mirror   1067
Masonic Record   1067
Mass Production   3218
Mass Spectrometry   1660
Mass Spectrometry Bulletin   1661
Master Baker   3417
Master Builders' Journal   3766
Master Painter   3806
Master Painter & Decorator   3806
Master Photographer   3933
Match Boxes   3344
Materials Handling   2560-2573
Materials Handling and Management   2569
Materials Handling News   2570
Materials Reclamation Weekly   2689
Materials Research Bulletin   1688
Material and Child Care   1049
Maternity Services   1049-1050
Mathematical Gazette   1570
Mathematical Pie   1571
Mathematical Spectrum   1572
Mathematics   1563-1580
   Teaching   1208-1209
Mathematics in School   1573
Mathematics Teaching   1209
Matrix and Tensor Quarterly   2382
Mayfair   211
Measurement and Control   3632
Measurement and Instrument Review   2424
Meat   2989-2993
Meat   2989
Meat   2990
Meat and Dairy Produce Bulletin   2991
Meat Industry   2990
Meat Marketing   2990
Meat Trader   2992
Meat Trades Journal   2993
Meccanica   1633
Mechanical Engineering   2405-2415, 4673
Mechanical Engineering News   4673
Mechanical Handling   2571
Mechanical Sciences Abstracts   2414
Mechanical Sciences Research Communications   4672
Mechanics   1628-1634
   See also Fluid Mechanics
Mechanised Accounting and Computer Management   3604
Medical and Biological Illustration   2070
Medical Bookman and Historian   2233

397

INDEX

Medical Electronics and Communications Abstracts 2479
Medical Equipment 2071
Medical Herbalist 2203
Medical History 2072
Medical Laboratory Technology 2252
Medical News 2073
Medical News-Tribune 2073
Medical Officer 1045
Medical Record 1036
Medical Sciences 2047-2102, 4663
Medical Secretary 952
Medical Section of the Library Association Bulletin 56
Medical Technician 2074
Medical Tribune 2073
Medical Welfare Services 1036
Medical Women's Federation Newsletter 2064
Medical World 2076
Medicine Illustrated 2233
Medicine Science and the Law 911
Medico-Chirurgical Transactions 2085
Medico-Legal Journal 922
Medieval Archaeology 4385
Medium 4226
Medium Aeuum 1464, 4328
Medway 1341
Members Circular 3101
Memo 3081
Memo Key 3084
Memoirs and Proceedings: Manchester Literary and Philosophical Society 1508
Memoirs of the Geological Society 1803
Mensa Journal 1154
Mental Disorders 2309-2322, 4669
  Health 2150
Mental Health 2320
Mental Health Magazine 2321
Mercantile Guardian 1309
Merchant Navy Journal 1413
Mercian Geologist 1804
Mercury 212
Meridian News 3721
Merlin 4227
Merseyside Business News 1342
Merseyside Industrial and Commercial News 1342
Metabolism 2124-2125
Metal Bulletin 3484
Metal Construction 2537
Metal Finishing 2541-2545
  Working 3523-3524
Metal Finishing Abstracts 2543
Metal Finishing Journal 2544
Metal Finishing Plant and Processes 2545
Metal Forming 3523
Metal Physics 1620
Metallurgia 3485
Metallurgical Abstracts 3483
Metallurgical Journal 3486
Metallurgy 3479-3493
Metals Abstracts 3487
Metals and Materials 3488
Metalworking Production 3489
Metalworking Production International 3490
Metaphilosophy 366
Meteorological Magazine 1844
Meteorology 1840-1847
Methodist Church Music Society Bulletin 3981
Methodist Churches 549-554
Metric Information Service Bulletin 1439
Metrication 1437-1440

Metrication News 1440
Metrology 1436
Metron 3633
Microbiology 1894-1904
Microbiology Abstracts 1900/2
Microbios 1903
Microdoc 3944
Microelectronics and Reliability 2480
Microinfo 3945
Microscope 1939
Microscope and Crystal Front 1939
Microscopy 1670-1671, 1936-1940
Midbank Chronicle 213
Middle East, History 4552-4555
Middle East Economic Digest 1356
Middle East International 4553
Middle Eastern Studies 4554
Middle Way 561
Midland Bank Review 1310
Midland History 4329
Midland Industrialist 3219
Midland Venture 213
Midlands Electricity News 207
Midlands Industry & Commerce 1343
Midwife and Health Visitor 2257
Midwives Chronicle 2343
Migraine 2307-2308
Migraine News 2308
Military Modelling Magazine 3740
Milk 2940
Milk Industry 2970-2983
Milk Industry 2978
Milk News 2979
Milk Producer 2980
Milkmade 2982
Millnotes 4386
Millinery 3722
Millinery and Boutique 3722
Milling 3419-3422
Milling 3422
Milling Flour & Feed 3422
Mind 367
Mind 2321
Mine and Quarry 2590
Mine and Quarry Engineering 2590
Mineral Water Trade Journal 3390
Mineralogical Abstracts 1788
Mineralogical Magazine 1788, 1789
Mineralogy 1787-1789
Miniature Auto 3742
Miniature Warfare and Model Soldiers 3741
Mining 2585-2598
Mining Engineer 2592
Mining and Minerals Engineering 2590
Mining Journal 2593
Mining Magazine 2594
Mining Research and Development Review 2595
Mining Technology 2596
Ministry of Labour Gazette 778
Mintel 3264
Minus One 214
Mirabelle 215
Mission 470
Missionary Herald 539
Missionary Messenger 470
Missions 465-473
Mobile Home 3895
Mode Magazine 3707
Model Aircraft 3738
Model Cars 3742
Model Engineer 3743
Model Maker and Model Boats 3744
Model Railway Constructor 2645
Model Shipwright 3745
Modelmaking 3738-3748

Modern Asian Studies 4545
Modern Caravan 3896
Modern Churchman 488
Modern English 1479
Modern English Teacher 1198
Modern Free Churchman 4612
Modern Geology 1805
Modern Geriatrics 2251
Modern Grassland Farming 2838
Modern Irish Printer 3102
Modern Language Review 1465, 4192
Modern Language Teaching 1193
Modern Languages 1193
Modern Law Review 912
Modern Living 216
Modern Medicine 2077
Modern Photographer 3934
Modern Plastering 3778
Modern Purchasing 2549
Modern Railways 2646
Modern Tramway 1425
Mole Express 217
Mole Express 4598
Molecular Chemistry 1785
Molecular Crystals and Liquid Crystals 1696
Molecular Physics 1696-1697
Molecular Physics 1697
Molluscs 1986-1988
Monarchist 928
Monarchist Guardian 928
Monarchy 928
Monasticism 481
Monatala Letro 1469
Monday Scot 218
Money 823
Money Management 809
Money Matters 813
Money which? 3301
Moneymaker 814
Moneysavers 4623
Monogram 4013
Monotype Bulletin 3103
Monotype Recorder 3104
Month 505
Month in Yorkshire 3834
Monthly Bulletin 3676
Monthly Bulletin of Construction Statistics 4627
Monthly Bulletin: Commonwealth Industries Association 1351
Monthly Digest of Statistics 629
Monthly Index of Medical Specialities 2078
Monthly Letter 1469
Monthly Letter: EMG 4703
Monthly Notes 1398
Monthly Notices of the Royal Astronomical Society 1589
Monthly Record 410
Monthly Review of Dental Surgery 2278
Monthly Review of the Institute of Weights and Measures Administration 1436
Monthly Soccer 4066
Monthly Statement of Balances of London Clearing Banks 815
Monthly Statistical Bulletin 3513
Moodies Information Services 1311
Moodies Japanese Review 4646
Moorgate and Wall Street 816
Moral Rearmament 461
Morgan's Magazine 219
Morgan's World 219
Mosses 1968
Mother 3068
Mother & Baby 3069
Mother and Child 3070
Mother Earth 2854

INDEX

Motor 2733
Motor Boat and Yachting 4137
Motor Business 2734
Motor Commerce 2735
Motor Cycle 4118
Motor Cycle and Cycle Trader 2749
Motor Cycle Mechanics 4119
Motor Cycle News 4120
Motorcycle Rider 4121
Motorcycle Scooter and 3-wheeler Mechanics 4119
Motorcycle Sport 4122
Motor Cycles 2749-2750
    Cycling 4117-4123
    Racing 4109-4116
Motor Cyclist Illustrated 4123
Motor Industry 2735
Motor Management 2736
Motor Market News 2737
Motor Service 2735
Motor Ship 2757
Motor Sport 4115
Motor Trade Equipment Monitor 2741
Motor Trade Executive 2738
Motoring Life 2739
Motoring Weekly Advertiser 2714
Motoring Which? 3302
Motorists Guide to New and Used Car Prices 2740
Mountain 4098
Mountain Craft 4098
Mountain Life 4099
Mountaineering 4095-4100
Mountaineering 4099
Movement 4599
Movie Maker 3950
Muck Shifter 2561
Multihull International 2758
Multinational Business 1312
Multinational Business 4688
Multiracial School 1199
Municipal and Public Services Journal 988
Municipal Engineering 989
Municipal Engineering & Sanitary Record 989
Municipal Journal 988
Municipal Officer 994
Municipal Review 990
Muscular Dystrophy 2298
Muscular Distrophy Journal 2298
Muse Magazine 4228
Museums 334-348
Museums Association Monthly Bulletin 341
Museums Calendar 342
Museums Journal 343
Mushrooms 2914
Music 3951-3972
    Teaching 1219-1220
Music and Letters 3959
Music and Musicians 3960
Music & Radio Retailer 3991
Music Box 3649
Music Business Weekly 3961
Music in Education 1219
Music in Schools 1219
Music Industry 3962
Music Student 1220
Music Teacher 1220
Music Tracks Review 3991
Music Week 3650
Musical Express 3653
Musical Opinion 3963
Musical Times 3964
Muslim Herald 560
Mycology 1957-1965
Mysl Polska 220

NA Journal 2750
NAAS Quarterly Review 2811
NACRO Information Bulletin 1024
Nalgo Action News 4621
NANTIS News 3079
NATE Bulletin 1196
NC News 222
NCC Members Newsletter 3897
NCC News 3897
NCCL Bulletin 932
NCET News 1155
NCR Post 223
NDT Info 2395
NERC News Journal 1931
NFCU Journal 1025
NFU Record 2839
NIIP Bulletin 3226
NLL Announcements Bulletin 4586
NLL Review 4587
NODA Bulletin 3977
NOP Bulletin 619
NPKS Bulletin 2864
NR Technology 3576
NU Newsletter 225
NU Norwich Newsletter 225
Naafi News 221
Names 1475-1476
Narrow Gauge 2647
Narrow Gauge News 2648
Narrow Gauge Telegraph 2649
Nasa Rec 226
Nash's Pall Mall 3019
National Association of Poultry Packers Ltd. Market Price Report 2957
National Association of Poultry Packers Ltd. Weekly Industry 2958
National Association Review 3413
National Begonia Society Bulletin 2924
National Builder 3767
National Cactus and Succulent Society Journal 2925
National Chamber of Trade Journal 1344
National Childbirth Trust Newsletter 1050
National Electronics Review 4679
National Guardian 3371
National Hamster Council Journal 2968
National Institute Economic Review 768
National Library of Wales Journal 38
National Master painter 3806
National Newsagent 3135
National Newsletter of the British Association of Colliery Management 2597
National Ports Council Bulletin 1400
National Rifle Association Journal 4180
National Trust News 4499
National Trust Newsletter 4499
National Westminster 1313
National Westminster Bank Quarterly Review 1314
NATNEWS 2258
Natural Gas and LPG 3364
Natural History 1523-1562
Natural History Transactions of Northumberland and Durham 1559
Nature 1509
Nature in Cambridgeshire 1540
Nature in Wales 1541
Nautical Magazine 1401
Naval Architect 2759

Naval Engineering 2604-2605
    See also Shipbuilding
Naval Record 2604
Naval Review 1013
Navigation 1610
Navvies 4647
Navy 1011-1014
Navy International 1014
Navy: The Journal of the Navy League 1014
Neddy in print 769
Needle 4637
Needlecraft Practical Journal 3922
Needlewoman and Needlecraft 3922
Needlework 3919-3923
Neptune 4155
Nerve Cell Biology 2138
Nerves 2138
Nestle Group News 227
Net 523
Netball 4060-4061
Netball 4061
Nettlefolds News 155
Neurology 2299-2304
Neuropharmacology 2214
Neuropharmacology 2214
Neurophysiology 2110
Neuropsychologia 2304
Neutron Activation Analysis Abstracts 1694
New Advance 228
New Africa 4567
New Beacon 1055
New Blackfriars 482
New Books 197
New Building 3768
New Cassettes 3651
New Civil Engineer 2621
New Civil Engineer 4680
New Community 703
New Consensus and Review 3652
New Contact 489
New Dawn 3082
New Departures 4229
New Diffusionist 1444-4387
New Direction 229
New Domestic Appliances 3355
New Earnings Survey 782
New Edinburgh Review 230
New Electronics 2481
New Epoch 231
New Era 1156
New Geographical Literature and Maps 4358
New Humanist 406
New Internationalist 4617
New Law Journal 913
New Left Review 735
New Library World 55
New Musical Express 3653
New Outlook 725
New Phytologist 1952
New Poetry 4230
New Quarterly Journal 2486
New Rambler 4281
New Records 3654
New Schoolmaster 1229
New Scientist and Science Journal 1510
New Secretary 4633
New Shetlander 4447
New Sixth 1157
New Society 588
New Stationer 3136
New Statesman 676
New Technology 1319
New Technology 2032
New Testament Studies 434
New Towns Bulletin 3848

INDEX

New Trade Names in the Rubber and Plastics Industries 3577
New Vision 574
New Window 232
New World News 461
New Zealand, History 4583
New Zealand News 4583
New World Antiquity 4575
News and Book Trade Review and Stationers Gazette 3143
News and Views 233
News and Views 1080
News and Views 1158
News Bulletin 2981
News Letter 2383
News Reel 3547
News Review 1034
News Sheet 2896
News Sheet 3309
Newsday 3779
Newsletter from Scotland 677
Newsletter of Cardiff and District Consumer Group 3303
Newsletter of the British Arachnological Society 1991
Newsletter: Cambridgeshire & Isle of Ely Naturalists Trust 1542
Newsletter of the Cave Research Group of Great Britain 1830
Newsletter: Confederate Historical Society 4576
Newsletter: Economic Development Committee for Electrical Engineering 2456
Newsletter: Irish league of Credit Unions 4626
Newsletter: Leicestershire & Rutland Trust for Nature Conservation 1543
Newsletter of the Library History Group 53
Newsletter of the Luso-Brazilian Section Association of British Hispanists 4579
Newsletter: Mental Health Association of Ireland 4669
Newsletter of the National Trolleybus Association 1428
Newsletter of the Perivale Bird Sanctuary 2019
Newsletter of the Scottish Society for Industrial Archaeology 4388
Newsletter of the Surrey Naturalists' Trust 1544
Newsletter of the Women's Group on Public Welfare and the Standing Conferences of Womens' Organisations 1447
Newspapers 349-354
Newspeace 454
News sheet, Electric Transport Development Society 2463
Nickel 3508
Nielsen Researcher 3265
Nigerian Law Journal 914
19 234
Nineteenth Century 306
Nitrogen 3343
Nitrogen 3343
Noise and Vibration Bulletin 1648
Non-Destructive Testing 2394
Non-ferrous Metals 3507
Non-Ionizing Radiation 1680
Norbertine 492
Nor-Easter 235
Norfolk Archaeology 4414
Norfolk Fair 4500
Norfolk Sailor 4475
Norgrass 2881
North Cheshire Family Historian 4368

North Magazine 4501
North Midland Bibliography 13
North 7 4448
North Staffordshire Journal of Field Studies 1545
North West Lancashire Chamber of Commerce Journal 1332
North Western Newsletter 57
Northampton and County Independent 4502
Northamptonshire & Bedfordshire Life 4503
Northamptonshire Archaeology 4415
Northamptonshire Past and Present 4504
Northern Architect 3877
Northern Club Trade News 1071
Northern Counties Magazine 4446
Northern Gardner 2911
Northern House Pamphlet Poets 4231
Northern Industry 3220
Northern Ireland Economic Report 770
Northern Ireland Education Statistics 1159
Northern Ireland Libraries 25
Northern Ireland Libraries 58
Northern Light 4705
Northern Notes 4416
Northern Perspective 3877
Northern Radical 726
Northern Scotland 4330
Northumbrian 4505
NORWEB News 224
Norwich Union Group Magazine 236
Notebooks of Pierre Menard 4232
Notes and Queries 1480
Notes and Records of the Royal Society 1511
Notes on Water Pollution 2677
Nottingham City News and Calendar 991
Nottingham Civic News 991
Nottingham French Studies 4298
Nottingham Medieval Studies 4331
Nottingham Topic 4506
Nottinghamshire Farmers' Journal 2839
Nova 237
Novena 506
Now 553
Nu-Swift Fire Fighting News 2188
Nuclear Energy 2416-2418
  Physics 1690-1695
Nuclear Energy 2417
Nuclear Engineering International 2418
Nuclear Magnetic Resonance 1662
Nuclear Magnetic Resonance Spectrometry Abstracts 1663
Nuclear Power 2418
Nucleic Acids Abstracts 1875
Nudism 2219
Numismatics 3902-3908
Nursery Journal 1264
Nursery World 3071
Nurseryman and Garden Centre 2860
Nurseryman and Seedsman 2860
Nurseryman, Seedsman & Glasshouse Grower 2860
Nursing 2253-2261
Nursing Bibliography 2259
Nursing Mirror 2260
Nursing Notes 2343
Nutrition 2117-2123
Nutrition 2119
Nutrition and Food Science 2121
Nutrition Abstracts and Reviews 2120

O Glaso Romano 4651
O & M Bulletin 3242
OMR-Organic Magnetic Resonance 1773
OSTI Newsletter 60
Oasis 4193
Obituary Notices of Fellows of the Royal Society 1501
Observatory 1590
Obstetrics 2343
Occasional Bulletin 857
Occupational Health 2146
Occupational Psychology 3227
Ocean Engineering 1836
Oceanography 1835-1838
O'Connel's Coal and Iron 3356
OFF-Licence Journal 3372
OFF Licence News 3373
Office Equipment 3085-3089
  Management 3081-3084
Office Magazine 3216
Office Management 3038
Office Management Association Bulletin 3083
Office Methods and Machines 3216
Office Skills 3084
Office Training 3081
Official Architecture and Planning 3761
Official Circular of the County Councils Association 983
Official Gazette 983
Official Journal (Patents) 2046
Offsets 4686
Offshore Services 4682
Oil and Colourmans' Journal 3468
Oil and Gas Firing 3797
Oil and Petrochemical Equipment News 3431
Oil Firing 3797
Old Catholic Church Herald 507
Old Cornwall 4417
Old Time Music 3965
Omega 4694
Omma 4507
On-Call 2079
On Course 1160
On The Road 3268
One 4600
One and All 1276
Onward 106
Onwards 4653
Open Access 59
Openings 4233
Opera 3975-3979
Opera 3978
Opera & Mundi-Europe 3078
Operational Research Quarterly 1586
Operations Research 1585-1586
Ophthalmic Literature 2337
Ophthalmic Optician 2338
Ophthalmology 2330-2341
Opportunities 992
Opportunity 238
Optica Acta 1650
Optical World 1651
Optics 1649-1653
Optics Technology 2339
Opto-Electronics 1652
Oral History 80
Orbis 4234
Ore 239
Ore 1454
Organ 3992-3995
Organ 3993
Organ Club Journal 3994
Organic Chemistry 1769-1777
Organic Compounds of Sulphur, Selenium, and Tellurium (Specialist Periodical Reports) 3339

Organic Mass Spectrometry 1664
Organics News 240
Organists Review 3995
Organometallic Chemistry 1774
Organophosphorus Chemistry (Specialist Periodical Reports) 3341
Oriental Art 3835
Orienteer 4361
Orpheus 241
Orthopaedics 2328
Oryx 1975
Orzel Bialy 678
Ostrich 4235
Our Dogs 2966
Our Zoo News 1973
Outdoors 1252
Outlook 1932
Outlook on Agriculture 2812
Outpost 61
Outposts 4236
Overseas Challenge 1230
Overseas Development 679
Overseas Geology and Mineral Resources 1806
Overseas Trade Accounts of the United Kingdom 1357
Overseas Trade Statistics of the United Kingdom 1357
Owen News 266
Oxford Agrarian Studies 2813
Oxford Consumer 3304
Oxford Economic Papers 771
Oxford Gazette 198
Oxford German Studies 4295
Oxford Guardian 723
Oxford Magazine 242
Oxford University Forest Society Journal 2892
Oyez Notes 915
Oz 243

PAC Bulletin 964
PERA Bulletin 3240
PIRA Marketing Abstracts 2550
PIRA News 3105
PIRA Packaging Journal 2551
PLA Monthly 1404
PLA Quarterly 62
PM Newsletter 244
PNEU 1161
PRT-Polymer Age 3578
PSAB News Bulletin 1243
PSI. Popular and Amateur Science Index 1512
PTS Journal 3169
Pacemaker 471
Pacific Sociological Review 607
Packaging 2546-2558
Packaging 2552
Packaging Abstracts 2553
Packaging News 2554
Packaging Technology 2555
Packaging Week 2556
Paediatrics 2249
Page 3622
Paint 3464-3472
Paint Journal 3470
Paint Manufacture 3466
Paint, Oil and Colour Journal 3468
Paint Technology 3467
Painting & Decorating 3804-3809
Painting & Decorating 3807
Painting & Decorating Journal 3807
Palaeontology 1850-1851
Palaeontology 1850
Palestine Exploration Quarterly 4555

Paper 3537
Paper and Board Abstracts 3538
Paper and Packaging Bulletin 3539
Paper Box and Bag Maker 2547
Paper Bulletin 3539
Paper Facts and Figures 3540
Paper Maker 3537
Paper Technology 3536-3542
Paper Technology 3541
Paper Training News 3542
Paperbacks in Print 3137
Paperboard Packaging International 2557
Parachuting 4156
Paraplegia 2305
Paraplegia 2305
Parasitology 1894-1904
Parasitology 1904
Parent-Teacher 1231
Parent-Teacher National Bulletin 1231
Parents Review 1161
Parish Council's Review 993
Parker's Car Price Guide 4683
Parkers Property Price Guide 4628
Parks and Recreation 3860
Parks, Golf Courses and Sports Grounds 3861
Parliament and Social Work 1026
Parliamentarian 713
Parliamentary Affairs 714
Parliaments 711-719, 4619
Parthenon 3870
Particle Accelerators 1625
Particle Dynamics 1635-1636
Particle Science and Technology Information Service Current Titles Bulletin 1636
Particulate Information 1636
Passenger Transport 1420-1428
Passenger Transport 1422
Past and Present 4332
Patent Law Review 916
Patents 2041-2046
Pathology 2231-2242
Patriot 4449
Pattern Making 2528-2529
Pattern Recognition 1621
Patterns of Prejudice 575
Pedestrian 2173
Pelargonium News 2926
Pelican 245
Pelican Record 246
Pembrokeshire Historian 4333
Pen & Ink 246
Penguin News 3138
Penguins in Print 3139
Pennant 247
Pensioner's Voice 1056
Penthouse 248
Perception 398
Perception 398
Perfumes 3473-3476
Periodicals News 22
Periscope 3291
Perkin-Elmer Analytical News (PELAN) 1754
Perkin-Elmer Electron Microscopy News 1940
Perkin-Elmer Instrument News 3634
Perkin-Elmer NMR Quarterly 1665
Permanent Light 858
Personnel & Training Abstracts 3233
Personnel & Training Management 3234

Personnel Management 3232-3237
Personnel Management 3234
Personnel Management & Methods 3234
Personnel Review 3235
Perspective East Yorkshire 3884
Pest Control 2866-2869
Pest Technology 2866
Pesticide Science 2867
Pet Product Marketing and Garden Supplies 2931
Pet Trade Journal and Garden Supplies 2931
Pet Fish Monthly 3014
Petroleum Chemistry USSR 3432
Petroleum Review 3433
Petroleum Technology 3427-3434
Petroleum Times 3434
Petrology 1848-1849
Petticoat 249
Phalanx 4194
Pharmaceutical Journal 2208
Pharmacy 2191-2213
Pharmacy Management 2209
Pharos 2167
Phenomenology 405
Philatelic Bulletin 3165
Philatelic Exporter 3166
Philatelic Fanfare 3172
Philatelic Magazine 3167
Philatelic Trader 3168
Philately 3159-3178
Philately 3170
Phillumatch 3344
Philology 1458-1466, 4653
Philosophical Books 368
Philosophical Magazine 1622
Philosophical Quarterly 370
Philosophical Transactions of the Royal Society 1574, 1876
Philosophy 359-374
Philosophy 371
Philosophy Forum 369
Philosophy of the Social Sciences 589
Phonetics 1477, 4654
Phorpres News 3776
Phosphorus 1765, 3341-3342
Phosphorus 1765
Phosphorus and Potassium 3342
Photochemistry 1732-1733
Photochemistry 1732
Photochemistry and Photobiology 1733
Photogrammetric Record 1609
Photogrammetry 1609
Photo Finisher 3935
Photofinisher 3938
Photographic Abstracts 3936
Photographic Journal 3932
Photographic Journal 3937
Photographic Processor 3938
Photography 3926-3942
Photography 3939
Photography Index for Amateurs 3940
Photoplay 4014
Photoscene 3941
Phycology 1956
Physical Chemistry 1722-1726
Physical Education 1249-1252
Physical Education 1249
Physical Structures 1687-1689
Physics 1611-1627
    Teaching 1210
    See also Biophysics, Infra-red Physics, Nuclear Physics, Solid-state Physics
Physics Abstracts 1623

INDEX

Physics and Chemistry of Glasses 3438C
Physics and Chemistry of Liquids 1637
Physics Bulletin 1624
Physics Education 1210
Physics in Medicine and Biology 2242
Physics of Metals and Metallography 3491
Physiological Plant Pathology 2868
Physiology 2106-2113
Physiology and Behaviour 2111
Physiotherapy 2215-2218
Physiotherapy 2218
Phytochemistry 1952-1953
Phytochemistry 1953
Piano 3991
Piano World & Music Trades International 3991
Piano World and Music Trades Review 3991
Pianomaker 3991
Pictorial Education 1232
Pictorial Education Quarterly 1233
Pig Breeders Gazette 2954
Pigeons 2961
Pigeons and Bantams 2961
Pigeons and Pigeon World 2961
Pigs 2952-2954
Pilot 4157
Pilot and Light Aeroplane 4157
Pipe Band 4001
Pipeline Industries Guild Bulletin 3155
Pipelines 3155-3156
Pipes (Musical Instruments) 4001
Pipes 3155-3156
Pipes and Pipelines International 3156
Piping Drumming & Highland Dancing 4001
Pitman Shorthand News 3081
Planet 680
Planet 4195
Planetary and Space Science 1599
Planets 1598-1599
Planned Savings 822
Planning Abstracts 3849
Planning & Transportation Abstracts 3849
Plant & Factory Maintenance 3251
Plant & Factory Maintenance Engineering 3251
Plant Breeding Abstracts 2861
Plant Equipment 3230-3231
Plant Hire 2562
Plant Pathology 2869
Plant Varieties and Seed Gazette 2814
Plantation Crops 2874
Plasma Physics 1695
Plasticheskie Massy 3591
Plastics 3572-3592
Plastics and Polymers 3579
Plastics & Rubber Weekly 3580
Plastics Applications 3773
Plastics RAPRA Abstracts 3585
Plastics, Rubbers, Textiles 3581
Playfair Cricket Monthly 4088
Playing Fields 3862
Plays and Players 4027
Ploughing 2862
Plumbing 3780-3785
Plumbing 3780
Plumbing and Heating Engineer 3782
Plumbing & Heating Journal 3783
Plumbing Equipment News and Heating Engineer 3781
Plumbing Trade Journal 3783

Poet 4237
Poetical Gazette 4239
Poetmeat 4203
Poetry 4199-4255
Poetry of the Circle in the Square 4238
Poetry Review 4239
Poetry Supplement 4240
Poetry Wales 4241
Point Three 490
Point to Point Communications 2487
Point to Point Telecommunications 2487
Pointe 4036
Pointer 576
Polanews 1402
Polar Record 4585
Police 973-978
Police 973
Police College Magazine 974
Police Federation Newsletter 973
Police Journal 975
Police Research Bulletin 976
Police Review 977
Police World 978
Policy 1094
Policy and Politics 681
Policy Holder Insurance Journal 1095
Policy Insurance Weekly 1094
Political Companion 715
Political Education 1188
Political Parties 720-722
Political Quarterly 682
Political Studies 683
Politics 645-695, 4614-4618
Politics and Money 817
Pollution 2686-2687
Pollution 2686
Pollution Monitor 2687
Polo 4086
Polymer 1738
Polymer News 1737
Polymer Science USSR 3582
Polymerism 1735-1738
Polymers, Paint and Colour Journal 3468
Pony 4165
Popular Arts Review 3836
Popular Camping 4102
Popular Flying 4158
Popular Hi-Fi 3655
Popular Motoring 2742
Popular Photography 3942
Population Projections 639
Population Registration 640
Population Studies 641
Poromerics Progress 3690
Port of Hull and Humber Ports Journal 1403
Port of London 1404
Port Sunlight Monthly Journal 250
Port Sunlight News 250
Port Watch 1402
Portico 3878
Portuguese and Colonial Bulletin 684
Post 3157-3158
Post Magazine 1096
Post Magazine & Insurance Monitor 1096
Post Office Electrical Engineers Journal 2488
Post Office Engineer 2490
Post Office Engineering Union Journal 2491
Post Office Magazine 3157
Post Office Telecommunications Journal 2489
Postal History International 1385

Postgraduate Medical Journal 2081
Postal Services 1385
Postcards 3543
Potato Post 2882
Potato Quarterly 2882
Potatoes 2882-2883
Pottery Gazette 3448
Poultry 2955-2960
Poultry Industry 2959
Poultry World 2960
Poverty and Human Resources Abstracts 608
Powder Metallurgy 2536
Powder Metallurgy 2536
Power Laundry and Cleaning News 3064
Power Quarterly 2457
Power Record 2457
Practical Boat Owner 4138
Practical Camper 4105
Practical Caravan 3898
Practical Education 1162
Practical Electronics 2482
Practical Home Building and Decorating 3055
Practical Householder 3055
Practical Motorist 2743
Practical Motorist and Motor Cyclist 2743
Practical Photography 3942
Practical Radio Engineer 2496
Practical Television 2518
Practical Wireless 2499
Practical Woodworking 3529
Practitioner 2082
Pram and Nursery Trader 2698
Pram Retailer 2699
Prams 2698-2699
Precast Concrete 3458
Prediction 402
Presbyterian Churches 535-541, 4612
Presbyterian Herald 539
Presbyterian Outlook 540
Prescribers Journal 2210
Preservation Technology 3423-3426
Press Association Link 251
Pressure Vessels 3332, 4674
Pressure Vessels and Piping 3332
Prevent 2083
Prevention 2084
Preventive Medicine 2162
Preview 252
Preview 344
Prices Current 3562
Prikladnaia Matematika i Mekhanika 1630
Primitive and Eastern Churches 495-496
Print 3106
Print Buyer 3107
Print Room 3108
Printer's Prophet 253
Printing 3092-3122, 4689-4690
   Processes 3123-3125
   Teaching 1215
Printing Abstracts 3109
Printing & Bookbinding Trade Review 3110
Printing Art 3111
Printing Art 4690
Printing Equipment and Materials 3112
Printing Journal 3113
Printing Technology 3117
Printing Trades Journal 3114
Printing World 3115
Prison Officers Magazine 941
Prison Service Journal 942
Prisons 941-942

Private Eye 254
Private Library 62
Private Printer and Private Press 3116
Private Wire 2458
Probability 1583-1584
Probation 943
Probation 943
Probe 2287
Problems of Society 609
Proceedings and Journal of the Electrophysiological Technologists Association 2112
Proceedings & Reports: Belfast Natural History and Philosophical Society 1546
Proceedings of the Association of Clinical Biochemists 1905
Proceedings of the Bristol Naturalists Society 1547
Proceedings of the British Society of Animal Production 2933
Proceedings of the British Speleological Association 1831
Proceedings of the Cambridge Antiquarain Society 4418
Proceedings of the Cambridge Philosophical Society 1575, 1859
Proceedings of the Central Asian Society 4540
Proceedings of the Chemical Societies 1712
Proceedings of the Classical Association 1486
Proceedings of the Cotteswold Naturalists Field Club 1548
Proceedings of the Croydon Microscopical and Natural History Club 1549
Proceedings of the Croydon Natural History and Scientific Society 1549
Proceedings of the Cumberland Geological Society 1807
Proceedings of the Dorset Natural History and Archaeological Society 1550
Proceedings of the Edinburgh Mathematical Society 1576
Proceedings of the Geological Society of Glasgow 1808
Proceedings of the Geological Society of Glasgow 4658
Proceedings of the Geologists Association 1809
Proceedings of the Huguenot Society of London 534
Proceedings of the IHVE 3794
Proceedings of the Institute of British Foundrymen 2532
Proceedings of the Institute of Psychophysical Research 391
Proceedings of the Institute of Refrigeration 2521
Proceedings of the Institution of Civil Engineers 2617
Proceedings of the Institution of Municipal Engineers 2378
Proceedings of the Institution of Electrical Engineers 2459
Proceedings of the Institution of Railway Signal Engineers 2650
Proceedings of the Lancashire and Cheshire Fauna Society 1551
Proceedings of the Linnean Society 1857, 1943, 1976
Proceedings of the London Mathematical Society 1577
Proceedings of the Malacological Society of London 1988

Proceedings of the Musical Association 3966
Proceedings of the Natural History Society of Glasgow 1531
Proceedings of the Nutrition Society 2122
Proceedings of the Philological Society 1466
Proceedings of the Physical Society 1615, 1693, 1701
Proceedings of the Prehistoric Society 4389
Proceedings of the Prehistoric Society of East Anglia 4389
Proceedings of the Royal Entomological Society 2003
Proceedings of the Royal Horticultural Society 2910
Proceedings of the Royal Institution of Great Britain 1513
Proceedings of the Royal Musical Association 3966
Proceedings of the Royal Society 1578, 1877
Proceedings of the Royal Society of Edinburgh 1514, 1878
Proceedings of the Royal Society of Medicine 2085
Proceedings of the Scottish Tartans Society 1446
Proceedings of the Society For Analytical Chemistry 1749
Proceedings of the Society for Applied Bacteriology 1897
Proceedings of the Society for Psychical Research 403
Proceedings of the Society for the Study of Fertility 1980
Proceedings of the Society for Water Treatment and Examination 2685
Proceedings of the Society of Agricultural Bacteriologists 1897
Proceedings of the Society of Antiquaries of Scotland 4392
Proceedings of the Society of Relay Engineers 2516
Proceedings of the Somerset Archaeological & Natural History Society 4422
Proceedings of the South Wales Institute of Engineers 2384
Proceedings of the Suffolk Institute of Archaeology 4419
Proceedings of the Virgil Society 4299
Proceedings of the Wesley Historical Society 554
Proceedings of the West Cornwall Field Club 4404
Proceedings of the Zoological Society of London 1974
Process Control and Automation 3629
Process Engineering 3328
Process Technology International 3329
Proclaimer 491
Produce Packaging 2548
Product Finishing 3469
Product Licensing Journal and Research Disclosure 884
Production & Export 2805
Production Engineer 3221
Production Equipment Digest 3241
Production Exchange 1345
Production Journal 352
Production Management 3238-3241
Production Technology 2583
Professional Administration 953
Professional Engineer 2385

Professional Printer 3117
Profile 255
Program 63
Programmed Learning and Educational Technology 1163
Progress 1057
Progress of Physics 1625
Progress Wales 4508
Project 2033
Project 2246
Project Scotland 2622
Property 832-847, 4627-4629
Property and Compensation Reports 917
Property and Investment Review 844
Property Journal 845
Property Market Review 835
Property News 4629
Property Survey 846
Prophecy 441
Prophetic Witness 441
Prospect 2558
Prospects 2574
Protection 2175
Province 530
Psionic Medicine 2086
Psychiatry 2309-2322, 4669
Psychic Phenomena 399-403
Psycho Analysis 404
Psychological Medicine 2322
Psychologist Magazine 392
Psychotherapy 2226-2227, 4667
Public Address 2493
Public Address Engineers Journal 2493
Public Address System 2493
 Administration 962-965
 Health 982, 2152-2160, 4664-4665
 Opinion 619
Public Administration 963
Public Administration Bulletin 964
Public Enterprise 3222
Public Expenditure 818
Public Health 2157
Public Health Inspector 982
Public Law 918
Public Lighting 2695
Public Pharmacist 2206
Public Road Transport Association Journal 1426
Public School Leaver 1244
Public Service 994
Publications of the Thoresby Society 4509
Publicity 3278
Publisher 3129
Publisher 3140
Publisher and Bookseller 3131
Publishers' Circular 3140
Puffin Post 3141
Pulse 2087
Pumps 2525-2526
Pumps 2525
Pumps and Other Fluids Machinery Abstracts 2526
Punch 256
Puppet Post 4016
Puppets 4016
Purchasing 3252
Purchasing Journal 3252
Pure and Applied Chemistry 1717
Purpose 472
Push and Pull 2651
Puzzler 3735
Pyramidology 3892
Pyrimidology Magazine 3892
Pyramids 3892

Quakers 557-559, 4613
Quality Control 3245-3246

INDEX

Quality Egg 2986
Quality Engineer 3245
Quality Matters 3246
Quantities 3770
Quantity Surveyor 3770
Quarry Managers Journal 2599
Quarrying 2599
Quarterly Bulletin [BSI] 1443
Quarterly Bulletin of the Alpine Garden Society 2927
Quarterly Bulletin of the Intelligence Unit, GLC. 995
Quarterly Economic Commentary 772
Quarterly Economic Reviews 1315
Quarterly Journal of Conchology 1987
Quarterly Journal of Engineering Geology 1810
Quarterly Journal of Experimental Physiology 2113
Quarterly Journal of Experimental Psychology 393
Quarterly Journal of Forestry 2893
Quarterly Journal of Mathematics 1579
Quarterly Journal of Mechanics and Applied Mathematics 1634
Quarterly Journal of Medicine 2088
Quarterly Journal of Microscopical Science 1890
Quarterly Journal of Pharmacy and Pharmacology 2207
Quarterly Journal of the Geological Society 1801
Quarterly Journal of the Royal Astronomical Society 1591
Quarterly Journal of the Royal Meteorological Society 1845
Quarterly Journal of the Sleep-Learning Association 2227
Quarterly List of Publications 3583
Quarterly Newsletter 2969
Quarterly Return of the Registrar General, Scotland 642
Quarterly Review 257
Quarterly Reviews 1711
Quarterly Reviews of Biophysics 1915
Quarterly Rubber Statistical News Sheet 3584
Quarterly Statement of the Palestine Exploration Fund 4555
Quarterly Weather Report 1847
Queen 169
Queen's Nurses Magazine 2253
Quest 258
Quest 546
Quest 610
Quest 1456
Question 407
Quick Freezing 3425
Quorum 4601

R & D Abstracts 2034
R & D Management 2035
RAC Motor Sport News 4116
RAEL Gazette 1164
RAPRA Abstracts 3585
RE Bulletin 1186
RIBA Annual Review of Periodical Articles 3879
RIBA Journal 3880
RIBA Library Bulletin 3881
RIC Reviews 1711
RMA Research Chronicle 3968
ROC News 509
RRE Journal 2509
RSGB Bulletin 2504
Ruma 3947

RYA Magazine 4145
Rabbit Keeper and Show Reporter 2930
Rabbits 2969
Racal Grapevine 259
Racal Review 2500
Race 704
Race Relations 696-708
Race Relations 705
Race Relations Abstracts 706
Race Relations Bulletin 707
Race Today 708
Racing & Football Outlook 4067
Radar 2509-2511
Radar and Electronics 2510
Radar Systems International 2511
Radiation 1677-1684, 4657
Radiation Botany 1949
Radiation Effects 1681
Radical Philosophy 372
Radio 2494-2508
Radio Amateur 2503
Radio and Electrical Retailing 2501
Radio and Electronic Components 2467
Radio and Electronic Engineer 2502
Radio and Electronics Constructor 2503
Radio Communication 2504
Radio Control Models and Electronics 3746
Radio Marketing 2495
Radio Perception 1822
Radio Relay Review 2515
Radiograph 2506
Radiography 2223
Radioimmunoassay 2224
Radiological Protection Bulletin 4657
Radiology 2220-2225
Radionic-Magnetic Centre Newsletter 1682
Railpower 2652
Railway Division (IME) Journal 2653
Railway Engineering 2631-2663
Railway Engineering Journal 2653
Railway Enthusiasts and Historians Guide to their Literature 2654
Railway Forum 2455
Railway Gazette 2656
Railway Invigoration Society Progress Report 2657
Railway Magazine 2658
Railway Modeller 3747
Railway Observer 2659
Railway Philately 3171
Railway Preservation Society Newsletter 2655
Railway Review 2660
Railway World 2661
Railways 1386
Railways 2661
Ram 4242
Ramblers News 4094
Rambling 4092-4094
Ramsbury Tree 260
Rangeability 2745
Ranger 1105
Rank and File 1165
Rank and File 1234
Rare Books 355-358
Rates and Rateable Values in Scotland 970
Rating 970-972
Rating and Income Tax 971
Rating and Valuation Reporter 971
Ratio 373
Rationalism 406-407
Rationalist Annual 407

Reader 524
Reader's Digest 261
Reader's News 262
Reading 4589
Reading 77
Reading Geographer 4359
Real Estate Journal 845
Realités 3837
Reality 455
Realtime 3623
Recall 1166
Reconciliation 456
Reconciliation Quarterly 456
Record 801
Record 1346
Record 2841
Record and Tape Retailer 3650
Record Bargains 3657
Record Collector 3642
Record Collector 3656
Record Collector for Good Listening 3657
Record Collectors Bulletin 3656
Record of the Save the Children Fund 1065
Recorded Sound 3658
Records and Recording 3659
Records of the Month 3660
Recruitment 1008
Recusant History 508
Red Barrel 319
Red Cross 1034-1035
Red Flag 685
Red Front 748
Red Machinery Guide 2852
Red Mole 263
Red Rag 4602
Red Rat 264
Red Rat 394
Red Vanguard 749
Redbridge Medical Journal 2089
Redemption Tidings 435
Redemptorist Record 455
Reed's Aircraft and Equipment News 2787
Reed's Marine Equipment News 2760
Referativnyy Zhurnal Kibernetika 1585
Referativnyy Zhurnal Korroziya i Zashchita ot Korrozii 2402
Reform 540
Reformation Today 547
Refractories Journal 3449
Refrigeration 2519-2523
Refrigeration and Air Conditioning 2522
Regional Catalogue of Earthquakes 1820
Regional Review 1046
Regional Studies 3850
Registered Accountant 3197
Registrar General's Annual Estimates of the Population of England and Wales of Local Authority Areas 643
Registrar General's Quarterly Return for England and Wales 630
Registrar Generals' Statistical Review for England and Wales 631
Registrar General's Weekly Return for England and Wales 632
Registry of Ships 1405
Rehabilitation 1058
Reinforced Plastics 3586
Reinsurance 1097
Relay Association Journal 2515
Relay Engineer 2516
Religion 414-427, 4606-4607

Religion 418
Religion 4606
Religion in Communist Countries 4607
Religion in Education 1185
Religious Education 1185-1186
Religious Studies 419
Remedial Education 1167
Remedial Gymnast 4090
Remedial Gymnastics and Recreational Therapy 4090
Removal Services 3179
Removals & Storage 3179
Renaissance and Modern Studies 4334
Renal Physiology 2127
Renal Transplantation and Dialysis 2128
Report by the Commission for Herring Fisheries 3010
Report of the Botanical Society and Exchange Club of the British Isles 1951
Report of the Commissioners of HM Customs and Excise 869
Report of the Commissioners of HM Inland Revenue 865
Report on Spain 4528
Report on the Administration of Home Office Services 965
Report on the Census of Production of Northern Ireland 885
Report on the Fisheries of Scotland 3010
Report on World Affairs 686
Reports & Communications of the Cambridge Antiquarian Society 4417
Reports of the Croydon Microscopical Club 1549
Reports on Progress in Physics 1626
Representation 934
Reprint Review 3142
Repro 3946
Reproduction 2129-2134
Reproduction 3118
Reprography 3944-3947
Reptiles 2007
Reptillian Review 3013
Resale Weekly 2415
Research Association of British Flour & Millers Bulletin 3420
Research Bulletin 1933
Research in Education 1168
Research in Education 1169
Research in Librarianship 64
Research in Progress in English and Historical Studies in the Universities of the British Isles 4335
Research in Reproduction 2134
Research in Special Education 1254
Research in Veterinary Science 2350
Research into Higher Education Abstracts 1289
Resources 1170
Resurgam 2168
Resurgence 4196
Retail Business 3273
Retail Confectioner 3410
Retail Fruit Trade Review 2900
Retail Jeweller 3522
Retail Newsagent 3143
Retail Newsagent, Bookseller and Stationer 3143
Resuscitation 2090
Retail Marketing 3269-3276
  Trade 1347
Retort 1718

Review 4243
Review for Addlestone, Byfleet, Chertsey, New Haw, Weybridge 4510
Review of Applied Mycology 1964
Review of Applied Entomology 2004
Review of Coal Tar Technology 3477
Review of Current Literature on the Paint and Allied Industries 3472
Review of Economic Studies 773
Review of English Literature 4282
Review of English Studies 1481
Review of International Co-operation 852
Review of Medical and Veterinary Mycology 1963
Review of Nutrition and Food Science 2121
Review of Parliament 4619
Review of Parliament and Parliamentary Digest 716
Review of Physics in Technology 1627
Review of Plant Pathology 1964
Rheumatic Diseases 2294-2297
Rheology 1703-1705
Rheology Abstracts 1705
Rheumatology and Physical Medicine 2297
Rhodes-Livingstone Institute Journal 596
Ribosomes 1913
Ricardian 4336
Rice 2879
Rice Bulletin 2879
Rickmansworth Historian 4337
Riding 4166
Riding School and Stable Management 2934
Ridings 4522
Ridleys Wine and Spirit Trade Circular 3377
Ringsport 4128
Ringing World 4002
Road Motor Vehicles 2665
Road Tar 3478
Road Traffic Reports 1414
Road Transport 1414-1419
Road Way 1415
Roads and Road Construction 2667
Rocksport 4100
Rod and Line 4173
Roman Catholic Church 497-513, 4610-4611
  Education 1187
Romano Drom 4652
Romford Record 4338
Ronin 4706
Roofing 3769
Roofing Contractor 3769
Ropeways 2664
Ros 1455
Rose Bulletin 2912
Rotary 1081
Rotary Service 1081
Rotary Wheel 1081
Round Table 687
Round the Table 859
Rowing 4140-4142
Rowing 4142
Rowntree Mackintosh News 265
Royal Aero Club Gazette 2786
Royal Association of British Dairy Farmers Journal 2975
Royal College of Music Magazine 3967
Royal Microscopical Society Proceedings 1671
Royal Naval Sailing Association Journal 4146

Royal Observatory Annals 1592
Royal Observatory Bulletins 1593
Royal Society of Health Journal 2158
Royal Stuart Papers 4339
Royalist Viewpoint 4340
RoyinForm 4340
Rubber and Plastics Age 3578
Rubber & Plastics Age 3581
Rubber and Plastics Weekly 3580
Rubber Developments 3587
Rubber Journal 3588
Rubber Journal and International Plastics 3580
Rubber RAPRA Abstracts 3585
Rubber Statistical Bulletin 3589
Rubber Trends 3590
Rubbers 3572-3592
Rubery Owen News 266
Rucksack 4094
Rugby 4071-4073
Rugby Leaguer 4071
Rugby World 4072
Rural District Review 996
Rural Life 3864
Rural Life 3038
Rural Medicine 2091
Russia Today 4531
Russian Castings Production 2534
Russian Chemical Reviews 1719
Russian Engineering Journal 2386
Russian Journal of Inorganic Chemistry 1764
Russian Journal of Physical Chemistry 1725
Russian Machine Tools 2583
Russian Metallurgy 3492
Russian Teaching 1202
Russian Ultrasonics 2396
Ryedale Historian 4420

SATIPS Newsletter 1158
SATIS 1498
SATRA Bulletin 3686
SCRATA Journal of Research 3500
SDC News 3463
SEED 1934
SERHB Magazine 267
SERHB News 267
SLA News 65
SLR Camera 3943
SMMB Bulletin 2981
SOGAT Journal 3121
SPAM (Soil-Plant-Animal-Man) 2858
SSEB News 268
SSHA Journal 847
SSRC Newsletter 590
SUC Bulletin 1601
Sad Traffic 4603
Safe Times 2176
Safer Motoring 2744
Safety 2171-2177
Safety and Rescue 2176
Safety at Sea International 795
Safety Equipment and Industrial Clothing 794
Safety in Mines Abstracts 2598
Saga Book of the Viking Society 4535
Sail 4147
Sailplane and Gliding 4159
St George's Hospital Gazette 1047
St. John Review 2190
St. Nicholas Review 448
St. Raphael Quarterly 515
St. Thomas' Hospital Gazette 1048
Salaries 790-791
Salemaker 269
Sales and Wants Advertiser 3114
Sales Engineer 3266
Sales Engineering 3266
Salmon and Trout Magazine 4174

INDEX

Salvesen News 3147
Samphire 4244
Sanitarian 982
Sanitary Record 989
Sanity 925
Satellite 471
Savings 822
Savoyard 3979
Scale Models 3748
Scan 528
Scandinavia, History 4535
Scandinavia, Literature 4296
Scandinavica 4296
Schiltrom 688
School Leaver 1245
School Librarian 66
School Music Record 1219
School Music Review 1219
School Science Review 1204
School Technology 1172
Schoolmaster 1237
Schoolmaster and Woman Teacher's Chronicle 1237
Schools Council Project Technology Bulletin 1172
Schuss 270
Sciath 2177
Science 1493-1522, 4655
Teaching 1203-1207
Science 1205
Science and General Quarterly 2436
Science and General Record 2436
Science Chelsea 2036
Science for People 1515
Science, Medicine and Man 4655
Science Policy 1516
Science Progress 1517
Science Teacher 1206
Science Teaching 1206
Science Teaching Equipment 1207
Scientific Era 1518
Scientific Horticulture 2913
Scientific Proceedings of the Cardiff Medical Society 2092
Scope 2093
Scope 3087
Scope 3365
Scotia Review 271
Scotia Review 4450
Scotland 72 997
Scotland 3080
Scotland, Archaeology 4391-4393
History 4444-4454
Scots Independent 4451
Scottish Abstract of Statistics 633
Scottish Agriculture 2815
Scottish Bankers Magazine 819
Scottish Birds 2020
Scottish Co-operator 853
Scottish Curler 4057
Scottish Dance Archives 4041
Scottish Decorators Quarterly Review 3808
Scottish Diver 4153
Scottish Economic Bulletin 774
Scottish Educational Journal 1171
Scottish Farmer 2840
Scottish Field 4452
Scottish Fisheries Bulletin 3009
Scottish Forestry 2894
Scottish Genealogist 4369
Scottish Geographical Magazine 4360
Scottish Health Statistics 2159
Scottish Historical Review 4341
Scottish Home and Country 1082
Scottish Inland Waterways Association Newsletter 4648
Scottish International Review 4283
Scottish Journal of Agriculture 2815

Scottish Journal of Political Economy 689
Scottish Journal of Theology 420
Scottish Licensed Trade News 3374
Scottish Literary News 4284
Scottish Marxist 736
Scottish Master Plumber 3785
Scottish Medical Journal 2094
Scottish Optician 2340
Scottish Pharmacist 2211
Scottish Plumber's Journal 3784
Scottish Plumbing and Heating Monthly 3785
Scottish Primary Quarterly 476
Scottish Public Services 2611
Scottish Schoolmaster 1236
Scottish Schools Science Equipment Research Centre Bulletin 1519
Scottish Sea Fisheries Statistical Tables 3010
Scottish Secondary Teachers' Association Bulletin 1268
Scottish Ski Club Journal 4130
Scottish Stamp News 3172
Scottish Studies 4453
Scottish Sunday School Teacher 477
Scottish Theatre 4028
Scottish Typographical Journal 3119
Scottish Wildlife Trust Newsletter 1552
Scottish Woodland Owners Association Newsletter 2895
Scottish Youth Review 1246
Scouter 1106
Screen 1247
Screen Education 1247
Screen 'n' Heard 3661
Screen Printing and Point of Sale News 3124
Scribe 577
Scrip 2212
Script 2505
Scripta Metallurgica 3493
Scipture Bulletin 436
Scipture in Church 510
Sea Breezes 1406
Sea Transport 1391-1413
Sea Board 2460
Seafarer 1407
Seal 272
Seals 2426
Seaman 1408
Sear 1173
Sechaba 4568
Second Aeon 4245
Secondary Education 1266-1270
Secondary Education 1290
Secretaries Journal 953
Secretary and Secretaries Chronicle 953
Security 979-981
Security and Protection 979
Security Gazette 980
Security Surveyor 981
Seddon Atkinson Magazine 2745
Sedimentation 1823
Sedimentology 1823
Seed 273
Seed 3406
Seed Potato 2883
Seismology 1817-1820
Selbourne Magazine 1553
Self Service Times and Modern Marketing 3274
Selling 3267
Selling Today 3268
Seniorscope 478
Service 457
Service Point 67
Service Station 2746

Sesame 1291
Seven Arts 274
765 Journal 345
1745 Association and Military History Society Quarterly Notes 4636
Severn & Wye Review 4342
Shadow 4197
Shakespeare Fellowship News-Letter 4286
Shakespeare Survey 4285
Shakespearean Authorship Review 4286
Shambala 4549
Shavian 4287
Shaws Price Guide 3046
She 275
Sheep 2950
Sheet Metal Industries 3524
Sheffield Consumer 3305
Sheffield Spectator 4511
Shetland Pony Stud Book Society Magazine 2936
Shield 591
Ship & Boat Builder 2761
Ship and Boat International 2761
Shipbuilding 2751-2767
See also
Naval Engineering
Shipbuilding & Marine Engineering International 2762
Shipbuilding & Shipping Record 2763
Shipbuilding International 2762
Shipping Statistics and Economics 1409
Shipping Studies 1410
Shipping World and Shipbuilder 1411
Ships' Telegraph 1413
Shirley Institute Summary of Current Literature 3557
Shirley Link 3555
Shoe and Leather News 3687
Shoe and Leather Record 3687
Shoe Manufacturer's Monthly 3689
Shoe Materials Progress 3690
Shoe Trade 3678-3690
Shoebiz 3688
Shoemaking Progress 3679
Shooting 4178-4181
Shop and Shopfitting Review 3889
Shop Equipment and Shopfitting News 3887
Shopfitting and Equipment Monitor 3888
Shop Fitting International 3889
Shop Property 1347
Shopfitting 3887-3889
Shopping and Homes Gazette 3030
Short Story 276
Shorthand 3090
Shorthand Teacher 1190
Shout 3662
Show Jumping 4164
Shropshire Newsletter 4421
Sierra Leone Language Review 1487
Sight and Sound 4015
Signal 2506
Signal 4288
Signature 277
Silent World 2139
Silver 2909
Silver Bulletin 3909
Simon Star 1027
Simulation and Games 3886
Single Tax 863
Sino British Trade 1358
Sir Thomas Beecham Society Newsletter 3969
Six-Monthly Statistical Bulletin 2988
Six Towns Magazine 4512
Six Towns Magazine 4513

INDEX

Skating *4130-4133*
Skating World 4131
Skefco News 278
Ski Notes & Queries 4132
Ski Survey 4132
Skier 4133
Skiing 4130-4133
Skill 2387
Skins 2996
Sky Blue 4068
Skytrader and Air Marketing International 1435
Slade Trade Gazette 3769
Slavonic and East European Review 4524
Slavonic Review 4524
Sleeping Sickness Bureau Bulletin 2161
Slimming 2123
Slimming and Family Nutrition 2123
Small Arms in Profile 2602
Small Boat 4139
Small Car 2712
Small Offset Printing 3125
Small Offset Supplies 3108
Small Pets 2930
Small Printer 3120
Small Trader & Wholesaler 3275
Smith Express 279
Smiths' Trade Circular 3144
Smiths' Trade News 3144
Soap, Perfumery and Cosmetics 3476
Soccer Star 4069
Social Action 1027
Social Relations 620-622
  Sciences 580-593
  Work 1015-1033, 4637
Social Science and Medicine 592
Social Service 1028
Social Service Quarterly 1028
Social Studies 612
Social Work 1029
Social Work Today 1030
Socialism 727-746, 4620
Socialist Affairs 737
Socialist Christian 652
Socialist Commentary 738
Socialist International Information 737
Socialist Standard 739
Socialist Vanguard 738
Socialist Woman 740
Socialist Worker 741
Society for the Preservation of the Fauna of the Empire Journal 1975
Society for the Study of Labour History Bulletin 613
Society of Engineers Journal 2388
Society of Friends 557-559, 4613
Socio-Economic Planning Sciences 887
Sociological Analysis 614
Sociological Review 615
Sociology 596-618
Sociology 616
Sociology of Education Abstracts 1174
Soft Drinks 3390
Soft Drinks Trade Journal 3390
Softwax Practice and Experience 3624
Software World 3625
Soil Biology and Biochemistry 2856
Soil Mechanics 2629
  Science 2853-2858
Soils and Fertilizers 2857
Solanus 68
Solar Energy 1600

Solar Energy 1600
Soldier 1007
Solid Fuel 3356
Solid-Liquid Flow Abstracts 1643
Solid State Communications 1702
Solid-State Electronics 1676
Solid-State Physics 1699-1702
Solidarity 280
Somerset Archaeology and Natural History Proceedings 4422
Somerset Life 4519
Le Soudage dans le Monde 2539
Soul Music 3662
Sound 1053
Sound and Picture Tape Recording 3663
Sound and Vision Broadcasting 2517
Sound Recording and Reproduction 3635-3664, 4703
Sounding Brass 3985
Soundings 3970
Sources of Finance 820
South African Studies 4569
South Asian Review 4546
South Lincolnshire Farmer 2841
South Place Magazine 410
Southampton and Solent Ports Journal 1412
Southend-on-Sea Consumer Group News 3307
Southern Arts 3838
Southern Farmer 2842
Soviet Jewish Affairs 578
Soviet Plastics 3591
Soviet Rubber Technology 3592
Soviet Science Review 1520
Soviet Studies 4533
Spaceflight 1598-1599
Spaceflight 2789-2794
Spaceflight 2792
Spacelink 2793
Spacewise 2794
Spain, History 4526-4528
Spain Today 4528
Spanish Language 1483
Spare Rib 281
Speak-out 933
Speaking of Women 1448
Spearhead 690
Spearhead 4618
Special Education 1255
Special Papers in Palaeontology 1851
Special Schools Journal 1255
Special Steels Review 3501
Spectator 282
Spectrochimica Acta 1666
Spectroscopic Properties of Inorganic and Organometallic Compounds 1667
Spectroscopy 1655-1669
Spectrum 1175
Speculative Builder 3768
Speech 2137
Speech 2137
Speech and Drama 1221
Speech Pathology and Therapy 2137
Speed 4115
Speleological Abstracts 1832
Speleology 1826-1834
Spiders 1990-1991
Spirax Topics 3798
Spiritualist News 376
Spokesman 742
Sport and Country 2843
Sport Parachutist 4156
Sports and Recreational Equipment 3692
Sports Dealer 3693
Sports Equipment 3691-3693

Sports Equipment News 3692
Sports Trader 3693
Sports Turf Bulletin 3863
Sportsworld 4055
Spotlight 69
Spotlight 283
Spotlight Casting Directory 4029
Spotlight Contacts 4030
Spread Eagle 284
Spring Journal 2420
Springs 2420
Squash 4074-4075
Squash Player 4075
Sruth 285
Stable Management 2934
Stable Management 2934
Staffordshire Magazine 4513
Stage 4031
Stage and Television Today 4031
Stained Glass 3439
Staines Local History Society Journal 4343
Stainless Steel 3502
Stamp Collecting 3173
Stamp Lover 3174
Stamp Magazine 3175
Stamp Monthly 3176
Stamp News 3172
Stamp Weekly 3177
Stamps of Ireland 3178
Stand 4246
Standard of Truth 458
Standard-Triumph News 2747
Standardization 1442-1443
Stanki i Instrument 2413
Starfish 1554
State Service 969
State Technology 969
Stationery Trade Review 3145
Statistical Abstract 4167
Statistical Record 634
Statistical Review 3285
Statistical Supplement 2865
Statistician 635
Statistics 623-635
Staybrite Chroncile 286
Steam and Heating Engineer 3799
Steam Engineer 3799
Steam Engineering 2427-2428
Steam Man 2428
Steel 3494-3506
Steel and Coal 2586
Steel and Coal 3505
Steel Castings Abstracts 3503
Steel in the USSR 3504
Steel Times 3505
Steel User News 3506
Steering Wheel 1416
Stereo Headphones 4247
Steroids 1782
Stitchcraft 3923
Stochastics 1744
Stock Breeding 2932-2933
Stock Exchange Journal 826
Stock Exchange Weekly Official Intelligence 827
Stock Market Research Reviews 4624
Stone Industries 3901
Stonemasonry 3901
Storage Handling Distribution 2572
Strad 3999
Strain 2397
Strata 3459
Street Farmer 287
Street Research 4630
Streetword 4248
Steros 4588
String Instruments 3997-3999
Structural Engineer 2623

407

INDEX

Structural Materials 2627-2628
Stud & Stable 4168
Studia Celtica 1491
Studies 374
Studies in Adult Education 1277
Studies in Comparative Religion 421
Studies in Conservation 346
Studies in Conservation 1935
Studies in Design Education and Craft 1176
Studies in Education 1177
Studies in Education and Craft 1176
Studies in Speleology 1833
Studies on Fertility 1980
Studio 3839
Studio International 3839
Studio Sound 3664
Stylops 2003
Sub-Postmaster 3158
Substrata 3460
Sugar 3407-3408
Sugar Cane 3407
Sugar Review 3408
Sulphur 1766, 3339-3340
Sulphur 3340
Sumatra, History 4577
Sunday Observance 462
   Schools 476-478
Sunrise News 440
Supervisor 3236
Supervisory Management 3237
Supply Estimates 1316
Surface and Defect Properties of Solids 1775
Surface Coatings 3464-3472
Surface Coatings 3470
Surface Wave Abstracts 2398
Surgery 2231-2242, 2325-2327
Surgo 2095
Surrey Naturalist 1555
Survey 1606
Survey of British and Commonwealth Affairs 691
Survey of Current Affairs 691
Survey Review 1607
Surveying 1603-1608
Surveyor 2624
Surveyor-Local Government Technology 1608
Sussex Archaeological Society Newsletter 4423
Sussex Industrial History 4424
Sussex Life 4514
Suzanne 4249
Sweet & Maxwell's Student's Law Reporter 919
Sweet and Tobacco Retailing 3135
Swift 473
Swimming 4152-4155
   Baths 3890
Swimming Pool Review 3890
Swimming Times 4154
Swinton Journal 692
Symons' Meteorological Magazine 1844
Symposia of the Faraday Society 1726
Synthesis 1745
Syren and Shipping 1411
Systematics 409
Systematization 409, 4605
Systems Technology 2492

TAB-Tyres Accessories Batteries 2697
TASS Journal 2527
TR Journal 288
TRE Journal 2509
TSB Gazette 821
TSF Bulletin 422

TV Action 289
Table Tennis 4059
Table Tennis 4059
Table Tennis News 4059
Tablet 511
Tableware International 3448
Tableware Times 290
Tackle & Guns 4175
Tailor and Cutter 4704
Talanta 1750
Taliesin 4289
Talk 1059
Talyllyn News 2662
Talyllyn Telegraph 2649
Tanker & Bulk Carrier 2764
Tanker Times 2764
Tape Recording Magazine 3663
Target 3306
Tarmac World 291
Tate & Lyle News 292
Tate & Lyle Times 293
Tax Clerks Journal 867
Taxation 861-868
Taxation 866
Taxes 867
Taymag 347
Taywood News 2625
Teach-in 2096
Teacher 1237
Teacher in Commerce 1190
Teacher in Wales 1238
Teacher of the Blind 1256
Teacher of the Deaf 1257
Teacher of the Deaf 4644
Teachers Abstracts 1498
Teacher's World 1265
Teaching 1226-1238
   See also under subjects eg. Mathematics
Teaching Adults 1278
Teaching and Training 1258
Teaching English 1200
Teaching History 1225
Teaching Politics 1188
Tech Air 2788
Technical Bulletin: Radiochemical Centre 1683
Technical Education 1283
Technical Education Abstracts 1269
Technical Instructor of the Society of Licensed Aircraft Engineers & Technologists 2788
Technical Journal 1270
Technical Notes 2626
Technologist 2037
Technology 2026-2040
Technology and Society 2037
Technology Ireland 2038
Teilhard Review 423
Telecommunications 2484-2492
Telegraph 1413
Telegraphic Journal and Electrical Review 2449
Telegraphy 3091
Television 2512-2518
Television 2518
Temperance 411
Temple Bar 1098
Tempo 3971
Tennis 4076
Tennyson Research Bulletin 4290
Teploenergetika 3801
Terpenes 1781
Terpenoids and Steroids 1781
Tertiary Times 1811
Testing Materials 2391-2399
Tetrahedron 1776
Tetrahedron Letters 1777
Textile Abstracts 3557
Textile History 3548

Textile Institute and Industry 3549
Textile Manufacturer 3550
Textile Month 3551
Textile News 3552
Textile Production 3553
Textile Progress 3554
Textiles 3544-3557
Textiles 3555
Textiles of Ireland and Linen Trade Circular 3556
Texture 1689
Thames Gas 294
Thames Valley Countryside 4460
Theatre 4018-4034
Theatre Nights 4032
Theatre Notebook 4033
Theatre Quarterly 4034
Then 353
Theological and Religious Index 424
Theology 414-427
Theology 425
Theoretical Chemical Engineering Abstracts 3330
Theoretical Cybernetics Abstracts 1585
Theoria to Theory 593
Theosophical Journal 377
Theosophical News and Notes 377
Thermal Abstracts 3800
Thermal Engineering 3801
Thermal Processes 3331
Thermochemistry 1727-1728
Thin Films 1784
Thin-layer Chromatography Abstracts 1755
Third World 743
Third World 1061
This England 4515
Thorax 2274
Thorncliffe News 222
Thornfield Journal 395
Three Banks Review 1317
Three Crowns 295
Throb 296
Tibet, History 4549
Ticket & Fare Collection Society Newsletter 3150
Tickets 3150
Tim 297
Timber and Plywood 3530
Timber Grower 2896
Timber Technology 3525-3535
Timber Trades Journal 3531
Time 1441
Time & Tide 298
Time Out 299
Time Sale 3626
Times Educational Supplement 1178
Times Higher Education Supplement 1292
Times Literary Supplement 78
Timken 300
Timken Times 300
Tin 3513-3515
Tin and Its Uses 3514
Tin International 3515
Tin-Printer and Box Maker 3122
Tin Printer and Box Maker 3515
Tissue and Cell 1893
Tobacco 3394-3396
Tobacco 3394
Tobacco Intelligence 3395
Toc H Journal 490
Today's Children 1062
Today's Cinema 4004
Today's Guide 1107
Together 525
Toilers of the Deep 3011
Tomorrow 421
Too Much 301

INDEX

Tooling 2584
Top Management Abstracts 3223
Topical Dates & Facts Newsletter 4516
Topology 1582
Topology 1582
Tourism 1324
Tower Times 1318
Town and Country Planning 3842-3856, 4705
Town and Country Planning 3851
Town Planning Review 3852
Toxicological and Environmental Chemistry Reviews 2229
Toxicology 2228-2230
Toxicon 2230
Toy Trader 3736
Toys 3729-3737
Toys International 3737
Trade 1296-1323
  See also *Export Trade, Import Trade, International Trade, Retail Trade*
Trade and Industry 1319
Trade Market 2044
Trade Marks 2041-2046
Trade Marks Journal 2045
Trade Partners 1359
Trade Unions 798-801, 4621
Trader 3275
Trading Accounts and Balance Sheets 1320
Trading and Other Accounts 1321
Traffic Engineering and Control 1417
Training Officer 1179
Trains Illustrated 2646
Trains Illustrated 2663
Tramway Review 1427
Transactions and Journal of the British Ceramic Society 3450
Transactions and Journal of the Plastics Institute 3579
Transactions & Proceedings of the Botanical Society of Edinburgh 1950
Transactions of Leeds Geological Association 1800
Transactions of the Ancient Monuments Society 3882
Transactions of the Anglesey Antiquarian Society and Field Club 4441
Transactions of the Architectural and Archaeological Society of Durham and Northumberland 4425
Transactions of the Association of Industrial Medical Officers 796
Transactions of the Baptist Historical Society 542
Transactions of the Birmingham & Warwickshire Archaeological Society 4426
Transactions Birmingham Archaeological Society 4426
Transactions of the Botanical Society of Edinburgh 1950
Transactions of the Bristol & Gloucestershire Archaeological Society 4427
Transactions of the British Bryological Society 1968
Transactions of the British Mycological Society 1965
Transactions of the Bronte Society 4291
Transactions of the Cambridge Bibliographical Society 23
Transactions of the Cardiff Naturalists Society 1556

Transactions of the Cardiganshire Antiquarian Society 4440
Transactions of the Cave Research Group of Great Britain 1834
Transactions: Chigwell Local History Society 4517
Transactions of the Cumberland and Westmorland Antiquarian and Archaeological Society 4428
Transactions of the English Arboricultural Society 2893
Transactions of the Faculty of Actuaries 1099
Transactions of the Faraday Society 1723
Transactions of the Glasgow Archaeological Society 4393
Transactions of the Grotius Society 923
Transactions of the Historic Society of Lancashire & Cheshire 4344
Transactions of the Honourable Society of Cymm Rodorion 4518
Transactions of the Institute of Brewing 3389
Transactions of the Institute of Credit Management 3277
Transactions: Institute of Marine Engineers 2765
Transactions of the Institute of Metal Finishing 3471
Transactions of the Institution of Chemical Engineers 3324
Transactions of the Institution of Engineers & Shipbuilders in Scotland 2767
Transactions of the Institution of Gas Engineers 3363
Transactions of the Institution of Mining and Metallurgy 1812
Transactions of the Institution of Mining Engineers 2592
Transactions of the Laboratory Club 3389
Transactions of the Lancashire & Cheshire Antiquarian Society 4429
Transactions of the Leicestershire Archaeological & Historical Society 4430
Transactions, Lichfield and South Staffordshire Archaeological and Historical Society 4433
Transactions, Lichfield Archaeological & Historical Society 4433
Transactions of the Lincolnshire Naturalists Union 1557
Transactions of the London & Middlesex Archaeological Society 4431
Transactions of the Natural History Society of Northumberland, Durham & Newcastle-on-Tyne 1559
Transactions of the Newcomen Society 2039
Transactions of the Norfolk and Norwich Naturalists Society 1558
Transactions of the North East Coast Institution of Engineers & Shipbuilders 2766
Transactions of the North Staffordshire Field Club 1545
Transactions of the Ophthalmological Societies of the United Kingdom 2341
Transactions of the Philological Society 1466
Transactions of the Radnorshire Society 4442
Transactions of the Royal Asiatic Society of Great Britain & Ireland 4544

Transactions of the Royal Entomological Society 2005
Transactions of the Royal Geological Society of Cornwall 1813
Transactions of the Royal Historical Society 4345
Transactions of the Royal Institution of Naval Architects 2759
Transactions of the Royal Society of Edinburgh 1521
Transactions of the St. John's Hospital Dermatological Society 2291
Transactions of the Shropshire Archaeological Society 4432
Transactions of the Society of Instrument Technology 3632
Transactions of the Society of Occupational Medicine 796
Transactions of the South Staffordshire Archeological & Historical Society 4433
Transactions of the Technical Section of BPBMA 3541
Transactions of the Thoroton Society of Nottinghamshire 4434
Transactions of the Tyneside Naturalists Field Club 1559
Transactions of the Unitarian Historical Society 555
Transactions of the Woolhope Naturalists Field Club 1560
Transactions of the Worcestershire Naturalists Club 1561
Transactions of the Yorkshire Dialect Society 1468
Transatlantic Review 4292
Translation 4256
Transport 1370-1384, 3147-3149
  See also *Air Transport, Passenger Transport, Road Transport, Sea Transport*
Transport 29
Transport and Materials Handling 2573
Transport Bookman 24
Transport Engineer 1418
Transport History 1383
Transport Training 1419
Transportation News 3148
Transportation Research 3149
Travel Trade Guide, Scotland 4454
Travel World 1372
Travelling 302
Trees 2897
Treffpunkt 1201
Trends & Topics 3840
Trends in Education 1180
Tribology 2575
Tribos 2576
Tribune 744
Trichologist 2292
Trichology 2292
Triple Trader 3411
Triton 4155
Tritsch-Tratsch 3974
Triumph News 2747
Trivium 4198
Trolleybus Magazine 1428
Tropical Agriculture 2816
Tropical Animal Health and Production 2351
Tropical Diseases Bulletin 2161
Tropical Doctor 2097
Tropical Products Quarterly 2817
Tropical Science 2818
Trout & Salmon 4176
True Magazine 303
Truman Times 304
Trumpet 4000
Trumpeter 4000

409

INDEX

Tubercle 2244
Tuberculosis 2243-2244
Tuesday Paper 305
Tunnels and Tunnelling 2630
Tunnels and Tunnelling 2630
Twentieth Century 306
Twice 307
Two Nations 693
Two Wheeler Dealer 2750
Tyndale Bulletin 426
Tyndale House Bulletin 426
Tyre Distributor 2697
Tyres 2696-2697

U.D. Notebook 2982
UK Exporter's Guide to Payments Risks and Import Regulations Abroad 1322
UKCIS Macroprofiles 1684
UKCIS Macroprofiles ESR—Chemical Aspects 1720
UKCIS Macroprofiles NMR—Chemical Aspects 1721
UKCIS Macroprofiles: Gas Chromatography 1756
UKCIS Macroprofiles: Paper and Thin-layer Chromatography 1757
UKCIS Macroprofiles: Steroids 1782
UKRA Bulletin 77
USA, History 4572-4576
USSR, History 4529-4533
USSR and Third World 4547
USSR Computational Mathematics and Mathematical Physics 1580
Ukapian 308
Ukrain, History 4534
Ukrainian Literature 4300
Ukrainian Review 4300
Ukrainian Thought 4534
Ulster Commentary 4455
Ulster Journal of Archaeology 4396
Ulster Medical Journal 2098
Ultrasonics 2399
Umbrella 3841
Undercurrents 2040
Underwater Science and Technology Information Bulletin 1837
Underwater Science and Technology Journal 1838
Underwear 3709-3710
Underwear and Stockings 3720
Uni Ropa 3224
Uniform and Industrial Clothing 794
Unigate News 2982
Unilever International 309
Union News 192
Unison 310
Unitarian 556
Unitarianism 555-556
Unity 4121
University College Hospital Magazine 2099
University Equipment 1293
University of Edinburgh Journal 311
University of Leeds Gazette 312
University of Leeds Reporter 313
University of London Bulletin 4604
University of London Institute of Education Library Bulletin 40
University of Wales Dictionary 79
Update 2100
Urban Affairs Quarterly 3853
Urban Design Bulletin 3854
Urban Education 1181
Urban Studies 3855
Urology 2293
Ushaw Magazine 512

VAT Newsletter 868
Vacher's European Companion 717
Vacuum 2419
Vacuum Technology 2419
Valentine 314
Valuation 970-972
Value 3307
Valuer 972
Vegan Action Newsletter 315
Vegetable Oils and Oilseeds 2875
Vegetarian 3049
Vegetarian Messenger 3049
Vegetarianism 3048-3049
Vending 3276
Vending Times 3272
Venereal Diseases 2323
Ventilating 3786-3802
Venture 472
Venture 745
Vernacular Architecture 3883
Vestnik Mashinostroeniya 2386
Veterinary Journal 2344
Veterinary News 2352
Veterinary Record 2353
Veterinary Science 2344-2354
Viator 4346
Vickers News 316
Victor Magazine 317
Victoria and Albert Museum Bulletin 348
Vietnam 4556
Vietnam, History 4556
Viewpoints 4250
Vigilance 797
Village 1031
Village Life 3038-3039
Village Life 3039
Vine 4588A
Virology 1954-1955
Virology Abstracts 1955
Vision 427
Vision 1323
Vision Research 1653
Visual Aids 1247-1248
Visual Education 1248
Vital Economic Trends in the United Kingdom 775
Vivisection 2114-2116
Viz 1475
Vocational Aspect of Education 1294
Vocational Aspect of Secondary and Further Education 1294
Voice 318
Voice 459
Voice of the People 746
Vole 4251
Vox 1360
Vulcan Journal 797
Vysokomolekulyarnge Soyedineniya 3582

WAGBI Magazine 4181
WEA News 1182
WIRA News 3566
WIRA Scan 3567
Wirascan for Clothier's 3568
WPR Summary of Current Literature 2681
WRA Digest 2678
WRVS Magazine 1032
Waddon Swimming News 4154
Wages 790-791
Wake Newsletter 4293
Wales, Archaeology 4439-4442
   History 4523
Wales Science Bulletin 1522

Wallpaper & Paint Retailers Journal 3809
Wallpaper, Paint and Wallcovering 3809
War 1009
Warm Air Heating and Environmental Engineering 3802
Warship Profile 2605
Warwickshire History 4347
Waste Disposal 2690
Waste Trade World 2689
Waste Treatment 2688-2690
Watchmaker, Jeweller and Silversmith 3596
Watchtower 4609
Water and Waste Treatment 2679
Water and Water Engineering 2680
Water Pollution Abstracts 2681
Water Pollution Control 2682
Water Power 2668
Water Research 2683
Water Research Newsheet 2684
Water Supply 2673-2685
Water Treatment and Examination 2685
Waterfowl 2021
Waterways News 1389
Waterways World 1390
Watneys News 319
Watsonia 1951
Waxing Moon 1457
Way Ahead 3043
Wear 3708
Weather 1846
Weather Report 1847
Webb Society Quarterly Journal 1594
Wedgwood Review 3451
Weed Abstracts 2870
Weed Research 2871
Weeds 2870-2871
Weekend 320
Weekend Mail 320
Weekly Circular of the Chair Frame Manufacturers Association 3677
Weekly Dairy Produce Supplies 2983
Weekly Fruit Supplies 2901
Weekly Law Reports 920
Weekly Return of the Registrar General, Scotland 644
Weights and Measures 1436
Weir Bulletin 321
Welding 2537-2540
Welding and Metal Fabrication 2538
Welding in the World 2539
Welding International Research and Development 2540
Welding Research International 2540
Welfare Officer 1033
Welfare Services to the Physically Handicapped 1051-1059 4638
   Poor 1060-1062, 4639
Welsh Churchman 531
Welsh Geological Quarterly 4659
Welsh History Review 4348
Welsh Labour History 710
Welsh Literature 4301
Welsh Medical Gazette 2101
Welsh Music 3972
Welsh Nation 720
Welsh Nationalist 720
Welsh Pony and Cob Society Journal 2937
Welsh Rugby 4073
Welsh Sociologist 617
Welwyn Digest 3452
Welwyn Newsletter 3452
Wessex Life 4519

INDEX

West Indian Review 1361
West India Committee Circular 1362
West Indies Chronicle 1362
West London Free Press 322
West Surrey Outlook 4479
Western Buddhist 562
Westminster 1313
Westminster Abbey Occasional Paper 526
Westminster Cathedral Journal 513
Westminster Summary 719
What's New 3231
Wheat Flour Bread 3418
Where 1183
Where to Go in London 323
Which? 3308
Which Course? 1295
Whip 324
Whitaker's Books of the Month & Books to Come 3146
White and Red 325
White Canons 492
White Eagle 678
Whiting 3452
Wholesale Confectioner 3412
Wholesale Grocer 3047
Wiadomosci Gospodarcze 326
Wiener Library Bulletin 4349
Wife and Citizen 1079
Wiggin Nickel Alloys 3508
Wildfowl 2022
Wildfowler & Rough Shooter 4181
Wills Worlds 327
Wiltshire Archaeological and Natural History Magazine 4435
Wiltshire Industrial Archaeology 4436
Wiltshire Life 4519
Wimpy Times 328
Window Cleaning 3065
Window Talk 3065
Wine and Food 3378
Wine and Spirit Trade International 3379
Wine and Spirit Trade Record 3379
Wine & Spirit Trade Review 3373
Wine—Butler 3380
Wine Magazine 3381
Wine Mine 3382
Wines 3375-3382, 4695
Wire 2421
Wire Industry 2421
Wireless World 2507
Witchcraft 1456-1457
Woking Offers 4520
Woking Review 4520
Woman 329
Woman and Home 3031
Woman Bride and Home 3032
Woman Engineer 2389
Woman Health Officer 2254
Woman's Journal 3033
Women's Liberation Review 4649
Woman's Own 3034
Woman's Realm Home Sewing & Knitting 3021
Women 1447-1448, 4649-4650
Women Speaking 1448
Women's Report 618
Women's Studies 4650
Women's Work 553

Wonderlands 548
Wood 3525-3535
Wood 3532
Wood and Equipment News 3533
Woodworker 3534
Woodworking Industry 3535
Wool 3566-3571
Wool Intelligence 3569
Wool Record and Textile World 3570
Wool Science Review 3571
Worcestershire Archaeology Newsletter 4437
Worcestershire Naturalists Club Newsletter 1561
World in Action 437
Work Study 3242-3244
Work Study 3243
Work Study & Industrial Engineering 3244
Work Study & Management 3244
Work Study and Management Service 3244
Working Class 710
Works Engineering 2390
Works Management 3225
Works World 139
Workshop 4252
Workshop New Poetry 4252
Workshop Poetry Magazine 4252
World Agricultural Economics and Rural Sociology Abstracts 2819
World and the School 1184
World Archaeology 4390
World Bowls 4058
World Crops 2820
Worlds Foods and Protein News 2863
World Fibre News 3563
World Fishing 3012
World Jewry 579
World Medicine 2102
World of Irish Nursing 2261
World of NPKS 2864
World Pentecost 493
World Refrigeration and Air Conditioning 2523
World Soccer 4070
World Sports 4055
World Surface Coatings Abstracts 3472
World Survey 694
World Textile Abstracts 3557
World Tobacco 3396
World Today 695
World Wildlife News 1562
World's Children 1065
World's Fair 4017
World's Paper Trade Review 3537
World's Press News 349
Worldwide Newspaper Collecting and Press History 354
Wrestler 4129
Wrestling 4125-4129
Writer 4258
Writers Forum 4253
Writers Journal 330
Writers Workshop 4252

X-Ray Fluorescence Spectroscopy Abstracts 1668

X-Ray Focus 2225
X-Ray Spectrometry 1669
Xenobiotica 2125

Y Ddolen 70
Y Draig Goch 721
Y Faner 722
Y Gwyddonydd 331
Y Llan 532
Y Tir (The Land) 2821
Y Traethodydd 4301
Y Tyst 541
Y Tyst Cymraeg 541
YLG News 69
YLS Activity 69
YLS News 69
YMCA 475
YMCA World 475
Yachting 4143-4151
Yachting & Boating Weekly 4148
Yachting Monthly 4149
Yachting World 4150
Yachts and Yachting 4151
Yoga 563-564
Yoga and Health 563
Yoga Quarterly Review 564
York Poetry 4254
Yorkshire Archaeological and Topographical Journal 4438
Yorkshire Archaeological Journal 4438
Yorkshire Architect 3884
Yorkshire Bulletin of Economic and Social Research 751
Yorkshire Cactus Journal 2925
Yorkshire Illustrated 4521
Yorkshire Librarian 71
Yorkshire Life 4521
Yorkshire Life Illustrated 4521
Yorkshire Ridings 4522
Yorkshire Ridings Magazine 4522
You and Your Health 2213
Young Elizabethan 148
Young People's Societies 1100-1107
Young Writer 4259
Your Environment 2160
Youth 594-595
Youth and Society 594
Youth Employment 1240
Youth Organisations 1066
Youth Service 595
Youth Travels 1384

Zaire Africa 4570
Zerone 4255
Zero One 332
Zhurnal Vychislitel 'noi Matematiki i Matematicheskoi Fiziki 1580
Zinc 3512
Zinc Abstracts 3512
Zion's Herald 460
Zodiac 212
Zodiac 2508
Zoo 3856
Zoo Federation News 1977
Zoo Magazine 1978
Zoological Journal of the Linnean Society 1976
Zoology 1970-1978
Zoophilist 2114

Ref
Folio
Z
6956
E5
W66
1973
v.1